MARKETING

Fifteenth Edition

Roger A. Kerin
Southern Methodist University

Steven W. Hartley
University of Denver

MARKETING: FIFTEENTH EDITION

Published by McGraw-Hill Education, 2 Penn Plaza, New York, NY 10121.

Some ancillaries, including electronic and print components, may not be available to customers outside the United States.

This book is printed on acid-free paper.

1 2 3 4 5 6 7 8 9 LWI 24 23 22 21 20

ISBN 978-1-260-26036-6 (bound edition)
MHID 1-260-26036-4 (bound edition)
ISBN 978-1-260-47123-6 (loose-leaf edition)
MHID 1-260-47123-3 (loose-leaf edition)

Executive Brand Manager: *Meredith Fossel*
Executive Marketing Manager: *Nicole Young*
Senior Product Developer: *Kelly I. Pekelder*
Lead Content Project Manager: *Christine Vaughan*
Senior Content Project Manager: *Keri Johnson*
Senior Buyer: *Susan K. Culbertson*
Senior Designer: *Matt Diamond*
Senior Content Licensing Specialist: *Ann Marie Jannette*
Cover Image: *©Glenn van der Knijff/Getty Images*
Compositor: *Aptara®, Inc.*

Library of Congress Cataloging-in-Publication Data

Names: Kerin, Roger A., author. | Hartley, Steven W., author.
Title: Marketing / Roger A. Kerin, Southern Methodist University, Steven W. Hartley, University of Denver.
Description: Fifteenth edition. | New York, NY : McGraw-Hill Education, [2021] | Includes index.
Identifiers: LCCN 2019041923 (print) | LCCN 2019041924 (ebook) | ISBN 9781260260366 (hardcover) | ISBN 9781260471236 (spiral bound) | ISBN 9781260471212 (ebook) | ISBN 9781260471199 (ebook other)
Subjects: LCSH: Marketing.
Classification: LCC HF5415 .M29474 2021 (print) | LCC HF5415 (ebook) | DDC 658.8–dc23
LC record available at https://lccn.loc.gov/2019041923
LC ebook record available at https://lccn.loc.gov/2019041924

mheducation.com/highered

WELCOME FROM THE AUTHORS!

A recent survey of the market for marketers revealed an incredible variety of new job titles including brand ambassador, digital marketing manager, content strategist, event coordinator, marketing analytics manager, and social media manager. These new titles reflect the exciting changes occurring in the marketplace and the integral role marketing professionals will play in businesses, nonprofit organizations, government agencies, and all parts of our economic and social environment. We are excited to have the opportunity to participate in your journey as a student of marketing, and we hope that this textbook will help you discover your personal goals related to a career of compassion and purpose in marketing or any of the fields it will influence!

The changes in the workplace are the result of new technologies, new consumer interests, and new social trends. For example, artificial intelligence, consumer demands for environmentally friendly products, and the growing movement toward a gender-neutral society all have dramatic implications for the practice of marketing. To help you see the links with marketing actions we have included many current, interesting, and relevant examples such as Elon Musk's Mission to Mars and Neuralink businesses, Chobani's efforts to create "better food for more people," IBM's "Let's Put Smart To Work" strategy, and Toyota's hydrogen fuel-cell vehicle, the Mirai. In addition, we have integrated many of the most popular marketing tools available to practitioners, including net promoter scores, customer lifetime value, and blue ocean strategy analysis.

The dynamic nature of the marketing discipline necessitates equally dynamic learning resources. As a result, we have focused our time and energy on ensuring that our textbook provides the most insightful and comprehensive coverage of the marketplace today. The dramatic changes in student learning styles—from traditional observational styles to contemporary collaborative styles—are also reflected in our efforts as we have included many features to match these interests. Our approach to presenting the complexities of marketing and facilitating the changes in learning is based on three important dimensions:

- **Engagement.** As professors we have benefited from interactions with many exceptional students, managers, and instructors. Their insights have contributed to our approach to teaching and, subsequently, to our efforts as textbook authors. One of the essential elements of our approach is a commitment to active learning through engaging, integrated, and timely materials. In-class activities, an interactive blog, marketing plan exercises, and in-text links to online ads and web pages are just a few examples of the components of our engagement model.
- **Leadership.** Our approach is also based on a commitment to taking a leadership role in the development and presentation of new ideas, principles, theories, and practices in marketing. This is more important now than ever before, as the pace of change in our discipline accelerates and influences almost every aspect of traditional marketing. We are certain that exposure to leading-edge material related to topics such as social media, data analytics, and marketing metrics can help students become leaders in their jobs and careers.
- **Innovation.** New educational technologies and innovative teaching tools have magnified the engagement and leadership aspects of our approach. Connect, LearnSmart, and SmartBook, for example, provide a digital and interactive platform that embraces the "anytime and anywhere" style of today's students. In addition, we have provided new videos and increased the visual impact of the text and PowerPoint materials to facilitate multimedia approaches to learning.

Through the previous 14 U.S. editions—and 20 international editions in 12 languages—we have been gratified by the enthusiastic feedback we have received from students and instructors. We are very excited to have this opportunity to share our passion for this exciting discipline with you today. Welcome to the 15th edition of *Marketing*!

Roger A. Kerin
Steven W. Hartley

PREFACE

Marketing utilizes a unique, innovative, and effective pedagogical approach developed by the authors through the integration of their combined classroom, college, and university experiences. The elements of this approach have been the foundation for each edition of *Marketing* and serve as the core of the text and its supplements as they evolve and adapt to changes in student learning styles, the growth of the marketing discipline, and the development of new instructional technologies. The distinctive features of the approach are illustrated below:

Marketing 15/e *Pedagogical Approach*

High-Engagement Style
Easy-to-read, high-involvement, interactive writing style that engages students through active learning techniques.

Rigorous Framework
A pedagogy based on the use of learning objectives, learning reviews, learning objectives reviews, and supportive student supplements.

Personalized Marketing
A vivid and accurate description of businesses, marketing professionals, and entrepreneurs—through cases, exercises, and testimonials—that allows students to personalize marketing and identify possible career interests.

Traditional and Contemporary Coverage
Comprehensive and integrated coverage of traditional and contemporary marketing concepts.

Marketing Decision Making
The use of extended examples, cases, and videos involving people making marketing decisions.

Integrated Technology
The use of powerful technical resources and learning solutions, such as Connect, LearnSmart, SmartBook, the Kerin & Hartley Blog (www.kerinmarketing.com), and in-text video links.

The goal of the 15th edition of *Marketing* is to create an exceptional experience for today's students and instructors of marketing. The development of *Marketing* was based on a rigorous process of assessment, and the outcome of the process is a text and package of learning tools that are based on *engagement*, *leadership*, and *innovation* in marketing education.

ENGAGEMENT

The author team has benefited from extraordinary experiences as instructors, researchers, and consultants, as well as the feedback of users of previous editions of *Marketing*—now more than 1 million students! The authors believe that success in marketing education in the future will require the highest levels of engagement. They ensure engagement by facilitating interaction between students and four learning partners—the instructor, other students, businesses, and the publisher. Some examples of the high-engagement elements of *Marketing*:

In-Class Activities and Digital In-Class Activities. The in-class activities, located in the *Instructor's Manual*, are designed to engage students in discussions with the instructor and among themselves. They involve surveys, online resources, out-of-class assignments, and personal observations. Each activity illustrates a concept from the textbook and can be done individually or as a team. Examples include: Designing a Candy Bar, Marketing Yourself, Pepsi vs. Coke Taste Test, and What Makes a Memorable TV Commercial? In addition, digital in-class activities have been added to selected chapters. These activities, located in the Instructor Resources, focus on the use of Web resources and the marketing data they can provide students.

Interactive Web Page and Blog (www.kerinmarketing.com). Students can access recent articles about marketing and post comments for other students. The site also provides access to a *Marketing* Twitter feed!

Building Your Marketing Plan. The Building Your Marketing Plan guides at the end of each chapter are based on the format of the Marketing Plan presented in Appendix A. On the basis of self-study or as part of a course assignment, students can use the activities to organize interactions with businesses to build a marketing plan. Students and employers often suggest that a well-written plan in a student's portfolio is an asset in today's competitive job market.

LEADERSHIP

The popularity of *Marketing* in the United States and around the globe is the result, in part, of the leadership role of the authors in developing and presenting new marketing content and pedagogies. For example, *Marketing* was the first text to meaningfully integrate ethics, interactive and social media marketing, and marketing metrics and dashboards. It was also the first text to develop custom-made videos to help illustrate marketing principles and practices and bring them to life for students as they read the text. The authors have also been leaders in developing new learning tools, such as a three-step learning process that includes learning objectives, learning reviews, and learning objectives reviews and new testing materials that are based on Bloom's learning taxonomy. Other elements that show how *Marketing* is a leader in the discipline include:

Chapter 20: Using Social Media and Mobile Marketing to Connect with Consumers. *Marketing* features a dedicated and up-to-date chapter for social media and mobile marketing. This new environment is rapidly changing and constantly growing. The authors cover the building blocks of social media and mobile marketing and provide thorough, relevant content and examples. The authors describe major social media platforms like Twitter, Facebook, LinkedIn, and YouTube. They explain how managers and companies can use those platforms for marketing purposes, including influencer marketing. Chapter 20 also includes a new section titled Social Media Marketing Programs and Customer Engagement that describes criteria for selecting social media platforms and social media content, how social media can produce sales, and methods of measuring a company's success with social media and mobile marketing. This chapter is an example of one of many ways *Marketing* is on the cutting edge of marketing practice.

Applying Marketing Metrics. The Applying Marketing Metrics feature in the text delivers two important measurement elements in business and marketing management today—performance metrics and the dashboards to visualize them. The text includes 15 examples of proven marketing performance metrics, including their purpose, calculation, application, interpretation, and display in marketing dashboards. Some of the metrics included are: net promoter scores (NPS), customer lifetime value (CLV), new product development index, category development index (CDI), brand development index (BDI), load factor (a capacity management metric), price premium, sales per square foot, same-store sales growth, promotion-to-sales ratio, cost per thousand (CPM) impressions, and customer engagement with social media. The feature is designed to encourage readers to learn, practice, display, and apply marketing metrics in a meaningful manner for decision-making purposes.

Color-Coded Graphs and Tables. The use of color in the graphs and tables enhances their readability and adds a visual level of learning to the textbook for readers. In addition, these color highlights increase student comprehension by linking the text discussion to colored elements in the graphs and tables.

New Video Cases. Each chapter ends with a case that is supported by a video to illustrate the issues in the chapter. New cases such as IBM, Toyota, Justin's, Fallon Worldwide, Body Glove, and Cascade Maverik, and recent cases such as GoPro and Coppertone, provide current and relevant examples that are familiar to students.

INNOVATION

In today's fast-paced and demanding educational environment, innovation is essential to effective learning. To maintain *Marketing*'s leadership position in the marketplace, the author team consistently creates innovative pedagogical tools that match contemporary students' learning styles and interests. The authors keep their fingers on the pulse of technology to bring real innovation to their text and package. Innovations such as in-text links, a Twitter feed, hyperlinked PowerPoint slides, and an online blog augment the McGraw-Hill Education online innovations such as Connect, LearnSmart, and SmartBook.

In-Text Links. You can see Internet links in magazine ads; on television programming; as part of catalogs, in-store displays, and product packaging; and throughout *Marketing*! These links bring the text to life with ads and videos about products and companies that are discussed in the text. These videos also keep the text even more current. While each link in the text has a caption, the links are updated to reflect new campaigns and market changes. In addition, the links allow readers to stream the video cases at the end of each chapter. You can simply click on the links in the digital book or use your smartphone or computer to follow the links.

Twitter Feed and Online Blog. Visit www.kerinmarketing.com to participate in *Marketing*'s online blog discussion and to see Twitter feed updates. You can also subscribe to the Twitter feed to receive the Marketing Question of the Day and respond with the #QotD hashtag.

Connect, LearnSmart, and SmartBook Integration. These McGraw-Hill Education products provide a comprehensive package of online resources to enable students to learn faster, study more efficiently, and increase knowledge retention. The products represent the gold standard in online, interactive, and adaptive learning tools and have received accolades from industry experts for their Library and Study Center elements, filtering and reporting functions, and immediate student feedback capabilities. In addition, the authors have developed book-specific interactive assignments, including (a) auto-graded applications based on the marketing plan exercises, and (b) activities based on the Applying Marketing Metrics boxes and marketing metrics presented in the text.

Innovative Test Bank. Containing more than 5,000 multiple-choice and essay questions, the *Marketing* Test Bank reflects more than two decades of innovations. The Test Bank also includes "visual test questions" in each chapter to reward students who made an effort to understand key graphs, tables, and images in the chapter.

FOR INSTRUCTORS

You're in the driver's seat.

Want to build your own course? No problem. Prefer to use our turnkey, prebuilt course? Easy. Want to make changes throughout the semester? Sure. And you'll save time with Connect's auto-grading too.

65%

Less Time Grading

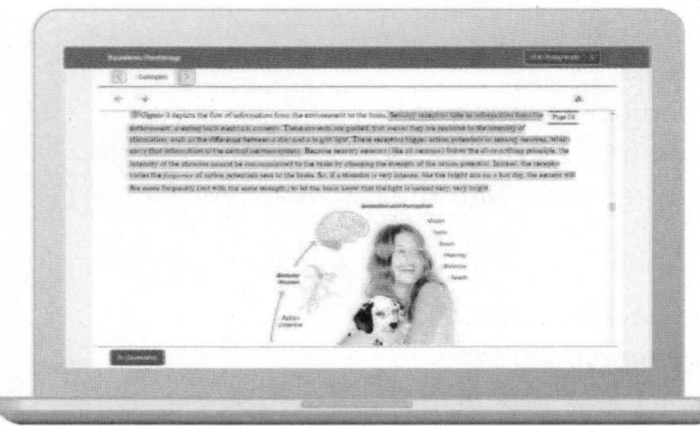

Laptop: McGraw-Hill; Woman/dog: George Doyle/Getty Images

They'll thank you for it.

Adaptive study resources like SmartBook® 2.0 help your students be better prepared in less time. You can transform your class time from dull definitions to dynamic debates. Find out more about the powerful personalized learning experience available in SmartBook 2.0 at **www.mheducation.com/highered/connect/smartbook**

Make it simple, make it affordable.

Connect makes it easy with seamless integration using any of the major Learning Management Systems—Blackboard®, Canvas, and D2L, among others—to let you organize your course in one convenient location. Give your students access to digital materials at a discount with our inclusive access program. Ask your McGraw-Hill representative for more information.

Padlock: Jobalou/Getty Images

Solutions for your challenges.

A product isn't a solution. Real solutions are affordable, reliable, and come with training and ongoing support when you need it and how you want it. Our Customer Experience Group can also help you troubleshoot tech problems—although Connect's 99% uptime means you might not need to call them. See for yourself at **status.mheducation.com**

Checkmark: Jobalou/Getty Images

FOR STUDENTS

Effective, efficient studying.

Connect helps you be more productive with your study time and get better grades using tools like SmartBook 2.0, which highlights key concepts and creates a personalized study plan. Connect sets you up for success, so you walk into class with confidence and walk out with better grades.

Study anytime, anywhere.

Download the free ReadAnywhere app and access your online eBook or SmartBook 2.0 assignments when it's convenient, even if you're offline. And since the app automatically syncs with your eBook and SmartBook 2.0 assignments in Connect, all of your work is available every time you open it. Find out more at **www.mheducation.com/readanywhere**

> ***"I really liked this app—it made it easy to study when you don't have your text-book in front of you."***
>
> \- Jordan Cunningham,
> Eastern Washington University

Calendar: owattaphotos/Getty Images

No surprises.

The Connect Calendar and Reports tools keep you on track with the work you need to get done and your assignment scores. Life gets busy; Connect tools help you keep learning through it all.

Learning for everyone.

McGraw-Hill works directly with Accessibility Services Departments and faculty to meet the learning needs of all students. Please contact your Accessibility Services office and ask them to email accessibility@mheducation.com, or visit **www.mheducation.com/about/accessibility** for more information.

Top: Jenner Images/Getty Images, Left: Hero Images/Getty Images, Right: Hero Images/Getty Images

McGraw Hill

Asset Alignment with Bloom's Taxonomy

Principles of Marketing

We Take Students Higher

As a learning science company we create content that supports higher order thinking skills. Interactive learning tools within *McGraw-Hill Connect* are tagged accordingly, so you can filter, search, assign, and receive reports on your students' level of learning. The result—increased pedagogical insights and learning proces efficiency that facilitate a stronger connection between the course material and the student.

The chart below shows a few of the key assignable marketing assets with *McGraw-Hill Connect* aligned with Bloom's Taxonomy. Take your students higher by assigning a variety of applications, moving them from sim memorization to concept application.

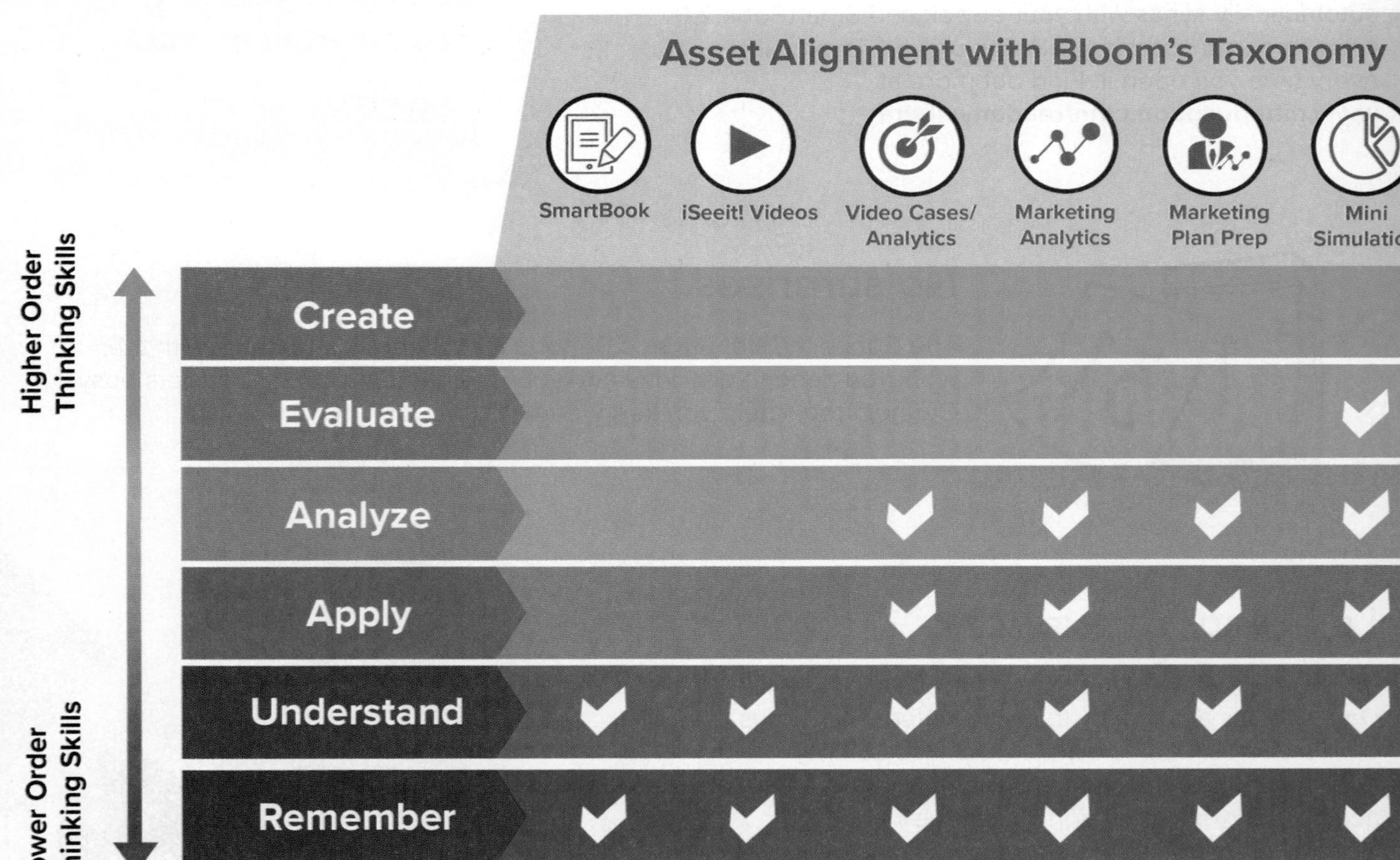

nartBook

- Adaptively aids students to study more efficiently by highlighting where in the chapter to focus, asking review questions and pointing them to resources until they understand.

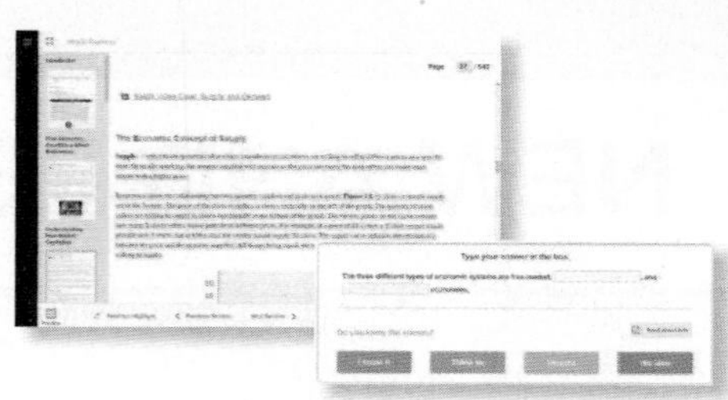

eeit! Videos

- Short, contemporary videos provide engaging, animated introductions to key course concepts. Available at the chapter level. Perfect for launching lectures and assigning pre- or post-lecture.

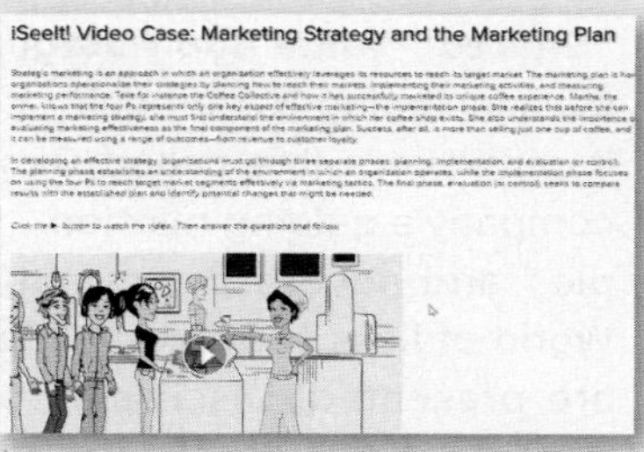

ideo Cases & Case Analyses

- Mini-cases and scenarios of real-world firms accompanied by questions that help students analyze and apply marketing theory and other core concepts.

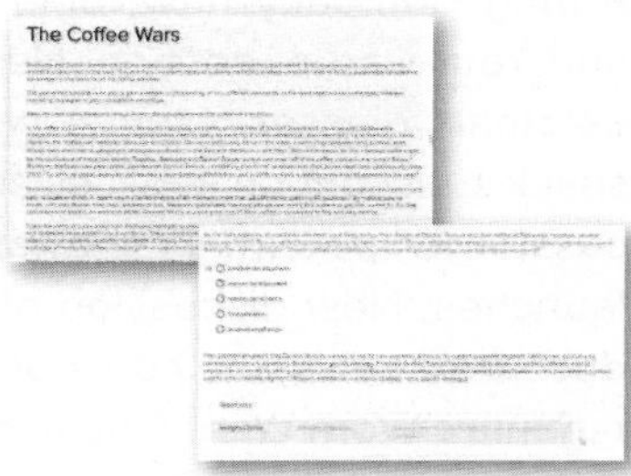

arketing Analytics

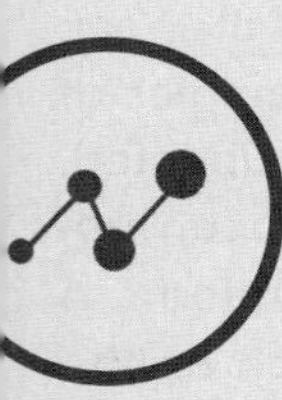

- These newest auto-graded, data analytics activities challenge students to make decisions using metrics commonly seen across Marketing professions. The goal of this activity is to give students practice analyzing and using marketing data to make decisions.

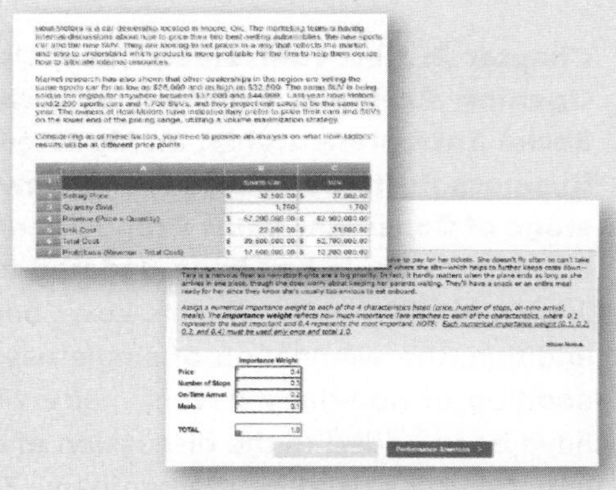

arketing Plan Prep

- These exercises use guided activities and examples to help students understand and differentiate the various elements of a marketing plan.

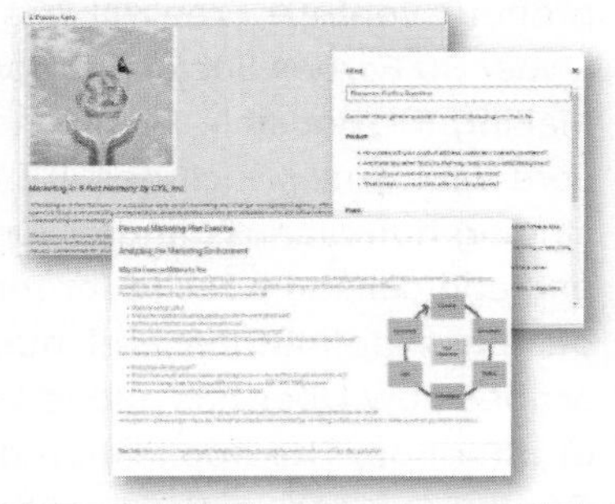

ini Simulation

- Marketing Mini Sims help students apply and understand the interconnections of elements in the marketing mix by having them take on the role of Marketing Manager for a backpack manufacturing company.
- Mini Sims can be assigned by topic or in its entirety.

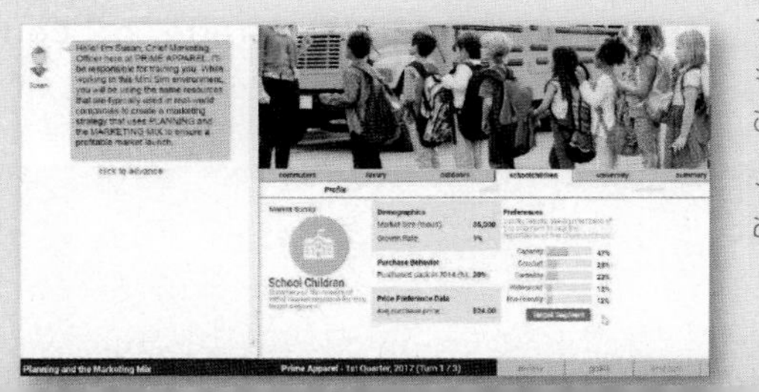

Photos: Shutterstock/P. Chinnapong; Monkey Business Images/Shutterstock

NEW AND REVISED CONTENT

Chapter 1: Update of Chobani's New Products, New Showstopper Analysis, and New Material on "Shared" Value and Patagonia. Chobani's new products, including its non-dairy, coconut-based yogurt, and its children's line called Gimmies are discussed. The company's guiding mission, "Better food for more people," and advertising campaigns such as "Wonderful World of Less," "Believe in Food," and "Love This Life" are presented. Discussion of Elon Musk's new businesses such as the Mission to Mars, Neuralink, and The Boring Company have been added to the Marketing and Your Career section. New-product examples such as smart glasses, stevia-sweetened soft drinks, and snack subscription services have been added to the discussion of potential "showstoppers" for new-product launches. New discussion of Facebook's efforts to reduce fake news, the concept of "shared" value, and Patagonia's Worn Wear initiative have also been added.

Chapter 2: New IBM Video Case, Updated Chapter Opening Example, Addition of a New Example of Social Entrepreneurship, an Updated Application of Business Portfolio Analysis, and New Extended Coverage of Consumer Value Propositions. The Chapter 2 opening example has been updated to discuss Ben & Jerry's familiar motto "Peace, Love, and Ice Cream." In addition, the elimination of single-use plastic and the addition of non-dairy flavors made with almond milk have been added to the discussion of creative marketing strategies used by the company. The social entrepreneur venture FreeWill has been added to the *30 Under 30 Forbes Social Entrepreneurs* discussion in the Making Responsible Decisions box. The discussion of core values now includes IKEA's seven core values including humbleness and willpower, daring to be different, and constant desire for renewal. The discussion of business definitions and business models now describes how Uber has added Uber Jump to its portfolio of offerings. The application of the Boston Consulting Group business portfolio model to Apple's product line has been updated to include changes related to the Apple Card, the iPhone, and the iPad/iPad mini tablet devices. Extended coverage of consumer value propositions includes criteria for their selection and a description of IKEA's consumer value proposition, which is central to it becoming the world's largest retailer. In addition, a new Gantt chart example has been added. The end-of-chapter video case is completely new and features the recent IBM campaign and strategy: "Let's Put Smart To Work."

Chapter 3: Update of Facebook's Response to the Changing Marketing Environment, Update of New Trends in Marketing, and Updated Discussion of Gender-Neutral Marketing Actions. The chapter opening example is updated to reflect the dramatic environmental changes Facebook is facing. The discussion of new trends, such as the growing popularity of biometric "watches," the new emphasis on the concept of a circular economy, the emergence of the Fourth Industrial Revolution, the shift from single transactions to ongoing relationships, and the increase in regulation related to privacy, cybersecurity, and online fraud, has been expanded. An update of Generation Z value formation has been added to the discussion of generational cohorts. Discussion of *Ad Age*'s Multicultural Agency of the Year, The Community, has been added and the examples of gender-neutral marketing actions have been updated. The Marketing Insights About Me box has been updated to reflect the new data.census.gov platform. A discussion of new trends in technology, such as the growth of facial recognition technology, blockchain, artificial intelligence, and wearable technology, has also been added. The Regulatory Forces discussion now includes the California Consumer Privacy Act.

Chapter 4: New Toyota Video Case, Updated Chapter Opening Example, and Expanded Description of Consumer Ethics and Sustainable Consumption. The chapter opening example highlights the decision by Anheuser-Busch to spend $1 billion on its social media program to reduce the harmful use of alcohol and its 2025 Sustainability Goals in the areas of air pollution, water conservation, and recycling. The role of consumers in becoming partners with business in ethical buying behavior and sustainable consumption is expanded. In addition, the chapter ends with a completely new video case about Toyota, its transition to a "mobility" company, and its marketing activities related to the hydrogen fuel-cell vehicle, the Mirai.

Chapter 5: Updated Consumer Lifestyle Discussion, a New Applying Marketing Metrics Box Featuring Net Promoter Scores™, and New Location of the Section on Social Class Influence. The section describing consumer lifestyle, the VALS framework, and the Marketing Insights About Me box has been expanded to reflect the latest marketing practices. The growing emphasis on consumer advocacy is highlighted with a new Applying Marketing Metrics box describing the calculation, application, interpretation, and display of Net Promoter Scores in a consumer advocacy context. The section on Social Class Influence has been moved to follow the section on Reference Group Influence.

Chapter 6: Updated Examples of IBM and Boeing Procurement, New Discussion of Mary Kay Pink Young Line, an Updated Marketing Insights About Me Box about Supplier Diversity, and a New Reverse Auction Example. The descriptions of organizational buying at IBM and Boeing have been updated. In addition, the Marketing Insights About Me box has been updated to reflect the latest publication of DiversityInc. A description of Nike's use of bids from advertising agencies for the company's multimillion-dollar media program has been added to the reverse auction discussion.

Chapter 7: New Discussion of Globalization and World Trade, including the passage of the United States, Mexico, Canada Agreement (USMCA) and Great Britain's exit from the European Union. The discussion on globalization has been updated to feature recent developments pertaining to economic protectionism, economic nationalism, and trade wars between nations. Their effect on world trade is described. The recent passage of the USMCA, which renegotiated the North American Fair Trade Agreement (NAFTA), and Great Britain's formal exit from the European Union are highlighted in this regard.

Chapter 8: Updated Chapter Opening Example, an Update of Nielsen Television Program Rankings, and an Updated Example of Forecasting Sales for a New Running Shoe. The chapter opening example has been updated to reflect the use of marketing research in Hollywood, and its potential influence on movies such as *Avengers: Endgame* and *Atomic Blonde*. The discussion of national TV ratings data collected by Nielsen, as an example of a mechanical method of data collection, has been updated. In addition, the discussion of direct forecasting has been updated to include the New Balance Zante Pursuit as an example.

Chapter 9: Update of Zappos's Use of Segmentation and Its Training Center, New Examples, New Section on Customer Lifetime Value, and a New Applying Marketing Metrics Box. The chapter opening example has been updated to describe how Zappos uses behavioral segmentation, and how the company training center, Zappos Insights, allows other companies to learn the techniques. The When and How to Segment Markets section offers an updated discussion of Ford's shift in strategy to reduce its product line by focusing on pickups, SUVs, and electric cars. The discussion of mass customization now includes the *Nike By You* service as an example. In addition, a new section titled The Financial Relevance of Customer Patronage: Customer Lifetime Value has been added. In addition, a new Applying Marketing Metrics box featuring the calculation, application, and interpretation of the lifetime value of a McDonald's, Burger King, and Wendy's customer using actual company data has been added.

Chapter 10: New Example of Open Innovation, a New Section on New Product Performance, a New Marketing Metric—the New Product Vitality Index, and New Images. The discussion on open innovation now includes Pepsi's entrepreneurial group, called "The Hive," as an example. A new section titled Tracking New Product Performance has been added. In addition, the New Product Vitality Index, used by many large companies, is described, calculated, interpreted, and displayed in a new Applying Marketing Metrics box. New images of Flamin' Hot Cheetos, the Pebble Smartwatch, the Google Glass Enterprise, and new product successes at General Mills have been added to the discussion.

Chapter 11: New Justin's Video Case, the Latest Brand Extension for Gatorade, an Expanded Example of the Product Life Cycle for All-Electric-Powered Vehicles, New Material on Brand Purpose in Brand Equity Development, and New Packaging Examples. The Chapter 11 discussion of Gatorade in the chapter opener now includes material on Gatorade's new sugar-free Gatorade Zero. An expanded discussion of the product life cycle for all-electric vehicles is included. The latest thinking on brand purpose in brand equity development is introduced. In addition, the Packaging and Labeling discussion includes the Tide Eco-Box and Starkist's single-serve pouches as examples. The chapter ends with a new video case titled Justin's: Managing a Successful Product with Passion, which describes the inspiring story of entrepreneur Justin Gold, and the application of product management concepts to the Justin's brand of organic nut butters.

Chapter 12: New Discussion of Airbnb's Efforts to Become a "21st Century Company," New Services Examples, and New Advertisements. Discussion of Airbnb's efforts to become a "21st Century Company" through new services such as Experiences, HotelTonight, and Backyard has been added to the chapter opener. New services examples include Babylon digital health care, Apple News, and Warby Parker. The Services in the Future section now includes a discussion of Valeo Voyage, which allows users to be virtual passengers in a car, and a discussion of *netnography*—the use of online information to better understand service consumers. In addition, new advertisements from American Airlines, United Airlines, Merrill Lynch, the American Red Cross, the March of Dimes, the United States Postal Service, Accenture, and Amazon Prime have been added.

Chapter 13: Updated Example of Final Price Calculation, New Example of Price Setting to Achieve a Market Share Objective, Update of Apple iPhone Pricing, and New Coverage of Estimating the Profit Impact of Price Changes. The example of the calculation of a final price for a Bugatti Chiron, with a Mini-Cooper trade-in, has been updated. An example of the use of price by P&G and Kimberly-Clark to achieve a market share objective has been added. The section on pricing a Single Product versus a Product Line now includes an updated example based on Apple iPhones. In addition, a new discussion highlighting how price changes affect profitability adds rigor to the understanding of the effect of raising and reducing prices and price elasticity of demand.

Chapter 14: Updated Odd-Even Pricing Example, Updated Applying Marketing Metrics Box, and Discussion of Apple's Approach to Product-Line Pricing. The updated odd-even pricing example now includes Lowe's offer of a DeWalt radial saw. The Applying Marketing Metrics box about above-, at-, or below-market pricing in the energy drink market has been updated. Apple's approach to product-line pricing is highlighted in the context of its models of new iPhones.

Chapter 15: New Section on Direct to Consumer Marketing and the Role of *BOPUS* and *BORIS* Multichannel Marketing Practices, New Starbucks Example of a Strategic Channel Alliance, and a New KFC Advertisement in the Logistics and Supply Chain Section. A new section highlights the popularity of direct to consumer marketing and the application of *BOPUS* (*b*uy *o*nline and *p*ick *u*p at a *s*tore) and *BORIS* (*b*uy *o*nline and *r*eturn a purchase *i*n *s*tore) that leverage the value-adding capabilities of retail stores in implementing multichannel practices. Starbucks's use of PepsiCo's distribution network has been added as an example of a strategic channel alliance. In addition, a new image related to the impact of KFC's change of distributors on customer service has been added.

Chapter 16: New Chapter Opening Example about Generation Z Shopping in Malls, Update of the Top Franchises, New Discussion about Amazon Go Stores, New Retail Positioning Matrix Example. Chapter 16 opens with a description of the surprising shopping preferences of Generation Z. They are combining traditional and contemporary approaches by using technology at the mall! The discussion of Contractual Systems in retailing has been updated to include new information about the top five franchises. The Self-Service retailing section now includes a description of the cashierless convenience stores, called Amazon Go. New topics such as geofencing, mobile app product scanning, personalized advertising, and online retailers with catalogs and storefronts, are also discussed. In addition, Ulta Beauty has been added as a new example in the discussion of the retail positioning matrix.

Chapter 17: Updated Terminology Describing the Marketspace as a Digital Environment, New Example of Choiceboard Technology, and a New Definition and Keyword on Marketing Attribution. Terminology related to the marketspace has been updated to include "digital natives" and the "digitally enabled" environment. A new example of Indochino's use of technology to allow customers to design their own products has been added to the section on Choiceboards. A new keyword, marketing attribution, has been added to the Monitor and Measure Multichannel Marketing Performance section. This chapter was previously located later in the sequence of chapters. It has been moved to follow coverage of marketing channels and supply chains (Chapter 15) and retailing and wholesaling (Chapter 16) given the convergence of these topics.

Chapter 18: Updated Chapter Opening Example, New Advertisements, Updated Marketing Matters Box, New Example of an IMC Program for a Movie, New Discussion of the Media Agency of the Year, and Addition of Opt-In Approaches to Direct Marketing Discussion. The chapter opening example has been completely updated to reflect Taco Bell's recent IMC activities. The company's Taco ReBELLion campaign, Taco Tuesday, Party Packs, Grubhub delivery service, the special Taco Bell edition of Xbox One, the Taco Bell Hotel and Resort, and Taco Hacks are all discussed. New advertisements include examples from The North Face, Oculus, Pepsi/Cheetos, and Otezla. The Marketing Matters box has been updated to describe marketing activities directed at the 20 million college students in the United States, including while they are on spring break! The IMC program used to promote the movie *Star Wars: The Rise of Skywalker* has been added to the Scheduling the Promotion section. The work of *Advertising Age*'s Media Agency of the Year, Assembly, is discussed. In addition, the Direct Marketing section has been updated to include the new emphasis on "opt-in" approaches.

Chapter 19: New Fallon Worldwide Video Case, New Chapter Opening Example about Advertising to "Over-The-Top" Media Users, New Advertisements and Sales Promotion Examples, New Discussion of the Advertising Agency of the Year, and Updated Examples of Sales Promotions. The consumer shift from viewing video programming through a cable or satellite connection to an Internet or "over-the-top" (OTT) connection is discussed in the chapter opening example. Examples of customized and addressable OTT campaigns include Cadillac and Toyota. New advertising examples from Hyundai, Flowers Victoria, IBM, KPMG, Milk Life, Under Armour, the NFL, Allstate, Louis Vuitton, and Nike, and new sales promotion examples from Kellogg's and Starbucks have been added. The Identifying the Target Audience section now includes the Under Armour Project Rock campaign as an example, and the Message Content section includes a discussion of the increasing use of gender-neutral advertising by firms such as CoverGirl, Zara, Guess, Mattel, and Louis Vuitton. The chapter also includes new discussion of *Advertising Age*'s Agency of the Year—Wieden+Kennedy. In addition, new sales promotion examples such as Pringles Mystery Flavor Contest, Starbucks's loyalty program, and Apple product placements in movies are discussed. The chapter ends with a new video case titled Fallon Worldwide: Creating a Competitive Advantage with Creativity, which describes the agency's approach to developing advertising such as the Arby's "We Have the Meats" campaign.

Chapter 20: New Body Glove Video Case, Updated Chapter Opening Example about Connected Cars, New Section on the Growth of Influencer Marketing, New Section on the Emergence of Social Commerce and Social Shopping, New Material about Misinformation Prevention and Privacy at Facebook, and New Applying Marketing Metrics Box on Measuring Customer Engagement on Social Media Platforms. Chapter 20 has been significantly revised. The chapter opening example has been updated to reflect the growth of connected cars, smart transportation, and intelligent mobility. In addition, a new section titled Emergence of Influencer Marketing addresses the role and growth of social media influencers such as Kendall Jenner, who has more than 110 million Instagram followers. Another new section titled Emergence of Social Commerce and Social Shopping introduces social shopping as a key term and discusses the idea that individuals are influenced by their peers' purchases and recommendations. New discussions about Facebook's Click-Gap metric, designed to prevent misinformation and fake news, and its new privacy protections related to the use of personal data, have been added to the section on Mobile Marketing at Facebook. The revised section titled Social Media Marketing Programs and Customer Engagement introduces new key terms and definitions for social media marketing programs, customer engagement and measurement, and social media content. The section now includes an Applying Marketing Metrics box to illustrate the calculation of customer engagement rate. The chapter features a new video case about Body Glove and the role social media play in the company's marketing plan.

Chapter 21: New Cascade Maverik video case, Updated Prospecting Discussion Now Includes Social Selling, New Images, and New and Updated Examples. The Prospecting section now includes social selling as part of the discussion about identifying leads and prospects. New images in the Marketing Matters box, the Close section, and the Making Responsible Decisions box communicate a contemporary perspective on personal selling and sales management. New and updated examples include college textbook publishers' use of a geographical sales organization, and Mary Kay Cosmetics's use of unconventional rewards for outstanding salespeople. The chapter ends with a new video case titled Cascade Maverik: Creating an Amazing Success Story with Exceptional Salespeople, which describes the sales management process and the personal selling process used by the firm to be "the fastest supplier of high-performance lacrosse gear."

Chapter 22: Update of Chapter Opening Example, New Coverage of Blue Ocean Strategies, Greater Emphasis on the Behavioral Aspects of the Strategic Marketing Process, and Updated Example of Starbucks in the Marketing Evaluation Section. The chapter opening example has been updated to include the General Mills "Consumer First" approach to strategic marketing, and examples of several of its new products such as Epic performance bars and Fruity Lucky Charms. In addition, a major addition to this chapter is the description of blue ocean strategies for reimagining industries and markets to achieve both cost and differentiation competitive advantages. The creation of smartphones illustrates the application of a blue ocean strategy. Also, the text has been revised to emphasize the behavioral aspects of the strategic marketing process, including pratfalls and pitfalls, to complement the more structural coverage of the strategic marketing process in Chapter 2. The discussion of actual results exceeding goals includes Starbucks's marketing actions to introduce new flavors such as S'mores Frappuccino, open new Reserve Roastery stores, launch a new loyalty program, and to build 10,000 "greener" stores by 2025.

INSTRUCTOR RESOURCES

Marketing 15/e
Instructor Resources

Test Bank
We offer more than 5,000 test questions categorized by topic, learning objectives, and level of learning.

Instructor's Manual
The IM includes lecture notes, video case teaching notes, and In-Class Activities.

Video Cases
A unique series of 22 marketing video cases includes new videos featuring Fallon Worldwide, Cascade Maverik, IBM, Toyota, Justin's and Body Glove.

In-Class Activities
Chapter-specific in-class activities for today's students who learn from active, participative experiences.

PowerPoint Slides
Media-enhanced and hyperlinked slides enable engaging and interesting classroom discussions.

Digital In-Class Activities
Digital In-Class Activities focus on the use of Web resources and the marketing data they can provide students.

Connect, LearnSmart, and SmartBook
The unique content platform delivering powerful technical resources and adaptive learning solutions. Includes new Marketing Analytics Exercises.

Blog
www.kerinmarketing.com
A blog written specifically for use in the classroom! Throughout each term we post new examples of marketing campaigns, along with a classroom discussion and participation guide.

Practice Marketing (Simulation)
Practice Marketing is a 3D, online, multiplayer game that enables students to gain practical experiences in an interactive environment.

Test Builder in Connect

Available within Connect, Test Builder is a Cloud-based tool that enables instructors to format tests that can be printed or administered within an LMS. Test Builder offers a modern, streamlined interface for easy content configuration that matches course needs, without requiring a download.

Test Builder allows you to:

- Access all Test Bank content from a particular title.
- Easily pinpoint the most relevant content through robust filtering options.
- Manipulate the order of questions or scramble questions and/or answers.
- Pin questions to a specific location within a test.
- Determine your preferred treatment of algorithmic questions.
- Choose the layout and spacing.
- Add instructions and configure default settings.

Test Builder provides a secure interface for better protection of content and allows for just-in-time updates to flow directly into assessments.

Tegrity: Lectures 24/7

Tegrity in Connect is a tool that makes class time available 24/7 by automatically capturing every lecture. With a simple one-click start-and-stop process, you capture all computer screens and corresponding audio in a format that is easy to search, frame by frame. Students can replay any part of any class with easy-to-use, browser-based viewing on a PC, Mac, iPod, or other mobile device.

Educators know that the more students can see, hear, and experience class resources, the better they learn. In fact, studies prove it. Tegrity's unique search feature helps students efficiently find what they need, when they need it, across an entire semester of class recordings. Help turn your students' study time into learning moments immediately supported by your lecture. With Tegrity, you also increase intent listening and class participation by easing students' concerns about note-taking. Using Tegrity in Connect will make it more likely you will see students' faces, not the tops of their heads.

Practice Marketing

Practice Marketing is a 3D, online, single or multiplayer game that helps students apply the four Ps by taking on the role of marketing manager for a backpack company. By playing the game individually and/or in teams, students come to understand how their decisions and elements of the marketing mix affect one another. Practice Marketing is easy to use, fully mobile, and provides an interactive alternative to marketing plan projects. Log in to mhpractice.com with your Connect credentials to access a demo, or contact your local McGraw-Hill representative for more details.

Marketing Mini Sims—Now Assignable within Connect!

Marketing Mini Sims are building-block sims based on our full Practice Marketing simulation that require students to take on the role of a marketing decision maker for a backpack manufacturing company. Each of the nine Mini Sims focuses on one aspect of the marketing mix and serves to both reinforce the understanding of key concepts as well as allow students to make business decisions.

To view a demonstration video and/or see a list of available simulations, please visit the McGraw-Hill Marketing Discipline Landing page at http://bit.ly/MHEmarketing

Acknowledgments

To ensure continuous improvement of our textbook and supplements we have utilized an extensive review and development process for each of our past editions. Building on that history, the *Marketing*, 15th edition development process included several phases of evaluation and a variety of stakeholder audiences (e.g., students, instructors, etc.).

Reviewers who were vital in the changes that were made to the 15th and previous editions of *Marketing* and its supplements include:

A. Diane Barlar
Abe Qastin
Abhay Shah
Abhi Biswas
Abhik Roy
Adrienne Hinds
Ahmed Maamoun
Al Holden
Alan Bush
Alexander Edsel
Alicia Revely
Allan Palmer
Allen Smith
Amy Frank
Anand Kumar
Andrei Strijnev
Andrew Dartt
Andrew Thacker
Andy Aylesworth
Angela Stanton
Anil Pandya
Ann Kuzma
Ann Little
Ann Lucht
Ann Veeck
Annette George
Anthony Koh
Anthony R. Fruzzetti
Aysen Bakir
Barbara Evans
Barbara Ribbens
Barnett Greenberg
Barry Bunn
Bashar Gammoh
Beibei Dong
Ben Oumlil
Beth Deinert
Bill Curtis
Bill Murphy
Bill Peterson
Blaise Waguespack Jr.
Bob Dahlstrom
Bob Dwyer
Bob E. Smiley
Bob McMillen
Bob Newberry
Brent Cunningham
Brian Kinard
Brian Murray
Bronis J. Verhage
Bruce Brown
Bruce Chadbourne
Bruce Ramsey
Bruce Robertson
Bryan Hayes
Carl Obermiller
Carmen Powers
Carmina Cavazos
Carol Bienstock
Carol M. Motley
Carolyn Massiah
Casey Donoho
Catherine Campbell
Cathie Rich-Duval
Cathleen H. Behan
Cathleen Hohner
Cecil Leonard
Cesar Maloles
Charla Mathwick
Charles Bodkin
Charles Ford
Charles Schewe
Cheryl Stansfield
Chiranjeev Kohli
Chris Anicich
Chris Ratcliffe
Christie Amato
Christine Lai
Christopher Blocker
Christopher Kondo
Christopher Ziemnowicz
Chuck Pickett
Cindy Leverenz
Clare Comm
Clark Compton
Clay Rasmussen
Clint Tankersley
Clyde Rupert
Connie Bateman
Corinne Asher
Craig Stacey
Cristanna Cook
Cydney Johnson
Dan Darrow
Dan Goebel
Dan Sherrel
Dan Toy
Daniel Butler
Daniel Rajaratnam
Darrell Goudge
Dave Olson
David Erickson
David Gerth
David J. Burns
David Jamison
David Kuhlmeier
David Smith
David Terry Paul
Deana Ray
Deb Jansky
Debbie Coleman
Debra Laverie
Deepa Pillai
Dennis Pappas
Diana Joy Colarusso
Diane Dowdell
Diane T. McCrohan
Don Weinrauch
Donald Chang
Donald F. Mulvihill

Donald Fuller
Donald G. Norris
Donald Hoffer
Donald Larson
Donald R. Jackson
Donald V. Harper
Donna Wertalik
Doris M. Shaw
Dotty Harpool
Douglas Kornemann
Duncan G. LaBay
Eberhard Scheuling
Ed Gonsalves
Ed Laube
Ed McLaughlin
Eddie V. Easley
Edna Ragins
Edwin Nelson
Elaine Notarantonio
Eldon L. Little
Elena Martinez
Elizabeth R. Flynn
Ellen Benowitz
Eric Ecklund
Eric Newman
Eric Shaw
Erin Baca Blaugrund
Erin Cavusgil
Erin Wilkinson
Ernan Haruvy
Eugene Flynn
Farrokh Moshiri
Fekri Meziou
Frances Depaul
Francis DeFea
Francisco Coronel
Frank A. Chiaverini
Fred Honerkamp
Fred Hurvitz
Fred Morgan
Fred Trawick
Gail M. Zank
Gary Carson
Gary F. McKinnon
Gary Law
Gary Poorman
Gary Tucker
George Kelley
George Miaoulis
George Young
Gerald O. Cavallo
Gerard Athaide
Gerald Waddle
Glen Brodowsky
Glen Gelderloos
Godwin Ariguzo
Gonca Soysal
Gordon Mosley
Greg Kitzmiller
Guy Lochiatto
Harlan Wallingford
Harold Lucius
Harold S. Sekiguchi
Havva Jale Meric
Heidi Rottier
Heikki Rinne
Helen Koons
Herbert A. Miller
Herbert Katzenstein
Howard Combs
Hsin-Min Tong
Hugh Daubek
Imran Khan
Irene Dickey
Irene Lange
Ismet Anitsal
J. Ford Laumer
Jacqueline Karen
Jacqueline Williams
James A. Henley Jr.
James A. Muncy
James C. Johnson
James Cross
James Garry Smith
James Gaubert
James Ginther
James Gould
James H. Barnes
James H. Donnelly
James L. Grimm
James Lollar
James Marco
James McAlexander
James Meszaros
James Munch
James Olver
James P. Rakowski
James V. Spiers
James Wilkins
James Zemanek
Jane Cromartie
Jane Lang
Jane McKay-Nesbitt
Janet Ciccarelli
Janet Murray
Janice Karlen
Janice Taylor
Janice Williams
Jarrett Hudnal
Jason Little
Jay Lambe
Jean Murray
Jean Romeo
Jeanne Munger
Jeff Blodgett
Jeff Finley
Jeffrey W. von Freymann
Jefrey R. Woodall
Jennie Mitchell
Jennifer Nelson
Jerry Peerbolte
Jerry W. Wilson
Jianfeng Jiang
Jim McHugh
Jo Ann McManamy
Joan Williams
Joanne Orabone
Jobie Devinney-Walsh
Joe Cronin
Joe Kim
Joe M. Garza
Joe Puzi
Joe Ricks
Joe Stasio
John Benavidez
John Brandon
John C. Keyt
John Coppett
John Cox
John Finlayson
John Fitzpatrick
John Gaskins
John H. Cunningham
John Kuzma
John Penrose
John Striebich
Jonathan Hibbard
Joseph Belonax
Joseph Defilippe
Joseph Myslivec
Joseph Wisenblit
Juan (Gloria) Meng
Judy Bulin

Judy Foxman
Judy Wagner
Julie Haworth
Julie Sneath
Jun Ma
June E. Parr
Karen Becker-Olsen
Karen Berger
Karen Flaherty
Karen Gore
Karen LeMasters
Kasia Firlej
Katalin Eibel-Spanyi
Kathleen Krentler
Kathleen Stuenkel
Kathleen Williamson
Kathryn Schifferle
Kathy Meyer
Katie Kemp
Kay Chomic
Kaylene Williams
Keith B. Murray
Keith Jones
Keith Murray
Kellie Emrich
Ken Crocker
Ken Fairweather
Ken Herbst
Ken Murdock
Ken Shaw
Kenneth Goodenday
Kenneth Jameson
Kenneth Maricle
Kerri Acheson
Kevin Feldt
Kevin W. Bittle
Kim Montney
Kim Richmond
Kim Sebastiano
Kim Wong
Kimberly D. Smith
Kimberly Grantham
Kin Thompson
Kirti Celly
Koren Borges
Kristen Regine
Kristine Hovsepian
Kristy McManus
Kumar Sarangee
Kunal Sethi
Lan Wu
Larry Borgen
Larry Carter
Larry Feick
Larry Goldstein
Larry Marks
Larry Rottmeyer
Laura Dwyer
Lauren Wright
Lawrence Duke
Lee Meadow
Leigh McAlister
Leon Zurawicki
Leonard Lindenmuth
Leslie A. Goldgehn
Leta Beard
Linda Anglin
Linda M. Delene
Linda Morable
Linda Munilla
Linda N. LaMarca
Linda Rochford
Lindell Phillip Chew
Lisa M. Sciulli
Lisa Siegal
Lisa Simon
Lisa Troy
Lisa Zingaro
Lori Feldman
Lowell E. Crow
Lynn Harris
Lynn Loudenback
Marc Goldberg
Maria McConnell
Maria Randazzo-Nardin
Maria Sanella
Marilyn Lavin
Mark Collins
Mark Weber
Mark Young
Martin Bressler
Martin Decatur
Martin St. John
Marton L. Macchiete
Martyn Kingston
Marva Hunt
Mary Ann McGrath
Mary Beth DeConinck
Mary Conran
Mary Joyce
Mary Schramm
Mary Tripp
Matt Meuter
Max White
Mayukh Dass
Melissa Clark
Melissa Moore
Michael Callow
Michael Drafke
Michael Fowler
Michael Mayo
Michael Peters
Michael Pontikos
Michael R. Luthy
Michael Swenson
Michelle Kunz
Michelle Wetherbee
Mike Hagan
Mike Hyman
Mike Luckett
Milton Pressley
Miriam B. Stamps
Nadia J. Abgrab
Nancy Bloom
Nancy Boykin
Nancy Grassilli
Nanda Kumar
Nathan Himelstein
Neel Das
Nikolai Ostapenko
Norman Smothers
Notis Pagiavlas
Ottilia Voegtli
Pamela Grimm
Pamela Hulen
Parimal Bhagat
Pat Spirou
Patricia Baconride
Patricia Bernson
Patricia Manninen
Paul Dion
Paul Dowling
Paul Jackson
Paul Londrigan
Paul Myer
Peter J. McClure
Philip Kearney
Philip Parron
Philip Shum
Phyllis Fein
Phyllis McGinnis
Poh-Lin Yeoh
Pola B. Gupta

Priscilla G. Aaltonen
Priyali Rajagopal
Rae Caloura
Rajesh Iyer
Rajiv Kashyap
Ram Kesaran
Randall E. Wade
Randy Stuart
Ravi Shanmugam
Raymond Marzilli
Reid Claxton
Renee Foster
Renee Pfeifer-Luckett
Rex Moody
Rhonda Mack
Rhonda Taylor
Richard C. Leventhal
Richard D. Parker
Richard Hansen
Richard Hargrove
Richard J. Lutz
Richard Lapidus
Richard M. Hill
Richard Penn
Rick Sweeney
Rita Dynan
Robert C. Harris
Robert Jones
Robert Lawson
Robert Luke
Robert Morris
Robert S. Welsh
Robert Swerdlow
Robert W. Ruekert
Robert Williams
Robert Witherspoon
Roberta Schultz
Roger McIntyre
Roger W. Egerton
Ron Dougherty
Ron Hasty
Ron Larson
Ron Weston
Ronald A. Feinberg
Ronald Michaels
Rosemary Ramsey
Roy Adler
Roy Klages
Ruth Ann Smith
Ruth Rosales
Ruth Taylor
S. Choi Chan
S. Tamer Cavusgil
Sally Sledge
Samuel E. McNeely
Sanal Mazvancheryl
Sandipan Sen
Sandra Robertson
Sandra Smith
Sandra Young
Sang Choe
Sanjay S. Mehta
Santhi Harvey
Scott Cragin
Scott Swan
Scott Thorne
Shabnam Zanjani
Sheila Wexler
Sherry Cook
Siva Balasubramanian
Soon Hong Min
Srdan Zdravkovic
Stacia Gray
Stan Garfunkel
Stan Scott
Starr F. Schlobohm
Stephen Calcich
Stephen Garrott
Stephen Pirog
Stephen W. Miller
Steve Hertzenberg
Steve Taylor
Steven Engel
Steven Moff
Sudhir Karunakaran
Sue Lewis
Sue McGorry
Sue Umashankar
Suman Basuroy
Sundaram Dorai
Sunder Narayanan
Susan Godar
Susan Peterson
Susan Sieloff
Susan Stanix
Susie Pryor
Suzanne Murray
Sylvia Keyes
Tamara Masters
Teri Root
Terrance Kevin McNamara
Terry Kroeten
Theodore Mitchell
Theresa Flaherty
Thom J. Belich
Thomas Brashear
Thomas L. Trittipo
Thomas M. Bertsch
Thomas Passero
Tim Aurand
Tim Landry
Timothy Donahue
Timothy Reisenwitz
Tina L. Williams
Tino DeMarco
Tom Castle
Tom Deckelman
Tom Marshall
Tom Rossi
Tom Stevenson
Tom Thompson
Tracy Fulce
Vahwere Kavota
Van R. Wood
Vicki Rostedt
Victoria Miller
Vincent P. Taiani
Vladimir Pashkevich
Vonda Powell
Walter Kendall
Wendy Achey
Wendy Wood
Wesley Johnston
William B. Dodds
William Brown
William D. Ash
William Foxx
William G. Browne
William G. Mitchell
William J. Carner
William Motz
William Pertula
William R. Wynd
William Rodgers
William S. Piper
Wilton Lelund
Yi He
Yue Pan
Yunchuan Liu

Thanks are due to many people, including current and past students, marketing educators around the globe, university staff, business journal and periodical authors, company representatives, and marketing professionals of every kind. Their assistance has been essential in our efforts to continue to provide the most comprehensive, up-to-date, and integrated teaching and learning package available. We have been fortunate to have so many people be part of our team! In particular, however, we continue to benefit from the insights and guidance of our long-time friend, colleague, and coauthor, William Rudelius. His contributions to the textbook are truly timeless.

Nancy Harrower of Concordia University, St. Paul, led our efforts on the *Instructor's Manual*, the PowerPoint slides, the In-Class Activities, and the new Digital In-Class Activities. In addition, she provides the content for our blog (kerinmarketing.com). Tia Quinlan-Wilder of the University of Denver was responsible for the Test Bank and Quizzes and the LearnSmart component of our interactive learning package. Erin Steffes of Towson University was responsible for the Connect application exercises and the new Marketing Analytics exercises. All of these professors are exceptional educators and we are very fortunate that they are part of our team. Michael Vessey, our long-time collaborator who recently passed away, also provided assistance in the preparation of materials that are still in use.

Thanks are also due to many other colleagues who contributed to the text, cases, and supplements. They include: Richard Lutz of the University of Florida; Linda Rochford of the University of Minnesota–Duluth; Kevin Upton of the University of Minnesota–Twin Cities; Nancy Nentl of Metropolitan State University; Leslie Kendrick of Johns Hopkins University; Lau Geok Theng of the National University of Singapore; and Leigh McAlister of the University of Texas at Austin. Rick Armstrong of Armstrong Photography, Dan Hundley and George Heck of Token Media, Nick Kaufman and Michelle Morgan of NKP Media, Bruce McLean of World Class Communication Technologies, Paul Fagan of Fagan Productions, Martin Walter of White Room Digital, Scott Bolin of Bolin Marketing, and Andrew Schones of Pure Imagination produced the videos.

Many businesspeople also provided substantial assistance by making available information that appears in the text, videos, and supplements—much of it for the first time in college materials. Thanks are due to Andy Rhode, Charlie Wolff, Jordan Hoffarber, Tiffany Luong, and Stacy Runkel of Fallon Worldwide; Tim Ellsworth, Debbie Errante, and Laura Edward of Cascade Maverik; Ann Rubin, Teresa Yoo, and Kathleen Cremmins of IBM; Jana Hartline, Rommel Momen, Joanie Swearingen, and Amy Ulloa of Toyota; Justin Gold and Mike Guanella of Justin's; Lisa Selk of CytoSport; Jeff Ettinger of Hormel; Russ Lesser, Billy Meistrell, Nick Meistrell, and Jenna Meistrell of Body Glove; Peter Maule of Marquee Brands; Daniel Jasper, Jill Renslow, and Sarah Schmidt of Mall of America; Mike Pohl of ACES Flight Simulation; Chris Klein, Jaime Cardenas, Casey Leppanen, Heather Peace, and Lori Nevares of LA Galaxy; Ian Wolfman and Jana Boone of meplusyou; David Ford and Don Rylander of Ford Consulting Group; Mark Rehborg of Tony's Pizza; Vivian Callaway, Sandy Proctor, and Anna Stoesz of General Mills; David Windorski, Tom Barnidge, and Erica Schiebel of 3M; Nicholas Skally, Jeremy Stonier, and Joe Olivas of Prince Sports; Brian Niccol of Pizza Hut; Tom Cassady of JCPenney, Inc.; Charles Besio of the Sewell Automotive Group, Inc.; Lindsey Smith of GE Healthcare; Beverly Roberts of the U.S. Census Bureau; Sheryl Adkins-Green of Mary Kay, Inc.; Mattison Crowe of Seven Cycles, Inc.; Alisa Allen, Kirk Hodgdon, Patrick Hodgdon, and Nick Naumann of Altus Marketing and Business Development; and Nelson Ng from Dundas Data Visualization, Inc.

Those who provided the resources for use in the *Marketing*, 15th edition textbook, *Instructor's Manual*, and/or PowerPoint presentations include: Todd Walker and Jean Golden of Million Dollar Idea; Karen Cohick of Susan G. Komen for the Cure; Liz Stewart of Ben & Jerry's; John Formella and Patricia Lipari of Kodak; Erica Schiebel of 3M; Joe Diliberti of *Consumer Reports;* Patricia Breman of Strategic Business Insights (VALS); Brian Nielsen of the Nielsen Company; David Walonick of StatPac; Mark Rehborg of Schwan's Consumer Brands (Tony's Pizza); Jennifer Olson of Experian Simmons; Kitty Munger and Mary Wykoff of Wendy's; Mark Heller of RetailSails;

Nicky Hutcheon of ZenithOptimedia; Amy Thompson and Jennifer Allison of Dell, Inc.; Adriana Carlton of Walmart and Rick Hill of Bernstein-Rein Advertising (Walmart); Janine Bolin of Saks, Inc.; Dr. Yory Wurmser of the Data and Marketing Association; and Elizabeth Clendenin of Unilever (Caress).

We also want to thank the following people who generously provided assistance with our *Marketing*, 15th edition In-Class Activities (ICAs) and associated PowerPoint presentations: Mitch Forster and Carla Silveira of Ghirardelli Chocolate Company; Karolyn Warfel and Betsy Boyer of Woodstream Corp. (Victor Pest); Leonard Fuld of Fuld & Co.; Maggie Jantzen of Starbucks Coffee Company; Michelle Green and Victoria Glazier of the U.S. Census Bureau; Lisa Castaldo of Pepsi; Muffie Taggert of General Mills; Robert M. McMath, formerly of NewProductWorks; Greg Rodriguez; Jeremy Tucker, Julia Wells, and Lisa Cone of Frito-Lay (Doritos); Susan Carroll and Bob Robinson of Apple, Inc.; Willard Oberton of Fastenal Company; Scott Wosniak and Jennifer Arnold of Toro; Kim Eskro of Fallon Worldwide (Gold'n Plump); Robin Grayson of TBWA/Chiat/Day (Apple); Katie Kramer of Valassis Communications, Inc. (Nutella/Advil); Triestina Greco of Nutella/Ferrero; Tim Stauber of Wyeth Consumer Healthcare (Advil); and Yvonne Pendleton and Lucille Storms of Mary Kay.

Staff support from the Southern Methodist University and the University of Denver was essential. We gratefully acknowledge the help of Jeanne Milazzo and Gabriela Barcenas for their many contributions.

Checking countless details related to layout, graphics, and photos, and managing last-minute text changes is essential for a sound and accurate textbook. This also involves coordinating activities of authors, designers, editors, compositors, and production specialists. Christine Vaughan, our lead content project manager, of McGraw-Hill Education's production staff provided the necessary oversight and attention to detail while retaining an extraordinary level of professionalism, often under tight deadlines. We are very fortunate that Christine was part of our team. Thank you again!

Finally, we acknowledge the professional efforts of the McGraw-Hill Education staff. Completion of our book and its many supplements required the attention and commitment of many editorial, production, marketing, and research personnel. Our McGraw-Hill team included Terri Schiesl, Meredith Fossel, Nicole Young, Kelly Pekelder, Danielle Clement, Susan Culbertson, Matt Diamond, Carrie Burger, and many others. In addition, we relied on David Tietz for constant attention regarding the photo elements of the text, and Claire Hunter for management of the details of the online authoring system. Handling the countless details of our text, supplement, and support technologies has become an incredibly complex challenge. We thank all these people for their efforts!

Roger A. Kerin
Steven W. Hartley

BRIEF CONTENTS

DETAILED CONTENTS

Part 1 Initiating the Marketing Process

John Minchillo/AP Images

Hatim Kaghat/AFP/Getty Images

Justin Sullivan/Getty Images

Richard Ulreich/ZUMA Press/Newscom

Part 2 Understanding Buyers and Markets

Whisson/Jordan/Getty Images

Source: JCPenney

Andrey Arkusha/Shutterstock

Part 3 Targeting Marketing Opportunities

Hilch/Shutterstock

Scott Olson/Getty Images

Part 4 Satisfying Marketing Opportunities

Shutterstock/tanuha2001

J. Meric/Getty Images

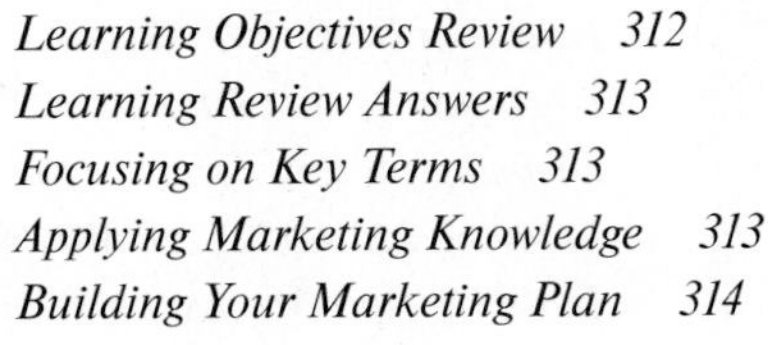

imageBROKER/Alamy Stock Photo

Art Konovalov/Shutterstock

Daniilantiq/Getty Images

JHVEPhoto/Shutterstock

MariaX/Shutterstock

calimedia/Shutterstock

Theo Wargo/Getty Images

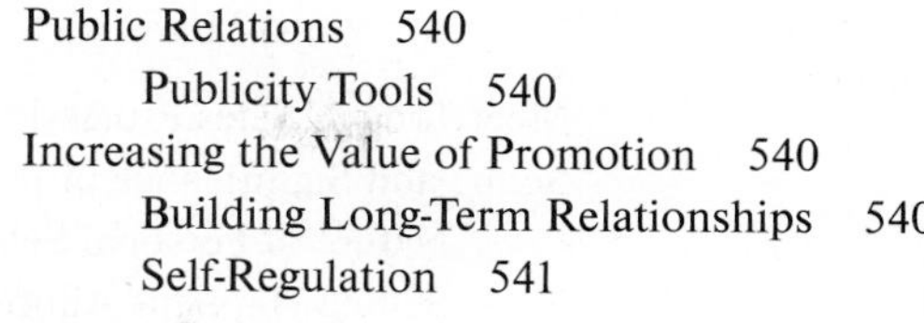

medvedsky.kz/Shutterstock

Hillsman Stuart Jackson

McGraw-Hill Education

Part 5 Appendices

MARKETING

Creating Customer Relationships and Value through Marketing

LEARNING OBJECTIVES

After reading this chapter you should be able to:

LO 1-1 Define marketing and identify the diverse factors that influence marketing actions.

LO 1-2 Explain how marketing discovers and satisfies consumer needs.

LO 1-3 Distinguish between marketing mix factors and environmental forces.

LO 1-4 Explain how organizations build strong customer relationships and customer value through marketing.

LO 1-5 Describe the characteristics of a market orientation.

At Chobani, Marketing Is All Natural!

Consumers around the globe are demanding healthy products made with natural ingredients. If you are one of those consumers you may have tried Chobani yogurt, a product created to offer you a good value through its nutritious and natural recipes!

The Chobani products you've seen on the shelves are the result of an extraordinary marketing success story. Just a few years ago the U.S. yogurt market was dominated by Dannon and Yoplait. Then Hamdi Ulukaya created Chobani with less sugar and more protein to better match the changing tastes of American consumers. Today Chobani has more than $2 billion in annual sales and was recently recognized as one of the most innovative companies in the world "for stirring it up in the grocery store."[1]

What is the secret to Chobani's success? Read on to hear the rest of the story!

Creating an Exceptional Product

The Chobani website proclaims that one of its guiding values is "better food for more people."[2] The process starts with milk from local sources and then uses a straining procedure that makes the yogurt extra thick and gives it twice as much protein. Finally, only real fruit and natural sweeteners are added. The recipe is the result of a commitment to a high-quality product. "I was very picky. It took us 18 months to get the recipe right. I knew I had only one shot, and it had to be perfect," says Ulukaya. To produce the yogurt, Ulukaya purchased a closed dairy in a small town in New York using a Small Business Administration loan. He remodeled the facility using sustainability as a theme to reflect a focus on environment and community.[3]

Connecting with Customers

Chobani had little money for traditional advertising, so it relied on positive word of mouth, with one happy customer telling another about the new style of yogurt. In addition, Chobani used social media such as Twitter and Facebook to connect with consumers and a mobile yogurt food truck called the CHOmobile to hand out free samples to encourage consumers to try Chobani's Greek Yogurt for the first time. One of Chobani's biggest breakthroughs in gaining public awareness was its sponsorship of the U.S. Olympic and Paralympic Teams.

Chobani also pushed for distribution in major grocery chains, rather than smaller niche stores, and encouraged placement of the product in the main dairy cases of the stores, not the specialty or health food sections. Ulukaya was convinced that Americans would really like Greek yogurt if they tried it and that they would try it if they heard about it and could find it easily in their grocery store.[4]

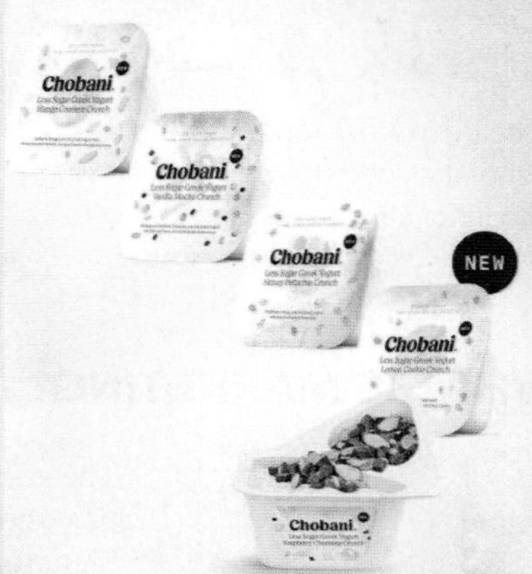

Here's to less.
NEW
Introducing Chobani® Less Sugar Greek Yogurt Crunch*
Only natural ingredients.
No artificial sweeteners.

Source: Chobani, LLC

Chobani Today

Chobani continues to monitor changing consumer tastes and offers new products to accommodate them. For example, the company recently introduced a non-dairy, coconut-based yogurt to address the growing consumer interest in plant-based food and a children's line of shakes, pouches, tubes, and bowls called Chobani Gimmies™. The products are designed for new and existing consumers and for new eating occasions.

VIDEO 1-1
Chobani Hungry Bear Ad
kerin.tv/15e/v1-1

One way Chobani stays in touch with consumer interests is through its yogurt cafés in New York's SoHo and Tribeca neighborhoods and in Houston. New ideas are continually tested on the

Located in New York City, Chobani SoHo is the brand's first-of-its-kind retail concept, serving yogurt creations with innovative toppings.
Diane Bondareff/Invision for Chobani/AP Images

menu and the feedback has been so useful that Chobani plans to open similar outlets in Los Angeles, San Francisco, Chicago, and other U.S. cities. Chobani also created the Chobani Food Incubator, which is designed to invest in and cultivate ideas from emerging food entrepreneurs.

Today, Chobani boasts a 54 percent market share of the Greek yogurt segment, which makes up almost 40 percent of the $8.5 billion yogurt market. Chobani advertising, such as the "Wonderful World of Less," "Believe in Food," "No Bad Stuff," and "Love This Life" campaigns, are featured on the Chobani YouTube channel. The company's success has even led to a Super Bowl ad featuring a 1,400-pound bear in search of a healthy snack![5]

Chobani, Marketing, and You

Will Hamdi Ulukaya and his Chobani Greek Yogurt continue this fantastic success story—especially with the recent appearance of competing Greek yogurts from Yoplait, Dannon, Zoi, The Greek Gods, and Fage? For Ulukaya, one key factor will be how well Chobani understands and uses marketing—the subject of this book.

WHAT IS MARKETING?

The good news is that you are already a marketing expert! You perform many marketing activities and make marketing-related decisions every day. For example, would you sell more LG Signature 65-inch 4K OLED Rollable TVs at $24,999 or $7,999? You answered $7,999, right? So your experience in shopping gives you some expertise in marketing. As a consumer, you've been involved in thousands of marketing decisions, mostly on the buying and not the selling side. But to test your expertise, answer the "marketing expert" questions posed in Figure 1–1. You'll find the answers within the next several pages.

The bad news is that good marketing isn't always easy. That's why every year thousands of new products fail in the marketplace and then quietly slide into oblivion.

Marketing and Your Career

Marketing affects all individuals, all organizations, all industries, and all countries. This book seeks to teach you marketing concepts, often by having you actually "do marketing"—by putting

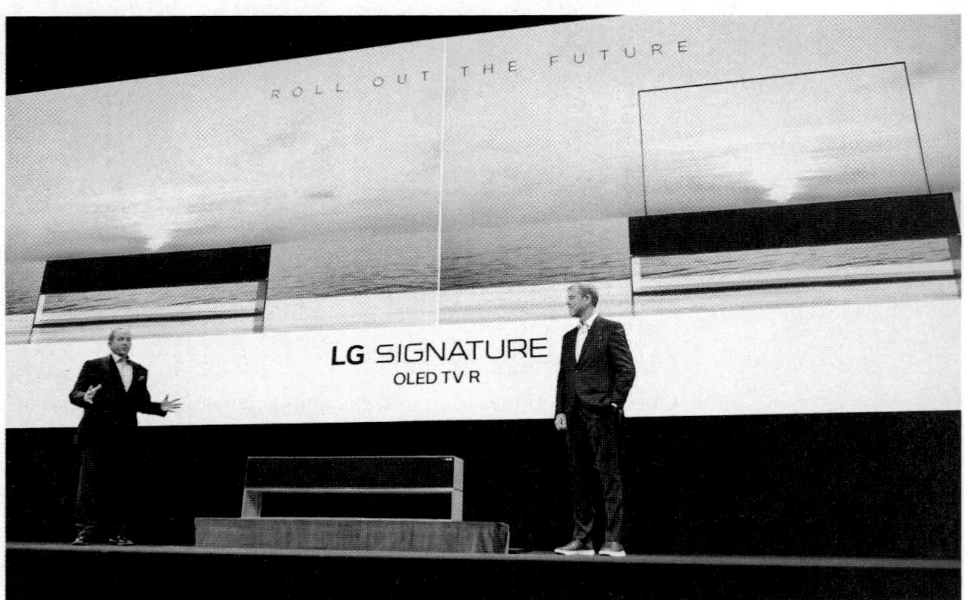

Are you a marketing expert? If so, what would you pay for this cutting-edge TV?
Robyn Beck/AFP/Getty Images

FIGURE 1–1
The see-if-you're-really-a-marketing-expert test.

Answer the questions below. The correct answers are given later in the chapter.

1. What is the name of the zero-calorie, no-sugar, naturally sweetened Coke beverage that Coca-Cola has released in some markets? (a) Coca-Cola Life, (b) Coke Zero Sugar, (c) Diet Coke, (d) Coca-Cola Stevia.

2. True or False: The 65-year lifetime value of a loyal auto repair center customer is $147,000.

3. To be socially responsible Patagonia encourages its customers to do which of the following with its products? (a) repair, (b) trade, (c) recycle, (d) all three.

The chief executive officer of Tesla and SpaceX began building businesses shortly after graduating from college.
John Raoux/AP Images

you in the shoes of a marketing manager facing actual marketing decisions. The book also shows marketing's many applications and how it affects our lives. This knowledge should make you a better consumer and enable you to be a more informed citizen, and it may even help you in your career planning.

Perhaps your future will involve doing sales and marketing for a large organization. Working for a well-known company—Apple, Ford, Facebook, or General Mills—can be personally satisfying and financially rewarding, and you may gain special respect from your friends.

Start-ups and small businesses also offer marketing careers. Small businesses are the source of the majority of new U.S. jobs. So you might become your own boss by being an entrepreneur and starting your own business.

Shortly after leaving Stanford, Elon Musk, for example, started and sold a web software company called Zip2. With the proceeds from that business he started another business which merged with another and became PayPal. When PayPal was purchased by eBay, Musk founded another venture called SpaceX, which develops and manufactures space launch vehicles and hopes to send a mission to Mars by 2024. Since those initial business start-ups, Musk also started the electric car company Tesla and a solar power company called SolarCity. In addition, he has started a design competition for a high-speed transportation system called Hyperloop, a not-for-profit artificial intelligence company called OpenAI, a neurotechnology company called Neuralink, and a tunnel construction firm called The Boring Company. Perhaps your interest in marketing will lead to new business successes like Musk's![6]

LO 1-1
Define marketing and identify the diverse factors that influence marketing actions.

Marketing: Delivering Value to Customers

The American Marketing Association represents individuals and organizations involved in the development and practice of marketing worldwide. It defines **marketing** as the activity, set of institutions, and processes for creating, communicating, delivering, and exchanging offerings that have value for customers, clients, partners, and society at large.[7] This definition shows that marketing is far more than simply advertising or personal selling. It stresses the need to deliver genuine value in the offerings of goods, services, and ideas marketed to customers. Also, notice that an organization's marketing activities should also create value for its partners and for society.

To serve both buyers and sellers, marketing seeks (1) to discover the needs and wants of prospective customers and (2) to satisfy them. These prospective customers include both individuals, buying for themselves and their households, and organizations, buying for their own use (such as manufacturers) or for resale (such as wholesalers and retailers). The key to

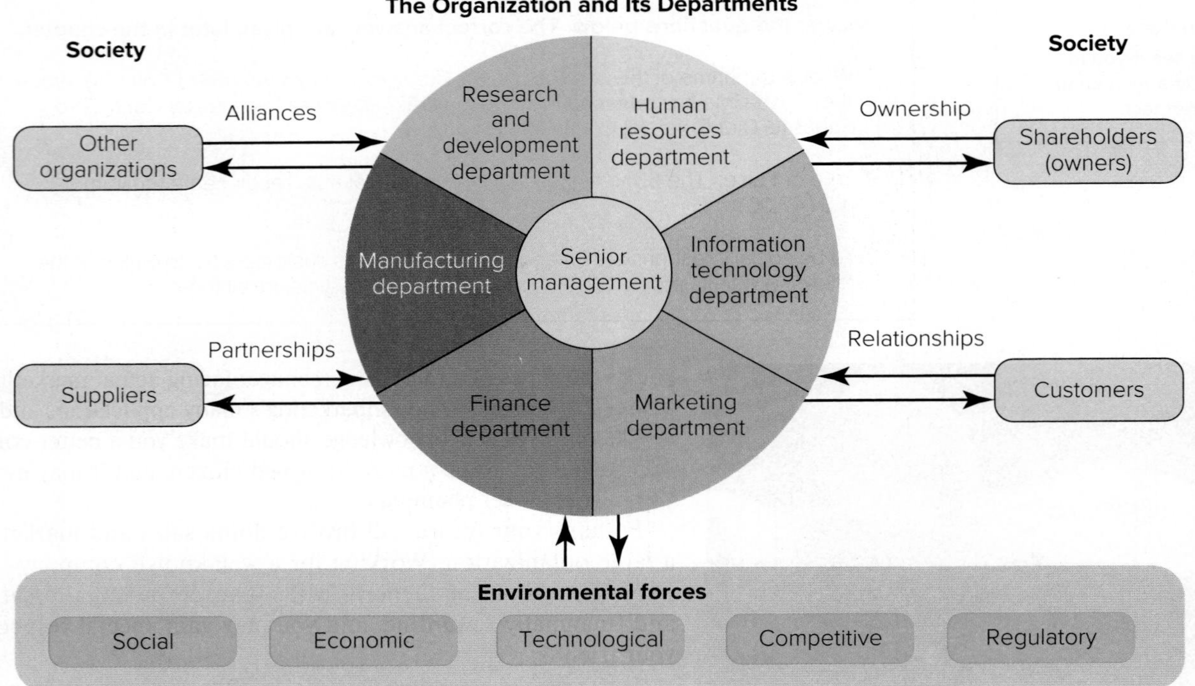

FIGURE 1–2
A marketing department relates to many people, organizations, and forces. Note that the marketing department both *shapes* and *is shaped by* its relationship with these internal and external groups.

achieving these two objectives is the idea of **exchange**, which is the trade of things of value between a buyer and a seller so that each is better off after the trade.[8]

The Diverse Elements Influencing Marketing Actions

Although an organization's marketing activity focuses on assessing and satisfying consumer needs, countless other people, groups, and forces interact to shape the nature of its actions (see Figure 1–2). Foremost is the organization itself, whose mission and objectives determine what business it is in and what goals it seeks. Within the organization, management is responsible for establishing these goals. The marketing department works closely with a network of other departments and employees to help provide the customer-satisfying products required for the organization to survive and prosper.

Figure 1–2 also shows the key people, groups, and forces outside the organization that influence its marketing activities. The marketing department is responsible for facilitating relationships, partnerships, and alliances with the organization's customers, its shareholders (or often representatives of nonprofit organizations), its suppliers, and other organizations. Environmental forces involving social, economic, technological, competitive, and regulatory considerations also shape an organization's marketing actions. Finally, an organization's marketing decisions are affected by and, in turn, often have an important impact on society as a whole.

The organization must strike a balance among the sometimes differing interests of these groups. For example, it is not possible to simultaneously provide the lowest-priced and highest-quality products to customers and pay the highest prices to suppliers, the highest wages to employees, and the maximum dividends to shareholders.

What Is Needed for Marketing to Occur

For marketing to occur, at least four factors are required: (1) two or more parties (individuals or organizations) with unsatisfied needs, (2) a desire and ability on their part to have their needs satisfied, (3) a way for the parties to communicate, and (4) something to exchange.

MIX & MATCH
CHOOSE ANY 2 OR MORE
FOR $5.99 EACH
OVEN BAKED SUBS
LOADED CHEESY BREAD
SPINACH & FETTA
PEPPERONI
BACON
JALAPENO
SPECIALTY CHICKEN
CLASSIC HOT BUFFALO
SWEET BBQ BACON
SPICY JALAPENO PINEAPPLE
CRISPY BACON & TOMATO
MEDIUM PEPPERONI PIZZA

Marketing doesn't happen in a vacuum. The text describes the four factors needed to buy a product from Domino's Mix & Match menu.
Source: Domino's IP Holder LLC

Two or More Parties with Unsatisfied Needs Suppose you've developed an unmet need—a desire for a late-night meal after studying for an exam—but you don't yet know that Domino's has a location in your area. Also unknown to you is that Domino's has a special "mix & match" offer for any two or more of its menu items, just waiting to be ordered and picked up or delivered. This is an example of two parties with unmet needs: you, desiring a meal, and your local Domino's owner, needing someone to place an order.

Desire and Ability to Satisfy These Needs Both you and the Domino's owner want to satisfy these unmet needs. Furthermore, you have the money to pay for a purchase and the time to place an order. The Domino's owner has the desire to sell its products but also the ability to do so since the items are easily made and delivered to (or picked up by) you.

A Way for the Parties to Communicate The marketing transaction of purchasing a Domino's pizza or one of its other products will never occur unless you are aware the product exists and you know how to make a purchase (at a Domino's location, on Dominos.com, or via a store phone number). Similarly, Domino's won't be able to sell its products unless there's a market of potential buyers nearby. When you receive a coupon on your phone or drive by and see the Domino's store location, this communication barrier between you (the buyer) and the Domino's owner (the seller) is overcome.

Something to Exchange Marketing occurs when the transaction takes place and both the buyer and seller exchange something of value. In this case, you exchange your money ($5.99) for each item ordered from Domino's Mix & Match menu. Both you and the Domino's owner have gained and also given up something, but you are both better off because each of you has satisfied the other's unmet needs. You have the opportunity to eat Domino's food items to satisfy your hunger, but you gave up some money to do so; the Domino's owner gave up the pizza, salad, and other items but received money, which will help the owner remain in business. The ethical and regulatory foundations of this exchange process are central to marketing and are discussed in Chapter 4.

LEARNING REVIEW

1-1. What is marketing?

1-2. Marketing focuses on __________ and __________ consumer needs.

1-3. What four factors are needed for marketing to occur?

HOW MARKETING DISCOVERS AND SATISFIES CONSUMER NEEDS

LO 1-2
Explain how marketing discovers and satisfies consumer needs.

The importance of discovering and satisfying consumer needs in order to develop and offer successful products is so critical to understanding marketing that we look at each of these two steps in detail next. Let's start by asking you to analyze the following three products.

Discovering Consumer Needs

The first objective in marketing is discovering the needs of prospective customers. Marketers often use customer surveys, concept tests, and other forms of marketing research (discussed

For these three products, identify (1) what benefits the product provides buyers and (2) what factors or "showstoppers" might doom the product in the marketplace. Answers are discussed in the text.

(Left): Sean Gallup/Getty Images; (Center): Source: The Coca-Cola Company; (Right): Source: Universal Yums LLC

Smart glasses.

A no-sugar soda.

A subscription service for snacks.

in detail in Chapter 8) to better understand customer ideas. Many firms also use "crowdsourcing" or "innovation tournaments" to solicit and evaluate ideas from customers. At LEGO Group, for example, ideas that are submitted to LEGO Ideas (www.ideas.lego.com) and receive 10,000 votes from site visitors are considered for possible addition to the product line. LEGO Group products that were discovered through the website (www.ideas.lego.com) include its Voltron robot, its Women of NASA set, its *Big Bang Theory* model, and a set based on the *Minecraft* video game! Sometimes, however, customers may not know or be able to describe what they need and want. Smartphones, connected homes, and electric cars are all examples of this, in which case an accurate long-term prediction of consumer needs is essential.[9]

The Challenge: Meeting Consumer Needs with New Products

While marketers are improving the ways they can generate new product ideas, experts estimate that it takes 3,000 raw ideas to generate one commercial success. Market intelligence agency Mintel estimates that 38,000 new products are introduced worldwide each month. In addition, studies of new-product launches indicate that about 40 percent of the products fail. Robert M. McMath, who has studied more than 110,000 new-product launches, has two key suggestions: (1) focus on what the customer benefit is, and (2) learn from past mistakes.[10]

The solution to preventing product failures seems embarrassingly obvious. First, find out what consumers need and want. Second, produce what they need and want, and don't produce what they don't need and want. The three products shown previously illustrate just how difficult it is to achieve new-product success, a topic covered in more detail in Chapter 10.

Without reading further, think about the potential benefits to customers and possible "showstoppers"—factors that might doom the product—for each of the three products pictured. Some of the products may come out of your past, and others may be on your horizon. Here's a quick analysis of the three products:

VIDEO 1-2
Google Glass Enterprise Edition
kerin.tv/15e/v1-2

VIDEO 1-3
Coca-Cola Stevia Ad
kerin.tv/15e/v1-3

- *Smart Glasses.* Several years ago Google launched a brand of smart glasses called Google Glass. The new product was head-mounted and similar in appearance to a pair of glasses. In addition, though, the glasses had Internet capabilities, a camera, phone, speaker, microphone, touchpad, and a heads-up display. While the product was popular among technology enthusiasts it did not attract a mass market. Showstoppers included its $1,500 price tag, a general perception that it looked "nerdy," and concerns that wearing the device might violate privacy rights. Google discontinued the product, although it has recently reintroduced the concept as an Enterprise Edition for businesses, and other brands such as Focals and Vuzix are offering models that are trying to attract the consumer market![11]
- *Coca-Cola Stevia No Sugar.* As consumer preferences have shifted, beverage companies have expanded their offerings to include drinks with less sugar. Soda producers, for example, have offered new products such as Pepsi True and Coca-Cola Life which

Studying late at night for an exam and being hungry, you decide to eat a Cool Mint Chocolate Clif Bar. Is this a need or a want? The text discusses the role of marketing in influencing decisions like this one.

Evelyn Nicole Kirksey/McGraw-Hill Education

are sweetened with sugar and stevia leaf extract. New products are also being developed as the U.S. Food & Drug Administration's new Nutrition Facts label requirements (effective 2020) provide more information about added sugars. Coca-Cola, for example, is testing Coca-Cola Stevia which will be sweetened only with the natural ingredient stevia, rather than the aspartame used in Coke Zero Sugar. A potential showstopper: In the past consumers reported that products with stevia sweetener had a bitter aftertaste. Will Coca-Cola Stevia be different? As always, as a consumer you will be the judge![12]

- *Universal Yums Subscription.* Approximately 5 million consumers buy brands through subscription services today. Universal Yums hopes to appeal to customers with a selection of snacks from a different country every month. Each delivery also includes a guidebook with trivia, games, and recipes about that month's snacks. The service is available in 3-, 6-, or 12-month options and three sizes. Past boxes have included snacks from Italy, Germany, Thailand, Brazil, the Netherlands, and many other countries! What are potential showstoppers? First, the competition is growing–there are already 400–600 subscription box services in the United States. Second, consumers may tire of receiving new products each month, particularly if they find several brands that meet their needs.[13]

Firms spend billions of dollars annually on marketing and technical research that significantly reduces, but doesn't eliminate, new-product failure. So meeting the changing needs of consumers is a continuing challenge for firms around the world.

Consumer Needs and Consumer Wants Should marketing try to satisfy consumer needs or consumer wants? Marketing tries to do both. Heated debates rage over this question, fueled by the definitions of needs and wants and the amount of freedom given to prospective customers to make their own buying decisions.

A *need* occurs when a person feels deprived of basic necessities such as food, clothing, and shelter. A *want* is a need that is shaped by a person's knowledge, culture, and personality. So if you feel hungry, you have developed a basic need and desire to eat something. Let's say you then want to eat a Cool Mint Chocolate Clif Bar because, based on your past experience, you know it will satisfy your hunger need. Effective marketing, in the form of creating an awareness of good products at fair prices and convenient locations, can clearly shape a person's wants.

Certainly, marketing tries to influence what we buy. A question then arises: At what point do we want government and society to step in to protect consumers? Most consumers would say they want government to protect them from harmful drugs and unsafe cars but not from candy bars and soft drinks. To protect college students, should government restrict their use of credit cards?[14] Such questions have no clear-cut answers, which is why legal and ethical issues are central to marketing. Because even psychologists and economists still debate the exact meanings of *need* and *want*, we shall use the terms interchangeably throughout the book.

As shown on the left side of Figure 1-3 on the next page, discovering needs involves looking carefully at prospective customers, whether they are children buying M&M's candy, college students buying Chobani Greek Yogurt, or firms buying Xerox color copiers. A principal activity of a firm's marketing department is to scrutinize its consumers to understand what they need and want and the forces that shape those needs and wants.

What a Market Is Potential consumers make up a **market**, which is people with both the desire and the ability to buy a specific offering. All markets ultimately are people. Even when we say a firm bought a Xerox copier, we mean one or several people in the firm decided to buy it. People who are aware of their unmet needs may have the desire to buy the product, but that alone isn't sufficient. People must also have the ability to buy, such as the authority, time, and money. People may even "buy" an idea that results in an action, such as having their blood pressure checked annually or switching to a reusable water bottle.

FIGURE 1–3
Marketing seeks first to discover consumer needs through extensive research. It then seeks to satisfy those needs by successfully implementing a marketing program possessing the right combination of the marketing mix—the four Ps.

LO 1-3
Distinguish between marketing mix factors and environmental forces.

Satisfying Consumer Needs

Marketing doesn't stop with the discovery of consumer needs. Because the organization obviously can't satisfy all consumer needs, it must concentrate its efforts on certain needs of a specific group of potential consumers. This is the **target market**—one or more specific groups of potential consumers toward which an organization directs its marketing program.

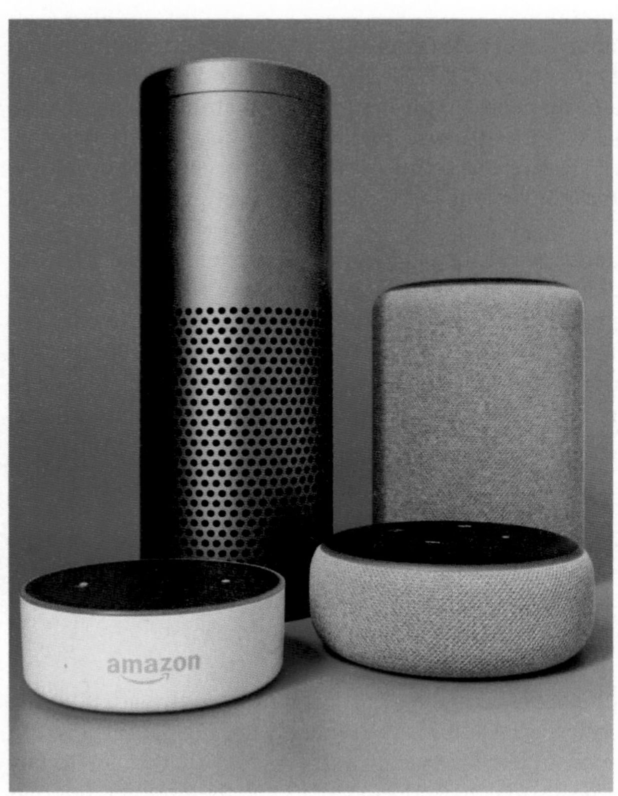

Firms can affect some environmental forces with breakthrough products such as AI assistants.
Malcolm Haines/Alamy Stock Photo

The Four Ps: Controllable Marketing Mix Factors Having selected its target market consumers, the firm must take steps to satisfy their needs, as shown on the right side of Figure 1-3. Someone in the organization's marketing department, often the marketing manager, must develop a complete marketing program to reach consumers by using a combination of four elements, often called "the four Ps"—a useful shorthand reference to them first published by Professor E. Jerome McCarthy:[15]

- *Product.* A good, service, or idea to satisfy the consumer's needs.
- *Price.* What is exchanged for the product.
- *Promotion.* A means of communication between the seller and buyer.
- *Place.* A means of getting the product to the consumer.

We'll define each of the four Ps more carefully later in the book, but for now it's important to remember that they are the elements of the **marketing mix**. These four elements are the controllable factors—product, price, promotion, and place—that can be used by the marketing manager to solve a marketing problem. For example, when a company puts a product on sale, it is changing one element of the marketing mix—namely, the price. The marketing mix elements are called *controllable factors* because they are under the control of the marketing department in an organization. Managing the marketing mix allows an organization to create a cluster of benefits that satisfies customers' needs.[16]

The Uncontrollable, Environmental Forces While marketers can control their marketing mix factors, there are forces that are mostly beyond their control (see Figure 1-2). These are the

environmental forces that affect a marketing decision, which consist of social, economic, technological, competitive, and regulatory forces. Examples are what consumers themselves want and need, changing technology, the state of the economy in terms of whether it is expanding or contracting, actions that competitors take, and government restrictions. Covered in detail in Chapter 3, these five forces may serve as accelerators or brakes on marketing, sometimes expanding an organization's marketing opportunities and at other times restricting them.

Traditionally, many marketing executives have treated these environmental forces as rigid, absolute constraints that are entirely outside their influence. However, recent studies and marketing successes have shown that a forward-looking, action-oriented firm can often affect some environmental forces by achieving technological or competitive breakthroughs, such as Amazon's AI assistant, Google's Duplex chatbot, and Alibaba's AliMe customer service technology.

THE MARKETING PROGRAM: HOW CUSTOMER RELATIONSHIPS ARE BUILT

LO 1-4
Explain how organizations build strong customer relationships and customer value through marketing.

An organization's marketing program connects it with its customers. To clarify this link, we will first discuss the critically important concepts of customer value, customer relationships, and relationship marketing. Then we will illustrate these concepts using 3M's marketing program for its Post-it® Flag Highlighter products.

Relationship Marketing: Easy to Understand, Hard to Do

Intense competition in today's fast-paced global markets has prompted many successful U.S. firms to focus on "customer value." Gaining loyal customers by providing unique value is the essence of successful marketing. What is new is a more careful attempt at understanding how a firm's customers perceive value and then actually creating and delivering that value to them.[17] **Customer value** is the unique combination of benefits received by targeted buyers that includes quality, convenience, on-time delivery, and both before-sale and after-sale service at a specific price. In addition, firms now actually try to place a dollar value on the purchases of loyal, satisfied customers during their lifetimes. For example, automobile collision repair centers estimate that loyal customers average $2,350 per repair, return eight times, and provide 50 referrals over 65 years, a value of $147,000![18]

Research suggests that firms cannot succeed by being all things to all people. Instead, firms seek to build long-term relationships with customers by providing unique value to them. Many successful firms deliver outstanding customer value with one of three value strategies: best price, best product, or best service.[19]

Target, Starbucks, and Nordstrom provide customer value using three very different approaches. For their strategies, see the text.
(Left) Source: Target Brands, Inc.; (Center) Source: Starbucks Coffee Company; (Right) Source: Nordstrom, Inc.

With the intense competition among U.S. businesses, being seen as "best" is admittedly difficult. Still, the three firms shown in the ads above have achieved great success as reflected in the mission, vision, and values statements they stress and live by:[20]

- *Best price: Target.* Target uses the brand promise of "Expect More, Pay Less®" to "make Target the preferred shopping destination for our guests by delivering outstanding value."
- *Best product: Starbucks.* Starbucks seeks "to inspire and nurture the human spirit—one person, one cup and one neighborhood at a time." Its ads remind customers that Starbucks coffee is "perfect."
- *Best service: Nordstrom.* As a leading fashion specialty retailer, Nordstrom works to "deliver the best possible shopping experience, helping our customers express their style—not just buy fashion." Nordstrom is "committed to providing our customers with the best possible service—and to improving it every day."

Remaining among the "best" is a continuing challenge for today's businesses.

A firm achieves meaningful customer relationships by creating connections with its customers through careful coordination of the product, its price, the way it is promoted, and how it is placed.

The hallmark of developing and maintaining effective customer relationships is today called **relationship marketing**, which links the organization to its individual customers, employees, suppliers, and other partners for their mutual long-term benefit. Relationship marketing involves a personal, ongoing relationship between the organization and its individual customers that begins before the sale and may evolve through different types of relationships after the sale.[21]

Information technology, along with cutting-edge manufacturing and marketing processes, better enable companies to form relationships with customers today. Smart, connected products, now elements of "the Internet of Everything," help create detailed databases about product usage. Then, using data analytics, or the examination of data to discover relevant patterns, companies can gain insights into how products create value for customers. For example, BMW receives data transmitted by each new vehicle it sells and General Electric collects information sent in by the jet engines it builds to help understand how customers use their products and when service may be needed. The Ritz-Carlton Hotel Company trains each of its employees to observe guest preferences and record them in the guest recognition system. In addition,

Ritz-Carlton hotels use relationship marketing concepts—tailoring the purchase experience to each individual—to create lifelong customers.
Paul Hilton/Bloomberg/Getty Images

the hotel's statement of values, called Gold Standards, guides employees to "build strong relationships and create Ritz-Carlton guests for life," and the website includes a variety of ways for customers to become part of its online community, including a Twitter-based concierge service.[22]

The Marketing Program and Market Segments

Effective relationship marketing strategies help marketing managers discover what prospective customers need and convert these ideas into marketable products (see Figure 1-3). These concepts must then be converted into a tangible **marketing program**—a plan that integrates the marketing mix to provide a good, service, or idea to prospective buyers. Ideally, they can be formed into **market segments**, which are relatively homogeneous groups of prospective buyers that (1) have common needs and (2) will respond similarly to a marketing action. This action might be a product feature, a promotion, or a price. As shown in Figure 1-3, in an effective organization this process is continuous: Consumer needs trigger product concepts that are translated into actual products that stimulate further discovery of consumer needs.

LEARNING REVIEW

1-4. An organization can't satisfy the needs of all consumers, so it must focus on one or more subgroups, which are its __________.

1-5. What are the four marketing mix elements that make up the organization's marketing program?

1-6. What are environmental forces?

3M's Strategy and Marketing Program to Help Students Study

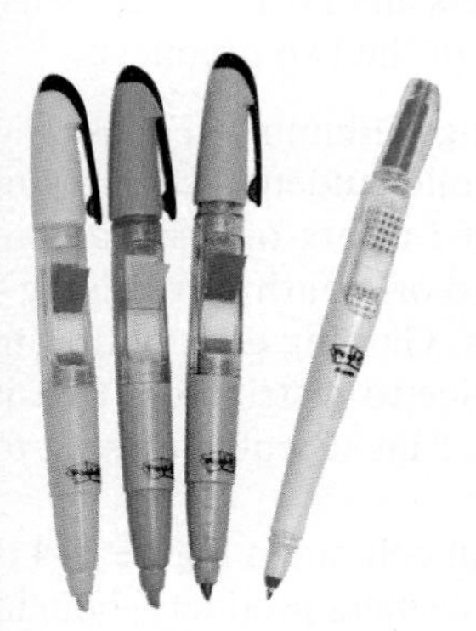

3M's initial product line of Post-it® Flag Highlighters and Post-it® Flag Pens included variations in color.

Mike Hruby/McGraw-Hill Education

VIDEO 1-4
3M Post-it® Flag Highlighters Ad
kerin.tv/15e/v1-4

"How do college students *really* study?" asked David Windorski, a 3M inventor of Post-it® brand products, when thinking about adding new items to the Post-it® line.[23]

To answer this question, Windorski hired a team of four college students. Their task was to observe and question other students about their study behavior, such as how they used their textbooks, took notes, wrote term papers, and reviewed for exams. As part of their research, the team observed that students often highlight a passage and then mark the page with a Post-it® Note or the smaller Post-it® Flag. Windorski realized there was an opportunity to merge the functions of two products—highlighters and Post-it® markers—into one product to help students study!

Moving from Ideas to Marketable Products After testing several models, Windorski concluded he had to build a highlighter product that would dispense Post-it® Flags because the Post-it® Notes were simply too large to put inside the barrel of a highlighter.

Next, hundreds of the highlighter prototypes with Post-it® Flags inside were produced and given to students—and also office workers—to get their reactions. This research showed that students loved the convenience of the Post-it® Flags in the highlighter. The research also suggested that many people in offices also need immediate access to Post-it® Flags but while writing with pens. So, the Post-it® Flag Pen was born! Students are a potential market for this product, too, but probably a smaller market segment than office workers.

A Marketing Program for the Post-it® Flag Highlighter and Post-it® Flag Pen After several years of research, development, and production engineering, 3M introduced its new products. Figure 1-4 outlines the strategies for each of the four marketing

MARKETING MIX ELEMENT	MARKETING PROGRAM ACTION TO REACH: COLLEGE STUDENT MARKET SEGMENT	OFFICE WORKER MARKET SEGMENT	RATIONALE FOR MARKETING PROGRAM ACTION
Product strategy	Offer Post-it® Flag Highlighter to help college students in their studying	Offer Post-it® Flag Pen to help office workers in their day-to-day work activities	Listen carefully to the needs and wants of potential customer segments to use 3M technology to introduce a useful, innovative product
Price strategy	Seek retail price of about $2.99 to $3.99 for a single Post-it® Flag Highlighter or $7.99 to $9.99 for a three-pack	Seek retail price of about $5.99 to $7.99 for a two-pack of Post-it® Flag Pens; wholesale prices are lower	Set prices that provide genuine value to the customer segment being targeted
Promotion strategy	Run limited promotion with a TV ad and some ads in college newspapers and then rely on student word-of-mouth messages	Run limited promotion among distributors to get them to stock the product	Increase awareness among potential users who have never heard of this new, innovative 3M product
Place strategy	Distribute Post-it® Flag Highlighters through college bookstores, office supply stores, and mass merchandisers	Distribute Post-it® Flag Pens through office wholesalers and retailers as well as mass merchandisers	Make it easy for prospective buyers to buy at convenient retail outlets (both products) or to get at work (Post-it® Flag Pens only)

FIGURE 1–4
Marketing programs for the launch of two Post-it® brand products targeted at two target market segments.

mix elements in 3M's program to market its Post-it® Flag Highlighters and Post-it® Flag Pens. Although similar, we can compare the marketing program for each of the two products:

- *Post-it® Flag Highlighter.* The target market shown in the orange column in Figure 1–4 is mainly college students, so 3M's initial challenge was to build student awareness of a product that they didn't know existed. The company used a mix of print ads in college newspapers and a TV ad and then relied on word-of-mouth advertising—students telling their friends about how great the product is. Gaining distribution in college bookstores was also critical. Plus, 3M charged a price to distributors that it hoped would give a reasonable bookstore price to students and an acceptable profit to distributors and 3M.
- *Post-it® Flag Pen.* The primary target market shown in the green column in Figure 1–4 is people working in offices. The Post-it® Flag Pens are mainly business products—bought by the purchasing department in an organization and stocked as office supplies for employees to use. So the marketing program for Post-it® Flag Pens emphasizes gaining distribution in outlets used by an organization's purchasing department.

Welcome to the most recent generation of Post-it® Flag Highlighters: the Post-it® Flag + Highlighter & Pen. The cap contains the Post-it® Flags.
McGraw-Hill Education

How well did these new 3M products do in the marketplace? They have done so well that 3M bestowed a prestigious award on David Windorski and his team. And in what must be considered any inventor's dream come true, Oprah Winfrey invited Windorski to appear on her TV show and thanked him in person. She told Windorski and her audience that the Post-it® Flag Highlighter is changing the way she does things at home and at work. "David, I know you never thought this would happen when you were in your 3M lab . . . but I want you to take a bow before America for the invention of this . . . (highlighter). It's the most incredible invention," she said.[24] The success of the Post-it® Flag Highlighter and the Post-it® Flag Pen encouraged Windorski to continue to conduct research about how the products were used. Feedback suggested there was another opportunity in the market: A 3-in-1 combination that has a highlighter on one end, a pen on the other, and 3M Post-it® Flags in the removable cap. The latest in the family of 3M product innovations is shown in the photo!

HOW MARKETING BECAME SO IMPORTANT

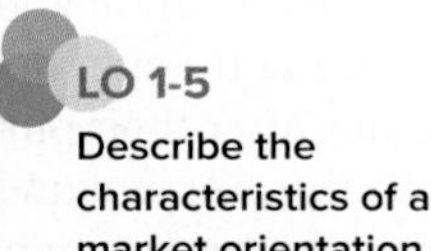

LO 1-5

Describe the characteristics of a market orientation.

To understand why marketing is a driving force in the modern global economy, let us look at (1) the evolution of the market orientation, (2) ethics and social responsibility in marketing, and (3) the breadth and depth of marketing activities.

Evolution toward a Market Orientation

Many American manufacturers have experienced four distinct stages in the life of their firms.[25] The first stage, the *production era*, covers the early years of the United States up until the 1920s. Goods were comparatively scarce and buyers were willing to accept virtually any goods that were available and make do with them.[26] In the *sales era* from the 1920s to the 1960s, manufacturers found they could produce more goods than buyers could consume. Competition grew. Firms hired more salespeople to find new buyers. This sales era continued into the 1960s for many American firms.

Starting in the late 1950s, marketing became the motivating force among many American firms and the *marketing concept era* dawned. The **marketing concept** is the idea that an organization should (1) strive to satisfy the needs of consumers while also (2) trying to achieve the organization's goals. General Electric probably launched the marketing concept and its focus on consumers when its 1952 annual report stated: "The concept introduces . . . marketing . . . at the beginning rather than the end of the production cycle and integrates marketing into each phase of the business."[27]

Firms such as Southwest Airlines, Marriott, and Facebook have achieved great success by putting a huge effort into implementing the marketing concept, giving their firms what has been called a *market orientation*. An organization that has a **market orientation** focuses its efforts on (1) continuously collecting information about customers' needs, (2) sharing this information across departments, and (3) using it to create customer value.[28] The *customer relationship era*, the brown bar in Figure 1–5, started in the 1980s and continues today as firms continuously seek to satisfy the high expectations of customers.

Focusing on Customer Relationship Management

A recent focus in the customer relationship era has been the advent of digital marketing, in which organizations and their customers develop relationships through applications (apps) and social media websites such as Instagram, Facebook, Twitter, and YouTube, among others.

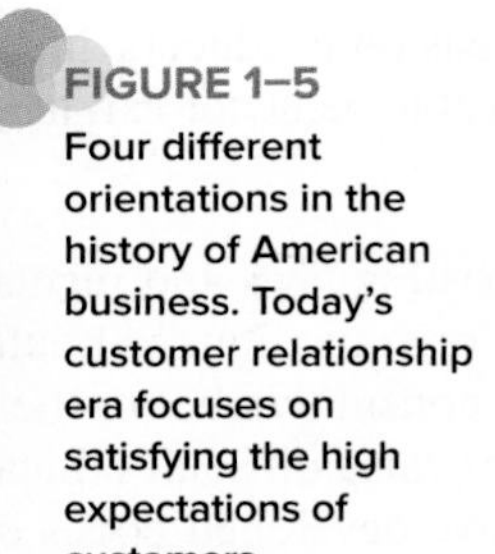

FIGURE 1–5

Four different orientations in the history of American business. Today's customer relationship era focuses on satisfying the high expectations of customers.

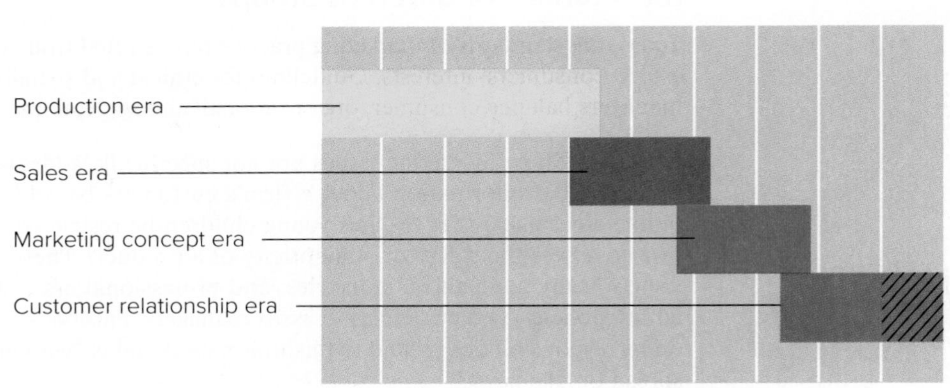

Trader Joe's is consistently ranked as one of America's favorite supermarket chains. This reflects the company's focus on providing a great customer experience, as described in the text.

Lannis Waters/ZUMA Press/ Newscom

This focus has allowed organizations to understand and market to current and prospective customers in ways that are still evolving.

An important outgrowth of this focus on the customer is the recent attention placed on **customer relationship management (CRM)**, the process of identifying prospective buyers, understanding them intimately, and developing favorable long-term perceptions of the organization and its offerings so that buyers will choose them in the marketplace and become advocates after their purchase.[29] This process requires the involvement and commitment of managers and employees throughout the organization[30] and a growing application of information, communication, and digital technology, as will be described throughout this book.

The foundation of customer relationship management is really **customer experience**, which is the internal response that customers have to all aspects of an organization and its offering. This internal response includes both the direct and indirect contacts of the customer with the company. Direct contacts include the customer's contacts with the seller through buying, using, and obtaining services. Indirect contacts most often involve unplanned "touches" with the company through word-of-mouth comments from other customers, reviewers, and news reports. In terms of outstanding customer experience, Trader Joe's is high on the list. Not surprisingly, it is ranked as one of America's favorite supermarket chains.[31]

What makes the customer experience at Trader Joe's unique? The reasons include:

- Setting low prices, made possible by offering its own brands rather than well-known national ones.
- Offering unusual, affordable products, like Organic Bolivia Yanaloma Small Lot Coffee and Trader Ming's Mandarin Orange Chicken, not available from other retailers.
- Encouraging employee "engagement" to help customers, like actually walking them to where the roasted chestnuts are–rather than saying "aisle five."

This commitment to providing an exceptional customer experience is what gives Trader Joe's its high rankings. It is also the reason why Trader Joe's doesn't authorize or sell its products online. According to a company spokesperson, "The store is our brand and our products work best when they're sold as part of the overall customer experience *within* the store. Part of that customer experience is the value we are committed to providing customers, each and every time they shop our stores–great products of the highest quality at great prices."[32]

Ethics and Social Responsibility in Marketing: Balancing the Interests of Different Groups

Today, the standards of marketing practice have shifted from an emphasis on producers' interests to consumers' interests. Guidelines for ethical and socially responsible behavior can help managers balance consumer, organizational, and societal interests.

Ethics Many marketing issues are not specifically addressed by existing laws and regulations. Should information about a firm's customers be sold to other organizations? Should online advertising that reaches young children be restricted? Should consumers be on their own to assess the safety or authenticity of a product? These questions raise difficult ethical issues. Many companies, industries, and professional associations have developed codes of ethics, policies, and guidelines to assist managers. Facebook, for example, is changing its view on its responsibilities related to misinformation and is "working hard to detect and reduce the spread of fake news."

Facebook's ads acknowledge the social impact of fake news and describe the company's efforts to detect and reduce its presence on the social network.
Source: Facebook, Inc.

Social Responsibility While many ethical issues involve only the buyer and seller, others involve society as a whole. For example, suppose you have the oil in your car changed at a local oil change center. Is this just a transaction between you and the service center? Not quite! The used oil and oil filter have potential to contaminate the environment if they are not recycled, and contamination represents a cost to society in terms of lost use of landfill space or eventual cleanup of the discarded waste products. To reduce the social cost of individual purchases today, many organizations use a variety of strategies that range from pure philanthropy, to environmentally friendly and sustainable practices, to creating "shared" value.[33] These strategies illustrate the issue of *social responsibility*, the idea that organizations are accountable to a larger society.

The well-being of society at large should also be recognized in an organization's marketing decisions. In fact, some marketing experts stress the **societal marketing concept**, the view that organizations should satisfy the needs of consumers in a way that provides for society's well-being. For example, Patagonia's Worn Wear program encourages its customers to repair, trade, and eventually recycle all of its products. Patagonia says, "One of the most responsible things we can do as a company is to make high-quality stuff that lasts for years and can be repaired, so you don't have to buy more of it."[34]

The Breadth and Depth of Marketing

Marketing today affects every person and organization. To understand this, let's analyze (1) who markets, (2) what is marketed, (3) who buys and uses what is marketed, (4) who benefits from these marketing activities, and (5) how consumers benefit.

Who Markets? Every organization markets. It's obvious that business firms involved in manufacturing (Patagonia), retailing (Trader Joe's), and providing services (Marriott) market their offerings. And nonprofit organizations such as museums (the Louvre), your local hospital or college, places (cities, states, countries), and even special causes (Race for the Cure) also engage in marketing. Finally, individuals such as political candidates often use marketing to gain voter attention and preference.

VIDEO 1-5
Hermitage Tour
kerin.tv/15e/v1-5

What Is Marketed? Goods, services, and ideas are marketed. *Goods* are physical objects, such as toothpaste, smartphones, or automobiles, that satisfy consumer needs. *Services* are intangible items such as airline trips, financial advice, or art museums. *Ideas* are thoughts about concepts, actions, or causes.

Strategies in marketing art museums can include new "satellite" museums such as this one for the Louvre in Abu Dhabi . . .
Source: Louvre Abu Dhabi

. . . or using an app to take an interactive tour of Russia's State Hermitage Museum.
Source: Hermitage Museum

In this book, goods, services, and ideas are all considered "products" that are marketed. So a **product** is a good, service, or idea consisting of a bundle of tangible and intangible attributes that satisfies consumers' needs and is received in exchange for money or something else of value.

Services like those offered by art museums, hospitals, and sports teams are relying more heavily on effective marketing. For example, financial pressures have caused art museums to innovate to market their unique services—the viewing of works of art by visitors—to increase revenues. This often involves levels of creativity unthinkable several decades ago.

This creativity ranges from establishing a global brand identity by launching overseas museums to offering sit-at-home video tours. France's Louvre, home to the *Mona Lisa* painting, opened a new satellite museum in Abu Dhabi, housed in a striking domed building.[35] Russia's world-class, 1,000-room State Hermitage Museum wanted to find a way to market itself to potential first-time visitors. So it developed a free app to guide visitors through the museum and provide information about events and exhibits.

Ideas are most often marketed by nonprofit organizations or the government. So The Nature Conservancy markets the cause of protecting the environment. Charities market the idea that it's worthwhile for you to donate your time or money. The Peace Corps markets to recruit qualified volunteers. And state governments in Arizona and Florida market taking a warm, sunny winter vacation in their states.

Who Buys and Uses What Is Marketed? Both individuals and organizations buy and use products that are marketed. **Ultimate consumers** are the people who use the products and services purchased for a household. In contrast, **organizational buyers** are those manufacturers, wholesalers, retailers, service companies, nonprofit organizations, and government agencies that buy products and services for their own use or for resale. Although the terms *consumers*, *buyers*, and *customers* are sometimes used for both ultimate consumers and organizations, there is no consistency on this. In this book you will be able to tell from the example whether the buyers are ultimate consumers, organizations, or both.

Marketing the idea of volunteering for the Peace Corps can benefit society.
Source: Peace Corps

Who Benefits? In our free-enterprise society, there are three specific groups that benefit from effective marketing: consumers who buy, organizations that sell, and society as a whole. True competition between products and services in the marketplace ensures that consumers can find value from the best products, the lowest prices, or exceptional service. Providing choices leads to the consumer satisfaction and quality of life that we expect from our economic system.

Organizations that provide need-satisfying products with effective marketing programs—for example, Amazon, Apple, and L'Oréal—have blossomed. But competition creates problems for ineffective competitors, including the many retailers such as Payless ShoeSource, Brookstone, Sears, and Toys "R" Us that recently filed for bankruptcy.

Finally, effective marketing benefits society.[36] It enhances competition, which both improves the quality of products and services and lowers their prices. This makes countries more competitive in world markets and provides jobs and a higher standard of living for their citizens.

How Do Consumers Benefit? Marketing creates **utility**, the benefits or customer value received by users of the product. This utility is the result of the marketing exchange process and the way society benefits from marketing. There are four different utilities: form, place, time, and possession. The production of the product or service constitutes *form utility*. *Place utility* means having the offering available where consumers need it, whereas *time utility* means having it available when needed. *Possession* *utility* is the value of making an item easy to purchase through the provision of credit cards or financial arrangements. Marketing creates its utilities by bridging space (place utility) and hours (time utility) to provide products (form utility) for consumers to own and use (possession utility).

LEARNING REVIEW

1-7. What are the two key characteristics of the marketing concept?

1-8. What is the difference between ultimate consumers and organizational buyers?

LEARNING OBJECTIVES REVIEW

LO 1-1 *Define marketing and identify the diverse factors that influence marketing actions.*
Marketing is an organizational function and a set of processes for creating, communicating, and delivering value to customers and for managing customer relationships in ways that benefit the organization and its stakeholders. This definition relates to two primary goals of marketing: (*a*) discovering the needs of prospective customers and (*b*) satisfying them. Achieving these two goals also involves the four marketing mix factors largely controlled by the organization and the five environmental forces that are generally outside its control.

LO 1-2 *Explain how marketing discovers and satisfies consumer needs.*
The first objective in marketing is discovering the needs and wants of consumers who are prospective buyers and customers. This is not easy because consumers may not always know or be able to describe what they need and want. A need occurs when a person feels deprived of basic necessities such as food, clothing, and shelter. A want is a need that is shaped by a person's knowledge, culture, and personality. Effective marketing can clearly shape a person's wants and tries to influence what he or she buys. The second objective in marketing is satisfying the needs of targeted consumers. Because an organization obviously can't satisfy all consumer needs, it must concentrate its efforts on certain needs of a specific group of potential consumers or target market—one or more specific groups of potential consumers toward which an organization directs its marketing program. It then selects its target market segment(s), which is a relatively homogeneous group of prospective buyers that (1) have common needs and (2) will respond similarly to a marketing action. Finally, the organization develops a set of marketing actions in the form of a unique marketing program to reach them.

LO 1-3 *Distinguish between marketing mix factors and environmental forces.*
Four elements in a marketing program designed to satisfy customer needs are product, price, promotion, and place. These elements are called the marketing mix, the four Ps, or the marketer's controllable variables. The marketing mix also provides a clear customer value proposition—a cluster of benefits that an offering satisfies. Environmental forces, also called uncontrollable variables, are largely beyond the organization's control. These include social, economic, technological, competitive, and regulatory forces.

LO 1-4 *Explain how organizations build strong customer relationships and customer value through marketing.*
The essence of successful marketing is to provide sufficient value to gain loyal, long-term customers. Customer value is the unique combination of benefits received by targeted buyers that usually includes quality, price, convenience, on-time delivery, and both before-sale and after-sale service. Marketers do this by using one of three value strategies: best price, best product, or best service.

LO 1-5 *Describe the characteristics of a market orientation.*
Many firms have achieved great success by putting huge effort into implementing the marketing concept—the idea that an organization should (1) strive to satisfy the needs of consumers while also (2) trying to achieve the organization's goals. Implementing the marketing concept creates a market orientation. An organization that has a market orientation focuses its efforts on (1) continuously collecting information about customers' needs, (2) sharing this information across departments, and (3) using it to create customer value.

LEARNING REVIEW ANSWERS

1-1 What is marketing?
Answer: Marketing is the activity for creating, communicating, delivering, and exchanging offerings that benefit customers, the organization, its stakeholders, and society at large.

1-2 Marketing focuses on __________ and __________ consumer needs.
Answer: discovering; satisfying

1-3 What four factors are needed for marketing to occur?
Answer: The four factors are: (1) two or more parties (individuals or organizations) with unsatisfied needs; (2) a desire and ability on their part to have their needs satisfied; (3) a way for the parties to communicate; and (4) something to exchange.

1-4 An organization can't satisfy the needs of all consumers, so it must focus on one or more subgroups, which are its ___________.
Answer: target market(s)

1-5 What are the four marketing mix elements that make up the organization's marketing program?
Answer: product, price, promotion, place

1-6 What are environmental forces?
Answer: Environmental forces are the uncontrollable forces that affect a marketing decision. They consist of social, economic, technological, competitive, and regulatory forces.

1-7 What are the two key characteristics of the marketing concept?
Answer: An organization should (1) strive to satisfy the needs of consumers while also (2) trying to achieve the organization's goals.

1-8 What is the difference between ultimate consumers and organizational buyers?
Answer: Ultimate consumers are the people who use the products and services purchased for a household. Organizational buyers are those manufacturers, wholesalers, retailers, and government agencies that buy products and services for their own use or for resale.

FOCUSING ON KEY TERMS

customer experience p. 16
customer relationship management (CRM) p. 16
customer value p. 11
environmental forces p. 11
exchange p. 6
market p. 9
market orientation p. 15
market segments p. 13
marketing p. 5
marketing concept p. 15
marketing mix p. 10
marketing program p. 13
organizational buyers p. 18
product p. 18
relationship marketing p. 12
societal marketing concept p. 17
target market p. 10
ultimate consumers p. 18
utility p. 18

APPLYING MARKETING KNOWLEDGE

1 What consumer wants (or benefits) are met by the following products or services? (*a*) 3M Post-it® Flag Highlighter, (*b*) Nike running shoes, (*c*) Hertz Rent-A-Car, and (*d*) Amazon online shopping.

2 Each of the four products, services, or programs in question 1 has substitutes. Respective examples are (*a*) a Bic™ highlighter, (*b*) regular tennis shoes, (*c*) an Uber or Lyft ride, and (*d*) a department store. What consumer benefits might these substitutes have in each case that some consumers might value more highly than those mentioned in question 1?

3 What are the characteristics (e.g., age, income, education) of the target market customers for the following products or services? (*a*) *National Geographic* magazine, (*b*) Chobani Greek Yogurt, (*c*) New York Giants football team, and (*d*) Facebook.

4 A college in a metropolitan area wishes to increase its evening offerings of business-related courses such as marketing, accounting, finance, and management. Who are the target market customers (students) for these courses?

5 What actions involving the four marketing mix elements might be used to reach the target market in question 4?

6 What environmental forces (uncontrollable variables) must the college in question 4 consider in designing its marketing program?

7 Does a firm have the right to "create" wants and try to persuade consumers to buy goods and services they didn't know about earlier? What are examples of "good" and "bad" want creation? Who should decide what is good and what is bad?

BUILDING YOUR MARKETING PLAN

If your instructor assigns a marketing plan for your class, we hope you will be excited–for two reasons. First, you will get insights into trying to actually "do marketing" that often go beyond what you can get by simply reading the textbook. Second, thousands of graduating students every year get their first job by showing prospective employers a "portfolio" of samples of their written work from college–often a marketing plan if they have one. This can work for you.

This "Building Your Marketing Plan" section at the end of each chapter suggests ways to improve and focus your marketing plan. You will use the sample marketing plan in Appendix A (following Chapter 2) as a guide, and this section after each chapter will help you apply those Appendix A ideas to your own marketing plan.

The first step in writing a good marketing plan is to have a business or product that enthuses you and for which you can get detailed information, so you can avoid glittering generalities. We offer these additional bits of advice in selecting a topic:

- *Do* pick a topic that has personal interest for you—a family business; a business, product, or service you or a friend might want to launch; or a student organization that needs marketing help.
- *Do not* pick a topic that is so large it can't be covered adequately or so abstract it will lack specifics.

1 Now to get you started on your marketing plan, list four or five possible topics and compare these with the criteria your instructor suggests and those shown above. Think hard, because your decision will be with you all term and may influence the quality of the resulting marketing plan you show to a prospective employer.

2 When you have selected your marketing plan topic, whether the plan is for an actual business, a possible business, or a student organization, write the "company description" in your plan, as shown in Appendix A (following Chapter 2).

VIDEO CASE 1 Chobani®: Making *Greek Yogurt* a Household Name

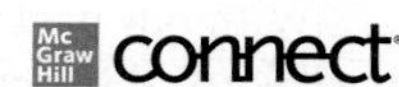

"Everybody should be able to enjoy a pure, simple cup of yogurt. And that's what Chobani is," says Hamdi Ulukaya, founder and chief executive officer of Chobani, LLC, in summarizing his vision for the company.

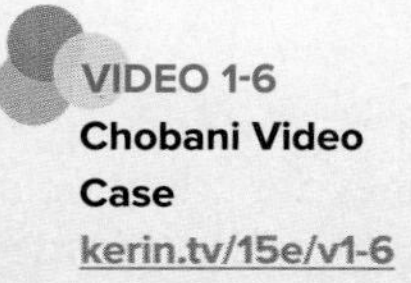

VIDEO 1-6
Chobani Video Case
kerin.tv/15e/v1-6

As the winner of an Ernst & Young World Entrepreneur of the Year award, his words and success story carry great credibility.

THE IDEA

Hamdi Ulukaya came to the United States in 1994 to learn English and study business. He started a feta cheese company, Euphrates, when his visiting father complained about the quality of American feta cheese. In 2005, Kraft Foods closed its New Berlin, New York, yogurt plant. While tidying up his office, Ulukaya stumbled upon a postcard about the sale of the shuttered Kraft plant and threw it out. After sleeping on the decision, he fished it out of the wastebasket, visited the plant, and purchased it with the help of a U.S. Small Business Administration loan.

Diane Bondareff/Invision for Chobani/AP Images

Ulukaya (center in photo) had no real experience in the yogurt business. He grew up milking sheep at his family's dairy in eastern Turkey and eating the thick, tangy yogurt of his homeland. Describing the regular yogurt he found on shelves in America, he has one comment: "Terrible!" In his view, it is too thin, too sweet, and too fake. So he decided to produce what is known as "Greek yogurt"—an authentic strained version that produces a thick texture, with high protein content and little or no fat. With the help of four former Kraft employees and yogurt master Mustafa Dogan, Ulukaya worked 18 months to perfect the recipe for Chobani Greek Yogurt.

The very first cup for sale of Ulukaya's Greek yogurt appeared on the shelves of a small grocer in Long Island, New York. The new-product launch focused on the classic four Ps elements of marketing mix actions: product, price, place, and promotion.

PRODUCT STRATEGY

From the start Ulukaya's Greek yogurt carried the brand name "Chobani." There was no room for error, and the product strategy for the Chobani brand focused on the separate elements of (1) the product itself and (2) its packaging.

The Chobani product strategy stresses its authentic straining process that removes excess liquid whey. This results in a thicker, creamier yogurt that yields 13 to 18 grams of protein per single-serve cup, depending on the flavor. Chobani is free of ingredients like milk protein concentrate and animal-based thickeners, which some manufacturers add to make "Greek-style" yogurts.

Chobani uses three pounds of milk to make one pound of Chobani Greek Yogurt. Some other features that make Chobani Greek Yogurt "nothing but good," to quote one of its advertising taglines:

- Higher in protein than regular yogurt.
- Made with real fruit and only natural ingredients.

- Preservative-free.
- No artificial flavors or artificial sweeteners.
- Contains five live and active cultures, including three probiotics.

Then, and still today, Ulukaya obsessed about Chobani's packaging of the original cups. While designing the cup, Ulukaya concluded that *not any cup* would do. He insisted on a European-style cup with a circular opening *exactly* 95 millimeters across. This made for a shorter, wider cup that was more visible on retailer's shelves. Also, instead of painted-on labels, Ulukaya chose shrink-on plastic sleeves that adhere to the cup and offer eye-popping colors.

"With our packaging people would say, 'You're making it all look different and why are you doing that?'" says Kyle O'Brien, executive vice president of sales. "If people pay attention to our cups—bright colors and all—we know we have won them, because what's inside the cup is different from anything else on the shelf."

PRICE STRATEGY

To keep control of their product, Ulukaya and O'Brien approached retailers directly rather than going through distributors. Prices were set high enough to recover Chobani's costs and give reasonable margins to retailers but not so high that future rivals could undercut its price. Today, prices remain at about $1.29 for a single-serve cup.

Source: Chobani, LLC

PLACE STRATEGY

The decision of Ulukaya and O'Brien to get Chobani Greek Yogurt into the conventional yogurt aisle of traditional supermarkets—not on specialty shelves or in health food stores—proved to be sheer genius. Today Chobani sees its Greek yogurt widely distributed in both conventional and mass supermarkets, club stores, and natural food stores. On the horizon: growing distribution in convenience and drugstores, as well as schools. Chobani is also focused on educating food service directors at schools across the United States about Greek yogurt's health benefits for schoolkids.

The Chobani growth staggers imagination. From the company's first order of 200 cases, its sales have grown to over 2 million cases per week. To increase capacity and bring new products to market faster, Chobani opened a nearly one million square foot plant in Idaho. Built in just 326 days, it is the largest yogurt manufacturing facility in the world.

Along the way Chobani faced a strange glitch: Demand for Chobani Greek Yogurt far surpassed supply, leading to unhappy retailers with no Chobani cups to sell. Kyle O'Brien launched Operation Bear Hug. "Instead of hiding behind letters to retailers, we decided to get on a plane and to communicate with them within 24 hours about the problem and what we proposed to do about it," says O'Brien. "So we found it critical to be very transparent and open with our communication at times like that."

PROMOTION STRATEGY

In its early years Chobani had no money for traditional advertising, so it relied on word-of-mouth recommendation from enthusiastic customers. The brand harnessed consumer passion on social media channels early on and found that people loved the taste of Chobani once they tried it. So Chobani kicked off its CHOmobile tour: a mobile vehicle sampling Chobani at events across the country, encouraging consumers to taste Greek yogurt for the first time. As Chobani grew, it began to launch new promotional activities tied to (1) traditional advertising, (2) social media, and (3) direct communication with customers.

Chobani's first national advertising campaign, called "Real Love Stories," was very successful. The only problem: apparently it was *too* successful! The resulting additional consumer demand for Chobani Greek Yogurt exceeded its production capacity, leaving retailers unhappy because of complaining consumers. What did Chobani do then? It stopped the advertising campaign and sent in another Operation Bear Hug team to communicate with retailers. Since then it has run other successful national advertising campaigns, including sponsorship of the U.S. Olympic Teams.

"Social media has been important to Chobani, which has embraced a high-touch model that emphasizes positive communication with its customers," says Sujean Lee, head of corporate affairs. Today, Chobani's Customer Loyalty Team receives about 7,000 inbound customer e-mails and phone calls a month and is able to make return phone calls to many of them. Consumers also sometimes get a handwritten note. Chobani launched its "Go Real Chobani" campaign to highlight that it is a *real* company making *real* products and engaging consumers through *real* conversations.

In addition to Facebook (www.Facebook.com/Chobani), the company interacts with its consumers through Twitter, Pinterest, Instagram, Foursquare, and other social media platforms. Chobani Kitchen (www.chobanikitchen.com) is an online resource with recipes, videos, and tips on how to use its Greek yogurt in favorite recipes.

AGGRESSIVE INNOVATION AND POSITIVE SOCIAL CHANGE

Dannon, Yoplait, and PepsiCo were shocked by the success of Chobani Greek Yogurt. Each now offers its own competing Greek yogurt. With giant competitors like these, what can Chobani do? Innovate and develop creative, new Greek yogurt products!

"Today we offer our Chobani Greek Yogurt in single-serve and multi-serve sizes, while expanding our authentic strained Greek yogurt to new occasions and forms," says Joshua Dean, vice president of brand advertising. Its recent new-product offerings include:

- Non-Dairy Chobani™—a coconut blend made from natural, non-GMO ingredients without artificial flavors, sweeteners, or preservatives. Sample flavors: blueberry, mango, peach, and vanilla chai.
- Chobani Gimmies™—pouches, tubes, and containers for kids, with protein, probiotics, and calcium and less sugar than other kids' yogurt products. Sample flavor: Cookies and Cream Crush.
- Chobani Flip™—a 5.3-ounce, two-compartment package that lets consumers bend or "flip" mix-ins like granola or hazelnuts into the Chobani Greek Yogurt compartment. Sample flavor: Almond Coco Loco, a coconut low-fat yogurt paired with dark chocolate and honey-roasted salted almonds.
- Drink Chobani™—a smooth, drinkable yogurt with 10 grams of protein in 10 flavors.

Chobani gives 10 percent of all profits to its Shepherd's Gift Foundation to support people and organizations working for positive, long-lasting change. The name comes from the "spirit of a shepherd," an expression in Turkey used to describe people who give without expecting anything in return. To date the foundation has supported over 50 projects—from local ones to international famine relief efforts.

WHERE TO NOW?

International operations and a unique test-market boutique in New York City give a peek at Chobani's future.

International markets provide a growth opportunity. Other countries have far greater annual per capita consumption of yogurt than the United States. For example,

John Minchillo/AP Images

some Europeans eat five or six times as much on average. So while entrenched competitors exist in many foreign countries, the markets are often huge, too.

How do you test ideas for new Greek yogurt flavors? In Chobani's case, it opened what it calls a "first-of-its-kind Mediterranean yogurt bar"—called Chobani SoHo—in a trendy New York City neighborhood. Here, customers can try new yogurt creations—from Strawberry + Granola to Toasted Coconut + Pineapple. The Chobani marketing team obtains consumer feedback at Chobani SoHo, leading to potential new flavors or products in the future.

Hmmm! Ready to schedule a visit to New York City and Chobani SoHo? And then sample a creation made with Pistachio + Chocolate (plain Chobani topped with pistachios, dark chocolate, honey, oranges, and fresh mint leaves), and perhaps influence what Chobani customers will be buying in the future?[37]

Questions

1 From the information about Chobani in the case and at the start of the chapter, (*a*) who did Hamdi Ulukaya identify as the target for his first cups of Greek yogurt and (*b*) what was his initial four Ps marketing strategy?

2 (*a*) What marketing actions would you expect the companies selling Yoplait, Dannon, and PepsiCo yogurts to take in response to Chobani's appearance and (*b*) how might Chobani respond?

3 What are (*a*) the advantages and (*b*) the disadvantages of Chobani's Customer Loyalty Team that handles communication with customers—from phone calls and e-mails to Facebook and Twitter messages?

4 As part of building its brand, Chobani opened a unique retail store in New York City: Chobani SoHo. Why did Chobani do this?

5 (*a*) What criteria might Chobani use when it seeks markets in new countries and (*b*) what three or four countries meet these criteria?

Chapter Notes

1. Remi Rosmarin, "The Chobani Food Incubator Helps Young Food Startups Off Their Feet," *Businessinsider.com,* March 4, 2019; "Chobani Unveils Major Brand Evolution in Celebration of 10th Anniversary," *Dairy Foods,* January 2018, p. 24; and "Why Chobani Is One of the Most Innovative Companies of 2017," *Fast Company,* March 2017, p. 44.
2. Chobani website, https://www.chobani.com/impact/.
3. "How Chobani Came to Be," www.chobani.com/about, March 12, 2019; and John Tamny, "The Story of Chobani Is about Much More Than Yogurt," *Forbes,* July 4, 2016, p. 1.
4. Arvinna Lee, "How Chobani Dominated the Yogurt Market in Just 8 Years," Referral Candy, http://www.referralcandy.com/blog/chobani-marketing-strategy/; and Mark Boshnack, "Chobani Executive Touts Company's Olympic Ties," *The Daily Star,* August 12, 2016.
5. Beth Kowitt, "Chobani Is Betting You Won't Miss the Dairy in Its New Yogurt," *Fortune.com,* January 9, 2019; Amy Barnes, "Chobani Gimmies Yogurt Gets Animated: Packaging Meets Character Promotion," *Forbes.com,* March 7, 2019; "Yogurt in the U.S.," *Statista,* September 2018; and Emily Steel, "Newcomers Buy Ad Time at Big Game," *The New York Times,* January 31, 2015, p. B1.
6. Don Reisinger, "Elon Musk's SpaceX Raptor Engine Is One Step Closer to Reaching Mars," *Fortune.com,* February 7, 2019; Natasha Bach, "Elon Musk Unveils Boring Company's Underground Test Tunnel," *Fortune.com,* December 19, 2018; Richard Robinson, "It's Time for Marketers to Start a Bonfire of the Legacies," *Marketing Week,* January 26, 2017, p. 13.
7. See http://www.marketing-dictionary.org/ama (definition approved by the American Marketing Association Board of Directors, July 2013).
8. Richard P. Bagozzi, "Marketing as Exchange," *Journal of Marketing,* October 1975, pp. 32–39; and Gregory T. Gundlach and Patrick E. Murphy, "Ethical and Legal Foundations of Relational Marketing Exchanges," *Journal of Marketing,* October 1993, pp. 35–46.
9. Nuno Camacho, Hyoryung Nam, P.K. Kannan, and Stefan Stremersch, "Tournaments to Crowdsource Innovation: The Role of Moderator Feedback and Participation Intensity," *Journal of Marketing,* March 2019, pp. 138–157; B. J. Allen, Deepa Chandrasekaran, and Suman Basuroy, "Design Crowdsourcing: The Impact on New Product Performance of Sourcing Design Solutions from the 'Crowd,'" *Journal of Marketing,* March 2018, pp. 106–123; "Building Together: How LEGO Leverages Crowdsourcing to Sustain Both Innovation and Brand Love," *digit.hbs.org,* March 26, 2018.
10. Mintel Global New Products Database, http://www.mintel.com/global-new-products-database, accessed March 3, 2019; George Castellion and Stephen K. Markham, "Perspective: New Product Failure Rates: Influence of Argumentum ad Populum and Self-Interest," *Journal of Product Innovation Management* 30, no. 5 (2013), pp. 976–79; and Robert M. McMath and Thom Forbes, *What Were They Thinking?* (New York: Times Business, 1998), pp. 3–22.
11. Ashley Carman, "North Focal Glasses Review: A $600 Smartwatch for Your Face," *Theverge.com,* February 14, 2019; Hugh Langley, "There's a New Google Glass on the Way–But It Probably Isn't for You," *Wareable.com,* November 14, 2018; and Ben Geier, "This Is Where Google Says Glass Went All Wrong," *Fortune.com,* March 23, 2015.
12. Nima Rajan, "Coca-Cola Finally Launches Their Patented No-Sugar Stevia-Sweetened Coke," *Xtalks.com,* May 15, 2018; Barbara Harfmann, "A Sweet Replacement Solution," *Beverage Industry,* March 2018, pp. 64, 66, and 68; and Megan Poinski, "FDA Proposes 2020 Compliance Deadline for Nutrition Facts Label," *www.fooddive.com,* September 29, 2017.
13. Sarah Steimer, "Subscription Box as Stratagem," *Marketing News,* January 2018, pp. 42–49; Universal Yums! website, www.universalyums.com, July 10, 2019.
14. Louis DeNicola, "Credit Card Use in College after the CARD Act," *The Clearpoint Blog,* www.clearpoint.org, May 1, 2017; and "Washington: Marketing to College Student Appears to Have Declined," *Plus Media Solutions,* February 27, 2014.
15. E. Jerome McCarthy, *Basic Marketing: A Managerial Approach* (Homewood, IL: Richard D. Irwin, 1960); and Walter van Waterschool and Christophe Van den Bulte, "The 4P Classification of the Marketing Mix Revisited," *Journal of Marketing,* October 1992, pp. 83–93.
16. Roger A. Kerin and Robert A. Peterson, *Strategic Marketing Problems: Cases and Comments,* 13th ed. (Upper Saddle River, NJ: Prentice Hall, 2013), p. 12.
17. Ashish Kothari and Joseph Lackner, "A Value-Based Approach to Management," *Journal of Business and Industrial Marketing* 21, no. 4, pp. 243–49; and James C. Anderson, James A. Narius, and Wouter van Rossum, "Customer Value Propositions in Business Markets," *Harvard Business Review,* March 2006, pp. 91–99.
18. Sheryl Driggers, "Retaining Customers Is Vital," www.abrn.com, September 2017; and V. Kumar and Werner Reinartz, "Creating Enduring Customer Value," *Journal of Marketing* 80 (November 2016), pp. 36–68.
19. Nicolas A. Zacharias, Edwin J. Nijssen, and Ruth Maria Stock, "Effective Configurations of Value Creation and Capture Capabilities: Extending Treacy and Wiersema's Value Disciplines," *Journal of Business Research,* October 2016, pp. 4121–31; and Michael Treacy and Fred D. Wiersema, *The Discipline of Market Leaders* (Reading, MA: Addison-Wesley, 1995).
20. Target. Mission Statement, corporate website; Starbucks Coffee Company. "Our Starbucks Mission Statement," accessed June 09, 2019. http://www.starbucks.in/about-us/company-information/mission-statement; Nordstrom, Mission Statement. https://shop.nordstrom.com/content/about-us.
21. Jonathan Z. Zhang, George F. Watson IV, Robert W. Palmatier, and Rajiv P. Dant, "Dynamic Relationship Marketing," *Journal of Marketing,* September 2016, pp. 53–75; Robert W. Palmatier, Rajiv P. Dant, Dhruv Grewal, and Kenneth R. Evans, "Factors Influencing the Effectiveness of Relationship Marketing: A Meta-Analysis," *Journal of Relationship Marketing,* October 2006, pp. 136–53; and William Boulding, Richard Staelin, Michael Ehret, and Wesley J. Johnson, "A Customer Relationship Management Roadmap: What Is Known, Potential Pitfalls, and Where to Go," *Journal of Marketing,* October 2005, pp. 155–66.
22. Jagdish Sheth, "Revitalizing Relationship Marketing," *Journal of Services Marketing,* no. 1 (2017), pp. 6–10; Michael E. Porter and James E. Hepplemann, "How Smart, Connected Products Are Transforming Competition," *Harvard Business Review,* November 2014, pp. 65–88; and Ritz-Carlton website, www.ritzcarlton.com/en/about/gold-standards.
23. The 3M Post-it® Flag Highlighter and 3M Post-it® Flag Pen examples are based on a series of interviews and meetings with 3M inventor and researcher David Windorski.
24. Oprah, "Making It Big," January 15, 2008. https://www.oprah.com/food/making-it-big_2/13; and "Post-it® Flags Co-Sponsors Oprah's Live Web Event," *3M Stemwinder,* March 4–17, 2008, p. 3.
25. Reservations about and elaborations of these simplified stages appear in D. G. Brian Jones and Eric H. Shaw, "A History of Marketing Thought," Chapter 2 in *Handbook of Marketing,* ed. Barton Weitz and Robin Wensley (London: Sage Publications, 2006), pp. 39–65; Frederick E. Webster Jr., "The Role of Marketing and the Firm," Chapter 3 in *Handbook of Marketing,* ed. Barton Weitz and Robin Wensley (London: Sage Publications, 2006), pp. 66–82; and Frederick E. Webster Jr., "Back to the Future: Integrating Marketing as Tactics, Strategy and Organizational Culture," *Journal of Marketing,* October 2005, pp. 4–8.
26. Robert F. Keith, "The Marketing Revolution," *Journal of Marketing,* January 1960, pp. 35–38.
27. Securities and Exchange Commission, *Annual Report* (New York: General Electric Company, 1952), p. 21.
28. John C. Narver, Stanley F. Slater, and Brian Tietje, "Creating a Market Orientation," *Journal of Market-Focused Management,* no. 2 (1998), pp. 241–55; Stanley F. Slater and John C. Narver, "Market Orientation

and the Learning Organization," *Journal of Marketing,* July 1995, pp. 63-74; and George S. Day, "The Capabilities of Market-Driven Organizations," *Journal of Marketing,* October 1994, pp. 37-52.

29. The definition of customer relationship management is adapted from Philip Kotler, Hermawan Kartajaya, and Iwan Setiawan, *Marketing 4.0* (Hoboken, NJ: Wiley, 2017); Rajendra K. Srivastava, Tasadduq A. Shervani, and Liam Fahey, "Marketing, Business Processes, and Shareholder Value: An Embedded View of Marketing Activities and the Discipline of Marketing," *Journal of Marketing,* special issue (1999), pp. 168-79; and Christopher Meyer and Andre Schwager, "Understanding Customer Experience," *Harvard Business Review,* February 2007, pp. 117-26.

30. Gary F. Gebhardt, Gregory S. Carpenter, and John F. Sherry Jr., "Creating a Market Orientation: A Longitudinal, Multifirm, Grounded Analysis of Cultural Transformation," *Journal of Marketing,* October 2006, pp. 37-55.

31. Marilyn Much, "How Joe Coulombe Built the Culture behind Trader Joe's Cult Status," *Investors Business Daily,* March 1, 2019; and Marketforce Information, https://www.marketforce.com/2018-americas-favorite-grocery-stores.

32. "Trader Joe's Sticks to Stores," *Dallas Morning News,* April 30, 2019, p. 3B.

33. Kasturi Rangan, Lisa Chase, and Sohel Karim, "The Truth about CSR," *Harvard Business Review,* January-February 2015, pp. 41-49.

34. Worn Wear Spring 2015 Tour–Free Clothing Repairs and More in 15 Cities across the Country; Jamie Feldman, "Patagonia Just Made Another Major Move to Save the Earth and Your Wallet," *www.huffpost.com,* January 30, 2017; Philip Kotler and Sidney J. Levy, "Broadening the Concept of Marketing," *Journal of Marketing,* January 1969, pp. 10-15; and Jim Rendon, "When Nations Need a Little Marketing," *The New York Times,* November 23, 2003, p. BU6.

35. Peter Gumbel, "Louvre, Inc." *Time,* August 11, 2008, pp. 51-52; and Stella Wai-Art Law, *A Branding Context: The Guggenheim and the Louvre,* M.A. Thesis, Columbus: The Ohio State University, 2008.

36. William L. Wilkie and Elizabeth S. Moore, "Marketing's Relationship to Society," in *Handbook of Marketing,* ed. Barton Weitz and Robin Wensley (London: Sage Publications, 2006), pp. 9-38.

37. Chobani, LLC: This case was written by William Rudelius, based on personal interviews with Chobani executives Joshua Dean, Sujean Lee, and Kyle O'Brien. Other sources include: Kate Bernot, "Chobani Hopes New Squeeze Bottles Turn Greek Yogurt into a Condiment," *thetakeout.com,* August 8, 2018; "The Chobani Story," MEDIA@CHOBANI.COM, 2013; Megan Durisin, "Chobani CEO: Our Success Has Nothing to Do with Yogurt," *Business Retail Insider,* May 3, 2013, p. 1; and Sarah E. Needleman, "Old Factory, Snap Decision Spawn Greek Yogurt Craze," *The Wall Street Journal,* June 21, 2012, pp. B1, B2.

Chapter 2 Developing Successful Organizational and Marketing Strategies

LEARNING OBJECTIVES

After reading this chapter you should be able to:

LO 2-1 Describe three kinds of organizations and the three levels of strategy in them.

LO 2-2 Describe core values, mission, organizational culture, business, and goals.

LO 2-3 Explain why managers use marketing dashboards and marketing metrics.

LO 2-4 Discuss how an organization assesses where it is now and where it seeks to be.

LO 2-5 Explain the three steps of the planning phase of the strategic marketing process.

LO 2-6 Describe the four components of the implementation phase of the strategic marketing process.

LO 2-7 Discuss how managers identify and act on deviations from plans.

Peace, Love, and Ice Cream

Chances are this is a familiar motto to you. It is also the belief that guided longtime friends Ben Cohen and Jerry Greenfield when they started their business, Ben & Jerry's ice cream shops!

Ben & Jerry's started in 1978 when the two men moved to Vermont to open an ice cream parlor in a renovated gas station. The venture was buoyed with enthusiasm, $12,000 in borrowed and saved money, and ideas from a $5 correspondence course in ice cream making. Their first flavor? Vanilla–because it's a universal best seller. Other flavors such as Chunky Monkey, Cherry Garcia, Peanut Butter Cup, and many others soon followed.

The ice cream flavors weren't the only extraordinary thing about the company though. Ben and Jerry embraced a concept they called "linked prosperity" which encouraged the success of all their constituents, including employees, suppliers, farmers, customers, franchisees, and neighbors. They set out to achieve linked prosperity with a three-part mission statement:

- *Product Mission*: To make, distribute, and sell the finest quality all-natural ice cream.
- *Economic Mission*: To operate the company for sustainable financial growth.
- *Social Mission*: To operate the company in ways that make the world a better place.

The mission statement guided the entrepreneurs' decisions related to many aspects of the business, including purchasing practices, ingredient sourcing, manufacturing, and involvement in the community.[1]

Ben and Jerry's mission-driven approach led them to successfully implement many highly creative organizational and marketing strategies. Some examples include:

- *Eliminate Single-Use Plastic.* Ben & Jerry's has announced that it will no longer offer plastic straws and spoons. Jenna Evans, Global Sustainability Manager, explains that recycling isn't enough, "we, and the rest of the world, need to get out of single-use plastic."
- *Free Cone Day*. One day each year Ben & Jerry's gives away free servings of ice cream to more than a million fans around the world. It's one way the company can give back to the communities it serves.
- *Fairtrade*. Ben & Jerry's believes that farmers who grow ingredients for their ice cream products (such as cocoa, coffee, and vanilla) should receive a fair price for their harvest. In return Fairtrade farmers agree to use sustainable farming practices, implement fair working standards, and invest in local communities.

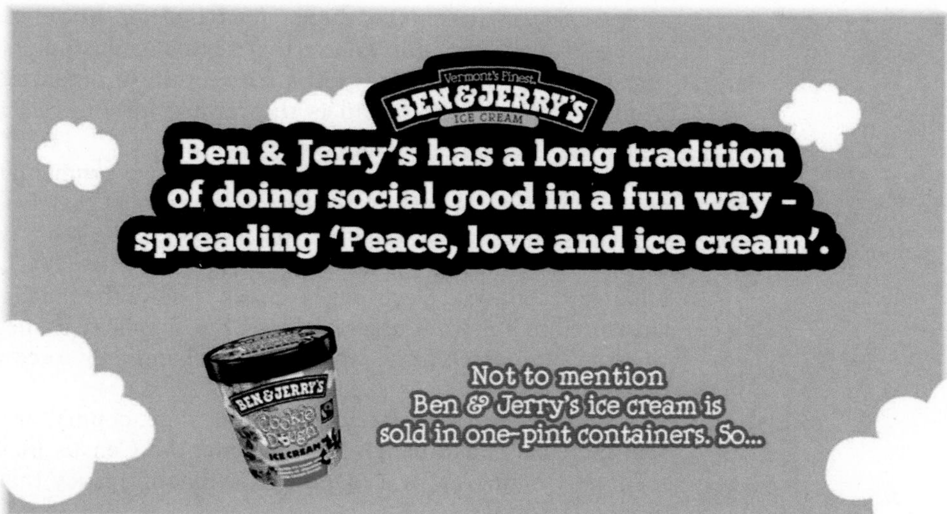

Source: Ben & Jerry's Homemade, Inc.

- *B-Corp Certification*. Ben & Jerry's was one of the first companies involved in the Benefit Corporation movement, which has developed a rigorous set of principles and standards on which to evaluate companies in terms of social and environmental performance, accountability, and transparency.

As you can see, Ben & Jerry's has a strong link between its mission and its strategies. CEO Matthew McCarthy explains that the brand's tradition is to promote sustainability and advocate for social causes while promoting ice cream![2]

Today, Ben & Jerry's is owned by Unilever, which is the market leader in the global ice cream industry—one that is expected to reach $74.9 billion by 2024. Ben & Jerry's recently added a line of non-dairy flavors made with almond milk that are certified 100 percent vegan, and it offered beer and ice cream flavor pairings in honor of St. Patrick's Day. In addition, the company supports a foundation that helps employees engage in philanthropy and activism. While customers love Ben & Jerry's flavors, many buy its products to support its social mission. As a testament to its success, Ben & Jerry's has over 8.7 million fans on Facebook![3]

VIDEO 2-1
Ben & Jerry's
kerin.tv/15e/v2-1

Chapter 2 describes how organizations set goals to provide an overall direction to their organizational and marketing strategies. The marketing department of an organization converts these strategies into plans that must be implemented and then evaluated so deviations can be exploited or corrected based on the marketing environment.

TODAY'S ORGANIZATIONS

In studying today's organizations, it is important to recognize (1) the kinds of organizations that exist, (2) what strategy is, and (3) how this strategy relates to the three levels of structure found in many large organizations.

LO 2-1

Describe three kinds of organizations and the three levels of strategy in them.

Kinds of Organizations

An *organization* is a legal entity that consists of people who share a common mission. This motivates them to develop *offerings* (goods, services, or ideas) that create value for both the organization and its customers by satisfying their needs and wants.[4] Today's organizations are of three types: (1) for-profit organizations, (2) nonprofit organizations, and (3) government agencies.

A *for-profit organization*, often called a *business firm*, is a privately owned organization such as Target, Nike, or Keurig that serves its customers to earn a profit so that it can survive. **Profit** is the money left after a for-profit organization subtracts its total expenses from its total revenues and is the reward for the risk it undertakes in marketing its offerings.

In contrast, a *nonprofit organization* is a nongovernmental organization that serves its customers but does not have profit as an organizational goal. Instead, its goals may be operational efficiency or client satisfaction. Regardless, it also must receive sufficient funds above its expenses to continue operations. Organizations like Teach For America, described in the Making Responsible Decisions box, seek to solve the practical needs of society and are often structured as nonprofit organizations.[5] For simplicity in the rest of the book, the terms *firm*, *company*, and *organization* are used interchangeably to cover both for-profit and nonprofit organizations.

Last, a *government agency* is a federal, state, county, or city unit that provides a specific service to its constituents. For example, the Census Bureau, a unit of the U.S. Department of Commerce, is a federal government agency that provides population and economic data.

Organizations that develop similar offerings create an *industry*, such as the computer industry or the automobile industry.[6] As a result, organizations make strategic decisions that reflect the dynamics of the industry to create a compelling and sustainable advantage for their offerings relative to those of competitors and achieve a superior level of performance.[7] Much of an organization's marketing strategy is having a clear understanding of the industry within which it competes.

What Is Strategy?

An organization has limited human, financial, technological, and other resources available to produce and market its offerings–it can't be all things to all people! Every organization must develop strategies to help focus and direct its efforts to accomplish its goals. However, the definition of strategy has been the subject of debate among management and marketing theorists. For our purpose, **strategy** is an organization's long-term course of action designed to deliver a unique customer experience while achieving its goals.[8] All organizations set a strategic direction. And marketing helps to both set this direction and move the organization there.

Keurig is an example of a for-profit organization. Its K-Mini Plus Single Serve Coffee Maker is slim, fast, and also travel mug friendly.
Source: Keurig Dr Pepper, Inc.

Making Responsible Decisions

Social Responsibility

New Types of Organizations Help Entrepreneurs Focus on Passion and Purpose

Filmmaker Pete Williams recently spent two years creating a documentary called *The New Breed* to describe the growing movement of people who are committed to using business concepts to change the world for good. These "social entrepreneurs" are using a variety of organizational models to address social needs about which they are passionate. The enterprises are sometimes organized as traditional for-profit companies with a for-purpose orientation. They can also be benefit corporations, which are for-profit organizations with legal requirements for social and environmental impact assessment. Finally, social entrepreneurs often create enterprises that are organized as nonprofit ventures. The issues they are focusing on range from health care delivery, to the cost of higher education, to agricultural efficiency.

Each year *Forbes* magazine recognizes some of the most innovative social ventures in its annual list of *30 Under 30: Social Entrepreneurs.* For example, Jenny Xia and Patrick Schmitt met in college, decided they wanted to have a positive impact on the world, and founded FreeWill. The social venture is an online service that makes estate planning warm, accessible, and totally free so that users can easily care for the people and causes they love. So, has the idea been a success? To date, more than 32,000 people have used the FreeWill service to create a will, and they have committed more than $373 million to charity!

Teach For America is another example of a creative social venture. Launched by college senior Wendy Kopp, Teach For America is the national corps of outstanding recent college graduates who commit to teach for two years in urban and rural public schools and become lifelong leaders in expanding educational opportunity. Each year more than 10,000 corps members teach 750,000 students.

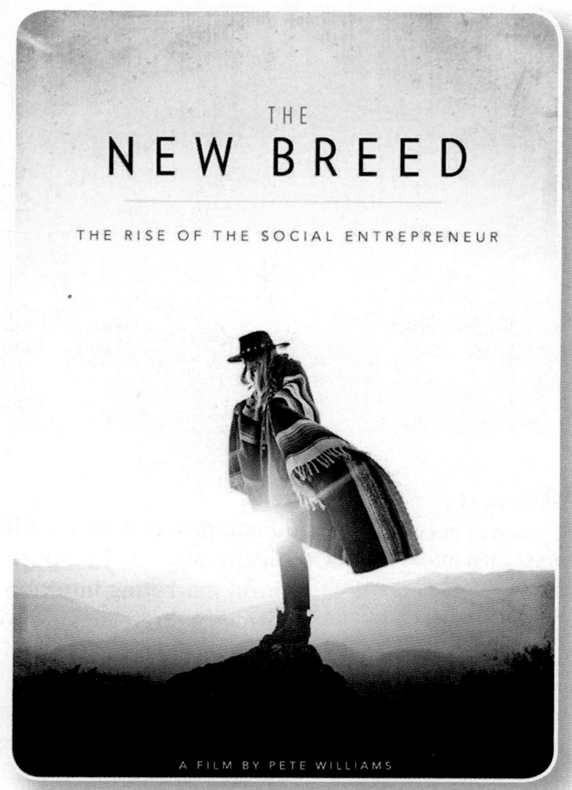

The New Breed/Stay Gold Studios

These examples illustrate how organizations are changing to create value for a broad range of constituents by addressing the needs and challenges of society.

The Structure of Today's Organizations

Large organizations are extremely complex. They usually consist of three organizational levels whose strategies are linked to marketing, as shown in Figure 2–1.

Corporate Level The *corporate level* is where top management directs overall strategy for the entire organization. "Top management" usually means the board of directors and senior management officers with a variety of skills and experiences that are invaluable in establishing the organization's overall strategy.

The president or chief executive officer (CEO) is the highest-ranking officer in the organization and is usually a member of its board of directors. This person must possess leadership skills ranging from overseeing the organization's daily operations to spearheading strategy planning efforts that may determine its very survival.

In recent years, many large firms have changed the title of the head of marketing from vice president of marketing to chief marketing officer (CMO). In fact, 70 percent of *Fortune*

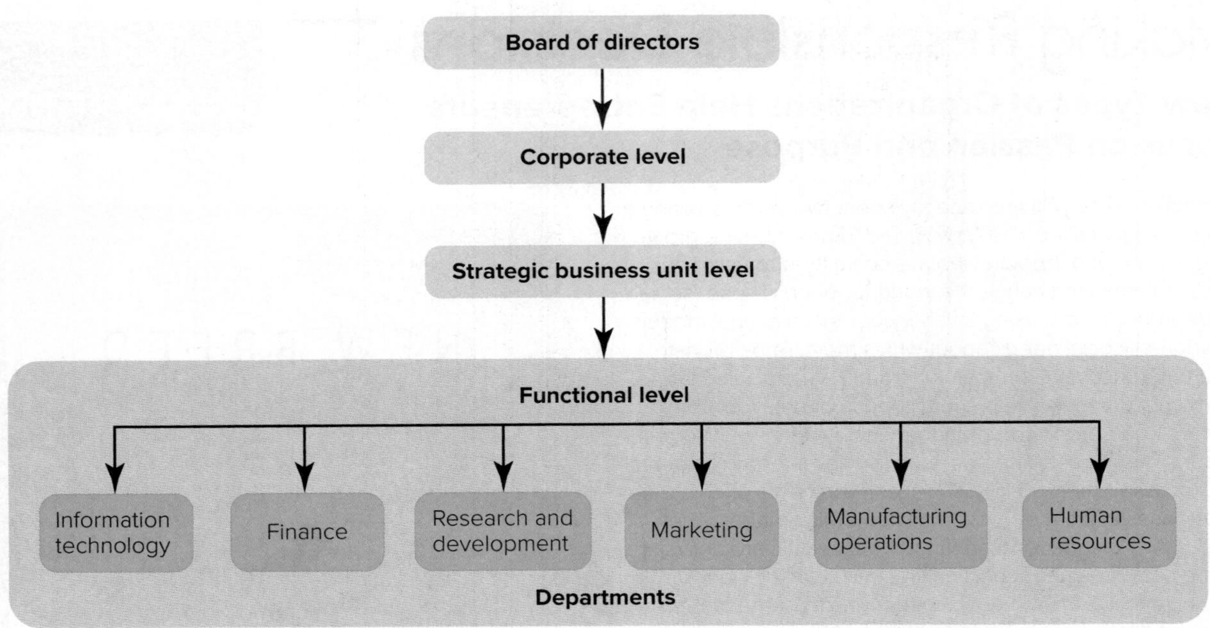

FIGURE 2–1
The board of directors oversees the three levels of strategy in organizations: corporate, strategic business unit, and functional.

500 companies have a CMO. These CMOs have an important role in top management and typically offer multi-industry backgrounds, cross-functional management expertise, and insightful marketing intuition as qualifications. In addition, they are increasingly called upon to bring "a strategic viewpoint, exceptional measurement and analytical capabilities, financial management rigor, and operational savviness to their role."[9]

Strategic Business Unit Level Some multimarket, multiproduct firms, such as Prada and Johnson & Johnson, manage a portfolio or group of businesses. Each group is a *strategic business unit (SBU)*, which is a subsidiary, division, or unit of an organization that markets a set of related offerings to a clearly defined target market. At the *strategic business unit level*,

Prada manages a portfolio or group of businesses—including clothing, perfume, leather goods, and footwear—each of which may be viewed as a strategic business unit (SBU).
Lintao Zhang/Getty Images

managers set a more specific strategic direction for their businesses to exploit value-creating opportunities. For less complex firms with a single business focus, such as Ben & Jerry's, the corporate and business unit levels may merge.

Functional Level Each strategic business unit has a *functional level,* where groups of specialists actually create value for the organization. The term *department* generally refers to these specialized functions such as marketing and finance (see Figure 2–1). At the functional level, the organization's strategic direction becomes its most specific and focused. Just as there is a hierarchy of levels within an organization, there is a hierarchy of strategic directions set by managers at each level.

A key role of the marketing department is to look outward by listening to customers, developing offerings, implementing marketing program actions, and then evaluating whether those actions are achieving the organization's goals. When developing marketing programs for new or improved offerings, an organization's senior management may form *cross-functional teams.* These consist of a small number of people from different departments who are mutually accountable to accomplish a task or a common set of performance goals. Sometimes these teams will have representatives from outside the organization, such as suppliers or customers, to assist them.

LEARNING REVIEW

2-1. What is the difference between a for-profit and a nonprofit organization?

2-2. What are examples of a functional level in an organization?

STRATEGY IN VISIONARY ORGANIZATIONS

LO 2-2
Describe core values, mission, organizational culture, business, and goals.

To be successful, today's organizations must be forward-looking. They must anticipate future events and then respond quickly and effectively to those events. In addition, they must thrive in today's uncertain, chaotic, rapidly changing environment. A visionary organization must specify its foundation (why does it exist?), set a direction (what will it do?), and formulate strategies (how will it do it?), as shown in Figure 2–2.[10]

Organizational Foundation: Why Does It Exist?

An organization's foundation is its philosophical reason for being—why it exists. At their most basic level organizations exist to create value for someone. Successful visionary organizations use this foundation to guide and inspire their employees through three elements: core values, mission, and organizational culture.

Core Values An organization's **core values** are the fundamental, passionate, and enduring principles that guide its conduct over time. A firm's founders or senior management develop these core values, which are consistent with their essential beliefs and character.

FIGURE 2–2
Today's visionary organizations use key elements to (1) establish a foundation and (2) set a direction using (3) strategies that enable them to develop and market their products successfully.

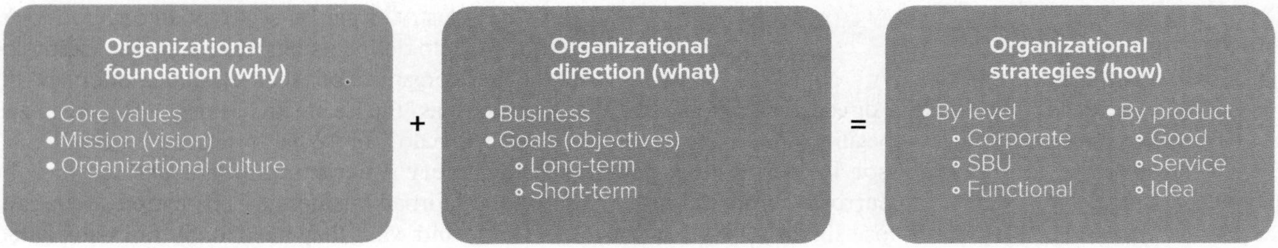

They capture the firm's heart and soul and serve to inspire and motivate its *stakeholders*—employees, shareholders, board of directors, suppliers, distributors, creditors, unions, government, local communities, and customers. Core values also are timeless and guide the organization's conduct. The seven core values at IKEA, for example, are (1) humbleness and willpower, (2) leadership by example, (3) daring to be different, (4) togetherness and enthusiasm, (5) cost-consciousness, (6) constant desire for renewal, and (7) accept and delegate responsibility. To be effective, an organization's core values must be communicated to and supported by its top management and employees.[11]

Mission By understanding its core values, an organization can take steps to define its **mission**, a statement of the organization's function in society that often identifies its customers, markets, products, and technologies. Often used interchangeably with *vision*, a *mission statement* should be clear, concise, meaningful, inspirational, and long-term.[12]

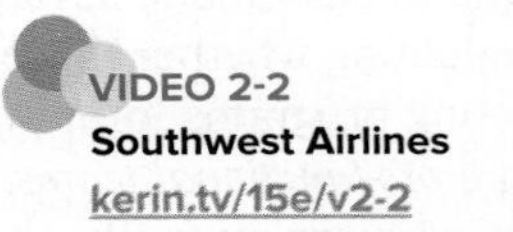
VIDEO 2-2
Southwest Airlines
kerin.tv/15e/v2-2

Inspiration and focus appear in the mission statements of for-profit organizations, as well as nonprofit organizations and government agencies. For example:

- *Southwest Airlines*: "Dedication to the highest quality of Customer Service delivered with a sense of warmth, friendliness, individual pride, and Company Spirit."[13]
- *American Red Cross*: "To prevent and alleviate human suffering in the face of emergencies by mobilizing the power of volunteers and the generosity of donors."[14]
- *Federal Trade Commission*: "To prevent business practices that are anticompetitive or deceptive or unfair to consumers; to enhance informed consumer choice and public understanding of the competitive process; and to accomplish this without unduly burdening legitimate business activity."[15]

Each statement exhibits the qualities of a good mission and provides a compelling picture of an envisioned future.

Recently, many organizations have added a social element to their mission statements to reflect an ideal that is morally right and worthwhile. This is what Ben & Jerry's social mission statement shows in the chapter opener. Stakeholders, particularly customers, employees, and now society, are asking organizations to serve two purposes—to create financial value while also paying attention to social goals.[16]

Organizational Culture An organization must connect with all of its stakeholders. Thus, an important corporate-level marketing function is communicating its core values and mission to them. These activities send clear messages to employees and other stakeholders about **organizational culture**—the set of values, ideas, attitudes, and norms of behavior that is learned and shared among the members of an organization.

Heart sets us apart
Introducing a vibrant look inspired by our love of People.
Southwest

"Heart sets us apart" ads emphasize how providing a warm, friendly experience is part of Southwest Airlines' organizational strategy.
Source: Southwest Airlines Co.

Organizational Direction: What Will It Do?

As shown in Figure 2–2, the organization's foundation enables it to set a direction in terms of (1) the "business" it is in and (2) its specific goals.

Business A **business** describes the clear, broad, underlying industry or market sector of an organization's offering. To help define its business, an organization looks at the set of organizations that sell similar offerings—those that are in direct competition with each other—such as "the ice cream business." The organization can then begin to answer the questions "What do we do?" or "What business are we in?"

Professor Theodore Levitt saw that 20th-century American railroads defined their business too narrowly, proclaiming, "We are in the railroad business!" This myopic focus caused them to lose sight of who their customers were and what they needed. So railroads failed to

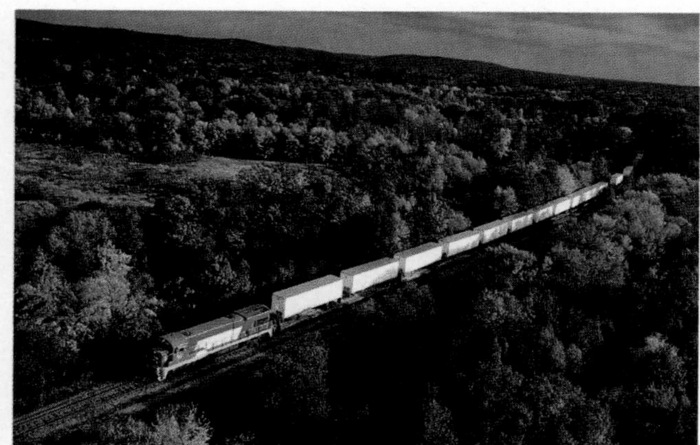

In the first half of the 20th century, what "business" did railroad executives believe they were in? The text reveals their disastrous error.
Digital Vision/Getty Images

develop strategies to compete with airlines, barges, pipelines, and trucks. As a result, many railroads merged or went bankrupt. Railroads should have realized they were in "the transportation business." Similarly, the publishing industry defined its business as being the printer of newspapers and magazines. The dramatic decline in demand for print publications, however, suggests that it should view itself as being in the information and entertainment business.[17]

With today's increased global competition, many organizations are rethinking their *business model*, the strategies an organization develops to provide value to the customers it serves. Technological innovation is often the trigger for this business model change, particularly when it is linked to consumer needs. Netflix, for example, changed its business model several times, shifting its original DVD rental model to a video streaming model, and then to an original content production model.[18] Bookstore retailer Barnes & Noble, too, is rethinking its *business model* as e-book readers like Amazon's Kindle and Apple's iPad have gained widespread popularity.[19]

Uber, known for its car transportation services, is continually redefining its business. The company started as a limousine service called UberCab. Soon the business was redefined as a ride-sharing service when it added UberX and UberPool apps which allowed drivers to use their own cars. The definition expanded further, to transportation, when UberRush was added to provide package delivery, Uber Eats was added to provide food delivery from restaurants, and Uber Jump was added to offer bicycles and scooters. Today, taking a lesson from Theodore Levitt, Uber sees itself as much more than a cab service or ride-sharing service or delivery service. In fact, *Forbes* magazine simply describes Uber's business model as a "frictionless middleman."[20]

Why is the definition of Uber's business changing? See the text for the answer.
Hatim Kaghat/AFP/Getty Images

VIDEO 2-3
Uber Video
kerin.tv/c15e/v2-3

Goals **Goals** or **objectives** (terms used interchangeably in this book) are statements of an accomplishment of a task to be achieved, often by a specific time. Goals convert an organization's mission and business into long- and short-term performance targets. Business firms can pursue several different types of goals:

- *Profit*. Most firms seek to maximize profits—to get as high a financial return on investment (ROI) as possible.
- *Sales*. If profits are acceptable, a firm may elect to maintain or increase its sales (dollars or units) even though profits may not be maximized.
- *Market share*. **Market share** is the ratio of sales revenue of the firm to the total sales revenue of all firms in the industry, including the firm itself.
- *Quality*. A firm may seek to offer a level of quality that meets or exceeds the cost and performance expectations of its customers.
- *Customer satisfaction*. Customers are the reason the organization exists, so their perceptions and actions are of vital importance. Satisfaction can be measured with surveys or by the number of customer complaints.
- *Employee welfare*. A firm may recognize the critical importance of its employees by stating its goal of providing them with good employment opportunities and working conditions.
- *Social responsibility*. Firms may seek to balance the conflicting goals of stakeholders to promote their overall welfare, even at the expense of profits.

Nonprofit organizations (such as museums and hospitals) also have goals, such as to serve consumers as efficiently as possible. Similarly, government agencies set goals that seek to serve the public good.

Organizational Strategies: How Will It Do It?

As shown in Figure 2-2, the organizational foundation sets the "why" of organizations and the organizational direction sets the "what." To convert these into actual results, the organizational strategies are concerned with the "how." These organizational strategies vary in at least two ways, depending on (1) a strategy's level in the organization and (2) the offerings an organization provides to its customers.

Variation by Level Moving down the levels in an organization involves creating increasingly specific, detailed strategies and plans. So, at the corporate level, top managers create a portfolio of market-product businesses (SBUs) that is consistent with the mission statement. At the strategic business unit level managers focus on specific value-creation activities such as improving quality, lowering cost, or adding services. Finally, at the functional level, the issue is who makes tomorrow's sales call.

Variation by Product Organizational strategies also vary by the organization's products. The strategy will be far different when marketing a very tangible physical good (Ben & Jerry's ice cream), a service (a Southwest Airlines flight), or an idea (a donation to the American Red Cross).

Most organizations develop a marketing plan as a part of their strategic marketing planning efforts. A **marketing plan** is a road map for the marketing actions of an organization for a specified future time period, such as one year or five years. The planning phase of the strategic marketing process (discussed later) usually results in a marketing plan that directs the marketing actions of an organization. Appendix A at the end of this chapter provides guidelines for writing a marketing plan.

LEARNING REVIEW

2-3. What is the meaning of an organization's mission?

2-4. What is the difference between an organization's business and its goals?

Tracking Strategic Performance with Marketing Analytics

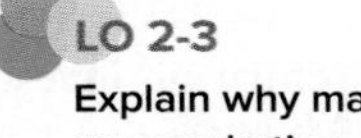

Explain why managers use marketing dashboards and marketing metrics.

Although marketing managers can set the strategic direction for their organizations, how do they know if they are making progress in getting there? As several industry experts have observed, "You can't manage what you don't measure."[21] One answer to this problem is the growing field of data analytics, or big data, which enables data-driven decisions by collecting data and presenting them in a visual format such as a marketing dashboard.

Car Dashboards and Marketing Dashboards A **marketing dashboard** is the visual display of the essential information related to achieving a marketing objective.[22] Today's business intelligence and artificial intelligence tools often provide real-time data to allow marketing mix changes, personalization, and evaluation of customer satisfaction. An example is when a chief marketing officer (CMO) wants to see daily what the effect of a new social media campaign is on a product's sales.[23]

The idea of a marketing dashboard really comes from the display of information found on a car's dashboard. On a car's dashboard, we glance at the fuel gauge and take action when our gas is getting low. With a marketing dashboard, a marketing manager glances at a graph or table to monitor key metrics and makes a decision to take action or analyze the problem further.[24]

Dashboards, Metrics, and Plans The marketing dashboard from Dundas Data Visualization, Inc. in Figure 2-3 is from Sonatica, a hypothetical hardware and software firm.

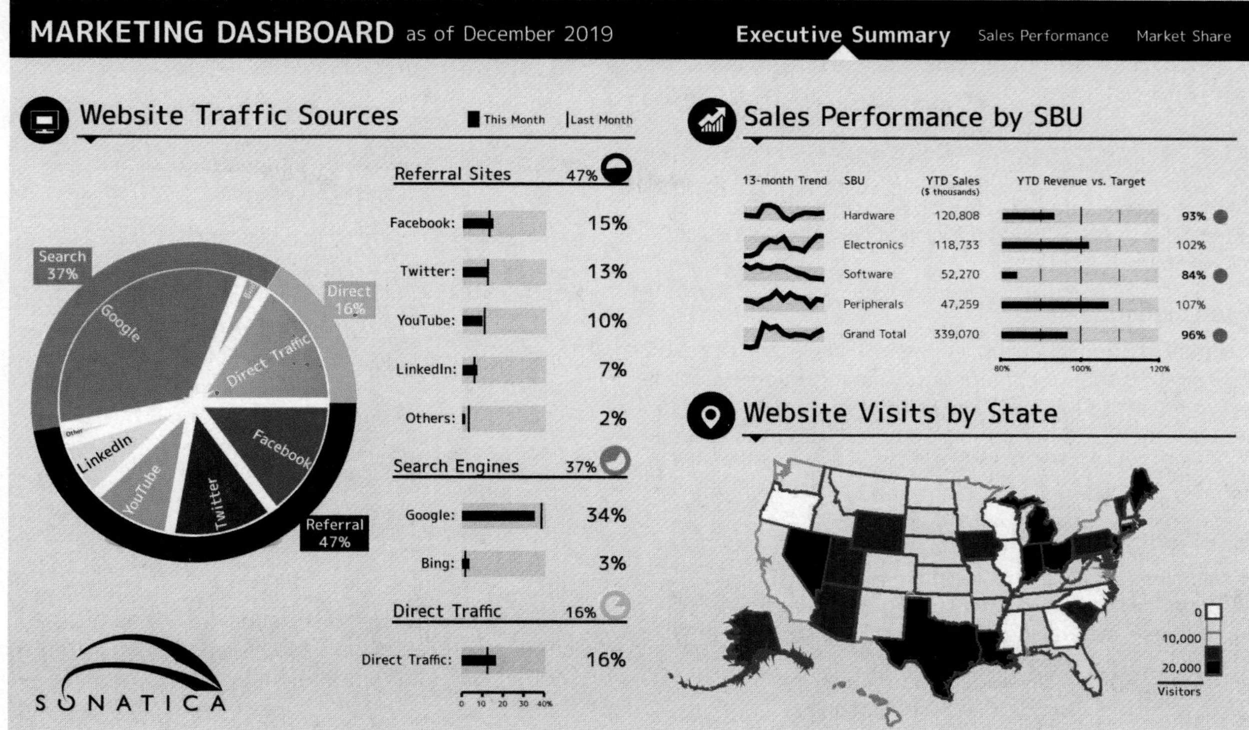

Source: Dundas Data Visualization, Inc.

FIGURE 2–3 An effective marketing dashboard, like this one from Dundas Data Visualization, Inc., helps managers assess a business situation at a glance.

This dashboard shows graphic displays of key performance indicators linked to Sonatica's product lines.[25] Each display in a marketing dashboard shows a **marketing metric**, which is a measure of the quantitative value or trend of a marketing action or result.[26] Choosing which marketing metrics to display is critical for a busy manager, who can be overwhelmed with irrelevant data.[27]

Today's marketers use *data visualization*, which presents information about an organization's marketing metrics graphically so marketers can quickly (1) spot deviations from plans during the evaluation phase and (2) take corrective actions.[28] This book uses data visualization in many figures to highlight in color key points described in the text. The Sonatica marketing dashboard in Figure 2–3 prepared by Dundas Data Visualization, Inc. effectively uses data visualization tools like a pie chart, a line or bar chart, and a map to show how parts of its business are performing as of December 2019:

- *Website Traffic Sources*. The color-coded perimeter of the pie chart shows the three main sources of website traffic (referral sites at 47 percent, search engines at 37 percent, and direct traffic at 16 percent). These three colors link to those of the circles in the column of website traffic sources. Of the 47 percent of traffic coming from referral sites, the horizontal *bullet graphs* to the right show that Sonatica's Facebook visits comprise 15 percent of total website traffic, up from a month ago (as shown by the vertical line).
- *Sales Performance by SBU*. The *spark lines* (the wavy lines in the far left column) show the 13-month trends of Sonatica's strategic business units (SBUs). For example, the trends in electronics and peripherals are generally up, causing their sales to exceed their YTD (year to date) targets. Conversely, both software and hardware sales failed to meet YTD targets, a problem quickly noted by a marketing manager seeing the red "warning" circles in their rows at the far right. This suggests that immediate corrective actions are needed for the software and hardware SBUs.
- *Website Visits by State*. The U.S. map shows that the darker the state, the greater the number of website visits for the current month. For example, Texas has close to 20,000 visits per month, while Illinois has none.

Applying Marketing Metrics

How Well Is Ben & Jerry's Doing?

As the marketing manager for Ben & Jerry's, you need to assess how it is doing within the United States in the super-premium ice cream market in which it competes. For this, you choose two marketing metrics: dollar sales and dollar market share.

Your Challenge

Scanner data from checkout counters in supermarkets and other retailers show the total industry sales of super-premium ice cream were \$1.25 billion in 2019. Internal company data show you that Ben & Jerry's sold 50 million units at an average price of \$5.00 per unit in 2019. A "unit" in super-premium ice cream is one pint.

Your Findings

Dollar sales and dollar market share for 2019 can be calculated using simple formulas and displayed on the Ben & Jerry's marketing dashboard as follows:

$$\text{Dollar sales (\$)} = \text{Average price} \times \text{Quantity sold} = \$5.00 \times 50 \text{ million units} = \$250 \text{ million}$$

$$\text{Dollar market share (\%)} = \frac{\text{Ben \& Jerry's sales (\$)}}{\text{Total industry sales (\$)}} = \frac{\$250 \text{ million}}{\$1.25 \text{ billion}} = 0.20 \text{ or } 20\%$$

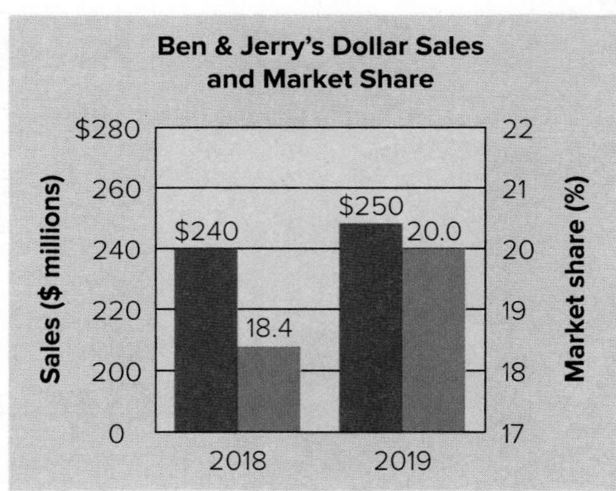

Your dashboard displays show that from 2018 to 2019 dollar sales increased from \$240 million to \$250 million and that dollar market share grew from 18.4 to 20.0 percent.

Your Action

The results need to be compared with the goals established for these metrics. In addition, they should be compared with previous years' results to see if the trends are increasing, flat, or decreasing. This will lead to marketing actions.

The Ben & Jerry's dashboard in the Applying Marketing Metrics box shows how the two widely used marketing metrics of dollar sales and dollar market share can help the company assess its growth performance from 2018 to 2019. The Applying Marketing Metrics boxes in later chapters highlight other key marketing metrics and how they can lead to marketing actions.

SETTING STRATEGIC DIRECTIONS

LO 2-4

Discuss how an organization assesses where it is now and where it seeks to be.

To set a strategic direction, an organization needs to answer two difficult questions: (1) Where are we now? and (2) Where do we want to go?

A Look Around: Where Are We Now?

Asking an organization where it is at the present time involves identifying its competencies, customers, and competitors.

Competencies Senior managers must ask the question: What do we do best? The answer involves an assessment of the organization's core *competencies*, which are its special capabilities—the skills, technologies, and resources—that distinguish it from other

Lands' End's unconditional guarantee for its products highlights its focus on customers.
Source: Lands' End

organizations and provide customer value. Exploiting these competencies can lead to success.[29] Competencies should be distinctive enough to provide a *competitive advantage*, a unique strength relative to competitors that provides superior returns, often based on quality, time, cost, or innovation.[30]

Customers Ben & Jerry's customers are ice cream and frozen yogurt customers who have different preferences (form, flavor, health, and convenience). Boeing's jet airliner customers include passenger airlines such as American, United, and Southwest who serve travelers that need this type of service. Lands' End communicates a remarkable commitment to its customers and its product quality with these unconditional words:

Guaranteed. Period.®

The Lands' End website points out that this guarantee has always been an unconditional one. It reads: "If you're not satisfied with any item, simply return it to us at any time for an exchange or refund of its purchase price." But to get the message across more clearly to its customers, it created the two-word guarantee. The point is that Lands' End's strategy must provide genuine value to customers to ensure that they have a satisfying experience.[31]

Competitors In today's global marketplace, the distinctions among competitors are increasingly blurred. Lands' End started as a catalog retailer. But today, Lands' End competes with not only other clothing catalog retailers such as L.L.Bean but also department stores, mass merchandisers, and specialty shops. In addition, well-known clothing brands such as Eddie Bauer have their own chain stores. Although only some of the clothing in any of these stores may directly compete with Lands' End offerings, all of these retailers have websites to sell their offerings online. This means there's a lot of competition out there.

Growth Strategies: Where Do We Want to Go?

Knowing where the organization is at the present time enables managers to set a direction for the firm and allocate resources to move in that direction. Two techniques to aid managers with these decisions are (1) business portfolio analysis and (2) diversification analysis.

Business Portfolio Analysis Successful organizations have a portfolio or range of offerings (products and services) that possess different growth rates and market shares within the industry in which they operate. The Boston Consulting Group (BCG), an internationally known management consulting firm, has developed **business portfolio analysis**. It is a technique that managers use to quantify performance measures and growth targets to analyze their firms' SBUs as though they were a collection of separate investments.[32] The purpose of this tool is to determine which SBU or offering generates cash and which one requires cash to fund the organization's growth opportunities.

As described in the Marketing Matters box, let's assume you are filling the shoes of Apple CEO Tim Cook. Based on your knowledge of Apple products, you are currently conducting a quick analysis of four major Apple SBUs through 2022. Try to rank them from highest to lowest in terms of percentage growth in expected unit sales. We will introduce you to business portfolio analysis as we look at the possible future of the four Apple SBUs.

Marketing Matters

Technology

Filling the Shoes of Apple CEO Tim Cook: Where Will Apple's Projected Future Growth for Its Major SBUs Come From?

Every CEO of a for-profit organization faces one problem in common: trying to find ways to increase future sales and profits to keep it growing!

Put yourself in Tim Cook's shoes. One of his jobs is to search for new growth opportunities. Using your knowledge about Apple products, do a quick analysis of the four SBUs shown below to determine where Apple should allocate its time and resources. Rate these growth opportunities from highest to lowest in terms of percentage growth in unit sales from 2019 to 2022:

1. ______________________ (Highest)
2. ______________________
3. ______________________
4. ______________________ (Lowest)

We'll walk you through possible answers. You then can evaluate your performance in the discussion that follows and decide whether you're really ready for Mr. Cook's job!

iPod

iPhone

iPad/iPad mini

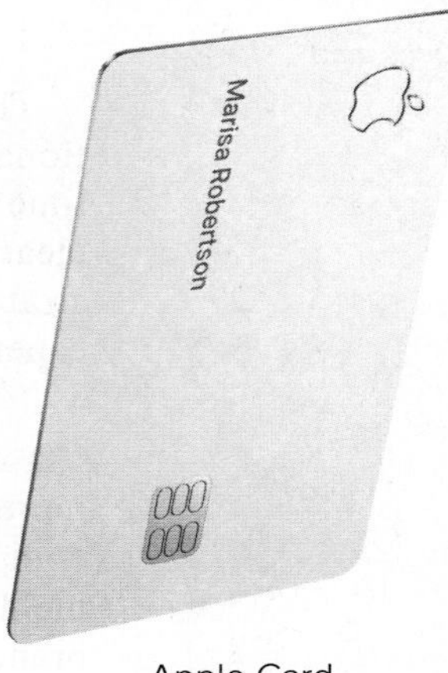

Apple Card

Photos: (iPod) oleganko/Shutterstock and Apple Inc.; (iPhoneX) Oleg GawriloFF/Shutterstock and Apple Inc.; (iPad) Zeynep Demir/Shutterstock and Apple Inc.; (Apple Card) Apple Inc.

The BCG business portfolio analysis requires an organization to locate the position of each of its SBUs on a growth-share matrix (see Figure 2–4). The vertical axis is the *market growth rate*, which is the annual rate of growth of the SBU's industry. The horizontal axis is the *relative market share*, defined as the sales of the SBU divided by the sales of the largest firm in the industry. A relative market share of 10× (at the left end of the scale) means that the SBU has 10 times the share of its largest competitor, whereas a share of 0.1× (at the right end of the scale) means it has only 10 percent of the share of its largest competitor.

The BCG has given specific names and descriptions to the four resulting quadrants in its growth-share matrix based on the amount of cash they generate for or require from the organization:

1. *Question marks* are SBUs with a low share of high-growth markets. They require large injections of cash just to maintain their market share, much less increase it. The name implies management's dilemma for these SBUs: choosing the right ones to invest in and phasing out the rest.
2. *Stars* are SBUs with a high share of high-growth markets that may need extra cash to finance their own rapid future growth. When their growth slows, they are likely to become cash cows.
3. *Cash cows* are SBUs that generate large amounts of cash, far more than they can use. They have dominant shares of slow-growth markets and provide cash to cover the organization's overhead and to invest in other SBUs.

FIGURE 2–4
Boston Consulting Group (BCG) business portfolio analysis for four of Apple's consumer-related SBUs. The red arrow indicates typical movement of a product through the matrix.

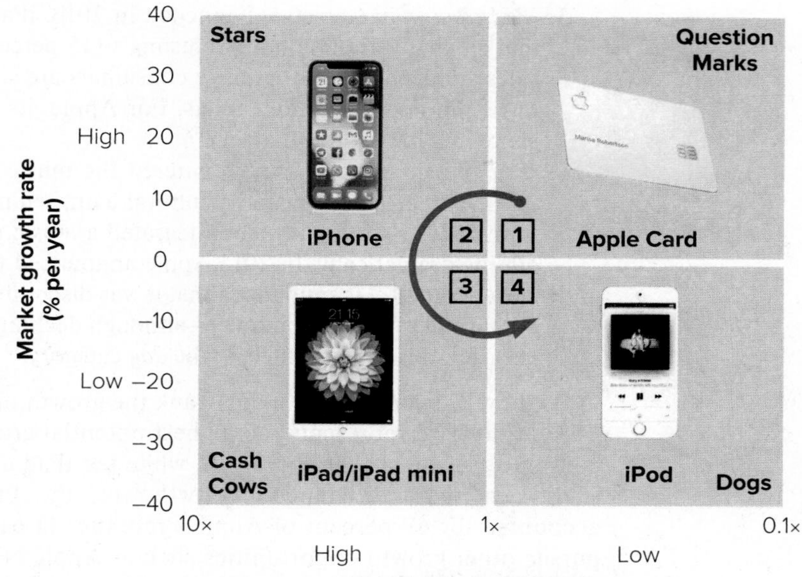

Photos: (iPhoneX) Oleg GawriloFF/Shutterstock and Apple Inc.; (Apple Card) Apple Inc.; (iPad) Zeynep Demir/Shutterstock and Apple Inc.; (iPod) olegganko/Shutterstock and Apple Inc.

What can Apple expect in future growth of sales revenues from its iPhone products . . .

Oleg GawriloFF/Shutterstock and Apple Inc.

4. *Dogs* are SBUs with low shares of slow-growth markets. Although they may generate enough cash to sustain themselves, they may no longer be or may not become real winners for the organization. Dropping SBUs that are dogs may be required if they consume more cash than they generate, except when relationships with other SBUs, competitive considerations, or potential strategic alliances exist.[33]

An organization's SBUs often start as question marks and go counterclockwise around Figure 2–4 to become stars, then cash cows, and finally dogs. Because an organization has limited influence on the market growth rate, its main objective is to try to change its relative dollar or unit market share. To do this, management decides what strategic role each SBU should have in the future and either injects cash into or removes cash from it.

According to Interbrand, a leading brand management consulting firm, Apple has been consistently cited as one of the top global brands over the past decade in its annual Best Global Brands survey. What has made Apple so iconic is not only its revolutionary products but also its commitment to infusing the "human touch" with its technology such that its customers connect with the brand on both a cognitive *and* an emotional level. The late Steve Jobs was instrumental in creating Apple's organizational culture and core values that will continue to guide its future.[34]

Using the BCG business portfolio analysis framework, Figure 2–4 shows that the Apple picture might look this way from 2019 to 2022 for four of its SBUs:[35]

. . . or its Apple Card financial services?

Source: Apple Inc.

1. *Apple Card.* Apple recently entered the financial services market with its version of a credit card, the Apple Card. The card competes with Citi, Chase, and Capital One credit cards and a wide range of other financial payment technologies such as PayPal, Venmo, and Android Pay. Industry analysts estimate that 6 out of 10 Americans have a credit card and that credit card use has grown by 42 percent in the past 7 years. The Apple Card enters the market as a *question mark*.[36]
2. *iPhone* (smartphones). Apple launched its revolutionary iPhone smartphone in 2007. iPhone unit sales skyrocketed and Apple's U.S. market share is now greater than 56 percent, exceeding the 24 percent market share of its largest competitor, Samsung. The smartphone market grew at double-digit rates through 2015 and has been slowing in recent years. U.S. and global smartphone sales are expected to grow at 1 to 2 percent through 2022. High market share and high growth suggest that Apple's iPhone has been a *star* and may become a *cash cow*.[37]

3. *iPad/iPad mini* (tablets). Launched in 2010, iPad unit sales now represent 35 percent market share—leading both Samsung's (15 percent) and Huawei's (10 percent). Tablet sales are declining, however, as consumers are substituting big-screen smartphones and ultra-thin computers for tablets. For Apple, its iPad SBU is a *cash cow* (high market share in a low-growth market).[38]
4. *iPod* (music players). Apple entered the music player market with its iPod device in 2001. The product became a cultural icon, selling more than 50 million units annually until 2010 when the iPhone integrated a music player. Since 2010, sales have been declining dramatically. In 2014 Apple announced that it was discontinuing the iPod classic, and in 2017 it announced that it was discontinuing the iPod shuffle and nano. Today Apple still sells the iPod touch—although declining sales and discontinued products suggest that this SBU is entering the *dog* category.[39]

So, how did you—as Tim Cook—rank the growth opportunity for each of the four SBUs? The Apple Card represents the highest potential growth rate The iPhone SBU is likely to continue growing at 1 to 2 percent, while the iPad and iPod are experiencing a decline in sales. Despite the difference in growth rates, the iPhone and iPad product lines together accounted for 69 percent of Apple's revenues in early 2019. These revenues are used to pursue other growth opportunities such as Apple News, Apple Arcade, Apple HomePod, Apple TV+, Apple Watch, a next-generation phone, and possibly an Apple-enabled car. A careful look at many of Apple's new offerings suggests a shift to services that complement its existing products.[40]

The primary strength of business portfolio analysis lies in forcing a firm to place each of its SBUs in the growth-share matrix, which in turn suggests which SBUs will be cash producers and cash users in the future. Weaknesses of this analysis arise from the difficulty in (1) getting the needed information and (2) incorporating competitive data into business portfolio analysis.[41]

Diversification Analysis **Diversification analysis** is a technique that helps a firm search for growth opportunities from among current and new markets as well as current and new products. For any market, there is both a current product (what the firm now sells) and a new product (what the firm might sell in the future). And for any product there is both a current market (the firm's existing customers) and a new market (the firm's potential customers). As Ben & Jerry's seeks to increase sales revenues, it considers all four market-product strategies shown in Figure 2–5:

VIDEO 2-4
B&J's Chocolate Chip Cookie Dough Video
kerin.tv/15e/v2-4

- *Market penetration* is a marketing strategy to increase sales of current products in current markets, such as selling more Ben & Jerry's Chocolate Chip Cookie Dough ice cream to U.S. consumers. There is no change in either the basic product line or the markets served. Increased sales are generated by selling either more ice cream (through better

FIGURE 2–5
Four market-product strategies: alternative ways to expand sales revenues for Ben & Jerry's using diversification analysis.

MARKETS	PRODUCTS: Current	PRODUCTS: New
Current	**Market penetration** Selling more Ben & Jerry's super-premium ice cream to Americans	**Product development** Selling a new product such as children's clothing under the Ben & Jerry's brand to Americans
New	**Market development** Selling Ben & Jerry's super-premium ice cream to Brazilians for the first time	**Diversification** Selling a new product such as children's clothing under the Ben & Jerry's brand to Brazilians for the first time

promotion or distribution) *or* the same amount of ice cream at a higher price to its current customers.

- *Market development* is a marketing strategy to sell current products to new markets. For Ben & Jerry's, Brazil is an attractive new market. There is good news and bad news for this strategy: As household incomes of Brazilians increase, consumers can buy more ice cream; however, the Ben & Jerry's brand may be unknown to Brazilian consumers.
- *Product development* is a marketing strategy of selling new products to current markets. Ben & Jerry's could leverage its brand by selling children's clothing in the United States. This strategy is risky because Americans may not see the company's expertise in ice cream as extending to children's clothing.
- *Diversification* is a marketing strategy of developing new products and selling them in new markets. This is a potentially high-risk strategy for Ben & Jerry's if it decides to try to sell Ben & Jerry's branded clothing in Brazil. Why? Because the firm has neither previous production nor marketing experience from which to draw in marketing clothing to Brazilian consumers.

Research shows that senior marketing executives prefer to invest in existing markets and products (market penetration) for growth. The second most preferred strategy is product development, followed by market development and diversification, respectively.[42]

LEARNING REVIEW

2-5. What is the difference between a marketing dashboard and a marketing metric?

2-6. What is business portfolio analysis?

2-7. Explain the four market-product strategies in diversification analysis.

THE STRATEGIC MARKETING PROCESS

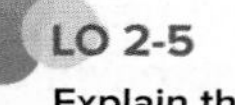

LO 2-5
Explain the three steps of the planning phase of the strategic marketing process.

After an organization assesses where it is and where it wants to go, management attention is focused on the strategic marketing process. The **strategic marketing process** involves the allocation of an organization's marketing mix resources to reach its target markets and achieve a competitive advantage. The process is guided by underlying principles and is divided into three phases: planning, implementation, and evaluation as shown in Figure 2–6.

Principles Underlying the Strategic Marketing Process

Four principles underlie the strategic marketing process.[43] Each principle represents a fundamental assumption about customers, competitors, and organizational resources. They are:

1. *Customers are different.* Customers are not alike. Rather, important differences exist and these differences affect how customers respond to different marketing mix elements.
2. *Customers change.* Customer preferences, needs, and behavior are not static. Customer preferences, needs, and behavior change over time and due to circumstances and are affected by competitor actions.
3. *Competitors change and react.* The sustainability of an organization's competitive advantage is affected by the conduct of present and future competitors and how they react to an organization's actions.
4. *Organizational resources are limited.* No organization has unlimited human, technological, and financial resources. Trade-offs have to be made when capitalizing on organizational opportunities and overcoming threats to their performance.

These principles are central to the concepts, techniques, and tools applied in each phase of the strategic marketing process.

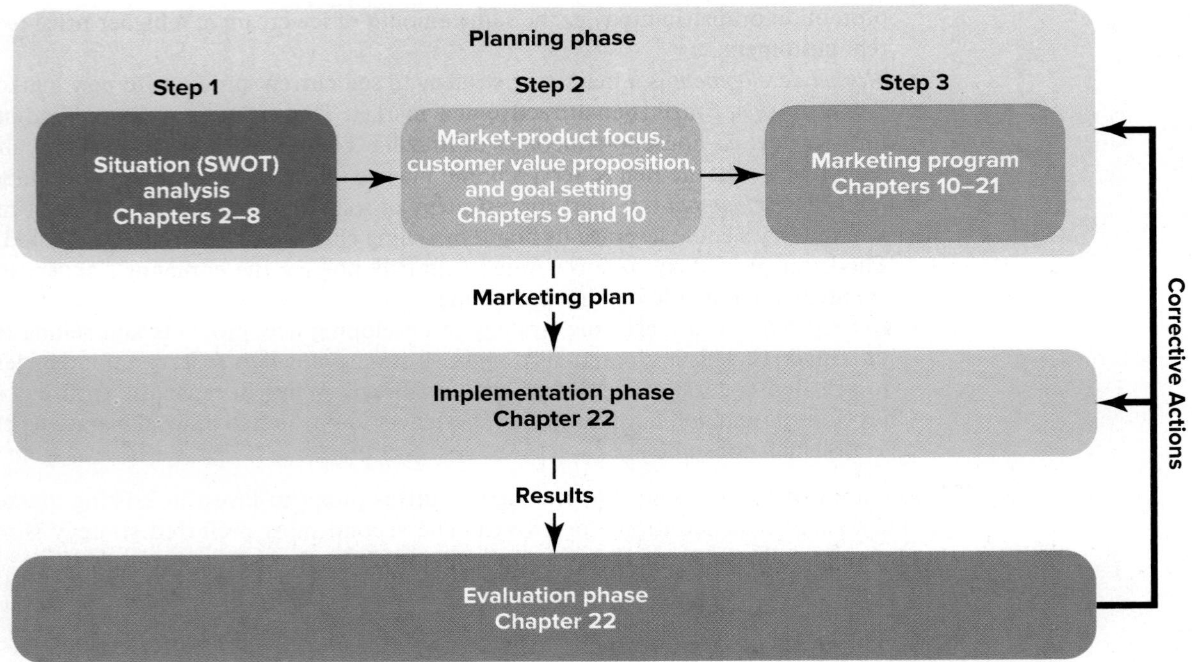

FIGURE 2–6
The strategic marketing process has three vital phases: planning, implementation, and evaluation. The figure also indicates the chapters in which these phases are discussed in the text.

The Planning Phase of the Strategic Marketing Process

Figure 2–6 shows the three steps in the planning phase of the strategic marketing process: (1) conduct a situation (SWOT) analysis; (2) develop a market-product focus, customer value proposition, and goals; and (3) design the marketing program.

Step 1: Conduct a Situation (SWOT) Analysis The essence of **situation analysis** is taking stock of where the firm or product has been recently, where it is now, and where it is headed in terms of the organization's marketing plans and the external forces and trends affecting it. An effective summary of a situation analysis is a **SWOT analysis**, an acronym describing an organization's appraisal of its internal **S**trengths and **W**eaknesses and its external **O**pportunities and **T**hreats.

The SWOT analysis is based on an exhaustive study of four areas that form the foundation upon which the firm builds its marketing program:

- Identify changes and trends in the organization's industry.
- Analyze the organization's current and potential competitors.
- Assess the organization itself, including available resources.
- Research the organization's present and prospective customers.

Assume you are responsible for doing the SWOT analysis for Ben & Jerry's shown in Figure 2–7. Note that the SWOT table has four cells formed by the combination of internal versus external factors (the rows) and favorable versus unfavorable factors (the columns) that identify Ben & Jerry's strengths, weaknesses, opportunities, and threats.

The task is to translate the results of the SWOT analysis into specific marketing actions that will help the firm grow. The ultimate goal is to identify the *critical* strategy-related factors that impact the firm and then build on vital strengths, correct glaring weaknesses, exploit significant opportunities, and avoid disaster-laden threats.

The Ben & Jerry's SWOT analysis in Figure 2–7 can be the basis for these kinds of specific marketing actions. An action in each of the four cells might be:

- *Build on a strength.* Find specific efficiencies in distribution with parent-company Unilever's existing ice cream brands.

FIGURE 2–7
Ben & Jerry's: A SWOT analysis to keep it growing. The picture painted in this SWOT analysis is the basis for management actions.

LOCATION OF FACTOR	TYPE OF FACTOR	
	Favorable	**Unfavorable**
Internal	**Strengths** • Prestigious, well-known brand name among U.S. consumers • Complements Unilever's other ice cream brands • Recognized for its social mission, values, and actions	**Weaknesses** • B&J's social responsibility actions could reduce focus • Experienced managers needed to help growth • Modest sales growth and profits in recent years
External	**Opportunities** • Growing demand for quality ice cream in overseas markets • Increasing U.S. demand for Greek-style yogurt • Many U.S. firms successfully use product and brand extensions	**Threats** • B&J customers read nutritional labels and are concerned with sugary and fatty desserts • Competes with General Mills and Nestlé brands • Increasing competition in international markets

How can Ben & Jerry's develop new products and social responsibility programs that contribute to its mission? The text describes how the strategic marketing process and its SWOT analysis can help.

Source: Ben & Jerry's Homemade, Inc.

- *Correct a weakness*. Recruit experienced managers from other consumer product firms to help stimulate growth.
- *Exploit an opportunity*. Develop new flavors of non-dairy frozen desserts to respond to changes in consumer tastes.
- *Avoid a disaster-laden threat*. Focus on less risky international markets, such as Brazil and Argentina.

Step 2: Develop a Market-Product Focus, Customer Value Proposition, and Goals Determining what products will be directed toward which customers (step 2 of the planning phase in Figure 2–6) is essential for designing an effective marketing program (step 3). This decision is often based on **market segmentation**, which involves aggregating prospective buyers into groups, or segments, that (1) have common needs and (2) will respond similarly to a marketing action. This enables an organization to tailor specific marketing programs for its target market segments.

Step 2 also involves developing a clear **customer value proposition**, which is a cluster of benefits that an organization promises customers (or segments) to satisfy their needs. An effective customer value proposition is a formal statement that meets three criteria. First, it is relevant. That is, it describes how an organization's products solve a customer (segment) problem or improve their situation. Second, it details specific benefits in clear terms. Finally, it states why targeted customers, or customer segments, should purchase your products and not your competitor's offerings. This comparison is often called **points of difference**, or those characteristics of a product that make it superior to competitive substitutes. The value proposition allows an organization to specify meaningful and measurable marketing goals to be achieved.

What does a customer value proposition look like? Consider IKEA, the world's largest home furnishings retailer. Its customer value proposition promises customers (1) a wide range of well-designed, ready-to-assemble, functional home furnishings at low prices, (2) a favorable and consistent shopping and buying experience in its stores, online, and from its catalogs, and (3) uniformity in product selection and quality workmanship across countries. It should not be surprising that IKEA's customer value proposition reflects the company's organizational values described earlier.

FIGURE 2–8
The four Ps elements of the marketing mix must be blended to produce a cohesive marketing program.

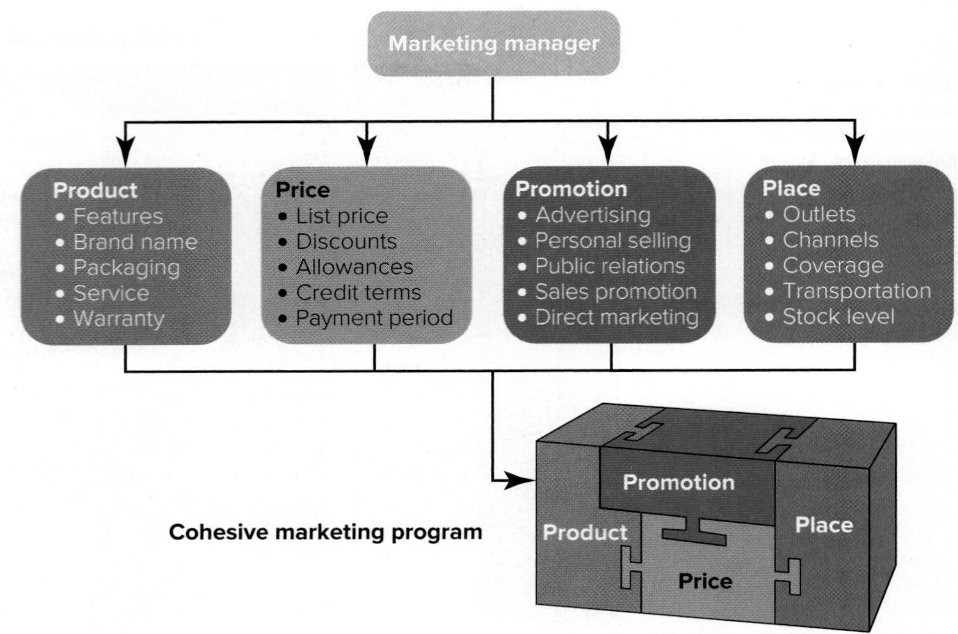

Step 3: Design a Marketing Program Activities in step 2 tell the marketing manager which customers to target and which customer needs the firm's product offerings can satisfy—the *who* and *what* aspects of the strategic marketing process. The *how* aspect—step 3 in the planning phase—involves designing the marketing program and mix (the four Ps) and its budget. Figure 2–8 shows that each marketing mix element is combined to provide a cohesive marketing program.

Putting a marketing program into effect requires that the firm commit time and money to it in the form of a sales forecast (see Chapter 8) and budget that must be approved by top management.

LEARNING REVIEW

2-8. What are the three steps of the planning phase of the strategic marketing process?

2-9. What are points of difference and why are they important?

The Implementation Phase of the Strategic Marketing Process

LO 2-6
Describe the four components of the implementation phase of the strategic marketing process.

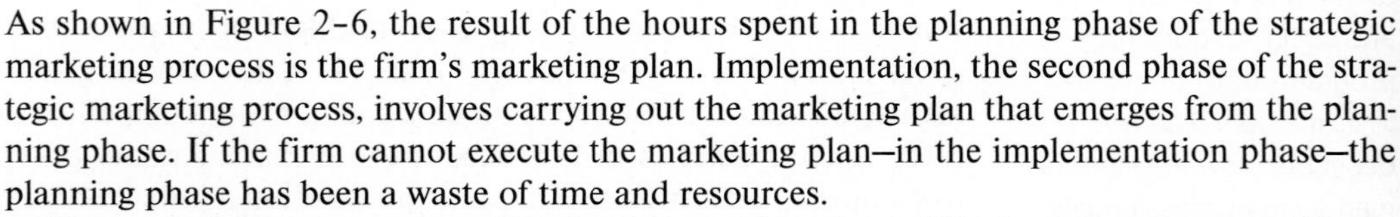

As shown in Figure 2–6, the result of the hours spent in the planning phase of the strategic marketing process is the firm's marketing plan. Implementation, the second phase of the strategic marketing process, involves carrying out the marketing plan that emerges from the planning phase. If the firm cannot execute the marketing plan—in the implementation phase—the planning phase has been a waste of time and resources.

There are four components of the implementation phase: (1) obtaining resources; (2) designing the marketing organization; (3) defining precise tasks, responsibilities, and deadlines; and (4) actually executing the marketing program designed in the planning phase.

Obtaining Resources A key task in the implementation phase of the strategic marketing process is obtaining and assembling sufficient human and financial resources to execute the marketing program successfully. Small business owners often obtain funds from savings, family, friends, and bank loans. Marketing managers in existing organizations obtain these

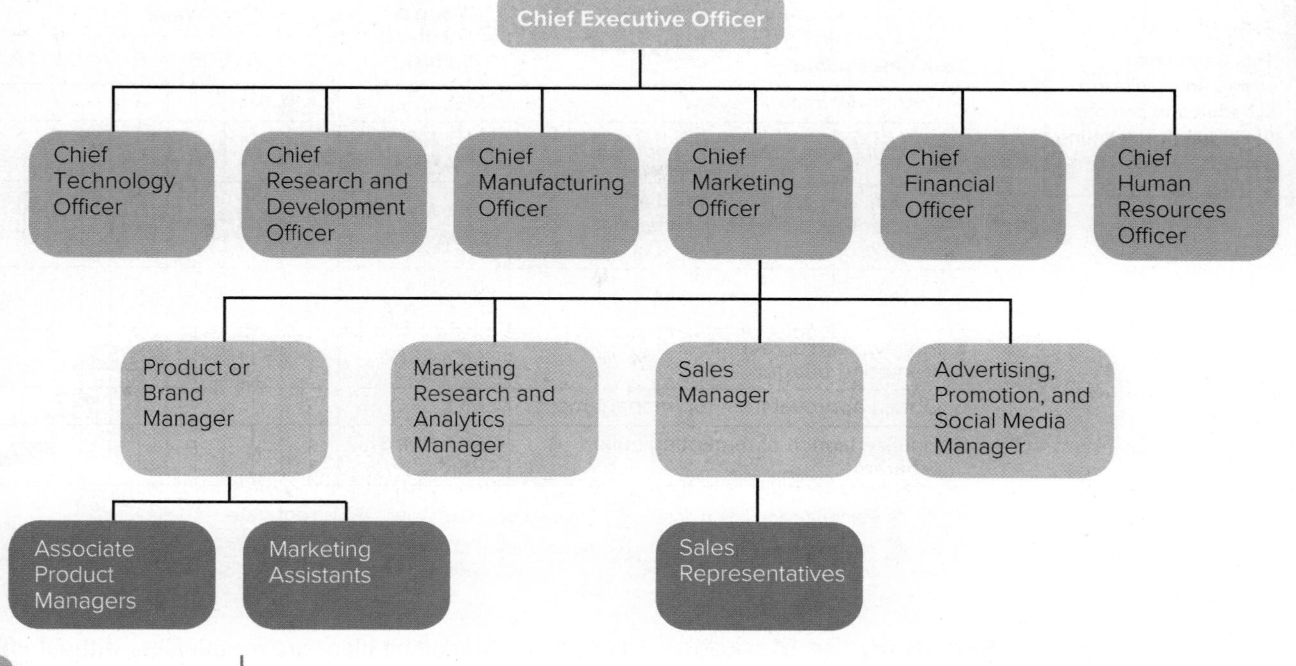

FIGURE 2–9
Organization of a typical manufacturing firm, showing a breakdown of the marketing department.

resources by getting top management to assign managerial talent and invest financial resources through approved marketing budgets.

Designing the Marketing Organization A marketing program needs a marketing organization to implement it. Figure 2–9 shows the organization chart of a typical manufacturing firm, giving some details of the marketing department's structure. Four managers of marketing activities are shown to report to the chief marketing officer or CMO. Sales representatives report to the manager of sales, possibly through several regional sales managers and an international sales manager based on the size of the salesforce. The product or brand managers and their subordinates help plan, implement, and evaluate the marketing plans for their offerings. However, the entire marketing organization is responsible for converting these marketing plans into realistic marketing actions.

Defining Precise Tasks, Responsibilities, and Deadlines Successful implementation requires that team members know the tasks for which they are responsible and the deadlines for completing them. Scheduling activities can be done efficiently with a *Gantt chart,* which is a graph of a program schedule. Figure 2–10 shows a Gantt chart–invented by Henry L. Gantt–used to schedule tasks involved in the strategic marketing process, demonstrating how the concurrent work on several tasks enables team members to deliver an executable marketing program on time. Software applications such as Microsoft Project simplify the task of developing a program schedule or Gantt chart.

Central features of a Gantt chart include: (1) the task, (2) the person or people responsible for completing the task, (3) the date to finish the task, and (4) what is to be delivered. In this example, the people involved include the CMO, the chief financial officer (CFO), marketing research personnel (MR), product managers (PM), sales professionals (SM), and advertising, promotion, and social media specialists (APSM).

The key to all scheduling techniques is to distinguish tasks that *must* be done sequentially from those that *can* be done concurrently. For example, Tasks 6 and 7 in Figure 2–10 *must* be done sequentially. This is because the marketing team must get formal top management approval (Task 6) before it can finalize the marketing mix program (Task 7). In contrast, Tasks 3 and 4 *can* be done somewhat concurrently because the choice of marketing mix program elements overlaps with market segmentation and consumer value proposition determination.

FIGURE 2–10 This Gantt chart shows how tasks are scheduled to complete the strategic marketing process on time.

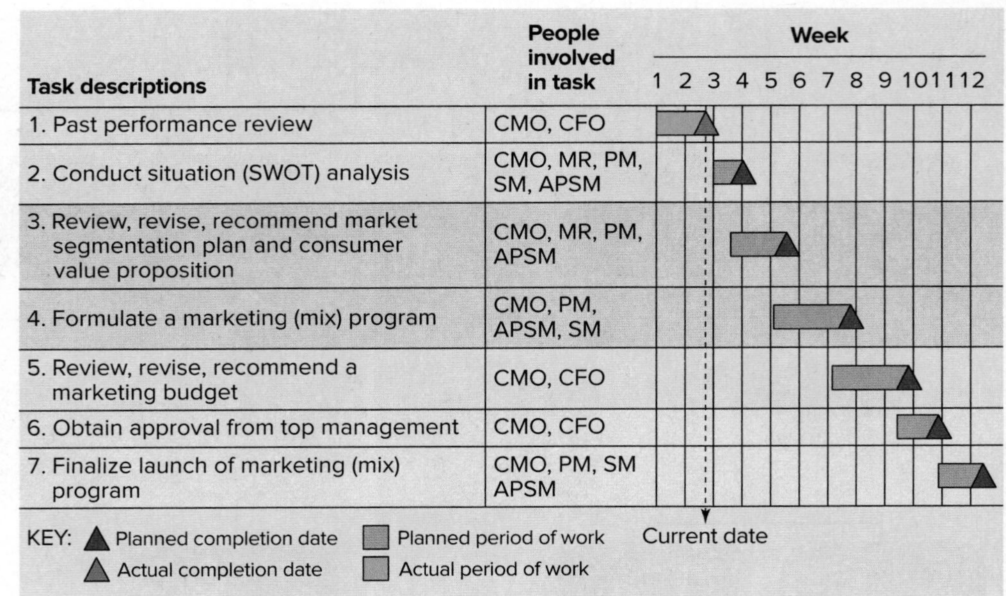

Task descriptions
People involved in task
Week
1 2 3 4 5 6 7 8 9 10 11 12
1. Past performance review
CMO, CFO
2. Conduct situation (SWOT) analysis
CMO, MR, PM, SM, APSM
3. Review, revise, recommend market segmentation plan and consumer value proposition
CMO, MR, PM, APSM
4. Formulate a marketing (mix) program
CMO, PM, APSM, SM
5. Review, revise, recommend a marketing budget
CMO, CFO
6. Obtain approval from top management
CMO, CFO
7. Finalize launch of marketing (mix) program
CMO, PM, SM APSM
Current date
KEY:
Planned completion date
Actual completion date
Planned period of work
Actual period of work

Executing the Marketing Program Marketing plans are meaningless without effective execution of those plans. This requires attention to detail for both marketing strategies and marketing tactics. A **marketing strategy** is the means by which a marketing goal is to be achieved, usually characterized by a specified target market and a marketing program to reach it. The term implies both the end sought (target market) and the means or actions to achieve it (marketing program).

To implement a marketing program successfully, hundreds of detailed decisions are often required to develop the actions that comprise a marketing program for an offering. These actions, called **marketing tactics**, are detailed day-to-day operational marketing actions for each element of the marketing mix that contribute to the overall success of marketing strategies. Writing ads and setting prices for new product lines are examples of marketing tactics.

The Evaluation Phase of the Strategic Marketing Process

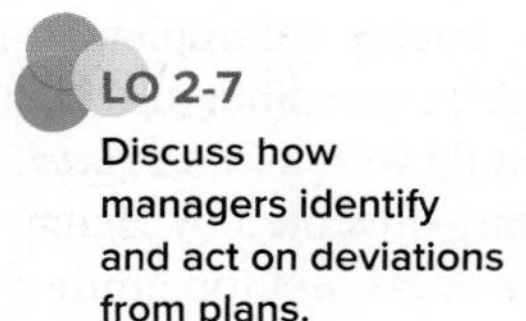

LO 2-7 Discuss how managers identify and act on deviations from plans.

The evaluation phase of the strategic marketing process seeks to keep the marketing program moving in the direction set for it (see Figure 2-6). Accomplishing this requires the marketing manager to (1) compare the results of the marketing program with the goals in the written plans to identify the presence and causes of deviations and (2) act on these deviations—exploiting positive deviations and correcting negative ones.

Comparing Results with Plans to Identify Deviations At the end of its fiscal year, which is September 30, Apple begins the evaluation phase of its strategic marketing process. Suppose you are on an Apple task force in 2009 that is responsible for making plans through 2018. You observe that extending the 2004-2009 trend of Apple's recent sales revenues (line AB in Figure 2-11) to 2018 along line BC shows an annual growth in sales revenue unacceptable to Apple's management.

Looking at potential new products in the Apple pipeline, your task force sets an aggressive annual sales growth target of 25 percent per year–line BD in Figure 2-11. This would give sales revenues of $130 billion in 2014 and $315 billion in 2018.

This reveals a white wedge-shaped gap DBC in the figure. Planners call this the *planning gap*, the difference between the projection of the path to reach a new sales revenue goal (line BD) and the projection of the path of a plan already in place (line BC). The ultimate purpose of the firm's marketing program is to "fill in" this planning gap–in the case of your Apple task

FIGURE 2–11
The evaluation phase of the strategic marketing process requires that the organization compare actual results with goals to identify and act on deviations to fill in its "planning gap." The text describes how Apple is working to fill in its planning gap

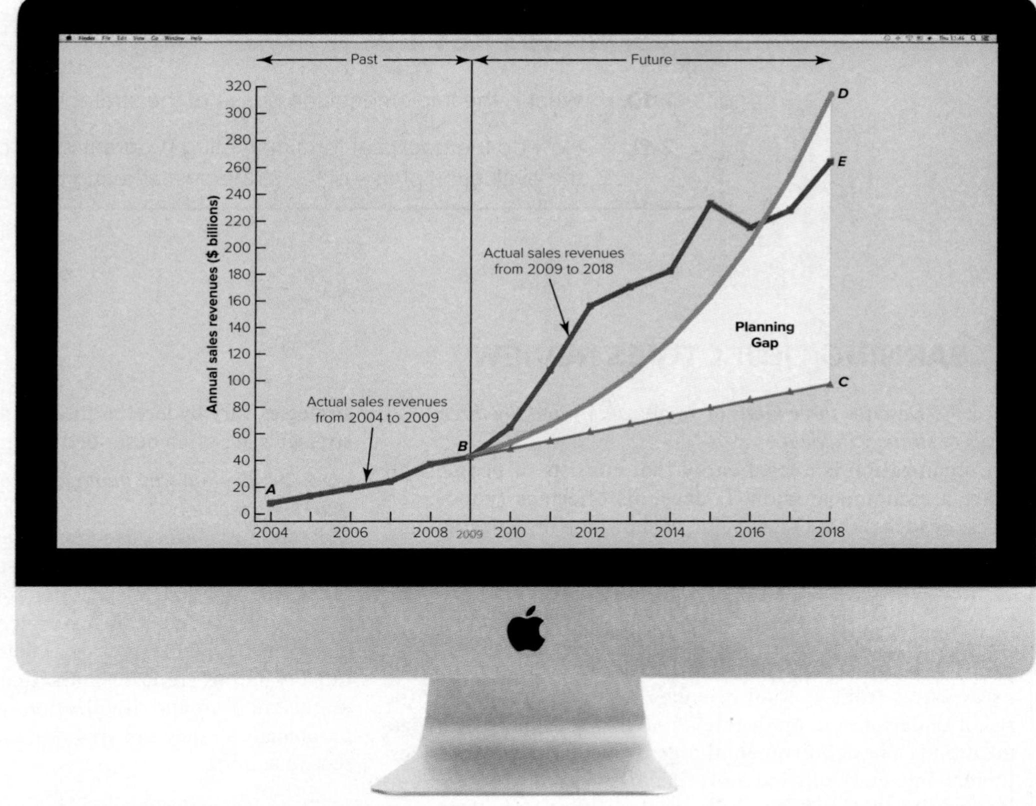

Computer: Joby Sessions/MacFormat Magazine via Getty Images

force, to move its future sales revenue line from the slow-growth line BC up to the more challenging target of line BD.

This is the essence of evaluation: comparing actual results with goals set. To reach aggressive growth targets in sales revenues, firms like Apple must continuously look for a new BCG SBU or product *cash cow* or *star*.

Acting on Deviations When evaluation shows that actual performance differs from expectations, managers need to take immediate marketing actions–exploiting positive deviations and correcting negative ones. Comparing the explosion in Apple's actual sales revenues from 2009 to 2018 (line BE in Figure 2-11) to its target sales revenues (line BD) shows Apple's rare, world-class ability to both generate and anticipate consumer demand and commercialize new technologies for its revolutionary offerings. Let's consider some of its marketing actions:

- *Exploiting a positive deviation*. Favorable customer reactions to Apple's iPhone (2007) and its iPad (2010) enable it to sell the products globally and to introduce improved versions and models, such as the iPad Air (2019) and the iPhone XT and XR (2018). Success of new versions and models also enables the introduction of new products such as the Apple Watch (2015), Apple AirPods (2016), the HomePod (2018), and Apple News (2019).
- *Correcting a negative deviation*. As Apple's desktop PCs became dated, it moved aggressively to replace them with new iMacs and MacBooks. Also, Apple refreshed its MacBook Air (2015, 2017) and MacBook Pro (2016, 2017) lines of laptops. Similarly, as demand for tablets has declined, Apple introduced next-generation versions of iPad Air (2019) and iPad mini (2019).

As we saw earlier in the BCG business portfolio analysis of the four Apple product lines, the firm has several *stars* and *cash cows* to fill in its planning gap. We shall explore Apple's market-product strategies in more detail later in Chapters 9 and 10.

LEARNING REVIEW

2-10. What is the implementation phase of the strategic marketing process?

2-11. How do the goals set for a marketing program in the planning phase relate to the evaluation phase of the strategic marketing process?

LEARNING OBJECTIVES REVIEW

LO 2-1 *Describe three kinds of organizations and the three levels of strategy in them.*

An organization is a legal entity that consists of people who share a common mission. It develops offerings (goods, services, or ideas) that create value for both the organization and its customers by satisfying their needs and wants. Today's organizations are of three types: for-profit organizations, nonprofit organizations, and government agencies. A for-profit organization serves its customers to earn a profit so that it can survive. Profit is the money left after a for-profit organization subtracts its expenses from its total revenues and is the reward for the risk it undertakes in marketing its offerings. A nonprofit organization is a nongovernmental organization that serves its customers but does not have profit as an organizational goal. Instead, its goals may be operational efficiency or client satisfaction. A government agency is a federal, state, county, or city unit that provides a specific service to its constituents. Most large for-profit and nonprofit organizations are divided into three levels of strategy: (*a*) the corporate level, where top management directs overall strategy for the entire organization; (*b*) the strategic business unit level, where managers set a more specific strategic direction for their businesses to exploit value-creating opportunities; and (*c*) the functional level, where groups of specialists actually create value for the organization.

LO 2-2 *Describe core values, mission, organizational culture, business, and goals.*

Organizations exist to accomplish something for someone. To give organizations direction and focus, they continuously assess their core values, mission, organizational culture, business, and goals. Today's organizations specify their foundation, set a direction, and formulate strategies—the "why," "what," and "how" factors, respectively. Core values are the organization's fundamental, passionate, and enduring principles that guide its conduct over time. The organization's mission is a statement of its function in society, often identifying its customers, markets, products, and technologies. Organizational culture is a set of values, ideas, attitudes, and norms of behavior that is learned and shared among the members of an organization. To answer the question, "What business are we in?" an organization defines its "business"—the clear, broad, underlying industry category or market sector of its offering. The organization's goals (or objectives) are statements of an accomplishment of a task to be achieved, often by a specific time. Finally, organizational strategies vary by level in the organization and by product. The strategies are often described in a marketing plan.

LO 2-3 *Explain why managers use marketing dashboards and marketing metrics.*

Marketing managers use marketing dashboards to visually display the essential information related to achieving a marketing objective. This information consists of key performance measures of a product category, such as sales or market share, known as marketing metrics, which are a measure of the quantitative value or trend of marketing actions or results. Today's marketers use data visualization to present marketing metrics graphically so they can spot deviations from plans and take corrective actions.

LO 2-4 *Discuss how an organization assesses where it is now and where it seeks to be.*

Managers of an organization ask two key questions to set a strategic direction. The first question, "Where are we now?" requires an organization to (*a*) assess its core competencies to understand how its special capabilities provide a competitive advantage; (*b*) identify its customers and how they receive genuine value and have a satisfying experience; and (*c*) analyze its competitors from a global perspective to determine the distinctions among them.

The second question, "Where do we want to go?" requires an organization to set a specific direction and allocate resources to move it in that direction. Business portfolio analysis and diversification analysis help an organization do this. Managers use business portfolio analysis to assess the organization's strategic business units (SBUs), product lines, or individual products as though they were a collection of separate investments (*cash cows, stars, question marks*, and *dogs*) to determine the amount of cash each should receive. Diversification analysis is a technique that helps a firm search for growth opportunities from among four strategies: market penetration (selling more of current products to current markets); market development (selling current products to new markets); product development (selling new products to current markets); and diversification (selling new products to new markets).

LO 2-5 *Explain the three steps of the planning phase of the strategic marketing process.*

An organization uses the strategic marketing process to allocate its marketing mix resources to reach its target markets and achieve a competitive advantage. This process is divided into three phases: planning, implementation, and evaluation. The planning phase consists of (*a*) a situation (SWOT) analysis, which involves taking stock of where the firm or product has been recently, where it is now, and where it is headed and focuses on the organization's internal factors (strengths and weaknesses) and the external forces and trends affecting it (opportunities and threats); (*b*) a market-product focus through market segmentation (grouping buyers into segments with common needs and similar responses to marketing programs) and customer value proposition, which in part requires identifying points of difference (those characteristics of a product that make it superior to competitive substitutes); and (*c*) a marketing program that specifies the budget and actions (marketing strategies and tactics) for each marketing mix element.

LO 2-6 *Describe the four components of the implementation phase of the strategic marketing process.*
The implementation phase of the strategic marketing process carries out the marketing plan that emerges from the planning phase. It has four key components: (*a*) obtaining resources; (*b*) designing the marketing organization to perform product management, marketing research, sales, and advertising and promotion activities; (*c*) developing schedules to identify the tasks that need to be done, the time that is allocated to each one, the people responsible for each task, and the deadlines for each task—often with an action item list and Gantt chart; and (*d*) executing the marketing strategies, which are the means by which marketing goals are to be achieved, and their associated marketing tactics, which are the detailed day-to-day marketing actions for each element of the marketing mix that contribute to the overall success of a firm's marketing strategies. These are the marketing program actions a firm takes to achieve the goals set forth in its marketing plan.

LO 2-7 *Discuss how managers identify and act on deviations from plans.*
The evaluation phase of the strategic marketing process seeks to keep the marketing program moving in the direction that was established in the marketing plan. This requires the marketing manager to compare the results from the marketing program with the marketing plan's goals to (*a*) identify deviations or "planning gaps" and (*b*) take corrective actions to exploit positive deviations or correct negative ones.

LEARNING REVIEW ANSWERS

2-1 What is the difference between a for-profit and a nonprofit organization?
Answer: A for-profit organization is a privately owned organization that serves its customers to earn a profit so that it can survive. A nonprofit organization is a nongovernmental organization that serves its customers but does not have profit as an organizational goal. Instead, its goals may be operational efficiency or client satisfaction.

2-2 What are examples of a functional level in an organization?
Answer: The functional level in an organization is where groups of specialists from the marketing, finance, manufacturing/operations, accounting, information systems, research and development, and/or human resources departments focus on a specific strategic direction to create value for the organization.

2-3 What is the meaning of an organization's mission?
Answer: A mission is a clear, concise, meaningful, inspirational, and long-term statement of the organization's function in society, often identifying its customers, markets, products, and technologies. It is often used interchangeably with *vision*.

2-4 What is the difference between an organization's business and its goals?
Answer: An organization's business describes the clear, broad, underlying industry or market sector of an organization's offering. An organization's goals (or objectives) are statements of an accomplishment of a task to be achieved, often by a specific time. Goals convert an organization's mission and business into long- and short-term performance targets to measure how well it is doing.

2-5 What is the difference between a marketing dashboard and a marketing metric?
Answer: A marketing dashboard is the visual display of the essential information related to achieving a marketing objective. Each variable displayed in a marketing dashboard is a marketing metric, which is a measure of the quantitative value or trend of a marketing action or result.

2-6 What is business portfolio analysis?
Answer: Business portfolio analysis is a technique that managers use to quantify performance measures and growth targets to analyze their firms' SBUs as though they were a collection of separate investments. The purpose of this tool is to determine which SBU or offering generates cash and which one requires cash to fund the organization's growth opportunities.

2-7 Explain the four market-product strategies in diversification analysis.
Answer: The four market-product strategies in diversification analysis are: (1) Market penetration, which is a marketing strategy to increase sales of current products in current markets. There is no change in either the basic product line or the markets served. Rather, selling more of the product or selling the product at a higher price generates increased sales. (2) Market development, which is a marketing strategy to sell current products to new markets. (3) Product development, which is a marketing strategy of selling new products to current markets. (4) Diversification, which is a marketing strategy of developing new products and selling them in new markets. This is a potentially high-risk strategy because the firm has neither previous production nor marketing experience on which to draw in marketing a new product to a new market.

2-8 What are the three steps of the planning phase of the strategic marketing process?
Answer: The three steps of the planning phase of the strategic marketing process are: (1) Conducting a situation analysis, which involves taking stock of where the firm or product has been recently, where it is now, and where it is headed in terms of the organization's marketing plans and the external forces and trends affecting it. To do this, an organization uses a SWOT analysis, an acronym that describes an organization's appraisal of its internal Strengths and Weaknesses and its external Opportunities and Threats. (2) Developing a market-product focus and customer value proposition, which determine what products an organization will offer to which

customers. This is often based on market segmentation—aggregating prospective buyers into groups or segments that have common needs and will respond similarly to a marketing action—and crafting a customer value proposition. (3) Designing a marketing program, which is where an organization develops the marketing mix elements and budget for each offering.

2-9 What are points of difference and why are they important?
Answer: Points of difference are those characteristics of a product that make it superior to competitive substitutes—offerings the organization faces in the marketplace. They are important factors in the success or failure of a new product.

2-10 What is the implementation phase of the strategic marketing process?
Answer: The implementation phase carries out the marketing plan that emerges from the planning phase and consists of (1) obtaining resources; (2) designing the marketing organization; (3) defining precise tasks, responsibilities, and deadlines; and (4) executing the marketing program designed in the planning phase.

2-11 How do the goals set for a marketing program in the planning phase relate to the evaluation phase of the strategic marketing process?
Answer: The planning phase goals or objectives are used as the benchmarks with which the actual performance results are compared in the evaluation phase to identify deviations from the written marketing plans and to act on those deviations—exploiting positive ones and correcting negative ones.

FOCUSING ON KEY TERMS

business p. 32
business portfolio analysis p. 37
core values p. 31
customer value proposition p. 43
diversification analysis p. 40
goals (objectives) p. 33
market segmentation p. 43
market share p. 33
marketing dashboard p. 34
marketing metric p. 35
marketing plan p. 34
marketing strategy p. 46
marketing tactics p. 46
mission p. 32
objectives (goals) p. 33
organizational culture p. 32
points of difference p. 43
profit p. 28
situation analysis p. 42
strategic marketing process p. 41
strategy p. 28
SWOT analysis p. 42

APPLYING MARKETING KNOWLEDGE

1 (*a*) Using Netflix as an example, explain how a mission statement gives it a strategic direction. (*b*) Create a mission statement for your own career.

2 What competencies best describe (*a*) your college or university and (*b*) your favorite restaurant?

3 Compare the advantages and disadvantages of Ben & Jerry's attempting to expand sales revenues by using (*a*) a product development strategy or (*b*) a market development strategy.

4 Select one strength, one weakness, one opportunity, and one threat from the Ben & Jerry's SWOT analysis shown in Figure 2-7. Suggest an action that a Ben & Jerry's marketing manager might take to address each factor.

5 What is the main result of each of the three phases of the strategic marketing process? (*a*) planning, (*b*) implementation, and (*c*) evaluation.

6 Parts of Tasks 4 and 5 in Figure 2-10 are done both concurrently and sequentially. (*a*) How can this be? (*b*) How does it help the team members meet the project deadline? (*c*) What is the main advantage of scheduling tasks concurrently rather than sequentially?

7 The goal-setting step in the planning phase of the strategic marketing process sets quantified objectives for use in the evaluation phase. What does a manager do if measured results fail to meet objectives? Exceed objectives?

BUILDING YOUR MARKETING PLAN

1 Read Appendix A, "Building an Effective Marketing Plan." Then write a 600-word executive summary for the Paradise Kitchens marketing plan using the numbered headings shown in the plan. When you have completed the draft of your own marketing plan, write a 600-word executive summary to go in the front of your own marketing plan.

2 Using Chapter 2 and Appendix A as guides, focus your marketing plan by (*a*) writing your mission statement in 25 words or less, (*b*) listing three nonfinancial goals and three financial goals, (*c*) writing your competitive advantage in 35 words or less, and (*d*) creating a SWOT analysis table.

3 Draw a simple organization chart for your organization.

Businesses of the world are changing the way they work and IBM has a strategy to help them. Ann Rubin, vice president of corporate marketing at IBM, explains: "IBM is in a constant state of innovation, preparing for a world that is infused with digital intelligence and a world where humans and machines work side-by-side to do things that humans simply cannot do alone." "'Let's Put Smart To Work' is our new brand platform," she continues, but "it's not just advertising, it's bigger than that. 'Let's Put Smart To Work' is an invitation. We're asking clients and partners to work with us to put smart to work to use innovative technologies to change businesses and industries and organizations."

VIDEO 2-5
IBM Video Case
kerin.tv/15e/v2-5

THE NEW IBM

IBM has a hundred-plus-year history of innovation. Since its early days as the Tabulating Machine Company, IBM has gone through many dramatic transformations. The company shifted from tabulation machines, to typewriters, to computers, to business services and consulting, to artificial intelligence in response to changes in technology, the global economy, and business practices. Along the way IBM developed several well-known products such as the automated teller machine (ATM), the hard disk drive, the magnetic stripe card, and the Universal Product Code (UPC). In addition, researchers at the company won four Nobel prizes and six Turing awards for contributions of lasting and major technical importance to the computer field. IBM is in the top 20 of the world's most valuable brands and in the top 50 of the world's most admired companies. Today IBM has $79 billion in sales and 380,000 employees, is ranked 34th on the *Fortune* 500, and is viewed as a cognitive solutions and cloud platform company. According to CEO Virginia Rometty, "IBM now possesses capabilities that are unmatched in our industry to address our clients' most pressing needs."

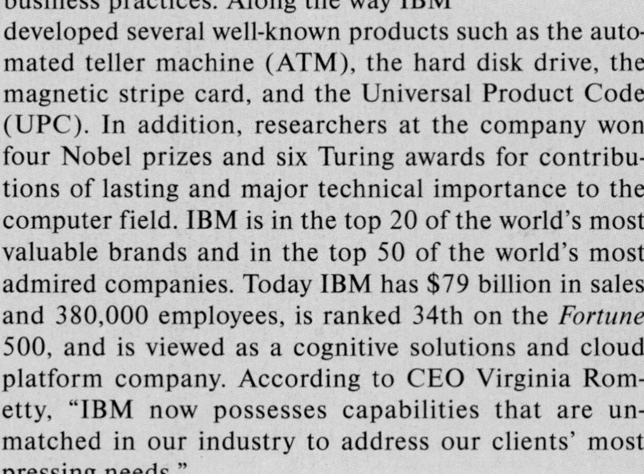

rvlsoft/Shutterstock

Strategy Based on Values

The forward-looking, visionary strategy at IBM is built on core values that are the fundamental, passionate, and enduring principles guiding its conduct. To articulate those values IBM held a global discussion event, called ValuesJam, among more than 50,000 employees. The results were three underlying values of IBM's business practices. Teresa Yoo, vice president of brand strategy and experience design, explains the outcome: "We weren't founded on or defined by a particular product or even a particular leader. It was what we believed and valued in the world, and what drove the decisions about everything that we do. So, those values have evolved over time and remain at the core of what we do. They are (1) a dedication to every client's success, (2) innovation that matters for our company and for the world, and (3) trust and personal responsibility in all our relationships."

The values influence IBM's use of strategic tools, such as portfolio analysis and SWOT analysis, in its assessment of marketplace opportunities around the globe. According to Rubin, "Using methodologies like business portfolio analysis is really important because you need to understand the opportunities in every country that you are going to and what is going to drive business in a certain area." The analysis "helps figure out what the revenue opportunity is and the growth opportunity for every one of our products in every one of our countries," she continues. Similarly, Teresa Yoo explains that "we use SWOT analysis when we're putting together a strategy for a particular brand we're building or a particular portfolio or product set. It makes a difference when you're trying to figure out what your value proposition is and you need to look at where you really stand in order to create a great strategy."

The analysis indicates fundamental changes in the business environment. IBM believes that in the near future businesses will need enterprise-strength cloud capabilities, artificial intelligence that is capable of analyzing all company and consumer data, industry-specific consulting services, and advanced cybersecurity. "Our brand strategy is to help IBM be easier to understand, consume, and navigate," says Yoo. "We have hundreds of products that span the whole gamut of what we do, from services to AI to cloud to research to security. So we have really focused around a few core brands that we want to be known for. They are IBM Watson for AI, IBM Cloud, IBM Security, IBM Services, and IBM Research." Overall, IBM sees these brands as the key to helping businesses become smarter businesses.

In her letter to IBM shareholders, Rometty described the trend toward smarter businesses as an "inflection point." She observed that (1) businesses are becoming smarter by leveraging intelligent digital platforms, (2) businesses are becoming smarter by making their systems and processes intelligent, and (3) businesses are becoming smarter by embedding AI and data to change how work is done, equipping themselves for an era of man + machine. The insights about the changes in businesses have led to IBM's strategy called "Let's Put Smart To Work."

The "Let's Put Smart To Work" Strategy

The "Let's Put Smart To Work" initiative was launched at IBM's annual conference, called IBM Think, at which partners, clients, industry representatives, and technology leaders meet to share information about the changing business environment and business needs. IBM seeks to be an "incumbent disruptor" as it continues its transformation to the new world of enterprise technology. "The evolution of 'Let's Put Smart To Work' is the result of technologies that are fundamentally different today. They are amazing. And we are directing them more specifically to business applications," explains Yoo. We can tell clients "so let's really put it to work in your business to accomplish whatever it is that you need to get done," she adds.

The strategy touches every aspect of IBM. "'Let's Put Smart To Work' is our rallying cry or call to action to partner with clients and to make the world a better place and to make businesses smarter," says Rubin. "IBM and our clients are putting smart to work across every industry," she adds. Industries where IBM is assisting businesses include agriculture, automotive, aviation, banking, health care, insurance, oil and gas, retail, and utilities. For example, in agriculture IBM's Watson analyzes temperature, soil pH, and other environmental factors to help farmers improve their harvest yields. In the automotive industry IBM technologies are helping combine data from IoT sensors to create better experiences for drivers in intelligent vehicles. Health care scientists are using IBM artificial intelligence to help accelerate research and find new uses for existing drugs. And in South Africa, IoT sensors are being used to monitor animal movements to help reduce rhinoceros poaching.

Source: IBM Corporation

Marketing "Let's Put Smart To Work"

The IBM marketing organization includes thousands of marketing professionals located in hundreds of countries. They are all adopting an approach they call "agile marketing," which is based on improvisation, testing and data, and collaboration, and which results in speed, adaptability, and creativity. "At IBM we use agile practices, agile methodologies," says Rubin. "It's the way that you best collaborate and the way that you best iterate and the way that you best create programs and products to move forward," she adds. The general strategy and the specific elements of the agile marketing approach all come together in a marketing plan. Rubin explains, "Everything is grounded in the marketing plan, in fact, everything is grounded in our overall corporate strategy and our values, and our strategic priorities."

The marketing plan includes a variety of marketing tools. "Our marketing plan leverages all kinds of elements from traditional to emerging technologies and emerging platforms. We use traditional advertising like TV and radio and print but we have to really understand how our clients consume media," says Rubin. For example, IBM customers tend to travel a lot so IBM places a lot of out-of-home advertising in airports. Digital advertising and social media are also part of the marketing plan. "The important thing about social [media] is understanding that every platform is different. You can't just take your TV spot and run it on Facebook and LinkedIn and Twitter and Instagram and think it's going to work. The more you look at the metrics and the data and the analytics, the more you learn those things. Then you uncover the insights and you can create the right content for the right platform," Rubin explains.

Events are also a very important part of the marketing plan. The reason, as Rubin explains, is that "it's hard to touch and feel our products so it's really important for our audience to engage with IBMers." The events give IBM managers an opportunity to engage one-on-one with their clients. Similarly, IBM sponsors events such as the Masters golf tournament, the US Open, many tennis tournaments around the world, and the Grammys, the Oscars, and the Tony awards. The reason, explains Yoo, is "the clients we are targeting tend to watch and go to those events" and the events are "an opportunity to make the technology we provide easier to understand."

The "Smart" Future

Innovative technologies and changing businesses have created an exciting combination for IBM's latest transformation. Ann Rubin describes the excitement in this way: "I feel like I have the best job in IBM and frankly one of the best jobs in the marketing industry overall. The marketing industry is changing every day, so you need to keep up, but it's so exiting, there's just nothing boring about it!" So what will the future bring? Teresa Yoo's advice is, "Keep your eyes on IBM, we're working on some incredible things that are going to change the world!"[44]

Questions

1 What is IBM's "Let's Put Smart To Work" strategy?
2 How does this strategy relate to IBM's values?
3 Conduct a SWOT analysis for IBM's "Let's Put Smart To Work" initiative. What are the relevant trends to consider?
4 What marketing tools described in Chapter 2 are prominent in IBM's strategic marketing process?
5 What is "agile" marketing at IBM? Why does IBM use the agile approach?

Chapter Notes

1. Ben & Jerry's, "Our Values," from Ben & Jerry's website, http://www.benjerry.com/values, March 23, 2019; and "Ice Cream History Revealed! What Was Ben & Jerry's First Ice Cream Flavor?" *BusinessWire,* November 15, 2011, http://www.businesswire.com/news/home/20111115007275/en/Ice-Cream-History-Revealed!-Ben-Jerry%E2%80%99s-Ice#.VR8B7J50yM8.
2. "The Final Straw for Ben & Jerry's," *Waste360*, January 30, 2019, p. 1; Vanessa Fuhrmans, "New CEO at Ben & Jerry's Plans to Whip Up Activism," *Wall Street Journal Online*, August 15, 2018; Mahita Gajanan, "You Can Get Unlimited Free Ben & Jerry's Ice Cream Tuesday for Free Cone Day," *Fortune.com*, April 10, 2018; Nick Craig and Scott Snook, "From Purpose to Impact," *Harvard Business Review*, May 2014, pp. 105–11; and Joe Van Brussel, "Ben & Jerry's Become B-Corp Certified, Adds Credibility to Impact Investing Movement," *Huffington Post: Business,* October 23, 2012.
3. "Size of the Global Ice Cream Market from 2013 to 2024," *Statista*, 2019; Madison Flager, "Ben & Jerry's Added Two New Vegan Flavors to Its Dairy-Free Line-up," www.delish.com, February 19, 2019; and "8 Ice Cream and Beer Pairings Perfect for St. Patrick's Day," www.benjerry.com/whats-new, March 14, 2019.
4. Roger A. Kerin and Robert A. Peterson, *Strategic Marketing Problems: Cases and Comments,* 13th ed. (Upper Saddle River, NJ: Prentice Hall, 2013), p. 140.
5. Steven Beroni and Alexandra Wilson, eds., "30 Under 30 Social Entrepreneurs," *Forbes*, November 30, 2018, p. 99; Tori Utley, "Can Business Change the World? This Filmmaker Says Yes–Through Social Entrepreneurship," www.forbes.com, February 28, 2018; and http://www.teachforamerica.org.
6. For a discussion of how industries are defined and offerings are classified, see the Census Bureau's Economic Classification Policy Committee Issues Paper #1 (http://www.census.gov/eos/www/naics/history/docs/issue_paper_1.pdf), which aggregates industries in the NAICS from a "production-oriented" view; see also the American Marketing Association definition at https://www.ama.org/resources/Pages/Dictionary.aspx?dLetter=I.
7. W. Chan Kim and Reneé Mauborgne, "Blue Ocean Strategy: From Theory to Practice," *California Management Review* 47, no. 3 (Spring 2005), p. 105; and Michael E. Porter, "What Is Strategy?" *Harvard Business Review*, November–December 1996, p. 2.
8. The definition of *strategy* reflects thoughts appearing in Porter, "What Is Strategy?" pp. 4 and 8; a condensed definition of strategy is found on the American Marketing Association website, https://www.ama.org/resources/Pages/Dictionary.aspx?dLetter=S; Gerry Johnson, Kevan Scholes, and Richard Wittington, *Exploring Corporate Strategy* (Upper Saddle River, NJ: Prentice Hall, 2005), p. 10; and Costas Markides, "What Is Strategy and How Do You Know If You Have One?" *Business Strategy Review* 15, no. 2 (Summer 2004), p. 5.
9. "The Vanishing CMO," *Advertising Age*, July 15, 2019, pp. 22–23; Hal Conick, "The Evolution and Awaking of the Modern CMO," *Marketing News*, March 2017, pp. 28–37; and Roger A. Kerin, "Strategic Marketing and the CMO," *Journal of Marketing,* October 2005, pp. 12–13.
10. Taken in part from Jim Collins and Morten T. Hansen, *Great by Choice* (New York: HarperCollins Publishers, 2011); Jim Collins and Jerry I. Porras, *Built to Last: Successful Habits of Visionary Companies* (New York: HarperCollins Publishers, 2002), p. 54; and Steve Hemsley, "How to Build a Visionary Company," *Marketing Week*, July 23, 2015, p. 1.
11. Patrick M. Lencioni, "Make Your Values Mean Something," *Harvard Business Review,* July 2002, p. 6; and https://www.ikea.com/ms/en_US/the_ikea_story/working_at_ikea/our_values.html.
12. Collins and Porras, *Built to Last*, pp. 94–95; and Tom Krattenmaker, "Write a Mission Statement That Your Company Is Willing to Live," *Harvard Management Communication Letter,* March 2002, pp. 3–4.
13. Southwest Airlines, "About Southwest," accessed April 13, 2019. https://www.southwest.com/html/about-southwest/.
14. American Red Cross, "Mission & Values," accessed April 13, 2019. https://www.redcross.org/about-us/who-we-are/mission-and-values.html.
15. Mission statement of Federal Trade Commission, see https://www.ftc.gov/about-ftc.
16. Adi Ignatius, "Profit and Purpose," *Harvard Business Review,* March–April 2019, p. 10; and Julie Battilana, Anne-Claire Pache, Metin Sendul, and Marissa Kimsey, "The Dual-Purpose Playbook," *Harvard Business Review,* March–April 2019, pp. 125–33.

17. Amy Gallo, "A Refresher on Marketing Myopia," *Harvard Business Review*, August 22, 2016, pp. 2–5; and Theodore Levitt, "Marketing Myopia," *Harvard Business* July–August 1960, pp. 45–56.
18. Stelios Kavadias, Kostas Ladas, and Christoph Loch, "The Transformative Business Model," *Harvard Business Review*, October 2016, pp. 90–98; Dan Radak, "Breaking Down the Netflix Business Model: The History and the Future of the VOD Giant," *Business 2 Community*, July 1, 2016; and Miriam Gottfried, "Eyeballs Are No Longer Enough for Netflix," *The Wall Street Journal*, January 17, 2017.
19. Jim Milliot, "What's Next for Barnes & Noble?" *Publishers Weekly*, August 22, 2016, p. 4; Jim Milliot, "E-books Gained, Online Retailers Slipped in 2014," *Publishers Weekly*, March 30, 2015, pp. 4–5; and Jeffrey A. Trachtenberg, "What's Barnes & Noble's Survival Plan?" *The Wall Street Journal*, April 18, 2014, p. B1.
20. Joshua Brustein, "A New Way to Uber," *Bloomberg Businessweek*, September 3, 2018, pp. 23–24; Alan Ohnsman and Brian Solomon, "Uber's Bold Move," *Forbes*, December 30, 2016, pp. 58–74; and Adam Lashinsky, "Classifying Uber's Business Model Is a Complicated Affair," *Fortune.com*, December 5, 2016, p. 73.
21. Andrew McAfee and Erik Brynjolfsson, "Big Data: The Management Revolution," *Harvard Business Review*, October 2012, pp. 61–68.
22. The definition is adapted from Stephen Few, *Information Dashboard Design: The Effective Visual Communication of Data* (Sebastopol, CA: O'Reilly Media, Inc., 2006), pp. 2–46.
23. Tim Fountaine, Brian McCarthy and Tamim Saleh, "Building the AI-Powered Organization," *Harvard Business Review*, July–August 2019, pp. 62–73; Pedro Hernandez, "Microsoft Enables Real-Time IoT Dashboards in Power BI," *eWeek*, February 1, 2017, p. 3; Michel Wedel and P. K. Kannan, "Marketing Analytics for Data-Rich Environments," *Journal of Marketing*, November 2016, pp. 97–121; and Koen Pauwels et al., *Dashboards & Marketing: Why, What, How and What Research Is Needed?* (Hanover, NH: Tuck School, Dartmouth, May 2008).
24. Vikal Mittal, "The Downside of Marketing Dashboards," *Marketing News*, January 2017, pp. 22–23; Few, *Information Dashboard Design:* Michael T. Krush, Raj Agnihotri, Kevin J. Trainor, and Edward L. Nowlin, "Enhancing Organizational Sensemaking: An Examination of the Interactive Effects of Sales Capabilities and Marketing Dashboards," *Industrial Marketing Management*, July 2013, pp. 824–35; Bruce H. Clark, Andrew V. Abela, and Tim Ambler, "Behind the Wheel," *Marketing Management,* May–June 2006, pp. 19–23; and Spencer E. Ante, "Giving the Boss the Big Picture," *BusinessWeek,* February 13, 2006, pp. 48–49.
25. Few, *Information Dashboard Design,* p. 13.
26. Mark Jeffery, *Data-Driven Marketing: The 15 Metrics Everyone in Marketing Should Know* (Hoboken, NJ: Wiley 2010), Chapter 1; Michael Krauss, "Balance Attention to Metrics with Intuition," *Marketing News,* June 1, 2007, pp. 6–8; John Davis, *Measuring Marketing: 103 Key Metrics Every Marketer Needs* (Singapore: Wiley [Asia], 2007); and Paul W. Farris, Neil T. Bendle, Phillip E. Pfeifer, and David J. Reibstein, *Marketing Metrics,* 2nd ed. (Upper Saddle River, NJ: Wharton School Publishing, 2010).
27. David Burrows, "Too Many Metrics: The Perils of Training Marketers to Calculate ROI," *Marketing Week*, September 11, 2014, p. 42; Art Weinstein and Shane Smith, "Game Plan," *Marketing Management,* Fall 2012, pp. 24–31; Alexander Chiang, "Special Interview with Stephen Few, Dashboard and Data Visualization Expert," *Dundas Dashboard,* July 14, 2011; Stephen Few, *Now You See It* (Oakland, CA: Analytics Press, 2009), Chapters 1–3; and Jacques Bughin, Amy Guggenheim Shenkan, and Mark Singer, "How Poor Metrics Undermine Digital Marketing," *The McKinsey Quarterly,* October 2008.
28. The now-classic reference on effective graphic presentation is Edward R. Tufte, *The Visual Display of Quantitative Information,* 2nd ed. (Cheshire, CT: Graphics Press, 2001); see also Few, *Information Dashboard Design*, Chapters 3–5.
29. George Stalk, Phillip Evans, and Lawrence E. Shulman, "Competing on Capabilities: The New Rules of Corporate Strategy," *Harvard Business Review,* March–April 1992, pp. 57–69; and Darrell K. Rigby, *Management Tools 2007: An Executive's Guide* (Boston: Bain & Company, 2007), p. 22.
30. Roger Kerin and Robert Peterson, *Strategic Marketing Problems: Cases and Comments,* 13th ed. (Upper Saddle River, NJ: Prentice Hall, 2013), pp. 2–3; and Derek F. Abell, *Defining the Business* (Englewood Cliffs, NJ: Prentice Hall, 1980), p. 18.
31. Donna Rosato, "Guide to Returning Gifts: Retailers with the Best and Worst Policies," *Consumer Reports, Inc*. (December 10, 2018); Robert D. Hof, "How to Hit a Moving Target," *BusinessWeek,* August 21, 2006, p. 3; and Peter Kim, *Reinventing the Marketing Organization* (Cambridge, MA: Forrester, July 13, 2006), pp. 7, 9, and 17.
32. Adapted from *The Experience Curve Reviewed, IV: The Growth Share Matrix of the Product Portfolio* (Boston: The Boston Consulting Group, 1973). See also https://www.bcgperspectives.com/content/classics/strategy_the_product_portfolio (registration and login required for access).
33. Roger A. Kerin, Vijay Mahajan, and P. Rajan Varadarajan, *Contemporary Perspectives on Strategic Marketing Planning* (Boston: Allyn & Bacon, 1990), p. 52.
34. "The Best Global Brands 2016 Rankings," *Interbrand*, http://interbrand.com/best-brands/best-global-brands/2016/ranking/.
35. See the Apple press release library at http://www.apple.com/pr/library/.
36. "Apple, Goldman to Test Joint Credit Card," *American Banker*, February 22, 2019, p. 1; Alaina Lee, "Apple Card vs Citi, Chase, and Capital One: Is Apple's New Credit Card as Good as It Seems?" www.macworld.com, March 26, 2019; and Andrew Latham, "2019 Consumer Credit Card Industry Study," www.supermoney.com, January 22, 2019.
37. "Mobile Vendor Market Share United States of America," *gs.statcounter.com*, February 2019; and Jake Swearingen, "We're No Longer in Smartphone Plateau. We're in the Smartphone Decline," www.nymag.com/intelligencer, December 4, 2018.
38. Peter Cao, "Tablet Shipments in Q2 Still Declining Despite Apple's Growth with iPad," www.9to5mac.com, August 2, 2018; "Tablet Shipments Continue to Decline," www.idc.com, August 2, 2018; and Matt Weinberger, "The World of Technology Is Changing and the iPad Is Getting Caught in the Middle," *Business Insider*, February 1, 2017.
39. Anita Balakrishnan, "Apple Is Discontinuing the iPod Shuffle and Nano," *CNBC*, www.cnbc.com, July 27, 2017; Jason Cipriani, "The Real Reason Apple Decided to Release a New iPod Touch," *Fortune.com*, July 15, 2015; Don Reisinger, "iPod History: 10 Milestones in This Wearable Music Player's Evolution," *eWeek,* October 31, 2014; James Hall, "MP3 Players Are Dead," *Business Insider,* December 26, 2012, http://www.businessinsider.com/mp3-players-are-dead-2012-12; and Zak Islam, "Smartphones Heavily Decrease Sales of iPod, MP3 Players," *Tom's Hardware,* December 31, 2012, http://www.tomshardware.com/news/SmartphonesiPod-MP3-Players-Sales,20062.html.
40. "Share of Apple's Revenue by Product Category from the First Quarter of 2012 to the First Quarter of 2019," *Statista*, 2019; and Heather Kelly, "Apple Event 2019: Everything Announced at Apple's Big March Presentation," www.cnn.com, March 26, 2019.
41. Strengths and weaknesses of the BCG technique are based on Derek F. Abell and John S. Hammond, *Strategic Market Planning: Problem and Analytic Approaches* (Englewood Cliffs, NJ: Prentice Hall, 1979); Yoram Wind, Vijay Mahajan, and Donald Swire, "An Empirical Comparison of Standardized Portfolio Models," *Journal of Marketing,*

Spring 1983, pp. 89–99; and J. Scott Armstrong and Roderick J. Brodie, "Effects of Portfolio Planning Methods on Decision Making: Experimental Results," *International Journal of Research in Marketing*, Winter 1994, pp. 73–84.

42. H. Igor Ansoff, "Strategies for Diversification," *Harvard Business Review*, September–October 1957, pp. 113–24; and Christine Moorman and Lauren Kirby, "The CMO Survey: Top Marketing Trends of the Decade," *Marketing News*, June–July 2019, pp. 36–41.

43. Robert W. Palmatier and Andrew T. Crecelus, "The 'First Principles' of Marketing Strategy," *Academy of Marketing Science Review*, June 2019, pp. 5–26.

44. This case was written by Steven Hartley and Roger Kerin. Sources: Interviews with IBM executives Ann Rubin and Teresa Yoo; Thomas Haigh, "Defining American Greatness: IBM from Watson to Trump," *Communication of the ACM*, January 2018, pp. 32–37; Yagmur Simsek, "IBM Has Introduced a New Brand Platform along with a New Campaign–'Let's Put Smart To Work,'" *Digital Agency Network*, April 2018; Jason Bloomberg, "IBM Bet Company on Exponential Innovation in AI, Blockchain, and Quantum Computing," *Forbes*, March 22, 2018; "Our Values at Work," https://www.ibm.com/ibm/values/us/; Adi Ignatius, "Don't Try to Protect the Past: A Conversation with IBM CEO Ginni Rometty," *Harvard Business Review*, July–August 2017, pp. 126–32; Avi Dan, "How Michele Peluso Is Redefining Marketing at IBM," *Forbes*, January 18, 2018; *IBM 2017 Annual Report;* IBM website, www.ibm.com; "The Fortune 500," *Fortune*, June 2018; "The World's Most Admired Companies," *Fortune*, January 19, 2018; and "The World's Most Valuable Brands," *Forbes*, May 23, 2018.

BUILDING AN EFFECTIVE MARKETING PLAN

"If you have a real product with a distinctive point of difference that satisfies the needs of customers, you may have a winner," says Arthur R. Kydd, who has helped launch more than 60 start-up firms. "And you get a real feel for this in a well-written marketing or business plan," he explains.[1]

This appendix (1) describes what marketing and business plans are, including the purposes and guidelines in writing effective plans, and (2) provides a sample marketing plan.

MARKETING PLANS AND BUSINESS PLANS

After explaining the meanings, purposes, and audiences of marketing plans and business plans, this section describes some writing guidelines for them and what external funders often look for in successful plans.

Meanings, Purposes, and Audiences

A **marketing plan** is a road map for the marketing actions of an organization for a specified future time period, such as one year or five years.[2] No single "generic" marketing plan applies to all organizations and all situations. Rather, the specific format for a marketing plan for an organization depends on the following:

- *The target audience and purpose.* Elements included in a particular marketing plan depend heavily on (1) who the audience is and (2) what its purpose is. A marketing plan for an internal audience seeks to point the direction for future marketing activities and is sent to all individuals in the organization who must implement the plan or who will be affected by it. If the plan is directed to an external audience, such as friends, banks, venture capitalists, or crowdfunding sources like Kickstarter and Indiegogo for the purpose of raising capital, it has the additional function of being an important sales document. So it contains elements such as the strategic focus, organizational structure, and biographies of key personnel that would rarely appear in an internal marketing plan. The elements of a marketing plan for each of these two audiences are compared in the two left-hand columns in Figure A-1.
- *The kind and complexity of the organization.* A neighborhood restaurant has a less detailed marketing plan than Apple, which serves international markets. The restaurant's plan would be relatively simple and directed at serving customers in a local market. In Apple's case, because there is a hierarchy of marketing plans, various levels of detail would be used—such as the entire organization, the strategic business unit, or the product/product line.
- *The industry.* Both the restaurant serving a local market and Apple, selling electronic devices globally, analyze elements of their industry. However, their geographic scopes are far different, as are the complexities of their offerings and, hence, the time periods likely to be covered by their plans. A one-year marketing plan may be adequate for the restaurant, but Apple may need a five-year planning horizon because product development cycles for complex, new electronic devices and services may be many years.

In contrast to a marketing plan, a **business plan** is a road map for the entire organization for a specified future period of time, such as one year or five years.[3] A key difference between a marketing plan and a business plan is that the business plan contains details on the research and development (R&D)/operations/manufacturing activities of the organization. Even for a manufacturing business, the marketing plan is probably 60 or 70 percent of the entire business plan. For firms like a small restaurant or an auto repair shop, their marketing and business plans are virtually identical. The elements of a business plan typically targeted at internal and external audiences appear in the two right-hand columns in Figure A-1.

Element of the plan	Marketing plan		Business plan	
	For internal audience (to direct the firm)	For external audience (to raise capital)	For internal audience (to direct the firm)	For external audience (to raise capital)
1. Executive summary	✓	✓	✓	✓
2. Description of company		✓		✓
3. Strategic plan/focus		✓		✓
4. Situation analysis	✓	✓	✓	✓
5. Market-product focus	✓	✓	✓	✓
6. Marketing program strategy and tactics	✓	✓	✓	✓
7. R&D and operations program			✓	✓
8. Financial projections	✓	✓	✓	✓
9. Organizational structure		✓		✓
10. Implementation plan	✓	✓	✓	✓
11. Evaluation	✓		✓	
Appendix A: Biographies of key personnel		✓		✓
Appendix B, etc.: Details on other topics	✓	✓	✓	✓

FIGURE A–1
Elements in typical marketing and business plans targeted at different audiences.

The Most-Asked Questions by Outside Audiences

Lenders and prospective investors reading a business plan or a marketing plan that is used to seek new capital are probably the toughest audiences to satisfy. Their most-asked questions include the following:

1. Is the business or marketing idea valid?
2. Is there something unique or distinctive about the product or service that separates it from substitutes and competitors?
3. Is there a clear market for the product or service?
4. Are the financial projections realistic?
5. Are the key management and technical personnel capable, and do they have a track record in the industry within which they must compete?
6. Does the plan clearly describe how those providing capital will get their money back and make a profit?

Rhonda Abrams, author of books on writing business plans, observes, "Although you may spend five months preparing your plan, the cold, hard fact is that an investor or lender can dismiss it in less than five minutes. If you don't make a positive impression in those critical first five minutes, your plan will be rejected."[4] While her comments apply to plans seeking to raise capital, the first five questions listed above apply equally well to plans prepared for internal audiences.

Writing and Style Suggestions

There are no magic one-size-fits-all guidelines for writing successful marketing and business plans. Still, the following writing and style guidelines generally apply:[5]

- Use a direct, professional writing style. Use appropriate business terms without jargon. Present and future tenses with active voice ("I will write an effective marketing plan") are generally better than past tense and passive voice ("An effective marketing plan was written by me").

- Be positive and specific to convey potential success. At the same time, avoid superlatives (*terrific*, *wonderful*). Specifics are better than glittering generalities.
- Use numbers for impact, justifying projections with reasonable quantitative assumptions, where possible.
- Use bullet points for succinctness and emphasis. As with the list you are reading, bullets enable key points to be highlighted effectively.
- Use A-level (the first level) and B-level (the second level) headings under the numbered section headings to help readers make easy transitions from one topic to another. This also forces the writer to organize the plan more carefully.
- Use visuals where appropriate. Photos, illustrations, graphs, and charts enable massive amounts of information to be presented succinctly.
- Shoot for a plan 15 to 35 pages in length, not including financial projections and appendices. An uncomplicated small business may require only 15 pages, while a high-technology start-up may require more than 35 pages.
- Use care in layout, design, and presentation. Use 11- or 12-point type (you are now reading 10-point type) in the text. Use a serif type (with "feet," like that you are reading now) in the text because it is easier to read, and sans serif (without "feet") in graphs and charts like Figure A–1. A bound report with a nice cover and a clear title page adds professionalism.

These guidelines are used, where possible, in the sample marketing plan that follows.

SAMPLE FIVE-YEAR MARKETING PLAN FOR PARADISE KITCHENS, INC.

To help interpret the marketing plan for Paradise Kitchens, Inc. that follows, we will describe the company and suggest some guidelines for interpreting the plan.[6]

Background on Paradise Kitchens, Inc.

Randall and Leah Peters have over 40 years of food industry experience with General Foods and Pillsbury, with a number of diverse responsibilities. With these backgrounds and their savings, they co-founded Paradise Kitchens, Inc. to produce and market a new line of high-quality frozen chili products.

Interpreting the Marketing Plan

The marketing plan that follows, based on an actual Paradise Kitchens plan, is directed at an external audience (see Figure A–1). For simplicity, let us assume it is early 2020, the Peters have company data through 2019, and they are developing a five-year marketing plan through 2024. Some details and dates have been altered, but the basic logic of the plan has been kept.

Notes in the margins next to the Paradise Kitchens plan fall into two categories:

1. ***Substantive notes*** are in blue boxes. These notes explain the significance of an element in the marketing plan and are keyed to chapter references in this textbook.
2. ***Writing style, format, and layout notes*** are in red boxes and explain the editorial or visual rationale for the element.

A word of encouragement: Writing an effective marketing plan is hard but also challenging and satisfying work. Dozens of the authors' students have used effective marketing plans they wrote for class in their interviewing portfolio to show prospective employers what they could do and to help them get their first job.

Color-Coding Legend

Blue boxes explain significance of marketing plan elements.

Red boxes give writing style, format, and layout guidelines.

The Table of Contents provides quick access to the topics in the plan, usually organized by section and subsection headings.

Seen by many experts as the single most important element in the plan, the two-page Executive Summary "sells" the plan to readers through its clarity and brevity. For space reasons, it is not shown here, but the Building Your Marketing Plan exercise at the end of Chapter 2 asks the reader to write an Executive Summary for this plan.

The Company Description highlights the recent history and recent successes of the organization.

The Strategic Focus and Plan sets the strategic direction for the entire organization, a direction with which proposed actions of the marketing plan must be consistent. This section is not included in all marketing plans. See Chapter 2.

The qualitative Mission statement focuses the activities of Paradise Kitchens for the stakeholder groups to be served. See Chapter 2.

FIVE-YEAR MARKETING PLAN
Paradise Kitchens,® Inc.

Table of Contents

1. Executive Summary

2. Company Description

Paradise Kitchens,® Inc. was started by co-founders Randall F. Peters and Leah E. Peters to develop and market Howlin' Coyote® Chili, a unique line of single serve and microwavable Southwestern/Mexican style frozen chili products. The Howlin' Coyote line of chili was first introduced into the Minneapolis–St. Paul market and expanded to Denver two years later and Phoenix two years after that.

To the Company's knowledge, Howlin' Coyote is the only premium-quality, authentic Southwestern/Mexican style frozen chili sold in U.S. grocery stores. Its high quality has gained fast, widespread acceptance in its targeted markets. In fact, same-store sales doubled in the last year for which data are available. The Company believes the Howlin' Coyote brand can be extended to other categories of Southwestern/Mexican food products, such as tacos, enchiladas, and burritos.

Paradise Kitchens believes its high-quality, high-price strategy has proven successful. This marketing plan outlines how the Company will extend its geographic coverage from 3 markets to 20 markets by the year 2024.

3. Strategic Focus and Plan

This section covers three aspects of corporate strategy that influence the marketing plan: (1) the mission, (2) goals, and (3) core competency/sustainable competitive advantage of Paradise Kitchens.

Mission

The mission of Paradise Kitchens is to market lines of high-quality Southwestern/Mexican food products at premium prices that satisfy consumers in this fast-growing food segment while providing challenging career opportunities for employees and above-average returns to stockholders.

The Goals section sets both the nonfinancial and financial targets—where possible in quantitative terms—against which the company's performance will be measured. See Chapter 2.

Lists use parallel construction to improve readability—in this case a series of infinitives starting with "To . . ."

Photos or sample ads can illustrate key points effectively, even if they are not in color as they appear here.

A brief caption on photos and sample ads ties them to the text and highlights their reason for being included.

Goals

For the coming five years Paradise Kitchens seeks to achieve the following goals:

- Nonfinancial goals
  1. To retain its present image as the highest-quality line of Southwestern/Mexican products in the food categories in which it competes.
  2. To enter 17 new metropolitan markets.
  3. To achieve national distribution in two convenience store or supermarket chains in 2020 and five by 2021.
  4. To add a new product line every third year.
  5. To be among the top five chili lines–regardless of packaging (frozen or canned)–in one-third of the metro markets in which it competes by 2021 and two-thirds by 2023.
- Financial goals
  1. To obtain a real (inflation-adjusted) growth in earnings per share of 8 percent per year over time.
  2. To obtain a return on equity of at least 20 percent.
  3. To have a public stock offering by the year 2021.

Core Competency and Sustainable Competitive Advantage

In terms of core competency, Paradise Kitchens seeks to achieve a unique ability to (1) provide distinctive, high-quality chilies and related products using Southwestern/Mexican recipes that appeal to and excite contemporary tastes for these products and (2) deliver these products to the customer's table using effective manufacturing and distribution systems that maintain the Company's quality standards.

To translate these core competencies into a sustainable competitive advantage, the Company will work closely with key suppliers and distributors to build the relationships and alliances necessary to satisfy the high taste standards of our customers.

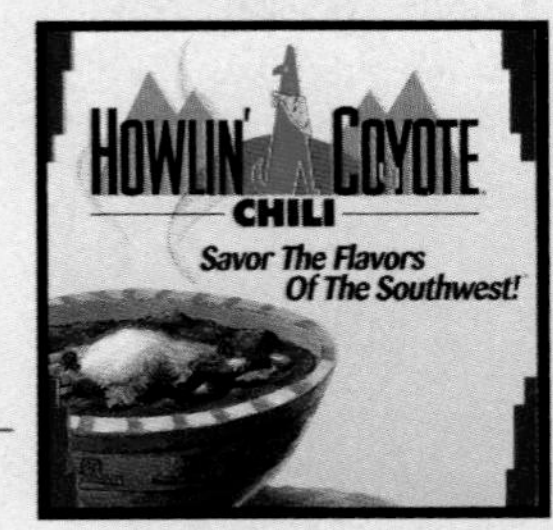

To help achieve national distribution through chains, Paradise Kitchens introduced this point-of-purchase ad that adheres statically to the glass door of the freezer case.

Photo: Source: Paradise Kitchens, Inc.

To improve readability, each numbered section usually starts on a new page. (This is not done in this plan to save space.)

The Situation Analysis is a snapshot to answer the question "Where are we now?" See Chapter 2.

The SWOT analysis identifies strengths, weaknesses, opportunities, and threats to provide a solid foundation, which is the springboard to identify subsequent actions in the marketing plan. See Chapter 2.

Each long table, graph, or photo is given a figure number and title. It then appears as soon as possible after the first reference in the text, accommodating necessary page breaks. This avoids breaking long tables like this one in the middle. Short tables or graphs are often inserted in the text without figure numbers because they don't cause serious problems with page breaks.

Effective tables seek to summarize a large amount of information in a short amount of space.

4. Situation Analysis

This situation analysis starts with a snapshot of the current environment in which Paradise Kitchens finds itself by providing a brief SWOT (strengths, weaknesses, opportunities, threats) analysis. After this overview, the analysis probes ever-finer levels of detail: industry, competitors, company, and consumers.

SWOT Analysis

Figure 1 shows the internal and external factors affecting the market opportunities for Paradise Kitchens. Stated briefly, this SWOT analysis highlights the great strides taken by the company since its products first appeared on grocers' shelves.

Figure 1. SWOT Analysis for Paradise Kitchens

Internal Factors	Strengths	Weaknesses
Management	Experienced and entrepreneurial management and board	Small size can restrict options
Offerings	Unique, high-quality, high-price products	Many lower-quality, lower-price competitors
Marketing	Distribution in three markets with excellent consumer acceptance	No national awareness or distribution; restricted shelf space in the freezer section
Personnel	Good workforce, though small; little turnover	Big gap if key employee leaves
Finance	Excellent growth in sales revenues	Limited resources may restrict growth opportunities when compared to giant competitors
Manufacturing	Sole supplier ensures high quality	Lack economies of scale of huge competitors
R&D	Continuing efforts to ensure quality in delivered products	Lack of canning and microwavable food processing expertise
External Factors	**Opportunities**	**Threats**
Consumer/Social	Upscale market, likely to be stable; Southwestern/Mexican food category is fast-growing segment due to growth in Hispanic American population and desire for spicier foods	Premium price may limit access to mass markets; consumers value a strong brand name
Competitive	Distinctive name and packaging in its markets	Not patentable; competitors can attempt to duplicate product; others better able to pay slotting fees
Technological	Technical breakthroughs enable smaller food producers to achieve many economies available to large competitors	Competitors have gained economies in canning and microwavable food processing
Economic	Consumer income is high; convenience important to U.S. households	More households "eating out," and bringing prepared take-out into home
Legal/Regulatory	High U.S. Food & Drug Administration standards eliminate fly-by-night competitors	Mergers among large competitors being approved by government

The text discussion of Figure 1 (the SWOT Analysis table) elaborates on its more important elements. This "walks" the reader through the information from the vantage point of the plan's writer.

The Industry Analysis section provides the backdrop for the subsequent, more detailed analysis of competition, the company, and the company's customers. Without an in-depth understanding of the industry, the remaining analysis may be misdirected. See Chapter 2.

Sales of Mexican entrees are significant and provide a variety of future opportunities for Paradise Kitchens.

Even though relatively brief, this in-depth treatment of sales of Mexican foods in the U.S. demonstrates to the plan's readers the company's understanding of the industry within which it competes.

The Competitor Analysis section demonstrates that the company has a realistic understanding of its major chili competitors and their marketing strategies. Again, a realistic assessment gives confidence that subsequent marketing actions in the plan rest on a solid foundation. See Chapters 2, 3, 8, and 9.

In the Company's favor internally are its strengths: an experienced management team and board of directors, excellent acceptance of its product line in the three metropolitan markets within which it competes, and a strong manufacturing and distribution system to serve these limited markets. Favorable external factors include the increasing appeal of Southwestern/Mexican foods, the strength of the upscale market for the Company's products, and food-processing technological breakthroughs that make it easier for smaller food producers to compete.

Among unfavorable factors, the main weakness is the limited size of Paradise Kitchens relative to its competitors in terms of the depth of the management team, the available financial resources, and the national awareness and distribution of product lines. Threats include the danger that the Company's premium prices may limit access to mass markets and competition from the "eating-out" and "take-out" markets.

Industry Analysis: Trends in Frozen and Mexican Foods

Frozen Foods. According to food industry observers, consumers are eating out less and buying more frozen food. The reasons: busy, health-conscious families want nutritious, convenient, and less wasteful meals, and there are a growing number of new frozen food products that meet these requirements.[7] In 2019, total sales of frozen food in supermarkets, drugstores, and mass merchandisers reached $33.5 billion. Prepared frozen meals, which are defined as meals or entrees that are frozen and require minimal preparation, accounted for about 35 percent of the total frozen food market.[8]

Sales of Mexican entrees now exceed $600 million. Heavy consumers of frozen meals, those who eat five or more meals every two weeks, tend to be kids, teens, and adults 35–44 years old.[9]

Mexican Foods. Currently, Mexican foods such as burritos, enchiladas, and tacos are used in two-thirds of American households. These levels of demand reflect a general trend toward spicy foods that include red chili peppers. The growing Hispanic population in the United States, over 59 million people with about $1.4 trillion in purchasing power, partly explains the increasing demand for Mexican food. Hispanic purchasing power is projected to be more than $1.9 trillion in 2022.[10]

Competitor Analysis: The Chili Market

The chili market represents over $500 million in annual sales. On average, consumers buy five to six servings annually, according to the NPD Group. The products fall primarily into two groups: canned chili (75 percent of sales) and dry chili (25 percent of sales).

This page uses a "block" style and does *not* indent each paragraph, although an extra space separates each paragraph. Compare this page with the opposite page, which has indented paragraphs. Most readers find that indented paragraphs in marketing plans and long reports are easier to follow.

The Company Analysis provides details of the company's strengths and marketing strategies that will enable it to achieve the mission and goals identified earlier. See Chapters 2 and 8.

The "A heading" for this section ("4. Situation Analysis") identifies the major section of the plan. The "B heading" of Customer Analysis has a more dominant typeface and position than the lower-level "C heading" of Customer Characteristics. These headings introduce the reader to the sequence and level of topics covered within each major "A level" section. The organization of this textbook uses this kind of structure and headings.

Satisfying customers and providing genuine value to them is why organizations exist in a market economy. This section addresses the question "Who are the customers for Paradise Kitchens's products?" See Chapters 5, 6, 7, 8, and 9.

Bluntly put, the major disadvantage of the segment's dominant product, canned chili, is that it does not taste very good. A taste test described in an issue of *Consumer Reports* magazine ranked 26 canned chili products "poor" to "fair" in overall sensory quality. The study concluded, "Chili doesn't have to be hot to be good. But really good chili, hot or mild, doesn't come out of a can."[11]

Company Analysis

The husband-and-wife team that co-founded Paradise Kitchens, Inc. has 44 years of experience between them in the food-processing business. Both have played key roles in the management of the Pillsbury Company. They are being advised by a highly seasoned group of business professionals, who have extensive understanding of the requirements for new-product development.

The Company now uses a single outside producer with which it works closely to maintain the consistently high quality required in its products. The greater volume has increased production efficiencies, resulting in a steady decrease in the cost of goods sold.

Customer Analysis

In terms of customer analysis, this section describes (1) the characteristics of customers expected to buy Howlin' Coyote products and (2) health and nutrition concerns of Americans today.

Customer Characteristics. Demographically, chili products in general are purchased by consumers representing a broad range of socioeconomic backgrounds. Howlin' Coyote chili is purchased chiefly by consumers who have achieved higher levels of education and whose income is $50,000 and higher. These consumers represent 50 percent of canned and dry mix chili users.

The household buying Howlin' Coyote has one to three people in it. Among married couples, Howlin' Coyote is predominantly bought by households in which both spouses work. While women are a majority of the buyers, single men represent a significant segment.

Because the chili offers a quick way to make a tasty meal, the product's biggest users tend to be those most pressed for time. Howlin' Coyote's premium pricing also means that its purchasers are skewed toward the higher end of the income range. Buyers range in age from 25 to 54 years old and often live in the western United States where spicy foods are more readily eaten.

The five Howlin' Coyote entrees offer a quick, tasty meal with high-quality ingredients.

Photo: Source: Paradise Kitchens, Inc.

This section demonstrates the company's insights into a major trend that has a potentially large impact.

Health and Nutrition Concerns. Coverage of food issues in the U.S. media is often erratic and occasionally alarmist. Because Americans are concerned about their diets, studies from organizations of widely varying credibility frequently receive significant attention from the major news organizations. For instance, a study of fat levels of movie popcorn was reported in all the major media. Similarly, studies on the healthfulness of Mexican food have received prominent play in print and broadcast reports. The high caloric levels of much Mexican and Southwestern-style food have been widely reported and often exaggerated. Some Mexican frozen-food competitors, such as Don Miguel, Mission Foods, Ruiz Foods, and José Olé, plan to offer or have recently offered more "carb-friendly" and "fat-friendly" products in response to this concern.

Howlin' Coyote is already lower in calories, fat, and sodium than its competitors, and those qualities are not currently being stressed in its promotions. Instead, in the space and time available for promotions, Howlin' Coyote's taste, convenience, and flexibility are stressed.

The size of headings should give a professional look to the report and not overwhelm the reader. These two headings are too large.

5. Market-Product Focus

This section describes the five-year marketing and product objectives for Paradise Kitchens and the target markets, points of difference, and positioning of its lines of Howlin' Coyote chilies.

Marketing and Product Objectives

As noted in Chapters 2, 9, and 10, the chances of success for a new product significantly increase if objectives are set for the product itself and if target market segments are identified for it. Diversification analysis, discussed in Chapter 2, helps identify the market segments to target. This section makes these explicit for Paradise Kitchens. The objectives also serve as the planned targets against which marketing activities are measured in program implementation and evaluation.

Howlin' Coyote's marketing intent is to take full advantage of its brand potential while building a base from which other revenue sources can be mined—both in and out of the retail grocery business. These are detailed in four areas below:

- *Current markets.* Current markets will be grown by expanding brand and flavor distribution at the retail level. In addition, same-store sales will be grown by increasing consumer awareness and repeat purchases, thereby leading to the more efficient broker/warehouse distribution channel.
- *New markets.* By the end of Year 5, the chili, salsa, burrito, and enchilada business will be expanded to a total of 20 metropolitan areas, which represent 53 percent of the 38 major U.S. metropolitan markets. This will represent 70 percent of U.S. food store sales.
- *Food service.* Food service sales will include chili products and smothering sauces. Sales are expected to reach $693,000 by the end of Year 3 and $1.5 million by the end of Year 5.
- *New products.* Howlin' Coyote's brand presence will be expanded at the retail

A heading should be spaced closer to the text that follows (and that it describes) than the preceding section to avoid confusion for the reader. This rule is not followed for the Target Markets heading, which now unfortunately appears to "float" between the preceding and following paragraphs.

This section identifies the specific niches or target markets toward which the company's products are directed. When appropriate and when space permits, this section often includes a market-product grid. See Chapter 9.

An organization cannot grow by offering only "me-too products." The greatest single factor in a new product's failure is the lack of significant "points of difference" that set it apart from competitors' substitutes. This section makes these points of difference explicit. See Chapter 10.

A positioning strategy helps communicate the unique points of difference of a company's products to prospective customers in a simple, clear way. This section describes this positioning. See Chapter 9.

level through the addition of new products in the frozen-foods section. This will be accomplished through new-product concept screening in Year 1 to identify new potential products. These products will be brought to market in Years 2 and 3.

Target Markets

The primary target market for Howlin' Coyote products is households with one to three people, where often both adults work, and with individual income typically above $50,000 per year. These households contain more experienced, adventurous consumers of Southwestern/Mexican food and want premium quality products.

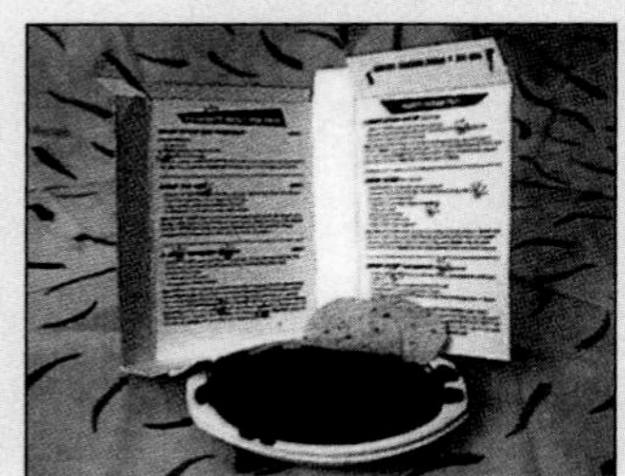

To help buyers see the many different uses for Howlin' Coyote chili, recipes are even printed on the *inside* of the packages.

Points of Difference

The "points of difference"–characteristics that make Howlin' Coyote chilies unique relative to competitors–fall into three important areas:

- *Unique taste and convenience.* No known competitor offers a high-quality, "authentic" frozen chili in a range of flavors. And no existing chili has the same combination of quick preparation and home-style taste that Howlin' Coyote does.
- *Taste trends.* The American palate is increasingly intrigued by hot spices. In response to this trend, Howlin' Coyote brands offer more "kick" than most other prepared chilies.
- *Premium packaging.* Howlin' Coyote's packaging graphics convey the unique, high-quality product contained inside and the product's nontraditional positioning.

Positioning

In the past, chili products have been either convenient or tasty, but not both. Howlin' Coyote pairs these two desirable characteristics to obtain a positioning in consumers' minds as very high-quality "authentic Southwestern/Mexican tasting" chilies that can be prepared easily and quickly.

Photo: Source: Paradise Kitchens, Inc.

Everything that has gone before in the marketing plan sets the stage for the marketing mix actions—the four Ps—covered in the marketing program. See Chapters 10 through 21.

This section describes in detail three key elements of the company's product strategy: the product line, its quality and how this is achieved, and its "cutting edge" packaging. See Chapters 10 and 11.

This Price Strategy section makes the company's price point very clear, along with its price position relative to potential substitutes. When appropriate and when space permits, this section might contain a break-even analysis. See Chapters 13 and 14.

This "introductory overview" sentence tells the reader the topics covered in the section—in this case in-store demonstrations, recipes, and cents-off coupons. While this sentence may be omitted in short memos or plans, it helps readers see where the text is leading. These sentences are used throughout this plan. This textbook also generally uses these introductory overview sentences to aid your comprehension.

6. Marketing Program

The four marketing mix elements of the Howlin' Coyote chili marketing program are detailed below. Note that "chile" is the vegetable and "chili" is the dish.

Product Strategy

After first summarizing the product line, this section describes Howlin' Coyote's approach to product quality and packaging.

Product Line. Howlin' Coyote chili, retailing for $3.99 for an 11-ounce serving, is available in five flavors: Green Chile Chili, Red Chile Chili, Beef and Black Bean Chili, Chicken Chunk Chili, and Mean Bean Chili.

Unique Product Quality. The flavoring systems of the Howlin' Coyote chilies are proprietary. The products' tastiness is due to extra care lavished upon the ingredients during production. The ingredients used are of unusually high quality. Meats are low-fat cuts and are fresh, not frozen, to preserve cell structure and moistness. Chilies are fire-roasted for fresher taste. Tomatoes and vegetables are of select quality. No preservatives or artificial flavors are used.

Packaging. Reflecting the "cutting edge" marketing strategy of its producers, Howlin' Coyote bucks conventional wisdom in its packaging. It specifically avoids placing predictable photographs of the product on its containers. Instead, Howlin' Coyote's package shows a southwestern motif that communicates the product's out-of-the-ordinary positioning. As noted earlier, both women and men represent significant segments of actual purchasers of Howlin' Coyote chili. The southwestern motif on the packaging is deliberately designed to appeal to both women and men.

The southwestern motif makes Howlin' Coyote's packages stand out in a supermarket's freezer case.

Price Strategy

At a $3.99 retail price for an 11-ounce package, Howlin' Coyote chili is priced comparably to the other frozen offerings but higher than the canned and dried chili varieties. However, the significant taste advantages it has over canned chilies and the convenience advantages over dried chilies justify this pricing strategy. This retail price also provides adequate margins for wholesalers and retailers in Howlin' Coyote's channel of distribution.

Promotion Strategy

Key promotion programs feature in-store demonstrations, recipes, and cents-off coupons.

Photo: Source: Paradise Kitchens, Inc.

Elements of the Promotion Strategy are highlighted in terms of the three key promotional activities the company is emphasizing: in-store demonstrations, recipes, and cents-off coupons. For space reasons, the company's online strategies are not shown in the plan. See Chapters 18, 19, and 20.

Another bulleted list adds many details for the reader, including methods of gaining customer awareness, trial, and repeat purchases as Howlin' Coyote enters new metropolitan areas.

The Place Strategy is described here in terms of both (1) the present method and (2) the new one to be used when the increased sales volume makes it feasible. See Chapters 15, 16, and 17.

All the marketing mix decisions covered in the just-described marketing program have both revenue and expense effects. These are summarized in this section of the marketing plan.

Note that this section contains no introductory overview sentence. While the sentence is not essential, many readers prefer to see it to avoid the abrupt start with Past Sales Revenues.

In-Store Demonstrations. In-store demonstrations enable consumers to try Howlin' Coyote products and discover their unique qualities. Demos will be conducted regularly in all markets to increase awareness and trial purchases.

Recipes. Because the products' flexibility of use is a key selling point, recipes are offered to consumers to stimulate use. The recipes are given at all in-store demonstrations, on the back of packages, through a mail-in recipe book offer, and in coupons sent by direct-mail or freestanding inserts.

Cents-Off Coupons. To generate trial and repeat purchase of Howlin' Coyote products, coupons are distributed in four ways:

- *In Sunday newspaper inserts.* These inserts are widely read and help generate awareness.
- *In-pack coupons.* Each box of Howlin' Coyote chili will contain coupons for $1 off two more packages of the chili. These coupons will be included for the first three months the product is shipped to a new market. Doing so encourages repeat purchases by new users.
- *Direct-mail chili coupons.* Those households that fit the Howlin' Coyote demographics described previously will be mailed coupons.
- *In-store demonstrations.* Coupons will be passed out at in-store demonstrations to give an additional incentive to purchase.

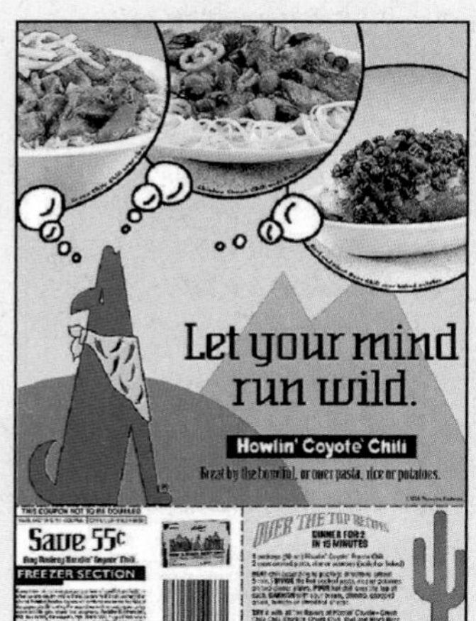

Sunday newspaper inserts encourage consumer trial and provide recipes to show how Howlin' Coyote chili can be used in summer meals.

Place (Distribution) Strategy

Howlin' Coyote is distributed in its present markets through a food distributor. The distributor buys the product, warehouses it, and then resells and delivers it to grocery retailers on a store-by-store basis. As sales grow, we will shift to a more efficient system using a broker who sells the products to retail chains and grocery wholesalers.

7. Financial Data and Projections

Past Sales Revenues

Historically, Howlin' Coyote has had a steady increase in sales revenues since its introduction in 2010. In 2015, sales jumped spectacularly, due largely to new

Photo: Source: Paradise Kitchens, Inc.

The graph shows more clearly the dramatic growth of sales revenue than data in a table would do.

The Five-Year Projections section starts with the judgment forecast of cases sold and the resulting net sales. Gross profit and then operating profit—critical for the company's survival—are projected. An actual plan often contains many pages of computer-generated spreadsheet projections, usually shown in an appendix to the plan.

Because this table is very short, it is woven into the text, rather than given a figure number and a title.

Because the plan proposes to enter 17 new metropolitan markets in the coming five years (for a total of 20), it is not possible to simply extrapolate the trend in Figure 2. Instead, management's judgment must be used. Methods of making sales forecasts—including the "lost horse" technique used here—are discussed in Chapter 8.

The Organization of Paradise Kitchens appears here. It reflects the bare-bones organizational structure of successful small businesses. Often a more elaborate marketing plan will show the new positions expected to be added as the firm grows.

promotion strategies. Sales have continued to rise, but at a less dramatic rate. Sales revenues appear in Figure 2.

Figure 2. Sales Revenues for Paradise Kitchens, Inc.

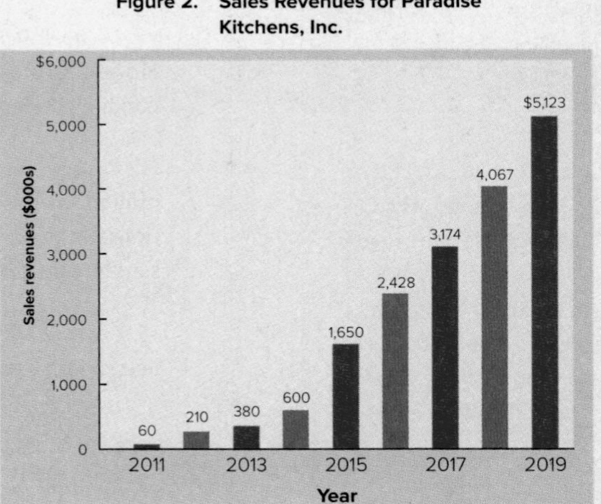

Five-Year Projections

Five-year financial projections for Paradise Kitchens appear below. These projections reflect the continuing growth in the number of cases sold (with eight packages of Howlin' Coyote chili per case).

		Projections (000s)				
Financial Element	Actual 2019	Year 1 2020	Year 2 2021	Year 3 2022	Year 4 2023	Year 5 2024
Cases sold (000s)	353	684	889	1,249	1,499	1,799
Net sales ($000s)	$5,123	$9,913	$12,884	$18,111	$21,733	$26,080
Gross profit ($000s)	$2,545	$4,820	$6,527	$8,831	$10,597	$12,717
Operating profit ($000s)	$339	$985	$2,906	$2,805	$3,366	$4,039

8. Organization

Paradise Kitchens's present organization appears in Figure 3. It shows the four people reporting to the President. Below this level are both the full-time and part-time employees of the Company.

Figure 3. The Paradise Kitchens Organization

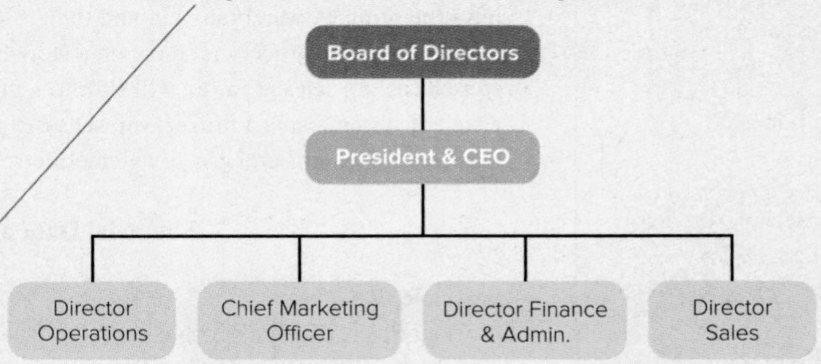

Board of Directors

President & CEO

Director Operations | Chief Marketing Officer | Director Finance & Admin. | Director Sales

The Implementation Plan shows how the company will turn its plan into results. Charts are often used to set deadlines and assign responsibilities for the many tactical marketing decisions needed to enter a new market.

At present, Paradise Kitchens operates with full-time employees in only essential positions. It now augments its full-time staff with key advisors, consultants, and subcontractors. As the firm grows, people with special expertise will be added to the staff.

9. Implementation Plan

Introducing Howlin' Coyote chilies to 17 new metropolitan markets is a complex task and requires that creative promotional activities gain consumer awareness and initial trial. Counting the three existing metropolitan markets in which Paradise Kitchens competes, by 2024 it will be in 20 metropolitan markets or 53 percent of the top 38 U.S. metropolitan markets. The anticipated rollout schedule to enter these metropolitan markets appears in Figure 4.

Figure 4. Rollout Schedule to Enter New U.S. Markets

Year	New Markets Added Each Year	Cumulative Markets	Cumulative Percentage of 38 Major U.S. Markets
Last (2019)	2	5	16
Year 1 (2020)	3	8	21
Year 2 (2021)	4	12	29
Year 3 (2022)	2	14	37
Year 4 (2023)	3	17	45
Year 5 (2024)	3	20	53

The essence of Evaluation is comparing actual sales with the targeted values set in the plan and taking appropriate actions. Note that the section briefly describes a contingency plan for alternative actions, depending on how successful the entry into a new market turns out to be.

The diverse regional tastes in chili will be monitored carefully to assess whether minor modifications may be required in the chili recipes. As the rollout to new metropolitan areas continues, Paradise Kitchens will assess manufacturing and distribution trade-offs. This is important in determining whether to start new production with selected high-quality regional contract packers.

10. Evaluation

Monthly sales targets in cases have been set for Howlin' Coyote chili for each metropolitan area. Actual case sales will be compared with these targets and tactical marketing programs modified to reflect the unique sets of factors in each metropolitan area.

Various appendices may appear at the end of the plan, depending on the plan's purpose and audience. For example, résumés of key personnel or detailed financial spreadsheets often appear in appendices. For space reasons these are not shown here.

Appendix A. Biographical Sketches of Key Personnel

Appendix B. Detailed Financial Projections

Sources: Five-Year Marketing Plan, Paradise Kitchens, Inc.; (mission statement) Paradise Kitchens, Inc., (1996), https://www.termpaperwarehouse.com/essay-on/Paradise-Kitchens-Inc/54894.

Appendix Notes

1. Personal interview with Arthur R. Kydd, St. Croix Management Group.
2. Examples of guides to writing marketing plans include William A. Cohen, *The Marketing Plan,* 5th ed. (New York: Wiley, 2006); and Roman G. Hiebing Jr. and Scott W. Cooper, *The Successful Business Plan: A Disciplined and Comprehensive Approach* (New York: McGraw-Hill, 2008).
3. Examples of guides to writing business plans include Rhonda Abrams, *Business Plan in a Day,* 3rd ed. (Palo Alto, CA: The Planning Shop, a Division of Rhonda, Inc., 2017); Rhonda Abrams, *Successful Business Plan: Secrets and Strategies,* 7th ed. (Palo Alto, CA: The Planning Shop, a Division of Rhonda, Inc., 2019); Joseph A. Covello and Brian J. Hazelgren, *The Complete Book of Business Plans,* 2nd ed. (Naperville, IL: Sourcebooks, 2006); Joseph A. Covello and Brian J. Hazelgren, *Your First Business Plan,* 5th ed. (Naperville, IL: Sourcebooks, 2005); and Mike McKeever, *How to Write a Business Plan,* 8th ed. (Berkeley, CA: Nolo, 2007).
4. Rhonda Abrams, *The Successful Business Plan,* 5th ed. (Palo Alto, CA: The Planning Shop, a Division of Rhonda, Inc., 2010), p. 41.
5. Some of these points are adapted from Rhonda M. Abrams, *The Successful Business Plan: Secrets & Strategies* (Running 'R' Media, 2000), pp. 41–49; others were adapted from William Rudelius, *Guidelines for Technical Report Writing* (Minneapolis: University of Minnesota, undated). See also William Strunk Jr. and E. B. White, *The Elements of Style,* 4th ed. (Needham Heights, MA: Allyn & Bacon, 2000).
6. Personal interviews with Randall F. and Leah E. Peters, Paradise Kitchens, Inc.
7. Sarah Karnaziewicz, "Why Serious Cooks Are in Love with Frozen Food," *Wall Street Journal Online*, February 1, 2019; Aaron Back, "Why the Frozen-Food Aisle Is Hot Right Now," *Wall Street Journal Online*, June, 2018; and Amy Reiter, "Americans Are Cooking More Meals at Home, Eating Out Less," www.foodnetwork.com, September 2018.
8. "NAICS 31141: Frozen Food Manufacturing Industry," *2019 U.S. Industry & Market Report*, Barnes Reports, 2019; and "Frozen Foods Heat Up," www.progressivegrocer.com, June 15, 2018.
9. "Frozen/Refrigerated Prepared Foods," *Progressive Grocer*, April 2015, p. 20; and Chuck Van Hyning, *NPD's National Eating Trends*, www.npdfoodworld.com.
10. Jeffrey M. Humphreys, *The Multicultural Economy*, Selig Center for Economic Growth, 2017; and Jens Manuel Krogstad, "Key Facts about How the U.S. Hispanic Population Is Changing," Pew Research Center, www.pewresearch.org, September 8, 2016.
11. "The Best Canned Chili: Our Taste Test Reveals There's Only One Worth Trying," *The Huffington Post*, February 7, 2014; and "This Is Chili?" *Consumer Reports*, Vol. 55, no. 10 (October 1990): http://connection.ebscohost.com/c/product-reviews/9010081102/this-chili.

Chapter 3 Scanning the Marketing Environment

LEARNING OBJECTIVES

After reading this chapter you should be able to:

LO 3-1 Explain how environmental scanning provides information about social, economic, technological, competitive, and regulatory forces.

LO 3-2 Describe how social forces such as demographics and culture can have an impact on marketing strategy.

LO 3-3 Discuss how economic forces such as macroeconomic conditions and consumer income affect marketing.

LO 3-4 Describe how technological changes can affect marketing.

LO 3-5 Discuss the forms of competition that exist in a market and the key components of competition.

LO 3-6 Explain the major legislation that ensures competition and regulates the elements of the marketing mix.

Facebook Responds to a Changing Environment

We have all heard a version of the Facebook story by now. Mark Zuckerberg started the social network in his Harvard dorm room. He built Facebook to accomplish a social mission–to make the world more open and connected. And the outcome: today Facebook has more than 2.3 billion monthly active users, nearly one-third of the world's population!

Facebook's incredible success was the result of many things, including its ability to observe and adapt to a rapidly changing marketing environment. The environment continues to change, however, and Facebook has recently faced a variety of challenges related to misinformation, election interference, and control of personal information. Let's take a look at the environmental forces that influence Facebook:

- *Social forces* created an extraordinary demand for information and real-time communication through messaging, photos, and video. Facebook's initial role was to provide a platform for exchange. Now the potential for fake news and offensive content has necessitated a proactive approach to preventing harm.
- *Economic* forces are also changing as the global standard of living improves and the cost of mobile devices and Internet access declines. Experts estimate that more than 50 percent of the world's population now has access to the Internet.
- *Technological* advances include voice recognition software, GPS-enabled apps, high-resolution cameras, cloud storage, and a variety of enhancements that increase use of Facebook. Facebook is one of the largest investors in the installation of new high-speed cable around the globe.
- *Competitive* forces include a variety of other social networks such as WhatsApp, WeChat, and Twitter. In addition, Facebook competes with Google, Amazon, and other platforms for digital advertising revenue. The company also faces a variety of malicious threats in the form of cyber attacks, spamming, hacking, and fraud.
- *Legal and regulatory* forces are likely to be a growing influence. Some legislators are suggesting that Facebook has become so large that antitrust laws may become relevant. And in the aftermath of the use of personal data by Cambridge Analytica, Zuckerberg was called to testify before Congress and a discussion of possible new privacy laws began.

Facebook has already responded to many of these trends. In a letter to users and shareholders Zuckerberg suggests that recent changes have "fundamentally altered our DNA."

Justin Sullivan/Getty Images

Facebook in the Future

Today Facebook's portfolio of services includes Facebook, Instagram, WhatsApp, Facebook Messenger, and Oculus virtual reality technology. In a recent interview Zuckerberg suggested that "The future of communication will increasingly shift to private encrypted services where people can be confident what they say to each other stays secure." This means there might be two types of services: public platforms or digital "town squares" such as Facebook and Instagram, and private platforms, or digital "living rooms" such as WhatsApp and Messenger. In addition, Facebook is developing procedures for removing harmful activity from its platforms, and the company is changing its guidelines for targeting advertising (to particular users by age, gender, or zip code) that might be discriminatory. New features will include groups that require paid subscriptions to maintain membership, and Community Finder, a tool to connect female entrepreneurs with their peers around the globe.[1] Chapter 20 provides additional discussion on social networks and social media.

Many businesses operate in environments where important forces change. Anticipating and responding to changes often means the difference between marketing success and failure. This chapter describes how the marketing environment has changed in the past and how it is likely to change in the future.

ENVIRONMENTAL SCANNING

LO 3-1
Explain how environmental scanning provides information about social, economic, technological, competitive, and regulatory forces.

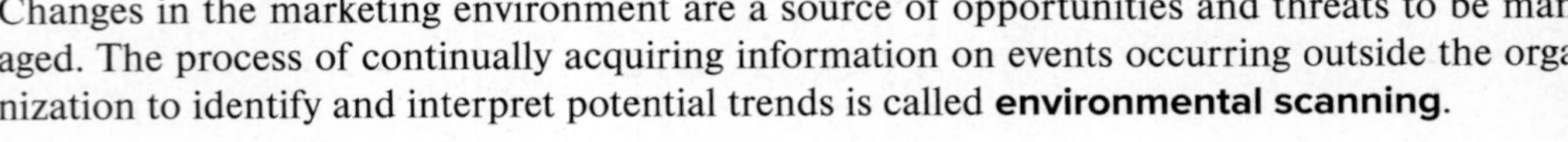

Changes in the marketing environment are a source of opportunities and threats to be managed. The process of continually acquiring information on events occurring outside the organization to identify and interpret potential trends is called **environmental scanning**.

Tracking Environmental Trends

Environmental trends typically arise from five sources: social, economic, technological, competitive, and regulatory forces. As shown in Figure 3–1 and described later in this chapter, these forces affect the marketing activities of a firm in numerous ways. To illustrate how environmental scanning is used, consider the following trends:[2]

VIDEO 3-1
Starbucks Roastery
kerin.tv/15e/v3-1

> Coffee industry marketers have observed that the percentage of adults who drink coffee declined slightly from 64 percent in 2012 to 62 percent today. The percentage of coffee consumed that is defined as "gourmet," however, has increased from 46 percent in 2012 to 59 percent today. The percentage of young adults (18–24 years) who drink coffee is 50 percent while the percentage for older adults (60+) is 68 percent.

The growth of gourmet coffee is one of the trends in the coffee industry.
AFP/Getty Images

What types of businesses are likely to be influenced by these trends? What future would you predict for coffee?

You may have concluded that these changes in coffee consumption are likely to influence coffee manufacturers, coffee shops, and supermarkets. If so, you are correct. Due to the decline in coffee consumption, manufacturers are offering new flavors and seasonal blends, coffee shops are offering online ordering systems and cold brew coffee, and supermarkets are

FIGURE 3–1
Environmental forces affect the organization, as well as its suppliers and customers.

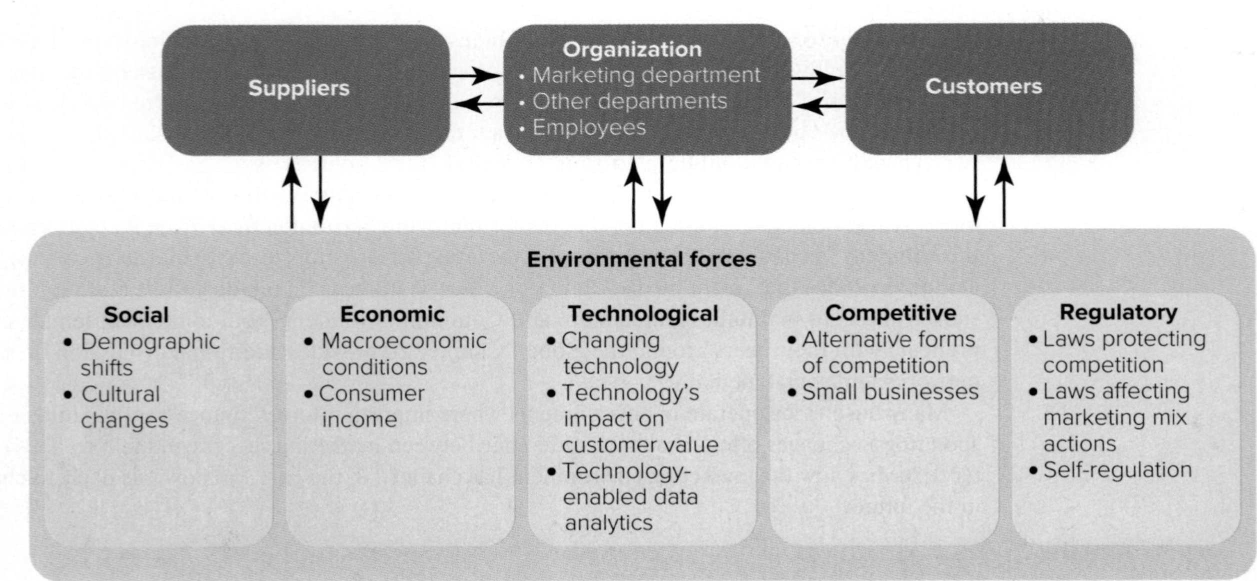

adding boutiques and ready-to-drink coffees. The shift toward gourmet coffee has also led to changes. Starbucks is testing three new formats: the Starbucks Roastery coffee tasting rooms, the Starbucks Reserve coffee stores, and the Starbucks Reserve Bar. Predicting the future requires assumptions about the number of years the trends will continue and their rate of increase or decline. Do you believe that gourmet coffee consumption will remain steady in the future?

Environmental scanning also involves explaining trends. Why is coffee consumption declining? One explanation is that consumers are switching from coffee to other beverages that are perceived to be healthier options. The decline might also be the result of increased use of single-cup coffee machines, which are much more efficient and result in less waste. Finally, the decline may be the result of economic forces that cause consumers to reduce discretionary expenditures. Identifying and interpreting trends, such as the changes in coffee consumption, and developing explanations (such as those offered in this paragraph) are essential to successful environmental scanning.[3]

FIGURE 3–2
An environmental scan of today's marketplace shows the many important trends that influence marketing.

An Environmental Scan of Today's Marketplace

What other trends might affect marketing in the future? A firm conducting an environmental scan of the marketplace might uncover key trends such as those listed in Figure 3–2 for each

ENVIRONMENTAL FORCE	TRENDS IDENTIFIED BY AN ENVIRONMENTAL SCAN
Social	• Interest in health and wellness is growing as biometric "watches" add heart, sleep, and remote monitoring capabilities. • Consumers are increasingly demanding personalized, one-to-one marketing that matches their interests and improves their customer experience. • There is an increasing expectation that companies should tell the stories of their brands with transparency and authenticity and that the brands should enable a positive social impact.
Economic	• The concept of a circular economy, which emphasizes reuse rather than disposal of resources, is gaining popularity among European and U.S. firms. • Expenditures for video advertising is growing, and will soon exceed $20 billion, as video now accounts for 85 percent of all Internet traffic. • New global trade agreements resulting from Brexit, the U.S.-China trade deal, USMCA, and other discussions will lead to changes in the availability and costs of many products and services.
Technological	• The Fourth Industrial Revolution, characterized by 5G networks, AI, the IoT, robotics, and other technologies, is gaining momentum. • Voice-connected devices such as Amazon's Alexa, Google's Assistant, and Apple's Siri are quickly becoming the natural way to interact with technology. • Visual searches, on platforms such as Pinterest and Google, are facilitating a growing interest in the ability to find information based on an image rather than keywords.
Competition	• Marketers are shifting their focus from single transactions to creating ongoing relationships through high-engagement, experiential customer journeys. • Machine intelligence is becoming a competitive strategy as businesses and consumers embrace chatbots and other forms of automation that can reach and respond to prospects and customers. • Companies are using faster and more flexible innovation strategies to create competitive advantage by bringing new smartphones, cars, and brands to the market faster.
Regulatory	• Changing laws related to industries such as ride sharing, cannabis, and health care will have increasing impact on marketing decisions related to advertising, pricing, and customer data collection. • Social media self-regulation is declining as privacy and cybersecurity are becoming the subject of many regulatory initiatives such as the GDPR in Europe and the CCPA in California. • Advertising platforms such as Facebook and Google will face increasing pressure to deter fraud and "fake" news, possibly through the use of blockchain technology.

of the five environmental forces.[4] Although the list of trends in Figure 3–2 is far from complete, it reveals the breadth of an environmental scan—from the growing popularity of personalized marketing, to the increasing emphasis on reuse rather than disposal of products and resources, to the importance of visual search, artificial intelligence, and blockchain technologies. These trends affect consumers and the organizations that serve them. Trends such as these are described in the following discussion of the five environmental forces.

SOCIAL FORCES

Describe how social forces such as demographics and culture can have an impact on marketing strategy.

The **social forces** of the environment include the demographic characteristics of the population and its culture. Changes in these forces can have a dramatic impact on marketing strategy.

Demographics

Describing a population according to selected characteristics such as age, gender, ethnicity, income, and occupation is referred to as **demographics**. Several organizations such as the Population Reference Bureau and the United Nations monitor the world population profile, while many other organizations such as the U.S. Census Bureau provide information about the American population.

The World Population at a Glance The most recent estimates indicate there are 7.6 billion people in the world today, and the population is likely to exceed 9.9 billion by 2050. While this growth has led to the term *population explosion*, the increases have not occurred worldwide; they are primarily in the developing countries of Africa and Asia. In fact, India is predicted to have the world's largest population in 2050 with 1.68 billion people, replacing the current largest country, China, which will have a population of 1.34 billion people. World population projections show that the populations of 38 countries, including China, Japan, Ukraine, Russia, Romania, Poland, Spain, and Taiwan, will be declining.[5]

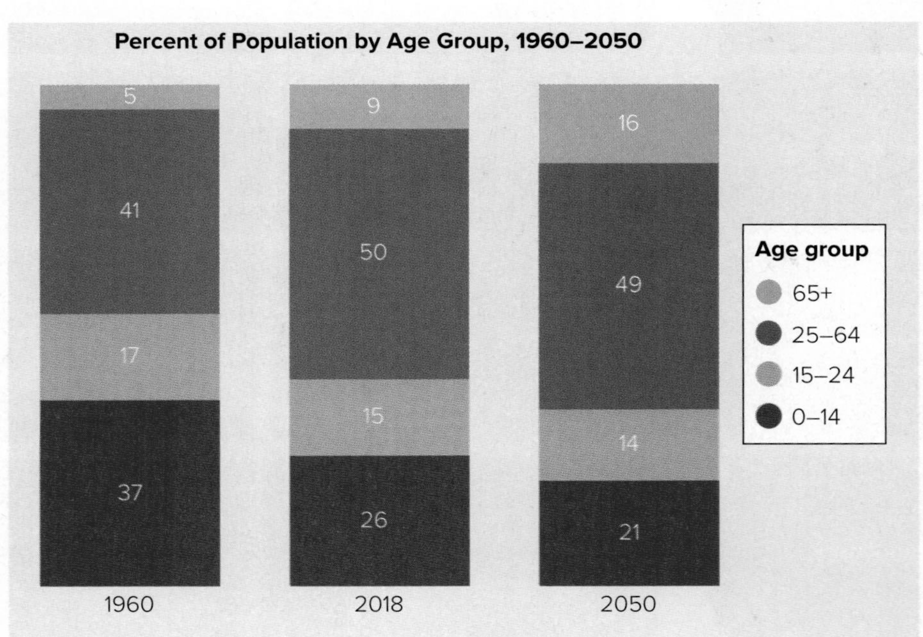

What are the implications of the changes in the world population?
Source: United Nations Population Division, World Population Prospects: The 2017 Revision. New York: United Nations, 2017.

Another important global trend is the shifting age structure of the world population. Worldwide, the number of people 60 years and older is expected to more than double in the coming decades and reach 2.1 billion by 2050. Again, the magnitude of this trend varies by country as South Korea, Japan, Bosnia, Singapore, China, Portugal, and Greece are expected to have the oldest populations by 2050. Global income levels and living standards also have been increasing, although the averages across countries are very different. Per capita income, for example, ranges from $80,560 in Switzerland, to $58,270 in the United States, to $740 in Ethiopia.[6]

For marketers, global trends such as these have many implications. Obviously, the relative size of countries such as India and China will mean they represent huge markets for many product categories. Elderly populations in developed countries are likely to save less and begin spending their funds on health care, travel, and other retirement-related products and services. Economic progress in developing countries will lead to growth in entrepreneurship; new markets for infrastructure related to manufacturing, communication, and distribution; and the growth of exports.

The U.S. Population Studies of the demographic characteristics of the U.S. population suggest several important trends. Generally, the population is becoming larger, older, and more diverse. The U.S. Census Bureau estimates that the current population of the United States is approximately 328 million people. If current trends in life expectancy, birthrates, and immigration continue, by 2030 and 2050 the U.S. population will exceed 355 and 389 million people, respectively. This growth suggests that niche markets based on age, life stage, family structure, geographic location, and ethnicity will become increasingly important.

The global trend toward an older population is particularly true in the United States. Today, there are more than 49 million people aged 65 and older. By 2050, this age group will include more than 85 million people, or 22 percent of the population. You may have noticed companies trying to attract older consumers by making wider car doors, lowering store shelves, and avoiding colors that are difficult to read (yellow and blue). Finally, the term *minority* as it is currently used is likely to become obsolete as the total size of all ethnic groups will grow from 37 percent of the population to 50 percent of the population in 2044.[7]

Brands such as Kellogg's Special K are intended to appeal to baby boomers' interest in health and fitness.
McGraw-Hill Education

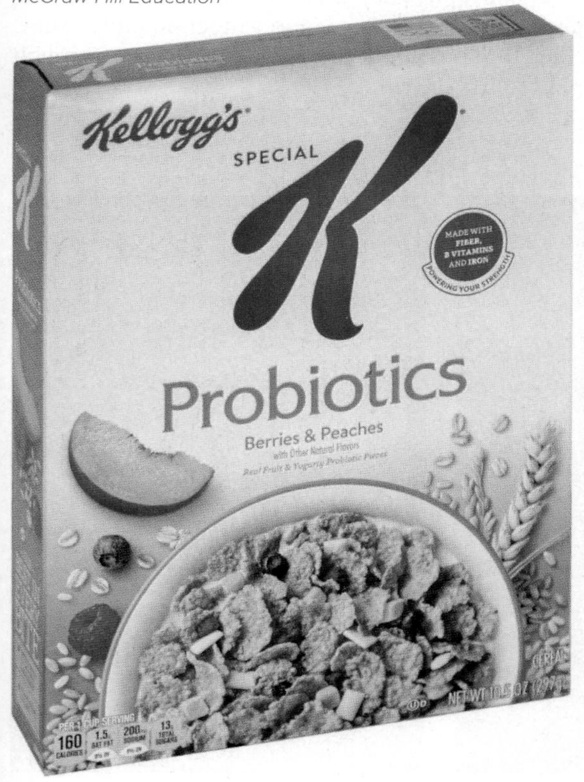

Generational Cohorts A major reason for the graying of America is that the generation referred to as the **baby boomers**—the 76 million children born between 1946 and 1964—are growing older. Baby boomers are retiring at a rate of 10,000 every 24 hours, and they will all be 65 or older by 2030. Their participation in the workforce has made them the wealthiest generation in U.S. history, accounting for an estimated 50 percent of all consumer spending.

Companies that target boomers will need to respond to their interests in health, fitness, retirement housing, financial planning, and appearance. Kellogg's Special K cereal, for example, attracts baby boomers with its fruit, fiber, and probiotics ingredients. Similarly, Prudential offers a retirement plan and Olay offers "age-defying" products for this age group. Baby boomers are also sometimes called the "sandwich generation" because they often find themselves balancing obligations to their parents and their children.[8]

The baby boom cohort is followed by **Generation X**, which includes the 55 million people born between 1965 and 1980. This period is also known as the *baby bust*, because during this time the number of children born each year was declining. This is a generation of consumers who are self-reliant, supportive of racial and ethnic diversity, and better educated than any previous generation. They are not prone to extravagance and are likely to pursue lifestyles that are a blend of caution, pragmatism, and traditionalism.

In terms of net worth, Generation X is the first generation to have less than the previous generation. As baby boomers move toward retirement, however, Generation X is becoming a dominant force in many markets. Generation X, for example, spends more on food, housing, apparel, and entertainment than other generations. In addition, this generation is on the Internet more than any other generation and also leads in terms of online spending. Surveys of Generation X consumers indicate they want websites that are comprehensive, professional, and interactive; services such as self-checkout and curbside pickup; and advertising that is authentic, family-oriented, and unique. Generation X is also replacing baby boomers as the largest segment of business travelers. In response, many airlines, such as Delta, are now offering travelers more comfortable seats, 110-volt and USB outlets, and larger entertainment screens.[9]

The generational cohort labeled **Generation Y** includes the 62 million Americans born between 1981 and 1996. This was a period of increasing births, which resulted from baby boomers having children, and it is often referred to as the *echo-boom*. Generation Y exerts influence on music, sports, computers, video games, and all forms of communication and networking related to smartphones. Generation Y members are interested in distinctive, memorable, and personal experiences and are very adept at managing their lives to create a work-life balance. They are strong-willed, passionate about the environment, and optimistic. This is also a group that is attracted to purposeful work where they have control. The term *millennials* is often used, with inconsistent definitions, to refer to members of Generation Y. The Making Responsible Decisions box describes how millennials' interest in sustainability is influencing product offerings, colleges, and employers. Based on immigration and death rate estimates, millennials have recently surpassed baby boomers as the largest living generation, with 75 million people.

The post-millennial generation is referred to as **Generation Z**, which includes consumers born between 1997 and 2010. Their values were formed by the Great Recession, ISIS, Sandy Hook, marriage equality, the first black president, and a growing interest in populism. They are hardworking, financially responsible, and independent multitaskers who embrace the broadest definitions of diversity and inclusivity. They prefer a "natural" look, discover and learn online, and expect a seamless use of digital and physical aspects of the marketplace. From a marketing perspective, Generation Z consumers say they will pay more for a product or brand if it promotes environmental issues, social justice, and gender equality. They, more than any other generation, say that they find out about products and services through social media.[10]

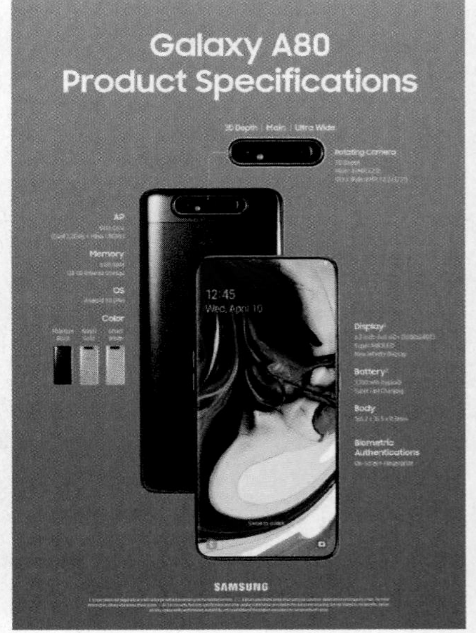

Which generational cohorts are these three advertisers trying to reach?

(Left) Source: Procter & Gamble; (Center) Source: Delta Air Lines, Inc.; (Right) Source: Samsung

Making Responsible Decisions — Sustainability

Balancing Profits and Purpose—Millennial Style

Millennials are technologically savvy, innovative, and ambitious. In addition, they are a generation that is determined to make the world a better place. They expect brands and companies to embrace social change, corporate social responsibility, and environmental stewardship, as well as profits. This focus on a higher purpose influences their choices as consumers, as students, and as early career employees.

Some companies are taking note of millennials' interests. Procter & Gamble, for example, recently introduced fully recyclable Head & Shoulders shampoo bottles made with 25 percent recycled plastic. Similarly, Unilever has launched its Sustainable Living Plan to create "brands with purpose," Apple's new headquarters is described as "the greenest building on the planet," and Whole Foods Market makes decisions only after considering the needs of all stakeholders.

Source: Net Impact

There are approximately 17 million undergraduate millennials who expect sustainable campus communities that include LEED (Leadership in Energy and Environmental Design)–certified housing, campus transit systems, and recycling programs. Graduate students are looking for programs with sustainability electives, case studies, and potential for involvement with organizations such as Net Impact (www.netimpact.org), a nonprofit for students who want to "use business to improve the world." Sara Hochman is a typical example. She was interested in environmental issues in college, and her first job was as an environmental consultant. To make a bigger impact on her clients, she enrolled in graduate school at the University of Chicago where she could take an elective on renewable energy and join the Energy Club.

Early career employees want "green" jobs such as social responsibility officer, corporate philanthropy manager, and sustainability database specialist. In addition they want to work at companies that advocate good corporate citizenship, responsible capitalism, and "B-Corp" status. They view themselves as part of a "positive business" movement that balances the interests of shareholders, employees, and society. Charlotte Moran, a mid-20s group marketing manager for Siemens Home Appliances, explains: "I'd find it very hard to work for a company that didn't understand its impact on the environment and didn't make an effort to change for the better."

How will your interests in being a force for good influence your education and career decisions? The world will know soon!

Because the members of each generation are distinctive in their attitudes and consumer behavior, marketers have been studying the many groups or cohorts that make up the marketplace and have developed *generational marketing* programs for them.

The American Household As the population age profile has changed, so has the structure of the American household. In 1960, 75 percent of all households consisted of married couples. Today, that type of household is 48 percent of the population. Twenty percent of households are married couples with children, and 10 percent are households with working fathers and stay-at-home moms. Some of the fastest-growing types of households are those with an adult child who has moved back home with his or her parents, those with unmarried partners, and those with same-sex partners.

Hallmark offers cards for the many types of American households.
Kristoffer Tripplaar/Alamy Stock Photo

In fact, for the first time, the number of young adults (18- to 34-year-olds) living with their parents exceeds the number living with a spouse or partner. One factor contributing to this circumstance is that many young people are postponing, or eschewing, marriage and parenthood. Some researchers estimate that as many as 25 percent of today's young adults may never marry. Businesses are adjusting to the changes because they have implications for purchases related to weddings, homes, baby and child products, and many other industries.[11]

The increase in cohabitation (households with unmarried partners) may be one reason the national divorce rate has declined during recent years. Even so, the likelihood that a couple will divorce exceeds 40 percent, and divorce among baby boomers—what is being called *gray divorce*—is increasing. The reasons for the increase of divorce in this age group may be related to increased longevity and increased economic independence. The majority of divorced people eventually remarry, which has created the **blended family**, one formed by merging two previously separated units into a single household. Today, one of every three Americans is a stepparent, stepchild, stepsibling, or some other member of a blended family. Hallmark Cards, Inc. now has specially designed cards and sentiments for blended families.[12]

Population Shifts A major regional shift in the U.S. population toward southern and western states is under way. The shift is the result of three components: natural population change (births minus deaths), state-to-state migration, and international migration (immigration minus emigration). The most recent Census Bureau estimates indicate that the populations of Nevada, Idaho, Utah, Arizona, Florida, and Washington grew at the fastest rates, while the population of Illinois declined at the greatest rate. Nearly a century ago each of the top 10 most populous cities in the United States was within 500 miles of the Canadian border. Today, 7 of the top 10 are in states that border Mexico. Last year, Texas gained more people than any other state–its population increased by more than 379,000![13]

Populations are also shifting within states. In the early 1900s, the population shifted from rural areas to cities. From the 1930s through the 2000s, the population shifted from cities to suburbs, and most recently there has been a shift from suburbs to more remote suburbs called *exurbs.* In fact, low mortgage rates and a growing population of millennials looking for child-friendly, affordable housing are driving demand in the exurbs surrounding large cities such as San Francisco where owning or renting a home may be difficult. In addition, young professionals and active retirees are moving to exurban communities that offer amenities such as equestrian centers, car clubs with racetracks, vineyards, and even "agrihoods" built around community-based farms. Today, 30 percent of all Americans live in central cities, 50 percent live in suburbs, and 20 percent live in rural locations.[14]

To assist marketers in gathering data on the population, the Census Bureau has developed a classification system to describe the varying locations of the population. The system consists of two types of *statistical areas*:

- A *metropolitan statistical area* has at least one urbanized area of 50,000 or more people and adjacent territory that has a high degree of social and economic integration.
- A *micropolitan statistical area* has at least one urban cluster of at least 10,000 but less than 50,000 people and adjacent territory that has a high degree of social and economic integration.

If a metropolitan statistical area contains a population of 2.5 million or more, it may be subdivided into smaller areas called *metropolitan divisions*. In addition, adjacent metropolitan statistical areas and micropolitan statistical areas may be grouped into *combined statistical areas*.[15]

There are currently 392 metropolitan statistical areas, which include about 86 percent of the population, and 546 micropolitan statistical areas, which include about 8.5 percent of the population.

Racial and Ethnic Diversity A notable trend is the changing racial and ethnic composition of the U.S. population. Approximately one in three U.S. residents belongs to the following racial or ethnic groups: African American, Native American or Alaska Native, Asian American, or Native Hawaiian or Pacific Islander. Diversity is further evident in the variety of peoples that make up these groups. For example, Asians consist of Asian Indians, Chinese, Filipinos, Japanese, Koreans, and Vietnamese.

The most recent Census allowed respondents to choose more than one of the five race options, and more than 5 million people reported more than one race. Hispanics, who may be from any race, currently make up 17 percent of the U.S. population and are represented by Mexicans, Puerto Ricans, Cubans, and others of Central and South American ancestry. While the United States is becoming more diverse, Figure 3–3 suggests that racial and ethnic groups tend to be concentrated in geographic regions.[16]

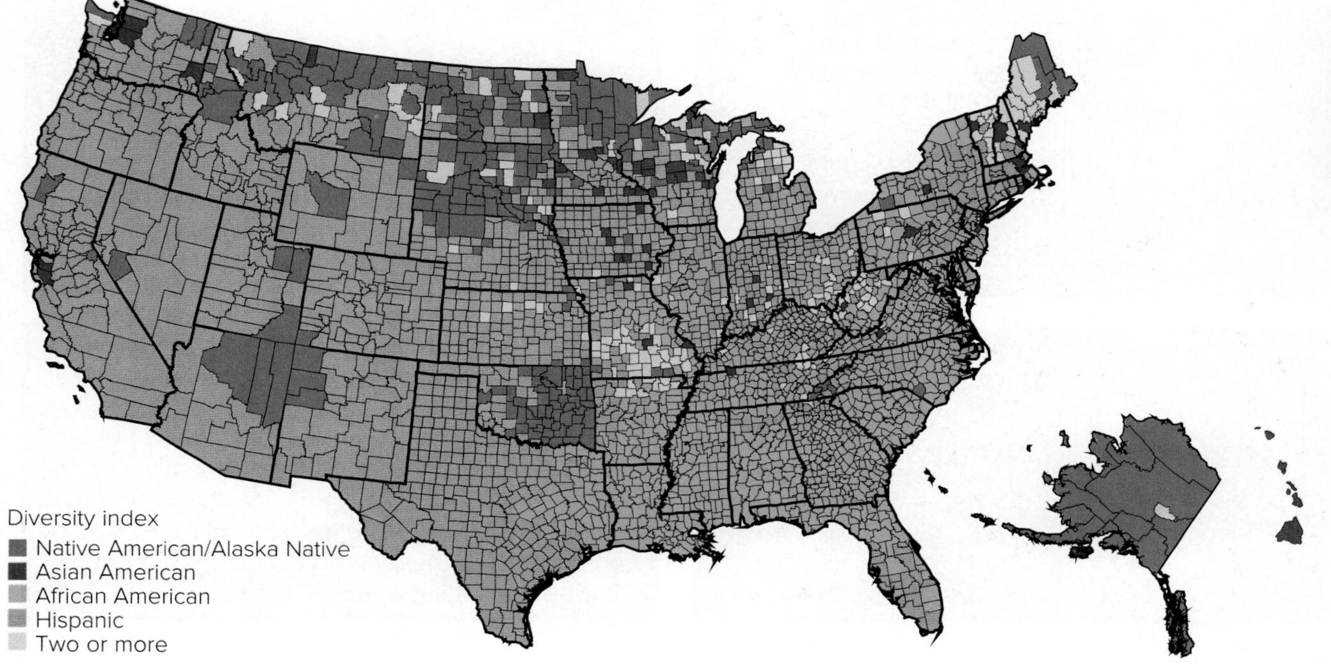

FIGURE 3–3
Racial and ethnic groups (excluding Caucasians) are concentrated in geographic regions of the United States.

The racial and ethnic composition of the United States is expected to change even more in the future. By 2030, the Hispanic population will grow to more than 74 million, or 21 percent of the population. The number of Asians in the United States will increase to 24 million, or 7 percent of the population, and the African American population will be approximately 49 million, or 14 percent of the population. The multiracial category currently makes up 2.6 percent of the population and is expected to grow to 3.6 percent. Overall, the trends in the composition of the population suggest that the U.S. market will no longer be dominated by one group and that non-Hispanic Caucasians will make up less than 50 percent of the U.S. population by 2044.

While the growing size of these groups has been identified through new Census data, their economic impact on the marketplace is also very noticeable. Hispanics, African Americans, and Asian Americans spend more than $1.5 trillion, $1.3 trillion, and $1.0 trillion each year, respectively. To adapt to this new marketplace, many companies are developing **multicultural marketing** programs, which are combinations of the marketing mix that reflect the unique attitudes, ancestry, communication preferences, and lifestyles of different races. Because businesses must now market their products to a consumer base with many racial and ethnic identities, in-depth marketing research that allows an accurate understanding of each culture is essential.[17]

Information about cultural preferences combined with information about geographic concentrations, such as the information shown in Figure 3-3, allows companies to combine their multicultural marketing efforts with regional marketing activities. Consider, for example, that 48 percent of Asian Americans live in Los Angeles, New York City, and San Francisco and that two-thirds of Hispanics live in Florida, Texas, and California. *Advertising Age*'s Multicultural Agency of the Year, The Community, is a global agency of people with diverse backgrounds with a mission "to create culturally-potent ideas for a multi-everything world." The agency creates campaigns for Domino's Pizza, Ferrero Rocher, Verizon, Coca-Cola, Google, and many others. For example, The Community created an ad for Verizon to appeal to Hispanic audiences.

Many other changes are facilitating multicultural marketing programs. Increasingly diverse television programming, such as *Black-ish*, *Empire*, *Atlanta*, *Insecure*, and *Fresh Off the Boat*, for example, is available for advertisers. Sports such as soccer, baseball, and basketball are implementing programs such as the NBA's Latin Nights events, which display team names as

Danny, deja de jugar en línea! Voy a video chat con la tía.

Salga de la línea! Estoy a punto de transmitir el partido.

Fios es una red 100% de fibra óptica. Podríamos estar en línea todos al mismo tiempo.

Red 100% fibra óptica
El Red 100% fiber óptico con las velocidades más rápidas por $79.99 por mes.

Verizon Fios combines ethnic and regional marketing by using Spanish-language promotions like this one in some states.
Source: Fios

spoken by bilingual fans (the Miami Heat is also El Heat). In addition, retailers often designate stores for bilingual signage and staff. Finally, marketers have learned that mobile devices and social media are often the best way to reach multicultural audiences. Facebook recently began using online information to designate Hispanic, African American, and Asian American affinity groups for advertisers.[18]

VIDEO 3-2
Verizon Fios
kerin.tv/15e/v3-2

Culture

A second social force, **culture**, incorporates the set of values, ideas, and attitudes that are learned and shared among the members of a group. Because many of the elements of culture influence consumer buying patterns, monitoring national and global cultural trends is important for marketing. Cross-cultural analysis needed for global marketing is discussed in Chapter 7.

The Changing Attitudes and Roles of Men and Women One of the most notable cultural changes in the United States in the past 30 years has been in the attitudes and roles of men and women in the marketplace. Some experts predict that as this trend continues, the buying patterns of men and women will eventually be very similar.

Your mothers and grandmothers probably remember advertising targeted at them that focused on the characteristics of household products—like laundry detergent that got clothes "whiter than white." In the 1970s and 1980s, ads began to create a bridge between genders with messages such as Secret's "Strong enough for a man, but made for a woman." In the 1990s, marketing to women focused on their challenge of balancing family and career interests. Since then, women and men have encouraged the slow movement toward equality in the marketplace. As a result, today's Generation Y represents the first generation of women who have no collective memory of the dramatic changes we have undergone. As one expert explains, "Feminism today is like fluoride; we scarcely notice that we have it."

Several factors have contributed to the shift in attitudes. First, many young women had career mothers who provided a reference point for lifestyle choices. Second, increased participation in organized sports eliminated one of the most visible inequalities in opportunities for women. And finally, the Internet has provided exposure to the marketplace through a mechanism that makes gender, race, and ethnicity invisible. Today millennials encourage "everyday feminism" through daily lifestyle decisions and online activism to work toward equal opportunities and treatment in the marketplace, the workplace, and politics.[19]

Calvin Klein introduced CK2 to appeal to women as well as men.
Source: Calvin Klein

Many companies that had a consumer base that was primarily women or primarily men in the past are preparing for growth from the other gender. Grocery stores, car dealers, investment services, video game developers, and many others hope to appeal to both groups in the future. Under Armour, for example, is trying to attract women with clothing specifically designed for them, while Lululemon is trying to attract men with lines that match their interests in running and training. Similarly, social media site Pinterest hopes to attract more men to the site by subtly making its search results more gender-neutral.

Some companies are moving away from traditional gender norms to avoid gender stereotypes. Target, for example, removed gender-based signage from its toy, entertainment, and home departments. Fashion leader Zara recently introduced a line of ungendered clothing which includes hoodies, Bermuda shorts, and crewneck tops, and Calvin Klein introduced fragrance CK2 for women and men. Gender-neutral advertising is also becoming more common. Jaden Smith recently modeled Louis Vuitton's new women's line with three female models, and one of Calvin Klein's advertising campaigns for CK2 uses the tagline, "a new scent for #the2ofus."[20]

Changing Values Culture also includes values that may differ over time and between countries. In the past, a list of values in the United States included achievement, work, efficiency, and material comfort. Today, commonly held values include personal control, continuous change, equality, individualism, self-help, competition, future orientation, and action. These values are useful in understanding most current behaviors of U.S. consumers, particularly when they are compared to values in other countries. Contrasting values outside the United States, for example, include belief in fate, the importance of tradition, the importance of rank and status, a focus on group welfare, and acceptance of birthright.

VIDEO 3-3
Bombas Video
kerin.tv/15e/v3-3

An increasingly important value for consumers in the United States and around the globe is sustainability and preserving the environment. In fact, 82 percent of today's shoppers consider themselves environmentally friendly. Concern for the environment is one reason consumers are buying hybrid gas-electric automobiles, such as the Toyota Prius, the Chevy Volt, and the Ford C-MAX. Companies are also changing their business practices to respond to trends in consumer values. Coca-Cola has been working on alleviating global water scarcity, Facebook has committed to reducing the carbon footprint of its data centers, and Wal-Mart Stores, Inc., has set ambitious goals to cut energy use by buying more local products, reducing packaging, and switching to renewable power. Recent research also indicates that consumers are committed to brands with a strong link to social action. For example, Bombas has donated more than 5 million pairs of socks to homeless shelters in its efforts to help "an under-publicized problem in the United States."[21]

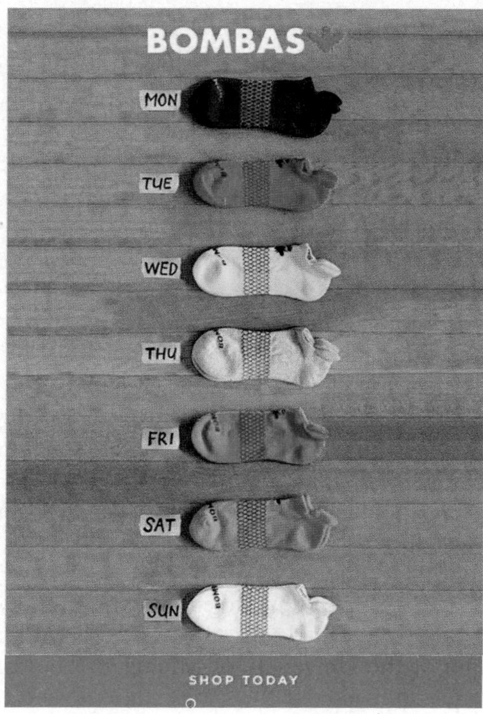

Bombas has donated millions of pairs of socks to homeless shelters, reflecting new consumer values related to social action.
Source: Bombas

Lester Balajadia/Shutterstock

A change in consumption orientation is also apparent. In the past, consumers often used debt to make many of their purchases. During the recent recession and global economic crisis, however, consumers changed their perspective. Today, U.S. consumers have become cautious buyers. **Value consciousness**—or the concern for obtaining the best quality, features, and performance of a product or service for a given price—is driving consumption behavior for many products at all price levels. For example, some consumers cut back on brand-name products such as toothpaste, shampoo, and toilet paper so that they could still afford discretionary products such as high-definition televisions and smartphones. In addition, the new aversion to spending prompted consumers to search for low prices at many types of stores and online.

Innovative marketers have responded to this new value-conscious orientation in numerous ways. Dollar General, for example, is opening 1,000 new small-format stores to attract consumers "who put a high premium on value." Similarly, Walmart purchased online retailer Jet.com for $3.3 billion to complement its existing e-commerce offering and offer lower prices and a broader assortment of products to customers who shop for bargains online.[22]

LEARNING REVIEW

3-1. Describe four generational cohorts.

3-2. Why are many companies developing multicultural marketing programs?

3-3. How are important values such as sustainability reflected in the marketplace today?

ECONOMIC FORCES

LO 3-3
Discuss how economic forces such as macroeconomic conditions and consumer income affect marketing.

The second component of the environmental scan, the **economy**, pertains to the income, expenditures, and resources that affect the cost of running a business and household. We'll consider two aspects of these economic forces: a macroeconomic view of the marketplace and a microeconomic perspective of consumer income.

Macroeconomic Conditions

Of particular concern at the macroeconomic level is the performance of the economy based on indicators such as GDP (gross domestic product), unemployment, and price changes (inflation or deflation). In an inflationary economy, the cost to produce and buy products and services escalates as prices increase. From a marketing standpoint, if prices rise faster than consumer incomes, the number of items consumers can buy decreases. This relationship is evident in the cost of a college education. The College Board reports that since 2000 college tuition and fees have increased 190 percent (from $3,510 to $10,230) while family incomes have increased by 2 percent. The share of family income required to pay for tuition at public four-year colleges has risen from 8 percent in 2000 to 16 percent today.[23]

Periods of declining economic activity are referred to as recessions. During recessions, businesses decrease production, unemployment rises, and many consumers have less money to spend. The U.S. economy experienced recessions from 1973–75, 1981–82, 1990–91, and in 2001. Most recently, a recessionary period began in 2007 and ended in 2009, becoming the longest in recent history.[24]

Consumer expectations about the economy are an important element of environmental scanning. Consumer spending, which accounts for two-thirds of U.S. economic activity, is affected by expectations of the future. The two most popular surveys of consumer expectations are the Consumer Confidence Index, conducted by a nonprofit business research organization called the Conference Board, and the Index of Consumer Sentiment (ICS), conducted by the Survey Research Center at the University of Michigan. The surveys track the responses of consumers to specific questions about their expectations, and the results are reported once

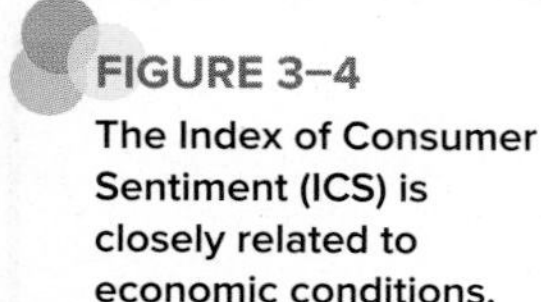

FIGURE 3–4
The Index of Consumer Sentiment (ICS) is closely related to economic conditions.

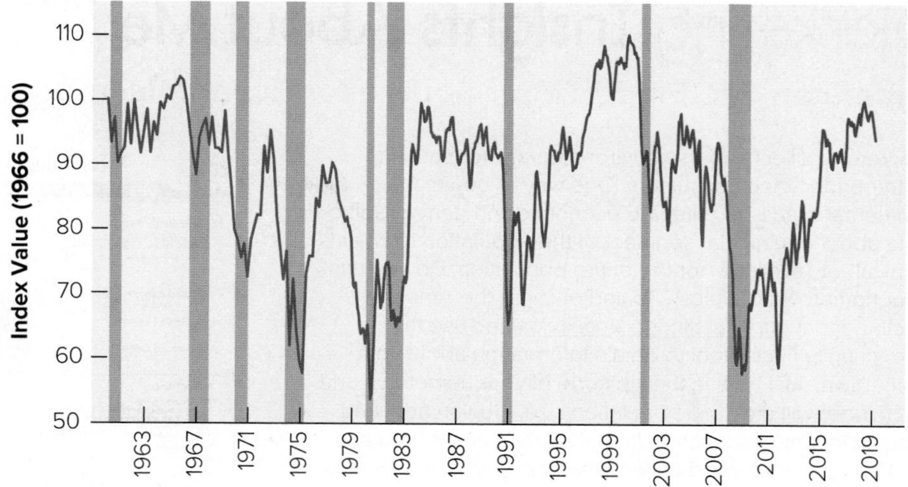

each month. For example, the Index of Consumer Sentiment asks, "Looking ahead, do you think that a year from now you will be better off financially, worse off, or just about the same as now?" The answers to the questions are used to construct an index. The higher the index, the more favorable are consumer expectations. Figure 3–4 shows the fluctuation in the ICS and its close relationship to economic conditions (green areas represent recessionary periods). The consumer expectations surveys are closely monitored by many companies, particularly manufacturers and retailers of cars, furniture, and major appliances.[25]

Consumer Income

The microeconomic trends in terms of consumer income are also important issues for marketers. Having a product that meets the needs of consumers may be of little value if they are unable to purchase it. A consumer's ability to buy is related to income, which consists of gross, disposable, and discretionary components.

Gross Income The total amount of money made in one year by a person, household, or family unit is referred to as **gross income** (or *money income* at the Census Bureau). While the typical U.S. household earned only about $8,700 of income in 1970, it earned about $61,300 in 2017. When gross income is adjusted for inflation, however, income of that typical U.S. household was relatively stable. In fact, inflation-adjusted income has only increased $12,000 since 1970. Approximately 50 percent of U.S. households have an annual income between $25,000 and $99,999.[26] Are you from a typical household? Read the Marketing Insights About Me box on the next page to learn how you can determine the median household income in your hometown.

Disposable Income The second income component, **disposable income**, is the money a consumer has left after paying taxes to use for necessities such as food, housing, clothing, and transportation. Thus, if taxes rise or fall faster than income, consumers are likely to have more or less disposable income. Similarly, dramatic changes in the prices of products can lead to spending adjustments. A decline in the price of gasoline, for example, often leads to increases in consumer spending in other categories. In addition, changes in home prices have a psychological impact on consumers, who tend to spend more when they feel their net worth is rising and postpone purchases when it declines. During a recessionary period, spending, debt, and the use of credit all decline.[27]

Discretionary Income The third component of income is **discretionary income**, the money that remains after paying for taxes and necessities. Discretionary income is used for luxury items such as a Cunard cruise. An obvious problem in defining discretionary versus disposable income is determining what is a luxury and what is a necessity.

Marketing Insights About Me

American FactFinder: Your Source for Economic Information

Marketers collect and use environmental information to better understand consumers. One way to begin an environmental scan is to compare economic and demographic data about a particular segment of the population to what is "typical" or "average" for the entire population. Do you think your hometown is typical? To find out, visit the American FactFinder at http://factfinder.census.gov and use the "Community Facts" tool to obtain information about your hometown. Just type in the zip code of your hometown and FactFinder will give you population size, median age, and median income information from the U.S. Census. You can also click on links listed under *American Community Survey* for more detailed information. Use the tool to look up information about your state or the United States to make comparisons.

Source: American Factfinder

The Department of Labor monitors consumer expenditures through its annual Consumer Expenditure Survey. The most recent report indicates that consumers spend about 13 percent of their income on food, 33 percent on housing, and 3 percent on clothes. While an additional 24 percent is often spent on transportation and health care, the remainder is generally viewed as discretionary. The percentage of income spent on food and housing typically declines as income increases, which can provide an increase in discretionary income. Discretionary expenditures also can be increased by reducing savings. The Bureau of Labor Statistics observed that during the 1990s and early 2000s the savings rate declined from a long-term average of 8 percent to less than 4 percent. Recent data on consumer expenditures indicate that the savings rate is now approximately 7.5 percent.[28]

As consumers' discretionary income increases, so does the opportunity to indulge in the luxurious leisure travel marketed by Cunard.
Courtesy of Cunard Line

TECHNOLOGICAL FORCES

LO 3-4
Describe how technological changes can affect marketing.

Our society is in a period of dramatic technological change. **Technology**, the third environmental force in Figure 3–2, refers to inventions or innovations from applied science or engineering research. Each new wave of technological innovation can replace existing products and companies. Perhaps you've had a favorite product such as a phone or a computer replaced by an improved version, or a product category such as digital music files or printed books replaced by completely new technology?

Technology of Tomorrow

Technological change is the result of research, so it is difficult to predict. Some of the most dramatic technological changes occurring now, however, include the following:

- New authentication technology based on facial recognition and fingerprint recognition will improve transactions by eliminating passwords.
- Digital ledger technology, or blockchain, will facilitate instant and efficient digital advertising by connecting advertisers directly with media platforms.
- Smart speakers, digital assistants, and artificial intelligence will combine to become convenient, knowledgeable, and always-available purchase influencers.
- Wearable technology will evolve from fitness monitors to health and wellness devices that provide remote monitoring, digital therapeutics, and even personalized healthy behavior guidance.

Some of these trends in technology are already being realized in today's marketplace. The Olympics, for example, uses facial recognition technology to reduce congestion in waiting lines. IBM has partnered with Salesforce.com to use artificial intelligence to enhance Salesforce's customer service software. Apple recently introduced a watch with electrocardiogram (ECG) capability. Other technologies, such as Google's Cloud Storage service, Slack's new software, and Nest doorbells, are likely to replace or become substitutes for existing products and services such as hard-drive storage, e-mail, and security cameras.[29]

Technology's Impact on Customer Value

Advances in technology have important effects on marketing. First, the cost of technology is plummeting, causing the customer value assessment of technology-based products to focus on

Technological change leads to new products. What products or services might be replaced by these innovations?

(Left) Source: Alphabet Inc.; (Center) Source: Slack; (Right) Source: Nest Labs

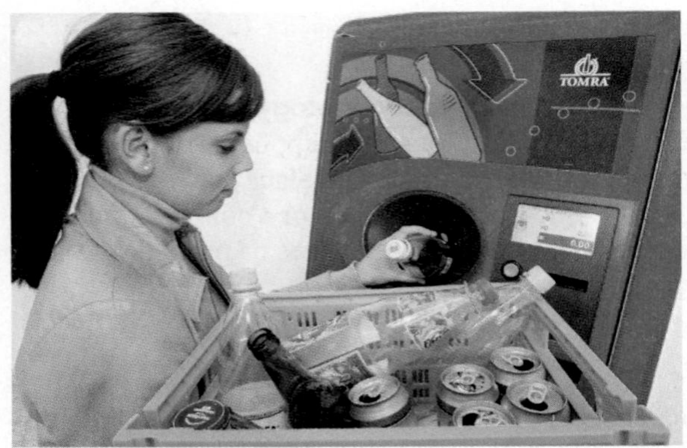

Tomra offers recycling through its kiosks.
dpa picture alliance/Alamy Stock Photo

other dimensions such as quality, service, and relationships. *PC Magazine* (www.pcmag.com) publishes an article titled "The Best Free Software" each year to tell readers about companies that give their software away, with the expectation that advertising or upgrade purchases will generate revenue. A similar approach is used by some cell phone service providers, who offer free or subsidized telephones if the consumer changes providers.[30]

Technology also provides value through the development of new products. More than 4,400 companies recently unveiled thousands of new products at the Consumer Electronics Show held in Las Vegas. New products included wireless earbuds that translate 37 languages in real time, a smart alarm clock that simulates a sunrise, a heated razor, and a personal robot that monitors your sleep, responds to hand gestures, and provides a daily briefing! *Better Homes and Gardens* magazine recently announced its Innovation Awards, which include anti-hacking software from Virtru, a washer and dryer combined into one unit by LG, and a 360-degree camera by Samsung. Other new products likely to be available soon include injectable health monitors that will send biometric information to a mobile monitor, such as a watch or a phone, and wireless charging systems that will send power to devices within five feet of the system.[31]

Technology can also change existing products and the ways they are produced. Many companies are using technological developments to recycle products through the manufacturing cycle several times. The National Association for PET Container Resources, for example, estimates that 30 percent of all plastic bottles are now recycled, usually to make polyester fibers that are spun into everything from sweaters to upholstery. Tomra Systems has installed more than 82,000 reverse vending machines in North America, Europe, Japan, South America, and the Middle East, facilitating the collection of more than 40 billion cans and bottles annually. In California, there are more than 350 rePLANET recycling centers where consumers can bring back their empty beverage containers and redeem them for the deposit paid when the products were purchased. Another approach is *precycling*, or efforts by manufacturers and consumers to avoid creating waste. For manufacturers, this includes decreasing the amount of packaging they use; and for consumers, it means buying products that last longer, avoiding products with excess packaging, and reusing as much as possible. According to marketing expert Melissa Lavigne, "It's about being conscious about products you buy in the first place. That's the idea behind precycling."[32]

The Internet of Things has contributed to the growth in data analytics.
Askold Romanov/Getty Images

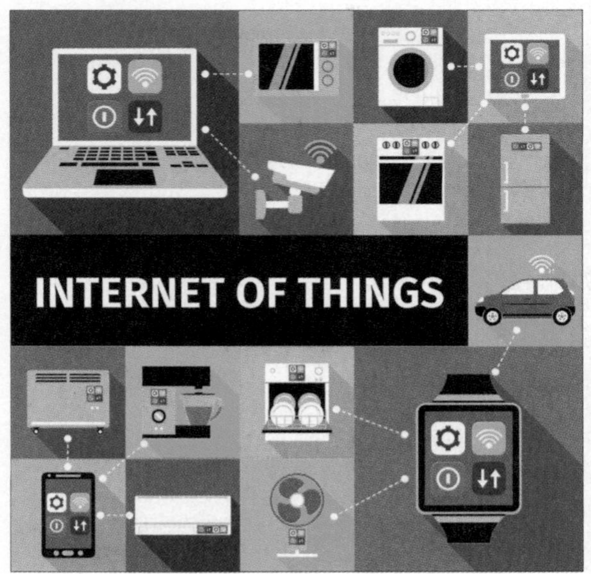

Technology Enables Data Analytics

Technology has also had a dramatic impact on the operations of marketing organizations. First, the development of online capabilities created the **marketspace**, an information- and communication-based electronic exchange environment occupied by sophisticated computer and telecommunication technologies and digital offerings. Second, these capabilities led to **electronic commerce** (*e-commerce*), or the activities that use electronic communication in the inventory, promotion, distribution, purchase, and exchange of products and services. Internet-based technology also allows companies to create *intranets* to communicate within the organization and *extranets* to communicate with suppliers, distributors, and other partners such as advertising agencies.

Today, technologies have advanced to allow computer chips to be placed in almost anything and to be connected to a network almost anywhere. This network of products embedded with connectivity-enabled electronics has come to be known as the **Internet of Things (IoT)**. The information generated by the Internet of Things has led to an explosion in interest in advanced analytics that can predict consumer preferences and behavior. A recent study by Forrester Research indicates that 74 percent of firms want to be "data-driven," while Wikibon Research estimates that expenditures on big data capabilities will reach $92 billion by 2026. Some experts suggest that the use of analytics is associated with success in the marketplace. Firms that have grown their revenues through analytical insights include Netflix, Google, Amazon, Dell, and eBay.[33]

COMPETITIVE FORCES

The fourth component of the environmental scan, **competition**, refers to the alternative firms that could provide a product to satisfy a specific market's needs. There are various forms of competition, and each company must consider its present and potential competitors in designing its marketing strategy.

Alternative Forms of Competition

LO 3-5

Discuss the forms of competition that exist in a market and the key components of competition.

Four basic forms of competition create a continuum from pure competition to monopolistic competition to oligopoly to pure monopoly. Chapter 13 contains further discussions on pricing practices under these four forms of competition.

At one end of the continuum is *pure competition*, in which there are many sellers and each has a similar product. Companies that deal in commodities common to agribusiness (for example, wheat, rice, and grain) often are in a pure competition position in which distribution (in the sense of shipping products) is important but other elements of marketing have little impact.

In the second point on the continuum, *monopolistic competition*, many sellers compete with substitutable products within a price range. For example, if the price of coffee rises too much, consumers may switch to tea. Coupons or sales are frequently used marketing tactics.

Oligopoly, a common industry structure, occurs when a few companies control the majority of industry sales. The wireless telephone industry, for example, is dominated by four carriers that serve more than 95 percent of the U.S. market. Verizon, AT&T, T-Mobile, and Sprint have 154, 150, 77, and 54 million subscribers, respectively. Similarly, the entertainment industry in the United States is dominated by Viacom, Disney, and Time Warner, and the major firms in the U.S. defense contractor industry are Boeing, Northrop Grumman, and Lockheed Martin. Critics of oligopolies suggest that because there are few sellers, price competition among firms is not desirable because it leads to reduced profits for all producers.[34]

The final point on the continuum, *pure monopoly*, occurs when only one firm sells the product. Monopolies are common for producers of products and services considered essential to a community: water, electricity, and cable service. Typically, marketing plays a small role in a monopolistic setting because it is regulated by the state or federal government. Government control usually seeks to ensure price protection for the buyer, although deregulation in recent years has encouraged price competition in the electricity market. Concern that Microsoft's 91 percent share of the PC operating system market was a monopoly that limited consumer access to competitors' Internet browsers led to lawsuits and consent decrees from the U.S. Justice Department and investigations and fines from the European Union. A recent Federal Trade Commission investigation of Google found that although the company's market share of the online search market exceeds 70 percent, it had not harmed competition in the marketplace. An investigation by the European Union, however, has led to $9 billion in antitrust fines.[35]

Components of Competition

In developing a marketing program, companies must consider the factors that drive competition: entry, the bargaining power of buyers and suppliers, existing rivalries, and substitution possibilities.[36] Scanning the environment requires a look at all of them. These factors relate to a firm's marketing mix decisions and may be used to create a barrier to entry, increase brand awareness, or intensify a fight for market share.

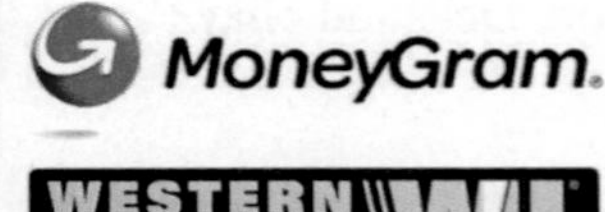
rvlsoft/Shutterstock

Entry In considering the competition, a firm must assess the likelihood of new entrants. Additional producers increase industry capacity and tend to lower prices. A company scanning its environment must consider the possible **barriers to entry** for other firms, which are business practices or conditions that make it difficult for new firms to enter the market. Barriers to entry can be in the form of capital requirements, advertising expenditures, product identity, distribution access, or the cost to customers of switching suppliers. The higher the expense of the barrier, the more likely it will deter new entrants. For example, Western Union and MoneyGram dominate the $600 billion money transfer market because of their huge distribution networks of branch offices and global pickup locations. Potential competitors find it difficult to enter the market because lack of distribution limits consumer access.[37]

Power of Buyers and Suppliers A competitive analysis must consider the power of buyers and suppliers. Powerful buyers exist when they are few in number, there are low switching costs, or the product represents a significant share of the buyer's total costs. This last factor leads the buyer to exert significant pressure for price competition. A supplier gains power when the product is critical to the buyer and when it has built up the switching costs.

Existing Competitors and Substitutes Competitive pressures among existing firms depend on the rate of industry growth. In slow-growth settings, competition is more heated for any possible gains in market share. High fixed costs also create competitive pressures for firms to fill production capacity. For example, airlines offer discounts for making early reservations and charge penalties for changes or cancellations in an effort to fill seats, which represent a high fixed cost.

Small Businesses as Competitors

While large companies provide familiar examples of the forms and components of competition, small businesses make up the majority of the competitive landscape for most businesses. Consider that there are approximately 30.2 million small businesses in the United States, which employ 48 percent of all private sector employees. In addition, small businesses generate 66 percent of all new jobs and 46 percent of the GDP. Research has shown a strong correlation between national economic growth and the level of new small business activity in previous years.[38]

LEARNING REVIEW

3-4. What is the difference between a consumer's disposable and discretionary income?

3-5. How does technology impact customer value?

3-6. In pure competition there are a ______________ number of sellers.

REGULATORY FORCES

LO 3-6 Explain the major legislation that ensures competition and regulates the elements of the marketing mix.

For any organization, the marketing and broader business decisions are constrained, directed, and influenced by regulatory forces. **Regulation** consists of restrictions state and federal laws place on business with regard to the conduct of its activities. Regulation exists to protect companies as well as consumers. Much of the regulation from the federal and state levels is the result of an active political process and has been passed to ensure competition and fair business practices. For consumers, the focus of legislation is to protect them from unfair trade practices and ensure their safety.

Protecting Competition

Major federal legislation has been passed to encourage competition, which is deemed desirable because it permits the consumer to determine which competitor will succeed and which will fail. The first such law was the *Sherman Antitrust Act* (1890). Lobbying by farmers in the Midwest against fixed railroad shipping prices led to the passage of this act, which forbids (1) contracts, combinations, or conspiracies in restraint of trade and (2) actual monopolies or attempts to monopolize any part of trade or commerce. Because of vague wording and government inactivity, however, there was only one successful case against a company in the nine years after the act became law, and the Sherman Act was supplemented with the *Clayton Act* (1914). This act forbids certain actions that are likely to lessen competition, although no actual harm has yet occurred.

In the 1930s, the federal government had to act again to ensure fair competition. During that time, large chain stores appeared, such as the Great Atlantic & Pacific Tea Company (A&P). Small businesses were threatened, and they lobbied for the *Robinson-Patman Act* (1936). This act makes it unlawful to discriminate in prices charged to different purchasers of the same product, where the effect may substantially lessen competition or help to create a monopoly.

Product-Related Legislation

Various federal laws in existence specifically address the product component of the marketing mix. Some are aimed at protecting the company, some at protecting the consumer, and at least one at protecting both.

A company can protect its competitive position in new and novel products under the patent law, which gives inventors the right to exclude others from making, using, or selling products that infringe the patented invention. The federal copyright law is another way for a company to protect its competitive position in a product. The copyright law gives the author of a literary, dramatic, musical, or artistic work the exclusive right to print, perform, or otherwise copy that work. Copyright is secured automatically when the work is created. However, the published work should bear an appropriate copyright notice, including the copyright symbol, the first year of publication, and the name of the copyright owner, and it must be registered under the federal copyright law.

Digital technology has necessitated additional copyright legislation, called the *Digital Millennium Copyright Act* (1998), to improve protection of copyrighted digital products. In addition, producers of DVD movies, music recordings, and software want protection from websites and devices designed to circumvent antipiracy elements of their products.[39]

There are many consumer-oriented federal laws regarding products. The various laws include more than 30 amendments and separate laws relating to food, drugs, and cosmetics, such as the *Infant Formula Act* (1980), the *Nutritional Labeling and Education Act* (1990), and new labeling requirements for dietary supplements (1997) and trans fats (2006). Recently, several states have proposed new legislation that would require the labeling of genetically modified food.[40] Various other consumer protection laws have a broader scope, such as the *Fair Packaging and Labeling Act* (1966), the *Child Protection Act* (1966), and the *Consumer Product Safety Act* (1972), which established the Consumer Product Safety Commission to monitor product safety and establish uniform product safety standards. Many of these laws came about because of **consumerism**, a grassroots movement started in the 1960s to increase the influence, power, and rights of consumers in dealing with institutions. This movement continues and is reflected in the growing consumer demand for ecologically safe products and ethical and socially responsible business practices. One hotly debated issue concerns liability for environmental abuse.

Trademarks are intended to protect both the firm selling a trademarked product and the consumer buying it. Senate report 1333 states:

> The purposes underlying any trademark statute [are] twofold. One is to protect the public so that it may be confident that, in purchasing a product bearing a particular trademark which it favorably knows, it will get the product which it asks for and wants to get. Secondly, where the owner of a trademark has spent energy, time, and money in presenting to the public the product, he is protected in this investment from misappropriation in pirates and cheats.

These products are identified by protected trademarks. Are any of these trademarks in danger of becoming generic?
Editorial Image, LLC

This statement was made in connection with another product-related law, the *Lanham Act* (1946), which provides for registration of a company's trademarks. Historically, the first user of a trademark in commerce had the exclusive right to use that particular word, name, or symbol in its business. Registration under the Lanham Act provides important advantages to a trademark owner that has used the trademark in interstate or foreign commerce, but it does not confer ownership. A company can lose its trademark if it becomes *generic*, which means that it has primarily come to be merely a common descriptive word for the product. *Coca-Cola*, *Whopper*, and *Xerox* are registered trademarks, and competitors cannot use these names. *Aspirin* and *escalator* are former trademarks that are now generic terms in the United States and can be used by anyone.

In 1988, the *Trademark Law Revision Act* resulted in a major change to the Lanham Act, allowing a company to secure rights to a name before actual use by declaring an intent to use the name.[41] In 2003, the United States agreed to participate in the *Madrid Protocol*, which is a treaty that facilitates the protection of U.S. trademark rights throughout the world. Currently, 95 nations are members of the Madrid Protocol, including the United States, Australia, China, the European Union, France, Germany, Japan, and the United Kingdom.[42]

An important change in trademark law is the U.S. Supreme Court's ruling that companies may obtain trademarks for colors that consumers associate with specific brands. Examples of products that benefit from this law include NutraSweet's sugar substitute in pastel blue packages and Owens Corning's pink fiberglass insulation.[43] Another addition to trademark law is the *Federal Trademark Dilution Act* (1995, 2006), which is used to prevent someone from using a trademark on a noncompeting product (e.g., "Cadillac" brushes). One of the newest developments in trademark law, though, is that the U.S. Patent and Trademark Office has begun issuing trademarks for hashtags used on social media. Recent court rulings, however, suggest that this form of trademark protection may not continue, leaving marketers with some uncertainty about these branding efforts.[44]

Pricing-Related Legislation

The pricing component of the marketing mix is the focus of regulation from two perspectives: price fixing and price discounting. Although the Sherman Act did not outlaw price fixing, the courts view this behavior as *per se illegal* (*per se* means "through or of itself"), which means the courts see price fixing itself as illegal.

Certain forms of price discounting are allowed. Quantity discounts are acceptable; that is, buyers can be charged different prices for a product provided there are differences in manufacturing or delivery costs. Promotional allowances or services may be given to buyers on an equal basis proportionate to volume purchased. Also, a firm can meet a competitor's price "in good faith." Legal and regulatory aspects of pricing are covered in more detail in Chapter 14.

Distribution-Related Legislation

The government has four concerns with regard to distribution–earlier referred to as "place" actions in the marketing mix–and the maintenance of competition. The first, *exclusive dealing*, is an arrangement a manufacturer makes with a reseller to handle only its products and not those of competitors. This practice is illegal under the Clayton Act only when it substantially lessens competition.

Requirement contracts require a buyer to purchase all or part of its needs for a product from one seller for a time period. These contracts are not always illegal but depend on the court's interpretation of their impact on distribution.

Exclusive territorial distributorships are a third distribution issue often under regulatory scrutiny. In this situation, a manufacturer grants a distributor the sole rights to sell a product in a specific geographical area. The courts have found few violations with these arrangements.

The fourth distribution strategy is a *tying arrangement*, whereby a seller requires the purchaser of one product to also buy another item in the line. These contracts may be illegal when the seller has such economic power in the tying product that the seller can restrain trade in the tied product. Legal aspects of distribution are reviewed in greater detail in Chapter 15.

VIDEO 3-4
Federal Trade Commission (FTC)
kerin.tv/15e/v3-4

Advertising- and Promotion-Related Legislation

Promotion and advertising are aspects of marketing closely monitored by the FTC, which was established by the *FTC Act of 1914*. The FTC is concerned with deceptive or misleading advertising and unfair business practices and has the power to (1) issue cease and desist orders and (2) order corrective advertising. In issuing a *cease and desist order*, the FTC orders a company to stop practices the commission considers unfair. With *corrective advertising*, the FTC can require a company to spend money on advertising to correct previous misleading ads. The enforcement powers of the FTC are so significant that often just an indication of concern from the commission can cause companies to revise their promotion.[45]

Source: Federal Trade Commission

Other laws have been introduced to regulate promotion practices. The *Deceptive Mail Prevention and Enforcement Act* (1999), for example, provides specifications for direct-mail sweepstakes, such as the requirement that the statement "No purchase is necessary to enter" be displayed in the mailing, in the rules, and on the entry form. Similarly, the *Telephone Consumer Protection Act* (1991) provides requirements for telemarketing promotions, including fax promotions. Telemarketing is also subject to a law that created the *National Do Not Call Registry*, which is a list of consumer phone numbers of people who do not want to receive unsolicited telemarketing calls.

Finally, laws such as the *Children's Online Privacy Protection Act* (1998), the *European Union Data Protection Act* (1998), and the *Controlling the Assault of Non-Solicited Pornography and Marketing (CAN-SPAM) Act* (2004) are designed to restrict information collection and unsolicited e-mail promotions and specify simple opt-out procedures on the Internet. See the Marketing Matters box on the next page to learn about the FTC's effort to create a "Do Not Track" system to ensure online privacy.[46] A related Internet issue, taxation, has generated an ongoing debate. Temporary laws, such as the *Internet Tax Freedom Act*, have recently become a permanent provision in the *Trade Facilitation and Trade Enforcement Act* (2015).[47]

Companies must meet certain requirements before they can display this logo on their websites.
Better Business Bureau logo. Used with permission.

Control through Self-Regulation

The government has provided much legislation to create a competitive business climate and protect the consumer. An alternative to government control is **self-regulation**, where an industry attempts to police itself. The major television networks, for example, have used self-regulation to set their own guidelines for TV ads for children's toys. These guidelines have generally worked well. There are two problems with self-regulation, however: noncompliance by members and enforcement. In addition, if attempts at self-regulation are too strong, they may violate the Robinson-Patman Act.

The best-known self-regulatory group is the Better Business Bureau (BBB). This agency is a voluntary alliance of companies whose goal is to help maintain fair practices. The BBB is a nonprofit corporation that tries to use "moral suasion" to encourage members to comply with its standards. The BBB offers an Accredited Business Seal Program to provide consumers assurance that an organization is part of a community of trustworthy businesses. Before it

Marketing Matters

Technology

Does Protecting Privacy Hurt the Web?

Have you ever wondered how your web browser determines which advertisements appear on your screen? The answer is that your actions are "tracked" to create a profile of your interests. Each of the major browser makers—Microsoft, Google, Mozilla, and Apple—can keep a record of the web pages you visit or the topics you discuss in your e-mail. The information allows advertisers to match their advertising specifically to you—a practice marketers call *online behavioral targeting (OBT)*. You see dog food ads if you are a dog owner and cat food ads if you are a cat owner, for example.

The collection of this information, however, has also raised the issue of privacy. Privacy advocates suggest that many consumers do not realize that the information is being collected and used without their consent. They also argue that in extreme situations the information could lead to unintended outcomes for the consumers—being turned down for a mortgage or a health insurance policy because of online book or food purchases, for example.

To facilitate the debate, the FTC released a report calling for better self-regulation of online information collection. In its report, the FTC suggests that each browser should offer users a "Do Not Track" option to signal a computer user's desire to not be tracked. This opt-out system would be very similar to the current "Do Not Call" system and is currently being considered in Congress. In Europe, the General Data Protection Regulation (2018) is more restrictive, requiring consumers to explicitly "opt in." The Interactive Advertising Bureau suggests that such restrictions might limit the effectiveness of advertising, which is "the number one funding model for the Internet." In California, however, the California Consumer Privacy Act (2018) specifies that residents must know what personal data are being collected about them.

The questions related to this issue are not simple. Consumers will need to decide if giving up some privacy by sharing data is a reasonable trade-off for targeted advertising, customized news sites, and online social networks. Organizations in the $24 billion advertising industry will need to evaluate their ability to self-regulate, and the FTC and Congress eventually will need to decide whether legislation is needed. The situation is likely to become even more complicated in the near future as consumers, and especially children, increase their use of smartphone mobile apps that generate tracking data. How do you think the debate will be resolved?

displays the BBB Accredited Business Seal, a participating company must, among other things, first agree to adhere to the BBB Code of Business Practices, have been in business for at least one year, respect the privacy and e-mail preferences of its online visitors, and commit to work with its customers and the BBB to resolve disputes that arise over products or services promoted or advertised on its site.[48]

LEARNING REVIEW

3-7. The ____________ Act was punitive toward monopolies, whereas the ____________ Act was preventive.

3-8. Describe some of the recent changes in trademark law.

3-9. How does the Better Business Bureau encourage companies to follow its standards for commerce?

LEARNING OBJECTIVES REVIEW

LO 3-1 *Explain how environmental scanning provides information about social, economic, technological, competitive, and regulatory forces.*

Many businesses operate in environments where important forces change. Environmental scanning is the process of acquiring information about these changes to allow marketers to identify and interpret trends. There are five environmental forces businesses must monitor: social, economic, technological, competitive, and regulatory. By identifying trends related to each of these forces, businesses can develop and maintain successful marketing programs. Several trends that most businesses are monitoring include the growing interest in health and wellness, the increasing popularity of the concept of a circular economy, and the momentum of new technologies such as 5G networks, AI, the IoT, and robotics.

LO 3-2 *Describe how social forces such as demographics and culture can have an impact on marketing strategy.*
Demographic information describes the world population; the U.S. population; the generational cohorts such as baby boomers, Generation X, Generation Y, and Generation Z; the structure of the American household; the geographic shifts of the population; and the racial and ethnic diversity of the population, which has led to multicultural marketing programs. Cultural factors include the trend toward fewer differences in male and female consumer behavior and the impact of values such as sustainability on consumer preferences.

LO 3-3 *Discuss how economic forces such as macroeconomic conditions and consumer income affect marketing.*
Economic forces include the strong relationship between consumers' expectations about the economy and their spending. Gross income has remained stable for more than 45 years although the rate of saving has fluctuated, declining to 4 percent before rising to 7.5 percent recently.

LO 3-4 *Describe how technological changes can affect marketing.*
Technological innovations can replace existing products and services. Changes in technology can also have an impact on customer value by reducing the cost of products, improving the quality of products, and providing new products that were not previously feasible. Electronic commerce is transforming how companies do business.

LO 3-5 *Discuss the forms of competition that exist in a market and the key components of competition.*
There are four forms of competition: pure competition, monopolistic competition, oligopoly, and monopoly. The key components of competition include the likelihood of new competitors, the power of buyers and suppliers, and the presence of competitors and possible substitutes. While large companies are often used as examples of marketplace competitors, there are 30.2 million small businesses in the United States, which have a significant impact on the economy.

LO 3-6 *Explain the major legislation that ensures competition and regulates the elements of the marketing mix.*
Regulation exists to protect companies and consumers. Legislation that ensures a competitive marketplace includes the Sherman Antitrust Act. Product-related legislation includes copyright and trademark laws that protect companies and packaging and labeling laws that protect consumers. Pricing- and distribution-related laws are designed to create a competitive marketplace with fair prices and availability. Regulation related to promotion and advertising reduces deceptive practices and provides enforcement through the Federal Trade Commission. Self-regulation through organizations such as the Better Business Bureau provides an alternative to federal and state regulation.

LEARNING REVIEW ANSWERS

3-1 Describe four generational cohorts.
Answer: (1) Baby boomers are the generation of 76 million children born between 1946 and 1964. These Americans are growing older and will all be 65 or older by 2030. (2) Generation X includes the 55 million people born between 1965 and 1980. These well-educated Americans, also known as the baby bust cohort because of declining birthrates during that time, are supportive of racial and ethnic diversity. (3) Generation Y, or millennials, are the 62 million Americans among the U.S. population born between 1981 and 1996. Based on immigration and death rate estimates, millennials are currently the largest generation, with 75 million people. (4) The post-millennial generation, which includes consumers born between 1997 and 2010, is referred to as Generation Z.

3-2 Why are many companies developing multicultural marketing programs?
Answer: Multicultural marketing programs consist of combinations of the marketing mix that reflect the unique attitudes, ancestry, communication preferences, and lifestyles of different races and ethnic groups. The reason for developing these programs is that the racial and ethnic diversity of the United States is changing rapidly due to the increases in the African American, Asian, and Hispanic populations, which increases their economic impact.

3-3 How are important values such as sustainability reflected in the marketplace today?
Answer: Many Americans desire and practice sustainability to preserve the environment. Specifically, these consumers buy products such as hybrid gas-electric cars. Consumers also prefer brands that have a strong link to social action (like Ben & Jerry's—see Chapter 2). Companies are responding to this consumer trend by producing products that use renewable energy and less packaging.

3-4 What is the difference between a consumer's disposable and discretionary income?
Answer: Disposable income is the money a consumer has left after paying taxes to use for necessities such as food, housing, clothing, and transportation. Discretionary income is the money that remains after paying for taxes and necessities and is usually spent on luxury items.

3-5 How does technology impact customer value?
Answer: (1) Because the cost of technology is plummeting, this allows consumers to assess the value of technology-based products on other dimensions, such as quality, service, and relationships. (2) Technology provides value through the development of new products. (3) Technology has changed the way existing products are produced through recycling and precycling. (4) Technology enables the collection of data used in the growing field of data analytics.

3-6 In pure competition there are a ____________ number of sellers.
Answer: large

3-7 The ____________ Act was punitive toward monopolies, whereas the ____________ Act was preventive.
Answer: Sherman Antitrust; Clayton

3-8 Describe some of the recent changes in trademark law.
Answer: Trademarks are intended to protect both the firm selling a trademarked product and the consumer buying it. The Lanham Act (1946) provides for registration of a company's trademarks. The Trademark Law Revision Act (1988), which modified the Lanham

Act, allows companies to secure rights to a name before its actual use by declaring an intent to use the name. In 2003, the United States agreed to participate in the Madrid Protocol, which is a treaty that facilitates the protection of U.S. trademark rights. Also, the U.S. Supreme Court recently ruled that a company may obtain trademarks for colors associated with its products. Finally, the Federal Dilution Act (1995, 2006) prevents someone from using a trademark on a noncompeting product (such as the "Cadillac" of brushes). The U.S. Patent and Trademark Office also recently began issuing trademarks for social media hashtags.

3-9 How does the Better Business Bureau encourage companies to follow its standards for commerce?

Answer: The Better Business Bureau (BBB) uses moral suasion to get members to comply with its standards. Companies, which join the BBB voluntarily, must agree to follow these standards before they are allowed to display the BBB Accredited Business logo.

FOCUSING ON KEY TERMS

baby boomers p. 77
barriers to entry p. 90
blended family p. 80
competition p. 89
consumerism p. 91
culture p. 82
demographics p. 76
discretionary income p. 85
disposable income p. 85
economy p. 84
electronic commerce p. 88
environmental scanning p. 74
Generation X p. 77
Generation Y p. 78
Generation Z p. 78
gross income p. 85
Internet of Things (IoT) p. 88
marketspace p. 88
multicultural marketing p. 81
regulation p. 90
self-regulation p. 93
social forces p. 76
technology p. 87
value consciousness p. 84

APPLYING MARKETING KNOWLEDGE

1 For many years Gerber has manufactured baby food in small, single-sized containers. In conducting an environmental scan, (*a*) identify three trends or factors that might significantly affect this company's future business, and (*b*) propose how Gerber might respond to these changes.

2 Describe the new features you would add to an automobile designed for consumers in the 55+ age group. In what magazines would you advertise to appeal to this target market?

3 The population shift from suburbs to exurbs and small towns was discussed in this chapter. What businesses and industries are likely to benefit from this trend? How will retailers need to change to accommodate these consumers?

4 New technologies are continuously improving and replacing existing products. Although technological change is often difficult to predict, suggest how the following companies and products might be affected by the Internet and digital technologies: (*a*) Timex watches, (*b*) American Airlines, and (*c*) the Metropolitan Museum of Art.

5 In recent years in the brewing industry, a couple of large firms that have historically had most of the beer sales (Anheuser-Busch and MillerCoors) have faced competition from many small "micro" brands. In terms of the continuum of competition, how would you explain this change?

6 The Johnson Company manufactures buttons and pins with slogans and designs. These pins are inexpensive to produce and are sold in retail outlets such as discount stores, hobby shops, and bookstores. Little equipment is needed for a new competitor to enter the market. What strategies should Johnson consider to create effective barriers to entry?

7 Why would Xerox be concerned about its name becoming generic?

8 Develop a "Code of Business Practices" for a new online vitamin store. Does your code address advertising? Privacy? Use by children? Why is self-regulation important?

BUILDING YOUR MARKETING PLAN

Your marketing plan will include a situation analysis based on internal and external factors that are likely to affect your marketing program.

1 To summarize information about external factors, create a table similar to Figure 3-2 and identify three trends related to each of the five forces (social, economic, technological, competitive, and regulatory) that relate to your product or service.

2 When your table is completed, describe how each of the trends represents an opportunity or a threat for your business.

"As long as there's innovation there is going to be new kinds of chaos," explains Robert Stephens, founder of the technology support company Geek Squad. The chaos Stephens is referring to is the difficulty we have all experienced trying to keep up with the many changes in our environment, particularly those related to computers, technology, software, communication, and entertainment. Generally, consumers have found it difficult to install, operate, and use many of the electronic products available today. "It takes time to read the manuals," Stephens says. "I'm going to save you that time because I stay home on Saturday nights and read them for you!"

VIDEO 3-5
Geek Squad Video Case
kerin.tv/15e/v3-5

THE COMPANY

The Geek Squad story begins when Stephens, a native of Chicago, passed up an Art Institute scholarship to pursue a degree in computer science. While Stephens was a computer science student he took a job fixing computers for a research laboratory, and he also started consulting. He could repair televisions, computers, and a variety of other items, although he decided to focus on computers. His experiences as a consultant led him to realize that most people needed help with technology and that they saw value in a service whose employees would show up at a specified time, be friendly, use understandable language, and solve the problem. So, with just $200, Stephens formed Geek Squad in 1994.

Geek Squad set out to provide timely and effective help with all computing needs regardless of the make, model, or place of purchase. Geek Squad employees were called "agents" and wore uniforms consisting of black pants or skirts, black shoes, white shirts, black clip-on ties, a badge, and a black jacket with a Geek Squad logo to create a "humble" attitude that was not threatening to customers. Agents drove black-and-white cars, or Geekmobiles, with a logo on the door, and charged fixed prices for services, regardless of how much time was required to provide the service. The "house call" services ranged from installing networks, to debugging a computer, to setting up an entertainment system, and cost from $100 to $300. "We're like 'Dragnet'; we show up at people's homes and help," Stephens says. "We're also like *Ghostbusters* and there's a pseudogovernment feel to it like *Men in Black*."

In 2002, Geek Squad was purchased by leading consumer electronics retailer Best Buy for about $3 million. Best Buy had observed very high return rates for most of its complex products. Shoppers would be excited about new products, purchase them and take them home, get frustrated trying to make them actually work, and then return them to the store demanding a refund. In fact, Best Buy research revealed that consumers were beginning to see service as a critical element of the purchase. The partnership was an excellent match. Best Buy consumers welcomed the help. Stephens became Geek Squad's chief inspector and a Best Buy vice president and began putting a Geek Squad "precinct" in every Best Buy store, creating some stand-alone Geek Squad Stores, and providing 24-hour telephone support. There are now more than 20,000 agents in 1,100 Best Buy stores in the United States, Canada, the United Kingdom, and China, and return rates have declined by 25 to 35 percent. Geek Squad service plans, called Geek Squad Protect & Support Plus, provide device setup, operating system and software installation, hardware repair, battery replacement, virus removal, and many other services. The Geek Squad website proclaims, "We're Here To Help" and "No One Stands Behind You Like Geek Squad."

Source: Best Buy

THE CHANGING ENVIRONMENT

Many changes in the environment occurred to create the need for Geek Squad's services. Future changes are also likely to change the way Geek Squad operates. An environmental scan helps illustrate the changes.

The most obvious changes may be related to technology. Wireless broadband technology, high-definition televisions, products with Internet interfaces, and a general trend toward computers, smartphones, entertainment systems, and even appliances being connected to the Internet are just a few examples of new products and applications for consumers to learn about. There are also technology-related problems such as viruses, spyware, lost data, and "crashed" or inoperable computers. New technologies have also created a demand for new types of maintenance such as password management, operating system updates, disk cleanup, and "defragging."

Source: Best Buy

Another environmental change that contributes to the popularity of Geek Squad is the change in social factors such as demographics and culture. In the past many electronics manufacturers and retailers focused primarily on men. Women, however, are becoming increasingly interested in personal computing and home entertainment and, according to the Consumer Electronics Association, are likely to outspend men in the near future. Best Buy's consumer research indicates that women expect personal service during the purchase as well as during the installation after the purchase—exactly the service Geek Squad is designed to provide.

Competition, economics, and the regulatory environment have also had a big influence on Geek Squad. As discount stores such as Walmart and PC makers such as Dell began to compete with Best Buy, new services such as in-home installation were needed to create value for customers. Now, just as change in competition created an opportunity for Geek Squad, it is also leading to another level of competition as Staples has introduced Tech Services and Office Depot has introduced its Workonomy suite of tech services. The economic situation for electronics continues to improve as prices decline and demand increases. Consumers purchase more than 38 million digital TVs annually, and sales of all consumer electronics exceed $285 billion as consumers purchase home theaters, Wi-Fi networks, and security systems, in addition to computing equipment. Finally, the regulatory environment continues to change with respect to the electronic transfer of copyrighted materials such as music and movies and software. Geek Squad must monitor the changes to ensure that its services comply with relevant laws.

THE FUTURE FOR GEEK SQUAD

The combination of many positive environmental factors helps explain the extraordinary success of Geek Squad. Today, it repairs more than 3,000 PCs a day and generates more than $2 billion in revenue. Because Geek Squad services have a high profit margin they contribute to the overall performance of Best Buy, and they help generate traffic in the store and create store loyalty. To continue to grow, however, Geek Squad will need to continue to scan the environment and try new approaches to creating customer value.

According to Best Buy CEO Hubert Joly, one possible new approach is to help consumers create "connected" homes. "We want to build a relationship over time, so if you want help with not just an individual product but a whole system . . . we can do that," Joly explains. Geek Squad is also using new technology to improve. Agents now use a smartphone to access updated schedules, log in their hours, and run diagnostics tests on clients' equipment. Finally, Best Buy is also testing a "Solutions Central" desk, similar to the Genius Bar concept in Apple stores, and staffing it with Geek Squad agents.

Other changes and opportunities are certain to appear soon. However, despite the success of the Geek Squad and the potential for additional growth, Robert Stephens is modest and claims, "Geeks may inherit the Earth, but they have no desire to rule it!"[49]

Questions

1 What are the key environmental forces that created an opportunity for Robert Stephens to start the Geek Squad?

2 What changes in the purchasing patterns of (*a*) all consumers and (*b*) women made the acquisition of Geek Squad particularly important for Best Buy?

3 Based on the case information and what you know about consumer electronics, conduct an environmental scan for Geek Squad to identify key trends. For each of the five environmental forces (social, economic, technological, competitive, and regulatory), identify trends likely to influence Geek Squad in the near future.

4 What promotional activities would you recommend to encourage consumers who currently use independent installers to switch to Geek Squad?

Chapter Notes

1. Cubano Pepper, "Facebook's Never-Ending Crisis," *Bloomberg Businessweek*, March 18, 2019, pp. 52–57; Michal Lev-Ram, "Facebook's Fix-It Team," *Fortune*, June 1, 2018, pp. 104–12; "Top Facebook Updates That You Can't Afford to Miss," www.adespresso.com, February 28, 2019; Mark Zuckerberg, Facebook Post, www.facebook.com/zuck/posts, December 28, 2018; Nicholas Thompson, "Mark Zuckerberg on Facebook's Future and What Scares Him Most," www.wired.com, March 6, 2019; David McLaughlin, "Why Were Facebook, Amazon, Apple, and Google Allowed to Get So Big?" www.fortune.com, March 16, 2019; and Josh Eidelson and Sarah Frier, "Facebook to Block Discriminatory Ads in 'Historic' Legal Accord," www.fortune.com, March 20, 2019.
2. Emily Jed, "NCA Drinking Trends Survey Show Daily Coffee Consumption Up Sharply," *Vending Times*, April 9, 2018; Julie Jargon, "Starbucks CEO Kevin Johnson Reins In Predecessor's Ambitions: 'I'm Not Howard,'" *Wall Street Journal Online*, January 8, 2019; Adam Campbell-Schmitt, "Roastery, Reserve Bar, Regular Starbucks: What's The Difference?" www.foodandwine.com, December 20, 2018.
3. Nikki Cutler, "The Hot News for Hot Brews," *Convenience Store*, September 21, 2018, pp. 47–60; Amanda Del Buono, "Liquid Energy," www.preparedfoods.com, March 2016; and D. Cvetan, "Bring the Coffee Shop Home," *Store Brands*, July 2016, p. 42.
4. Michael Stoddart, "Four Creative Trends for Marketers This Year," *CMO Innovation*, March 8, 2019; Patty Odell and Sven Lubek, "Top 2019 Digital Marketing Trends and Predictions," *Promotional Marketing*, January 7, 2019, p. 3; Max Dawes, "3 Augmented Reality Trends That Will Define Marketing in 2019," *Promotional Marketing*, January 8, 2019, p. 1; Chris Pemberton, "4 Hidden Forces That Will Shape Marketing in 2019," www.gartner.com, January 10, 2019; "11 Trends That Will Shape Marketing in 2019," www.forbes.com, January 15, 2019; Andrew Lo, "Top Tech Trends," www.canadianunderwriter.com, March 2019; "The Key Trends That Will Impact Marketers' Jobs in 2019," www.marketingweek.com, December 12, 2018; Giselle Abramovich, "The 5 Biggest Marketing Trends for 2019," www.cmo.com, December 17, 2018; Deep Patel, "10 Marketing Trends to Watch in 2019," www.entrepreneur.com, December 26, 2018; and "What Is the Circular Economy?" www.activesustainability.com.
5. *2018 World Population Data Sheet with Focus on Changing Age Structures* (Washington, DC: Population Reference Bureau, 2018).
6. "GNI per Capita, Atlas Method," *World Development Indicators Database* (Washington, DC: World Bank Group, 2017); and *World Population Prospects: The 2015 Revision,* Key Finding and Advance Tables (New York: United Nations, Department of Economic and Social Affairs, Population Division, 2016).
7. National Population Projections Tables, United States Census Bureau, https://www.census.gov/programs-surveys/popproj/data/tables.html; Dan Tynan, "Future Tense: Brands Look to Futurists to Foresee Trends and Anticipate Disruption," *Adweek*, December 3, 2018, pp. 18–19; and Sandra L. Colby and Jennifer M. Ortman, "Projections of the Size and Composition of the U.S. Population: 2014 to 2060, Current Population Reports," U.S. Department of Commerce, March 2015.
8. "Consumer Insights: Baby Boomers," www.fona.com, May 11, 2018; Bill McPherson, "The 'Sandwich Generation' Feels the Squeeze," *Franchising World,* November 2016, pp. 55–56; and Sandra L. Colby and Jennifer M. Ortman, "The Baby Boom Cohort in the United States: 2012 to 2060," United States Census Bureau, Current Population Reports, May 2014.
9. "Millennials vs. Gen X vs. Baby Boomers," *Convenience Store News*, January 2019, p. 98; Chris Matthews, "America's Most Indebted Generation, Gen X," *Fortune.com*, August 29, 2014; Michele Hammond, "Gen X Pips Boomers to Lead Online Retail Spending," www.startupsmart.com.au, January 10, 2013; Chris Johns, "Hotels for Hipsters," *The Globe and Mail,* November 13, 2012, p. E1; and Piet Levy, "Segmentation by Generation," *Marketing News,* May 15, 2011, p. 20.
10. Richard Fry, "Millennials Projected to Overtake Baby Boomers as America's Largest Generation," www.pewresearch.org, March 1, 2018; Ave Rio, "Searching for a Higher Purpose," www.CLOmedia, April 2019; Helena Wasserman, "Managing Millennials," *Finweek*, March 2, 2017, pp. 44–45; and "Gen Zero," *Bloomberg Businessweek*, April 29, 2019, pp. 18–19.
11. Kim Parker, Rich Morin, and Juliana Manasce Horowitz, "Views of Demographic Changes," www.pewsocialtrends.org, March 21, 2019; Emily Schondelmyer, "Demographics and Living Arrangements," *Current Population Reports*, October 2017; Richard Fry, "For the First Time in Modern Era, Living with Parents Edges Out Other Living Arrangements for 18- to 34-Year-Olds," www.pewsocialtrends.org, Pew Research Center, May 24, 2016; Jonathan Vespa, Jamie M. Lewis, and Rose M. Kreider, "America's Families and Living Arrangements: 2012," U.S. Census Bureau, August 2013; and "Household Characteristics of Opposite-Sex and Same-Sex Couple Households," *2015 American Community Survey*, Table 1, ACS 2015.
12. Belinda Luscombe, "The Divorce Rate Is Dropping. That May Not Actually Be Good News," www.time.com, November 26, 2018; "National Marriage and Divorce Rate Trends," National Center for Health Statistics, National Vital Statistics System, November 23, 2015; Renee Stepler, "Led by Baby Boomers, Divorce Rates Climb for America's 50+ Population," www.pewresearch.org, Pew Research Center, March 9, 2017; and Caryl Rivers and Rosalind C. Barnett, "Gray Divorce: Why Your Grandparents Are Finally Calling It Quits," www.latimes.com, September 28, 2016.
13. "Washington, D.C., Tops 700,000 People for the First Time since 1975," www.census.gov, December 20, 2018; Lori Dorn, "Shifting Cities: An Interactive Map That Shows the Most Populous U.S. Cities by Decade," https://laughingsquid.com, August 26, 2015; and "Estimates of Resident Population Change for the United States, Regions, States, and Puerto Rico and Region and State Rankings: July 1, 2016 to July 1, 2016," U.S. Census Bureau, Population Division, December 2016, Table 3.
14. Laura Kusisto, "A Decade after the Housing Bust, the Exurbs Are Back," *Wall Street Journal Online*, March 26, 2019; Randall Reid, "Coexisting at the Edges, Meet the New Exurban," *Public Management*, April 2018, pp. 6–9; and Joel Kotkin, "So Much for the Death of Sprawl: America's Exurbs Are Booming," www.forbes.com, November 3, 2015.
15. "Revised Delineations of Metropolitan Statistical Areas, Micropolitan Statistical Areas, and Combined Statistical Areas, and Guidance on Uses of the Delineations of These Areas," OMB Bulletin No. 18-04, Office of Management and Budget, September 14, 2018; "2010 Standards for Delineating Metropolitan and Micropolitan Statistical Areas," Office of Management and Budget, *Federal Register* 75, no. 123, June 28, 2010; and "About Metropolitan and Micropolitan Statistical Areas," U.S. Census Bureau, www.census.gov/population/www/estimates/aboutmetro.html.
16. Sandra L. Colby and Jennifer M. Ortman, "Projections of the Size and Composition of the U.S. Population: 2014 to 2060," *Current Population Reports,* U.S. Census Bureau, March 2015; "2010 Census Shows America's Diversity," U.S. Census Bureau, CB11-CN.125, March 24, 2011; "An Older and More Diverse Nation by Midcentury," Public Information Office, U.S. Census Bureau, Last Revised: February 2, 2011; Table 4: Projections of the Population by Sex, Race, and Hispanic Origin for the United States: 2010 to 2050 (NP2008-T4), Population Division, U.S. Census Bureau, August 14, 2008; and "Mapping Census 2000: The Geography of U.S. Diversity," Population Division, U.S. Census Bureau.
17. Matt Weeks, "Minority Markets See Economic Growth," www.news.uga.edu, March 21, 2019; Johnathan Vespa, David M. Armstrong, and Lauren Medina, "Demographic Turning Points for the United States: Population Projections for 2020 to 2060," *Current Population Reports,* U.S. Census Bureau, March 2018; and Jens Manuel Krogstad, "With

Fewer New Arrivals, Census Lowers Hispanic Population Projections," www.pewresearch.org, Pew Research Center, December 16, 2014.

18. Adrianne Pasquarelli, "Multicultural Agency of the Year," *Advertising Age*, February 19, 2018, p. 36; Madeline Berg, "Note to Networks: Diversity on TV Pays Off," *Forbes.com*, February 27, 2017; Laurel Wentz, "Welcome to the Multicultural Mainstream," *Advertising Age*, April 6, 2015, p. 18; and Michael Sebastian, "Where's the Multicultural Mainstream? Looking at Their Phones," *Advertising Age*, April 6, 2015, p. 21.

19. Alison Dahl Crossley, "Finding Feminism: Millennial Activists and the Unfinished Gender Revolution," *Publishers Weekly*, February 27, 2017, p. 90; Mindi Chahal, "Five Trends Marketers Need to Know for 2015," *Marketing Week*, December 3, 2014, p. 1; "Salary Survey 2011: Taking a Lead on Gender Issues," *Marketing Week*, January 13, 2011, p. 17; "From 18 to 80: Women on Politics and Society," 2008 Women's Monitor Study, *PR Newswire*, August 20, 2008; and Rebecca Gardyn, "Granddaughters of Feminism," *American Demographics*, April 2001, p. 42.

20. Kelvin Claveria, "Ungendered: Why Forward-Thinking Marketers Are Embracing Gender Fluidity," www.visioncritical.com, March 14, 2019; March Bain, "Lululemon's Next Target Is Mindfulness for Men," www.qz.com, January 10, 2019; Evan Clark, "Women's Still in Focus during Under Armour Restructuring," *Women's Wear Daily*, July 27, 2018, p. 4; Tanya Dua, "From Coca-Cola to Barbie: The Fierce Rise of Gender-Neutral Advertising," *Digiday*, March 29, 2015; Kristina Monllos, "Brands Are Throwing Out Gender Norms to Reflect a More Fluid World," *Adweek*, October 17, 2016; Sam Frizell, "Here's How Pinterest Is Trying to Attract More Men," *Time.com*, January 23, 2015, p. 1.

21. "Socks Are the #1 Most Requested Clothing Item at Homeless Shelters," www.bombas.com, April 10, 2019; Blake Gladman, "2017: The Trends to Know," *Checkout*, January 2017, pp. 16–18; Robin M. Williams Jr., *American Society: A Sociological Interpretation,* 3rd ed. (New York: Knopf, 1970); L. Robert Kohls, "Why Do Americans Act Like That?" International Programs, San Francisco State University; Eric Pooley, David Welch, and Alan Ohnsman, "Charged for Battle," *Bloomberg Businessweek*, January 3, 2011, pp. 48–56.

22. Claire Williams, "Nearly a Third of Consumers Say They Plan to Spend Less This Holiday Season," www.morningconsult.com, November 30, 2018; "Aggressive Expansion Still Works," *MMR*, March 25, 2019, pp. 1–2; Jack Neff, "Chain Defies the Retail Odds by Reinventing and Reinvesting," *Advertising Age*, December 3, 2018, p. 28; Justin McCarthy, "US Consumers' February Spending Highest since 2008," *Gallup News Service*, March 6, 2017; and "Dollar General Unveils Small-Format Concept," *Establishment Review*, February 20, 2017.

23. "Tuition and Fees and Room and Board Charges over Time in Current Dollars and 2018 Dollars," College Board, http://trends.collegeboard.org/college-pricing/figures-tables/tuition-fees-room-board-time; and Kayla Fontenot, Jessica Semega, and Melissa Kollar, "Income and Poverty in the United States: 2017," *Current Population Reports* (Washington, DC: U.S. Census Bureau, September 12, 2018), Table A-1.

24. Azhar Iqbal and Mark Vitner, "The Deeper the Recession, the Stronger the Recovery: Is It Really That Simple?" *Business Economics,* January 2011, pp. 22–31.

25. "The Index of Consumer Sentiment," data from Surveys of Consumers (Ann Arbor, MI: Survey Research Center, University of Michigan, June 2012). Copyright © 2017, The regents of the University of Michigan, www.sca.isr.umich.edu.

26. Kayla Fontenot, Jessica Semega, and Melissa Kollar, "Income and Poverty in the United States: 2017," *Current Population Reports* (Washington, DC: U.S. Census Bureau, September 12, 2018), Table A-1.

27. Doug Handler and Nariman Behravesh, *U.S. Economic Environment,* IHS Economics, March 3, 2015; and Nick Timiraos and Kris Hudson, "The Demand Divide: Two-Tier Economy Reshapes U.S. Marketplace," *The Wall Street Journal,* January 29, 2015.

28. "Consumer Expenditures in 2017," U.S. Department of Labor, Bureau of Labor Statistics, September 11, 2018, Table 1300; and "Personal Income," U.S. Department of Commerce, Bureau of Economic Analysis, March 29, 2019.

29. Lawrence A. Crosby, "Marketing Faces Shifts in Technology, Demographics in 2019," *Marketing News*, January 2019, pp. 18–19; "Dream Less, Do More: 2019 Marketing Predictions," *Marketing News*, January 2019, pp. 28–35; Andrew Lo, "Top Tech Trends," www.canadianunderwriter.ca, March 2019, p. 11; Hal Conick, "From Knowing Alexa, to Following @Alexa, to 'Hey, Alexa'," *Marketing News*, April 2019, pp. 40–49; and Beau Jerome, "Our Faces Are Replacing Alphanumeric Passwords," www.medium.com, August 13, 2018.

30. Eric Griffith, "The Best Free Software of 2017," *PCMag.com,* February 21, 2017; "Get Select 4G LTE Smartphones for Free When You Switch," Cricket web page, https://www.cricketwireless.com/free-cell-phones.html, accessed March 24, 2017; and Koen Pauwels and Allen Weiss, "Moving from Free to Fee: How Online Firms Market to Change Their Business Model Successfully," *Journal of Marketing,* May 2008, pp. 14–31.

31. CES website, https://www.ces.tech/About-CES/CES-by-the-Numbers.aspx; "Best of CES Awards," www.engadget.com, January 10, 2019; "Mymanu Clik Smart Earbuds Are Coming to Translate Languages in Real Time," www.wareable.com, January 9, 2017; "*Better Homes and Gardens* Editors' Choice 2017 Innovation Awards," www.bhg.com, 2017; and Dave Gershgorn, "The Future of Wireless Charging Is Here," *qz.com*, January 9, 2017.

32. Rick Moore, Kate Eagles, and Steve Alexander, "PET Recylcers Stay Strong in Challenging Market," National Association for PET Container Resources, October 13, 2016; Tomra website, https://www.tomra.com/en/solutions-and-products/collection-solutions/reverse-vending/; Steve Richerson, "Sustainability: It Delivers Four Benefits," *Sales and Service Excellence*, September 2012, p. 16; and Becky Ebenkam, "'Precycling' Catches On with Consumers," *Brandweek.com,* August 12, 2008.

33. Hal Conick, "Turning Big Data into Big Insights," *Marketing News*, January 2017, pp. 12–13; Ralph Finos, "2016-2026 Worldwide Big Data Market Forecast," www.wikibon.com, March 30, 2016; Marco Vriens and Patricia Kidd, "The Big Data Shift," *Marketing Insights*, November–December 2014, pp. 22–29; and Cliff Saran, "Big Data Technology Has Its Work Cut Out to Harness Web Analytics," *Computer Weekly*, May 13–19, 2014, p. 12.

34. "How Verizon, AT&T, T-Mobile, Sprint and More Stacked Up in Q3 2018," http://www.fiercewireless.com/wireless/how-verizon-at-t-t-mobile-sprint-and-more-stacked-up-q3-2018-top-7-carriers, November 6, 2018; and "Economic Consequences of Armaments Production: Institutional Perspectives of J. K. Galbraith and T. B. Veblen," *Journal of Economic Issues,* March 1, 2008, p. 37.

35. Charles Rile and Ivana Kottasov, "Europe Hits Google with a Third, $1.7 Billion Antitrust Fine," www.cnn.com, March 20, 2019; "Desktop Operating System Market Share," www.marketshare.com, February 2017; James Kanter, "E.U. Accuses Microsoft of Violating Antitrust Deal," *The International Herald Tribune,* October 25, 2012, p. 17; and "Google Wins an Antitrust Battle," *The New York Times,* January 6, 2013, p. 10.

36. Michael Porter, *Competitive Advantage* (New York: Free Press, 1985); and Michael Porter, *Competitive Strategy* (New York: Free Press, 1980).

37. Gautam Begde, "Key Trends in the Money Transfer Industry for 2016," https://www.infosys.com/industries/cards-and-payments/resources/Documents/money-transfer-industry-2016.pdf, 2016; and Jessica Silver-Greenberg, "New Rules for Money Transfers, but Few Limits," *The New York Times,* www.nytimes.com, June 1, 2012.

38. "Frequently Asked Questions," Small Business Administration, Office of Advocacy, www.sba.gov/advocacy, August 2018; "Small Business Trends," Small Business Administration, www.sba.gov/content/small-business-trends; and Kathryn Kobe, "Small Business GDP: Update 2002–2010," Small Business Administration, Office of Advocacy, January 2012.

39. "One Year Later, SOPA Activists Reignite Copyright Conversation," *CBS News,* January 18, 2013; and "Legal Roundup," *Billboard,* January 31, 2009.

40. Thomas A. Hemphill and Syagnik Banerjee, "Mandatory Food Labeling for GMOs," *Regulation,* Winter 2014–2105, p. 7; and Julie Ann Grimm, "Bill Would Require Labeling of Genetically Modified Food," *Las Cruces Sun-News,* January 19, 2013.
41. Dorothy Cohen, "Trademark Strategy Revisited," *Journal of Marketing,* July 1991, pp. 46–59.
42. Matthew Himich, "United States: Madrid Protocol: Is It for You?" *Mondaq Business Briefing,* February 10, 2012; and "Madrid System for the International Registration of Marks," World Intellectual Property Organization, http://www.wipo.int/madrid/en/, January 25, 2013.
43. Paul Barrett, "High Court Sees Color as Basis for Trademarks," *The Wall Street Journal,* March 29, 1995, p. A6; Paul Barrett, "Color in the Court," *The Wall Street Journal,* January 5, 1995, p. A1; and David Kelly, "Rainbow of Ideas to Trademark Color," *Advertising Age,* April 24, 1995, pp. 20, 22.
44. Carrie L. Kiedrowski and Charlotte K. Murphy, "Are Hashtags Capable of Trademark Protection under U.S. Law?" *INTA Bulletin*, February 1, 2016; Vasilios Peros, "Famous Trademarks: Dilution versus Confusion," *Mondaq,* April 18, 2011; and Maxine L. Retsky, "Dilution of Trademarks Hard to Prove," *Marketing News,* May 12, 2003, p. 6.
45. Lesley Fair, "Federal Trade Commission Advertising Enforcement," https://www.ftc.gov/sites/default/files/attachments/training-materials/enforcement.pdf, March 1, 2008.
46. Sarah Vizard, "New Online Ad Laws 'Put Future of the Web in Danger,'" *Marketing Week*, January 11, 2017; Sarah Vizard, "One in Four Businesses 'Unprepared' for New Data Laws," *Marketing Week*, February 14, 2017; Robert J. Aalberts, Alexander Nill, Percy S. Poon, "Online Behavioral Targeting: What Does the Law Say?" *Journal of Current Issues & Research in Advertising*, May 25, 2016, pp. 95–112; Dawn Chmielewski, "How 'Do Not Track' Ended Up Going Nowhere," www.recode.net, January 4, 2016; Cotton Delo, "You Are Big Brother (but That Isn't So Bad)," *Advertising Age,* April 23, 2012, p. 1; Ana Radelat, "Online Privacy, Postal Hikes Top List of DMA Concerns," *Advertising Age,* April 23, 2012, p. 3; Kate Kaye, "Capitol Hill Focuses on Mobile Privacy with Spate of Actions," *Advertising Age,* December 17, 2012, p. 9; "The Internet Browsing Cops," *The Wall Street Journal,* January 21, 2011, p. A12; and Edmund Lee, "Government Says Self-Regulation of Online Privacy Is Coming Up Short," *Advertising Age,* December 6, 2010, p. 1.
47. Jeffrey M. Stupak, "The Internet Tax Freedom Act: In Brief," Congressional Research Service, April 13, 2016; "Internet Tax Reprieve," *The Wall Street Journal,* December 15, 2014, p. A12; "The New Internet Tax Freedom Act," *JD Supra,* May 16, 2008.
48. BBB Online Program Standards, http://us.bbb.org, accessed January 25, 2013.
49. Geek Squad: This case was written by Steven Hartley. Sources: "Digital Television Unit Shipments in the United States," www.statista.com, 2019; Kevin Kelleher, "How the Geek Squad Could Be Best Buy's Secret Weapon," www.time.com, July 19, 2016; Phil Wahba, "Best Buy's Geek Squad Is Trading In Its VW Beetles," www.fortune.com, July 8, 2016; Phil Wahba, "Best Buy Brings Geek Squad to Minneapolis Airport in Holiday Shopping Push," www.fortune.com, January 21, 2016; "2016 a Banner Year for 4K UHD TV," press release, Consumer Technology Association, November 9, 2016; "New Tech to Drive CE Industry Growth in 2015," *Business Wire*, July 15, 2015; Jen Wieczner, "The New Geek Squad," *Fortune*, November 1, 2015, pp. 142–48; Thomas Lee, "Best Buy Stakes Big Share of Its Future on Geek Squad," *San Jose Mercury News,* August 7, 2012; Natalie Zmuda, "Best Buy Gets Back in the Game with New Tagline," *Advertising Age,* June 25, 2012, p. 4; "Best Buy Continues to Diversify by Selling Geek Squad Services," *Trefis,* October 9, 2012; Mary Ellen Lloyd, "Camp Teaches Power of Geekdom," *The Wall Street Journal,* July 11, 2007; and information contained on the Best Buy website (www.bestbuy.com).

Chapter 4 Ethical and Social Responsibility for Sustainable Marketing

LEARNING OBJECTIVES

After reading this chapter you should be able to:

LO 4-1 Explain the differences between legal and ethical behavior in marketing.

LO 4-2 Identify factors that influence ethical and unethical marketing decisions.

LO 4-3 Describe the different concepts of social responsibility.

LO 4-4 Recognize unethical and socially irresponsible consumer behavior.

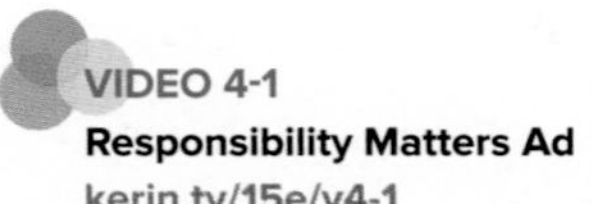
VIDEO 4-1
Responsibility Matters Ad
kerin.tv/15e/v4-1

Anheuser-Busch: Becoming the Best Beer Company in a Better World

Why would a company spend billions of dollars trying to persuade people to use its products responsibly and tens of millions of dollars more to protect and preserve the environment? Ask Anheuser-Busch, the leading American brewer.

Responsible Drinking

Anheuser-Busch has been an advocate for responsible drinking for almost four decades. The company began an aggressive campaign to fight alcohol misuse and underage drinking with its landmark "Know When to Say When" campaign in 1982. This campaign was the forerunner of programs, advertising, and partnerships that promoted responsible drinking; helped prevent drunk driving; and helped curb underage drinking before it starts. For example, the company's *Family Talk About Drinking* program provided a guide to help parents, educators, and other adults talk with children about underage drinking. This program now includes social media with a dedicated Facebook Page (see www.facebook.com/ABFamilyTalk).

Anheuser-Busch expanded its alcohol awareness and education efforts with the launch of its "Responsibility Matters" campaign. This effort emphasized and implemented programs that promoted responsibility and responsible behaviors. Anheuser-Busch believes these efforts have helped contribute–at least in part–to declines in drunk-driving fatalities, underage drinking, and other forms of alcohol misuse since 1982.

In 2013, Budweiser launched its first-ever responsible drinking blimp. The airship, which carried the "Designate a Driver" message, toured the United States. The blimp's flight plan coincided with major festivals, outdoor celebrations, and sporting events in tour cities.

Anheuser-Busch also implements programs to help prevent underage drinking by providing retailers with tools to properly check IDs and help prevent sales to minors. The company also helps parents start and continue conversations about alcohol with their children; supports law enforcement in upholding the law; and, through a variety of community speakers, assists schools in building self-esteem among teens. In 2015, the company announced it would invest another $1 billion in social media campaigns and programs to further reduce the harmful use of alcohol by the end of 2025.

Environmental Sustainability

Anheuser-Busch is committed to brewing the highest quality beers, improving its environmental performance, and making a positive impact in communities throughout the

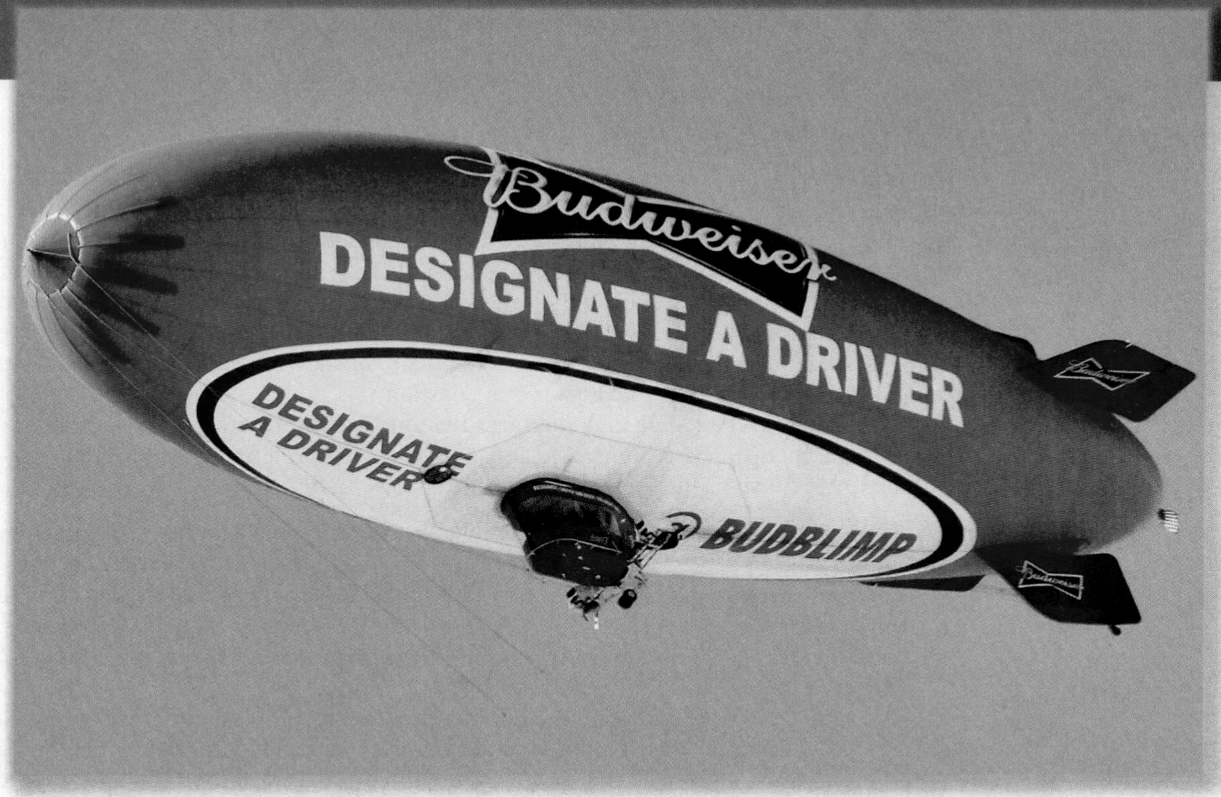

Richard Ulreich/ZUMA Press/Newscom

United States. The company's commitment to the environment is reflected in its 2025 U.S. Sustainability Goals:

- *Renewable electricity and carbon reduction*. By 2025, all of the company's purchased electricity from renewable sources and carbon dioxide emissions will be reduced by 25 percent.
- *Water stewardship*. All Anheuser-Busch facilities will be engaged in water efficiency efforts and communities in high-stress areas will have measurably improved water availability and quality.
- *Smart agriculture*. All direct farmers of its product ingredients will be "highly skilled, connected and financially empowered"; 98 percent of the company's product ingredients are currently grown in the United States.
- *Circular packaging*. All packaging for the company's products will be made from majority recycled content or will be returnable.

Anheuser-Busch clearly acts on what it views as an ethical obligation to its customers and the general public with its alcohol awareness and education programs and community support. At the same time, the company's efforts to protect the natural environment and improve societal well-being reflect its broader social responsibility. Not surprisingly, Anheuser-Busch is recognized as one of the world's most admired companies.[1]

NATURE AND SIGNIFICANCE OF MARKETING ETHICS

LO 4-1
Explain the differences between legal and ethical behavior in marketing.

Ethics are the moral principles and values that govern the actions and decisions of an individual or group.[2] They serve as guidelines on how to act rightly and justly when faced with moral dilemmas.

An Ethical/Legal Framework for Marketing

A good starting point for understanding the nature and significance of ethics is the distinction between the legality and the ethicality of marketing decisions. Figure 4–1 helps visualize the relationship between laws and ethics.[3] Whereas ethics deals with personal moral principles and values, **laws** are society's values and standards that are enforceable in the courts. This distinction can sometimes lead to the rationalization that if a behavior is within reasonable ethical and legal limits, then it is not really illegal or unethical. When surveys ask the question, "Is it OK to get around the law if you don't actually break it?" about half of businesspeople respond "yes."[4] How would you answer this question?

Judgment plays a large role in numerous situations in defining ethical and legal boundaries. Consider the following situations. After reading each, assign it to the cell in Figure 4–1 that you think best fits the situation along the ethical–legal continuum.[5]

1. More than 70 percent of the physicians in the Maricopa County (Arizona) Medical Society agreed to establish a maximum fee schedule for health services to curb rising medical costs. All physicians were required to adhere to this schedule as a condition for membership in the society. The U.S. Supreme Court ruled that this agreement to set prices violated the Sherman Act and represented price fixing, which is illegal. Was the society's action ethical?
2. A company in California sells a computer program to auto dealers showing that car buyers should finance their purchase rather than pay cash. The program omits the effect of income taxes and misstates the interest earned on savings over the loan period. The finance option always provides a net benefit over the cash option. Company employees agree that the program does mislead buyers, but they say the company will "provide what [car dealers] want as long as it is not against the law." Is this practice ethical?
3. China is the world's largest tobacco-producing country and has 300 million smokers. Approximately 1 million Chinese die annually from smoking-related illnesses. This

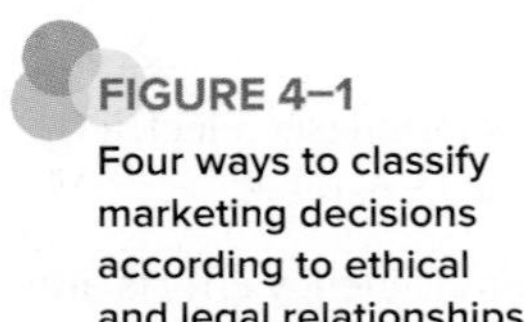

FIGURE 4–1
Four ways to classify marketing decisions according to ethical and legal relationships.

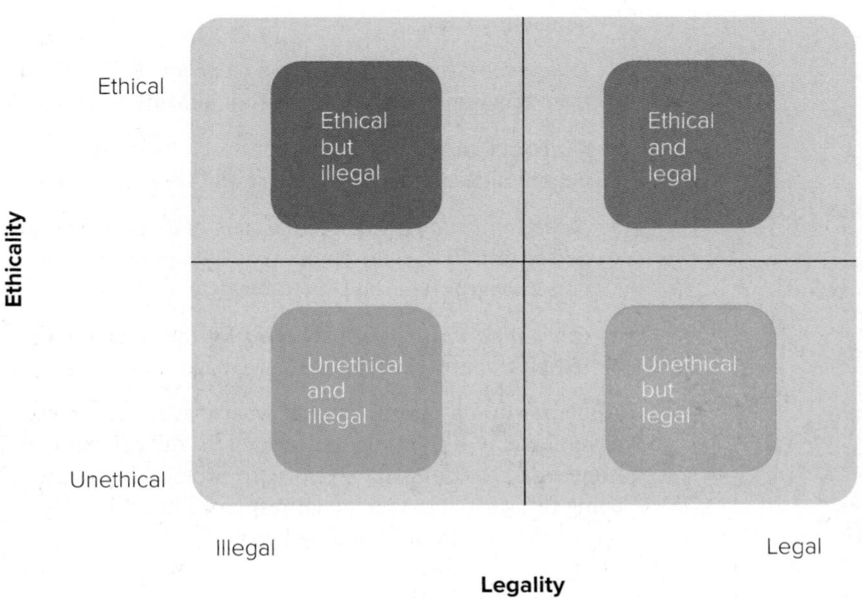

figure is expected to rise to more than 3 million by 2050. China legally restricts tobacco imports. U.S. trade negotiators advocate free trade, thus allowing U.S. tobacco companies to market their products in China. Is the Chinese trade position ethical?

4. A group of college students recorded movies at a local theater and then uploaded the movies to the Internet. Federal statutes state that the unauthorized reproduction, distribution, or exhibition of copyrighted motion pictures is illegal. The students then directed friends and family to a peer-to-peer Internet network that allowed them to download the movies for free, which they did. Is the students' behavior ethical? Is the behavior of their friends and family ethical?

Did these situations fit neatly into Figure 4–1 as clearly ethical and legal or unethical and illegal? Probably not. As you read further in this chapter, you will be asked to consider other ethical dilemmas faced by marketers and consumers.

Critical Perceptions of Ethical Behavior

There has been a public outcry about the ethical practices of businesspeople.[6] Public opinion surveys show that 16 percent of U.S. adults rate the ethical standards of business executives as "very high" or "high." Advertising practitioners, insurance agents, telemarketers, and car salespeople are thought to be among the least ethical occupations. Nursing is thought to be the most ethical profession. Surveys of corporate employees generally confirm this public perception. When asked if they are aware of ethical misconduct in their companies, 41 percent say "yes."

There are at least four possible reasons the state of perceived ethical business conduct is at its present level. First, there is increased pressure on businesspeople to make decisions in a society characterized by diverse value systems. Second, there is a growing tendency for business decisions to be judged publicly by groups with different values and interests. Third, the public's expectations of ethical business behavior have increased. Finally, and most disturbing, ethical business conduct may have declined.

LEARNING REVIEW

4-1. What are ethics?

4-2. What are four possible reasons for the present state of ethical conduct in the United States?

FOUR FACTORS AFFECT ETHICAL MARKETING BEHAVIOR

LO 4-2
Identify factors that influence ethical and unethical marketing decisions.

Researchers have identified four factors that influence ethical marketing behavior.[7] Figure 4–2 presents a framework that shows these factors and their relationships.

Societal Culture and Norms

As described in Chapter 3, *culture* refers to the set of values, ideas, and attitudes that are learned and shared among the members of a group. Culture also serves as a socializing force that dictates what is morally right and just. This means that moral standards are relative to particular societies.[8] These standards often reflect the laws and regulations that affect social and economic behavior, which can create ethical dilemmas. Companies that compete in the global marketplace recognize this fact. Consider UPS, the world's largest package delivery company operating in more than 220 countries and territories worldwide.[9] According to UPS's global compliance and ethics coordinator, "Although languages and cultures around the world may be different, we do not change our ethical standards at UPS. Our ethics program is

FIGURE 4–2
A framework for understanding ethical behavior. Each of these influences has an effect on ethical marketing behavior, as described in the text.

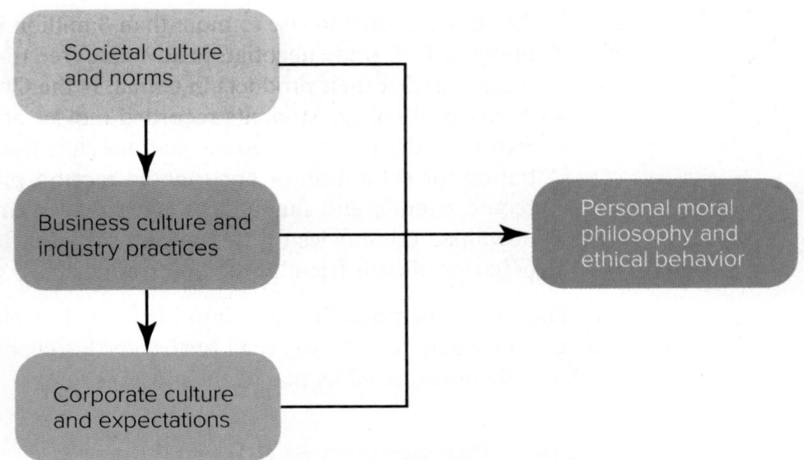

global in nature." Not surprisingly, UPS is consistently ranked among the world's most ethical companies.

Societal values and attitudes also affect ethical and legal relationships among individuals, groups, and business institutions and organizations. Consider the copying of another's copyright, trademark, or patent. These are viewed as intellectual property. Unauthorized use, reproduction, or distribution of intellectual property is illegal in the United States and most countries and can result in fines and prison terms for perpetrators. The owners of intellectual property also lose. For example, annual worldwide lost sales from the theft of intellectual property amount to $14 billion in the music industry, $37 billion in the TV and movie industry, and $69 billion in the software industry.[10] Lost sales, in turn, result in lost jobs, royalties, wages, and tax revenue.

But what about downloading copyrighted music, movies, books, and software over the Internet or from peer-to-peer file-sharing programs without paying the owner of this property? Is this an ethical or unethical act? It depends on who you ask. Surveys of the U.S. public indicate that the majority consider these acts unethical. However, only a third of U.S. college students say these acts are unethical.[11]

Business Culture and Industry Practices

Societal culture provides a foundation for understanding moral behavior in business activities. *Business cultures* "comprise the effective rules of the game, the boundaries between competitive and unethical behavior, [and] the codes of conduct in business dealings."[12] Consumers have witnessed instances where business cultures in the financial (insider trading), insurance and banking (deceptive sales practices), and defense (bribery) industries went awry. Business culture affects ethical conduct both in the exchange relationship between sellers and buyers and in the competitive behavior among sellers.

Ethics of Exchange The exchange process is central to the marketing concept. Ethical exchanges between sellers and buyers should result in both parties being better off after a transaction.

Before the 1960s, the legal concept of ***caveat emptor***—let the buyer beware—was pervasive in the American business culture. In 1962, President John F. Kennedy outlined a **Consumer Bill of Rights** that codified the ethics of exchange between buyers and sellers. These were the right (1) to safety, (2) to be informed, (3) to choose, and (4) to be heard. Consumers expect and often demand that these rights be protected, as have American businesses.

The *right to safety* manifests itself in industry and federal safety standards for most products sold in the United States. In fact, the U.S. Consumer Product Safety Commission routinely monitors the safety of 15,000 consumer products. However, even the most vigilant efforts to

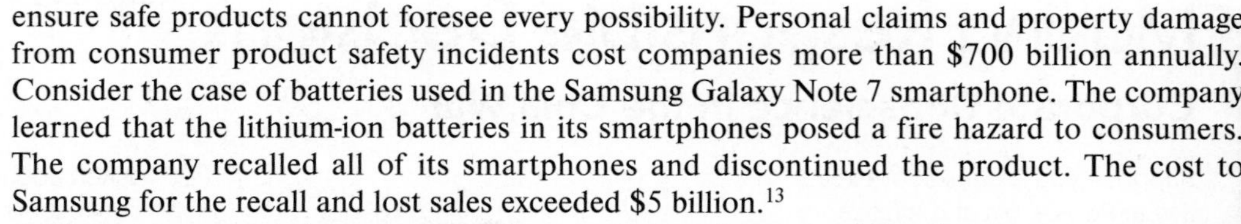

The Federal Trade Commission plays an active role in educating consumers and businesses about the importance of personal information privacy on the Internet. FTC initiatives, including proposals concerning children's online privacy, are detailed on its website.
Lisa F. Young/iStock/Getty Images

ensure safe products cannot foresee every possibility. Personal claims and property damage from consumer product safety incidents cost companies more than $700 billion annually. Consider the case of batteries used in the Samsung Galaxy Note 7 smartphone. The company learned that the lithium-ion batteries in its smartphones posed a fire hazard to consumers. The company recalled all of its smartphones and discontinued the product. The cost to Samsung for the recall and lost sales exceeded $5 billion.[13]

The *right to be informed* means that marketers have an obligation to give consumers complete and accurate information about products and services. This right also applies to the solicitation of personal information over the Internet and its subsequent use by marketers.[14] An FTC survey of websites indicated that 92 percent collect personal information such as consumer e-mail addresses, telephone numbers, shopping habits, and financial data. Yet, only two-thirds of websites inform consumers of what is done with this information once obtained. The FTC wants more than posted privacy notices that merely inform consumers of a company's data-use policy, which critics say are often vague, confusing, or too legalistic to be understood. This view is shared by two-thirds of consumers who worry about protecting their personal information online. The consumer right to be informed has spawned much federal legislation, such as the *Children's Online Privacy Protection Act* (1998) and self-regulation initiatives restricting disclosure of personal information. The FTC recently fined YouTube $170 million for violating provisions of this act.

Relating to the *right to choose*, today many supermarket chains demand "slotting allowances" from manufacturers, in the form of cash or free goods, to stock new products.[15] This practice could limit the number of new products available to consumers and interfere with their right to choose. One critic of this practice remarked, "If we had had slotting allowances a few years ago, we might not have had granola, herbal tea, or yogurt."

Finally, the *right to be heard* means that consumers should have access to public policymakers regarding complaints about products and services. This right is illustrated in limitations put on telemarketing practices. The FTC established the Do Not Call Registry for consumers who do not want to receive unsolicited telemarketing calls. Today, over 250 million U.S. landline and cell phone numbers are listed in the registry, which is managed by the FTC. A telemarketer can be fined up to $16,000 for each call made to a telephone number posted on the registry.

Ethics of Competition Business culture also affects ethical behavior in competition. Two kinds of unethical behavior are most common: (1) economic espionage and (2) corruption.

Economic espionage is the clandestine collection of trade secrets or proprietary information about a company's competitors. This practice is illegal and unethical and carries serious criminal penalties for the offending individual or business. Espionage activities include illegal trespassing, theft, fraud, misrepresentation, electronic hacking, the search of a competitor's trash, and violations of written and implicit employment agreements with noncompete clauses. More than half of the largest firms in the world have uncovered espionage in some form, costing them $445 billion annually in lost sales.[16]

Economic espionage is most prevalent in high-technology industries, such as electronics, specialty chemicals, industrial equipment, aerospace, and pharmaceuticals, where technical know-how and trade secrets separate industry leaders from followers. But espionage can occur anywhere—even in the soft drink industry! Read the Making Responsible Decisions box to learn how Pepsi-Cola responded to an offer to obtain confidential information about its archrival's marketing plans.[17]

Corruption is a second form of unethical behavior. Corruption involves unethical conduct by a person entrusted with a position of authority, often to acquire a personal benefit. The giving and receiving of bribes, kickbacks, and graft are the most common forms of corruption. These practices are more common in business-to-business and government marketing than in consumer marketing.

Making Responsible Decisions — Ethics

Corporate Conscience in the Cola War

Suppose you are a senior executive at Pepsi-Cola and a Coca-Cola employee offers to sell you the marketing plan and sample for a new Coke product at a modest price. Would you buy it knowing Pepsi-Cola could gain a significant competitive edge in the cola war?

When this question was posed in an online survey of marketing and advertising executives, 67 percent said they would buy the plan and product sample if there were no repercussions. What did Pepsi-Cola do when this offer actually occurred? The company immediately contacted Coca-Cola, which contacted the FBI. An undercover FBI agent paid the employee $30,000 in cash stuffed in a Girl Scout cookie box as a down payment and later arrested the employee and accomplices. When asked about the incident, a Pepsi-Cola spokesperson said: "We only did what any responsible company would do. Competition must be tough, but must always be fair and legal."

©Cliff Tew

Why did the 33 percent of respondents in the online survey say they would decline the offer? Most said they would prefer competing ethically so they could sleep at night. According to a senior advertising agency executive who would decline the offer: "Repercussions go beyond potential espionage charges. As long as we have a conscience, there are repercussions."

So what happened to the Coca-Cola employee and her accomplices? She was sentenced to eight years in prison and ordered to pay $40,000 in restitution. Her accomplices were each sentenced to five years in prison.

In general, bribery is most evident in industries experiencing intense competition and in countries in the earlier stages of economic development or facing economic and political turmoil. According to a United Nations study, 15 percent of all companies in industrialized countries have to pay bribes to win or retain business. In Asia, this figure is 40 percent. In Eastern Europe, 60 percent of all companies must pay bribes to do business. Analysts at the World Bank estimate that the equivalent of $2.6 trillion is offered in bribes and kickbacks every year in the global arena.[18] Corruption on a worldwide scale is monitored by Transparency International (see the Marketing Insights About Me box). Visit its website to view country rankings on its Corruption Perception Index.

The prevalence of economic espionage and bribery in international marketing has prompted laws to curb these practices. Two significant laws, the *Economic Espionage Act* (1996) and the *Foreign Corrupt Practices Act* (1977), address these practices in the United States. Both are detailed in Chapter 7.

Corporate Culture and Expectations

A third influence on ethical practices is corporate culture. *Corporate culture* is the set of values, ideas, and attitudes that is learned and shared among the members of an organization. The culture of a company demonstrates itself in the dress ("We don't wear ties"), sayings ("The IBM Way"), and manner of work (team efforts) of employees. Culture is also apparent in the expectations for ethical behavior present in formal codes of ethics and the ethical actions of top management and co-workers.

Codes of Ethics A **code of ethics** is a formal statement of ethical principles and rules of conduct. It is estimated that 85 to 90 percent of U.S. companies have some sort of ethics code and one of every four large companies has corporate ethics officers. Ethics codes typically address contributions to government officials and political parties, customer and supplier

Marketing Insights About Me

Is Corruption More or Less Common in My Country?

Corruption as a means to win and retain business varies widely by country. Transparency International periodically polls employees of multinational firms and institutions and political analysts and ranks countries on the basis of their perceived level of corruption to win or retain business. To obtain the most recent ranking, visit the Transparency International website at www.transparency.org, and click "Corruption Perceptions Index."

Scroll the Corruption Perceptions Index to see where the United States stands in the worldwide rankings. How does the United States compare in relation to its neighbors, Canada and Mexico? Any surprises? Which country listed in the index has the highest ranking and which has the lowest ranking?

webphotographer/E+/Getty Images

relations, conflicts of interest, and accurate recordkeeping. At United Technologies, for example, 500 business practices officers distribute the company's ethics code, translated into 31 languages, to about 200,000 employees who work for this defense and engineering giant in some 180 countries.[19]

However, an ethics code is rarely enough to ensure ethical behavior. Coca-Cola has an ethics code and emphasizes that its employees be ethical in their behavior. But that did not stop some Coca-Cola employees from rigging the results of a test market for a frozen soft drink to win Burger King's business. Coca-Cola subsequently agreed to pay Burger King and its operators more than $20 million to settle the matter.[20]

Lack of specificity is a major reason for the violation of ethics codes. Employees must often judge whether a specific behavior is unethical. The American Marketing Association has addressed this issue by providing a detailed statement of ethics, which all members agree to follow. This statement is shown in Figure 4–3.

Ethical Behavior of Top Management and Co-Workers A second reason for violating ethics codes rests in the perceived behavior of top management and co-workers.[21] Observing peers and top management and gauging responses to unethical behavior play an important role in individual actions. A study of business executives reported that 47 percent had witnessed ethically troubling behavior. About 44 percent of those who reported unethical behavior were penalized, through either outright punishment or a diminished status in the company.[22] Clearly, ethical dilemmas can bring personal and professional conflict. For this reason, states have enacted laws designed to protect **whistle-blowers**, employees who report unethical or illegal actions of their employers.

Your Personal Moral Philosophy and Ethical Behavior

Ultimately, ethical choices are based on the personal moral philosophy of the decision maker. Moral philosophy is learned through the process of socialization with friends and family and by formal education. It is also influenced by the societal, business, and corporate culture in which a person finds him- or herself. Two prominent personal moral philosophies have direct bearing on marketing practice: (1) moral idealism and (2) utilitarianism.

Moral Idealism **Moral idealism** is a personal moral philosophy that considers certain individual rights or duties as universal, regardless of the outcome. This philosophy exists in the Consumer Bill of Rights and is favored by moral philosophers and consumer interest

AMERICAN MARKETING ASSOCIATION STATEMENT OF ETHICS

Preamble

The American Marketing Association commits itself to promoting the highest standard of professional ethical norms and values for its members. Norms are established standards of conduct that are expected and maintained by society and/or professional organizations. Values represent the collective conception of what people find desirable, important, and morally proper. Values serve as the criteria for evaluating the actions of others. Marketing practitioners must recognize that they not only serve their enterprises but also act as stewards of society in creating, facilitating, and executing the efficient and effective transactions that are part of the greater economy. In this role, marketers should embrace the highest ethical norms of practicing professionals and the ethical *values* implied by their responsibility toward stakeholders (e.g., customers, employees, investors, channel members, regulators, and the host community).

General Norms

1. *Marketers must do no harm.* This means doing work for which they are appropriately trained or experienced so that they can actively add value to their organizations and customers. It also means adhering to all applicable laws and regulations and embodying high ethical standards in the choices they make.
2. *Marketers must foster trust in the marketing system.* This means that products are appropriate for their intended and promoted uses. It requires that marketing communications about goods and services are not intentionally deceptive or misleading. It suggests building relationships that provide for the equitable adjustment and/or redress of customer grievances. It implies striving for good faith and fair dealing so as to contribute toward the efficacy of the exchange process.
3. *Marketers must embrace, communicate, and practice the fundamental ethical values that will improve consumer confidence in the integrity of the marketing exchange system.* These basic *values* are intentionally aspirational and include honesty, responsibility, fairness, respect, openness, and citizenship.

Ethical Values

Honesty—to be truthful and forthright in our dealings with customers and stakeholders.

- We will tell the truth in all situations and at all times.
- We will offer products of value that do what we claim in our communications.
- We will stand behind our products if they fail to deliver their claimed benefits.
- We will honor our explicit and implicit commitments and promises.

Responsibility—to accept the consequences of our marketing decisions and strategies.

- We will make strenuous efforts to serve the needs of our customers.
- We will avoid using coercion with all stakeholders.
- We will acknowledge the social obligations to stakeholders that come with increased marketing and economic power.

FIGURE 4–3
American Marketing Association Statement of Ethics.

Reprinted with permission from American Marketing Association Statement of Ethics, published by the American Marketing Association, www.marketingpower.com

groups. For example, the right to know applies to probable defects in an automobile that relate to safety.

This philosophy also applies to ethical duties. A fundamental ethical duty is to do no harm. Adherence to this duty prompted the recent decision by 3M executives to phase out production of a chemical 3M had manufactured for nearly 40 years. The substance, used in far-ranging products from pet food bags, candy wrappers, carpeting, and 3M's popular Scotchgard fabric protector, had no known harmful health or environmental effect. However, the company discovered that the chemical appeared in minuscule amounts in humans and animals around the world and accumulated in tissue. Believing that the substance could be possibly harmful in large doses, 3M voluntarily stopped the production of the chemical, resulting in a $200 million loss in annual sales.[23]

Utilitarianism An alternative perspective on moral philosophy is **utilitarianism**, which is a personal moral philosophy that focuses on "the greatest good for the greatest number" by assessing the costs and benefits of the consequences of ethical behavior. If the benefits exceed the costs, then the behavior is ethical. If not, then the behavior is unethical. This philosophy underlies the economic tenets of capitalism and, not surprisingly, is embraced by many business executives and students.[24]

FIGURE 4–3
(Continued)

- We will recognize our special commitments to economically vulnerable segments of the market such as children, the elderly, and others who may be substantially disadvantaged.

Fairness—to try to balance justly the needs of the buyer with the interests of the seller.

- We will represent our products in a clear way in selling, advertising, and other forms of communication; this includes the avoidance of false, misleading, and deceptive promotion.
- We will reject manipulations and sales tactics that harm customer trust.
- We will not engage in price fixing, predatory pricing, price gouging, or "bait-and-switch" tactics.
- We will not knowingly participate in material conflicts of interest.

Respect—to acknowledge the basic human dignity of all stakeholders.

- We will value individual differences even as we avoid stereotyping customers or depicting demographic groups (e.g., gender, race, sexual orientation) in a negative or dehumanizing way in our promotions.
- We will listen to the needs of our customers and make all reasonable efforts to monitor and improve their satisfaction on an ongoing basis.
- We will make a special effort to understand suppliers, intermediaries, and distributors from other cultures.
- We will appropriately acknowledge the contributions of others, such as consultants, employees, and co-workers, to our marketing endeavors.

Openness—to create transparency in our marketing operations.

- We will strive to communicate clearly with all our constituencies.
- We will accept constructive criticism from our customers and other stakeholders.
- We will explain significant product or service risks, component substitutions, or other foreseeable eventualities that could affect customers or their perception of the purchase decision.
- We will fully disclose list prices and terms of financing as well as available price deals and adjustments.

Citizenship—to fulfill the economic, legal, philanthropic, and societal responsibilities that serve stakeholders in a strategic manner.

- We will strive to protect the natural environment in the execution of marketing campaigns.
- We will give back to the community through volunteerism and charitable donations.
- We will work to contribute to the overall betterment of marketing and its reputation.
- We will encourage supply chain members to ensure that trade is fair for all participants, including producers in developing countries.

Implementation

Finally, we recognize that every industry sector and marketing subdiscipline (e.g., marketing research, e-commerce, direct selling, direct marketing, advertising) has its own specific ethical issues that require policies and commentary. An array of such codes can be accessed through links on the AMA website. We encourage all such groups to develop and/or refine their industry and discipline-specific codes of ethics to supplement these general norms and values.

What does 3M's Scotchgard have to do with ethics, social responsibility, and a $200 million loss in annual sales? Read the text to find out.
Mike Hruby/McGraw-Hill Education

Utilitarian reasoning was apparent in Nestlé Food Corporation's marketing of Good Start infant formula, sold by Nestlé's Carnation Company. The formula, promoted as hypoallergenic, was designed to prevent or reduce colic caused by an infant's allergic reaction to cow's milk, a condition suffered by 2 percent of babies. However, some severely milk-allergic infants experienced serious side effects after using Good Start, including convulsive vomiting. Physicians and parents charged that the hypoallergenic claim was misleading, and the Food and Drug Administration investigated the matter.

A Nestlé vice president defended the claim and product, saying, "I don't understand why our product should work in 100 percent of cases. If we wanted to say it was foolproof, we would have called it allergy-free. We call it hypo-, or less, allergenic."[25] Nestlé officials seemingly believed that most allergic infants would benefit from Good Start–"the greatest good for the greatest number." But, other views prevailed. The claim was dropped from the product label.

An appreciation for the nature of ethics, coupled with a basic understanding of why unethical behavior arises, alerts a person to when and how ethical issues arise in marketing decisions. Ultimately, ethical behavior rests with the individual, but the consequences affect many.

LEARNING REVIEW

4-3. What rights are included in the Consumer Bill of Rights?

4-4. Economic espionage includes what kinds of activities?

4-5. What is meant by moral idealism?

UNDERSTANDING SOCIAL RESPONSIBILITY FOR SUSTAINABLE MARKETING

LO 4-3
Describe the different concepts of social responsibility.

As we saw in Chapter 1, the societal marketing concept stresses marketing's social responsibility by not only satisfying the needs of consumers but also providing for society's welfare. **Social responsibility** means that organizations are part of a larger society and are accountable to that society for their actions. Like ethics, agreement on the nature and scope of social responsibility is often difficult to come by, given the diversity of values present in different societal, business, and corporate cultures.

Three Concepts of Social Responsibility

Figure 4–4 shows three concepts of social responsibility: (1) profit responsibility, (2) stakeholder responsibility, and (3) societal responsibility.

Profit Responsibility *Profit responsibility* holds that companies have a simple duty: to maximize profits for their owners or stockholders. This view is expressed by Nobel Laureate Milton Friedman, who said, "There is one and only one social responsibility of business–to

FIGURE 4–4
Three concepts of social responsibility. Each concept of social responsibility relates to particular constituencies. There is often conflict in satisfying all three constituencies at the same time.

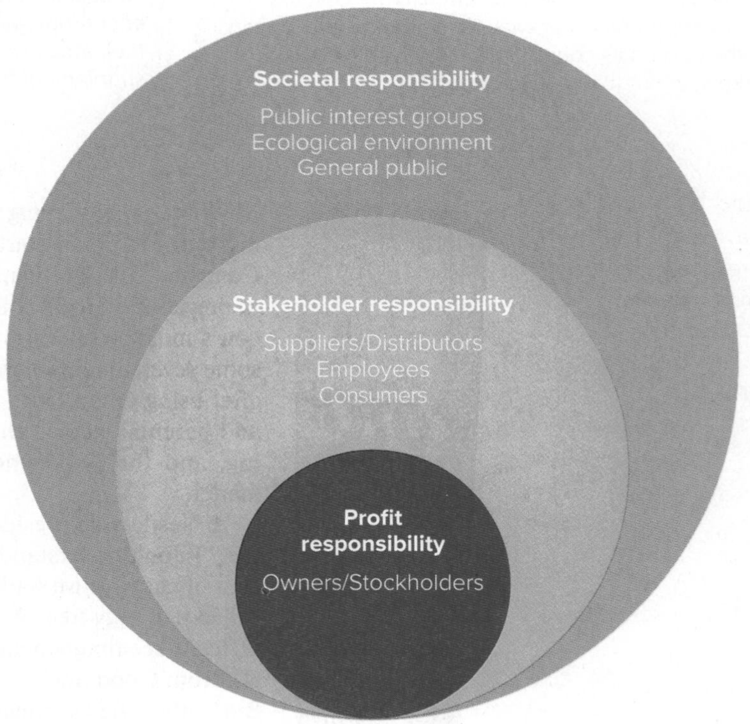

use its resources and engage in activities designed to increase its profits so long as it stays within the rules of the game, which is to say, engages in open and free competition without deception or fraud."[26]

Genzyme, the maker of Cerdelga, a drug that treats a genetic illness called Gaucher disease that affects 10,000 people worldwide, has been criticized for apparently adopting this view in its pricing practices. Genzyme charges up to $300,000 for a year's worth of Cerdelga. A Genzyme spokesperson responded saying the company spends millions of dollars annually to manufacture Cerdelga and freely gives the drug to patients without insurance. Also, the company invested considerable dollars in research over several years to develop Cerdelga, and the drug's profits are reinvested in ongoing R&D programs.[27]

Stakeholder Responsibility Criticism of the profit view has led to a broader concept of social responsibility. *Stakeholder responsibility* focuses on the obligations an organization has to those who can affect achievement of its objectives. These constituencies include consumers, employees, suppliers, and distributors. Failure to consider a company's broader constituencies when making decisions can have dire consequences.

For example, Volkswagen AG was widely criticized for employing sophisticated software on selected Volkswagen, Audi, and Porsche models that impaired its diesel emissions devices required by the U.S. Environmental Protection Agency. Volkswagen had installed the emissions software on more than half a million diesel cars sold in the United States and about 10.5 million cars worldwide. This software disguised the amount of smog pollutants emitted from selected cars.[28]

Volkswagen AG executives admitted that the company engaged in emissions deception practices and agreed to pay up to $25 billion in settlement fees. The company's CEO acknowledged that "We know that we still have a great deal of work to earn back the trust of the American people." Following this episode, Volkswagen sales fell in the United States, which affected company employees, suppliers, shareholders, and distributors.[29]

Societal Responsibility An even broader concept of social responsibility has emerged in recent years. *Societal responsibility* refers to obligations that organizations have (1) to the preservation of the ecological environment and (2) to the general public. Emphasis is placed on the **triple bottom line**—recognition of the need for organizations to improve the state of people, the planet, and profit simultaneously if they are to achieve sustainable, long-term growth.[30] Marketers have embraced societal responsibility through **sustainable marketing**, which seeks to meet today's (global) economic, environmental, and social needs without compromising the opportunity for future generations to meet theirs. Green marketing, cause marketing, social audits, and sustainable development reflect this recognition.

Green marketing—marketing efforts to produce, promote, and reclaim environmentally sensitive products—takes many forms.[31] At 3M, product development opportunities emanate both from consumer research and its "Pollution Prevention Pays" (3P) program. This program solicits employee suggestions on how to reduce pollution and recycle materials. This program has generated over 11,000 3P projects that have eliminated more than 2 billion tons of air, water, and solid-waste pollutants from the environment. Levi Strauss & Co. uses eight recycled plastic bottles in each pair of Waste<Less jeans, which are composed of at least 20 percent recycled plastic. This practice has eliminated millions of discarded plastic bottles from landfills and reduced the water consumed in the manufacturing process.

Walmart has instituted buying practices that encourage its suppliers to use containers and packaging made from corn, not oil-based, resins. The company expects this initiative will save 800,000 barrels of oil annually. These voluntary responses to environmental issues have been implemented with little or no additional cost to consumers and have resulted in cost savings to companies.

A global undertaking to further green marketing efforts is the ISO 14000 initiative developed by the International Standards Organization (ISO) in Geneva, Switzerland. ISO 14000 consists of worldwide standards for environmental quality and green marketing practices. These standards are embraced by 171 countries, including the United States. More than 300,000 companies have met ISO 14000 standards for environmental quality and green marketing.[32]

Pampers.
unicef
1 pack =
1 life-saving
vaccine*
against newborn tetanus
Learn more

A cause marketing pioneer for more than three decades, Procter & Gamble focuses on supporting disadvantaged youth and disaster relief. A successful brand campaign in partnership with UNICEF includes the Pampers 1 Pack = 1 Vaccine initiative, protecting over 300 million women and their babies against maternal and neonatal tetanus over the past decade.

Source: Procter & Gamble Babycare Western Europe and Unicef/United Nations Children's Fund

Sustainable marketing efforts on behalf of the general public are becoming more common. A formal practice is **cause marketing**, which occurs when the charitable contributions of a firm are tied directly to the customer revenues produced through the promotion of one of its products.[33] This definition distinguishes cause marketing from a firm's standard charitable contributions, which are outright donations. For example, when consumers purchase selected company products, Procter & Gamble directs part of that revenue toward programs that support disadvantaged youth and provide disaster relief. MasterCard International links usage of its card with fund-raising for institutions that combat cancer, heart disease, child abuse, drug abuse, and muscular dystrophy. Barnes & Noble promotes literacy, and Coca-Cola sponsors local Boys and Girls Clubs. Avon Products, Inc. focuses on different issues in different countries, including breast cancer, domestic violence, and disaster relief, among many others.

Cause marketing programs incorporate all three concepts of social responsibility by addressing public concerns and satisfying customer needs. They can also enhance corporate sales and profits, as described in the Marketing Matters box.[34]

The Social Audit and Sustainable Development: Doing Well by Doing Good

Converting socially responsible ideas into actions involves careful planning and monitoring of programs. Many companies develop, implement, and evaluate their social responsibility efforts by means of a **social audit**, which is a systematic assessment of a firm's objectives, strategies, and performance in terms of social responsibility. Frequently, marketing and social responsibility programs are integrated. Consider McDonald's. The company's concern for the needs of families with children who are chronically or terminally ill was converted into over 350 Ronald McDonald Houses around the world. These facilities, located near treatment centers, enable families to stay together during the child's care. In this case, McDonald's is contributing to the welfare of a portion of its target market.

A social audit consists of five steps:[35]

1. Recognition of a firm's social expectations and the rationale for engaging in social responsibility endeavors.
2. Identification of social responsibility causes or programs consistent with the company's mission.

Marketing Matters

Customer Value

Will Consumers Switch Brands for a Cause? Yes, If . . .

American Express Company pioneered cause marketing when it sponsored the renovation of the Statue of Liberty. This effort raised $1.7 million for the renovation, increased card usage among cardholders, and attracted new cardholders. General Mills has raised over $882 million since 1996 for schools with its popular "Box Tops for Education" cause marketing program. It is estimated that cause marketing raised over $12 billion in 2018.

Source: General Mills

Cause marketing benefits companies as well as causes. Research indicates that 85 percent of U.S. consumers say they have a more favorable opinion of companies that support causes they care about. Also, 80 percent of consumers say they will switch to a brand or retailer that supports a good cause if the price and quality of brands or retailers are equal. In short, cause marketing may be a valued point of difference for brands and companies, all other things being equal.

For more information, including cause marketing news, links, and case studies, visit https://engageforgood.com.

3. Determination of organizational objectives and priorities for programs and activities it will undertake.
4. Specification of the type and amount of resources necessary to achieve social responsibility objectives.
5. Evaluation of social responsibility programs and activities undertaken and assessment of future involvement.

Corporate attention to social audits will increase as companies seek to achieve sustainable development and improve the quality of life in a global economy. **Sustainable development** involves conducting business in a way that protects the natural environment while making economic progress.

Ecologically responsible initiatives such as green marketing represent one such initiative. Recent initiatives related to working conditions at offshore manufacturing sites that produce goods for U.S. companies focus on quality-of-life issues. Public opinion surveys show that 90 percent of U.S. citizens are concerned about working conditions under which products are made in Asia

Marketing and social responsibility programs are often integrated, as is the case with McDonald's.
Source: Ryan Fischer /The Herald-Dispatch/AP Images

and Latin America. Companies such as Reebok, Nike, Liz Claiborne, Levi Strauss, and Mattel have responded by imposing codes of conduct to reduce unsafe, harsh, or abusive working conditions at offshore manufacturing facilities. Still, poor working conditions exist.[36]

Companies that evidence sustainable marketing have been rewarded for their efforts. Research has shown that these companies (1) benefit from favorable word of mouth among consumers and (2) typically outperform less responsible companies in terms of financial performance.[37]

Turning the Table: Consumer Ethics and Social Responsibility

LO 4-4
Recognize unethical and socially irresponsible consumer behavior.

Consumers also have an obligation to act ethically and responsibly in the exchange process and in the use and disposition of products. Unfortunately, consumer behavior is spotty on both counts.

Unethical practices of consumers are a serious concern to marketers.[38] These practices include filing warranty claims after the claim period; misredeeming coupons; making fraudulent returns of merchandise; providing inaccurate information on credit applications; buying counterfeit products; pirating music, movies, and software from the Internet; and submitting phony insurance claims.

The cost to marketers of such unethical behavior in lost sales and prevention expenses is huge. For example, consumers who redeem coupons for unpurchased products or use coupons for other products cost manufacturers over $1 billion each year. The willing purchase of counterfeit products by consumers—from phony designer watches, handbags, and sunglasses to automobile parts—costs companies another $1.3 billion each year. Fraudulent automobile insurance claims cost insurance companies more than $10 billion annually. In addition, retailers lose about $49 billion yearly from shoplifting and worker theft and $16 billion annually from fraudulent returns of merchandise. Consumers also act unethically toward each other. According to the FBI, consumer complaints about online auction fraud, in which consumers misrepresent their goods to others, outnumber all other reports of online crime.

Research on unethical consumer behavior indicates that these acts are rarely motivated by economic need. This behavior appears to be influenced by (1) a belief that a consumer can get away with the act and it is worth doing and (2) the rationalization that the act is justified or driven by forces outside the individual—"everybody does it." These reasons were vividly expressed by a 24-year-old who pirated a movie and was sentenced to six months of house arrest, three years of probation, and a $7,000 fine. He said, "I didn't like paying for movies," and added, "so many people do it, you never think you're going to get caught."[39]

Fake designer clothes and accessories are made by companies using trademarks stolen from legitimate companies. The purchase of counterfeit products is not illegal, but is it ethical?
Source: National Crime Prevention Council

WHAT DO YOUR FAKE FASHIONS SAY ABOUT YOU?
counterfeit watch
counterfeit bracelet
counterfeit purse
counterfeit sunglasses
counterfeit scarf
"I'm a phony."
Fake designer clothes and products say more than you think. Buying counterfeit products amounts to stealing. The dollars you save come at a cost to others. These products are often cheaply made under sub-standard conditions using trademarks stolen from legitimate companies that pay taxes and fair wages to workers. What kind of fashion statement is that?
Counterfeits Hurt. You Have the Power to Stop Them.
Avoid counterfeit products. Visit NCPC.ORG/GETREAL

©2011 National Crime Prevention Council

Consumer purchase, use, and disposition of environmentally sensitive products relate to consumer social responsibility. Research indicates that consumers are sensitive to ecological issues.[40] For example, 65 percent of U.S. consumers say they want to buy brands that advocate environmental sustainability, yet only 26 percent actually do so and are personally willing to change their lifestyle to improve the environment. Related research shows that consumers (1) may be unwilling to sacrifice convenience and pay higher prices to protect the environment and (2) lack the knowledge to make informed decisions dealing with the purchase, use, and disposition of products.

Consumer confusion over which products are environmentally safe is also apparent, given marketers' rush to offer "green products." For example, few consumers realize that nonaerosol "pump" hair sprays are the second-largest cause of air pollution, after drying paint. And some environmentally safe claims made by marketers have been labeled *greenwashing*—the practice of making an unsubstantiated or misleading claim about the environmental benefits of a product, service, technology, or company practice. Companies that engage in greenwashing usually incur a decline in corporate legitimacy and reputation.[41]

VIDEO 4-2
Corporate Greenwashing
kerin.tv/15e/v4-2

To address such claims, the FTC has drafted guidelines that describe the circumstances under which environmental claims can be made without constituting misleading information in regard to recyclable, biodegradable, and sustainable products and processes.[42] For example, an advertisement or product label touting a package as "50 percent more recycled content than before" could be misleading if the recycled content has increased from 2 percent to 3 percent.

Ultimately, marketers and consumers alike are accountable for ethical and socially responsible behavior. The years ahead will prove to be a testing period for both.

LEARNING REVIEW

4-6. What is meant by social responsibility?

4-7. Marketing efforts to produce, promote, and reclaim environmentally sensitive products are called ________________.

4-8. What is a social audit?

LEARNING OBJECTIVES REVIEW

LO 4-1 *Explain the differences between legal and ethical behavior in marketing.*

A good starting point for understanding the nature and significance of ethics is the distinction between the legality and the ethicality of marketing decisions. Whereas ethics deal with personal moral principles and values, laws are society's values and standards that are enforceable in the courts. This distinction can lead to the rationalization that if a behavior is within reasonable ethical and legal limits, then it is not really illegal or unethical. Judgment plays a large role in defining ethical and legal boundaries in marketing. Ethical dilemmas arise when acts or situations are not clearly ethical and legal or unethical and illegal.

LO 4-2 *Identify factors that influence ethical and unethical marketing decisions.*

Four factors influence ethical marketing behavior. First, societal culture and norms serve as socializing forces that dictate what is morally right and just. Second, business culture and industry practices affect ethical conduct in both the exchange relationships between buyers and sellers and the competitive behavior among sellers. Third, corporate culture and expectations are often defined by corporate ethics codes and the ethical behavior of top management and co-workers. Finally, an individual's personal moral philosophy, such as moral idealism or utilitarianism, will dictate ethical choices. Ultimately, ethical behavior rests with the individual, but the consequences affect many.

LO 4-3 *Describe the different concepts of social responsibility.*

Social responsibility means that organizations are part of a larger society and are accountable to that society for their actions. There are three concepts of social responsibility. First, profit responsibility holds that companies have a simple duty: to maximize profits for their owners or stockholders. Second, stakeholder responsibility focuses on the obligations an organization has to those who can affect achievement of its objectives. Those constituencies include consumers, employees, suppliers, and distributors. Finally, societal responsibility focuses on obligations that organizations have to the preservation of the ecological environment and the general public. Companies are placing greater emphasis on sustainable marketing today and are reaping the rewards of positive word of mouth from their consumers and favorable financial performance.

LO 4-4 *Recognize unethical and socially irresponsible consumer behavior.*

Consumers, like marketers, have an obligation to act ethically and responsibly in the exchange process and in the use and disposition of products. Unfortunately, consumer behavior is spotty on both counts. Unethical consumer behavior includes filing warranty claims after the claim period; buying counterfeit products; misredeeming coupons; pirating music, movies, and software from the Internet; and submitting phony insurance claims, among other behaviors. Unethical behavior is rarely motivated by economic need. Rather, research indicates that this behavior is influenced by (*a*) a belief that a consumer can get away with the act and it is worth doing and (*b*) the rationalization that such acts are justified or driven by forces outside the individual—"everybody does it." Consumer purchase, use, and disposition of environmentally sensitive products relate to consumer social responsibility. Even though consumers are sensitive to ecological issues they (*a*) may be unwilling to sacrifice convenience and pay potentially higher prices to protect the environment and (*b*) lack the knowledge to make informed decisions dealing with the purchase, use, and disposition of products.

LEARNING REVIEW ANSWERS

4-1 What are ethics?
Answer: Ethics are the moral principles and values that govern the actions and decisions of an individual or group. They serve as guidelines on how to act rightly and justly when faced with moral dilemmas.

4-2 What are four possible reasons for the present state of ethical conduct in the United States?
Answer: (1) Increased pressure on businesspeople to make decisions in a society with diverse value systems. (2) A growing tendency for business decisions to be judged publicly by groups with different values and interests. (3) The public's expectations of ethical business behavior have increased. (4) Ethical business conduct may have actually declined.

4-3 What rights are included in the Consumer Bill of Rights?
Answer: The Consumer Bill of Rights (1962) codified the ethics of exchange between buyers and sellers. These are the rights to safety, to be informed, to choose, and to be heard.

4-4 Economic espionage includes what kinds of activities?
Answer: Economic espionage is the illegal and unethical clandestine collection of trade secrets or proprietary information about a company's competitors. This practice includes trespassing, theft, fraud, misrepresentation, electronic hacking, searching of competitors' trash, and violations of written and implicit employment agreements with noncompete clauses.

4-5 What is meant by moral idealism?
Answer: Moral idealism is a personal moral philosophy that considers certain individual rights or duties as universal, regardless of the outcome; it is the philosophy embodied in the Consumer Bill of Rights and favored by consumer interest groups.

4-6 What is meant by social responsibility?
Answer: Social responsibility means that organizations are part of a larger society and are accountable to that society for their actions. It comprises three concepts: (1) profit responsibility–maximizing profits for the organization's owners or shareholders; (2) stakeholder responsibility–focusing on the obligations of the organization to those who can affect the achievement of its objectives; and (3) societal responsibility–focusing on the obligations of the organization to the preservation of the ecological environment and to the general public.

4-7 Marketing efforts to produce, promote, and reclaim environmentally sensitive products are called ________.
Answer: green marketing

4-8 What is a social audit?
Answer: A social audit is a systematic assessment of a firm's objectives, strategies, and performance in terms of social responsibility. It consists of five steps: (1) Recognition of a firm's social expectations and the rationale for engaging in social responsibility endeavors. (2) Identification of social responsibility causes or programs consistent with the company's mission. (3) Determination of organizational objectives and priorities for programs and activities it will undertake. (4) Specification of the type and amount of resources necessary to achieve social responsibility objectives. (5) Evaluation of social responsibility programs and activities undertaken and assessment of future involvement.

FOCUSING ON KEY TERMS

cause marketing p. 114
caveat emptor p. 106
code of ethics p. 108
Consumer Bill of Rights p. 106
economic espionage p. 107
ethics p. 104
green marketing p. 113
laws p. 104
moral idealism p. 109
social audit p. 114
social responsibility p. 112
sustainable development p. 115
sustainable marketing p. 113
triple bottom line p. 113
utilitarianism p. 110
whistle-blowers p. 109

APPLYING MARKETING KNOWLEDGE

1 What concepts of moral philosophy and social responsibility are applicable to the practices of Anheuser-Busch described in the introduction to this chapter? Why?

2 Five ethical situations were presented in this chapter: (*a*) a medical society's decision to set fee schedules, (*b*) the use of a computer program by auto dealers to arrange financing, (*c*) smoking in China, (*d*) downloading movies, and (*e*) the pricing of Cerdelga for the treatment of a rare genetic illness. Where would each of these situations fit in Figure 4-1?

3 The American Marketing Association Statement of Ethics shown in Figure 4-3 details the rights and duties of parties in the marketing exchange process. How do these rights and duties compare with the Consumer Bill of Rights?

4 Compare and contrast moral idealism and utilitarianism as alternative personal moral philosophies.

5 How would you evaluate Milton Friedman's view of the social responsibility of a firm?

6 The text lists several unethical practices of consumers. Can you name others? Why do you think consumers engage in unethical conduct?

7 Cause marketing programs have become popular. Describe two such programs with which you are familiar.

BUILDING YOUR MARKETING PLAN

Consider these potential stakeholders that may be affected in some way by the marketing plan on which you are working: shareholders (if any), suppliers, employees, customers, and society in general. For each group of stakeholders:

1 Identify what, if any, ethical and social responsibility issues might arise.
2 Describe, in one or two sentences, how your marketing plan addresses each potential issue.

VIDEO CASE 4 Toyota: Where the Future Is Available Today

Akio Toyoda, president of Toyota Motor Corporation, recently announced, "It's my goal to transition Toyota from an automobile company to a mobility company." What exactly does that mean? According to Jana Hartline, Mirai and Prius Prime marketing manager at Toyota, "It means that the days of traditional vehicle models are ending and the way we move is going to change in the future. We are looking at autonomous vehicles, we are looking at shared transportation, and we are looking at how we help people move across their living room and across the city. It's not just about vehicles anymore, it's about how you move people and that is what Toyota is focusing on." Welcome to the future; it's already here at Toyota!

VIDEO 4-3
Toyota Video Case
kerin.tv/15e/v4-3

THE COMPANY

Akio's grandfather, Kiichiro Toyoda, started the company in Japan as a manufacturer of weaving looms. Research on gasoline-powered engines led to the construction of an automobile manufacturing facility and the company's first vehicle, the "Toyopet." Subsequent vehicles included the Toyota Corolla, which is still one of the best-selling cars in the world and recently exceeded 44 million purchases in more than 150 countries. Other brands were also developed, including Lexus, Hino, Ranz, and Daihatsu.

Toyota grew to become one of the largest automobile manufacturers in the world, regularly vying for first place with Volkswagen. The company is ranked number five on *Fortune*'s list of the world's largest corporations, with sales of $254 billion and 369,000 employees. In addition, Toyota ranks ninth on the *Forbes* list of the world's most valuable brands.

What factors have contributed to the company's success? First, the Toyoda family advocates an inspiring corporate philosophy:

Seeking harmony between people, society, and the global environment, and sustainable development of society through manufacturing.

This philosophy has been supported by several statements of business values. They include The Toyota Way and The Toyota Effect.

The Toyota Way

"The corporate culture here at Toyota is guided by what we call the Toyota Way," explains Rommel Momen, Mirai manager at Toyota. "The Toyota Way is made up of two pillars, respect for people and continuous improvement," he adds. The two pillars are supported by five business practices: challenge, kaizen, genchi genbutsu, respect, and teamwork. Momen says kaizen means "continuously improving by getting suggestions from the end user and tweaking our product to make it better and better," and genchi genbutsu means to "go look and see, go to the source, talk to the consumer, and use your own eyes, feelings, and experiences to make a great and successful product." He adds, "We try to make sure that all parties are in agreement with a strategy so that we are more cohesive, work better as a team, and show respect for people."

The Toyota Effect

The Toyota Effect describes the company's approach to creating a positive impact. According to Hartline, "The Toyota Effect is Toyota's ability to use our resources and our know-how to better society, and people, and the planet." She explains, "For example, after Superstorm Sandy, the Food Bank was having a problem fulfilling the needs of all the displaced residents, so we implemented a Toyota production system to help them package and distribute food more efficiently." Another example of the Toyota Effect is Toyota's "Mothers of Invention" program which recognizes and supports women who are driving positive change in the world through innovation, entrepreneurship, and innovation. Toyota provides grants, networking opportunities, and access to intellectual capital as part of this program.

Today, as Toyota continues its emphasis on the environment and sustainability and transitions to a mobility company, there are a wide variety of new initiatives under

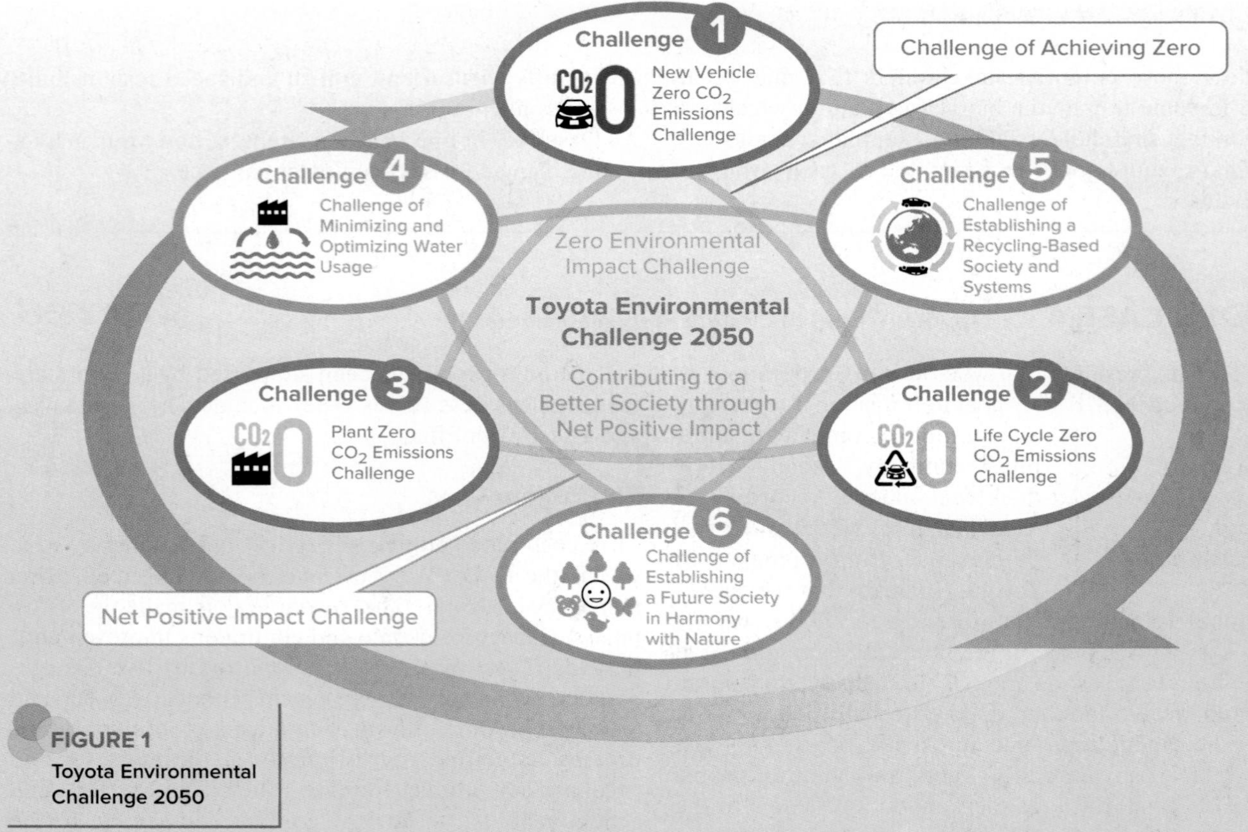

FIGURE 1
Toyota Environmental Challenge 2050

way. "We have a lot of business models that we are exploring," says Hartline, "from autonomous vehicles to ride sharing." She adds, "We have all kinds of things going on around the globe where we are looking at how people are going to move from A to B in the future."

TOYOTA'S ENVIRONMENTAL CHALLENGE 2050

To guide the company's environmental efforts, Akio Toyoda launched the Toyota Environmental Challenge 2050. This global initiative seeks to reduce negative factors associated with automobiles and create a net positive impact on society and the planet. The blueprint for the future is articulated in six specific actions and includes performance benchmarks through 2050 (see Figure 1). The actions are:

1. Eliminate almost all CO_2 emissions from new Toyota vehicles.
2. Eliminate all CO_2 emissions from the manufacturing of new Toyota vehicles.
3. Eliminate all CO_2 emissions from Toyota facilities, logistics, and processes.
4. Ensure all Toyota facilities conserve and protect water resources.
5. Ensure all Toyota facilities support a recycling-based society.
6. Ensure all Toyota facilities operate in harmony with nature.

"The first three incorporate having cars that emit zero emissions, and factories that build them without any emission, and ultimately the disposal of those vehicles with zero emissions," explains Momen. "The other three incorporate the use of more biodegradable materials, the use of less water, and the overall focus to be environmentally responsible." "Corporate social responsibility means being a great steward of not just the people who work for the company but for the world," he adds.

Toyota's past efforts at sustainability have provided a good start toward these goals. The Toyota Prius, a hybrid vehicle that combines an internal combustion engine and an electric motor, for example, is the longest and best-selling vehicle of its kind on the market. "Now Toyota has 30-plus hybrid models around the globe and we are considered the hybrid leader," Hartline says. Another example of Toyota's focus on sustainability includes its investment in zero-emission and hydrogen-fueled vehicles.

Hydrogen is the most abundant element in the universe and represents a future source of electricity that can be harnessed through fuel-cell technology without emitting greenhouse gases. Toyota's first hydrogen fuel-cell vehicle, the Mirai, literally means "the future."

THE MIRAI

"Mirai is the hydrogen fuel-cell vehicle that we have on sale today," says Momen, and it represents one step toward the Toyota Environmental Challenge goals. The Mirai has a 300-mile driving range and takes only 5 minutes to refuel at a hydrogen fueling station. The technology works by mixing oxygen from the surrounding air with hydrogen stored in a tank. Then the chemical reaction creates electricity, which is used to power an electric motor. The only by-product of the process is water, which drains out the tailpipe. Toyota has already sold more than 4,000 Mirai vehicles in California. The California Energy Commission seeks to have 5 million zero-emission vehicles, including hydrogen fuel-cell vehicles like the Mirai, on the road by 2030.

"What people don't realize about hydrogen fuel-cell technology is that when Toyota started developing the Prius, a group was also started at the same time to work on fuel-cell technology," says Hartline. "So, Toyota has been working on the development of fuel-cell technology for well over 20 years. We were looking at how we could bring this technology to market, how we could make a reliable and safe and convenient and affordable vehicle for the mass market, and that's what became the Toyota Mirai," she adds. Over the years of development, engineers have addressed issues of convenience, safety, and range to create a product that has everything consumers would expect from a Toyota vehicle.

Source: Toyota Motor Sales, U.S.A. Inc.

MARKETING THE MIRAI

The many unique aspects of fuel-cell technology make the marketing planning process for the Mirai unique. Hartline offers her perspective: "Mirai is really unique right now because we're at the very beginning of this technology. It's not like marketing a Camry or a Corolla because consumers know how they work. We are trying to educate consumers about the technology and about a particular vehicle. So we worked on the marketing plan for several years prior to launch. As we developed the campaign we wanted to understand who was going to purchase the vehicle, who were our competitors, and what were the unique aspects of the vehicle. The joke at Toyota was that nothing about Mirai is normal!"

At Toyota, marketing is organized in tiers designated to specific segments. Each segment typically has specific vehicles and a senior manager, a product manager, a product planner, and brand ambassadors. Much of the marketing function is centralized at Toyota headquarters where large-scale and national campaigns are managed. For example, Toyota recently ran ads during the Super Bowl that support its sponsorship of the Olympics and Paralympics. You might remember some of the ads, which feature taglines such as, "Start Your Impossible" and "Let's Go Places." Some marketing activities are also coordinated by smaller groups placed at regional locations.

Joanie Swearingen, a product planner in Vehicle Marketing and Communications at Toyota, describes some of the specific marketing activities she manages. "As a product planner," she says, "I'm interfacing with multiple event and dealer teams daily, using e-mail and our database management platform which consolidates all of our audience targeting." Swearingen adds, "So, integrated marketing is what I do each and every day." The integrated marketing programs include traditional advertising, such as the national television advertising campaigns, and many forms of social and online media. Swearingen says, "We see social media as part of online paid media," and explains, "we like to think of it holistically because the customer is seeing our communications holistically." What is her secret to success as a product planner? "I think to be successful in marketing you have to be comfortable getting uncomfortable," she reveals.

THE FUTURE OF MOBILITY AT TOYOTA

The future has many paths for Toyota. For example, the company is expanding the application of its zero-emission fuel-cell technology to heavy-duty trucks, buses, and power stations. Toyota has also invested in ride-sharing companies Uber and Grab, a self-driving car company, and the Partner Robot Group, which is developing products to assist people with visual impairments. "With all of these initiatives that we have at Toyota to try and make the environment cleaner and greener and better for everyone, we're excited and very proud to be part of this company," says Momen. Similarly, Swearingen says, "I'm really excited that I get to be part of the future and that this 'mobility for all' is just the starting point of something really great." And Hartline confirms that "Toyota is truly the mobility company for the future!"[43]

Questions

1 Describe Toyota's transition from an automobile company to a mobility company.

2 How does Toyota's corporate philosophy relate to the concepts of profit responsibility, stakeholder responsibility, and societal responsibility?

3 How does Toyota's Mirai fit with the goals of the Challenge 2050 initiative?

4 What new mobility products and services is Toyota considering for the future? What activities would you recommend for Toyota as it prepares for the future?

Chapter Notes

1. www.anheuser-busch.com, downloaded January 15, 2019; "Anheuser-Busch Announces U.S. 2025 Sustainability Goals," Anheuser-*Busch News Release,* April 18, 2018; and "America's Most Admired Companies," *Fortune,* February 1, 2019, pp. 75ff.
2. Bruce Weinstein, "Is There a Difference between Ethics and Morality in Business?" *Forbes.com,* February 18, 2018.
3. Verne E. Henderson, "The Ethical Side of Enterprise," *Sloan Management Review,* Spring 1982, pp. 37–47. See also Joseph L. Badaracco Jr., *Defining Moments: When Managers Must Choose between Right and Right* (Boston: Harvard Business School Press, 1997).
4. Ron Carucci, "Why Ethical People Make Unethical Choices," *hbr.org,* December 16, 2016.
5. Andrew Martin, "The Chinese Government Is Getting Rich Selling Cigarettes," *Bloombergbusinessweek.com,* December 11, 2014; Roger O. Crockett, "Hauling in the Hollywood Hackers," *Businessweek,* May 15, 2006, pp. 80–82; Ray O. Werner, "Marketing and the Supreme Court in Transition, 1982–1984," *Journal of Marketing,* Summer 1985, pp. 97–105; and Jane Bryant Quinn, "Computer Program Deceives Consumers," *Dallas Morning News,* March 2, 1998, p. B3.
6. *The 2016 National Business Ethics Survey* (Washington, DC: Ethics Resource Center, 2017); "America's 43 Most and Least Trusted Professions,"*msn.com,* downloaded December 28, 2018.
7. See, for example, Linda K. Trevino and Katherine A. Nelson, *Managing Business Ethics: Straight Talk about How to Get It Right,* 7th ed. (New York: John Wiley & Sons, 2016).
8. Thomas Donaldson, "Values in Tension: Ethics Away from Home," *Harvard Business Review,* September–October 1996, pp. 48–62.
9. Ethisphere Institute, "World's Most Ethical Companies," www.ethisphere.com, accessed January 3, 2018.
10. These statistics were obtained from Recording Industry Association of America (www.riaa.com), Motion Picture Association of America (www.mpaa.com), and the Business Software Alliance (www.bsa.org).
11. June Jamich Parsons and Dan Oja, *Computer Concepts 2010* (Florence, KY: Cengage Publishing, 2009), p. 171.
12. Vern Terpstra and David H. Kenneth, *The Cultural Environment of International Business,* 3rd ed. (Cincinnati: South-Western Publishing, 1991), p. 12.
13. "Samsung Galaxy Note 7 Recall by the Numbers," *usatoday.com,* October 12, 2016.
14. "Child Web Privacy Law Gets Updated," *The Wall Street Journal,* December 20, 2012, pp. B1, B2; and "YouTube Agrees to Bolster Children's Privacy," *The Wall Street Journal,* September 5, 2019, pp. B1, B4.
15. For an extensive examination of slotting fees, see Paul N. Bloom, Gregory T. Gundlach, and Joseph P. Cannon, "Slotting Allowances and Fees: Schools of Thought and Views of Practicing Managers," *Journal of Marketing,* April 2000, pp. 92–109. Also see K. Sudhir and Vithala R. Rao, "Do Slotting Allowances Enhance Efficiency or Hinder Competition?" *Journal of Marketing Research* (May 2006), pp. 137–55.
16. "Report: Cybercrime and Espionage Costs $445 Billion Annually," www.washingtonpost.com, accessed January 2, 2017.
17. For a detailed description of this episode, see Zachary Crockett, "The Botched Coca-Cola Heist," http://thehustle.co/coca-cola-stolen-recipe, April 28, 2018.
18. "Global Cost of Corruption at Least 5 Percent of World Gross Domestic Product," United Nations press release, September 10, 2018.
19. United Technologies Ethics Code, accessed March 1, 2019.
20. "Coca-Cola Unit Head Resigns after Rigged Test," www.forbes.com, downloaded August 25, 2003.
21. *Global Business Ethics Survey: The State of Ethics & Compliance in the Workplace* (Arlington, VA: Ethics & Compliance Initiative, March 2018).
22. *Global Business Ethics Survey.*
23. "Scotchgard Working Out Recent Stain on Its Business," www.mercurynews.com, downloaded June 22, 2003; and "3M Will Pay $850 Million in Minnesota Water Pollution Case," *money.cnn.com,* February 21, 2018.
24. James Q. Wilson, "Adam Smith on Business Ethics," *California Management Review,* Fall 1989, pp. 57–72.
25. Alix M. Freedman, "Bad Reaction: Nestlé's Bid to Crash Baby-Formula Market in U.S. Stirs a Row," *The Wall Street Journal,* February 16, 1989, pp. A1, A6; and Alix Freedman, "Nestlé to Drop Claim on Label of Its Formula," *The Wall Street Journal,* March 13, 1989, p. B5. For an update on this topic, see "FTC Challenges Gerber Baby Formula Claims in Court," www.ftc.gov, October 30, 2014.
26. Milton Friedman, *Capitalism and Freedom* (University of Chicago Press, 1962); and Harvey S. James and Farhad Rassekh, "Smith, Friedman, and Self-Interest in Ethical Society," *Business Ethics Quarterly,* July 2000, pp. 659–74.
27. "FDA Approves Sanofi's Gaucher Disease Drug Cerdelga," www.news.yahoo, August 19, 2014.
28. "VW Executive Is Arrested in U.S.," *The Wall Street Journal,* January 10, 2017, pp. B1, B6; and "Everything You Need to Know about the VW Diesel-Emissions Scandal," www.caranddriver.com, December 22, 2016.
29. Quote by Mathias Muller, "Volkswagen Faces Up to Penalties," *The Wall Street Journal,* March 11–12, 2017, pp. B1, B2; and "Guide to the Volkswagen Emissions Recall," www.consumerreports.com, January 6, 2016.
30. Shelby Hunt, "Strategic Marketing, Sustainability, the Triple Bottom Line, and Resource-Advantage (R-A) Theory," *AMS Review,* June 2017, pp. 52–66.
31. "3M 2018 Sustainability Report," downloaded May 25, 2019; "Shades of Green," *Advertising Age,* March 4, 2019, pp. 18ff; and "Change the World," *Fortune,* September 25, 2018, pp. 74–89.

32. "Achieving Environmental Focus with ISO 14000," *ISO Focus*, November–December 2018, pp. 22–29.

33. For a seminal discussion on this topic, see P. Rajan Varadarajan and Anil Menon, "Cause-Related Marketing: A Coalignment of Marketing Strategy and Corporate Philanthropy," *Journal of Marketing*, July 1988, pp. 58–74.

34. "Even as Cause Marketing Grows, 83 Percent of Consumers Still Want to See More," press release, Cone LLC, September 15, 2016; and "Second Annual National Box Tops for Education Week Kicks Off Coast-to-Coast Collection Drive," General Mills News Release, September 17, 2018.

35. These steps are adapted from J. J. Corson and G. A. Steiner, *Measuring Business's Social Performance: The Corporate Social Audit* (New York: Committee for Economic Development, 1974). See also William David Chandler, *Strategic Corporate Social Responsibility* (Thousand Oaks, CA: Sage Publications, 2006).

36. "The Toll of Cheap Clothing," *Bloomberg Businessweek*, October 31–November 6, 2016, pp. 10–11.

37. For a thorough assessment of sustainable marketing, see M. B. Lunde, "Sustainability in Marketing: A Systematic Review Unifying 20 Years of Theoretical and Substantive Contributions (1997–2016)," *Academy of Marketing Science Review*, December 2018, pp. 85–110.

38. This discussion is based on Wayne D. Hoyer, Deborah J. Mac-Innis, and Rik Pieters, *Consumer Behavior,* 7th ed. (New York: Houghton Mifflin, 2018), pp. 535–37; "Shop Online? You've Likely Bought Fake Goods," *Dallas Morning News*, May 16, 2019, p. 6B; *2017 Consumer Returns in the Retail Industry* (New York: National Retail Federation, 2018); and "When Lost Sales Have Nothing to Do with Lost Customers," *emarketer.com*, November 16, 2017.

39. Roger O. Crockett, "Hauling in the Hollywood Hackers," *BusinessWeek,* May 15, 2006, pp. 80–82.

40. Katherine White, David J. Hardisty, and Rishad Habib, "The Elusive Green Consumer," *Harvard Business Review*, July–August, 2019, pp. 125–33; and Hal Conick, "How Brands Can Help Consumers Green Up Their Act," *Marketing News*, August 2019, pp. 42–51.

41. Pascual Berrone, "Getting Beyond Greewashing," *Strategy + Business*, Winter 2018, pp. 21–32.

42. Jack Neff, "FTC Green Guidelines May Leave Marketers Red-Faced," *Advertising Age,* August 23, 2010, pp. 1, 21.

43. Toyota: This case was written by Steven Hartley and Roger Kerin. Sources: Interviews with Toyota executives Jana Hartline, Rommel Momen, and Joanie Swearingen; "Toyoda, President and Member of the Board of Directors, Toyota Motor Corporation: 2018 CES Remarks," Toyota press release, January 8, 2018; Dave Leggett, "Toyota Surpasses 3,000 Mirai Hydrogen Fuel Cell Vehicle Sales in California," *Just-Auto.com,* January 27, 2018, p. 1; Darrell Etherington, "Toyota's Mobility Business Shifts into High Gear at CES," *techcrunch.com*, January 8, 2018; Robert Klara, "Why Toyota, the Car Company, Now Wants to Be Known More as a 'Mobility' Company," *Adweek,* November 16, 2017; Chris Martin and Lynn Doan, "This Miracle Fuel Has a Few Problems," *Bloomberg Businessweek,* March 12, 2018, pp. 23–25; "Fortune Global 500," *Fortune,* August 1, 2017, p. F1; Kurt Bandenhausen, "The World's Most Valuable Brands," *Forbes,* May 23, 2018; Brian Bremner, Craig Trudell, and Yuki Hagiwara, "Remaking Toyota," *Bloomberg Businessweek,* January 14, 2015; "Toyota Corolla: World's Most Popular Car," Toyota Global Newsroom, https://newsroom.toyota.co.jp/en/detail/62516/, September 5, 2013.

Chapter 5 Understanding Consumer Behavior

LEARNING OBJECTIVES

After reading this chapter you should be able to:

LO 5-1 Describe the stages in the consumer purchase decision process.

LO 5-2 Distinguish among three variations of the consumer purchase decision process: extended, limited, and routine problem solving.

LO 5-3 Identify the major psychological influences on consumer behavior.

LO 5-4 Identify the major sociocultural influences on consumer behavior.

Enlightened Carmakers Know What Custom(h)ers and Influenc(h)ers Value

Who makes 60 percent of new-car-buying decisions? Who influences 87 percent of new-car-buying decisions? Women. Yes, women.

Women are a driving force in the U.S. automobile industry. Enlightened carmakers have hired women designers, engineers, and marketing executives to better understand and satisfy this valuable car buyer and influencer. What have they learned? While car price, reliability, and technology are important, women and men think and feel differently about car features and key elements of the new-car-buying decision process and experience.

- *The sense of styling*. Women and men care about styling. For men, styling is more about a car's exterior lines and accents or "curb appeal." Women are more interested in interior design and finishes. Designs that fit their proportions, provide good visibility, offer ample storage space, and make for effortless parking are particularly important.
- *The need for speed*. Both sexes want speed, but for different reasons. Men think about how many seconds it takes to get from 0 to 60 miles per hour. Women want to feel secure that the car has enough acceleration to outrun an 18-wheeler trying to pass them on a freeway entrance ramp.
- *The substance of safety*. Safety for men is about features that help avoid an accident, such as antilock brakes and responsive steering. For women, safety is about features that help to survive an accident. These features include passenger airbags and reinforced side panels.
- *The shopping experience*. The new-car-buying experience differs between men and women in important ways. Generally, men decide up front what car they want and set out alone to find it. By contrast, women approach it as an intelligence-gathering expedition. Referred to as *CROPing*, women shoppers look for *CR*edible *OP*inions. They actively seek information and postpone a purchase decision until all options have been evaluated. Women, more frequently than men, visit auto-buying websites, read car-comparison articles, and scan car advertisements. Still, recommendations of friends and relatives matter most to women. Women typically shop three dealerships before making a purchase decision—one more than men.

Carmakers have learned that women, more than men, dislike the car-buying experience—specifically, the experience of dealing with car salespeople. In contrast to many male car buyers, women do not typically revel in the gamesmanship of car buying. "Men get all excited about going out to buy a car and talk about how they're going to one-up the salesman and get a great deal," says Anne Fleming, president of

Whisson/Jordan/Getty Images

www.women-drivers.com, a consumer ratings site. "I've never heard or seen any comments from women like that." In particular, women dread the price negotiations that are often involved in buying a new car. Not surprisingly, about half of women car buyers take a man with them to finalize the terms of sale.[1]

This chapter examines **consumer behavior**, the actions a person takes in purchasing and using products and services, including the mental and social processes that come before and after these actions. This chapter shows how the behavioral sciences help answer questions such as why people choose one product or brand over another, how they make these choices, and how companies use this knowledge to provide value to consumers.

CONSUMER PURCHASE DECISION PROCESS AND EXPERIENCE

LO 5-1
Describe the stages in the consumer purchase decision process.

Behind the visible act of making a purchase lies an important decision process and consumer experience that must be investigated. The stages a buyer passes through in making choices about which products and services to buy is the **purchase decision process**. This process has the five stages shown in Figure 5-1: (1) problem recognition, (2) information search, (3) alternative evaluation, (4) purchase decision, and (5) postpurchase behavior.

FIGURE 5–1
The purchase decision process consists of five stages.

The experience a consumer seeks (or avoids) and enjoys (or endures) at each stage of the purchase decision process often dictates whether she or he will continue or discontinue to engage in the buying process. Equally relevant, a consumer's favorable or unfavorable experience has important marketing consequences. Experience can influence consumer satisfaction, consumer loyalty, and consumer willingness to speak positively or negatively about a company, product, service, or brand.

Problem Recognition: Perceiving a Need

Problem recognition, the initial step in the purchase decision process, is perceiving a difference between a person's ideal and actual situations big enough to trigger a decision.[2] This can be as simple as finding an empty milk carton in the refrigerator; noting, as a first-year college student, that your high school clothes are not in the style that other students are wearing; or realizing that your notebook computer may not be working properly.

In marketing, advertisements or salespeople can activate a consumer's decision process by showing the shortcomings of competing (or currently owned) products or brands. For instance, an advertisement for a new-generation smartphone could stimulate problem recognition because it emphasizes "maximum use from one device."

Information Search: Seeking Value

After recognizing a problem, a consumer begins to search for information, the next stage in the purchase decision process. First, you may scan your memory for previous experiences with products or brands.[3] This action is called *internal search*. For frequently purchased products such as shampoo and conditioner, this may be enough.

In other cases, a consumer may undertake an *external search* for information.[4] This is needed when past experience or knowledge is insufficient, the perceived risk of making a wrong purchase decision is high, and the cost of gathering information is low. The primary sources of external information are (1) *personal sources*, such as relatives and friends, as well as social networking websites that the consumer trusts; (2) *public sources*, including various product-rating organizations such as *Consumer Reports*, government agencies, and TV "consumer programs"; and (3) *marketer-dominated sources*, such as information from sellers including advertising, company websites, salespeople, and point-of-purchase displays in stores.

Suppose you are considering buying a new smartphone. You will probably tap several of these information sources: friends and relatives, advertisements, brand and company websites, and stores carrying these phones (for demonstrations). You also might study the comparative evaluation of selected smartphones from independent rating agencies, such as the one shown in Figure 5–2.[5]

Alternative Evaluation: Assessing Value

The alternative evaluation stage clarifies the information gathered by (1) suggesting criteria to use for the purchase, (2) yielding brand names that might meet the criteria, and (3) developing consumer value perceptions. Given only the information shown in Figure 5–2, which selection criteria would you use in buying a smartphone? Would you use price, phone display, audio quality, text messaging, web capability, camera image quality, battery life, or some other combination of these or other criteria?

Common Selection Criteria	Apple 11 Pro	HTC U12+	LG V50	Moto Z4	Samsung Galaxy S10 5G
Retail price (without contract)	$999	$790	$850	$500	$1,300
Phone display	★★★	★★★	★★★	★★★	★★★
Audio quality	★★	★★	★★	★	★★
Text messaging	★★★	★★★	★★★	★★★	★★★
Web capability	★★★	★★★	★★★	★★★	★★★
Camera quality	★★★	★	★★	★★★	★★
Battery	★★	★★	★★	★★	★★
Composite smartphone evaluations by testing organizations	★★★ Superior	★★ Above average	★ Average		

(Column group heading: Brand and Model Name)

FIGURE 5–2
Common consumer selection criteria for the evaluation of smartphones.

For some of you, the information provided may be inadequate because it does not contain all the factors you might consider when evaluating smartphones. These factors are a consumer's *evaluative criteria*, which represent both the objective attributes of a brand (such as display) and the subjective ones (such as prestige) you use to compare different products and brands.[6] Firms try to identify and capitalize on both types of criteria to create the best value for the money paid by you and other consumers. These criteria are often displayed in advertisements.

Consumers often have several criteria for evaluating brands. Knowing this, companies seek to identify the most important evaluative criteria that consumers use when comparing brands. For example, among the seven criteria shown in Figure 5–2, suppose you initially use three in considering smartphones: (1) a retail price under $800, (2) superior text messaging, and (3) superior web capability. These criteria establish the brands in your *consideration set*—the group of brands a consumer considers acceptable from among all the brands in the product class of which he or she is aware.[7]

Your evaluative criteria result in two brands/models in your consideration set: the HTC U12 Plus and the Moto Z4. If the brand alternatives are equally attractive based on your original criteria, you might expand your list of desirable features. For example, you might decide that camera and audio quality are also important and compare the alternatives based on those criteria as well.

Purchase Decision: Buying Value

Having examined the alternatives in the consideration set, you are almost ready to make a purchase decision. Two choices remain: (1) from whom to buy and (2) when to buy. For a product like a smartphone, the information search process probably involved visiting retail stores, seeing different brands advertised on television, the Internet, and newspapers, and viewing a smartphone on a seller's website. The choice of which seller to buy from will depend on such considerations as the terms of sale, your past experience buying from the seller, and the return policy. Often a purchase decision involves a simultaneous evaluation of both product attributes and seller characteristics. For example, you might choose the second-most preferred smartphone brand at a store or website with a liberal refund and return policy versus the most preferred brand from a seller with more conservative policies.

Shoppers routinely browse online and shop retail stores, often during the same shopping trip.
g-stockstudio/Shutterstock

Deciding when to buy is determined by a number of factors. For instance, you might buy sooner if one of your preferred brands is on sale or its manufacturer offers a rebate. Other factors such as the store atmosphere, pleasantness or ease of the shopping experience, salesperson assistance, time pressure, and financial circumstances could also affect whether a purchase decision is made now or postponed.[8]

Use of the Internet to gather information, evaluate alternatives, and make buying decisions adds a technological dimension to the consumer purchase decision process and buying experience. For example, 45 percent of consumers with price comparison smartphone apps routinely compare prices for identical products across different sellers at the point of purchase prior to making a purchase decision.[9]

Postpurchase Behavior: Realizing Value

After buying a product, the consumer compares it with his or her expectations and is either satisfied or dissatisfied. If the consumer is dissatisfied, marketers must determine whether the product was deficient or consumer expectations were too high. Product deficiency may require a design change. If expectations are too high, a company's advertising or the salesperson may have oversold the product's features and benefits.

Sensitivity to a customer's consumption or use experience is extremely important in a consumer's value perception. For example, research on telephone and Internet services provided by Sprint, AT&T, and others indicates that satisfaction or dissatisfaction affects consumer value perceptions.[10] Studies show that satisfaction or dissatisfaction affects consumer communications and repeat-purchase behavior. Satisfied buyers tell three other people about their experience. In contrast, about 90 percent of dissatisfied buyers will not buy a product again and will complain to nine people.[11] Satisfied buyers also tend to buy from the same seller each time a purchase occasion arises. The financial impact of repeat-purchase behavior is significant, as described in the Marketing Matters box.[12]

Firms such as General Electric (GE), Johnson & Johnson, Coca-Cola, and British Airways focus attention on postpurchase behavior to maximize customer satisfaction and retention. These firms, among many others, now provide toll-free telephone numbers, offer liberal return and refund policies, and engage in extensive staff training to handle complaints, answer questions, record suggestions, and solve consumer problems. For example, GE has a database that stores 750,000 answers regarding about 8,500 of its models in 120 product lines to handle 3 million calls annually. Such efforts produce positive postpurchase communications among consumers and foster relationship building between sellers and buyers.

Often a consumer is faced with two or more highly attractive alternatives, such as the choice between the Moto Z4 and an HTC U12 Plus. If you choose the Moto Z4, you might think, "Should I have purchased the HTC U12 Plus?" This feeling of postpurchase psychological tension or anxiety is called *cognitive dissonance*. To alleviate it, consumers often attempt to applaud themselves for making the right choice. So after your purchase, you may seek information to confirm your choice by asking friends questions like, "Don't you like my new phone?" or by reading ads for the brand you have chosen. You might even look for negative features about the brands you didn't buy and decide that the HTC U12 Plus smartphone did not feel right. Firms often use ads or follow-up calls from salespeople in this postpurchase behavior stage to reassure buyers that they made the right decision. For many years, Buick ran an advertising campaign with the message, "Aren't you really glad you bought a Buick?"

Marketing Matters

Customer Value

How Much Is a Satisfied Customer Worth?

Customer satisfaction and experience underlie the marketing concept. But how much is a satisfied customer worth?

This question has prompted firms to calculate the financial value of a satisfied customer over time. Frito-Lay, for example, estimates that the average loyal consumer in the southwestern United States eats 21 pounds of snack chips a year. At a price of $2.50 a pound, this customer spends $52.50 annually on the company's snacks such as Lay's and Ruffles potato chips, Doritos and Tostitos tortilla chips, and Fritos corn chips. Exxon estimates that a loyal customer will spend $500 annually for its branded gasoline, not including candy, snacks, oil, or repair services purchased at its gasoline stations. Kimberly-Clark reports that a loyal customer will buy 6.7 boxes of its Kleenex tissues each year and will spend $994 on facial tissues over 60 years, in today's dollars.

These calculations have focused marketers' attention on their customers' (1) buying experience, (2) satisfaction, and (3) retention. Consider General Motors (GM), the maker of Cadillac, Chevrolet, Buick, and GMC brands. GM estimates that a retail customer is worth $276,000 over a lifetime of buying cars (11 or more), parts, and service. GM's customer retention rate is 69 percent. Also, GM estimates that its company revenue increases $700 million for every percentage point that sales retention increases.

rvlsoft/Shutterstock

This calculation is not unique to General Motors. Research shows that a 5 percent improvement in customer retention can increase a company's profits by 70 to 80 percent.

Consumer Involvement Affects Problem Solving

LO 5-2
Distinguish among three variations of the consumer purchase decision process: extended, limited, and routine problem solving.

Sometimes consumers don't engage in the five-stage purchase decision process. Instead, they skip or minimize one or more stages depending on the level of **involvement**, the personal, social, and economic significance of the purchase to the consumer.[13] High-involvement purchase occasions typically have at least one of three characteristics: The item to be purchased (1) is expensive, (2) can have serious personal consequences, or (3) could reflect on one's social image. For these occasions, consumers engage in extensive information searches, consider many product attributes and brands, form attitudes, and participate in word-of-mouth communication. Low-involvement purchases, such as toothpaste and soap, barely involve most of us, but audio and video systems and automobiles are very involving.

There are three general variations in the consumer purchase decision process based on consumer involvement and product knowledge. Figure 5–3 shows some of the important differences between the three problem-solving variations.

Extended Problem Solving In extended problem solving, each of the five stages of the consumer purchase decision process is used and considerable time and effort are devoted to the search for external information and the identification and evaluation of alternatives. Several brands are in the consideration set, and these are evaluated on many attributes. Extended problem solving exists in high-involvement purchase situations for items such as automobiles and audio systems.

Limited Problem Solving In limited problem solving, consumers typically seek some information or rely on a friend to help them evaluate alternatives. Several brands might be

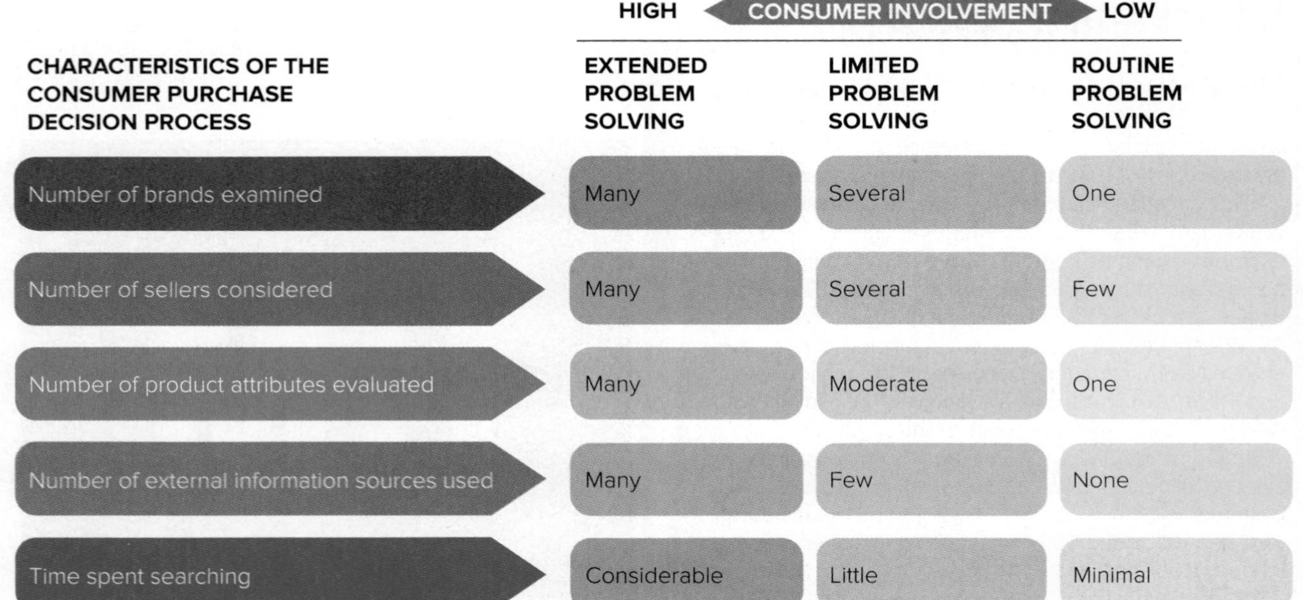

HIGH
CONSUMER INVOLVEMENT
LOW
CHARACTERISTICS OF THE CONSUMER PURCHASE DECISION PROCESS
EXTENDED PROBLEM SOLVING
LIMITED PROBLEM SOLVING
ROUTINE PROBLEM SOLVING
Number of brands examined
Many
Several
One
Number of sellers considered
Many
Several
Few
Number of product attributes evaluated
Many
Moderate
One
Number of external information sources used
Many
Few
None
Time spent searching
Considerable
Little
Minimal

FIGURE 5–3
Comparison of problem-solving variations: extended problem solving, limited problem solving, and routine problem solving.

evaluated using a moderate number of attributes. Limited problem solving is appropriate for purchase situations that do not merit a great deal of time or effort, such as choosing a toaster or a restaurant for lunch.

Routine Problem Solving For products such as table salt and milk, consumers recognize a problem, make a decision, and spend little effort seeking external information and evaluating alternatives. The purchase process for such items is virtually a habit and typifies low-involvement decision making. Routine problem solving is typically the case for low-priced, frequently purchased grocery products.

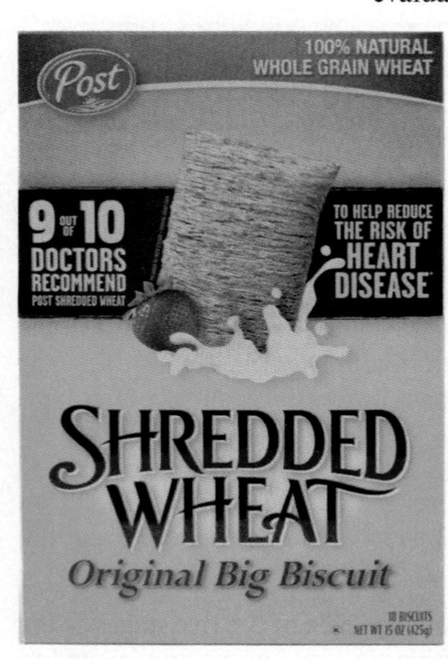

What is a behavioral explanation for why Post Cereals prominently displays heart-healthy claims on its Shredded Wheat brand packaging?
Mike Hruby/McGraw-Hill Education

Consumer Involvement and Marketing Strategy Low and high consumer involvement have important implications for marketing strategy. If a company markets a low-involvement product and its brand is a market leader, attention is placed on (1) maintaining product quality, (2) avoiding stockout situations so that buyers don't substitute a competing brand, and (3) using repetitive advertising messages that reinforce a consumer's knowledge or assure buyers they made the right choice. Market challengers have a different task. They must break buying habits by using free samples, coupons, and rebates to encourage trial of their brand. Advertising messages will focus on getting their brand into a consumer's consideration set. For example, Campbell's V8 vegetable juice advertising message—"Could've Had a V8"—was targeted at consumers who routinely considered only fruit juices and soft drinks for purchase. Marketers can also link their brand attributes with high-involvement issues. Post Cereals does this by linking consumption of its whole grain cereals with improved heart health and protection against major diseases.

Marketers of high-involvement products know that their consumers constantly seek and process information about objective and subjective brand attributes, form evaluative criteria, rate product attributes of various brands, and combine these ratings for an overall brand evaluation—like the purchase decision process described in the smartphone example. Market leaders ply consumers with product information through advertising and personal selling and use social media to create online experiences for their company or brand. Market challengers capitalize on this behavior through comparative advertising that focuses on existing product attributes and often introduce novel evaluative criteria for judging competing brands. Challengers also benefit from Internet search engines such as Microsoft Bing and Google that assist buyers of high-involvement products.

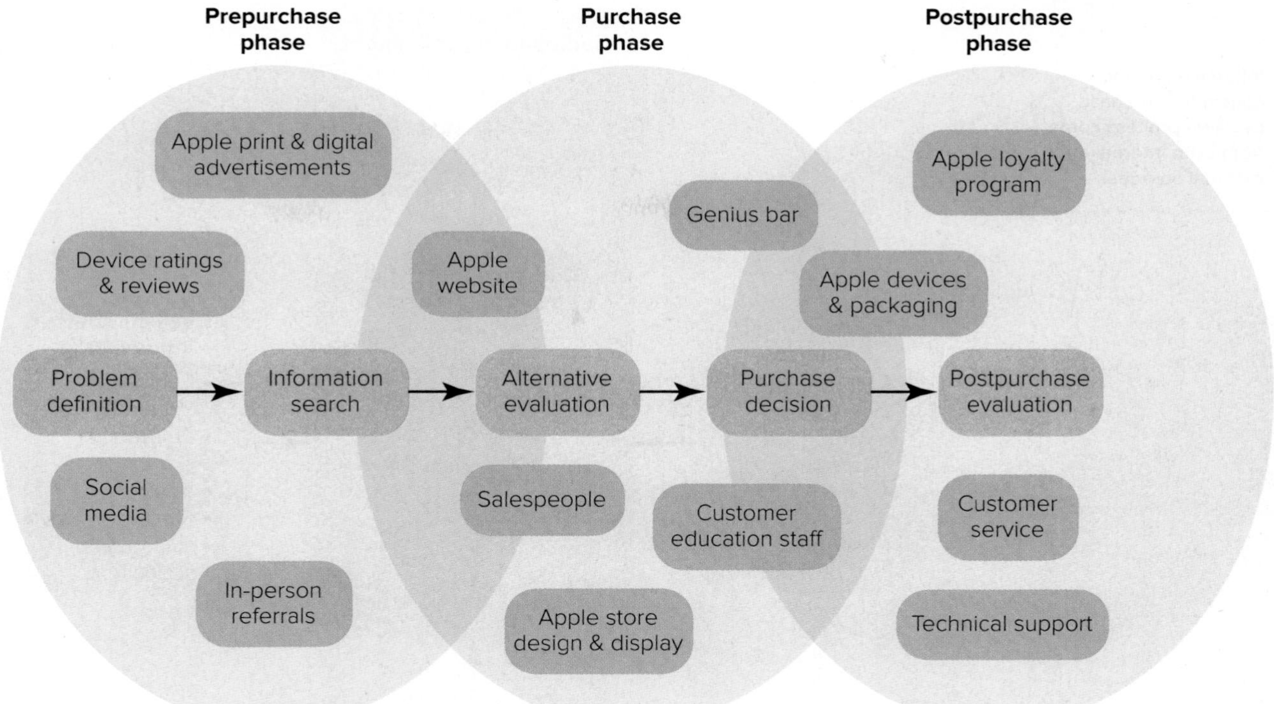

FIGURE 5–4
Apple consumer journey map and consumer touchpoints for electronic devices sold in Apple stores.

Situational Influences That Affect Purchase Decisions

Often the purchase situation will affect the purchase decision process. Five *situational influences* have an impact on the purchase decision process: (1) the purchase task, (2) social surroundings, (3) physical surroundings, (4) temporal effects, and (5) antecedent states.[14]

The purchase task is the reason for engaging in the decision. The search for information and the evaluation of alternatives may differ depending on whether the purchase is a gift, which often involves social visibility, or for the buyer's own use. Social surroundings, including the other people present when a purchase decision is made, may also affect what is purchased. Consumers accompanied by children buy about 40 percent more items than consumers shopping by themselves. Physical surroundings such as décor, music, and crowding in retail stores may alter how purchase decisions are made. Temporal effects such as time of day or the amount of time available will influence where consumers have breakfast and lunch and what is ordered. Finally, antecedent states, which include the consumer's mood or the amount of cash on hand, can influence purchase behavior and choice. For example, consumers with credit cards purchase more than those with cash or debit cards.

Putting the Purchase Decision Process into Practice: Consumer Touchpoints and Consumer Journey Maps

Marketing practitioners today focus on the complete consumer purchase decision process and consumer experience.[15] Their objective is ambitious: To be present at those moments in time and place that most influence what, when, where, and how purchase decisions are triggered, information is sought and evaluated, purchase transactions are made and services are delivered, and postpurchase outcomes affect later consumer behavior. Marketers call these moments in time and place "moments of truth" because each can form or change a consumer's impression about a particular product, service, or brand.

Marketers view the purchase decision process and consumer experience through the lens of consumer touchpoints and consumer journey maps (see Figure 5-4). **Consumer touchpoints** are a marketer's product, service, or brand points of contact with a consumer from start to

FIGURE 5–5
Influences on the consumer purchase decision process come from both internal and external sources.

finish in the purchase decision process. For example, consumers may see a company's offerings online, in print and digital advertisements, or in a catalog; shop for a company's products online or in a store; or call a company's customer service or technical support department. But consumer touchpoints are not always controlled by a company. Independent rating and review services and conversations with other consumers, including social media, are also touchpoints if they include reference to a company's products, services, or brands. Not surprisingly, social media posts are tracked by many marketers. Collectively, touchpoints create a consumer experience whenever consumers and companies engage to exchange information, provide service, or handle transactions.

A **consumer journey map** is a visual representation of all the touchpoints for a consumer who comes into contact with a company's products, services, or brands before, during, and after a purchase. Figure 5–4 illustrates a consumer journey map for electronic devices sold by Apple in its stores, such as smartphones, computers, and wearable technology. Representative touchpoints are shown along with the underlying consumer purchase decision process stages. A consumer journey map also shows what, when, and where different touchpoints play a central role before, during, and after a purchase. In this regard, consumer journey maps can locate and illuminate "pain points" that detract from a consumer experience. A website that is difficult to navigate is a pain point, with severe consequences. Research indicates that consumers will abandon a website that is difficult to navigate after eight seconds.

Figure 5–5 shows the many influences that affect the consumer purchase decision process. In addition to situational influences, the decision to buy a product also involves and is affected by important psychological and sociocultural influences. These two influences are covered in the remainder of this chapter. Marketing mix influences are described later in Part 4 of the book. Chapter 17 elaborates on consumer behavior in the context of online information search and buying.

LEARNING REVIEW

5-1. What is the first stage in the consumer purchase decision process?

5-2. The brands a consumer considers buying out of the set of brands in a product class of which the consumer is aware are collectively called the ____________________.

5-3. What is the term for postpurchase anxiety?

PSYCHOLOGICAL INFLUENCES ON CONSUMER BEHAVIOR

LO 5-3
Identify the major psychological influences on consumer behavior.

Psychology helps marketers understand why and how consumers behave as they do. In particular, psychological concepts such as motivation and personality; perception; learning; values, beliefs, and attitudes; and lifestyle are useful for interpreting buying processes and directing marketing efforts.

Consumer Motivation and Personality

Motivation and personality are two familiar psychological concepts that have specific meanings and marketing implications. These concepts are closely related and are used to explain why people do some things and not others.

VIDEO 5-1
Match.com
kerin.tv/15e/v5-1

Motivation

Motivation is the energizing force that stimulates behavior to satisfy a need. Because consumer needs are the focus of the marketing concept, marketers try to arouse these needs.

An individual's needs are boundless. People possess physiological needs for basics such as water, shelter, and food. They also have learned needs, including self-esteem, achievement, and affection. Psychologists point out that these needs may be hierarchical; that is, once physiological needs are met, people seek to satisfy their learned needs.

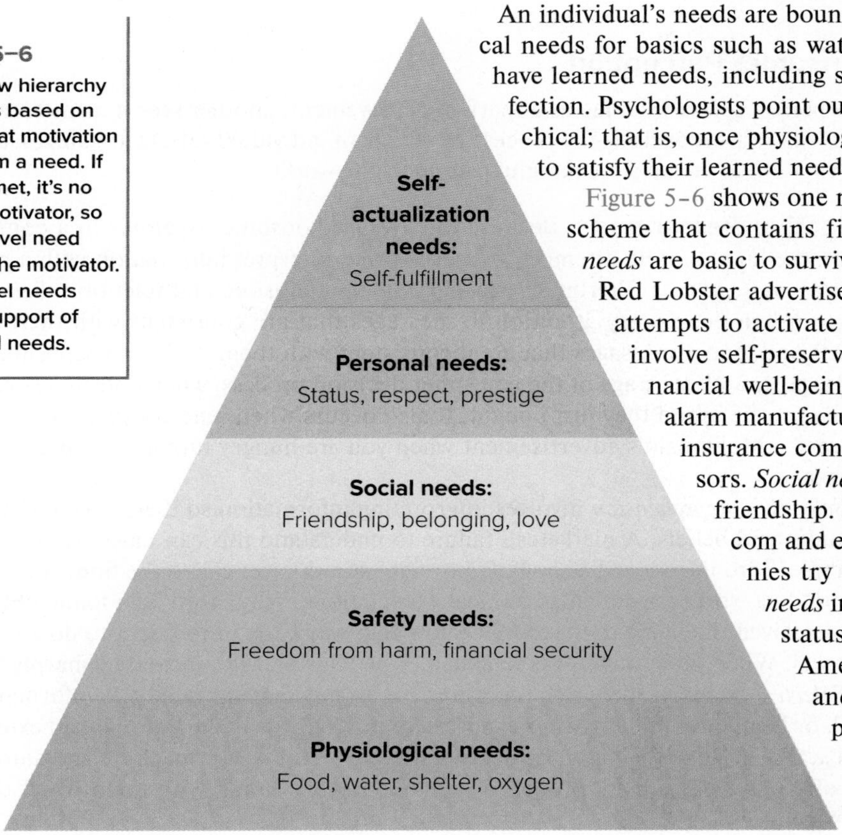

FIGURE 5–6
The Maslow hierarchy of needs is based on the idea that motivation comes from a need. If a need is met, it's no longer a motivator, so a higher-level need becomes the motivator. Higher-level needs demand support of lower-level needs.

Self-actualization needs: Self-fulfillment

Personal needs: Status, respect, prestige

Social needs: Friendship, belonging, love

Safety needs: Freedom from harm, financial security

Physiological needs: Food, water, shelter, oxygen

Figure 5–6 shows one need hierarchy and classification scheme that contains five need classes.[16] *Physiological needs* are basic to survival and must be satisfied first. A Red Lobster advertisement featuring a seafood salad attempts to activate the need for food. *Safety needs* involve self-preservation as well as physical and financial well-being. Smoke detector and burglar alarm manufacturers focus on these needs, as do insurance companies and retirement plan advisors. *Social needs* are concerned with love and friendship. Dating services, such as Match.com and eHarmony, and fragrance companies try to arouse these needs. *Personal needs* include the need for achievement, status, prestige, and self-respect. The American Express Centurion Card and Brooks Brothers Clothiers appeal to these needs. Sometimes firms try to arouse multiple needs to stimulate problem recognition. Michelin has combined safety with parental love to promote tire replacement for automobiles. *Self-actualization needs* involve personal fulfillment. For example, a recent Under Armour advertising campaign challenged consumers to "Rule Yourself!"

Personality While motivation is the energizing force that makes consumer behavior purposeful, a consumer's personality guides and directs behavior. **Personality** refers to a person's consistent behaviors or responses to recurring situations.

Although many personality theories exist, most identify *key traits*—enduring characteristics within a person or in his or her relationships with others. Such traits include assertiveness, extroversion, compliance, dominance, and aggression, among others. These traits are inherited or formed at an early age and change little over the years. Research suggests that compliant people prefer known brand names and use more mouthwash and toilet soaps. Aggressive types use razors, not electric shavers, apply more cologne and aftershave lotions, and purchase signature goods such as Gucci and Yves St. Laurent as an indicator of status. Also, extroversion and neuroticism have been shown to be associated with impulsive buying.[17]

Personality characteristics often reveal a person's *self-concept*, which is the way people see themselves and the way they believe others see them. Marketers recognize that people have an actual self-concept and an ideal self-concept. The actual self-concept refers to how people actually see themselves. The ideal self-concept describes how people would like to see themselves.

These two self-images—actual and ideal—are reflected in the products and brands a person buys, including automobiles, home appliances and furnishings, magazines, consumer electronics, clothing, and grooming and leisure products. Frequently, these two self-images are also reflected in the stores in which a person shops. The importance of self-concept is summed up by a senior marketing executive at Lenovo, a global supplier of notebook computers: "The notebook market is getting more like cars. The car you drive reflects you, and notebooks are becoming a form of self-expression as well."[18]

Consumer Perception

One person sees a Cadillac as a mark of achievement; another sees it as ostentatious. This is the result of **perception**—the process by which an individual selects, organizes, and interprets information to create a meaningful picture of the world.

Selective Perception Because the average consumer operates in a complex environment, the human brain attempts to organize and interpret information with a process called *selective perception*, a filtering of exposure, comprehension, and retention. *Selective exposure* occurs when people pay attention to messages that are consistent with their attitudes and beliefs and ignore messages that are inconsistent with them. Selective exposure often occurs in the postpurchase stage of the consumer decision process, when consumers read advertisements for the brand they just bought. It also occurs when a need exists—you are more likely to "see" a McDonald's advertisement when you are hungry rather than after you have eaten a pizza.

Selective comprehension involves interpreting information so that it is consistent with your attitudes and beliefs. A marketer's failure to understand this can have disastrous results. For example, Toro introduced a small, lightweight snowblower called the Snow Pup. Even though the product worked, sales failed to meet expectations. Why? Toro later found out that consumers perceived the name to mean that Snow Pup was a toy or too light to do any serious snow removal. When the product was renamed Snow Master, sales increased sharply.[19]

Selective retention means that consumers do not remember all the information they see, read, or hear, even minutes after exposure to it. This affects the internal and external information search stage of the purchase decision process. This is why furniture and automobile retailers often give consumers product brochures to take home with them when they leave the showroom.

Making Responsible Decisions

Ethics

The Ethics of Subliminal Messages

For over 60 years, the topic of subliminal perception and the presence of subliminal messages and images embedded in commercial communications have sparked heated debate.

The Federal Communications Commission has denounced subliminal messages as deceptive. Still, consumers spend $50 million a year for subliminal messages designed to help them raise their self-esteem, stop compulsive buying, quit smoking, or lose weight. Almost two-thirds of U.S. consumers think subliminal messages are present in commercial communications; about half are firmly convinced that this practice can cause them to buy things they don't want.

Subliminal messages are not illegal in the United States, however, and marketers are often criticized for pursuing opportunities to create these messages in both electronic and print media. A book by August Bullock, *The Secret Sales Pitch*, is devoted to this topic. Bullock identifies images and advertisements that he claims contain subliminal messages and describes techniques that can be used for conveying these messages. Do you "see" the subliminal message that is embedded in the book's cover?

Do you believe that a marketer's attempts to implant subliminal messages in electronic and print media are a deceptive practice and are unethical, regardless of their intent?

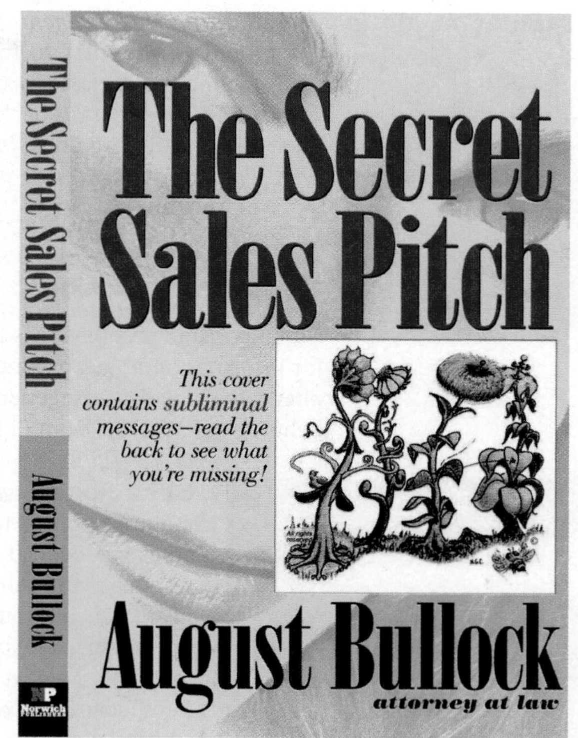

2004 by August Bullock. All Rights Reserved. Used with permission. The SecretSalesPitch.com

How did Colgate-Palmolive marketers allay consumers' perceived risk and change consumers' attitudes toward Colgate Total toothpaste to create a brand with over $1 billion in sales worldwide? The answers appear in the text.

McGraw-Hill Education

Because perception plays an important role in consumer behavior, it is not surprising that the topic of subliminal perception is a popular item for discussion. *Subliminal perception* means that you see or hear messages without being aware of them. The presence and effect of subliminal perception on behavior is a hotly debated issue, with more popular appeal than scientific support. Indeed, evidence suggests that such messages have limited effects on behavior.[20] If these messages did influence behavior, would their use be an ethical practice? (See the Making Responsible Decisions box.)[21]

Perceived Risk Perception plays a major role in the perceived risk in purchasing a product or service. **Perceived risk** represents the anxiety felt because the consumer cannot anticipate the outcomes of a purchase but believes there may be negative consequences. Examples of possible negative consequences are the size of the financial outlay required to buy the product (can I afford $900 for those skis?), the risk of physical harm (is bungee jumping safe?), and the performance of the product (will the whitening toothpaste work?). A more abstract form is psychosocial (what will my friends say about my tattoo?).

Perceived risk affects a consumer's information search. The greater the perceived risk, the more extensive the external search stage is likely to be. For example, the average car shopper spends about 14 hours online researching cars and almost 4 hours visiting car dealerships when choosing a car.[22]

Recognizing the importance of perceived risk, companies develop strategies to reduce the consumer's perceived risk and encourage purchases. Some of these strategies and examples of firms using them include the following:

- *Obtaining seals of approval*: The Good Housekeeping Seal for Fresh Step cat litter.
- *Securing endorsements from influential people*: Colgate-Palmolive secured the endorsements of dentists to make the claim that Colgate Total toothpaste is the #1 recommended toothpaste by most dentists.
- *Providing free trials of the product*: Samples of Mary Kay's Velocity fragrance.
- *Giving extensive usage instructions*: Clairol hair coloring.
- *Providing warranties and guarantees*: Kia Motors's 10-year, 100,000-mile limited powertrain warranty.

Consumer Learning

Much consumer behavior is learned. Consumers learn which information sources to consult for information about products and services, which evaluative criteria to use when assessing alternatives, and, more generally, how to make purchase decisions. **Learning** refers to those behaviors that result from (1) repeated experience and (2) reasoning.

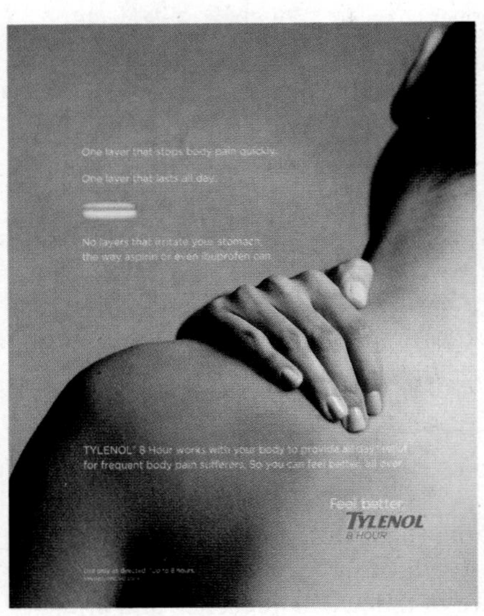

How does this advertisement for Tylenol 8-Hour apply to cognitive learning? Read the text to find out.

Source: McNeil Consumer Healthcare Division of McNeil-PPC, Inc.

Behavioral Learning *Behavioral learning* is the process of developing automatic responses to a situation built up through repeated exposure to it. Four variables are central to how consumers learn from repeated experience: drive, cue, response, and reinforcement. A *drive* is a need that moves an individual to action. Drives, such as hunger, might be represented by motives. A *cue* is a stimulus or symbol perceived by consumers. A *response* is the action taken by a consumer to satisfy the drive. *Reinforcement* is the reward. Being hungry (drive), a consumer sees a cue (a billboard), takes action (buys a sandwich), and receives a reward (it tastes great!).

Marketers use two concepts from behavioral learning theory. *Stimulus generalization* occurs when a response elicited by one stimulus (cue) is generalized to another stimulus. Using the same brand name for different products is an application of this concept, such as Tylenol Cold & Flu and Tylenol PM. *Stimulus discrimination* refers to a person's ability to perceive differences in stimuli. Consumers' tendency to perceive all light beers as being alike led to Budweiser Light commercials that distinguished between many types of "light beers" and Bud Light.

Cognitive Learning Consumers also learn through thinking, reasoning, and mental problem solving without direct experience. This type of learning, called *cognitive learning*, involves making connections between two or more ideas or simply observing the outcomes of others' behaviors and adjusting your own accordingly. Firms also influence this type of learning. Through repetition in advertising, messages such as "1 Shade Whiter Teeth in 1 Week" link a brand (Colgate Visible White) and an idea (teeth stain removal) by showing someone using the brand and getting whiter teeth. In the same way, McNeil Consumer Healthcare links its Tylenol 8-Hour brand and an idea (pain reliever) by showing someone using the brand and finding relief.

Brand Loyalty Learning is also important to marketers because it relates to habit formation—the basis of routine problem solving. Furthermore, there is a close link between habits and **brand loyalty**, which is a favorable attitude toward and consistent purchase of a single brand over time. Brand loyalty results from the positive reinforcement of previous actions. A consumer reduces risk and saves time by consistently purchasing the same brand of shampoo and has favorable results—healthy, shiny hair. There is evidence of brand loyalty in many commonly purchased products in the United States and the global marketplace. However, the incidence of brand loyalty appears to be declining in North America, Western Europe, and Japan.[23]

Consumer Values, Beliefs, and Attitudes

Values, beliefs, and attitudes play a central role in consumer decision making and related marketing actions.

Attitude Formation An **attitude** is a "learned predisposition to respond to an object or class of objects in a consistently favorable or unfavorable way."[24] Attitudes are shaped by our values and beliefs, which are learned. Values vary by level of specificity. We speak of American core values, including material well-being and humanitarianism. We also have personal values, such as thriftiness and ambition. Marketers are concerned with both but focus mostly on personal values. Personal values affect attitudes by influencing the importance assigned to specific product attributes. Suppose thriftiness is one of your personal values. When you evaluate cars, fuel economy (a product attribute) becomes important. If you believe a specific car brand has this attribute, you are likely to have a favorable attitude toward it.

Beliefs also play a part in attitude formation. **Beliefs** are a consumer's subjective perception of how a product or brand performs on different attributes. Beliefs are based on personal experience, advertising, and discussions with other people. Beliefs about product attributes are important because, along with personal values, they create the favorable or unfavorable attitude the consumer has toward certain products, services, and brands.

Attitude Change Marketers use three approaches to try to change consumer attitudes toward products and brands, as illustrated in the following examples.[25]

1. *Changing beliefs about the extent to which a brand has certain attributes.* To allay mothers' concerns about ingredients in its mayonnaise, Hellmann's successfully communicated the product's high omega-3 content, which is essential to human health.
2. *Changing the perceived importance of attributes.* Pepsi-Cola made freshness an important product attribute when it stamped freshness dates on its cans. Before doing so, few consumers considered cola freshness an issue. After Pepsi spent about $25 million on advertising and promotion, a consumer survey found that 61 percent of cola drinkers believed freshness dating was an important attribute.
3. *Adding new attributes to the product.* Colgate-Palmolive included a new antibacterial ingredient, triclosan, in its Colgate Total toothpaste and spent $100 million marketing the brand. The result? Colgate Total toothpaste is now a billion-dollar-plus global brand.

These are both 40 year old married college graduates with two children, similar income, and own their own businesses. But you can't motivate and communicate to them the same way. This is the benefit of consumer lifestyle analysis.
Source: FabCom

Consumer Lifestyle

Lifestyle is a mode of living that is identified by how people spend their time and resources, what they consider important in their environments, and what they think of themselves and the world around them. The analysis of consumer lifestyles, called *psychographics*, provides insights into consumer needs and wants. Lifestyle analysis has proven useful in segmenting and targeting consumers for new and existing products and services (see Chapter 9).

Psychographics is a catchall label used to describe a variety of segmentation approaches such as those based on behaviors, attitudes, activities, interests, opinions, and social values. The practice of combining psychology, lifestyle, and demographics to uncover consumer motivations has been formalized by Strategic Business Insights (SBI), a consulting company, and its VALS™ (Values And Life Style) proprietary methodology.[26] Using a stand-alone survey and a proprietary algorithm, VALS measures the enduring differences between U.S. adults aged 18 and older that help explain and predict consumer behavior. Eight primary population segments—mindsets—are identified on the basis of motivations and resources.

Marketing **Insights About Me**

What Motivates You? Identifying Your VALS Type

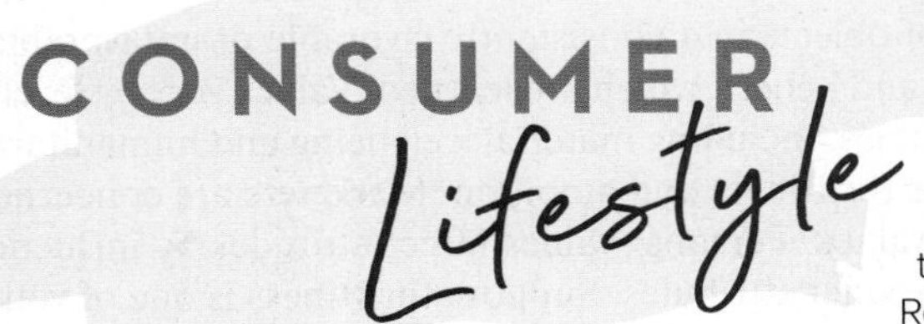

VALS™ identifies eight unique consumer segments—mindsets—based on a person's primary motivation and resources. The text provides a brief description of each segment.

Do you wish to know your VALS profile? If you do, respond to the questions on the VALS survey at www.strategicbusinessinsights.com/vals. Simply click on "Take the VALS Survey" to obtain your type in real time. From the VALS home page click on US VALS Types to view brief descriptions of all eight types, read about Motivations and Resources, and compare and contrast characteristics and behaviors of your own and other types in greater detail.

According to SBI, consumers are motivated to buy products and services and to seek life experiences that give shape, substance, and satisfaction to their lives. Different consumer groups will often exhibit different behavior; equally as often, different consumer groups will exhibit the same behavior for different reasons based on their motivations and resources.

- *Consumer motivations*. The majority of consumers are driven by one of three primary motivations–ideals, achievement, and self-expression. Consumers motivated by ideals include Thinkers and Believers. Consumers motivated by achievement include Achievers and Strivers. Consumers motivated by self-expression include Experiencers and Makers.
- *Consumer resources*. Different levels of resources enhance or constrain a person's primary motivation. The VALS resource dimension includes measures of key demographics and income in addition to psychological, emotional, and material capacities such as self-confidence, curiosity, information seeking, and risk-taking. Before reading further, visit the VALS website discussed in the Marketing Insights About Me box. Complete the short survey to learn which segment best describes you.

A brief description of each of the eight VALS consumer groups follows. A more complete overview of each segment can be found at www.strategicbusinessinsights.com/vals.

- *Ideals-motivated groups*. Consumers motivated by ideals are guided by knowledge and principles. High-resource *Thinkers* tend to be mature, motivated, practical, and well-informed. They have "ought" and "should" benchmarks for social conduct. Low-resource *Believers* are not looking to change society. They believe in right/wrong for a good life and have a strong connection to church and family.
- *Achievement-motivated groups*. Consumers motivated by achievement look for products and services that demonstrate success to their peers or a group to which they aspire. High-resource *Achievers* have a me-first, my-family-first attitude. They are successful and work-oriented and get satisfaction from their jobs. They are anchors of the status quo. Low-resource *Strivers* live in the moment. Although they would like to better their lives, they have difficulty doing so.
- *Self-expression-motivated groups*. Consumers motivated by self-expression want to make an impact on their world. High-resource *Experiencers* are social and spontaneous. They are first in, first out of trend adoption. Low-resource *Makers* protect what they think they own. They value self-sufficiency and practical and functional products.
- *High- and low-resource groups*. Two segments stand apart from a single primary motivation. High-resource *Innovators* are future oriented and value change. They are confident

enough to experiment—to try, fail, and try again. Low-resource *Survivors* are the quiet rank and file focused on meeting basic needs. They are analog, not digital.

Each segment exhibits unique media preferences. For example, Experiencers are the most likely to visit Facebook and to read fashion magazines. Makers and Achievers drive the most miles each week; therefore, they are the most likely segment to view outdoor advertising. Innovators and Thinkers are the most likely to read national newspapers such as *USA Today*. Survivors watch more hours of television in an average week compared to other groups.

LEARNING REVIEW

5-4. The problem with the Toro Snow Pup was an example of selective ____________.

5-5. What three attitude-change approaches are most common?

5-6. What does *lifestyle* mean?

SOCIOCULTURAL INFLUENCES ON CONSUMER BEHAVIOR

LO 5-4
Identify the major sociocultural influences on consumer behavior.

Sociocultural influences, which evolve from a consumer's formal and informal relationships with other people, also exert a significant impact on consumer behavior. They involve personal influence, reference groups, family influence, social class, culture, and subculture.

Personal Influence

A consumer's purchases are often influenced by the views, opinions, or behaviors of others. Two aspects of personal influence are very important to marketing: opinion leadership and word-of-mouth activity.

Opinion Leadership Individuals who exert direct or indirect social influence over others are called **opinion leaders**. Opinion leaders are considered to be knowledgeable about or

Companies use world-class athletes and music stars as spokespersons to represent their products, as in these ads featuring country music star Kelly Clarkson (for Citizen watches) and tennis star Roger Federer (for Rolex watches).

(Left): Source: Citizen Watch Company of America; (Right): Source: Rolex

Marketing Matters — Customer Value

BzzAgent—The Buzz Experience

Have you recently heard about a new product, movie, website, book, or restaurant from someone you know . . . or a complete stranger? If so, you may have had a word-of-mouth experience.

Marketers recognize the power of word of mouth. The challenge has been to harness that power. BzzAgent does just that. Its worldwide volunteer army of one million natural-born talkers channel their chatter toward products and services they deem authentically worth talking about, either online or in person. "Our goal is to capture honest word of mouth," says BzzAgent's founder, David Balter, "and to build a network that turns passionate customers into brand evangelists."

Courtesy of BzzAgent

BzzAgent's method is simple. Once a client signs on with BzzAgent, the company searches its network of "agents" for those who match the demographic and psychographic profile of the target market for a client's offering. Agents then opt in through an invitation e-mail and receive a sample product and online training for buzz-creating strategies. Online activities, such as Facebook and Instagram posts, are completed through BzzAgent.com. Each time an agent completes an offline activity, he or she is expected to file a BzzReport describing the nature of the buzz and its effectiveness. BzzAgent moderators respond with encouragement and feedback on additional techniques, including flagging any nondisclosed content.

Agents keep the products they promote. Who are the agents? All are gregarious and genuinely like the product or service, otherwise they wouldn't participate in the BzzCampaign.

Nestlé, Procter & Gamble, Danone, L'Oréal, and Unilever are a sampling of the companies that have used BzzAgent. Are you interested in BzzAgent? Visit its website at www.bzzagent.com or www.facebook.com/bzzagent.

users of particular products and services, so their opinions influence others' choices.[27] Opinion leadership is widespread in the purchase of cars and trucks, entertainment, clothing and accessories, club membership, consumer electronics, children's toys, food, vacation destinations, and financial investments. A study by *Popular Mechanics* magazine identified 18 million opinion leaders who influence the purchases of some 85 million consumers for do-it-yourself products.

About 10 percent of U.S. adults are opinion leaders. Identifying, reaching, and influencing opinion leaders is a major challenge for companies. Some firms use music stars, actors, or sports figures as spokespersons to represent their products. Others promote their products in media believed to reach opinion leaders. Still others use more direct approaches. For example, a carmaker recently invited influential community leaders and business executives to test-drive its new models. Some 6,000 accepted the offer, and 98 percent said they would recommend their tested car. The company estimated that the number of favorable recommendations totaled 32,000.

The importance of personal influence has popularized *influencer marketing*—the practice of focusing on the identification and recruitment of influencers to advocate products, services, and brands rather than focusing exclusively on prospective buyers. Social media, notably Instagram and YouTube, are the primary platforms used in influencer marketing because they are easily and quickly shared with prospective buyers. Influencer marketing is elaborated upon in Chapter 20.

Word of Mouth and Consumer Advocacy The influencing of people during conversations is called **word of mouth**. Word of mouth is the most powerful and authentic information source for consumers because it typically involves friends viewed as trustworthy. About 75 percent of all consumer conversations about brands happen face-to-face, 15 percent

Applying **Marketing Metrics**

Are Your Customers Recommending Your Company or Brand?

Marketers are attuned to the importance of favorable and unfavorable customer word of mouth and whether or not customers are inclined to recommend their company or brand to others. The Net Promoter Score™ is a popular marketing metric used by many *Fortune* 500 companies.

Your Challenge

As a marketing manager at a large TV and Internet service provider, you are interested in how current customers perceive a recent program to bundle and reprice the company's service that was rolled out over the past 12 months. You requested a review of quarterly Net Promoter Scores produced by the Consumer Insights and Research Group.

A Net Promoter Score (NPS) is based on a single question posed to current customers either by phone or e-mail: "On a scale of 0 to 10, how likely is it that you would recommend a (company or brand) to a friend or colleague?" Based on their response to this question, customers are divided into three groups:

Promoters—the percentage of current customers who say they are very willing to recommend the company or brand to others (those customers gave a rating of 9 or 10).

Passives—the percentage of current customers who are satisfied, but unenthusiastic customers (a rating of 7 or 8).

Detractors—the percentage of current customers who are unwilling to recommend the company or brand, or may actually disparage the company or brand (ratings from 0 to 6).

The Net Promoter Score is created by subtracting the percentage of detractors among current customers from the percentage of promoters among current customers:

Net Promoter Score = Percentage (%) of promoters − Percentage (%) of distractors

For example, with 30 percent promoters, 55 percent passives, and 15 percent detractors, the NPS would be 15 (30 – 15). The NPS ranges from +100 to –100. A score above zero (0) is considered "good," 50 is "excellent," and 70 is "world class."

Your Findings

The two-year summary of quarterly scores indicated that your company's NPS ranged from 9 to 11, with an average score of 10. As a benchmark, the average NPS for TV and Internet service providers was 6, with a range of –1 to 7. Therefore, your company NPS was stable and above the industry average. But a closer look yielded a troubling signal. The pattern of promoters, passives, and detractors had noticeably changed. The company's NPS had remained at 10 for the past two years (eight quarters). However, since the bundling and repricing program was rolled out, the promoter percentage had dropped from 40 percent to 30 percent and the passive percentage increased from 30 percent to 50 percent as shown in the bar charts.

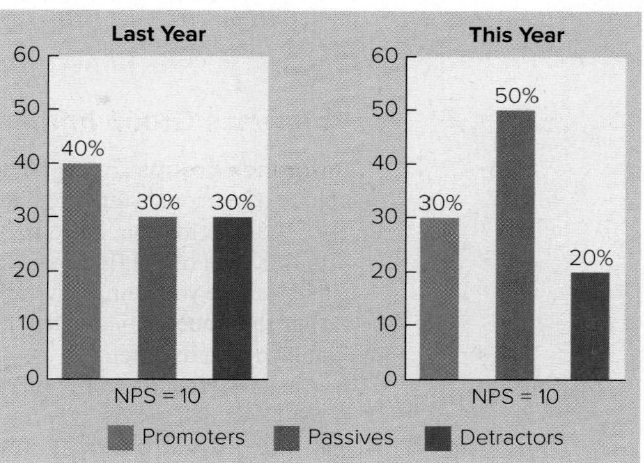

Your Action

An increase in passives means that a sizable percentage of current customers may be susceptible to offers from competitors. A closer look is necessary. Are these passives customers who simply rolled over to the new program as a matter of convenience? Or are they new customers who are satisfied, but not enthusiastic about the program once purchased. In either case, they might become detractors and do more harm than good for the company in the longer term.

happen over the phone, and 10 percent happen online.[28] Research indicates that 67 percent of U.S. consumer product sales are directly based on word-of-mouth activity among friends, family, and colleagues.[29]

The power of personal influence has prompted firms to promote positive and retard negative word of mouth. For instance, "teaser" advertising campaigns are run in advance of new-product introductions to stimulate conversations. Other techniques such as advertising slogans, music, and humor also heighten positive word of mouth. Many commercials shown during the Super Bowl are created expressly to initiate conversations about the advertisements and their featured products or services the next day. Increasingly, companies recruit and

VIDEO 5-2
Dove
kerin.tv/15e/v5-2

deploy people to produce *buzz*—popularity created by consumer word of mouth. Read the Marketing Matters box to learn how this is done by BzzAgent.[30] Then go to the link in Video 5-2 to see BzzAgent's campaign for Dove hair care products.

Unfortunately, word of mouth can also be a source of negative information. For example, consider the damaging (and untrue) rumors that have plagued Kmart (snake eggs in clothing), Taco Bell (beef content in taco meat filling), Corona Extra beer (contamination), and Snickers candy bars in Russia (a cause of diabetes). Overcoming or neutralizing negative word of mouth is difficult and costly. However, supplying factual information, providing toll-free numbers for consumers to call the company, and giving appropriate product demonstrations have proven helpful.

The power of word of mouth is magnified by the Internet through online forums, blogs, social media, and websites. In fact, companies use special software to monitor online messages and find out what consumers are saying about their products, services, and brands. They have found that 30 percent of people spreading negative information have never owned or used the product, service, or brand and "likes" on Facebook and Instagram and product reviews on Amazon are sometimes gotten by fraudulent means![31]

Many large companies use a Net Promoter Score™ to track the likelihood of their current customers engaging in positive and negative word-of-mouth behavior.[32] An illustration of how a Net Promoter Score is calculated, applied, and interpreted appears in the Applying Marketing Metrics box.[33]

Reference Group Influence

Reference groups are people to whom an individual looks as a basis for self-appraisal or as a source of personal standards. Reference groups affect consumer purchases because they influence the information, attitudes, and aspiration levels that help set a consumer's standards. For example, one of the first questions one asks others when planning to attend a social occasion is, "What are you going to wear?" Reference groups influence the purchase of luxury products rather than necessities—particularly when the use or consumption of a chosen brand will be highly visible to others.

Consumers have many reference groups, but three groups have clear marketing implications.[34] An *associative group* is one to which a person actually belongs, including fraternities and sororities and alumni associations. Such groups are easily identifiable and are targeted by firms selling insurance, insignia products (including tattoos), and charter vacations.

Associative reference groups can also form around a brand, as is the case with clubs like the HOG (Harley Owners Group), which is made up of Harley-Davidson fans. A **brand community** is a specialized group of consumers with a structured set of relationships involving a particular brand, fellow customers of that brand, and the product in use. A consumer who is a member of a brand community thinks about brand names (e.g., Harley-Davidson), the product category (e.g., motorcycles), other customers who use the brand (e.g., HOG members), and the marketer that makes and promotes the brand.

The Harley Owners Group (HOG) has over 1 million members and is a prototypical brand community. Read the text to learn about the characteristics of a brand community.

Joseph Eid/AFP/Getty Images

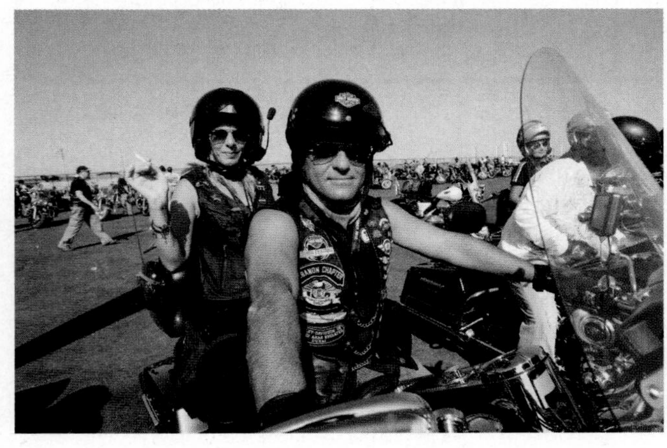

An *aspiration group* is one that a person wishes to be a member of or wishes to be identified with, such as a professional society or sports team. Firms frequently rely on spokespeople or settings associated with their target market's aspiration group in their advertising.

A *dissociative group* is one that a person wishes to maintain a distance from because of differences in values or behaviors. Firms often avoid dissociative reference groups in their marketing. For example, retailer Abercrombie & Fitch once offered to pay cast members of a controversial TV reality show to *not* wear its clothing. "We understand that the show is for entertainment purposes, but believe this association is contrary to the aspirational nature of our brand, and may be distressing to many of our fans," the retailer stated.[35]

Social Class Influence

A subtler influence on consumer behavior than direct contact with others is the social class to which people belong. **Social class** may be defined as the relatively permanent, homogeneous divisions in a society into which people sharing similar values, interests, and behavior can be grouped. A person's occupation, source of income (not level of income), and education determine his or her social class. Generally speaking, three major social class categories exist—upper, middle, and lower—with subcategories within each. This structure has been observed in the United States, Great Britain, Western Europe, and Latin America.[36]

To some degree, persons within social classes exhibit common values, attitudes, beliefs, lifestyles, and buying behaviors. Compared with the middle classes, people in the lower classes have a more short-term time orientation, think in concrete rather than abstract terms, and see fewer personal opportunities. Members of the upper classes focus on achievements and the future and think in abstract or symbolic terms.

Companies use social class as a basis for identifying and reaching particularly good prospects for their products and services. For instance, JCPenney has historically appealed to the middle classes. *New Yorker* magazine reaches the upper classes. In general, people in the upper classes are targeted by companies for items such as financial investments, expensive cars, and formal evening wear. The middle classes represent a target market for home improvement centers, automobile parts stores, and personal hygiene products. Firms also recognize differences in media preferences among classes: lower and working classes prefer tabloid magazines; middle classes read fashion, romance, and celebrity (*People*) magazines; and upper classes tend to subscribe to literary, travel, and news magazines.

Family Influence

Family influences on consumer behavior result from three sources: consumer socialization, passage through the family life cycle, and decision making within the family or household.

Consumer Socialization The process by which people acquire the skills, knowledge, and attitudes necessary to function as consumers is called *consumer socialization*.[37] Children learn how to purchase (1) by interacting with adults in purchase situations and (2) through their own purchasing and product usage experiences. Research shows that children evidence brand preferences at age two, and these preferences often last a lifetime. This knowledge prompted the licensing of Time Inc.'s *Sports Illustrated Kids* magazine to Microsoft's kid-friendly news site, MSN Kids.

Family Life Cycle Consumers act and purchase differently as they go through life. The concept **family life cycle** describes the distinct phases that a family progresses through from formation to retirement, each phase bringing with it identifiable purchasing behaviors.[38] Figure 5–7 illustrates the traditional progression as well as contemporary variations of the family life cycle. Today, the *traditional family*—a married couple with children younger than 18 years—constitutes just 20 percent of all U.S. households. The remaining 80 percent of U.S. households includes single parents; unmarried couples; divorced, never-married, or widowed individuals; and older married couples whose children no longer live at home.

Young singles' buying preferences are for nondurable items, including prepared foods, clothing, personal care products, and entertainment. They represent a target market for recreational travel, automobile, and consumer electronics firms. Young married couples without children are typically more affluent than young singles because usually both spouses are employed. These couples exhibit preferences for furniture, housewares, and gift items for each other. Young marrieds with children are driven by the needs of their children. They make up a sizable market for life insurance, various children's products, and home furnishings. Single

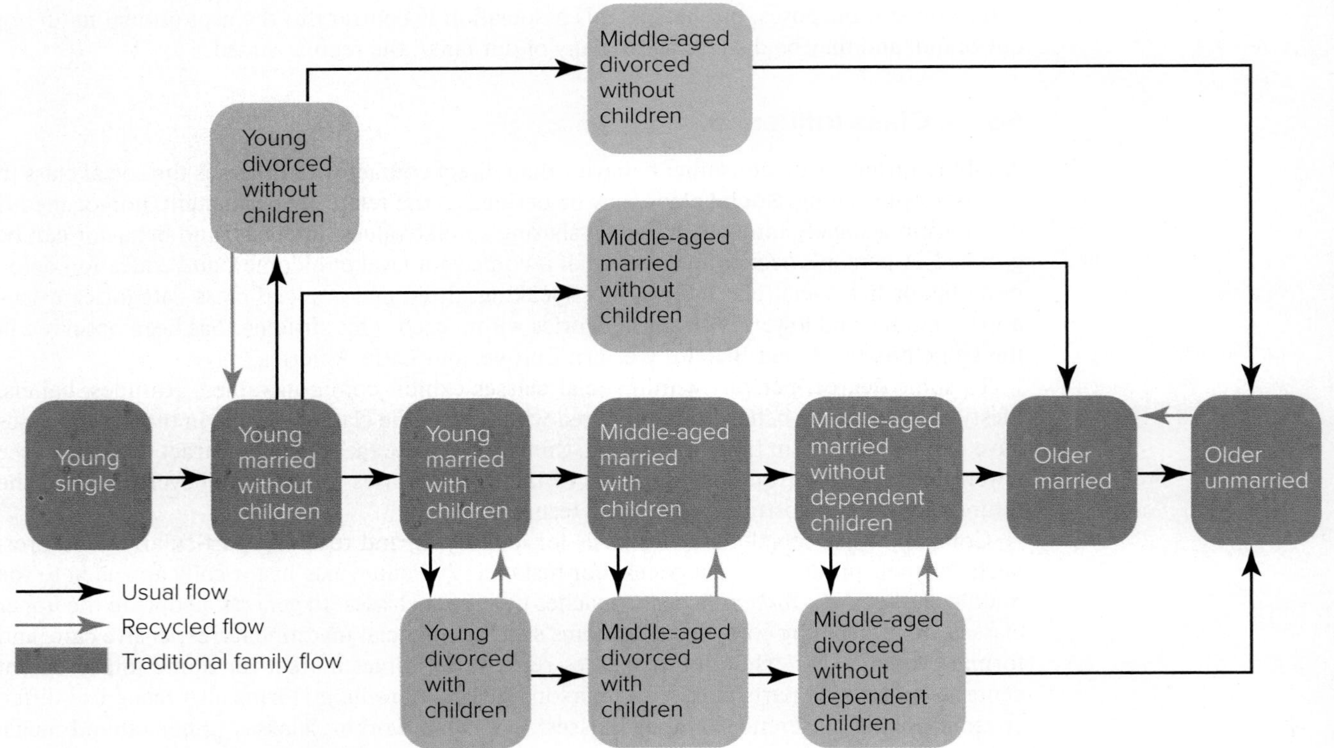

FIGURE 5–7
Modern family life-cycle stages and flows. Can you identify people you know in different stages? Do they follow the purchase patterns described in the text?

parents with children are the least financially secure of households with children. Their buying preferences are often affected by a limited economic status and tend toward convenience foods, child care services, and personal care items.

Middle-aged married couples with children are typically better off financially than their younger counterparts. They are a significant market for leisure products and home improvement items. Middle-aged couples without children typically have a large amount of discretionary income. These couples buy better home furnishings, status automobiles, and financial services. Persons in the last two phases–older married and older unmarried–make up a sizable market for prescription drugs, medical services, vacation trips, and gifts for younger relatives.

Family Decision Making A third source of family influence on consumer behavior involves the decision-making process that occurs within the family.[39] Two decision-making styles exist: spouse-dominant and joint decision making. With a joint decision-making style, most decisions are made by both husband and wife. Spouse-dominant decisions are those for which either the husband or the wife is mostly responsible. Research indicates that wives tend to have more say when purchasing groceries, children's toys, clothing, and medicines. Husbands tend to be more influential in home and car maintenance purchases. Joint decision making is common for cars, vacations, houses, home appliances and electronics, family finances, and medical care. As a rule, joint decision making increases with the education of the spouses.

Roles of individual family members in the purchase process are another element of family decision making. Five roles exist: (1) information gatherer, (2) influencer, (3) decision maker, (4) purchaser, and (5) user. Family members assume different roles for different products and services. This knowledge is important to firms. For example, 89 percent of wives either influence or make outright purchases of men's clothing. Even though women are often the grocery decision makers, they are not necessarily the purchasers. Today, 31 percent of men are the primary grocery shoppers in their households.

Increasingly, preteens and teenagers are the information gatherers, influencers, decision makers, and purchasers of products and services for the family, given the prevalence of

Today, 31 percent of men in the United States are the primary grocery shoppers in their households. Marketers that supply the $560 billion retail food industries are now adjusting store layouts and shelf placements to cater to men.
Jochen Sand/Getty Images

working parents and single-parent households. The market for products bought by or for preteens and teenagers surpasses $210 billion annually. These figures help explain why, for example, Johnson & Johnson, Apple, Kellogg, P&G, Nike, Sony, and Oscar Mayer, among countless other companies, spend more than $70 billion annually in digital, electronic, and print media that reach preteens and teens.

Culture and Subculture Influences

VIDEO 5-3
Nissan Ad
kerin.tv/15e/v5-3

As described in Chapter 3, *culture* refers to the set of values, ideas, and attitudes that are learned and shared among the members of a group. Thus, we often refer to the American culture, the Latin American culture, or the Japanese culture. Cultural underpinnings of American buying patterns were described in Chapter 3; Chapter 7 will explore the role of culture in global marketing.

Subgroups within the larger, or national, culture with unique values, ideas, and attitudes are referred to as **subcultures**. Various subcultures exist within the American culture. The three largest racial/ethnic subcultures in the United States are Hispanics, African Americans, and Asian Americans. Collectively, they are expected to account for more than one in four U.S. consumers and to spend over $4 trillion for products and services in 2025, which will represent about 30 percent of the United States' total buying power.[40] Each group exhibits sophisticated social and cultural behaviors that affect buying patterns, which we describe next.

Why does ACH Food Companies, Inc. advertise its Mazola Corn Oil in Spanish? Read the text for the answer. Mazola Corn Oil, www.mazola.com
Source: MAZOLA®, a registered trademark of ACH FOOD COMPANIES, Inc.

Hispanic Buying Patterns Hispanics represent the largest racial/ethnic subculture in the United States in terms of population and spending power. About 35 percent of Hispanics in the United States are immigrants, and the majority are under the age of 30. About 25 percent of Hispanics are younger than 18.

Research on Hispanic buying practices has uncovered several consistent patterns:[41]

1. Hispanics are quality and brand conscious. They are willing to pay a premium price for premium quality and are often brand loyal.
2. Hispanics prefer buying American-made products, especially those offered by firms that cater to Hispanic needs.
3. Hispanic buying preferences are strongly influenced by family and peers.
4. Hispanics consider advertising a credible product information source, and U.S. firms spend about $10 billion annually on advertising to Hispanics.
5. Convenience is not an important product attribute to Hispanic homemakers with respect to food preparation or consumption, nor is low caffeine in coffee and soft drinks, low fat in dairy products, or low cholesterol in packaged foods.

Despite some consistent buying patterns, marketing to Hispanics has proven to be a challenge for two reasons. First, the Hispanic subculture is diverse and composed of Mexicans, Puerto Ricans, Cubans, and others of Central and South American ancestry. Cultural differences among these nationalities often affect product preferences. For example, Goya Foods markets soups, beans, and sauces using different recipes to appeal to Puerto Ricans on the East Coast and Mexicans in the Southwest. Second, a language barrier exists, and commercial messages are frequently misinterpreted when translated into Spanish. Volkswagen learned this lesson when the Spanish translation of its "Drivers Wanted" slogan suggested "chauffeurs wanted." The Spanish slogan was changed to "*Agarra Calle*," a slang expression that can be loosely translated as "let's hit the road."

Sensitivity to the unique needs of Hispanics by firms has paid huge dividends. For example, Metropolitan Life Insurance is the largest insurer of Hispanics. Goya Foods dominates the market for ethnic food products sold to Hispanics. Mazola Corn Oil captures two-thirds of the Hispanic market for this product category. Meredith Corporation has 6.2 million readers of its Spanish-language *People en Español* magazine.

African American Buying Patterns African Americans have the second-largest spending power of the three racial/ethnic subcultures in the United States. Consumer research on African American buying patterns has focused on similarities and differences with Caucasians. When socioeconomic status differences between African Americans and Caucasians are removed, there are more similarities than points of difference. Differences in buying patterns are greater within the African American subculture, due to levels of socioeconomic status, than between African Americans and Caucasians of similar status.

African American women represent a large market for health and beauty products. Cosmetics companies like CoverGirl actively seek to serve this market.
Source: Procter & Gamble

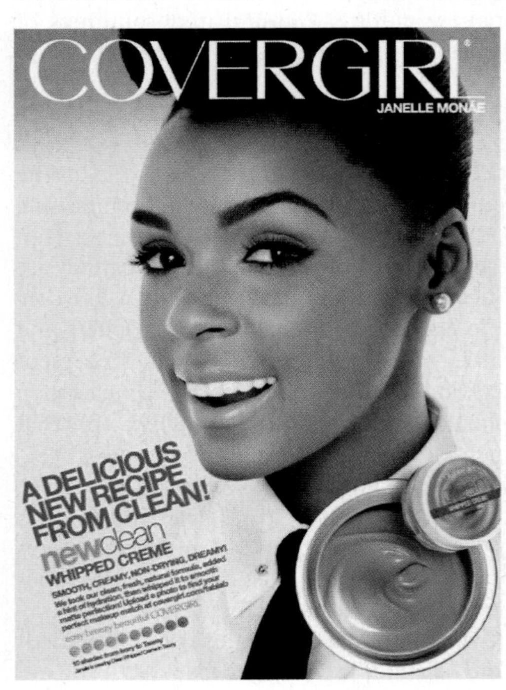

Even though similarities outweigh differences, there are consumption patterns that do differ between African Americans and Caucasians.[42] For example, African Americans spend far more than Caucasians on boys' clothing, rental goods, smartphones, and audio equipment. African American women spend three times more on health and beauty products than Caucasian women. Furthermore, the typical African American family is five years younger than the typical Caucasian family. This factor alone accounts for some of the observed differences in preferences for clothing, music, shelter, cars, and many other products, services, and activities. Finally, it must be emphasized that, historically, African Americans have been deprived of employment and educational opportunities in the United States. Both factors have resulted in income disparities between African Americans and Caucasians, which influence purchase behavior.

Recent research indicates that while African Americans are price conscious, they are strongly motivated by quality and choice. They respond more to products and advertising that appeal to African American cultural images, as well as address their ethnic features and needs, regardless of socioeconomic status. African Americans are much more likely to tell their friends about products and services they like than the general public as a whole.

Asian American Buying Patterns Asian Americans are the fastest-growing racial/ethnic subculture in the United States. About 66 percent of Asian Americans are immigrants. Most are under the age of 30. Asian Americans tend to live in multigenerational households.

The Asian American subculture is composed of Chinese, Japanese, Filipinos, Koreans, Asian Indians, people from Southeast Asia, and Pacific Islanders. The diversity of this subculture is so great that generalizations about buying patterns of this group are difficult to make.[43] Consumer research on Asian Americans suggests that individuals and families can be divided into two groups. *Assimilated* Asian Americans are conversant in English, are highly educated, hold professional and managerial positions, and exhibit buying patterns very much like the typical American consumer. *Nonassimilated* Asian Americans are recent immigrants who still cling to their native languages and customs.

The diversity of Asian Americans, evident in language, customs, and tastes, requires marketers to be sensitive to different Asian nationalities. And, for the majority of each nationality, preserving their cultural heritage is important. As a consequence, Anheuser-Busch's agricultural products division sells eight varieties of California-grown rice, each with a different Asian label to cover a range of nationalities and tastes. The company's advertising also addresses the preferences of Chinese, Japanese, and Koreans for different kinds of rice bowls. McDonald's actively markets to Asian Americans. According to a company executive, "We recognize diversity in this market. We try to make our messages in the language they prefer to see them."

Studies show that the Asian American subculture as a whole is characterized by hard work, strong family ties, appreciation for education, and median family incomes exceeding those of any other ethnic group. This subculture is also the most entrepreneurial in the United States, as evidenced by the number of Asian-owned businesses. These qualities led Metropolitan Life Insurance to identify Asian Americans as a target for insurance following the company's success in marketing to Hispanics.

LEARNING REVIEW

5-7. What are the two primary forms of personal influence?

5-8. Marketers are concerned with which types of reference groups?

5-9. What two challenges must marketers overcome when marketing to Hispanic consumers?

LEARNING OBJECTIVES REVIEW

LO 5-1 *Describe the stages in the consumer purchase decision process.*
The consumer purchase decision process consists of five stages: (1) problem recognition, (2) information search, (3) alternative evaluation, (4) purchase decision, and (5) postpurchase behavior. Problem recognition is perceiving a difference between a person's ideal and actual situation big enough to trigger a decision. Information search involves remembering previous purchase experiences (internal search) and external search behavior such as seeking information from other sources. Alternative evaluation clarifies the problem for the consumer by (*a*) suggesting the evaluative criteria to use for the purchase, (*b*) yielding brand names that might meet the criteria, and (*c*) developing consumer value perceptions. The purchase decision involves the choice of an alternative, including from whom to buy and when to buy. Postpurchase behavior involves the comparison of the chosen alternative with a consumer's expectations, which leads to satisfaction or dissatisfaction and subsequent purchase behavior. Marketing practitioners study the consumer purchase process by identifying consumer touchpoints and consumer journey maps.

LO 5-2 *Distinguish among three variations of the consumer purchase decision process: extended, limited, and routine problem solving.*
Consumers don't always engage in the five-stage purchase decision process. Instead, they skip or minimize one or more stages depending on the level of involvement–the personal, social, and economic significance of the purchase. For high-involvement purchase occasions, each of the five stages of the consumer purchase decision process is used and considerable time and effort are devoted to the search for external information and the identification and evaluation of alternatives. With limited problem

solving, consumers typically seek some information or rely on a friend to help them evaluate alternatives. For low-involvement purchase occasions, consumers engage in routine problem solving. They recognize a problem, make a decision, and spend little effort seeking external information and evaluating alternatives.

LO 5-3 *Identify the major psychological influences on consumer behavior.*
Psychology helps marketers understand why and how consumers behave as they do. In particular, psychological concepts such as motivation and personality; perception; learning; values, beliefs, and attitudes; and lifestyle are useful for interpreting buying processes. Motivation is the energizing force that stimulates behavior to satisfy a need. Personality refers to a person's consistent behaviors or responses to recurring situations. Perception is the process by which an individual selects, organizes, and interprets information to create a meaningful picture of the world. Consumers filter information through selective exposure, comprehension, and retention.

Much consumer behavior is learned. Learning refers to those behaviors that result from (*a*) repeated experience and (*b*) reasoning. Brand loyalty results from learning. Values, beliefs, and attitudes are also learned and influence how consumers evaluate products, services, and brands. A more general concept is lifestyle. Lifestyle, also called psychographics, combines psychology and demographics and focuses on how people spend their time and resources, what they consider important in their environment, and what they think of themselves and the world around them.

LO 5-4 *Identify the major sociocultural influences on consumer behavior.*
Sociocultural influences, which evolve from a consumer's formal and informal relationships with other people, also affect consumer behavior. These involve personal influence, reference groups, social class, family, culture, and subculture. Opinion leadership and word-of-mouth behavior are two major sources of personal influence on consumer behavior. Reference groups are people to whom an individual looks as a basis for self-approval or as a source of personal standards. Social class influences consumer values, attitudes, beliefs, and lifestyle. Family influences on consumer behavior result from three sources: consumer socialization, passage through the family life cycle, and decision making within the family or household. Finally, a person's culture and subculture have been shown to influence product preferences and buying patterns.

LEARNING REVIEW ANSWERS

5-1 What is the first stage in the consumer purchase decision process?
Answer: problem recognition—perceiving a need

5-2 The brands a consumer considers buying out of the set of brands in a product class of which the consumer is aware are collectively called the ______.
Answer: consideration set

5-3 What is the term for postpurchase anxiety?
Answer: cognitive dissonance

5-4 The problem with the Toro Snow Pup was an example of selective ______.
Answer: comprehension—consumers perceived the name to mean that Snow Pup was a toy that was too light to do any serious snow removal.

5-5 What three attitude-change approaches are most common?
Answer: (1) Change beliefs about the extent to which a brand has certain attributes. (2) Change the perceived importance of these attributes. (3) Add new attributes to the product.

5-6 What does *lifestyle* mean?
Answer: Lifestyle is a mode of living that is identified by how people spend their time and resources, what they consider important in their environment, and what they think of themselves and the world around them.

5-7 What are the two primary forms of personal influence?
Answer: (1) Opinion leadership—persons considered to be knowledgeable about or users of particular products and services and (2) word of mouth—the influencing of people (friends, family, and colleagues) during conversations.

5-8 Marketers are concerned with which types of reference groups?
Answer: Three reference groups have clear marketing implications: (1) associative groups—ones to which a person actually belongs, such as a brand community that consists of a specialized group of consumers with a structured set of relationships involving a particular brand; (2) aspiration groups—ones that people wish to be a member of or identified with; and (3) dissociative groups—ones that people wish to maintain a distance from because of differences in values or behaviors.

5-9 What two challenges must marketers overcome when marketing to Hispanic consumers?
Answer: (1) The diversity of nationalities among this subculture that affect product preferences and (2) the language barrier that can lead to misinterpretation or mistranslation of commercial messages when translated into Spanish.

FOCUSING ON KEY TERMS

attitude p. 137
beliefs p. 137
brand community p. 142
brand loyalty p. 136
consumer behavior p. 125
consumer journey map p. 132
consumer touchpoints p. 131
family life cycle p. 143
involvement p. 129
learning p. 136
motivation p. 133
opinion leaders p. 139
perceived risk p. 135
perception p. 134
personality p. 134
purchase decision process p. 125
reference groups p. 142
social class p. 143
subcultures p. 145
word of mouth p. 140

APPLYING MARKETING KNOWLEDGE

1 Review Figure 5-2, which shows common smartphone attributes. Which attributes are important to you? What other attributes might you consider? Which brand would you prefer?

2 Suppose research at Panasonic reveals that prospective buyers are anxious about buying high-definition television sets. What strategies might you recommend to the company to reduce consumer anxiety?

3 Assign one or more levels of the Maslow hierarchy of needs described in Figure 5-6 to the following products: (*a*) life insurance, (*b*) cosmetics, (*c*) *The Wall Street Journal*, and (*d*) hamburgers.

4 With which stage in the family life cycle would the purchase of the following products and services be most closely identified? (*a*) bedroom furniture, (*b*) life insurance, (*c*) a Caribbean cruise, (*d*) a house mortgage, and (*e*) children's toys.

BUILDING YOUR MARKETING PLAN

To conduct a consumer analysis for the product—the good, service, or idea—in your marketing plan:

1 Identify the consumers who are most likely to buy your product—the primary target market—in terms of (*a*) their demographic characteristics and (*b*) any other kind of characteristics you believe are important.

2 Describe (*a*) the main points of difference of your product for this group and (*b*) what problem they help solve for the consumer in terms of the first stage in the consumer purchase decision process in Figure 5-1.

3 For each of the four outside boxes in Figure 5-5 (marketing mix, psychological, sociocultural, and situational influences), identify the one or two key influences with respect to your product.

This consumer analysis will provide the foundation for the marketing mix actions you develop later in your plan.

VIDEO CASE 5 Coppertone: Creating the Leading Sun Care Brand by Understanding Consumers

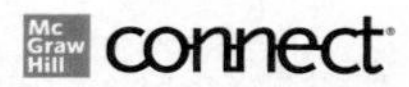

How do you create the leading sun care brand in the United States? "I would say love the consumer," explains Tracy Nunziata, marketing vice president at Coppertone. "The consumer is at the basis of everything that you're going to do, and so the more that you can understand what is going on in their minds, their behaviors, their attitudes, the more you will understand how to best market your brand and meet all of their needs," she adds.

VIDEO 5-4
Coppertone Video Case
kerin.tv/15e/v5-4

COPPERTONE AND THE SUN CARE INDUSTRY

Coppertone has a long and interesting history of meeting the changing needs of consumers. It was developed by pharmacist Benjamin Green who observed that red petroleum was used to protect the skin of service men and women in the Air Force. He added cocoa butter and coconut oil to create Coppertone Suntan Cream—the first consumer sun care product in the United States. As Coppertone marketing director Lisa Perez explains, "Coppertone actually started off as a tanning brand. If I think back to some of the taglines the business used to use, one of the most popular was 'Tan, Don't Burn.'" Soon the company introduced the now iconic Coppertone Girl in advertising that showed a young girl surprised by a Cocker Spaniel as it tugs at her swimsuit to reveal a tan line. Little Miss Coppertone contests followed, and young celebrities such as Jodi Foster often debuted in Coppertone commercials. One of the original outdoor billboards can still be seen in Miami Beach, Florida!

As public awareness of skin care preferences increased, consumer interests shifted from tanning to protection, and Coppertone developed new products to match those interests. "What's been so great," Perez observes, is that "we've continuously evolved to meet consumer needs." For example, Coppertone created a research center that developed an objective system for measuring sun protection. This system provided the basis for the SPF (Sun Protection Factor) ratings that the Food and Drug Administration created for the sun care industry. In addition,

Coppertone developed the first sunscreen product for babies, introduced the first water-resistant lotion, and launched the first continuous spray sunscreens. Coppertone has also developed the MyUV Alert™ app to provide reapplication reminders tailored to individual family members.

Today, Coppertone is the market leader with 18 percent share of an industry that has grown to $9 billion in global sales. Coppertone's success is extraordinary considering the large number of competitors in the category. Nunziata explains: "You need to understand who your competition is and what their offerings are, so understanding Neutrogena, Banana Boat, and even private-label products is essential. They all play different roles within the category, so understanding what innovations they have, how they are supporting their product, and what targets they are going after" are all important. The industry is changing also as the distinction between sun care and skin care is becoming less obvious. Many sun care products have added ingredients such as vitamin B3 and ginkgo biloba, while many skin care products now offer SPF protection, creating "multifunctional products" as a new source of competition.

Source: Bayer

THE SUN CARE PRODUCT PURCHASE DECISION PROCESS

Coppertone managers are very attentive to the path that sun care product consumers follow as they make a purchase. According to Perez, the first stage—problem recognition—begins in two ways. "First is the understanding and heightened awareness of the importance to protect their skin against sun exposure," she says. Second is the circumstance when consumers are "going somewhere" such as the beach, the pool, or on vacation. Both situations lead consumers to conclude that they need a sun care product. Coppertone research has revealed that 80 percent of its customers decide to purchase a sun care product before they even get into a store.

After recognizing the need, sun care product customers gather information from a wide range of places. They often ask peers what they use. Consumers also go online to collect information. "They look at different brands, they look at what kind of sun protection factors they will need while using the product," observes Nunziata. "They also search to see what are the new innovations. News is very important in this category, so they're out there searching for the best sunscreen they should be using for their different needs," she continues. To facilitate customers' information search Coppertone allocates a significant part of its marketing budget to make sure Coppertone products appear in any online searches. In addition, Coppertone uses traditional advertising, public relations activities, and announcements on its web page to ensure that new information is readily available.

The sun care product category has many options so alternative evaluation can be complicated for consumers. One of the first things consumers evaluate is the product form—spray versus lotion. Then there is a range of SPF protection levels to choose from, and a wide variety of brands. Finally, price can also be an attribute that influences the evaluation process. Coppertone is continually adding new attributes such as water resistance (Coppertone SPORT), citrus scent (Coppertone CLEARLYSheer Faces), antioxidant blends (Coppertone CLEARLYSheer AfterSun), and a portable travel size option, to match consumers' interests. Prices are frequently adjusted to ensure that Coppertone is considered by value shoppers. As Lisa Perez observes, "there are a lot of decision criteria that consumers consider."

Once consumers have examined the alternatives they can make a purchase online or in a retail store. Coppertone's website (www.coppertone.com), for example, sometimes offers links to make purchases from Walgreens, Target, Kmart, CVS, Amazon.com, Soap.com, and drugstore.com. If a consumer elects to go to a retail store, the Coppertone brand is also sold in food retailers such as Kroger, Safeway, and Publix, and in club stores such as Costco and Sam's. As Perez describes the situation, "consumers are looking for what they want, when they want it." Because in-store personnel do not typically participate in a sun care product purchase, point-of-purchase displays are an important way for Coppertone to help consumers find the location of their product. In some cases Coppertone may partner with a retailer to provide training and information to a "beauty advisor" who works at a cosmetics counter in the store.

Nunziata believes that the postpurchase evaluation happens quickly and on two dimensions. She explains: "One, did they get burned? I think that's the biggest telltale sign of whether they are satisfied with the product. The second is how it feels. So if you have a very greasy, oily formula that's really sticky, they're not going to be happy with it." Coppertone solicits feedback about all of its products on its website and by e-mail, mail, and telephone. In addition, Coppertone's marketing activities include engagement with consumers on Facebook and Instagram and with beauty websites and bloggers. The goal is to participate in authentic conversations about the Coppertone brand.

There are many other influences on the consumer decision process. Consumers are likely to select different products, for example, in different situations such as purchases for themselves or for their children, or in different weather conditions. Similarly, psychological influences, such as outdoor and indoor lifestyles, and perceptions of health and wellness can influence sun care product preferences. Perez comments, "I think it really depends on where our consumers are in their life stage or what their lifestyle is like." Finally, sociocultural influences such as peers and reference groups are important. Coppertone has observed that female consumers are interested in their friends' product preferences particularly when it is related to skin care and cosmetics.

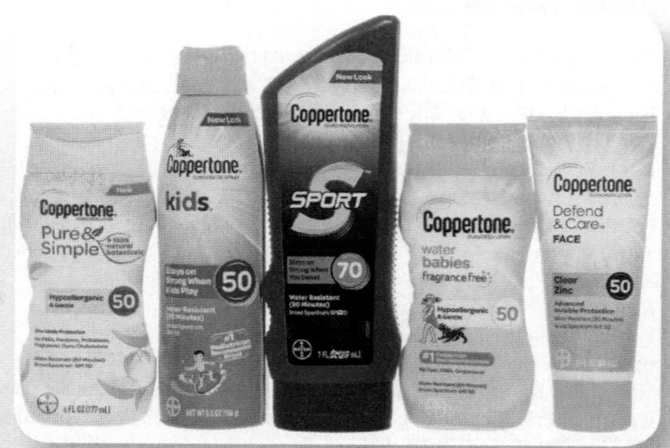

McGraw-Hill Education

MARKETING AT COPPERTONE

Together, Tracy Nunziata and Lisa Perez are responsible for managing a comprehensive integrated marketing program for Coppertone products. The program includes traditional mass media such as TV and print, and a variety of social media and digital advertising outlets. In addition, the Coppertone brand is supported with many types of coupons. These include free standing inserts (FSIs) in Sunday papers, digital coupons that are available online, and instant redeemable coupons (IRCs) that consumers can find on Coppertone packaging. Another important aspect of the Coppertone marketing program is its sponsorship of the U.S. women's and U.S. men's soccer teams. In addition, Coppertone has a partnership with Disney which has led to promotions related to movies such as *Finding Dory*. Coppertone's marketing activities also include sampling, displays, and signage throughout the United States.

COPPERTONE IN THE FUTURE

Coppertone faces several unique opportunities and challenges in the future. First, demand for Coppertone products is very seasonal. In fact, the majority of Coppertone sales currently occur in just 100 days. Second, consumers have traditionally thought about Coppertone products as solutions to a particular event such as a visit to the beach or a vacation. However, as consumers become more engaged in their own health and wellness, Coppertone must help consumers think about its products as a part of their everyday routine. Finally, Coppertone recently partnered with Vision Ease to launch a line of sunglasses with Coppertone polarized lenses and a line of contact lenses as part of its commitment to develop new products to meet consumers' needs.

Now and in the future Coppertone's strategies will require continued attention to understanding consumers. Perez explains: "Coppertone is a fast-moving business that's changing on a daily basis. Consumers are really on trend, they're smart, they're savvy, and they're looking for information. So, for me as a marketer, what's really important is how do I get ahead of that? And the answer is constantly evaluating trends, talking to consumers, and figuring out how we can have our marketing activities sync up and be relevant to them."[44]

Questions

1 How has an understanding of consumer behavior helped Coppertone grow in the United States and around the globe?

2 Describe the five-stage purchase decision process for a Coppertone customer.

3 What are the possible situational, psychological, and sociocultural influences on the Coppertone consumer purchase decision process?

4 What specific marketing activities does Coppertone utilize to help the company grow in the marketplace?

5 What challenges does Coppertone face in the future? What actions would you recommend related to each challenge?

Chapter Notes

1. "Driving by Gender," *Consumer Reports*, April 2019, p. 99; "2019 U.S. Women's Car Dealership Report," www.women-drivers.com, February 9, 2019; and "2019 Women's Car Buying Report," www.cbtnews.com, April 8, 2019.
2. Roger D. Blackwell, Paul W. Miniard, and James F. Engel, *Consumer Behavior,* 10th ed. (Mason, OH: South-Western Publishing, 2006).
3. For thorough descriptions of consumer expertise, see Joseph W. Alba and J. Wesley Hutchinson, "Knowledge Calibration: What Consumers Know and What They Think They Know," *Journal of Consumer Research,* September 2000, pp. 123–57.
4. For representative in-depth studies on external information search patterns, see Sungha Jang, Ashutosh Prasad, and Brian T. Ratchford, "Consumer Search of Multiple Information Sources and Its Impact on Consumer Price Satisfaction," *Journal of Interactive Marketing,* November 2017, pp. 24–40; and Joel E. Urbany, Peter R. Dickson, and William L. Wilkie, "Buyer Uncertainty and Information Search," *Journal of Consumer Research,* March 1992, pp. 452–63.
5. "Get Smart about Your Smartphone," *Consumer Reports*, February 2019, pp. 26–33; "Better Battery Life Tops 5G on Wish List of Smartphone Users," *USA Today*, February 20, 2019, pp. B1–B2; and "The Best Phones for 2019," www.pcmag.com, July 2019.
6. For an extended discussion on evaluative criteria, see David L. Mothersbaugh and Delbert Hawkins, *Consumer Behavior: Building Marketing Strategy,* 13th ed. (Burr Ridge, IL: McGraw-Hill/Irwin, 2016).
7. John A. Howard, *Buyer Behavior in Marketing Strategy,* 2nd ed. (Englewood Cliffs, NJ: Prentice Hall, 1994). For an extended discussion on consumer choice sets, see Allan D. Shocker, Moshe Ben-Akiva, Brun Boccara, and Prakesh Nedungadi, "Consideration Set Influences on Consumer Decision Making and Choice: Issues, Models, and Suggestions," *Marketing Letters,* August 1991, pp. 181–98.
8. Robert J. Donovan, John R. Rossiter, Gillian Marcoolyn, and Andrew Nesdale, "Store Atmosphere and Purchasing Behavior," *Journal of Retailing,* Fall 1994, pp. 283–94; and Eric A. Greenleaf and Donald R. Lehmann, "Reasons for Substantial Delay in Consumer Decision Making," *Journal of Consumer Research,* September 1995, pp. 186–99.
9. "Webrooming and Mobile Showrooming in 2015," *multichannelmerchant.com,* January 19, 2016.
10. Sunil Gupta and Valarie Zeithaml, "Customer Metrics and Their Impact on Financial Performance," *Marketing Science,* November–December 2006, pp. 718–39.
11. These estimates are given in Jagdish N. Sheth and Banwari Mitral, *Consumer Behavior,* 2nd ed. (Mason, OH: South-Western Publishing, 2003), p. 32.
12. Francis Buttle and Stan Maklan, *Customer Relationship Management,* 3rd ed. (London: Routledge, 2015); "Customer Retention Is Top Concern for 64% of Dealers," www.autoremarketing.com, May 1, 2016; and "GM at Top for Customer Loyalty," www.thedrive.com, January 18, 2018.
13. For an overview of research on involvement, see Wayne D. Hoyer, Deborah J. MacInnis, and Rik Pieters, *Consumer Behavior,* 7th ed. (Independence, KY: Cengage Publishing, 2018).
14. Russell Belk, "Situational Variables and Consumer Behavior," *Journal of Consumer Research,* December 1975, pp. 157–63. The examples in this section are taken from Martin Lindstrom, *buy.ology: Truth and Lies about Why We Buy* (New York: Doubleday Publishing, 2008).
15. For a thorough discussion of consumer experience and the consumer journey, see Katherine N. Lemon and Peter C. Verhoef, "Understanding Customer Experience and the Customer Journey," *Journal of Marketing,* November 2016, pp. 69–96.
16. A. H. Maslow, *Motivation and Personality* (New York: Harper & Row, 1970). For an update on this need hierarchy, see Douglas T. Kendrick et al., "Renovating the Pyramid of Needs: Contemporary Extensions Built upon Ancient Foundations," *Perspectives on Psychological Sciences* 5, no. 3 (2010), pp. 292–314.
17. Bernardo J. Carducci, *The Psychology of Personality,* 2nd ed. (Oxford, UK: Wiley, 2009), pp. 182–84; and D. Bratko, A. Butkovic, and M. Bosnjak, "Twin Study of Impulsive Buying and Its Overlap with Personality, *Journal of Individual Differences* 34, no. 1 (2013), pp. 8–14.
18. Jane Spencer, "Lenovo Puts Style in New Laptop," *The Wall Street Journal,* September 28, 2009.
19. Julie Sedivy and Greg Carlson, *Sold on Language: How Advertisers Talk to You and What This Says about You* (New York: Wiley, 2011).
20. "Myth: Subliminal Messages Can Change Your Behavior," www.psychologicalscience.org, March 29, 2019.
21. Adrian Furnham, "Hidden Persuaders: The Psychology of Subliminal Perception," www.psychologytoday.com, July 20, 2015; Ian Zimmerman, "Subliminal Ads, Unconscious Influence, and Consumption," www.pschologytoday.com, June 9, 2014; and August Bullock, *The Secret Sales Pitch* (San Jose, CA: Norwich Publishers, 2004).
22. "Death of a Car Salesman," *The Economist,* August 22, 2015, pp. 52–54.
23. "The Death of Brand Loyalty: Cultural Shifts Mean It's Gone Forever," www.forbes.com, July 26, 2016; and "Deloitte Survey: Shoppers Continue to Leave National Brands," www.prnewswire.com, June 23, 2015.
24. Martin Fishbein and I. Aizen, *Belief, Attitude, Intention and Behavior: An Introduction to Theory and Research* (Reading, MA: Addison-Wesley, 1975), p. 6.
25. Richard J. Lutz, "Changing Brand Attitudes through Modification of Cognitive Structure," *Journal of Consumer Research,* March 1975, pp. 49–59.
26. This discussion is based on "The VALS™ Types," www.strategicbusinessinsights.com, downloaded February 1, 2019.
27. This discussion is based on Ed Keller and Jon Berry, *The Influentials* (New York: Simon and Schuster, 2003); "The Kids Who Rule Toyland," *Bloomberg Businessweek,* October 23, 2017; and "For Influencers, Instagram Is the Clear-Cut Favorite," www.emarketer.com, January 30, 2018.
28. Ed Keller and Brad Fay, "Word-of-Mouth Advocacy: A New Key to Advertising Effectiveness," *Journal of Advertising Research,* December 2012, pp. 459–64.
29. "What Really Shapes the Customer Experience," www.bcg.perspectives.com, September 10, 2015.
30. Correspondence with Rebecca A. Hall, Marketing Manager, BzzAgent, April 28, 2017; and www.BzzAgent.com, downloaded April 22, 2019.
31. "Sizing Up Reviews on Amazon," *The Wall Street Journal*, December 21, 2018, pp. B1, B4; "Instagram Strips Out Fake 'Likes' Tied to 3rd-Party Apps," *marketingland.com*, November 19, 2018; and "Why Facebook Hates and Likes Fake Likes," www.forbes.com, October 6, 2014.
32. Net Promoter Score is a registered trademark of Frederick R. Reichheld, Bain & Company, and Satmetrix. Bendle et al., *Marketing Metrics*, 3rd ed. (Upper Saddle Ridge, NJ: Pearson Education, 2016).
33. Net Promoter Score is a registered trademark of Frederick R. Reichheld, Bain & Company, and Satmetrix. Bendle et al., *Marketing Metrics*.
34. Wayne D. Hoyer, Deborah J. MacInnis, and Rik Pieters, *Consumer Behavior,* 7th ed. (Independence, KY: Cengage Publishing, 2018).
35. Caroline Bankoff, "Abercrombie & Fitch Will Pay The Situation to Not Wear Their Clothes," *Vulture*, August 16, 2011; Elizabeth Holmes, "Abercrombie and Fitch Offers to Pay 'The Situation' to Stop Wearing Its Clothes," *The Wall Street Journal,* August 16, 2011, p. B2.
36. For a recent overview of social class and consumer behavior, see Sharon Shavitt, Duo Jiang, and Hyewon Cho, "Stratification and Segmentation: Social Class in Consumer Behavior," *Journal of Consumer Psychology,* October 2016, pp. 583–93.
37. For an extensive review on consumer socialization of children, see Deborah Roedder John, "Consumer Socialization of Children: A Retrospective Look at Twenty-Five Years of Research," *Journal of Consumer Research,* December 1999, pp. 183–213. Also see Elizabeth S. Moore, William L. Wilkie, and Richard J. Lutz, "Passing the Torch: Intergenerational

Influences as a Source of Brand Equity," *Journal of Marketing,* April 2002, pp. 17–37.

38. "America's Families and Living Arrangements: 2018" (Washington, DC: U.S. Department of Commerce, August 2019); "Supermarkets Lure in Male Shoppers," *The Wall Street Journal,* July 10, 2018, p. A9; and Rich Morin and D'Vera Cohn, "Women Call the Shots at Home: Public Mixed on Gender Roles in Jobs," www.pewresearch.org, downloaded February 4, 2011. Also see Rex Y. Du and Wagner A. Kamakura, "Household Life Cycles and Lifestyles in the United States," *Journal of Marketing Research,* February 2006, pp. 121–32.

39. David L. Mothersbaugh, Delbert I. Hawkins, and Susan Kleiser, *Consumer Behavior: Building Marketing Strategy,* 14th ed. (Burr Ridge, IL: McGraw-Hill/Irwin, 2016); "New Kids on the Block," *Advertising Age,* January 21, 2019, pp. 22–24; and "62% Rise in Millennial Dads Buying Groceries: Study," *progressivegrocer.com,* June 13, 2016.

40. Jeffrey M. Humphreys, "The Multicultural Economy in 2018," Selig Center for Economic Growth, Terry College of Business, The University of Georgia.

41. The remainder of this discussion is based on Hoyer et al., *Consumer Behavior*; and *15th Annual Hispanic Fact Pack* (New York: Advertising Age, 2019).

42. The remainder of this discussion is based on Hoyer et al., *Consumer Behavior*; and *Powerful, Growing, Influential: The African-American Consumer* (New York: The Nielsen Company, 2016).

43. The remainder of this discussion is based on *Asian-Americans Are Expanding Their Footprint in the U.S. and Making an Impact* (New York: The Nielsen Company, 2016); and *Asian American Women: Digitally Fluent with Intercultural Mindset* (New York: The Nielsen Company, 2017).

44. Coppertone: This case was written by Steven Hartley and Roger Kerin. Sources: Interviews with Coppertone executives Tracy Nunziata and Lisa Perez; information from the Coppertone website, www.coppertone.com; "A New Day for Sun Care," *GCI Magazine,* January–February 2016, pp. 32–35; "Consumers Embrace Multifunction Sun Products," *Chain Drug Review,* July 6, 2015, p. 43; Jayme Cyk, "Sun Care's New Wave," *WWB,* April 10, 2015, p. 6; Antoinette Alexander, "Raising Awareness about Sun Safety," *Drug Store News,* August 25, 2014, p. 128; Lisa Samalonis, "Sun Care: It's All about Convenience," *Beauty Packaging,* April–May 2012, p. 42–46; "Coppertone Polarized Lenses," *20/20,* 2016, p. 108; Andrew Karp, "Vision Ease Intros Coppertone Polarized Lenses in Green," *Vision Monday,* January 18, 2016, p. 27; and Mercedes M. Cardona, "Coppertone Brings Back Ad Icon for $15 Mil Effort," *Advertising Age,* February 15, 1999, p. 16.

Chapter 6 Understanding Organizations as Customers

LEARNING OBJECTIVES

After reading this chapter you should be able to:

LO 6-1 Distinguish among industrial, reseller, and government organizational markets.

LO 6-2 Describe the key characteristics of organizational buying that make it different from consumer buying.

LO 6-3 Explain how buying centers and buying situations influence organizational purchasing.

LO 6-4 Recognize the importance and nature of online buying in industrial, reseller, and government organizational markets.

Organizational Buying Is Marketing, Too! Purchasing Publication Paper for JCPenney

Executives at JCPMedia, Inc. view paper differently than most people do. And for good reason. JCPMedia purchasing professionals buy over 100,000 tons of publication paper–annually.

JCPMedia is responsible for print and paper purchasing at JCPenney, one of the largest department store retailers in the United States. JCPMedia buys publication paper for JCPenney newspaper inserts and direct-mail pieces, which is a serious responsibility. Some 10 companies from around the world–including Verso Paper in the United States, Catalyst Paper Corporation in Canada, Norske Skog in Norway, and UPM-Kymmene, Inc. in Finland–supply paper to JCPenney.

"The choice of paper and suppliers is also a significant marketing decision given the sizable revenue and expense consequences," notes the Vice President-Marketing Production at JCPMedia, Inc. JCPMedia paper buyers work closely with senior JCPenney marketing executives and within budget constraints to ensure that the right appearance, quality, and quantity of publication paper is purchased at the right price point for merchandise featured in the millions of JCPenney newspaper inserts and direct-mail pieces distributed every year in the United States.

In addition to paper appearance, quality, quantity, and price, JCPMedia paper buyers formally evaluate paper supplier capabilities, often by extended visits to supplier facilities in the United States, Canada, and Europe. Supplier capabilities include the capacity to deliver on-time selected grades of paper from specialty items to magazine papers, the availability of specific types of paper to meet printing deadlines, and formal programs focused on the life cycle of paper products. For example, a supplier's forestry management and sustainability practices are considered in the paper buying process. In fact, paper bought by JCPMedia is certified through the Sustainable Forestry Initiative, Forest Stewardship Council, or the Programme for the Endorsement of Forest Certification–three prominent certification programs for forest management.[1]

The next time you thumb through a JCPenney newspaper insert or direct-mail piece, take a moment to notice the paper. Considerable effort and attention were given to this selection and purchase decision by JCPMedia paper buyers.

Purchasing paper for JCPMedia is one example of organizational buying. This chapter examines the different types of organizational buyers; key characteristics of organizational buying, including online buying; buying situations; unique aspects of the organizational buying process compared with the consumer purchase process; and some typical buying procedures and decisions in today's organizational markets.

Source: JCPenney

BUSINESS-TO-BUSINESS MARKETING AND ORGANIZATIONAL BUYERS

LO 6-1
Distinguish among industrial, reseller, and government organizational markets.

Understanding organizational markets and buying behavior is a necessary prerequisite for effective business-to-business marketing. **Business-to-business marketing** is the marketing of products and services to companies, governments, or not-for-profit organizations for use in the creation of products and services that they can produce and market to others. Because over half of all U.S. business school graduates take jobs in firms that engage in business marketing, it is important to understand the characteristics of organizational buyers and their buying behavior.

Organizational Buyers

Organizational buyers are those manufacturers, wholesalers, retailers, service companies, not-for-profit organizations, and government agencies that buy products and services for their own use or for resale. For example, these organizations buy computers and telephone services for their own use. However, manufacturers buy raw materials and parts that they reprocess into the finished goods they sell. Wholesalers and retailers resell the goods they buy without reprocessing them.

Organizational buyers include all buyers in a nation except ultimate consumers. These organizational buyers purchase and lease large volumes of capital equipment, raw materials, manufactured parts, supplies, and business services. In fact, because they often buy raw materials and parts, process them, and sell the upgraded product several times before it is purchased by the final organizational buyer or ultimate consumer, the total annual purchases of organizational buyers are far greater than those of ultimate consumers. IBM alone buys over $300 billion in products and services each year for its own use or resale.[2]

Organizational Markets

Organizational buyers are divided into three markets: (1) industrial, (2) reseller, and (3) government.[3] Each market is described next.

Industrial Markets There are about 7.5 million firms in the industrial, or business, market. These *industrial firms* in some way reprocess a product or service they buy before selling it again to the next buyer. This is certainly true of Corning, Inc., which transforms an exotic blend of materials to create optical fiber capable of carrying much of the telephone traffic in the United States on a single strand. It is also true (if you stretch your imagination) of a firm selling services, such as a bank that takes money from its depositors, reprocesses it, and "sells" it as loans to borrowers.

Companies that primarily sell physical goods (manufacturing; mining; construction; and farms, timber, and fisheries) represent 25 percent of all the industrial firms. The services market sells diverse services such as legal advice, auto repair, and dry cleaning. Service companies–finance, insurance, and real estate businesses; transportation, communication, and public utility firms; and not-for-profit organizations–represent 75 percent of all industrial firms.

Reseller Markets Wholesalers and retailers that buy physical products and resell them again without any reprocessing are *resellers*. In the United States there are about 1.1 million retailers and 435,000 wholesalers. In Chapters 15 and 16, you will see how manufacturers use wholesalers and retailers in their distribution ("place") strategies as channels through which their products reach ultimate consumers. In this chapter, we look at these resellers mainly as organizational buyers in terms of (1) how they make their own buying decisions and (2) which products they choose to carry.

VIDEO 6-1
NASA
kerin.tv/15e/v6-1

Government Markets *Government units* are the federal, state, and local agencies that buy goods and services for the constituents they serve. There are about 89,500 of these government units in the United States. These purchases include the $20.4 billion the National Aeronautics and Space Administration (NASA) intends to pay Lockheed Martin through 2023 to develop the Orion Multi-Purpose Crew Vehicle to explore asteroids and Mars.[4]

Measuring Organizational Markets

The measurement of industrial, reseller, and government markets is an important first step for a firm interested in gauging the size of one, two, or all three of these markets in the United States and around the world. This task has been made easier with the **North American Industry Classification System (NAICS)**. The NAICS provides common industry definitions for Canada, Mexico, and the United States.

The NAICS groups economic activity to permit studies of market share, demand for products and services, import competition in domestic markets, and similar studies. It designates industries with a numerical code in a defined structure. A six-digit coding system is used. The

The Orion spacecraft to be designed, developed, tested, and evaluated by Lockheed Martin Corp. is an example of a purchase by a government unit, namely, NASA. Read the text to find out how much NASA will pay for Orion's development, test flights, and its first manned mission.
Courtesy of Lockheed Martin Company

first two digits designate a sector of the economy, the third digit designates a subsector, and the fourth digit represents an industry group. The fifth digit designates a specific industry and is the most detailed level at which comparable data are available for Canada, Mexico, and the United States. The sixth digit designates individual country-level national industries.

LEARNING REVIEW

6-1. Organizational buyers are ___________.

6-2. What are the three main types of organizational buyers?

CHARACTERISTICS OF ORGANIZATIONAL BUYING

LO 6-2
Describe the key characteristics of organizational buying that make it different from consumer buying.

Organizations are different from individuals, so buying for an organization is different from buying for yourself or your family. In both cases the objective in making the purchase is to solve the buyer's problem—to satisfy a need or want. However, the unique objectives and policies of an organization put special constraints on how it makes buying decisions. Understanding the characteristics of organizational buying is essential in designing effective marketing programs to reach these buyers. Key characteristics of organizational buying are listed in Figure 6-1 and discussed next.[5]

Demand Characteristics

Consumer demand for products and services is affected by their price and availability and by consumers' personal tastes and discretionary income. By comparison, industrial demand is derived. **Derived demand** means that the demand for industrial products and services is driven by, or derived from, demand for consumer products and services. For example, the demand for Weyerhaeuser's pulp and paper products is based on consumer demand for newspapers, FedEx packages, and disposable diapers. Derived demand is based on expectations of future consumer demand. For instance, Whirlpool buys parts for its washers and dryers in

CHARACTERISTICS	DIMENSIONS
Market characteristics	• Demand for industrial products and services is derived. • Few customers typically exist, and their purchase orders are large.
Product or service characteristics	• Products or services are technical in nature and purchased on the basis of specifications. • Many of the goods purchased are raw and semifinished. • Heavy emphasis is placed on delivery time, technical assistance, and postsale service.
Buying process characteristics	• Technically qualified and professional buyers follow established purchasing policies and procedures. • Buying objectives and criteria are typically spelled out, as are procedures for evaluating sellers and their products or services. • There are multiple buying influences, and multiple parties participate in purchase decisions. • There are reciprocal arrangements, and negotiation between buyers and sellers is commonplace. • Online buying over the Internet is widespread.
Marketing mix characteristics	• Direct selling to organizational buyers is the rule, and distribution is very important. • Advertising and other forms of promotion are technical in nature. • Price is often negotiated, evaluated as part of broader seller and product/service qualities, and frequently affected by quantity discounts.

FIGURE 6–1
Key characteristics and dimensions of organizational buying behavior.

anticipation of consumer demand, which is affected by the replacement cycle for these products and by consumer income.

Size of the Order or Purchase

The size of the purchase involved in organizational buying is typically much larger than that in consumer buying. The dollar value of a single purchase made by an organization can amount to millions or billions of dollars. For example, Siemens was paid $1 billion to build a natural-gas-fired power plant in Texas.[6] The Boeing Company, the world's largest aerospace company, charges about $111 million for its "average" Boeing 737 commercial jetliner, $375 million for its Boeing 777, and $293 million for the Boeing 787.[7]

With so much money at stake, most organizations place constraints on their buyers in the form of purchasing policies or procedures. Buyers must often get competitive bids from at least three prospective suppliers when the order is above a specific amount, such as $5,000. When the order is above an even higher amount, such as $50,000, it may require the review and approval of a vice president or even the president of the company. Knowing how order size affects buying practices is important in determining who will participate in the purchase decision, who will make the final decision, and the length of time that will be required to arrive at a purchase agreement.

Buying commercial aircraft is time-consuming, involved, and expensive. Read the text to find out how much a new Boeing 777 airplane costs.
Karie Hamilton/Bloomberg/Getty Images

Number of Potential Buyers

Firms marketing consumer products or services often try to reach thousands or millions of individuals or households. For

Marketing Insights About Me

Do I Buy from Organizations That Promote Diversity among Their Suppliers and in Their Workplaces?

Supplier diversity is a strategic initiative in many organizations. More often than not, an organization's emphasis on supplier diversity goes hand in hand with an emphasis on workplace diversity.

Few consumers are aware of which organizations actively engage minority- and women-owned suppliers and vendors and promote diversity in their workplace. DiversityInc is a valuable source of contemporary information about company diversity practices. Its mission is to bring education and clarity to the business benefits of diversity. Each year, DiversityInc publishes a list of companies recognized for their workplace and supplier diversity practices.

To access this list, visit www.diversityinc.com and click "Top 50 Lists" at the top of the home page. Here you will find valuable information on the wide variety of diversity issues as well as the Top 12 companies for supplier diversity.

Source: DiversityInc

Supplier Diversity Program

Pitney Bowes is a leader in supplier diversity. The company has hundreds of diverse suppliers that account for millions of dollars in annual purchases. To learn more about companies that have successful supplier diversity, and corporate diversity overall, visit www.diversityinc.com.

Source: Pitney Bowes Inc.

example, your local supermarket or bank probably serves thousands of people. Kellogg tries to reach 80 million North American households with its breakfast cereals and probably succeeds in selling to a third or half of these in any given year. Firms marketing to organizations are often restricted to far fewer buyers. Gulfstream Aerospace Corporation can sell its business jets to a few thousand organizations throughout the world, and Goodyear sells its original equipment tires to fewer than 10 car manufacturers.

Organizational Buying Objectives

For business firms, the buying objective is usually to increase profits through reducing costs or increasing revenues. For example, 7-Eleven buys automated inventory systems to increase the number of products that can be sold through its convenience stores and to keep them fresh. Nissan Motor Company switched its advertising agency because it expects the new agency to devise a more effective ad campaign to help it sell more cars and increase revenues. To improve executive decision making, many firms buy advanced computer systems to process data. The objectives of nonprofit firms and government agencies are usually to meet the needs of the groups they serve.

Many companies today have broadened their buying objectives to include an emphasis on buying from minority- and women-owned suppliers and vendors. Companies such as Pitney Bowes, PepsiCo, AT&T, Coors, and JCPenney report that sales, profits, and customer satisfaction have increased because of their minority- and women-owned supplier and vendor initiatives. To learn more about companies that have successful supplier diversity programs and corporate diversity overall, visit www.diversityinc.com described in the Marketing Insights About Me box.

Other companies include environmental sustainability initiatives. For example, Lowe's and The Home Depot no longer purchase lumber from companies that harvest timber from the world's endangered forests. Successful business marketers recognize that understanding a company's buying objectives is a necessary first step in marketing to organizations.

Organizational Buying Criteria

In making a purchase, the buying organization must weigh key buying criteria that apply to the potential supplier and what it wants to sell. *Organizational buying criteria* are the objective attributes of the supplier's products and services and the capabilities of the supplier itself. These criteria serve the same purpose as the evaluative criteria used by consumers and described in Chapter 5. The most commonly used criteria are (1) price, (2) ability to meet the quality specifications required for the item, (3) ability to meet required delivery schedules, (4) technical capability, (5) warranties and claim policies in the event of poor performance, (6) past performance on previous contracts, and (7) production facilities and capacity.[8] Suppliers that meet or exceed these criteria create customer value.

As a practical example, Figure 6–2 shows the actual buying criteria employed by organizational buyers when choosing among machine vision system products and suppliers, as well as the frequency with which these criteria are used. Interestingly, of the various selection criteria listed, a machine vision system's price is among the least frequently mentioned.[9]

Many organizational buyers today are transforming their buying criteria into specific requirements that are communicated to prospective suppliers. This practice, called *supplier development,* involves the deliberate effort by organizational buyers to build relationships that shape suppliers' products, services, and capabilities to fit a buyer's needs and those of its customers. Consider Deere & Company, the maker of John Deere farm, construction, and lawn-care equipment. Deere employs supplier-development engineers who work full-time with the company's suppliers to improve their efficiency and quality and reduce their costs. According to a Deere senior executive, "Their quality, delivery, and costs are, after all, our quality, delivery, and costs."[10]

Buyer–Seller Relationships and Supply Partnerships

Another distinction between organizational and consumer buying behavior lies in the nature of the relationship between organizational buyers and suppliers. Specifically, organizational

FIGURE 6–2
Product and supplier selection criteria for buying machine vision equipment emphasize factors other than price.
(Photo): Courtesy of Keyence Corporation of America

A machine vision inspection camera is used in the automotive industry to perform a gear inspection—in this case, to check if the notches are correctly angled and sized.

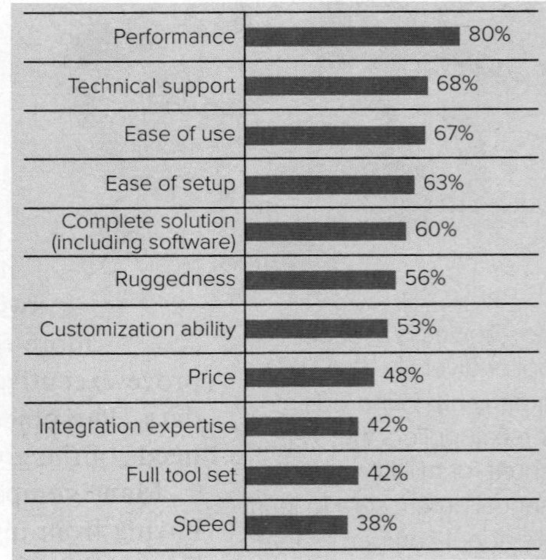

Individual selection criteria cited as most important by machine vision buyers making a product or supplier decision.

Marketing Matters — Customer Value

At Milsco Manufacturing, "Our Marketing Philosophy Is Designed to Develop Partnerships" and Deliver a Great Ride for Customers' Seats

Form, fit, and functionality are the hallmarks of a proper seating solution. Just ask the executives and engineers at Milsco Manufacturing, which produces more than 3 million seats annually in more than 200 unique variations.

ChameleonsEye/Shutterstock

Whether you are cruising the wide open spaces on your Harley-Davidson motorcycle or mowing your backyard on a John Deere lawn tractor, you're getting a comfortable ride thanks to a company you may have never heard of. Milsco is a Wisconsin-based designer and producer of seating solutions. Its customers include Harley-Davidson, John Deere, Yamaha, Caterpillar, Arctic Cat, Kubata, Toro, and Toyota, as well as numerous other well-known and respected household names in the motorcycle, power sports, agricultural, construction, marine recreation, turf care, industrial lift, golf cart, and mobility markets.

Milsco's marketing philosophy is designed to develop partnerships with its customers. The 85-year partnership between Harley-Davidson and Milsco is a case in point. Since 1934, Milsco has been the sole source of original equipment motorcycle seats and a major supplier of aftermarket parts and accessories, such as saddlebags, for Harley-Davidson. Milsco engineers and designers work closely with their Harley counterparts in the design of each year's new products.

In fact, Milsco partners with each of its customers to design and manufacture the most effective and functional seating solution. Every year, the company launches over 100 new products, many of which are crafted by hand, in response to new and changing customer requirements.

The next time you sit down on a Harley or a John Deere lawn tractor (or any other product involving a partnership with Milsco Manufacturing), notice the seat and remember that it was designed and manufactured for your form, fit, and functionality—and, of course, comfort.

buying is more likely to involve complex negotiations concerning delivery schedules, price, technical specifications, warranties, and claim policies. These negotiations also can last for an extended period. This was the case when the U.S. Department of Energy's Oak Ridge National Laboratory acquired an IBM Summit supercomputer at a cost of about $200 million. In terms of processing speed, the Summit can perform 200,000 trillion calculations a second![11]

Reciprocal arrangements also exist in organizational buying. *Reciprocity* is an industrial buying practice in which two organizations agree to purchase each other's products and services. The U.S. Justice Department disapproves of reciprocal buying because it restricts the normal operation of the free market. However, the practice exists and can limit the flexibility of organizational buyers in choosing alternative suppliers.

Long-term contracts are also prevalent. For example, GT Advanced Technology has a multiyear, $578 million contract with Apple to supply material used in iPhone camera lenses and screens.[12]

In some cases, buyer–seller relationships evolve into supply partnerships. A *supply partnership* exists when a buyer and its supplier adopt mutually beneficial objectives, policies, and procedures for the purpose of lowering the cost or increasing the value of products and services delivered to the ultimate consumer. A classic example of a supply partnership is the one between Harley-Davidson and Milsco Manufacturing. Milsco has designed and manufactured Harley-Davidson motorcycle seats since 1934. The importance of supply partnerships for Milsco is described in the Marketing Matters box.[13]

VIDEO 6-2
Starbucks Sustainability
kerin.tv/15e/v6-2

Retailers, too, have forged partnerships with their suppliers. Walmart has such a relationship with Procter & Gamble for ordering and replenishing P&G's products in its stores. By using computerized cash register scanning equipment and direct electronic linkages to P&G, Walmart can tell P&G what merchandise is needed, along with how much, when, and to which store to deliver it on a daily basis.

Making Responsible Decisions

Sustainability

Sustainable Procurement for Sustainable Growth at Starbucks

saravutpics/Shutterstock

Manufacturers, retailers, wholesalers, and governmental agencies are increasingly sensitive to how their buying decisions affect the environment. Concerns about the depletion of natural resources; air, water, and soil pollution; and the social consequences of economic activity have given rise to the concept of sustainable procurement. Sustainable procurement aims to integrate environmental considerations into all stages of an organization's buying process with the goal of reducing the negative impact on human health and the physical environment.

Starbucks is a pioneer and worldwide leader in sustainable procurement. The company's attention to quality coffee extends to its coffee growers located in more than 20 countries. This means that Starbucks pays coffee farmers a fair price for the beans; that the coffee is grown in an ecologically sound manner; and that Starbucks invests in the farming communities where its coffees are produced. In this way, Starbucks focuses on the sustainable growth of its suppliers.

Supply partnerships often include provisions for what is called *sustainable procurement*. To learn more about this buying practice and how it has been embraced at Starbucks, see the Making Responsible Decisions box.[14]

THE ORGANIZATIONAL BUYING FUNCTION, PROCESS, AND BUYING CENTER

Organizational buyers, like consumers, engage in a decision process when selecting products and services. **Organizational buying behavior** is the decision-making process that organizations use to establish the need for products and services and identify, evaluate, and choose among alternative brands and suppliers. There are important similarities and differences between the two decision-making processes. To better understand the nature of organizational buying behavior, we first describe the buying function in organizations. Next, the organizational buying process itself is detailed by comparing it with consumer buying behavior. We then describe a unique feature of organizational buying–the buying center.

The Buying Function in Organizations

The buying function in an organization is primarily responsible for facilitating the selection and purchase of products and services for the organization's own use or resale to consumers. The buying function involves gathering and screening information about products and services, prices, and suppliers, called *vendors*. The buying function is often responsible for the formal solicitation of bids from suppliers (vendors) and the awarding of purchasing contracts.

STAGE IN THE BUYING DECISION PROCESS	CONSUMER PURCHASE: SMARTPHONE FOR A STUDENT	ORGANIZATIONAL PURCHASE: EARBUD HEADSET FOR A SMARTPHONE
Problem recognition	Student doesn't like the features of the smartphone now owned and desires a new one.	Marketing research and sales departments observe that competitors are improving the earbud headsets for their smartphones. The firm decides to improve the earbud headsets on its own new models, which will be purchased from an outside supplier.
Information search	Student uses personal past experience and that of friends, ads, the Internet, and *Consumer Reports* to collect information and uncover alternatives.	Design and production engineers draft specifications for earbud headsets. The purchasing department identifies suppliers of earbud headsets.
Alternative evaluation	Alternative smartphones are evaluated on the basis of important attributes desired in a phone, and several stores are visited.	Purchasing and engineering personnel visit with suppliers and assess (1) facilities, (2) capacity, (3) quality control, and (4) financial status. They drop any suppliers not satisfactory on these attributes.
Purchase decision	A specific brand of smartphone is selected, the price is paid, and the student leaves the store.	They use (1) quality, (2) price, (3) delivery, and (4) technical capability as key buying criteria to select a supplier. Then they negotiate terms and award a contract.
Postpurchase behavior	Student reevaluates the purchase decision and may return the phone to the store if it is unsatisfactory.	They evaluate suppliers using a formal vendor rating system and notify a supplier if the earbud headsets do not meet their quality standard. If the problem is not corrected, they drop the firm as a future supplier.

FIGURE 6–3
Comparing the stages in a consumer and organizational purchase decision process.

Individuals responsible for the selection and purchase of goods and services are typically called purchasing managers or agents, procurement managers, or sourcing managers. Their role in the organizational buying process is described below.

Stages in the Organizational Buying Process

As shown in Figure 6–3, the five stages a student might use in buying a smartphone also apply to organizational purchases. However, comparing the two columns in Figure 6–3 reveals some key differences. For example, when a manufacturer buys an earbud headset for its units from a supplier, more individuals are involved, supplier capability becomes more important, and the postpurchase evaluation behavior is more formal. The earbud headset buying decision process is typical of the steps made by organizational buyers.

The Buying Center: A Cross-Functional Group

LO 6-3
Explain how buying centers and buying situations influence organizational purchasing.

For routine purchases with a small dollar value, a single buyer or purchasing manager often makes the purchase decision alone. In many instances, however, several people in the organization participate in the buying process. The individuals in this group, called a **buying center**, share common goals, risks, and knowledge important to a purchase decision. For most large multistore chain resellers, such as Target, 7-Eleven convenience stores, or Safeway, the buying center is highly formalized and is called a *buying committee*. However, most industrial firms or government units use informal groups of people or call meetings to arrive at buying decisions.

The importance of the buying center requires that a firm marketing to many industrial firms and government units understand the structure, the technical and business functions represented, and the behavior of these groups.[15] Four questions provide guidance in understanding the buying center in these organizations:

1. Which individuals are in the buying center for the product or service?
2. What is the relative influence of each member of the group?
3. What are the buying criteria of each member?
4. How does each member of the group perceive our firm, our products and services, and our salespeople?

People in the Buying Center The composition of the buying center in a given organization depends on the specific item being bought. Although a buyer or purchasing manager is almost always a member of the buying center, individuals from other functional areas are included, depending on what is to be purchased. In buying a million-dollar machine tool, the president (because of the size of the purchase) and the production vice president or manager would probably be members. For key components to be included in a final manufactured product, a cross-functional group of individuals from research and development (R&D), engineering, and quality control are likely to be added. For new word-processing software and equipment, experienced secretaries who will use the equipment would be members. Still, a major question in penetrating the buying center is finding and reaching the people who will initiate, influence, and actually make the buying decision.

Roles in the Buying Center Researchers have identified five specific roles that an individual in a buying center can play.[16] In some purchases the same person may perform two or more of these roles. In other purchases, two or more people may perform these roles.

- *Users* are the people in the organization who actually use the product or service, such as a secretary who will use a new word processor.
- *Influencers* affect the buying decision, usually by helping define the specifications for what is bought. The information technology manager would be a key influencer in the purchase of a new mainframe computer.
- *Buyers* have formal authority and responsibility to select the supplier and negotiate the terms of the contract. Senior purchasing managers perform this role at JCPMedia, as described in the chapter opening example.
- *Deciders* have the formal or informal power to select or approve the supplier that receives the contract. In routine orders the decider is usually the buyer or purchasing manager; in important technical purchases it is more likely to be someone from R&D, engineering, or quality control. The decider for a key component being incorporated in a final manufactured product might be any of these three people.
- *Gatekeepers* control the flow of information in the buying center. Purchasing personnel, technical experts, and secretaries can all keep salespeople or information from reaching people performing the other four roles.

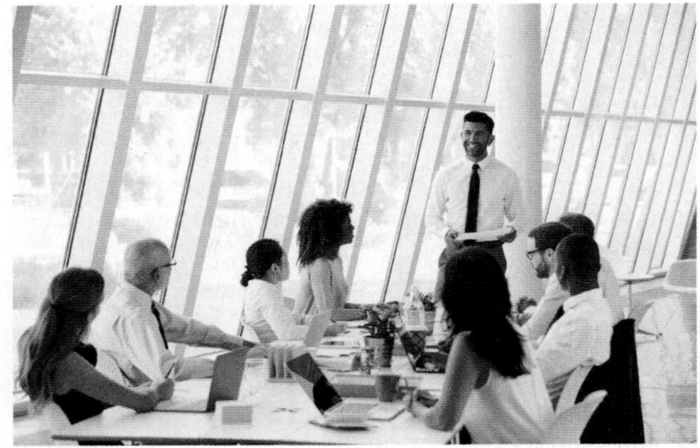

Effective marketing to organizations requires an understanding of buying centers and their role in purchase decisions.
Monkeybusinessimages/Getty Images

Buying Situations and the Buying Center The number of people in the buying center largely depends on the specific buying situation. Researchers who have studied organizational buying identify three types of buying situations, called **buy classes**. These buy classes vary from the routine reorder, or *straight rebuy*, to the completely new purchase, termed *new buy*. In between these extremes is the *modified rebuy*. Figure 6–4 summarizes how buy classes affect buying center tendencies in different ways. Some examples will clarify the differences.[17]

- *New buy*. Here the organization is a first-time buyer of the product or service. This involves greater potential risks in the purchase, so the buying center is enlarged to include

BUYING CENTER DIMENSION	NEW BUY	STRAIGHT REBUY	MODIFIED REBUY
	BUY-CLASS SITUATION		
People involved	Many	One	Two to three
Decision time	Long	Short	Moderate
Problem definition	Uncertain	Well-defined	Minor modifications
Buying objective	Good solution	Low-priced supplier	Low-priced supplier
Suppliers considered	New/present	Present	Present
Buying influence	Technical/operating personnel	Purchasing agent	Purchasing agent and others

FIGURE 6–4
The buying situation affects buying center behavior in different ways. Understanding these differences can pay huge dividends for companies that market to organizations.

all those who have a stake in the new buy. BMW's recent purchase of a multimillion-dollar cloud-based data management system from IBM represents a new buy.

- *Straight rebuy*. Here the buyer or purchasing manager reorders an existing product or service from the list of acceptable suppliers, probably without even checking with users or influencers from the engineering, production, or quality control departments. Office supplies and maintenance services are usually obtained as straight rebuys.
- *Modified rebuy*. In this buying situation the users, influencers, or deciders in the buying center want to change the product specifications, price, delivery schedule, or supplier. Although the item purchased is largely the same as with the straight rebuy, the changes usually necessitate enlarging the buying center to include people outside the purchasing department.

LEARNING REVIEW

6-3. What one department is almost always represented by a person in the buying center?

6-4. What are the three types of buying situations or buy classes?

ONLINE BUYING IN BUSINESS-TO-BUSINESS MARKETING

LO 6-4
Recognize the importance and nature of online buying in industrial, reseller, and government organizational markets.

Organizational buying behavior and business-to-business marketing continue to evolve with the application of Internet technology. Organizations dwarf consumers in terms of online transactions made, average transaction size, and overall purchase volume. In fact, organizational buyers account for about 70 percent of the global dollar value of all online transactions.

Prominence of Online Buying in Organizational Markets

Online buying in organizational markets is prominent for three major reasons.[18] First, organizational buyers depend heavily on timely supplier information that describes product

Marketing Matters — Entrepreneurship

eBay Means Business for Business-to-Business Marketing Entrepreneurs, Too!

San Jose, California–based eBay Inc. is a true Internet phenomenon. By any measure, it is the predominant person-to-person trading community in the world. But there is more.

eBay offers a trading platform for 6 million small businesses in the United States engaged in business-to-business marketing and even greater numbers around the world. For example, 81 percent of small businesses on eBay Business Supply sell to five or more foreign countries. eBay Business Supply does some $4 billion per year in gross merchandise sales.

rvlsoft/Shutterstock

The eBay trading platform has proven to be a boon for small businesses. According to an eBay-commissioned survey conducted by Nielsen, 82 percent of small businesses using eBay report that it has helped their business grow and expand, 78 percent say it has helped to reduce their costs, and 79 percent say it has helped their business become more profitable.

In addition, eBay promotes entrepreneurship. According to a spokesperson from the American Enterprise Institute for Public Policy Research, "The potential for entrepreneurs to realize success through eBay is significant."

availability, technical specifications, application uses, price, and delivery schedules. This information can be conveyed quickly via Internet technology. Second, this technology has been shown to substantially reduce buyer order processing costs. At General Electric, online buying has cut the cost of a purchase transaction from $50 to $100 to about $5. Third, business marketers have found that Internet technology can reduce marketing costs, particularly sales and advertising expense, and broaden their potential customer base for many types of products and services.

For these reasons, online buying is popular in all three kinds of organizational markets. For example, airlines electronically order over $15 billion in spare parts from the Boeing Company each year. Customers of W. W. Grainger, a large U.S. wholesaler of maintenance, repair, and operating supplies, buy almost $5 billion worth of these products annually online. Supply and service purchases totaling about $50 billion each year are made online by the U.S. government.

E-Marketplaces: Virtual Organizational Markets

A significant development in organizational buying has been the creation of online trading communities, called **e-marketplaces**, that bring together buyers and supplier organizations. These online communities go by a variety of names, including *B2B exchanges* and *e-hubs*, and make possible the real-time exchange of information, money, products, and services.

E-marketplaces can be independent trading communities or private exchanges. Independent e-marketplaces act as a neutral third party and provide an Internet technology trading platform and a centralized market that enable exchanges between buyers and sellers. They charge a fee for their service and exist in settings that have one or more of the following features: (1) thousands of geographically dispersed buyers and sellers, (2) volatile prices caused by demand and supply fluctuations, (3) time sensitivity due to perishable offerings and changing technologies, and (4) easily comparable offerings between a variety of sellers.

Examples of independent e-marketplaces include Amazon Business (general business equipment and supplies), PlasticsNet (plastics), Hospital Network.com (health care supplies and equipment), and TextileWeb (garment and apparel products). Small business buyers and sellers, in particular, benefit from independent e-marketplaces. These e-marketplaces offer them an economical way to expand their customer base and reduce the cost of products and services. For example, eBay provides an electronic platform for entrepreneurs and the small business market in the United States and other countries. Read the Marketing Matters box to learn more about how eBay promotes business-to-business sales and entrepreneurship.[19]

Large companies tend to favor private exchanges that link them with their network of qualified suppliers and customers. Private exchanges focus on streamlining a company's purchase transactions with its suppliers and customers. Like independent e-marketplaces, they provide a technology trading platform and central market for buyer–seller interactions. However, unlike independent e-marketplaces, they are not a neutral third party; private exchanges represent the interests of their owners. For example, NeoGrid is an international business-to-business private exchange. It connects more than 250 retail customers with 80,000 suppliers. Its members include Best Buy, Campbell Soup, Costco, Safeway, Target, Tesco, and Walgreens. The Global Healthcare Exchange engages in the buying and selling of health care products for over 4,000 hospitals and more than 400 health care suppliers, such as Abbott Laboratories, GE Medical Systems, Johnson & Johnson, Medtronic USA, and McKesson Corporation in North America.

Online Auctions in Organizational Markets

Online auctions have grown in popularity among organizational buyers and business marketers. Many e-marketplaces offer this service. Two general types of auctions are common: (1) a traditional auction and (2) a reverse auction.[20] Figure 6–5 shows how buyer and seller participants and price behavior differ by type of auction. Let's look at each auction type more closely to understand the implications of each for buyers and sellers.

In a **traditional auction** a seller puts up an item for sale and would-be buyers are invited to bid in competition with each other. As more would-be buyers become involved, there is an upward pressure on bid prices. Why? Bidding is sequential. Prospective buyers observe the bids of others and decide whether or not to increase the bid price. The auction ends when a single bidder remains and "wins" the item with its highest price. Traditional auctions are often used to dispose of excess merchandise. For example, Dell Inc. sells surplus, refurbished, or closeout computer merchandise at its www.dellauction.com website.

A reverse auction works in the opposite direction from a traditional auction. In a **reverse auction**, a buyer communicates a need for a product or service and would-be suppliers are invited to bid in competition with each other. As more would-be suppliers become involved, there is a downward pressure on bid prices for the buyer's business. Why? Like traditional auctions, bidding is sequential and prospective suppliers observe the bids of others and decide whether or

FIGURE 6–5
Buyer and seller participants and price behavior differ by type of online auction. As an organizational buyer, would you prefer to participate in a traditional auction or a reverse auction?

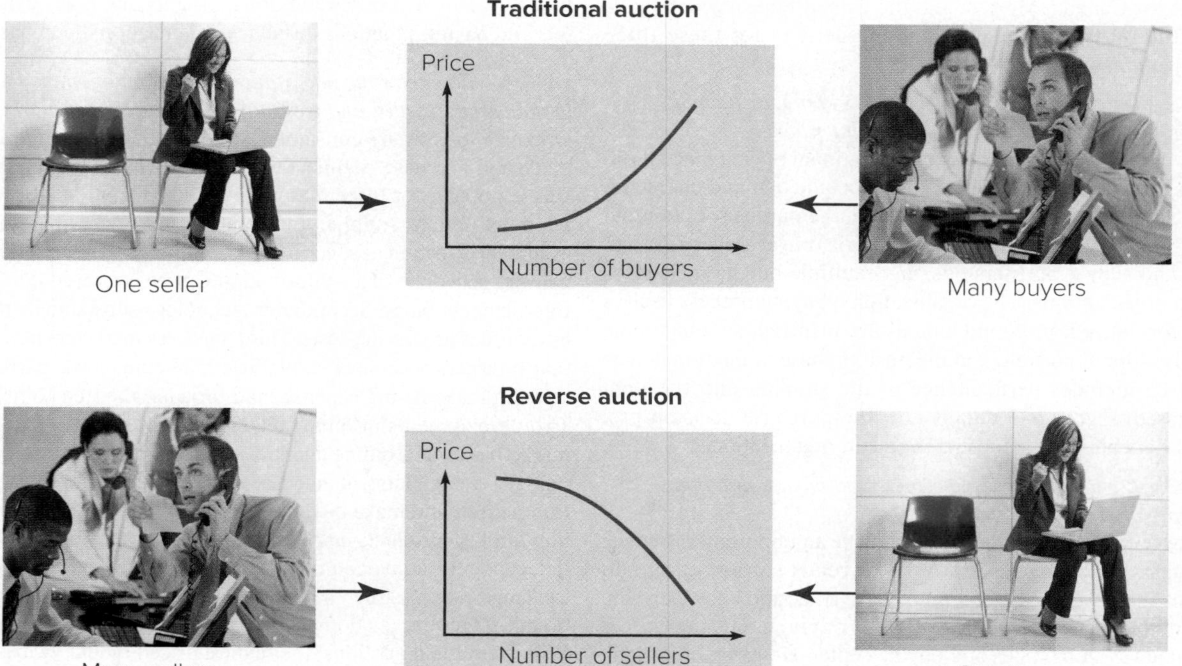

(Top left, bottom right): ©Jim Esposito/blend Images/Getty Images; (Top right, bottom left): ©Comstock Images/Getty Images

not to decrease the bid price. The auction ends when a single bidder remains and "wins" the business with its lowest price. Reverse auctions benefit organizational buyers by reducing the cost of their purchases. As an example, Nike has elected to have advertising agencies submit their bids for the company's multimillion-dollar media program using a reverse auction to reduce cost.[21]

Clearly, buyers welcome the lower prices generated by reverse auctions. Suppliers often favor reverse auctions because they give them a chance to capture business that they might not have otherwise had, perhaps because of a long-standing purchase relationship between the buyer and another supplier. On the other hand, suppliers say reverse auctions put too much emphasis on prices, discourage consideration of other important buying criteria, and may threaten supply partnership opportunities.[22]

LEARNING REVIEW

6-5. What are e-marketplaces?

6-6. In general, which type of online auction creates upward pressure on bid prices and which type creates downward pressure on bid prices?

LEARNING OBJECTIVES REVIEW

LO 6-1 *Distinguish among industrial, reseller, and government organizational markets.*
There are three different organizational markets: industrial, reseller, and government. Industrial firms in some way reprocess a product or service they buy before selling it to the next buyer. Resellers—wholesalers and retailers—buy physical products and resell them again without any reprocessing. Government agencies at the federal, state, and local levels buy goods and services for the constituents they serve. The North American Industry Classification System (NAICS) provides common industry definitions for Canada, Mexico, and the United States, which facilitates the measurement of economic activity for these three organizational markets.

LO 6-2 *Describe the key characteristics of organizational buying that make it different from consumer buying.*
Seven major characteristics of organizational buying make it different from consumer buying. These include demand characteristics, the size of the order or purchase, the number of potential buyers, buying objectives, buying criteria, buyer–seller relationships and supply partnerships, and multiple buying influences within organizations. The organizational buying process itself is more formalized, more individuals are involved, supplier capability is more important, and the postpurchase evaluation behavior often includes performance of the supplier and the item purchased. Figure 6–3 details how the purchase decision process differs between a consumer and an organization.

LO 6-3 *Explain how buying centers and buying situations influence organizational purchasing.*
Buying centers and buying situations have an important influence on organizational purchasing. A buying center consists of a group of individuals who share common goals, risks, and knowledge important to a purchase decision. A buyer or purchasing manager is almost always a member of a buying center. However, other individuals may affect organizational purchasing due to their unique roles in a purchase decision. Five specific roles that a person may play in a buying center include users, influencers, buyers, deciders, and gatekeepers. The specific buying situation will influence the number of people and the different roles played in a buying center. For a routine reorder of an item—a straight rebuy situation—a purchasing manager or buyer will typically act alone in making a purchasing decision. When an organization is a first-time purchaser of a product or service—a new buy situation—a buying center is enlarged and all five roles in a buying center often emerge. A modified rebuy situation lies between these two extremes. Figure 6–4 offers additional insights into how buying centers and buying situations influence organizational purchasing.

LO 6-4 *Recognize the importance and nature of online buying in industrial, reseller, and government organizational markets.*
Organizations dwarf consumers in terms of online transactions made and purchase volume. Online buying in organizational markets is popular for three reasons. First, organizational buyers depend on timely supplier information that describes product availability, technical specifications, application uses, price, and delivery schedules. This information can be conveyed quickly via Internet technology. Second, this technology substantially reduces buyer order processing costs. Third, business marketers have found that Internet technology can reduce marketing costs, particularly sales and advertising expense, and broaden their customer base. Two developments in online buying have been the creation of e-marketplaces and online auctions. E-marketplaces provide a technology trading platform and a centralized market for buyer–seller transactions and make possible the real-time exchange of information, money, products, and services. These e-marketplaces can be independent trading communities, such as PlasticsNet, or private exchanges, such as the Global Healthcare Exchange. Online traditional and reverse auctions represent a second major development. With traditional auctions, the highest-priced bidder "wins." Conversely, the lowest-priced bidder "wins" with reverse auctions.

LEARNING REVIEW ANSWERS

6-1 Organizational buyers are ________.
Answer: those manufacturers, wholesalers, retailers, service companies, not-for-profit organizations, and government agencies that buy products and services for their own use or for resale.

6-2 What are the three main types of organizational buyers?
Answer: (1) Industrial firms, which in some way reprocess a product or service they buy before selling it again to the next buyer; (2) resellers, which are wholesalers and retailers that buy physical products and resell them again without any reprocessing; and (3) government units, which are the federal, state, and local agencies that buy products and services for the constituents they serve.

6-3 What one department is almost always represented by a person in the buying center?
Answer: purchasing department

6-4 What are the three types of buying situations or buy classes?
Answer: (1) New buy—the organization is a first-time buyer of the product or service; (2) straight rebuy—the organization reorders an existing product or service from a list of acceptable suppliers; and (3) modified rebuy—an organization's buying center changes the product's specifications, price, delivery schedule, or supplier.

6-5 What are e-marketplaces?
Answer: E-marketplaces are online trading communities that bring together buyers and supplier organizations to make possible the real-time exchange of information, money, products, and services.

6-6 In general, which type of online auction creates upward pressure on bid prices and which type creates downward pressure on bid prices?
Answer: traditional auction; reverse auction

FOCUSING ON KEY TERMS

business-to-business marketing p. 155
buy classes p. 164
buying center p. 163
derived demand p. 157
e-marketplaces p. 166
North American Industry Classification System (NAICS) p. 156
organizational buyers p. 155
organizational buying behavior p. 162
reverse auction p. 167
traditional auction p. 167

APPLYING MARKETING KNOWLEDGE

1 Describe the major differences among industrial firms, resellers, and government units in the United States.

2 List and discuss the key characteristics of organizational buying that make it different from consumer buying.

3 What is a buying center? Describe the roles assumed by people in a buying center and what useful questions should be raised to guide any analysis of the structure and behavior of a buying center.

4 A firm that is marketing multimillion-dollar wastewater treatment systems to cities has been unable to sell a new type of system. This setback has occurred even though the firm's systems are cheaper than competitive systems and meet U.S. Environmental Protection Agency (EPA) specifications. To date, the firm's marketing efforts have been directed to city purchasing departments and the various state EPAs to get on approved bidders' lists. Talks with city-employed personnel have indicated that the new system is very different from current systems and therefore city sanitary and sewer department engineers, directors of these two departments, and city council members are unfamiliar with the workings of the system. Consulting engineers, hired by cities to work on the engineering and design features of these systems and paid on a percentage of system cost, are also reluctant to favor the new system. (*a*) What roles do the various individuals play in the purchase process for a wastewater treatment system? (*b*) How could the firm improve the marketing effort behind its new system?

BUILDING YOUR MARKETING PLAN

Your marketing plan may need an estimate of the size of the market potential or industry potential (see Chapter 8) for a particular product market in which you compete. Use these steps:

1 Define the product market precisely, such as ice cream.
2 Visit the NAICS website at www.census.gov.
3 Click "NAICS Lookup" and enter a keyword that describes your product market (e.g., ice cream).
4 Follow the instructions to find the specific NAICS code for your product market and the economic Census data that detail the dollar sales and provide the estimate of market or industry potential.

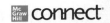

"Let me tell you a little bit about the history of Trek," says Mark Joslyn, vice president of human resources at Trek Bicycle Corporation. "It's a fantastic story," he continues proudly. "It's a story about a business that started in response to a market opportunity." That opportunity was to build bicycles with the highest-quality frames. In fact, Trek's mission was simple: "Build the best bikes in the world." To do this Trek needed to find the best raw materials from the best vendors. Michael Leighton, a Trek product manager, explains, "Our relationship with our vendors is incredibly important, and one of our recipes for success!"

VIDEO 6-3
Trek Video Case
kerin.tv/15e/v6-3

THE COMPANY

Trek Bicycle was founded in 1976 by Richard Burke and Bevill Hogg. With just five employees they began manufacturing bicycles in a Wisconsin barn. From the beginning they targeted the high-quality, prestige segment of the bicycle market, using only the best materials and components for their bicycles. The first year they manufactured 900 custom-made bicycles which sold quickly. Soon, Trek exceeded its manufacturing capacity. It built a new 26,000-square-foot factory and corporate headquarters to help meet growing demand.

Trek's focus on quality meant that it was very sensitive to the materials used to manufacture the bicycles. The first models, for example, used hand-brazed steel for the frames. Then, borrowing ideas from the aerospace industry, Trek soon began making frames out of bonded aluminum. Following on the success of its aluminum bicycles, Trek began manufacturing bicycles out of carbon fiber. The idea was to be "at the front of technology," explains Joslyn.

The company also expanded its product line. Its first bikes were designed to compete directly with Japanese and Italian bicycles and included road racing models. In 1983 Trek manufactured its first mountain bike. In 1990 Trek developed a new category of bicycle—called a multitrack—that combined the speed of road bikes with the ruggedness of mountain bikes. The company also began manufacturing children's bikes, tandem bikes, BMX bikes, and models used by police departments and the U.S. Secret Service. In addition, it added a line of cycling apparel called Trek Wear and cycling accessories such as helmets. Recently, Trek also undertook an Eco Design initiative to build bicycles and parts that are "green" in terms of the environmental impact of manufacturing them, how long they last, and how they can be recycled. To accommodate these production demands, Trek expanded its facilities two more times.

As Trek's popularity increased, it began to expand outside of the United States. For example, the company acquired a Swiss bicycle company called Villiger and the oldest bicycle company in Germany, Diamant. It also expanded into China, opening two stores and signing deals with 20 Chinese distributors.

Today, Trek is one of the leading manufacturers of bicycles and cycling products, with more than $800 million in sales and 2,000 employees. Trek's products are now marketed through 1,700 dealers in North America and wholly owned subsidiaries in seven countries and through distributors in 90 other countries. Its brands include Trek, Gary Fisher, and Bontrager. As a global company, Trek's mission has evolved also, and today the mission is to "help the world use the bicycle as a simple solution to complex problems." Trek employees believe that the bicycle is the most efficient form of human transportation and that it can combat climate change, ease urban congestion, and build human fitness. Their motto: "We believe in bikes." Mark Joslyn explains:

> In the world today we are faced with a number of challenges. We are faced with congestion, issues with mobility, issues with the environment, and quite frankly, issues with health. We believe that the bicycle is a simple solution to all of those things. We are clearly an alternative to other forms of transportation and that's evident in the way that people are embracing cycling not just for recreation but also for transportation. And more and more, particularly in the United States, we are seeing people move to the bike as a way to get around and get to the places they need to ultimately get their life done.

ORGANIZATIONAL BUYING AT TREK

Trek's success at accomplishing its mission is the result of many important business practices, including its organizational buying process. The process begins when managers specify types of materials such as carbon fiber, component parts such as wheels and shifters, and finishing materials such as paint and decals needed to produce a Trek product. In addition, they specify quality requirements, sizing standards, and likely delivery schedules. According to Leighton, once the requirements are known, the next step is to "go to our buying center and say 'can you help us find this piece?'"

The buying center is the group of individuals who are responsible for finding the best suppliers and vendors for the organization's purchases. At Trek the buying center consists of a purchasing manager, buyers who identify

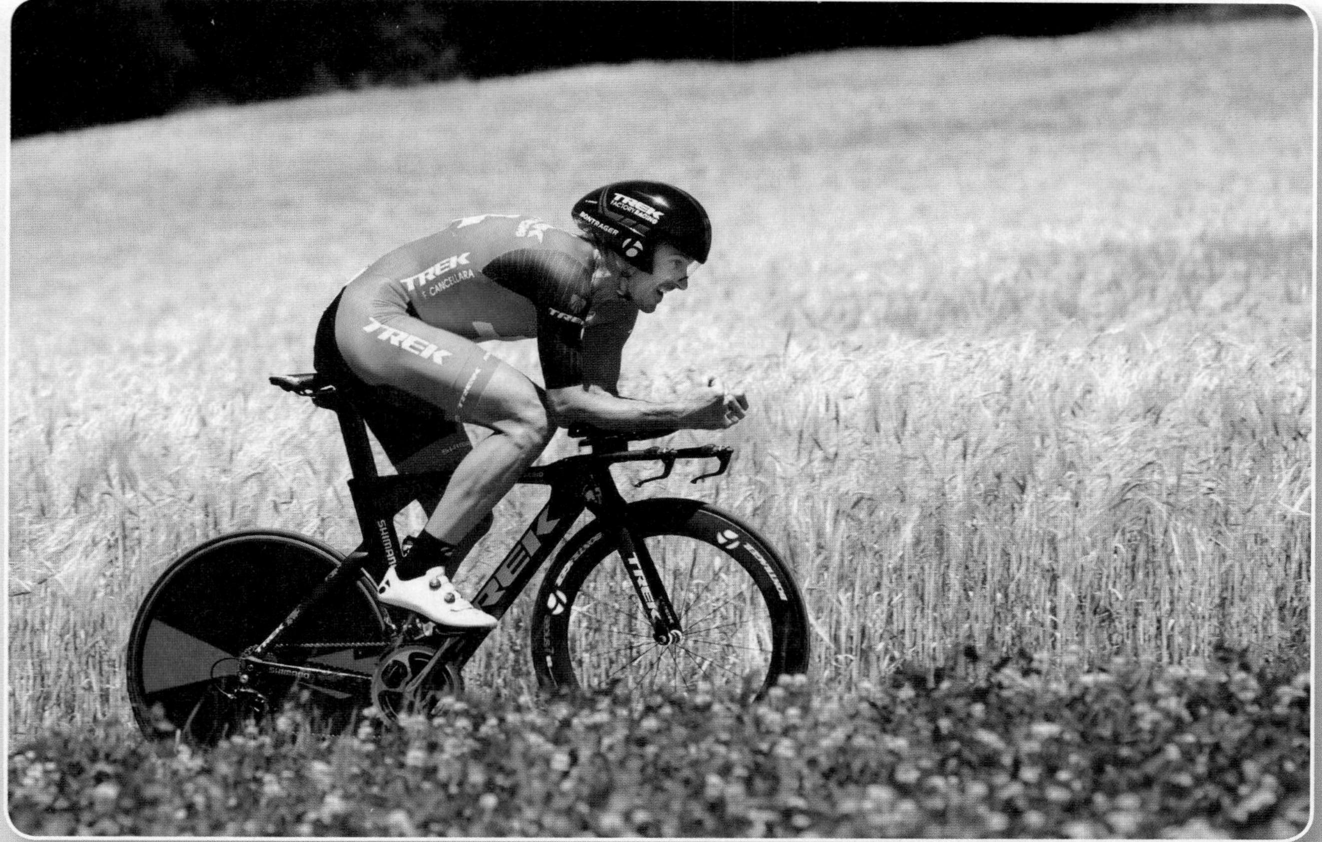

Jean Christophe Bott/Keystone/AP Images

domestic and international sources of materials and components, and representatives from research and development, production, and quality control. The communication between the product managers and the buying center is important. "I work very closely with our buying centers to ensure that we're partnering with vendors who can supply reliable quality, and they are actually the ones who, with our quality control team, go in and say, 'yes this vendor is building product to the quality that meets Trek's standards,' and they also negotiate the pricing. Our buying center domestically is a relatively small team of people and they are focused on specific components."

When potential suppliers are identified, they are evaluated on four criteria—quality, delivery capabilities, price, and environmental impact of their production process. This allows Trek to compare alternative suppliers and to select the best match for Trek and its customers. Once a business is selected as a Trek supplier, it is continuously evaluated on elements of the four criteria. For example, current suppliers might receive scores on the number of defects in a large quantity of supplies, whether just-in-time orders made their deadlines, if target prices were maintained, and if recycled packaging was used. At Trek the tool that is used to record information about potential and existing suppliers is called a "white paper." Michael Leighton describes how this works: "Our buying center is tasked with developing what we call white papers. It's a sheet that managers can look at that shows issues and benefits related to working with these people." Every effort is made to develop long-term relationships with suppliers so that they become partners with Trek. These partnerships mean that Trek's success also contributes to the partner's success.

Trek's product managers and the buying center are involved in three types of organizational purchases. First, new buys are purchases that are made for the first time. Second, modified rebuys involve changing some aspect of a previously ordered product. Finally, straight rebuys are reorders of existing products from the list of acceptable suppliers. Leighton offers examples of each type of purchase at Trek:

> So, [for] a new buy, we work with our buying centers to find new products, something we've never done before whether it's a new saddle with a new material or a new technology that goes into the frame that damps vibration or gives a better ride. Another case might be electric bikes—maybe we

are putting a motor in a bike, that's a new thing, so our buying center will help us go find those vendors. A modified rebuy is basically a saddle with a little bit different material but we are sharing some components of it, so the existing components of the saddle [are the same] but the cover is new, so it's a little bit different, but it's just the evolution of the product. A straight rebuy is looking at our strategic vision for the component further on down the line where we are just buying the same component and the volume goes up. We look at how can we make this a better business; can we save some money or can we make it more worth our while to keep buying the same product rather than buying something new.

While each of the types of purchases may occur frequently at Trek, the criteria that are used to select or evaluate a vendor may vary by the type of purchase and the type of product, making the buying process a dynamic challenge for managers.

ECO BUYING AND THE FUTURE AT TREK

One of Trek's criteria for evaluating existing and potential vendors is their environmental impact. Joslyn says it well: "We evaluate our vendors on many criteria including, increasingly, the elements that we would consider to be the 'green' part" of their offering. For example, Trek recently selected a supplier that (1) owned a quarry for extracting material, (2) used its own manufacturing facilities, and (3) used natural gas instead of coal in its production process. This was appealing to Trek because it suggested that the supplier had a "thorough understanding" of the impact of the product on the environment from start to finish.

Trek's organizational buying reflects the growing importance of its "Eco" perspective. Its bikes are becoming "smarter" as it adds electric-assist components to help them become a practical transportation alternative. Its bikes are also becoming "greener" as more low-impact materials and components are used and as packaging size and weight are reduced. Trek is also addressing the issue of recycling by building the bikes to last longer, using its dealers to help recycle tires and tubes, and funding a nonprofit organization called Dream Bikes to teach youth to fix and repair donated bikes.

In addition to changing bikes and the way it makes them, Trek faces several other challenges as it strives to improve its organizational buying process. For example, the growing number of suppliers and vendors necessitates constant, coordinated, and real-time communication to ensure that all components are available when they are needed. In addition, changes in consumer interests and economic conditions mean that Trek must anticipate fluctuations in demand and make appropriate changes in order sizes and delivery dates. As Mark Joslyn explains, "Everything we do all the time can and should be improved. So the search for ideas inside of our business and outside of our business, always looking for ways that we can improve and bring new technology and new solutions to the marketplace, is just a core of who we are."[23]

Questions

1 What is the role of the buying center at Trek? Who is likely to comprise the buying center in the decision to select a new supplier at Trek?

2 What selection criteria does Trek utilize when it selects a new supplier or evaluates an existing supplier?

3 How has Trek's interest in the environmental impact of its business influenced its organizational buying process?

4 Provide an example of each of the three buying situations—straight rebuy, modified rebuy, and new buy—at Trek.

Chapter Notes

1. Personal correspondence with Cheryl J. Welker, JCPenney, February 25, 2019; and "Catalog Makes a Comeback at Penney," *The Wall Street Journal,* January 20, 2015, pp. B1, B2.
2. "How IBM Uses Watson for Procurement," www.supplymanagement.com, April 27, 2018.
3. Figures reported in this discussion are provided by the U.S. Department of Commerce at www.commerce.gov, March 10, 2019.
4. "How NASA Is Prepping Its New Megarocket to Shoot for the Moon in 2019," www.space.com, January 5, 2018; and "Orion Update for January 2017," www.spaceflightinsider.com, January 18, 2017.
5. This list of characteristics and portions of the discussion in this section are based on Michael D. Hutt and Thomas W. Speh, *Business Marketing Management: B2B,* 12th ed. (Independence, KY: Cengage, 2017).
6. "Panda's New Power Plant Up and Running in Texas," *Power Engineering,* November 2014, pp. 23–24.
7. "About Boeing Commercial Airplanes," www.boeing.com, February 19, 2019.
8. Hutt and Speh, *Business Marketing Management.* For a more expansive view on this topic, see Eric Almquist, Jamie Cleghorn, and Lori Sherer, "The B2B Elements of Value," *Harvard Business Review,* March–April 2018, pp. 72–81.
9. *Global Machine Vision Market 2018–2025* (Ann Arbor: Automated Imaging Association, September 2018).
10. This example is found in Sandy D. Jap and Jakki J. Mohr, "Leveraging Internet Technologies in B2B Relationships," *California Management Review,* Summer 2002, pp. 24–38.
11. "IBM Supercomputer Vies for No. 1," *The Wall Street Journal,* June 9–10, 2018, p. B3.
12. "Apple Signs $578M Sapphire Deal with GT Advanced Technology," *appleinsider.com,* accessed February 19, 2017.

13. "About Us," www.milsco.com, downloaded January 25, 2019; "Top Seating: Milsco," *Industry Today,* January 2018, pp. 60–69; and "Milsco Manufacturing Co. to Welcome Harley-Davidson Riders at World Headquarters for Three-Day Seating Experience," Company press release, August 30, 2018.
14. *Starbucks Global Responsibility Report 2018,* downloaded January 5, 2019.
15. Nicolas Toman, Brent Adamson, and Christina Gomez, "The Sales Imperative," *Harvard Business Review*, March–April, 2017, pp. 118–25; Wesley J. Johnson and Jennifer Chandler, "The Organizational Buying Center: Innovation, Knowledge Management, and Brand," in Gary L. Lilien and Rajdeep Grewal, eds., *Handbook of Business-to-Business Marketing* (Northhampton, MA: Edward Elgar Publishing, 2013), pp. 386–99.
16. These definitions are adapted from Frederick E. Webster Jr. and Yoram Wind, *Organizational Buying Behavior* (Englewood Cliffs, NJ: Prentice Hall, 1972), p. 6.
17. Jeffrey E. Lewin and Naveen Donthu, "The Influence of Purchase Situation on Buying Center Structure and Involvement: A Select Meta-Analysis of Organizational Buying Behavior Research," *Journal of Business Research,* October 2005, pp. 81–90.
18. This discussion is based on "E-Commerce Accounts for 56% of 2017 Revenue for Grainger," www.b2becommerceworld.com, January 24, 2018; "Feds to Ramp Up Online Purchasing Presence," www.ecommercetimes.com, January 22, 2018; and "Boeing Takes On Peers, Partners in Bid for Replacement Parts Business," www.reuters.com, October 24, 2016.
19. "eBay's Global Marketplace Focuses on Minority Business," www.forbes. com, September 11, 2018; "Global McKinsey Institute Report Confirms eBay, Inc. Research on Small Business Cross Border Trade," www.ebaymainstreet.com, April 24, 2014; and "eBay Launches eBay Business Supply," www.digitalcommerce.com, July 12, 2016.
20. This discussion is based on Robert J. Dolan and Youngme Moon, "Pricing and Market Making on the Internet," *Journal of Interactive Marketing,* Spring 2000, pp. 56–73; and Ajit Kambil and Eric van Heck, *Making Markets: How Firms Can Benefit from Online Auctions and Exchanges* (Boston: Harvard Business School Press, 2002).
21. "Nike's Reverse Auction Review Is Bad Omen for Agencies," www.adage.com, January 5, 2018.
22. Shawn P. Daley and Prithwiraz Nath, "Reverse Auctions for Relationship Marketers," *Industrial Marketing Management,* February 2005, pp. 157–66; and Sandy Jap, "The Impact of Online Reverse Auction Design on Buyer–Seller Relationships," *Journal of Marketing,* January 2007, pp. 146–59.
23. Trek: This case was written by Steven Hartley. Sources: "Trek Bicycle Corporation," *Hoovers*, 2012; "Alliance Data Signs Long-Term Extension Agreement with Trek Bicycle Corporation," *PR Newswire,* November 22, 2010; Lou Massante, "Trek Bicycle Buys Villiger, a Leader in the Swiss Market," *Bicycle Retailer & Industry News,* January 1, 2003, p. 10; "Trek Bicycle Corporation," *Wikipedia*, accessed September 4, 2011; and Trek website, http://www.trekbikes.com/us/en/company/believe, accessed September 4, 2012.

Chapter 7 Understanding and Reaching Global Consumers and Markets

LEARNING OBJECTIVES

After reading this chapter you should be able to:

- **LO 7-1** Describe the nature and scope of world trade from a global perspective.
- **LO 7-2** Identify the major developments that have influenced world trade and global marketing.
- **LO 7-3** Identify the environmental forces that shape global marketing efforts.
- **LO 7-4** Name and describe the alternative approaches companies use to enter global markets.
- **LO 7-5** Explain the distinction between standardization and customization when companies craft worldwide marketing programs.

Transforming the Way India Sells and Transforming the Way India Buys: Amazon India Builds a Multibillion-Dollar Operation from the Ground up to the Cloud

"The opportunity (in India) is so large it will be measured in trillions, not billions—trillions of U.S. dollars, that is, not Indian rupees," says Diego Piacentini, Amazon's senior vice president retail operations in Asia and Europe. "But," he added, "we know that in order to win in India we need to do things we have never done in any other country. We need great people, a great platform, and honestly, a lot of money." How much money? Amazon is currently investing about $1 billion annually to build its business in India.

Amazon initiated operations in India seven years ago when retail e-commerce totaled $2.3 billion. Amazon executives are enthusiastic about the opportunity that India represents. But doing business in India presents unique challenges.

Amazon's Awesome Opportunity in India

Why is India seen as a huge opportunity for Amazon, already the world's largest e-commerce company? Consider the following:

- India is the second most populous country in the world and the world's second-largest English-speaking country.
- India is the world's fastest-growing major economy and the total purchasing power of its economy ranks third behind China and the United States.
- India has the second-largest Internet user base in the world today and will have 850 million users in 2025.

Amazon's Awesome Challenges in India

Amazon executives admit the company's future in India is fraught with challenges to face and overcome. "What we do in India will affect Amazon's future in a very, very big way," says Amit Agarwal, the head of Amazon in India.

So what challenges does Amazon India face and how has it dealt with them? Here are a few examples.

Trade Regulations. Amazon has had to modify its operating platform in India due to Indian trade regulations. Specifically, foreign companies, like Amazon, are prohibited from holding their own inventory and selling products directly to Indian consumers. Therefore, instead of Amazon buying products at wholesale prices in bulk and selling them through its online store, Amazon must rely on local manufacturers and retailers for its products. This means that Amazon stocks merchandise

Andrey Arkusha/Shutterstock

owned by Indian manufacturers and retailers in its distribution warehouses and provides an order fulfillment function for them. It is common for Amazon to pick up purchased items at a seller's location, pack them into boxes and bags with the Amazon logo, and deliver the goods to buyers on Amazon motorbikes. This practice can cost Amazon more money than it makes on the transaction.

Payment Systems. Barely 60 percent of Indian consumers have bank accounts. And only 12 percent have credit or debit cards. So Amazon's payment systems in India are drastically different from any the company has attempted before. About half of Indian buyers pay cash only when their purchases are delivered. In response, Amazon has partnered with thousands of small shop owners across India to act as pickup points in exchange for receiving a small commission per package.

Entrenched Competition. Amazon faces well-financed and capable domestic competitors in India. Two companies patterned after Amazon—Flipkart (owned by Walmart) and Snapdeal—already operate sizable distribution systems, advanced electronic platforms, and online stores in India. Tata Group, the largest retailer in India, has its own e-commerce platform and has linked it to thousands of its retail stores. These competitors have invested billions of dollars in their e-commerce technology and warehouses as well. And, they don't face the trade regulations imposed on Amazon as a foreign company.

Cloud Technology Expansion. Amazon expanded its cloud computing platform in India in 2017 to improve its service for Indian customers. This sizable financial and technological investment was made to address increasingly complicated server and infrastructure demands that only a localized cloud computing platform for India can provide.

Failure Is Not an Option

Despite the challenges, Amazon executives believe that failure is not an option in India. E-commerce industry analysts generally agree that India represents the last major e-commerce opportunity in the world. They expect that Indian retail e-commerce sales could reach $72 billion by 2025.

If Amazon transforms the way India sells and transforms the way India buys, as it expects to do, company executives predict that India will be the company's biggest market after the United States within a decade.[1]

This chapter describes today's complex and dynamic global marketing environment. It begins with a description of world trade. Attention is then focused on prominent cultural, economic, and political-regulatory factors that present both an opportunity and a challenge for global marketers. Four major global market entry strategies are then detailed, including a discussion of the advantages and disadvantages of each. Finally, the task of designing, implementing, and evaluating worldwide marketing for companies is described.

DYNAMICS OF WORLD TRADE

LO 7-1
Describe the nature and scope of world trade from a global perspective.

The dollar value of world trade has almost doubled in the past decade. Manufactured products and commodities account for 85 percent of world trade. Service industries, including telecommunications, transportation, insurance, education, banking, and tourism, represent the other 15 percent.

All nations and regions of the world do not participate equally in world trade. World trade flows reflect interdependencies among industries, countries, and regions. These flows manifest themselves in country, company, industry, and regional exports and imports. The dynamics of world trade are constantly evolving. China is the biggest country measured by world trade. Asia is the largest region measured by world trade.[2]

Global Perspective on World Trade

The United States, China, Japan, Western Europe, and Canada together account for more than two-thirds of world trade in manufactured products and commodities. China is the world's leading exporter, followed by the United States and Germany. The United States is the world's leading importer, followed by China and Germany. China, Germany, and the United States remain well ahead of other countries in terms of imports and exports, as shown in Figure 7–1.

A global perspective on world trade views exports and imports as complementary economic flows: A country's imports affect its exports and a country's exports affect its imports. Every nation's imports arise from the exports of other nations. As the exports of one country increase, its national output and income rise, which in turn leads to an increase in the demand for imports. This nation's greater demand for imports stimulates the exports of other countries. Increased demand for exports of other nations energizes their economic activity, resulting in higher national income, which stimulates their demand for imports. In short, imports affect exports and vice versa. This phenomenon is called the *trade feedback effect* and is one argument for free trade among nations.

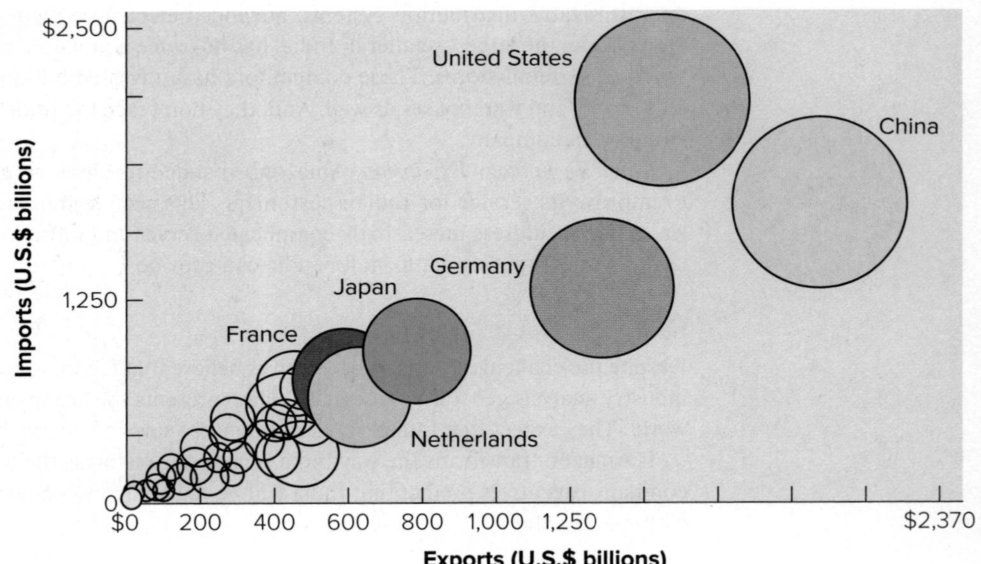

FIGURE 7–1
The United States, China, and Germany are the leaders in global merchandise trade by a wide margin. China exports more manufactured products and commodities than it imports. The United States imports more manufactured products and commodities than it exports. Read the text to learn about trends worldwide and in U.S. exports and imports.

Not all trade involves the exchange of money for products or services. In a world where 70 percent of all countries do not have convertible currencies or where government-owned enterprises lack sufficient cash or credit for imports, other means of payment are used. An estimated 10 to 15 percent of world trade involves **countertrade**, the practice of using barter rather than money for making global sales.

Countertrade is popular with many Eastern European nations and Asian and African countries. For example, Daimler AG agreed to sell 30 trucks to Romania in exchange for 150 Romanian-made jeeps. Daimler then sold the jeeps in Ecuador in exchange for bananas, which it brought back to Germany and sold to a German supermarket chain in exchange for cash. China's state-owned firms agreed to a $9 billion deal to build railways, hospitals, and health centers in the Democratic Republic of Congo in exchange for 10 million tons of copper and 400,000 tons of cobalt, a critical metal used in electric car batteries.

United States' Perspective on World Trade

The role of the United States in world trade can be viewed from two perspectives: (1) gross domestic product and (2) balance of trade.

Gross Domestic Product The United States has been a perennial world leader in terms of *gross domestic product* (*GDP*), which is the monetary value of all products and services produced in a country during one year. The United States is also among the world's leaders in exports due in large part to its global prominence in the aerospace, chemical, office equipment, information technology, pharmaceutical, telecommunications, and professional service industries. However, the U.S. percentage share of world exports has shifted downward over the past 40 years, whereas its percentage share of world imports has increased. Therefore, the relative position of the United States as a supplier to the world has diminished despite an absolute growth in exports. In fact, as a percentage of its GDP, U.S. exports are the lowest among industrial countries in the world. At the same time, its relative role as a marketplace for the world has increased, particularly for automobile, textile, apparel, and consumer electronics products.

Balance of Trade The difference between the monetary value of a nation's exports and imports is called the **balance of trade**. When a country's exports exceed its imports, it incurs a surplus in its balance of trade. When imports exceed exports, a deficit results. World trade trends in U.S. exports and imports are reflected in the U.S. balance of trade.

Two important things have happened in U.S. exports and imports over the past 40 years. First, imports have exceeded exports each year, indicating that the United States has a continuing balance of trade deficit. Second, the volume of both exports and imports has increased dramatically, showing why almost every American is significantly affected. The effect varies from the products they buy (Samsung smartphones from South Korea, Waterford crystal from Ireland, Louis Vuitton luggage from France) to those they sell (Cisco Systems's communication technology to Europe, Boeing aircraft to Asia, DuPont's chemicals to the Far East, Merck pharmaceuticals to Africa) and the jobs and improved standard of living that result.

World trade flows to and from the United States reflect demand and supply interdependencies for products and services among nations and industries. The four largest importers of U.S. products and services are, in order: Canada, Mexico, China, and Japan. These individual countries purchase approximately two-thirds of U.S. exports. The four largest exporters to the United States are, in order: China, Canada, Mexico, and Japan. The United States has a balance of trade deficit with all four major trading partners. China alone accounts for about 40 percent of the total U.S. balance of trade deficit.

LEARNING REVIEW

7-1. What country is the biggest as measured by world trade?

7-2. What is the trade feedback effect?

MARKETING IN A DYNAMIC GLOBAL ECONOMY

LO 7-2

Identify the major developments that have influenced world trade and global marketing.

Global marketing continues to be affected by a dynamic world economy motivated by globalization. **Globalization** is the focus on creating economic, cultural, political, and technological interdependence among individual national institutions and economies. Five developments have significantly influenced the landscape of global marketing and globalization over the past decade:

1. Economic protectionism by individual countries.
2. Economic integration among countries.
3. Global competition among global companies for global consumers.
4. The presence of a networked global marketspace.
5. The growing prevalence of economic espionage.

Economic Protectionism by Individual Countries

Protectionism is the practice of shielding one or more industries within a country's economy from foreign competition through the use of tariffs or quotas. The argument for protectionism is that it limits the outsourcing of jobs, protects a nation's political security, discourages economic dependency on other countries, and promotes development of domestic industries and employment. The prevalence of protectionist practices has become more commonplace due to growing economic nationalism and populism.[3] Setting aside economic issues, read the Making Responsible Decisions box and decide for yourself if protectionism has an ethical dimension.[4]

Tariffs and quotas can discourage world trade, as depicted in Figure 7–2. In fact, tariffs and quotas, among other restrictive trade measures, have slowed the growth of world trade for the past decade.

Tariffs, which are a government tax on products or services entering a country, primarily serve to raise prices on imports. The average tariff on manufactured products in industrialized countries is 4 percent. However, wide differences exist across nations and industries. For example, EU countries have a 10 percent tariff on cars imported from the United States, which is about four times higher than the tariff imposed by the United States on cars from the European Union.

FIGURE 7–2

How does protectionism affect world trade? Protectionism hinders world trade through tariff and quota policies of individual countries. Tariffs increase prices and quotas limit supply.

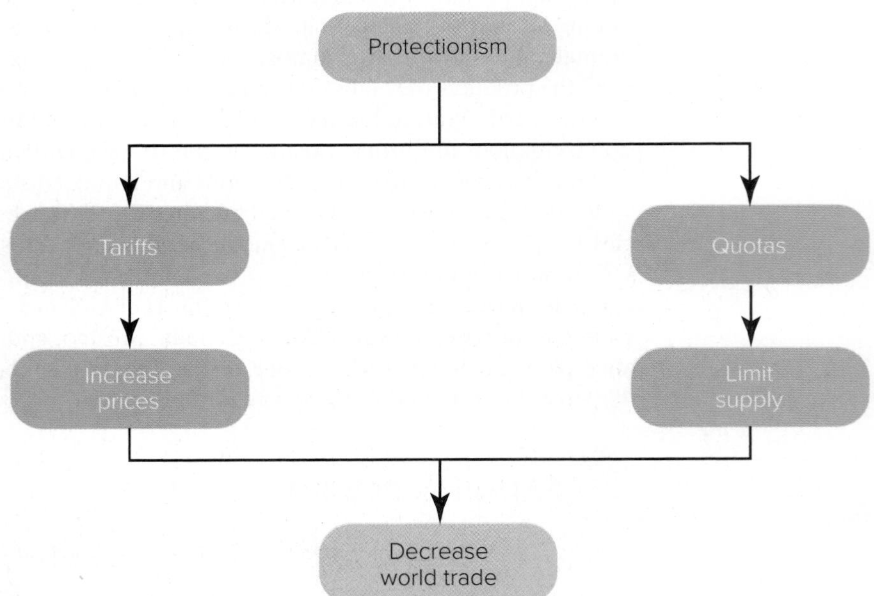

Making Responsible Decisions

Ethics

Global Ethics and Global Economics—The Case of Protectionism

World trade benefits from free and fair trade among nations. Nevertheless, governments of many countries continue to use tariffs and quotas to protect their various domestic industries. Why? Protectionism earns profits for domestic producers and tariff revenue for the government. There is a cost, however. Protectionist policies cost Japanese consumers between $75 billion and $110 billion annually. U.S. consumers pay about $70 billion each year in higher prices because of tariffs and other protective trade restrictions.

Sugar and textile import quotas in the United States, automobile and banana import tariffs in European countries, shoe and automobile tire import tariffs in the United States, beer import tariffs in Canada, and rice import tariffs in Japan have protected domestic industries but also interfered with world trade for these products. Regional trade agreements, such as those found in the provisions of the European Union (EU), may also pose a situation whereby member nations can obtain preferential treatment in quotas and tariffs but nonmember nations cannot.

Vanatchanan/Shutterstock

Protectionism, in its many forms, raises an interesting global ethical question. Is protectionism, no matter how applied, an ethical practice?

The effect of tariffs on consumer prices is substantial. Consider U.S. rice exports to Japan. The U.S. Rice Millers' Association claims that if the Japanese rice market were opened to imports by lowering tariffs, lower prices would save Japanese consumers $6 billion annually, and the United States would gain a large share of the Japanese rice market. Tariffs imposed on bananas by EU countries cost consumers $2 billion a year. U.S. consumers pay $3 billion annually for tariffs on imported shoes. Incidentally, 99 percent of shoes worn in the United States are imported.[5]

A **quota** is a restriction placed on the amount of a product allowed to enter or leave a country. Quotas can be mandated or voluntary and may be legislated or negotiated by governments. Import quotas seek to guarantee domestic industries access to a certain percentage of their domestic market. For example, there is a limit on Chinese dairy products sold in India, and in Italy there is a quota on Japanese motorcycles. China has import quotas on corn, cotton, rice, and wheat.

The United States also imposes quotas. For instance, U.S. sugar import quotas have existed for more than 70 years and preserve about half of the U.S. sugar market for domestic producers. American consumers pay $3 billion annually in extra food costs because of this quota. U.S. quotas on textiles are estimated to add 50 percent to the wholesale price of clothing for American consumers–which, in turn, raises retail prices.

The major industrialized nations of the world formed the **World Trade Organization (WTO)** in 1995 to address an array of world trade issues arising from globalization. There are 164 WTO member countries, including the United States, which account for 98 percent of world trade. The WTO is a permanent institution that sets rules governing trade between its members through panels of trade experts who decide on trade disputes between members and issue binding decisions.

The WTO has decided over 500 trade disputes for the purpose of mitigating trade wars between countries. A **trade war** is a situation in which countries try to damage each other's trade, typically by imposition of tariff and quota restrictions. The most recent example of a trade war is the dispute between the United States and China.

Economic Integration among Countries

A number of countries with similar economic goals have formed transnational trade groups or signed trade agreements for the purpose of promoting free trade among member nations and enhancing their individual economies. Two of the best-known examples are the European Union (or simply EU) and the United States–Mexico–Canada Agreement (USMCA). About 46 percent of all U.S. exports go to its free trade partners.

European Union The European Union consists of 27 member countries that have eliminated most barriers to the free flow of products, services, capital, and labor across their borders (see Figure 7–3).[6] This single market houses about 510 million consumers with a combined gross domestic product larger than that of the United States. In addition, 16 countries have adopted a common currency called the *euro*. Adoption of the euro has been a boon to electronic commerce in the EU by eliminating the need to continually monitor currency exchange rates.

The EU creates abundant marketing opportunities because firms do not need to market their products and services on a nation-by-nation basis. Rather, pan-European marketing strategies are possible due to greater uniformity in product and packaging standards; fewer regulatory restrictions on transportation, advertising, and promotion imposed by countries; and the removal of most tariffs that affect pricing practices. For example, Colgate-Palmolive Company markets its Colgate toothpaste with one formula and package across EU countries at one price. Stanley Black & Decker–the maker of electrical hand tools, appliances, and other consumer products–now produces 8, not 20, motor sizes for the European market, resulting in production and marketing cost savings. These practices were previously impossible because of

FIGURE 7–3 The European Union in mid-2019 consists of 27 countries with about 510 million consumers. The United Kingdom is in discussions to formally withdraw from the European Union.

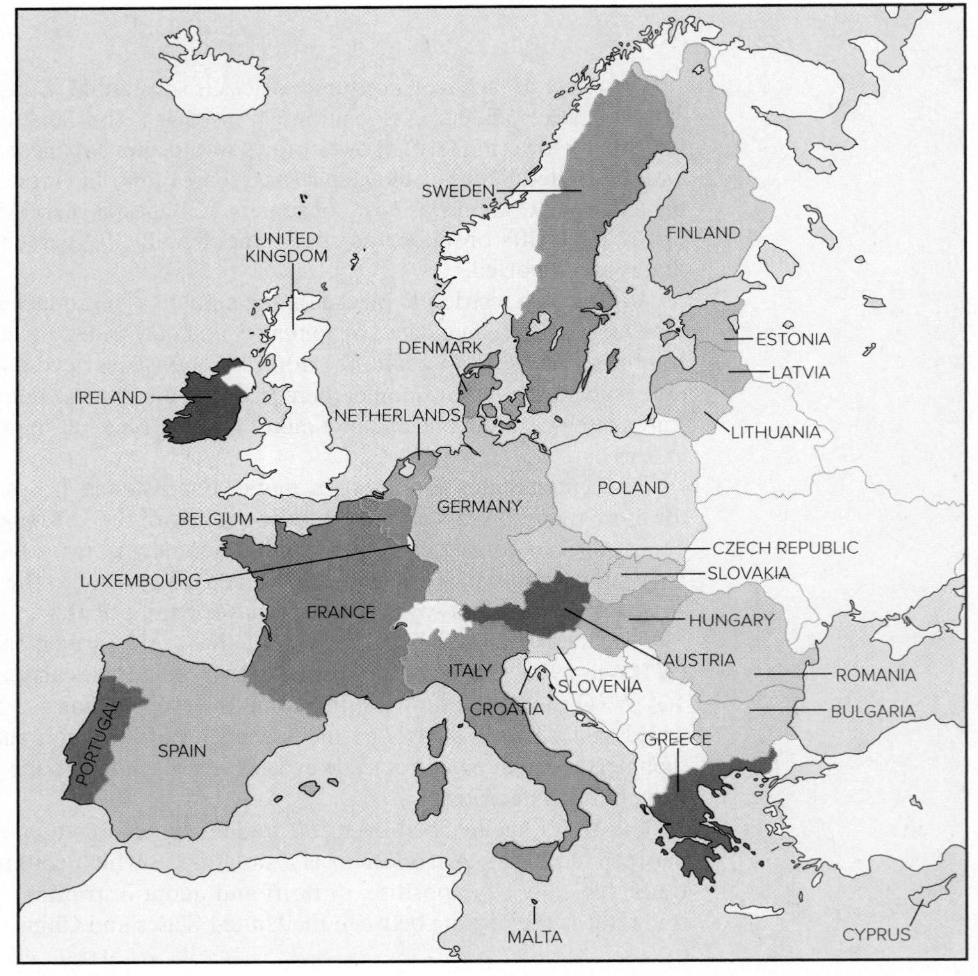

different government and trade regulations. European-wide distribution from fewer locations is also feasible given open borders. French tire maker Michelin closed 180 of its European distribution centers and now uses just 20 to serve all EU countries.

The United Kingdom (England, Northern Ireland, Scotland, and Wales) voted to formally withdraw from the EU in 2019. The United Kingdom and the EU continue to resolve disputes related to trade.

United States–Mexico–Canada Agreement The United States–Mexico–Canada Agreement (USMCA) recently renegotiated aspects of the North American Free Trade Agreement (NAFTA) that was established in 1994. These agreements have much in common and were created to govern trade relationships among member nations as well as cross-border retailing, manufacturing, and investment. For example, NAFTA paved the way for Walmart to move into Mexico and for Mexican supermarket giant Gigante and Mexican bakery giant Grupo Bimbo to move operations into the United States. Whirlpool Corporation's Canadian subsidiary stopped making washing machines in Canada and moved that operation to the United States. Whirlpool then shifted the production of kitchen ranges and compact dryers to Canada. Ford invested $60 million in its Mexico City manufacturing plant to produce smaller cars and light trucks for global sales.[7]

The USMCA modernized NAFTA by updating trade practices pertaining to each country's regulatory practices, advances in cross-border electronic commerce, labor practices, the protection of intellectual property, environmental issues, and the mechanisms for resolving trade disputes. In addition, the USMCA changed tariff policies between the United States, Canada, and Mexico for selected products.

Mary Kay, Inc. operates in more than 40 countries on five continents. This ad features the Pink Young line of cosmetics sold exclusively in China and Hong Kong since April 2019. Mary Kay, Inc. employs a global marketing strategy and is a global brand. Read the text to learn what constitutes a global marketing strategy and what makes a global brand.

Courtesy of Mary Kay, Inc.

Mary Kay, Inc.
www.marykay.com

Global Competition among Global Companies for Global Consumers

Economic integration among countries has created a new reality for marketers of all shapes and sizes. Today, world trade is driven by global competition among global companies for global consumers.

Global Competition **Global competition** exists when firms originate, produce, and market their products and services worldwide. The automobile, pharmaceutical, apparel, electronics, aerospace, and telecommunication fields represent well-known industries with sellers and buyers on every continent. Other industries that are increasingly global in scope include soft drinks, cosmetics, ready-to-eat cereals, snack chips, and retailing.

Global competition broadens the competitive landscape for marketers. The familiar "cola war" waged by Pepsi-Cola and Coca-Cola in the United States has been repeated around the world, including in India, China, Myanmar, and Argentina. Procter & Gamble's Pampers and Kimberly-Clark's Huggies have taken their disposable diaper rivalry from the United States to Western Europe. Boeing and Europe's Airbus vie for lucrative commercial aircraft contracts on virtually every continent.

Global Companies Three types of companies populate and compete in the global marketplace: (1) international firms, (2) multinational firms, and (3) transnational firms.[8] All three employ people in different countries, and many have administrative, marketing, and manufacturing operations (often called *divisions* or *subsidiaries*) around the world. However, a firm's orientation toward and strategy for global markets and marketing defines the type of company it is or attempts to be.

An *international firm* engages in trade and marketing in different countries as an extension of the marketing strategy in its home country. Generally, these firms market their existing products and services in other countries the same way they do in their home country. Avon, for example, distributes its product line through direct selling in Asia, Europe, and South America, employing virtually the same marketing strategy used in the United States.

A *multinational firm* views the world as consisting of unique parts and markets to each part differently. Multinationals use a **multidomestic marketing strategy**, which means that they have as many different product variations, brand names, and advertising programs as countries in which they do business.

For example, Procter & Gamble markets Mr. Clean, its popular multipurpose cleaner, in North America and Asia. But you won't necessarily find the Mr. Clean brand name in other parts of the world. In Mexico and Puerto Rico, Mr. Clean is Maestro Limpio, and it is Don Limpio in Spain. Mr. Clean is Monsieur Propre in France and Belgium, Mastro Lindo in Italy, Pan Proper in Poland, and Mister Proper in Eastern Europe, the Middle East, and Russia.

A *transnational firm* views the world as one market and emphasizes cultural similarities across countries or universal consumer needs and wants rather than differences. Transnational marketers employ a **global marketing strategy**—the practice of standardizing marketing activities when there are cultural similarities and adapting them when cultures differ. This approach benefits marketers by allowing them to realize economies of scale from their production and marketing activities.

Global marketing strategies are popular among many business-to-business marketers such as Caterpillar and Komatsu (heavy construction equipment) and Texas Instruments, Intel, and Hitachi (semiconductors). Consumer product marketers such as Apple and Samsung (smartphones), Seiko and Swatch (watches), Coca-Cola and Pepsi-Cola (cola soft drinks), Mattel and LEGO (children's toys), Nike and Adidas (athletic shoes), Gillette (personal care products), L'Oréal and Shiseido (cosmetics), and McDonald's (quick-service restaurants) successfully execute this strategy.

Mr. Clean has a different name in different countries and regions in the world. However, his image remains the same.
Source: Procter & Gamble

Marketing Matters — Customer Value

The Global Teenager—A Market of Voracious Consumers

The "global teenager" market consists of 13- to 19-year-olds in Europe, North and South America, and industrialized nations of Asia, Africa, and the Pacific Rim who have experienced intense exposure to television (MTV broadcasts to 372 million households worldwide on 60 branded TV channels), movies, travel, social media, and global advertising by companies such as Apple, Sony, Nike, and Coca-Cola. The similarities among teens across these countries are greater than their differences. For example, a global study of middle-class teenagers' rooms in 25 industrialized countries indicated it was difficult, if not impossible, to tell whether the rooms were in Los Angeles, Hong Kong, Mexico City, Tokyo, Rio de Janeiro, Sydney, or Paris. Why? Teens spend about $820 billion annually for a common gallery of products: Nintendo video games, Levi's blue jeans, Nike and Adidas athletic shoes, Swatch watches, Apple and Samsung smartphones, and CoverGirl cosmetics. Facebook, Snapchat, and Instagram are the most popular social media.

Kim Petersen/Alamy

Teenagers around the world appreciate fashion and music, and they desire novelty and trendier designs and images. They also acknowledge an Americanization of fashion and culture based on another study of 6,500 teens in 26 countries. When asked what country had the most influence on their attitudes and purchase behavior, 54 percent of teens from the United States, 87 percent of those from Latin America, 80 percent of the Europeans, and 80 percent of those from Asia named the United States. This phenomenon has not gone unnoticed by parents. As one parent in India said, "Now the youngsters dress, talk, and eat like Americans."

Each of these companies markets a **global brand**—a brand marketed under the same name in multiple countries with similar and centrally coordinated marketing programs.[9] Global brands have the same product formulation or service concept, deliver the same benefits to consumers, and use consistent advertising across multiple countries and cultures. This isn't to say that global brands are not sometimes tailored to specific cultures or countries. However, adaptation is used only when necessary to better connect the brand to consumers in different markets.

Consider McDonald's.[10] This global marketer has adapted its proven formula of "food, fun, and families" across 101 countries on six continents. Although the Golden Arches and Ronald McDonald appear worldwide, McDonald's tailors other aspects of its marketing program. It serves beer in Germany, wine in France, and coconut, mango, and tropical mint shakes in Hong Kong. Hamburgers are made with different meat and spices in Japan, Thailand, India, and the Philippines. But McDonald's world-famous french fry is standardized. Its french fry in Beijing, China, tastes like the one in Paris, France, which tastes like the one in your hometown.

Global Consumers Global competition among global companies often focuses on the identification and pursuit of global consumers, as described in the Marketing Matters box.[11] **Global consumers** consist of consumer groups living in many countries or regions of the world who have similar needs or seek similar features and benefits from products or services. Evidence suggests the presence of a global middle-income class, a youth market, and an elite segment, each consuming or using a common assortment of products and services, regardless of geographic location.

A variety of companies have capitalized on the global consumer. Whirlpool, Sony, and IKEA have benefited from the growing global middle-income class desire for kitchen appliances, consumer electronics, and home furnishings, respectively. Levi Strauss, Nike, Adidas, Coca-Cola, and Apple have tapped the global youth market. De Beers, Rolex, Chanel, Gucci, Rolls-Royce, and Sotheby's and Christie's, the world's largest fine art and antique auction houses, cater to the elite segment for luxury products worldwide.

The Presence of a Networked Global Marketspace

The use of Internet technology as a tool for exchanging products, services, and information on a global scale is the fourth development affecting globalization and world trade. Over 7 billion businesses, educational institutions, government agencies, and households worldwide are projected to have Internet access in 2025. The broad reach of this technology attests to its potential for promoting world trade.

VIDEO 7-1
Nestlé Hungary Ad
kerin.tv/15e/v7-1

A networked global marketspace enables the exchange of products, services, and information from sellers *anywhere* to buyers *anywhere* at *any time* and at a lower cost. In particular, companies engaged in business-to-business marketing have spurred the growth of global electronic commerce.[12] Ninety percent of global electronic commerce revenue arises from business-to-business transactions among a dozen countries in North America, Western Europe, and the Asia/Pacific Rim region.

Marketers recognize that the networked global marketspace offers unprecedented access to prospective buyers on every continent. Companies that have successfully capitalized on this access manage multiple country and language websites that customize content and communicate with consumers in their native tongue. Nestlé, the world's largest packaged food manufacturer, coffee roaster, and chocolate maker, is a case in point. The company operates 65 individual country websites in more than 20 languages that span five continents.

The Prevalence of Economic Espionage

The dynamic global economy also has a dark side—economic espionage.[13] **Economic espionage** is the clandestine collection of trade secrets or proprietary information about a company's competitors. This practice is common in high-technology industries such as electronics, specialty chemicals, industrial equipment, aerospace, and pharmaceuticals, where technical know-how and trade secrets separate global industry leaders from followers.

It is estimated that foreign economic espionage costs U.S. firms upward of $600 billion a year. The intelligence services of some 23 nations routinely target U.S. firms for information about research and development efforts, manufacturing and marketing plans, and customer lists.

Sweden's IKEA is capitalizing on the home-improvement trend sweeping through China. The home-furnishings retailer is courting young Chinese consumers who are eagerly updating their housing with modern, colorful, but inexpensive furniture. IKEA entered China in 1998. The company currently has 21 stores in China and plans to open another 4 to 5 stores per year through 2022.
Imaginechina/AP Images

IKEA
www.ikea.com

To counteract this threat, the *Economic Espionage Act* (1996) makes the theft of trade secrets by foreign entities a federal crime in the United States. This act prescribes prison sentences of up to 15 years and fines of up to $500,000 for individuals. Agents of foreign governments found guilty of economic espionage face a 25-year prison sentence and a $10 million fine.

LEARNING REVIEW

7-3. What is protectionism?

7-4. The United States–Mexico–Canada Agreement replaced what trade agreement?

7-5. What is the difference between a multidomestic marketing strategy and a global marketing strategy?

A GLOBAL ENVIRONMENTAL SCAN

LO 7-3
Identify the environmental forces that shape global marketing efforts.

Global companies conduct continuing environmental scans of the five sets of environmental factors described earlier in Chapter 3 in Figure 3–1 (social, economic, technological, competitive, and regulatory forces). This section focuses on three kinds of uncontrollable environmental variables—cultural, economic, and political-regulatory—that affect global marketing practices in strikingly different ways than those in domestic markets.

Cultural Diversity

Marketers must be sensitive to the cultural underpinnings of different societies if they are to initiate and consummate mutually beneficial exchange relationships with global consumers. A necessary step in this process is **cross-cultural analysis**, which involves the study of similarities and differences among consumers in two or more nations or societies.[14] A thorough cross-cultural analysis involves an understanding of and an appreciation for the values, customs, symbols, and language of other societies.

Values A society's *values* represent personally or socially preferable modes of conduct or states of existence that tend to persist over time. Understanding and working with these aspects of a society are important factors in global marketing. For example,

- McDonald's does not sell beef hamburgers in its restaurants in India because the cow is considered sacred by almost 85 percent of the population. Instead, McDonald's sells the Maharaja Mac: two all-chicken patties, special sauce, lettuce, cheese, pickles, onions on a sesame-seed bun. For the 40 percent of Indian consumers who eat no meat of any kind, McDonald's offers the McAloo Tikki burger, which features a spicy breaded potato patty, and the McPuff, a vegetable and cheese pastry.
- Germans have not been overly receptive to the use of credit cards, such as Visa or MasterCard, or the use of installment debt to purchase products and services. Indeed, the German word for debt, *schuld*, is the same as the German word for "guilt."

You will have to visit India to sample McDonald's Maharaja Mac or the McAloo Tikki burger described in the text.
Source: McDonald's

Cultural values become apparent in the personal values of individuals that affect their attitudes and beliefs and the importance assigned to specific behaviors and attributes of products and services. These personal values affect consumption-specific values, such as an aversion toward the use of installment debt by Germans, and product-specific values, such as the importance assigned to credit card interest rates.

Customs **Customs** are what is considered normal and expected about the way people do things in a specific country. Clearly customs can vary significantly from country to country.

Consider, for example, that in France, men wear more than twice the number of cosmetics than women do and that Japanese women give Japanese men chocolates on Valentine's Day.

The custom of giving token business gifts is popular in many countries where they are expected and accepted. However, bribes, kickbacks, and payoffs offered to entice someone to commit an illegal or improper act on behalf of the giver for economic gain is considered corrupt in any culture.

The prevalence of bribery in global marketing has led to an agreement among the world's major exporting nations to make bribery of foreign government officials a criminal offense. This agreement is patterned after the **Foreign Corrupt Practices Act (1977)**, as amended by the *International Anti-Dumping and Fair Competition Act* (1998). These acts make it a crime for corporations to bribe an official of a foreign government or political party to obtain or retain business in a foreign country. For example, the German engineering company Siemens AG paid an $800 million fine and Walmart paid a $282 million fine for alleged bribery of foreign government officials.[15]

Cultural Symbols **Cultural symbols** are things that represent ideas and concepts in a specific culture. Symbols and symbolism play an important role in cross-cultural analysis because different cultures attach different meanings to things. So important is the role of symbols that a field of study, called *semiotics*, has emerged that examines the correspondence between symbols and their role in the assignment of meaning for people. By adroitly using cultural symbols, global marketers can tie positive symbolism to their products, services, and brands to enhance their attractiveness to consumers. However, improper use of symbols can spell disaster. A culturally sensitive global marketer will know that:

- North Americans are superstitious about the number 13, and Japanese feel the same way about the number 4. *Shi*, the Japanese word for "four," is also the word for "death." Knowing this, Tiffany & Company sells its fine glassware and china in sets of five, not four, in Japan.
- "Thumbs-up" is a positive sign in the United States. However, in Russia and Poland, this gesture has an offensive meaning when the palm of the hand is shown, as AT&T learned. The company reversed the gesture depicted in ads, showing the back of the hand, not the palm.

Cultural symbols evoke deep feelings. Consider how executives at Coca-Cola Company's Italian office learned this lesson. In a series of advertisements directed at Italian vacationers, the Eiffel Tower, the Empire State Building, and the Tower of Pisa were turned into the familiar Coca-Cola bottle. However, when the white marble columns in the Parthenon that crowns the Acropolis in Athens were turned into Coca-Cola bottles, the Greeks were outraged. Greeks

Cultural symbols evoke deep feelings. What cultural lesson did Coca-Cola executives learn when they used the Eiffel Tower in Paris, France, and the Parthenon in Athens, Greece, in a global advertising campaign? Read the text to find the answer.

(Eiffel Tower): Sylvain Sonnet/Getty Images; (Parthenon): Bruno Cossa/SOPA/Corbis

refer to the Acropolis as the "holy rock," and a government official said the Parthenon is an "international symbol of excellence" and that "whoever insults the Parthenon insults international culture." Coca-Cola apologized for the ad.[16]

VIDEO 7-2
Nestlé Japan Ad
kerin.tv/15e/v7-2

Language Global marketers should know not only the native tongues of countries in which they market their products and services but also the nuances and idioms of a language. Even though about 100 official languages exist in the world, anthropologists estimate that at least 3,000 different languages are spoken. There are 24 official languages spoken in the European Union, and Canada has two official languages (English and French). Twenty major languages are spoken in India alone.

English, French, and Spanish are the principal languages used in global diplomacy and commerce. However, the best language to use to communicate with consumers is their own, as any seasoned global marketer will attest to. Brand names and messages with unintended meanings have ranged from the absurd to the obscene:

- When the advertising agency responsible for launching Pert shampoo in Canada realized that the name means "lost" in French, it substituted the brand name Pret, which means "ready."
- The Vicks brand name common in the United States is German slang for sexual intimacy; therefore, Vicks is called Wicks in Germany.

Experienced global marketers use **back translation**, where a translated word or phrase is retranslated into the original language by a different interpreter to catch errors. For example, IBM's first Japanese translation of its "Solutions for a Small Planet" advertising message yielded "Answers that make people smaller." The error was corrected. Nevertheless, unintended translations can produce favorable results. Consider Kit Kat bars marketed by Nestlé worldwide. Kit Kat is pronounced "kitto katsu" in Japanese, which roughly translates to "Surely win." Japanese teens eat Kit Kat bars for good luck, particularly when taking crucial school exams.[17]

The Mini is marketed in many countries using many languages, such as English and Italian. The Italian translation is "Stop Looking at My Rear."
Source: BMW

What does the Nestlé Kit Kat bar have to do with academic achievement in Japan? Read the text to find out.
CB2/ZOB/WENN/Newscom

Cultural Ethnocentricity The tendency for people to view their own values, customs, symbols, and language favorably is well known. However, the belief that aspects of one's culture are superior to another's is called *cultural ethnocentricity* and is a sure impediment to successful global marketing.

An outgrowth of cultural ethnocentricity exists in the limited purchase and use of products and services produced outside of a country. Global marketers are acutely aware that certain groups within countries disfavor imported products, not on the basis of price, features, or performance, but purely because of their foreign origin.

Consumer ethnocentrism is the tendency to believe that it is inappropriate, indeed immoral, to purchase foreign-made products.[18] Ethnocentric consumers believe that buying imported products is wrong because such purchases are unpatriotic, harm domestic industries, and cause domestic unemployment. Consumer ethnocentrism has been observed among a segment of the population in the United States, France, Japan, Korea, and Germany as well as other parts of Europe and Asia. Consumer ethnocentrism makes the task of global marketers more difficult.

Consumer ethnocentrism is common in many countries. This bumper sticker is just one illustration of how ethnocentric consumers express themselves in the United States.

Economic Considerations

Global marketing is also affected by economic considerations. Therefore, a scan of the global marketplace should include (1) an assessment of the economic infrastructure in these countries, (2) measurement of consumer income in different countries, and (3) recognition of a country's currency exchange rates.

Economic Infrastructure The *economic infrastructure*—a country's communications, transportation, financial, and distribution systems—is a critical consideration in determining whether to try to market to a country's consumers and organizations. Parts of the infrastructure that North Americans or Western Europeans take for granted can be huge problems elsewhere—not only in developing nations but even in Eastern Europe, the Indian subcontinent, and China, where such an infrastructure is assumed to be in place. For example, PepsiCo

PepsiCo has made a huge financial investment in bottling and distribution facilities in China.
ChinaFotoPress/ZUMA Press/Newscom

has invested $1.5 billion in transportation and manufacturing systems in China and India since 2010.

The communication infrastructures in these countries also differ. This infrastructure includes telecommunication systems and networks in use, such as telephones, cable television, broadcast radio and television, computers, satellites, and cell phones. In general, the communication infrastructure in many developing countries is limited or antiquated compared with that of developed countries. For example, some 800 million people do not have Internet access, with the majority of them living in African countries.[19]

Even the financial and legal system can cause problems. Formal operating procedures among financial institutions and the notion of private property are still limited. As a consequence, it is estimated that two-thirds of the commercial transactions in Russia involve nonmonetary forms of payment. The legal red tape involved in obtaining titles to buildings and land for manufacturing, wholesaling, and retailing operations also has been a huge problem. Still, the Coca-Cola Company has invested $1 billion for bottling facilities in Russia. Frito-Lay spent $60 million to build a plant outside Moscow to make Lay's potato chips.

Consumer Income and Purchasing Power A global marketer selling consumer products must also consider what the average per capita or household income is among a country's consumers and how the income is distributed to determine a nation's purchasing power. Per capita income varies greatly between nations. Average yearly per capita income in EU countries is about $36,000 while it is less than $800 in some developing countries such as Liberia. A country's income distribution is important because it gives a more reliable picture of a country's purchasing power. Generally, as the proportion of middle-income households in a country increases, the greater that nation's purchasing capability tends to be.

VIDEO 7-3
Denizen
kerin.tv/15e/v7-3

Seasoned global marketers recognize that people in developing countries often have government subsidies for food, housing, and health care that supplement their income. So people with seemingly low incomes are actually promising customers for a variety of products. For instance, a consumer in South Asia earning the equivalent of $250 per year can afford Gillette razors. When that consumer's income rises to $1,000, a Sony television becomes affordable, and a new Nissan automobile can be bought with an annual income of $10,000. In developing countries of Eastern Europe, a $1,000 annual income makes a refrigerator affordable, and $2,000 brings an automatic washer within reach–good news for Whirlpool, the world's leading manufacturer and marketer of major home appliances.

Levi Strauss & Co. launched its Denizen brand jeans in China. Created for teens and young adults in emerging markets who cannot afford Levi-branded jeans, Denizen is now sold in North America.
Eugene Hoshiko/AP Images

Income growth in developing countries of Asia, Latin America, and Eastern Europe stimulates world trade. The number of consumers in these countries earning the equivalent of $10,000 per year exceeds the number of consumers in the United States, Japan, and Western Europe combined. By one estimate, half of the world's population has now achieved "middle-class" status and 63 percent will achieve middle-class status by 2030.[20] For this reason, developing countries represent a prominent marketing opportunity for global companies.

Currency Exchange Rates Fluctuations in exchange rates among the world's currencies are of critical importance in global marketing. Such fluctuations affect everyone, from international tourists to global companies.

A **currency exchange rate** is the price of one country's currency expressed in terms of another country's currency, such as the U.S. dollar expressed in Japanese yen, euros, Swiss francs, or the British pound. Failure to consider exchange rates when pricing products for global markets can have dire consequences. Mattel learned this lesson the hard way. The company was recently unable to sell its popular Holiday Barbie doll and accessories in some international markets because they were too expensive. Why? Barbie prices, expressed in U.S. dollars, were set without regard for how they would convert into foreign currencies and were too high for many buyers.[21]

Exchange rate fluctuations affect the sales and profits made by global companies. When foreign currencies can buy more U.S. dollars, for example, U.S. products are less expensive for the foreign customer. Short-term fluctuations, however, can have a significant effect on the profits of global companies.[22] Hewlett-Packard recently gained nearly a half million dollars of additional profit through exchange rate fluctuations in one year. On the other hand, Procter & Gamble recently lost $550 million on its operations in Russia due to devaluation of the Russian ruble.

Political-Regulatory Climate

Assessing the political and regulatory climate for marketing in a country or region of the world involves not only identifying the current climate but also determining how long a favorable or unfavorable climate will last. An assessment of a country or regional political-regulatory climate includes an analysis of its political stability and trade regulations.

Political Stability Trade among nations or regions depends on political stability. Billions of dollars in trade have been lost in the Middle East and Africa as a result of internal political strife, terrorism, and war. Losses such as these encourage careful selection of politically stable countries and regions of the world for trade.

Political stability in a country is affected by numerous factors, including a government's orientation toward foreign companies and trade with other countries. These factors combine to create a political climate that is favorable or unfavorable for marketing and financial investment in a country or region of the world. Marketing managers monitor political stability using a variety of measures and often track country risk ratings supplied by agencies such as the PRS Group, Inc. Visit the PRS Group, Inc. website described in the Marketing Insights About Me box to see political risk ratings for 100 countries, including your own. Expect to be surprised by the ranking of countries, including the United States.

Trade Regulations Countries have a variety of rules that govern business practices within their borders. These rules often serve as trade barriers. For example, Japan has some 11,000 trade regulations. Japanese car safety rules effectively require all automobile replacement parts to be Japanese and not American or European; public health rules make it illegal to sell aspirin or cold medicine without a pharmacist present. The Malaysian government has advertising regulations stating that "advertisements must not project or promote an excessively aspirational lifestyle," Sweden outlaws all advertisements to children, Iran prohibits Mattel's Barbie dolls because they are a symbol of Western decadence, and Cuba and North Korea ban Coca-Cola because of U.S. trade embargoes. And recall from the chapter introduction that India has imposed regulations on Amazon regarding the sourcing and inventorying of Indian-made products.

Marketing Insights About Me

Checking Your Country's Political Risk Rating—Are You Surprised?

The political climate in every country is regularly changing. Governments can make new laws or enforce existing policies differently. Numerous consulting firms prepare political risk analyses that incorporate a variety of variables such as the risk of internal turmoil, external conflict, government restrictions on company operations, and tariff and nontariff trade barriers.

The PRS Group, Inc. maintains multiple databases of country-specific information and projections, including country political risk ratings for 100 countries. These ratings can be accessed at www.prsgroup.com. Click "Political Risk Index."

Which three countries have the highest rating (lowest risk), and which three have the lowest rating (highest risk)? Which countries have risk ratings closest to the United States?

Source: The PRS Group

LEARNING REVIEW

7-6. Cross-cultural analysis involves the study of ___________.

7-7. When foreign currencies can buy more U.S. dollars, are U.S. products more or less expensive for a foreign consumer?

COMPARING GLOBAL MARKET-ENTRY STRATEGIES

LO 7-4
Name and describe the alternative approaches companies use to enter global markets.

Once a company has decided to enter the global marketplace, it must select a means of market entry. Four general options exist: (1) exporting, (2) licensing, (3) joint venture, and (4) direct investment.[23] As Figure 7–4 demonstrates, the amount of financial commitment, risk, marketing control, and profit potential increases as the firm moves from exporting to direct investment.

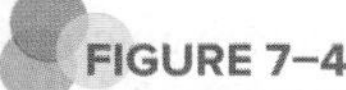

FIGURE 7–4
A firm's profit potential and control over marketing activities increase as it moves from exporting to direct investment as a global market-entry strategy. But so does a firm's financial commitment and risk. Firms often engage in exporting, licensing, and joint ventures before pursuing a direct investment strategy.

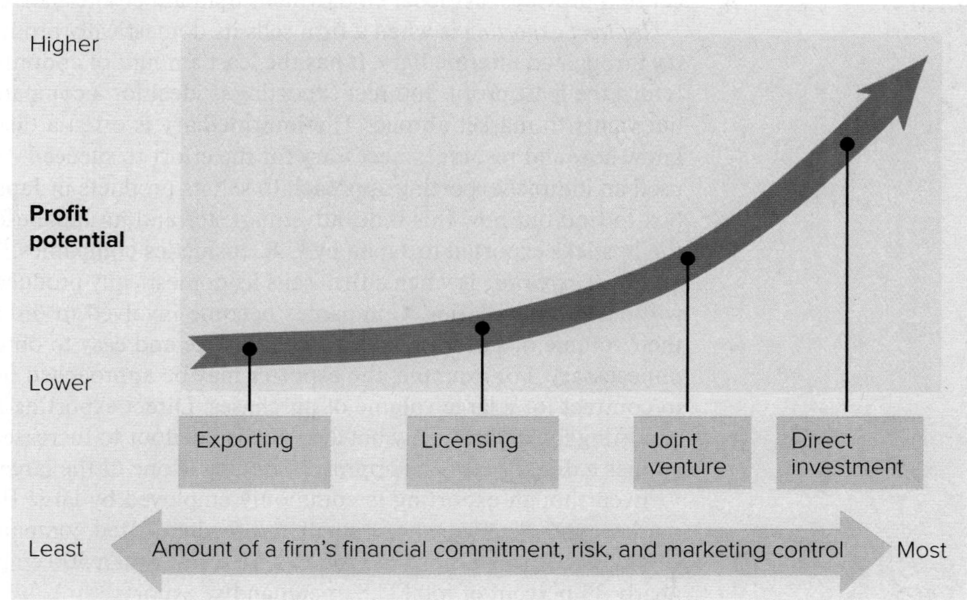

Marketing Matters — Entrepreneurship

Creative Cosmetics and Creative Export Marketing in Japan

How does a medium-sized U.S. cosmetics firm sell 1.5 million tubes of lipstick in Japan annually? Fran Wilson Creative Cosmetics can attribute its success to a top-quality product, effective advertising, and a novel export marketing program. The firm's Moodmatcher lip coloring comes in green, orange, silver, black, and six other hues that change to a shade of pink, coral, or red, depending on a woman's chemistry when it's applied.

The company does not sell to department stores. According to a company spokesperson, "Shiseido and Kanebo (two large Japanese cosmetics firms) keep all the other Japanese or import brands out of the major department stores."[24] Rather, the company sells its Moodmatcher lipstick through a network of Japanese distributors that reach Japan's 40,000 beauty salons.

The result? The company, with its savvy Japanese distributors, accounted for 20 percent of the lipsticks exported annually to Japan by U.S. cosmetics companies.

Source: Fran Wilson, Creative Cosmetics.

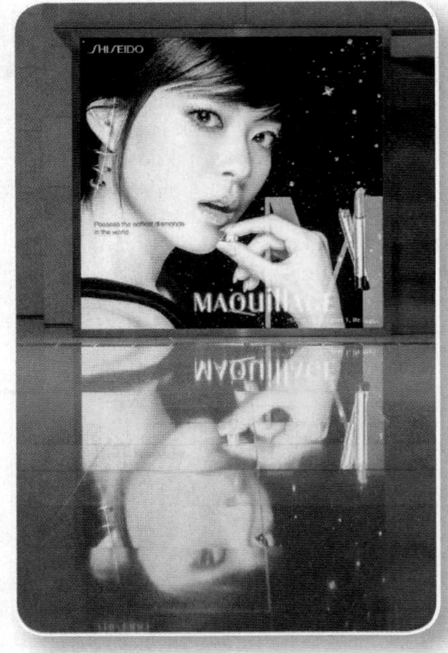

Markus Sepperer/Anzenberger/Redux

Exporting

Exporting is producing products in one country and selling them in another country. This entry option allows a company to make the least number of changes in terms of its product, its organization, and even its corporate goals. Host countries usually do not like this practice because it provides less local employment than under alternative means of entry.

Indirect exporting is when a firm sells its domestically produced products in a foreign country through an intermediary. It has the least amount of commitment and risk but will probably return the least profit. Indirect exporting is ideal for a company that has no overseas contacts but wants to market abroad. The intermediary is often a distributor that has the marketing know-how and resources necessary for the effort to succeed. Fran Wilson Creative Cosmetics used an indirect exporting approach to sell its products in Japan. Read the Marketing Matters box to find out how this innovative marketer and its Japanese distributors sell 20 percent of the lipsticks exported to Japan by U.S. cosmetics companies.[25]

Direct exporting is when a firm sells its domestically produced products in a foreign country without intermediaries. Companies become involved in direct exporting when they believe their volume of sales will be sufficiently large and easy to obtain, thus making intermediaries unnecessary. For example, the exporter may be approached by foreign buyers that are willing to contract for a large volume of purchases. Direct exporting involves more risk than indirect exporting for the company but also opens the door to increased profits. The Boeing Company applies a direct exporting approach. Boeing is one of the largest U.S. exporters.

Even though exporting is commonly employed by large firms, it is the prominent global market-entry strategy among small and medium-sized companies. For example, about 98 percent of U.S. firms exporting products have fewer than 500 employees. These firms account for nearly 33 percent of total U.S. merchandise exports.[26]

McDonald's uses franchising as a market-entry strategy, and about two-thirds of the company's sales come from non-U.S. operations. Note that the Golden Arches appear prominently—one aspect of its global brand promise.
China/Alamy Stock Photo

Licensing

Under licensing, a company offers the right to a trademark, patent, trade secret, or other similarly valued item of intellectual property in return for a royalty or a fee. The advantages to the company granting the license are low risk and a capital-free entry into a foreign country. The licensee gains information that allows it to start with a competitive advantage, and the foreign country gains employment by having the product manufactured locally. For instance, Yoplait yogurt is licensed from Sodima, a French cooperative, by General Mills for sales in the United States.

There are some serious drawbacks to this mode of entry, however. The licensor forgoes control of its product and reduces the potential profits gained from it. In addition, while the relationship lasts, the licensor may be creating its own competition. Some licensees are able to modify the product somehow and enter the market with product and marketing knowledge gained at the expense of the company that got them started. To offset this disadvantage, many companies strive to stay innovative so that the licensee remains dependent on them for improvements and successful operation. Finally, should the licensee prove to be a poor choice, the name or reputation of the company may be harmed.

A variation of licensing is *franchising*. Franchising is one of the fastest-growing market-entry strategies. Over 75,000 franchises of U.S. firms are located in countries throughout the world. Franchises include soft drink, motel, retailing, fast-food, and car rental operations and a variety of business services. McDonald's is a premier global franchiser, with some 14,000 franchised units outside the United States.

Joint Venture

When a foreign company and a local firm invest together to create a local business, it is called a **joint venture**. These two companies share the ownership, control, and profits of the new company. For example, the Strauss Group has a joint venture with PepsiCo to market Frito-Lay's Cheetos, Doritos, and other snacks in Israel and the Strauss Group's Sabra hummus in North America.[27]

The advantages of this option are twofold. First, one company may not have the necessary financial, physical, or managerial resources to enter a foreign market alone. The joint venture between Ericsson, a Swedish telecommunications firm, and CGCT, a French switch maker, enabled them together to beat out AT&T for a $100 million French contract. Ericsson's money and technology combined with CGCT's knowledge of the French market helped them to win the contract. Second, a government may require or strongly encourage a joint venture before it allows a foreign company to enter its market. For example, in China, international giants such as Procter & Gamble, Starbucks, and General Motors operate wholly or in part through joint ventures.

Sabra is the best-selling hummus brand in the U.S. and Canada. Read the text to learn which two companies formed a joint venture to manufacture and distribute the brand in North America.
McGraw-Hill Education

The disadvantages arise when the two companies disagree about policies or courses of action for their joint venture or when governmental bureaucracy bogs down the effort. For example, U.S. firms often prefer to reinvest earnings gained, whereas some foreign companies may want to spend those earnings. Or a U.S. firm may want to return profits earned to the United States, while the local firm or its government may oppose this–a problem faced by many potential joint ventures. The collapse of the joint venture between France's Group Danone and a local company in China is a case in point. The joint venture partners could not agree on the distribution of profits.[28]

Direct Investment

The biggest commitment a company can make when entering the global market is *direct investment*, which entails a domestic firm actually investing in and owning a foreign subsidiary or division. Examples of direct investment are Nissan's Smyrna, Tennessee, plant that produces pickup trucks and the Mercedes-Benz factory in Vance, Alabama, that makes the M-Class sport-utility vehicle. Many U.S.-based global companies also use this mode of entry. Reebok entered Russia by creating a subsidiary known as Reebok Russia.

For many companies, direct investment often follows one of the other three market-entry strategies.[29] For example, both FedEx and UPS entered China through joint ventures with Chinese companies. Each subsequently purchased the interests of its partner and converted the Chinese operations into a division.

The advantages to direct investment include cost savings, a better understanding of local market conditions, and fewer local restrictions. Firms entering foreign markets using direct investment believe that these advantages outweigh the financial commitments and risks involved. However, sometimes they don't. U.S.-based Target Stores entered Canada in 2013 only to withdraw in 2015 after sizable operating losses and an investment of $5.7 billion; Uber and Amazon departed China in 2016 and 2019, respectively, after posting significant losses.[30]

LEARNING REVIEW

7-8. What mode of entry could a company follow if it has no previous experience in global marketing?

7-9. How does licensing differ from a joint venture?

CRAFTING A WORLDWIDE MARKETING PROGRAM

LO 7-5
Explain the distinction between standardization and customization when companies craft worldwide marketing programs.

The choice of a market-entry strategy is a necessary first step for a marketer when joining the community of global companies. The next step involves the challenging task of planning, implementing, and evaluating marketing programs worldwide.

Successful global marketers standardize global marketing programs whenever possible and customize them wherever necessary. The extent of standardization and customization is often rooted in a careful global environment scan supplemented with judgment based on experience and marketing research.

Product and Promotion Strategies

Global companies have five strategies for matching products and their promotion efforts to global markets. As Figure 7-5 shows, the strategies focus on whether a company extends or adapts its product and promotion message for consumers in different countries and cultures.

A product may be sold globally in one of three ways: (1) in the same form as in its home market, (2) with some adaptations, or (3) as a totally new product:[31]

1. *Product extension*. Selling virtually the same product in other countries is a product extension strategy. It works well for products such as Coca-Cola, Gillette razors, Samsung consumer electronics, Nike apparel and shoes, and Apple smartphones. As a general rule, product extension seems to work best when the consumer market target for the product is alike across countries and cultures—that is, consumers share the same desires, needs, and uses for the product.
2. *Product adaptation*. Changing a product in some way to make it more appropriate for consumer preferences or a country's climate is a product adaptation strategy. Wrigley's offers grapefruit, cucumber, and tea-flavored chewing gum in China. Frito-Lay produces

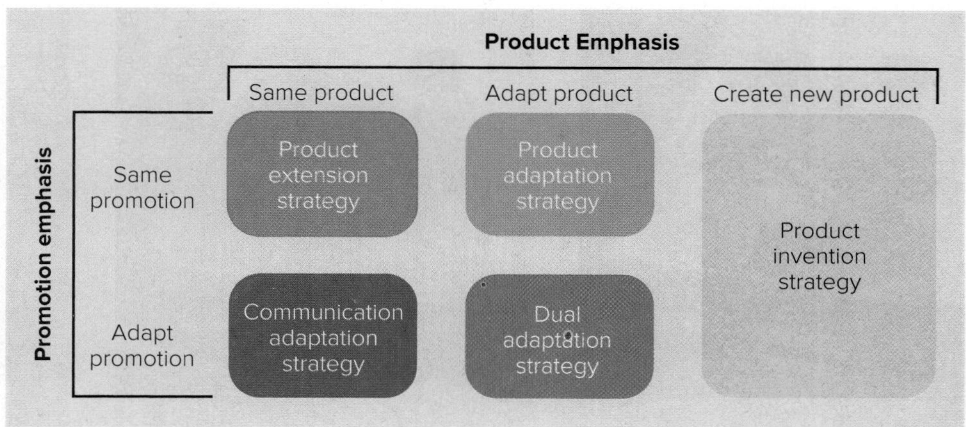

FIGURE 7–5
Five product and promotion strategies for global marketing exist based on whether a company extends or adapts its product and promotion message for consumers in different countries and cultures. Read the text to learn how different companies employ these strategies.

and markets its potato chips in Russia, but don't expect them to taste like the chips eaten in North America. Russians prefer dairy-, meat-, and seafood-flavored potato chips. Listerine mouthwash comes in different varieties outside the United States. There is the alcohol-free Listerine Zero, popular in Muslim countries where alcohol is forbidden, and Green Tea Listerine, made especially for Asian markets. Maybelline's makeup is adapted to local skin types and weather across the globe, including an Asia-specific mascara that doesn't run during the rainy season.

3. *Product invention*. Alternatively, companies can invent totally new products designed to satisfy common needs across countries. Stanley Black & Decker did this with its Snake Light flexible flashlight. Created to address a global need for portable lighting, the product became a best-seller in North America, Europe, Latin America, and Australia and became one of the most successful new products developed by Stanley Black & Decker. Similarly, Whirlpool developed a compact, automatic clothes washer specifically for households in developing countries with annual household incomes of $2,000. Called Ideale, the washer features bright colors because washers are often placed in home living areas, not hidden in laundry rooms (which don't exist in many homes in developing countries).

An identical promotion message is used for the product extension and product adaptation strategies around the world. Gillette uses the same global message for its men's toiletries: "Gillette, the Best a Man Can Get."[32] Even though Exxon adapts its gasoline blends for different countries based on climate, the promotion message is unchanged: "Put a Tiger in Your Tank."[33]

VIDEO 7-4
Nescafé China
kerin.tv/15e/v7-4

Global companies may also adapt their promotion message. For instance, the same product may be sold in many countries but advertised differently. As an example, L'Oréal, a French health and beauty products marketer, introduced its Golden Beauty brand of sun care products through its Helena Rubenstein subsidiary in Western Europe with a *communication adaptation strategy*. Recognizing the existence of differing cultural and buying motives related to skin care and tanning, Golden Beauty advertising features dark tanning for northern Europeans, skin protection to avoid wrinkles among Latin Europeans, and beautiful skin for Europeans living along the Mediterranean Sea, even though the products are the same.

Other companies use a *dual adaptation strategy* by modifying both their products and promotion messages. Nestlé does this with Nescafé coffee. Nescafé is marketed using different coffee blends and promotional campaigns to match consumer preferences in different countries. For example, Nescafé, the world's largest brand of coffee, generally emphasizes the taste, aroma, and warmth of shared moments in its advertising around the world. However, Nescafé is advertised in Thailand as a way to relax from the pressures of daily life.

These examples illustrate the simple rule applied by global companies: Standardize product and promotion strategies whenever possible and customize them wherever necessary. This is the art of global marketing.[34]

Gillette delivers the same global message whenever possible, as shown in the Gillette for Women Venus ads from the United States, Mexico, and France.

(All): Source: Procter & Gamble

Distribution Strategy

Distribution is of critical importance in global marketing. The availability and quality of retailers and wholesalers as well as transportation, communication, and warehousing facilities are often determined by a country's stage of economic development. Figure 7–6 outlines the channel through which a product manufactured in one country must travel to reach its destination in another country. The first step involves the seller; its headquarters is the starting point and is responsible for the successful distribution to the ultimate consumer.

The next step is the channel between two nations, moving the product from one country to another. Intermediaries that can handle this responsibility include resident buyers in a foreign country, independent merchant wholesalers who buy and sell the product, or agents who bring buyers and sellers together.

Once the product is in the foreign nation, that country's distribution channels take over. These channels can be very long or surprisingly short, depending on the product line. In Japan, fresh fish go through three intermediaries before getting to a retail outlet. Conversely, shoes go through only one intermediary.

Pricing Strategy

Global companies also face many challenges in determining a pricing strategy as part of their worldwide marketing effort. Individual countries, even those with free trade agreements, may impose considerable competitive, political, and legal constraints on the pricing latitude of global companies. For example, antitrust authorities in Germany limited Walmart from selling some items below cost to lure shoppers. Without this advantage, Walmart was unable to compete against German discount stores. This, and other factors, led Walmart to leave Germany following eight years without a profit.[35]

Pricing too low or too high can have dire consequences. When prices appear too low in one country, companies can be charged with dumping, a practice subject to severe penalties and fines. *Dumping* is when a firm sells a product in a foreign country below its domestic price or

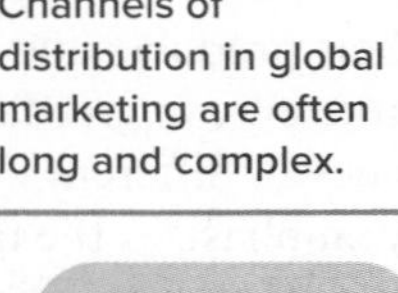

FIGURE 7–6
Channels of distribution in global marketing are often long and complex.

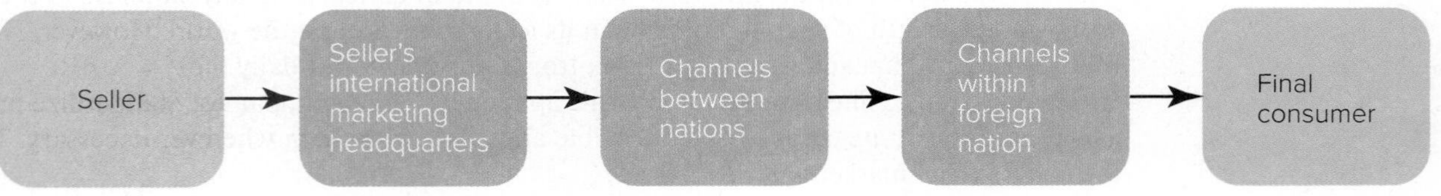

below its actual cost. This is often done to build a company's share of the market by pricing at a competitive level. Another reason is that the products being sold may be surplus or cannot be sold domestically and, therefore, are already a burden to the company. The firm may be glad to sell them at almost any price.

When companies price their products very high in some countries but competitively in others, they face a gray market problem. A *gray market*, also called *parallel importing*, is a situation where products are sold through unauthorized channels of distribution. A gray market comes about when individuals buy products in a lower-priced country from a manufacturer's authorized retailer, ship them to higher-priced countries, and then sell them below the manufacturer's suggested retail price through unauthorized retailers. Many well-known brands have been sold through gray markets, including Seiko watches, Chanel perfume, and Mercedes-Benz cars. Parallel importing is legal in the United States. It is illegal in the European Union.

LEARNING REVIEW

7-10. Products may be sold globally in three ways. What are they?

7-11. What is *dumping*?

LEARNING OBJECTIVES REVIEW

LO 7-1 *Describe the nature and scope of world trade from a global perspective.*
A global perspective on world trade views exports and imports as complementary economic flows: A country's imports affect its exports and exports affect its imports. Trade flows reflect interdependencies among industries, countries, and regions.

LO 7-2 *Identify the major developments that have influenced world trade and global marketing.*
Five major developments have influenced the landscape of global marketing in the past decade. First, there has been a gradual increase of economic protectionism by individual countries, leading to tariffs and quotas. Second, economic integration and free trade among nations is being challenged. Third, there exists global competition among global companies for global consumers, resulting in firms adopting global marketing strategies and promoting global brands. Fourth, a networked global marketspace has emerged using Internet technology as a tool for exchanging products, services, and information on a global scale. And finally, economic espionage has grown among countries and companies because technical know-how and trade secrets separate global industry leaders from followers.

LO 7-3 *Identify the environmental forces that shape global marketing efforts.*
Three major environmental forces shape global marketing efforts. First, there are cultural forces, including values, customs, cultural symbols, and language. Economic forces also shape global marketing efforts. These include a country's stage of economic development and economic infrastructure, consumer income and purchasing power, and currency exchange rates. Finally, political-regulatory forces in a country or region of the world create a favorable or unfavorable climate for global marketing efforts.

LO 7-4 *Name and describe the alternative approaches companies use to enter global markets.*
Companies have four alternative approaches for entering global markets. These are exporting, licensing, joint venture, and direct investment. Exporting involves producing products in one country and selling them in another country. Under licensing, a company offers the right to a trademark, patent, trade secret, or similarly valued item of intellectual property in return for a royalty or fee. In a joint venture, a foreign company and a local firm invest together to create a local business. Direct investment entails a domestic firm actually investing in and owning a foreign subsidiary or division.

LO 7-5 *Explain the distinction between standardization and customization when companies craft worldwide marketing programs.*
Companies distinguish between standardization and customization when crafting worldwide marketing programs. Standardization means that all elements of the marketing program are the same across countries and cultures. Customization means that one or more elements of the marketing program are adapted to meet the needs or preferences of consumers in a particular country or culture. Global marketers apply a simple rule when crafting worldwide marketing programs: Standardize marketing programs whenever possible and customize them wherever necessary.

LEARNING REVIEW ANSWERS

7-1 **What country is the biggest as measured by world trade?**
Answer: China

7-2 **What is the trade feedback effect?**
Answer: The phenomenon in which one country's imports affect the exports of other countries and vice versa, thus stimulating trade among countries.

7-3 **What is protectionism?**
Answer: Protectionism is the practice of shielding one or more industries within a country's economy from foreign competition through the use of tariffs or quotas.

7-4 **The United States–Mexico–Canada Agreement replaced what trade agreement?**
Answer: North American Free Trade Agreement

7-5 **What is the difference between a multidomestic marketing strategy and a global marketing strategy?**
Answer: Multinational firms view the world as consisting of unique markets. As a result, they use a multidomestic marketing strategy because they have as many different product variations, brand names, and advertising programs as countries in which they do business. Transnational firms view the world as one market. As a result, they use a global marketing strategy, which involves standardizing marketing activities when there are cultural similarities and adapting them when cultures differ.

7-6 **Cross-cultural analysis involves the study of ________.**
Answer: similarities and differences among consumers in two or more nations or societies.

7-7 **When foreign currencies can buy more U.S. dollars, are U.S. products more or less expensive for a foreign consumer?**
Answer: less expensive

7-8 **What mode of entry could a company follow if it has no previous experience in global marketing?**
Answer: indirect exporting through intermediaries

7-9 **How does licensing differ from a joint venture?**
Answer: Under licensing, a company offers the right to a trademark, patent, trade secret, or other similarly valued item of intellectual property in return for a fee or royalty. In a joint venture, a foreign company and a local firm invest together to create a local business to produce some product or service. The two companies share ownership, control, and profits of the new entity.

7-10 **Products may be sold globally in three ways. What are they?**
Answer: Products can be sold: (1) in the same form as in their home market (product extension); (2) with some adaptations (product adaptation); and (3) as totally new products (product invention).

7-11 **What is *dumping*?**
Answer: *Dumping* is when a firm sells a product in a foreign country below its domestic price or below its actual cost to produce.

FOCUSING ON KEY TERMS

back translation p. 187
balance of trade p. 177
consumer ethnocentrism p. 188
countertrade p. 177
cross-cultural analysis p. 185
cultural symbols p. 186
currency exchange rate p. 190
customs p. 185
economic espionage p. 184
exporting p. 192
Foreign Corrupt Practices Act (1977) p. 186
global brand p. 183
global competition p. 181
global consumers p. 183
globalization p. 178
global marketing strategy p. 182
joint venture p. 193
multidomestic marketing strategy p. 182
protectionism p. 178
quota p. 179
tariffs p. 178
trade war p. 179
World Trade Organization (WTO) p. 179

APPLYING MARKETING KNOWLEDGE

1 Explain what is meant by this statement: "Quotas are a hidden tax on consumers, whereas tariffs are a more obvious one."

2 How successful would a television commercial in Japan be if it featured a husband surprising his wife in her dressing area on Valentine's Day with a small box of chocolates containing four candies? Explain.

3 As a novice in global marketing, which global market-entry strategy would you be likely to start with? Why? What other alternatives do you have for a global market entry?

4 Coca-Cola is sold worldwide. In some countries, Coca-Cola owns the bottling facilities; in others, it has signed contracts with licensees or relies on joint ventures. When selecting a licensee in each country, what factors should Coca-Cola consider?

BUILDING YOUR MARKETING PLAN

Does your marketing plan involve reaching global customers outside the United States? If the answer is no, read no further and do not include a global element in your plan.

If the answer is yes, try to identify the following:

1 What features of your product are especially important to potential customers?
2 In which countries do these potential customers live?
3 What special marketing issues are involved in trying to reach these customers?

Answers to these questions will help you develop the more detailed marketing mix strategies described in later chapters.

VIDEO CASE 7 Mary Kay, Inc.: Building a Brand in India

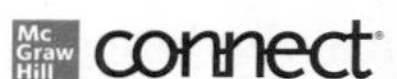

Sheryl Adkins-Green couldn't ask for a better assignment. As the newly appointed vice president of brand development at Mary Kay, Inc. she is responsible for development of the product portfolio around the world, including global initiatives and products specifically formulated for global markets. She is enthusiastic about her position, noting that "There is tremendous opportunity for growth. Even in these economic times, women still want to pamper themselves, and to look good is to feel good."

VIDEO 7-5
Mary Kay Video Case
kerin.tv/15e/v7-5

Getting up to speed on her new company and her new position topped her short-term agenda. She was specifically interested in the company's efforts to date to build the Mary Kay brand in India.

THE MARY KAY WAY

Mary Kay Ash founded Mary Kay Cosmetics in 1963 with her life savings of $5,000 and the support of her 20-year-old son, Richard Rogers, who currently serves as executive chair of Mary Kay, Inc. Mary Kay, Inc. is one of the largest direct sellers of skin care and color cosmetics in the world, with more than $2.5 billion in annual sales. Mary Kay brand products are sold in more than 35 markets on five continents. The United States, China, Russia, and Mexico are the top four markets served by the company. The company's global independent sales force exceeds 2 million. About 65 percent of the company's independent sales representatives reside outside the United States.

Mary Kay Ash's founding principles were simple, time-tested, and remain a fundamental company business philosophy. She adopted the Golden Rule as her guiding principle, determining the best course of action in virtually any situation could be easily discerned by "doing unto others as you would have them do unto you." She also steadfastly believed that life's priorities should be kept in their proper order, which to her meant "God first, family second, and career third." Her work ethic, approach to business, and success have resulted in numerous awards and recognitions, including, but not limited to, the Horatio Alger American Citizen Award, recognition as one of "America's 25 Most Influential Women," and induction into the National Business Hall of Fame.

Mary Kay, Inc. engages in the development, manufacture, and packaging of skin care, makeup, spa and body, and fragrance products for men and women. It offers anti-aging, cleanser, moisturizer, lip and eye care, body care, and sun care products. Overall, the company produces more than 200 premium products in its state-of-the-art manufacturing facilities in Dallas, Texas, and Hangzhou, China. The company's approach to direct selling employs the "party plan," whereby independent sales representatives host parties to demonstrate or sell products to consumers.

GROWTH OPPORTUNITIES IN ASIA-PACIFIC MARKETS

Asia-Pacific markets represent major growth opportunities for Mary Kay, Inc. These markets for Mary Kay, Inc. include Australia, China, Hong Kong, India, Korea, Malaysia, New Zealand, the Philippines, Singapore, and Taiwan.

China accounts for the largest sales revenue outside the United States, representing about 25 percent of annual Mary Kay, Inc. worldwide sales. The company entered China in 1995 and currently has some 200,000 independent sales representatives or "beauty consultants" in that country.

Part of Mary Kay's success in China has been attributed to the company's message of female empowerment and femininity, which has resonated in China, a country where young women have few opportunities to start their own businesses. Speaking about the corporate philosophy at Mary Kay, Inc., KK Chua, president, Asia-Pacific, said, "Mary Kay's corporate objective is not only to create a market, selling skin care and cosmetics; it's all about enriching women's lives by helping women reach their full potential, find their inner beauty and discover how truly great they are."[36] This view is echoed by Sheryl Adkins-Green, who notes that the Mary Kay brand has "transformational and aspirational" associations for users and beauty consultants alike.

Mary Kay, Inc. learned that adjustments to its product line and message for women were necessary in some Asia-Pacific markets. In China, for example, the order of life's priorities—"God first, family second, and career third"—has been modified to "Faith first, family second, and career third." Also, Chinese women aren't heavy users of makeup. Therefore, the featured products include skin cream, anti-aging cream, and whitening creams. As a generalization, whitening products are popular among women in China, India, Korea, and the Philippines, where lighter skin is associated with beauty, class, and privilege.

MARY KAY INDIA

Mary Kay, Inc. senior management believed that India represented a growth opportunity for three reasons. First, the Indian upper and consuming classes were growing and were expected to total over 500 million individuals. Second, the population was overwhelmingly young and optimistic. This youthful population continues to push consumerism as the line between luxury and basic items continues to blur. Third, a growing number of working women have given a boost to sales of cosmetics, skin care, and fragrances in India's urban areas, where 70 percent of the country's middle-class women reside.

Senior management also believed that India's socioeconomic characteristics in 2007 were similar in many ways to China's in 1995, when the company entered that market (see Figure 1). The Mary Kay culture was viewed as a good fit with the Indian culture, which would benefit the company's venture into this market. For example, industry research has shown that continuing modernization of the country has led to changing aspirations. As a result, the need to be good-looking, well-groomed, and stylish has taken on a newfound importance.

Mary Kay initiated operations in India in September 2007 with a full marketing launch in early 2008. The initial launch was in Delhi, the nation's capital and the second most populated metropolis in India, and Mumbai, the nation's most heavily populated metropolis. Delhi, with per capita income of U.S.$1,420, and Mumbai, with per capita income of $2,850, were among the wealthiest metropolitan areas in India.

According to Rhonda Shasteen, chief marketing officer at Mary Kay, Inc., "For Mary Kay to be successful in India, the company had to build a brand, build a sales force, and build an effective supply chain to service the sales force."

Building a Brand

Mary Kay, Inc. executives believed that brand building in India needed to involve media advertising; literature describing the Mary Kay culture, the Mary Kay story, and the company's image; and educational material for Mary Kay independent sales representatives. In addition, Mary Kay, Inc. became the cosmetics partner of the Miss India Worldwide Pageant. At this event, Mary Kay Miss Beautiful Skin was crowned.

Brand building in India also involved product mix and pricing. Four guidelines were followed:

1 Keep the offering simple and skin care focused for the new Indian sales force and for a new operation.
2 Open with accessibly priced basic skin care products in relation to the competition in order to establish Mary Kay product quality and value.
3 Avoid opening with products that would phase out shortly after launch.
4 Address the key product categories of Skin Care, Body Care, and Color based on current market information.

FIGURE 1
Social and economic statistics for India in 2007 and China in 1995.

	India 2007	China 1995
Population (million)	1,136	1,198
Population age distribution (0–24; 25–49; 50+)	52%, 33%, 15%	43%, 39%, 18%
Urban population	29.2%	29.0%
Population/square mile	990	332
Gross domestic product (U.S.$ billion)	3,113	728
Per capita income (U.S.$)	$950	$399
Direct selling sales percent of total cosmetics/skin care sales	3.3%	3.0%

Courtesy of Mary Kay, Inc.

Brand pricing focused on offering accessibly priced basic skin care to the average middle-class Indian consumer between the ages of 25 and 54. This strategy, called "masstige pricing," resulted in product price points that were above mass but below prestige competitive product prices. Following an initial emphasis on offering high-quality, high-value products, Mary Kay introduced more technologically advanced products that commanded higher price points. For example, the company introduced the Mary Kay MelaCEP Whitening System, consisting of seven products, which was specifically formulated for Asian skin in March 2009. This system was "priced on the lower price end of the prestige category with a great value for money equation," said Hina Nagarajan, country manager for Mary Kay India.

Building a Sales Force

According to Adkins-Green, "Mary Kay's most powerful marketing vehicle is the direct selling organization," which is a key component of the brand's marketing strategy. Mary Kay relied on its Global Leadership Development Program directors and National Sales directors and the Mary Kay Sales Education staff from the United States and Canada for the initial recruitment and training of independent sales representatives in India. New independent sales representatives received two to three days of intensive training and a starter kit that included not only products, but also information pertaining to product demonstrations, sales presentations, professional demeanor, the company's history and culture, and team building.

"Culture training is very important to Mary Kay (independent sales representatives) because they are going to be the messengers of Mary Kay," said Hina Nagarajan. "As a direct-selling company that offers products sold person-to-person, we recognize that there's a personal relationship between consultant and client with every sale," added Rhonda Shasteen. By late 2009, there were some 4,000 independent sales representatives in India present in some 200 cities mostly in the northern, western, and northeastern regions of the country.

Creating a Supply Chain

Mary Kay India imported products into India from China, Korea, and the United States. Products were shipped to regional distribution centers in Delhi and Mumbai, India, where Mary Kay Beauty Centers were located. Beauty Centers served as order pickup points for the independent sales representatives. Mary Kay beauty consultants purchased products from the company and, in turn, sold them to consumers.

LOOKING AHEAD

Mary Kay, Inc. plans to invest around $20 million in the next five years on product development, company infrastructure, and building its brand in India. "There is a tremendous opportunity for growth," says Sheryl Adkins-Green. India represents a particularly attractive opportunity. Developing the brand and brand portfolio and specifically formulating products for Indian consumers will require her attention to brand positioning and brand equity.[37]

Questions

1 Is Mary Kay an international firm, a multinational firm, or a transnational firm based on its marketing strategy? Why?

2 What global market-entry strategy did Mary Kay use when it entered India?

3 Is Mary Kay a global brand? Why or why not?

Chapter Notes

1. "India's Web Rules Bite Amazon," *The Wall Street Journal*, February 2–3, 2019, p. B3; "A Package to India," *Bloomberg Businessweek*, October 22, 2018, pp. 42–47; "The Elephant in the Room," *The Economist*, January 13, 2018, pp. 20–22; "India's Ecommerce Market Continues to Surge," www.emarketer.com, June 7, 2018; and *Pocket World in Figures, 2020 Edition* (London: The Economist, 2019).
2. Unless otherwise indicated, all trade statistics and practices are provided by the World Trade Organization, www.wto.org, downloaded May 10, 2019; "The Catch-22 for Globalization," *The Wall Street Journal*, January 22, 2019, p. R2; U.S. Bureau of Economic Analysis, www.bea.gov, downloaded May 10, 2019; "Global Economies and the $9B Barter Deal," *barternews.com*, February 1, 2017; and "A Fractured World: Nationalism Is Growing and Changing," *The Wall Street Journal*, January 23, 2018, pp. R1, R15.
3. Jan-Benedict Steenkamp, "The Uncertain Future of Globalization," *International Marketing Review* 36, no. 2 (2019), pp. 25–37.
4. Alfred J. Field and Dennis R. Appleyard, *International Economics*, 9th ed. (Burr Ridge, IL: McGraw-Hill/Irwin, 2016), Chapter 15; "EU Trade Outlook Alarms Africa's Banana Exporters," www.politico.eu, April 19, 2019; Yuri Kageyama, "Selling Rice to Japan? U.S. Plans to Try," www.msnbc.com, March 7, 2004; "A Shoe Tariff with a Big Footprint," *The Wall Street Journal*, November 23, 2012, p. A13; and *Economic Report of the President* (Washington, DC: U.S. Government Printing Office, 2019).
5. "Almost All Shoes in the U.S. Are Imported," www.washingtonpost.com, July 24, 2018.
6. This discussion on the European Union is based on information provided at www.europa.eu, downloaded March 5, 2019.
7. https://ustr.gov/trade-agreements, accessed December 12, 2019.
8. For an overview of different types of global companies and marketing strategies, see, for example, Masaaki Kotabe and Kristiaan Helsen, *Global Marketing Management*, 6th ed. (New York: Wiley, 2015); Warren J. Keegan and Mark C. Green, *Global Marketing*, 4th ed. (Upper Saddle River, NJ: Prentice Hall, 2005); and Michael Czinkota and Ilkka A. Ronkainen, *International Marketing*, 10th ed. (Mason, OH: South-Western, 2013).
9. Johnny K. Johansson and Ilkka A. Ronkainen, "The Brand Challenge," *Marketing Management*, March–April 2004, pp. 54–55.
10. Kevin Lane Keller, *Strategic Brand Management*, 4th ed. (Upper Saddle River, NJ: Prentice Hall, 2013); and "Here's What It's Like to Eat at McDonald's in Countries around the World," www.businessinsider.com, July 11, 2018.
11. "Number of TV Households Receiving MTV Programming Worldwide in the Fiscal Years 2007–2016," www.statistica.com, downloaded February 3, 2018; "These Are Teens' Favorite Brands of 2017," *fortune.com*, April 11, 2017; and "Global Social Media Statistics for 2017," www.digitalinformationworld.com, February 8, 2017.
12. *Pocket World in Figures, 2020 Edition.*
13. *The Report of the Commission on the Theft of American Intellectual Property* (Seattle, WA: National Bureau of Asian Research, 2017); "2016 Cost of Data Breach Study: United States," www.ibm.com/security/data-breach, June 2016; and "No Sign China Has Stopped Hacking U.S. Companies, Official Says," www.bloomberg.com, November 18, 2016.
14. For comprehensive references on cross-cultural aspects of marketing, see Paul A. Herbig, *Handbook of Cross-Cultural Marketing* (New York: Haworth Press, 1998); Jean Claude Usunier and Julie Anne Lee, *Marketing across Cultures*, 6th ed. (London: Prentice Hall Europe, 2013); and Philip K. Cateora, R. Bruce Money, Mary C. Gilly, and John L. Graham, *International Marketing*, 19th ed. (Burr Ridge, IL: McGraw-Hill, 2021). Unless otherwise indicated, examples found in this section appear in these excellent sources.
15. "SEC Enforcement Actions: FCPA Cases," www.sec.gov, downloaded March 16, 2018; and "Walmart to Pay $282 Million in Settlement of Bribery Probe," *The Wall Street Journal*, June 21, 2019, p. B3.
16. Michael White, *A Short Course in International Marketing Blunders* (Novato, CA: World Trade Press, 2002).
17. Erika Fry, "How Japanese Kit Kat Got So Hot," *Fortune*, April 3, 2018, p. 12.
18. Terence A. Shimp and Subhash Sharma, "Consumer Ethnocentrism: Construction and Validation of the CETSCALE," *Journal of Marketing Research*, August 1987, pp. 280–89. For a review of research on this topic, see Nicoletta-Theofania and George Balabanis, "Revisiting Consumer Ethnocentrism: Review, Reconceptualization, and Empirical Testing," *Journal of International Marketing*, September 2015, pp. 66–86.
19. Shira Ovide, "How to Connect 800 Million People with a $20 Phone," *Bloomberg Businessweek*, June 10, 2019, pp. 56–63.
20. "More Than Half of World's Population Is Now Middle Class," www.ft.com, September 30, 2016.
21. "Mattel Plans to Double Sales Abroad," *The Wall Street Journal*, February 11, 1998, pp. A3, A11.

22. "Strong Dollar Squeezes U.S. Firms," *The Wall Street Journal*, January 28, 2015, pp. A1, A2.
23. For an extensive and recent examination of these market-entry options, see, for example, Johnny K. Johansson, *Global Marketing: Foreign Entry, Local Marketing, and Global Management*, 5th ed. (Burr Ridge, IL: McGraw-Hill/Irwin, 2008).
24. YouSigma, "Fran Wilson's Indirect Exporting," www.yousigma.com.
25. Based on an interview with Pamela Viglielmo, Director of International Marketing, Fran Wilson Creative Cosmetics; and "Foreign Firms Think Their Way into Japan," www.successstories.com/nikkei, downloaded March 24, 2003.
26. *Profile of U.S. Importing and Exporting Companies* (Washington, DC: International Trade Administration, April 2018).
27. "About Us," www.strauss-group.com, downloaded March 15, 2019.
28. "Dannon Pulls Out of Disputed China Venture," *The Wall Street Journal*, October 1, 2009, p. B1.
29. Kate Gillespie and H. David Hennessey, *Global Marketing*, 4th ed. (New York: Taylor & Francis, 2016), Chapter 9.
30. "Target's New CEO Makes a Bold Decision to Leave Canada," www.forbes.com, January 15, 2015; "Ride-Hailing in China," *The Economist*, August 4, 2016, p. 77; and "Amazon Quits Chinese Business," *The Wall Street Journal*, April 19, 2019, p. B3.
31. This discussion is based on Kevin Lane Keller, *Strategic Brand Management*, 4th ed. (Upper Saddle River, NJ: Prentice Hall, 2013), pp. 709–10; "Adapting Listerine to a Global Market," www.nytimes.com, September 12, 2014; "Gum Makers Cater to Chinese Tastes," *The Wall Street Journal*, February 26, 2014, p. B9; "Global Sales of Lay's Chips Top $10 Billion in '11," *Dallas Morning News*, March 12, 2012, pp. D1, 10D; "Machines for the Masses," *The Wall Street Journal*, December 9, 2003, pp. A19, A20; "The Color of Beauty," *Forbes*, November 22, 2000, pp. 170–76; Donald R. Graber, "How to Manage a Global Product Development Process," *Industrial Marketing Management*, November 1996, pp. 483–98; and Herbig, *Handbook of Cross-Cultural Marketing*.
32. Procter & Gamble.
33. Slogan of Esso Extra.
34. Jagdish N. Sheth and Atul Parvatiyar, "The Antecedents and Consequences of Integrated Global Marketing," *International Marketing Review* 18, no. 1 (2001), pp. 16–29. Also see D. Szymanski, S. Bharadwaj, and R. Varadarajan, "Standardization versus Adaptation of International Marketing Strategy: An Empirical Investigation," *Journal of Marketing*, October 1993, pp. 1–17.
35. "Where Wal-Mart Isn't: Four Countries the Retailer Can't Conquer," www.businessweek.com, October 10, 2013.
36. KK Chua, president, Asia-Pacific corporate philosophy at Mary Kay, Inc.
37. Mary Kay, India: This case was prepared by Roger A. Kerin based on company interviews.

Marketing Research: From Customer Insights to Actions

LEARNING OBJECTIVES

After reading this chapter you should be able to:

LO 8-1 Identify the reason for conducting marketing research.

LO 8-2 Describe the five-step marketing research approach that leads to marketing actions.

LO 8-3 Explain how marketing uses secondary and primary data.

LO 8-4 Discuss the uses of observations, questionnaires, panels, experiments, and newer data collection methods.

LO 8-5 Explain how data analytics and data mining lead to marketing actions.

LO 8-6 Describe three approaches to developing a company's sales forecast.

Hollywood Loves Marketing Research!

Avengers: Endgame, *Avatar*, and *Titanic* are the top three blockbuster movies that have attracted millions of moviegoers worldwide. The theater ticket revenues they generated each exceeded $2 billion, well above the $200+ million budgets needed to produce them. Unfortunately, not every movie has such favorable results. Movies such as *John Carter*, *The Lone Ranger*, and *47 Ronin*, for example, each lost more than $100 million. So what can studios do to try to reduce the risk that a movie will be a box-office flop? Marketing research![1]

VIDEO 8-1
Avengers: Endgame **Movie Trailer**
kerin.tv/15e/v8-1

A Film Industry Secret

Bad titles, poor scripts, temperamental stars, costly special effects, competing movies, and ever-changing consumers are just a few of the risks studio executives face. They try to reduce their risk through a largely secretive process of marketing research that involves small sample audiences selected to be representative of the larger population.

Fixing bad movie names, for example, can turn potential disasters into successful blockbusters. Many studios use title testing—a form of marketing research—to choose a name. Here are a few examples:

- *Atomic Blonde* originally went by the title *Coldest City*. The name was changed, though, to better match the performance of the movie's star, Charlize Theron.
- *Edge of Tomorrow*, starring Tom Cruise and Emily Blunt, first used the name of the book on which it was based, *All You Need Is Kill*. The word *kill*, however, was unpopular.
- *War Dogs* started out as *Arms and the Dudes*, which was confusing and too complicated.
- *Begin Again*, with Keira Knightley and Mark Ruffalo, began as *Can a Song Save Your Life?* but test audiences didn't like that title.

Generally, filmmakers want movie titles that are short, memorable, appealing to consumers, and without legal restrictions—the same factors that make a good brand name.[2]

Studios also try to reduce their risks with additional forms of marketing research such as:

- *Concept testing and script assessment*. These techniques are used to assess early ideas for proposed new films. In addition, because many scripts and films today are part of a series such as *Avengers*, *Star Wars*, and *Spider-Man*, these forms of research can ensure that sequels are consistent with expectations created by the past movies.[3]

Walt Disney Studios Motion Pictures/Photofest

- *Test (or preview) screenings*. In test screenings, 300 to 400 prospective moviegoers are recruited to attend a "sneak preview" of a film before its release. After viewing the movie, the audience completes a survey to critique its title, plot, characters, music, and ending to identify improvements to make in the final edit. James Cameron, for example, used a test screening of *Titanic* to cut the length of the movie from 4 hours to 194 minutes, and to change the ending.[4]

The text describes how social listening is used to help movies become a success.
(Composite image): vvs1976/Getty Images; Hilch/Shutterstock

- *Tracking studies*. Before an upcoming film's release, studios will ask prospective moviegoers in the target audience three questions: (1) Are you aware of the film? (2) Are you interested in seeing the film? (3) Will you see the film? Studios also use "social listening" to understand what potential moviegoers are saying on Twitter, YouTube, Tumblr, Facebook, Instagram, and other social media sites. Studios use these data to monitor a promotional campaign, forecast the movie's opening weekend box-office sales, and, if necessary, add additional marketing activities to promote the film.[5]

These examples show how marketing research leads to effective marketing actions, the main topic of this chapter. Also, marketing research is often used to help a firm develop its sales forecasts, the final topic of this chapter.

THE ROLE OF MARKETING RESEARCH

LO 8-1
Identify the reason for conducting marketing research.

Let's (1) look at what marketing research is, (2) identify some difficulties with it, and (3) describe the five steps marketers use to conduct it.

What Is Marketing Research?

Marketing research is the process of defining a marketing problem and opportunity, systematically collecting and analyzing information, and recommending actions.[6] Although imperfect, marketers conduct marketing research to reduce the risk of—and thereby improve—marketing decisions.

The Challenges in Doing Good Marketing Research

Whatever the marketing issue involved—whether discovering consumer tastes or setting the right price—good marketing research is challenging. For example:

- Suppose your firm is developing a product that is completely new to the marketplace, and you are charged with estimating demand for the product. How can marketing

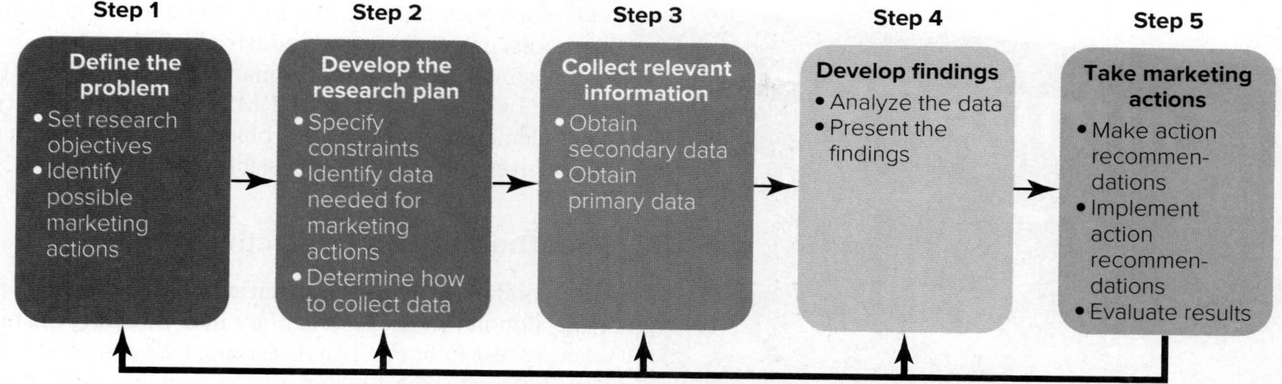
Step 1
Define the problem
• Set research objectives
• Identify possible marketing actions
Step 2
Develop the research plan
• Specify constraints
• Identify data needed for marketing actions
• Determine how to collect data
Step 3
Collect relevant information
• Obtain secondary data
• Obtain primary data
Step 4
Develop findings
• Analyze the data
• Present the findings
Step 5
Take marketing actions
• Make action recommen-dations
• Implement action recommen-dations
• Evaluate results
Feedback to learn lessons for future research

FIGURE 8–1
Five-step marketing research approach leading to marketing actions. Lessons learned from past research mistakes are fed back to improve each of the steps.

research determine if consumers will buy a product they have never seen, and never thought about, before?

- Understanding why consumers purchase some products often requires answers to personal questions. How can marketing research obtain answers that people know but are reluctant to reveal?
- Past purchase behaviors may help firms understand the influence of marketing actions. How can marketing research help people accurately remember and report their interests, intentions, and purchases?

Marketing research must overcome these difficulties and obtain the information needed so that marketers can assess what consumers want and will buy.

Five-Step Marketing Research Approach

LO 8-2
Describe the five-step marketing research approach that leads to marketing actions.

A *decision* is a conscious choice from among two or more alternatives. All of us make many such decisions daily. At work we choose from alternative ways to accomplish an assigned task. At college we choose from alternative courses. As consumers we choose from alternative brands. No magic formula guarantees correct decisions.

Managers and researchers have tried to improve the outcomes of decisions by using more formal, structured approaches to *decision making*, the act of consciously choosing from among alternatives. In this chapter, we describe a systematic marketing research approach used to collect information to improve marketing decisions and actions. This five-step approach is shown in Figure 8–1. Although our focus in this chapter is on marketing decisions, this approach provides a systematic checklist for making both business and personal decisions.

STEP 1: DEFINE THE PROBLEM

Every marketing problem faces its own research challenges. For example, the marketing strategy used by LEGO Group's toy researchers and designers in Denmark illustrates the wide variations possible in collecting marketing research data to build better toys.

LEGO Group's definition of *toy* has changed dramatically in the past 55 years—from interlocking plastic bricks to construction sets that create figures, vehicles, buildings, and even robots. One new version of a LEGO Group toy is the MINDSTORMS® kit, which integrates electronics, computers, and robots with traditional LEGO Group bricks. Developed with the help of the Media Lab at the Massachusetts Institute of Technology, the MINDSTORMS® kit appeals to a diverse market—from elementary school kids to world-

Marketing research helps LEGO Group identify possible marketing actions for products such as its MINDSTORMS® EV3 building system.
Source: LEGO Group

class robotics experts. The kits can be found in homes, schools, universities, and industrial laboratories.[7]

A simplified look at the marketing research for the LEGO Group's MINDSTORMS® EV3 shows the two key elements in defining a problem: setting the research objectives and identifying possible marketing actions.

Set the Research Objectives

Research objectives are specific, measurable goals the decision maker seeks to achieve in conducting the marketing research. For LEGO Group, let's assume the immediate research objective is to decide which of two new MINDSTORMS® designs should be selected for marketing.

In setting research objectives, marketers have to be clear on the purpose of the research that leads to marketing actions. The three main types of marketing research are as follows:

1. *Exploratory research* provides ideas about a vague problem or question. LEGO Group, for example, was concerned that middle school kids might be overwhelmed by the 500-plus pieces in MINDSTORMS® kits and quickly lose interest. LEGO Group's marketing researchers used exploratory research techniques such as interviews and focus groups to reveal that kids need to have a basic device up, running, and doing tricks in 20 minutes.
2. *Descriptive research* generally involves trying to find the frequency with which something occurs or the extent of a relationship between two factors. So if LEGO Group wants to know which of the two MINDSTORMS® kits is of greatest interest to middle school versus high school students, it might ask them specific questions about preference. LEGO Group can then assess the relationship by doing a cross tabulation (discussed later in the chapter) of school level versus kit preference.
3. *Causal research* tries to determine the extent to which the change in one factor changes another one. Changing key pieces in a MINDSTORMS® kit affects how quickly the newly built device can do tricks–affecting acceptance by kit users. Test markets, discussed later, use causal research.

LEGO Group's MINDSTORMS® EV3 TRACK3R can operate after only 20 minutes of assembly.
Source: LEGO Group

Identify Possible Marketing Actions

Effective decision makers develop specific **measures of success**, which are criteria or standards used in evaluating proposed solutions to the problem. Different research outcomes, based on the measure of success, lead to different marketing actions. For LEGO Group, assume the measure of success is the total time spent with each of the two potential new MINDSTORMS® kits until a device that can do simple tricks is produced. This measure of success leads to a clear-cut marketing action: Market the kit that produces an acceptable device in the least amount of playing time.

Marketing researchers know that defining a problem is an incredibly difficult task. If the objectives are too broad, the problem may not be researchable. If they are too narrow, the value of the research results may be seriously diminished. This is why marketing researchers spend so much time defining a marketing problem precisely and writing a formal proposal that describes the research to be done.[8]

STEP 2: DEVELOP THE RESEARCH PLAN

The second step in the marketing research process requires that the researcher (1) specify the constraints on the marketing research activity, (2) identify the data needed for marketing actions, and (3) determine how to collect the data.

Specify Constraints

The **constraints** in a decision are the restrictions placed on potential solutions to a problem. Examples include the limitations on the time and money available to solve the problem.

What constraints might LEGO Group set in developing new LEGO Group MINDSTORMS® EV3 products? LEGO Group might establish the following constraints on its decision to select one of the two new designs: The decision (1) must be made in five weeks (2) using 10 teams of middle school students playing with the two alternative MINDSTORMS® kits.

Identify Data Needed for Marketing Actions

Effective marketing research studies focus on collecting data that will lead to effective marketing actions. In the MINDSTORMS® case, LEGO Group's marketers might want to know students' math skills, time spent playing video games, and so on. But that information, while nice to know, is largely irrelevant because the study should focus on collecting only those data that will help them make a clear choice between the two MINDSTORMS® designs.

Determine How to Collect Data

Determining how to collect useful marketing research data is often as important as actually collecting the data—step 3 in the process, which is discussed later. Two key elements to consider in deciding how to collect the data are (1) concepts and (2) methods.

Concepts In the world of marketing, *concepts* are ideas about products or services. To find out about consumer reactions to a potential new product, marketing researchers frequently develop a *new-product concept*, which is a picture or verbal description of a product or service the firm might offer for sale. For example, the LEGO Group designers might develop a new-product concept for a new MINDSTORMS® EV3 robot that uses a color sensor, responds to voice commands, or uses GPS navigation software.

Methods *Methods* are the approaches that can be used to collect data to solve all or part of a problem. To collect data, LEGO Group marketing researchers might use a combination of (1) observing the behavior of MINDSTORMS® users and (2) asking users questions about their opinions of the MINDSTORMS® kits. Observing people and asking them questions—the two main data collection methods—are discussed in the section that follows.

How successful is LEGO Group's marketing research and design strategy for its MINDSTORMS® products? Among younger users alone, tens of thousands of elementary and middle school teams face off in competitions around the world each year.

How can you find and use the methods that other marketing researchers have found successful? Information on useful methods is available in tradebooks, textbooks, and handbooks that relate to marketing and marketing research. Some periodicals and technical journals, such as the *Journal of Marketing* and the *Journal of Marketing Research*, both published by the American Marketing Association, summarize methods and techniques valuable in addressing marketing problems.

Special methods vital to marketing are (1) sampling and (2) statistical inference. For example, marketing researchers often use *sampling* by selecting a group of distributors, customers, or prospects; asking them questions; and treating their answers as typical of all those in whom they are interested. They may then use *statistical inference* to generalize the results from the sample to much larger groups of distributors, customers, or prospects to help decide on marketing actions.

LEARNING REVIEW

8-1. What is marketing research?

8-2. What is the five-step marketing research approach?

8-3. What are constraints, as they apply to developing a research plan?

STEP 3: COLLECT RELEVANT INFORMATION

LO 8-3
Explain how marketing uses secondary and primary data.

Collecting enough relevant information to make a rational, informed marketing decision sometimes simply means using your knowledge to decide immediately. At other times it entails collecting an enormous amount of information at great expense.

Figure 8–2 shows how the different kinds of marketing information fit together. **Data**, the facts and figures related to the project, are divided into two main parts: secondary data and primary data. **Secondary data** are facts and figures that have already been recorded prior to the project at hand. As shown in Figure 8–2, secondary data are divided into two parts—internal and external secondary data—depending on whether the data come from inside or outside the organization needing the research. **Primary data** are facts and figures that are newly collected for the project. Figure 8–2 shows that primary data can be divided into observational data, questionnaire data, and other sources of data.

Secondary Data: Internal

The internal records of a company generally offer the most easily accessible marketing information. These internal sources of secondary data may be divided into two related parts: (1) marketing inputs and (2) marketing outcomes.

FIGURE 8–2
Types of marketing information. Researchers must choose carefully among these to get the best results, considering time and cost constraints.

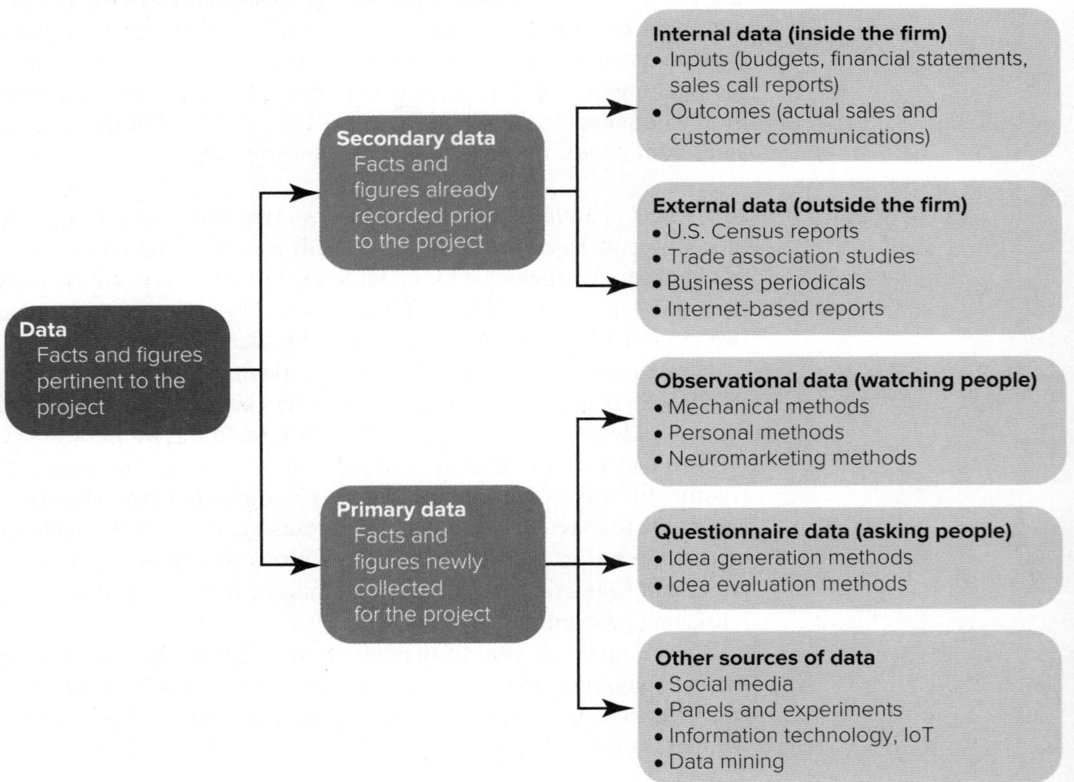

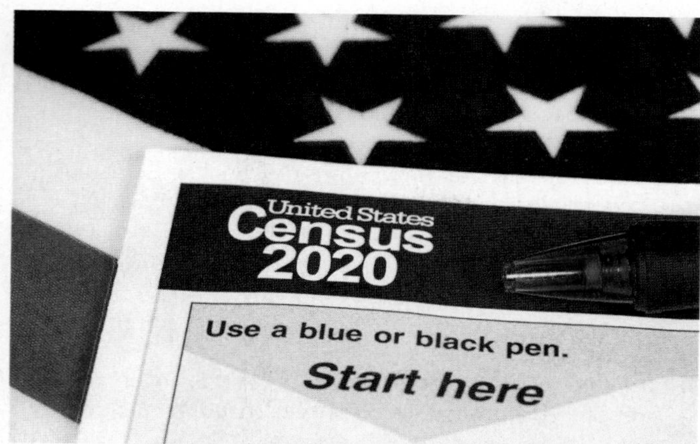

The U.S. Census provides valuable information for marketing decisions.
Maria Dryfhout/Shutterstock

Marketing input data relate to the effort expended to make sales. These range from marketing budget reports, which include advertising expenditures, to salespeople's call reports, which describe the number of sales calls per day, who was visited, and what was discussed.

Marketing outcome data relate to the results of the marketing efforts. These involve accounting records on shipments and include sales and repeat sales, often broken down by sales representative, industry, and geographic region. In addition, e-mails, phone calls, and social media posts from customers can reveal both complaints and what is working well.[9]

Secondary Data: External

Published data from outside the organization are external secondary data. The U.S. Census Bureau publishes a variety of useful reports. Census 2020, which is the twenty-fourth census, is the most recent count of the U.S. population that occurs every 10 years. Recently, the Census Bureau began collecting data annually from a smaller number of people through the American Community Survey. Both surveys contain detailed information on American households, such as the number of people per household and the age, sex, race/ethnic background, income, occupation, and education of individuals within the household. Marketers use these data to identify characteristics and trends of ultimate consumers.

VIDEO 8-2
U.S. Census
kerin.tv/15e/v8-2

The Census Bureau also publishes the Economic Census, which is conducted every five years. These reports are vital to business firms selling products and services to organizations. The 2017 Economic Census contains data on the number and sales of establishments in the United States that produce a product or service based on each firm's geography (state, county, zip code, etc.), industry sector (manufacturing, retail trade, etc.), and North American Industry Classification System (NAICS) code. Data from the 2017 Economic Census are released from September 2019 through December 2021. The 2017 Economic Census was the first to collect responses completely through an electronic survey.

Several market research companies pay households and businesses to record all their purchases using a paper or electronic diary. Such *syndicated panel* data economically answer questions that require consistent data collection over time, such as, "How many times did our customers buy our products this year compared to last year?" Examples of syndicated panels that provide a standard set of data on a regular basis are the Nielsen TV ratings and J.D. Power's automotive quality and customer satisfaction surveys.

Some data services provide comprehensive information on household demographics and lifestyle, product purchases, TV viewing behavior, responses to coupon and free-sample promotions, and social media use. Their advantage is that a single firm can collect, analyze, interrelate, and present all this information. For consumer product firms such as Procter & Gamble, sales data from various channels help them allocate scarce marketing resources. As a result, they use tracking services such as IRI's InfoScan to collect product sales and coupon/free-sample redemptions that have been scanned at the checkout counters of supermarket, drug, convenience, and mass merchandise retailers.

Finally, trade associations, universities, and business periodicals provide detailed data of value to market researchers and planners. These data are often available online and can be identified and located using a search engine such as Google or Bing. The Marketing Matters box on the next page provides examples.

Advantages and Disadvantages of Secondary Data

A general rule among marketing researchers is to obtain secondary data first and then collect primary data. Two important advantages of secondary data are (1) the tremendous time savings because the data have already been collected and published or exist internally and (2) the

Marketing Matters — Technology

Online Databases and Internet Resources Useful to Marketers

Marketers in search of secondary data can utilize a wide variety of online databases and Internet resources. These resources provide access to articles in periodicals; statistical or financial data on markets, products, and organizations; and reports from commercial information companies.

Sources of news and articles include:

- LexisNexis Academic (www.lexisnexis.com), which provides comprehensive news and company information from regional, national, and international sources.
- *The Wall Street Journal* (www.wsj.com), *CNBC* (www.cnbc.com), and *Bloomberg* (www.bloomberg.com), which provide up-to-the-minute business news and video clips about companies, industries, and trends.

Sources of statistical and financial data on markets, products, and organizations include:

- The Census Bureau (www.census.gov) and the Bureau of Economic Analysis (www.bea.gov) of the U.S. Department of Commerce, which provide information on U.S. business, economic, and trade activity collected by the federal government.

Portals and search engines include:

- USA.gov (www.usa.gov), the portal to all U.S. government websites. Users can click on links to browse by topic or enter keywords for specific searches.
- Google (www.google.com), the most popular portal to the entire Internet. Users enter keywords for specific searches and then click on results of interest.

Some of these websites are accessible only if you or your educational institution have paid a subscription fee. Check with your institution's website.

low cost, such as free or inexpensive Census reports. Furthermore, a greater level of detail is often available through secondary data, especially U.S. Census Bureau data.

However, these advantages must be weighed against some significant disadvantages. First, the secondary data may be out of date, especially if they are U.S. Census data collected only every 5 or 10 years. Second, the definitions or categories might not be quite right for a researcher's project. For example, the age groupings or product categories might be wrong for the project. Also, because the data have been collected for another purpose, they may not be specific enough for the project. In such cases, it may be necessary to collect primary data.

LEARNING REVIEW

8-4. What is the difference between secondary and primary data?

8-5. What are some advantages and disadvantages of secondary data?

Primary Data: Watching People

LO 8-4
Discuss the uses of observations, questionnaires, panels, experiments, and newer data collection methods.

Observing people and asking them questions are the two principal ways to collect new or primary data for a marketing study. Facts and figures obtained by watching how people actually behave is the way marketing researchers collect **observational data**. Observational data can be collected by mechanical (including electronic), personal, or neuromarketing methods.

Mechanical Methods National TV ratings, such as those of Nielsen shown in Figure 8-3, are an example of mechanical observational data collected by a "people meter." The device measures what channel and program are tuned in and who is watching. The people meter (1) is a box that is attached to a television, DVR, cable box, or satellite dish in about 30,000 households across the country; (2) has a remote control unit that is used to indicate when a viewer begins and finishes watching a TV program; and (3) stores and then transmits the viewing information to Nielsen each night. Data about TV viewing are also collected using diaries (a paper-pencil recording system).[10]

What determines if *Young Sheldon* stays on the air? For the importance of the TV "ratings game," see the text.
CBS/Photofest

Obtaining an accurate picture of television viewing behavior is complicated, however, as audiences are increasingly delaying their viewing and watching on multiple devices. More than 55 percent of the viewing of *The Bachelor*, for example, takes place on a delayed basis, while more than 50 percent of TV viewers watch on devices other than televisions each month. To address these issues, Nielsen introduced a cross-platform television rating system called Total Content Rating that combines Nielsen's existing TV ratings with its new online ratings. These ratings include traditional consumer viewing of TV programs and programming that is streamed on PCs, smartphones, tablets, and video game consoles.[11]

On the basis of all these observational data, Nielsen then calculates the rating of each TV program. With 119 million TV households in the United States, a single rating point equals 1 percent, or 1,190,000 TV households.[12] In some situations, ratings are reported as share points, or the percentage of television households with a television in use that are tuned to the program. Because TV and cable networks sell over $67 billion annually in advertising and set advertising rates to advertisers on the basis of those data, precision in the Nielsen data is critical.[13]

A change of 1 percentage point in a rating can mean gaining or losing millions of dollars in advertising revenues because advertisers pay rates on the basis of the size of the audience for a TV program. So as shown by the green rows in Figure 8–3, we might expect to pay more for a 30-second TV ad on *NCIS* than one on *The Voice*. Broadcast and cable networks may change the time slot or even cancel a TV program if its ratings are consistently poor and advertisers are unwilling to pay a rate based on a higher rating.

Personal Methods Watching consumers in person is another approach to collecting observational data. Procter & Gamble, for example, invests millions of dollars in observational research to identify new innovations. As several industry experts have observed, "Odds are that as you're reading this, P&G researchers are in a store somewhere observing shoppers, or even in a consumer's home." While observing consumers using its Gillette shavers in India, P&G noticed that many consumers shaved with a small cup of cold water, which caused the blades to clog. As a result, P&G introduced the Gillette Guard razor with a single blade and an easy-rinse design. Similarly, IKEA noticed that customers often stopped shopping when their baskets or carts were full, so additional shopping bags are now placed throughout IKEA stores.[14]

FIGURE 8–3
Nielsen Television Index Ranking Report for network TV primetime households. The difference of a few share points in Nielsen TV ratings affects the cost of a TV ad on a show and even whether the show remains on the air.

Rank	Program	Network	Rating	Viewers (000)
1	*The Big Bang Theory*	CBS	3.2	18,534
2	*Young Sheldon*	CBS	2.1	13,604
3	*NCIS*	CBS	1.7	11,701
4	*Big Bang Theory Farewell*	CBS	1.7	11,612
5	*American Idol*	ABC	1.5	8,739
6	*FBI*	CBS	1.5	8,562
7	*60 Minutes*	CBS	1.5	8,420
8	*Chicago Med*	NBC	1.1	7,982
9	*Chicago Fire*	NBC	1.1	7,960
10	*The Voice*	NBC	1.1	7,696

Source: Nielsen. Primetime Broadcast Programs. Viewing estimates on this page include live viewing and DVR playback on the same day, defined as 3 A.M. to 3 A.M. Ratings are the percentage of TV homes in the United States tuned in to television.

Observational data led P&G to develop Gillette Guard razors.
Editorial Image, LLC

Another method of collecting observational data is through the use of mystery shoppers. Companies pay researchers to shop at their stores, outlets, or showrooms to obtain the point of view of actual customers. Mystery shoppers can check on the availability and pricing of products and services and on the quality of the customer service provided by employees. Supermarkets, electronics stores, banks, theme parks, and many other businesses use this technique as part of their *customer experience management* efforts, thus evaluating customer service, store cleanliness, and staff appearance and conduct. This process provides unique marketing research information that can be obtained in no other way.[15]

Ethnographic research is a specialized observational approach in which trained observers seek to discover subtle behavioral and emotional reactions as consumers encounter products in their "natural use environment," such as in their home or car.[16] For example, Best Buy studied in-home use of fitness equipment and conducted "shop-alongs" to better understand purchase decisions and preferences. Best Buy discovered that consumers wanted integration of consumer electronics with fitness equipment that provided feedback on health and fitness.[17]

Personal observation is both useful and flexible, but it can be costly and unreliable if different observers report different conclusions when watching the same event. And while observation can reveal *what* people do, it cannot easily determine *why* they do it.

Neuromarketing Methods Marketing researchers are also utilizing neuromarketing methods to observe responses to nonconscious stimuli. Neuromarketing is a relatively new field of study that merges technologies used to study the brain with marketing's interest in understanding consumers. Aradhna Krishna, one of the foremost experts in the field, suggests that "many companies are just starting to recognize how strongly the senses affect the deepest parts of our brains." Another expert, Martin Lindstrom, has used brain scanning to analyze the buying processes of more than 2,000 people. The findings of his research are summarized in his book *Buyology.* Other neuroscience tools such as eye tracking, biometric monitoring, and facial coding are also being used to complement brain studies.[18]

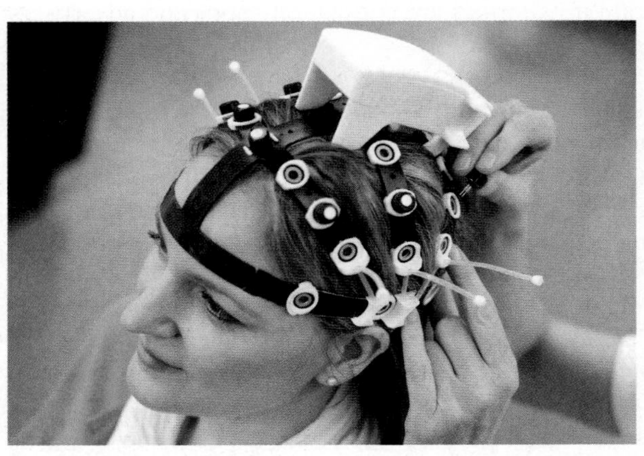
"Neuromarketing" often uses a headset with sensors to measure brain waves to try to understand consumers better. For some changes made by Campbell Soup Company based on neuromarketing, see the text.
Ronny Hartmann/picture-alliance/dpa/AP Images

Neuromarketing can provide insights for many elements of a marketing program, including media options, advertising content, packaging, and labeling. Based on the results of neuromarketing studies, for example, Campbell Soup Company changed the labels of most of its soup cans. Some of the changes: Steam now rises from more vibrant images of soup; the "unemotional spoons" have disappeared; and the script logo is smaller and has been moved to the bottom of the can.[19]

Primary Data: Asking People

How many times have you responded to some kind of a questionnaire? Maybe it was a short survey at school rating your course or your professor, or perhaps it was a telephone or e-mail survey asking if you were pleased with some type of service you received. Asking consumers questions and recording their answers is the second principal way of gathering information.

We can divide this primary data collection task into (1) idea generation methods and (2) idea evaluation methods, although they sometimes overlap and each has a number of special techniques.[20] Each survey method results in valuable **questionnaire data**, which are facts and figures obtained by asking people about their attitudes, awareness, intentions, and behaviors.

Idea Generation Methods—Coming Up with Ideas In the past, the most common way of collecting questionnaire data to generate ideas was through an *individual interview*, which involves a single researcher asking questions of one respondent. This approach has many advantages, such as being able to probe for additional ideas using follow-up questions to a respondent's initial answers. However, this method is very expensive. Later in the chapter we'll discuss some alternatives.

Focus groups of students and instructors were used in developing this textbook. To see the specific suggestion that may help you study, read the text.
Spencer Grant/PhotoEdit

General Mills sought ideas about why Hamburger Helper didn't fare well when it was introduced. Initial instructions called for cooking a half-pound of hamburger separately from the noodles or potatoes, which were later mixed with the hamburger. So General Mills researchers used a special kind of individual interview, called a *depth interview*, in which they ask lengthy, free-flowing kinds of questions to probe for underlying ideas and feelings. These depth interviews discovered that consumers (1) didn't think it contained enough meat and (2) didn't want the hassle of cooking in two different pots. The Hamburger Helper product manager changed the recipe to call for a full pound of meat and to allow users to prepare it in one dish, leading to product success.

Focus groups are informal sessions of 6 to 10 past, present, or prospective customers in which a discussion leader, or moderator, asks for opinions about the firm's products and those of its competitors, including how they use these products and special needs they have that these products don't address. Often recorded and conducted in special interviewing rooms with a one-way mirror, these groups enable marketing researchers and managers to hear and watch consumer reactions.

The informality and peer support in an effective focus group help uncover ideas that are often difficult to obtain with individual interviews. For example, to improve understanding and learning by students using this textbook, focus groups were conducted among both marketing instructors and students. Both groups recommended providing answers to each chapter's set of Learning Review questions. This suggestion was followed, so you can see the answers by going to the section at the end of the chapter or by tapping your finger on the question in the SmartBook version.

VIDEO 8-3
Trend Hunter
kerin.tv/15e/v8-3

Finding "the next big thing" for consumers has caused marketing researchers to turn to some less traditional techniques. For example, "fuzzy front end" methods attempt early identification of elusive consumer tastes or trends. Trend Hunter is a firm that seeks to anticipate and track "the evolution of cool." Trend hunting (or watching) is the practice of identifying "emerging shifts in social behavior," which are driven by changes in pop culture that can lead to new products. Trend Hunter has identified about 252,000 cutting-edge ideas through its global network of 155,000 members, and it features these new ideas on its daily Trend Hunter TV broadcast via its YouTube channel (trendhuntertv).[21]

Wendy's spent over two years remaking its 42-year-old burger. The result: Dave's Single (also available in Double and Triple), named after Wendy's founder, Dave Thomas. See Figure 8–4 on the next page for some questions that Wendy's asked consumers in a survey to discover their fast-food preferences, behaviors, and demographics.
Source: Wendy's International, LLC

Idea Evaluation Methods—Testing an Idea In idea evaluation, the marketing researcher tries to test ideas discovered earlier to help the marketing manager recommend marketing actions. Idea evaluation methods often involve conventional questionnaires using personal, mail, telephone, and online (e-mail or Internet) surveys of a large sample of past, present, or prospective consumers. In choosing among them, the marketing researcher balances the cost of the particular method against the expected quality of the information and the speed with which it can be obtained.

Personal interview surveys enable the interviewer to be flexible in asking probing questions or getting reactions to visual materials but are very costly. *Mail surveys* are usually biased because those most likely to respond have had especially positive or negative experiences with the product or brand. While *telephone interviews* allow flexibility, unhappy respondents may hang up on the interviewer, even with the efficiency of computer-assisted telephone interviewing (CATI). Advances in natural language processing (NLP) have led marketing researchers to begin to use chatbots or surveybots, which mimic human interviewers, to conduct telephone surveys.

Increasingly, marketing researchers have begun to use *online surveys* (e-mail and Internet) to collect primary data. The reason: Online methods can reach most audiences while telephone landlines and mail offer declining access. Marketers can embed a survey in an e-mail sent to targeted respondents. When they open the e-mail, consumers can either see the survey or click on a link to access it from a website. Marketers can also ask consumers to complete a "pop-up" survey in a separate browser window when they access an organization's website. Many organizations use this method to have consumers assess their products and services or evaluate the design and usability of their websites.

The advantages of online surveys are that the cost is relatively minimal and the turnaround time from data collection to report presentation is much quicker than the traditional methods discussed earlier. However, online surveys have serious drawbacks: Some consumers may view e-mail surveys as "junk" or "spam" and may either choose to not receive them (if they have a "spam blocker") or purposely or inadvertently delete them, unopened. For Internet surveys, some consumers have a "pop-up blocker" that prohibits a browser from opening a separate window that contains the survey; thus, they may not be able to participate in the research. For both e-mail and Internet surveys, consumers can complete the survey multiple times, creating a significant bias in the results. This is especially true for online panels. In response, research firms such as Qualtrics and SurveyMonkey have developed sampling technology to prohibit this practice.[22]

The foundation of all research using questionnaires is developing precise questions that get clear, unambiguous answers from respondents.[23] Figure 8–4 shows a number of formats for questions taken from a Wendy's survey that assessed fast-food restaurant preferences among present and prospective consumers.

FIGURE 8–4
To obtain the most valuable information from consumers, this Wendy's survey utilizes four different kinds of questions discussed in the text.

1. What things are most important to you when you decide to eat out at a fast-food restaurant?

____

____

____

2. Have you eaten at a fast-food restaurant in the past month?

○ Yes ○ No

3. If you answered yes to question 2, how often do you eat at a fast-food restaurant?

○ Once a week or more ○ 2 to 3 times a month ○ Once a month or less

4. How important is it to you that a fast-food restaurant satisfies you on the following characteristics?
[Check the response that describes your feelings for each characteristic listed.]

Characteristic	Very Important	Somewhat Important	Important	Unimportant	Somewhat Unimportant	Very Unimportant
• Taste of food	○	○	○	○	○	○
• Cleanliness	○	○	○	○	○	○
• Price	○	○	○	○	○	○
• Variety of menu	○	○	○	○	○	○

5. For each of the characteristics listed below check the space on the scale that describes how you feel about Wendy's. Mark an X on only one of the five spaces for each characteristic listed.

Characteristic		**Check the space that describes the degree to which Wendy's is . . .**					
• Taste of food	Tasty	___	___	___	___	___	Not Tasty
• Cleanliness	Clean	___	___	___	___	___	Dirty
• Price	Inexpensive	___	___	___	___	___	Expensive
• Variety of menu	Broad	___	___	___	___	___	Narrow

6. Check the response that describes your agreement or disagreement with each statement listed below:

Statement	Strongly Agree	Agree	Don't Know	Disagree	Strongly Disagree
• Adults like to take their families to fast-food restaurants	◉	◉	◉	◉	◉
• Our children have a say in where the family chooses to eat	◉	◉	◉	◉	◉

7. How important are each of the following sources of information to you when selecting a fast-food restaurant at which to eat? [Check one response for each source listed.]

Source of Information	Very Important	Somewhat Important	Not at All Important
• Television	◉	◉	◉
• Newspapers	◉	◉	◉
• Radio	◉	◉	◉
• Billboards	◉	◉	◉
• Internet	◉	◉	◉
• Social networks	◉	◉	◉

8. How often do you eat out at each of the following fast-food restaurants? [Check one response for each restaurant listed.]

Restaurant	Once a Week or More	2 to 3 Times a Month	Once a Month or Less
• Burger King	◉	◉	◉
• McDonald's	◉	◉	◉
• Wendy's	◉	◉	◉

9. As head of the household, please answer the following questions about you and your household. [Check only one response for each question.]

a. What is your gender? ◉ Male ◉ Female

b. What is your marital status? ◉ Single ◉ Married ◉ Other (widowed, divorced, etc.)

c. How many children under age 18 live in your home? ◉ 0 ◉ 1 ◉ 2 ◉ 3 or more

d. What is your age? ◉ Under 25 ◉ 25–44 ◉ 45 or older

e. What is your total annual individual or household income?

◉ Less than $15,000 ◉ $15,000–$49,000 ◉ Over $49,000

Question 1 is an example of an *open-ended question*, which allows respondents to express opinions, ideas, or behaviors in their own words without being forced to choose among alternatives that have been predetermined by a marketing researcher. This information is invaluable to marketers because it captures the "voice" of respondents, which is useful in understanding consumer behavior, identifying product benefits, or developing advertising messages.

In contrast, *closed-end* or *fixed alternative questions* require respondents to select one or more response options from a set of predetermined choices. Question 2 is an example of a *dichotomous question*, the simplest form of a fixed alternative question that allows only a "yes" or "no" response.

A fixed alternative question with three or more choices uses a *scale*. Question 5 is an example of a question that uses a *semantic differential scale*, a five-point scale in which the

Frito-Lay used social media to ask people to show their preferences by voting on new potato chip flavors.
Source: Frito-Lay's/Instagram, Inc.

opposite ends have one- or two-word adjectives that have opposite meanings. For example, depending on the respondent's opinion regarding the cleanliness of Wendy's restaurants, he or she would check the left-hand space on the scale, the right-hand space, or one of the three other intervening points. Question 6 uses a *Likert scale*, in which the respondent indicates the extent to which he or she agrees or disagrees with a statement.

The questionnaire in Figure 8–4 provides valuable information to the marketing researcher at Wendy's. Questions 1 to 8 inform him or her about the respondent's likes and dislikes in eating out, frequency of eating out at fast-food restaurants generally and at Wendy's specifically, and sources of information used in making decisions about fast-food restaurants. Question 9 gives details about the respondent's personal or household characteristics, which can be used in trying to segment the fast-food market, a topic discussed in Chapter 9.

Marketing research questions must be worded precisely so that all respondents interpret the same question similarly. For example, in a question asking whether you eat at fast-food restaurants regularly, the word *regularly* is ambiguous. Two people might answer "yes" to the question, but one might mean "once a day" while the other means "once or twice a month." However, each of these interpretations suggests that dramatically different marketing actions be directed to these two prospective consumers.

The high cost of using personal interviews in homes has increased the use of *mall intercept interviews*, which are personal interviews of consumers visiting shopping centers. These face-to-face interviews reduce the cost of personal visits to consumers in their homes while providing the flexibility to show respondents visual cues such as ads or actual product samples. A disadvantage of mall intercept interviews is that the people interviewed may not be representative of the consumers targeted, giving a biased result.

Electronic technology has revolutionized traditional concepts of interviews or surveys. Today, respondents can walk up to a kiosk in a shopping center, read questions off a screen, and key their answers into a computer on a touchscreen. Fully automated telephone interviews exist in which respondents key their replies on a touch-tone telephone.

Primary Data: Other Sources

Four other methods of collecting primary data exist that overlap somewhat with the methods just discussed. These involve using (1) social media, (2) panels and experiments, (3) data analytics, and (4) data mining.

Social Media Instagram, Facebook, Twitter, and other social media are revolutionizing the way today's marketing research is done. In developing a new potato chip flavor, Frito-Lay substituted social media research for its usual focus groups. Three new flavor alternatives were distributed in stores and people were asked to vote via Twitter, Instagram, and Snapchat. All they had to do was click or swipe to show their preferences and help Frito-Lay decide what new flavor to add to its product mix. And Estée Lauder asked social media users to vote on which discontinued shades to bring back.[24]

Carmex's Facebook account allows it to respond to consumers' comments and to follow daily consumer experiences. For how it uses social media marketing research, see the Applying Marketing Metrics box.
Source: Carma Labs Inc./Facebook

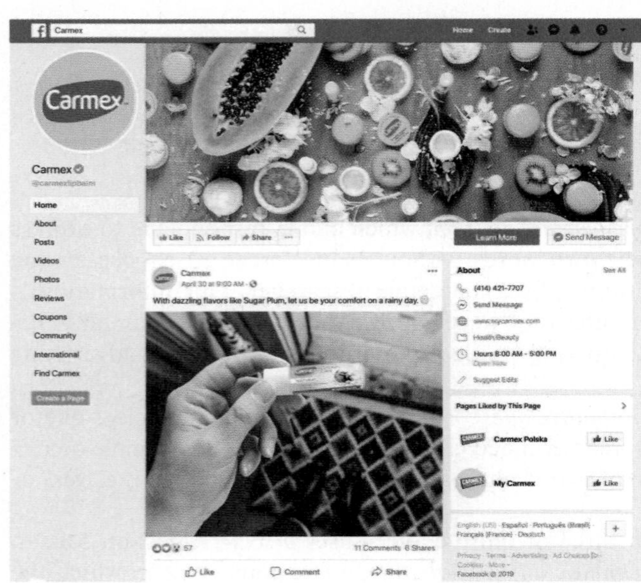

Carma Laboratories, Inc., the maker of Carmex lip balm, is a third-generation, family-owned business with a history of accessibility to customers. In fact, founder Alfred Woelbing personally responded to every letter he received from customers. Today, Carma Labs relies on social media programs to help promote its products.[25]

One opportunity for Carmex (www.mycarmex.com) is to conduct marketing research using social media listening tools to understand the nature of online lip balm conversations. The Applying Marketing Metrics box shows how Carmex uses marketing metrics to assess its social media programs for its line of products. Data have been modified to protect proprietary information.

Applying Marketing Metrics

Are the Carmex Social Media Programs Working Well?

As a marketing consultant to Carmex, you've just been asked to assess its social media activities for its lip balm product line.

Carmex has recently launched new social media programs and promotions to tell U.S. consumers more about its line of lip balm products. These include Facebook and Twitter contests that allow Carmex fans and followers to win free samples by connecting with Carmex. A creative "Carmex Kiss" widget allows users to upload their photo and to send an animated kiss to a friend.

Your Challenge

To assess how the Carmex social media programs are doing, you choose these five metrics: (1) Carmex conversation velocity—total Carmex mentions on the Internet; (2) Facebook fans—the number of Facebook users in a time period who have liked Carmex's Facebook brand page; (3) Twitter followers—the number of Twitter users in a time period who follow Carmex's Twitter feed; (4) Carmex share of voice—Carmex mentions on the Internet as a percentage of mentions of all major lip balm brands; and (5) Carmex sentiment—the percentage of Internet Carmex share-of-voice mentions that are (*a*) positive, (*b*) neutral, or (*c*) negative.

Your Findings

Analyzing the marketing dashboard here, you reach these conclusions. First, the number of both Facebook fans and Twitter followers for Carmex is up significantly for 2019 compared to 2018, which is good news. Second, the Carmex share of voice of 35 percent is good, certainly relative to the 48 percent for the #1 brand ChapStick. But especially favorable is Carmex's 12 percent increase in share of voice compared to a year ago. Third, the Carmex sentiment dashboard shows 80 percent of the mentions are positive, and only 5 percent are negative. Even more significant is that positive mentions are up 23 percent over last year.

Your Actions

You conclude that Carmex's social media initiatives are doing well. Your next step is to probe deeper into the data to see which ones—such as free samples or the Carmex Kiss—have been especially effective in triggering the positive results and build on these successes in the future.

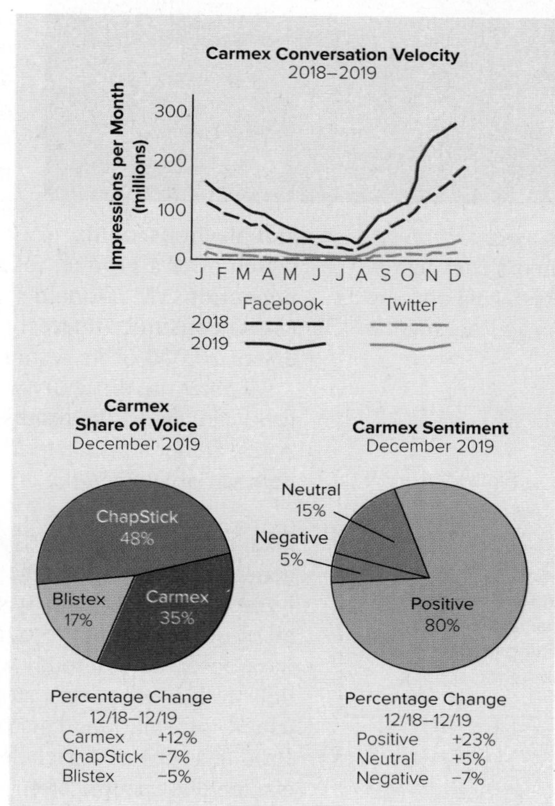

Carmex uses several social media metrics, such as *conversation velocity*, *share of voice*, and *sentiment*.[26] These metrics are tracked by electronic search engines that comb the Internet for consumers' behaviors and "brand mentions" to calculate share of voice and determine whether these brand mentions appear to be "positive," "neutral," or "negative" in order to calculate "sentiment." A widely used Facebook metric measures the number of *likes*, which refers to the number of Facebook users opting in to a brand's messages and liking the brand.

Marketing researchers increasingly want to glean information from sites to "mine" their raw consumer-generated content in real time. However, when relying on this consumer-generated content, the sample of individuals from whom this content is gleaned may not be statistically representative of the marketplace.[27]

Panels and Experiments Two special ways that observations and questionnaires are sometimes used are panels and experiments.

Marketing researchers often want to know if consumers change their behavior over time, so they take successive measurements of the same people. A *panel* is a sample of consumers or stores from which researchers take a series of measurements. For example, the NPD Group collects data about consumer purchases such as apparel, food, and electronics from its online Consumer Panel, which consists of nearly 2 million individuals worldwide. So a firm like General Mills can count the frequency of consumer purchases to measure switching behavior from one brand of its breakfast cereal (Wheaties) to another (Cheerios) or to a competitor's brand (Kellogg's Special K). A disadvantage of panels is that the marketing research firm needs to recruit new members continually to replace those who drop out. These new recruits must match the characteristics of those they replace to keep the panel representative of the marketplace.

To discover how McDonald's used test markets to help develop its delivery service, see the text.
Source: McDonald's

An *experiment* involves obtaining data by manipulating factors under tightly controlled conditions to test cause and effect. The interest is in whether changing one of the independent variables (a cause) will change the behavior of the dependent variable that is studied (the result). In marketing experiments, the independent variables of interest–sometimes called the marketing *drivers*–are often one or more of the marketing mix elements, such as a product's features, price, or promotion (like advertising messages or coupons). The ideal dependent variable usually is a change in the purchases (incremental unit or dollar sales) of individuals, households, or organizations. For example, food companies often use *test markets*, which offer a product for sale in a small geographic area to help evaluate potential marketing actions. McDonald's, for example, tested its delivery service in three Florida cities to assess consumer interest before deciding to expand. Recently, McDonald's expanded delivery to 20,000 of its restaurants.[28]

A potential difficulty with experiments is that outside factors (such as actions of competitors) can distort the results of an experiment and affect the dependent variable (such as sales). A researcher's task is to identify the effect of the marketing variable of interest on the dependent variable when the effects of outside factors in an experiment might hide it.

LO 8-5
Explain how data analytics and data mining lead to marketing actions.

Big Data, Data Analytics, and Artificial Intelligence *Big data* is a vague term generally used to describe large amounts of data collected from a variety of sources and analyzed with an increasingly sophisticated set of technologies. **Information technology** includes all of the computing resources that collect, store, and analyze the data. Marketing researchers have observed that today we live in an era of data deluge. The challenge facing managers is not data collection or even storage but how to efficiently transform the huge amount of data into useful information. This transformation is accomplished through the use of data analytics. Products such as Apache's Hadoop and Google's Bigtable are examples of the analytical tools available for people often referred to as data scientists. Their work is also creating a new field of marketing research that focuses on *data visualization*, or the presentation of the results of the analysis.

Today, businesses can obtain data from many sources such as barcode scanners at checkout counters, online tracking software on computers and tablets, and usage histories on your telephone. In fact, the growth of the Internet of Things (IoT) now allows data collection from almost any device a consumer might use. Marketing managers must use a combination of data, technology, and analytics to convert the data into useful information that will answer marketing questions and lead to effective marketing actions. An organization that accomplishes this successfully is often referred to as an *intelligent enterprise*.[29]

As shown in Figure 8-5, the elements of an intelligent marketing enterprise platform interact to facilitate the work of the marketing researcher or data scientist. The top half of the figure shows how big data are created through a sophisticated communication network that collects data from internal and external sources. These data are stored, organized, and managed in databases. Collectively, these databases form a data warehouse. Data storage (and computing) may also take place in "the cloud," which is simply a collection of servers accessed through an Internet connection. Large databases are also subject to *artificial intelligence* platforms which undertake reasoning and commonsense tasks to allow computers to "behave" intelligently. IBM, Tesla, and Amazon, for example, are using artificial intelligence

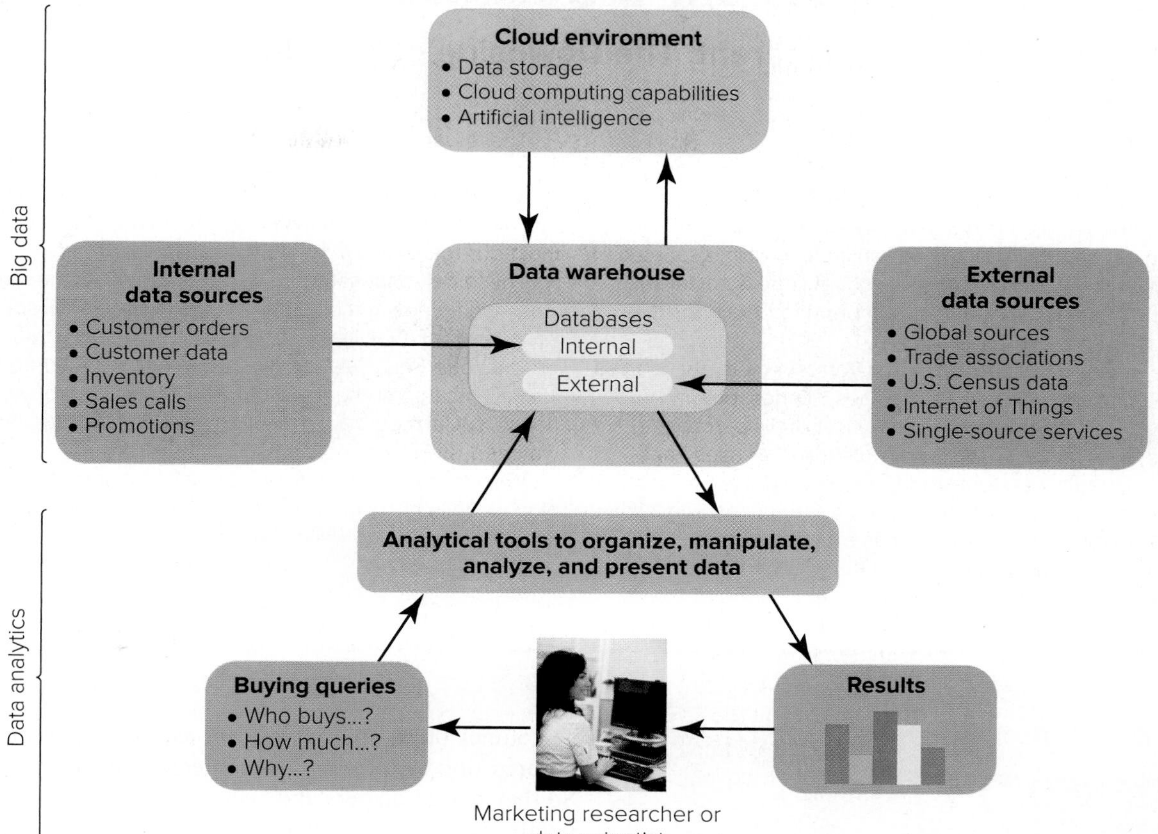

FIGURE 8–5
How marketing researchers and managers use an intelligent enterprise platform to turn data into action.

(Photo): Todd Warnock/Lifesize/Getty Images

to operate Watson, guide self-driving cars, and make purchase recommendations, respectively.[30]

As shown at the bottom of Figure 8-5, data analytics consists of several elements. Marketers use computers to specify important marketing queries or questions and to access the databases in the warehouse (or the cloud). Analytical tools are used to organize and manipulate the data to identify any managerial insights that may exist. The results are then presented using tables and graphics for easier interpretation. When accessing a database, marketers can use sensitivity analysis to ask "what if" questions to determine how hypothetical changes in product or brand drivers—the factors that influence the buying decisions of a household or organization—can affect sales.

Traditional marketing research typically involves identifying possible drivers and then collecting data. For example, we might collect data to test the hypothesis that increasing couponing (the driver) during spring will increase trials by first-time buyers (the result). As marketers develop increasingly sophisticated intelligent marketing enterprise platforms the need to ask respondents specific questions may decline. The artificial intelligence and predictive analytics components of the platforms will offer answers by identifying behavioral patterns in the data.

Data Mining In contrast, *data mining* is the extraction of hidden predictive information from large databases to find statistical links between consumer purchasing patterns and marketing actions. Some of these are common sense: Since many consumers buy peanut butter and grape jelly together, why not run a joint promotion between Skippy peanut butter and Welch's grape jelly? But would you have expected that men buying diapers in the evening

Making Responsible Decisions

Ethics

Your Digital Life Is Transparent: The Downside of Data Mining

Amazon, Google, Yahoo!, eBay, YouTube, reputation.com, . . . yes . . . and Facebook and Twitter, too!

The common denominator for all these is their sophisticated data mining techniques that reveal an incredible amount of personal information about almost anyone. *Time* journalist Joel Stein, using both online and offline sources, discovered how easily outsiders could find his social security number and then found a number of other things about himself—some correct, some not.

For example, his data mining effort revealed that he likes hockey, rap, rock, parenting, recipes, clothes, beauty products, and movies. He makes most of his purchases online, averaging only $25 per purchase. He uses Facebook, LinkedIn, Pandora, and StumbleUpon. He bought his house in November, which is when his home insurance is up for renewal. His dad's wife has a traffic ticket.

And, some sources predicted that he is an 18- to 19-year-old woman!

OK, OK, sometimes data mining errors occur!

These data are collected in many ways—from tracking devices (like cookies, discussed in Chapter 17) on websites, to apps downloaded on a cell phone, PC, or tablet device that reveal a user's contact list and location, to algorithms that aggregate data from multiple online sources.

These personal details have huge benefits for marketers. Data mining now enables advertisers to target individual consumers and facilitates the design of personalized product offerings. This involves using not only demographics such as age and gender but also "likes," past buying habits, social media used, brands bought, TV programs watched, stores visited, and so on.

Want to do some sleuthing yourself? Download Ghostery at www.ghostery.com. It tells you all the companies grabbing your data when you visit a website.

At 10 P.M., what is this man likely to buy besides these diapers? For the curious answer that data mining reveals, see the text.

Brent Jones

sometimes buy a six-pack of beer as well? Supermarkets discovered this when they mined checkout data from scanners. So they placed diapers and beer near each other, then placed potato chips between them—and increased sales on all three items! For how much online data mining can reveal about you personally and the ethical issues involved, see the Making Responsible Decisions box.[31]

Advantages and Disadvantages of Primary Data

Compared with secondary data, primary data have the advantages of being more flexible and more specific to the problem being studied. The main disadvantages are that primary data are usually far more costly and time-consuming to collect than secondary data.

Analyzing Primary Data Using Cross Tabulations

Suppose top management at Wendy's wants to use the questionnaire in Figure 8–4 to survey a sample of U.S. households to assess how often customers of different ages eat at fast-food restaurants. Management suspects that as the age of the head of the household increases, visits to fast-food restaurants decline. The data provided by the questionnaire confirm this, but the information is not in a format that suggests ideas for viable marketing actions. Using cross tabulations will provide answers leading to actions.

Developing Cross Tabulations A **cross tabulation**, or *cross tab*, is a method of presenting and analyzing data involving two or more variables to discover relationships in the data.

The Wendy's questionnaire in Figure 8–4 includes many questions that might be paired to understand the fast-food business better. For example, to try to answer the question in which

Customer Satisfaction Survey

	Extremely Dissatisfied			Neither			Extremely Satisfied
Overall how satisfied were you with THIS experience at THIS Wendy's restaurant?	O	O	O	O	O	O	O
	Extremely Unlikely			Neither			Extremely Likely
Based on THIS experience, would you be likely to recommend THIS Wendy's restaurant to friends and family?	O	O	O	O	O	O	O
Based on THIS experience, would you be likely to return to THIS Wendy's restaurant?	O	O	O	O	O	O	O
	Extremely Dissatisfied			Neither			Extremely Satisfied
How satisfied were you that this visit to Wendy's was worth the money you spent?	O	O	O	O	O	O	O

Clear Next

Wendy's Customer Satisfaction Survey allows customers to provide feedback on their meal experience. To take the survey, go to www.talktowendys.com. You'll need a receipt from a recent visit, which has an 8-digit code to start the survey. Your reward? A printable coupon that can be used on your next visit!

Source: Wendy's International, LLC

Wendy's top management is interested, we can pair the question regarding the age of the head of the household in Figure 8–4 (question 9d) with the question that asks how often the respondent eats at a fast-food restaurant (question 3).

Using the answers to question 3 as the column headings and the answers to question 9d as the row headings gives the cross tabulation shown in Figure 8–6, based on answers from 586 respondents. The figure shows two forms of cross tabulations:

- The raw data or answers to the specific questions are shown in Figure 8–6A. For example, this cross tab shows that 144 households in the sample whose head was under 25 (shaded red) ate at fast-food restaurants once a week or more. It also shows the loyalty of many customers of fast-food restaurants; the number of customers who visit them once a week or more is more than double the number who visit them once a month or less, as indicated by the totals shaded brown in Figure 8–6A.
- Answers on a percentage basis, with the percentages running horizontally, are shown in Figure 8–6B. Of the 215 households headed by someone under 25, 67.0 percent ate at a fast-food restaurant at least once a week and only 8.8 percent ate there once a month or less. Also, across all age groups, 46.5 percent—almost half—ate in a fast-food restaurant once a week or more.

Two other forms of cross tabulation using the raw data shown in Figure 8–6A are described in problem 7 in Applying Marketing Knowledge at the end of the chapter.

Interpreting Cross Tabulations A careful analysis of Figures 8–6A and 8–6B shows that patronage of fast-food restaurants is related to the age of the head of the household. The percentages on the diagonal (in orange) in Figure 8–6B reveal that younger households are far more likely than older households to visit fast-food restaurants once a week or more.

So if we want to reach frequent users of fast-food restaurants, we should target those whose head of household is under 25 years of age and who tend to visit these restaurants once a week

FIGURE 8–6
Two forms of a cross tabulation relating age of head of household to frequency of fast-food restaurant patronage.

A. ABSOLUTE FREQUENCIES

Age of Head of Household (Years)	Frequency of Visiting Fast-Food Restaurants: Once a Week or More	2 to 3 Times a Month	Once a Month or Less	Total
Under 25	144	52	19	215
25 to 44	46	58	29	133
45 or Older	82	69	87	238
Total	272	179	135	586

B. ROW PERCENTAGES: RUN HORIZONTALLY

Age of Head of Household (Years)	Frequency of Visiting Fast-Food Restaurants: Once a Week or More	2 to 3 Times a Month	Once a Month or Less	Total
Under 25	67.0%	24.2%	8.8%	100.0%
25 to 44	34.6%	43.6%	21.8%	100.0%
45 or Older	34.5%	29.0%	36.5%	100.0%
Total	46.5%	30.5%	23.0%	100.0%

or more, as shown in Figure 8-6B. Marketers often use special efforts to reach these loyal, frequent users. So Wendy's might advertise to the segment of households headed by a man or woman under 25 years old. But Figures 8-6A and 8-6B *do not* tell us what media to use to reach them—such as by television ads or social networks. For those answers, we need to relate the age of the head of household again to the answers given to question 7 in Figure 8-4—the source of information that households use.

Probably the most widely used technique for organizing and presenting marketing data, cross tabulations have some important advantages. The simple format permits direct interpretation and an easy means of communicating data to management. Cross tabs offer great flexibility and can be used to summarize questionnaire, observational, and experimental data.

Cross tabulations also have some disadvantages. For example, they can be misleading if the percentages are based on too few observations. Also, cross tabulations can hide some relationships because each cross tab typically shows only two or three variables. Balancing both advantages and disadvantages, more marketing decisions are probably made using cross tabulations than any other method of analyzing data.

LEARNING REVIEW

8-6. What is the difference between observational and questionnaire data?

8-7. Which type of survey provides the greatest flexibility for asking probing questions: mail, telephone, or personal interview?

8-8. What is cross tabulation?

STEP 4: DEVELOP FINDINGS

Mark Twain once observed, "Data is like garbage. You'd better know what you're going to do with it before you collect it." So, marketing data have little more value than garbage unless they are analyzed carefully and translated into information and findings, step 4 in the marketing research approach.[32]

How are sales doing? To see how marketers at Tony's Pizza assessed this question and the results, read the text.

Schwan's Consumer Brands, Inc

Analyze the Data

Schwan's produces millions of frozen pizzas a day under brand names that include Tony's, Red Baron, and Freschetta. Let's see how Teré Carral, the marketing manager for the Tony's brand, might address a market segment question. We will use hypothetical data to protect Tony's proprietary information.

Teré is concerned about the limited growth in the Tony's brand over the past four years. She hires a consultant to collect and analyze data to explain what's going on with her brand and to recommend ways to improve its growth. Teré asks the consultant to put together a proposal that includes the answers to two key questions:

1. How are Tony's sales doing on a household basis? For example, are fewer households buying Tony's pizzas, or is each household buying fewer Tony's pizzas? Or both?
2. What factors might be contributing to Tony's very flat sales over the past four years?

Facts uncovered by the consultant are vital. For example, is the average household consuming more or less Tony's pizza than in previous years? Is Tony's flat sales performance related to a specific factor? With answers to these questions Teré can take actions to address the issues in the coming year.

Present the Findings

Findings should be clear and understandable from the way the data are presented. Managers are responsible for *actions*. Often it means delivering the results in clear pictures and, if possible, in a single page.

The consultant gives Teré the answers to her questions using the marketing dashboards in Figure 8–7, a creative way to present findings graphically. Let's look over Teré's shoulder as she interprets these findings:

- Figure 8–7A, *Annual Sales*–This shows the annual growth of Tony's Pizza is stable but virtually flat from 2016 through 2019.
- Figure 8–7B, *Average Annual Sales per Household*–Look closely at this graph. At first glance, it seems like sales in 2019 are *half* what they were in 2016, right? But be careful to read the numbers on the vertical axis. They show that household purchases of Tony's pizzas have been steadily declining over the past four years, from an average of 3.4 pizzas per household in 2016 to 3.1 pizzas per household in 2019. (Significant, but hardly a 50 percent drop.) Now the question is, if Tony's annual sales are stable, yet the average individual household is buying fewer Tony's pizzas, what's going on? The answer is, more households are buying pizzas–it's just that each household is buying fewer Tony's pizzas. That households aren't choosing Tony's is a genuine source of concern. But again, here's

FIGURE 8–7 These marketing dashboards present findings to Tony's marketing manager that will lead to recommendations and actions.

Source: Teré Carral, Tony's Pizza.

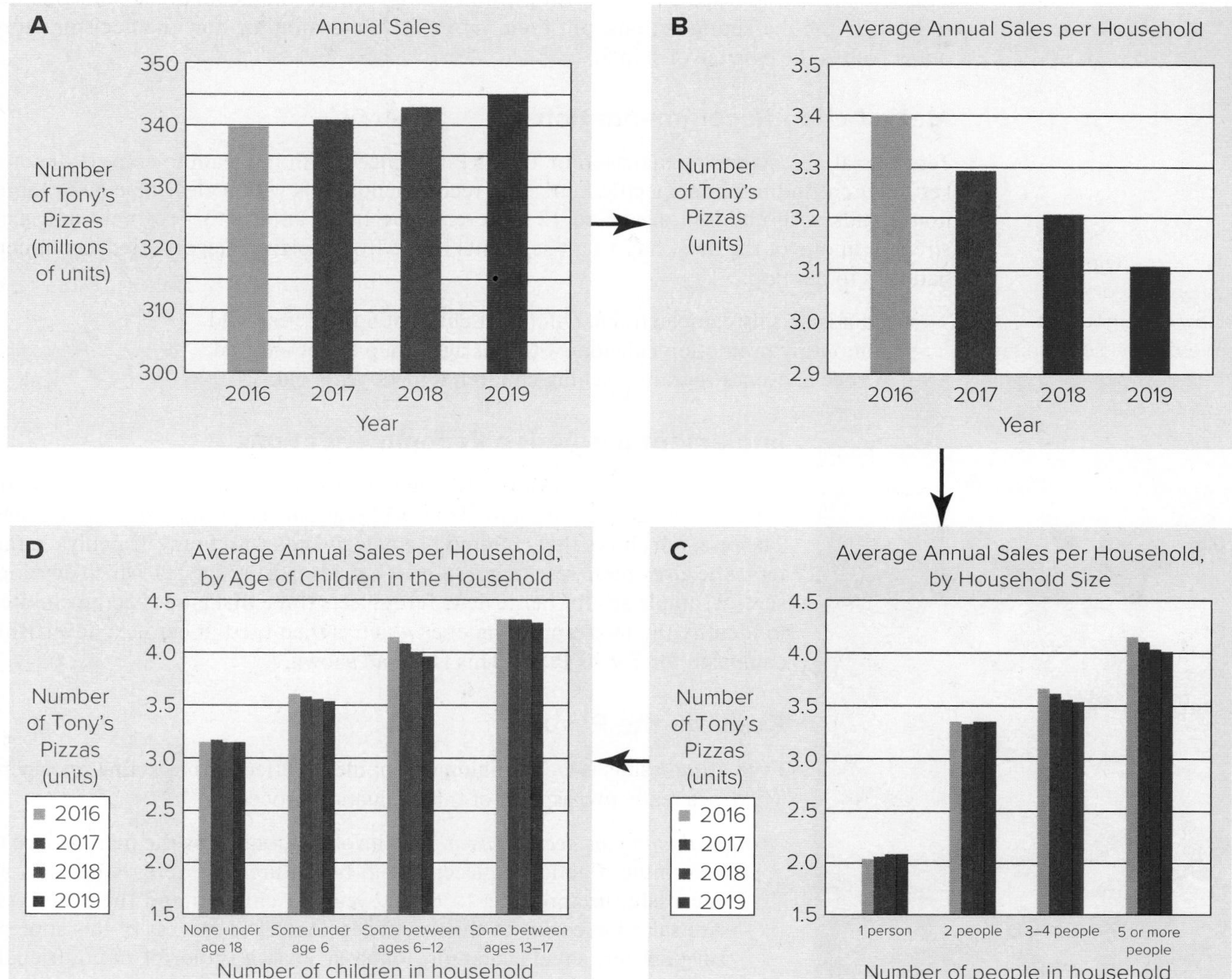

a classic example of a marketing problem representing a marketing opportunity. The number of households buying pizza is *growing*, and that's good news for Tony's.

- Figure 8–7C, *Average Annual Sales per Household, by Household Size*—This chart starts to show a source of the problem: Even though average sales of pizza to households with only one or two people are stable, households with three or four people and those with five or more are declining in average annual pizza consumption. Which households tend to have more than two people? Answer: Households *with children*. Therefore, we should look more closely at the pizza-buying behavior of households with children.
- Figure 8–7D, *Average Annual Sales per Household, by Age of Children in the Household*—The real problem that emerges is the serious decline in average consumption in the households with younger children, especially in households with children in the 6-to-12-year-old age group.

Identifying a sales problem in households with children 6 to 12 years old is an important discovery, as Tony's sales are declining in a market segment that is known to be one of the heaviest in buying pizzas.

STEP 5: TAKE MARKETING ACTIONS

Effective marketing research doesn't stop with findings and recommendations—someone has to identify the marketing actions, put them into effect, and monitor how the decisions turn out, which is the essence of step 5.

Make Action Recommendations

Teré Carral, the marketing manager for Tony's Pizza, meets with her team to convert the market research findings into specific marketing recommendations with a clear objective: Target households with children ages 6 to 12 to reverse the trend among this segment and gain strength in one of the most important segments in the frozen pizza category. Her recommendation is to develop:

- An advertising campaign that will target children 6 to 12 years old.
- A monthly promotion calendar with this age group target in mind.
- A special event program reaching children 6 to 12 years old.

Marketing research at Tony's Pizza helped develop this colorful, friendly ad targeted at families with children in the 6-to-12-year-old age group.
Schwan's Consumer Brands, Inc

Implement the Action Recommendations

As her first marketing action, Teré undertakes advertising research to develop ads that appeal to children in the 6-to-12-year-old age group and their families. The research shows that children like colorful ads with funny, friendly characters. She gives these research results to her advertising agency, which develops several sample ads for her review. Teré selects three that are tested on children to identify the most appealing one, which is then used in her next advertising campaign for Tony's Pizza. This is the ad shown.

Evaluate the Results

Evaluating results is a continuing way of life for effective marketing managers. There are really two aspects of this evaluation process:

- *Evaluating the decision itself.* This involves monitoring the marketplace to determine if action is necessary in the future. For Teré, is her new ad successful in appealing to 6-to-12-year-old children and their families? Are sales increasing to this target segment? The success of this strategy suggests Teré should add more follow-up ads with colorful, funny, friendly characters.

- *Evaluating the decision process used.* Was the marketing research and analysis used to develop the recommendations effective? Was it flawed? Could it be improved for similar situations in the future? Teré and her marketing team must be vigilant in looking for ways to improve the analysis and results—to learn lessons that might apply to future marketing research efforts at Tony's.

Again, systematic analysis does not guarantee success. But, as in the case of Tony's Pizza, it can improve a firm's success rate for its marketing decisions.

LEARNING REVIEW

8-9. In the marketing research for Tony's Pizza, what is an example of (*a*) a finding and (*b*) a marketing action?

8-10. In evaluating marketing actions, what are the two dimensions on which they should be evaluated?

SALES FORECASTING TECHNIQUES

LO 8-6
Describe three approaches to developing a company's sales forecast.

Forecasting, or estimating potential sales, is often a key goal in a marketing research study. Good sales forecasts are important for a firm as it schedules production. The term **sales forecast** refers to the total sales of a product that a firm expects to sell during a specified time period under specified environmental conditions and its own marketing efforts. For example, Betty Crocker might develop a sales forecast of 4 million cases of cake mix for U.S. consumers in 2020, assuming consumers' dessert preferences remain constant and competitors don't change prices.

Three main sales forecasting techniques are often used: (1) judgments of the decision maker, (2) surveys of knowledgeable groups, and (3) statistical methods.

Judgments of the Decision Maker

Probably 99 percent of all sales forecasts are simply the judgment of the person who must act on the results of the forecast—the individual decision maker. *A direct forecast* involves estimating the value to be forecast without any intervening steps. Examples appear daily: How many quarts of milk should I buy? How much money should I withdraw at the ATM?

How might a marketing manager for the New Balance Zante Pursuit running shoe create a sales forecast through 2022? Read the text to find out.

A *lost-horse forecast* involves starting with the last known value of the item being forecast, listing the factors that could affect the forecast, assessing whether they have a positive or negative impact, and making the final forecast. The technique gets its name from how you'd find a lost horse: Go to where it was last seen, put yourself in its shoes, consider those factors that could affect where you might go (to the pond if you're thirsty, the hayfield if you're hungry, and so on), and go there.

For example, New Balance recently introduced its Fresh Foam Zante Pursuit, a shoe with firm cushioning and a sticky grip. It is designed to be a light, comfortable shoe and uses a socklike upper. Suppose a New Balance marketing manager in early 2020 needs to make a sales forecast through 2022. She would take the known value of 2019 sales and list positive factors (new "Hypoknit" material used to provide stretch and support, positive wear-tester comments) and the negative factors (increased competition, slow economic growth) to arrive at the final sales forecast.

Surveys of Knowledgeable Groups

If you wonder what your firm's sales will be next year, ask people who are likely to know something about future sales. Two common groups that are surveyed to develop sales forecasts are prospective buyers and the firm's salesforce.

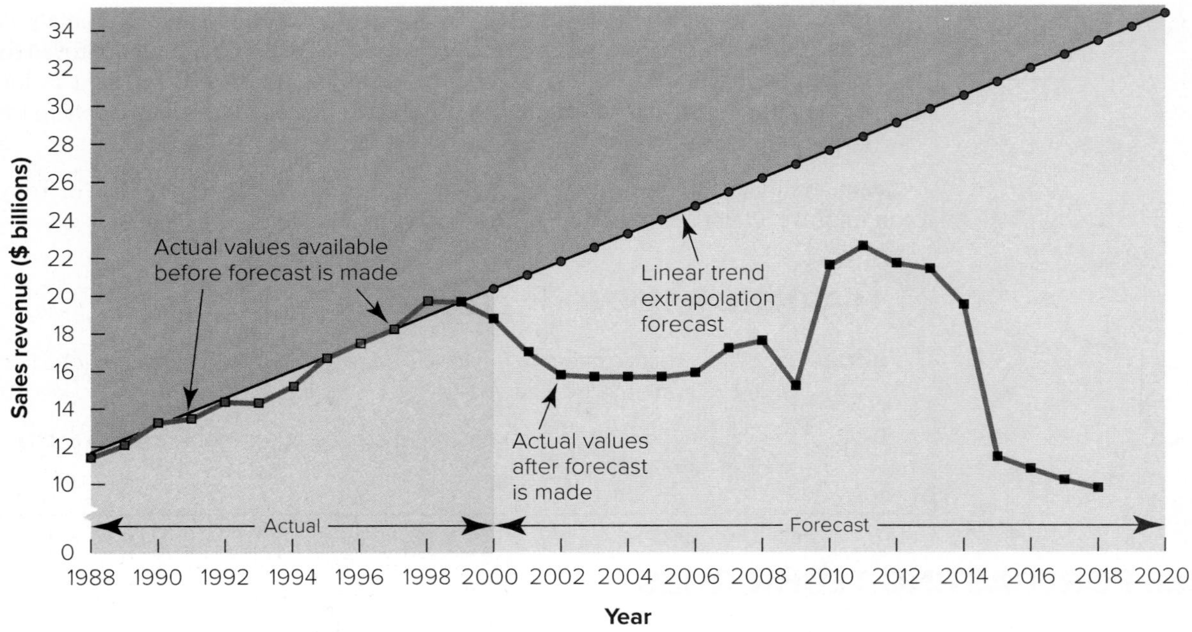

FIGURE 8–8
Linear trend extrapolation of sales revenues at Xerox, made at the start of 2000.

A *survey of buyers' intentions forecast* involves asking prospective customers if they are likely to buy the product during some future time period. For industrial products with few prospective buyers, this can be effective. There are only a few hundred customers in the entire world for Boeing's large airplanes, so Boeing surveys them to develop its sales forecasts and production schedules.

A *salesforce survey forecast* involves asking the firm's salespeople to estimate sales during a forthcoming period. Because these people are in contact with customers and are likely to know what customers like and dislike, there is logic to this approach. However, salespeople can be unreliable forecasters—painting too rosy a picture if they are enthusiastic about a new product or too grim a forecast if their sales quota and future compensation are based on it.

Statistical Methods

The best-known statistical method of forecasting is *trend extrapolation*, which involves extending a pattern observed in past data into the future. When the pattern is described with a straight line, it is *linear trend extrapolation*. Suppose that in early 2000 you were a sales forecaster for the Xerox Corporation and had actual sales data running from 1988 to 1999 (see Figure 8–8). Using linear trend extrapolation, you draw a line to fit the past sales data and project it into the future to give the forecast values shown for 2000 through 2020.

If in 2019 you want to compare your forecasts with actual results, you are in for a surprise—illustrating the strength and weakness of trend extrapolation. Trend extrapolation assumes that the underlying relationships in the past will continue into the future, which is the basis of the method's key strength: simplicity. If this assumption proves correct, you have an accurate forecast. However, if this proves wrong, the forecast is likely to be wrong. In this case, your forecasts from 2000 through 2018 were too high, as shown in Figure 8–8, largely because of fierce competition in the photocopying industry.

LEARNING REVIEW

8-11. What are the three kinds of sales forecasting techniques?

8-12. How do you make a lost-horse forecast?

LEARNING OBJECTIVES REVIEW

LO 8-1 *Identify the reason for conducting marketing research.*
To be successful, products must meet the wants and needs of potential customers. So marketing research reduces risk by providing the vital information to help marketing managers understand those wants and needs and translate them into marketing actions.

LO 8-2 *Describe the five-step marketing research approach that leads to marketing actions.*
Marketing researchers engage in a five-step decision-making process to collect information that will improve marketing decisions. The first step is to define the problem, which requires setting the research objectives and identifying possible marketing actions. The second step is to develop the research plan, which involves specifying the constraints, identifying data needed for marketing decisions, and determining how to collect the data. The third step is to collect the relevant information, which includes considering pertinent secondary data (both internal and external) and primary data (by observing and questioning consumers) as well as using information technology and data mining to trigger marketing actions. The fourth step is to develop findings from the marketing research data collected. This involves analyzing the data and presenting the findings of the research. The fifth and last step is to take marketing actions, which involves making and implementing the action recommendations and then evaluating the results.

LO 8-3 *Explain how marketing uses secondary and primary data.*
Secondary data have already been recorded prior to the start of the project and consist of two parts: (*a*) internal secondary data, which originate from within the organization, such as sales reports and customer comments, and (*b*) external secondary data, which are created by other organizations, such as the U.S. Census Bureau (which provides data on the country's population, manufacturers, retailers, and so on) or business and trade publications (which provide data on industry trends, market size, etc.). Primary data are collected specifically for the project and are obtained by either observing or questioning people.

LO 8-4 *Discuss the uses of observations, questionnaires, panels, experiments, and newer data collection methods.*
Marketing researchers observe people in various ways, such as electronically using Nielsen people meters to measure TV viewing behavior or personally using mystery shoppers or ethnographic techniques. A recent electronic innovation is neuromarketing–using brain scanning to record the responses of a consumer's brain to marketing stimuli like packages or TV ads. Questionnaires involve asking people questions (*a*) in person using interviews or focus groups or (*b*) via a questionnaire using a telephone, print, e-mail, Internet, or social media survey. A cross tabulation is often used with questionnaire data to analyze the relationships among two or more variables to lead to marketing actions. Panels involve a sample of consumers or stores that are repeatedly measured through time to see if their behaviors change. Experiments, such as test markets, involve measuring the effect of marketing variables such as price or advertising on sales. Collecting data from social networks like Instagram, Facebook, or Twitter is increasingly important because users can share their opinions about products and services with countless "friends" around the globe.

LO 8-5 *Explain how data analytics and data mining lead to marketing actions.*
Marketing researchers have observed that today we live in an era of data deluge. Information technology enables this massive amount of marketing data to be stored, accessed, and processed. Transforming the data into useful information is accomplished through the use of data analytics, which uses specific queries or questions to guide the analysis. In contrast, data mining is the extraction of hidden information from the databases to find statistical relationships useful for marketing decisions and actions.

LO 8-6 *Describe three approaches to developing a company's sales forecast.*
One approach uses the subjective judgments of the decision maker, such as direct or lost-horse forecasts. A direct forecast involves estimating the value to be forecast without any intervening steps. A lost-horse forecast starts with the last known value of the item being forecast and then lists the factors that could affect the forecast, assesses whether they have a positive or negative impact, and makes the final forecast. Surveys of knowledgeable groups, a second method, involve obtaining information such as the intentions of potential buyers or estimates provided by the salesforce. Statistical methods involving extending a pattern observed in past data into the future are a third approach. The best-known statistical method is linear trend extrapolation.

LEARNING REVIEW ANSWERS

8-1 What is marketing research?
Answer: Marketing research is the process of defining a marketing problem and opportunity, systematically collecting and analyzing information, and recommending actions to reduce the risk of and thereby improve marketing decisions.

8-2 What is the five-step marketing research approach?
Answer: The five-step marketing research approach provides a systematic checklist for making marketing decisions and actions. The five steps are: (1) define the problem; (2) develop the research plan; (3) collect relevant information (data); (4) develop findings; and (5) take marketing actions.

8-3 What are constraints, as they apply to developing a research plan?
Answer: Constraints in a decision are the restrictions placed on potential solutions to a problem, such as time and money. These set the parameters for the research plan–due dates, budget, and so on.

8-4 What is the difference between secondary and primary data?
Answer: Secondary data are facts and figures that have already been recorded prior to the project at hand, whereas primary data are facts and figures that are newly collected for the project.

8-5 What are some advantages and disadvantages of secondary data?
Answer: Advantages of secondary data are the time savings, the low cost, and the greater level of detail that may be available. Disadvantages of secondary data are that the data may be out of date, unspecific, or have definitions, categories, or age groupings that are wrong for the project.

8-6 What is the difference between observational data and questionnaire data?
Answer: Observational data are facts and figures obtained by watching, either mechanically or in person, how people actually behave. Questionnaire data are facts and figures obtained by asking people about their attitudes, awareness, intentions, and behaviors.

8-7 Which type of survey provides the greatest flexibility for asking probing questions: mail, telephone, or personal interview?
Answer: personal interview (or individual/depth interview)

8-8 What is cross tabulation?
Answer: Cross tabulation, or *cross tab*, is a method of presenting and analyzing data involving two or more variables to discover relationships in the data. As the most widely used technique for organizing and presenting marketing data, the simple format and flexibility of cross tabulations permit the direct interpretation of and an easy means to communicate the data.

8-9 In the marketing research for Tony's Pizza, what is an example of (*a*) a finding and (*b*) a marketing action?
Answer: (*a*) Figure 8-7A depicts annual sales from 2016 to 2019; the finding is that annual sales are relatively flat, rising only 5 million units over the four-year period. (*b*) Figure 8-7D shows a finding (the decline in pizza consumption) that leads to a recommendation to develop an ad targeting children 6 to 12 years old (the marketing action).

8-10 In evaluating marketing actions, what are the two dimensions on which they should be evaluated?
Answer: There are two aspects marketers use to evaluate the results of marketing actions: (1) evaluate the decision itself, which involves monitoring the marketplace to determine if action is necessary in the future, and (2) evaluate the decision process used to determine (*a*) whether the marketing research and analysis used to develop the recommendations were effective or flawed in some way and (*b*) whether the process could be improved for similar situations in the future.

8-11 What are the three kinds of sales forecasting techniques?
Answer: They are: (1) judgments of the decision maker who acts on the results of a sales forecast; (2) surveys of knowledgeable groups, those who are likely to know something about future sales; and (3) statistical methods such as trend extrapolation, which involves extending a pattern observed in past data into the future.

8-12 How do you make a lost-horse forecast?
Answer: To make a lost-horse forecast, begin with the last known value of the item being forecast, list the factors that could affect the forecast, assess whether they have a positive or negative impact, and then make the final forecast.

FOCUSING ON KEY TERMS

constraints p. 209
cross tabulation p. 222
data p. 210
information technology p. 220
marketing research p. 206
measures of success p. 208
observational data p. 212
primary data p. 210
questionnaire data p. 214
sales forecast p. 227
secondary data p. 210

APPLYING MARKETING KNOWLEDGE

1 Suppose your dean of admissions is considering surveying high school seniors about their perceptions of your school to design better informational brochures for them. What are the advantages and disadvantages of doing (*a*) telephone interviews and (*b*) an Internet survey of seniors requesting information about the school?

2 Wisk detergent decides to run a test market to see the effect of coupons and in-store advertising on sales. The index of sales is as follows:

Element in Test Market	Weeks before Coupon	Week of Coupon	Week after Coupon
Without in-store ads	100	144	108
With in-store ads	100	268	203

What are your conclusions and recommendations?

3 Nielsen obtains ratings of local TV stations in small markets by having households fill out diary questionnaires. These give information on (*a*) who is watching TV and (*b*) the program being watched. What are the limitations of this questionnaire method?

4 The format in which information is presented is often vital. (*a*) If you were a harried marketing manager and queried your information system, would you rather see the results in tables or charts and graphs? (*b*) What are one or two strengths and weaknesses of each format?

5 (*a*) Why might a marketing researcher prefer to use secondary data rather than primary data in a study? (*b*) Why might the reverse be true?

6 Look back at Figure 8-4. Which questions would you pair to form a cross tabulation to uncover the following relationships? (*a*) Frequency of fast-food restaurant

patronage and restaurant characteristics important to the customer; (*b*) Age of the head of household and source of information used about fast-food restaurants; (*c*) Frequency of patronage of Wendy's and source of information used about fast-food restaurants; and (*d*) How much children have to say about where the family eats and number of children in the household.

7 Look back at Figure 8-6A. (*a*) Run the percentages vertically and explain what they mean. (*b*) Express all numbers in the table as a percentage of the total number of people sampled (586) and explain what the percentages mean.

8 Which of the following variables would linear trend extrapolation be more accurate for? (*a*) Annual population of the United States or (*b*) annual sales of cars produced in the United States by Ford. Why?

BUILDING YOUR MARKETING PLAN

To help you collect the most useful data for your marketing plan, develop a three-column table:

1 In column 1, list the information you would ideally like to have to fill holes in your marketing plan.

2 In column 2, identify the source for each bit of information in column 1, such as doing an Internet search, talking to prospective customers, looking at internal data, and so forth.

3 In column 3, set a priority on information you will have time to spend collecting by ranking each item: 1 = most important; 2 = next most important; and so forth.

VIDEO CASE 8 Carmex® (A): Leveraging Facebook for Marketing Research

"What makes social media 'social' is its give and take," says Jeff Gerst of Bolin Marketing, who manages the Carmex® social media properties. By "give" Gerst is referring to the feedback consumers send on social media; "take" is what they receive–such as news and coupons. "For Carmex, Facebook isn't just a way to share coupons or the latest product news, but it is also a marketing research resource. We have instantaneous access to the opinions of our consumers."

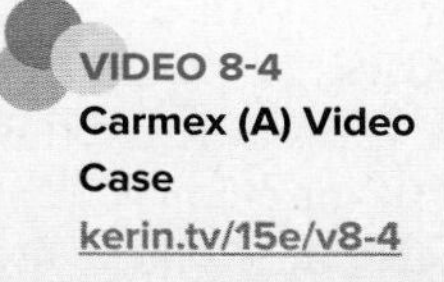

VIDEO 8-4
Carmex (A) Video Case
kerin.tv/15e/v8-4

"While some people think of social media as 'free,' that is not true. However, almost everything in social media can be faster and cheaper than in the offline world," adds Dane Hartzell, general manager of Bolin Digital. "Many platforms have been prebuilt and we marketers only need to modify them slightly."

CARMEX AND ITS PRODUCT LINE

Although Carmex has been making lip balm since 1937, only in the last five years has it made serious efforts to stress growth and become more competitive. For example, Carmex has:

- Extended its lip balm products into new flavors and varieties.
- Expanded into nearly 30 international markets.
- Developed the Carmex Moisture Plus line of premium lip balms for women.
- Launched a line of skin care products, its first venture outside of lip care.

Carmex has used social media tools in developing all of these initiatives, but the focus of this case is how Carmex might use Facebook marketing research to grow its lip balm varieties in the United States.

FACEBOOK MARKETING RESEARCH: TREND SPOTTING

Brands can leverage Facebook and all social media platforms to test what topics and themes its audience engages with the most as well as validate concepts and ideas. In 2012 Carmex identified the growing trend of consumers seeking product customization. Carmex combined research with Facebook engagement data, which helped to validate consumer interest and led it to develop two new lines of limited-edition lip balm products that launched in 2013.

The first line was a set of three different Carmex "City Sticks" featuring New York, Chicago, and Las Vegas versions of the Carmex lip balm stick with recognizable

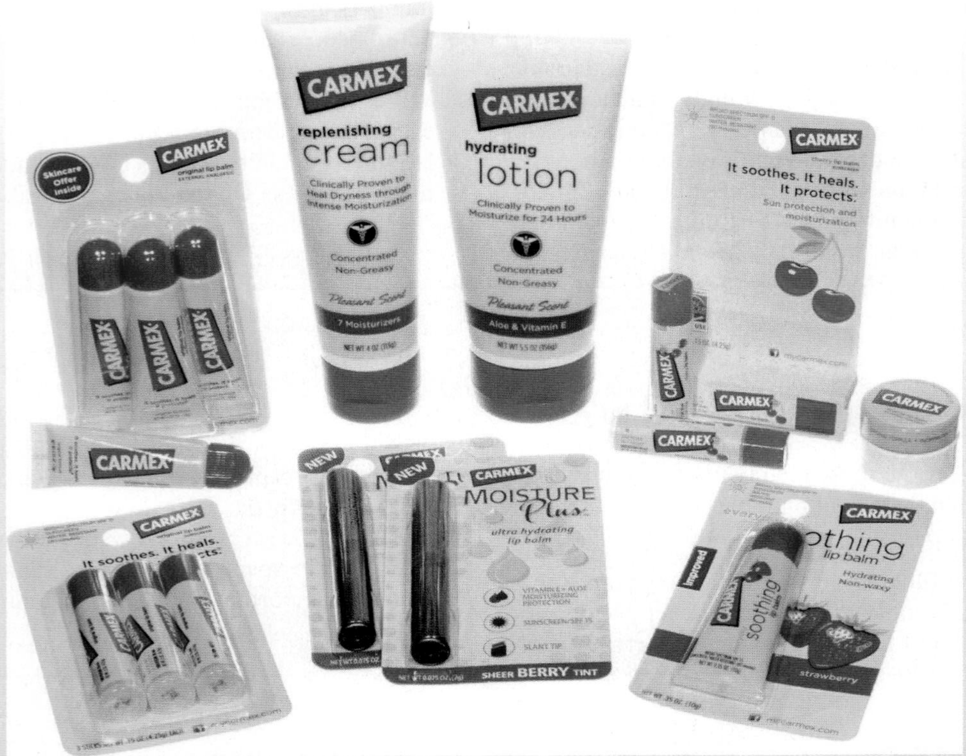

Editorial Image, LLC/McGraw-Hill

landmarks from each city on them. The brand partnered with Walgreens to exclusively sell the "City Sticks" in each of the three cities. During this time Carmex leveraged its social media channels on Facebook and Instagram to solicit photos of fans holding up their favorite style of Carmex in front of a landmark in their own city. Carmex then used these photos to help it decide on new locations for future limited-edition "City Sticks."

Carmex's second line of new products was four fashion-forward "glamorous" designs of Carmex Moisture Plus. Carmex researched current design trends in the women's fashion industry to come up with the four different styles, and it had seen good engagement from its Facebook community on "fashion themed" posts, which helped validate the concept. The four styles were: "Chic," a black and white houndstooth; "Fab," with bright purple circles; "Adventurous," a leopard print; and "Whimsical," with blue, orange, green, and pink intertwined ribbons. Carmex first announced the line to its Facebook fans to generate interest and they were brought to market in the summer of 2013.

FACEBOOK MARKETING RESEARCH: TWO KEY METRICS

"We have three potential new flavors and we can only put two into quantitative testing," explains Jeff Gerst to his team. "So we have two goals in doing marketing research on this. One is to use Facebook to help us determine which two flavors we should move forward with. The second goal is to drive our Facebook metrics."

The two key Facebook metrics the Carmex marketing team has chosen to help narrow the flavor choices from three to two are "likes" and "engagement." "Likes" are the number of new "likers" to the brand's Facebook Page. This metric measures the size of the brand's Facebook audience. In contrast, "engagement" measures how active its Facebook audience is with Carmex. Anytime a liker posts a comment on the Carmex Wall, likes its status, or replies to one of its posts, the engagement level increases.

The easiest way for Carmex to grow the number of "likes" on its Facebook Page is through contests and promotions. If it gives away prizes, people will be drawn to its site and its likes will increase. However, these people may not actually be fans of the Carmex product so at the end of the promotion, they may "unlike" Carmex or they may remain fans but not engage with the Carmex Page at all.

"One of the biggest challenges facing Facebook Community Managers for brands is how to grow your likes without hurting the level of engagement," says Holly Matson, director of experience planning at Bolin Marketing.

"Depending on how we go about conducting the research," Gerst adds, "we can drive engagement with our existing Facebook community, we can use this as an opportunity to grow our Facebook community or, potentially, we could do both." The benefits of this Carmex Facebook strategy are twofold: (1) narrowing the number of flavors to be researched from three to two and (2) enhancing the connections with the Carmex Facebook community.

HOW THE METRICS MIGHT BE USED

Carmex's Facebook activity can benefit (1) by using a poll to increase engagement, (2) by launching a contest to increase the number of likers, and (3) by trying to increase both engagement and likers through combining a poll with a contest.

The "Engagement" Strategy: Use a Poll

Let's look at two ways to use the engagement strategy showing actual Facebook screens. First, Carmex can post a somewhat open-ended question on its Facebook Wall, such as, "Which Carmex lip balm flavor would you most like to see next: Watermelon, Green Apple, or Peach Mango?" (Figure 1). However, consumers are less likely to respond to a question if they have to type in a response and have their name attached to it.

Alternatively, Carmex can post the same question on its Wall as a fixed-alternative poll question (Figure 2).

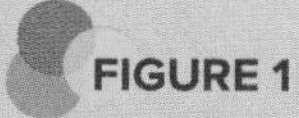

FIGURE 1
Facebook Open-Ended Poll Question
Carma Labs Inc.

CARMEX
Carmex
Which Carmex lip balm flavor would you most like to see next: Watermelon, Green Apple, or Peach Mango?
Like Comment

FIGURE 2
Facebook Fixed-Alternative Poll Question
Carma Labs Inc.

CARMEX
Carmex
Which Carmex lip balm flavor would you most like to see next?
Watermelon
Green Apple
Peach Mango

Then consumers need only click on a flavor to vote; this is quick, anonymous, and will drive more people to vote, where more votes means more engagement. Within five minutes Carmex will have several dozen votes and, by the end of a business day, Carmex can very easily have over 500 responses.

In this scenario, the consumers are content because they are able to engage with a brand they like and have their opinions heard. Carmex is content because it has engaged hundreds of its fans on its Facebook Page, and it gains results that are very helpful in deciding which flavors to put into testing. This scenario gets an answer quickly and drives fan engagement with existing fans but does not drive new likers to the Carmex Facebook Page.

The "Likes" Strategy: Use a Contest

If Carmex wants to grow the size of its Facebook community, which means the number of its brand page "likes," it can adopt a different strategy. Carmex can announce a contest where, if consumers "like" Carmex on Facebook and share a comment, they will be entered to win three limited-edition flavors. The chance to win limited-edition flavors is exciting to Carmex enthusiasts, and a contest like this will draw new consumers to the page. Carmex can ask the winners to review the limited-edition flavors and see if there is a consensus on which flavors should move on to quantitative testing. Setting up a contest, developing official rules, promoting the contest through Facebook ads, and fulfilling a contest can be costly and time-consuming.

The Combined Strategy: Use Poll and Contest

Carmex can also choose to layer these two strategies into a combined strategy where it runs the limited-edition flavor contest to promote new likes and meanwhile posts the poll question on its Facebook Wall to drive engagement.

REACHING A DECISION

Figure 3 shows the potential results from the three Facebook strategies being considered—the poll only, the contest only, or both strategies together. Assume the Carmex marketing team has sought your help in selecting a strategy and needs your answers to the questions below.[33]

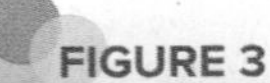

FIGURE 3
Potential Results from Three Possible Facebook Strategies
Carma Labs Inc.

FACEBOOK STRATEGY	POTENTIAL IMPACT ON...		
	Increased "Engagement"	Increased "Likes"	Cost
Poll Only	High	Low	Low
Contest Only	Low	High	Moderate
Poll + Contest	High	High	Moderate to High

Favorable Neutral Unfavorable

Questions

1 What are the advantages and disadvantages for the Carmex marketing team in collecting data to narrow the flavor choices from three to two using (*a*) an online survey of a cross section of Internet households or (*b*) an online survey of Carmex Facebook likers?

2 (*a*) On a Facebook brand page, what are "engagement" and "likes" really measuring? (*b*) For Carmex, which is more important and why?

3 (*a*) What evokes consumers' "engagement" on a brand page on Facebook? (*b*) What attracts consumers to "like" a brand page on Facebook?

4 (*a*) What are the advantages of using a fixed-alternative poll question on Facebook? (*b*) When do you think it would be better to use an open-ended question?

5 (*a*) If you had a limited budget and two weeks to decide which two flavors to put into quantitative testing, would you choose a "poll only" or a "contest only" strategy? Why? (*b*) If you had a sizable budget and two months to make the same decision, which scenario would you choose? Why?

Chapter Notes

1. "Worldwide Grosses," Box Office Mojo, http://www.boxofficemojo.com/alltime/world/, accessed August 10, 2019; and Tim Dirks, "Greatest Box-Office Bombs, Disasters and Film Flops of All-Time," AMC Filmsite, http://www.filmsite.org/greatestflops.html, 2018.
2. Hilary Lewis, "8 Movies with Major Title Changes," *Hollywood Reporter*, August 26, 2016; Rachel Dodes, "Movies: What's in a Name?" *The Wall Street Journal*, October 19, 2012, p. D1; and John Horn, "Studios Play Name Games," *Star Tribune*, August 10, 1997, p. F11.
3. Kathryn Lunte, "Screening Success: Marketing Research for Movies," *Film and Digital Media*, https://filmanddigitalmedia.wordpress.com/?s=screening+success, February 28, 2015.
4. Rudie Obias, "11 Movies That Changed Because of Test Audiences," *mentalfloss.com*, April 4, 2016; and Willow Bay, "Test Audiences Have Profound Effect on Movies," *CNN Newsstand & Entertainment Weekly*, September 28, 1998.
5. Natalie Robehmed, "How Hollywood Monitors Social Media to Help Movies Make Money," www.forbes.com, April 30, 2015; Brooks Barnes, "Hollywood Tracks Social Media Chatter to Target Hit Films," *The New York Times*, www.nytimes.com, December 7, 2014; and Carl Diorio, "Tracking Projections: Box Office Calculations an Inexact Science," *Variety*, May 24, 2001.
6. A lengthier, expanded definition is found on the American Marketing Association's website. See https://www.ama.org/AboutAMA/Pages/Definition-of-Marketing.aspx; and for a researcher's comments on this and other definitions of marketing research, see Lawrence D. Gibson, "Quo Vadis, Marketing Research?" *Marketing Research*, Spring 2000, pp. 36–41.
7. Lindsay Kolowich, "Building a Playful Brand, Brick by Brick: The History of Lego Marketing," *Hubspot*, August 10, 2015; Parmy Olson, "Gadgets We Love: LEGO Mindstorms EV3," www.forbes.com, December 2, 2014, p. 1; and Harry McCracken, "Build-A-Bot," *Time*, January 21, 2013, pp. 52–53.
8. Lawrence D. Gibson, "Defining Marketing Problems," *Marketing Research*, Spring 1998, pp. 4–12; and Martin Meister, "How to Define a Marketing Research Problem," *Business Insights Review*, July 11, 2012.
9. David A. Aaker, V. Kumar, George S. Day, and Robert P. Leone, *Marketing Research*, 10th ed. (Hoboken, NJ: John Wiley & Sons, 2010), pp. 114–16.
10. Adapted from "TV Ratings," Nielsen website, https://www.nielsen.com/us/en/top-ten/ and Alex Welch, "NBC Wins the Season in 18–49, CBS Wins in Viewers: Broadcast Top 25 and Network Rankings for May 13–19," https://tvbythenumbers.zap2it.com; Miriam Gottfried, "Nielsen Isn't Leaving the Living Room Soon," *The Wall Street Journal*, January 20, 2015, p. C8; and Meg James, "Nielsen 'People Meter' Changed the TV Ratings Game 25 Years Ago," *Los Angeles Times*, August 31, 2012.
11. Joe Otterson, "Delayed Viewing Ratings: Reality Shows Stay on Top during Winter Olympics," www.variety.com, March 12, 2018; Jason Lynch, "Here Are the TV Shows and Networks People Watch Live Most and Least Often," www.adweek.com, October 7, 2016; Jeanine Poggi, "TV's New Ratings Aren't What Advertisers Want," *Advertising Age*, January 23, 2017, p. 36; and George Winslow, "Researchers Tackle Cross-Platform Measurement," *Broadcasting & Cable*, September 15, 2014, p. 22.

12. "Nielsen Estimates More Than 119.9 Million TV Homes in the U.S. for the 2018–19 TV Season," The Nielsen Company website, September 7, 2018, https://www.nielsen.com/us/en/search.html?q=tv+homes&sp_cs=UTF-8.
13. "Zenith's 2019 U.S. Media and Marketing Services Spending Forecast," *Advertising Age, Marketing Fact Pack*, December 17, 2019, p. 14.
14. Suhit Anantula, "How Gillette Learned Design-Led Consumer Research from P&G," *Humanomics*, March 2, 2015; Bruce Brown and Scott Anthony, "How P&G Tripled Its Innovation Success Rate," *Harvard Business Review*, June 2011, pp. 64–72; and "Observe and Learn from Consumers," *Managing People at Work*, April 2011, p. 4.
15. Elka Torpey, "Mystery Shopper," *Career Outlook*, February 2016, p. 1; Jim Dudlicek, "Mystery Machine," *Progressive Grocer*, May 2015, p. 10; and Clive R. Boddy, "'Hanging Around with People': Ethnography in Marketing Research and Intelligence Gathering," *The Marketing Review* 11, no. 2 (2011), pp. 151–63.
16. "How to Use Ethnography for In-Depth Consumer Insight," *Marketing Week*, May 22, 2014, p. 4; and Gavin Johnson and Melinda Rea-Holloway, "Ethnography: How to Know If It's Right for Your Study," *Alert! Magazine*, Marketing Research Association, 47, no. 2 (February 2009), pp. 1–4.
17. Kenneth Chang, "Enlisting Science's Lessons to Entice More Shoppers to Spend More," *The New York Times*, September 19, 2006, p. D3; and Janet Adamy, "Cooking Up Changes at Kraft Foods," *The Wall Street Journal*, February 20, 2007, p. B1.
18. Zach Brooke, "Marketing's Mind Readers," *Marketing News*, January, 2017, pp. 38–41; Kyle Hilton, "The Science of Sensory Marketing," *Harvard Business Review*, March 2015, pp. 28–29; Roger Dooley, "Nielsen Doubles Down on Neuro," *Forbes*, June 3, 2015; Aradhna Krishna, *Customer Sense* (New York: Palgrave Macmillan, 2013); Lluis Martinez-Ribes, "The Power of the Senses," http://www.martinez-ribes.com/the-power-ofthe-senses-sensory-applications-in-retail/, April 24, 2013; and Martin Lindstrom, *Buyology: Truth and Lies about Why We Buy* (New York: Doubleday, 2008), pp. 8–36.
19. Jack Neff, "Neuromarketing Exits the 'Hype Cycle,' Starts Shaping TV Commercials," *Advertising Age*, April 18, 2016, p. 17; and Ilan Brat, "The Emotional Quotient of Soup Shopping," *The Wall Street Journal*, February 17, 2010, p. B6.
20. For a more complete discussion of questionnaire methods, see Joseph F. Hair Jr., Mary Wolfinbarger, Robert P. Bush, and David J. Ortinau, *Essentials of Marketing Research*, 3rd ed. (New York: McGraw-Hill/Irwin, 2013), Chapters 4 and 8.
21. See www.trendhunter.com/about-trend-hunter.
22. "Are Chatbots the Future of Market Research?" www.d8aspring.com, May 16, 2108; and "What Is Online Research?" Marketing Research Association at http://www.marketingresearch.org/?q=node/221. See also www.surveymonkey.com.
23. For more discussion on wording questions effectively, see Gilbert A. Churchill Jr., Tom J. Brown, and Tracy A. Suter, *Basic Marketing Research*, 7th ed. (Mason, OH: South-Western, Cengage Learning, 2010), pp. 289–307.
24. David Kirkpatrick, "Lay's Latest Flavor Contest Lets Fans Cast Votes via Snapchat," www.marketingdive.com, July 19, 2017; and Stephanie Clifford, "Social Media Act as a Guide for Marketers," *The New York Times*, July 31, 2012, pp. A1, A3.
25. Jeff Gerst of Bolin Marketing provided the Carmex example, with the permission of Carma Laboratories, Inc.
26. Mark Jeffery, *Data-Driven Marketing: The 15 Metrics Everyone in Marketing Should Know* (Hoboken, NJ: John Wiley & Sons, Inc., 2010), pp. 156–86.
27. Gordon Wyner, "The Uncertain Future of Market Research," *Marketing News*, June 2017, pp. 18–19; Douglas D. Bates, "The Future of Qualitative Research Is Online," *Alert! Magazine*, Marketing Research Association 47, no. 2 (February 2009); Jack Neff, "The End of Consumer Surveys?" *Advertising Age*, September 15, 2008; Jack Neff, "Marketing Execs: Researchers Could Use a Softer Touch," *Advertising Age*, January 27, 2009; Bruce Mendelsohn, "Social Networking: Interactive Marketing Lets Researchers Reach Consumers Where They Are," *Alert! Magazine*, Marketing Research Association 46, no. 4 (April 2008); Toby, "Social Media Research: Interview with Joel Rubinson of ARF: Part 1," *Diva Marketing Blog*, February 16, 2009; and Toby, "Social Media Research: Interview with Joel Rubinson of ARF: Part 2," *Diva Marketing Blog*, February 23, 2009.
28. Erik Adams, "McDonald's Delivery Business Is Booming," *Skift Table*, July 26, 2018; Hannah E. Smith, "On-Demand Meal Delivery Risks," PropertyCasualty360, April 25, 2019; and Bill Peters, "Happy Meals on Wheels: McDonald's Touts '3-Mile' Delivery Advantage," *Investors Business Daily*, March 1, 2017, p.1.
29. Janakiraman Moorthy, Rangin Lahiri, Neelanjan Biswas, Dipyaman Sanyal, Jayanthi Ranjan, Krishnadas Nanath, and Pulak Ghosh, "Big Data: Prospects and Challenges," *Vikalpa*, January–March 2015, pp. 74–96; Karthik Kambatla, Giorgos Kollias, Vipin Kumar, and Ananth Grama, "Trends in Big Data Analytics," *Journal of Parallel and Distributed Computing*," January 2014, pp. 2561–73; Steve LaValle, Eric Lesser, Rebecca Shockley, Michael S. Hopkins, and Nina Kruschwitz, "Big Data, Analytics and the Path from Insights to Value," *Sloan Management Review*, Winter 2011, pp. 21–31; and "Big Data: Before You Start Restricting It, Be Aware of All the Opportunities," *The Wall Street Journal*, November 19, 2012, p. R10.
30. Zach Brooke, "The Market Research Arms Race," *Marketing News*, June–July 2018, pp. 78–87; and Hal Conick, "The Past, Present and Future of AI in Marketing," *Marketing News*, January 2017, pp. 26–35.
31. "How Social Media Data Mining Could Shape the Products of Tomorrow," www.phys.org, February 15, 2017; Joni R. Jackson, "Big Data: Goldmine or Minefield?" *AMA Winter Conference Proceedings*, 2016, p. 41; Joel Stein, "Your Data, Yourself," *Time*, March 21, 2011, pp. 39–46; Ryan Flinn, "The Big Business of Sifting through Social Media Data," *Bloomberg Businessweek*, October 25–October 31, 2010, pp. 20–22; and Michael Lev-Ram, "The Hot New Gig in Tech," *Fortune*, September 5, 2011, p. 29.
32. The step 4 discussion was written by David Ford and Don Rylander of Ford Consulting Group, Inc.; the Tony's Pizza example was provided by Teré Carral of Tony's Pizza.
33. Carmex: This case was written by Jeff Gerst of Bolin Marketing.

Chapter 9 Market Segmentation, Targeting, and Positioning

LEARNING OBJECTIVES

After reading this chapter you should be able to:

LO 9-1 Explain what market segmentation is and when to use it.

LO 9-2 Identify the five steps involved in segmenting and targeting markets.

LO 9-3 Recognize the bases used to segment consumer and organizational (business) markets.

LO 9-4 Develop a market-product grid to identify a target market and recommend resulting marketing actions.

LO 9-5 Explain how marketing managers position products in the marketplace.

"On a Scale of 1 to 10, How Weird Are You?"

This is one of the questions Zappos founder and CEO, Tony Hsieh, asks prospective employees in job interviews. Why? To find personalities that fit well with his company's culture. Hsieh's philosophy is to balance profits, passion, and purpose to create a unique company culture and an extraordinary customer experience. If you have purchased a pair of shoes online, you may be one of millions of people who agree that the Zappos experience, created by "weird" employees, is truly extraordinary![1]

Segmentation Is Zappos's Secret to Success

Zappos began with the idea of creating a website that would offer the best selection of shoes. The key to the success of the new venture was Hsieh's segmentation strategy: Focus on people who like to use mobile technology and who will shop for and buy shoes online. While this focus on the segment of online shoe buyers generated more than $1 billion in annual sales, the Zappos vision soon evolved to include consumers of anything in the one-third of all retail transactions that are likely to occur online. The segmentation strategy also evolved as Zappos implemented behavioral segmentation to match relevant products from other categories based on past shoe purchases. Some recommendations are even based on the type of device consumers use to shop.[2]

In addition to a huge selection of shoes and personalized recommendations of other products, Zappos provides 24-hour customer service with no wait times, as well as free shipping and free returns. Pamela Leo, a New Jersey customer, says "With Zappos I can try the shoes in the comfort of my own home . . . it's fabulous."[3]

Delivering WOW through Customer Service

"We try to spend most of our time on stuff that will improve customer-service levels," Hsieh explains. This customer-service obsession for its market segment of online customers means that all new Zappos.com employees go through four weeks of customer-loyalty training. Hsieh offers $2,000 to anyone completing the training who wants to leave Zappos.com, and another $1,000 per year of work at Zappos up to $5,000. The theory: If you take the money, you're not right for Zappos.com. Few take the money![4]

Ten "core values" are the foundation for the Zappos.com culture, brand, and business strategies. Some examples:[5]

#1. Deliver WOW through service.
#3. Create fun and a little weirdness.
#6. Build open and honest relationships with communication.

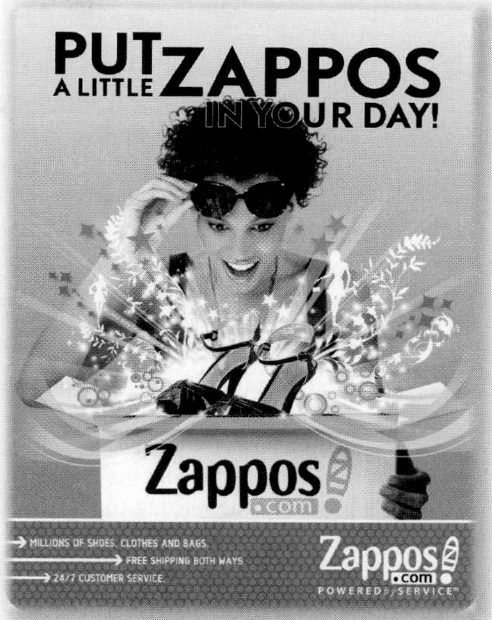

Source: Zappos.com, Inc.

The other Zappos.com core values appear on its website: www.zappos.com. Hsieh's interest in the company culture also led him to implement a structure called "holocracy," which emphasizes self-management by eliminating traditional hierarchical reporting lines and replacing them with "work circles." The Zappos model has been so successful the company created Zappos Insights, a training center for other companies to learn how to attract and retain customers through excellent service.[6]

The Zappos.com strategy illustrates successful market segmentation and targeting, the first topics in this chapter. The chapter concludes with the topic of positioning the organization, product, or brand.

WHY SEGMENT MARKETS?

LO 9-1
Explain what market segmentation is and when to use it.

A business firm segments its markets so it can respond more effectively to the wants of groups of potential buyers and thus increase its sales and profits. Not-for-profit organizations also segment the clients they serve so they can satisfy client needs more effectively while achieving the organization's goals. Let's describe (1) what market segmentation is and (2) when to segment markets, sometimes using the Zappos.com segmentation strategy as an example.

What Market Segmentation Means

People have different needs and wants, even though it would be easier for marketers if they didn't. **Market segmentation** involves aggregating prospective buyers into groups, or segments, that (1) have common needs and (2) will respond similarly to a marketing action. As defined in Chapter 1, *market segments* are the relatively homogeneous groups of prospective

FIGURE 9–1
Market segmentation links market needs to an organization's marketing program—its specific marketing mix actions designed to satisfy those needs.

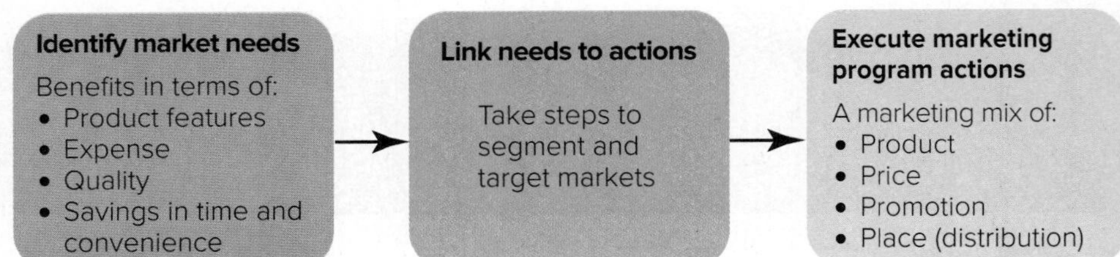

buyers that result from the market segmentation process. Each market segment consists of people who are relatively similar to each other in terms of their consumption behavior.

Identify market needs
Benefits in terms of:
• Product features
• Expense
• Quality
• Savings in time and convenience
Link needs to actions
Take steps to segment and target markets
Execute marketing program actions
A marketing mix of:
• Product
• Price
• Promotion
• Place (distribution)

The existence of different market segments has caused firms to use a marketing strategy of **product differentiation**. This strategy involves a firm using different marketing mix actions, such as product features and advertising, to help consumers perceive the product as being different and better than competing products. The perceived differences may involve physical features, such as size or color, or nonphysical ones, such as image or price.

Segmentation: Linking Needs to Actions The process of segmenting a market and selecting specific segments as targets is the link between the various buyers' needs and the organization's marketing program, as shown in Figure 9–1. Market segmentation is only a means to an end: It leads to tangible marketing actions that can increase sales and profitability.

VIDEO 9-1
Zappos Video
kerin.tv/15e/v9-1

Market segmentation first stresses the importance of grouping people or organizations in a market according to the similarity of their needs and the benefits they are looking for in making a purchase. Second, such needs and benefits must be related to specific marketing actions that the organization can take, such as providing a new product or offering a special promotion.

The Zappos.com Segmentation Strategy The Zappos.com target customer segment originally consisted of people who wanted to (1) have a wide selection of shoes, (2) shop online in the convenience of their own homes, and (3) receive quick delivery and free returns. Zappos's actions include offering a huge inventory of shoes using an online selling strategy and providing overnight delivery. These actions have enabled Zappos.com to create a positive customer experience and generate repeat purchases. Zappos's success in selling footwear has enabled it to add lines of clothing, handbags, accessories (such as sunglasses), and housewares to reach new segments of buyers.

Zappos.com is reaching new market segments with new products and edgy, attention-getting ads.
Source: Zappos.com, Inc.

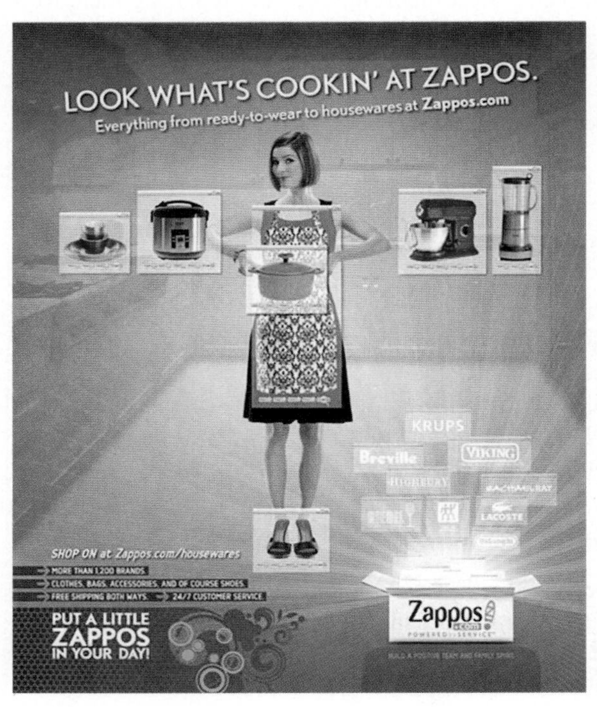

With millions of customers and thousands of calls daily to Zappos's service center, its executives believe the speed with which a customer receives an online purchase plays a big role in gaining repeat customers.[7] The company continues to stress this point of difference of providing the absolute best service among online sellers.

Using Market-Product Grids How do you sleep—on your side, your back, or your stomach? These are really the key market segments of sleepers. Sleep researchers have discovered that you'll probably get a better night's sleep if you have the right firmness of pillow under your head. Using this research, we can develop the market-product grid shown in Figure 9–2.[8]

A **market-product grid** is a framework to relate the market segments of potential buyers to products offered or potential marketing actions. The market-product grid in Figure 9–2 shows the different market segments for bed pillows—side, back, and stomach sleepers—in the horizontal rows. The product offerings—the pillows—appear in the vertical columns and are based on three different pillow firmnesses—firm, medium, and soft.

FIGURE 9–2
This market-product grid shows the kind of sleeper that is targeted for each of the bed pillow products. The sizes of the circles show that side sleepers are the dominant market segment and that they prefer firm pillows.

MARKET SEGMENTS	BED PILLOW PRODUCTS		
	Firm Pillows	Medium Pillows	Soft Pillows
Side sleepers	●		
Back sleepers		●	
Stomach sleepers			●

Marketing research reveals the size of each sleeper segment, as shown by both the percentages and the circles in Figure 9-2. This tells pillow manufacturers the relative importance of each of the three market segments, which is critical information when scheduling production. It also emphasizes the importance of firm pillows, a product targeted at the side sleeper market segment. As Figure 9-2 shows, this segment is almost three times the size of the other two combined. Therefore, meeting the needs of this market segment with the right firmness of pillow is especially important.

When and How to Segment Markets

A business goes to the trouble and expense of segmenting its markets when it expects that this extra effort will increase its sales, profit, and return on investment. P&G, for example, offers multiple brands in the same product category to serve different market segments.[9] When expenses are greater than the potentially increased sales from segmentation, a firm should not attempt to segment its market. Three specific segmentation strategies that illustrate this point are (1) one product and multiple market segments, (2) multiple products and multiple market segments, and (3) segments of one, or mass customization.

One Product and Multiple Market Segments When an organization produces only a single product or service and attempts to sell it to two or more market segments, it avoids the extra costs of developing and producing additional versions of the product. In this case, the incremental costs of taking the product into new market segments are typically those of a separate promotional campaign or a new channel of distribution.

Magazines are single products frequently directed at two or more distinct market segments. The annual *Street & Smith's Baseball* uses 15 different covers featuring a baseball star from each of its regions in the United States. Yet each regional issue has the same magazine content.

Other examples of a single offering for multiple segments include books, movies, and many services. Book series such as *The Mortal Instruments*, *Harry Potter*, *The Twilight Saga*, *Divergent*,

These *different* covers for the *same* magazine issue show a very effective market segmentation strategy. For which strategy it is and why it works, see the text.
Source: American City Business Journals

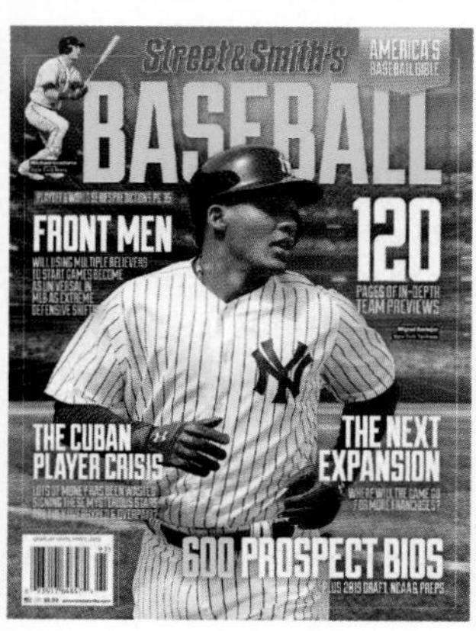

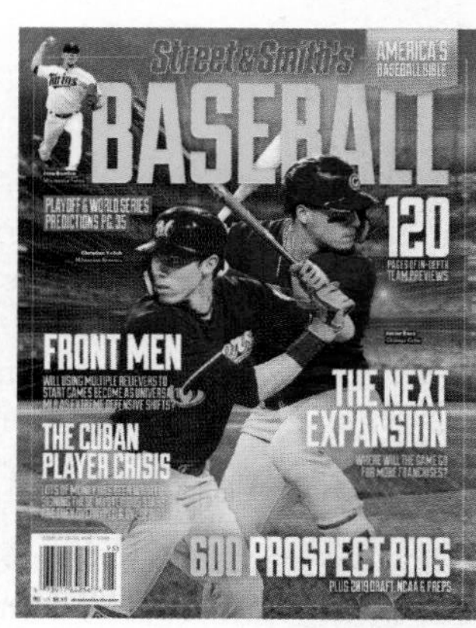

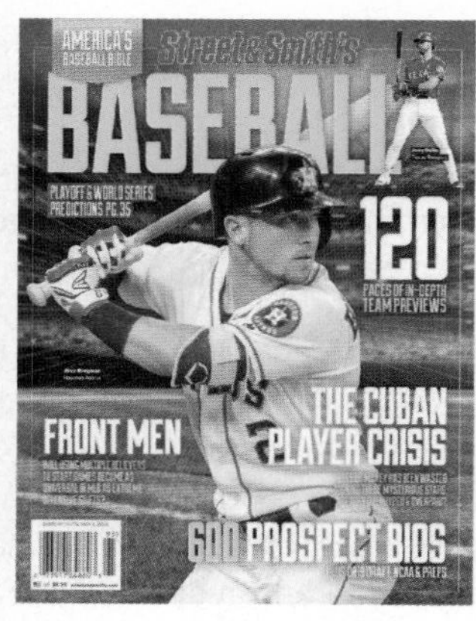

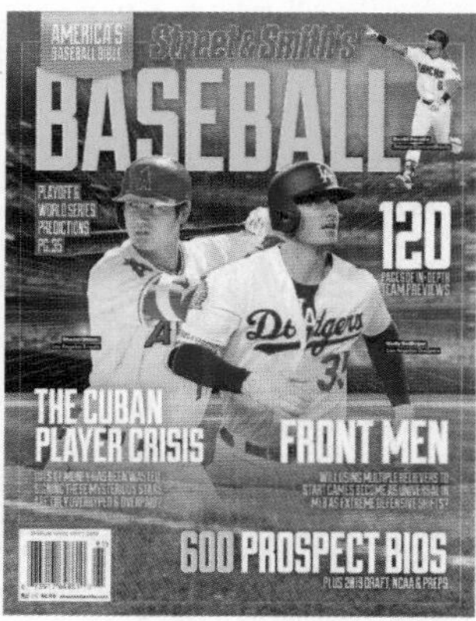

and *The Hunger Games* have phenomenal success in part due to their publishers' creativity in marketing to preteen, teen, and adult segments. Movies have a similar challenge, particularly since different segments are reached through different channels such as movie theaters, streaming services, and pay-per-view cable channels. Finally, services such as Disney's resorts offer the same basic experience to at least three distinct segments—children, parents, and grandparents. Although separate advertising, promotion, and distribution for these offerings can be expensive, these expenses are minor compared with the costs of producing a different version of the offerings for each segment.[10]

Multiple Products and Multiple Market Segments For an example of multiple products aimed at multiple market segments, consider the products of Ford Motor Company. Each of its different lines of cars, SUVs, trucks, crossovers, and hybrids are targeted at a different type of customer. Producing these different vehicles is clearly more expensive than producing only a single vehicle. But this strategy is very effective *if* it meets customers' needs better, doesn't reduce quality or increase price, and adds to Ford's sales revenues and profits.

Unfortunately, this product differentiation strategy in the auto industry has a huge potential downside: The proliferation of different brands, models, and options can raise prices and reduce quality. Several years ago Ford offered vehicles under a variety of brand names, including Ford, Lincoln, Mercury, Jaguar, Aston Martin, Volvo, and Land Rover. In addition, each of the brands offered different models and many options for each model, which often meant thousands of combinations were possible. The huge number of combinations led to limited production volume, which increased prices.[11]

Today Ford is pursuing a different strategy. The company has discontinued or sold all of its brands except Ford and Lincoln and it has discontinued its sedans to focus on pickups, SUVs, and electric vehicles. In addition, it now offers many options but only in packages. Although there are fewer choices, Ford's simplified product line provides two benefits to consumers: (1) lower prices because producing a higher volume is more efficient and (2) higher quality because of the ability to debug fewer basic designs.[12]

Segments of One: Mass Customization American marketers are rediscovering today what their predecessors running the corner general store knew a century ago: Each customer has unique needs and wants and desires exceptional customer service. Economies of scale in manufacturing and marketing during the past century made mass-produced products so affordable that most customers were willing to compromise their individual tastes and settle for standardized products. Today's Internet ordering and flexible manufacturing and marketing processes have made *mass customization* possible, which means tailoring products or services to the tastes of individual customers on a high-volume scale.

Mass customization is the next step beyond *build-to-order* (*BTO*), which involves manufacturing a product only when there is an order from a customer. Apple uses BTO systems that trim work-in-progress inventories and shorten delivery times to customers. To do this, Apple restricts its computer manufacturing line to only a few basic models that can be assembled in four minutes. This gives customers a good choice with quick delivery. Similarly, Nike offers its *Nike By You* service which configures shoes to a customer's specific preferences for colors, soles, logos, and can even add initials and numbers.

The Segmentation Trade-Off: Synergies versus Cannibalization The key to successful product differentiation and market segmentation strategies is finding the ideal balance between satisfying a customer's individual wants and achieving *organizational synergy*, the increased customer value achieved through performing organizational functions such as marketing or manufacturing more efficiently. The "increased customer value" can take many forms: more products, improved quality of existing products, lower prices, easier access to products through improved distribution, and so on. So the ultimate criterion for an organization's marketing success is that customers should be better off as a result of the increased synergies.

The organization should also achieve increased revenues and profits from the product differentiation and market segmentation strategies it uses. When the increased customer value

ANN INC.'s LOFT chain tries to reach younger, value-conscious women with a casual lifestyle, while its Ann Taylor chain targets more sophisticated and relatively affluent women. For the potential dangers of this two-segment strategy, see the text.
JHVEPhoto/Shutterstock

involves adding new products or a new chain of stores, the product differentiation–market segmentation trade-off raises a critical issue: Are the new products or new chain simply stealing customers and sales from the older, existing ones? This is known as *cannibalization*.

Marketers increasingly emphasize a two-tier, "Tiffany/Walmart" strategy. Many firms now offer different variations of the same basic offering to high-end and low-end segments. Gap Inc.'s Banana Republic chain sells blue jeans for $58, whereas its Old Navy stores sell a slightly different version for $22.

Unfortunately, the lines between customer segments can often blur and lead to problems. For example, consider the competition within the ANN INC. organization between stores in its two chains—Ann Taylor and LOFT. The Ann Taylor chain targets "successful, relatively affluent, fashion-conscious women," while its sister chain, LOFT, targets "value-conscious women who want a casual lifestyle at work and home." The LOFT stores wound up stealing sales from the Ann Taylor chain. The result: More than 100 stores from both chains were closed.[13] Both chains are now aggressively targeting their customers by stressing online sales and opening new factory outlets—Ann Taylor Factory and LOFT Outlet stores.

The smaller Walmart Neighborhood Market format offers convenient locations to discount shoppers.
Scott Olson/Getty Images

Walmart has been opening Walmart Neighborhood Market stores that are about one-fifth the size of its supercenters. These smaller stores are intended to compete for the segments that shop at discount chains such as Dollar General. Walmart Neighborhood Markets are designed to meet a range of needs by offering fresh produce, health and beauty supplies, household items, gasoline, and a pharmacy. Walmart currently has 698 of the small format stores and plans to open new stores in the future. Will its own Tiffany/Walmart strategy—or perhaps "Walmart/Dollar General" strategy—prove successful or lead to cannibalization of the larger stores? Watch for new stores near you during the next few years to determine the answer.[14]

LEARNING REVIEW

9-1. Market segmentation involves aggregating prospective buyers into groups that have two key characteristics. What are they?

9-2. In terms of market segments and products, what are the three market segmentation strategies?

STEPS IN SEGMENTING AND TARGETING MARKETS

LO 9-2
Identify the five steps involved in segmenting and targeting markets.

Figure 9–3 on the next page identifies the five-step process used to segment a market and select the target segments on which an organization wants to focus. Segmenting a market requires both detailed analysis and large doses of common sense and managerial judgment. So market segmentation is both science and art!

For the purposes of our discussion, assume that you have just purchased a Wendy's restaurant. Your Wendy's is located next to a large urban university, one that offers both day and evening classes. Your restaurant offers the basic Wendy's fare: hamburgers, chicken and deli sandwiches, salads, french fries, and Frosty desserts. Even though you are part of a chain that

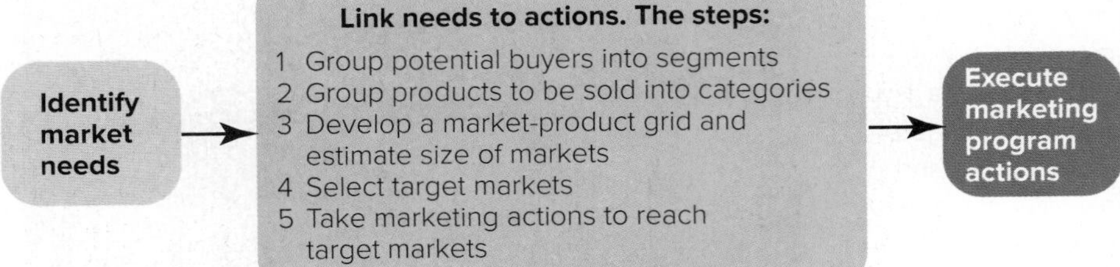

Identify market needs
Link needs to actions. The steps:
1 Group potential buyers into segments
2 Group products to be sold into categories
3 Develop a market-product grid and estimate size of markets
4 Select target markets
5 Take marketing actions to reach target markets
Execute marketing program actions

FIGURE 9–3
The five key steps in segmenting and targeting markets link the market needs of customers to the organization's marketing program.

A local Wendy's restaurant—like yours!
Reed Saxon/AP Images

has some restrictions on menu and decor, you are free to set your hours of business and to develop local advertising. How can market segmentation help? In the sections that follow, you will apply the five-step process for segmenting and targeting markets to arrive at marketing actions for your Wendy's restaurant.

Step 1: Group Potential Buyers into Segments

It's not always a good idea to segment a market. Grouping potential buyers into meaningful segments involves meeting some specific criteria that answer the questions, "Would segmentation be worth doing?" and "Is it possible?" If so, a marketer must find specific variables that can be used to create these various segments.

Criteria to Use in Forming the Segments A marketing manager should develop market segments that meet five essential criteria:[15]

- *Simplicity and cost-effectiveness of assigning potential buyers to segments.* A marketing manager must be able to put a market segmentation plan into effect. This means identifying the characteristics of potential buyers in a market and then cost-effectively assigning them to a segment.
- *Potential for increased profit.* The best segmentation approach is the one that maximizes the opportunity for future profit and return on investment (ROI). If this potential is maximized without segmentation, don't segment. For nonprofit organizations, the criterion is the potential for serving clients more effectively.
- *Similarity of needs of potential buyers within a segment.* Potential buyers within a segment should be similar in terms of common needs that, in turn, lead to common marketing actions, such as product features sought or advertising media used.
- *Difference of needs of buyers among segments.* If the needs of the various segments aren't very different, combine them into fewer segments. A different segment usually requires a different marketing action that, in turn, means greater costs. If increased sales don't offset extra costs, combine segments and reduce the number of marketing actions.
- *Potential of a marketing action to reach a segment.* Reaching a segment requires a simple but effective marketing action. If no such action exists, don't segment.

LO 9-3
Recognize the bases used to segment consumer and organizational (business) markets.

Ways to Segment Consumer Markets Four general bases of segmentation can be used to segment U.S. consumer markets. These four segmentation bases are (1) *geographic segmentation*, which is based on where prospective customers live or work (region, city size); (2) *demographic segmentation*, which is based on some *objective* physical (gender, race), measurable (age, income), or other classification attribute (birth era, occupation) of prospective customers; (3) *psychographic segmentation*, which is based on some *subjective* mental or emotional attributes (personality), aspirations (lifestyle), or needs of prospective customers; and (4) *behavioral segmentation*, which is based on some observable actions or attitudes by

Marketing Insights About Me

To Which "Flock" Do You Belong?

There is an old saying that "birds of a feather flock together." This also applies to the formation of market segments and gives rise to the following questions marketers must ask and answer: Who are your target customers? What are they like? Where do they live? How can you reach them?

These questions are answered in part by Claritas, whose PRIZM® consumer segmentation system classifies every household into 1 of 66 demographically and behaviorally distinct neighborhood segments to identify lifestyles and purchase behavior within a defined geographic market area, such as zip code. Many organizations today use these neighborhood segments, especially with social media.

Source: Claritas

Want to know what your neighborhood is like? Go to https://claritas360.claritas.com/mybestsegments/?_ga=2.126683789.1886065759.1565840454-226569367.1565840454#zipLookup to reach the MyBestSegments home page. Enter your zip code in the "ZIP Code Look-up" box and click the "Submit" button to find out what the most common segments are in your neighborhood.

For a description of these segments, click the "Segment Details" tab. Is this your "flock"? What specific product or service organizations might be interested in targeting these segments?

prospective customers—such as where they buy, what benefits they seek, how frequently they buy, and why they buy. Some examples are:

- *Geographic segmentation*: *Region*. Campbell Soup Company found that its canned nacho cheese sauce, which could be heated and poured directly onto nacho chips, was too spicy for Americans in the East and not spicy enough for those in the West and Southwest. The result: Campbell's plants in Texas and California now produce a hotter nacho cheese sauce to serve their regions better.
- *Demographic segmentation*: *Household size*. More than half of all U.S. households are made up of only one or two persons, so Campbell Soup Company packages meals with only one or two servings for this market segment.
- *Psychographic segmentation*: *Lifestyle*. Lifestyle segmentation is based on the belief that "birds of a feather flock together." Thus, people of similar lifestyles tend to live near one another, have similar interests, and buy similar offerings. This is of great value to marketers. Claritas PRIZM® classifies every household in the United States into 1 of 66 unique market segments. See the Marketing Insights About Me box for a profile of where you live.
- *Behavioral segmentation*: *Product features*. Understanding what features are important to different customers is a useful way to segment markets because it can lead directly to specific marketing actions, such as a new product, an ad campaign, or a distribution channel. For example, college dorm residents frequently want to keep and prepare their own food to save money or have a late-night snack. However, their dorm rooms are often woefully short of space. MicroFridge understands this and markets a combination microwave, refrigerator, freezer, smoke sensor, and charging station appliance targeted to these students.
- *Behavioral segmentation*: *Usage rate*. **Usage rate** is the quantity consumed or patronage—store visits—during a specific period. It varies significantly among different customer groups. Airlines have developed frequent-flyer programs to encourage passengers to use the same airline repeatedly to create loyal customers. This technique, sometimes called *frequency marketing*, focuses on usage rate.

This MicroFridge appliance includes everything from a small refrigerator, freezer, and microwave oven to a smoke sensor and a charging station for laptops and mobile phones. To which market segment might this appeal? The answer appears in the text.
Source: Intirion Corporation

Simmons continuously surveys over 25,000 adults each year to obtain quarterly, projectable usage rate data from the U.S. national population for more than

FIGURE 9–4

Patronage of fast-food restaurants by adults 18 years and older. The table shows the critical importance of attracting heavy users and medium users to a fast-food restaurant.

User or Nonuser	Specific Segment	Number (1,000s)	Percent	Actual Consumption Percent	Usage Index per Person	Importance of Segment
Users	Heavy users (15 + per month)	69,327	30.2%	56.8%	560	High
	Medium users (6–14 per month)	78,321	34.1%	37.8%	330	
	Light users (1–5 per month)	45,164	19.6%	5.4%	100	
Total Users		—	**83.9%**	—	—	
Nonusers	Prospects	2,221	1.0%	—	—	
	Nonprospects	34,800	15.1%	—	—	
Total Nonusers		**37,021**	**16.1%**	—	—	Low
Total	Users + Nonusers	**229,833**	**100%**	—	—	

Source: Simmons National Consumer Survey Spring 2014 Adult Survey OneView[SM] Crosstabulation Report, Simmons Research LLC.

500 consumer product categories and 8,000-plus brands. Its purpose is to discover how the products and services they buy and the media they use relate to their behavioral, psychographic, and demographic characteristics.

Patronage of Fast-Food Restaurants Figure 9–4 shows the results of a question Simmons asked about adult respondents' frequency of use (or patronage) of fast-food restaurants.[16] As shown by the arrow in the far right column of Figure 9–4, the importance of the segment increases as we move up the table. Among nonusers of these restaurants, prospects (who might become users) are more important than nonprospects (who are never likely to become users). Moving up the rows to users, it seems logical that light users of these restaurants (1 to 5 times per month) are important but less so than medium users (6 to 14 times per month), who, in turn, are a less important segment than the critical group: heavy users (15 or more times per month). The Actual Consumption column in Figure 9–4 shows how much of the total monthly usage of these restaurants is accounted for by heavy, medium, and light users.

Usage rate is sometimes referred to in terms of the **80/20 rule**, a concept that suggests 80 percent of a firm's sales are obtained from 20 percent of its customers. The percentages in the 80/20 rule are not really fixed at exactly 80 percent and 20 percent, but they suggest that a small fraction of customers provides most of a firm's sales. For example, the orange shading in Figure 9–4 shows that the 30.2 percent of the U.S. population who are heavy users of fast-food restaurants provide 56.8 percent of the actual consumption volume. This high percentage illustrates the situation where one group of customers is responsible for a disproportionately high percentage of sales.

The Usage Index per Person column in Figure 9–4 emphasizes the importance of the heavy-user segment even more. Giving the light users (1 to 5 restaurant visits per month) an index of 100, the heavy users have an index of 560. In other words, for every $1.00 spent by a light user in one of these restaurants in a month, each heavy user spends $5.60. This is the reason that as a Wendy's restaurant owner, you want to focus most of your marketing efforts on reaching the highly attractive heavy-user market segment.

As part of its survey, Simmons asked adults which fast-food restaurant(s) was (were) (1) the sole or only restaurant, (2) the primary one, or (3) one of several secondary ones they patronized. As a Wendy's restaurant owner, the information depicted in Figure 9–5 should

FIGURE 9–5
Comparison of various kinds of users and nonusers for Wendy's, Burger King, and McDonald's fast-food restaurants. This figure gives Wendy's restaurants a snapshot of its customers compared to those of its major competitors.

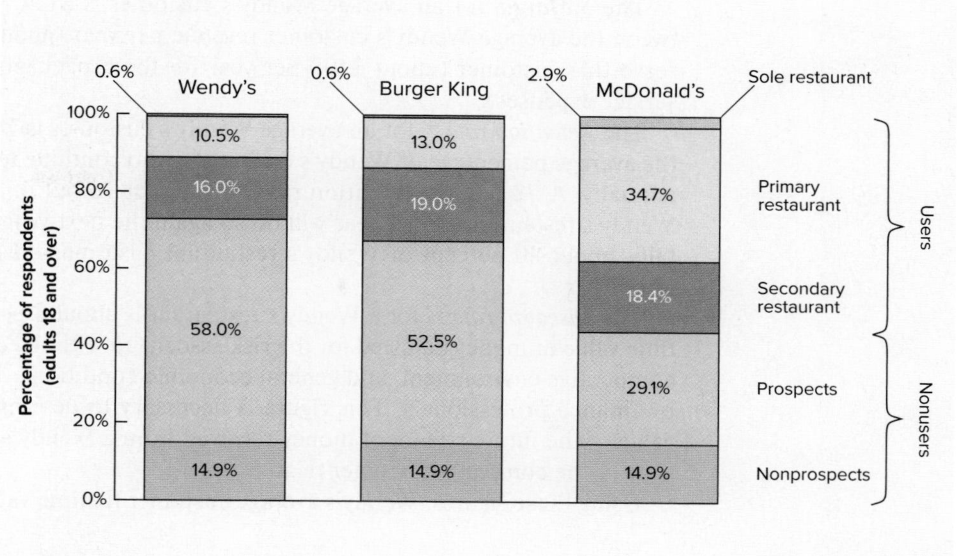

Source: Simmons National Consumer Survey Spring 2014 Adult Survey OneView[SM] Crosstabulation Report, Simmons Research LLC.

give you some ideas in developing a marketing program for your local market. For example, the Wendy's bar graph in Figure 9–5 shows that your sole (0.6 percent) and primary (10.5 percent) user segments are somewhat behind Burger King and far behind McDonald's. Thus, your challenge is to look at these two competitors and devise a marketing program to win customers from them.

The nonusers part of the Wendy's bar graph in Figure 9–5 shows that 14.9 percent of adult Americans don't go to fast-food restaurants in a typical month and are really nonprospects—unlikely to ever patronize any fast-food restaurant. However, 58.0 percent of nonusers are prospects who may be worth a targeted marketing program. These adults use the product category (fast food) but do not yet patronize Wendy's. New menu items or promotional strategies may succeed in converting these prospects into users that patronize Wendy's.

The Financial Relevance of Customer Patronage: Customer Lifetime Value

Customer patronage has long-term financial consequences. Today, companies look beyond an individual purchase from a customer (the average single customer purchase transaction at a quick-service burger restaurant ranges between \$5.00 and \$7.00). Instead, companies pursue continuing and mutually beneficial relationships with customers. The financial relevance of customer patronage is captured by the concept of customer lifetime value.

Customer lifetime value (CLV) represents the financial worth of a customer to a company over the course of their relationship. The concept explicitly considers a customer's product or service *usage rate*, loyalty to a company that provides them, and the company's cost to serve that customer over time, be it months or years. Customer lifetime value is useful in comparing the financial worth of heavy versus light users and loyal versus fickle customers. As a rule, loyal heavy users have the highest customer lifetime value consistent with the *80/20 rule* described earlier.

As a recent purchaser of a Wendy's restaurant, you are interested in the customer lifetime value of an average Wendy's customer.[17] The most common approach for calculating customer lifetime value is shown below:

$$\text{Customer lifetime value} = \$\ \text{Margin} \times \frac{\text{retention rate }\%}{1 + \text{Discount rate }\% - \text{Retention rate }\%}$$

The *$ Margin* for an average Wendy's customer is $132. This figure is the difference between the average Wendy's customer revenue per year (about $240) and the average cost to serve this customer (about $108 per year for food, packaging, labor, and related customer service expenses).

The *Retention rate %* for an average Wendy's customer is 78 percent. This figure represents the average percentage of Wendy's customers who continue to patronize a Wendy's restaurant annually. A 78 percent retention rate means that 78 out of 100 customers who patronize a Wendy's restaurant in one year will do so again the next year; 22 customers will not. Incidentally, about 80 percent of Wendy's restaurant customers also patronize McDonald's in any given year

The *Discount rate %* for a Wendy's restaurant is about 6 percent. This figure represents the time value of money adjusted for the risk associated with the company's competitive status, its competitive environment, and general economic conditions. The *Discount rate %* is calculated by finance professionals. This figure is necessary to determine the present (today's) dollar value of the future stream of money received from a Wendy's customer's *$ Margin* during the time of the company–customer relationship.

Using these figures, Wendy's average customer lifetime value is:

$$\text{Wendy's average customer lifetime value} = \$132 \times \frac{0.78}{1 + 0.06 - 0.78} = \$368$$

The average customer lifetime value of $368 represents a blend of heavy, medium, and light users of fast food as described in Figure 9–5. It also includes a mixture of customers who treat Wendy's as their sole, primary, and secondary restaurant as shown in Figure 9–6. In short, customer lifetime value puts a dollar value on consumer consumption behavior and brand (restaurant) preference. This average can be compared to that of major competitors as well using publicly available information as shown in the Applying Marketing Metrics box.[18]

Variables to Use in Forming Segments for Wendy's To analyze your Wendy's customers, you need to identify which variables to use to segment them. Because the restaurant is located near a large urban university, the most logical starting point for segmentation is really behavioral: Are the prospective customers students or nonstudents?

To segment the students, you could try a variety of (1) geographic variables, such as city or zip code; (2) demographic variables, such as gender, age, year in school, or college major; or (3) psychographic variables, such as personality or needs. But none of these variables really meets the five criteria listed previously—particularly, the fifth criterion about leading to a doable marketing action to reach the various segments. The behavioral basis of segmentation for the "students" segment really combines two variables: (1) where students live and (2) when they are on campus. This results in four "student" segments:

- Students living in dormitories (residence halls, sororities, fraternities).
- Students living near the university in apartments.
- Day commuter students living outside the area.
- Night commuter students living outside the area.

The three main segments of "nonstudents" include:

- Faculty and staff members who work at the university.
- People who live in the area but aren't connected with the university.
- People who work in the area but aren't connected with the university.

People in each of these nonstudent segments aren't quite as similar as those in the student segments, which makes them harder to reach with a marketing program or action. Think about (1) whether the needs of all these segments are different and (2) how various advertising media can be used to reach these groups effectively.

Segmenting Organizational (Business) Markets A number of variables can be used to segment organizational (business) markets. For example, a product manager at Xerox

Applying **Marketing Metrics**

What Is the Lifetime Value of a McDonald's and Burger King Customer?

As a recent purchaser of a Wendy's restaurant, you are interested in comparing the customer lifetime values of major competitors. This information will be helpful as a benchmark.

Your Challenge

Using publicly available information in *QSR (Quick Service Restaurant) Magazine,* trade publications such as Simmons Research, and company annual reports, you have estimated the average customer lifetime value of $368 for a Wendy's restaurant. Using these same sources, you can estimate customer lifetime values for McDonald's and Burger King.

Recall from the text, the factors used in computing customer lifetime value (CLV) are:

$$\text{Customer lifetime value} = \$\text{ Margin} \times \frac{\text{Retention rate \%}}{1 + \text{Discount rate \%} - \text{Retention rate \%}}$$

Your Findings

Your findings are shown in the following table. It is immediately clear why McDonald's is the dominant restaurant among its competitors. Its average annual customer revenue ($312) and retention rate (88 percent) far exceed comparable figures for Wendy's and Burger King. Its customer lifetime value is $908. Interestingly, McDonald's customer cost of service as a percent of customer revenue per year is highest among the three major competitors.

The fact that McDonald's is the sole or primary restaurant for 38 percent of its customers is reflected in its retention rate. Also, McDonald's probably serves a higher percentage of heavy fast-food users given its high average customer revenue.

Your Actions

Your findings highlight the importance of two variables affected by marketing actions; namely, average customer revenue and customer retention. Targeting heavy users and delivering a positive customer experience with an attractive menu and service at the point of sale are critical in building a customer base with a high lifetime value.

Company	Revenue/ Year	Cost of Service	$Margin	Retention Rate %	Discount Rate %	CLV
McDonald's	$312	$147	$165	88%	4%	$908
Burger King	$225	$ 95	$130	73%	7%	$279

responsible for its new line of multifunction color printers (MFPs) might use these segmentation bases and corresponding variables:

- *Geographic segmentation*: *Statistical area*. Firms located in a metropolitan statistical area might receive a personal sales call, whereas those in a micropolitan statistical area might be contacted by telephone.
- *Demographic segmentation*: *NAICS code*. Firms categorized by the North American Industry Classification System (NAICS) code as manufacturers that deal with customers throughout the world might have different document printing needs than retailers or lawyers serving local customers.
- *Demographic segmentation*: *Number of employees*. The size of the firm is related to the volume of digital documents produced, so firms with varying numbers of employees might be specific target markets for different Xerox MFPs.
- *Behavioral segmentation*: *Usage rate*. Similar to this segmentation variable for consumer markets, features are often of major importance in organizational markets. So Xerox can target organizations needing fast printing, copying, faxing, and scanning in color—the benefits and features emphasized in the ad for its Xerox WorkCentre 4265 Multifunction Printer.

What variables might Xerox use to segment organizational markets to respond to a firm's color copying needs? For the possible answer and related marketing actions, see the text.
Source: Xerox

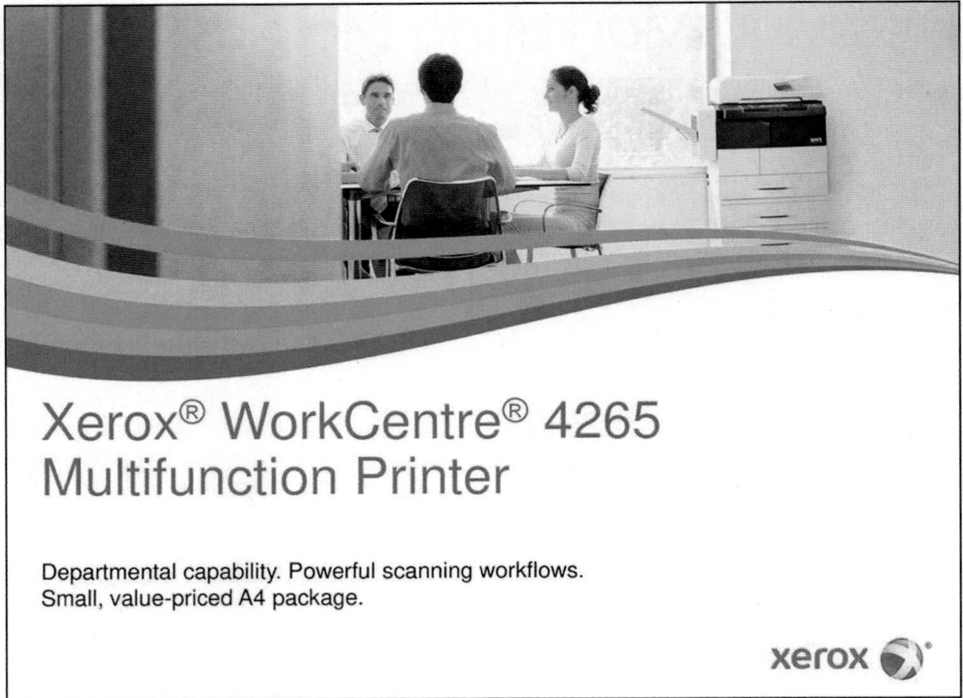

LEARNING REVIEW

9-3. The process of segmenting and targeting markets is a bridge between which two marketing activities?

9-4. What is the difference between the demographic and behavioral bases of market segmentation?

VIDEO 9-2
Dave's Hot 'N Juicy Ad
kerin.tv/15e/v9-2

Step 2: Group Products to Be Sold into Categories

What does your Wendy's restaurant sell? Of course you are selling individual products such as Frostys, hamburgers, and fries. But for marketing purposes you're really selling combinations of individual products that become a "meal." This distinction is critical, so let's discuss both (1) individual Wendy's products and (2) groupings of Wendy's products.

Individual Wendy's Products When Dave Thomas founded Wendy's in 1969, he offered only four basic items: "Hot 'N Juicy" hamburgers (now called Dave's hamburgers), Frosty Dairy Desserts (Frostys), french fries, and soft drinks. Since then, Wendy's has introduced many new products and innovations to compete for customers' fast-food dollars. Some of these are shown in Figure 9–6. New products include baked potatoes, fresh-made salads, the Baconator, chili cheese fries, and a Peppercorn Mushroom Melt sandwich. But there are also nonproduct innovations to increase consumer convenience like drive-thru services and the Wendy's mobile app.

Figure 9–6 also shows that each product or innovation is not targeted equally to all market segments based on gender, needs, or university affiliation. The cells in Figure 9–6 labeled "P" represent Wendy's primary target market segments when it introduced each product or innovation. The boxes labeled "S" represent the secondary target market segments that also bought these products or used these innovations. In some cases, Wendy's discovered that large numbers of people in a segment not originally targeted for a particular product or innovation bought or used it anyway.

MARKET SEGMENT		PRODUCT OR INNOVATION								
GENERAL	GROUP WITH NEED	HOT 'N JUICY HAMBURGER (1969)	DRIVE-THRU (1970)	BAKED POTATO (1983)	SUPER VALUE MEALS (1989)	FRESH-MADE SALADS (2002)	BACONATOR® (2007)	CHILI CHEESE FRIES (2012)	MY WENDY'S MOBILE APP (2015)	PEPPERCORN MUSHROOM MELT (2019)
GENDER	Male	P	P	P	P	S	P	P	P	P
	Female			P		P		P	P	P
NEEDS	Price/Value				P	S				
	Health-Conscious			S		P				P
	Convenience	S	P	P		S	P	P	P	S
	Meat Lovers	P			S		S			
UNIVERSITY AFFILIATION	Affiliated (students, faculty, staff)	P	S	P	P	P	S	P	P	P
	Nonaffiliated (residents, workers)	S	P	S	S	S	P	S	S	S

Key: P = Primary market; S = Secondary market

(Photos): Source: Wendy's International, LLC

FIGURE 9–6
Wendy's new products and other innovations target specific market segments based on a customer's gender, needs, or university affiliation.

Groupings of Wendy's Products: Meals Finding a means of grouping the products a firm sells into meaningful categories is as important as grouping customers into segments. If the firm has only one product or service, this isn't a problem. But when it has many, these must be grouped in some way so buyers can relate to them. This is why department stores and supermarkets are organized into product groups, with the departments or aisles containing related merchandise. Likewise, manufacturers organize products into groupings in the catalogs they send to customers.

What are the product groupings for your Wendy's restaurant? It could be the item purchased, such as hamburgers, salads, Frostys, and french fries. This is where judgment–the qualitative aspect of marketing–comes in. Customers really buy an eating experience–a meal occasion that satisfies a need at a particular time of day. So the product groupings that make the most marketing sense are the five "meals" based on the time of day consumers buy them: breakfast, lunch, between-meal snack, dinner, and after-dinner snack. These groupings are more closely related to the way purchases are actually made and permit you to market the entire meal, not just your individual items such as french fries or hamburgers.

Step 3: Develop a Market-Product Grid and Estimate the Size of Markets

LO 9-4
Develop a market-product grid to identify a target market and recommend resulting marketing actions.

As noted earlier in the chapter, a market-product grid is a framework to relate the market segments of potential buyers to products offered or potential marketing actions by an organization. In a complete market-product grid analysis, each cell in the grid can show the estimated market size of a given product sold to a specific market segment. Let's first look at forming a market-product grid for your Wendy's restaurant and then estimate market sizes.

Forming a Market-Product Grid for Wendy's Developing a market-product grid means identifying and labeling the markets (or horizontal rows) and product groupings (or vertical columns), as shown in Figure 9–7 on the next page. From our earlier discussion, we've chosen to

FIGURE 9–7

A market-product grid for your Wendy's fast-food restaurant next to an urban university. The numbers in the grid show the estimated size of the market in each cell, which leads to selecting the shaded target market.

MARKET SEGMENTS		PRODUCT OR INNOVATION				
General	Where They Live	Breakfast	Lunch	Between-Meal Snack	Dinner	After-Dinner Snack
Student	Dormitory	0	1	3	0	3
	Apartment	1	3	3	1	1
	Day Commuter	0	3	2	1	0
	Night Commuter	0	0	1	3	2
Nonstudent	Faculty or Staff	0	3	1	1	0
	Live in Area	0	1	2	2	1
	Work in Area	1	3	0	1	0

Key: 3 = Large market; 2 = Medium market; 1 = Small market; and 0 = No market

divide the market segments into students versus nonstudents, with subdivisions of each. The columns—or "products"—are really the meals (or eating occasions) customers enjoy at the restaurant.

Estimating Market Sizes for Wendy's Now the size of the market in each cell (the unique market-product combination) of the market-product grid must be estimated. For your Wendy's restaurant, this involves estimating the sales of each kind of meal expected to be sold to each student and nonstudent market segment.

The market size estimates in Figure 9-7 vary from a large market ("3") to no market at all ("0") for each cell in the market-product grid. These may be simple guesstimates if you don't have the time or money to conduct formal marketing research (as discussed in Chapter 8). But even such estimates of the size of specific markets using a market-product grid are helpful in determining which target market segments to select and which product groupings to offer.

Step 4: Select Target Markets

A firm must take care to choose its target market segments carefully. If it picks too narrow a set of segments, it may fail to reach the volume of sales and profits it needs. If it selects too broad a set of segments, it may spread its marketing efforts so thinly that the extra expense exceeds the increased sales and profits.

Wendy's has been aggressive in introducing new menu items—such as its Bacon Maple Chicken sandwich—to appeal to fast-food customers.

Source: Wendy's International, LLC

Criteria to Use in Selecting the Target Segments Two kinds of criteria in the market segmentation process are those used to (1) divide the market into segments (discussed earlier) and (2) actually pick the target segments. Even experienced marketing executives often confuse them. Five criteria can be used to select the target segments for your Wendy's restaurant:

- *Market size.* The estimated size of the market in the segment is an important factor in deciding whether it's worth going after. There is really no market for breakfasts among dormitory students with meal plans, so you should not devote any marketing effort toward reaching this tiny segment. In your market-product grid (Figure 9-7), this market segment is given a "0" to indicate there is no market.

- *Expected growth*. Although the size of the market in the segment may be small now, perhaps it is growing significantly or is expected to grow in the future. Sales of fast-food meals eaten outside the restaurants are projected to exceed those eaten inside. And Wendy's has been shown to be the fast-food leader in average time to serve a drive-thru order—faster than McDonald's. This speed and convenience is potentially very important to night commuters in adult education programs.
- *Competitive position*. Is there a lot of competition in the segment now or is there likely to be in the future? The less competition, the more attractive the segment is. For example, if the college dormitories announce a new policy of "no meals on weekends," this segment is suddenly more promising for your restaurant. Wendy's recently introduced the "My Wendy's" mobile app for ordering and making payments at its restaurants to keep up with a similar service at Burger King.
- *Cost of reaching the segment*. A segment that is inaccessible to a firm's marketing actions should not be pursued. For example, the few nonstudents who live in the area may not be reachable with ads in newspapers or other media. As a result, you should not waste money trying to advertise to them.
- *Compatibility with the organization's objectives and resources*. If your Wendy's restaurant doesn't yet have the cooking equipment to make breakfasts and has a policy against spending more money on restaurant equipment, then don't try to reach the breakfast segment. As is often the case in marketing decisions, a particular segment may appear attractive according to some criteria and very unattractive according to others.

Choose the Wendy's Segments Ultimately, a marketing executive has to use these criteria to choose the segments for special marketing efforts. As shown in Figure 9–7, let's assume you've written off the breakfast product grouping for two reasons: It's too small a market and it's incompatible with your objectives and resources. In terms of competitive position and cost of reaching the segment, you focus on the four student segments and *not* the three nonstudent segments (although you're certainly not going to turn their business away!). This combination of market-product segments—your target market—is shaded in Figure 9–7.

Step 5: Take Marketing Actions to Reach Target Markets

The purpose of developing a market-product grid is to trigger marketing actions to increase sales and profits. This means that someone must develop and execute an action plan in the form of a marketing program.

Your Immediate Wendy's Segmentation Strategy With your Wendy's restaurant, you've already reached one significant decision: There is a limited market for breakfast, so you won't open for business until 10:00 A.M. In fact, Wendy's first attempt at a breakfast menu was a disaster and was discontinued. However, that strategy has changed yet again with a limited breakfast menu now being offered in some locations.

Another essential decision is where and what meals to advertise to reach specific market segments. If you choose three segments for special attention (Figure 9–8 on the next page), advertising actions to reach them might include:

- *Day commuters* (an entire market segment). Run ads inside commuter buses and purchase signage near parking lots or in parking structures used by day commuters. These ads promote all the meals at your restaurant to the day commuter segment of students, a horizontal orange row through the product groupings or "meals" in your market-product grid.
- *Between-meal snacks* (directed to all four student market segments). To promote eating during this downtime for your restaurant, offer "Ten percent off all purchases between 2:00 and 4:30 P.M. during spring semester." This ad in the school newspaper promotes a single meal to all four student segments, a vertical blue column through the market-product grid.

FIGURE 9–8 Advertising actions to market various meals to a range of possible market segments of students.

MARKET SEGMENTS	PRODUCT GROUPINGS: MEAL OCCASION			
Behavioral: Where They Live	Lunch	Between-Meal Snack	Dinner	After-Dinner Snack
Dormitory Students	1	3	0	3
Apartment Students	3	3	1	1
Day Commuter Students	3	2	1	0
Night Commuter Students	0	1	3	2

Ads in buses: signage near parking lots and in parking structures.

Ad campaign: "10% off all purchases between 2:00 and 4:30 P.M. during spring semester"

Ads distributed by campus ambassadors, bookstore signage, and targeted mobile ads.

Key: 3 = Large market; 2 = Medium market; 1 = Small market; and 0 = No market

- *Dinners to night commuters* (selecting a unique market-product combination). The most focused of all three campaigns, this strategy promotes a single meal to the single segment of night commuter students shaded green. The campaign uses ads distributed by campus ambassadors, bookstore signage, and targeted mobile ads. To encourage eating dinner at Wendy's, offer a free Frosty when the person buys a meal between 5:00 and 8:00 P.M. using the drive-thru window.

Depending on how your advertising actions work, you can repeat, modify, or drop them and design new campaigns for other segments you deem are worth the effort. This advertising example is just a small piece of a complete marketing program for your Wendy's restaurant.

Keeping an Eye on Competition Competitors will not be sitting still, so in running your Wendy's you must be aware of their strategies as well. McDonald's, for example, continues to expand its popular all-day breakfast menu, and recently added Donut Sticks. In addition, McDonald's is testing Cheesy Bacon Fries, self-order kiosks, and artificial intelligence technology in its drive-thru displays to show menu items based on the time of day and weather. Meanwhile, Burger King launched its BK Cafe Subscription app to allow you to pick up a coffee every day for $5 per month, and is testing its Impossible Burger in response to a growing interest in plant-based meatless burger options.[19]

There's always plenty of competition in the hamburger business. Five Guys Burgers and Fries has grown to more than 1,500 outlets.

ZUMA Press, Inc/Alamy

New or small hamburger chains such as The Habit Burger Grill, Bobby's Burger Palace, Whataburger, Bareburger, and Larkburger are growing. For example, in 1986, a Virginia husband-and-wife team started the Five Guys Burgers and Fries hamburger restaurant and 15 years later had only five restaurants in the Washington, DC, area. But from 2003 to 2019, Five Guys exploded, with almost 1,500 locations in the United States, Canada, the U.K., and Europe, and another 1,500 new restaurants planned. Some of its points of difference: simple menu and decor, modest prices, only fresh ground beef (none frozen), and a trans-fat-free menu (cooking with peanut oil). But who's keeping track? The Big Three of McDonald's, Burger King, and Wendy's certainly are.[20]

In addition to competition from traditional hamburger chains like Five Guys, all three are responding aggressively to reach the new "fast-casual" market segment. These customers want healthier food and lower prices in sit-down restaurants–a market segment being successfully targeted by fast-casual restaurants like Chipotle Mexican Grill, Noodles and Company, and Panera Bread. Then, between the fast-food options and the fast-casual options is Chick-fil-A, which positions itself as "premium fast food," and will likely surpass Burger King and Wendy's in sales in the near future.[21]

Finally, a new source of competition is emerging from a variety of chains that aren't necessarily classified as restaurants at all. These include convenience store chains like 7-Eleven, coffee shops like Starbucks, smoothie outlets like Jamba Juice, and gas stations with prepared and reheatable packaged food.[22] Many of these outlets are now selling food items and trying to gain market share from the Big Three.

Future Strategies for Your Wendy's Restaurant Changing customer tastes and competition mean you must alter your strategies when necessary. This involves looking at (1) what Wendy's headquarters is doing, (2) what competitors are doing, and (3) what might be changing in the area served by your restaurant.

Wendy's recently introduced aggressive new marketing programs that include:[23]

- Announcing its partnership with the NextGen Consortium to address single-use food packaging waste and its *Squarely Sustainable* approach to using sustainable practices and materials.
- Advertising its use of fresh beef that has not been frozen; switching to eggs from cage-free hens; and testing new menu items such as a Bacon Maple Chicken sandwich.
- Increasing convenience for customers by adding more than 1,000 self-service kiosks; and testing fast pass drive-thru for orders placed on a mobile device.

The Wendy's strategy has been remarkably successful, alternating with Burger King as the number 2 or number 3 burger chain in terms of sales behind McDonald's. In addition, a recent *Consumer Reports* survey of the best and worst fast-food restaurants in America ranked Wendy's burgers higher than McDonald's, Burger King, and three other burger chain options.[24]

With Wendy's corporate plans and new actions from competitors, maybe you'd better rethink your market segmentation decisions on hours of operation. Also, if new businesses have moved into your area, what about a new strategy to reach people that work in the area? Or you might consider a new promotion for the night owls and early birds–the 12:00 A.M. to 5:00 A.M. customers.

VIDEO 9-3
Apple's 1984 Super Bowl Ad
kerin.tv/15e/v9-3

Apple's Ever-Changing Segmentation Strategy Steve Jobs and Steve Wozniak didn't realize they were developing today's multibillion-dollar PC industry when they invented the Apple I in the garage of Jobs' childhood home in California. However, when the Apple II was displayed at a computer trade show, consumers loved it and Apple Computer was born. Typical of young companies, Apple focused on its products and had little concern for its markets. Its creative, young engineers were often likened to "Boy Scouts without adult supervision."[25] Yet the Apple Macintosh revolutionized computers, and its 1984 Super Bowl TV ad is generally recognized as the best TV ad in history.

How has Apple moved from its 1977 Apple II to today's iMac? The Marketing Matters box provides insights.
SSPL via Getty Images

Steve Jobs detailed his vision for Apple by describing a market segmentation strategy that he called the "Apple Product Matrix." This strategy consisted of developing two general types of computer products (desktops and laptops) targeted at two market segments–the consumer and professional sectors.

In most segmentation situations, a single product does not fit into an exclusive market niche. Rather, product lines and market segments overlap. So Apple's market segmentation strategy enables it to offer different products to meet the needs of different market segments, as shown in the Marketing Matters box.

Marketing Matters

Technology

Apple's Segmentation Strategy—Camp Runamok No Longer

Camp Runamok was the nickname given to Apple in its early years because the innovative company had no coherent series of product lines directed at identifiable market segments. Today, Apple has targeted its various lines of Macintosh computers at specific market segments, as shown in the accompanying market-product grid.

The market-product grid shifts as a firm's strategy changes, so the one here is based on Apple's current computer products. The grid suggests the market segmentation strategy Apple is using to compete in the digital age.

MARKETS		COMPUTER PRODUCTS						
SECTOR	SEGMENT	MacBook	MacBook Air	MacBook Pro	iMac	iMac Pro	Mac Mini	Mac Pro
CONSUMER	Individuals	✓	✓		✓		✓	
	Small/ home office		✓	✓	✓	✓		
	Students	✓	✓		✓		✓	
	Teachers			✓	✓			
PROFESSIONAL	Medium/ large business		✓	✓	✓	✓		✓
	Creative			✓	✓	✓		✓
	College faculty		✓	✓	✓			
	College staff				✓	✓		

(Photos): Source: Apple Inc.

What market-product synergies does Apple's iMac satisfy? Read the text to find out.
Source: Apple Inc.

Market-Product Synergies: A Balancing Act

Recognizing opportunities for key synergies–that is, efficiencies–is vital to success in selecting target market segments and making marketing decisions. Market-product grids illustrate where such synergies can be found. How? Let's consider Apple's market-product grid in the Marketing Matters box and examine the difference between marketing synergies and product synergies shown there.

- *Marketing synergies*. Running horizontally across the grid, each row represents an opportunity for efficiency in terms of a market segment. Were Apple to focus on just one group of consumers, such as the medium/large business segment, its marketing efforts could be streamlined. Apple would not have to spend time learning about the buying habits of students or college faculty. So it could probably create a single ad to reach the medium/large business target segment (the yellow row), highlighting only those products it would need to worry about developing: the MacBook Air, the MacBook Pro, the iMac, the iMacPro, and the Mac Pro. Although clearly not Apple's strategy today, new firms often focus only on a single customer segment.

- *Product synergies*. Running vertically down the market-product grid, each column represents an opportunity for efficiency in research and development (R&D) and production. If Apple wanted to simplify its product line, reduce R&D and production expenses, and manufacture only one computer, which might it choose? Based on the market-product grid, Apple might do well to focus on the iMac (the orange column), because every segment purchases it.

Marketing synergies often come at the expense of product synergies because a single customer segment will likely require a variety of products, each of which will have to be designed and manufactured. The company saves money on marketing but spends more on production. Conversely, if product synergies are emphasized, marketing will have to address the concerns of a wide variety of consumers, which costs more time and money. Marketing managers responsible for developing a company's product line must balance both product and marketing synergies as they try to increase the company's profits.

LEARNING REVIEW

9-5. What factor is estimated or measured for each of the cells in a market-product grid?

9-6. What are some criteria used to decide which segments to choose for targets?

9-7. How are marketing and product synergies different in a market-product grid?

POSITIONING THE PRODUCT

LO 9-5
Explain how marketing managers position products in the marketplace.

When a company introduces a new product, a decision critical to its long-term success is how prospective buyers view it in relation to those products offered by its competitors. **Product positioning** refers to the place a product occupies in consumers' minds based on important attributes relative to competitive products. By understanding where consumers see a company's product or brand today, a marketing manager can seek to change its future position in their minds. This requires **product repositioning**, or *changing* the place a product occupies in a consumer's mind relative to competitive products.

Two Approaches to Product Positioning

Marketers follow two main approaches to positioning a product in the market. *Head-to-head positioning* involves competing directly with competitors on similar product attributes in the same target market. Using this strategy, Dollar Rent A Car competes directly with Avis and Hertz.

Differentiation positioning involves seeking a less-competitive, smaller market niche in which to locate a brand. Whole Foods, for example, differentiates itself from large supermarket chains with its "wholesome" and organic selection of products, unique store design, local ambiance, and promotion of a "greener" lifestyle.

Writing a Product Positioning Statement

Marketing managers often convert their product positioning ideas into a succinct written positioning statement. These positioning statements are derived from the company's *customer value proposition* described in Chapter 2 which directs the company's overall marketing strategy. Positioning statements apply to specific products. Ideally, a product positioning statement identifies the target market and needs satisfied, the product (service) class or category in which the organization's offering competes, and the offering's unique benefits or attributes provided. The positioning statement is used not only internally within the marketing department but also outside the organization, for example in working with research and development engineers or advertising agencies.[26] Here is the Volvo product positioning statement for the North American passenger car market:

> ***For upscale American families, who desire a carefree driving experience (target market and need), Volvo is a premium-priced automobile (product category) that offers the utmost in safety and dependability (benefits).***

More "zip" for chocolate milk? The text and Figure 9–9 describe how American dairies have successfully repositioned chocolate milk to appeal to adults.
Editorial Image, LLC/ McGraw-Hill

This positioning statement directs Volvo's North American passenger car marketing strategy and focuses its product development efforts, such as the inclusion of side door airbags in its automobiles. The statement also directs Volvo's passenger car marketing communications message. So Volvo advertising stresses safety and dependability–the two benefits that underlie its award-winning "Volvo for life" slogan. Not surprisingly, this positioning statement for passenger cars is derived from Volvo's customer value proposition that focuses on "putting people first." The formal positioning statement for Volvo's North American trucks would be different due to the target market and need, product category (trucks), and benefits.

Product Positioning Using Perceptual Maps

A key to positioning a product or brand effectively is discovering the perceptions in the minds of potential customers by taking four steps:

1. Identify the important attributes for a product or brand class.
2. Discover how target customers rate competing products or brands with respect to these attributes.
3. Discover where the company's product or brand is on these attributes in the minds of potential customers.
4. Reposition the company's product or brand in the minds of potential customers.

As shown in Figure 9–9, from these data it is possible to develop a **perceptual map**, a means of displaying in two dimensions the location of products or brands in the minds of consumers. This enables a manager to see how consumers perceive competing products or brands, as well as the firm's own product or brand.

A Perceptual Map to Reposition Chocolate Milk for Adults

Recently, U.S. dairies decided to reposition chocolate milk in the minds of American adults to increase its sales. This is how dairies repositioned chocolate milk for American adults using the four steps listed above:

1. *Identify the important attributes (or scales) for adult drinks.* Research reveals the key attributes adults use to judge various drinks are (*a*) low versus high nutrition and (*b*) children's drinks versus adult drinks, as shown by the two axes in Figure 9–9.
2. *Discover how adults see various competing drinks.* Locate various adult drinks on these axes, as shown in Figure 9–9.
3. *Discover how adults see chocolate milk.* Figure 9–9 shows adults see chocolate milk as moderately nutritious (on the vertical axis) but as mainly a child's drink (on the horizontal axis).
4. *Reposition chocolate milk to make it more appealing to adults.* What actions did U.S. dairies take to increase sales? They repositioned chocolate milk to the location of the red star shown in the perceptual map in Figure 9–9.

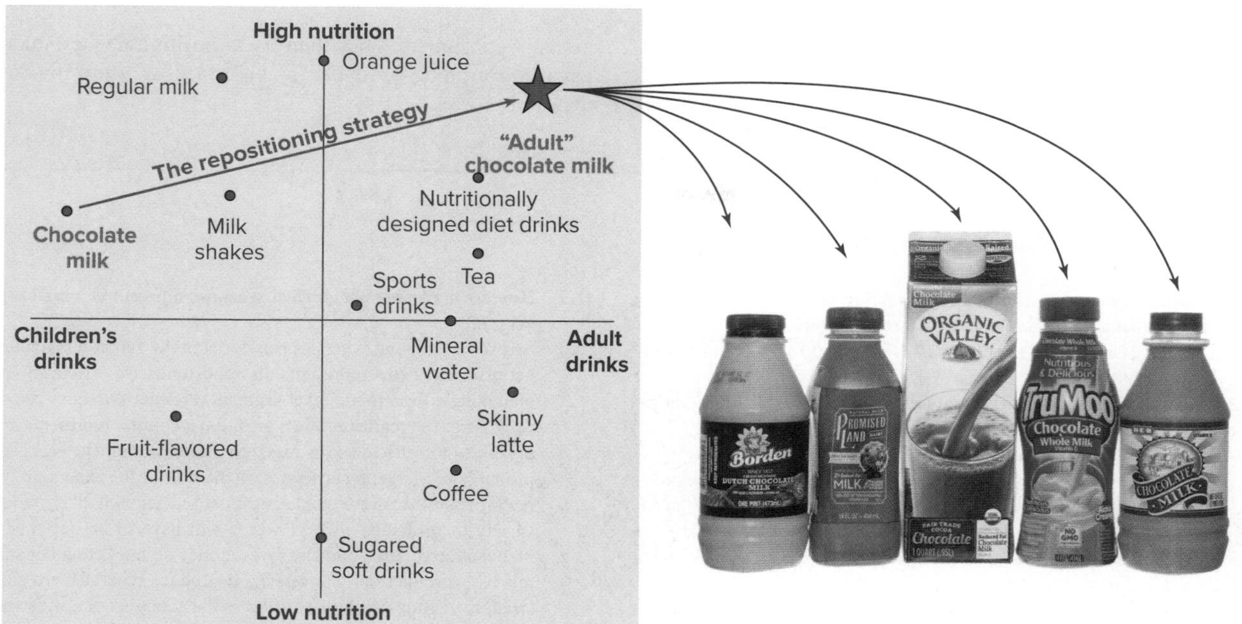

FIGURE 9–9 The strategy American dairies are using to reposition chocolate milk to reach adults: Have adults view chocolate milk as both more nutritional and more "adult."

(Photo): Editorial Image, LLC/McGraw-Hill

The dairies' arguments are nutritionally powerful. For women, chocolate milk provides calcium, critically important in female diets. And dieters get a more filling, nutritious beverage than with a soft drink for about the same calories. The result: Chocolate milk sales increased dramatically, much of it because of adult consumption.[27] Part of this is due to giving chocolate milk "nutritional respectability" for adults, but another part is due to the innovative packaging that enables many new chocolate milk containers to fit in a car's cup holders.

LEARNING REVIEW

9-8. What is the difference between product positioning and product repositioning?

9-9. Why do marketers use perceptual maps in product positioning decisions?

LEARNING OBJECTIVES REVIEW

LO 9-1 *Explain what market segmentation is and when to use it.*
Market segmentation involves aggregating prospective buyers into groups that (*a*) have common needs and (*b*) will respond similarly to a marketing action. Organizations go to the expense of segmenting their markets when it increases their sales, profits, and ability to serve customers better.

LO 9-2 *Identify the five steps involved in segmenting and targeting markets.*
Step 1 is to group potential buyers into segments. Buyers within a segment should have similar characteristics to each other and respond similarly to marketing actions like a new product or a lower price. Step 2 involves putting related products to be sold into meaningful groups. In step 3, organizations develop a market-product grid with estimated sizes of markets in each of the market-product cells of the resulting table. Step 4 involves selecting the target market segments on which the organization should focus. Finally, step 5 involves taking marketing mix actions—often in the form of a marketing program—to reach the target market segments.

LO 9-3 *Recognize the bases used to segment consumer and organizational (business) markets.*
The four bases used to segment consumer markets are: geographic, demographic, psychographic, and behavioral. Organizational markets use the same bases except for the psychographic one.

LO 9-4 *Develop a market-product grid to identify a target market and recommend resulting marketing actions.*
Organizations use five key criteria to segment markets, whose groupings appear in the rows of the market-product grid. Groups of related products appear in the columns. After estimating the size of the market in each cell in the grid, they select the target market segments on which to focus. They then identify marketing mix actions—often in a marketing program—to reach the target market most efficiently.

LO 9-5 *Explain how marketing managers position products in the marketplace.*
Marketing managers often locate competing products on two-dimensional perceptual maps to visualize the products in the minds of consumers. They then try to position new products or reposition existing products in this space to attain maximum sales and profits.

LEARNING REVIEW ANSWERS

9-1 **Market segmentation involves aggregating prospective buyers into groups that have two key characteristics. What are they?**
Answer: The groups should (1) have common needs and (2) respond similarly to a marketing action.

9-2 **In terms of market segments and products, what are the three market segmentation strategies?**
Answer: The three market segmentation strategies are: (1) one product and multiple market segments; (2) multiple products and multiple market segments; and (3) "segments of one," or mass customization–the next step beyond build-to-order.

9-3 **The process of segmenting and targeting markets is a bridge between which two marketing activities?**
Answer: identifying market needs and executing the marketing program

9-4 **What is the difference between the demographic and behavioral bases of market segmentation?**
Answer: Demographic segmentation is based on some objective physical (gender, race), measurable (age, income), or other classification attribute (birth era, occupation) of prospective customers. Behavioral segmentation is based on some observable actions or attitudes by prospective customers–such as where they buy, what benefits they seek, how frequently they buy, and why they buy.

9-5 **What factor is estimated or measured for each of the cells in a market-product grid?**
Answer: Each cell in the grid shows the estimated market size of a given product sold to a specific market segment.

9-6 **What are some criteria used to decide which segments to choose for targets?**
Answer: Possible criteria include market size, expected growth, competitive position, cost of reaching the segment, and compatibility with the organization's objectives and resources.

9-7 **How are marketing and product synergies different in a market-product grid?**
Answer: Marketing synergies run horizontally across a market-product grid. Each row represents an opportunity for efficiency in the marketing efforts to a market segment. Product synergies run vertically down the market-product grid. Each column represents an opportunity for efficiency in research and development (R&D) and production. Marketing synergies often come at the expense of product synergies because a single customer segment will likely require a variety of products, each of which will have to be designed and manufactured. The company saves money on marketing but spends more on production. Conversely, if product synergies are emphasized, marketing will have to address the concerns of a wide variety of consumers, which costs more time and money.

9-8 **What is the difference between product positioning and product repositioning?**
Answer: Product positioning refers to the place a product occupies in consumers' minds based on important attributes relative to competitive products. Product repositioning involves changing the place a product occupies in a consumer's mind relative to competitive products.

9-9 **Why do marketers use perceptual maps in product positioning decisions?**
Answer: Perceptual maps are a means of displaying in two dimensions the location of products or brands in the minds of consumers. Marketers use perceptual maps to see how consumers perceive competing products or brands as well as their own product or brand. Then they can develop marketing actions to move their product or brand to the ideal position.

FOCUSING ON KEY TERMS

80/20 rule p. 244
customer lifetime value (CLV) p. 245
market segmentation p. 237
market-product grid p. 238
perceptual map p. 256
product differentiation p. 238
product positioning p. 255
product repositioning p. 255
usage rate p. 243

APPLYING MARKETING KNOWLEDGE

1 What variables might be used to segment these consumer markets? (*a*) smartphones, (*b*) frozen pizzas, (*c*) breakfast cereals, and (*d*) soft drinks.

2 What variables might be used to segment these industrial markets? (*a*) cleaning supplies, (*b*) photocopiers, (*c*) production control systems, and (*d*) car rental agencies.

3 In Figure 9–7, the dormitory market segment includes students living in college-owned residence halls, sororities, and fraternities. What market needs are common to these students that justify combining them into a single segment in studying the market for your Wendy's restaurant?

4 You may disagree with the estimates of market size given for the rows in the market-product grid in Figure 9–7. Estimate the market size, and give a brief justification for these market segments: (*a*) dormitory

students, (*b*) day commuters, and (*c*) people who work in the area.

5 Suppose you want to increase revenues for your fast-food restaurant even further. Referring to Figure 9-8, what advertising actions might you take to increase revenues from (*a*) dormitory students, (*b*) dinners, and (*c*) after-dinner snacks consumed by night commuter students?

6 Locate these drinks on the perceptual map in Figure 9-9: (*a*) cappuccino, (*b*) beer, and (*c*) soy milk.

BUILDING YOUR MARKETING PLAN

Your marketing plan needs a market-product grid to (*a*) focus your marketing efforts and (*b*) help you create a forecast of sales for the company. Use these steps:

1. Define the market segments (the rows in your grid) using the bases of segmentation used to segment consumer and organizational markets.
2. Define the groupings of related products (the columns in your grid).
3. Form your grid and estimate the size of the market in each market-product cell.
4. Select the target market segments on which to focus your efforts with your marketing program.
5. Use the information and the lost-horse forecasting technique (discussed in Chapter 8) to make a sales forecast (company forecast).
6. Draft your positioning statement.

VIDEO CASE 9 Prince Sports, Inc.: Tennis Racquets for Every Segment

VIDEO 9-4
Prince Sports Video Case
kerin.tv/15e/v9-4

"Over the last decade we've seen a dramatic change in the media to reach consumers," says Linda Glassel, vice president of sports marketing and brand image of Prince Sports, Inc.

PRINCE SPORTS IN TODAY'S CHANGING WORLD

"Today—particularly in reaching younger consumers—we're now focusing so much more on social marketing and social networks, be it Facebook, Twitter, or internationally with Hi5, Bebo, and Orkut," she adds.

Linda Glassel's comments are a snapshot look at what Prince Sports faces in the changing world of tennis in the 21st century.

Prince Sports is a racquet sports company whose portfolio of brands includes Prince (tennis, squash, and badminton), Ektelon (racquetball), and Viking (platform/paddle tennis). Its complete line of tennis products alone is astounding: more than 150 racquet models; more than 50 tennis strings; over 50 footwear models; and countless types of bags, apparel, and other accessories.

Prince prides itself on its history of innovation in tennis—including inventing the first "oversize" and "longbody" racquets, the first "synthetic gut" tennis string, and the first "Natural Foot Shape" tennis shoe. Its challenge today is to continue to innovate to meet the needs of all levels of tennis players.

"One favorable thing for Prince these days is the dramatic growth in tennis participation—higher than it's been in many years," says Nick Skally, senior marketing manager. A recent study by the Sporting Goods Manufacturers Association confirms this point: Tennis participation in the United States was up 43 percent—the fastest-growing traditional individual sport in the country.

TAMING TECHNOLOGY TO MEET PLAYERS' NEEDS

Every tennis player wants the same thing: to play better. But they don't all have the same skills, or the same ability to swing a racquet fast. So adult tennis players fall very broadly into three groups, each with special needs:

- *Those with shorter, slower strokes*. They want maximum power in a lightweight frame.
- *Those with moderate to full strokes*. They want the perfect blend of power and control.
- *Those with longer, faster strokes*. They want greater control with less power.

To satisfy all these needs in one racquet is a big order.

"When we design tennis racquets, it involves an extensive amount of market research on players at all levels," explains Tyler Herring, global business director for performance tennis racquets. Prince's research led it to introduce its breakthrough O^3 technology. "Our O^3 technology solved an inherent contradiction between racquet speed and sweet spot," he says. Never before had a racquet been designed that simultaneously delivers faster racquet speed with a dramatically increased "sweet spot." The "sweet spot" in a racquet is the middle of the frame that gives the most power and consistency when hitting. Recently, Prince introduced its latest evolution of the O^3 platform called EXO^3. Its newly patented design suspends the string bed from the racquet frame–thereby increasing the sweet spot by up to 83 percent while reducing frame vibration up to 50 percent.

SEGMENTING THE TENNIS MARKET

"The three primary market segments for our tennis racquets are our performance line, our recreational line, and our junior line," says Herring. He explains that within each of these segments Prince makes difficult design trade-offs to balance (1) the price a player is willing to pay, (2) what playing features (speed versus spin, sweet spot versus control, and so on) they want, and (3) what technology can be built into the racquet for the price point.

Within each of these three primary market segments, there are at least two subsegments–sometimes overlapping! Figure 1 gives an overview of Prince's market segmentation

MARKET SEGMENTS				PRODUCT FEATURES IN RACQUET		
Main Segments	Subsegments	Segment Characteristics (Skill level, age)	Brand Name	Length (Inches)	Unstrung Weight (Ounces)	Head Size (Sq. in.)
Performance	Precision	For touring professional players wanting great feel, control, and spin	EXO^3 Ignite 95	27.0	11.8	95
	Thunder	For competitive players wanting a bigger sweet spot and added power	EXO^3 Red 95	27.25	9.9	105
Recreational	Small head size	For players looking for a forgiving racquet with added control	AirO Lightning MP	27.0	9.9	100
	Larger head size	For players looking for a larger sweet spot and added power	AirO Maria Lite OS	27.0	9.7	110
Junior	More experienced young players	For ages 8 to 15; somewhat shorter and lighter racquets than high school or adult players	AirO Team Maria 23	23.0	8.1	100
	Beginner	For ages 5 to 11; much shorter and lighter racquets; tennis balls with 50 percent to 75 percent less speed for young beginners	Air Team Maria 19	19.0	7.1	82

FIGURE 1
Prince targets racquets at specific market segments.

strategy and identifies sample racquet models. The three right-hand columns show the design variations of length, unstrung weight, and head size. The figure shows the complexities Prince faces in converting its technology into a racquet with physical features that satisfy players' needs.

DISTRIBUTION AND PROMOTION STRATEGIES

"Prince has a number of different distribution channels—from mass merchants like Walmart and Target, to sporting goods chains, to smaller specialty tennis shops," says Nick Skally. For the large chains, Prince contributes co-op advertising for its in-store circulars, point-of-purchase displays, in-store signage, consumer brochures, and even "space planograms" to help the retailer plan the layout of Prince products in its tennis area. Prince aids for small tennis specialty shops include a supply of demo racquets, detailed catalogs, posters, racquet and string guides, merchandising fixtures, and hardware, such as racquet hooks and footwear shelves, in addition to other items. Prince also provides these shops with "player standees," which are corregated life-size cutouts of professional tennis players.

Consumer Trends/Alamy

Prince reaches tennis players directly through its website (www.princetennis.com), which gives product information, tennis tips, and the latest tennis news. Besides using social networks like Facebook and Twitter, Prince runs ads in regional and national tennis publications and develops advertising campaigns for online sites and broadcast outlets.

In addition to its in-store activities, advertising, and online marketing, Prince invests heavily in its Teaching Pro program. These sponsored teaching pros receive all the latest product information, demo racquets, and equipment from Prince, so they can truly be Prince ambassadors in their community. Aside from their regular lessons, instructors and teaching professionals hold local "Prince Demo events" around the country to give potential customers a hands-on opportunity to see and try various Prince racquets, strings, and grips.

Prince also sponsors over 100 professional tennis players who appear in marquee events such as the four Grand Slam tournaments (Wimbledon and the Australian, French, and U.S. Opens). TV viewers can watch Russia's Maria Sharapova walk onto a tennis court carrying a Prince racquet bag or France's Gaël Monfils hit a service ace using his Prince racquet.

Where is Prince headed in the 21st century? "As a marketer, one of the biggest challenges is staying ahead of the curve," says Glassel. And she stresses, "It's learning, it's studying, it's talking to people who understand where the market is going."[28]

Questions

1 In the 21st century, what trends in the environmental forces (social, economic, technological, competitive, and regulatory) (*a*) work for and (*b*) work against success for Prince Sports in the tennis industry?

2 Because sales of Prince Sports in tennis-related products depend heavily on growth of the tennis industry, what marketing activities might it use in the United States to promote tennis playing?

3 What promotional activities might Prince use to reach (*a*) recreational players and (*b*) junior players?

4 What might Prince do to gain distribution and sales in (*a*) mass merchandisers like Target and Walmart and (*b*) specialty tennis shops?

5 In reaching global markets outside the United States (*a*) what are some criteria that Prince should use to select countries in which to market aggressively, (*b*) what three or four countries meet these criteria best, and (*c*) what are some marketing actions Prince might use to reach these markets?

Chapter Notes

1. Veronika Kero, "How to Answer Zappos CEO Tony Hsieh's Quirky Interview Question," www.cnbc.com, January 25, 2019; Aimee Groth, *The Kingdom of Happiness: Inside Tony Hsieh's Zapponean Utopia* (New York: Touchstone, 2017); Tony Hsieh, *Delivering Happiness* (New York: Hatchette Book Group, 2010); and information from the "About Zappos" section of the Zappos.com website.
2. Greg Bensinger, "How We Shop: Shoppers' Move to Apps Changes Game for Retailers," *The Wall Street Journal,* April 14, 2106, p. B1; Deborah L. Cowles, Jan P. Owens, and Kristen L. Walker, "Ensuring a Good Fit: Fortifying Zappos' Customer Service and User Experience," *International Journal of Integrated Marketing Communications,* Fall 2013, pp. 57–66; and Amanda Green, "Know Thy Customer: Behavioral Tracking Brings New Granularity to Segmentation," *On the Beat,* October 19, 2011, p. 11.
3. Susan Adams, "Seven Lessons from the Failure of Shoes.com," *Forbes.com,* March 17, 2017; Chris Paradixo, "Improving Customer Experience

with Digital Marketing," *Insurance Advocate,* December 22, 2014, p. 18; and quoted in Kimberly Weisal, "A Shine in Their Shoes," *BusinessWeek,* December 5, 2005, p. 84.

4. Dan Percival, "Why Zappos Pays People to Quit," *medium.com*, August 1, 2017; and Duff McDonald, "Zappos.com: Success through Simplicity," *CIO-Insight,* November 10, 2006.

5. Jon Wolske, "Ten Core Values Drive Zappos," *Credit Union Magazine,* July 2014, p. 12; Jena McGregor, "Zappos' Secret: It's an Open Book," *Bloomberg Businessweek,* March 23 and 30, 2009, p. 62; and Jeffrey M. O'Brien, "The 10 Commandments of Zappos," *Fortune,* January 22, 2009; see http://money.cnn.com/2009/01/21/news/companies/obrien_zappos10.fortune and www.zappos.com.

6. Shahira Raineri, "Zappos Embraces Digital Tech, Customer Service for Success," www.thebalancesmb.com, December 16, 2018; Elaine Low, "At Amazon's Zappos, CEO Tony Hsieh Delivers on Being Different," *Investors Business Daily,* August 6, 2016, p. 18; Jennifer Reingold, "The Zappos Experiment," *Fortune,* March 15, 2016, pp. 206–14; and Motoko Rich, "Why Is This Man Smiling?" *The New York Times,* April 10, 2011, pp. ST1, ST10.

7. Dan Pontefract, "What Is Happening at Zappos?" www.forbes.com, May 11, 2015; and Natalie Zmuda, "Marketer of the Year: Zappos," *Advertising Age,* October 20, 2008, p. 36.

8. Eric N. Berkowitz, Roger A. Kerin, and William Rudelius, *Marketing* (St. Louis, MO: Times Mirror/Mosby College Publishing, 1986), pp. 189–91; Sleep Research Institute, the National Sleep Foundation, and the International Sleep Products Association (March 20, 2007); and Frederick G. Crane, Roger A. Kerin, Steven W. Hartley, and William Rudelius, *Marketing,* 8th Canadian ed. (Toronto, Canada: McGraw-Hill Ryerson Ltd., 2011), pp. 229–32.

9. Gigi DeVault, "The History of Procter & Gamble's Brand Strategy," www.thebalancesmb.com, November 30, 2018.

10. John Patrick Pullen, "Hey, Millennials: Here's Where You Can Stream Your Favorite Movies," *Time.com,* April 29, 2015; John Stone, "Disney's Grand Adventure," *Travel Agent,* November 17, 2014, pp. 38, 40; and Jeffrey A. Trachtenberg and Ann Paul Sonne, "Rowling Casts E-Book Spell," *The Wall Street Journal,* June 24, 2011, pp. B1, B2.

11. Jason Lancaster, "What Makes Luxury Cars So Expensive?" *The Huffington Post,* May 19, 2015; and Kathleen Kerwin and Keith Naughton, "Remaking Ford," *BusinessWeek,* October 11, 1999, pp. 132–42.

12. Michael Martinez, "Sedans Make Way for More Utilities, Electrification," *Automotive News*, August 27, 2018, p. 22; Gordon Wyner, "Why Segment?" *Marketing News,* June 2016, pp. 24–25; Doug DeMuro, "Buying a Car: Why Do So Many Options Come in Packages?" www.autotrader.com, June 2015; and "Company Timeline," Ford website, https://corporate.ford.com/history.html.

13. Trefis Team, "What's Driving Ann Taylor's Store Count?" *Forbes,* July 17, 2014; 2010 *Ann Taylor Annual Report;* and selected press releases.

14. "Neighborhood Markets Show Ability to Drive Sales," *MMR,* December 19, 2016, p. 59; "Discounters Aim to Extend Reach with Small Formats," *Chain Drug Review,* April 27, 2015, p. 75; and Jonathan Hipp, "The Strategy behind Walmart Neighborhood Market Stores," *GlobeSt.com,* http://www.globest.com/blogs/netleaseinsider/netlease/TheStrategy-Behind-Walmart-Neighborhood-Market-Stores-358653–1.html, June 5, 2015.

15. The relation of these criteria to implementation is discussed in Jacqueline Dawley, "Making Connections: Enhance the Implementation of Value of Attitude-Based Segmentation," *Marketing Research,* Summer 2006, pp. 16–22.

16. The discussion of fast-food trends and market share is based on Simmons National Consumer Survey Spring 2014 Adult Survey OneView[SM] Crosstabulation Report, Simmons Research LLC, 2017.

17. The average revenue and retention data are provided in "Report: Chick-fil-A, McDonald's Are Winning Fast Food's Battle," *QSR Magazine*, January 5, 2019, pp. 17–21. The data for Wendy's gross profit margin and discount rate are provided in "Wendy's Co. Gross Margin %" and "The Wendy's Co. WACC," www.gurufocus.com, accessed January 8, 2019.

18. The average revenue and retention data are provided in "Report: Chick-fil-A, McDonald's Are Winning Fast Food's Battle." The data for Wendy's gross profit margin and discount rate are provided in "Wendy's Co. Gross Margin %" and "The Wendy's Co. WACC," accessed January 8, 2019; and "Fast Food Industry Analysis 2019: Costs and Trends," www.franchisehelp.com, accessed January 10, 2019.

19. Chris Morris, "McDonald's Adds Donut Sticks to Breakfast Menu," www.fortune.com, February 11, 2019; Bill Peters, "McDonald's Biggest Deal Since Chipotle Is for This Artificial Intelligence Tech," *Investor's Business Daily*, March 26, 2019, p. 1; Leslie Patton, "McDonald's Is Buying a Decision-Logic Tech Company to Personalize Your Drive-Thru Experience," www.fortune.com, March 26, 2019; Jonathan Maze, "Burger King Is Testing an Impossible Whopper," www.restaurantbusinessonline.com, April 1, 2019; and Caitlyn Hitt, "Burger King Is Taking on McDonald's and Starbucks with a New $5/Month Coffee Subscription," www.thrillist.com, March 15, 2019.

20. Beth Mattson-Teig, "Burger Battle," *Shopping Center Today,* February 2017, pp. 20–21; Jack Dickey and Bill Saporito, "Beefed Up," *Time,* February 23, 2015, pp. 56–62; and "About Us," Five Guys Burger and Fries website, http://www.fiveguys.com/about-us.aspx, accessed April 25, 2019.

21. Jonathan Maze, "Chick-fil-A Is McDonald's Biggest Competitor," *Restaurant Business*, February 2019, p. 61; Nick Setyan, "Supply Outpacing Demand in Fast Casual and Casual Dining Restaurants," *Wall Street Transcript,* March 24, 2017, pp. 12–14; and Mallory Schlossberg, "Chick-fil-A Has One Advantage over Chipotle," www.businessinsider.com, October 1, 2015.

22. Kerry Close, "McDonald's Is Making a Power Move to Compete with Starbucks," *Money,* March 10, 2016; Keith O'Brien, "Supersize," *The New York Times Magazine,* May 6, 2012, pp. 44–48; and "A Look Ahead: 2011–Fast Food," *Advertising Age,* January 20, 2011, p. 4.

23. Emily Cappiello, "10 Fast Food Items Coming to Your Favorite Restaurant Next Year," www.rd.com, April 23, 2019; "Wendy's Partners with NextGen Consortium to Boost Sustainability," *Waste360*, March 19, 2019, p. 1; Brian Sozzi, "Wendy's CEO: Future of Fast Food Will Include Kiosks and Fast Pass Drive-Thrus," www.street.com, June 11, 2018; Maureen Morrison, "Wendy's Has a Beef with Rivals' Frozen Burgers," *Advertising Age,* February 8, 2016, p. 6; and Michal Addady, "Wendy's Announces Plans to Use Cage-Free Eggs," *Fortune.com,* January 21, 2016.

24. "The QSR 50," www.qsrmagazine.com, April 2019; "Best Fast-Food Restaurant Buying Guide," *Consumer Reports*, April 7, 2016.

25. Glen Sanford and the discussion of Apple's segmentation strategies through the years is based on information from its website, www.apple.com and www.apple-history.com/history.html.

26. Much of the discussion about positioning and perceptual maps is based on Roger A. Kerin and Robert A. Peterson, *Strategic Marketing Problems: Cases and Comments,* 13th ed. (Upper Saddle River, NJ: Prentice Hall, 2013), pp. 146–47; Orville C. Walker Jr. and John W. Mullins, *Marketing Strategy: A Decision-Focused Approach,* 8th ed. (Burr Ridge, IL: McGraw-Hill Education, 2014), p. 202; and "Volvo for Life," http://businessscandinavia.org/volvo-for-life, June 5, 2016.

27. Kimberly J. Decker, "Chocolate Milk Helps Dairy Industry Recover," *Dairy Foods,* October 2016, pp. 32–36; John Shepherd, "Nestle Launches Nesquik Protein Plus for Adults," *Just-food.com,* September 30, 2016, p. 4; and Nicholas Zamiska, "How Milk Got a Major Boost by Food Panel," *The Wall Street Journal,* August 30, 2004, pp. B1, B5.

28. Prince Sports: This case was written by William Rudelius and is based on personal interviews with Linda Glassel, Tyler Herring, and Nick Skally.

Chapter 10 Developing New Products and Services

Learning Objectives

After reading this chapter you should be able to:

LO 10-1 Recognize the various terms that pertain to products and services.

LO 10-2 Identify the ways in which consumer and business products and services can be classified.

LO 10-3 Explain the significance of "newness" in new products and services as it relates to the degree of consumer learning involved.

LO 10-4 Describe the factors contributing to the success or failure of a new product or service.

LO 10-5 Explain the purposes of each step of the new-product development process.

Apple: The World-Class New-Product Machine

How does a company become one of the most admired *and* financially valuable organizations in the world? Just look to Apple Inc. and its legendary product innovations that have touched the lives of people on every continent for 40 years.

Apple's New-Product Development Successes

Apple's new-product successes, orchestrated by its late co-founder, Steve Jobs, revolutionized five different industries: personal computing, music, smartphones, tablet computing, and digital publishing. A sampling of Apple's market-disrupting innovations includes:

- Apple II—the first commercial personal computer (1977).
- Macintosh—the first personal computer with a mouse and a graphical user interface (1984).
- iPod—the first and most successful MP3 music player (2001).
- iPhone—the world's best multitouch smartphone and media player with more than 1 million apps (2007).
- iPad (2010) and iPad mini (2012)—the thin tablet devices that allow users to read books, newspapers, magazines, and even textbooks.
- CarPlay—a device that allows you to use your iPhone while driving your car to make calls, listen to music, and access messages by voice or touch (2014).
- Apple Watch—a smartwatch that is a market share leader in wearable technology (2015).
- Apple AirPods—wireless Bluetooth earbuds that revolutionized the headphone market (2017).
- HomePod—a Siri-powered premium speaker and smart home hub (2018).

Apple's New-Product Development Stumbles

But Apple has stumbled at times too in its relentless pursuit of innovation. Examples of notable failures are:

- Apple III (1980) and Apple Lisa (1983)—two products intended for business users that failed due to design flaws. Each product was discontinued four years after introduction.

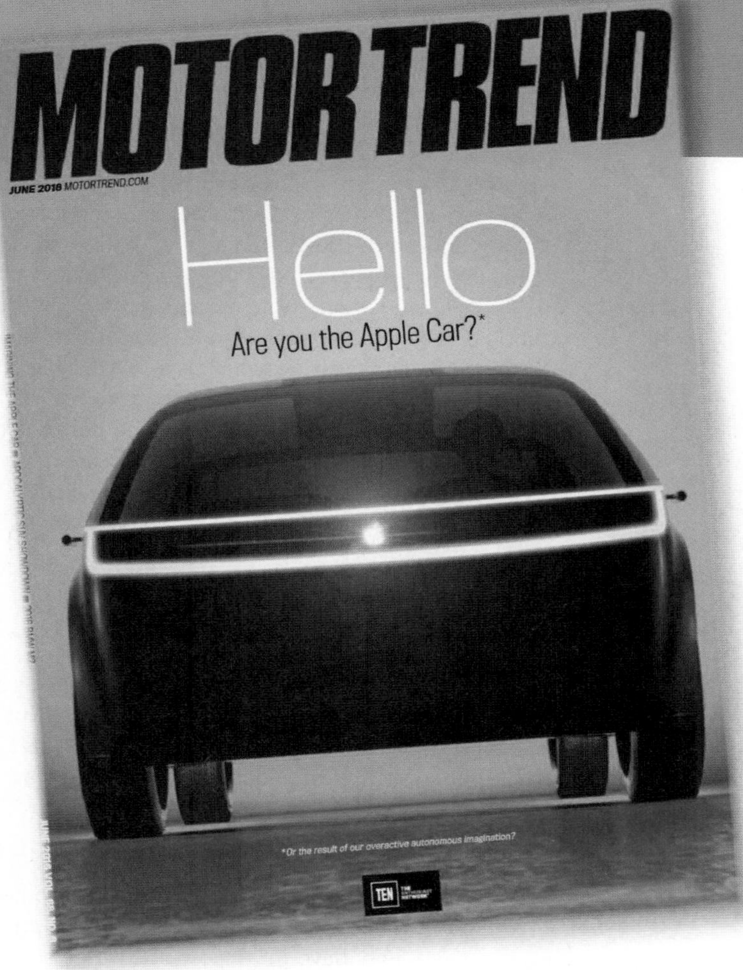

Source: Motor Trend

- Apple Newton (1987)–a personal digital assistant (PDA) that featured handwriting recognition software. Newton was discontinued 10 years later because of its limited battery life and hard-to-read screen.
- Macintosh Portable (1989)–Apple's first attempt to create a battery-powered portable computer. Its high price, coupled with an "un-portable" weight of 16 pounds, led to its demise two years later.
- "Hockey Puck" Mouse (1998)–the first commercially released Apple Mouse to use a USB connection. The mouse's round shape made it difficult to hold and use. It was discontinued in 2000.

These examples illustrate that new-product development is a challenge, even for Apple. Apple learned from each stumble and applied valuable insights from its failures to produce subsequent successes. In short, when a new-product development effort fails, Apple fails wisely. For example, the Macintosh was born from the failure of Apple Lisa. Apple's iPhone was a direct result of Apple's failed original music phone, produced in conjunction with Motorola.

The Next Chapter in Apple's Story: An Apple-Enabled iCar?

What major innovation is next on Apple's product development horizon? A car? Yes, an Apple-enabled iCar may debut between 2023 and 2025 with a list price of $55,000.

According to industry insiders, Apple has assembled a team of automotive, design, and computer software engineers to become a player in the automotive industry. The team has the task of applying expertise that Apple has honed in developing its iPhones–in areas such as batteries, sensors, and hardware-software integration–to the next generation of automobiles.

Details on Apple's development efforts are sketchy. It is thought that Apple will partner with an existing car manufacturer to build the actual electric car. Apple is currently testing its technology on Lexus sport-utility vehicles and Volkswagen vans. The car will have distinctive features: the ability to work with other Apple devices and autonomous capability, including driving, parking, and braking. Expect to learn more about Apple's plans and progress at its newly registered Internet domain name, www.AppleCar.com, when it goes live.

Independent automotive engineers have provided *Motor Trend* magazine with their conceptualization of what an Apple-enabled iCar might look like. These features are vividly displayed in a recent issue of the magazine, which is also available online. Is the image shown on the *Motor Trend* magazine cover what you might expect from Apple's design engineers?

The life of an organization depends on how it conceives, produces, and markets *new* products and services. This chapter describes the nature of products and services, highlights why new products succeed or fail, and details the new-product development process. Chapter 11 will discuss how organizations manage *existing* products, services, and brands.[1]

WHAT ARE PRODUCTS AND SERVICES?

LO 10-1
Recognize the various terms that pertain to products and services.

The essence of marketing is in developing products and services to meet buyer needs. A **product** is a good, service, or idea consisting of a bundle of tangible and intangible attributes that satisfies consumers' needs and is received in exchange for money or something else of value. Let's clarify the meanings of goods, services, and ideas.

A Look at Goods, Services, and Ideas

Nondurable goods like chewing gum are easily consumed and rely on consumer advertising.
Mike Hruby/McGraw-Hill Education

A *good* has tangible attributes that a consumer's five senses can perceive. For example, the Apple Watch can be touched and its features can be seen and heard. A good also may have intangible attributes consisting of its delivery or warranties and embody more abstract concepts, such as becoming healthier or wealthier. Goods also can be divided into nondurable goods and durable goods. A *nondurable* good is an item consumed in one or a few uses, such as food products and fuel. A *durable* good is one that usually lasts over many uses, such as appliances, cars, and smartphones. This classification method also provides direction for marketing actions. For example, nondurable goods, such as Wrigley's gum, rely heavily on consumer advertising. In contrast, costly durable goods, such as cars, generally emphasize personal selling.

Services are intangible activities or benefits that an organization provides to satisfy consumers' needs in exchange for money or something else of value. Services have become a significant part of the U.S. economy and often augment products. For example, Apple's iPhone is a product and Verizon is a wireless network service provider.

Finally, in marketing, an *idea* is a thought that leads to a product or action, such as a concept for a new invention or for getting people out to vote.

Throughout this book, *product* generally includes not only physical goods but services and ideas as well. When *product* is used in its narrower meaning of "goods," it should be clear from the example or sentence.

LO 10-2
Identify the ways in which consumer and business products and services can be classified.

Classifying Products

Two broad categories of products widely used in marketing relate to the type of user. **Consumer products** are products purchased by the ultimate consumer, whereas **business products** (also called *B2B products* or *industrial products*) are products organizations buy that assist in providing other products for resale. Some products can be considered both consumer and business items. For example, an Apple iMac computer can be sold to consumers for personal use or to business firms for office use. Each classification results in different marketing actions. Viewed as a consumer product, the iMac would be sold through Apple's retail stores or directly from its online store. As a business product, an Apple salesperson might contact a firm's purchasing department directly and offer discounts for large volume purchases.

Consumer Products The four types of consumer products shown in Figure 10–1 differ in terms of (1) the effort the consumer spends on the decision, (2) the attributes used in making the purchase decision, and (3) the frequency of purchase. **Convenience products** are items that the consumer purchases frequently, conveniently, and with a minimum of shopping effort. **Shopping products** are items for which the consumer compares several alternatives on criteria such as price, quality, or style. **Specialty products** are items that the consumer makes a special effort to search out and buy. **Unsought products** are items that the consumer does not know about or knows about but does not initially want.

Figure 10–1 shows how each type of consumer product stresses different marketing mix actions, degrees of brand loyalty, and shopping effort. But how a consumer product is classified depends on the individual. One consumer may view a smartphone as a shopping product and visit several stores and websites before deciding on a brand, whereas another consumer may view a smartphone as a specialty product and make a special effort to buy only an iPhone.

FIGURE 10–1
How a consumer product is classified significantly affects which products consumers buy and the marketing strategies used.

Business Products A major characteristic of business products is that their sales are often the result of *derived demand*; that is, sales of business products frequently result (or are derived) from the sale of consumer products. For example, as consumer demand for Toyota cars (a consumer product) increases, the company may increase its demand for paint spraying equipment (a business product).

	TYPE OF CONSUMER PRODUCT			
BASIS OF COMPARISON	**CONVENIENCE PRODUCT**	**SHOPPING PRODUCT**	**SPECIALTY PRODUCT**	**UNSOUGHT PRODUCT**
Product	Toothpaste, cake mix, hand soap, ATM cash withdrawal	Cameras, TVs, briefcases, airline tickets	Rolls-Royce cars, Rolex watches, heart surgery	Burial insurance, thesaurus
Price	Relatively inexpensive	Fairly expensive	Usually very expensive	Varies
Place (distribution)	Widespread; many outlets	Large number of selective outlets	Very limited	Often limited
Promotion	Price, availability, and awareness stressed	Differentiation from competitors stressed	Uniqueness of brand and status stressed	Awareness is essential
Brand loyalty of consumers	Aware of brand but will accept substitutes	Prefer specific brands but will accept substitutes	Very brand loyal; will not accept substitutes	Will accept substitutes
Purchase behavior of consumers	Frequent purchases; little time and effort spent shopping	Infrequent purchases; needs much comparison shopping time	Infrequent purchases; needs extensive search and decision time	Very infrequent purchases; some comparison shopping

Business products may be classified as components or support products. *Components* are items that become part of the final product. These include raw materials such as lumber, as well as assemblies such as a Toyota car engine. *Support products* are items used to assist in producing other products and services. These include:

- *Installations*, such as buildings and fixed equipment.
  - *Accessory equipment*, such as tools and office equipment.
  - *Supplies*, such as stationery, paper clips, and brooms.
- *Industrial services*, such as maintenance, repair, and legal services.

Strategies to market business products reflect both the complexities of the product involved (paper clips versus private jets) and the buy-class situations discussed in Chapter 6.

Classifying Services

Services can be classified according to whether they are delivered by (1) people or equipment, (2) business firms or nonprofit organizations, or (3) government agencies. These classifications are more thoroughly discussed in Chapter 12.

Product Classes, Forms, Items, Lines, and Mixes

Most organizations offer a range of products and services to consumers. Each set of offerings can be categorized according to the *product class* or industry to which they belong, like the iPad, which is classified as a tablet device. Products can exist in various *product forms* within a product class (see Chapter 11). A **product item** is a specific product that has a unique brand, size, or price. For example, Ultra Downy softener for clothes comes in different forms (liquid for the washer and sheets for the dryer) and load sizes (40, 60, etc.). Each of the different product items represents a separate *stock keeping unit* (*SKU*), which is a unique identification number that defines an item for ordering or inventory purposes.

VIDEO 10-1
Crapola
kerin.tv/15e/v10-1

A **product line** is a group of product or service items that are closely related because they satisfy a class of needs, are used together, are sold to the same customer group, are distributed through the same outlets, or fall within a given price range. Nike's product lines include shoes and clothing, whereas the Mayo Clinic's service lines consist of inpatient hospital care and outpatient physician services. Each product line has its own marketing strategy.

What company cheerfully tells its customers to "Have a crappy day"? Read the text to find out about this "tasty" offering!
Source: Brainstorm Bakery

The "Crapola Granola" product line started as an edgy party joke from Brian and Andrea Strom, owners of tiny Brainstorm Bakery. The dried **CR**anberries and **AP**ples gran**OLA**–hence the "Crapola" name–also contains nuts and five organic grains sweetened with maple syrup and honey. Its package promises that Crapola "Makes Even Weird People Regular."

Crapola is sold in retail outlets in the Midwest, California, and Oregon as well as online at www.crapola.us. Currently, the company offers other recipes: "Number Two," "Colon-ial Times," and "Kissapoo." These product line extensions enable both consumers and retailers to simplify their buying decisions. So a family liking Crapola might buy another product in the line. With a broader product line, the Stroms may obtain distribution in supermarket chains, which strive to increase efficiencies by dealing with fewer suppliers.[2]

Many firms offer a **product mix**, which consists of all of the product lines offered by an organization. For example, Cray Inc. has a small product mix of three lines (supercomputers, storage systems, and a "data appliance") that are mostly sold to governments and large businesses. Procter & Gamble, however, has a large product mix that includes product lines such as beauty and grooming (Crest toothpaste and Gillette razors) and household care (Downy fabric softener, Tide detergent, and Pampers diapers).

LEARNING REVIEW

10-1. What are the four main types of consumer products?

10-2. What is the difference between a product line and a product mix?

NEW PRODUCTS AND WHY THEY SUCCEED OR FAIL

LO 10-3
Explain the significance of "newness" in new products and services as it relates to the degree of consumer learning involved.

New products are the lifeblood of a company and keep it growing, but the financial risks can be large. Before discussing how new products reach the market, we'll begin by looking at *what* a new product is.

What Is a New Product?

The term *new* is difficult to define. Will a Sony PlayStation 5 be *new* when there was already a PlayStation 4? Perhaps—because Sony's PlayStation 5, Nintendo's Switch, and Microsoft's Xbox One X have all been positioned as entertainment "hubs" rather than just game consoles. What does *new* mean for new-product marketing? Newness from several points of view are discussed next.

Newness Compared with Existing Products If a product is functionally different from existing products, it can be defined as new. Sometimes this newness is revolutionary and creates a whole new industry, as was the case with the Apple smartphone. At other times, more features are added to an existing product to try to appeal to more customers. And as smart TVs, smartphones, smart cars, and smartwatches become more sophisticated, consumers' lives can get far more complicated. This proliferation of extra features—sometimes called product "feature bloat"—overwhelms many consumers and creates an unintended consequence: namely, consumer "feature fatigue." The Marketing Matters box describes the causes of feature bloat and the effect of feature fatigue.[3]

Newness from the Consumer's Perspective A second way to define new products is in terms of their effects on consumption. This approach classifies new products according to the degree of learning required by the consumer, as shown in Figure 10–2.

With a *continuous innovation*, consumers don't need to learn new behaviors. Toothpaste manufacturers can add new attributes or features like "whitens teeth" or "removes plaque" when they introduce a new or improved product, such as Colgate Total Advanced Gum Defense toothpaste. But the extra features in the new toothpaste do not require buyers to learn new tooth-brushing behaviors, so it is a continuous innovation. The benefit of this simple innovation is that effective marketing mainly depends on generating awareness, not re-educating customers.

With a *dynamically continuous innovation*, only minor changes in behavior are required. Procter & Gamble's Swiffer WetJet all-in-one mopping solution is a successful dynamically continuous innovation. Its novel design eliminates mess, elbow grease, and heavy lifting of floor cleaning materials without requiring any substantial behavioral change. So the marketing strategy here is to educate prospective buyers on the product's benefits, advantages, and proper use. Procter & Gamble did this with Swiffer. The result? Over a billion dollars in annual sales.

FIGURE 10–2
The degree of "newness" in a new product affects the amount of learning effort consumers must exert to use the product and the resulting marketing strategy.

LOW ← Degree of New Consumer Learning Needed → HIGH

BASIS OF COMPARISON	CONTINUOUS INNOVATION	DYNAMICALLY CONTINUOUS INNOVATION	DISCONTINUOUS INNOVATION
Definition	Requires no new learning by consumers	Disrupts consumer's normal routine but does not require totally new learning	Requires new learning and consumption patterns by consumers
Examples	New improved shaver, detergent, and toothpaste	Electric toothbrush, LED HDTVs, and smartphones	Wireless router, digital video recorder, and electric car
Marketing strategy	Gain consumer awareness and wide distribution	Advertise points of difference and benefits to consumers	Educate consumers through product trial and personal selling

Marketing Matters — Customer Value

Too Much of a Good Thing: Feature Bloat and Feature Fatigue in New-Product Development

Adding more features to a product to satisfy more consumers seems like a no-brainer strategy for success. Right?

Feature Bloat

In fact, most marketing research with potential buyers of a product shows that while they *say* they want more features, in actuality they are overwhelmed with the mind-boggling complexity—or "feature bloat"—of some new products. *Feature bloat* is the tendency for some product developers to add additional features or functionality to a product that are not of any benefit to most consumers and unnecessarily add to the cost of the product.

For example, consumers today can purchase a single product that functions as a cell phone, game console, calculator, text-messaging device, wireless Internet connection, digital camera, MP3 player, and global positioning system. The addition of each feature allows product developers to make claim to a new product . . . and rightly so!

Feature Fatigue

But, research shows that while feature bloat can increase the capability of a new product (relative to existing products) and encourage a purchase, the actual usage experience after purchase can result in consumer dissatisfaction, or feature fatigue. According to researchers at the University of Maryland, *feature fatigue* occurs because "consumers give more weight to capability and less weight to usability before use (of the product) than after use (of the product), they tend to choose overly complex products that do not maximize their satisfaction when they use them."[4]

A common result of feature fatigue is annoyance and a reduced likelihood of repurchase and consumer retention. This phenomenon has been observed in the domain of wearable technology, including digital watches, smart glasses, and smartphones. The figure shows the feature bloat to feature fatigue trajectory from a consumer's point of view. The critical tipping point occurs when the addition of another feature annoys rather than engages a consumer.

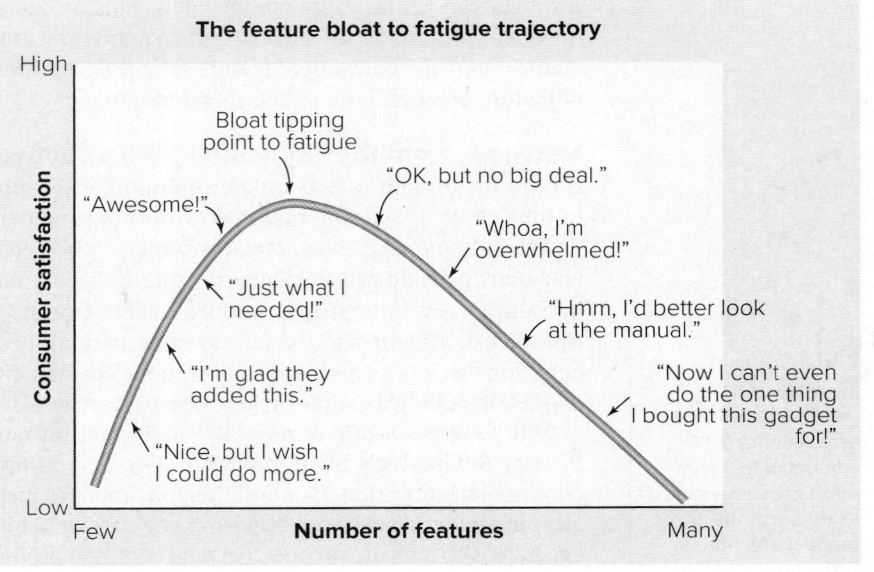

A *discontinuous innovation* involves making the consumer learn entirely new consumption patterns to use the product. Have you bought a "smart home" gadget from Amazon or Google that controls household systems like security, heating, and lighting? Congratulations if you successfully installed it yourself! Best Buy's Geek Squad and Amazon's Smart Home Services have a thriving business installing and activating these gadgets because they can be complicated to set up and operate appropriately.[5] Marketing efforts for discontinuous innovations usually involve not only gaining initial consumer awareness but also educating consumers on both the benefits and proper use of the innovative product.

Newness in Legal Terms The U.S. Federal Trade Commission (FTC) advises that the term *new* be limited to use with a product up to six months after it enters regular distribution. The difficulty with this suggestion is in the interpretation of the term *regular distribution*.

Newness from the Organization's Perspective Successful organizations view newness and innovation in their products at three levels. The lowest level, which usually

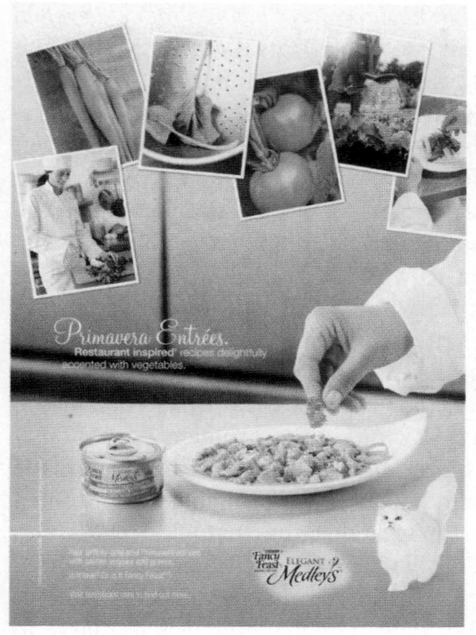

The text describes the potential benefits and dangers of an incremental innovation such as Purina's Elegant Medleys, its restaurant-inspired food for cats.
Source: Nestlé

involves the least risk, is a *product line extension*. This is an incremental improvement of an existing product line the company already sells. For example, Purina added its "new" line of Elegant Medleys, a "restaurant-inspired food for cats," to its existing line of 50 varieties of its Fancy Feast gourmet cat food. This has the potential benefit of adding new customers but the twin dangers of increasing expenses and cannibalizing products in its existing line.

At the next level is (1) a significant jump in innovation or technology or (2) a *brand extension* involving putting an established brand name on a new product in an unfamiliar market. In the first case, the significant jump in technology might be when a manufacturer offers new smartphones or digital cameras.

The second case—using an existing brand name to introduce a new product into an unfamiliar market—looks deceptively easy for companies with a powerful, national brand name. Colgate thought so. It put its brand name on a line of frozen dinners called Colgate's Kitchen Entrees. The product line died quickly. A marketing expert calls this "one of the most bizarre brand extensions ever," observing that the Colgate brand name, which is strongly linked to toothpaste in people's minds, does not exactly get their "taste buds tingling."[6]

The third and highest level of innovation involves a radical invention, a truly revolutionary new product. The 3D printer, invented and commercialized by Chuck Hull, the founder of 3D Systems, is an example of a radical invention. Effective new-product development in firms exists at all three levels.

Why Products and Services Succeed or Fail

LO 10-4
Describe the factors contributing to the success or failure of a new product or service.

We all know the giant product and service successes—such as Apple's iPhone and Netflix. Yet the thousands of product failures every year that slide quietly into oblivion cost American businesses billions of dollars. Ideally, a new product or service needs a precise **protocol**, a statement that, before product development begins, identifies (1) a well-defined target market; (2) specific customers' needs, wants, and preferences; and (3) what the product will be and do to satisfy consumers.

Research reveals how difficult it is to produce a single commercially successful new product, especially among consumer packaged goods (CPG) that appear on supermarket shelves one month and are gone forever a few months later. Most American families buy the same 150 items over and over again—making it difficult to gain buyers for new products. So less than 3 percent of new consumer packaged goods exceed first-year sales of $50 million—the benchmark of a successful CPG launch.[7]

The Keurig Kold cold beverage maker produced great-tasting carbonated drinks. So why did it fail? Read the text to find out.
Suzanne Kreiter/The Boston Globe/Getty Images

To learn marketing lessons and convert potential failures to successes, we can analyze why new products fail and then study several failures in detail. As we go through the new-product development process later in the chapter, we can identify ways such failures might have been avoided—admitting that hindsight is clearer than foresight.

Marketing Reasons for New-Product Failures Both marketing and nonmarketing factors contribute to new-product failures. Using the research results from several studies on new-product success and failure, we can identify the critical marketing factors—which sometimes overlap—that often separate new-product winners and losers:[8]

1. *Insignificant point of difference*. Research shows that a distinctive point of difference is the single most important factor for a new product to defeat competing ones—having superior characteristics that deliver unique benefits to the user. Consider General Mills's launch of Fingos, a sweetened cereal flake about the size of a corn chip, with a $34 million promotional budget. Consumers were supposed to snack on them dry, but they didn't.[9] The point of difference was not important enough to get consumers to stop eating competing snacks such as popcorn and potato chips.

The Hewlett-Packard Tablet was late in its introduction and a generation behind in functionality compared to the Apple iPad 2. The result? Discontinuance two months after its introduction.
David Paul Morris/Bloomberg via Getty Images

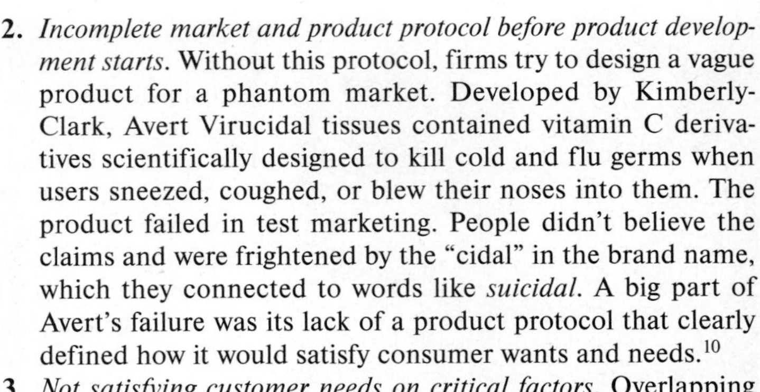

2. *Incomplete market and product protocol before product development starts.* Without this protocol, firms try to design a vague product for a phantom market. Developed by Kimberly-Clark, Avert Virucidal tissues contained vitamin C derivatives scientifically designed to kill cold and flu germs when users sneezed, coughed, or blew their noses into them. The product failed in test marketing. People didn't believe the claims and were frightened by the "cidal" in the brand name, which they connected to words like *suicidal.* A big part of Avert's failure was its lack of a product protocol that clearly defined how it would satisfy consumer wants and needs.[10]
3. *Not satisfying customer needs on critical factors.* Overlapping somewhat with point 1, this factor stresses that problems on one or two critical factors can kill the product, even though the general quality is high. Consider the failure of Kold made by Keurig Green Mountain, Inc. The company discontinued its Kold-brand countertop soda machine that allowed users to make chilled Coca-Cola, Dr Pepper, and other carbonated beverages at home. Despite making a great-tasting cold carbonated drink, Kold didn't deliver on other factors consumers considered critical. The machine was too large to fit on most kitchen countertops, the time necessary to produce the drink was too long, and the price was too high. Kold was priced at $370 and the cost per 8-ounce drink was $1.25.[11]
4. *Bad timing.* This results when a product is introduced too soon, too late, or when consumer tastes and preferences are shifting dramatically. Bad timing gives new-product managers nightmares. Hewlett-Packard, for example, introduced its HP Tablet a few years after Apple launched its original iPad, about the same time Apple introduced its next-generation iPad 2 that featured multiple apps. Hewlett-Packard was late and its HP Tablet was significantly behind in apps compared to the iPad 2. Failure to deliver a product that satisfied consumer preferences in a timely manner caused Hewlett-Packard to abandon its HP Tablet two months after its launch.

What dog or cat wouldn't want to drink vitamin-enriched, carbonated bottled water? As it happens, we may never know. Due to a lack of demand by their human companions, the product was short-lived on supermarket shelves.
Patrick FarrellKRT/Newscom

5. *No economical access to buyers.* Grocery products provide an example of this factor. Today's mega-supermarkets carry more than 60,000 different SKUs. With about 40,000 new consumer packaged goods (food, beverage, health and beauty aids, household, and pet items) introduced annually in the United States, the cost to gain access to retailer shelf space is huge. Because shelf space is judged in terms of sales per square foot, Thirsty Dog! (a zesty, beef-flavored, vitamin-enriched, mineral-loaded, lightly carbonated bottled water for your dog) must displace an existing product on the supermarket shelves, a difficult task with the high sales-per-square-foot demands of these stores. Thirsty Dog! and its companion product Thirsty Cat! failed to generate enough sales to meet these requirements.
6. *Poor execution of the marketing mix: brand name, package, price, promotion, distribution.* Somewhere in the marketing mix there can be a showstopper that kills the product. Introduced by Gunderson & Rosario, Inc., Garlic Cake was supposed to be served as an hors d'oeuvre with sweet breads, spreads, and meats, but somehow the company forgot to tell this to potential consumers. Garlic Cake died because consumers were left to wonder just what a Garlic Cake is and when on earth a person would want to eat it.

Product quality has hampered the commercial potential of hoverboards. Sales suffered after product safety issues were discovered.
B Christopher/Alamy Stock Photo

7. *Too little market attractiveness.* The ideal is a large target market with high growth and real buyer need. But often the target market is too small or competitive to warrant the huge expenses necessary to reach it. OUT! International's Hey! There's A Monster In My Room spray was designed to rid scary creatures from a kid's bedroom and had a bubble-gum fragrance. While a creative and cute product, the brand name probably kept the kids awake at night more than their fear of the monsters because it implied the monster was still hiding in the bedroom. Also, was this a real market?
8. *Poor product quality.* This factor often results when a product is not thoroughly tested. The costs to an organization for poor quality can be staggering and include the labor, materials, and other expenses to fix the problem—not to mention the lost sales, profits, and market share that usually result. Consider self-balancing scooters, commonly referred to as "hoverboards." After gaining widespread attention with the media, as well as popularity with teens, hoverboards made by a variety of manufacturers were found to catch fire or explode. Needless to say, hoverboard sales suffered greatly as a result.[12]

Simple marketing research could have revealed the problems in these new-product disasters. Developing successful new products may sometimes involve luck, but more often it involves having a product that really meets a need and has significant points of difference over competitive products.

Organizational Inertia in New-Product Failures Organizational problems and attitudes can also cause new-product disasters. Two key ones are:

- *Encountering "groupthink" in task force and committee meetings.*[13] Someone in the new-product planning team meeting knows or suspects the product concept is a dumb idea. But that person is afraid to speak up for fear of being cast as a "negative thinker" or "not a team player" and then ostracized from real participation in the group. Do you think someone on the General Mills's Fingo's new-product team suspected a sweetened cereal the size of a corn chip wasn't a good idea but was afraid to speak up? Probably yes, but they didn't, and the product failed. In the same way, a strong public commitment to a new product by its key advocate may make it difficult to kill the product even when new negative information comes to light. Groupthink can be minimized when team leaders encourage team members to challenge assumptions, express constructive dissent, and offer alternatives.
- *Avoiding the "NIH problem."* A great idea is a great idea, regardless of its source. Yet in the bureaucracy that can occur in large organizations, ideas from outside often get rejected simply because they come from outside—what has been termed the "not-invented-here (NIH) problem." Forward-looking companies attempt to deal with this problem by embracing the policy of open innovation.

Open innovation consists of practices and processes that encourage the use of external as well as internal ideas and internal as well as external collaboration when conceiving, producing, and marketing new products and services. For example, PepsiCo recently formed "The Hive." Described as "a small entrepreneurial sort of agile group" which includes talent from both inside and outside the company, this group

Applying Marketing Metrics

Do Your New Products Have Vitality?

You have been hired by Parvaderm, Inc. as a summer intern. Parvaderm's product line includes facial creams, hand and body lotions, and a variety of women's toiletries sold under different brand names through U.S. drugstores and supermarkets. Company sales have plateaued at $1 billion over the past three years following seven consecutive years of sales growth.

Your Challenge

Your internship project focused on constructing a New Product Vitality Index. The index calculation is shown below for Parvaderm. This index puts emphasis on the percentage of total company sales that came from new products each year. Originated by the 3M Company, this index is used by 62 percent of large U.S. companies. Its purpose is to track the "vitality" of a company's new-product development effort. An index between 20 and 30 percent is considered "good."

The index calculation is shown below:

$$\text{New Product Vitality Index} = \frac{\text{Company sales revenues due to new products released in the past three years}}{\text{Total current-year company sales revenue}} \times 100$$

While simple to calculate, the index requires some thought in its construction. First, it is necessary to define a "new product." For Parvaderm, new products are those new to the company and product and brand extensions. Second, the length of time a product is considered new has to be determined. About 60 percent of companies use a three-year period. After three years from the release date, a product's sales are dropped from the calculation and more recent new-product sales replace them.

Your Findings

Your calculation is displayed in the figure. The percentage of total Parvaderm sales that came from new products each year has been declining for the past three years—a period when company sales have plateaued. In constructing the index, you observed that the number and type of new products introduced by Parvaderm have not changed over the previous seven years. Also, the index itself has fallen below the threshold considered "good."

Your Action

Your recommendation to management is to revisit Parvaderm's new-product development process in its entirety. While the number and type of new products has not changed, the impactfulness or "vitality" of new products has declined and company sales revenues have plateaued, perhaps as a result.

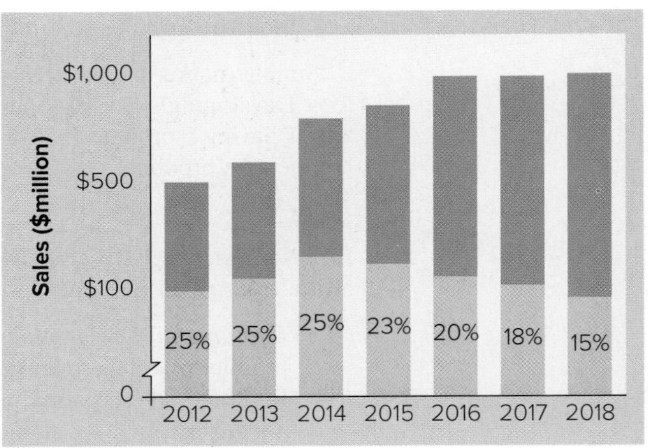

identifies and nurtures new-product concepts that would otherwise be overlooked or undervalued by existing policies and procedures.[14] Approaches to open innovation are highlighted in the description of the new-product development process discussed shortly.

These organizational problems can contribute to the eight marketing reasons for new-product failures just described.

Tracking New-Product Performance

Marketers monitor the impact of their new products on company sales to gauge the effectiveness of their new-product development effort. One measure used by 62 percent of large U.S. companies is the New Product Vitality Index. This index tracks the percentage of total company sales that come from new products each year. The calculation and interpretation of the New Product Vitality Index is described in the Applying Marketing Metrics box.[15]

LEARNING REVIEW

10-3. What kind of innovation would an improved electric toothbrush be?

10-4. Why can an "insignificant point of difference" lead to new-product failure?

10-5. What marketing metric might you use to assess the effectiveness of a new-product program?

THE NEW-PRODUCT DEVELOPMENT PROCESS

LO 10-5

Explain the purposes of each step of the new-product development process.

To develop new products efficiently, companies such as General Mills and 3M use a specific sequence of steps to make their products ready for market. Figure 10–3 shows the **new-product development process**, the seven stages an organization goes through to identify opportunities and convert them into salable products or services. Today many firms use a formal Stage-Gate® process to evaluate whether the results at each stage of the new-product development process are successful enough to warrant proceeding to the next stage. If problems in a stage can't be corrected, the project doesn't proceed to the next stage and product development is killed.[16]

Stage 1: New-Product Strategy Development

For companies, **new-product strategy development** is the stage of the new-product development process that defines the role for a new product in terms of the firm's overall objectives. During this stage, the firm uses both a SWOT analysis (Chapter 2) and environmental scanning (Chapter 3) to assess its strengths and weaknesses relative to the trends it identifies as opportunities or threats. The outcome not only defines the vital "protocol" for each new-product idea but also identifies the strategic role it might serve in the firm's product portfolio.

Occasionally a firm's Stage 1 activities can be blindsided by a revolutionary new product or technology that completely disrupts its business, sometimes called a "disruptive innovation." For example:

- *Wikipedia*. This free and community-edited online encyclopedia caused Encyclopedia Britannica to cease print production after 244 years.
- *Digital photography*. Even though they were invented by Kodak, digital cameras made film and film cameras obsolete by the mid-2000s and drove Kodak into bankruptcy. Kodak did not actively market its digital cameras because it wanted to protect its film business.

Clearly, a firm's new-product strategy development must be on the lookout for innovative products or technology that might disrupt its plans.

FIGURE 10–3 Carefully using the seven stages in the new-product development process increases the chances of new-product success.

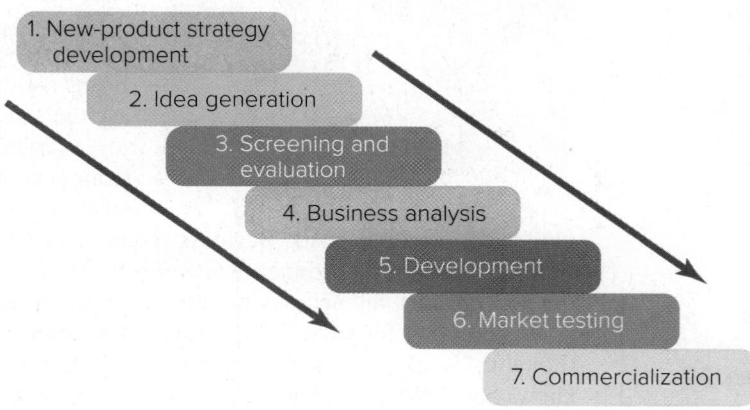

Read the text to learn about the history behind "Flamin' Hot" Cheetos and their inventor at Frito-Lay. Company employees are often a valuable source of product innovations.
LunaseeStudios/Shutterstock

New-product development for services, such as buying a stock or airline ticket or watching a National Football League game, is often difficult. Why? Because services are intangible and performance-oriented. Nevertheless, service innovations can have a huge impact on our lives. For example, the online brokerage firm E*TRADE revolutionized the financial services industry through its online investment trading.

Stage 2: Idea Generation

Idea generation, the second stage of the new-product development process, involves developing a pool of concepts to serve as candidates for new products, building upon the previous stage's results. Many forward-looking organizations have discovered that they are not generating enough useful new-product ideas. One internal approach for getting ideas within the firm is to train employees in the art and science of asking specific, probing questions. The goal in generating new-product ideas and strategies is to move from "what is" questions that describe the present situation to "what if" questions that focus on solutions and marketing actions. The following discussion suggests methods of generating new-product ideas both internally and externally, the latter often using open innovation.

Suggestions from Employees and Friends Businesses often get successful new-product ideas from employees who ask the "what if" question. For example, a janitor at a Frito-Lay manufacturing plant asked himself, "What if I put chili on a Cheeto?" He then tinkered with a spicy and hot chili-powder recipe at home in his kitchen and asked senior Frito-Lay executives to taste his flavor. The result? Flamin' Hot Cheetos became one of the best-selling snack products in the company's history. As for the janitor, Richard Montanez, he became an executive vice president at the company.[17]

VIDEO 10-2
Life Is Good
kerin.tv/15e/v10-2

The breakthrough for the Life Is Good T-shirt business started with a keg party the company founders, brothers Bert and John Jacobs, had with friends. At their parties the brothers often posted drawings with sayings for possible T-shirt ideas on their living room wall and asked their friends to jot down their reactions on the drawings.[18] At one party the drawing of a smiling, beret-wearing stick figure with the phrase "Life is good" got the most favorable comments. They named the character "Jake," printed 48 T-shirts with a smiling Jake and the words "Life is good," and sold out in less than an hour at a local street fair. Today Life Is Good, with its positive, upbeat messages, has $100 million in annual sales. The company sells Life Is Good T-shirts, hats, and other items for men, women, children, and pets in 4,500 retail stores and online in 30 countries.[19]

Brothers Bert and John Jacobs are constantly looking for positive, upbeat messages to print on their Life Is Good T-shirts.
Michael Dwyer/AP Images

Customer and Supplier Suggestions Firms ask their salespeople to talk to customers and ask their purchasing personnel to talk to suppliers to discover new-product ideas. Whirlpool gets ideas from customers on ways to standardize components so that it can cut the number of different product platforms to reduce costs. Business researchers tell firms to actively involve customers and suppliers in the new-product development process. This means the focus should be on what the new product will actually do for them rather than simply what they want.

VIDEO 10-3
P&G's Tide Pods Ad
kerin.tv/15e/v10-3

A. G. Lafley, former CEO of Procter & Gamble (P&G), gave his executives a *revolutionary* thought: "Look outside the company for solutions to problems rather than insisting P&G knows best." When he ran P&G's laundry detergent business, he had to redesign the laundry

Procter & Gamble's new Tide Pods launch shows how it has improved both planning and implementation by involving consumers earlier in its innovation activities.
Mike Hruby/McGraw-Hill Education

boxes so they were easier to open. Why? While consumers *said* P&G's laundry boxes were "easy to open," cameras they agreed to have installed in their laundry rooms showed they opened the boxes with *screwdrivers*![20]

With a $150 million marketing budget, P&G launched Tide Pods, a revolutionary three-chamber liquid dose of detergent that cleans, fights stains, and brightens. P&G describes Tide Pods as "its biggest laundry innovation in more than a quarter century." P&G says the Tide Pods product has produced the highest consumer-satisfaction scores the company has ever seen for a new laundry product. Following its successful new-product launch, however, P&G redesigned its packaging after discovering that some children thought the pods were candy and tried to eat them. How successful has Tide Pods been for P&G? The product now produces over $2 billion in annual sales—making it one of the company's most successful product launches![21]

"Crowdsourcing" is another creative idea generation method if an R&D marketing team wants ideas from 10,000 or 20,000 customers or suppliers. *Crowdsourcing* involves generating insights leading to actions based on ideas from massive numbers of people. This open innovation practice requires a precise question to focus the idea generation process. Dell Technologies used crowdsourcing to develop an online site to generate 13,464 ideas for new products as well as website and marketing improvements, of which 402 were implemented.[22]

An IDEO innovation: A five-section, single-serve package for salads. Visit IDEO's website (www.ideo.com) to view its recent innovations.
Source: IDEO

Research and Development Laboratories Another source of new products is a firm's own research and development laboratories. Apple's sleek, cutting-edge designs for the iPad, iPhone, iMac, Apple Watch, and AirPods came out of its Apple Industrial Design Group. What is the secret to Apple's world-class ability to convert vague concepts into tangible products? An action-item list from every meeting that focuses on *who* does *what* by *when*![23]

Professional R&D and innovation laboratories that are *outside* the walls of large corporations are also sources of open innovation and can provide new-product ideas. IDEO is a world-class new-product development firm that uses "design thinking," which involves incorporating human behavior as well as building upon the ideas of others in the innovation-design process. As the most prolific and influential design firm in the world, IDEO has created thousands of new products for its clients. Brainstorming sessions conducted at IDEO can generate 100 new ideas in an hour!

IDEO designs include developing the standing Crest Neat Squeeze toothpaste dispenser and improving the original Apple mouse. Recently, Fresh Express asked IDEO to design an innovative single-serve package for salads. IDEO's solution: A five-section package—one large section for the salad greens and four smaller ones for proteins, dressings, and so on—with each section sealed in plastic (see the photo).[24]

Inventor Aaron Krause has the distinction of introducing the most successful new product on the TV reality show *Shark Tank*.
John Ziomek/Courier-Post via USA TODAY NETWORK

Competitive Products Analyzing the competition can lead to new-product ideas. General Motors targeted Tesla Motors as a reference for its Chevrolet Bolt—a $30,000 all-electric vehicle. The Bolt is capable of driving 200 miles in a single charge and features a hatchback design to look more like a crossover vehicle. According to a General Motors executive, the Bolt will "completely shake up the status quo for electric vehicles as the first affordable long-range EV in the market." The Bolt was designed to be a direct competitor to Tesla's Model 3 target price at $35,000.[25]

Smaller Firms, Universities, and Inventors Many firms look for outside visionaries that have inventions or innovative ideas that can become products. Some sources and outcomes of this open innovation strategy include:[26]

- *Smaller, nontraditional firms.* Small technology firms and even small, nontraditional firms in adjacent industries provide creative advances. General Mills partnered with Weight Watchers to develop Progresso Light soups, the first consumer packaged product in any grocery category to carry the Weight Watchers endorsement.

Crowdfunder Kickstarter.com enabled Pebble to develop and market one of the first commercially successful smartphone-connected smartwatches two years before the Apple Watch.
artjazz/Shutterstock

- *Universities*. Many universities have technology transfer centers that often partner with businesses to commercialize faculty inventions. The first-of-its-kind carbonated yogurt Go-Gurt Fizzix was launched as a result of General Mills partnering with Brigham Young University to license the university's patent to put the "fizz" into yogurt.
- *Inventors*. Many lone inventors and entrepreneurs develop brilliant new-product ideas—like Aaron Krause's Scrub Daddy. This sponge, in the shape of a smiley face, changes its texture in water: hard in cold, soft in hot. Scrub Daddy was pitched on the TV reality show *Shark Tank* and became the most successful product introduced on the program, with total revenues surpassing $100 million.

Early-stage financing is almost always a problem for inventors and those starting a new business because of the risk involved. *Crowdfunding* is a way to gather an online community of supporters to financially rally around a specific project that is unlikely to get resources from traditional sources such as banks or venture capital firms. For example, Kickstarter.com raised $1.2 million for start-up SmartThings to introduce a product that allows users to monitor their homes by remote control. But its biggest crowdfunding success was for the Pebble smartwatch with iPhone and Android smartphone integration. More than 70,000 backers contributed over $30 million to develop and market this product between 2012 and 2016. Nevertheless, Pebble became insolvent and its assets were acquired by Fitbit. If you are interested in crowdfunding projects, you should know that for every $10 pledged, about $1 goes toward failed projects. The average Kickstarter donor gives $25.[27]

Great ideas can come from almost anywhere—a central idea behind open innovation. The challenge is recognizing and implementing them. According to Sergey Brin, the co-founder of Google,[28] "The fact is coming up with an idea is the least important part of creating something great. The execution and delivery are what's key."

Stage 3: Screening and Evaluation

Screening and evaluation is the stage of the new-product development process that internally and externally evaluates new-product ideas to eliminate those that warrant no further effort.

Internal Approach In this approach to screening and evaluation, a firm's employees evaluate the technical feasibility of a proposed new-product idea to determine whether it meets the objectives defined in the new-product strategy development stage. For example, 3M scientists develop many world-class innovations in the company's labs. A recent innovation was its microreplication technology—one that has 3,000 tiny gripping "fingers" per square inch. An internal assessment showed 3M that this technology could be used to improve the gripping of both batting and work gloves.

Organizations that develop service-dominated offerings need to ensure that employees have the commitment and skills to meet customer expectations and sustain customer loyalty—an important criterion in screening a new-service idea. This is the essence of *customer experience management* (*CEM*), which is the process of managing the entire customer experience within the company. Marketers must consider employees' interactions with customers so that the new services are consistently delivered and experienced, clearly differentiated from other service offerings, and relevant and valuable to the target market.

External Approach Firms that take an external approach to screening and evaluation use *concept tests*, external evaluations with consumers that consist of preliminary testing of a new-product idea rather than an actual finished product. Generally, these tests are more useful with minor modifications of existing products than with new, innovative products with which consumers are not familiar.

Concept tests rely on written descriptions of the product but may be augmented with sketches, mockups, or promotional literature. Key questions for concept testing include: How does the customer perceive the product? Who would use it? and How would it be used? Failure to address these questions can lead to disastrous results. Consumer response to Google Glass is a case in point, as detailed in the Marketing Matters box.[29]

Marketing Matters

Technology

Was the Google Glass Half Full or Half Empty?

How did the Google Glass morph from being one of *Time* magazine's best inventions of the year to an embarrassing failure? Perhaps Google's product development team failed to ask three simple questions: How would consumers perceive Google Glass? Who would use it? and How would it be used?

Google Glass resembled a pair of eyeglasses with a small screen visible to the wearer (see the photo). Its notable features included a touchpad that allowed the wearer to "see" current and past events, such as phone calls, photos, and updates, and a camera to take pictures and record video. The sound, video, and graphics accessed through the screen created an *augmented reality* that overlaid the physical, real-world environment at the same time.

Google started selling a prototype (not the finished product) to 8,000 qualified "Glass Explorers" for $1,500. The intent was to collect feedback on the device and then quickly update and fix problems before a planned launch of the product for the same price. Unfortunately, by releasing Google Glass widely, the public believed the device to be a finished product, not a prototype. It quickly became apparent that the prototype suffered from a short battery life, poor sound quality, and distorted images.

The technical problems could be fixed. But Google Glass had more severe problems—all of which related to incomplete concept testing. For example, Google never really understood how consumers would perceive the device. Was it simply a "cool" geeky gadget or wearable, chic eyeglass technology for a broader audience? How would wearers use the technology? As it happened, users immediately embraced the photo and video capabilities, and Google Glass wearers were thrown out of clubs and banned from theaters because of privacy and intellectual property concerns. More troubling, Google Glass wearers were derisively called "Glassholes."

The result? Google Glass was withdrawn from the market. A new version of Google Glass, called Glass Enterprise Edition 2, was introduced in 2019 for use by tech workers at a price of $999. Stay tuned on its success.

Peppinuzzo/Shutterstock

LEARNING REVIEW

10-6. What is the new-product strategy development stage in the new-product development process?

10-7. What are the main sources of new-product ideas?

10-8. How do internal and external screening and evaluation approaches differ?

Stage 4: Business Analysis

Business analysis specifies the features of the product or service and the marketing strategy needed to bring it to market and make financial projections. This is the last checkpoint before significant resources are invested to create a *prototype*–a full-scale operating model of the product or service. The business analysis stage assesses the total "business fit" of the proposed new product with the company's mission and objectives–from whether the product or service can be economically produced to the marketing strategy needed to have it succeed in the marketplace.

This process requires not only detailed sales and profit financial projections but also assessments of the marketing and product synergies related to the company's existing operations. Will the new product require a lot of new equipment or technology to produce it or can it be made using existing machines? Will the new product cannibalize sales of existing products or will it increase revenues by reaching new market segments? Can the new product be protected with patents or copyrights?

Carmakers in North America, Europe, and Asia had to address these and other questions when the initial business analysis for driverless vehicles began a decade ago. The business analysis included R&D and manufacturing expenditures, investments in the acquisition of technology, and production scheduling and product marketing timelines.

The Cruise AV is designed to operate safely on its own, with no driver, steering wheel, pedals, or other manual controls when it goes on the road in 2021.
Source: General Motors

Stage 5: Development

Development is the stage of the new-product development process that turns the idea on paper into a prototype. This results in a demonstrable, producible product that involves not only manufacturing the product efficiently but also performing laboratory and consumer tests to ensure the product meets the standards established for it in the protocol.

Google's driverless car initiative is an extreme example of the complexity of the Stage 5 development process for a durable consumer good. The Google development team relies on a fleet of vehicles as test models, among them the Toyota Prius and the Lexus RX 450h. Google's driverless cars have completed over 3 million miles of driving. These miles are "driven" by a nonhuman driver with an impressive driving record behind the wheel and a Google engineer in the passenger seat. A spinning, roof-mounted laser range finder and sophisticated software navigated the streets of San Francisco and the curvy Pacific Coast Highway.

In 2017, the Google driverless car became part of Waymo, a subsidiary of Google's parent company, Alphabet. Waymo will not commercialize the vehicle itself but intends to market the self-driving technology to carmakers, such as Fiat Chrysler. But there is more to the story. General Motors will introduce the Cruise AV, the first mass-produced self-driving car built from the ground up, in 2021 pending approval by the U.S. National Highway Traffic Safety Administration. This is not surprising. The Cruise AV will have no steering wheel, gas or brake pedals, or other manual controls.[30]

Stage 6: Market Testing

Market testing is the stage of the new-product development process that involves exposing actual products to prospective consumers under realistic purchase conditions to see if they will buy. If the budget permits, consumer packaged goods firms often do this by *test marketing*, which involves offering a product for sale on a limited basis in a defined area for a specific time period. The three main kinds of test markets are (1) standard, (2) controlled, and (3) simulated.[31] Because standard test markets are so time-consuming and expensive and can alert competitors to a firm's plans, some firms skip test markets entirely or use controlled or simulated test markets.

Standard Test Markets In a *standard test market*, a company develops a product and then attempts to sell it through normal distribution channels in a number of test-market cities. Test-market cities must be demographically representative of markets targeted for the new product, have cable TV systems that can deliver different ads to different homes, and have retailers with checkout counter scanners to measure sales. A distinguishing feature of a standard test market is that the producer sells the product to distributors, wholesalers, and retailers, just as it would do for other products.

Depending on the results of a test market, companies will take one of three actions. If the results don't meet expectations, a product is discontinued. If the results are favorable, a full-fledged national product introduction may be undertaken. Alternatively, a company may choose to undertake a *regional rollout,* in which a product is introduced sequentially into geographical areas to allow production levels and marketing activities to build up gradually to support the product.

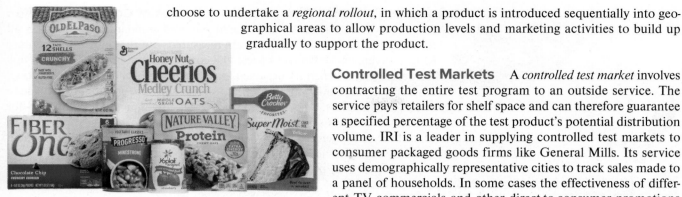

Consumer products, such as those from General Mills, often use controlled test markets to assess the likely success of new-product, promotional, or pricing strategies.
McGraw-Hill Education

Controlled Test Markets A *controlled test market* involves contracting the entire test program to an outside service. The service pays retailers for shelf space and can therefore guarantee a specified percentage of the test product's potential distribution volume. IRI is a leader in supplying controlled test markets to consumer packaged goods firms like General Mills. Its service uses demographically representative cities to track sales made to a panel of households. In some cases the effectiveness of different TV commercials and other direct-to-consumer promotions can be measured.

Simulated Test Markets To save time and money, companies often turn to *simulated (or laboratory) test markets (STMs),* a technique that somewhat replicates a full-scale test market. STMs are often run in shopping malls, to find consumers who use the product class being tested. Next, qualified participants are shown the product or the product concept and asked about usage, reasons for purchase, and important product attributes. They then see the company's and competitors' ads for the test product. Finally, participants are given money and allowed to choose between buying the firm's product or the products of competitors in a real or simulated store environment.

Stage 7: Commercialization

Finally, the product is brought to the point of **commercialization**—the stage of the new-product development process that positions and launches a new product in full-scale production and sales. This is the most expensive stage for most new products. If competitors introduce a product that leapfrogs the firm's own new product or if cannibalization of its own existing products appears significant, the firm may halt the new-product launch. Companies can face disasters at the commercialization stage, regardless of whether they are selling business products or consumer products. Examples are Boeing's 787 Dreamliner and Burger King's french fries, which are discussed next.

Takeaway new-product lesson from the Boeing 787 Dreamliner: "Innovation . . . can get messy." See the text for details.
KiyoshiOta/Bloomberg/Getty Images

The Boeing 787 Dreamliner Experience When Boeing announced the design for its Boeing 787 Dreamliner commercial airplane, its technical advances would mean the plane would burn 20 percent less fuel and cost 30 percent less to maintain than present airliners. Boeing invested billions of dollars in the 787's development, and airlines subsequently placed orders for almost 1,300 Dreamliners. But there is more to the story.

As the Dreamliner entered its commercialization stage, airlines around the world began taking deliveries. But with all the new technology in the Dreamliner, the new airplane was plagued by technical nightmares—even after extensive testing. Its wings, made with plastic-reinforced carbon fiber instead of aluminum, proved difficult to produce and attach to the fuselage. And the Dreamliner's new "high-tech skin" failed to dissipate lightning like the old aluminum skin. But an even more serious problem arose: Lithium-ion batteries, which provide electrical power, caught fire on two Dreamliner aircraft, prompting regulators to ground all Dreamliners in service around the world. Perhaps *The Wall Street Journal* gave the best new-product lesson from the Boeing 787 Dreamliner example: "Innovation—for all its value—doesn't come as easily as a catchphrase. It can get messy."[32]

Burger King's French Fries: The Complexities of Commercialization McDonald's french fries are considered the gold standard against which all other fries in the fast-food industry are measured. But that didn't deter Burger King in taking on McDonald's fries. The company spent millions of R&D dollars developing a french fry designed to retain heat longer and add crispiness.

The result was a thick-cut french fry. It had a new "coating" on the outside to create a "crispy, golden-brown deliciousness" while retaining the heat longer—for at least 10 minutes—because 75 percent of customers eat their fries "on the go" in their cars, offices, or homes. Burger King also launched the largest TV advertising campaign in its history to promote the new fries. The launch turned into a disaster. The reason: Except under ideal conditions, the new fry proved too complicated to get right day after day in Burger King restaurants.

Then, Burger King introduced its "Satisfries" as the french fries in its kids meals. These were intended to help address concerns about nutrition for and obesity in children. Satisfries had about 20 percent fewer calories and 25 percent less fat than its regular fries. But Burger King's effort failed. Burger King discontinued its Satisfries at most of its restaurants because it couldn't communicate a meaningful point of difference to its customers and Satisfries cost more than its regular fries.[33]

To discover the downs and ups of commercializing a new product, see the text discussion of Burger King's multiyear search for a french fry recipe that can compete with McDonald's.
Mike Hruby/McGraw-Hill Education

LEARNING REVIEW

10-9. How does the development stage of the new-product development process involve testing the product inside and outside the firm?

10-10. What is a test market, and what are the three kinds?

10-11. What is the commercialization of a new product?

LEARNING OBJECTIVES REVIEW

LO 10-1 *Recognize the various terms that pertain to products and services.*
A product is a good, service, or idea consisting of a bundle of tangible and intangible attributes that satisfies consumers and is received in exchange for money or something else of value.

A good has tangible attributes that a consumer's five senses can perceive and intangible ones such as warranties; a laptop computer is an example. Goods also can be divided into nondurable goods, which are consumed in one or a few uses, and durable goods, which usually last over many uses.

Services are intangible activities or benefits that an organization provides to satisfy consumer needs in exchange for money or something else of value, such as an airline trip. An idea is a thought that leads to a product or action, such as eating healthier foods.

LO 10-2 *Identify the ways in which consumer and business products and services can be classified.*
Classified by type of user, the major distinctions are consumer products, which are products purchased by the ultimate consumer, and business products, which are products that assist an organization in providing other products for resale.

Consumer products can be classified further based on the effort involved in the purchase decision process, marketing mix attributes used in the purchase, and the frequency of purchase: (*a*) convenience products are items that consumers purchase frequently and with a minimum of shopping effort; (*b*) shopping products are items for which consumers compare several alternatives on selected criteria; (*c*) specialty products are items that consumers make special efforts to seek out and buy; and (*d*) unsought products are items that consumers either do not know about or do not initially want.

Business products can be broken down into (*a*) components, which are items that become part of the final product, such as raw materials or parts, and (*b*) support products, which are items used to assist in producing other goods and services and include installations, accessory equipment, supplies, and industrial services.

Services can be classified in terms of whether they are delivered by (*a*) people or equipment, (*b*) business firms or nonprofit organizations, or (*c*) government agencies.

Firms can offer a range of products, which involve decisions regarding the product item, product line, and product mix.

LO 10-3 *Explain the significance of "newness" in new products and services as it relates to the degree of consumer learning involved.*
From the important perspective of the consumer, "newness" is often seen as the degree of learning that a consumer must engage in to use the product. With a continuous innovation, no new behaviors must be learned. With a dynamically continuous innovation, only minor behavioral changes are needed. With a discontinuous innovation, consumers must learn entirely new consumption patterns.

LO 10-4 *Describe the factors contributing to the success or failure of a new product or service.*
A new product or service often fails for these marketing reasons: (1) insignificant points of difference, (2) incomplete market and product protocol before product development starts, (3) a failure to satisfy customer needs on critical factors, (4) bad timing, (5) no economical access to buyers, (6) poor execution of the marketing mix, (7) too little market attractiveness, and (8) poor product quality.

LO 10-5 *Explain the purposes of each step of the new-product development process.*
The new-product development process consists of seven stages a firm uses to develop salable products or services: (1) *New-product strategy development* involves defining the role for the new product within the firm's overall objectives. (2) *Idea generation* involves developing a pool of concepts from consumers, employees, basic R&D, and competitors to serve as candidates for new products. (3) *Screening and evaluation* involves evaluating new-product ideas to eliminate those that are not feasible from a technical or consumer perspective. (4) *Business analysis* involves defining the features of the new product, developing the marketing strategy and marketing program to introduce it, and making a financial forecast. (5) *Development* involves not only producing a prototype product but also testing it in the lab and with consumers to see that it meets the standards set for it. (6) *Market testing* involves exposing actual products to prospective consumers under realistic purchasing conditions to see if they will buy the product. (7) *Commercialization* involves positioning and launching a product in full-scale production and sales with a specific marketing program.

LEARNING REVIEW ANSWERS

10-1 What are the four main types of consumer products?
Answer: They are: (1) convenience products–items that the consumer purchases frequently, conveniently, and with a minimum of shopping effort; (2) shopping products–items for which the consumer compares several alternatives on criteria such as price, quality, or style; (3) specialty products–items that the consumer makes a special effort to search out and buy; and (4) unsought products–items that the consumer does not know about or knows about but does not initially want.

10-2 What is the difference between a product line and a product mix?
Answer: A product line is a group of product or service items that are closely related because they satisfy a class of needs, are used together, are sold to the same customer group, are distributed through the same outlets, or fall within a given price range. The product mix consists of all the product lines offered by an organization.

10-3 What kind of innovation would an improved electric toothbrush be?
Answer: continuous innovation–no new learning is required by consumers

10-4 Why can an "insignificant point of difference" lead to new-product failure?
Answer: The new product must have superior characteristics that deliver unique benefits to the user; compared to competitors, its benefits must be sufficient enough to motivate a change in consumption behavior. Without these points of difference, the product will probably fail.

10-5 What marketing metric might you use to assess the effectiveness of a new-product program?
Answer: The New Product Development Index, which shows the percentage of total company sales that come from new products each year.

10-6 What is the new-product strategy development stage in the new-product development process?
Answer: New-product strategy development is the first stage of the new-product process that defines the role for a new product in terms of the firm's overall objectives. During this stage, the firm uses both a SWOT analysis and environmental scanning to assess its strengths and weaknesses relative to the trends it identifies as opportunities or threats. The outcome not only defines the vital "protocol" for each new-product idea but also identifies the strategic role it might serve in the firm's business portfolio.

10-7 What are the main sources of new-product ideas?
Answer: Many firms obtain ideas externally using open innovation, in which an organization finds and executes creative new-product ideas by developing strategic relationships with outside individuals and organizations. Some of these sources include employee and co-worker suggestions; customer and supplier suggestions (either directly, through the firm's salesforce or purchasing department or through crowdsourcing–soliciting ideas via the Internet from large numbers of people); R&D laboratories (both internal to the firm and professional innovation firms such as IDEO); competitive products (analyzing their points of difference that lead to a competitive advantage for them); and smaller, nontraditional technology firms, university technology transfer centers that partner with business firms to commercialize faculty inventions, and lone inventors or entrepreneurs.

10-8 How do internal and external screening and evaluation approaches differ?
Answer: In internal screening, company employees evaluate the technical feasibility of new-product ideas to determine whether they meet the objectives defined in the new-product strategy development stage. For services, employees are assessed to determine whether they have the commitment and skills to meet customer expectations and sustain customer loyalty. In external screening, evaluation consists of preliminary concept testing of the new-product idea (not the actual product itself) using written descriptions, sketches, mockups, or promotional literature with consumers.

10-9 How does the development stage of the new-product development process involve testing the product inside and outside the firm?
Answer: Development is the stage of the new-product process that turns the idea on paper into a prototype–a demonstrable, producible

product that can be efficiently manufactured. Internally, laboratory tests are done to see if the product achieves the physical, quality, and safety standards set for it. Externally, market testing is done to expose actual products to prospective consumers under realistic purchase conditions to see if they will buy.

10-10 What is a test market, and what are the three kinds?
Answer: Test marketing involves offering a product for sale on a limited basis in a defined area for a specific time period. The three main kinds of test markets are: (1) standard, (2) controlled, and (3) simulated. In a standard test market, a city (or cities) is selected that is viewed as being demographically representative of the markets targeted for the new product. Standard test markets must have both cable TV systems that can deliver different ads to different homes and retailers with checkout counter scanners to measure sales results. In a controlled test market, the firm contracts the entire test program to an outside service, which pays retailers for shelf space to guarantee a specified percentage of the test product's potential distribution volume. In a simulated (or laboratory) test market (STM), the firm attempts to replicate a full-scale test market by creating a fictitious storefront in a shopping mall and exposing prospective customers to the product (or concept) and ads from both it and its competitors to see if they will buy.

10-11 What is the commercialization of a new product?
Answer: Commercialization, the most expensive stage for most new products, is the last stage of the new-product development process. It involves positioning and launching a new product in full-scale production and sales.

FOCUSING ON KEY TERMS

business analysis p. 279
business products p. 266
commercialization p. 281
consumer products p. 266
convenience products p. 267
development p. 280
idea generation p. 276
market testing p. 280
new-product development process p. 275
new-product strategy development p. 275
open innovation p. 273
product p. 266
product item p. 268
product line p. 268
product mix p. 268
protocol p. 271
screening and evaluation p. 278
services p. 266
shopping products p. 267
specialty products p. 267
unsought products p. 267

APPLYING MARKETING KNOWLEDGE

1 Products can be classified as either consumer or business products. How would you classify the following products? (*a*) Johnson's baby shampoo, (*b*) a Stanley Black & Decker two-speed drill, and (*c*) an arc welder.
2 Are Nature Valley granola bars and Eddie Bauer hiking boots convenience, shopping, specialty, or unsought products?
3 Based on your answer to question 2, how would the marketing actions differ for each product and the classification to which you assigned it?
4 In terms of the behavioral effect on consumers, how would a computer, such as an Apple iMac, be classified? In light of this classification, what actions would you suggest to the manufacturers of these products to increase their sales in the market?
5 What methods would you suggest to assess the potential commercial success of the following new products? (*a*) a new, improved ketchup; (*b*) a three-dimensional television system that has taken the company 10 years to develop; and (*c*) a new children's toy on which the company holds a patent.
6 Concept testing is an important step in the new-product development process. Outline the concept tests for (*a*) an electrically powered car and (*b*) a new loan payment system for automobiles that is based on a variable interest rate. What are the differences in developing concept tests for products as opposed to services?

BUILDING YOUR MARKETING PLAN

In fine-tuning the product strategy for your marketing plan, do these two things:

1 Develop a simple three-column table in which (*a*) market segments of potential customers are in the first column and (*b*) the one or two key points of difference of the product to satisfy the segment's needs are in the second column.
2 In the third column of your table, write ideas for specific new products for your business in each of the rows in your table.

GoPro CEO Nick Woodman and his college friends loved to surf. It was a passion. As GoPro Vice President of Brand Integrity, Justin Wilkenfeld, explains, "We would run down to the beach to surf every day, trying to balance that with going to classes." The passion turned into a great new-product idea when Woodman was surfing in Australia and wanted to capture the experience but couldn't get photographers close enough to obtain good photos. The result was the first GoPro camera, which attached to a wrist strap. "The idea was that you could capture that experience hands-free and really focus on enjoying your passion as opposed to worrying about what's on the other side of a screen," Wilkenfeld says.

VIDEO 10-4
GoPro Video Case
kerin.tv/15e/v10-4

Chances are that you've viewed some of the millions of videos created by surfers, snowboarders, rock stars, hockey players, parents, sky divers, scuba divers, pilots, and just about anyone with a passion for their life. In fact, GoPro estimates that more than 1 billion minutes of GoPro video are viewed each year, just on YouTube! Woodman and his friends call it "the GoPro movement."

"Joining the GoPro movement is all about joining the GoPro community around the world," says Wilkenfeld. "This is a group of passionate people that live a big life and love to experience things." GoPro's success at attracting customers from around the world is supported by its commitment to developing new products that meet their needs. According to Wilkenfeld, "One of the biggest challenges of developing technology is getting ahead of the consumer and developing things that you think they are going to need."

Source: GoPro Inc.

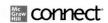

THE COMPANY

GoPro's history of new-product development is truly inspirational, particularly when the current product line is compared to the first offering. As Kelly Baker, Director of Media Relations, explains, "The first product out on the market was in this big, kind of clunky, plastic housing attached to your wrist that you could flip up and down. It captured images on 35mm film that you would take into a pharmacy or photography studio and get your pictures printed." That product was replaced by the Digital HERO camera which was powered by one AAA battery and provided silent 10-second VGA videos.

Other new products soon followed. GoPro added audio capabilities, wide-angle lenses, and time lapse features. In addition, mountable versions that included Helmet HERO, Motorsports HERO, and Surf HERO expanded its market beyond the wrist-camera positioning. The biggest shift in popularity, however, occurred when GoPro added the HD HERO featuring 1080p images. Complementary products such as removable battery packs, video editing tools, a GoPro app, and Wi-Fi remote controls were also added to the product line.

As the popularity of GoPro products grew so did the company, leading to its IPO on the Nasdaq stock exchange. According to Baker, "the most impressive statistics are the growth in employees and the growth in sales." Today the company has more than 1,300 employees and $1.5 billion in sales.

THE PRODUCT DEVELOPMENT PROCESS AT GOPRO

The stream of new products is essential to GoPro. "What's special for GoPro is that we're a company built on passion and, ultimately, on the shoulders of our consumers," remarks Wilkenfeld. Generally, the company follows a rigorous sequence of steps or stages to maintain its offerings for consumers.

The first stage, new-product strategy development, reflects GoPro's environmental scanning efforts. Initially Woodman and his friends observed the social trend toward sharing experiences. This trend was facilitated through its cameras and the growth of social media. GoPro also recognized a growing interest in capturing unique situations and camera angles where the use of other cameras such as smartphones isn't feasible. To build on this trend the company announced a developer program that allows third-party companies to build GoPro compatibility into their products. BMW, for example, created an application that combines GoPro video with telemetry data and location data to add value for its customers, while Fisher-Price is planning to build GoPro mounts into its Jumperoo and Walker products to provide a child's perspective.

The second stage is idea generation, which is the result of several distinct activities at GoPro. "When we're developing new products there are two different sources—one being just a crazy idea that an engineer or Nick or somebody on the team has, and then there is a more formulaic approach," say Wilkenfeld. Both approaches work well at GoPro, where employees are so passionate about GoPro they are constantly thinking of new ideas and where an open innovation perspective encourages ideas from consumers, retailers, and a team of amateur and professional athletes. GoPro even offers awards for the best content submitted to its website—in a variety of categories such as action, adventure, music, animals, family, travel, and science—where new and creative ideas are often found.

Screening and evaluation involves an assessment of each idea to determine if it warrants further effort. Although this stage assesses a variety of quantitative requirements of new technologies, GoPro is also careful to assess qualitative aspects of new ideas. "If you are all about the data and you're completely data-driven, then you're only going to be doing things that the consumer is asking you to do, and you're not exploring and experimenting and really coming up with ideas that the customer didn't necessarily know that they needed or wanted," Wilkenfeld explains.

Once an idea is approved, GoPro begins its business analysis step, which involves building a "business case" for the idea. One of the key considerations in this step is the potential for cannibalization. For example, when GoPro introduced its HERO Session camera at a price much lower than other GoPro models it had to consider the possibility of cannibalizing sales of its own products. The amount of time needed to reach break-even points and the likely timing for competitors to respond to new products must also be considered. "Life cycles are definitely a consideration," says Wilkenfeld.

GoPro begins to turn the idea into a prototype in the development stage. The team often produces a prototype with 3D printers to check the aesthetics and the dimensions of new products. Once the final design is determined, functional prototypes are developed. Wilkenfeld explains, "Our product teams test early prototypes to see if the functionality is there, if it's a viable product to take to market, before we get too far down the path."

Once production-quality prototypes are available, GoPro begins stage six, market testing. The first element of the testing engages GoPro's employees. According to Wilkenfeld, "We have a program every Thursday called Live It, Eat It, Love It, which is about living the brand." Employees go out and test GoPro products to provide feedback to the product development teams. A second element of the testing process sends prototypes to social media advocates, professional photographers, athletes, and past consumers to identify final changes to the products.

Changes from market testing lead to the final stage of the new-product development process, commercialization. At this point a good marketing plan is important. According to Wilkenfeld, "To be successful at the launch of a new product you've got to be very cognizant of what the right levers are to pull and what the audiences are, with digital marketing specifically." Stephanie Miller, senior manager of the GoPro Social Team, agrees: "Social media play a huge role in the go-to-market strategies for product releases and product launches. First and foremost, it starts with using social as a listening tool to understand the macro climate and key business trends that we are going to be launching the product into."

Providing its customers with a steady stream of new products means that the new-product development process is an ongoing activity at GoPro. The process varies for different types of products, though. "The typical product development life cycle is really going to depend on the type of product," explains Wilkenfeld. "You have products that could take a few months turnaround time, and then you have products that could take a couple of years, it really just depends on the complexity of the product," he adds. Although GoPro's success has certainly been related to the products it develops, there is also another element to its success. Wilkenfeld smiles and explains that to be successful "you also have to market the products!"

MARKETING AT GOPRO

As you might expect, GoPro is also exceptional at marketing. The fast-moving industry and highly engaged customers necessitate a comprehensive toolbox of marketing activities. Kelly Baker explains, "Consumers want to believe in brands that they feel are authentic and organic in their category. GoPro is about being passionate and exciting and engaging and living a big life and I think that comes across as genuine to our users."

GoPro's marketing activities include traditional media such as print ads in *Outside Magazine* and even a Super Bowl ad. In addition, GoPro uses social media, sponsorships, and an increasing emphasis on content marketing. Stephanie Miller manages all social media channels,

Source: GoPro Inc.

including Facebook, Instagram, Twitter, Pinterest, Periscope, and YouTube. "GoPro has a fantastically large social audience. We are over 22 million strong around the world, and we have a presence in over 17 countries," explains Miller. It's not easy, though. Miller describes the situation: "What we share on Facebook could be different than what we share on Twitter, which could differ from our Instagram strategy. It's a very fine-tuned approach."

VIDEO 10-5
GoPro Super Bowl Ad
kerin.tv/15e/v10-5

Sponsorships are also a large part of GoPro's marketing program. Baker and her team maintain a roster of about 140 athletes from a wide variety of sports. For example, Kelly Slater (surfing), Chris Cole (skateboarding), Sage Kotsenburg (snowboarding), Lindsey Vonn (skiing), and many others are sponsored by GoPro. "GoPro's athlete sponsorship program often starts very organically, meaning we look for athletes that are already using our camera," Baker explains. "We want people that are heroes in the sport and in their community" because "we know that is going to make them a wonderful ambassador for our brand," she adds.

A relatively new part of GoPro's marketing program is the growth of content marketing–the creation and distribution of content (e.g., videos, web pages, podcasts, infographics, etc.) for a specific audience. For example, GoPro often buys the rights to self-shot videos with inspiring content, edits them, and posts them to its own channels for additional distribution. Yara Khakbaz, executive producer at GoPro, observes that user-generated content (UGC) and "storytelling" are a unique and powerful aspect of GoPro's program. This new emphasis is the result of additional attention to new target markets. GoPro started with extreme sports enthusiasts, of course, and then added professional markets such as movie directors and producers, and then moms and families, and now travel and adventure enthusiasts. All of these markets are interested in telling their own interesting and powerful stories. As Khakbaz explains, content marketing is "really about building our audience and inspiring our users and our consumers to continue capturing and sharing their stories." "These genuine moments, that raw authenticity, is GoPro," she adds.

The future promises much more authenticity and excitement from GoPro. New products such as the Fusion (a 360-degree video camera) and apps for Cloud connectivity and virtual reality are in development. "GoPro has really helped enable modern storytelling in ways that we didn't even dream of, and what makes it so special for us is that we're constantly validated by people using our products," says Wilkenfeld. "That's what I love about it, is that it's an inspirational place to work."[34]

Questions

1 What are the points of difference, or unique attributes, for GoPro products?

2 What are GoPro's primary target markets? How does content marketing influence these markets?

3 Describe the new-product development process used at GoPro. What are the similarities and differences to the process described in Figure 10-3?

4 Which of the eight reasons for new-product failure did GoPro avoid to ensure the success of its products?

5 Identify one new-product idea you would suggest that GoPro evaluate.

Chapter Notes

1. "Apple iCar Release Date Rumors, Features and Images," www.macworld.co.uk, March 6, 2019; "Apple Car: What You Need to Know about Project Titan," www.digitaltrends.com, August 15, 2018; "The Apple Car, as Imagined by *Motor Trend*," www.wsj.com, April 14, 2016; "It Is Prime Time for Smartwatches," *The Wall Street Journal*, March 7, 2019, p. B12; and "Has Apple Lost Its Design Mojo?" *Fortune*, January 1, 2018, pp. 46–55.
2. www.crapola.us, retrieved July 20, 2019; "When Selling a Bunch of 'Crapola' Is a Good Thing," www.forbes.com, July 22, 2015; and "On the Run with Crapola Granola," *Star Tribune*, January 14, 2013, p. D2.
3. Debora Viana Thompson, Rebecca W. Hamilton, and Roland Rust, "Feature Fatigue: When Product Capabilities Become Too Much of a Good Thing," *Journal of Marketing Research*, November 2005, pp. 431–42; Ronald T. Rust, Debora Viana Thompson, and Rebecca W. Hamilton, "Defeating Feature Fatigue," *Harvard Business Review*, February 2006, pp. 98–107; Rebecca W. Hamilton, Roland T. Rust, and Chekitan S. Dev, "Which Features Increase Customer Retention?" *MIT Sloan Management Review*, Winter 2017, pp. 41–50; "eMarketer Releases New Report on Declining Interest in Wearables," *emarketer.com*, March 17, 2017; and "Apple's Rare Sales Warning Sparks iPhone Fatigue Fear," www.cnet.com, January 4, 2019.
4. Thompson et al., "Feature Fatigue: When Product Capabilities Become Too Much of a Good Thing."
5. "Amazon Is Quietly Rolling Out Its Own Geek Squad to Set Up Gadgets in Your Home," www.recode.net, July 30, 2017.
6. Unless otherwise noted, the examples described in this section appear in "The 25 Biggest Product Flops of All Time," www.walletpop.com/photos/top-25-biggest-product-flops-of-all-time, accessed March 21, 2019; and Zac Frank and Tania Khadder, "The 20 Worst Product Failures," www.saleshq.monster.com/news/articles/2655-the-20-worst-product-failures, accessed March 21, 2019.
7. Joan Schneider and Julie Hall, "Why Most Product Launches Fail," *Harvard Business Review*, April 2011, pp. 21–23.
8. Robert G. Cooper, "New Products: What Separates the Winners from the Losers?" in *The PDMA Handbook of New Product Development*, Kenneth B. Kahn, ed. (New York: Wiley, 2013), pp. 3–34; and Merle Crawford and Anthony Di Benedetto, *New Products Management*, 11th ed. (New York: McGraw-Hill/Irwin, 2015). The examples described in this section come from these sources unless otherwise indicated.
9. Martin Gitlin and Topher Ellis, *The Great American Cereal Book: How Breakfast Got Its Crunch* (New York: Harry N. Abrams, Inc., 2011).
10. The Avert Virucidal tissues and Garlic Cake examples discussed are described in Robert M. McMath and Thom Forbes, *What Were They Thinking?* (New York: Random House, 1998).
11. "Keurig Will Stop Selling Its $370 Kold Soda Machine," www.fortune.com, June 7, 2016.
12. "Thousands of Kids Injured by Hoverboards in Their First 2 Years on the Market," www.cbsnews.com, March 26, 2018.
13. The remaining discussion is based on D. Deichmann, L. Rozentale, and R. Barnhorn, "Open Innovation Generates Great Ideas, So Why Aren't Companies Adopting Them?" *hbr.org*, December 20, 2017; "The 25 Biggest Product Flops of All Time," www.walletpop.com/photos/top-25-biggest-product-flops-of-all-time, accessed March 21, 2019; "Innovation as a Team Wins, Study Finds," *The Wall Street Journal*, August 9, 2018, p. B6; and Cass Sunstein and Reid Hastie, *Wiser: Getting beyond Groupthink to Make Groups Smarter* (Boston: Harvard Business Review Press, 2015).
14. "PepsiCo Is Creating a New Unit to Deliver Smaller Brands," www.fortune.com, August 14, 2018.
15. "R&D: One of the Driving Factors behind 3M's Growth," www.forbes.com, December 20, 2016; "Innovation Measure #7: Innovation Vitality Index," http://thechiefinnovationofficer.com, November 11, 2014; and Bradford L. Goldense, "Do You Know Your Research Quotient for R&D Spending?" www.rdmag.com, May 23, 2018.
16. For an overview of the Stage-Gate process, see Robert G. Cooper, "The Drivers of Success in New Product Development," *Industrial Marketing Management*, March 2019, pp. 36-47; and Robert G. Cooper and Anita F. Summer, "Agile-Stage-Gate: New Idea-to-Launch Method for Manufactured New Products Is Faster, More Responsive," *Industrial Marketing Management*, November 2016, pp. 167–80.
17. "Flamin' Hot Cheetos: How a Frito-Lay Janitor Created One of the Most Popular Snacks," www.washingtonpost.com, February 23, 2018.
18. Dinah Eng, "Life Is Good in the T-Shirt Business," *Fortune*, May 19, 2014, pp. 39–42.
19. www.lifeisgood.com; and "Life Is Good's $100 Million Ad-Free Global Success Story," www.cnbc.com, May 19, 2015.
20. Sarah Ellison, "P&G Chief's Turnaround Recipe: Find Out What Women Want," *The Wall Street Journal*, June 1, 2005, pp. A1, A16.
21. "Tide Pods: Despite 'The Challenge,' P&G Doubles Down on Detergent Pouches," www.cincinnati.com, February 8, 2018.
22. Barry Bayus, "Crowdsourcing New Product Ideas over Time: An Analysis of the Dell IdeaStorm Community," *Management Science*, January 2013, pp. 226–44.
23. "Rethinking Apple's Recipe for Success," www.nytimes.com, May 26, 2016.
24. Charlie Rose, "How to Design Breakthrough Inventions," *CBS 60 Minutes*, air date January 6, 2013.
25. www.tesla.com, March 1, 2017; and "With Electric Cars, GM Targets Tesla," *The Wall Street Journal*, January 15, 2015, p. B2.
26. The examples are found in Kevin J. Boudreau and Karim R. Lakhani, "Using the Crowd as an Innovation Partner," *hbr.org*, April 2013; Peter Erickson, "One Food Company's Foray into Open Innovation," *PDMA Visions Magazine*, June 2008, pp. 12–14; and Stephen Key, "Want to Invent Best-Selling Products? Innovate Like the Founder of Scrub Daddy," www.inc.com, September 25, 2017.
27. "The Biggest Crowdfunding Campaigns: Where Are They Now?" *The Wall Street Journal*, May 1, 2018, pp. R1, R2; and "A Concise History of the Smartwatch," *bloombergbusiness.com*, January 8, 2018.
28. Quoted in Paul Trott, *Innovation Management and New Product Development*, 6th ed. (Harlow, UK: Pearson Education Ltd., 2017), p. 30.
29. "Google Glass: What Went Wrong," www.cnn.com, January 20, 2015; "The Reason Why Google Glass, Amazon Fire Phone, and Segway All Failed," www.forbes.com, February 12, 2015; and "Google Takes Another Stab at Google Glass, Updates the AR Headsets for Business Customers," www.usatoday.com, May 21, 2019.
30. "GM's Spending on Autonomous Vehicles Comes in below Forecast," www.autonews.com, February 6, 2019.
31. Tom J. Brown, Tracy A. Suter, and Gilbert A. Churchill, *Basic Marketing Research*, 9th ed. (Mason, OH: South-Western, Cengage Learning, 2018).

32. Daniel Michaels, "Innovation Is Messy Business," *The Wall Street Journal,* January 24, 2013, pp. B1, B2; and Christopher Drew, "Dreamliner Troubles Put Boeing on Edge," *The New York Times,* January 20, 2013.
33. "These Were the Biggest Menu Flops in Fast Food," www.businessinsider.com, July 17, 2018; Maureen Morrison, "Burger King Adds Satisfries Meals," www.adage.com, March 23, 2014; and "Burger King Stores Discontinue Satisfries and Sales Sizzle," www.bloombergbusiness.com, August 13, 2014.
34. GoPro: This case was written by Steven Hartley and Roger Kerin. Sources: Interviews with GoPro executives Justin Wilkenfeld, Yara Khakbaz, Kelly Baker, and Stephanie Miller; "We Are GoPro: A Guide to the DNA of Our Brand," GoPro, 2016; "GoPro Hires Veteran Apple Designer Seeking to Spur Growth," www.bloomberg.com, April 13, 2016; "GoPro Buys Pair of Video Editing Apps," www.fortune.com, March 1, 2016; and "GoPro Finally Starting to 'Get It,'" www.fool.com, April 18, 2016.

Chapter 11 Managing Successful Products, Services, and Brands

LEARNING OBJECTIVES

After reading this chapter you should be able to:

LO 11-1 Explain the product life-cycle concept.

LO 11-2 Identify ways that marketing executives manage a product's life cycle.

LO 11-3 Recognize the importance of branding and alternative branding strategies.

LO 11-4 Describe the role of packaging and labeling in the marketing of a product.

Gatorade: Bringing Science to Sweat for More Than 50 Years

Why is the thirst for Gatorade unquenchable? Look no further than constant product innovation and masterful brand management.

Like Kleenex in the tissue market and Jell-O among gelatin desserts, Gatorade is synonymous with sports drinks. Concocted in 1965 at the University of Florida as a rehydration beverage for the school's football team, the drink was coined "Gatorade" by an opposing team's coach after watching his team lose to the Florida Gators in the Orange Bowl. The name stuck, and a new beverage product class was born. Stokely-Van Camp, Inc. bought the Gatorade formula in 1967 and commercialized the product.

Creating the Gatorade Brand

The Quaker Oats Company acquired Stokely-Van Camp in 1983 and quickly increased Gatorade sales through a variety of means. More flavors were added. Multiple package sizes were offered using different containers. Distribution expanded from convenience stores and supermarkets to mass merchandisers such as Walmart. Consistent advertising effectively conveyed the product's unique performance benefits and links to athletic competition. Global expansion was vigorously pursued.

Today, Gatorade is a global brand and is sold in more than 80 countries. It is also the official sports drink of NASCAR, the National Football League, Major League Baseball, the National Basketball Association, the National Hockey League, Major League Soccer, and the Women's National Basketball Association.

Masterful brand management spurred Gatorade's success. Gatorade entered the bottled-water category with Propel Fitness Water, a lightly flavored water fortified with vitamins, in 1999. The Gatorade Performance Series was introduced in 2001, featuring an Energy Bar, Energy Drink, and a Nutritional Shake.

Building the Gatorade Brand

Brand development accelerated after PepsiCo bought Quaker Oats and the Gatorade brand in 2001. Gatorade Endurance Formula was created for serious runners, construction workers, and other people doing long, sweaty workouts. A low-calorie Gatorade called G2 appeared in 2008.

In 2009, Gatorade executives unleashed a bevy of enhanced beverages in bold new packaging. "Just like any good athlete, Gatorade is taking it to the next level," said Gatorade's chief marketing officer. "Whether you're in it for the win, for the

VIDEO 11-1
Gatorade Ad
kerin.tv/15e/v11-1

TO STOP IS TO FAIL
G
WINFROMWITHIN

Source: PepsiCo

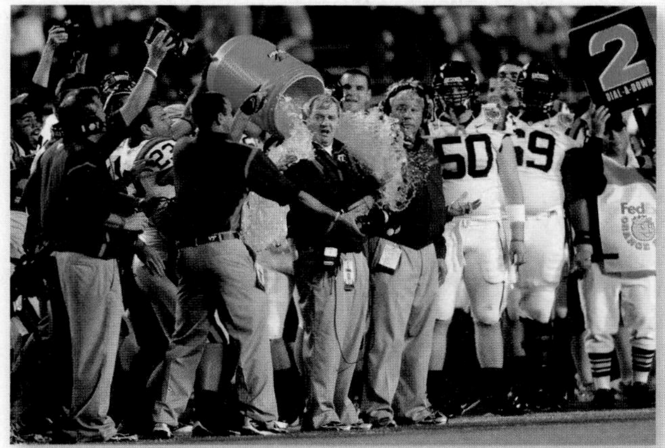

Gatorade's marketing performance is a direct result of continuous product improvement and masterful brand management as defined by the "Gatorade bath."
J. Meric/Getty Images

thrill or for better health, if your body is moving, Gatorade sees you as an athlete, and we're inviting you into the brand." According to a company announcement, "The new Gatorade attitude would be most visible through a total packaging redesign." For example, Gatorade Thirst Quencher now displays the letter *G* front and center along with the brand's iconic bolt. "For Gatorade, G represents the heart, hustle, and soul of athleticism and will become a badge of pride for anyone who sweats, no matter where they're active."[1]

Continuing product development efforts guided the creation of the G Series of products in 2010 and 2011. At the time, Gatorade underwent a brand repositioning during which it developed different Gatorade products targeted at different types of athletes. These lines included the traditional G Series for athletes and the G Series Endurance for extreme sports athletes. Product development within these lines continues today as evidenced by the launch of new Gatorade chews, bars, powders, shakes, and yogurt. Organic Gatorade was introduced in 2016. Gatorade Flow, a hydrating drink with fewer calories, was launched in 2017, followed by Gatorade Zero, a sugar-free drink, in 2018.

Gatorade introduced a microchip-fitted "smart cap" bottle and sweat patch that communicate digitally and provide athletes and fitness buffs constant updates on how much they should drink in 2018. New flavors (such as Peach Blitz) were introduced in 2019.[2]

The marketing of Gatorade illustrates continuous product development and masterful brand management in a dynamic marketplace. Gatorade remains a vibrant multibillion-dollar brand more than 50 years after its creation. This chapter shows how the actions taken by Gatorade executives exemplify those made by successful marketers.

CHARTING THE PRODUCT LIFE CYCLE

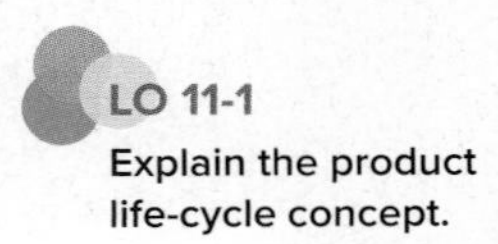

LO 11-1

Explain the product life-cycle concept.

Products, like people, are viewed as having a life cycle. The concept of the **product life cycle** describes the stages a new product goes through in the marketplace: introduction, growth, maturity, and decline (Figure 11-1).[3] The two curves shown in this figure, total industry sales revenue and total industry profit, represent the sum of sales revenue and profit of all firms producing the product. The reasons for the changes in each curve and the marketing decisions involved are detailed next.

Introduction Stage

The introduction stage of the product life cycle occurs when a product is introduced to its intended target market. During this period, sales grow slowly and profit is minimal. The lack of profit is often the result of large investment costs in product development, such as the millions of dollars spent by Gillette to develop the Gillette Fusion shaving system. The marketing objective for the company at this stage is to create consumer awareness and stimulate *trial*–the initial purchase of a product by a consumer.

Companies often spend heavily on advertising and other promotion tools to build awareness and stimulate product trial among consumers in the introduction stage. For example, Gillette budgeted $200 million in advertising to introduce the Fusion shaving system to male shavers. The result? Over 60 percent of male shavers became aware of the new razor within six months and 26 percent tried the product.[4]

Advertising and promotion expenditures in the introduction stage are often made to stimulate *primary demand*, the desire for the product class rather than for a specific brand, since there are few competitors with the same product. As more competitors launch their own products and the product progresses along its life cycle, company attention is focused on creating *selective demand*, the preference for a specific brand.

Other marketing mix variables also are important at this stage. Gaining distribution can be a challenge because channel intermediaries may be hesitant to carry a new product. Also, a company often restricts the number of variations of the product to ensure control of product quality. As an example, the original Gatorade came in only one flavor–lemon-lime.

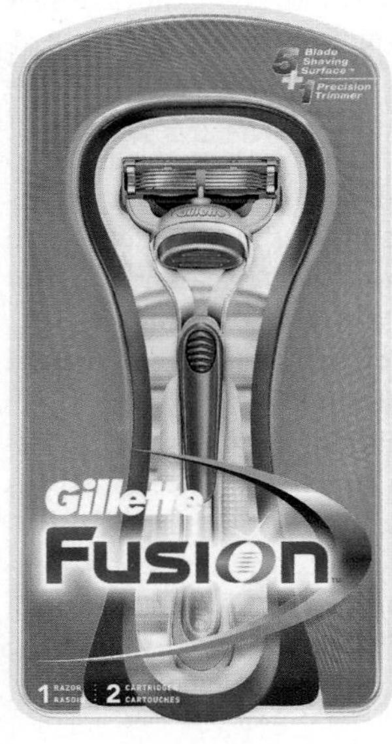

The success of the Gillette Fusion shaving system can be understood using product life-cycle concepts, as discussed in the text.
Mike Hruby/McGraw-Hill Education

During introduction, pricing can be either high or low. A high initial price may be used as part of a *skimming* strategy to help the company recover the costs of development as well as capitalize on the price insensitivity of early buyers. A master of this strategy is 3M. According to a 3M manager, "We hit fast, price high, and get the heck out when the me-too products pour in."[5] High prices tend to attract competitors eager to enter the market because they see the opportunity for profit. To discourage competitive entry, a company can price low, referred to as *penetration pricing*. This pricing strategy helps build unit volume, but a company must closely monitor costs. These and other pricing techniques are covered in Chapter 14.

Figure 11-2 on page 294 charts the stand-alone fax machine product life cycle for business use in the United States from the early 1970s to early 2020.[6] Sales grew slowly in the 1970s and early 1980s after Xerox pioneered the first portable fax machine. Fax machines were first sold direct to businesses by company salespeople and were premium priced. The average price for a fax machine in 1980 was a hefty $12,700, or about $39,000 in today's dollars! Those fax machines were primitive by today's standards. They contained mechanical parts, not electronic circuitry, and offered few features seen in today's models.

Several product classes are in the introductory stage of the product life cycle today. These include smart TVs and all-electric-powered automobiles.

Growth Stage

The growth stage of the product life cycle is characterized by rapid increases in sales. It is in this stage that competitors appear. For example, Figure 11-2 shows the dramatic increase in

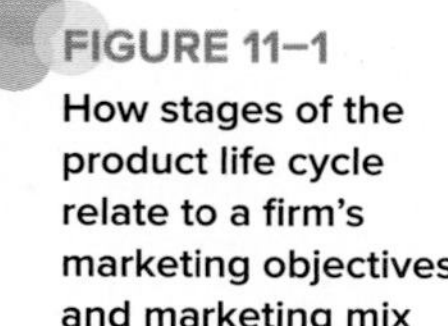

FIGURE 11–1
How stages of the product life cycle relate to a firm's marketing objectives and marketing mix actions.

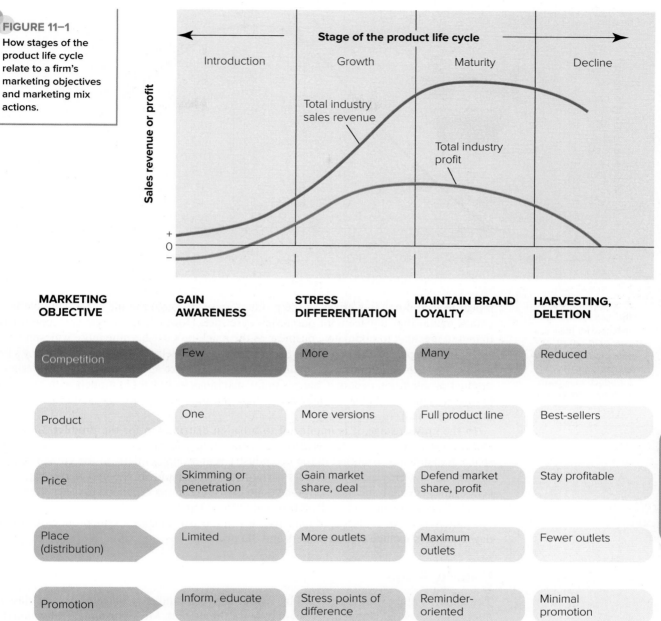

MARKETING OBJECTIVE	GAIN AWARENESS	STRESS DIFFERENTIATION	MAINTAIN BRAND LOYALTY	HARVESTING, DELETION
Competition	Few	More	Many	Reduced
Product	One	More versions	Full product line	Best-sellers
Price	Skimming or penetration	Gain market share, deal	Defend market share, profit	Stay profitable
Place (distribution)	Limited	More outlets	Maximum outlets	Fewer outlets
Promotion	Inform, educate	Stress points of difference	Reminder-oriented	Minimal promotion

fax machine sales from 1986 to 1998. The number of companies selling fax machines also increased, from one in the early 1970s to seven manufacturers in 1983, which sold nine brands. By 1998 there were some 25 manufacturers and 60 brands from which to choose.

The result of more competitors and more aggressive pricing is that profit usually peaks during the growth stage. For instance, the average price for a fax machine plummeted from $3,300 in 1985 to $500 in 1995. At this stage, advertising shifts emphasis to stimulating selective demand; product benefits are compared with those of competitors' offerings for the purpose of gaining market share.

Product sales in the growth stage grow at an increasing rate because of new people trying or using the product and a growing proportion of *repeat purchasers*—people who tried the product, were satisfied, and bought again. For the Gillette Fusion razor, over 60 percent of men who tried the razor adopted the product permanently. For successful products, the ratio of

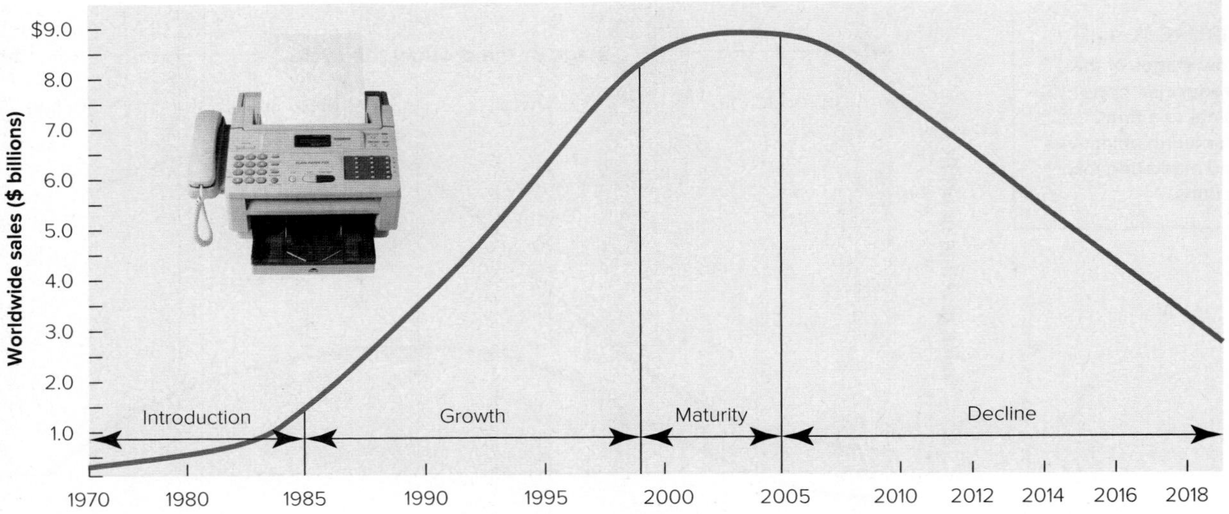

FIGURE 11–2
Product life cycle for the stand-alone fax machine for business use: 1970–2020. All four product life-cycle stages appear: introduction, growth, maturity, and decline.
EyeWire/Getty Images

repeat to trial purchases grows as the product moves through the life cycle. Durable fax machines meant that replacement purchases were rare. However, it became common for more than one machine to populate a business as the machine's use became more widespread.

Changes appear in the product in the growth stage. To help differentiate a company's brand from competitors, an improved version or new features are added to the original design and product proliferation occurs. Changes in fax machines included (1) models with built-in telephones; (2) models that used plain, rather than thermal, paper for copies; and (3) models that integrated e-mail.

In the growth stage, it is important to broaden distribution for the product. In the retail store, for example, this often means that competing companies fight for display and shelf space. Expanded distribution in the fax industry is an example. Early in the growth stage, just 11 percent of office machine dealers carried this equipment. By the mid-1990s, over 70 percent of these dealers sold fax equipment, and distribution was expanded to other stores selling electronic equipment, such as Best Buy and Office Depot.

Numerous product classes or industries are in the growth stage of the product life cycle today. Examples include e-book readers and 3D printers.

Maturity Stage

The maturity stage is characterized by a slowing of total industry sales or product class revenue. Also, marginal competitors begin to leave the market. Most consumers who would buy the product are either repeat purchasers of the item or have tried and abandoned it. Sales increase at a decreasing rate in the maturity stage as fewer new buyers enter the market. Profit declines due to fierce price competition among many sellers, and the cost of gaining new buyers at this stage rises.

Marketing attention in the maturity stage is often directed toward holding market share through further product differentiation and finding new buyers and uses. For example, Gillette modified its Fusion shaving system with the addition of Fusion ProGlide, a five-blade shaver with an additional blade on the back for trimming. Fax machine manufacturers developed Internet-enabled multifunctional models with new features such as scanning, copying, and color reproduction. They also designed fax machines suitable for small and home businesses, which today represent a substantial portion of sales. Still, a major consideration in a company's strategy in this stage is to control overall marketing cost by improving promotional and distribution efficiency.

Fax machines entered the maturity stage in the late 1990s. At the time, about 90 percent of industry sales were captured by five producers (Hewlett-Packard, Brother, Sharp, Epson, and Samsung), reflecting the departure of marginal competitors. By 2004, some 200 million stand-

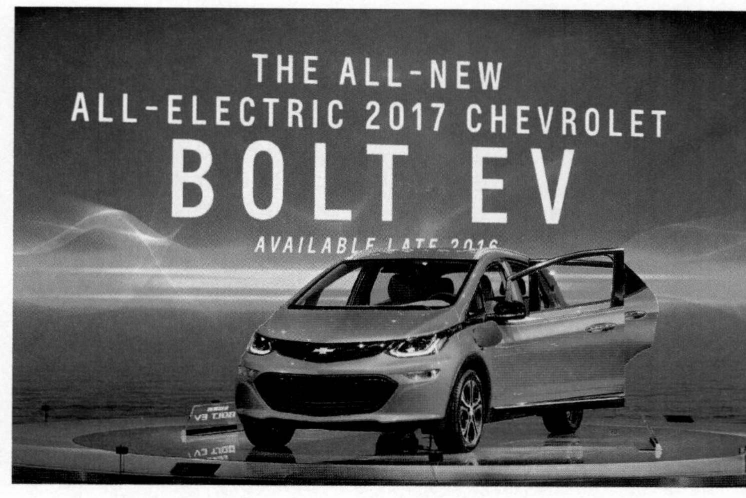

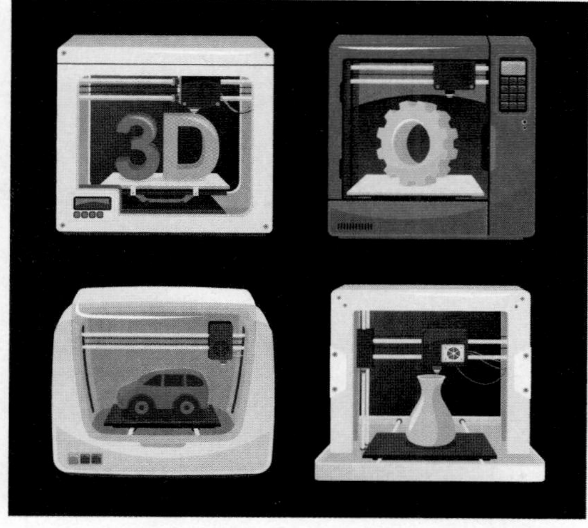

Electric automobiles like the Chevrolet Bolt made by General Motors are in the introductory stage of the product life cycle. By comparison, 3D printers are in the growth stage of the product life cycle. Each product faces unique challenges based on its product life-cycle stage.
(Left): Darren Brode/Shutterstock; (Right): Tomacco/Getty Images

General Motors Company
www.gm.com

alone fax machines were installed throughout the world, sending more than 120 billion faxes annually.

Numerous product classes and industries are in the maturity stage of their product life cycle. These include carbonated soft drinks and presweetened breakfast cereals.

Decline Stage

The decline stage occurs when sales drop. Fax machines entered this stage in early 2005 and the average price for a fax machine had sunk below $100. There are 46 million fax machines installed throughout the world today, sending over 20 billion faxes in 2019. Frequently, a product enters this stage not because of any wrong strategy on the part of companies, but because of environmental changes. For example, digital music pushed compact discs into decline in the recorded music industry. Will Internet technology and e-mail make fax machines extinct anytime soon? The Marketing Matters box on the next page offers one perspective on this question that may surprise you.[7]

Numerous product classes or industries are in the decline stage of their product life cycle. Two prominent examples include analog TVs and desktop personal computers.

Products in the decline stage tend to consume a disproportionate share of management and financial resources relative to their future worth. A company will follow one of two strategies to handle a declining product: deletion or harvesting.

Deletion Product *deletion*, or dropping the product from the company's product line, is the most drastic strategy. Because a residual core of consumers still consume or use a product even in the decline stage, product elimination decisions are not taken lightly. For example, Sanford Corporation continues to sell its Liquid Paper correction fluid for use with typewriters in the era of word-processing equipment.

Harvesting A second strategy, *harvesting*, is when a company retains the product but reduces marketing costs. The product continues to be offered, but salespeople do not allocate time in selling nor are advertising dollars spent. The purpose of harvesting is to maintain the ability to meet customer requests. Coca-Cola, for instance, still sells Tab, its first diet cola, to a small group of die-hard fans. According to Coke's CEO, "It shows you care. We want to make sure those who want Tab, get Tab."[8]

Three Aspects of the Product Life Cycle

Some important aspects of product life cycles are (1) their length, (2) the shape of their sales curves, and (3) the difference between product classes and forms.

Marketing Matters

Customer Value

Will E-Mail Spell Extinction for Fax Machines?

Technological substitution that creates value for customers often causes the decline stage in the product life cycle. Will e-mail replace fax machines?

This question has been debated for years. Even though e-mail continues to grow with broadening Internet access, millions of fax machines are still sold each year. Industry analysts estimated that the number of e-mail mailboxes worldwide would be 5.2 billion in 2019. However, the phenomenal popularity of e-mail has not brought fax machines to extinction. Why? The two technologies do not directly compete for the same messaging applications.

E-mail is used for text messages. Faxing is predominately used for communicating formatted documents by business users, notably doctors, other health care providers, and lawyers concerned about Internet security. Fax usage is expected to increase through 2025, even though unit sales of fax machines have declined on a worldwide basis. Internet technology and e-mail may eventually replace facsimile technology and paper and make fax machines extinct, but not soon.

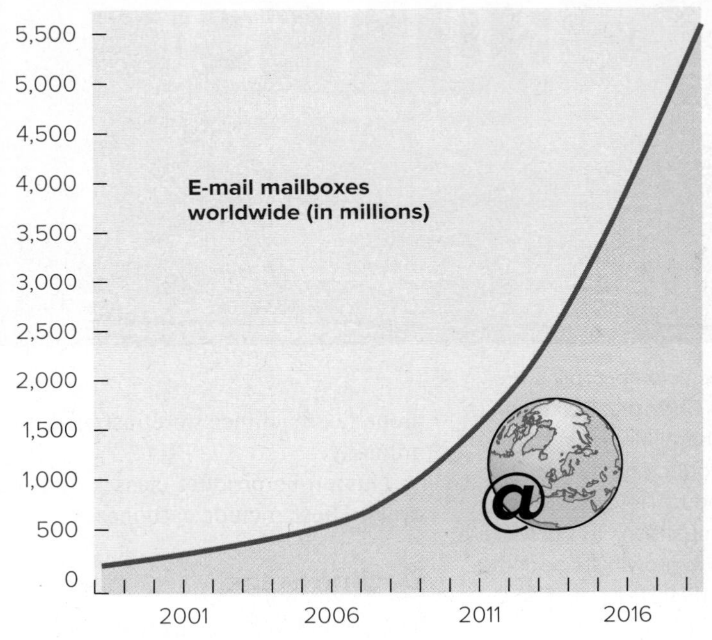

Length of the Product Life Cycle There is no set time that it takes a product to move through its life cycle. As a rule, consumer products have shorter life cycles than business products. For example, many new consumer food products such as Frito-Lay's Baked Lay's potato chips move from the introduction stage to maturity in 18 months. The availability of mass communication vehicles informs consumers quickly and shortens life cycles. Technological change shortens product life cycles as new-product innovation replaces existing products. For instance, smartphones have largely replaced digital cameras in the amateur photography market.

Shape of the Life-Cycle Curve The product life-cycle sales curve shown in Figure 11–1 is the *generalized life cycle*, but not all products have the same shape to their curve. In fact, there are several life-cycle curves, each type suggesting different marketing strategies. Figure 11–3 shows the shape of life-cycle sales curves for four different types of products: high-learning, low-learning, fashion, and fad products.

A *high-learning product* is one for which significant customer education is required and there is an extended introductory period (Figure 11–3A). It may surprise you, but personal computers had this life-cycle curve. Consumers in the 1980s had to learn the benefits of owning the product or be educated in a new way of performing familiar tasks. Convection ovens for home use required consumers to learn a new way of cooking and alter familiar recipes used with conventional ovens. As a result, these ovens spent years in the introductory period. The same can be said for all-electric-powered cars and trucks today.

In contrast, sales for a *low-learning product* begin immediately because little learning is required by the consumer and the benefits of purchase are readily understood (Figure 11–3B). This product often can be easily imitated by competitors, so the marketing strategy is to broaden distribution quickly. In this way, as competitors rapidly enter, most retail outlets

FIGURE 11–3
Alternative product life-cycle curves based on product types. Note the long introduction stage for a high-learning product compared with a low-learning product. Read the text for an explanation of the different product life-cycle curves.

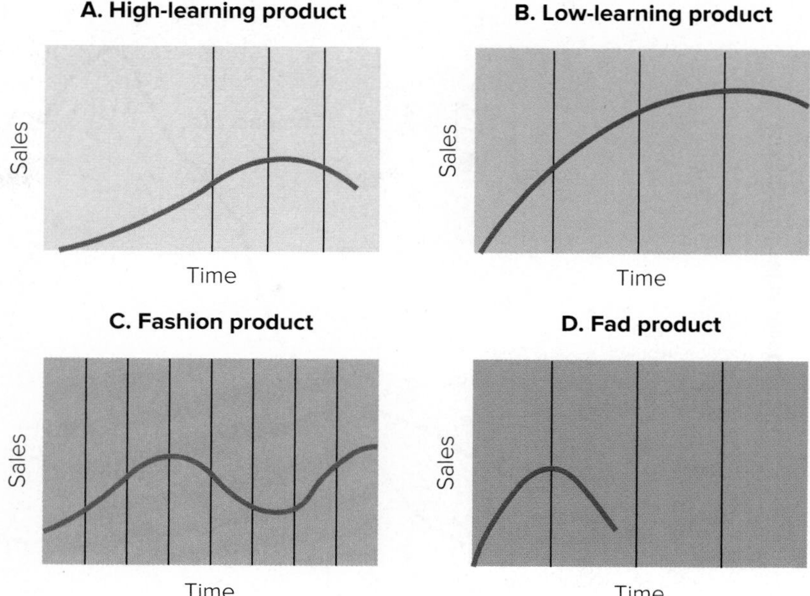

already have the innovator's product. It is also important to have the manufacturing capacity to meet demand. A successful low-learning product is Gillette's Fusion razor. This product achieved $1 billion in worldwide sales in less than three years and remains the best-selling razor in the world.

A *fashion product* (Figure 11–3C) is a style of the times. Life cycles for fashion products frequently appear in women's and men's apparel. Fashion products are introduced, decline, and then seem to return. The length of the cycles may be months, years, or decades. Consider women's hosiery. Product sales have been declining for years. Women consider it more fashionable to not wear hosiery—bad news for Hanes brands, the leading marketer of women's sheer hosiery. According to an authority on fashion, "Companies might as well let the fashion cycle take its course and wait for the inevitable return of pantyhose."[9]

A *fad product* experiences rapid sales on introduction and then an equally rapid decline (Figure 11–3D). These products are typically novelties and have a short life cycle. They include fidget spinners, car tattoos described as the first removable and reusable graphics for automobiles, and vinyl dresses and fleece bikinis made by a Minnesota clothing company.[10]

The Product Level: Class and Form The product life cycle shown in Figure 11–1 is a total industry or generalized product class sales curve. Yet, in managing a product it is often important to distinguish among the multiple life cycles (class and form) that may exist.

Product class refers to the entire product category or industry, such as prerecorded music. **Product form** pertains to variations of a product within the product class. For prerecorded music, product form exists in the technology used to provide the music, such as cassette tapes, compact discs, and digital music downloading and streaming. Figure 11–4 on the next page shows the life cycles for these three product forms and demonstrates the impact of technological innovation on sales.[11]

The Product Life Cycle and the Diffusion of Innovations

The life cycle of a product depends on sales to consumers. Not all consumers rush to buy a product in the introductory stage, and the shapes of the life-cycle curves indicate that most sales occur after the product has been on the market for some time. In essence, a product diffuses, or spreads, through the population, a concept called the *diffusion of innovation*.[12]

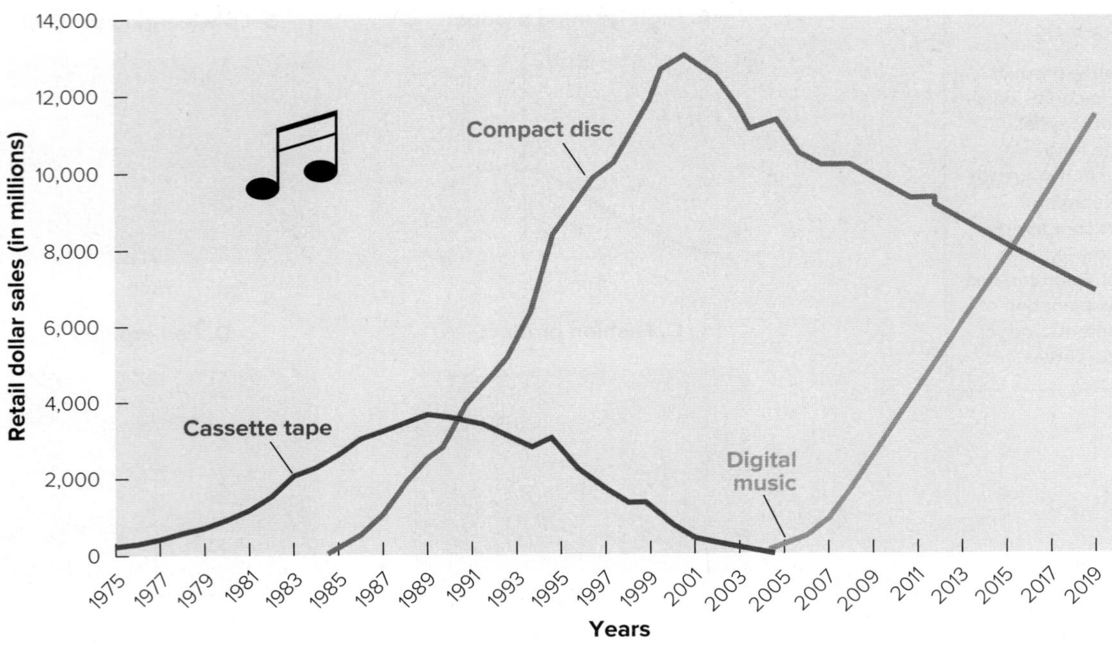

FIGURE 11–4
Prerecorded music product life cycles by product form illustrate the effect of technological innovation on sales. Compact discs replaced cassette tapes, and digital music and streaming replaced compact discs in 2015. Do you even remember the cassette tape?

The Diffusion of Innovations Some people are attracted to a product early. Others buy it only after they see their friends or opinion leaders with the item. Figure 11–5 shows the consumer population divided into five categories of product adopters based on when they adopt a new product. Brief profiles accompany each category. For any product to be successful, it must be purchased by innovators and early adopters. This is why manufacturers of new pharmaceuticals try to gain adoption by respected hospitals, clinics, and physicians. Once accepted by innovators and early adopters, successful new products move on to the early majority, late majority, and laggard categories.

Several factors affect whether a consumer will adopt a new product or not. Common reasons for resisting a product in the introduction stage are *usage barriers* (the product is not compatible with existing habits), *value barriers* (the product provides no incentive to change), *risk barriers* (physical, economic, or social), and *psychological barriers* (cultural differences or image).[13]

The Case of Electric-Powered Automobiles Three of these four factors help to explain the slow adoption of all-electric-powered vehicles in the United States. About 1 percent of cars sold in 2020 are expected to be all-electric-powered vehicles. Industry analysts cite the usage barrier for disappointing sales. They note that prospective buyers believe these cars are not compatible with existing driving habits. Analysts also mention a value barrier. Consumers have not recognized the superiority of all-electric cars over vehicles with internal combustion engines. Third, a risk barrier exists in large measure due to buyer uncertainty about the actual cost of all-electric-powered car ownership. According to one auto industry analyst, "The innovators and early adopters have purchased all-electric vehicles, but mainstream consumers have not followed." Not surprisingly, all-electric-powered vehicles remain in the introductory stage of the product life cycle. They are forecasted to remain in this stage until 2027 when they are expected to enter the growth stage.[14]

Companies attempt to overcome these barriers in numerous ways. For example, manufacturers of all-electric-powered automobiles provide low-cost leasing options to overcome usage, value, and risk barriers. Other companies provide warranties, money-back guarantees, extensive usage instructions, demonstrations, and free samples to stimulate initial trial of new products. For instance, software developers offer demonstrations downloaded from the Internet. Skin care consumers can browse through the Skin Advisor site at www.olay.com to find out

FIGURE 11–5
Five categories and profiles of product adopters. For a product to be successful, it must be purchased by innovators and early adopters.

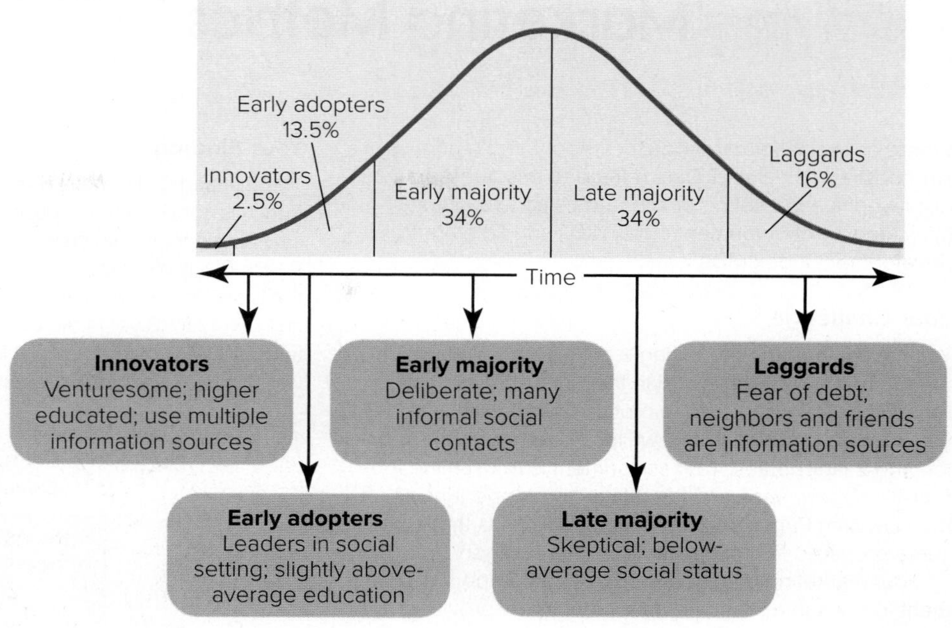

how certain skin care products will look based on a selfie submitted by the consumer. Free samples are one of the most popular means to gain consumer trial. In fact, 71 percent of consumers consider a sample to be the best way to evaluate a new product.[15]

LEARNING REVIEW

11-1. Advertising plays a major role in the __________ stage of the product life cycle, and __________ plays a major role in the maturity stage.

11-2. How do high-learning and low-learning products differ?

11-3. What are the five categories of product adopters in the diffusion of innovations?

MANAGING THE PRODUCT LIFE CYCLE

LO 11-2
Identify ways that marketing executives manage a product's life cycle.

An important task for a firm is to manage its products through the successive stages of their life cycles. This section describes the role of the product manager, who is usually responsible for this, and presents three ways to manage a product through its life cycle: modifying the product, modifying the market, and repositioning the product.

Role of a Product Manager

The product manager, sometimes called a *brand manager*, manages the marketing efforts for a close-knit family of products or brands. The product manager style of marketing organization is used by consumer goods firms, including General Mills and PepsiCo, and by technology companies such as Intel and Hewlett-Packard.

All product managers are responsible for managing existing products through the stages of the life cycle. Some are also responsible for developing new products. Product managers' marketing responsibilities include developing and executing a marketing program for the product line described in an annual marketing plan and approving ad copy, media selection, and package design.

Applying **Marketing Metrics**

Knowing Your CDI and BDI

Where are sales for my product category and brand strongest and weakest? Data related to this question are displayed in a marketing dashboard using two indexes: (1) a category development index (CDI) and (2) a brand development index (BDI).

Your Challenge

You have joined the marketing team for Hawaiian Punch, the top fruit punch drink sold in the United States. The brand has been marketed to mothers with children under 13 years old. The majority of Hawaiian Punch sales are in gallon and 2-liter bottles. Your assignment is to examine the brand's performance and identify growth opportunities for the Hawaiian Punch brand among households that consume prepared fruit drinks (the product category).

Your marketing dashboard displays a category development index and a brand development index provided by a syndicated marketing research firm. Each index is based on the calculations below:

$$\text{Category development index (CDI)} = \frac{\text{Percent of a product category's total U.S. sales in a market segment}}{\text{Percent of the total U.S. population in a market segment}} \times 100$$

$$\text{Brand development index (BDI)} = \frac{\text{Percent of a brand's total U.S. sales in a market segment}}{\text{Percent of the total U.S. population in a market segment}} \times 100$$

A CDI over 100 indicates above-average product category purchases by a market segment. A number under 100 indicates below-average purchases. A BDI over 100 indicates a strong brand position in a segment; a number under 100 indicates a weak brand position.

You are interested in CDI and BDI displays for four household segments that consume prepared fruit drinks: (1) households without children; (2) households with children 6 years old or under; (3) households with children aged 7 to 12; and (4) households with children aged 13 to 18.

Your Findings

The BDI and CDI metrics displayed below show that Hawaiian Punch is consumed by households with children, and particularly households with children under age 12. The Hawaiian Punch BDI is over 100 for both segments—not surprising since the brand is marketed to these segments. Households with children 13 to 18 years old evidence high fruit drink consumption with a CDI over 100. But Hawaiian Punch is relatively weak in this segment, with a BDI under 100.

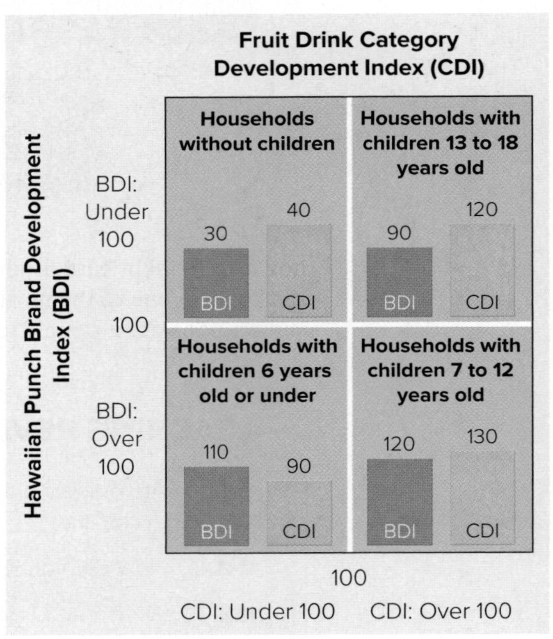

Your Action

An opportunity for Hawaiian Punch exists among households with children 13 to 18 years old—teenagers. You might propose that Hawaiian Punch be repositioned for teens. In addition, you might recommend that Hawaiian Punch be packaged in single-serve cans or bottles to attract this segment, much like soft drinks. Teens might also be targeted for advertising and promotions.

Product managers also engage in extensive data analysis related to their products and brands. Sales, market share, and profit trends are closely monitored. Managers often supplement these data with two measures: (1) a category development index (CDI) and (2) a brand development index (BDI). These indexes help to identify strong and weak market segments (usually demographic or geographic segments) for specific consumer products and brands and provide direction for marketing efforts. The calculation, visual display, and interpretation of these two indexes for Hawaiian Punch are described in the Applying Marketing Metrics box.

Harley-Davidson redesigned some of its motorcycle models to feature smaller hand grips, a lower seat, and an easier-to-pull clutch lever to create a more comfortable ride for women. According to Genevieve Schmitt, founding editor of WomenRidersNow.com, "They realize that women are an up-and-coming segment and that they need to accommodate them."
Gary Gardiner/Bloomberg/Getty Images

Harley-Davidson, Inc.
www.harley-davidson.com

VIDEO 11-2
Gillette Ad
kerin.tv/15e/v11-2

Modifying the Product

Product modification involves altering one or more of a product's characteristics, such as its quality, performance, or appearance, to increase the product's value to customers and increase sales. Wrinkle-free and stain-resistant clothing made possible by nanotechnology revolutionized the men's and women's apparel business and stimulated industry sales of casual pants, shirts, and blouses. A common approach to product modification to increase a product's value to consumers is called *product bundling*—the sale of two or more separate products in one package. For example, Microsoft Office is sold as a bundle of computer software, including Word, Excel, and PowerPoint.

New features, packages, or scents can be used to change a product's characteristics and give the sense of a revised product. Procter & Gamble revamped Pantene shampoo and conditioner with a new vitamin formula and relaunched the brand with a multimillion-dollar advertising and promotion campaign. The result? Pantene, a brand first introduced in the 1940s, remains a top-selling shampoo and conditioner in the United States in an industry with more than 1,000 competitors.

Modifying the Market

With **market modification** strategies, a company tries to find new customers, increase a product's use among existing customers, or create new use situations.

Finding New Customers As part of its market modification strategy, LEGO Group is offering a new line of products to attract consumers outside of its traditional market. Known for its popular line of construction toys for young boys, LEGO Group has introduced a product line for young girls called LEGO Friends. Harley-Davidson has tailored a marketing program to encourage women to take up biking, thus doubling the number of potential customers for its motorcycles.

Increasing a Product's Use Promoting more frequent usage has been a strategy of Campbell Soup Company. Because soup consumption rises in the winter and declines during the summer, the company now advertises more heavily in warm months to encourage consumers to think of soup as more than a cold-weather food. Similarly, the Florida Orange Growers Association advocates drinking orange juice throughout the day rather than for breakfast only.

Creating a New Use Situation Finding new uses for an existing product has been the strategy behind Gillette, the world leader for men's shaving products. The company now markets its Gillette Body line of razors, blades, and shaving gels for "manscaping"—the art of shaving body hair in areas below the neckline—a new use situation.

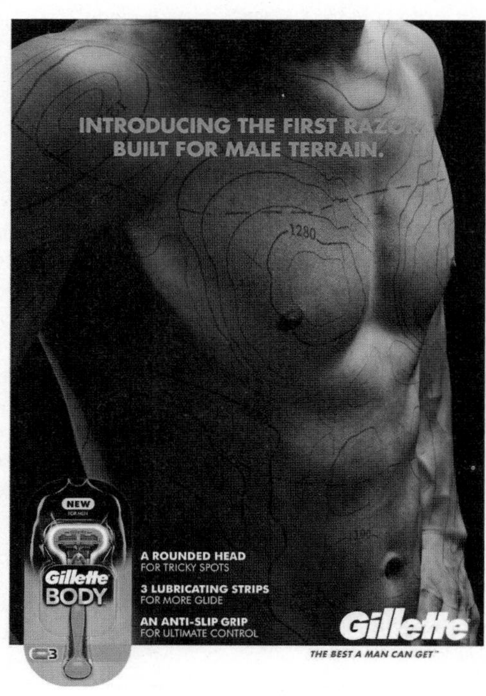

INTRODUCING THE FIRST
BUILT FOR MALE TERRAIN.
NEW
Gillette
BODY
A ROUNDED HEAD
FOR TRICKY SPOTS
3 LUBRICATING STRIPS
FOR MORE GLIDE
AN ANTI-SLIP GRIP
FOR ULTIMATE CONTROL
Gillette
THE BEST A MAN CAN GET

Gillette razors, blades, and gels have been adapted for shaving men's body hair in areas below the neckline. This new use situation for its shaving products is called "manscaping."
Source: Procter & Gamble

Repositioning the Product

Often a company decides to reposition its product or product line in an attempt to bolster sales. *Product repositioning* changes the place a product occupies in a consumer's mind relative to competitive products. A firm can reposition a product by changing one or more of the four marketing mix elements. Four factors that trigger the need for a repositioning action are discussed next.

Changing the Value Offered In repositioning a product, a company can decide to change the value it offers buyers and trade up or down. **Trading up** involves adding value to the product (or line) through additional features or higher-quality materials. Michelin, Bridgestone, and Goodyear have done this with a "run-flat" tire that can travel up to 50 miles at 55 miles per hour after suffering total air loss. Dog food manufacturers, such as Ralston Purina, also have traded up by offering super-premium foods based on "life-stage nutrition." Mass merchandisers, such as Target and Walmart, can trade up by adding a designer clothes section to their stores.

Trading down involves reducing a product's number of features, quality, or price. For example, airlines have added more seats, thus reducing legroom, and limited meal service by offering only snacks on most domestic flights. Trading down also exists when companies engage in *downsizing*—reducing the package content without changing package size and maintaining or increasing the package price. Companies are criticized for this practice, as described in the Making Responsible Decisions box.[16]

Reacting to a Competitor's Position One reason to reposition a product is because a competitor's entrenched position is adversely affecting sales and market share. New Balance, Inc. successfully repositioned its athletic shoes to focus on fit, durability, and comfort rather than competing head-on against Nike on performance and Adidas on fashion. The company offers an expansive range of shoes and networks with podiatrists, not sports celebrities.

Reaching a New Market When Unilever introduced iced tea in Britain, sales were disappointing. British consumers viewed it as leftover hot tea, not suitable for drinking. The company made its tea carbonated and repositioned it as a cold soft drink to compete as a carbonated beverage and sales improved. Johnson & Johnson effectively repositioned its St. Joseph aspirin from a product for infants to an adult low-strength aspirin to reduce the risk of heart problems or strokes.

Catching a Rising Trend Changing consumer trends can also lead to product repositioning. Growing consumer interest in foods that offer health and dietary benefits is an example. Many products have been repositioned to capitalize on this trend. Quaker Oats makes the FDA-approved claim that oatmeal, as part of a low-saturated-fat, low-cholesterol diet, may reduce the risk of heart disease. Calcium-enriched products, such as Kraft American cheese and Uncle

Making Responsible Decisions

Ethics

Consumer Economics of Downsizing—Get Less, Pay More

For more than 30 years, StarKist put 6.5 ounces of tuna into its regular-sized can. Today, StarKist puts 6.125 ounces of tuna into its can but charges the same price. Frito-Lay (Doritos and Lay's snack chips), PepsiCo (Tropicana orange juice), and Häagen-Dazs (ice cream) have whittled away at package contents 5 to 10 percent while maintaining their products' package sizes, dimensions, and prices.

Procter & Gamble recently kept its retail price on its jumbo pack of Pampers and Luvs diapers, but reduced the number of diapers per pack from 140 to 132. Similarly, Unilever reduced the number of Popsicles in each package from 24 to 20 without changing the package price. Georgia-Pacific reduced the content of its Brawny paper towel six-roll pack by 20 percent without lowering the price.

McGraw-Hill Education

Consumer advocates charge that downsizing the content of packages while maintaining prices is a subtle and unannounced way of taking advantage of consumer buying habits. They also say downsizing is a price increase in disguise and a deceptive, but legal, practice. Some manufacturers argue that this practice is a way of keeping prices from rising beyond psychological barriers for their products. Other manufacturers say prices are set by individual stores, not by them.

Is downsizing an unethical practice if manufacturers do not inform consumers that the package contents are less than they were previously?

Ben's Calcium Plus rice, emphasize healthy bone structure for children and adults. Weight-conscious consumers have embraced low-fat and low-calorie diets in growing numbers. Today, most food and beverage companies offer reduced-fat and low-calorie versions of their products.

LEARNING REVIEW

11-4. How does a product manager manage a product's life cycle?

11-5. What does "creating a new use situation" mean in managing a product's life cycle?

11-6. Explain the difference between trading up and trading down in product repositioning.

BRANDING AND BRAND MANAGEMENT

LO 11-3
Recognize the importance of branding and alternative branding strategies.

A basic decision in marketing products is **branding**, in which an organization uses a name, phrase, design, symbols, or combination of these to identify its products and distinguish them from those of competitors. A **brand name** is any word, device (design, sound, shape, or color), or combination of these used to distinguish a seller's products or services. Well-known devices used to distinguish brands apart from a name include symbols (the Nike swoosh), logos (the white apple used by Apple), and characters (Charlie the Tuna for StarKist).

A *trademark* identifies that a firm has legally registered its brand name or trade name so the firm has its exclusive use, thereby preventing others from using it. For example, Coca-Cola and Procter & Gamble have trademarked hashtags (#) that make reference to their brands. In the United States, trademarks are registered with the U.S. Patent and Trademark Office and protected under the *Lanham Act*. A well-known trademark can help a company advertise its offerings to customers and develop their brand loyalty. Consider Kylie and Kendall Jenner, cast members of the reality television show *Keeping Up with the Kardashians*. They filed to have their first names trademarked for use in "entertainment, fashion, and pop culture." Their filing was withdrawn after entertainer Kylie Minogue objected to the use of her name.[17]

Consumers may benefit most from branding. Recognizing competing products by distinct trademarks allows them to be more efficient shoppers. Consumers can recognize and avoid products with which they are dissatisfied, while becoming loyal to other, more satisfying brands. As discussed in Chapter 5, brand loyalty often eases consumers' decision making by eliminating the need for an external search.

Are you interested in creating a business using your name? If you are, you might first check to see if your name has been registered with the U.S. Patent and Trademark Office by visiting its website. See the Marketing Insights About Me box on the next page for details.

Brand Personality and Brand Equity

VIDEO 11-3
Dr Pepper Ad
kerin.tv/15e/v11-3

Product managers recognize that brands offer more than product identification and a means to distinguish their products from those of competitors.[18] Successful and established brands take on a **brand personality**, a set of human characteristics associated with a brand name. Research shows that consumers assign personality traits to products–traditional, romantic, rugged, sophisticated, rebellious–and choose brands that are consistent with their own or desired self-image.

Marketers can and do imbue a brand with a personality through advertising that depicts a certain user or usage situation and conveys emotions or feelings associated with the brand. For example, personality traits linked with Coca-Cola are all-American and real; with Pepsi, young and exciting; and with Dr Pepper, nonconforming and unique. The traits often linked to Harley-Davidson are masculinity, defiance, and rugged individualism.

Brand name importance to a company has led to a concept called **brand equity**, the added value a brand name gives to a product beyond the functional benefits provided. This added value

Marketing **Insights About Me**

Do You Want to Start a Business Using Your Own Name? Better Check First!

More than a million brand names or trade names are registered with the U.S. Patent and Trademark Office. Thousands more are registered each year.

An important step in choosing a brand or trade name is to determine whether the name has been registered already. The U.S. Patent and Trademark Office (www.uspto.gov) offers a valuable service by allowing individuals and companies to quickly check to see if a name has been registered.

Do you have an idea for a business that features your name? Check to see if your name has been registered by clicking "Trademarks," then "Search Trademark Database." Enter your name to find out if someone has registered it. You may already be a trademark!

Burke/Triolo Productions/Brand X Pictures/Getty Images

has two distinct advantages. First, brand equity provides a competitive advantage. The Sunkist brand implies quality fruit. The Disney name defines children's entertainment. Patagonia means environmental responsibility. A second advantage is that consumers are often willing to pay a higher price for a product with brand equity. Brand equity, in this instance, is represented by the premium a consumer will pay for one brand over another when the functional benefits provided are identical. Gillette razors and blades, Bose audio systems, Duracell batteries, Cartier jewelry, and Louis Vuitton luggage all enjoy a price premium arising from brand equity.

Creating Brand Equity Brand equity doesn't just happen. It is carefully crafted and nurtured by marketing programs that forge strong, favorable, and unique customer associations and experiences with a brand. Brand equity resides in the minds of consumers and results from what they have learned, felt, seen, and heard about a brand over time.

Companies today seek to create and sustain brand equity by communicating and acting upon the purpose of a brand. **Brand purpose** is the reason why a brand exists, the place it has in consumers' lives, the solution it provides to consumers, and the brand's role in making society better off. Brand purpose focuses on a brand's underlying values and beliefs and its identity and meaning. For example, Nike's purpose is to bring inspiration and innovation to every athlete in the world. Patagonia's brand purpose is to deliver quality apparel, forge

The strong brand equity for the Reebok brand name permits the company to charge premium prices for its products.
Source: Reebok

relationships based on integrity and respect, and promote responsible environmental behavior. Viewed broadly, the emphasis on a brand's purpose reflects the movement among companies to embrace the basic tenets of stakeholder and societal responsibility described in Chapter 4.[19]

Marketers recognize that brand equity is not easily or quickly achieved. Rather, it arises from a sequential building process consisting of four steps (see Figure 11–6).[20]

- The first step is to develop positive brand awareness and an association of the brand in consumers' minds with a product class or need to give the brand an identity. Gatorade and Kleenex have achieved this in the sports drink and facial tissue product classes, respectively.
- Next, a marketer must establish a brand's meaning in the minds of consumers. Meaning arises from what a brand stands for and has two dimensions—a functional, performance-related dimension and an abstract, imagery-related dimension. Nike has done this through continuous product development and improvement and its links to peak athletic performance in its marketing communications.
- The third step is to elicit the proper consumer responses to a brand's identity and meaning. Here attention is placed on how consumers think and feel about a brand. Thinking focuses on a brand's perceived quality, credibility, and superiority relative to other brands. Feeling relates to the consumer's emotional reaction to a brand. Michelin elicits both responses for its tires. Not only is Michelin thought of as a credible and superior-quality brand, but consumers also acknowledge a warm and secure feeling of safety, comfort, and self-assurance without worry or concern about the brand.
- The final, and most difficult, step is to create a consumer–brand connection evident in an intense, active loyalty relationship between consumers and the brand. A deep psychological bond characterizes a consumer–brand connection and the personal identification customers have with the brand. Brands that have achieved this status include Harley-Davidson and Apple.

Valuing Brand Equity Brand equity also provides a financial advantage for the brand owner.[21] Successful, established brand names, such as Gillette, Louis Vuitton, Nike, Gatorade, and Apple, have an economic value in the sense that they are intangible assets. The Apple brand name alone is valued at $205 billion. The recognition that brands are assets is apparent in the decision to buy and sell companies. For instance, when Procter & Gamble bought the

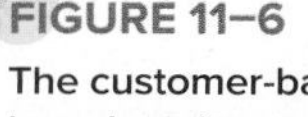

FIGURE 11–6

The customer-based brand equity pyramid shows the four-step building process that forges strong, favorable, and unique customer associations with a brand.

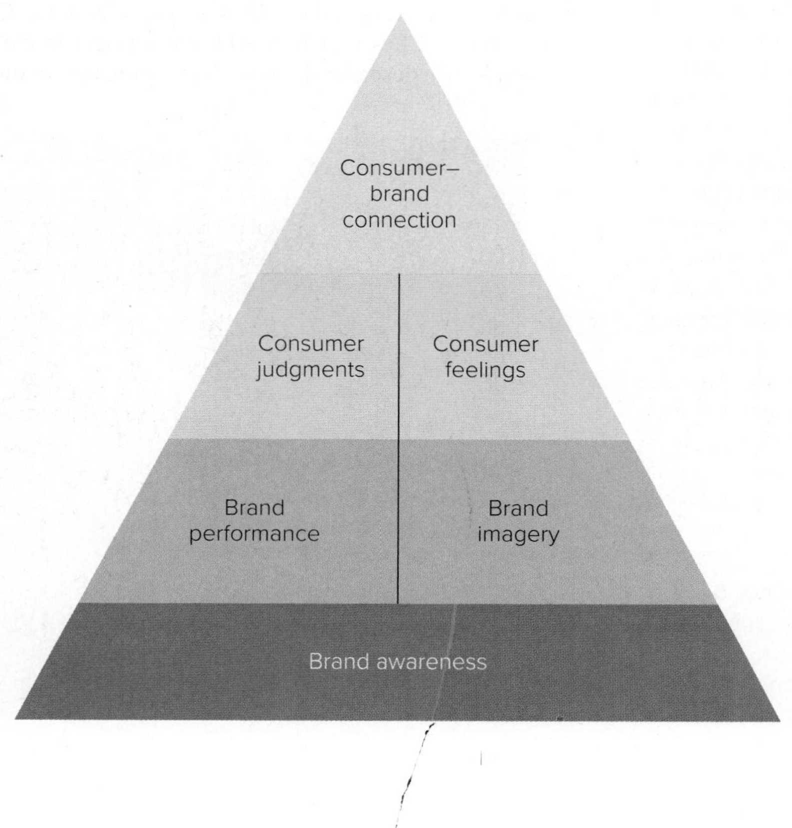

Gillette Company for $57 billion, the Gillette brand name alone was valued at $24 billion, or 42 percent of the company's purchase price. When Amazon bought Whole Foods, the Whole Foods name alone accounted for 70 percent of the acquisition price of the company.

Brands alone can be bought and sold by a company. For example, Triarc Companies bought the Snapple brand from Quaker Oats for $300 million and sold it three years later to Cadbury Schweppes for $900 million. This example illustrates that brands, unlike physical assets that depreciate with time and use, can appreciate in value when effectively marketed. However, brands can lose value when they are not managed properly. Consider the purchase and sale of Lender's Bagels. Kellogg bought the brand for $466 million only to sell it to Aurora Foods for $275 million three years later following deteriorating sales and profits.

Financially lucrative brand licensing opportunities arise from brand equity.[22] **Brand licensing** is a contractual agreement whereby one company (licensor) allows its brand name(s) or trademark(s) to be used with products or services offered by another company (licensee) for a royalty or fee. For example, the National Football League (NFL) and the National Basketball Association (NBA) each earn about $3.5 billion annually by licensing team names and logos for merchandise. The Peanuts brand characters, including Charlie Brown, Snoopy, and Lucy, generate almost $100 million annually in licensing fees.

Successful brand licensing requires careful marketing analysis to ensure a proper fit between the licensor's brand and the licensee's products. World-renowned designer Ralph Lauren earns over $2.5 billion each year by licensing his Ralph Lauren, Polo, and Chaps brands for dozens of products, including paint by Glidden, furniture by Henredon, footwear by Rockport, eyewear by Luxottica, and fragrances by L'Oréal.[23] Kleenex diapers, Bic perfume, and Domino's fruit-flavored bubble gum are a few examples of poor matches and licensing failures.

Picking a Good Brand Name

We take brand names such as Red Bull, iPad, Android, and Axe for granted, but it is often a difficult and expensive process to pick a good name. Companies will spend between $25,000 and $100,000 to identify and test a new brand name. Six criteria are mentioned most often when selecting a good brand name.[24]

- *The name should suggest the product benefits.* For example, Accutron (watches), Easy-Off (oven cleaner), Glass Plus (glass cleaner), Cling-Free (antistatic cloth for drying clothes), Chevrolet Bolt and Spark (electric cars), and Tidy Bowl (toilet bowl cleaner) all clearly describe the benefits of purchasing the product.

Ralph Lauren has a long-term licensing agreement with Luxottica Group, S.p.A. of Milan for the design, production, and worldwide distribution of prescription frames and sunglasses under the Ralph Lauren brand. The agreement is an ideal fit for both companies. Ralph Lauren is a leader in the design, marketing, and distribution of premium lifestyle products. Luxottica is the global leader in the premium and luxury eyewear sector.

Rebecca Sapp/WireImage for Mediaplacement/Getty Images

Luxottica Group, S.p.A.
www.luxottica.com

Ralph Lauren Corporation
www.ralphlauren.com

- *The name should be memorable, distinctive, and positive.* In the auto industry, when a competitor has a memorable name, others quickly imitate. When Ford named a car the Mustang, the Pinto and Bronco soon followed. The Thunderbird name led to the Phoenix, Eagle, Sunbird, and Firebird from other car companies.
- *The name should fit the company or product image.* Sharp is a name that can apply to audio and video equipment. Bufferin, Excedrin, Anacin, and Nuprin are scientific-sounding names, good for analgesics. Eveready, Duracell, and DieHard suggest reliability and longevity—two qualities consumers want in a battery.
- *The name should have no legal or regulatory restrictions.* Legal restrictions produce trademark infringement suits, and regulatory restrictions arise through the improper use of words. For example, the U.S. Food and Drug Administration discourages the use of the word *heart* in food brand names. This restriction led to changing the name of Kellogg's Heartwise cereal to Fiberwise, and Clorox's Hidden Valley Ranch Take Heart Salad Dressing had to be modified to Hidden Valley Ranch Low-Fat Salad Dressing. Increasingly, brand names need a corresponding website address on the Internet. This further complicates name selection because over 330 million domain names are already registered globally.
- *The name should be simple and emotional.* Examples that illustrate the former include Bold laundry detergent, Axe deodorant and body spray, and Bic pens; examples illustrating the latter include Joy and Obsession perfumes and Caress soap, shower gel, and lotion.
- *The name should have favorable phonetic and semantic associations in other languages.* In the development of names for international use, having a nonmeaningful brand name has been considered a benefit. A name such as Exxon does not have any prior impressions or undesirable images among a diverse world population of different languages and cultures. The 7UP name is another matter. In Shanghai, China, the phrase means "death through drinking" in the local dialect. Sales have suffered as a result.

Branding Strategies

Companies can choose from among several different branding strategies, including multiproduct branding, multibranding, private branding, and mixed branding (see Figure 11–7).

Multiproduct Branding Strategy With **multiproduct branding**, a company uses one name for all its products in a product class. This approach is sometimes called *family branding* or *corporate branding* when the company's name is used. For example, Microsoft, Samsung, Gerber, and Sony engage in corporate branding—the company's trade name and brand name are identical. Church & Dwight uses the Arm & Hammer family brand name for all its products featuring baking soda as the primary ingredient.

There are several advantages to multiproduct branding. Capitalizing again on brand equity, consumers who have a good experience with the product will transfer this favorable attitude to

FIGURE 11–7
Alternative branding strategies present both advantages and disadvantages to marketers. See the text for details.

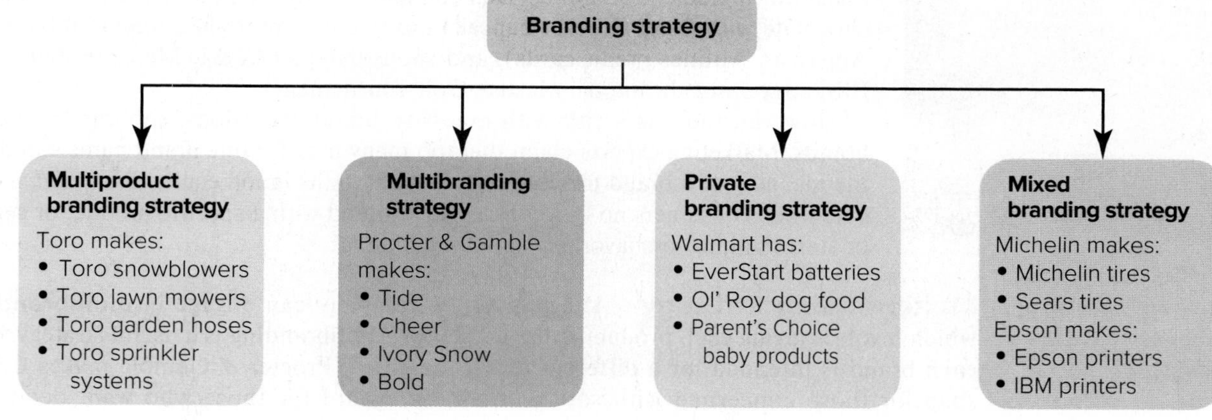

For how Kimberly-Clark has used a brand extension strategy to leverage its Huggies brand equity among mothers, see the text.
Mike Hruby/McGraw-Hill Education

Kimberly-Clark Corporation
www.kimberly-clark.com

What branding concept is American Express using with its multicolored cards?
Peter Jobst/Alamy Stock Photo

other items in the product class with the same name. Therefore, this brand strategy makes possible *product line extensions*, the practice of using a current brand name to enter a new market segment in its product class.

Campbell Soup Company employs a multiproduct branding strategy with soup line extensions. It offers regular Campbell's soup, home-cooking style, and chunky varieties and more than 100 soup flavors. This strategy can result in lower advertising and promotion costs because the same name is used on all products, thus raising the level of brand awareness. A risk with line extension is that sales of an extension may come at the expense of other items in the company's product line. Line extensions work best when they provide incremental company revenue by taking sales away from competing brands or attracting new buyers.

Some multiproduct branding companies employ *subbranding*, which combines a corporate or family brand with a new brand, to distinguish a part of its product line from others. Consider American Express. It has applied subbranding with its American Express Green, Gold, Platinum, Blue, and Centurion black charge cards, with unique service offerings for each. Similarly, Porsche successfully markets its higher-end Porsche Carrera and its lower-end Porsche Boxster.

A strong brand equity also allows for *brand extension*: the practice of using a current brand name to enter a different product class. For instance, equity in the Huggies family brand name has allowed Kimberly-Clark to successfully extend its name to a full line of baby and toddler toiletries. This brand extension strategy generates $500 million in annual sales globally for the company. Honda's established name for motor vehicles has extended easily to snowblowers, lawn mowers, snowmobiles, and business jets.

Co-branding opportunities also arise from a strong brand equity. *Co-branding* is the practice of pairing two or more strong brands to facilitate the marketing of a joint product or service for their mutual benefit. For example, companies use component or ingredient branding (Dell computers with Intel processors, or Hershey's chocolate with Betty Crocker cupcake mix), joint venture branding (Citibank and American Airlines credit cards), and sponsorships (AT&T, Mercedes-Benz, and IBM co-sponsor the annual Masters Golf Tournament).

However, there is a risk with excessive brand extensions, subbrands, and co-brands. Marketing experts claim that too many uses for one brand name can dilute the meaning of a brand for consumers and harm its brand equity. *Brand dilution* occurs when consumers no longer associate a brand with a specific product or service or start thinking less favorably about the brand.[25]

What branding concept is illustrated by this pairing of the Hershey's and Betty Crocker brands?
Keith Homan/Alamy Stock Photo

Multibranding Strategy Alternatively, a company can engage in **multibranding**, which involves giving each product a distinct name. Multibranding is a useful strategy when each brand is intended for a different market segment. Procter & Gamble makes Camay soap for those concerned with soft skin and Safeguard for those who want deodorant

Stanley Black & Decker uses a multibranding strategy to reach different market segments. It markets its tool line for the do-it-yourself (DIY) household segment using the Black & Decker name, but it uses the DeWalt name for professionals.

Source: Stanley Black & Decker, Inc.

Black & Decker
www.stanleyblackanddecker.com

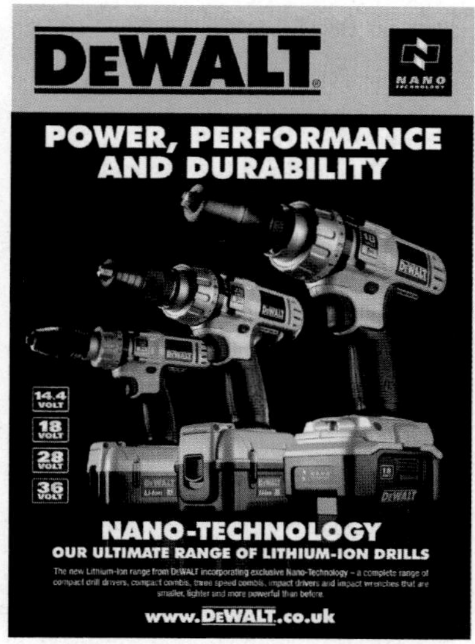

protection. Stanley Black & Decker markets its line of tools for the do-it-yourself (DIY) household segment with the Black & Decker name but uses the DeWalt name for its professional tool line.

Multibranding is applied in a variety of ways. Some companies array their brands on the basis of price–quality segments. Marriott International offers 18 hotel and resort brands, each suited for a particular traveler experience and budget. To illustrate, Marriott EDITION hotels and Vacation Clubs offer luxury amenities at a premium price. Marriott and Renaissance hotels offer medium- to high-priced accommodations. Courtyard hotels and TownePlace Suites appeal to economy-minded travelers, whereas the Fairfield Inn is for those on a very low travel budget.

Other multibrand companies introduce new product brands as defensive moves to counteract competition. Called *fighting brands*, their chief purpose is to confront competitor brands.[26] For instance, Frito-Lay introduced Santitas brand tortilla chips to go head-to-head against regional tortilla chip brands that were biting into sales of its flagship Doritos and Tostitos brand tortilla chips.

Compared with the multiproduct strategy, advertising and promotion costs tend to be higher with multibranding. The company must generate awareness among consumers and retailers for each new brand name without the benefit of any previous impressions. The advantages of this strategy are that each brand is unique to each market segment and there is no risk that a product failure will affect other products in the line. Still, some large multibrand firms have found that the complexity and expense of implementing this strategy can outweigh the benefits. For example, Procter & Gamble has pruned about 100 of its brands through product deletion and sales to other companies in the past decade.[27]

Private Branding Strategy A company uses **private branding**, often called *private labeling* or *reseller branding*, when it manufactures products but sells them under the brand name of a wholesaler or retailer. Rayovac, Paragon Trade Brands, and ConAgra Foods are major suppliers of private-label alkaline batteries, diapers, and grocery products, respectively. Costco, Amazon, Walmart, and Kroger are large retailers that have their own brand names. Private branding is popular because it typically produces high profits for manufacturers and resellers. Consumers also buy them. It is estimated that one of every five items purchased at U.S. supermarkets, drugstores, and mass merchandisers bears a private brand.[28]

Mixed Branding Strategy A fourth branding strategy is **mixed branding**, where a firm markets products under its own name(s) and that of a reseller because the segment attracted to the reseller is different from its own market. Diverse companies such as Del Monte, Whirlpool, and Dial produce private brands of pet foods, home appliances, and soap, respectively.

Marketing Matters — Customer Value

Creating Customer Value through Packaging—Pez Heads Dispense More Than Candy

Customer value can assume numerous forms. For Pez Candy, Inc. (www.pez.com), customer value manifests itself in some 550 Pez character candy dispensers. Each refillable dispenser ejects tasty candy tablets in a variety of flavors that delight preteens and teens alike in more than 80 countries—including China, which it entered in 2017.

Pez was formulated in 1927 by Austrian food mogul Eduard Haas III and successfully sold in Europe as an adult breath mint. The name *Pez,* which comes from the German word for "peppermint," *pfefferminz,* was originally packaged in a hygienic, headless plastic dispenser. Pez first appeared in the United States in 1953 with a headless dispenser, marketed to adults. After conducting extensive marketing research, Pez was repositioned with fruit flavors, repackaged with licensed character heads on top of the dispenser, and remarketed as a children's product in the mid-1950s. Since then, most top-level licensed characters and hundreds of other characters have become Pez heads. Consumers buy about 70 million Pez dispensers and 5 billion Pez tablets a year, and company sales growth exceeds that of the candy industry as a whole.

Blank Archives/Getty Images

The unique Pez package dispenses a "use experience" for its customers beyond the candy itself, namely, fun. And fun translates into a 98 percent awareness level for Pez among teenagers and an 89 percent awareness level among mothers with children. Pez has not advertised its product for years. With that kind of awareness, who needs advertising?

PACKAGING AND LABELING PRODUCTS

LO 11-4
Describe the role of packaging and labeling in the marketing of a product.

The **packaging** component of a product refers to any container in which it is offered for sale and on which label information is conveyed. A **label** is an integral part of the package and typically identifies the product or brand, who made it, where and when it was made, how it is to be used, and package contents and ingredients. To a great extent, the customer's first exposure to a product is the package and label, and both are an expensive and important part of marketing strategy. For Pez Candy, Inc., the central element of its marketing strategy is the character-head-on-a-stick plastic container that dispenses a miniature candy tablet. For more on how packaging creates customer value for Pez Candy, see the Marketing Matters box.[29]

Creating Customer Value and Competitive Advantage through Packaging and Labeling

Packaging and labeling cost U.S. companies about 15 cents of every dollar spent by consumers for products.[30] Despite their cost, packaging and labeling are essential because both provide important benefits for the manufacturer, retailer, and ultimate consumer. Packaging and labeling also can provide a competitive advantage.

Communication Benefits A major benefit of packaging is the label information it conveys to the consumer, such as directions on how, where, and when to use the product and the source and composition of the product, which is needed to satisfy legal requirements of product disclosure. For example, the labeling system for packaged and processed foods in the United States provides a uniform format for nutritional and dietary information. Many packaged foods contain informative recipes to promote usage of the product. Campbell Soup estimates that the green bean casserole recipe on its cream of mushroom soup can accounts for \$20 million in soup sales each year![31] Other information consists of seals and symbols, either government-required or commercial seals of approval (such as the Good Housekeeping Seal).

For the functional benefits provided by Pringles's cylindrical packaging, see the text.
Mike Hruby/McGraw-Hill Education

Functional Benefits Packaging often plays a functional role—providing storage, convenience, or protection or ensuring product quality. Stackable food containers are one example of how packaging can provide functional benefits. For example, beverage companies have developed lighter and easier ways to stack products on shelves and in refrigerators. Examples include Coca-Cola beverage packs designed to fit neatly onto refrigerator shelves and Ocean Spray's rectangular cranberry juice bottles that allow 10 units per package versus 8 of its former round bottles.

The convenience dimension of packaging is increasingly important. Kraft Miracle Whip salad dressing, Heinz ketchup, and Skippy Squeez'It peanut butter are sold in squeeze bottles; microwave popcorn is a major market success; and Folgers coffee is packaged in single-serving portions. Nabisco offers portion-control package sizes for the convenience of weight-conscious consumers. It offers 100-calorie packs of Oreos, Cheese Nips, and other products in individual pouches.

Consumer protection is another important function of packaging, including the development of tamper-resistant containers. Today, companies commonly use safety seals or pop-tops that reveal previous opening. Consumer protection through labeling exists in "open dating," which states the expected shelf life of the product.

Functional features of packaging also can affect product quality. Pringles, with its cylindrical packaging, offers uniform chips, minimal breakage, and for some consumers, a better value than chips packaged in flex-bags.

Perceptual Benefits A third component of packaging and labeling is the perception created in the consumer's mind. Package and label shape, color, and graphics distinguish one brand from another, convey a brand's positioning, and build brand equity. According to the director of marketing for L'eggs hosiery, "Packaging is important to the positioning and equity of the L'eggs brand."[32] Why? Packaging and labeling have been shown to enhance brand recognition and facilitate the formation of strong, favorable, and unique brand associations.

Packaging has been a major element of L'eggs hosiery positioning since the brand's launch 50 years ago.
Mike Hruby/McGraw-Hill Education

Hanes Brands, Inc.
www.leggs.com

Successful marketers recognize that changes in packages and labels can update and uphold a brand's image in the customer's mind. Pepsi-Cola has embarked on a packaging change to uphold its image among teens and young adults, introducing new package graphics that change every few weeks to reflect different themes, such as sports, music, fashion, and cars.

Because labels list a product's source, brands competing in the global marketplace can benefit from "country of origin or manufacture" perceptions, as described in Chapter 7. Consumers tend to hold stereotypes about country-product pairings that they judge "best"—English tea, French perfume, Italian leather, and Japanese electronics—which can affect a brand's image. Increasingly, Chinese firms are adopting the English language and Roman letters for their brand labels sold in China. This is being done because of a common perception in many Asian countries that "things Western are good."[33]

Packaging and Labeling Challenges and Responses

Package and label designers face four challenges. They are (1) the continuing need to connect with customers; (2) environmental concerns; (3) health, safety, and security issues; and (4) cost reduction.

Connecting with Customers Packages and labels must be continually updated to connect with customers. The challenge lies in creating aesthetic and functional design features that attract customer attention and deliver customer value in their use. If done right, the rewards can be huge. For example, the marketing team responsible for Kleenex tissues converted its standard rectangular box into an oval shape with colorful seasonal graphics. Sales soared with this aesthetic change in packaging. After months of in-home research, Kraft product managers discovered that consumers often transferred Chips Ahoy! cookies to jars for easy access and to avoid staleness. The company solved both problems by creating a patented resealable opening on the top of the bag. The result? Sales of the new package doubled that of the old package.

Environmental Concerns Because of widespread global concern about the growth of solid waste and the shortage of viable landfill sites, the amount, composition, and disposal of packaging material continue to receive much attention. For example, PepsiCo, Coca-Cola, and Nestlé have decreased the amount of plastic in their beverage bottles to reduce solid waste. Recycling packaging material is another major thrust. Procter & Gamble's Tide Eco-Box has 60 percent less plastics in its packaging, and its Spic and Span liquid cleaner is packaged in 100 percent recycled material. Other firms, such as Walmart, are emphasizing the use of less packaging material. Over the past decade, the company has worked with its 600,000 global suppliers to reduce overall packaging and shipping material by 5 percent.

Health, Safety, and Security Issues A third challenge involves the growing health, safety, and security concerns of packaging materials. Today, most consumers believe companies should make sure products and their packages are safe and secure, regardless of the cost, and companies are responding in numerous ways. Most butane lighters sold today, like those made by Scripto, contain a child-resistant safety latch to prevent misuse and accidental fire. Childproof caps on pharmaceutical products and household cleaners and sealed lids on food packages are now common. New packaging technology and materials that extend a product's *shelf life* (the time a product can be stored) and prevent spoilage continue to be developed.

Cost Reduction About 80 percent of packaging material used in the world consists of paper, plastics, metal, and glass. As the cost of these materials rises, companies are constantly challenged to find innovative ways to cut packaging costs while delivering value to their customers. Many food and personal care companies have replaced bottles and cans with sealed foil packages, such as StarKist's tuna, salmon, and chicken single-serve pouches. Pouches cut packaging costs by 10 to 15 percent.[34]

LEARNING REVIEW

11-7. What is the difference between a line extension and a brand extension?

11-8. Explain the role of packaging in terms of perception.

LEARNING OBJECTIVES REVIEW

LO 11-1 *Explain the product life-cycle concept.*
The product life cycle describes the stages a new product goes through in the marketplace: introduction, growth, maturity, and decline. Product sales growth and profitability differ at each stage, and marketing managers have marketing objectives and marketing mix strategies unique to each stage based on consumer behavior and competitive factors. In the introductory stage, the need is to establish primary demand, whereas the growth stage requires selective demand strategies. In the maturity stage, the need is to maintain market share; the decline stage necessitates a deletion or harvesting strategy. Some important aspects of product life cycles are (*a*) their length, (*b*) the shape of the sales curves, and (*c*) the rate at which consumers adopt products.

LO 11-2 *Identify ways that marketing executives manage a product's life cycle.*
Marketing executives manage a product's life cycle in three ways. First, they can modify the product itself by altering its characteristics, such as product quality, performance, or appearance. Second, they can modify the market by finding new customers for the product, increasing a product's use among existing customers, or creating a new use situation for the product. Finally, they can reposition the product using any one or a combination of marketing mix elements. Four factors trigger a repositioning action. They include reacting to a competitor's position, reaching a new market, catching a rising trend, and changing the value offered to consumers.

LO 11-3 *Recognize the importance of branding and alternative branding strategies.*
A basic decision in marketing products is branding, in which an organization uses a name, phrase, design, symbols, or a combination of these to identify its products and distinguish them from those of its competitors. Product managers recognize that brands offer more than product identification and a means to distinguish their products from competitors. Successful and established brands take on a brand personality and acquire brand equity–the added value a given brand name gives to a product beyond the functional benefits provided–that is crafted and nurtured by marketing programs that forge strong, favorable, and unique consumer associations with a brand. A good brand name should suggest the product benefits, be memorable, fit the company or product image, be free of legal restrictions, and be simple and emotional. Companies can and do employ several different branding strategies. With multiproduct branding, a company uses one name for all its products in a product class. A multibranding strategy involves giving each product a distinct name. A company uses private branding when it manufactures products but sells them under the brand name of a wholesaler or retailer. Finally, a company can employ mixed branding, where it markets products under its own name(s) and that of a reseller.

LO 11-4 *Describe the role of packaging and labeling in the marketing of a product.*
Packaging and labeling play numerous roles in the marketing of a product. The packaging component of a product refers to any container in which it is offered for sale and on which label information is conveyed. Manufacturers, retailers, and consumers acknowledge that packaging and labeling provide communication, functional, and perceptual benefits. Contemporary packaging and labeling challenges include (1) the continuing need to connect with customers, (2) environmental concerns, (3) health, safety, and security issues, and (4) cost reduction.

LEARNING REVIEW ANSWERS

11-1 **Advertising plays a major role in the ________ stage of the product life cycle, and ________ plays a major role in the maturity stage.**
Answer: introductory; product differentiation

11-2 **How do high-learning and low-learning products differ?**
Answer: A high-learning product requires significant customer education and there is an extended introductory period. A low-learning product requires little customer education because the benefits of purchase are readily understood, resulting in immediate sales.

11-3 **What are the five categories of product adopters in the diffusion of innovations?**
Answer: The five categories of product adopters based on the diffusion of innovation are: (1) innovators–2.5 percent; (2) early adopters–13.5 percent; (3) early majority–34 percent; (4) late majority–34 percent; and (5) laggards–16 percent.

11-4 **How does a product manager manage a product's life cycle?**
Answer: A product manager shepherds a product through its life cycle by (1) modifying the product, which involves altering one or more of its characteristics to increase its value to customers and thus increase sales; (2) modifying the market, which involves finding new customers, increasing a product's use among existing customers, or creating new use situations; and (3) repositioning the product, which involves changing the place it occupies in consumers' minds relative to competitive products.

11-5 **What does "creating a new use situation" mean in managing a product's life cycle?**
Answer: Creating a new use situation means finding new uses or applications for an existing product.

11-6 **Explain the difference between trading up and trading down in product repositioning.**
Answer: Trading up involves adding value to the product (or line) through additional features or higher-quality materials. Trading down involves reducing the number of features, quality, or price or downsizing–reducing the content of packages without changing package size and maintaining or increasing the package price.

11-7 **What is the difference between a line extension and a brand extension?**
Answer: A line extension uses a current brand name to enter a new market segment in its product class, whereas a brand extension uses a current brand name to enter a completely different product class.

11-8 **Explain the role of packaging in terms of perception.**
Answer: A package's shape, color, and graphics distinguish one brand from another, convey a brand's positioning, and build brand equity.

FOCUSING ON KEY TERMS

brand equity p. 303
brand licensing p. 306
brand name p. 303
brand personality p. 303
branding p. 303
brand purpose p. 304
label p. 310
market modification p. 301
mixed branding p. 309
multibranding p. 308
multiproduct branding p. 307
packaging p. 310
private branding p. 309
product class p. 297
product form p. 297
product life cycle p. 292
product modification p. 301
trading down p. 302
trading up p. 302

APPLYING MARKETING KNOWLEDGE

1 Listed here are three different products in various stages of the product life cycle. What marketing strategies would you suggest to these companies? (*a*) Canon digital cameras–maturity stage, (*b*) Hewlett-Packard tablet computers–growth stage, and (*c*) handheld manual can openers–decline stage.

2 It has often been suggested that products are intentionally made to break down or wear out. Is this strategy a planned product modification approach?

3 The product manager at GE is reviewing the penetration of trash compactors in American homes. After more than two decades in existence, this product is in relatively few homes. What problems can account for this poor acceptance? What is the shape of the trash compactor life cycle?

4 For years, Ferrari has been known as a manufacturer of expensive luxury automobiles. The company plans to attract the major segment of the car-buying market that purchases medium-priced automobiles. As Ferrari considers this trading-down strategy, what branding strategy would you recommend? What are the trade-offs to consider with your strategy?

BUILDING YOUR MARKETING PLAN

For the product offering in your marketing plan,

1 Identify (*a*) its stage in the product life cycle and (*b*) key marketing mix actions that might be appropriate, as shown in Figure 11-1.

2 Develop (*a*) branding and (*b*) packaging strategies, if appropriate for your offering.

VIDEO CASE 11 Justin's: Managing a Successful Product with Passion

"If you don't start somewhere, you'll never end up anywhere," explains Justin Gold, entrepreneur and founder of the Justin's brand of organic nut butters and peanut butter cups. It was this mantra that helped Gold turn his passion for good-tasting organic food into his now-famous brand and a growing portfolio of successful products. In fact, the Justin's website proclaims that Justin's is "Making a Butter World!"

VIDEO 11-4
Justin's Video Case
kerin.tv/15e/v11-4

THE COMPANY

The idea for better nut butter came from Gold's personal experiences. "I'm an active vegetarian and I was mountain biking, running, and skiing," he explains. The combination meant that nut butter was a staple in his diet. "I was curious," he adds, "why is it that peanut butter is only available in two flavors–smooth and crunchy? Why can't you flavor a peanut butter?" So, Justin bought a basic food processor and natural ingredients and began experimenting at home in his kitchen. He filled jars with his new flavors, and to deter his roommates from eating them he labeled the jars "Justin's." That simple decision was the beginning of the brand name for his products and for the company!

Everyone who tried the homemade nut butters encouraged Justin to start selling them. As a result he created a business plan based on research about consumers and advice from a network of mentors. According to Gold, "As an entrepreneur you basically think about things in four sections–sales, marketing, operations, and finance." The first sales of the product were through a farmer's market, and popularity there led to distribution in select retailers, including Whole Foods. The big breakthrough, however, came when Justin decided to package nut butter in a squeeze pack. The packages were placed next to the jars on the shelf in the stores, and consumers would buy them as a trial size and then come back and buy a jar. "That squeeze pack really put us on the map as an innovator in the nut butter category," says Gold. "It set us apart from all the competitors out there because we had a point of differentiation."

Courtesy of Justin's

Justin's continued to grow and was ranked in the Top 15 on the *Inc.* Fastest Growing Companies list for the Food and Beverage category. In addition, Justin was recognized as Entrepreneur of the Year by Ernst & Young. Three key values have contributed to the company's success. They include:

- *Passion* for natural and organic foods.
- *Consciousness* of sustainable and environmentally friendly practices and concern for the community.

- *Product* quality based on production innovation, nutrition, and amazing taste.

Eventually Justin decided that he needed a partner to continue the company's growth. Justin's was sold to Hormel Foods Corporation, a multinational manufacturer and marketer of consumer-branded food products, including Skippy peanut butter. "We felt that they were the perfect partner for us, we felt that Hormel was buying into our values and our mission," says Gold.

Today Justin's product line includes 10 flavors of nut butters, eight variations of nut butter cups, four types of snack packs, and a cookbook titled *Justin My Kitchen.* In addition to the initial distribution through Whole Foods stores, retail partners now include Safeway, Costco, Target, REI, Natural Grocers, King Soopers, Sprouts, and Walmart. Online retailers also include Amazon.com, Jet.com, and Thrivemarket.com. Sales have grown to include millions of jars and squeeze packs of nut butter! Recently, Justin's received a Most Innovative New Product Award from the National Confectioners Association for its new Organic White Chocolate Mini Peanut Butter Cups.

PRODUCT AND BRAND MANAGEMENT AT HORMEL

Hormel's acquisition of Justin's provided the growing nut butter company with a variety of resources. First, the acquisition provided Justin's with access to national distribution channels in the food industry. Second, it provided access to a wide variety of suppliers to ensure that many of the ingredients of Justin's existing and future products could be organic. Finally, Hormel provided sophisticated brand management expertise.

Lisa Selk, CEO of another Hormel acquisition, CytoSport, and the previous marketing director of Skippy brand peanut butter, describes the brand management orientation. "Hormel is a $9 billion company. We have a long legacy of developing brands and creating great products for American consumers and across the globe. We have 35 number one or two brands and over 20,000 employees in our company. We have passion around all of our brands," she says. The company has developed an organizational brand structure that utilizes a variety of management tools to ensure the success of the brands.

The product life cycle, for example, provides guidance for many of Hormel's brand managers as some products have a long history with the 120-year-old company while other products are much newer to the marketplace. "If you think about the product life cycle of Skippy, it's definitely a mature product and brand," explains Selk. "The typical marketing strategy for a mature brand is mass media reminder messages. It is really about how many impressions you can get across TV, print, social, and digital spaces." Product managers can guide their brands through the product life cycle by modifying the product, modifying the market, and repositioning the product. Skippy, for example, is using these approaches by creating PB Bites, finding new consumers through online channels, and positioning the product as a source of protein.

Hormel also uses a combination of branding strategies. A multiproduct branding strategy, using one name for many products, is applied to products such as Hormel Bacon, Hormel Chili, Hormel Deli Meats, and Hormel Pepperoni. A multibranding strategy, using a distinct name for each product, is also used by Hormel for many of its brands such as Jennie-O, Muscle Milk, Skippy, and Justin's. The combination of products and brands creates a portfolio that must be managed.

Another important brand management tool is package design and labeling. "Design is extremely important in the early development of a product," explains Selk, "because you cannot change during its life cycle." The package design helps consumers identify the product and they become accustomed to searching for the familiar appearance on the shelf. Occasionally small changes are warranted, however. According to Selk, "Benefits are going to change." For example, "Protein is one of those things that consumers are looking for in their daily diet so we're calling out how many grams of protein on the front of the package," she continues. The label also provides essential information, particularly as regulations about nutritional facts change.

MARKETING AT JUSTIN'S

There are many traditional and unique aspects to the marketing organization at Justin's. "Marketing at Justin's is organized on two paths," explains Mike Guanella, president of Justin's. "We have the brand managers who own all elements of the product line, all the four Ps, and we have master brand managers who own all of the communications that touch on all elements of the brand, not just the products," he continues. The brand managers serve in a traditional role by assuming responsibility for developing and executing the specific elements of the marketing program, while the master brand managers provide a creative solution to communication activities that influence the entire brand name.

Justin's brand managers are typically responsible for a category such as nut butters or butter cups. "The brand manager owns a specific product line, either spreads or confection, and they would own all elements of that brand, the decision making around strategy, and tactics," says Guanella. "Think about the brand manager being the hub of all the spokes that come out to deliver a product to

Courtesy of Justin's

the market. Our brand managers own every element of the four Ps from our promotional strategy, to everyday pricing, to working with our sales team." The master brand managers must take a broader perspective. According to Guanella, "Our master brand managers own elements that cut across all our product lines." For example, "Our website and our media campaigns focus on Justin's as a master brand as opposed to specific product lines."

The brand managers and master brand managers work together on new and existing products. New products are developed and typically launched in the natural food retailer channel with samples, demos, and event marketing. As the products grow, their distribution is expanded to conventional retailer channels with traditional promotion. Finally, "some of our products are approaching the mature phase," says Guanella, which becomes "an opportunity to refresh those products with different flavor offerings or different size offerings.

THE FUTURE

The team at Justin's is very excited about the future. Lisa Selk observes that "as a marketer the best feeling you can have is to create a product and put it on the shelf and watch it be consumed by people." Mike Guanella comments, "I work for a company that makes products that I love and does it in a meaningful way. A company that's focused on sustainability and corporate responsibility. It's the perfect combination. I love what I do!" And as Justin himself discloses, "at Justin's we call it the Nuthouse because you want to go somewhere where you're not only working but you love to come to work and you feel like you're making a difference!"[35]

Questions

1 How are passion, consciousness, and product quality part of the product management process at Justin's?

2 How does the stage of the product life cycle influence marketing decisions at Hormel and Justin's?

3 What roles are served by the brand managers and master brand managers of Justin's products and brands?

4 Describe the branding strategies used by Hormel and how Justin's products fit into the Hormel product line.

5 How are sustainability and corporate responsibility considerations likely to influence the future at Justin's?

Chapter Notes

1. Quote by Sarah Robb O'Hagan.
2. "Pepsi Needs a Win with Gatorade," *The Wall Street Journal*, July 27–28, 2019: David Robertson, "How Gatorade Invented New Products by Revisiting Old Ones," *hbr.org*, August 17, 2017; "Gatorade Taps into Tech-Thirsty Consumers," *The Wall Street Journal*, March 11, 2016, pp. B1, B2; "How Gatorade Plans to Reinvent Sports Drinks Again," www.fastcompany.com, January 11, 2016; Darren Rovell, *First in Thirst: How Gatorade Turned the Science of Sweat into a Cultural Phenomenon* (New York: AMACOM, 2005); and www.Gatorade.com.

3. For an extended discussion of the generalized product life cycle, see Donald R. Lehmann and Russell S. Winer, *Product Management,* 5th ed. (Burr Ridge, IL: McGraw-Hill, 2008).
4. *Gillette Fusion Case Study* (New York: Datamonitor, June 6, 2008). All subsequent references to Gillette Fusion are based on this case study and "Men's Shaving in the U.S.," www.statista.com, accessed April 1, 2017.
5. Orville C. Walker Jr. and John W. Mullins, *Marketing Management: A Strategic Decision-Making Approach,* 8th ed. (Burr Ridge, IL: McGraw-Hill/Irwin, 2014), p. 209.
6. Portions of this discussion on the fax machine product life cycle are based on Jonathan Coopersmith, *Faxed: The Rise and Fall of the Fax Machine* (Baltimore: Johns Hopkins University Press, 2015); "Why Fax Won't Die," www.fastcompany.com, February 10, 2018, pp. 10–12; and "Global Fax Machines Market Data Survey Report, 2013-2025" www.allmarketinsights.com, April 2019.
7. "*Email Statistics Report, 2018–2022* (Palo Alto, CA: The Radicati Group, 2018); and "Global Fax Machines Market Data Survey Report, 2013–2025.
8. "Where Has All the Tab Gone? A Shortage Panics Fans," www.nytimes.com, October 17, 2018.
9. "Hosiery Sales Hit Major Snag," *Dallas Morning News,* December 18, 2006, p. 50.
10. Arthur Asa Berger, *Ads, Fads, and Consumer Culture: Advertising's Impact on American Character and Society,* 5th ed. (Lanham, MD: Rowman & Littlefield, 2015).
11. *Year-End Marketing Reports on U.S. Recorded Music Shipments* (New York Recording Industry Association of America) and "How the Net Saved the Record Labels," *The Economist,* February 11, 2019, pp. 19–20.
12. Everett M. Rogers, *Diffusion of Innovations,* 5th ed. (New York: Free Press, 2003).
13. Jagdish N. Sheth and Banwari Mittal, *Consumer Behavior: A Managerial Perspective,* 2nd ed. (Mason, OH: South-Western, 2003).
14. "Charged Up," *The Economist,* April 20, 2019, pp. 57–58; "4 U.S. Electric Vehicle Trends to Watch," www.forbes.com, January 4, 2019; and "Car Makers Race to Go Electric Cheaply," *The Wall Street Journal,* February 24–25, 2018, p. B2.
15. "When Free Samples Become Saviors," *The Wall Street Journal,* August 14, 2001, pp. B1, B4.
16. *What To Do When the Cost of Goods Goes Up: Make the Product Smaller or Raise the Price?* (New York: Nielsen Co., 2018); Pierre Chandon, "Research: Customers Notice When Products Shrink More Than When They Get Bigger," *hbr.org,* March 7, 2017; "Supermarket Products Get Smaller . . . but Prices Stay the Same," www.theguardian.com, April 19, 2017; and "Same Package, Same Price, Less Product," *The Wall Street Journal,* June 12, 2015, pp. B1, B2.
17. "We Came to an Agreement and It's All Fine," www.standard.co.uk, March 29, 2018.
18. This discussion is based on Kevin Lane Keller, *Strategic Brand Management,* 4th ed. (Upper Saddle River, NJ: Prentice Hall, 2013). Also see Kevin Lane Keller, "Reflections on Customer-Based Brand Equity: Perspectives, Progress, and Priorities," *AMS Review,* June 2016, pp. 1–16.
19. Jim Stengel, Matt Carcier, and Renee Dunn, "Leveraging the Power of Brand Purpose," in Alice M. Tybout and Tim Calkings, eds., *Kellogg on Branding in a Hyper-Connected World* (New York: John Wiley, 2019), pp. 20–36; and "A Purpose-Driven Brand Is a Successful Brand," www.forbes.com, January 16, 2019.
20. Keller, *Strategic Brand Management.*
21. This discussion is based on "Apple Heads the World's Most Valuable Brands," www.forbes.com, May 22, 2019; *Amazon Annual Report: 2018*; "Untouchable Intangibles," *The Economist,* August 30, 2014, p. 58; John Deighton, "How Snapple Got Its Juice Back," *Harvard Business Review,* January 2002, pp. 47–53; and "Breakfast King Agrees to Sell Bagel Business," *The Wall Street Journal,* September 28, 1999, pp. B1, B6.
22. The examples in this section are taken from "The Global Top 150 Licensors," *License Global,* May 2019, pp. T3ff; and "Its the Great White North, Charlie Brown," *The Wall Street Journal,* May 27–28, 2017, p. A11.
23. "The Global Top 150 Licensors," pp. T3ff.
24. Marc Fetscherin et al., "In China? Pick Your Brand Name Carefully," *Harvard Business Review,* September 2012, p. 26; Beth Snyder Bulik, "What's in a (Good) Product Name? Sales," *Advertising Age,* February 2, 2009, p. 10; and Keller, *Strategic Brand Management.*
25. Keller, *Strategic Brand Management.*
26. Mark Ritson, "Should You Launch a Fighter Brand?" *Harvard Business Review,* October 2009, pp. 87–94.
27. Tim Calkins, "Creating a Powerful Brand Portfolio," in Alice Tybout and Tim Calkins, eds, *Kellogg on Branding in a Hyper-Connected World* (New York: Wiley, 2019).
28. *Store Brand Facts* (New York: Private Label Manufacturers Association, 2019); and "Store Brands Pinch Food Makers," *The Wall Street Journal,* July 29, 2019, pp. B1, B2.
29. www.pez.com, downloaded September 1, 2019; and Shawn Peterson, *PEZ: From Austrian Invention to American Icon* (Charleston, SC: The History Press, 2016).
30. "Market Statistics," www.Packaging-Gateway.com, downloaded March 25, 2018.
31. "Inventing a Thanksgiving Favorite," *The Wall Street Journal,* November 17–18, 2018, p. C4.
32. "Iconic L'eggs Sheer Energy Egg Package Returns," *Package World,* March 6, 2014, pp. 16–17.
33. "Here Comes the Modern Chinese Consumer," www.mckinsey.com, March 2016.
34. *2018 State of the U.S. Flexible Packaging Industry* (Annapolis, MD: Flexible Packaging Association, 2018).
35. Justin's: This case was written by Steven Hartley and Roger Kerin. Sources: Interviews with Justin's executives Justin Gold, Mike Guanella, and Lisa Selk; Elaine Low, "Natural Foods Are Mainstream, but Startups Now Face a Big Choice," *Investor's Business Daily,* March 12, 2018; "Hormel Foods Corporation Appoints Lisa Selk as Chief Executive Officer, CytoSport, Inc.," *PR Newswire,* August 18, 2017; Danielle Romano, "Welcome to the Latest & Greatest," *Convenience Store News,* June 2018; "Hormel Foods Launches New Justin's Nut Butter Cups," *FoodBev Media,* June 21, 2018; "Hormel Foods Announces Closing of Acquisition of Justin's LLC and COO Appointment," company press release, May 31, 2016; Robin D. Schatz, "How to Go from Farmer's Market to Whole Foods," *Inc.,* July–August 2013; and Justin's website, www.justins.com.

Chapter 12 Services Marketing

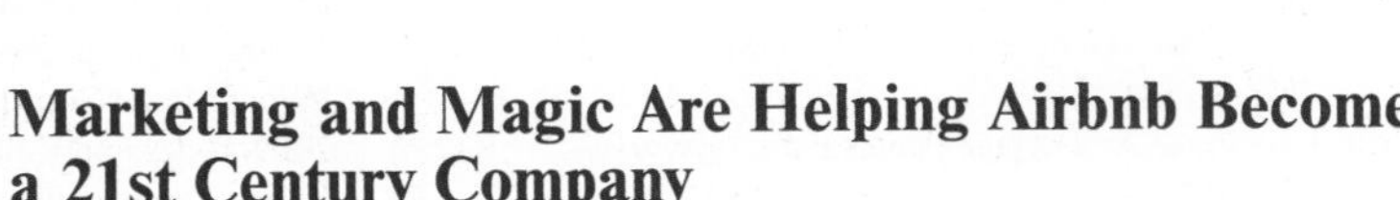

Learning Objectives

After reading this chapter you should be able to:

LO 12-1 Describe four unique elements of services.

LO 12-2 Recognize how services differ and how they can be classified.

LO 12-3 Explain how consumers purchase and evaluate services.

LO 12-4 Develop a customer contact audit to identify service advantages.

LO 12-5 Explain the role of the seven Ps in the services marketing mix.

LO 12-6 Discuss the important roles of internal marketing and customer experience management in service organizations.

Marketing and Magic Are Helping Airbnb Become a 21st Century Company

Airbnb founders Brian Chesky, Joe Gebbia, and Nathan Blecharczyk are thrilled with the incredible success of their "home-sharing" business. Currently, the company has more than 6 million listings in 81,000 cities in 191 countries. Now their challenge is to continue to grow while maintaining the customer experience that led to Airbnb's success. They want to become what they call a "21st Century Company."

How will they accomplish this ambitious goal? First, to grow, CEO Chesky hopes to create a one-stop shop for travelers that will attract 1 billion customers per year by 2028. New services such as Experiences, which offers local guided tours, and a last-minute booking platform called HotelTonight, will help attract new customers. In addition, Backyard, which helps homeowners design and build homes with space available for sharing, is intended to attract new hosts.

To preserve the magic that Airbnb guests have experienced in the past, the company is guided by its mission statement: to create a world where anyone can belong anywhere. As a result, Airbnb's marketing activities focus on using technology to create community, relationships, and a sense of belonging in an industry that is often standardized and impersonal. The key to the strategy is to encourage hosts not to simply offer their spaces as rentals but to work hard to offer unique experiences. Airbnb employees, for example, travel to many cities to offer seminars about how to become an Airbnb host. The company has also created a blog, a newsletter, an online community center, and a mentoring program where new hosts learn from experienced hosts.

Airbnb is also the genesis for what has come to be known as the sharing economy. Peer-to-peer sharing, or collaborative consumption, is a perfect match with recent changes in consumer attitudes about ownership. Today's consumers are much more likely to borrow, rent, and share than previous generations of consumers. As a result, many new services are being offered to accommodate these preferences. Uber and Lyft now offer peer-to-peer ride sharing, while Turo and Getaround offer peer-to-peer car sharing. Pavemint allows drivers to find homeowners who want to rent extra space in their driveway, and Rover helps pet owners find friendly pet sitting, dog boarding, and dog walking services. Rentoid and Spinlister help people rent products, tools, and bicycles rather than purchase them. Similarly, TaskRabbit allows users to outsource small jobs and tasks to people in their neighborhood. There are even sharing sites that encourage free exchanges, such as couchsurfing.com, which is a network of volunteers who offer free hospitality, advice, and accommodation to international travelers.

Experts estimate that hundreds of new peer-to-peer sharing services now in operation will grow to $335 billion in revenue by 2025. Neil Turner, the founder and CEO of adverCar, a service that allows drivers to rent out advertising space on their cars, suggests that "this is the way of the future." As we move from a perspective based on

Source: Airbnb, Inc.

VIDEO 12-1
Airbnb
kerin.tv/15e/v12-1

ownership to this new approach based on sharing and renting, traditional businesses will need to make changes. Avis Budget Group, for example, recently paid $500 million for Zipcar, while General Motors invested $500 million in Lyft. Home Depot has introduced product rental in about half of its stores.[1]

As these examples illustrate, services represent a dynamic and exciting component of our economy. In this chapter, we discuss how services differ from traditional products (goods), how service consumers make purchase decisions, and the ways in which the marketing mix is used for services.

THE UNIQUENESS OF SERVICES

Services are intangible activities or benefits (such as airline trips, financial advice, or automobile repair) that an organization provides to satisfy consumers' needs in exchange for money or something else of value.

Services today are a significant component of the global economy—and one of the most important components of the U.S. economy. The World Trade Organization estimates that, for all countries combined, exported merchandise and commercial services total $19.4 trillion and $5.2 trillion, respectively. As shown in Figure 12–1, on the next page, more than 47 percent of the U.S. gross domestic product (GDP) now comes from services, exceeding goods and the three other components of GDP—business investment, government spending, and net exports (not shown in the figure). The value of services in the economy has increased more

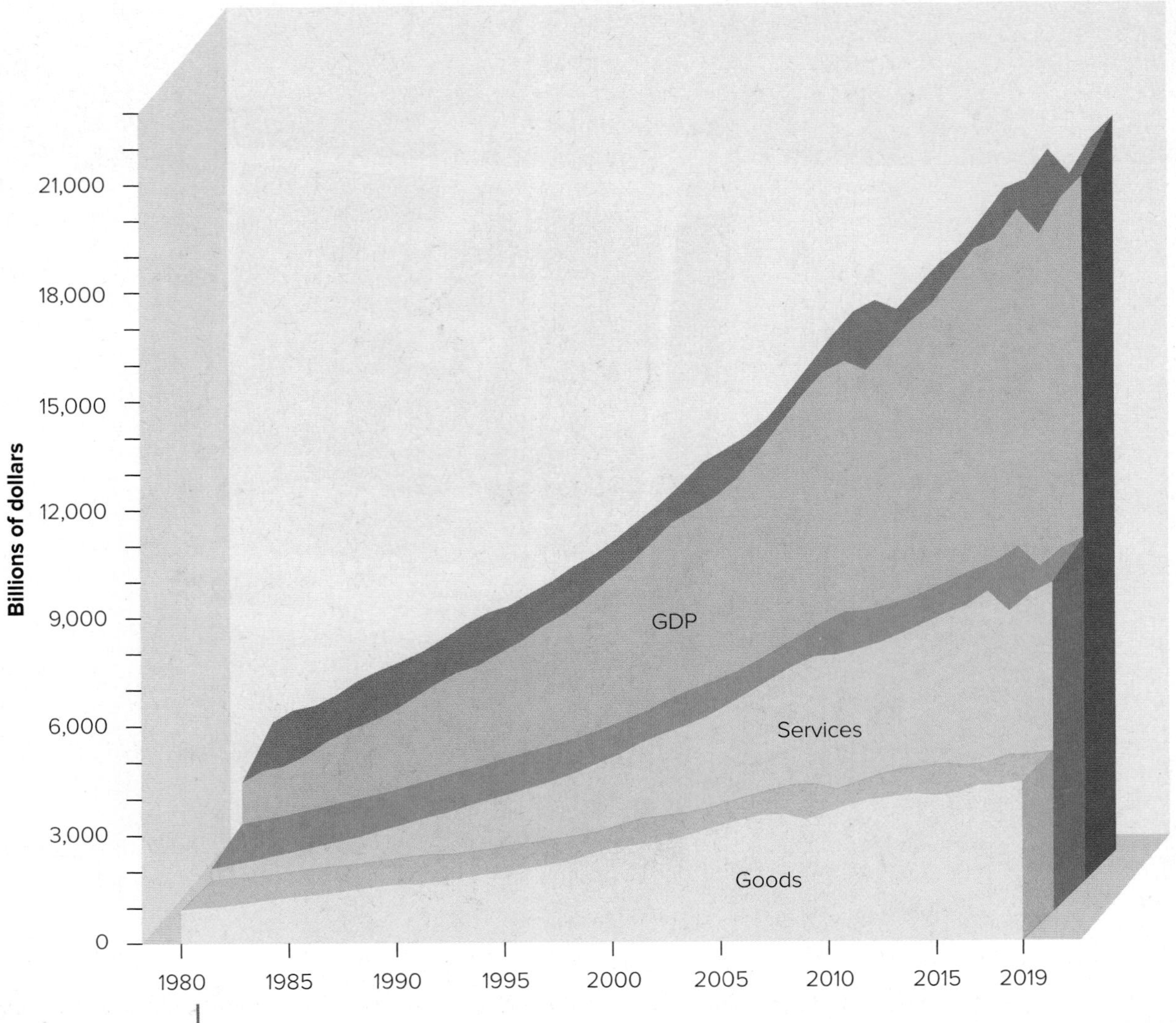

FIGURE 12–1
Services are now a larger part of the U.S. gross domestic product (GDP) than goods.

than 100 percent since 2000. Projections indicate that by 2026, goods-producing firms and service firms will employ 19.9 million people and more than 135.8 million people, respectively. Services also represent a large export business—the $783 billion of service exports in 2019 is one of the few areas in which the United States has a trade surplus.[2]

The growth of this sector is the result of increased demand for services that have been available in the past and an increasing interest in new services. Familiar services include transportation, education, health care, accounting, advertising, entertainment, and many others. Some traditional offerings, such as concierge services in hotels, are evolving. The Breakers in Palm Beach, Florida, and the Ritz-Carlton, for example, now offer club floors and lounges with dedicated concierges. At Hilton, its suite of digital concierge services is expanding to include a mobile app for exploring the area surrounding the hotel and an artificial intelligence chatbot to forge better relationships with its 34 million guests each year. Similarly, new health care concierge services, such as Babylon, offer AI-powered chatbots to provide remote diagnosis, consultation, and monitoring. Other new services include: Apple News, which provides digital access to 300 magazines for a monthly subscription fee; Virgin Galactic, which offers space travel to tourists (700 people have already made deposits!); and Warby Parker, which recently began offering facial mapping to recommend eyeglass frames specifically for your face and an app that can check prescriptions at home. These firms and many others like them are providing the types of imaginative services that will play a role in our economy in the future.[3]

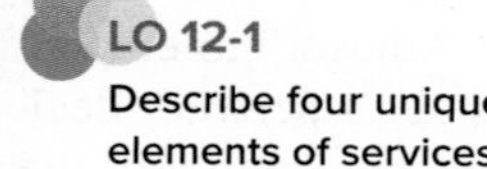

LO 12-1

Describe four unique elements of services.

The Four I's of Services

There are four unique elements to services—*intangibility*, *inconsistency*, *inseparability*, and *inventory*—referred to as the **four I's of services**.

Intangibility Services are intangible; that is, they can't be held, touched, or seen before the purchase decision. In contrast, before purchasing a traditional product, a consumer can touch a box of laundry detergent, kick the tire of an automobile, or sample a new breakfast cereal. Because services tend to be a performance rather than an object, they are much more difficult for consumers to evaluate. To help consumers assess and compare services, marketers try to make them tangible or show the benefits of using the service.

For example, American Airlines's marketing focuses on the airline's "wider seats, noise-reducing headphones, and sleeping amenities." United focuses on the tangible benefits provided by its MileagePlus loyalty program, which allows participants to earn points that can be redeemed for airline tickets, electronics, and a variety of other products.

Inconsistency Developing, pricing, promoting, and delivering services is challenging because the quality of a service is often inconsistent. Because services depend on the people who provide them, their quality varies with each person's capabilities and day-to-day job performance. Inconsistency is much more of a problem in services than it is with tangible products. Tangible products can be good or bad in terms of quality, but with modern production lines the quality will at least be consistent. In contrast, the Philadelphia Phillies baseball team may have great hitting and pitching and look like a pennant winner one day—and the next day they may lose by 10 runs. Or a soprano at New York's Metropolitan Opera may have a bad cold and give a less-than-perfect performance on the night that you attend. Whether the service involves tax assistance at H&R Block or guest relations at the Ritz-Carlton, organizations attempt to reduce inconsistency through standardization and training.[4]

Inseparability A third difference between services and products, which is also related to problems of consistency, is inseparability. In most cases, the consumer cannot (and does not)

Why does American Airlines's advertising emphasize wider seats and noise-reducing headphones? Why does United's MileagePlus loyalty program offer rewards for accumulated award miles? The answers appear in the text.

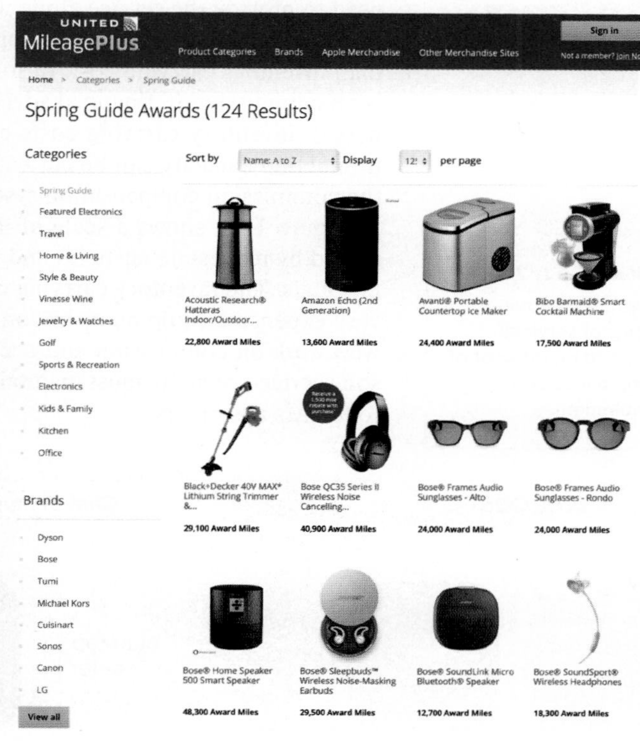

(Left): Source: American Airlines, Inc.; (Right): Source: United Airlines, Inc.

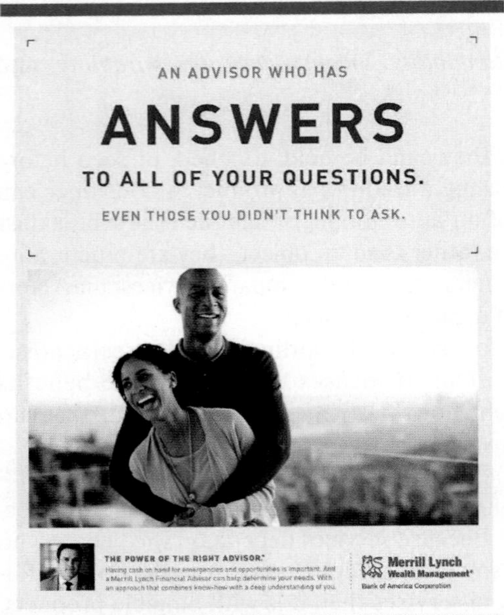

People play an important role in the delivery of many services. Many services ads emphasize the personal element of the offering.

Source: Bank of America Corporation

Merrill Lynch
www.wealthmanagement.ml.com

separate the deliverer of the service from the service itself. For example, Merrill Lynch ads describe "The Power of the Right Advisor" to emphasize the importance of its employees. Similarly, consider a person's decision to attend a university to receive higher education. The quality of the education may be high, but if the student has difficulty interacting with instructors, finds counseling services poor, or does not receive adequate career planning assistance, he or she may not be satisfied with the educational experience. Students' evaluations of their education will be influenced primarily by their perceptions of instructors, teaching assistants, counselors, and other people at the university. This interaction between the service provider and the consumer means that they often *co-create* value together.[5]

The amount of interaction between the consumer and the service provider depends on the extent to which the consumer must be physically present to receive the service. Some services, such as haircuts, golf lessons, medical diagnoses, and food service, require the customer to participate in the delivery of the services. Other services, such as car repair, dry cleaning, and waste disposal, process tangible objects with less involvement from the customer. Finally, services such as banking, consulting, and insurance are often delivered electronically, requiring no face-to-face customer interaction. Even pharmacies may soon be automated for shoppers who are willing to submit to a fingerprint scan. While this approach can create value for consumers, a disadvantage of some *self-service technologies* such as ATMs, grocery store scanning stations, and self-service gas station pumps is that they are perceived as being less personal.[6]

Inventory Inventory of services is different from that of products. Inventory problems exist with products because many items are perishable and because there are costs associated with handling inventory. With services, inventory carrying costs are more subjective and are related to **idle production capacity**, which is when the service provider is available but there is no demand for the service. The inventory cost of a service is the cost of paying the person used to provide the service along with any needed equipment. If a physician is paid to see patients but no one schedules an appointment, the fixed cost of the idle physician's salary is a high inventory carrying cost. In some service businesses, however, the provider of the service is on commission (a financial advisor) or is a part-time employee (a store clerk). In these businesses, inventory carrying costs can be significantly lower or nonexistent because the idle production capacity can be cut back by reducing hours or having no salary to pay because of the commission compensation system.

Figure 12–2 shows a scale of inventory carrying costs for services; the low end is represented by real estate agencies and hair salons and the high end is represented by airlines and hospitals. The inventory carrying costs of airlines are high because of high-salaried pilots and very expensive equipment. In contrast, real estate agencies and hair salons have employees who work on commission and need little expensive equipment to conduct business. One reason service providers must maintain production capacity is because of the importance of time to today's customers.

FIGURE 12–2
Inventory carrying costs of services depend on the cost of employees and equipment.

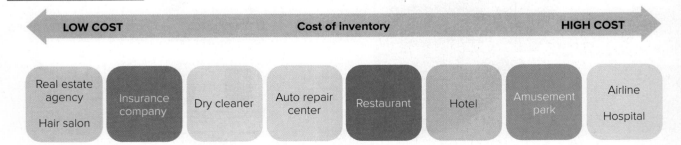

LOW COST			Cost of inventory				HIGH COST
Real estate agency Hair salon	Insurance company	Dry cleaner	Auto repair center	Restaurant	Hotel	Amusement park	Airline Hospital

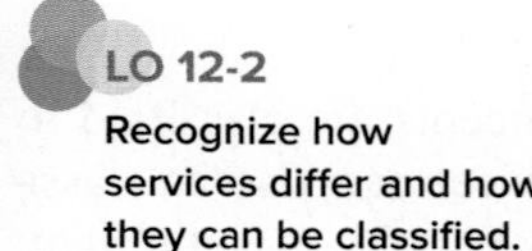

LO 12-2

Recognize how services differ and how they can be classified.

The Service Continuum

The four I's differentiate services from products in most cases, but many companies are not clearly service-based or product-based organizations. Is IBM a manufacturer or a service provider? Although IBM manufactures mainframe servers, data storage systems, and other products, more than half of the company's revenue is from its consulting, cloud, and AI services.[7] What companies bring to the market ranges from the tangible to the intangible. This range of product-dominant to service-dominant offerings is referred to as the **service continuum** (see Figure 12–3).

rvlsoft/Shutterstock

Teaching, nursing, and the theater are intangible, service-dominant activities, and intangibility, inconsistency, inseparability, and inventory are major concerns in their marketing. Salt, neckties, and dog food are tangible products, and the problems represented by the four I's are not relevant in their marketing. However, some businesses are a mix of intangible services and tangible product factors. A clothing tailor provides a service but also a product, the finished suit. How pleasant, courteous, and attentive the tailor is to the customer is an important component of the service, and how well the clothes fit is an important part of the product. As shown in Figure 12–3, a fast-food restaurant is about half tangible products (the food) and half intangible services (courtesy, cleanliness, speed, and convenience).

For many businesses today, it is useful to distinguish between their core offering—either a product or a service—and supplementary services. A core service offering such as a savings account, for example, also has supplementary services such as a mobile deposit app, parking or drive-thru availability, ATMs, and online statements. Supplementary services often allow service providers to differentiate their offering from competitors, and they may add value for consumers. While there are many potential supplementary services, key categories of supplementary services include consultation, finance, shipping, installation, maintenance, and upgrades. Innovation in core services today often relies on the creative efforts of the organization. Understanding the impact of supplementary services, however, may be best accomplished through input from customers.[8]

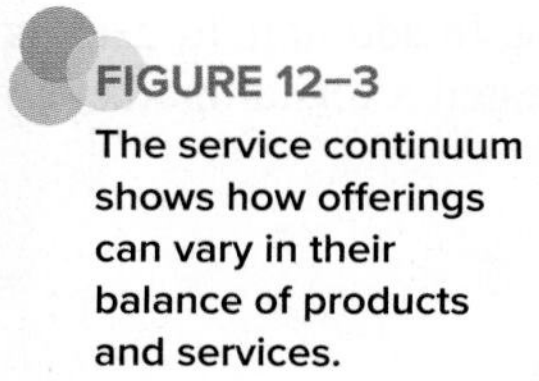

FIGURE 12–3

The service continuum shows how offerings can vary in their balance of products and services.

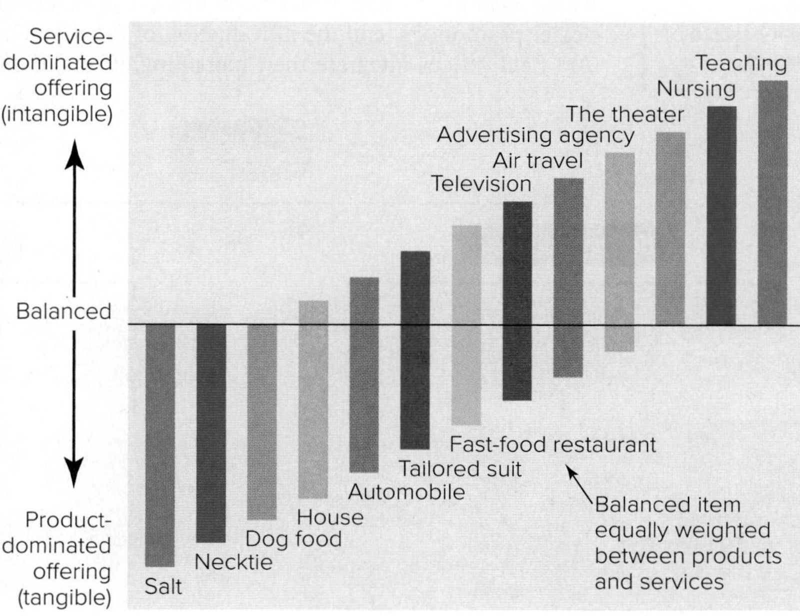

Classifying Services

Throughout this book, marketing organizations, techniques, and concepts are classified to show the differences and similarities in an organized framework. Services can also be classified in several ways, according to whether (1) they are delivered by people or equipment, (2) they are for-profit or nonprofit, or (3) they are government sponsored.

Delivery by People or Equipment As seen in Figure 12–4, many companies offer services. Professional services include management consulting firms such as Booz Allen Hamilton or Accenture. Skilled labor is required by Geek Squad to offer services such as cell phone, computer, and appliance repair and by Sheraton to offer its catering service. Unskilled labor such as that used by Brink's store-security forces is also a service provided by people.

Grzegorz Knec/Alamy Stock Photo

Equipment-based services do not have the marketing concerns of inconsistency because people are removed from the provision of the service. Electric utilities, for example, can provide service without frequent personal contact with customers. Movie theaters have projector operators that consumers never see. A growing number of customers use company-controlled *self-service technologies* such as Home Depot's self checkout, Southwest Airlines's self check-in, and Schwab's online stock trading without interacting with any service employees. In addition, customer-controlled *self-service devices* such as smartwatches, sport trackers, and smart home assistants allow access to and use of many services. An interesting outcome of customers' growing preference for self-service is that when a service representative is needed, it is typically for a complicated issue or transaction.[9]

For-Profit or Nonprofit Organizations Many organizations involved in services also distinguish themselves by their tax status as for-profit or nonprofit organizations. Unlike for-profit organizations, *nonprofit organizations'* excesses in revenue over expenses are not taxed or distributed to shareholders. When excess revenue exists, the money goes back into the organization's treasury to allow continuation of the service. Based on the corporate structure of the nonprofit organization, it may pay tax on revenue-generating holdings not directly related to its core mission. Nonprofit organizations in the United States now have revenue of $1.9 trillion and account for 9 percent of all wages and salaries.[10]

United Way, Greenpeace, Outward Bound, The Salvation Army, and Girl Scouts are examples of nonprofit organizations. In recent years nonprofit organizations have turned to marketing to help achieve their goals. The American Red Cross is a good example. To increase blood donations it partnered with HBO and *Game of Thrones* to create its "Bleed For The Throne" campaign, which included TV and print ads, an immersive experience at the SXSW Film Festival, T-shirt and poster promotions, and the introduction of the #ForTheThrone hashtag. In addition, to help its 700 field offices integrate their marketing efforts, the organization created a digital marketing

FIGURE 12–4
Services can be classified as equipment-based or people-based.

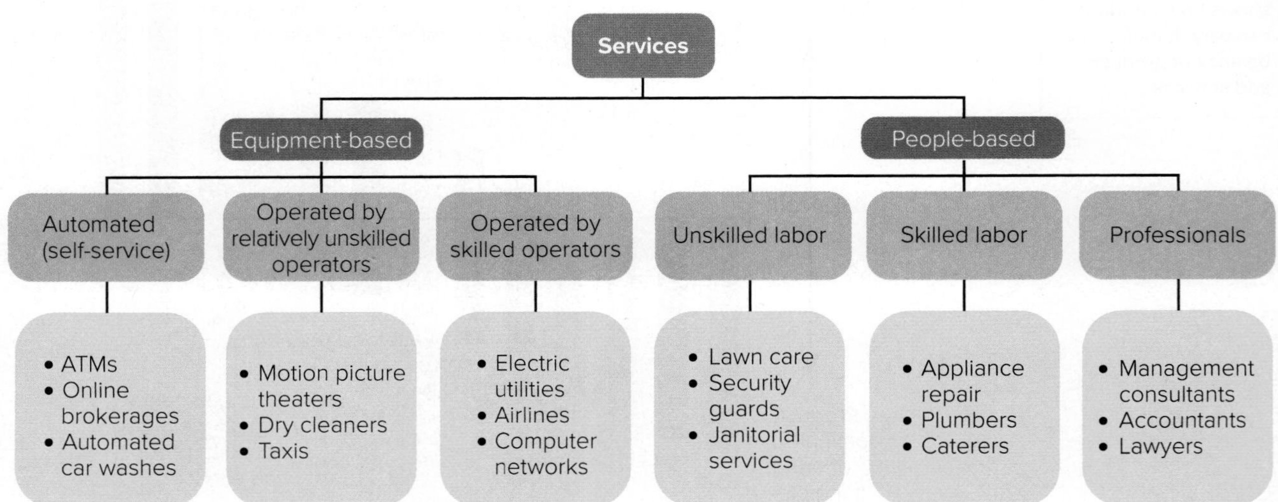

Nonprofit service organizations often advertise to help achieve their goals.

(Left): Source: Outward Bound; (Right): Source: The American National Red Cross

VIDEO 12-2
American Red Cross
kerin.tv/15e/v12-2

platform to consolidate its data. According to Banafsheh Ghassemi, VP of customer experience, "Data is the fuel for marketing." Other promotional activities include the development of mobile apps and the creation of the National Celebrity Cabinet, which currently includes Trace Adkins, Amy Grant, Pierce Brosnan, LL Cool J, Heidi Klum, Peyton Manning, and Raven-Symoné. Similarly, Outward Bound uses advertising to promote its "experience of a lifetime."[11]

Other nonprofits have also been successful in using marketing to help achieve their goals. The American Marketing Association recently selected Artis Stevens as the recipient of the Nonprofit Marketer of the Year award for his extraordinary leadership of the National 4-H Council, which reaches 6 million youth each year with programming related to STEM education, healthy living, and civic engagement.[12] See the Marketing Matters box on the next page to learn more about the social marketing activities of other nonprofit organizations, including Susan G. Komen for the Cure, the American Red Cross, and the March of Dimes.[13]

What are some of the many marketing activities being adopted by the United States Postal Service? See the text to find out.

Source: United States Postal Service

Government Sponsored A third way to classify services is based on whether or not they are government sponsored. Although there is no direct ownership and they are nonprofit organizations, governments at the federal, state, and local levels provide a broad range of services. The United States Postal Service, for example, has adopted many marketing activities. First-class postage revenue has declined as postal service customers have increased their use of the Internet to send e-mail, pay bills, and file taxes. Rather than fight the trend, however, the U.S. Postal Service is embracing the Internet. Its website, www.usps.com, allows consumers to pay for postage, print shipping labels, and request a free package pickup. In addition, new post office boxes are being designed in sizes to better meet the needs of consumers who shop online. You may have noticed that many post offices are now also retail outlets that sell supplies, collector stamps, and even neckties. The postal service is also developing new services such as Informed Delivery which will send people a visual notification of what is in their mailbox. These marketing activities are designed to increase consumer use and to compete with UPS, FedEx, DHL, and foreign postal services for package delivery business. The U.S. Postal Service is also promoting online mailing list management and the use of USPS Marketing Mail™.[14] The Peace Corps is another example of a government-sponsored service, which often recruits marketing specialists with skills in social media marketing, branding, design thinking, and sustainability.

Marketing Matters

Technology

Social Marketing Is a Must for Nonprofits

"Make It Social" is the mantra for many nonprofit organizations today. Recent changes in the tax code have reduced the total number of donors, so many of the 1.56 million public charities, private foundations, universities, religious congregations, and other nonprofit organizations have turned to social marketing and social media to engage potential contributors.

The Susan G. Komen for the Cure organization has been one of the most successful in using new approaches. In addition to its familiar walks and races, the Komen Foundation uses Facebook, Twitter, YouTube, and Instagram to promote its cause and fund-raising activities. Its merchandise is promoted on ShopKomen.com, Amazon, and other websites. It also allows mobile giving by texting the word KOMEN from a mobile phone. The success of the Komen organization's marketing actions has allowed it to raise more than $2 billion for breast cancer research and community outreach programs.

The American Red Cross has also been quick to adopt social marketing tools. The organization recently opened a Digital Disaster Operations Center in Washington, DC, to help it communicate with the general public, volunteers, and donors. In addition, the Red Cross has created tools such as its blood donation app and crowdfunding websites which have raised millions in contributions for disaster victims. Social media tools such as these are playing an increasingly important role in Red Cross operations as they become familiar to most people.

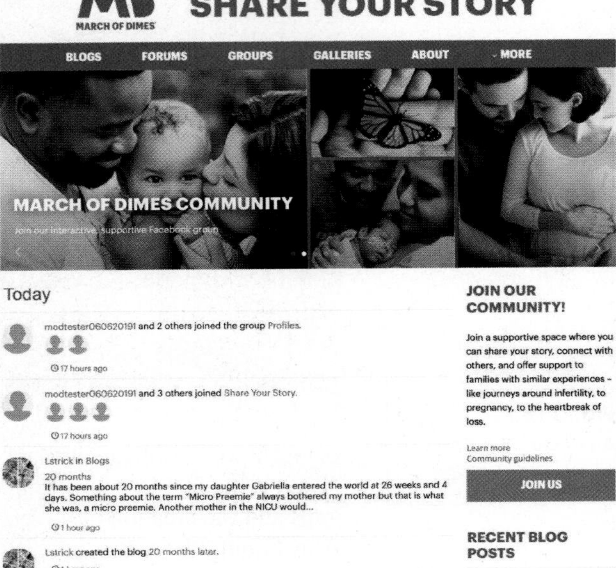

Source: March of Dimes Foundation

Nonprofit organizations should follow many of the same principles businesses use to engage people with social media. First, they should understand what motivates people to take up causes. One of the most important reasons is usually to feel like they are doing something, even if it is as simple as clicking the "like" button on Facebook. Second, nonprofit organizations need to be creative in their use of social media and incorporate digital photos, video, and gaming skills. As Jamie Henn, communications director for 350.org/ explains, "By using images and video we have been able to convey stories with emotional impact." The United Way, for example, partnered with CNN to deliver a live online panel discussion about its education goals. Finally, nonprofit campaigns should allow information sharing. The March of Dimes, for example, has created an online forum called "Share Your Story," where people can participate in blogs, forums, and discussion groups, and it now has an average of 8,100 posts each month.

Social marketing campaigns and social media offer nonprofit organizations very effective tools for engaging their members, fans, friends, and the public. While the number of success stories is growing, it is important to remember to have a goal and measure progress toward that goal. Participation rates, donations, number of texts, posts on a blog, and other dimensions of effectiveness all contribute to the perception of the brand!

LEARNING REVIEW

12-1. What are the four I's of services?

12-2. To eliminate service inconsistencies, companies rely on __________ and __________.

12-3. Would inventory carrying costs for an accounting firm with certified public accountants be (*a*) high, (*b*) low, or (*c*) nonexistent?

HOW CONSUMERS PURCHASE SERVICES

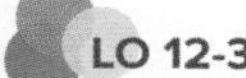

LO 12-3

Explain how consumers purchase and evaluate services.

Colleges, hospitals, hotels, and even charities are facing an increasingly competitive environment. Successful service organizations, like successful product-oriented firms, must (1) understand how the consumer makes a service purchase decision, (2) understand how the consumer evaluates quality, and (3) determine how to present a differential advantage relative to competing offerings.

The Purchase Process

Many aspects of services affect the consumer's evaluation of the purchase. Because services cannot be displayed, demonstrated, or illustrated, consumers cannot make a prepurchase evaluation of all the characteristics of services.[15] Similarly, because service providers may vary in their delivery of a service, an evaluation of a service may change with each purchase. Figure 12–5 portrays how different types of products and services are evaluated by consumers. Tangible products such as clothing, jewelry, and furniture have *search* properties, such as color, size, and style, which can be determined before purchase. Services such as restaurants and child care have *experience* properties, which can be discerned only after purchase or during consumption. Finally, services provided by specialized professionals such as medical diagnoses and legal services have *credence* properties, or characteristics that the consumer may find impossible to evaluate even after purchase and consumption.[16] To reduce the uncertainty created by these properties, service consumers turn to personal sources of information such as early adopters, opinion leaders, and reference group members during the purchase decision process. Research indicates that consumers search for much more information and they place an emphasis on trust, commitment, expertise, and competence when trying to evaluate services with credence properties.[17] In response to this need for more information, the Mayo Clinic uses an organized, explicit approach called "evidence management" to present customers with concrete and convincing evidence of its strengths.[18]

Assessing Service Quality

Once a consumer tries a service, how is it evaluated? Primarily, a consumer assesses service quality by comparing expectations about a service offering to his or her actual experience with the service.[19] Differences between the consumer's expectations and experience are identified through **gap analysis**. This type of analysis asks consumers to assess their expectations and

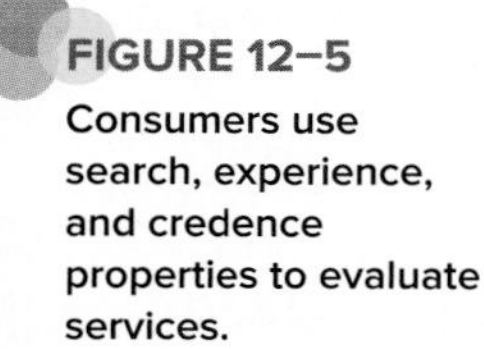

FIGURE 12–5

Consumers use search, experience, and credence properties to evaluate services.

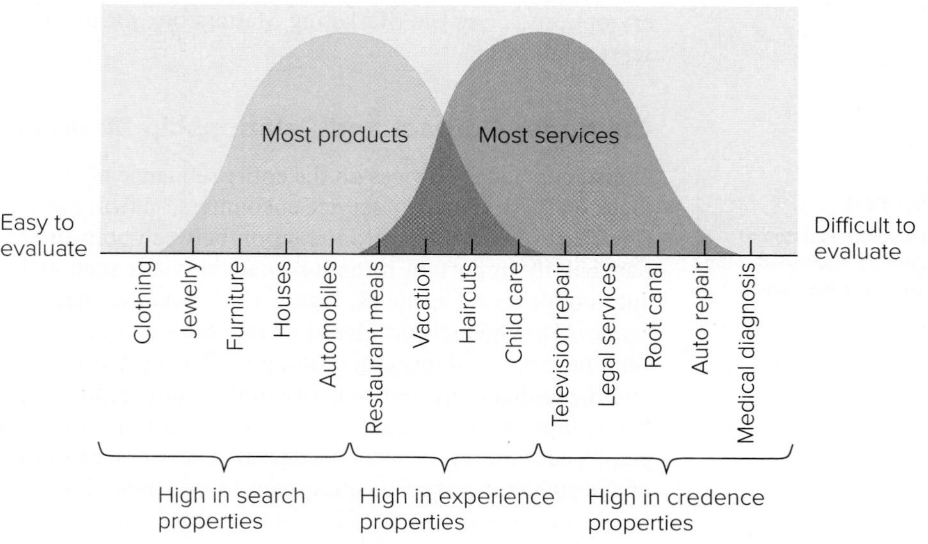

DIMENSION	DEFINITION	EXAMPLES OF QUESTIONS AIRLINE CUSTOMERS MIGHT ASK
Reliability	Ability to perform the promised service dependably and accurately	Is my flight on time?
Tangibility	Appearance of physical facilities, equipment, personnel, and communication materials	Are the gate, the plane, and the baggage area clean?
Responsiveness	Willingness to help customers and provide prompt service	Are the flight attendants willing to answer my questions?
Assurance	Knowledge and courtesy of employees and their ability to convey trust and confidence	Are the ticket counter attendants, flight attendants, and pilots knowledgeable about their jobs?
Empathy	Caring, individualized attention provided to customers	Do the employees determine if I have special seating, meal, baggage, transfer, or rebooking needs?

FIGURE 12–6
The five dimensions of service quality.

experiences on dimensions of service quality such as those described in Figure 12-6.[20] Expectations are influenced by word-of-mouth communications, personal needs, past experiences, and promotional activities, while actual experiences are determined by the way an organization delivers its service, particularly through interpersonal competencies.[21] The relative importance of the various dimensions of service quality varies by the type of service.[22] What if someone is dissatisfied and complains? Recent studies suggest that customers who experience a "service failure" will increase their satisfaction if the service provider makes a highly interactive service recovery effort, although they may not increase their intent to repurchase. In addition, service operators can increase customer satisfaction by identifying and responding to customer emotions (e.g., frustration, irritation, anger, disappointment, regret, uncertainty), explaining the cause of the service failure, and letting customers choose between several recovery options.[23] See the Marketing Matters box for ideas about monitoring and responding to service failures.[24]

Customer Contact and Relationship Marketing

LO 12-4
Develop a customer contact audit to identify service advantages.

Consumers judge services on the entire sequence of steps that make up the service process. To focus on these steps, or "service encounters," a firm can develop a **customer contact audit**—a flowchart of the points of interaction between consumers and the service provider.[25] This is particularly important in high-contact services such as hotels, educational institutions, and automobile rental agencies. Figure 12-7 is a customer contact audit prepared for a car rental agency. The interactions identified in a customer contact audit often serve as the basis for developing relationships with customers. Recent research suggests that employees' competence and the authenticity and sincerity of their interactions affect the success of their customer relationships. Another version of a customer contact audit, called a *service blueprint*, includes all employee actions and acknowledges that services are designed to be "experiences." Evaluation of the customer experience requires an understanding of the "touchpoints" that create value for the customer.[26]

Marketing Matters

Technology

Managing Service Failures: The Importance of Monitoring and Guarantees

Only 5 to 10 percent of dissatisfied customers choose to complain—the rest switch companies or make negative comments to other people. Increasingly, the forum for personal comments is on the many social media now available to consumers. Companies can search for comments and images using search engines such as Google News (click on "Tools" and "Blogs") and Google Images, and they can search for videos on YouTube. Domino's Pizza, for example, discovered that consumers were publishing comments that its pizza was "like cardboard." In addition, social media listening tools such as Hootsuite or Socialmention can monitor Twitter, Instagram, Facebook, LinkedIn, and other platforms. Web services such as www.reputationdefender.com are also available to manage the online reputations of individuals and businesses.

Source: Reputation Defender LLC

Most marketing experts agree that it is best to respond to service failures, particularly when the failure is viewed to be the result of a controllable factor. Regarding its product's comparison to cardboard, Domino's posted a response on YouTube and Twitter, and posted the real-time Twitter feed on a billboard in Times Square! Recent research also suggests that service providers should offer a service guarantee with two parts: (1) a commitment to good service, and (2) a promise to compensate the customer if good service is not provided.

To find out what consumers are saying about your favorite brands, try your own search now.

FIGURE 12–7

Customer contact audit for a car rental agency (green shaded boxes indicate customer activity).

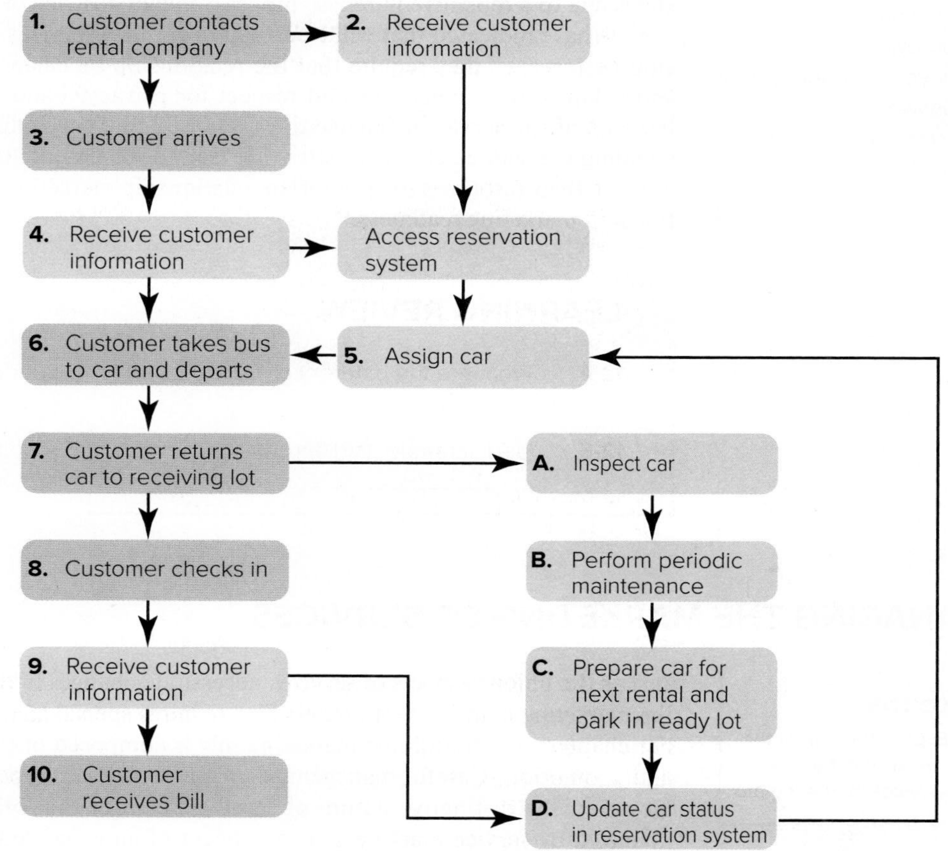

Car rental agencies like Hertz can create a service advantage by managing customer contact points.
B.O Kane/Alamy Stock Photo

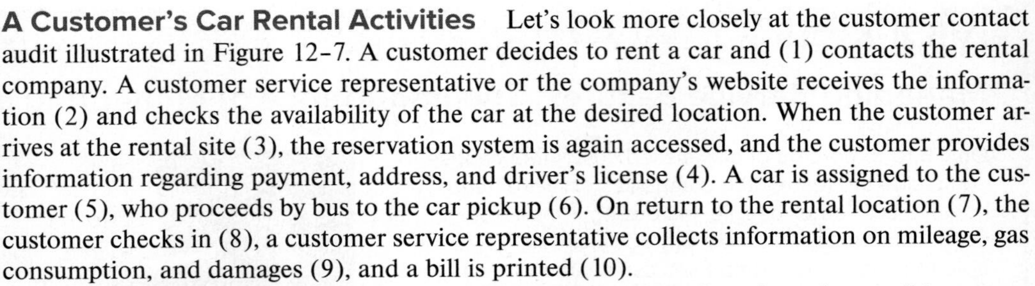

A Customer's Car Rental Activities Let's look more closely at the customer contact audit illustrated in Figure 12–7. A customer decides to rent a car and (1) contacts the rental company. A customer service representative or the company's website receives the information (2) and checks the availability of the car at the desired location. When the customer arrives at the rental site (3), the reservation system is again accessed, and the customer provides information regarding payment, address, and driver's license (4). A car is assigned to the customer (5), who proceeds by bus to the car pickup (6). On return to the rental location (7), the customer checks in (8), a customer service representative collects information on mileage, gas consumption, and damages (9), and a bill is printed (10).

Each of the steps numbered 1 to 10 is a customer contact point where the tangible aspects of the company's service are seen by the customer. Figure 12–7, however, also shows a series of steps lettered A to D that involve an inspection, maintenance, preparation for the next customer, and an update of the reservation system. These steps are essential in providing a clean, well-maintained car, but they are not points of customer interaction. To create a service advantage, a car rental agency—like any service company—must create a competitive advantage in the sequence of interactions with the customer. For example, Hertz has attempted to eliminate steps 4, 8, and 9 for some customers with its Gold Plus Rewards program. These customers simply pick up the car keys when they arrive and use an expedited drop-off when they return.

How many times will a Disney park visitor encounter a Disney employee? See the text for the answer.
imageBROKER/Alamy Stock Photo

Relationship Marketing The contact between a service provider and a customer represents a service encounter that is likely to influence the customer's assessment of the purchase. The number of encounters in a service experience may vary. Disney, for example, estimates that a park visitor will have 74 encounters with Disney employees in a single visit. These encounters represent opportunities to develop social bonds, or relationships, with customers. The relationship may also be developed through loyalty incentives such as airline frequent flyer programs. Relationship marketing provides several benefits for service customers, including the continuity of a single provider, customized service delivery, reduced stress due to a repetitive purchase process, and an absence of switching costs. Surveys of consumers have indicated that while customers of many services are interested in being "relationship customers," they require that the relationship be balanced in terms of loyalty, benefits, value, kinds of connections, and respect for privacy,[27] and their expectations of the future benefits of the service influence the likelihood that they continue the relationship.[28] Understanding the service characteristics that lead to repeat purchases can help services managers allocate their resources to appropriate relationship marketing activities and improve their relationship marketing readiness.[29]

LEARNING REVIEW

12-4. What are the differences between search, experience, and credence properties?

12-5. Hertz created its differential advantage at the points of ____________________ in its customer contact audit.

MANAGING THE MARKETING OF SERVICES

LO 12-5
Explain the role of the seven Ps in the services marketing mix.

Just as the unique aspects of services necessitate changes in the consumer's purchase process, the marketing management process also requires special adaptation.[30] As we have seen in earlier chapters, the traditional marketing mix is composed of the four Ps: product, price, place, and promotion. Careful management of the four Ps is important when marketing services. However, the distinctive nature of services requires that other variables also be effectively managed by service marketers. The concept of an expanded marketing mix for services has been adopted by many service-marketing organizations. In addition to the four Ps, the services marketing mix includes people, the physical environment, and the process, or the **seven Ps of services marketing**.[31]

Logos and brand names help consumers identify services.

(McDonald's): tanuha2001/ Shutterstock; (Sprint): Don Emmert/AFP/Getty Images; (Red Cross): Steve Allen/ Shutterstock

Product (Service)

The concepts of the product component of the marketing mix discussed in Chapters 10 and 11 apply equally well to Cheerios (a product) and American Express (a service). Managers of products and services must design the product concept with the features and benefits desired by customers. An important aspect of the product concept is branding. Because services are intangible, and more difficult to describe, the brand name or identifying logo of the service organization is particularly important when a consumer makes a purchase decision.[32] Therefore, service organizations, such as banks, hotels, rental car companies, and restaurants, rely on branding strategies to distinguish themselves in the minds of consumers. Strong brand names and symbols are important for service marketers, not only as a means of differentiation, but also to convey an image of quality. A service firm with a well-established brand reputation will also find it easier to introduce new services than firms without a brand reputation.[33]

Many services have undertaken creative branding activities. Hotels, for example, have begun to extend their branding efforts to consumers' homes through services such as *Hotels at Home*, an in-room catalog that offers Westin's "Heavenly Bed," Hilton's bathrobes, and even artwork from Sheraton hotel rooms for consumers to buy and use at home. Similarly, Fairmont Hotels has formed co-branding partnerships with Reebok, which provides fitness apparel and equipment to loyalty program members, and BMW, which offers automobiles and bicycles for guest use.[34] Look at the nearby logos to determine how successful some companies have been in branding their service with a name and symbol.

Price

In service businesses, price is referred to in many ways. Hospitals refer to *charges*; consultants, lawyers, physicians, and accountants to *fees*; airlines to *fares*; hotels to *rates*; and colleges and universities to *tuition*. Because of the intangible nature of services, price is often perceived by consumers as a possible indicator of the quality of the service. Do you expect higher quality from an expensive restaurant? Would you wonder about the quality of a $100 surgery? In many cases, there may be few other available cues for the customer to judge, so price becomes very important as a quality indicator.[35]

Pricing of services goes beyond the traditional tasks of setting the selling price. When customers buy a service, they also consider nonmonetary costs, such as the mental and physical efforts required to consume the service. Service marketers must try to minimize the effort required to purchase and use the service. Pricing also plays a role in balancing consumer demand for services. Many service businesses use **off-peak pricing**, which consists of charging different prices during different times of the day or during different days of the week to reflect variations in demand for the service. Airlines, for example, offer discounts for weekend travel, while movie theaters offer matinee prices.

Price influences perceptions of the quality of services.

Courtesy of The Redirections Group

Place (Distribution)

Place, or distribution, is a major factor in developing a service marketing strategy because of the inseparability of services from the producer. Rarely are intermediaries involved in the distribution of a service; the distribution site and the service deliverer are the tangible components of the service. Until recently, customers generally had to go to the service provider's physical location to purchase the service. Increased competition, however, has forced many service firms to consider the value of convenient distribution and to find new ways of distributing services to customers. Hairstyling chains such as Cost Cutters Family

Hair Salon, tax preparation offices such as H&R Block, and accounting firms such as EY (Ernst & Young) all use multiple locations for the distribution of services. Technology is also being used to deliver services beyond the provider's physical locations. In the banking industry, for example, customers of participating banks using the Cirrus system can access any one of 2 million automated teller machines in 93 countries. The availability of electronic distribution through the Internet also allows for global reach and coverage for a variety of services, including travel, education, entertainment, and insurance. With speed and convenience becoming increasingly important to customers when they select service providers, service firms can leverage the use of the Internet to deliver services on a 24/7 basis, in real time, on a global scale. This advantage varies by type of service, however: British grocery retailer Tesco has 1 million customers who shop online, while most health care services still rely on face-to-face interaction.[36]

Promotion

VIDEO 12-3
Amazon Prime Now Video
https://www.youtube.com/watch?v=3omjuYY_4gAk

The value of promotion, especially advertising, for many services is to show consumers the benefits of purchasing the service. It is valuable to stress availability, location, consistent quality, and efficient, courteous service[37] and to provide a physical representation of the service or a service encounter.[38] The Accenture ad, for example, describes the benefits available to its customers—"High performance. Delivered." The Amazon ad features its two-hour delivery option, Prime Now, by describing the benefit as "What you need, when you need it." In most cases, promotional concerns of services are similar to those of products.

Another form of promotion, *publicity*, has played a major role in the promotional strategy of many service organizations. Nonprofit organizations such as public schools, religious organizations, and hospitals, for example, often use publicity to disseminate their messages. For many of these organizations, the most common form of publicity is the *public service announcement* (*PSA*) because it is free.[39] As discussed in Chapter 19, however, using PSAs as the foundation of a promotion program is unlikely to be effective because the timing and location of the PSA are under the control of the medium, not the organization.

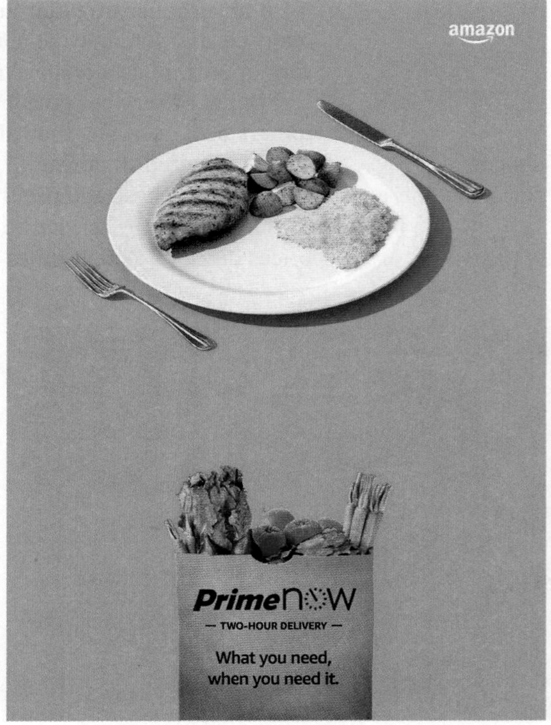

Services use promotional programs to communicate benefits and provide a representation of the service encounter.
(Left): Source: Accenture; (Right): Source: Amazon.com

Personal selling, sales promotion, and direct marketing also can play an important role in services marketing. Service firm representatives, such as hotel employees handling check-in services or waitstaff in restaurants, are often responsible for selling their services. Similarly, sales promotions such as coupons, free trials, and contests are often effective tools for service firms. Finally, direct marketing activities are often used to reach specific audiences with interest in specific types of services. Increasingly, service firms are adopting an integrated marketing communications approach (see Chapter 18), similar to the approach used by many consumer packaged goods firms, to ensure that the many forms of promotion are providing a consistent message and contributing to a common objective.

People

LO 12-6
Discuss the important roles of internal marketing and customer experience management in service organizations.

Many services depend on people for the creation and delivery of the customer service experience.[40] The nature of the interaction between employees and customers strongly influences the customer's perceptions of the service experience. Customers will often judge the quality of the service experience based on the performance of the people providing the service. This aspect of services marketing has led to a concept called *internal marketing.* In addition, employee participation in activities that identify, generate, and enhance value creation leads to an *internal market orientation*.[41]

Internal marketing is based on the notion that a service organization must focus on its employees, or internal market, before successful programs can be directed at customers. In fact, the relationships between internal marketing, internal service quality, employee productivity, and firm profitability have come to be known as the *service-profit chain*.[42] Service firms need to ensure that employees have the attitude, skills, and commitment needed to meet customer expectations and to sustain customer loyalty. Employees with a commitment to mutually beneficial relationships with customers are most suitable for services today. This idea suggests that employee development through recruitment, training, communication, coaching, management, and leadership is critical to the success of service organizations.[43] Finally, many service organizations, such as educational institutions and athletic teams, must recognize that individual customer behavior may also influence the service outcome for other customers. These interactions suggest that the people element in services includes employees and all customers.

Once internal marketing programs have prepared employees for their interactions with customers, organizations can better manage the services they provide. **Customer experience management (CEM)**, introduced in Chapter 10, is the process of managing the entire customer experience with the company. CEM experts suggest that the process should be intentional and planned, consistent so that every experience is similar, differentiated from other service offerings, and relevant and valuable to the target market. Companies such as Disney, Southwest Airlines, the Ritz-Carlton, and Starbucks all manage the experience they offer customers. They integrate their activities to connect with customers at each contact point to move beyond customer relationships to customer loyalty.[44] For example, Zappos.com, the online retailer profiled in the opener to Chapter 9, requires that all employees complete a four-week customer loyalty training program to help deliver one of the company's core concepts—"Deliver WOW through Service."[45]

Zappos provides training programs to help employees improve the customer experience.
Ethan Miller/Getty Images

Physical Environment

The appearance of the environment in which the service is delivered and where the firm and customer interact can influence the customer's perception of the service. The physical evidence of the service includes all the tangibles surrounding the service: the buildings, landscaping, vehicles, furnishings, signage, brochures, and equipment. Service firms need to manage physical evidence carefully and systematically to convey the proper impression of the service to the customer. This is sometimes referred to as impression, or evidence, management.[46] For many services, the physical environment provides an opportunity for the firm to send consistent and strong messages about the nature of the service to be delivered.

Process

Process refers to the actual procedures, mechanisms, and flow of activities by which the service is created and delivered. The actual creation and delivery steps that the customer experiences provide customers with evidence on which to judge the service. These steps involve not only "what" gets created but also "how" it is created. The customer contact audit discussed earlier in the chapter is relevant to understanding the service process discussed here. The customer contact audit can serve as a basis for ensuring better service creation and delivery processes. Grease Monkey believes that it has the right process in the vehicle oil change and fluid exchange service business. Customers do not need appointments, stores are open six days per week, the service is completed in 15–20 minutes, and a waiting room allows customers to read or work while the service is being completed.

Most services have a limited capacity due to the inseparability of the service from the service provider and the perishable nature of the service. For example, to "buy" an appendectomy, a patient must be in the hospital at the same time as the surgeon and only one patient can be helped at that time. Similarly, no additional surgery can be conducted tomorrow because of an unused operating room or an available surgeon today—the service capacity is lost if it is not used. So the service component of the marketing mix must be integrated with efforts to influence consumer demand.[47] This is referred to as **capacity management**.

Service organizations must manage the availability of the offering so that (1) demand matches capacity over the duration of the demand cycle (for example, one day, week, month, or year), and (2) the organization's assets are used in ways that will maximize the return on investment (ROI).[48] Figure 12–8 shows how a hotel tries to manage its capacity during the high and low seasons. Differing price structures are assigned to each segment of consumers to help moderate or adjust demand for the service. Airline contracts fill a fixed number of rooms throughout the year. In the low season, when more rooms are available, tour packages at appealing prices are used to attract groups or conventions, such as an offer for seven nights in Orlando at a reduced price. Weekend packages are also offered to vacationers. In the high-demand season, groups are less desirable because guests who will pay high prices travel to Florida on their own. The Applying Marketing Metrics box demonstrates how JetBlue Airways uses a capacity management measure called *load factor* to assess its profitability.

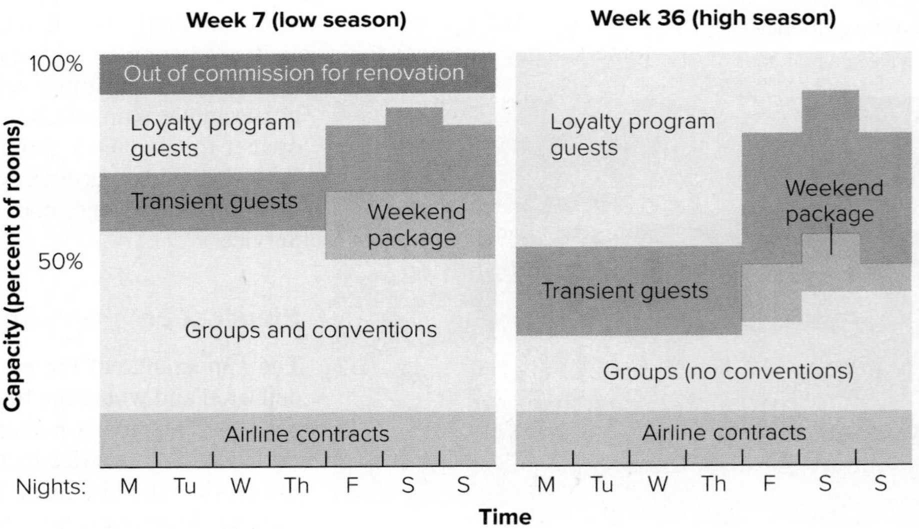

FIGURE 12–8
Different prices and packages help match hotel demand to capacity.

Applying Marketing Metrics

Are JetBlue's Flights Profitably Loaded?

Capacity management is critical in the marketing of many services. For example, having the right number of airline seats or hotel rooms available at the right time, price, and place can spell the difference between a profitable or unprofitable service operation.

Airlines feature *load factor* as a capacity management measure on their marketing dashboards, along with two other measures, namely, the *operating expense* per available seat flown one mile and the revenue generated by each seat flown one mile, called *yield*. Load factor is the percentage of available seats flown one mile occupied by a paying customer.

These three measures combine to show airline operating income or loss per available seat flown one mile:

Operating income (loss) per available seat flown one mile
= [Yield × Load factor] − Operating expense

Your Challenge

As a marketing analyst for New York City–based JetBlue Airways, you have been asked to determine the operating income or loss per available seat flown one mile for the past six months. In addition, you have been asked to determine what load factor JetBlue must reach to break even assuming its current yield and operating expense will not change in the immediate future.

Your Findings

JetBlue's yield, load factor, and operating expense marketing dashboard displays are shown below.

You can conclude from these measures that JetBlue Airways posted about a 0.21¢ loss per available seat flown one mile in the past six months:

Operating loss per available seat flown one mile
= [9.83¢ × 82.1%] − 8.28¢ = −0.2096¢

Assuming JetBlue's yield and operating expenses will not change and using a little algebra, the airline's load factor will have to increase from 82.1 percent to 84.23 percent to break even:

Operating income (loss) per available seat flown one mile
= [9.83¢ × Load factor] − 8.28¢ = 0¢
Load factor = 84.23%

Your Action

Assuming yield and operating expenses will not change, you should recommend that JetBlue consider revising its flight schedules to better accommodate traveler needs and advertise these changes. Consideration also might be given to how JetBlue utilizes its existing airplane fleet to serve its customers and produce a profit.

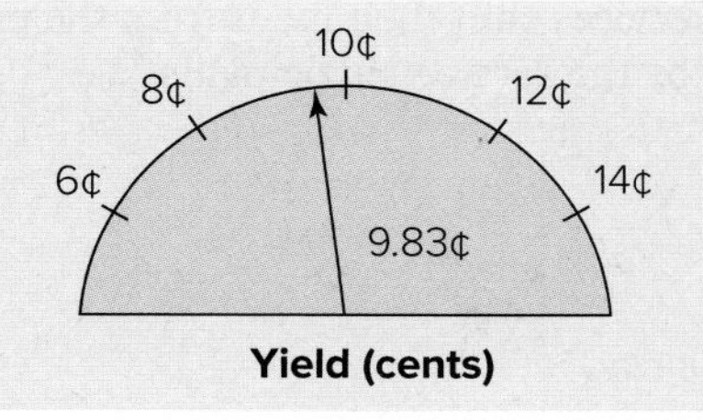

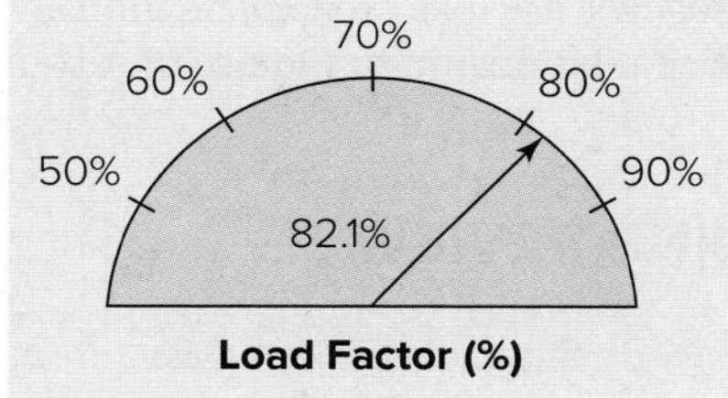

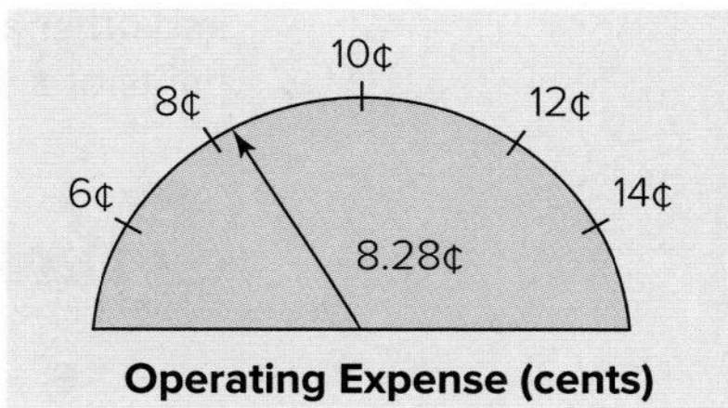

SERVICES IN THE FUTURE

Valeo Voyage is one example of how services are changing. Read the text to learn more.
Source: Valeo

What can we expect from the services industry in the future? New and better services, of course, and an unprecedented variety of choices. Many of the changes will be the result of three factors: technological development, improved understanding of service delivery and consumption, and the social imperative for sustainability.

Technological advances are rapidly changing the services industry. The introduction of the 5G broadband network, for example, is quickly improving mobile communications, facilitating the viability of autonomous vehicles, and increasing the effectiveness of the Internet of Things.

Similarly, advances in artificial intelligence are making customer service centers more efficient by giving agents more time to focus on high-level service requests. New technologies are also creating new services such as Google Interpreter, which can provide real-time translation in more than 27 languages, and Valeo Voyage, which allows someone to be a virtual passenger in your car.[49] Changes such as these also give an early indication of the likely changes coming to other components of the service ecosystem including regulation, employee training, and customer expectations.[50]

VIDEO 12-4
Valeo Voyage Video
kerin.tv/15e/v12-4

New data and information about service consumers and providers is also leading to changes in service delivery and consumption. Physicians at the University of Virginia Health System discovered that cardiac patients learned more and reported 98 percent satisfaction when they shared a 90-minute appointment with other patients, rather than meeting the doctor in the traditional, shorter, one-on-one format. Other studies of services have discovered that in some businesses, such as retailing, restaurants, and repair and installation, customer satisfaction levels are inflated because employees often engage in "service sweethearting"—giving unauthorized free products or services to customers. Many of these businesses are now changing employee recruiting and training activities to limit this type of behavior. Both examples emphasize how understanding the details of service transactions will lead to new forms of service in the future. In addition, service marketers are increasing their use of *netnography*—the use of online information about consumer opinions, experiences, and behaviors—to better understand service consumers.[51]

Finally, a growing interest in sustainability and "green" businesses is also changing the services industry. This trend began when consumers became aware of the environmental impact of many products such as automobiles, appliances, and cleaning solutions. Today, this trend has expanded to include consumers' assessment of services. Recent surveys indicate that green practices influence many consumer purchase decisions for services, including those provided by dry cleaners, contractors, and hotels. In response, many service providers are developing new approaches to their offerings. Hilton has set conservation goals to help its hotels achieve environmental management certification from the International Organization for Standardization (ISO). Similarly, the U.S. Postal Service has introduced sustainability initiatives to reduce energy, water, and petroleum use and to increase its recycling activities.[52] These and other approaches are likely to expand globally as services shift their focus from the participants of a service relationship to the use of resources by the service participants.[53]

LEARNING REVIEW

12-6. How does a movie theater use off-peak pricing?

12-7. Matching demand with capacity is the focus of ____________ management.

12-8. What factors will influence future changes in services?

LEARNING OBJECTIVES REVIEW

LO 12-1 *Describe four unique elements of services.*
The four unique elements of services—the four I's—are intangibility, inconsistency, inseparability, and inventory. Intangibility refers to the tendency of services to be a performance that cannot be held or touched, rather than an object. Inconsistency is a characteristic of services because they depend on people to deliver them, and people vary in their capabilities and in their day-to-day performance. Inseparability refers to the difficulty of separating the deliverer of the service (hair stylist) from the service itself (hair salon). Inventory refers to the need to have service production capability when there is service demand.

LO 12-2 *Recognize how services differ and how they can be classified.*
Services differ in terms of the balance of the part of the offering that is based on products and the part of the offering that is

based on service. Services can be delivered by people or equipment, they can be provided by for-profit or nonprofit organizations, and they can be government sponsored.

LO 12-3 *Explain how consumers purchase and evaluate services.*
Because services are intangible, prepurchase evaluation is difficult for consumers. To choose a service, consumers use search, experience, and credence qualities to evaluate the product and service elements of an offering. Once a consumer tries a service, it is evaluated by comparing expectations with the actual experience on five dimensions of quality: reliability, tangibility, responsiveness, assurance, and empathy. Differences between expectations and experience are identified through gap analysis.

LO 12-4 *Develop a customer contact audit to identify service advantages.*
A customer contact audit is a flowchart of the points of interaction between a consumer and a service provider. The interactions identified in a customer contact audit often serve as the basis for developing relationships with customers.

LO 12-5 *Explain the role of the seven Ps in the services marketing mix.*
The services marketing mix includes seven Ps. An important aspect of the *product* element is branding—the use of a brand name or logo to help consumers identify a service. *Pricing* is reflected in charges, fees, fares, and rates and can be used to influence perceptions of the quality of a service and to balance demand for services. *Place* (or distribution) is used to provide access and convenience. *Promotional* tools such as advertising and publicity are a means of communicating the benefits of a service. *People* are responsible for the creation and delivery of the service. Internal marketing and customer experience management are concepts that result from a focus on people within the service organization and their interactions with customers. *Physical* environment refers to the appearance of the place where the services are delivered. *Process* refers to the actual procedures, mechanisms, and activities by which a service is created and delivered.

LO 12-6 *Discuss the important roles of internal marketing and customer experience management in service organizations.*
Because the employee plays a central role in creating the service experience and building and maintaining relationships with customers, services have adopted a concept called internal marketing. This concept suggests that services need to ensure that employees (the internal market) have the attitude, skills, and commitment needed to meet customer expectations. Customer experience management is the process of managing the entire customer experience with the company to ensure customer loyalty.

LEARNING REVIEW ANSWERS

12-1 What are the four I's of services?
Answer: The four I's of services are: (1) intangibility, which means that they can't be held, touched, or seen; (2) inconsistency, which means that their quality varies with each person's capabilities and day-to-day job performance; (3) inseparability, which means that the consumer cannot (and does not) separate the deliverer of the service from the service itself; and (4) inventory, which means that inventory carrying costs are more subjective and are related to idle production capacity, which occurs when the service provider is available but there is no demand for the service.

12-2 To eliminate service inconsistencies, companies rely on ______________ and ______________.
Answer: standardization; training

12-3 Would inventory carrying costs for an accounting firm with certified public accountants be (*a*) high, (*b*) low, or (*c*) nonexistent?
Answer: Inventory carrying costs are related to idle production capacity, which is when the service provider is available but there is no demand. A CPA typically earns a high fixed cost salary. Therefore, if he/she is available but there is no demand for his/her service, the inventory cost of this service is (*a*) high, because the cost of the accountant's salary must be paid regardless of whether or not the service is performed.

12-4 What are the differences between search, experience, and credence properties?
Answer: Search properties, such as color, size, and style, can be determined before purchase. Experience properties, such as with restaurants, can only be assessed during or after consumption. Credence properties are characteristics of services provided by specialized professionals, such as legal advice or medical diagnostics, and may be impossible to evaluate even after purchase and consumption.

12-5 Hertz created its differential advantage at the points of ______________ in its customer contact audit.
Answer: interaction between consumer and service provider

12-6 How does a movie theater use off-peak pricing?
Answer: Off-peak pricing consists of charging different prices during different times of the day or during different days of the week to reflect variations in demand for the service. Movie theaters reduce prices for matinees and often reduce prices for Monday through Thursday shows as well, due to the lower demand during this time of the day and these days of the week.

12-7 Matching demand with capacity is the focus of ______________ management.
Answer: capacity

12-8 What factors will influence future changes in services?
Answer: Technology advances, improved understanding of service delivery and consumption, and the social imperative for sustainability are factors that will influence future changes in services.

FOCUSING ON KEY TERMS

- **capacity management** p. 334
- **customer contact audit** p. 328
- **customer experience management (CEM)** p. 333
- **four I's of services** p. 321
- **gap analysis** p. 327
- **idle production capacity** p. 322
- **internal marketing** p. 333
- **off-peak pricing** p. 331
- **service continuum** p. 323
- **services** p. 319
- **seven Ps of services marketing** p. 331

APPLYING MARKETING KNOWLEDGE

1 Explain how the four I's of services would apply to a Marriott hotel.

2 Idle production capacity may be related to inventory or capacity management. How would the pricing component of the marketing mix reduce idle production capacity for (*a*) a car wash, (*b*) a stage theater group, and (*c*) a university?

3 Look back at the service continuum in Figure 12–3. Explain how the following points in the continuum differ in terms of consistency: (*a*) salt, (*b*) automobile, (*c*) advertising agency, and (*d*) teaching.

4 What are the search, experience, and credence properties of an airline for (*a*) the business traveler and (*b*) the pleasure traveler? What properties are most important to each group?

5 Outline the customer contact audit for the typical deposit you make at your neighborhood bank.

6 How does off-peak pricing influence demand for services?

7 Draw the channel of distribution for the following services: (*a*) a restaurant, (*b*) a hospital, and (*c*) a hotel.

8 The text suggests that internal marketing is necessary before a successful marketing program can be directed at consumers. Why is this particularly true for service organizations?

9 Outline the capacity management strategies that an airline must consider.

10 In recent years, many service businesses have begun to provide their employees with uniforms. Explain the rationale behind this strategy in terms of the concepts discussed in this chapter.

BUILDING YOUR MARKETING PLAN

In this section of your marketing plan you should distinguish between your core product—a good or a service—and supplementary services.

1 Develop an internal marketing program that will ensure that employees are prepared to deliver the core and supplementary services.

2 Using the flowchart in Figure 12–7 as a guide, create a customer contact audit to identify specific points of interaction with customers.

3 Describe marketing activities that will (*a*) address each of the four I's as they relate to your service and (*b*) encourage the development of relationships with your customers.

Add this section as an appendix to your marketing plan and use the results to develop your marketing mix strategy.

VIDEO CASE 12 LA Galaxy: Where Sports Marketing Is a Kick!

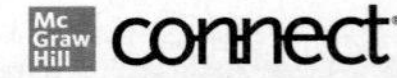

VIDEO 12-5
LA Galaxy Video Case
kerin.tv/15e/v12-5

"We have a unique product for people," exclaims Chris Klein, president of the LA Galaxy soccer club. Soccer combines many elements of athleticism, teamwork, and competition to make it fast, exciting, engaging, fun, and increasingly popular. Klein goes on to explain, "This is a cool sport, and it's something that's growing." His enthusiasm is supported by a sophisticated strategy that Klein and his marketing team have designed to help people "experience the excitement" of their product!

THE LA GALAXY

The LA Galaxy is a professional soccer club competing in Major League Soccer (MLS). The club was one of 10 charter clubs when the league began and is now part of the league's Western Conference. "The LA Galaxy was founded in 1996," says Klein, and "through the course of the League's history, the Galaxy has been the most successful franchise in Major League Soccer." The team has been conference champions nine times, regular season champions eight times, and the MLS championship winners five times.

The first Galaxy games were played at the Rose Bowl in Pasadena, California, until the team moved to its current location in the soccer-specific stadium Dignity Health Sports Park in Carson, California. Players are primarily from the United States but also represent countries such as Brazil, Ireland, Italy, and Panama. "We have signed some of the biggest players, not only in our country, like Cobi Jones and Landon Donovan, but we've also signed some of the biggest players in the world," explains Klein. English soccer superstar David Beckham joined the LA Galaxy in 2007 and played through 2012, helping the team win two championships during that period.

R Heyes Design/Alamy Stock Photo

Today, the LA Galaxy attracts an average of 23,000 fans to each of its games. While the hard-core fans tend to be 18- to 34-year-old men, the team also appeals to many other segments. For example, because soccer is the largest participant sport in the United States, many kids and youth soccer teams come to the games. In addition, many college students and families attend. According to Klein, it's a welcoming environment where "you can paint your face and yell" or you can bring your kids and just "have fun at the game." The team's mascot, Cozmo, is a froglike extraterrestrial who entertains fans at the games and throughout Southern California.

MAJOR LEAGUE SOCCER

As part of its negotiation to hold the 1994 FIFA (Fédération Internationale de Football Association) World Cup in the United States, the U.S. Soccer Federation promised to establish a professional soccer league. The result was Major League Soccer. Since its beginning with 10 teams in 1996, Major League Soccer has expanded to 24 teams, including 3 teams in Canada. Each team plays 34 games during the regular season from March to October, and the top 14 teams participate in the playoffs, which end with the MLS Cup in December.

Even though soccer is popular around the world, introducing professional soccer in the United States presented some difficulties. Klein describes the problem:

> Soccer is the biggest sport in the world, but here in the U.S. we have a lot of competition. Major League Soccer is the equivalent to Major League Baseball, the NFL, the NBA, and the NHL. These are established leagues and MLS is the fifth major sport. In 1996, we started thinking that we had to get every baseball fan, basketball fan, and football fan to enjoy our sport.

To attempt to attract fans from other sports, MLS experimented with changes to traditional soccer rules. For example, MLS added shootouts to resolve tie games, used a countdown (to zero) clock rather than a progressive clock, allowed extra substitutions, and even considered making the goals bigger to increase the scoring. Eventually, the league concluded that the changes had alienated some traditional soccer fans without attracting new fans from other sports, so it went back to the traditional rules for MLS games.

As the league shifted from an "attract all sports fans" philosophy to a focus on people with some existing interest in soccer, it made several other changes. First, it began moving MLS games from large, rented, football facilities to new, smaller, more intimate soccer-specific stadiums. In addition, the league made efforts to internationalize the teams by allowing up to eight players per team from outside of the United States. Finally, MLS encouraged all teams to create youth development programs to help find talented local players. To complement these efforts, each team manages its own marketing program.

THE LA GALAXY MARKETING PROGRAM

"The primary marketing objective for the Galaxy is ticket sales," says Casey Leppanen, senior director of marketing and broadcasting. "Our product is soccer," he goes on to explain, "but we are more than that. We are an experience." So, to sell single-game tickets and season tickets, the Galaxy developed a comprehensive marketing program. According to Leppanen, "Our marketing mix is pretty similar to any other sports team or company you're going to find." The key difference in marketing a sport, or any service, is that every game offers a different experience to fans. The players, the opponents, the weather, and the outcomes of the games change constantly.

How does the Galaxy sell a product that is constantly changing? The first step is to understand that different segments may attend a soccer game for different types of experiences. For example:

- *Supporter clubs*. Attend to watch the strategy of a game and see the Galaxy score.
- *Families*. Want to have fun, see the mascot, and get a souvenir.

- *Latino community.* Enjoys watching soccer and forming connections with players from Central and South America.
- *Trendsetting youth.* Attend to meet friends, enjoy an event, and see star players.
- *Groups* (teams, corporations, religious groups, etc.). Want an opportunity for networking and team building.

The different interests combined with the changing "product" create a special marketing challenge.

The experience the Galaxy provides to fans is much more than watching a soccer game. It includes the quality of play, the individual members of the team, the merchandise, food, facilities, activities, and interactions with staff, other fans, and players. Some of the specific elements of the Galaxy game experience include:

- *Star players.* Romain Alessandrini, Sebastian Lletget, and Giovani dos Santos are all soccer stars that attract fans.
- *Team LA Store.* Offers LA Galaxy merchandise at StubHub Center and other locations.
- *Supporter clubs.* Three clubs–the Angel City Brigade, the Riot Squad, and the Galaxians–offer the opportunity to participate in an intense and festive fan experience, complete with songs and chants!
- *Promotional nights.* Special events include Family Nights, Bobblehead Nights, Jersey-Off-The-Back Auctions, and Student Nights.
- *"Name in Lights."* A donation gets your message on the home game scoreboard.
- *"Cozmo."* The team mascot who entertains all fans at every game.
- *StubHub Center.* The soccer-specific stadium offers a great atmosphere, amazing sight lines, event suites, terrace cabanas, restaurants, assigned seating, general admission seating, and an inclined lawn (also called the berm) for picnic-style seating.

Of course, there are many other elements that are all part of the experience the Galaxy marketing team manages and delivers at every game!

Next, the Galaxy must deliver relevant messages to each segment. Leppanen explains that the Galaxy

Shaun Clark/Getty Images

marketing team "want[s] to make sure that we're delivering an authentic message." One way they accomplish this is through direct marketing, which consists of e-mail messages and direct-mail literature. These messages are complemented with traditional media advertising, outdoor advertising, and digital advertising. The traditional media include radio, TV, and print. The outdoor advertising includes billboards and bus wraps. The digital platforms, which have a total of 1.3 million Galaxy fan users, include Facebook, Twitter, YouTube, Google+, Instagram, Pinterest, Flickr, and Foursquare. Digital is a very important part of the mix because "we can get really granular and sophisticated in who we're targeting and how we speak to them," explains Leppanen.

The Galaxy also uses personal selling as part of its marketing program. A team of 25 people makes personal phone calls to help sell single-game tickets, family packs, group tickets, and season tickets. There are also two teams of brand ambassadors called the Star Squad and the Galaxy Street Team who are involved in about 500 events in the community each year. Lori Nevares, a marketing coordinator at Galaxy and former Street Team member, explains that "We got to go out and do all kinds of promotional events for different communities and see the fans and how much they were devoted to the Galaxy." A skills team called the Galaxy Futboleros provides high-energy performances throughout the community as well. Finally, Cozmo makes many appearances to deliver the Galaxy soccer message to current and potential fans.

One of the final steps in the ticket sales process is setting the price. According to Heather Pease, director of ticketing, "Every year we conduct a very in-depth analysis of our ticket sales. We go seat-by-seat, row-by-row, and category-by-category to see how many people have purchased seats and at what price." The analysis also includes a comparison of ticket prices for other sports teams in the area. Pease then uses the information to create a price and a package for every possible type of fan, ranging from Champions Lounge members, to season ticket holders, to groups or families, to single-game fans. She also offers discounted tickets for students and children.

There are a lot of marketing activities taking place at the Galaxy. In fact, Casey Leppanen says, "My role here at the Galaxy is to integrate all the pieces of our marketing department." The integration is paying off, as attendance at LA Galaxy games is well above the league average. In addition, the team currently has 8,500 season ticket holders and plans to reach 12,500 in three years!

Matthew Ashton - AMA/Getty Images

THE BUSINESS OF SOCCER

While ticket sales represent a substantial source of revenue for the Galaxy, there are several other important elements of the soccer "business"—broadcast rights, sponsorships, and merchandise—that the team must manage. Early in the league's history, MLS had to pay television and cable networks to broadcast its games. As the number of viewers increased, however, the league was able to attract coverage from ESPN, ABC, NBC, and Fox. The Galaxy recently began a 10-year, $55 million deal with the Time Warner Cable Sports network. Currently, all games have television and radio coverage in English and Spanish, and there is play-by-play coverage and webchat on LAGalaxy.com.

Sponsorships are also essential to the financial success of MLS and the Galaxy. Pepsi is the official soft drink and Aquafina is the official water of MLS. Similarly, Herbalife is the official nutrition company of the LA Galaxy. In addition, Herbalife recently announced a 10-year agreement to be the official jersey sponsor of the Galaxy. Herbalife pays $4 million annually to sponsor the team and place its logo on the front of the team jerseys. Other team sponsors include Chevrolet, Nestlé, Alaska Airlines, Shasta, and Buffalo Wild Wings. The sponsors participate in many of the team's contests, promotions, and events to support the team and to gain exposure to customers with similar values and interests.

The marketing team at the LA Galaxy is always busy. "There is a business to run," says Pease. "It is about driving revenue at the end of the day," she continues, "but the best part about it is you get to walk out on a game day and see a sold-out stadium." Seeing the sold-out stadium is a thrill not only because it's a business, however, but also because the marketing team loves soccer. Galaxy president Chris Klein, who studied business and marketing in college, is a good example of the attitude at Galaxy. "I went to college on a soccer scholarship," says Klein, "then I played professionally in our league, and I'm now president of a major club." He is thrilled by "the challenge of marketing a sport that I love, a sport that I've played, and a sport that has so much potential."[54]

Questions

1 What is the LA Galaxy "product"?

2 Which of the seven elements of the service marketing mix are most important in the LA Galaxy marketing program?

3 How is promotion (advertising, personal selling, public relations, sales promotion, direct marketing) used by the LA Galaxy? Do these activities depend on the specific target markets?

4 How are social media integrated into the LA Galaxy's marketing strategy?

5 How does the LA Galaxy assess the impact of its marketing activities? Has its program been successful?

Chapter Notes

1. Biz Carson, "New Tricks for an Old Unicorn," *Forbes*, October 31, 2018, pp. 40-50; Pei-Ru Keh, "To Power Its Transportation Ambitions, Airbnb Looks to Design," www.fortune.com, March 19, 2019; Emily Price, "Airbnb Isn't Just for Vacation Rentals Anymore," www.fortune.com, November 30, 2018; Biz Carson, "Airbnb to Buy HotelTonight as It Pushes Deeper into Hotel Booking Business," www.forbes.com, March 7, 2019; Derek Miller, "What Is the Sharing Economy?" www.thebalancesmb.com, August 27, 2018; Shamika Ravi, "The Current and Future State of the Sharing Economy," *Brookings Report*, December 29, 2016; and "General Motors Invests $500M in Lyft, Forms Partnership," www.chicagotribune.com, January 4, 2016.
2. "International Trade and Market Access Data," World Trade Organization, www.stat.wto.org.; "Gross Domestic Product: First Quarter 2019," news release, Bureau of Economic Analysis, U.S. Department of Commerce, April 26, 2019; and "Table 2.1 Employment by Major Industry Sector," Bureau of Labor Statistics, U.S. Department of Labor, October 24, 2017.
3. Arielle Pardes, "Here Are All the New Services Apple Announced Today," www.wired.com, March 25, 2019; "Hilton Introduces New Feature to Its Concierge App," www.insights.ehotelier.com, December 9, 2018; Eric M. Johnson, "Virgin Galactic Completes Crewed Space Test, More Flights Soon," www.reuters.com, December 13, 2018; "10 New Services That'll Make You Say, 'Why Didn't I Think of That?'" www.entrepreneur.com, May 31, 2018; Inga Shugalo, "Top 3 Healthcare Chatbots to Stop You from Googling Symptoms Online," www.readwrite.com, March 25, 2019; and The Breakers Palm Beach website, www.thebreakers.com.
4. Alfonso Pulido, Dorian Stone, and John Strevel, "The Three C's of Customer Satisfaction: Consistency, Consistency, Consistency," McKinsey article, www.mckinsey.com, March 2014; Janet R. McColl-Kennedy and Tina White, "Service Provider Training Programs at Odds with Customer Requirements in Five Star Hotels," *Journal of Services Marketing* 11, no. 4 (1997), pp. 249-64; Ellyn A. McColgan, "How Fidelity Invests in Service Professionals," *Harvard Business Review*, January-February 1997, pp. 137-43; and Frederick F. Reichheld and W. Earl Sasser Jr., "Zero Defections: Quality Comes to Services," *Harvard Business Review*, September-October 1990, pp. 105-11.
5. Lance A. Bettencourt, "How to Make Customer Work More Appealing," *Marketing News*, May 2016, pp. 14-15; Christian Gronroos, "Value Co-Creation in Service Logic: A Critical Analysis," *Marketing Theory*, September 2011, pp. 279-301; and Stephen L. Vargo and Robert F. Lusch, "Evolving to a New Dominant Logic for Marketing," *Journal of Marketing*, January 2004, p. 1.
6. Nichola Robertson, Heath McDonald, Civilai Leckie, and Lisa McQuilken, "Examining Customer Evaluations across Different Self-Service Technologies," *Journal of Services Marketing*, January 1, 2016, pp. 88-102; Alana Semuels, "Self-Service Machines Replacing Retail Workers," *The Star-Ledger*, March 13, 2011, p. 1; Zhen Zhu, Cheryl Nakata, and K.

Sivakumar, "Self-Service Technology Effectiveness: The Role of Design Features and Individual Traits," *Journal of the Academy of Marketing Science,* Winter 2007, pp. 492–506; and Lawrence F. Cunningham, Clifford E. Young, and James Gerlach, "A Comparison of Consumer Views of Traditional Services and Self-Service Technologies," *Journal of Services Marketing* 23, no. 1 (2009), pp. 11–23.

7. Pushkala Aripaka, "Cloud, Services Fuel IBM's Profit Beat, Robust Outlook; Shares Jump," www.reuters.com, January 22, 2019; and Jordan Novet, "IBM Earnings and 2019 Guidance Beat Estimates—Stock Jumps," www.cnbc.com, January 22, 2019.
8. Christopher Lovelock and Jochen Wirtz, *Services Marketing: People, Technology, Strategy,* 7th ed. (Upper Saddle River, NJ: Pearson Prentice-Hall, 2011); Lance A. Bettencourt, Stephen W. Brown, and Nancy J. Sirianni, "The Secret to True Service Innovation," *Business Horizons,* February 2013, pp. 13–22; and Thomas J. DeLong and Vineeta Vijayaraghavan, "Should You Listen to the Customer?" *Harvard Business Review,* September 2012, pp. 129–33.
9. Johanna Gummerus, Michaela Lipkin, Apramey Dube, and Kristina Heinonen, "Technology in Use—Characterizing Customer Self-Service Devices (SSDS)," *Journal of Services Marketing,* 1 (2019), pp. 44–56; Matthew Dixon, Lara Ponomareff, Scott Turner, and Rick DeLisi, "Kick-Ass Customer Service," *Harvard Business Review*, January–February 2017, pp. 110–17; Suzanne C. Makarem, Susan M. Mudambi, and Jeffrey S. Podoshen, "Satisfaction in Technology-Enabled Service Encounters," *Journal of Services Marketing* 3 (2009), p. 134; and Matthew L. Meuter, Amy L. Ostrom, Robert I. Roundtree, and Mary Jo Bitner, "Self-Service Technologies: Understanding Customer Satisfaction with Technology-Based Service Encounters," *Journal of Marketing,* July 2000, pp. 50–64.
10. Brice S. McKeever, Nathan E. Dietz, and Sanuji D. Fyffe, *The Nonprofit Almanac: The Essential Facts and Figures for Managers, Researchers, and Volunteers,* 9th ed. (Urban Institute Press, Rowman & Littlefield, 2016); and Brice McKeever, "The Nonprofit Sector in Brief 2018," National Center for Charitable Statistics, January 3, 2019.
11. "HBO Invites *Game of Thrones* Fans to Bleed for the Throne in National American Red Cross Blood Drive," www.medium.com, February 19, 2019; "Apps for Donors," *Marketing Health Services*, Winter 2014, p. 4; Christine Birkner, "The American Red Cross Took a Centralized Approach to Protect Its Brand Message," *Marketing News,* July 30, 2011, p. 10; and "Celebrity Cabinet," www.redcross.org, May 2, 2019.
12. "National 4-H Council Chief Marketing Officer Artis Stevens Named 2018 National Nonprofit Marketer of the Year," www.prnewswire.com, June 7, 2018.
13. Naomi Jagoda, "Charitable Giving Up, Number of Donors Down, in First Year under Trump's Tax Law," www.thehill.com, February 25, 2019; Brice McKeever, "The Nonprofit Sector in Brief"; Patty Odell, "Susan G. Komen Ignites Campaign around Reality of Breast Cancer Deaths," *Promotional Marketing*, February 21, 2019, p. 1; Cindy Waxer, "American Red Cross Breathes New Life into Its Marketing," www.dmnews.com, April 2014, pp. 26–29; and Maureen West, "How Nonprofits Can Use Social Media to Spark Change," *The Chronicle of Philanthropy,* February 20, 2011.
14. Jim Simay, "Standard Mail to USPS Marketing Mail™ Transition," www.tensionenvelope.com, January 30, 2018; Al Urbanski, "USPS' Informed Delivery Will Go Nationwide in 2017," dmnews.com, May 2016, p. 12; and "United States Postal Service Reports Losses and Diminished Income for First Half of Fiscal Year 2017," *The Seybold Report*, May 8, 2017, p. 2.
15. Keith B. Murray, "A Test of Services Marketing Theory: Consumer Information Acquisition Activities," *Journal of Marketing,* January 1991, pp. 10–25.
16. Dawn Iacobucci, "An Empirical Examination of Some Basic Tenets in Services: Goods-Services Continua," in *Advances in Services Marketing and Management,* vol. 1, eds. Teresa Swartz, David E. Bowen, and Stephen W. Brown (Greenwich, CT: JAI Press), pp. 23–52; and Valarie A. Zeithaml, "How Consumer Evaluation Processes Differ between Goods and Services," in *Marketing of Services,* eds. James H. Donnelly and William R. George (Chicago: American Marketing Association, 1981).
17. Amna Kirmani, Rebecca W. Hamilton, Debora V. Thompson, and Shannon Lantzy, "Doing Well versus Doing Good: The Differential Effect of Underdog Positioning on Moral and Competent Service Providers," *Journal of Marketing*, January 2017, pp. 103–17; Jason Oliver, "The Consumer's Perspective on Evaluating Products: Service Is the Key" *Journal of Services Marketing* 3 (2015), pp. 200–210; Ebrahim Mazaheri, Richard Marie-Odile, and Michel Laroche, "The Role of Emotions in Online Consumer Behavior: A Comparison of Search, Experience, and Credence Services," *Journal of Services Marketing* 7 (2012), pp. 535–50; Michael J. Dorsch, Stephen J. Grove, and William Darden, "Consumer Intentions to Use a Services Category," *Journal of Services Marketing* 2 (2000), pp. 92–117; and Murray, "A Test of Services Marketing Theory: Consumer Information Acquisition Activities."
18. Leonard L. Berry and Neeli Bendapudi, "Clueing in Customers," *Harvard Business Review,* February 2003, pp. 100–106.
19. John Ozment and Edward Morash, "The Augmented Service Offering for Perceived and Actual Service Quality," *Journal of the Academy of Marketing Science,* Fall 1994, pp. 352–63.
20. A. Parasuraman, Valarie A. Zeithaml, and Leonard L. Berry, "Reassessment of Expectations as a Comparison Standard in Measuring Service Quality: Implications for Further Research," *Journal of Marketing,* January 1994, pp. 111–24; and Leonard L. Berry, *On Great Service* (New York: Free Press, 1995).
21. Yu-Chi Wu, Chin-Shih Tsai, Hsiao-Wen Hsiung, and Kuan-Ying Chen, "Linkage between Frontline Employee Service Competence Scale and Customer Perceptions of Service Quality," *Journal of Services Marketing* 3 (2015), pp. 224–34; Valarie A. Zeithaml, A. Parasuraman, and Leonard L. Berry, *Delivering Quality Service* (New York: Free Press, 1990); and Stephen W. Brown and Teresa Swartz, "A Gap Analysis of Professional Service Quality," *Journal of Marketing,* April 1989, pp. 92–98.
22. Amy Ostrom and Dawn Iacobucci, "Consumer Trade-Offs and the Evaluation of Services," *Journal of Marketing,* January 1995, pp. 17–28; and J. Joseph Cronin Jr. and Steven A. Taylor, "Measuring Service Quality: A Reexamination and Extension," *Journal of Marketing,* July 1992, pp. 55–68.
23. L. Jean Harrison-Walker, "The Effect of Consumer Emotions on Outcome Behaviors following Service Failure," *Journal of Services Marketing*, 3 (2019), pp. 285–302; Teresa Fernandes, Marta Morgado, and Maria Antonia Rodrigues, "The Role of Employee Emotional Competence in Service Recovery Encounters," *Journal of Services Marketing*, 32 (2018), pp. 835–49; L. Jean Harrison-Walker, "The Role of Cause and Affect in Service Failure," *Journal of Services Marketing* 2 (2012), pp. 115–23; Kriengsin Prasongsukarn and Paul G. Patterson, "An Extended Service Recovery Model: The Moderating Impact of Temporal Sequence of Events," *Journal of Services Marketing* 7 (2012), pp. 510–20; Leslie M. Fine, "Service Marketing," *Business Horizons,* May–June 2009, pp. 163–68; and James G. Maxham III and Richard G. Netermeyer, "A Longitudinal Study of Complaining Customers' Evaluations of Multiple Service Failures and Recovery Efforts," *Journal of Marketing,* October 2002, pp. 57–71.
24. Ruxandra Mindruta, "The Top Social Media Monitoring Tools," www.brandwatch.com, February 1, 2019; Alexandra K. Abney, Mark J. Pelletier, Toni-Rochelle S. Ford, and Alisha B. Horky, "#IHateYourBrand: Adaptive Service Recovery Strategies on Twitter," *Journal of Services Marketing* 3 (2017), pp. 281–94; Amy L. Ostrom and Dawn Iacobucci, "Retrospective: the Effect of Guarantees on Consumers' Evaluation of Services," *Journal of Services Marketing* 4 (2016), pp. 373–76; and "How to Earn Extreme Trust: The True Story of Domino's Pizza," *Fearless Competitor,* June 27, 2012.
25. Vicki Clift, "Everyone Needs Service Flow Charting," *Marketing News,* October 23, 1995, pp. 41, 43; Mary Jo Bitner, Bernard H. Booms, and Mary Stanfield Tetreault, "The Service Encounter: Diagnosing Favorable and Unfavorable Incidents," *Journal of Marketing,* January 1990, pp. 71–84; Eberhard Scheuing, "Conducting Customer Service Audits," *Journal of Consumer Marketing,* Summer 1989, pp. 35–41; and W. Earl

Susser, R. Paul Olsen, and D. Daryl Wyckoff, *Management of Service Operations* (Boston: Allyn & Bacon, 1978).

26. Abdullah J. Sultan, "Orchestrating Service Brand Touchpoints and the Effects on Relational Outcomes," *Journal of Services Marketing*, 32 (2018), pp. 777–88; Chi Kin (Bennett) Yim, Kimmy Wa Chan, and Simon S. K. Lam, "Do Customers and Employees Enjoy Service Participation? Synergistic Effect of Self- and Other-Efficacy," *Journal of Marketing*, November 2012, pp. 121–40; Joseph Pine and James H. Gilmore, *The Experience Economy,* Revised Edition (Boston: Harvard Business School Publishing, 2011); and Mary Jo Bitner, Amy L. Ostrom, and Felicia N. Morgan, "Service Blueprinting: A Practical Technique for Service Innovation," *California Management Review,* Spring 2008, pp. 66–94.

27. Lance A. Bettencourt, Christopher P. Blocker, Mark B. Houston, and Daniel J. Flint, "Rethinking Customer Relationships," *Business Horizons* 58 (2015), pp. 99–108; Jill Avery, Susan Fournier, and John Wittenbraker, "Unlock the Mysteries of Your Customer Relationships," *Harvard Business Review*, July–August 2014, pp. 72–81; Leonard L. Berry, "Relationship Marketing of Services—Growing Interest, Emerging Perspectives," *Journal of the Academy of Marketing Science,* Fall 1995, pp. 236–45; Mary Jo Bitner, "Building Service Relationships: It's All about Promises," *Journal of the Academy of Marketing Science,* Fall 1995, pp. 246–51; Kevin P. Gwinner, Dwayne D. Gremler, and Mary Jo Bitner, "Relational Benefits in Servivces Industries: The Customer's Perspective," *Journal of the Academy of Marketing Science,* Spring 1998, pp. 101–14; Susan Fournier, Susan Dobscha, and David Glen Mick, "Preventing the Premature Death of Relationship Marketing," *Harvard Business Review,* January–February 1998, pp. 42–51; and John V. Petrof, "Relationship Marketing: The Wheel Reinvented?" *Business Horizons,* November–December 1997, pp. 26–31.

28. Katherine N. Lemon, Tiffany Barnett White, and Russell S. Winer, "Dynamic Customer Relationship Management: Incorporating Future Considerations into the Service Retention Decision," *Journal of Marketing,* January 2002, pp. 1–14.

29. Christian Gronroos, "Relationship Marketing Readiness: Theoretical Background and Measurement Directions," *Journal of Services Marketing* 3 (2017), pp. 218–25; Michael Paul, Thorsten Hennig-Thurau, Dwayne D. Gremler, Kevin P. Gwinner, and Caroline Wiertz, "Toward a Theory of Repeat Purchase Drivers for Consumer Services," *Journal of the Academy of Marketing Science,* Summer 2009, pp. 215–37.

30. Thomas S. Gruca, "Defending Service Markets," *Marketing Management* 1 (1994), pp. 31–38; and Leonard L. Berry, Jeffrey S. Conant, and A. Parasuraman, "A Framework for Conducting a Services Marketing Audit," *Journal of the Academy of Marketing Science,* Summer 1991, pp. 255–68.

31. Lovelock and Wirtz, *Services Marketing; People, Technology, Strategy,* 7th ed.; Valarie A. Zeithaml, Mary Jo Bitner, and Dwayne D. Gremler, *Services Marketing,* 6th ed. (New York: McGraw-Hill, 2013), p. 26; and Brian Solis, "Exploring the Fifth and Sixth Ps of Marketing," *Marketing News*, January 2013, p. 7.

32. Dan R. E. Thomas, "Strategy Is Different in Service Businesses," *Harvard Business Review,* July–August 1978, pp. 158–65.

33. Sundar G. Bharedwaj, P. Rajan Varadarajan, and John Fahy, "Sustainable Competitive Advantage in Service Industries: A Conceptual Model and Research Propositions," *Journal of Marketing,* October 1993, pp. 83–99.

34. "Partners and Programs," www.fairmont.com, May 2, 2019; Chuck Chiang, "Hotels See Growing High-End Guest List," *National Post's Financial Post*, April 16, 2016, p. B11; "Fairmont Hotels and Resorts to Offer Local Shuttle Service with BMW Vehicles," *Entertainment Close-Up,* January 30, 2013; and www.hotelsathome.com, May 2, 2019.

35. Kent B. Monroe, "Buyers' Subjective Perceptions of Price," *Journal of Marketing Research,* February 1973, pp. 70–80; and Jerry Olson, "Price as an Informational Cue: Effects on Product Evaluation," in *Consumer and Industrial Buying Behavior,* eds. A. G. Woodside, J. N. Sheth, and P. D. Bennett (New York: Elsevier North-Holland, 1977), pp. 267–86.

36. Hean Tat Keh and Jun Pang, "Customer Reactions to Service Separation," *Journal of Marketing,* March 2010, pp. 55–70; Leonard L. Berry, Kathleen Seiders, and Dhruv Grewal, "Understanding Service Convenience," *Journal of Marketing* 66 (July 2002), pp. 1–17.

37. Robert E. Hite, Cynthia Fraser, and Joseph A. Bellizzi, "Professional Service Advertising: The Effects of Price Inclusion, Justification, and Level of Risk," *Journal of Advertising Research* 30 (August–September 1990), pp. 23–31; William R. George and Leonard L. Berry, "Guidelines for the Advertising of Services," *Business Horizons,* July–August 1981, pp. 52–56; and Eugene M. Johnson, Eberhard E. Scheuing, and Kathleen A. Gaida, *Profitable Service Marketing* (Homewood, IL: Dow Jones-Irwin, 1986).

38. Kathleen Mortimer, "Identifying the Components of Effective Service Advertisements," *Journal of Services Marketing* 22 (2008), pp. 104–13.

39. Joe Adams, "Why Public Service Advertising Doesn't Work," *Adweek,* November 17, 1980, p. 72.

40. Patriya Tansuhaj, Donna Randall, and Jim McCullough, "A Services Marketing Management Model: Integrating Internal and External Marketing Functions," *Journal of Sciences Marketing,* Winter 1998, pp. 31–38.

41. Christian Gronroos, "Internal Marketing Theory and Practice," in *Services Marketing in a Changing Environment,* eds. Thomas Bloch, G. D. Upah, and V. A. Zeithaml (Chicago: American Marketing Association, 1984); and Achilleas Boukis, "Internal Market Orientation as a Value Creation Mechanism," *Journal of Services Marketing*, 2 (2019), pp. 233–44.

42. Jens Hogreve, Anja Iseke, Klause Derfuss, and Tonnjes Eller, "The Service-Profit Chain: A Meta-Analytic Test of a Comprehensive Theoretical Framework," *Journal of Marketing*, May 2017, pp. 41–61; Gronroos, "Internal Marketing Theory and Practice," in *Services Marketing in a Changing Environment.*

43. Rita Di Mascio, "The Service Models of Frontline Employees," *Journal of Marketing,* July 2010, pp. 63–80; Yong-Ki Lee, Jung-Heon Nam, Dae-Hwan Park, and Kyung Ah Lee, "What Factors Influence Customer-Oriented Prosocial Behavior of Customer-Contact Employees?" *Journal of Services Marketing* 20, no. 4 (2006), pp. 251–64; Stephen W. Brown, "The Employee Experience," *Marketing Management* 12 (March–April 2003), pp. 12–13; Lawrence A. Crosby and Sheree L. Johnson, "Watch What I Do," *Marketing Management* 12 (November–December 2003), pp. 10–11; and March C. Gilly and Mary Wolfinbarger, "Advertising's Internal Audience," *Journal of Marketing,* January 1998, pp. 69–88.

44. Adrian Palmer, "Customer Experience Management: A Critical Review of an Emerging Idea," *Journal of Service Marketing* 3 (2010), pp. 196–208; Gabriel M. Gelb and John M. McKeever, "In Their Shoes," *Marketing Management,* July–August 2006, pp. 40–45; Lynette Ryals, "Making Customer Relationship Management Work: The Measurement and Profitable Management of Customer Relationships," *Journal of Marketing,* October 2005, pp. 252–61; Bernd H. Schmitt, *Customer Experience Management* (Hoboken, NJ: Wiley and Sons, 2003); and Shaun Smith and Joe Wheeler, *Managing the Customer Experience* (Englewood Cliffs, NJ: Prentice Hall, 2002).

45. Lance A. Bettencourt, "Fundamental Tenets of Service Excellence," *Marketing Management,* Fall 2012, pp. 19–23; "Zappos Family Core Values," Zappos website, http://about.zappos.com/our-unique-culture/zappos-core-values, accessed February 5, 2013; and Paula Andruss, "Delivering WOW through Service," *Marketing News,* October 15, 2008, p. 10.

46. F. G. Crane, *Professional Services Marketing: Strategy and Tactics* (London: Haworth Press, 1993); and Leonard L. Berry and Neeli Bendapudi, "Clueing in Customers," pp. 100–106.

47. Frederick H. deB. Harris and Peter Peacock, "Hold My Place, Please," *Marketing Management,* Fall 1995, pp. 34–46.

48. Christopher Lovelock and Jochen Wirtz, *Services Marketing*, 6th ed. (Englewood Cliffs, NJ: Prentice Hall, 2007), pp. 260–84.

49. Christian de Looper, "What Is 5G? Here's Everything You Need to Know," www.digitaltrends.com, March 22, 2019; Mikhail Naumov, "5 Predictions on the Future of Customer Service," www.forbes.com,

April 23, 2018; and "Valeo Voyage XR: Teletransportation in the Vehicle Cabin," www.valeo.com, January 8, 2019.

50. Tarun Khanna, "When Technolgoy Gets Ahead of Society," *Harvard Business Review*, July–August 2018, pp. 86–95.

51. Kristina Heinonen and Gustav Medberg, "Netnography as a Tool for Understanding Consumers: Implications for Service Research and Practice," *Journal of Services Marketing*, 32 (2018), pp. 657–79; Kamalini Ramdas, Elizabeth Teisberg, and Amy L. Tucker, "4 Ways to Reinvent Service Delivery," *Harvard Business Review,* December 2012, pp. 99–106; and Michael K. Brady, Clay M. Voorhees, and Michael J. Brusco, "Service Sweethearting: Its Antecedents and Customer Consequences," *Journal of Marketing,* March 2012, pp. 81–98.

52. "How Hilton Is Going Green," *International Organization for Standardization*, www.iso.org, September 11, 2018; and "2018 Annual Sustainability Report" *United States Postal Service*, www.about.usps.com.

53. Helge Lobler, "Humans' Relationship to Nature—Framing Sustainable Marketing," *Journal of Services Marketing*, 31 (2017), pp. 73–82; and Mary Jo Bitner and Stephen W. Brown, "The Service Imperative," *Business Horizons,* January–February 2008, pp. 39–46.

54. LA Galaxy: This case was written by Steven Hartley. Sources: "Landon Donovan Retires a Champion as Galaxy Win MLS Cup," Time.com, December 8, 2014; "Galaxy's Home Has New Name," *The Daily News of Los Angeles,* March 5, 2013, p. A1; Kevin Baxter, "Beckham Will Hang Up His Boots: A Star in Europe, His Late Career Move to the Galaxy Brought U.S. Fans to Soccer and Put MLS on Map," *Los Angeles Times,* May 17, 2013, p. C2; "Galaxy, Tim Warner Strike 10-Year, $55 Million Deal," *The Daily News of Los Angeles,* November 16, 2011, p. C6; denz@rslsoapbox, "For Major League Soccer It Is All about the Numbers, TV, Attendance, and Season Tickets," rslsoapbox.com, May 18, 2012; Karl Greenberg, "Chevrolet Cleats Up for L.A. Galaxy Sponsorship," *Marketing Daily,* May 28, 2013; LA Galaxy website, www.lagalaxy.com, accessed July 26, 2013; and personal interviews with LA Galaxy personnel.

Chapter 13 Building the Price Foundation

LEARNING OBJECTIVES

After reading this chapter you should be able to:

LO 13-1 Identify the elements that make up a price.

LO 13-2 Recognize the objectives a firm has in setting prices and the constraints that restrict the range of prices a firm can charge.

LO 13-3 Explain what a demand curve is and its role in pricing decisions.

LO 13-4 Describe what price elasticity of demand means to a manager facing a pricing decision.

LO 13-5 Explain the role of costs in pricing decisions and describe how various combinations of price, fixed cost, and unit variable cost affect a firm's break-even point.

VIZIO, Inc.—Building a Smart TV Brand at a Great Value

Can you name the largest U.S.-based TV maker? Stumped? It's VIZIO, Inc., an entrepreneurial Irvine, California, company. The VIZIO brand was created by William Wang, VIZIO's co-founder, who was born in Taiwan, immigrated to the United States at age 13, and learned the English language watching television.

Twenty years ago, Wang was struck by an ad for a $10,000 flat-panel HDTV set and immediately saw an opportunity. Instead of marketing these sets as luxury items, Wang thought he could make and market an HDTV that would be affordable for the average customer.

Like many entrepreneurs, he borrowed money from friends and family and mortgaged his home. Within a year, he and his partners delivered the company's first VIZIO HDTV to Costco for distribution through that company's stores. VIZIO HDTVs are now sold through Costco, Walmart, BJ's Wholesale, Best Buy, Sam's Club, and Target stores nationwide, along with authorized online partners such as Amazon. VIZIO has sold more than 50 million HDTVs since its founding.

VIZIO's ability to deliver affordable HDTVs to the average customer is based on a novel strategy. VIZIO didn't invest in expensive manufacturing facilities but instead relied on contract manufacturers to build its products. Product development and marketing specialists in the United States handle product design and marketing. "The whole goal is to ensure that we have the right product at the right time and the right price and really drive a seamless end-to-end value chain," says a Vizio spokesperson.

"Consumers want to save money without sacrificing quality or technology," says VIZIO's chief technology officer, who emphasizes that VIZIO's strategy is to make affordable products with innovative features. He adds, "We're far from the cheapest brand on the market at present. Everybody deserves the latest technology, too."[1]

VIZIO's visionary commitment to delivering high-quality technology at a great value to consumers is evident by its pioneering role in launching smart TVs a decade ago. Smart TVs make it possible for viewers to watch content from the Internet directly on their TVs, for a more interactive TV watching experience. VIZIO is the smart TV market leader in North America.

VIZIO's powerful and profitable value-based pricing strategy clearly resonates with consumers. VIZIO is frequently ranked among the "Highest in Customer Satisfaction" with HDTVs by J.D. Power and Associates. VIZIO has the second-largest market share for televisions and smart televisions in the United States.[2]

VIDEO 13-1
VIZIO
kerin.tv/15e/v13-1

Welcome to the fascinating—and intense—world of pricing. This chapter describes the important factors organizations consider when they go about setting prices for their products and services.

Source: Vizio, Inc.

Source: Vizio, Inc.

The chapter begins with a description of the nature and importance of price for consumers and companies. Attention is then focused on the price setting process used by marketers. Emphasis is first placed on identifying company pricing objectives and understanding pricing constraints. This discussion is followed by the role of demand and revenue estimation in pricing, including the relevance of price elasticity of demand. Finally, the determination of product and service cost, unit volume, and profitability is detailed. Break-even analysis and its application are highlighted.

NATURE AND IMPORTANCE OF PRICE

LO 13-1
Identify the elements that make up a price.

The price paid for products and services goes by many names. You pay *tuition* for your education, *rent* for an apartment, *interest* on a bank credit card, and a *premium* for car insurance. Your dentist or physician charges you a *fee*, a professional or social organization charges *dues*, and airlines charge a *fare*. In business, an executive is given a *salary*, a salesperson receives a *commission*, and a worker is paid a *wage*. And what you pay for clothes or a haircut is termed a *price*.

Among all marketing and operations factors in a business firm, price has a unique role. It is the place where all other business decisions come together. The price must be "right"—in the sense that customers must be willing to pay it; it must generate enough sales dollars to pay for the cost of developing, producing, and marketing the product; *and* it must earn a profit for the company. Small changes in price can have big effects on both the number of units sold and company profit.

What Is a Price?

From a marketing viewpoint, **price (P)** is the money or other considerations (including other products and services) exchanged for the ownership or use of a product or service. The practice of exchanging products and services for other products and services rather than for money is called **barter**. Barter transactions account for billions of dollars annually in domestic and international trade. In the United States alone, $16 billion of products and services are traded every year without any money changing hands.[3]

The Price Equation For most products, money is exchanged. However, the amount paid is not always the same as the list, or quoted, price because of discounts, allowances, and extra fees. Today's pricing tactic involves using "special fees" and "surcharges." This practice is driven by consumers' zeal for low prices combined with the ease of making price comparisons on the Internet. Buyers are more willing to pay extra fees than a higher list price, so sellers use add-on charges as a way of having the consumer pay more without raising the list price.

All the factors that increase or decrease the final price of an offering help construct a "price equation," which is shown for a few products in Figure 13–1. These are key considerations if you want to buy a 2020 Bugatti Chiron.[4] This all-wheel-drive car accelerates from 0 to 60 mph in just 2.4 seconds. With its 1,500-horsepower engine, top speed is electronically limited—limited!—to 261 mph! The aerodynamic body is made out of carbon fiber to safely handle the speed.

Calculating a Final Price The Bugatti Chiron U.S. list price is a cool $3.4 million, give or take a dollar or two. But the dealer has agreed to give you a trade-in allowance of $7,000 based on the trade-in value for your 2008 Mini-Cooper four-door sedan that is in good condition.

Are you interested in trading in your 2008 Mini-Cooper shown on the right for a 2020 Bugatti Chiron shown on the left, the world's most expensive car? Read the text to find out the true cost of purchasing a new car.
(Left): Art Konovalov/Shutterstock; (Right): Drive Images/Alamy Stock Photo

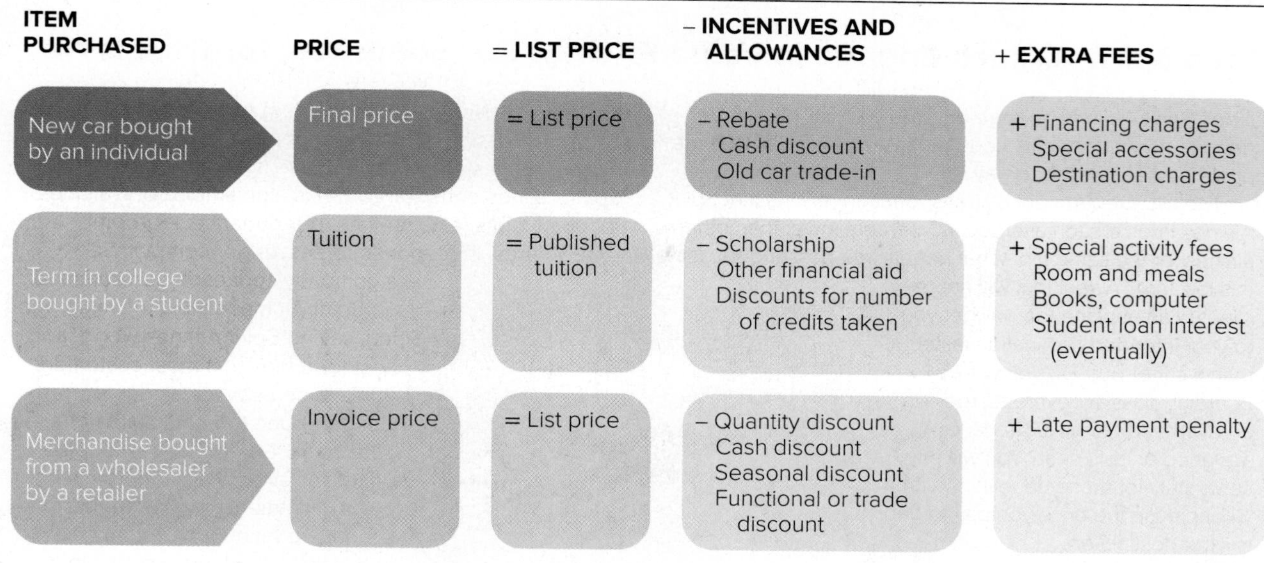

PRICE EQUATION
ITEM PURCHASED
PRICE
= LIST PRICE
– INCENTIVES AND ALLOWANCES
+ EXTRA FEES
New car bought by an individual
Final price
= List price
– Rebate
Cash discount
Old car trade-in
+ Financing charges
Special accessories
Destination charges
Term in college bought by a student
Tuition
= Published tuition
– Scholarship
Other financial aid
Discounts for number of credits taken
+ Special activity fees
Room and meals
Books, computer
Student loan interest (eventually)
Merchandise bought from a wholesaler by a retailer
Invoice price
= List price
– Quantity discount
Cash discount
Seasonal discount
Functional or trade discount
+ Late payment penalty

FIGURE 13–1
The "price" a buyer pays can take different names depending on what is purchased, and it can change depending on the price equation.

And your great-uncle has offered to give you a five-year interest-free loan. Other charges include: (1) an import duty of $85,000; (2) a gas-guzzler tax of $7,700; (3) a 7.5 percent sales tax of $225,000; (4) an auto registration fee of $7,000 to the state; and (5) a $54,000 destination charge to ship the car to you from France.

Applying the price equation shown in Figure 13–1 to your Bugatti Chiron purchase, your final price is:

$$\begin{aligned}
\text{Final price} &= [\text{List price}] - [\text{Allowances}] + [\text{Extra fees}] \\
&= [\$3{,}400{,}000] - [\$7{,}000] \\
&\quad + [\$85{,}000 + \$7{,}700 + \$225{,}000 + \$7{,}000 + \$54{,}000] \\
&= \$3{,}400{,}000 - \$7{,}000 + \$378{,}700 \\
&= \$3{,}771{,}700
\end{aligned}$$

Note that your final price is $371,700 more than the list price! Are you still interested in buying the 2020 Bugatti Chiron? If so, put yourself on the waiting list and expect delivery in 2022.

Price Is What a Consumer Pays, Value Is What a Consumer Receives

From a consumer's standpoint, price is often used to indicate value when it is compared with perceived benefits, such as the quality or durability of a product or service. Specifically, **value** is the ratio of perceived benefits to price, or[5]

$$\text{Value} = \frac{\text{Perceived benefits}}{\text{Price}}$$

This relationship shows that for a given price, as perceived benefits increase, value increases. Not surprisingly, if you're used to paying $7.99 for a medium frozen cheese pizza, wouldn't a large one at the same price be more valuable? Conversely, for a given price, value decreases when perceived benefits decrease. The reduced contents in many consumer packaged products sold in supermarkets without a comparable drop in price decreases value to consumers.

Marketing Matters — Customer Value

Does Spirit Airlines Engage in Value Pricing? For Some Yes, for Others No

Does Spirit Airlines engage in value pricing? Well, it depends on what benefits certain passengers seek and the price they are willing to pay.

The U.S. Department of Transportation reports that Spirit Airlines fares are, on average, 40 percent lower than other airlines for the same trip. What benefits do passengers get for this low fare? A seat that will not recline on an airplane that will get you to your intended destination faster than a car or bus. Do you want a boarding pass, a beverage, room in an overhead bin for luggage, or an assigned or aisle seat? You will pay separately for those benefits, which will increase the price you pay to get to your destination.

So, does Spirit Airlines engage in value pricing? The answer is yes for those who wish to get to their destination as cheaply as currently possible. For others, no. They expect to get more (benefits) for what they give (fare). Not surprisingly, Spirit Airlines consistently ranks high among U.S. airlines for complaints (e.g., on-time, performance, legroom), except fares. In response to passenger complaints, a company spokesperson summed up Spirit Airlines's view on value pricing, saying Spirit Airlines won't "add cost for things that most customers don't value as much as our low fares just to reduce the complaints of a few customers. Doing that would raise prices for everyone, compromising our commitment to what our customers have continuously told us they truly value—the lowest possible price."

Philip Pilosian/Shutterstock

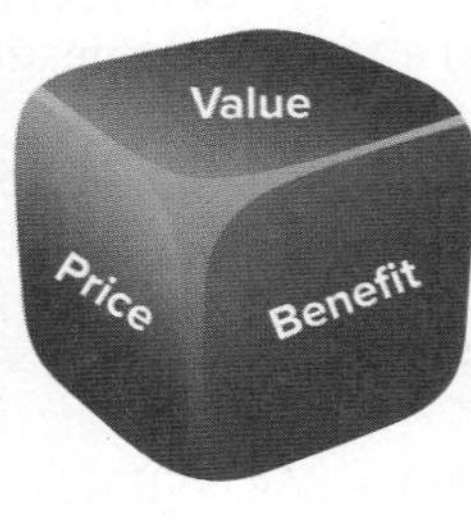

Using Value Pricing Creative marketers engage in **value pricing**, the practice of simultaneously increasing product and service benefits while maintaining or decreasing price. For some products, price influences consumers' perception of overall quality and ultimately its value to them.[6] In a survey of home furnishing buyers, 84 percent agreed with the statement: "The higher the price, the higher the quality."[7] For example, Kohler introduced a walk-in bathtub that is safer for children and older adults. Although priced higher than conventional step-in bathtubs, the product is successful because buyers are willing to pay a bit more for what they perceive as the value of extra safety.

In this context, "value" involves the judgment by a consumer of the worth of a product or service relative to substitutes that satisfy the same need. Through the process of comparing the costs and benefits of substitute items, a "reference value" emerges. For many consumers, the posted airfares of competing airlines serving the same cities become reference values. Based on airfare alone, Spirit Airlines usually offers the lowest price. But value assessments also include benefits received at a given price. Read the Marketing Matters box and decide whether or not Spirit Airlines offers value pricing.[8]

Price in the Marketing Mix

Pricing is a critical decision made by a marketing executive because price has a direct effect on a firm's profits. This is apparent from a firm's **profit equation**, where:

$$\begin{aligned}\text{Profit} &= \text{Total revenue} - \text{Total cost}\\ &= (\text{Unit price} \times \text{Quantity sold}) - (\text{Fixed cost} + \text{Variable cost})\end{aligned}$$

What makes this relationship even more complicated is that price affects the quantity sold, as illustrated with demand curves later in this chapter. Furthermore, since the quantity sold usually affects a firm's costs because of efficiency of production, price also indirectly affects costs. Thus, pricing decisions influence both total revenue (sales) and total cost, which makes pricing one of the most important decisions marketing executives face.

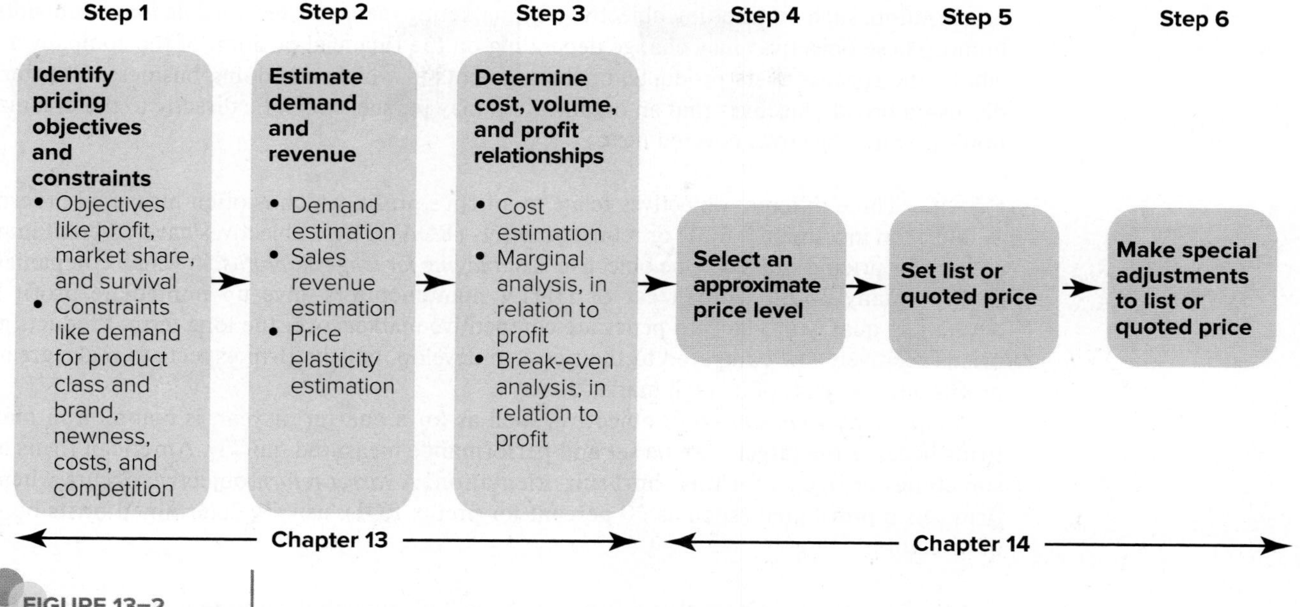

FIGURE 13–2
The six steps in setting price. The first three steps are covered in this chapter, and the last three steps are covered in Chapter 14.

The importance of price in the marketing mix necessitates an understanding of six major steps in the process organizations go through in setting prices (see Figure 13–2):

1. Identify pricing objectives and constraints.
2. Estimate demand and revenue.
3. Determine cost, volume, and profit relationships.
4. Select an approximate price level.
5. Set list or quoted price.
6. Make special adjustments to list or quoted price.

The first three steps are covered in this chapter, and the last three are discussed in Chapter 14.

LEARNING REVIEW

13-1. What is price?

13-2. What factors impact the list price to determine the final price?

13-3. What is the profit equation?

STEP 1: IDENTIFY PRICING OBJECTIVES AND CONSTRAINTS

LO 13-2
Recognize the objectives a firm has in setting prices and the constraints that restrict the range of prices a firm can charge.

With such a variety of alternative pricing strategies available, a marketing manager must consider the pricing objectives and constraints that will narrow the range of choices. While pricing objectives frequently reflect corporate goals, pricing constraints often relate to conditions existing in the marketplace.

Identifying Pricing Objectives

Pricing objectives involve specifying the role of price in an organization's marketing and strategic plans. To the extent possible, these pricing objectives are carried to lower levels in the organization, such as in setting objectives for marketing managers responsible for an individual brand. These objectives may change depending on the financial position of the company as a whole, the success of its products, or the segments in which it is doing business. Chapter 2 discussed broad objectives that an organization may pursue, which tie directly to the organization's pricing objectives covered next.

Profit Three different objectives relate to a firm's profit, which is often measured in terms of return on investment (ROI) or return on assets (ROA). These objectives have different implications for pricing strategy. One objective is *managing for long-run profits*, in which companies—such as many South Korean car or HDTV manufacturers—give up immediate profit by developing quality products to penetrate competitive markets over the long term. Products are priced relatively low compared to their cost to develop, but the firm expects to make greater profits later because of its high market share.

A *maximizing current profit* objective, such as for a quarter or year, is common in many firms because the targets can be set and performance measured quickly. American firms are sometimes criticized for this short-run orientation. A *target return* objective occurs when a firm sets a profit goal (such as 20 percent for pretax ROI), usually determined by its board of directors.

Sales Revenue Given that a firm's profit is high enough for it to remain in business, an objective may be to increase sales revenue, which can lead to increases in market share and profit. Objectives related to dollar sales revenue or unit sales have the advantage of being translated easily into meaningful targets for marketing managers responsible for a product line or brand. However, while lowering the price on one product in a firm's line may increase its sales revenue, it may also reduce the sales revenue of related products.

Market Share *Market share* is the ratio of the firm's sales revenues or unit sales to those of the industry (competitors plus the firm itself). Companies often pursue a market share objective when industry sales are relatively flat or declining. For example, Procter & Gamble (Pampers) and Kimberly-Clark (Huggies), which combined account for 80 percent of U.S. diaper sales, cut their U.S. prices for disposable baby diapers to maintain their respective U.S. market shares given the continuing decline in the U.S. birthrate.

Unit Volume Many firms use *unit volume*, the quantity produced or sold, as a pricing objective. These firms often sell multiple products at very different prices and need to match the unit volume demanded by customers with price and production capacity. Using unit volume as an objective can be counterproductive if a volume objective is achieved, say, by drastic price cutting that drives down profit.

Survival In some instances, profits, sales, and market share are less important objectives of the firm than mere survival. For example, RadioShack, an electronics retail chain, faced survival problems because it couldn't compete with the prices offered by other retailers. The company enacted price matching programs and promoted large discounts on its merchandise to raise cash and hopefully stave off bankruptcy. These efforts failed and RadioShack declared bankruptcy.

Companies in financial distress use pricing as a means to survival. Survival was the pricing objective for RadioShack when it faced bankruptcy.
Victor J. Blue/Bloomberg/Getty Images

Social Responsibility A firm may forgo a higher profit on sales and follow a pricing objective that recognizes its obligations to customers and society in general. For example, Gerber supplies a specially formulated product free of charge to children who cannot tolerate foods containing cow's milk.

Identifying Pricing Constraints

Factors that limit the range of prices a firm may set are referred to as **pricing constraints**. Consumer demand for the product clearly affects the price that can be

The price for a specific brand—like the Toyota Camry here—is also affected by general demand for its product class (cars) and product group (family sedans), as discussed in the text.
OvuOng/Shutterstock

charged. Other constraints on price vary from factors within the organization to competitive factors outside the organization. Legal and regulatory constraints on pricing are discussed in Chapter 14.

Demand for the Product Class, Product Group, and Brand The number of potential buyers for the product class (cars), product group (family sedans), and specific brand (Toyota Camry) clearly affects the price a seller can charge. Likewise, whether the item is a luxury—like the Bugatti Chiron—or a necessity—like bread and somewhere to live—also affects the price that can be charged. Generally, the greater the demand for a product, the higher the price that can be set. For example, the New York Mets have set different ticket prices for their games based on the appeal of their opponent—prices are higher when they play the New York Yankees and lower when they play the Pittsburgh Pirates.[9]

Newness of the Product: Stage in the Product Life Cycle The newer a product and the earlier it is in its life cycle, the higher the price that can usually be charged. Are you willing to spend $4,500 for a Samsung 65-inch 8K UHD Smart TV that offers four times the resolution of current HDTVs? The high initial price is possible because of patents and limited competition early in its product life cycle. By the time you read this, the price probably will be lower.

Sometimes—when nostalgia or fad factors come into play—prices may rise later in the product's life cycle. For example, collectibles can experience skyrocketing prices. Recently, consumers on eBay paid $250 for a Zip the Cat Beanie Baby (with black paws) and $29,500 for a 1963 copy of the first issue of *The Amazing Spider-Man*. But these prices can nosedive, too, when the fad wears off or a recession appears. To play it safe—and perhaps finance your retirement—save your perfect-condition, in-the-box Barbies, Hot Wheels, and Star Wars lightsabers.[10]

Who makes how much on a pair of designer denim jeans? Read the text to find out.
Amanda Edwards/Getty Images

Cost of Producing and Marketing the Product Another profit consideration for marketers is to ensure that firms in their channels of distribution make an adequate profit. Without profits for channel members, a marketer is cut off from its customers. For example, of the $200 a customer spends for a pair of designer denim jeans, 50 percent of each dollar spent goes to a specialty retailer to cover its costs and profit. The other 50 percent goes to the marketer (34 percent) and manufacturers and suppliers (16 percent).[11] So, the next time you buy a $200 pair of designer denim jeans, remember that $100 goes to the specialty retailer that stocked, displayed, and sold the jeans to you.

Cost of Changing Prices and Time Period They Apply If American Airlines asks General Electric (GE) to provide spare jet engines to power the new Boeing 777 it just bought, GE can easily set a new price for the engines to reflect its latest information since only one buyer has to be informed. But if L.L.Bean decides that sweater prices in its catalog are too low after thousands of catalogs have been mailed to customers, it has a big problem. It must consider the cost of changing prices, including determining which prices apply to which time periods, as well as the cost of revising its price list and reprinting and mailing another edition of its catalog. However, for many of today's consumer products, prices can change from minute to minute due to the transparency of prices afforded online.

Single Product versus a Product Line When Apple introduced its first iPhone, it was not only unique and in the introductory stage of its product life cycle, but it was also the first commercially successful smartphone sold. As a result, Apple had great latitude in setting the price for this single product.

Ever since Apple began unveiling multiple new iPhone models at once, it had to price these new models relative to each other and the existing iPhones they

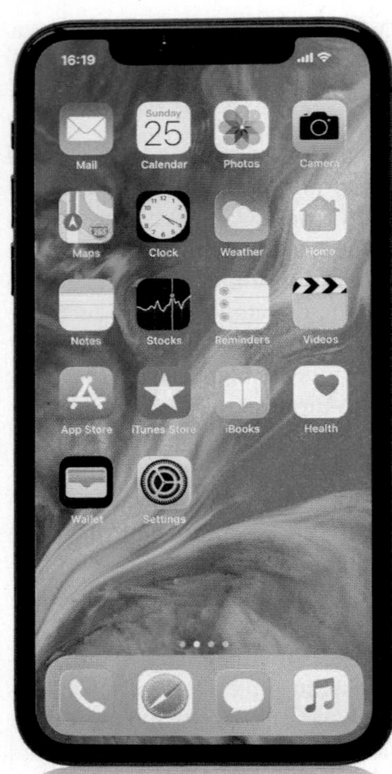

What was the pricing challenge Apple faced with introducing multiple iPhone models at the same time? Read the text to find out.
Kaspars Grinvalds/Shutterstock

replaced. Industry analysts called the launch of multiple products at the same time "threading the needle" because Apple now has to simultaneously consider the product cost and each phone's perceived value from a functionality point of view . . . and get the pricing just right![12] Product-line pricing is discussed further in Chapter 14.

Type of Competitive Market The seller's price is constrained by the type of market in which it competes. Economists generally delineate four types of competitive markets, as introduced in Chapter 3. From most competitive to least competitive, these are pure competition, monopolistic competition, oligopoly, and pure monopoly. Figure 13–3 shows that the type of competition dramatically influences the range of price competition and, in turn, the nature of product differentiation and the extent of advertising. A firm must recognize the general type of competitive market it is in to understand the range of both its price and nonprice strategies. Examples of how prices can be affected by the four competitive situations follow:

- *Pure competition*. Hundreds of local grain elevators sell corn whose price per bushel is set by the marketplace. Within strains, the corn is identical, so advertising only informs buyers that the seller's corn is available.
- *Monopolistic competition*. Dozens of regional, private brands of peanut butter compete with national brands like Skippy and Jif. Both price competition (regional, private brands being lower than national brands) and nonprice competition (product features and advertising) exist.
- *Oligopoly*. The few sellers of aluminum (Chalco, Alcoa) or large jetliners (Boeing, Airbus) try to avoid price competition because it can lead to disastrous price wars in which they all lose money. Yet firms in such industries stay aware of a competitor's price cuts or increases and may follow suit. The products can be undifferentiated (aluminum) or differentiated (large jetliners), and informative advertising that avoids head-to-head price competition is used. In the early stages of the video game market, the Microsoft Xbox's oligopolistic competition with Sony and Nintendo was so severe that Microsoft lost $126 on every unit sold at its $399 introductory price.[13]
- *Pure monopoly*. Johnson & Johnson (J&J) revolutionized the treatment of coronary heart disease by introducing the stent–a tiny mesh tube "spring" that props open clogged arteries. Initially a monopoly, J&J stuck with its early $1,595 price and achieved $1 billion in sales and 91 percent market share in two years. But its reluctance to give price reductions to hospitals for large-volume purchases turned out to be a poor strategy. When competitors like Medtronic introduced an improved stent at lower prices, J&J's market share plummeted to 8 percent two years later.[14]

Read how Amazon priced the hot-selling *Dance Central 3* video game, available for the Xbox.
Kevork Djansezian/Getty Images

Competitors' Prices and Consumers' Awareness of Them A company must know what specific prices its present and potential competitors are charging now as well as what they are likely to charge in the near future. The company then develops a marketing mix strategy–including setting prices–to respond to its competitors' prices. Today, the Internet has increased the number of "present and potential competitors" exponentially for many products.

Competitors' prices are important only if a prospective buyer both (1) knows about those prices and (2) can act to purchase them easily. Competitor changes and price transparency through the Internet and efficient distribution make possible (1) consumer-driven pricing actions and (2) seller- or retailer-driven pricing actions.

- *Consumer-Driven Pricing Actions*. With consumers able to compare prices on the Internet, they can make more efficient buying decisions. This occurs, say, when a consumer visits the HDTV section of a store to actually examine a TV–and then goes home and orders it online at a lower price.

STRATEGIES AVAILABLE	TYPE OF COMPETITIVE MARKET: PURE COMPETITION (Many sellers who follow the market price for identical, commodity products)	MONOPOLISTIC COMPETITION (Many sellers who compete on nonprice factors)	OLIGOPOLY (Few sellers who are sensitive to each other's prices)	PURE MONOPOLY (One seller who sets the price for a unique product)
Extent of price competition	Almost none: market sets price	Some: compete over range of prices	Some: price leader or follower of competitors	None: sole seller sets price
Extent of product differentiation	None: products are identical	Some: differentiate products from competitors	Various: depends on industry	None: no other producers
Extent of advertising	Little: purpose is to inform prospects that seller's products are available	Much: purpose is to differentiate firm's products from competitors	Some: purpose is to inform but avoid price competition	Little: purpose is to increase demand for product class

FIGURE 13–3
Pricing, product, and advertising strategies available to firms in four types of competitive markets.

- *Seller- or Retailer-Driven Pricing Actions.* Aggressive price changes through the Internet started with the airline industry, when airlines began constantly changing ticket prices to fill the seats on their planes using their yield management systems. Today, many sellers are changing online prices even faster.

For example, Amazon.com sold the hugely popular *Dance Central 3* (*DC3*) Xbox video game for $49.96—the same price as Walmart and 3 cents lower than Target. Then the pricing "dance moves" began. On Thanksgiving Day, Amazon lowered the game's price to $24.99, matching Best Buy. That same day, it dropped *DC3*'s price to $15.00 to match Walmart. Then, over the next several days, Amazon raised and lowered the price *seven* times. If you were lucky, you paid a price that was two-thirds lower than those who were unlucky and bought *DC3* at its highest price during that week![15]

Legal and Ethical Considerations Setting a final price is clearly a complex process. The task is further complicated by legal and ethical issues. Five pricing practices that have received special scrutiny are price fixing, price discrimination, deceptive pricing, geographical pricing, and predatory pricing, each of which is described more fully in Chapter 14.

LEARNING REVIEW

13-4. What is the difference between pricing objectives and pricing constraints?

13-5. How does the type of competitive market a firm is in affect its range in setting prices?

13-6. What are examples of (1) consumer-driven and (2) seller- or retailer-driven pricing actions made possible through price transparency on the Internet?

STEP 2: ESTIMATE DEMAND AND REVENUE

LO 13-3
Explain what a demand curve is and its role in pricing decisions.

Basic to setting a product's price is estimating the extent of customer demand for it. Marketing executives must also translate this estimate of customer demand into estimates of revenues the firm expects to receive.

Estimating Demand

How much will you pay for a frozen cheese pizza you can pop in the oven for a quick dinner while you are studying for a marketing exam? $6? $8? $10? And what are some of the factors affecting this decision? Your preference for pizza compared to other quick-service food? The ease with which you can call Domino's or your local Chinese restaurant for an already-prepared meal delivered to your residence? How much money you have available in your credit card account while you're thinking about the tuition payment that's due next month? All these factors affect demand.

What key factors affect the demand for Red Baron frozen cheese pizzas? Read the text to find out.

VIDEO 13-2
Red Baron
kerin.tv/15e/v13-2

To illustrate the fundamentals of estimating demand, let's assume you are a consultant to the marketing manager at Red Baron® pizza and your job is to start analyzing the demand for its Red Baron frozen cheese pizzas. In the process, you'll have to consider what the demand curve for frozen cheese pizza might look like, how it affects Red Baron's sales revenues, and the price elasticity of demand.

The Demand Curve A **demand curve** is a graph that relates the quantity sold and price, showing the maximum number of units that will be sold at a given price. Based on secondary research you conducted regarding the annual demand for Red Baron frozen cheese pizza under circumstances that existed in early 2020, you are able to construct the demand curve D_1 in Figure 13–4A, which you now need to update because market conditions have changed by late 2021. Note the following relationship: As price falls, more people decide to buy Red Baron frozen cheese pizza, which increases its unit sales. But price is not the complete story when estimating demand. Economists emphasize three other key factors that influence demand for a product:

1. *Consumer tastes.* As we saw in Chapter 3, these depend on many forces such as demographics, culture, and technology. Because consumer tastes can change quickly, up-to-date marketing research is essential to estimate demand. For example, if research by nutritionists concludes that some pizzas are healthier (because they are now gluten-free or vegetarian), demand for them will probably increase.
2. *Price and availability of similar products.* If the price of a competitor's pizza that is a substitute for yours–like Tombstone® pizza–falls, more people will buy it; its demand will rise and the demand for Red Baron pizza will fall. Other low-priced dinners are also substitutes for pizza. For example, if you want something fast so you can study, you could call Domino's or a local Chinese restaurant and order a meal for home delivery. So, as the price of a substitute falls or its availability increases, the demand for your Red Baron frozen cheese pizza will fall.
3. *Consumer income.* In general, as real consumers' incomes increase (allowing for inflation), demand for a product will also increase. So, if you get a scholarship and have extra cash for discretionary spending, you might eat more Red Baron frozen cheese pizzas and fewer peanut butter and jelly sandwiches to satisfy your appetite.

The first two factors influence what consumers *want* to buy, and the third factor affects what they *can* buy. Along with price, these are often called **demand factors**, or factors that determine consumers' willingness and ability to pay for products and services. As discussed in Chapters 8 and 10, it can be challenging to estimate demand for new products, especially because consumer likes and dislikes are often so difficult to read clearly. For example,

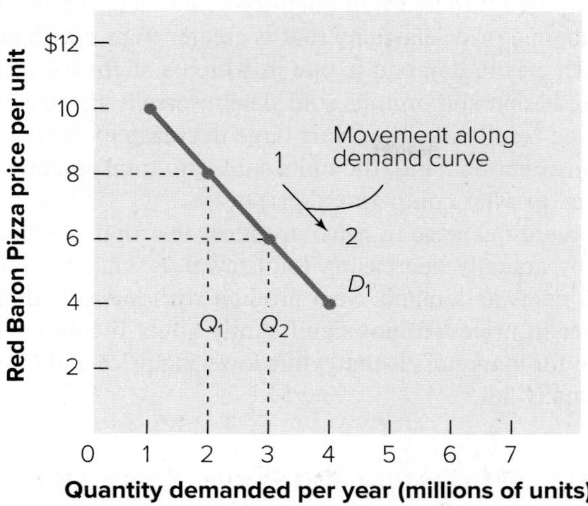

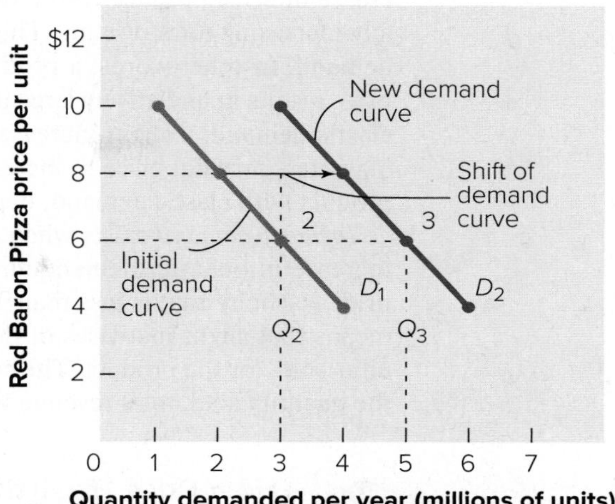

FIGURE 13–4

Demand curves for Red Baron frozen cheese pizza showing the effect on annual sales (quantity demanded per year) by change in price caused by (A) a movement along the demand curve and (B) a shift of the demand curve.

Campbell's (yes, the soup company) spent seven years and $55 million on a super secret project to produce a line of Intelligent Quisine (IQ) food products "scientifically proven to lower high levels of cholesterol, blood sugar, and blood pressure." After 15 months in an Ohio test market, Campbell's yanked the entire IQ line because customers found the line too pricey and lacking in variety.[16]

Movement along versus Shift of a Demand Curve The 2020 demand curve D_1 for Red Baron frozen cheese pizzas in Figure 13–4A shows that as its price is lowered from $8 (point 1) to $6 (point 2), the quantity sold (demanded) increases from 2 million (Q_1) to 3 million (Q_2) units per year. This is an example of a *movement along a demand curve* and it assumes that other factors (consumer tastes, price and availability of substitutes, and consumers' incomes) remain unchanged.

What if some of these factors do change? For example, if advertising causes more people to want Red Baron frozen cheese pizzas, demand will increase. Now the initial demand curve, D_1 (the blue line in Figure 13–4B), no longer represents the demand. Instead, the new demand curve, D_2 (the red line in Figure 13–4B) represents the new demand for Red Baron frozen cheese pizzas. Economists call this a *shift in the demand curve*—in this case, a shift to the right from D_1 to D_2. This increased demand means that more Red Baron frozen cheese pizzas are wanted for a given price. At a price of $6 (point 3), the demand is 5 million units per year (Q_3) on D_2 rather than 3 million units per year (Q_2) on D_1.

Price Elasticity of Demand

LO 13-4

Describe what price elasticity of demand means to a manager facing a pricing decision.

With a downward-sloping demand curve, marketing managers are especially interested in how sensitive consumer demand and the firm's revenues are to changes in the product's price. This can be conveniently measured by **price elasticity of demand**, or the percentage change in quantity demanded relative to a percentage change in price. Price elasticity of demand (E) is expressed as follows:

$$\text{Price elasticity of demand (E)} = \frac{\text{Percentage change in quantity demanded}}{\text{Percentage change in price}}$$

Because quantity demanded usually decreases as price increases, price elasticity of demand is usually a negative number. However, for the sake of simplicity and by convention, elasticity figures are shown as positive numbers. Finally, price elasticity of demand assumes two forms discussed here: elastic demand and inelastic demand.

Elastic Demand and Inelastic Demand *Elastic demand* exists when a 1 percent decrease in price produces more than a 1 percent increase in quantity demanded, thereby actually increasing total revenue. This results in a price elasticity that is greater than 1 with elastic demand. In other words, a product with elastic demand is one in which a slight decrease in price results in a relatively large increase in demand or units sold. The reverse is also true; with elastic demand, a slight increase in price results in a relatively large decrease in demand. So marketers may cut price to increase consumer demand, the units sold, and total revenue for a product with elastic demand, depending on what competitors' prices are.

Inelastic demand exists when a 1 percent decrease in price produces less than a 1 percent increase in quantity demanded, thereby actually decreasing total revenue. This results in a price elasticity that is less than 1 with inelastic demand. So a product with inelastic demand means that slight increases or decreases in price will not significantly affect the demand, or units sold, for the product. The concern for marketers is that while lowering price will increase the quantity sold, total revenue will actually fall.

A consumer product that is a necessity, like toothpaste, has inelastic demand, which can result in an *increase* in price even during a recession.

How Price Elasticity Affects Marketing and Public Policy Decisions Price elasticity of demand is determined by a number of factors. The more substitutes a product or service has, the more likely it is to be price elastic. For example, a new sweater, shirt, or blouse has many possible substitutes and is price elastic, but gasoline has almost no substitutes and is price inelastic. In fact, given America's love affair with cars and driving, we are surprisingly insensitive to price increases in gasoline: One study showed a 10 percent increase in price results in only a 0.6 percent decrease in gasoline consumption.[17] This could change in the future as hybrid and all-electric cars become even more cost competitive.

Products and services considered to be necessities are price inelastic, so open-heart surgery is price inelastic, whereas airline tickets for a vacation are price elastic. Toothpaste is an example of a consumer product with inelastic demand. So even during recessions, Procter & Gamble's and Colgate's toothpastes often show price *increases* on the shelves of retailers. Items that require a large cash outlay compared with a person's disposable income are price elastic. Accordingly, cars are price elastic; soft drinks tend to be price inelastic.

Price elasticity is not only a relevant concept for marketing managers; it is also important for pricing practices involving public policy. The Marketing Matters box describes how price elasticity has been applied to curb cigarette smoking.[18]

Fundamentals of Estimating Revenue

While economists may talk about "demand curves," marketing executives are more likely to speak in terms of "revenue generated." Demand curves lead directly to an essential revenue concept critical to pricing decisions: **total revenue (TR)**, or the total money received from the sale of a product. Total revenue (TR) equals the unit price (P) times the quantity sold (Q). Using this equation, let's recall our Red Baron pizza example and assume our annual demand has improved, our price is $6 per unit, and we sell 5 million per year. So,

$$\begin{aligned} TR &= P \times Q \\ &= \$6 \times 5{,}000{,}000 \\ &= \$30{,}000{,}000 \end{aligned}$$

This combination of price and quantity sold annually will give us a total revenue of $30,000,000 per year. Is that good? Are you making a profit? Alas, total revenue is only part of the profit equation that we saw earlier:

$$\text{Total profit} = \text{Total revenue} - \text{Total cost}$$

The next section covers the other part of the profit equation: cost.

Marketing Matters

Customer Value

Using Big Data to Curb Smoking: Uncovering the Price Elasticity of Demand for Cigarettes

Price elasticity of demand is often studied to gauge consumer response to taxes and fees imposed by federal, state, and local government agencies. Public concern about cigarette smoking and tobacco-related diseases has resulted in hundreds of studies dealing with changes in the price of cigarettes and the incidence of smoking. This research has shown that where consumers live and their education, income, and age can affect price elasticity of demand.

As an example, a recent large-scale study with some 34,000 consumers between the ages of 15 and 29 was conducted in the United States. The study demonstrated that the price elasticity of cigarettes was inelastic and varied inversely with age: 0.83 for ages 15–17; 0.52 for ages 18–20; 0.37 for ages 21–23; 0.20 for ages 24–26; and 0.09 for ages 27–29. Thus, younger consumers (ages 15–17) were more likely to reduce the number of cigarettes smoked in response to increased prices than older consumers (ages 27–29).

To test these findings, New York City recently increased the combined taxes from federal, state, and local governments on a pack of Marlboro Light King cigarettes to $6.86. So the typical retail price in that city was more than $12 a pack. As a result of these inflated prices, the number of high school students smoking in New York City has hit a new low of 13.8 percent, far below the national average.

LEARNING REVIEW

13-7. What is the difference between a movement along a demand curve and a shift of a demand curve?

13-8. What is the difference between elastic demand and inelastic demand?

13-9. What is total revenue and how is it calculated?

STEP 3: DETERMINE COST, VOLUME, AND PROFIT RELATIONSHIPS

LO 13-5

Explain the role of costs in pricing decisions and describe how various combinations of price, fixed cost, and unit variable cost affect a firm's break-even point.

While revenues are the monies received by the firm from selling its products or services to customers, costs or expenses are the monies the firm pays out to its employees and suppliers. Marketing managers often use break-even analysis to relate revenues and costs, topics covered in this section.

The Importance of Costs and Margins

Understanding the role and behavior of cost and margin concepts is critical for all marketing decisions, particularly pricing decisions. These concepts are: **total cost (TC)**, **fixed cost (FC)**, **variable cost (VC)**, **unit variable cost (UVC)**, and **contribution margin (CM)** (see Figure 13–5 on the next page).

Many firms go bankrupt because their costs get out of control, causing their total costs—the sum of their fixed costs and variable costs—to exceed their total revenues over an extended period of time. This is why sophisticated marketing managers make pricing decisions that balance both revenues and costs.

FIGURE 13–5
Fundamental cost and margin concepts are important for marketing decisions.

Total cost (TC) is the total expense incurred by a firm in producing and marketing a product. Total cost is the sum of fixed cost and variable cost.

Fixed cost (FC) is the sum of the expenses of the firm that are stable and do not change with the quantity of a product that is produced and sold. Examples of fixed costs are rent on the building, executive salaries, and insurance.

Variable cost (VC) is the sum of the expenses of the firm that vary directly with the quantity of a product that is produced and sold. For example, as the quantity sold doubles, the variable cost doubles. Examples are the direct labor and direct materials used in producing the product and the sales commissions that are tied directly to the quantity sold. As mentioned above,

$$TC = FC + VC$$

Unit variable cost (UVC) is expressed on a per unit basis, or $UVC = \frac{VC}{Q}$

Contribution margin (CM) is expressed on a per unit basis as the difference between unit selling price (**P**) and unit variable cost (**UVC**), or as a percent:

$$CM = \frac{UVC}{P} \times 100$$

Break-Even Analysis

Break-even analysis is a technique that analyzes the relationship between total revenue and total cost to determine profitability at various levels of output. Figure 13–6 provides the data needed to conduct a break-even analysis. The **break-even point (BEP)** is the quantity at which total revenue and total cost are equal. Profit then comes from all units sold beyond the BEP. In terms of the definitions in Figure 13–5:

$$BEP_{\text{Quantity}} = \frac{\text{Fixed cost}}{\text{Unit price} - \text{Unit variable cost}} = \frac{FC}{P - UVC}$$

FIGURE 13–6
Calculating a break-even point for the picture frame shop in the text example shows that its profit starts at 400 pictures sold per year.

Calculating a Break-Even Point Suppose you are the owner of a picture frame shop and you wish to identify how many pictures you must sell to cover your fixed cost at a given price. Let's assume demand for your pictures is strong, so the average price customers are willing to pay for each picture is $120. Your unit variable cost (UVC) for a picture is $40. Therefore, your contribution margin is $80 ($120 – $40). Your fixed cost (FC) is $32,000 (real estate taxes, interest on a bank loan, etc.).

Quantity of Pictures Sold (Q)	Price per Picture (P)	Total Revenue (TR = P × Q)	Unit Variable Cost (UVC)	Total Variable Cost (VC = UVC × Q)	Fixed Cost (FC)	Total Cost (TC = FC + VC)	Profit (TR – TC)
0	$120	$0	$40	$0	$32,000	$32,000	($32,000)
400	$120	$48,000	$40	$16,000	$32,000	$48,000	$0
800	$120	$96,000	$40	$32,000	$32,000	$64,000	$32,000
1,200	$120	$144,000	$40	$48,000	$32,000	$80,000	$64,000
1,600	$120	$192,000	$40	$64,000	$32,000	$96,000	$96,000
2,000	$120	$240,000	$40	$80,000	$32,000	$112,000	$128,000

Your break-even quantity (BEP) is 400 pictures, as follows:

$$BEP_{Quantity} = \frac{\$32{,}000}{\$120 - \$40}$$

$$BEP_{Quantity} = 400 \text{ pictures}$$

Developing a Break-Even Chart The row shaded in orange in Figure 13–6 shows that your break-even quantity at a price of $120 per picture is 400 pictures. At less than 400 pictures, your picture frame shop incurs a loss, and at more than 400 pictures, it makes a profit. Figure 13–7 depicts a graphic presentation of the break-even analysis, called a **break-even chart**. It shows that total revenue (line DE) and total cost (line AC) intersect and are equal at a quantity of 400 pictures sold, which is the break-even point (F) at which profit is exactly $0. You want to do better? If your picture frame shop could increase the quantity sold annually to 2,000 pictures, the graph in Figure 13–7 shows you can earn an annual profit of $128,000 ($240,000 – $112,000 or line EC), shown by the row shaded in green in Figure 13–6.

The Profit Impact of Price Changes Cost, volume, and profit analysis is also used to assess the effect of price changes on a company's dollar profit. For example, suppose the owner of our picture frame shop is considering a price reduction. Recall from Figure 13–6 that the current unit price (P) for a picture frame is $120. The unit variable cost (UVC) is $40. The contribution margin (CM) is $80 ($120 – $40 = $80).

Suppose the owner is thinking about a $20 decrease in the price of picture frames from $120 to $100. The owner is concerned about what minimum unit sales volume increase is necessary to maintain the shop's current dollar profit, assuming no change in the shop's fixed cost. A simple formula for determining the minimum percentage unit sales volume increase is shown below:

$$\text{Percent unit sales volume change} = \frac{-(\text{Change in price})}{(\text{Contribution margin}) + (\text{Change in price})}$$

$$= \frac{-(-\$20)}{(\$80) + (-\$20)} = \frac{\$20}{\$60} = .333, \text{ or } 33.3\%$$

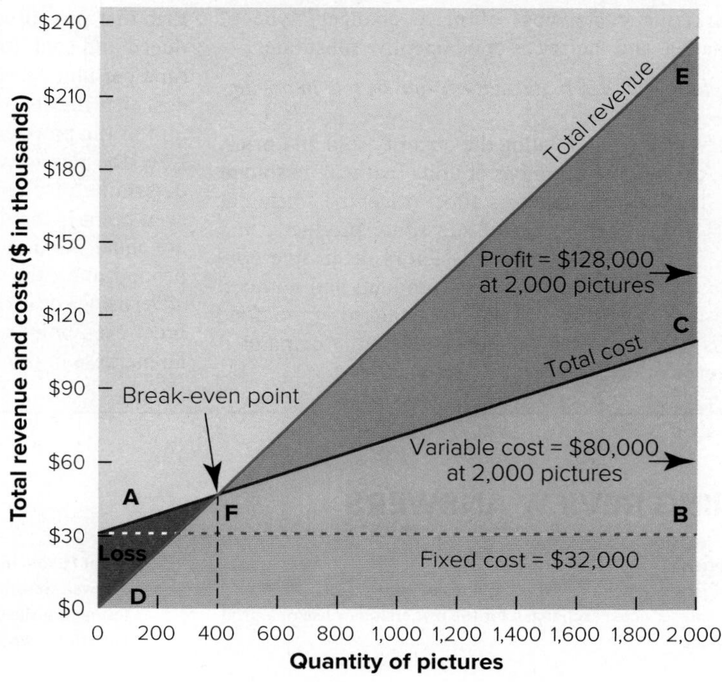

FIGURE 13–7 This break-even chart for a picture frame shop shows the break-even point at 400 pictures and the annual profit at 2,000 pictures.

This calculation shows that a 16.7 percent reduction in the picture from price requires a 33.3 percent increase in picture frame unit volume to maintain the shop's profit before the price change. In short, the percentage increase in unit volume is double the percentage decrease in picture frame price for the shop to not see a decrease in profit. Not surprisingly, companies are hesitant to reduce prices.

LEARNING REVIEW

13-10. What is the difference between fixed costs and variable costs?

13-11. What is a break-even point?

LEARNING OBJECTIVES REVIEW

LO 13-1 *Identify the elements that make up a price.*
Price is the money or other considerations (such as barter) exchanged for the ownership or use of a product or service. Although price typically involves money, the amount exchanged is often different from the list or quoted price because of incentives (rebates, discounts, etc.), allowances (trade-ins), and extra fees (finance charges, surcharges, etc.). The price of an offering is often used to indicate value, which is the ratio of perceived benefits to price. Pricing has a direct effect on a firm's profits, which is determined by the profit equation: Profit = Total revenue − Total cost.

LO 13-2 *Recognize the objectives a firm has in setting prices and the constraints that restrict the range of prices a firm can charge.*
Pricing objectives specify the role of price in a firm's marketing strategy and may include profit, sales revenue, market share, unit volume, survival, or some socially responsible price level. Pricing constraints that restrict a firm's pricing flexibility include demand, product newness, other products sold by the firm, production and marketing costs, cost of price changes, type of competitive market, and the prices of competitive substitutes.

LO 13-3 *Explain what a demand curve is and its role in pricing decisions.*
A demand curve is a graph relating the quantity sold and price, which shows the maximum number of units that will be sold at a given price. Three demand factors affect price: (*a*) consumer tastes, (*b*) price and availability of substitute products, and (*c*) consumer income. These demand factors determine consumers' willingness and ability to pay for products and services. Assuming these demand factors remain unchanged, if the price of a product is lowered or raised, then the quantity demanded for it will increase or decrease, respectively.

LO 13-4 *Describe what price elasticity of demand means to a manager facing a pricing decision.*
Price elasticity of demand measures the responsiveness of units of a product sold to a change in price, which is expressed as the percentage change in the quantity of a product demanded divided by the percentage change in price. Price elasticity is important to marketing managers because a change in price usually has an important effect on the number of units of the product sold and on total revenue.

LO 13-5 *Explain the role of costs in pricing decisions and describe how various combinations of price, fixed cost, and unit variable cost affect a firm's break-even point.*
Five important costs impact a firm's pricing decisions: (*a*) *total cost*, or *total expenses*, is the sum of fixed cost and variable cost incurred by a firm in producing and marketing a product; (*b*) *fixed cost* is the sum of expenses of the firm that are stable and do not change with the quantity of a product that is produced and sold; (*c*) *variable cost* is the sum of expenses of the firm that vary directly with the quantity of a product that is produced and sold; (*d*) *unit variable cost* is variable cost expressed on a per unit basis; and (*e*) *marginal cost* is the change in total cost that results from producing and marketing one additional unit of the product. Break-even analysis is a technique that analyzes the relationship between total revenue and total cost to determine profitability at various levels of output. The break-even point is the quantity at which total revenue and total cost are equal. Assuming no change in price, if the costs of a firm's product increase due to higher fixed costs (manufacturing or advertising) or variable costs (direct labor or materials), then its break-even point will be higher. And if total cost is unchanged, an increase in price will reduce the break-even point.

LEARNING REVIEW ANSWERS

13-1 What is price?
Answer: Price is the money or other considerations (including other products and services) exchanged for the ownership or use of a product or service.

13-2 What factors impact the list price to determine the final price?
Answer: Several factors increase or decrease the final price of an offering that the consumer pays. These factors help construct the price equation, which includes incentives, such as cash discounts,

allowances, and rebates, which decrease the final price, and extra fees or surcharges, which increase the final price.

13-3 What is the profit equation?
Answer: Price has a direct effect on a firm's profits, which can be expressed in the following profit equation: Profit = Total revenue − Total cost or [(Unit price × Quantity sold) − (Fixed cost + Variable cost)].

13-4 What is the difference between pricing objectives and pricing constraints?
Answer: Pricing objectives involve specifying the role of price in an organization's marketing and strategic plans whereas pricing constraints are factors that limit the range of prices a firm may set.

13-5 How does the type of competitive market a firm is in affect its range in setting prices?
Answer: The seller's price is constrained by the type of market in which it competes. Economists generally delineate four types of competitive markets: (1) With pure competition, there are many sellers who follow the market price for identical, commodity products. (2) With monopolistic competition, there are many sellers who compete on nonprice factors such as product features and advertising. (3) With an oligopoly, there are (*a*) a few sellers who are sensitive to each other's prices and (*b*) a firm that is a price leader that sets the market price that other firms follow. The firms that are price followers set a price based on the prices set by their competitors to avoid a price war. (4) With a pure monopoly, there is one seller in the market who can set any price it wants for its unique product.

13-6 What are examples of (1) consumer-driven and (2) seller- or retailer-driven pricing actions made possible through price transparency on the Internet?
Answer: Price transparency occurs as a result of a consumer's near-instantaneous access to competitors' prices for the same offering through the Internet. Two dimensions of price transparency are: (1) Consumer-driven pricing actions, in which consumers make more efficient buying decisions by comparing the price of an item first in the store and then on the Internet using a smartphone. If the price is lower on the Internet, they'll ask the store to match the price or go home and buy the item online. (2) Seller- or retailer-driven pricing actions, in which sellers can quickly change their online prices. This is made possible by Internet-based dynamic pricing, in which the seller changes prices in response to its existing inventory and the prices of its competitors.

13-7 What is the difference between a movement along a demand curve and a shift of a demand curve?
Answer: A demand curve is a graph that relates the quantity sold and price, showing the maximum number of units that will be sold at a given price. A movement along a demand curve (up or down) for a product occurs when its price is lowered or increased and the quantity demanded for it correspondingly increases or decreases, assuming that other factors such as consumer tastes, promotion (advertising and/or sales promotion), price and availability of substitute products, and/or consumer incomes remain unchanged. However, if one or more of these factors do change, then the demand curve for a product will shift to the right or left based on whether the change(s) was favorable or not. This means that there will be either an increase or a decrease in demand for the product based on the change in the factor(s).

13-8 What is the difference between elastic demand and inelastic demand?
Answer: Price elasticity of demand is the percentage change in the quantity demanded relative to a percentage change in price and is expressed as follows: Price elasticity of demand (E) = Percentage change in quantity demanded ÷ Percentage change in price. Elastic demand exists when a 1 percent decrease in price produces more than a 1 percent increase in quantity demanded, thereby actually increasing total revenue. This results in a price elasticity that is greater than 1. Inelastic demand exists when a 1 percent decrease in price produces less than a 1 percent increase in quantity demanded, thereby actually decreasing total revenue. This results in a price elasticity that is less than 1.

13-9 What is total revenue and how is it calculated?
Answer: Total revenue (TR) is the total money received from the sale of a product. Total revenue (TR) equals the product's unit price (P) times the quantity sold (Q) or TR = P × Q.

13-10 What is the difference between fixed costs and variable costs?
Answer: Fixed cost (FC) is the sum of the expenses of the firm that are stable and do not change with the quantity of a product that is produced and sold. Examples of fixed costs are rent on the building, executive salaries, and insurance. Variable cost (VC) is the sum of the expenses of the firm that vary directly with the quantity of a product that is produced and sold. Examples are the direct labor and direct materials used in producing the product and the sales commissions that are tied directly to the quantity sold.

13-11 What is a break-even point?
Answer: Break-even analysis is a technique that analyzes the relationship between total revenue and total cost to determine profitability at various levels of output. The break-even point (BEP) is the quantity at which total revenue and total cost are equal. Profit then comes from all units sold beyond the BEP. Break-even point (BEP) = [Fixed cost ÷ (Unit price − Unit variable cost)].

FOCUSING ON KEY TERMS

barter p. 348
break-even analysis p. 360
break-even chart p. 361
break-even point (BEP) p. 360
contribution margin (CM) p. 359
demand curve p. 356
demand factors p. 356
fixed cost (FC) p. 359
price (P) p. 348
price elasticity of demand p. 357
pricing constraints p. 352
pricing objectives p. 351
profit equation p. 350
total cost (TC) p. 359
total revenue (TR) p. 358
unit variable cost (UVC) p. 359
value p. 349
value pricing p. 350
variable cost (VC) p. 359

APPLYING MARKETING KNOWLEDGE

1 How would the price equation apply to the purchase price of (*a*) gasoline, (*b*) an airline ticket, and (*c*) a checking account?

2 What would be your response to the statement, "Profit maximization is the only legitimate pricing objective for the firm"?

3 How is a downward-sloping demand curve related to total revenue?

4 A marketing executive once said, "If the price elasticity of demand for your product is inelastic, then your price is probably too low." What is this executive saying in terms of the economic principles discussed in this chapter?

5 A marketing manager reduced the price on a brand of cereal by 10 percent and observed a 25 percent increase in quantity sold. The manager then thought that if the price were reduced by another 20 percent, a 50 percent increase in quantity sold would occur. What would be your response to the marketing manager's reasoning?

6 A student theater group at a university has developed a demand schedule that shows the relationship between ticket prices and demand based on a student survey (see the table that follows). (*a*) Graph the demand curve and the total revenue curve based on these data. What ticket price might be set based on this analysis? (*b*) What other factors should be considered before the final price is set?

Ticket Price	Number of Students Who Would Buy
$1	300
2	250
3	200
4	150
5	100

7 Touché Toiletries, Inc. has developed an addition to its Lizardman Cologne line tentatively branded Ode d'Toade Cologne. Unit variable costs are 45 cents for a three-ounce bottle, and heavy advertising expenditures in the first year would result in total fixed costs of $900,000. Ode d'Toade Cologne is priced at $7.50 for a three-ounce bottle. How many bottles of Ode d'Toade must be sold to break even?

8 Suppose that marketing executives for Touché Toiletries (see problem 7) reduced the price to $6.50 for a three-ounce bottle of Ode d'Toade and the fixed costs were $1,100,000. Suppose further that the unit variable cost remained at 45 cents for a three-ounce bottle. (*a*) How many bottles must be sold to break even? (*b*) What dollar profit level would Ode d'Toade achieve if 200,000 bottles were sold?

9 Executives of Random Recordings, Inc. produced a digital album titled *Sunshine/Moonshine* by the Starshine Sisters Band. (*a*) Using the price and cost information that follows, prepare a chart like that in Figure 13–6 showing total cost, fixed cost, and total revenue for album quantity sold levels starting at 10,000 through 100,000, using intervals of 10,000 for quantity of albums sold (i.e.,10,000, 20,000, 30,000, and so on). (*b*) What is the break-even point for the digital album?

Selling price	$10.00 per album
Album cover	$1.00 per album
Songwriter's royalties	$0.30 per album
Recording artists' royalties	$0.70 per album
Direct material and labor costs to produce the album	$1.00 per album
Fixed cost of producing an album (advertising, studio fee, etc.)	$100,000

BUILDING YOUR MARKETING PLAN

In starting to set a final price:

1 List two pricing objectives and three pricing constraints.

2 Think about your customers and competitors and set three possible prices.

3 Assume a fixed cost and unit variable cost and (*a*) calculate the break-even points and (*b*) plot a break-even chart for the three prices specified in step 2.

VIDEO CASE 13 Washburn Guitars: Using Break-Even Points to Make Pricing Decisions

VIDEO 13-3
Washburn Guitars Video Case
kerin.tv/15e/v13-3

"We offer a guitar at every price point for every skill level," explains Kevin Lello, vice president of marketing at Washburn Guitars. Washburn is one of the most prestigious guitar manufacturers in the world, offering instruments that range from one-of-a-kind, custom-made acoustic and electric guitars and basses to less-expensive, mass-produced guitars. Lello has responsibility for marketing Washburn's products and ensuring that the price of each product matches the company's objectives related to sales, profit, and market share. "We do pay attention to break-even points," adds Lello. "We need to know exactly how much a guitar costs us, and how much the overhead is for each guitar."

Paul Kane/Getty Images

THE COMPANY

The modern Washburn Guitars company started 40 years ago when a small Chicago firm bought the century-old Washburn brand name and a small inventory of guitars, parts, and promotional supplies. At that time, annual company sales of about 2,500 guitars generated revenues of $300,000. Washburn's first catalog told a frightening truth:

> Our designs are translated by Japan's most experienced craftsmen, assuring the consistent quality and craftsmanship for which they are known.

At that time, the American guitar-making craft was at an all-time low. Guitars made by Japanese firms, such as Ibanez and Yamaha, were in use by an increasing number of professionals.

Times have changed for Washburn. Today, the company sells about 50,000 guitars each year and annual revenues exceed $40 million. All this resulted from Washburn's aggressive marketing strategies to develop product lines with different price points targeted at musicians in distinctly different market segments.

THE PRODUCTS AND MARKET SEGMENTS

One of Washburn's early successes was the trendsetting Festival Series of cutaway, thin-bodied flattops, with built-in bridge pickups and controls. This guitar became the standard for live performances as its popularity with rock and country stars increased. Over the years, several generations of musicians have used Washburn guitars. Early artists included Bob Dylan, Dolly Parton, Greg Allman, and the late George Harrison of The Beatles. In recent years, Mike Kennerty of The All-American Rejects, Rick Savage of Def Leppard, and Hugh McDonald of Bon Jovi have been among the many musicians who use Washburn products.

Until 1991, all Washburn guitars were manufactured in Asia. That year Washburn started building its high-end guitars in the United States. Today, Washburn marketing executives divide its product line into four categories to appeal to different market segments. From high-end guitars to low-end ones, these product groupings are:

- One-of-a-kind, custom instruments.
- Batch-custom instruments.
- Mass-customized instruments.
- Mass-produced instruments.

The one-of-a-kind custom products appeal to the many stars who use Washburn instruments as well as to collectors. The batch-custom products appeal to professional musicians. The mass-customized products appeal to musicians with intermediate skill levels who may not yet be professionals. Finally, the mass-produced units are targeted at first-time buyers and are still manufactured in Asian factories.

PRICING ISSUES

Setting prices for its various lines presents a continuing challenge for Washburn. Not only do the prices have to reflect the changing tastes of its various segments of musicians, but the prices must also be competitive with the prices of other guitars manufactured and marketed globally. The price elasticity of demand, or price sensitivity, for Washburn's products varies between its segments. To reduce the price sensitivity for some of its products, Washburn uses endorsements by internationally known musicians who play its instruments and lend their names to lines of Washburn signature guitars. Stars playing

Washburn guitars, such as Nuno Bettencourt of Extreme, Paul Stanley of KISS, Scott Ian of Anthrax, and Dan Donegan of Disturbed, have their own lines of signature guitars—the "batch-custom" units mentioned earlier. These guitars receive excellent reviews. *Total Guitar* magazine, for example, recently said, "If you want a truly original axe that has been built with great attention to detail . . . then the Washburn Maya Pro DD75 could be the one."

Source: Washburn Guitars

Bill Abel, Washburn's vice president of sales, is responsible for reviewing and approving prices for the company's lines of guitars. Setting a sales target of 2,000 units for a new line of guitars, he is considering a suggested retail price of $349 per unit for customers at one of the hundreds of retail outlets carrying the Washburn line. For planning purposes, Abel estimates half of the final retail price will be the price Washburn nets when it sells its guitar to the wholesalers and dealers in its channel of distribution.

Looking at Washburn's financial data for its present plant, Abel estimates that this line of guitars must bear these fixed costs:

Rent and taxes	= $14,000
Depreciation of equipment	= $ 4,000
Management and quality control program	= $20,000

In addition, he estimates the variable costs for each unit to be:

Direct materials	= $25/unit
Direct labor	= 15 hours/unit @ $8/hour

Carefully kept production records at Washburn's plant make Abel believe that these are reasonable estimates. He explains, "Before we begin a production run, we have a good feel for what our costs will be. The U.S.-built N-4, for example, simply costs more than one of our foreign-produced electrics."

Caught in the global competition for guitar sales, Washburn continually searches for ways to reduce and control costs. For example, Washburn recently purchased Parker Guitar, another guitar manufacturer that designed products for professionals and collectors, and will combine the two production facilities in a new location. Washburn expects the acquisition to lower its fixed and variable costs. Specifically, Washburn projects that its new factory location will reduce its rent and taxes expense by 40 percent, and the new skilled employees will reduce the hours of work needed for each unit by 15 percent.

By managing the prices of its products, Washburn also helps its dealers and retailers. In fact, Abel believes it is another reason for Washburn's success: "We have excellent relationships with the independent retailers. They're our lifeblood, and our outlet to sell our product. We sell through chains and online dealers, but it's the independent dealer that sells the guitars. So we take a smaller margin from them because they have to do more work. They appreciate it, and they go the extra mile for us."[19]

Questions

1 What factors are most likely to affect the demand for the lines of Washburn guitars (*a*) bought by a first-time guitar buyer and (*b*) bought by a sophisticated musician who wants a signature model?

2 For Washburn, what are examples of (*a*) shifting the demand curve to the right to get a higher price for a guitar line (movement of the demand curve) and (*b*) pricing decisions involving moving along a demand curve?

3 In Washburn's factory, what is the break-even point for the new line of guitars if the retail price is (*a*) $349, (*b*) $389, and (*c*) $309? Also, (*d*) if Washburn achieves the sales target of 2,000 units at the $349 retail price, what will its profit be?

4 Assume that the merger with Parker leads to the cost reductions projected in the case. What will be the (*a*) new break-even point at a $349 retail price for this line of guitars and (*b*) new profit if it sells 2,000 units?

5 If, for competitive reasons, Washburn eventually has to move all its production back to Asia, (*a*) which specific fixed and variable costs might be lowered and (*b*) what additional fixed and variable costs might it expect to incur?

Chapter Notes

1. Quote by Laynie Newsome.
2. "The Vizio Story," www.vizio.com, downloaded May 15, 2019; "The Best TVs of 2019," www.usatoday.com, January 31, 2019; "Share of Smart TVs by Manufacturer in U.S. in 2017 and 2018," www.statista.com, accessed March 2, 2019; *VIZIO, Inc. Form S-1 Registration Statement* (Washington, DC: U.S. Securities and Exchange Commission, July 24, 2015); and "How Vizio Conquered TV," www.fortune.com, July 25, 2012.
3. International Reciprocal Trade Association press release, February 20, 2019.

4. "2020 Bugatti Chiron First Drive: The Benchmark," www.motortrend.com, March 23, 2019.
5. Adapted from Kent B. Monroe, *Pricing: Making Profitable Decisions,* 3rd ed. (New York: McGraw-Hill, 2003).
6. Numerous studies have examined the price-quality-value relationship. See, for example, Jacob Jacoby and Jerry C. Olsen, eds., *Perceived Quality* (Lexington, MA: Lexington Books, 1985); and Roger A. Kerin, Ambuj Jain, and Daniel Howard, "Store Shopping Experience and Consumer Price-Quality-Value Perceptions," *Journal of Retailing,* Winter 1992, pp. 235–45. For a thorough review of the price-quality-value relationship, see Valarie A. Zeithaml, "Consumer Perceptions of Price, Quality, and Value," *Journal of Marketing,* July 1998, pp. 2–22.
7. Roger A. Kerin and Robert A. Peterson, "Haverwood Furniture, Inc. (A)," *Strategic Marketing Problems: Cases and Comments,* 13th ed. (Upper Saddle River, NJ: Prentice Hall, 2013), pp. 294–305.
8. "Spirit's New Strategy: Be Less Terrible Airline," www.msn.com, June 14, 2019; "The Best and Worst U.S. Airlines," www.wsj.com, January 16, 2019; "How Low-Cost Airlines Alter the Economics of Flying," www.msn.com, September 2, 2017; and "America's Least Favorite Airline (Hint: It's not United)," www.money.com, April 25, 2017.
9. Ken Belson, "Mets Going for the Gold on Tickets for More Games," *The New York Times,* April 8, 2009, p. B13.
10. Prices quoted on eBay.com on February 17, 2019.
11. Christina Binkley, "How Can Jeans Cost $300?" *The Wall Street Journal,* July 7, 2011, pp. D1–D2.
12. "Apple Gambles on Allure of Premium Pricing," *The Wall Street Journal,* September 13, 2017, pp. A1, A8.
13. Arik Hesseldahl, "For Every Xbox, a Big Fat Loss," *BusinessWeek,* December 5, 2005, p. 13; and Akshay R. Rao, Mark E. Bergen, and Scott Davis, "How to Fight a Price War," *Harvard Business Review,* March–April 2000, pp. 107–16.
14. Ron Winslow, "How a Breakthrough Quickly Broke Down for Johnson & Johnson," *The Wall Street Journal,* September 18, 1988, pp. A1, A5.
15. "Websites Vary Prices, Deals Based on Users' Information," *The Wall Street Journal,* December 24, 2012, p. B1.
16. John B. Ford, "New Product Failure and Success," in Aaron L. Brody and John B. Ford, eds., *Developing New Food Products for a Changing Marketplace,* 2nd ed. (Boca Raton, FL: CRC Press, 2008), Chapter 3.
17. Eliana Eitches and Vera Crain, "Using Gasoline Data to Explain Inelasticity," *Beyond the Numbers: Prices and Spending* 5, no. 5 (Washington, DC: U.S. Bureau of Labor Statistics, March 2016).
18. "Cigarette Smoking Price Elasticity of Demand," in Irvin Tucker, *Microeconomics for Today,* 10th ed. (Boston, MA: Cengage, 2019), p. 141; "Big Tobacco Takes Its Last Drag as Economic Change Looms," www.forbes.com, September 6, 2013; and "Message Is Clear: Higher Prices Deter Smoking," *USA Today,* April 9, 2009, p. 10A.
19. Washburn Guitar: This case was edited by Steven Hartley. Sources: Burkhard Bilger, "String Theory, Building a Better Guitar," *The New Yorker,* May 14, 2007, p. 79; and the Washburn Guitar website, www.washburn.com.

Chapter 14 Arriving at the Final Price

LEARNING OBJECTIVES

After reading this chapter you should be able to:

LO 14-1 Describe how to establish the "approximate price level" using demand-oriented, cost-oriented, profit-oriented, and competition-oriented approaches.

LO 14-2 Recognize the major factors considered in deriving a final list or quoted price from the approximate price level.

LO 14-3 Identify the adjustments made to the approximate price level on the basis of discounts, allowances, and geography.

LO 14-4 Name the principal laws and regulations affecting specific pricing practices.

E-Books and E-Conomics: A Twisted Tale of Pricing for Profit

Have you ever wondered why e-book prices are set a few dollars or cents under an even number, such as $19.99? Or, from a business standpoint, does a publisher make less profit on an e-book than a printed book given the price difference? These questions may not keep you awake at night, but the answers may surprise you.

Setting the Stage with e-Readers: Amazon's Kindle

One of the most disruptive changes in the book publishing industry has been the transition from print to electronic books, or e-books. The change wasn't initiated by book publishers, but by Amazon with the introduction of its Kindle e-reader. Its innovation was quickly followed by Barnes & Noble, with its Nook e-reader, and Apple, with the iPad.

Amazon executives knew that for Kindle e-readers to be successful, printed books had to be converted to e-books quickly. This conversion would supply content for Kindle e-readers, thus increasing their value to consumers. One way to do this was to make e-books cheaper than printed books through advances in digital technology. However, the traditional approach to print book pricing stood in the way. The solution? Change the approach to book pricing, of course! This is where the twisted tale of e-book pricing for profit begins.

Printed Book Pricing Practices

The approach for pricing printed books was steeped in tradition. Based on forecasted demand, a publisher would set a price to a distributor like Amazon (usually 50 percent of the publisher's suggested retail price). The distributor would sell the book to consumers at whatever price the distributor chose. A publisher would then subtract its unit variable costs, such as unit manufacturing (paper and ink), freight and handling cost, and author royalties (about 15 percent of the price) to arrive at its contribution margin per printed book. At a $20.00 suggested retail price ($10.00 to the distributor), the publisher would typically record a $4.40 contribution margin. This amount would be used to pay the total fixed costs assigned to the printed book and produce a profit.

Enter e-Books

The dynamics in the e-book market proved to be quite different from the printed book market. For example, traditional distributors, such as bookstores, had an incentive to set a printed book's retail price from the publisher higher. In contrast, e-reader suppliers, such as Amazon, wanted lower retail prices for e-books to build the e-reader business. Therefore, Amazon initially decided to set a retail price for e-books at $9.99–a decision based on the belief that this act would stimulate e-book volume. This meant that

Daniilantiq/Getty Images

Amazon would lose money on many e-book transactions: paying $10.00 for an item and then selling it for $9.99 presented a problem. At the same time, publishers believed that low e-book prices promoted by Amazon and other distributors would erode consumers' perception of the value of books, cannibalize printed book sales, and eventually result in lower prices charged to distributors. In short, neither party benefited. So what should be done?

Pricing e-Books . . . Profitably

Book publishers changed their pricing approach. Publishers would set e-book retail list prices, and distributors, like Amazon, Barnes & Noble, or Apple, would get a commission on every e-book sold. The commission was usually 30 percent. Distributors could still set their own retail prices, but with a restriction. Distributors could set prices below a publisher's retail list price so long as they did not exceed the commission received from a publisher. Therefore, the most a publisher's retail list price of $20.00 could be discounted was $14.00. But consumers didn't see that retail price. Amazon and Apple usually set a price with an odd-ending number like 5, 7, or 9 as a matter of policy. The zeros in $14.00 would be replaced by one or more of these numbers, or $14.99.

So how do publishers and distributors make a profit using this approach to pricing? Suppose a publisher's retail list price for an e-book is $20.00. The distributor's e-book retail price is set at $14.99. The publisher would get 70 percent of $14.99, or $10.49, and the distributor would get $4.50. The publisher has no unit manufacturing, freight, or handling cost, just an author royalty, which drops to about $2.62. Therefore, the publisher's contribution margin per e-book is $7.87 ($10.49 − $2.62) to pay the total fixed costs assigned to the e-book and record a profit. Remember that a publisher's contribution margin for a printed book was $4.40. In short, both e-book distributors and publishers benefit from this pricing approach because both parties make a profit. Now you know a little bit more about e-book economics and the twisted tale of profitable pricing.[1]

STEP 4: SELECT AN APPROXIMATE PRICE LEVEL

LO 14-1

Describe how to establish the "approximate price level" using demand-oriented, cost-oriented, profit-oriented, and competition-oriented approaches.

This chapter describes how companies set an approximate price level for their offerings, highlights important considerations in setting a list or quoted price, and identifies various price adjustments that can be made to prices set by a company—the last three steps involved in setting prices (Figure 14–1). Legal and regulatory aspects of pricing are also described.

A key for a marketing manager setting a final price for a product is to find an approximate price level to use as a reasonable starting point. Four common approaches to helping find this approximate price level are (1) demand-oriented, (2) cost-oriented, (3) profit-oriented, and (4) competition-oriented (see Figure 14–2). Although these approaches are discussed separately below, some of them overlap, and a seasoned marketing manager will consider several in selecting an approximate price level.

Demand-Oriented Pricing Approaches

Demand-oriented approaches weigh factors underlying expected customer tastes and preferences more heavily than such factors as cost, profit, and competition when selecting a price level.

Skimming Pricing A firm introducing a new or innovative product can use **skimming pricing**, setting the highest initial price that customers who really desire the product are willing to pay. These customers are not very price sensitive because they weigh the new product's price, quality, and ability to satisfy their needs against the same characteristics of substitutes. As the demand of these customers is satisfied, the firm lowers the price to attract another, more price-sensitive segment. Thus, skimming pricing gets its name from skimming successive layers of "cream," or customer segments, as prices are lowered in a series of steps.

Skimming pricing is an effective strategy when (1) enough prospective customers are willing to buy the product immediately at the high initial price to make these sales profitable, (2) the high initial price will not attract competitors, (3) lowering price has only a minor effect on increasing the sales volume and reducing the unit costs, and (4) customers interpret the high price as signifying high quality. These four conditions are most likely to exist when the new product is protected by patents or copyrights or its uniqueness is understood and valued by consumers. Microsoft, for example, adopted a skimming strategy for its Xbox One X video game console since many of these conditions applied. The original Xbox One X was priced about $100 more than Sony's PlayStation 4 Pro.

Penetration Pricing Setting a low initial price on a new product to appeal immediately to the mass market is **penetration pricing**, the exact opposite of skimming pricing. Amazon

FIGURE 14–1

The six steps in setting price. The first three steps were covered in Chapter 13, and the last three steps are covered in this chapter.

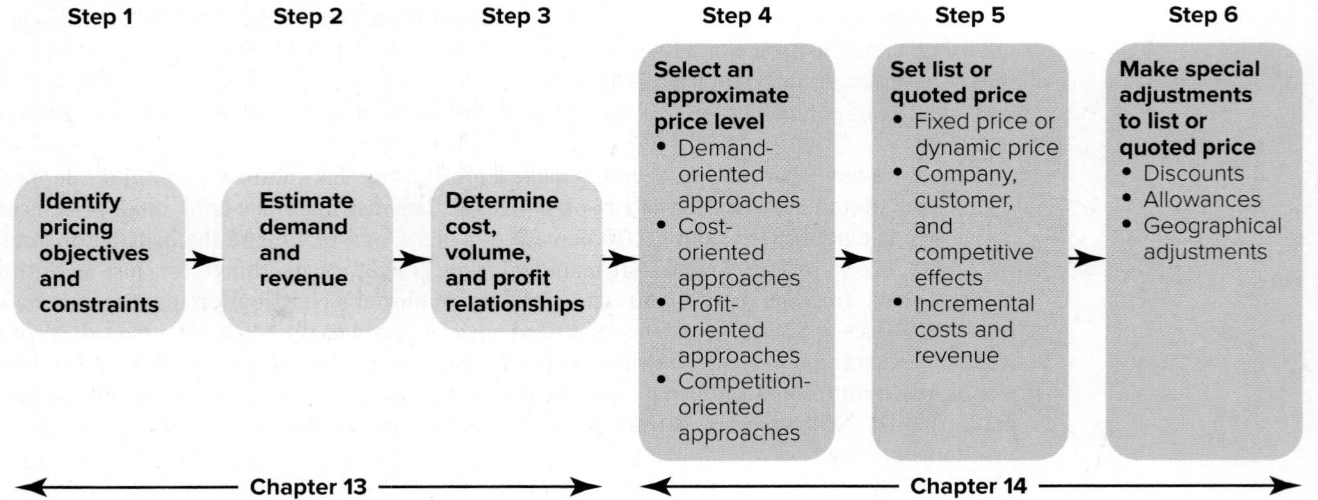

Select an approximate price level

Demand-oriented approaches	Cost-oriented approaches	Profit-oriented approaches	Competition-oriented approaches
• Skimming • Penetration • Prestige • Price lining • Odd-even • Target • Bundle • Yield management	• Standard markup • Cost-plus • Experience curve	• Target profit • Target return on sales • Target return on investment	• Customary • Above, at, or below market • Loss leader

FIGURE 14–2 Four approaches for selecting an approximate price level.

consciously chose a penetration strategy when it introduced its new generation Amazon Kindle Fire tablet computer at $49.99. The average price of competitive models was $323.

The conditions favoring penetration pricing are the reverse of those supporting skimming pricing: (1) many segments of the market are price sensitive, (2) a low initial price discourages competitors from entering the market, and (3) unit production and marketing costs fall dramatically as production volumes increase. A firm using penetration pricing may (1) maintain the initial price for a time to gain profit lost from its low introductory level or (2) lower the price further, counting on the new volume to generate the necessary profit.

In some situations, penetration pricing may follow skimming pricing. A company might initially price a product high to attract price-insensitive consumers and recoup initial research and development costs and introductory promotional expenditures. Once this is done, penetration pricing is used to appeal to a broader segment of the population and increase market share.[2]

VIDEO 14-1
Rolex Ad
kerin.tv/15e/v14-1

Prestige Pricing As noted in Chapter 13, consumers may use price as a measure of the quality or prestige of an item so that as price is lowered beyond some point, demand for the item actually falls. **Prestige pricing** involves setting a high price so that quality- or status-conscious consumers will be attracted to the product and buy it. As shown in Figure 14–3, the demand curve for prestige pricing slopes downward and to the right between points *A* and *B* but turns back to the left between points *B* and *C* because demand is actually reduced between points *B* and *C*. From *A* to *B*, buyers see the lowering of price as a bargain and buy more; from *B* to *C*, they become dubious about the quality and prestige and buy less. A marketing manager's pricing strategy here is to stay above price P_0 (the initial price).

Rolls-Royce cars, Chanel perfume, Cartier jewelry, Lalique crystal, and Swiss watches, such as Rolex, have an element of prestige pricing in them and may sell worse at lower prices than at higher ones.[3] The recent success of Swiss watchmaker TAG Heuer is an example. The company quadrupled the average price of its watches and its sales volume jumped sevenfold.[4] Recently, Energizer learned that buyers of high-performance alkaline batteries tend to link a lower price with lower quality. The Marketing Matters box on the next page describes the pricing lesson learned by Energizer.[5]

FIGURE 14–3 For prestige pricing, the demand curve for high-quality products bought by status-conscious consumers is backward sloping.

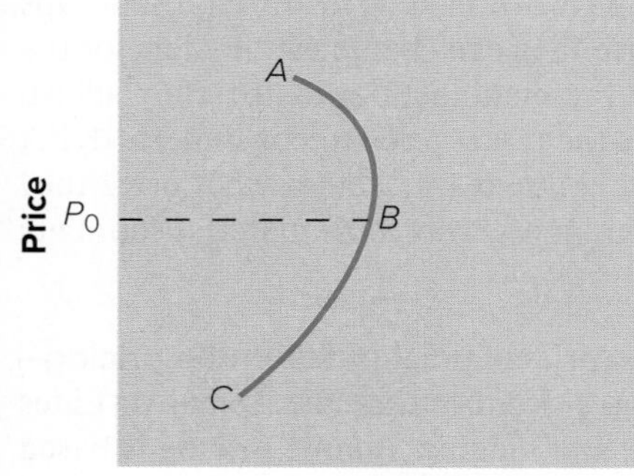

Price Lining Often a firm that is selling not just a single product but a line of products may price them at a number of different specific pricing points, which is called **price lining**. For example, a department store manager may price a line of women's casual slacks at $59, $79, and $99. As shown in Figure 14–4 on the next page, this assumes that demand is elastic at each of these price points but inelastic between these price points. In some instances, all the items might be purchased for the same cost and then marked up at different percentages to

Marketing Matters — Customer Value

Energizer's Lesson in Price Perception—Value Lies in the Eye of the Beholder

Battery manufacturers are as tireless as a certain drum-thumping bunny in their efforts to create products that perform better, last longer, and, not incidentally, outsell the competition. The commercialization of new alkaline battery technology at a price that creates value for consumers is not always obvious or easy. Just ask the marketing executives at Energizer about their experience with pricing Energizer Advanced Formula and Energizer e² AA alkaline batteries.

When Duracell launched its high-performance Ultra brand AA alkaline battery with a 25 percent price premium over standard Duracell batteries, Energizer quickly countered with its own high-performance battery—Energizer Advanced Formula. Believing that consumers would not pay the premium price, Energizer priced its Advanced Formula brand at the same price as its standard AA alkaline battery, expecting to gain market share from Duracell. It did not happen. Why? According to industry analysts, consumers associated Energizer's low price with inferior quality in the high-performance segment. Instead of gaining market share, Energizer lost market share to Duracell and Rayovac, the number three battery manufacturer.

Having learned its lesson, Energizer subsequently released its e² high-performance battery, this time priced 4 percent higher than Duracell Ultra and about 50 percent higher than Advanced Formula. The result? Energizer recovered lost sales and market share. The lesson learned? Value lies in the eye of the beholder.

chutima kuanamon/Alamy Stock Photo

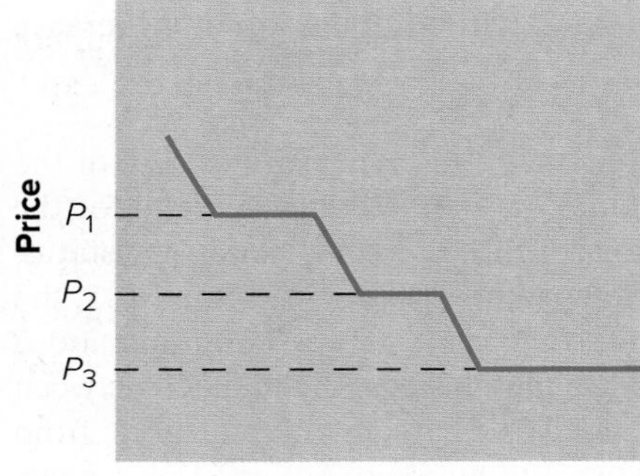

FIGURE 14–4 For price lining, the demand curve is elastic at each price point but inelastic between price points.

achieve these price points based on color, style, and expected demand. In other instances, manufacturers design products for different price points, and retailers apply approximately the same markup percentages to achieve the three or four different price points offered to consumers. Sellers often feel that a limited number of price points (such as 3 or 4) are preferable to 8 or 10, which may only confuse prospective buyers.[6]

Odd-Even Pricing Apple priced its iPhone 11 model at $699, Lowe's offers a DeWalt radial saw for $599.99, and the suggested retail price for the Gillette Fusion shaving system is $11.99. Why not simply price these items at $1,000, $600, and $12, respectively? These firms are using **odd-even pricing**, which involves setting prices a few dollars or cents under an even number. Recall that Amazon uses odd-even pricing for its e-books. The presumption is that consumers see the DeWalt radial saw as priced at "something over $500" rather than "about $600." In theory, demand increases if the price drops from $600 to $599.99. There is some evidence to suggest this does happen. However, research suggests that overuse of odd-ending prices tends to mute its effect on demand.[7]

Target Pricing Manufacturers will sometimes estimate the price that the ultimate consumer would be willing to pay for a product. They then work backward through markups taken by retailers and wholesalers to determine what price they can charge wholesalers for the product. This practice, called **target pricing**, results in the manufacturer deliberately adjusting the composition and features of a product to achieve the target price to consumers. IKEA uses target pricing for its home furnishings. IKEA's marketing team decides what price they want to sell a specific product for, and then company designers work with material suppliers and manufacturers to deliver the product at that price.

Bundle Pricing A frequently used demand-oriented pricing practice is **bundle pricing**—the marketing of two or more products in a single package price. For example, Delta Air Lines offers vacation packages that include airfare, car rental, and lodging. Bundle pricing is based on the idea that consumers value the package more than the individual items. This is due to

Which pricing strategy is used by DIRECTV? Read the text to find out which one and why.
Source: DIRECTV

benefits received from not having to make separate purchases and enhanced satisfaction from one item given the presence of another. This is the idea behind McDonald's Extra Value Meal and AT&T and DIRECTV's TV, phone, and Internet bundles. Moreover, bundle pricing often provides a lower total cost to buyers and lower marketing costs to sellers.[8]

Yield Management Pricing Have you noticed seats on airline flights are priced differently within coach class? This is **yield management pricing**—the charging of different prices to maximize revenue for a set amount of capacity at any given time. As described in Chapter 12, service businesses engage in capacity management, and an effective way to do this is by varying prices by time, day, week, or season. Yield management pricing is a complex approach that continually matches demand and supply to customize the price for a service. Airlines, hotels, cruise ships, and car rental companies frequently use it. American Airlines estimates that yield management pricing produces an annual revenue that exceeds $500 million.[9]

LEARNING REVIEW

14-1. In pricing a new product, what circumstances might support skimming or penetration pricing?

14-2. What is odd-even pricing?

Cost-Oriented Pricing Approaches

With cost-oriented approaches, a price setter stresses the cost side of the pricing problem, not the demand side. Price is set by looking at the production and marketing costs and then adding enough to cover direct expenses, overhead, and profit.

Standard Markup Pricing Managers of supermarkets and other retail stores have such a large number of products that estimating the demand for each product as a means of setting price is impossible. Therefore, they use **standard markup pricing**, which entails adding a fixed percentage to the cost of all items in a specific product class. This percentage markup varies depending on the type of retail store (such as furniture, clothing, or grocery) and the product involved. High-volume products usually have smaller markups than low-volume products.

Supermarkets such as Kroger and Safeway have different markups for staple items and discretionary items. The markup on staple items such as sugar, flour, and dairy products varies from 10 percent to 23 percent. Markups on discretionary items like snack foods and candy range from 27 percent to 47 percent. These markups must cover all of the expenses of the store, pay for overhead costs, and contribute something to profits. Although these markups may appear very large, they result in only a 1 percent profit on sales revenue, assuming the supermarket is operating efficiently.

What standard markups are used for the soft drinks, candy, and popcorn at your local movie theater? Read the text to find out.
Andresr/Getty Images

By comparison, consider the markups on snacks and beverages purchased at your local movie theater. The markup is 593 percent on soft drinks, 104 percent on candy bars, and 806 percent on popcorn. These markups might sound high, but consider the consequences. "If we didn't charge as much for concessions as we did, a movie ticket would cost $20," says the CEO of Regal Entertainment, the largest U.S. theater chain.[10]

Cost-Plus Pricing Many manufacturing, professional services, and construction firms use a variation of standard markup pricing. **Cost-plus pricing** involves summing the total unit cost of providing a product or service and adding a specific

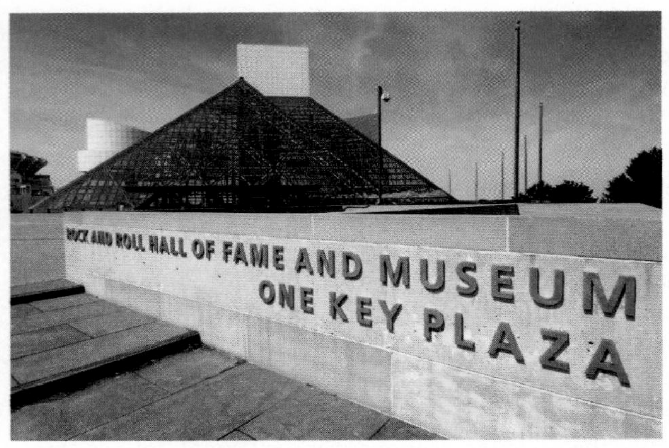

How was the price of the Rock and Roll Hall of Fame and Museum determined? Read the text to find out.
Ilene MacDonald/Alamy Stock Photo

amount to the cost to arrive at a price. Cost-plus pricing generally assumes two forms. With *cost-plus percentage-of-cost pricing*, a fixed percentage is added to the total unit cost. This is often used to price one- or few-of-a-kind items, as when an architectural firm charges a percentage of the construction costs of, say, the $92 million Rock and Roll Hall of Fame and Museum in Cleveland, Ohio.

In buying highly technical, few-of-a-kind products such as hydroelectric power plants or space satellites, governments have found that general contractors are reluctant to specify a formal, fixed price for the procurement. Therefore, they use *cost-plus fixed-fee pricing*, which means that a supplier is reimbursed for all costs, regardless of what they turn out to be, but is allowed only a fixed fee as profit that is independent of the final cost of the project. For example, suppose the National Aeronautics and Space Administration agreed to pay Lockheed Martin $4 billion as the cost for its Orion lunar spacecraft and agreed to a $6.5 billion fee for providing the lunar spacecraft. Even if Lockheed Martin's cost increased to $7 billion for the lunar spacecraft, its fee would remain at $6.5 billion.

Cost-plus pricing is the most commonly used method to set prices for business products. Increasingly, however, this method is finding favor among business-to-business marketers in the service sector. For example, the rising cost of legal fees has prompted some law firms to adopt a cost-plus pricing approach. Rather than billing business clients on an hourly basis, lawyers and their clients agree on a fixed fee based on expected costs plus a profit for the law firm. Many advertising agencies now use this approach. Here, the client agrees to pay the agency a fee based on the cost of its work plus some agreed-on profit, which is often a percentage of total cost.

The Caplow Company specializes in high-quality custom framing of fine art and photography as well as antique frame restoration for its customers. Read the text to find out how it would apply various target pricing approaches.
Jane Westerlund

Experience Curve Pricing The method of **experience curve pricing** is based on the learning effect, which holds that the unit cost of many products and services declines by 10 to 30 percent each time a firm's experience at producing and selling them doubles. This reduction is regular or predictable enough that the average cost per unit can be mathematically estimated. For example, if the firm estimates that costs will fall by 15 percent each time volume doubles, then the cost of the 100th unit produced and sold will be about 85 percent of the cost of the 50th unit, and the cost of the 200th unit will be 85 percent of the cost of the 100th unit. Therefore, if the cost of the 50th unit is $100, then the cost of the 100th unit will be $85, the cost of the 200th unit will be $72.25, and so on. Because prices often follow costs with experience curve pricing, a rapid decline in price is possible.

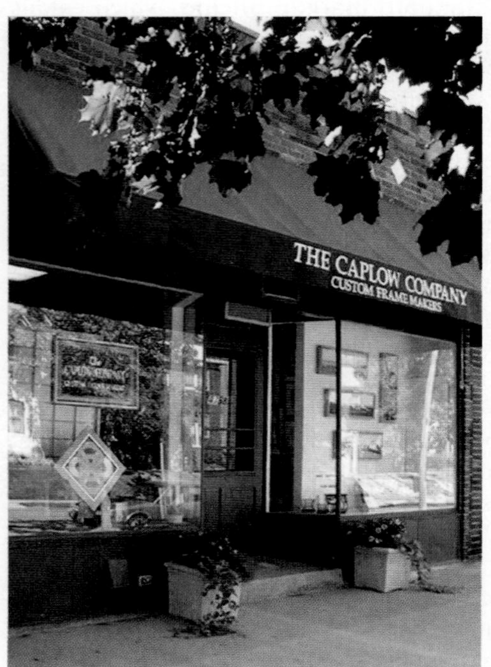

Japanese, Korean, and U.S. firms in the electronics industry often adopt this pricing approach. This cost-based pricing approach complements the demand-based pricing strategy of skimming followed by penetration pricing. For example, Sony, Samsung, LG, and other television manufacturers use experience curve pricing for HDTV sets. Consumers benefit because prices decline as cumulative sales volume grows. In fact, HDTV prices have fallen by over 40 percent in the past decade.[11]

Profit-Oriented Pricing Approaches

A price setter may choose to balance both revenues and costs to set price using profit-oriented approaches. These might either involve setting a target of a specific dollar volume of profit or expressing this target profit as a percentage of sales or investment.

Target Profit Pricing A firm that sets an annual target of a specific dollar volume of profit is using a **target profit pricing** approach. As the owner of The Caplow Company, a picture framing shop, suppose you decide to use target profit pricing to establish a price for a typical framed picture. First, you need to make some assumptions, such as:

- Variable cost is a constant $22 per unit.
- Fixed cost is a constant $26,000.
- Demand is insensitive to price up to $60 per unit.
- A target profit of $7,000, at an annual volume of 1,000 units (framed pictures).

You can then calculate price as follows:

$$\begin{aligned}
\text{Profit} &= \text{Total revenue} - \text{Total cost} \\
\text{Profit} &= (\text{P} \times \text{Q}) - [\text{FC} + (\text{UVC} \times \text{Q})] \\
\$7{,}000 &= (\text{P} \times 1{,}000) - [\$26{,}000 + (\$22 \times 1{,}000)] \\
\$7{,}000 &= 1{,}000\text{P} - (\$26{,}000 + \$22{,}000) \\
1{,}000\text{P} &= \$7{,}000 + \$48{,}000 \\
\text{P} &= \$55
\end{aligned}$$

Note that a critical assumption is that this higher average price for a framed picture will not cause the demand to fall.

Target Return-on-Sales Pricing A shortcoming with target profit pricing is that although it is simple and the target involves only a specific dollar volume, there is no benchmark of sales or investment used to show how much of the firm's effort is needed to achieve the target. Firms such as supermarket chains often use **target return-on-sales pricing** to set typical prices that will give them a profit that is a specified percentage, say, 1 percent, of the sales volume. Suppose, as the owner of The Caplow Company, you decide to use target return-on-sales pricing. To establish a price for a typical framed picture, you would begin by making the same first three assumptions shown previously. However, for the fourth assumption, your target is now a 20 percent return on sales at an annual volume of 1,250 units. This results in the following price:

$$\begin{aligned}
\text{Target return on sales} &= \frac{\text{Target profit}}{\text{Total revenue}} \\
20\% &= \frac{\text{TR} - \text{TC}}{\text{TR}} \\
0.20 &= \frac{\text{P} \times \text{Q} - [\text{FC} + (\text{UVC} \times \text{Q})]}{\text{TR}} \\
0.20 &= \frac{\text{P} \times 1{,}250 - [\$26{,}000 + (\$22 \times 1{,}250)]}{\text{P} \times 1{,}250} \\
\text{P} &= \$53.50
\end{aligned}$$

So at a price of $53.50 per unit and an annual quantity of 1,250 frames,

$$\begin{aligned}
\text{TR} &= \text{P} \times \text{Q} = \$53.50 \times 1{,}250 = \$66{,}875 \\
\text{TC} &= \text{FC} + (\text{UVC} \times \text{Q}) = \$26{,}000 + (\$22 \times 1{,}250) = \$53{,}500 \\
\text{Profit} &= \text{TR} - \text{TC} = \$66{,}875 - \$53{,}500 = \$13{,}375
\end{aligned}$$

As a check,

$$\text{Target return on sales} = \frac{\text{Target profit}}{\text{Total revenue}} = \frac{\$13{,}375}{\$66{,}875} = 20\%$$

Target Return-on-Investment Pricing Large, publicly owned corporations and many public utilities set annual return-on-investment (ROI) targets such as an ROI of 20 percent. **Target return-on-investment pricing** is a method of setting prices to achieve this target.

As the owner of The Caplow Company, suppose you decide to set a target ROI of 10 percent, which is twice that achieved the previous year. You consider raising the average price of a framed picture to $54 or $58—up from last year's average of $50. To do this, you might improve product quality by offering better frames and higher-quality matting. This is likely to increase the cost, but higher prices will probably offset the decreased revenue from the lower number of units you are likely to sell next year.

To handle this wide variety of assumptions, managers use spreadsheets to project operating statements based on a set of assumptions. Figure 14–5 shows the results of a spreadsheet simulation, with assumptions shown at the top and the projected results at the bottom. A previous year's operating statement results are shown in the column headed "Last Year." The assumptions and spreadsheet results for four different sets of assumptions are shown in columns A, B, C, and D.

In choosing a price or another action using spreadsheet results, a manager must (1) study the results of the simulation projections and (2) assess the realism of the assumptions underlying each set of projections. For example, as the owner of The Caplow Company, you would look at the bottom row of Figure 14–5 and see that all four spreadsheet simulations exceed the after-tax target ROI of 10 percent. But after more thought, you might decide that it would be more realistic to set an average price of $58 per unit, allow the unit variable cost to increase by 20 percent to account for more expensive framing and matting, and settle for the same unit sales as the 1,000 units sold last year. Therefore, you would select simulation

FIGURE 14–5
Results of a spreadsheet simulation used to select a price that will achieve a target return on investment.

			SPREADSHEET SIMULATION			
Assumptions or Results	**Financial Element**	**Last Year**	**A**	**B**	**C**	**D**
ASSUMPTIONS	Price per unit (P)	$50	$54	$54	$58	$58
	Units sold (Q)	1,000	1,200	1,100	1,100	1,000
	Change in unit variable cost (UVC)	0%	+10%	+10%	+20%	+20%
	Unit variable cost	$22.00	$24.20	$24.20	$26.20	$26.40
	Total expenses	$8,000	Same	Same	Same	Same
	Owner's salary	$18,000	Same	Same	Same	Same
	Investment	$20,000	Same	Same	Same	Same
	State and federal taxes	50%	Same	Same	Same	Same
SPREADSHEET RESULTS	Net sales (P × Q)	$50,000	$64,800	$59,400	$63,800	$58,000
	Less: COGS (Q × UVC)	$22,000	$29,040	$26,620	$29,040	$26,400
	Gross margin	$28,000	$35,760	$32,780	$34,760	$31,600
	Less: Total expenses	$26,000	$26,000	$26,000	$26,000	$26,000
	Net profit before taxes	$2,000	$9,760	$6,780	$8,760	$5,600
	Less: Taxes	$1,000	$4,880	$3,390	$4,380	$2,800
	Net profit after taxes	$1,000	$4,880	$3,390	$4,380	$2,800
	Investment	$20,000	$20,000	$20,000	$20,000	$20,000
	Return on investment	5.0%	24.4%	17.0%	21.9%	14.0%

D in this spreadsheet approach to target ROI pricing, settling on a goal of 14 percent after-tax ROI.

Has Red Bull's price premium among energy-drink brands sold in convenience stores increased or decreased? The Applying Marketing Metrics box answers this question.
McGraw-Hill Education

Competition-Oriented Pricing Approaches

Rather than emphasize demand, cost, or profit factors, a price setter can stress what "the market" is doing by using competition-oriented approaches.

Customary Pricing For some products where tradition, a standardized channel of distribution, or other competitive factors dictate the price, **customary pricing** is used. For example, tradition prevails in the pricing of Swatch watches. The $50 customary price for the basic model has changed little in 10 years. Candy bars offered through standard vending machines have a customary price of $1. A significant departure from this price may result in a loss of sales for the manufacturer. Hershey changes the amount of chocolate in its candy bars depending on the price of raw chocolate rather than varying its customary retail price so that it can continue selling through vending machines.

Above-, At-, or Below-Market Pricing For most products, it is difficult to identify a specific market price for a product or product class. Still, marketing managers often have a subjective feel for the competitors' price or market price. Using this benchmark, they then may deliberately choose a strategy of **above-, at-, or below-market pricing**.

Among watch manufacturers, Rolex takes pride in emphasizing that it makes one of the most expensive watches you can buy, a clear example of above-market pricing. Manufacturers of national brands of clothing such as Hart Schaffner Marx and Christian Dior and retailers such as Neiman Marcus deliberately set premium prices for their products.

Revlon cosmetics and Arrow brand shirts are generally priced "at market." As such, they also provide a reference price for competitors that use above- and below-market pricing.

A number of firms use below-market pricing. Manufacturers and retailers that offer private brands of products ranging from peanut butter to shampoo deliberately set prices for these products about 8 to 10 percent below the prices of nationally branded competitive products such as Skippy peanut butter and Vidal Sassoon shampoo. Below-market pricing also exists in business-to-business marketing. Hewlett-Packard, for instance, initially priced its office personal computers below those of competitors to promote a value image among corporate buyers.[12]

Companies use a "price premium" to assess whether their products and brands are above, at, or below the market. An illustration of how the price premium measure is calculated, displayed, and interpreted appears in the Applying Marketing Metrics box on the next page.[13]

Loss-Leader Pricing For a special promotion, retail stores deliberately sell a product below its customary price to attract attention to it. The purpose of this **loss-leader pricing** is not to increase sales but to attract customers in hopes they will buy other products as well, particularly the discretionary items with large markups. For example, supermarkets often use milk as a loss leader.

LEARNING REVIEW

14-3. What is standard markup pricing?

14-4. What profit-based pricing approach should a manager use if he or she wants to reflect the percentage of the firm's resources used in obtaining the profit?

14-5. What is the purpose of loss-leader pricing when used by a retail firm?

Applying Marketing Metrics

Are Red Bull Prices Above, At, or Below the Market?

How would you determine whether a firm's retail prices are above, at, or below the market? You might visit retail stores and record what prices retailers are charging for products or brands. However, this laborious activity can be simplified by combining dollar market share and unit volume market share measures to create a "price premium" display on your marketing dashboard.

Your Challenge

Red Bull is a leading energy-drink brand in the United States in terms of dollar market share and unit market share (see the table). Company marketing executives have research showing that Red Bull has a strong brand equity. What they want to know is whether the brand's price premium resulting from its brand equity has eroded due to heavy price discounting in convenience stores. Convenience stores account for 60 percent of U.S. energy-drink sales.

A price premium is the percentage by which the actual price charged for a specific brand exceeds (or falls short of) a benchmark established for a similar product or basket of products (such as energy drinks). As such, a price premium shows whether a brand is priced above, at, or below the market. This premium is calculated as follows:

$$\text{Price premium (\%)} = \frac{\text{Dollar sales market share for a brand}}{\text{Unit volume market share for a brand}} - 1$$

Your Findings

Using energy-drink brand dollar and unit market share data for U.S. convenience stores, the Red Bull price premium was 1.25, or 25 percent, in 2018, calculated as follows: (35 percent ÷ 28 percent) − 1 = 0.25. Red Bull's average price was 25 percent higher than the average price for energy-drink brands sold in convenience stores. Red Bull's price premium based on 2017 brand market share data was 1.12, or 12 percent, calculated as follows: (36 percent ÷ 29 percent) − 1 = 0.12. Red Bull's price premium has increased relative to its competitors. Its major competitor, Monster Energy, is priced "at market" since its dollar market share and unit market share in 2017 and 2018 are identical. Other brands are priced "below market" in both years. The price premiums for Red Bull, Monster Energy, and other brands for 2017 and 2018 are displayed in the marketing dashboard.

Your Action

Red Bull has improved its price premium with little erosion in unit volume share, which is favorable news for the brand given evidence of price discounting by other brands. Clearly, Red Bull's brand-building effort, reflected in sponsorships and a singular focus on brand attributes valued by consumers, should be continued.

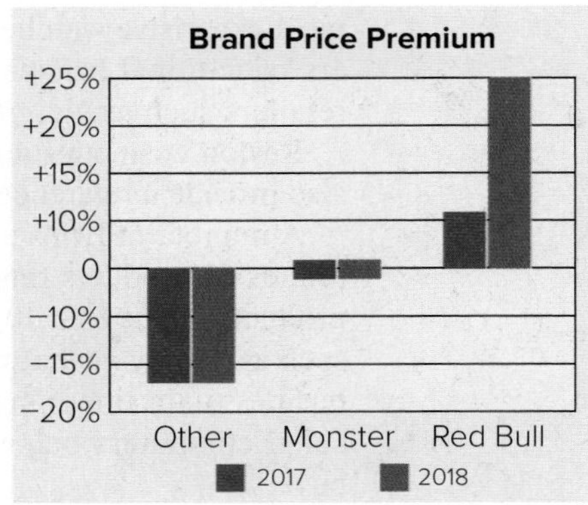

	Dollar Sales Market Share		Unit Volume Market Share	
Brand	**2018**	**2017**	**2018**	**2017**
Red Bull	35%	28%	36%	29%
Monster	30	30	30	30
Other brands	35	42	34	41
	100%	100%	100%	100%

STEP 5: SET THE LIST OR QUOTED PRICE

LO 14-2 Recognize the major factors considered in deriving a final list or quoted price from the approximate price level.

So far, we have covered four of the six steps involved in setting a price—steps 1-3, covered in Chapter 13, and step 4, covered in the preceding section. The result of these four steps is an approximate price level for the product that appears reasonable. But it still remains for the manager to set a specific list or quoted price in light of all relevant factors. In deciding upon the specific price for a product, the manager must choose a price policy; consider company, customer, and competitive effects on pricing; and balance incremental costs and revenues.

VIDEO 14-2
CarMax Ad
kerin.tv/15e/v14-2

Choose a Price Policy

Choosing a price policy is important in setting a list or quoted price. Two options are common—a fixed-price policy or a dynamic pricing policy.

Fixed-Price Policy Most companies use a fixed-price policy. A **fixed-price policy**, also called a *one-price policy*, is setting one price for all buyers of a product or service. For example, when you buy a Wilson Blade 98 tennis racquet from a sporting goods store, you are offered the product at a single price. You can buy it or not, but there is no variation in the price under the seller's fixed-price policy. CarMax uses this approach in its stores and features a "no haggle, one price" price for cars. Some retailers have married this policy with a below-market approach. Dollar Value Stores and 99¢ Only Stores sell everything in their stores for $1 or less. Family Dollar Stores sell everything for $2.

Dynamic Pricing Policy In contrast, a **dynamic pricing policy**, also called a *flexible-price policy*, involves setting different prices for products and services in real time in response to supply and demand conditions. A dynamic pricing policy gives sellers considerable discretion in setting the final price in light of demand, cost, and competitive factors. Yield management pricing described earlier is a form of dynamic pricing because prices vary by an individual buyer's purchase situation, company cost considerations, and competitive conditions. Dell Technologies uses dynamic pricing. It continually adjusts prices in response to changes in its own costs, competitive pressures, and demand from customers, from one segment of the personal computer market to another. "Our flexibility allows us to be [priced] different even within a day," says a Dell spokesperson.[14]

Dynamic pricing has grown in popularity because of increasingly sophisticated information technology. Today, many marketers have the ability to customize a price for an individual on the basis of his or her purchasing patterns, product preferences, and price sensitivity, all of which are stored in company data warehouses.[15] For example, online marketers, like Amazon, described in Chapter 13, routinely adjust prices in response to purchase situations and past purchase behaviors of online buyers. Some online marketers monitor an online shopper's *clickstream*—the way that person navigates through the website. If the visitor behaves like a price-sensitive shopper—perhaps by comparing many different products and prices—that person may be offered a lower price.

Dynamic pricing means that some customers pay more and others pay less for the same product or service. Dynamic pricing is not without its critics. One frequent criticism of dynamic pricing lies in the realm of "surge" pricing, which occurs when a company raises the price of its product or service if there is a spike in demand. Read the Making Responsible Decisions box on the next page to learn about the ethics and economics of surge pricing used by Uber and Lyft and decide where you stand on this practice.[16]

Consider Company, Customer, and Competitive Effects on Pricing

In determining a final list or quoted price, the manager must next assess company, customer, and competitive effects on pricing.

Company Effects For a firm with more than one product, a decision on the price of a single product must consider the price of other items in its product line or related product lines in its product mix. Within a product line or mix there are usually some products that are substitutes for one another and some that complement each other. Frito-Lay recognizes that its Baked Tostitos, Tostitos, and Doritos brands are partial substitutes for one another and its bean and cheese dips and salsas complement the products in its tortilla chip line.

A manager's challenge when marketing multiple products is **product-line pricing**, the setting of prices for all items in a product line. When setting prices, the manager seeks to cover the total cost and produce a profit for the complete line, not necessarily for each item. For example, the penetration price for Sony's PlayStation 4 Pro video game console was probably at or below its cost, but the prices of its video games (complementary products) were set high enough to cover any loss and deliver a handsome profit for the product line.

Making Responsible Decisions

Ethics

The Ethics and Economics of Surge Pricing

Uber and Lyft have changed the way local taxi service operates. Using independent drivers and driver-owned vehicles, both companies serve as intermediaries using digital technology to provide on-demand transportation services to consumers. Nevertheless, Uber and Lyft customers often complain about the practice of "surge" or "prime-time" pricing used by these companies during periods of peak demand. From a classical economics perspective, this form of dynamic pricing makes sense based on supply and demand relationships. Fare increases in periods of high demand—a shift in the demand curve to the right—in turn increase the supply of drivers available for passengers.

Imaginechina/AP Images

From an ethical perspective, supporters of surge or prime-time pricing argue from a utilitarian view that this type of pricing increases the supply of drivers and more people get a ride. Remember from Chapter 4 that utilitarianism focuses on "the greatest good for the greatest number" by assessing the costs and benefits of the behavior, in this case, dynamic pricing.

Critics of surge or prime-time pricing argue that this practice is flagrant price gouging by Uber and Lyft. Where do you stand on the economics versus ethics debate related to surge or prime-time pricing?

Product-line pricing involves determining (1) the lowest-priced product and price, (2) the highest-priced product and price, and (3) price differentials for all other products in the line.[17] The lowest- and highest-priced items in the product line play important roles. The highest-priced item is typically positioned as the premium item in quality and features. The lowest-priced item is the traffic builder designed to capture the attention of the hesitant or first-time buyer. Price differentials between items in the line should make sense to customers and reflect differences in the perceived value of the products offered.

Consider Apple's pricing of its new iPhones in 2019. The iPhone 11 model had a price of $699. The iPhone 11 Pro was priced at $999. The top-of-the-line iPhone 11 Pro Plus was priced at $1,099.

Customer Effects In setting a price, marketers pay close attention to factors that satisfy the perceptions or expectations of ultimate consumers, such as the customary prices for a variety of consumer products. For example, retailers have found that they should not price their store brands 20 to 25 percent below manufacturers' brands.[18] When they do, consumers often view the lower price as a signal of lower quality and don't buy.

Frito-Lay recognizes that its tortilla chip products are partial substitutes for one another. Its bean and cheese dips and salsas complement tortilla chips. This knowledge is used by Frito-Lay in its product-line pricing.
McGraw-Hill Education

Manufacturers and wholesalers must choose prices that result in profit for resellers in the channel to gain their cooperation and support. Toro learned this lesson the hard way when it decided to augment its traditional hardware outlet distribution by also selling its lawn mower and snow thrower product lines through mass merchandisers. To do so, it set mass merchandiser prices far below those for its traditional hardware outlets. Unhappy hardware stores abandoned Toro products in favor of mowers and snow throwers from competitors.

Competitive Effects A manager's pricing decision is immediately apparent to most competitors, who may retaliate with price changes of their own. Therefore, a manager who sets a final list or quoted price must anticipate potential price responses from competitors. Regardless of whether a firm is a price leader or follower, it wants to avoid cutthroat price wars in which no firm in the industry makes a profit.

A **price war** involves successive price cutting by competitors to increase or maintain their unit sales or market share. Price wars erupt in a variety of industries, from consumer electronics to disposable diapers, from soft drinks to airlines, and from grocery retailing to smartphone services. Managers who engage in price wars do so expecting that a lower price will result in a larger market share, higher unit sales, and greater profit for their company. These results may occur. But, if competitors match the lower price, other things being equal, the expected market share, sales, and profit gain are lost. According to an analysis of large U.S. companies, a 1 percent price cut–assuming no change in unit volume or costs–lowers a company's net profit by an average of 8 percent.[19]

Marketers are advised to consider price cutting only when one or more conditions exist: (1) the company has a cost or technological advantage over its competitors, (2) primary demand for a product class will grow if prices are lowered, and (3) the price cut is confined to specific products or customers (as with airline tickets) and is not across the board.

Balance Incremental Costs and Revenues

When a price is changed or new advertising or personal selling programs are planned, their effect on the quantity sold must be considered. This assessment involves a continuing, concise trade-off of incremental costs incurred against incremental revenues received.

Think about these managerial questions:

- How many extra units do we have to sell to pay for that $1,000 advertisement?
- Should we hire three more salespeople or not?

Figure 14–6 uses an example of a picture frame store owner to illustrate the advantages and disadvantages of using incremental analysis to make marketing decisions. The owner in this

FIGURE 14–6
Expected incremental revenue from pricing and other marketing actions must more than offset incremental costs to achieve an incremental profit.

Suppose The Caplow Company is considering buying a series of magazine ads to reach its upscale target market. The cost of the ads is $1,000, the average price of a framed picture is $50, and the unit variable cost (materials plus labor) is $30.

This is a direct application of marginal analysis that an astute manager uses to estimate the incremental revenue or incremental number of units that must be obtained to at least cover the incremental cost. In this example, the number of extra picture frames that must be sold is obtained as follows:

$$\text{Incremental number of frames} = \frac{\text{Extra fixed cost}}{\text{Price} - \text{Unit variable cost}}$$

$$= \frac{\$1{,}000 \text{ of advertising}}{\$50 - \$30}$$

$$= 50 \text{ frames}$$

Unless there are other benefits of the ads, such as long-term goodwill, the company should buy the ads only if it expects picture frame sales to increase by at least 50 units.

example is considering an ad campaign; to go forward with the campaign, the owner must be able to conclude that the ad campaign will more than pay for itself in additional sales. If not, the campaign should not be undertaken. A decision could also be made to increase the average price of a framed picture to cover the cost of the campaign, but the principle still applies: Expected incremental revenues from pricing and other marketing actions must more than offset incremental costs.

The example in Figure 14–6 shows both the main advantage and the difficulty of incremental analysis. The advantage is its commonsense usefulness, and the difficulty is obtaining the necessary data to make the decisions involved. The owner can measure the cost quite easily, but the incremental revenue that will be generated by the ads is difficult to measure. To get a general idea, she might offer $10 off the purchase price with use of a coupon printed in the ad to see which sales resulted from the ad.

STEP 6: MAKE SPECIAL ADJUSTMENTS TO THE LIST OR QUOTED PRICE

LO 14-3
Identify the adjustments made to the approximate price level on the basis of discounts, allowances, and geography.

When you pay $1 for a bag of M&M's in a vending machine or receive a quoted price of $10,000 from a contractor to renovate a kitchen, the pricing sequence ends with the last step just described: setting the list or quoted price. But when you are a manufacturer of M&M's candies or Nike apparel and you sell your product to dozens or hundreds of wholesalers and retailers in your marketing channel, you may need to make special adjustments to the list or quoted price. Wholesalers adjust the list or quoted prices they set for retailers. Retailers, in turn, do the same for consumers. Three special adjustments to the list or quoted price are (1) discounts, (2) allowances, and (3) geographical adjustments (see Figure 14–7).

Discounts

Discounts are reductions from the list price that a seller gives a buyer as a reward for some activity of the buyer that is favorable to the seller. Four kinds of discounts are especially important in marketing strategy: (1) quantity, (2) seasonal, (3) trade (functional), and (4) cash.[20]

Quantity Discounts To encourage customers to buy larger quantities of a product, firms at all levels in the marketing channel offer **quantity discounts**, which are reductions in unit costs for a larger order. For example, a photocopying service such as AlphaGraphics might set a price of 10 cents a copy for 1 to 25 copies, 9 cents a copy for 26 to 100, and 8 cents a copy for 101 or more. Because the photocopying service gets more of the buyer's business and has longer production runs that reduce its order-handling costs, it is willing to pass on some of the cost savings in the form of quantity discounts to the buyer.

Quantity discounts are of two general kinds: noncumulative and cumulative. *Noncumulative quantity discounts* are based on the size of an individual purchase order. They encourage large individual purchase orders, not a series of orders. This discount is used by FedEx to encourage

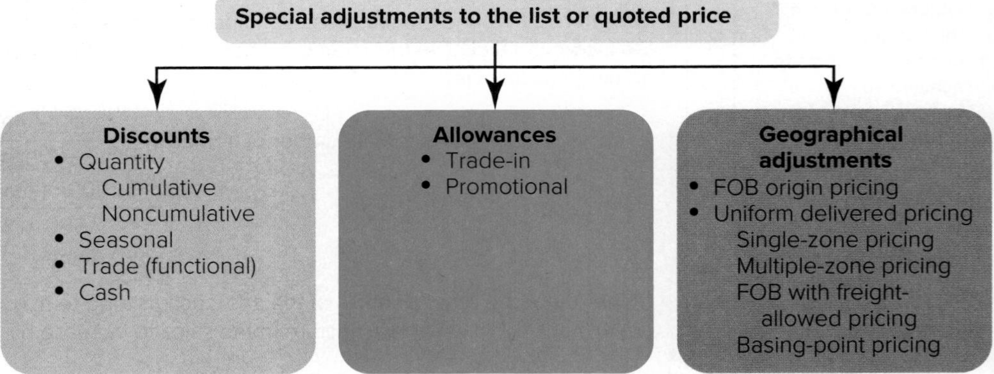

FIGURE 14–7
Three special adjustments to the list or quoted price include discounts, allowances, and geographical adjustments. Each can substantially change the final price.

Discounts are a common adjustment to list prices. They are used to give a buyer a reward for some activity of the buyer that is favorable to the seller, as described in the text.

companies to ship a large number of packages at one time. *Cumulative quantity discounts* apply to the accumulation of purchases of a product over a given time period, typically a year. Cumulative quantity discounts encourage repeat buying by a single customer to a far greater degree than do noncumulative quantity discounts.

Seasonal Discounts To encourage buyers to stock inventory earlier than their normal demand would require, manufacturers often use *seasonal discounts*. A firm such as Honda that manufactures lawn mowers and snow throwers offers seasonal discounts to encourage wholesalers and retailers to stock up on lawn mowers in January and February and on snow throwers in July and August—five or six months before the seasonal demand by ultimate consumers. This enables Honda to smooth out seasonal manufacturing peaks and troughs, thereby contributing to more efficient production. It also rewards wholesalers and retailers for the risk they accept in assuming increased inventory carrying costs and having supplies in stock at the time they are wanted by customers.

Trade (Functional) Discounts To reward wholesalers and retailers for marketing functions they will perform in the future, a manufacturer often gives *trade*, or *functional, discounts*. These reductions off the list or base price are offered to resellers in the marketing channel on the basis of (1) where they are in the channel and (2) the marketing activities they are expected to perform in the future.

Suppose a manufacturer quotes price in the following form: list price—$100 less 30/10/5. The first number in the percentage sequence always refers to the retail end of the channel. The last number always refers to the wholesaler or jobber closest to the manufacturer in the channel. The trade discounts are simply subtracted one at a time. This price quote shows $100 is the manufacturer's suggested retail price; 30 percent of the suggested retail price is available to the retailer to cover costs and provide a profit of $30 ($100 × 0.3 = $30); wholesalers closest to the retailer in the channel get 10 percent of their selling price ($70 × 0.1 = $7); and the final group of wholesalers in the channel (probably jobbers) that are closest to the manufacturer get 5 percent of their selling price ($63 × 0.05 = $3.15). Thus, starting with the manufacturer's suggested retail price and subtracting the three trade discounts shows that the manufacturer's selling price to the wholesaler or jobber closest to it is $59.85 (see Figure 14–8 on the next page).

Traditional trade discounts have been established in various product lines such as hardware, food, and pharmaceutical items. Although the manufacturer may suggest the trade discounts shown in the example just cited, the sellers are free to alter the discount schedule depending on their competitive situation.

Cash Discounts To encourage retailers to pay their bills quickly, manufacturers offer them *cash discounts*. Suppose a retailer receives a bill quoted at $1,000, 2/10 net 30. This means that the bill for the product is $1,000, but the retailer can take a 2 percent discount ($1,000 × 0.02 = $20) if payment is made within 10 days and send a check for $980. If the

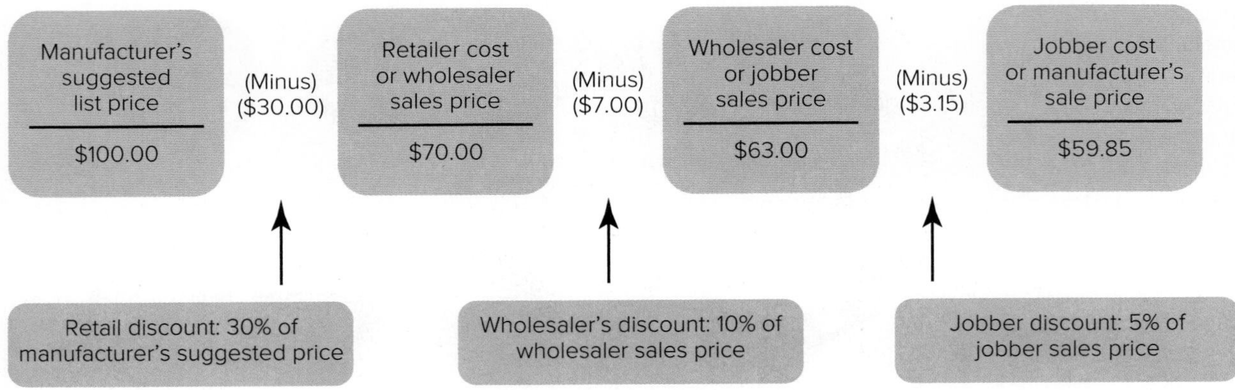

FIGURE 14–8
The structure of trade discounts affects the manufacturer's selling price and the margins made by resellers in a marketing channel.

payment cannot be made within 10 days, the total amount of $1,000 is due within 30 days. It is usually understood by the buyer that an interest charge will be added after the first 30 days of free credit.

Retailers provide cash discounts to consumers as well to eliminate the cost of credit granted to consumers. These discounts take the form of discount-for-cash policies.

Allowances

Allowances, like discounts, are reductions from list or quoted prices to buyers for performing some activity. They include trade-in and promotional allowances.

Trade-in Allowances Apple and Samsung offer a reduction in the list price of their new smartphone models by offering you a trade-in allowance on your current smartphone. A *trade-in allowance* is a price reduction given when a used product is accepted as part of the payment on a new product. Trade-ins are an effective way to lower the price a buyer has to pay without formally reducing the list price.

Promotional Allowances Sellers in the marketing channel can qualify for **promotional allowances** by undertaking certain advertising or selling activities to promote a product. Various types of allowances include an actual cash payment or an extra amount of "free goods" (as with a free case of Red Baron frozen cheese pizzas to a retailer for every dozen cases purchased). Frequently, a portion of these savings is passed on to the consumer by retailers.

Some companies, such as Procter & Gamble, have chosen to reduce promotional allowances for retailers by using everyday low pricing. **Everyday low pricing (EDLP)** is the practice of replacing promotional allowances with lower manufacturer list prices. EDLP promises to reduce the average price to consumers while minimizing promotional allowances that cost manufacturers billions of dollars every year. However, EDLP does not necessarily benefit supermarkets, as described in the Marketing Matters box.[21]

Geographical Adjustments

Geographical adjustments to list or quoted prices are made by manufacturers or even wholesalers to reflect the cost of transportation of the products from seller to buyer. The two general methods for quoting prices related to transportation costs are (1) FOB origin pricing and (2) uniform delivered pricing.

FOB Origin Pricing FOB means "free on board" some vehicle at some location, which means the seller pays the cost of loading the product onto the vehicle that is used (such as a barge, railroad car, or truck). **FOB origin pricing** usually involves the seller's naming the

Marketing Matters

Customer Value

Everyday Low Prices at the Supermarket = Everyday Low Profits—Creating Customer Value at a Cost

Who wouldn't welcome low retail prices every day? The answer is supermarket chains—76 percent of U.S. grocery stores have not adopted this practice. Supermarkets prefer Hi-Lo pricing based on frequent specials where prices are temporarily lowered and then raised again. Hi-Lo pricing reflects allowances that manufacturers give supermarkets to push their products. Consider a supermarket that sells Bumble Bee white tuna. It regularly pays $1.15 for a can of Bumble Bee white tuna ($55.43 ÷ 48 = $1.15), but the allowances reduce the cost to 96 cents. A price special of 99 cents still provides a 3 cent retail markup ($0.99 retail price in ad − $0.96 cost). When the price on tuna returns to its regular level, the store's gross margin on tuna increases substantially on those cans that were bought with the allowance but not sold during the special price promotion.

Everyday low pricing (EDLP) eliminates manufacturer allowances and can reduce average retail prices by up to 10 percent. While EDLP provides lower average prices than Hi-Lo pricing, EDLP does not allow for deeply discounted price specials. EDLP can create everyday customer value and modestly increase supermarket sales—but at a cost. Already slim supermarket chain profits can slip by 18 percent with EDLP without the benefit of allowances as described earlier. Also, some argue that EDLP without price specials is boring for many grocery shoppers who welcome price specials.

EDLP has been hailed as "value pricing" by manufacturers, but supermarkets view it differently. For them, EDLP means "Everyday Low Profits!"

location of this loading as the seller's factory or warehouse (such as "FOB Detroit" or "FOB factory"). The title to the goods passes to the buyer at the point of loading, so the buyer becomes responsible for picking the specific mode of transportation, for all the transportation costs, and for subsequent handling of the product. Buyers farthest from the seller face the big disadvantage of paying higher transportation costs.

Uniform Delivered Pricing When a **uniform delivered pricing** method is used, the price the seller quotes includes all transportation costs. It is quoted in a contract as "FOB buyer's location," and the seller selects the mode of transportation, pays the freight charges, and is responsible for any damage that may occur because the seller retains title to the goods until they are delivered to the buyer. Although they go by various names, there are four kinds of uniform delivered pricing methods: (1) single-zone pricing, (2) multiple-zone pricing, (3) FOB with freight-allowed pricing, and (4) basing-point pricing.

In *single-zone pricing*, all buyers pay the same delivered price for the products, regardless of their distance from the seller. So, although a retail store offering free delivery in a metropolitan area incurs varying transportation costs depending on a customer's location in relation to the store, all customers pay the same delivered price.

In *multiple-zone pricing*, a firm divides its selling territory into geographical areas or zones. The delivered price to all buyers within any one zone is the same, but prices across zones vary depending on the transportation cost to each particular zone and the level of competition and demand within each zone.

With *FOB with freight-allowed pricing*, also called *freight absorption pricing*, the price is quoted by the seller as "FOB plant—freight allowed." The buyer is allowed to deduct freight expenses from the list price of the goods, so the seller agrees to pay, or "absorb," the transportation costs.

Basing-point pricing involves selecting one or more geographical locations (basing point) from which the list price for products plus freight expenses are charged to the buyer. For example, a company might designate St. Louis as the basing point and charge all buyers a list price of $100 plus freight from St. Louis to their location. Basing-point pricing methods have been used in the steel, cement, and lumber industries where freight expenses are a significant part of the total cost to the buyer and products are largely undifferentiated.

Legal and Regulatory Aspects of Pricing

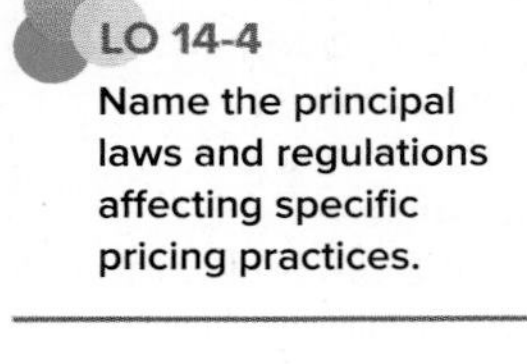

LO 14-4
Name the principal laws and regulations affecting specific pricing practices.

Arriving at a final price is clearly a complex process. The task is further complicated by legal and regulatory restrictions. Five pricing practices have received the most scrutiny: (1) price fixing, (2) price discrimination, (3) deceptive pricing, (4) geographical pricing, and (5) predatory pricing (see Figure 14–9).

Price Fixing A conspiracy among firms to set prices for a product is termed **price fixing**. Price fixing is illegal per se under the Sherman Act (*per se* means "in and of itself"). When two or more competitors explicitly or implicitly set prices, this practice is called *horizontal price fixing*. For example, in a landmark case, six foreign vitamin companies pled guilty to price fixing in the human and animal vitamin industry and paid the largest criminal fine in U.S. history, a hefty $500 million.[22]

Vertical price fixing involves controlling agreements between independent buyers and sellers (a manufacturer and a retailer) whereby sellers are required to not sell products below a minimum retail price. This practice, called *resale price maintenance*, was declared illegal per se in 1975 under provisions of the *Consumer Goods Pricing Act*. Nevertheless, this practice is not uncommon. For example, shoe supplier Nine West was charged with restricting competition by coercing retailers to adhere to its resale prices. As part of its settlement, Nine West agreed to pay $34 million.[23] Although this type of coercive price fixing is illegal per se, manufacturers and wholesalers can set the maximum retail price for their products provided the price agreement does not create an "unreasonable restraint of trade" and is not anticompetitive.

It is important to recognize that a "manufacturer's suggested retail price," or MSRP, is not illegal per se. The issue of legality arises only when manufacturers enforce such a practice by

FIGURE 14–9 Several pricing practices are affected by legal and regulatory restrictions. These restrictions seek to benefit both consumers and companies.

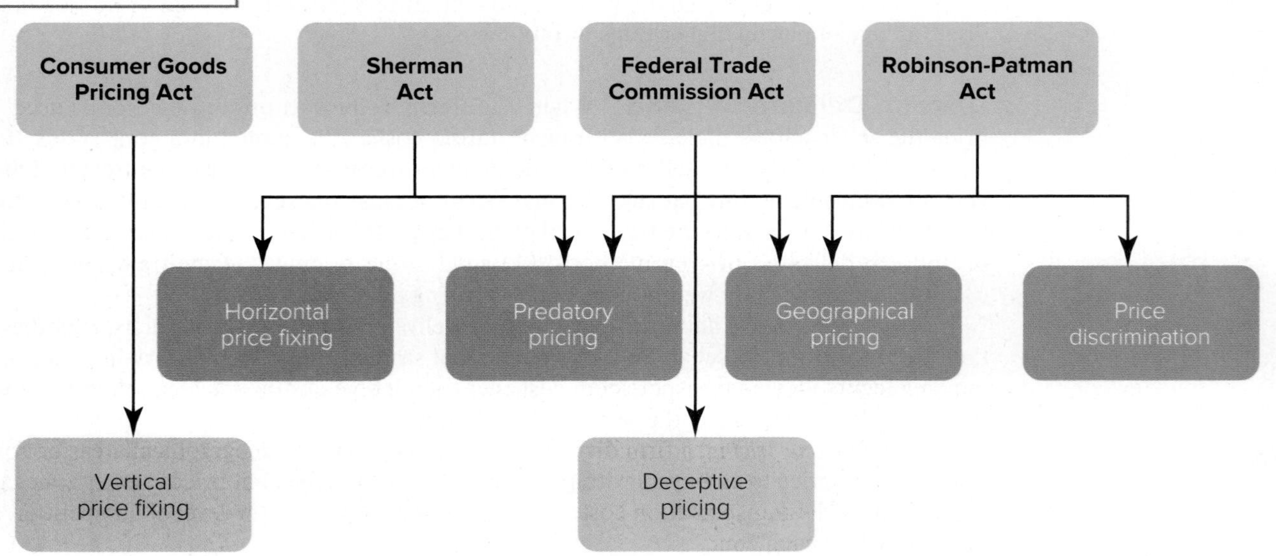

coercion. Furthermore, there appears to be a movement toward a "*rule of reason*" in horizontal and vertical price fixing cases.[24] This rule holds that circumstances surrounding a practice must be considered before making a judgment about its legality. The rule of reason perspective is the direct opposite of the per se rule.

Price Discrimination The Clayton Act as amended by the Robinson-Patman Act prohibits **price discrimination**—the practice of charging different prices to different buyers for goods of like grade and quality. However, not all price differences are illegal; only those that substantially lessen competition or create a monopoly are deemed unlawful. Moreover, "goods" is narrowly defined and does not include discrimination in services.

A unique feature of the Robinson-Patman Act is that it allows for price differentials to different customers under the following conditions:

1. When price differences charged to different customers do not exceed the differences in the cost of manufacture, sale, or delivery resulting from differing methods or quantities in which such goods are sold or delivered to buyers. This condition is called the *cost justification defense*.
2. When price differences result from changing market conditions, avoiding obsolescence of seasonal merchandise, including perishables, or closing out sales.
3. When price differences are quoted to selected buyers in good faith to meet competitors' prices and are not intended to injure competition. This condition is called the *meet-the-competition defense*.

The Robinson-Patman Act also covers promotional allowances. To legally offer promotional allowances to buyers, the seller must do so on a proportionally equal basis to all buyers distributing the seller's products. In general, the rule of reason applies frequently in price discrimination disputes and is often applied to cases involving firms that use dynamic pricing policies.

Buy one, get one free promotions are common. However, these promotions can be viewed as deceptive by the Federal Trade Commission. Read the text to learn when these promotions may be deceptive.
DBurke/Alamy Stock Photo

Deceptive Pricing Price deals that mislead consumers fall into the category of *deceptive pricing*. Deceptive pricing is outlawed by the Federal Trade Commission Act. The FTC monitors such practices and has published a regulation titled "Guides against Deceptive Pricing" to help businesspeople avoid a charge of deception. The five most common deceptive pricing practices are described in Figure 14–10 on the next page. As you read about these practices it should be clear that laws cannot be passed and enforced to protect consumers and competitors against all of these practices. So it is essential to rely on the ethical standards of those making and publicizing pricing decisions.

Geographical Pricing FOB origin pricing is legal, as are FOB freight-allowed pricing practices, providing no conspiracy to set prices exists. Basing-point pricing can be viewed as illegal under the Robinson-Patman Act and the Federal Trade Commission Act if there is clear-cut evidence of a conspiracy to set prices. In general, geographical pricing practices have been immune from legal and regulatory restrictions, except in those instances in which a conspiracy to lessen competition exists under the Sherman Act or price discrimination exists under the Robinson-Patman Act.

Predatory Pricing **Predatory pricing** is the practice of charging a very low price for a product with the intent of driving competitors out of business. Once competitors have been

DECEPTIVE PRICING PRACTICE	DESCRIPTION
Bait and switch	This deceptive practice exists when a firm offers a very low price on a product (the bait) to attract customers to a store. Once in the store, the customer is persuaded to purchase a higher-priced item (the switch) using a variety of tricks, including (1) downgrading the promoted item, (2) not having the item in stock, or (3) refusing to take orders for the item.
Bargains conditional on other purchases	This practice may exist when a buyer is offered "1-Cent Sales," "Buy 1, Get 1 Free," and "Get 2 for the Price of 1." Such pricing is legal only if the first items are sold at the regular price, not a price inflated for the offer. Substituting lower-quality items on either the first or second purchase is also considered deceptive.
Comparable value comparisons	Advertising such as "Retail Value $100.00, Our Price $85.00" is deceptive if a verified and substantial number of stores in the market area do not price the item at $100.
Comparisons with suggested prices	A claim that a price is below a manufacturer's suggested or list price may be deceptive if few or no sales occur at that price in a retailer's market area.
Former price comparisons	When a seller represents a price as reduced, the item must have been offered in good faith at a higher price for a substantial previous period. Setting a high price for the purpose of establishing a reference for a price reduction is considered deceptive.

FIGURE 14–10
Five most common deceptive pricing practices used by businesses. Have you ever witnessed or experienced one or more of these practices?

driven out, the firm raises its prices. This practice is illegal under the Sherman Act and the Federal Trade Commission Act. Proving the practice of predatory pricing is difficult and expensive, because it must be shown that the predator explicitly attempted to destroy a competitor and the predatory price was below the defendant's average cost.

LEARNING REVIEW

14-6. Why would a seller choose a dynamic pricing policy over a fixed-price policy?

14-7. If a firm wished to encourage repeat purchases by a buyer throughout a year, would a cumulative or a noncumulative quantity discount be a better strategy?

14-8. Which pricing practices are covered by the Sherman Act?

LEARNING OBJECTIVES REVIEW

LO 14-1 *Describe how to establish the "approximate price level" using demand-oriented, cost-oriented, profit-oriented, and competition-oriented approaches.*
Demand, cost, profit, and competition influence the initial consideration of the approximate price level for a product or service. Demand-oriented pricing approaches stress consumer demand and revenue implications of pricing and include eight types: skimming, penetration, prestige, price lining, odd-even, target, bundle, and yield management. Cost-oriented pricing approaches emphasize the cost aspects of pricing and include three types: standard markup, cost-plus, and experience curve pricing. Profit-oriented pricing approaches focus on a balance between revenues and costs to set a price and include three types: target profit, target return-on-sales pricing, and target return-on-investment pricing. Finally, competition-oriented pricing approaches stress what competitors or the marketplace are doing and include three types: customary; above-, at-, or below-market; and loss-leader pricing. Although these approaches are described

separately, some of them overlap, and an effective marketing manager will consider several in searching for an approximate price level.

LO 14-2 *Recognize the major factors considered in deriving a final list or quoted price from the approximate price level.*
Given an approximate price level for a product or service, a manager sets a list or quoted price by considering three additional factors. First, a manager must decide whether to follow a fixed-price versus a dynamic pricing policy. Second, the manager should consider the effects of the proposed price on the company, customer, and competitors. Finally, consideration should be given to balancing incremental costs and revenues, particularly when price and cost changes are planned.

LO 14-3 *Identify the adjustments made to the approximate price level on the basis of discounts, allowances, and geography.*
Numerous adjustments can be made to the approximate price level. Discounts are reductions from the list or quoted price that a seller gives a buyer as a reward for some activity of the buyer that is favorable to the seller. These include quantity, seasonal, trade (functional), and cash discounts. Allowances offered to buyers also reduce list or quoted prices. Trade-in allowances and promotional allowances are most common. Finally, geographical adjustments are made to list or quoted prices to reflect transportation costs from sellers to buyers. The two general methods for quoting prices related to transportation costs are FOB origin pricing and uniform delivered pricing.

LO 14-4 *Name the principal laws and regulations affecting specific pricing practices.*
There are four principal laws that affect six major pricing practices. The Sherman Act specifically prohibits horizontal price fixing and predatory pricing. The Consumer Goods Pricing Act makes it illegal for companies to engage in vertical price fixing (also called resale price maintenance agreements). The Federal Trade Commission Act outlaws deceptive pricing. Provisions in this act also address aspects of predatory pricing and geographical pricing. Finally, the Robinson-Patman Act prohibits price discrimination for goods of like grade and quality, covers the use of promotional allowances, and addresses certain aspects of geographical pricing.

LEARNING REVIEW ANSWERS

14-1 In pricing a new product, what circumstances might support skimming or penetration pricing?
Answer: Skimming pricing is an effective strategy when: (1) enough prospective customers are willing to buy the product immediately at the high initial price to make these sales profitable because they are not very price-sensitive; (2) the high initial price will not attract competitors; (3) lowering the price has only a minor effect on increasing the sales volume and reducing the unit costs; and (4) customers interpret the high price as signifying high quality. These conditions are most likely to exist when the new product is protected by patents or copyrights or its uniqueness is understood and valued by consumers. Penetration pricing is an effective strategy when: (1) used after a skimming strategy to appeal to a broader segment of the population and increase market share; (2) many segments of the market are price sensitive; (3) a low initial price discourages competitors from entering the market; (4) unit production and marketing costs fall dramatically as production volumes increase; (5) a firm wants to maintain the initial price for a time to gain profit lost from its low introductory level; and (6) a firm wants to lower the price further, counting on the new volume to generate the necessary profit.

14-2 What is odd-even pricing?
Answer: Odd-even pricing involves setting prices a few dollars or cents under an even number. Psychologically, a $499.99 price feels lower than $500.00, even though the difference is just 1 cent.

14-3 What is standard markup pricing?
Answer: Standard markup pricing entails adding a fixed percentage to the cost of all items in a specific product class. The price varies based on the type of product and the retail store within which it is sold.

14-4 What profit-based pricing approach should a manager use if he or she wants to reflect the percentage of the firm's resources used in obtaining the profit?
Answer: target return-on-investment pricing

14-5 What is the purpose of loss-leader pricing when used by a retail firm?
Answer: Loss-leader pricing involves deliberately selling a product below its customary price not to increase sales but to attract customers in hopes they will buy other products as well, such as discretionary items with large markups.

14-6 Why would a seller choose a dynamic pricing policy over a fixed-price policy?
Answer: A dynamic pricing policy sets different prices for products and services in real time in response to supply and demand conditions. Sellers have considerable discretion in setting the final price in light of demand, cost, and competitive factors. Moreover, sellers can continually adjust prices due to the implementation of sophisticated information technology that gives them the ability to customize a price on the basis of customer purchasing patterns, product preferences, and price sensitivity. A fixed-price policy sets one price for all buyers of a product or service. Consumers can choose to buy or not buy, but there is no variation in the price from the seller.

14-7 If a firm wished to encourage repeat purchases by a buyer throughout a year, would a cumulative or a noncumulative quantity discount be a better strategy?
Answer: Cumulative quantity discounts apply to the accumulation of purchases of a product over a given time period (typically a year) and encourage repeat buying by a single customer to a far greater degree than do noncumulative quantity discounts.

14-8 Which pricing practices are covered by the Sherman Act?
Answer: The Sherman Act prohibits (1) horizontal price fixing, which is when two or more competitors explicitly or implicitly set prices and (2) predatory pricing, which is the practice of charging a very low price for a product with the intent of driving competitors out of business. Once competitors have been driven out, the firm raises its prices.

FOCUSING ON KEY TERMS

above-, at-, or below-market pricing p. 377
basing-point pricing p. 386
bundle pricing p. 372
cost-plus pricing p. 373
customary pricing p. 377
dynamic pricing policy p. 379
everyday low pricing (EDLP) p. 384
experience curve pricing p. 374
fixed-price policy p. 379
FOB origin pricing p. 384
loss-leader pricing p. 377
odd-even pricing p. 372
penetration pricing p. 370
predatory pricing p. 387
prestige pricing p. 371
price discrimination p. 387
price fixing p. 386
price lining p. 371
price war p. 381
product-line pricing p. 379
promotional allowances p. 384
quantity discounts p. 382
skimming pricing p. 370
standard markup pricing p. 373
target pricing p. 372
target profit pricing p. 374
target return-on-investment pricing p. 375
target return-on-sales pricing p. 375
uniform delivered pricing p. 385
yield management pricing p. 373

APPLYING MARKETING KNOWLEDGE

1 Under what conditions would a digital camera manufacturer adopt a skimming price approach for a new product? A penetration approach?

2 What are some similarities and differences between skimming pricing, prestige pricing, and above-market pricing?

3 A producer of microwave ovens has adopted an experience curve pricing approach for its new model. The firm believes it can reduce the cost of producing the model by 20 percent each time volume doubles. The cost to produce the first unit was $1,000. What would be the approximate cost of the 4,096th unit?

4 The Hesper Corporation is a leading manufacturer of high-quality upholstered sofas. Current plans call for an increase of $600,000 in the advertising budget. If the firm sells its sofas for an average price of $850 and the unit variable costs are $550, then what dollar sales increase will be necessary to cover the additional advertising?

5 Suppose executives estimate that the unit variable cost for their DVD recorder is $100, the fixed cost related to the product is $10 million annually, and the target volume for next year is 100,000 recorders. What sales price will be necessary to achieve a target profit of $1 million?

6 A manufacturer of motor oil has a trade discount policy whereby the manufacturer's suggested retail price is $30 per case with the terms of 40/20/10. The manufacturer sells its products through jobbers, who sell to wholesalers, who sell to gasoline stations. What will the manufacturer's sale price be?

7 Suppose a manufacturer of exercise equipment sets a suggested price to the consumer of $395 for a particular piece of equipment to be competitive with similar equipment. The manufacturer sells its equipment to a sporting goods wholesaler who receives 25 percent of the selling price and a retailer who receives 50 percent of the selling price. What demand-oriented pricing approach is being used, and at what price will the manufacturer sell the equipment to the wholesaler?

8 Is there any truth in the statement, "Geographical pricing schemes will always be unfair to some buyers"? Why or why not?

BUILDING YOUR MARKETING PLAN

To arrive at the final price(s) for your offering(s):

1 In Chapter 13, you considered your customers and competitors and set three possible prices. Now, modify those three prices in light of (*a*) pricing considerations for demand-, cost-, profit-, and competition-oriented approaches described in this chapter, and (*b*) possibilities for discounts, allowances, and geographical adjustments.

2 Perform a break-even analysis for each of these three new prices.

3 Choose the final price(s).

VIDEO CASE 14 Carmex (B): Setting the Price of the Number One Lip Balm

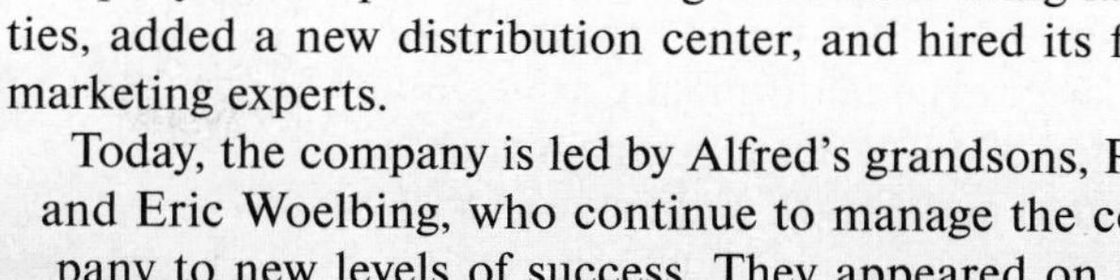

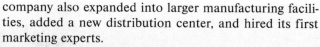

"Carmex is dedicated to providing consumers with superior lip balm formulas–that heal, soothe and protect–while ensuring lips remain healthy and hydrated," exclaims Paul Woelbing, president of Carma Laboratories, Inc.

VIDEO 14-3
Carmex (B) Video Case
kerin.tv/15e/v14-3

It's an ambitious mission, but the company has been extraordinarily successful with its 75-year-old product. Woelbing and his management team at Carma Laboratories can attribute their success to a strong brand, a loyal customer base, a growing product line, financial strength, and an exceptional talent for setting prices that achieve company objectives and still provide value to customers. Even during the recession and periods of slow growth the company has been successful. "In a rough economy, shopping habits change," Woelbing says. "People buy smaller quantities more frequently, but they still need personal care products."

McGraw-Hill Education

THE COMPANY

Carmex was created by Paul's grandfather, Alfred Woelbing, in his kitchen in Wauwatosa, Wisconsin, in 1937. Alfred had an entrepreneurial spirit and experimented with ingredients such as camphor, menthol, phenol, lanolin, salicylic acid, and cocoa seed butter to make the new product. The name didn't have any meaning other than Alfred liked the sound of "Carma" and "ex" was a popular suffix for many brands at the time. He packaged the balm in small glass jars and sold the product for 25 cents from the trunk of his car by making personal sales calls to pharmacies in Wisconsin, Illinois, and Indiana. From the beginning, price and value were important to the product's success. If pharmacies weren't initially interested in Carmex, Alfred would leave a dozen jars for free. The samples would sell quickly and soon the pharmacies would place orders for more!

As the company grew, Alfred's son, Don, joined the business and helped add new products to the company's offerings. For example, in the 1980s Carmex made its first significant packaging change by also offering the balm in squeezable tubes. In the 1990s Carmex became available in stick form, which had been used by two of Carma's major competitors–ChapStick and Blistex. In the 2000s Carmex became available in mint, cherry, and strawberry flavors (see Chapter 8 for a description of the research techniques used to identify new flavors). The company also expanded into larger manufacturing facilities, added a new distribution center, and hired its first marketing experts.

Today, the company is led by Alfred's grandsons, Paul and Eric Woelbing, who continue to manage the company to new levels of success. They appeared on *The Oprah Winfrey Show* to announce the sale of their billionth jar of Carmex. The governor of Wisconsin declared a Carmex commemoration day to celebrate its 75th anniversary. NBA all-star LeBron James became a promotional partner. In addition, *Pharmacy Times* magazine recently named Carmex the number one pharmacist-recommended brand of lip balm for the 15th consecutive year. "We are honored to receive this unprecedented acknowledgement," said Woelbing.

Industry observers estimate that Carma Labs holds approximately 10 percent of the lip balm market. The company distributes its products through major drug, food, and mass merchant retailers, convenience stores, and online in more than 25 countries around the world. The company's most recent products—Carmex Healing Cream and Carmex Hydrating Lotion—represent a significant step from lip care to skin care. The expanded product line, multichannel distribution, growing volume, international trade, and direct competition make pricing decisions even more important today than when Alfred started the business many years ago.

SETTING PRICES OF CARMEX PRODUCTS

"There are many factors that go into what results in the retail price in the store," explains Kirk Hodgdon of Bolin Marketing. As one of the marketing experts who helps Carma Labs with advertising, marketing research, and pricing decisions, Hodgdon uses information about consumer demand, production and material costs, profit goals, and competition to help Woelbing and Carmex retailers arrive at specific prices. The many factors often overlap and lead to different prices for different products, channels, and target markets. "It's a challenge!" says Hodgdon.

Consumers' tastes and preferences, for example, influence the price of Carmex products. Bolin director of marketing, Alisa Allen, explains: "Consumers will tell you that they love Carmex because it's a great value. That doesn't necessarily mean that it's the absolute lowest price. It means that it does so much; they pay a dollar and they get all kinds of benefits from the product above and beyond what they would expect." A single jar of original formula Carmex may sell for $0.99 at mass retailers such as Walmart and Target, and between $1.59 and $1.79 in drug and food retailers such as Walgreens and Kroger. These prices are a good indication of how important it is to understand consumers when setting prices. "There are magic price points for consumers," says Allen, "Any time you can drop a penny off, the consumer responds to that price."

Source: Carma Labs Inc.

Carmex has also introduced a premium lip balm product, Carmex Moisture Plus, at a retail price between $2.49 and $2.99. Moisture Plus is a lip balm that is packaged in a sleek silver tube, offers a slant tip like lipstick, and is targeted toward women. The formula offers women a satin gloss shine and includes vitamin E and aloe for richer moisturization. The upscale package and additional product benefits help Carmex Moisture Plus command a higher price than the traditional Carmex jar and tube.

The cost of the ingredients that make up the Carmex lip balm formulas, the packaging, the manufacturing equipment, and the staffing are also factored into the price of the products. Volumes are a key driver of the cost of packaging and ingredients. For example, Carmex purchases up to 12 million yellow tubes each year for the traditional product, and 2 million sticks each year for the newer Moisture Plus product. The difference in quantities leads to a lower price for the traditional yellow tubes. Similarly, ingredient suppliers, label suppliers, and box suppliers all provide discounts for larger quantities. It is also more efficient for Carmex's manufacturing facility to make a large batch of traditional formula than it is to make a small batch of Moisture Plus. Carmex has also reduced its costs with efforts such as its new environmentally friendly Carmex jar which holds the same amount of lip balm but uses 20 percent less plastic, eliminating 35 tons of raw material costs and the related shipping costs!

Carmex also considers retailer margins when it sets its prices. According to Allen, "We typically sell our product to two types of retailers." There are everyday low pricing (EDLP) retailers such as Walmart, and high-low retailers such as Walgreens. EDLP retailers offer consumers the lowest price every day without discounting through promotions. High-low retailers charge consumers a higher price, but they occasionally discount the product through special promotions which Carmex often supports with "marketing discretionary funds." Carmex typically offers its products at different prices to EDLP and high-low retailers to allow each retailer to achieve its profit margin goals and to account for Carmex's promotion expenditures. When the additional expenditures are considered, however, the cost to both types of retailer is similar.

Finally, Carmex considers competitors' prices when setting its prices. Burt's Bees, ChapStick, Blistex, and many other brands offer lip balm products and consumers often compare their prices to the price of Carmex. "We have found through research that it is extremely important that the price gap is not too great," explains Allen. "If that gap becomes too wide consumers will leave the Carmex brand and purchase a competitor's product." When Carmex was preparing to launch its premium Moisture Plus product it conducted a thorough analysis of similar products to ensure that Moisture Plus was in an acceptable price range.

CARMEX IN THE FUTURE

The original, and now legendary, Carmex formula and packaging will continue into the future with occasional changes to its pricing practices. New products, however, are on the horizon and likely to challenge the perceptions of the traditional products and prices in the Carmex line. Carmex Moisture Plus products, for example, will be offered in limited-edition designs that ask consumers, "Which personality are you?" Paul Woelbing explains the new approach:

> Lip care is an important component of a daily beauty regimen and consumers need a product they can rely on that protects and serves as an important foundation. The goal of the new Carmex Moisture Plus line is to offer our consumers a hard-working lip balm line that represents and reflects their unique style.

Some of the new styles include: *Chic* in houndstooth, *Fab* in a groovy retro look, *Adventurous* in a leopard print, and *Whimsical* in an art deco design.

"We are so excited about the future of Carmex," says Hodgdon. "We are planning new products, we have new plans for retailers, and the future is nothing but bright!"[25]

Questions

1 Which of the four approaches to setting a price does Carmex use for its products? Should one approach be used exclusively?

2 Why do many Carmex product prices end in "9"? What type of pricing is this called? What should happen to demand when this approach is used?

3 Should cost be a factor in Carmex's prices? What do you think is a reasonable markup for Carmex and for its retailers?

4 What is the difference between an EDLP retailer and a high-low retailer? Why does Carmex charge them different prices?

5 Conduct an online search of lip balm products and compare the price of a Carmex product with three similar products from competitors. How do you think the competitors are setting their prices?

Chapter Notes

1. This example is based on information and data contained in "Amazon Pricing Rewrites Publishing by Pushing Its Own Books," *The Wall Street Journal*, January 17, 2019, pp. A1, A8; "The State of Ebooks 2019" www.econtentmag.com, January 18, 2019; and Lin Hao and Ming Fan, "An Analysis of Pricing Models in the Electronic Book Market," *MIS Quarterly* 38, no. 4 (2014), pp. 1017–32.
2. The conditions favoring skimming versus penetration pricing are described in Kent B. Monroe, *Pricing: Making Profitable Decisions*, 3rd ed. (Burr Ridge, IL: McGraw-Hill/Irwin, 2003).
3. Jean-Noel Kapferer, *The New Strategic Brand Management: Advanced Insights and Strategic Thinking*, 5th ed. (London: Kogan Page Ltd., 2012).
4. Kapferer, *The New Strategic Brand Management*.
5. "Premium AA Alkaline Batteries," *Consumer Reports*, March 21, 2002, p. 54; Kemp Powers, "Assault and Batteries," *Forbes*, September 4, 2000, pp. 54, 56; and "Razor Burn at Gillette," *BusinessWeek*, June 18, 2001, p. 37.
6. Michael Levy and Barton A. Weitz, *Retailing Management*, 10th ed. (Burr Ridge, IL: McGraw-Hill/Irwin, 2019), Chapter 13.
7. "The Psychological Difference between $12.00 and $11.67," www.theatlantic.com, January 30, 2015. For further reading on odd-even pricing, see Mark Stiving and Russell S. Winer, "An Empirical Analysis of Price Endings with Scanner Data," *Journal of Consumer Research*, June 1997, pp. 57–67.
8. Thomas T. Nagle and George Muller, *The Strategy and Tactics of Pricing*, 6th ed. (New York: Routledge, 2018), pp. 243–49.
9. "The Evolution of Airline Revenue Management: Defining the Next Generation Approach," www.sabre.com, May 24, 2017.
10. "We Did the Math: Here's How Much Movie Theaters Mark Up Your Popcorn and Snacks," www.businessinsider.com, April 26, 2015; and "What Popcorn Prices Mean for Movies," *Advertising Age*, May 19, 2008, p. 4.
11. "Can the TV Industry Sustain Falling Prices?" www.ecommercetimes.com, January 30, 2017.
12. "In Lean Times, Big Companies Make a Grab for Market Share," *The Wall Street Journal*, September 5, 2003, pp. A1, A6.
13. "Monster's Energy-Drink Grip Weakens," *The Wall Street Journal*, April 18, 2019, p. B3; and "2018 Convenience Store Sales Data," www.cspdailynews.com, April 21, 2018.
14. "The Promise–and Perils–of Dynamic Pricing," *Knowledge@Wharton*, February 23, 2016.
15. Utpal M. Dholakia, "The Risks of Changing Your Prices Too Often," www.hbr.org, July 5, 2015.
16. "Decoding the Drive to Dynamic Pricing," www.forbes.com, October 15, 2018; and "A Fare Shake," *The Economist*, May 14, 2016, p. 68.
17. This discussion is based on Rafi Mohammed, "The Good-Better-Best Approach to Pricing," *Harvard Business Review*, September–October, 2018, pp. 106–15.
18. Raj Sethuraman and Jagmohan S. Raju, "Private Label Strategies: Myths and Realities," in Venkatesh Shankar and Gregory S. Carpenter, eds., *Handbook of Marketing Strategy* (Northhampton, MA: Edward Elgar, 2012), pp. 318–38; and Akshay R. Rao, "The Quality of Price as a Quality Cue," *Journal of Marketing Research*, November 2005, pp. 401–5.
19. Tim J. Smith, *Pricing Strategy* (Mason, OH: South-West Cengage Learning, 2012). Also see Kevin P. Coyne and John Horn, "Predicting Your Competitor's Reaction," *Harvard Business Review*, April 2009, pp. 90–97.
20. Monroe, *Pricing: Making Profitable Decisions*, Chapters 16 and 17.
21. "Do Shoppers Benefit When Stores Use Everyday Low Pricing?" www.psychologytoday.com, June 27, 2016; and "Everyday Low Prices in Spotlight," www.insiderrretail.com, April 29, 2015.
22. "Cartels: Just One More Fix," *The Economist*, March 24, 2014, p. 64.
23. "Price Fixing," *USA Today*, March 7, 2000, p. C1.
24. "The Rule of Reason as a Bar to Criminal Antitrust Enforcement," www.law.com/newyorklawjournal, December 12, 2018.
25. Carmex (B): This case was written by Steven Hartley and Alisa Allen. Sources: Kristen Scheuing, "The Man Behind Carmex," *Wisconsin Trails*, March/April 2011; "Carmex and Carma Laboratories: *Pharmacy Times* Names Carmex Number One Recommended Lip Balm," *IndiaPharma News*, June 21, 2013; "New Lip Balm Offers Sun Protection While Drenching Lips in Moisture," *Postmedia Breaking News*, May 21, 2013; Carma Laboratories website, www.mycarmex.com, accessed September 2, 2013; and interviews with Bolin Media personnel.

APPENDIX B

FINANCIAL ASPECTS OF MARKETING

Basic concepts from accounting and finance provide valuable tools for marketing executives. This appendix describes an actual company's use of accounting and financial concepts and illustrates how they assist the owner in making marketing decisions.

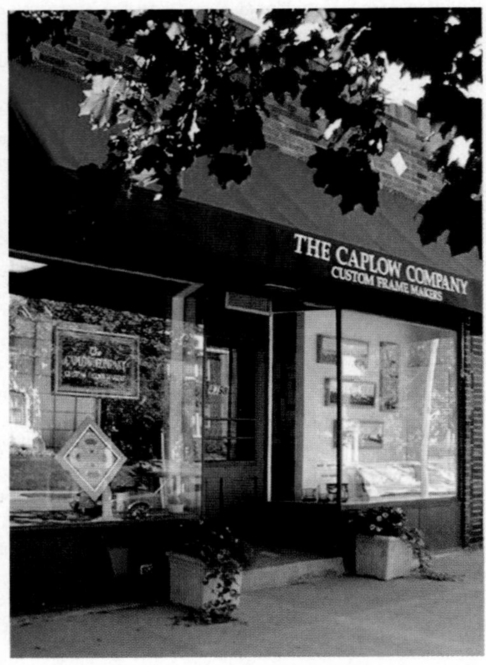

The Caplow Company specializes in high-quality custom framing of fine art and photography as well as antique frame restoration for its customers. Read the text to find out how it would apply various target pricing approaches.
Jane Westerlund

THE CAPLOW COMPANY

An accomplished artist and calligrapher, Jane Westerlund decided to apply some of her experience to the picture framing business in Minneapolis, Minnesota. She bought an existing retail frame store, The Caplow Company, from a friend who owned the business and wanted to retire. She avoided the do-it-yourself end of the framing business and chose three kinds of business activities: (1) cutting the frame, mats, and glass for customers who brought in their own pictures or prints to be framed; (2) selling prints and posters that she had purchased from wholesalers; and (3) restoring high-quality frames and paintings.

To understand how accounting, finance, and marketing relate to one another, let's analyze (1) the operating statement for her frame shop, (2) some general ratios of interest that are derived from the operating statement, and (3) some ratios that pertain specifically to her pricing decisions.

The Operating Statement

The *operating statement* (also called an *income statement* or *profit-and-loss statement*) summarizes the profitability of a business firm for a specific time period, usually a month, quarter, or year. The title of the operating statement for The Caplow Company shows it is for a one-year period (Figure B-1). The purpose of an operating statement is to show the profit of the firm and the revenues and expenses that led to that profit. This information tells the owner or manager what has happened in the past and suggests actions to improve future profitability.

The left side of Figure B-1 shows that there are three key elements to all operating statements: (1) sales of the firm's products and services, (2) costs incurred in making and selling these products and services, and (3) profit or loss, which is the difference between sales and costs.

Sales Elements The sales elements of Figure B-1 have four terms that need explanation:

- *Gross sales* represent the total amount billed to customers. Dissatisfied customers or errors may reduce the gross sales through returns or allowances.
- *Returns* occur when a customer gives the item purchased back to the seller, who either refunds the

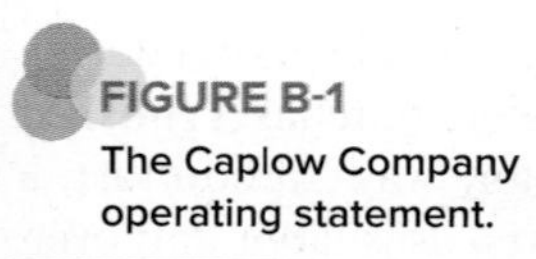

FIGURE B-1
The Caplow Company operating statement.

THE CAPLOW COMPANY
Operating Statement
For the Year Ending December 31, 2020

Sales	Gross sales			$80,500
	Less: Returns and allowances			500
	Net sales			$80,000
Costs	Cost of goods sold:			
	Beginning inventory at cost		$ 6,000	
	Purchases at billed cost	$21,000		
	Less: Purchase discounts	300		
	Purchases at net cost	20,700		
	Plus: freight-in	100		
	Net cost of delivered purchases		20,800	
	Direct labor (framing)		14,200	
	Cost of goods available for sale		41,000	
	Less: Ending inventory at cost		5,000	
	Cost of goods sold			36,000
	Gross margin (gross profit)			$44,000
	Expenses:			
	Selling expenses:			
	Sales salaries	2,000		
	Advertising expense	3,000		
	Total selling expense		5,000	
	Administrative expenses:			
	Owner's salary	18,000		
	Bookkeeper's salary	1,200		
	Office supplies	300		
	Total administrative expense		19,500	
	General expenses:			
	Depreciation expense	1,000		
	Interest expense	500		
	Rent expense	2,100		
	Utility expenses (heat, electricity)	3,000		
	Repairs and maintenance	2,300		
	Insurance	2,000		
	Social Security taxes	2,200		
	Total general expense		13,100	
	Total expenses			37,600
Profit or loss	Profit before taxes			$ 6,400

purchase price or allows the customer a credit on subsequent purchases. In any event, the seller now owns the item again.

- *Allowances* are given when a customer is dissatisfied with the item purchased and the seller reduces the original purchase price. Unlike returns, in the case of allowances the buyer owns the item.
- *Net sales* are simply gross sales minus returns and allowances.

The operating statement for The Caplow Company shows that:

Gross sales	$80,500
Less: Returns and allowances	500
Net sales	$80,000

The low level of returns and allowances shows the shop generally has done a good job in satisfying customers, which is essential in building the repeat business necessary for success.

Cost Elements The *cost of goods sold (COGS)* is the total cost of the products sold during the period. This item varies according to the kind of business. A retail store purchases finished products and resells them to customers without reworking them in any way. In contrast, a manufacturing firm combines raw and semifinished materials and parts, uses labor and overhead to rework these into finished products, and then sells them to customers. All these activities are reflected in the cost of goods sold item on a manufacturer's operating statement. Note that The Caplow Company has features of both a pure retailer (prints and posters it buys that are resold without alteration) and a pure manufacturer (assembling the raw materials of molding, matting, and glass to form a completed frame).

Some terms that relate to cost of goods sold need clarification:

- *Inventory* is the physical material that is purchased from suppliers, may or may not be reworked, and is available for sale to customers. In the frame shop, inventory includes molding, matting, glass, prints, and posters.
- *Purchase discounts* are reductions in the original billed price for reasons such as prompt payment of the bill or the quantity bought.
- *Direct labor* is the cost of the labor used in producing the finished product. For Caplow, this is the cost of producing the completed frames from the molding, matting, and glass.
- *Gross margin (gross profit)* is the money remaining to manage the business, sell the products or services, and provide some profit. Gross margin is net sales minus cost of goods sold.

The two right-hand columns in Figure B-1 between "Net sales" and "Gross margin" calculate the cost of goods sold:

Net sales		$80,000
Cost of goods sold		
Beginning inventory at cost	$ 6,000	
Net cost of delivered purchases	20,800	
Direct labor (framing)	14,200	
Cost of goods available for sale	41,000	
Less: Ending inventory at cost	5,000	
Cost of goods sold		36,000
Gross margin (gross profit)		$44,000

This section considers the beginning and ending inventories, the net cost of purchases delivered during the year, and the cost of the direct labor going into making the frames. Subtracting the $36,000 cost of goods sold from the $80,000 net sales gives the $44,000 gross margin.

Three major categories of expenses are shown in Figure B-1 below the gross margin:

- *Selling expenses* are the costs of selling the product or service produced by the firm. For The Caplow Company there are two such selling expenses: sales salaries of part-time employees waiting on customers and the advertising expense of simple newspaper ads and direct-mail ads sent to customers.
- *Administrative expenses* are the costs of managing the business, which for The Caplow Company include three expenses: the owner's salary, a part-time bookkeeper's salary, and office supplies expense.
- *General expenses* are miscellaneous costs not covered elsewhere; for the frame shop these include seven items: depreciation expense (on equipment), interest expense, rent expense, utility expenses, repairs and maintenance expense, insurance expense, and Social Security taxes.

As shown in Figure B-1, selling, administrative, and general expenses total $37,600 for The Caplow Company.

Jane Westerlund (left) and an assistant assess the restoration of a gold frame for regilding.
Jane Westerlund

Profit Element What the company has earned, the *profit before taxes*, is found by subtracting cost of goods sold and expenses from net sales. For The Caplow Company, Figure B-1 shows that profit before taxes is $6,400.

General Operating Ratios to Analyze Operations

Looking only at the elements of Caplow's operating statement that extend to the right-hand column highlights the firm's performance on some important dimensions. Using operating ratios such as *expense-to-sales ratios* for expressing basic expense or profit elements as a percentage of net sales gives further insights:

Element in Operating Statement	Dollar Value	Percentage of Net Sales
Gross sales	$80,500	
Less: Returns and allowances	500	
Net sales	80,000	100%
Less: Cost of goods sold	36,000	45
Gross margin	44,000	55
Less: Total expenses	37,600	47
Profit (or loss) before taxes	$ 6,400	8%

Westerlund can use this information to compare her firm's performance from one time period to the next. To do so, it is especially important that she keep the same definitions for each element of her operating statement, also a significant factor in using the electronic spreadsheets discussed in Chapter 14. Performance comparisons between periods will be more difficult if she changes definitions for the accounting elements in the operating statement.

Westerlund can use either the dollar values or the operating ratios (the value of the element of the operating statement divided by net sales) to analyze the firm's performance. However, the operating ratios are more valuable than the dollar values for two reasons: (1) the simplicity of working with percentages rather than dollars and (2) the availability of operating ratios of typical firms in the same industry, which are published by Dun & Bradstreet and trade associations. Thus, Westerlund can compare her firm's performance not only with that of *other* frame shops but also with that of *small* frame shops that have annual net sales, for example, under $100,000. In this way, she can identify where her operations are better or worse than other similar firms. For example, if trade association data show a typical frame shop of her size has a ratio of cost of goods sold to net sales of 37 percent, compared with her 45 percent, she might consider steps to reduce this cost through purchase discounts, reducing inbound freight charges, finding lower-cost suppliers, and so on.

Ratios to Use in Setting and Evaluating Price

Using The Caplow Company as an example, we can study four ratios that relate closely to setting a price: (1) markup, (2) markdown, (3) stockturns, and (4) return on investment. These terms are defined in Figure B–2 and explained below.

Markup Both *markup* and gross margin refer to the amount added to the cost of goods sold to arrive at the selling price, and they may be expressed in either dollar or percentage terms. However, the term *markup* is more commonly used in setting retail prices. Suppose the average price Westerlund charges for a framed picture is $80. Then in terms of the first two definitions in Figure B–2 and the earlier information from the operating statement,

Element of Price	Dollar Value
Selling price	$80
Cost of goods sold	$36
Markup (or gross margin)	$44

FIGURE B–2
How to calculate selling price, markups, markdown, stockturn rate, and return on investment.

Name of Financial Element or Ratio	What It Measures	Equation
Selling price ($)	Price customer sees	Cost of goods sold (COGS) + Markup
Markup ($)	Dollars added to COGS to arrive at selling price	Selling price − COGS
Markup on selling price (%)	Relates markup to selling price	$\frac{\text{Markup}}{\text{Selling price}} \times 100 = \frac{\text{Selling price} - \text{COGS}}{\text{Selling price}} \times 100$
Markup on cost (%)	Relates markup to cost	$\frac{\text{Markup}}{\text{COGS}} \times 100 = \frac{\text{Selling price} - \text{COGS}}{\text{Selling price}} \times 100$
Markdown (%)	Ability of firm to sell its products at initial selling price	$\frac{\text{Markdowns}}{\text{Net sales}} \times 100$
Stockturn rate	Ability of firm to move its inventory quickly	$\frac{\text{COGS}}{\text{Average inventory at cost}}$ or $\frac{\text{Net sales}}{\text{Average inventory at selling price}}$
Return on investment (%)	Profit performance of firm compared with money invested in it	$\frac{\text{Net income}}{\text{Investment}} \times 100$

The third definition in Figure B-2 gives the percentage markup on selling price:

$$\text{Markup on selling price (\%)} = \frac{\text{Markup}}{\text{Selling price}} \times 100$$

$$= \frac{44}{80} \times 100 = 55\%$$

And the percentage markup on cost (the fourth definition in Figure B-2) is obtained as follows:

$$\text{Markup on cost (\%)} = \frac{\text{Markup}}{\text{Cost of goods sold}} \times 100$$

$$= \frac{44}{36} \times 100 = 122.2\%$$

Inexperienced retail clerks sometimes fail to distinguish between the two definitions of markup, which (as the preceding calculations show) can represent a tremendous difference, so it is essential to know whether the base is cost or selling price. Marketers generally use selling price as the base for talking about markups unless they specifically state that they are using cost as a base.

Retailers and wholesalers that rely heavily on markup pricing (discussed in Chapter 14) often use standardized tables that convert markup on selling price to markup on cost, and vice versa. The two equations below show how to convert one to the other:

$$\text{Markup on selling price (\%)} = \frac{\text{Markup on cost (\%)}}{100\% + \text{Markup on cost (\%)}} \times 100$$

$$\text{Markup on cost (\%)} = \frac{\text{Markup on selling price (\%)}}{100\% - \text{Markup on selling price (\%)}}$$

Using the data from The Caplow Company gives:

$$\text{Markup on selling price (\%)} = \frac{\text{Markup on cost (\%)}}{100\% + \text{Markup on cost (\%)}} \times 100$$

$$= \frac{122.2}{100 + 122.2} \times 100 = 55\%$$

$$\text{Markup on cost (\%)} = \frac{\text{Markup on selling price (\%)}}{100\% - \text{Markup on selling price (\%)}} \times 100$$

$$= \frac{55}{100 - 55} \times 100 = 122.2\%$$

Consider the use of an incorrect markup base in Westerlund's business. A markup of 122.2 percent on her cost of goods sold for a typical frame she sells gives 122.2% × \$36 = \$44 of markup. Added to the \$36 cost of goods sold, this gives her a selling price of \$80 for the framed picture. However, a new clerk working for her who erroneously prices the framed picture at 55 percent of cost of goods sold sets the final price at \$55.80 (\$36 of cost of goods sold plus 55% × \$36 = \$19.80). The error, if repeated, could be disastrous: frames would be accidentally sold at \$55.80, or \$24.20 below the intended selling price of \$80.

Markdown A *markdown* is a reduction in a retail price that is necessary if the item will not sell at the full selling price to which it has been marked up. The item might not sell for a variety of reasons; perhaps the selling price was set too high or the item is out of style or has become soiled or damaged. The seller "takes a markdown" by lowering the price to sell it, thereby converting it to cash to buy future inventory that will sell faster.

The markdown percentage cannot be calculated directly from the operating statement. As shown in the fifth item of Figure B-2, the numerator of the markdown percentage is the total

Jane Westerlund discusses framing and matting choices with a customer.
Jane Westerlund

dollar markdowns. Markdowns are reductions in the prices of products that are purchased by customers. The denominator is net sales.

Suppose The Caplow Company had a total of $700 in markdowns on the prints and posters that are stocked and available for sale. Since the frames are custom made for individual customers, there is little reason for a markdown there. Caplow's markdown percentage is then:

$$\begin{aligned}\text{Markdown (\%)} &= \frac{\text{Markdowns}}{\text{Net sales}} \times 100 \\ &= \frac{\$700}{\$80{,}000} \times 100 \\ &= 0.875\%\end{aligned}$$

Other kinds of retailers often have markdown ratios several times this amount. For example, women's dress stores have markdowns of about 25 percent, and menswear stores have markdowns of about 2 percent.

Stockturn Rate A business firm is eager to have its inventory move quickly, or "turn over." *Stockturn rate*, or simply *stockturns*, measures this inventory movement. For a retailer, a slow stockturn rate may show it is buying merchandise customers don't want, so this is a critical measure of performance. When a firm sells only a single product, one convenient way to measure stockturn rate is simply to divide its cost of goods sold by average inventory at cost. The sixth item in Figure B-2 shows how to calculate stockturn rate using information in the operating statement:

$$\text{Stockturn rate} = \frac{\text{Cost of goods sold}}{\text{Average inventory at cost}}$$

The dollar amount of average inventory at cost is calculated by adding the beginning and ending inventories for the year and dividing by 2 to get the average. From Caplow's operating statement, we have:

$$
\begin{aligned}
\text{Stockturn rate} &= \frac{\text{Cost of goods sold}}{\text{Average inventory at cost}} \\
&= \frac{\text{Cost of goods sold}}{\dfrac{\text{Beginning inventory} + \text{Ending inventory}}{2}} \\
&= \frac{\$36{,}000}{\dfrac{\$6{,}000 + \$5{,}000}{2}} \\
&= \frac{\$36{,}000}{\$5{,}500} \\
&= 6.5 \text{ stockturns per year}
\end{aligned}
$$

What is considered a "good stockturn" varies by industry. For example, supermarkets have limited shelf space for thousands of new products from manufacturers each year, so they watch stockturn carefully by product line. The stockturn rate in supermarkets for breakfast foods is about 17 times per year, for pet food about 22 times per year, and for paper products about 25 times per year.

Return on Investment A better measure of the performance of a firm than the amount of profit it makes in a year is its *return on investment (ROI)*, which is the ratio of net income to the investment used to earn that net income. To calculate ROI, it is necessary to subtract income taxes from profit before taxes to obtain net income, then divide this figure by the investment that can be found on a firm's balance sheet (which is another accounting statement that shows the firm's assets, liabilities, and net worth). While financial and accounting experts have many definitions for *investment*, an often-used definition is "total assets."

For our purposes, let's assume that Westerlund has total assets (investment) of $20,000 in The Caplow Company, which covers inventory, store fixtures, and framing equipment. If she pays $1,000 in income taxes, her store's net income is $5,400. Therefore, using the return on investment ratio illustrated in the last item in Figure B–2, The Caplow Company's ROI is:

$$
\begin{aligned}
\text{Return on investment} &= \text{Net income/Investment} \times 100 \\
&= \$5{,}400/\$20{,}000 \times 100 \\
&= 27\%
\end{aligned}
$$

If Westerlund wants to improve her store's ROI next year, the strategies she might take are found in this alternative equation for ROI:

$$
\begin{aligned}
\text{ROI} &= \text{Net sales/Investment} \times \text{Net income/Net sales} \\
&= \text{Investment turnover} \times \text{Profit margin}
\end{aligned}
$$

This equation suggests that The Caplow Company's ROI can be improved by raising investment turnover or increasing profit margin. Increasing stockturns will accomplish the former, whereas lowering cost of goods sold to net sales will cause the latter.

Managing Marketing Channels and Supply Chains

LEARNING OBJECTIVES

After reading this chapter you should be able to:

LO 15-1 Explain what is meant by a marketing channel of distribution and why intermediaries are needed.

LO 15-2 Distinguish among traditional marketing channels, digital marketing channels, and different types of vertical marketing systems.

LO 15-3 Describe factors that marketing executives consider when selecting and managing a marketing channel, including legal restrictions.

LO 15-4 Explain what supply chain and logistics management are and how they relate to marketing strategy.

Eddie Bauer: The "Brick, Click, and Flip" Pick for the Active Outdoor Enthusiast

Are you an "active outdoor enthusiast"? If so, Eddie Bauer is the outdoor lifestyle apparel and gear company and brand for you.

Eddie Bauer is an iconic and authentic outdoor lifestyle brand with a 100-year heritage. It can trace its origins to Eddie Bauer, its founder and legendary sportsman, merchant, and apparel designer. He started his company in 1920 in Seattle, Washington, with a promise: "To give you such outstanding quality, value, service, and guarantee that we may be worthy of your high esteem & trade." This promise is now *The Eddie Bauer Creed* and still guides the company.[1]

Eddie Bauer's Multichannel Marketing Strategy

But there is more to Eddie Bauer than the promise of premium-quality products, great value, and superb service. Eddie Bauer has the distinction of being one of the first companies to fully implement a "brick, click, and flip" multichannel strategy. This strategy features an integrated mix of retail stores ("brick"), a website ("click"), and seasonal catalogs ("flip") that responds to where, when, and how its customers wish to browse and buy Eddie Bauer outdoor lifestyle apparel and gear.

Equally important, every effort is made to ensure that customers' apparel and gear shopping and purchase experience is the same across its retail store, website, and catalog marketing channels. According to an Eddie Bauer marketing manager, "We don't distinguish between channels because it's all Eddie Bauer to our customers." Company executives recognize that a "brick, click, and flip" multichannel strategy relies on measuring customer satisfaction across its store, website (www.eddiebauer.com), and catalog consumer touchpoints to better manage, maintain, and improve them.

Eddie Bauer integrates purchasing data from each of its channels to provide insights into evolving customer needs, preferences, and perceived value. This practice often illuminates unique product and market opportunities. For example, Eddie Bauer's CEO recently noted that when the company examined data from its website channel it uncovered that Eddie Bauer had at least 20,000 customers in New York City and thousands more in adjacent areas. This led to opening a retail store in downtown Manhattan, the most densely populated borough of New York City.

Supply Chain Dynamics at Eddie Bauer

Eddie Bauer executives understand and effectively manage supply chain dynamics common with its "brick, click, and flip" multichannel strategy. These executives are

(Top): JHVEPhoto/Shutterstock; (Left): Source: Eddie Bauer, LLC; (Bottom Right) Mike Hruby/ McGraw-Hill Education

responsible for a vast network of apparel and gear suppliers for its 370 Eddie Bauer stores in the United States and Canada and its website and catalog operations.

Managing a multichannel supply chain is a complex task due to the starkly different objectives and priorities of retail stores and online and catalog operations. For example, the supply chain for retail stores focuses on efficiently keeping the products most desired by customers displayed on store shelves, with rapid replenishment from distribution centers. For online and catalog operations, the focus is on providing wider product assortments and even customized products that are shipped from a central distribution center or a supplier's inventory.

Eddie Bauer has mastered the delicate balance between effectiveness and efficiency in managing its multichannel marketing channel supply chain.[2]

This chapter first focuses on marketing channels of distribution and why they are an important component in the marketing mix. It then shows how such channels benefit consumers and the sequence of firms that make up a marketing channel. Finally, it describes factors that influence the choice and management of marketing channels, including channel conflict and cooperation.

The chapter concludes with a discussion of logistics and supply chain management. In particular, attention is placed on the necessary alignment between supply chain management and marketing strategy and the trade-offs managers make between total distribution costs and customer service.

NATURE AND IMPORTANCE OF MARKETING CHANNELS

LO 15-1
Explain what is meant by a marketing channel of distribution and why intermediaries are needed.

Reaching prospective buyers, either directly or indirectly, is a prerequisite for successful marketing. At the same time, buyers benefit from distribution systems used by companies.

What Is a Marketing Channel of Distribution?

You see the results of distribution every day. You may have purchased Lay's potato chips at a 7-Eleven convenience store, a book online through Amazon.com, and Levi's jeans at a Kohl's department store. Each of these items was brought to you by a marketing channel of distribution, or simply a **marketing channel**, which consists of individuals and firms involved in the process of making a product or service available for use or consumption by consumers or industrial users.

Marketing channels can be compared to a pipeline through which water flows from a source to a terminus. Marketing channels make possible the flow of products and services from a producer, through intermediaries, to a buyer. Intermediaries go by various names (see Figure 15–1) and perform various functions. Some intermediaries purchase items from the seller, store them, and resell them to buyers. For example, Celestial Seasonings produces specialty teas and sells them to food wholesalers. The wholesalers then sell these teas to supermarkets and grocery stores, which, in turn, sell them to consumers. Other intermediaries such as brokers and agents represent sellers but do not actually take title to products—their role is to bring a seller and buyer together. Century 21 real estate agents are examples of this type of intermediary.

How Customer Value Is Created by Intermediaries

The importance of intermediaries is made even clearer when we consider the functions they perform and the value they create for buyers.

Important Functions Performed by Intermediaries Intermediaries make possible the flow of products from producers to ultimate consumers by performing three basic functions (see Figure 15–2). Intermediaries perform a *transactional function* when they buy and

FIGURE 15–1
Terms used for marketing intermediaries vary in specificity and use in consumer and business markets.

TERM	DESCRIPTION
Middleman	Any intermediary between the manufacturer and end-user markets
Agent or broker	Any intermediary with legal authority to act on behalf of the manufacturer
Wholesaler	An intermediary who sells to other intermediaries, usually to retailers; term usually applies to consumer markets
Retailer	An intermediary who sells to consumers
Distributor	An imprecise term, usually used to describe intermediaries who perform a variety of distribution functions, including selling, maintaining inventories, extending credit, and so on; a more common term in business markets but may also be used to refer to wholesalers
Dealer	A more imprecise term than *distributor* that can mean the same as distributor, retailer, wholesaler, and so forth

TYPE OF FUNCTION	ACTIVITIES RELATED TO FUNCTION
Transactional function	• *Buying*: Purchasing products for resale or as an agent for supply of a product • *Selling*: Contacting potential customers, promoting products, and seeking orders • *Risk taking*: Assuming business risks in the ownership of inventory that can become obsolete or deteriorate
Logistical function	• *Assorting*: Creating product assortments from several sources to serve customers • *Storing*: Assembling and protecting products at a convenient location to offer better customer service • *Sorting*: Purchasing in large quantities and breaking into smaller amounts desired by customers • *Transporting*: Physically moving a product to customers
Facilitating function	• *Financing*: Extending credit to customers • *Grading*: Inspecting, testing, or judging products and assigning them quality grades • *Marketing information and research*: Providing information to customers and suppliers, including competitive conditions and trends

FIGURE 15–2
Marketing channel intermediaries perform these fundamental functions, each of which consists of different activities.

sell products or services. But an intermediary such as a wholesaler also performs the function of sharing risk with the producer when it stocks merchandise in anticipation of sales. If the stock is unsold for any reason, the intermediary—not the producer—suffers the loss.

The logistics of a transaction (described at length later in this chapter) involve the details of preparing and getting a product to buyers. Gathering, sorting, and dispersing products are some of the *logistical functions* of the intermediary—imagine the several books required for a literature course sitting together on one shelf at your college bookstore! Finally, intermediaries perform *facilitating functions* that, by definition, make a transaction easier for buyers. For example, Macy's issues credit cards to consumers so they can buy now and pay later.

All three functions must be performed in a marketing channel, even though each channel member may not participate in all three. Channel members often negotiate which specific functions they will perform and for what price.

Consumer Benefits Consumers also benefit from intermediaries. Having the products and services you want, when you want them, where you want them, and in the form you want them is the ideal result of marketing channels.

In more specific terms, marketing channels help create value for consumers through the four utilities described in Chapter 1: time, place, form, and possession. *Time utility* refers to having a product or service when you want it. For example, FedEx provides next-morning delivery. *Place utility* means having a product or service available where consumers want it, such as having a Chevron gas station located on a long stretch of lonely highway. *Form utility* involves enhancing a product or service to make it more appealing to buyers. Consider the importance of bottlers in the soft-drink industry. Coca-Cola and Pepsi-Cola manufacture the flavor concentrate (cola, lemon-lime) and sell it to bottlers—intermediaries—which then add sweetener and the concentrate to carbonated water and package the beverage in bottles and cans, which are then sold to retailers. *Possession utility* entails efforts by intermediaries to help buyers take possession of a product or service, such as having airline tickets delivered by a travel agency.

LEARNING REVIEW

15-1. What is meant by a marketing channel?

15-2. What are the three basic functions performed by intermediaries?

MARKETING CHANNEL STRUCTURE AND ORGANIZATION

LO 15-2
Distinguish among traditional marketing channels, digital marketing channels, and different types of vertical marketing systems.

A product can take many routes on its journey from a producer to buyers. Marketers continually search for the most efficient route from the many alternatives available. As you'll see, there are some important differences between the marketing channels used for consumer products and business products.

Marketing Channels for Consumer Products and Services

Figure 15–3 shows the four most common marketing channels for consumer products and services. It also shows the number of levels in each marketing channel, as evidenced by the number of intermediaries between a producer and ultimate buyers. As the number of intermediaries between a producer and buyer increases, the channel is viewed as increasing in length. Thus, the producer → wholesaler → retailer → consumer channel is longer than the producer → consumer channel.

Direct Channel Channel A represents a *direct channel* because the producer and the ultimate consumers deal directly with each other. Many products and services are distributed this way. Many insurance companies sell their services using a direct channel and branch sales offices. The Schwan's Company of Marshall, Minnesota, the largest direct-to-home provider of foods in the United States, uses route sales representatives who sell from refrigerated trucks. Because there are no intermediaries with a direct channel, the producer performs all channel functions.

Indirect Channel The remaining three channel forms in Figure 15–3 are *indirect channels* because intermediaries are inserted between the producer and consumers and perform numerous channel functions. Channel B, with a retailer added, is most common when a retailer is large and can buy in large quantities from a producer or when the cost of inventory makes it too expensive to use a wholesaler. Automobile manufacturers such as Toyota use this channel, and a local car dealer acts as a retailer. Why is there no wholesaler? So many variations exist in the product that it would be impossible for a wholesaler to stock all the models required to satisfy buyers; in addition, the cost of maintaining an inventory would be too high. However, large retailers such as Target, 7-Eleven, Safeway, and The Home Depot buy in sufficient quantities to make it cost effective for a producer to deal with only a retail intermediary.

FIGURE 15–3
Common marketing channels for consumer products and services differ by the kind and number of intermediaries involved.

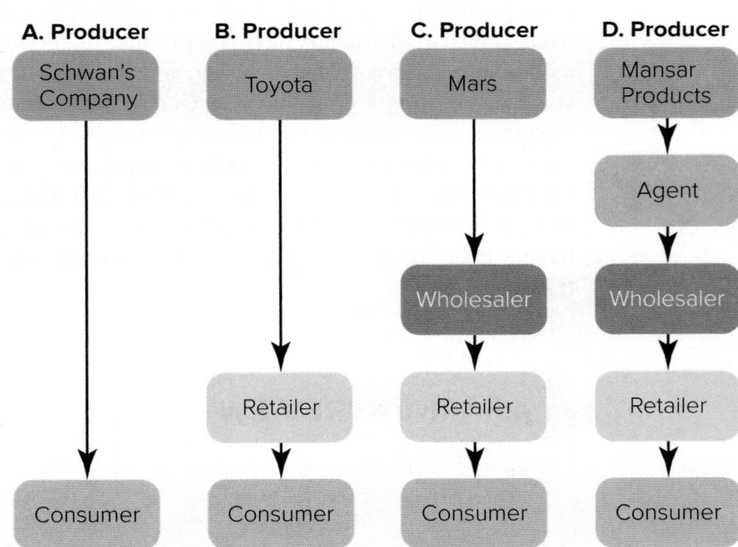

What kind of marketing channel does IBM use for its Watson supercomputer—an artificially intelligent computer system capable of answering questions in natural language? Read the text to find out.
Ben Hider/Getty Images

Adding a wholesaler in Channel C is most common for low-cost, low-unit-value items that are frequently purchased by consumers, such as candy, confectionary items, and magazines. For example, Mars sells case quantities of its line of candies to wholesalers, who then break down (sort) the cases so that individual retailers can order in boxes or much smaller quantities.

Channel D, the most indirect channel, is employed when there are many small manufacturers and many small retailers; in this type of channel, an agent is used to help coordinate a large supply of the product. Mansar Products, Ltd. is a Belgian producer of specialty jewelry that uses agents to sell to wholesalers in the United States, who then sell to many small independent jewelry retailers.

Marketing Channels for Business Products and Services

The four most common channels for business products and services are shown in Figure 15–4. In contrast with channels used for consumer products, business channels typically are shorter and rely on one intermediary or none at all because business users are fewer in number, tend to be more concentrated geographically, and buy in larger quantities.

Direct Channel Channel A in Figure 15–4, represented by IBM's large, mainframe computer business, is a direct channel. Firms using this channel maintain their own salesforce and perform all channel functions. This channel is employed when buyers are large and well-defined, the sales effort requires extensive negotiations, and the products are of high unit value and require hands-on expertise in terms of installation or use. Not surprisingly, IBM's Watson supercomputer, priced at $3 million, is sold and delivered directly to buyers.

Indirect Channel Channels B, C, and D in Figure 15–4 are indirect channels with one or more intermediaries between the producer and the industrial user. In Channel B, an industrial distributor performs a variety of marketing channel functions, including selling, stocking, delivering a full product assortment, and financing. In many ways, industrial distributors are like wholesalers in consumer channels. Caterpillar uses 500 industrial distributors to sell its construction and mining equipment in over 180 countries. In addition to selling, Caterpillar distributors stock 40,000 to 50,000 parts and service equipment using highly trained technicians.

FIGURE 15–4
Common marketing channels for business products and services differ by the kind and number of intermediaries involved.

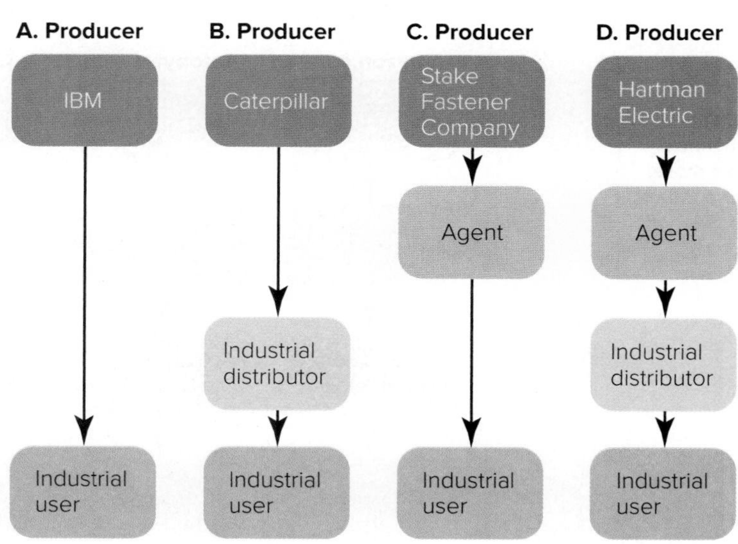

Channel C introduces a second intermediary, an agent, who serves primarily as the independent selling arm of producers and represents a producer to industrial users. For example, Stake Fastener Company, a producer of industrial fasteners, has an agent call on industrial users rather than employing its own salesforce.

Channel D is the longest channel and includes both agents and industrial distributors. For instance, Hartman Electric, a producer of electric products, uses agents to call on electrical distributors who sell to industrial users.

Digital Marketing Channels

These common marketing channels for consumer and business products and services are not the only routes to the marketplace. *Digital marketing channels* also make products and services available for consumption or use by consumers or organizational buyers. A unique feature of these channels is that they combine electronic and traditional intermediaries to create time, place, form, and possession utility for buyers.

Figure 15–5 shows the digital marketing channels for books (Amazon.com), automobiles (Autobytel.com), reservation services (Orbitz.com), and personal computers (Dell.com). Are you surprised that they look a lot like common consumer product marketing channels? An important reason for the similarity resides in the channel functions detailed in Figure 15–2. Electronic intermediaries can and do perform transactional and facilitating functions effectively and at a relatively lower cost than traditional intermediaries because of efficiencies made possible by digital technology. But electronic intermediaries are incapable of performing elements of the logistical function, particularly for products such as automobiles. This function remains with traditional intermediaries or with the producer, as is evident with Dell Inc. and its direct channel.

Many services can be distributed through digital marketing channels, such as car rental reservations marketed by Alamo.com, financial securities by E*TRADE, and insurance by Esurance.com. However, many other services, such as health care and auto repair, still involve traditional intermediaries.

Direct to Consumer and Multichannel Marketing

Many firms also use direct to consumer and multichannel marketing to reach buyers. **Direct to consumer marketing channels** allow consumers to buy products by interacting with various print or electronic media without a face-to-face meeting with a salesperson. Direct marketing channels include mail-order selling, direct-mail sales, catalog sales, telemarketing, interactive media, and televised home shopping (e.g., the Home Shopping Network). Some

FIGURE 15–5
Consumer digital marketing channels look much like those for consumer products and services. Read the text to learn why.

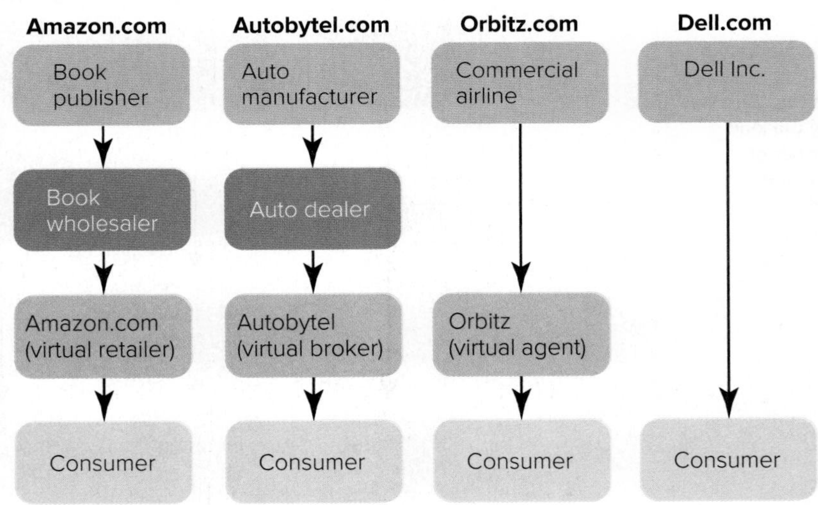

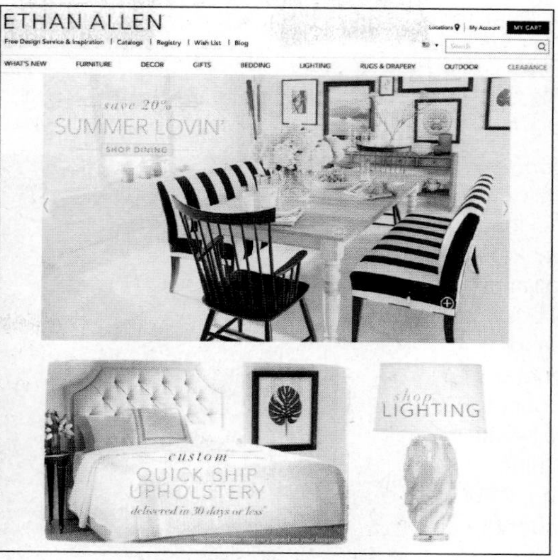

Ethan Allen successfully engages in multichannel marketing through its 300 design centers in the United States and Canada, its website, and its catalogs.

(Left): Rob Crandall/Shutterstock; (Center and right): Source: Ethan Allen Global, Inc.

firms sell products almost entirely through direct to consumer marketing. These firms include L.L.Bean (apparel), Dollar Shave Club (shaving and personal care products), and Newegg.com (consumer electronics). Marketers such as Nestlé, in addition to using traditional channels composed of intermediaries, also employ direct to consumer marketing channels through catalogs and telemarketing to reach more buyers. So does Nike, which sells its products directly to consumers through Nike Direct.

Multichannel marketing, sometimes called *omnichannel marketing*, is the *blending* of different communication and delivery channels that are *mutually reinforcing* in attracting, retaining, and building relationships with consumers who shop and buy in traditional intermediaries and online. Multichannel marketing seeks to integrate a firm's electronic marketing and delivery channels. Few companies have truly mastered multichannel marketing. Not surprisingly, improving multichannel marketing practices is considered a top priority among marketers.[3]

Multichannel marketing also leverages the value-adding capabilities of different channels. For example, retail stores leverage their physical presence through *BOPUS* (customers *b*uy *o*nline and *p*ick *u*p at a *s*tore) and *BORIS* (customers *b*uy *o*nline and *r*eturn purchases *i*n a *s*tore) capabilities. Catalogs can serve as shopping tools for online purchasing, as they do for store purchasing. Websites can help consumers do their homework before visiting a store. As described in the chapter-opening example, Eddie Bauer has done this. While its retail stores still account for the majority of its sales revenue, its website and catalog account for the remainder of company sales.[4]

Dual Distribution and Strategic Channel Alliances

In some situations, producers use **dual distribution**, an arrangement whereby a firm reaches different buyers by employing two or more different types of channels for the same basic product. For example, GE large appliances are sold directly to home and apartment builders while retail stores, including Lowe's home centers, sell to consumers. In some instances, firms pair multiple channels with a multibrand strategy (see Chapter 11). This is done to minimize cannibalization of the firm's family brand and differentiate the channels. For example, Hallmark sells its Hallmark greeting cards through Hallmark stores and select department stores and its Ambassador brand of cards through discount and drugstore chains.

VIDEO 15-1
Honey Nut Cheerios Ad
kerin.tv/15e/v15-1

An innovation in marketing channels is the use of *strategic channel alliances*, whereby one firm's marketing channel is used to sell another firm's products. As an example, Starbucks relies on PepsiCo's expansive distribution network in the United States to sell its cold, ready-to-drink coffee products in supermarkets and convenience stores.

Marketing Matters — Customer Value

Nestlé and General Mills—Cereal Partners Worldwide

Picture alliance/Daniel Kalker/Newscom

Can you say Nestlé Cheerios *miel amandes?* Millions in France start their day with this European equivalent of General Mills's Honey Nut Cheerios, made possible by Cereal Partners Worldwide (CPW). CPW is a strategic alliance designed from the start to be a global business. It combines the cereal manufacturing and marketing capability of U.S.-based General Mills with the worldwide distribution clout of Swiss-based Nestlé. The photo shows Nestlé's Trix cereal (not General Mills) sold in China.

From its headquarters in Switzerland, CPW first launched General Mills cereals under the Nestlé label in France, the United Kingdom, Spain, and Portugal in 1991. Today, CPW competes in more than 130 international markets.

The General Mills–Nestlé strategic channel alliance also increased the ready-to-eat cereal worldwide market share of these companies, which are already rated as the two best-managed firms in the world. CPW is expected to account for more than 10 percent of the projected $55 billion worldwide hot- and cold-cereal market in 2025.

Strategic alliances are popular in global marketing, where the creation of marketing channel relationships is expensive and time-consuming. For example, Kroger, the largest U.S supermarket chain, recently partnered with Alibaba, China's largest e-commerce marketer, to sell Kroger's organic private-branded food products. General Mills and Nestlé have an extensive alliance that spans about 140 international markets from Mexico to China. Read the Marketing Matters box so you won't be surprised when you are served Nestlé (not General Mills) Cheerios when traveling outside North America.[5]

Vertical Marketing Systems

The traditional marketing channels described so far represent a loosely knit network of independent producers and intermediaries brought together to distribute products and services. However, other channel arrangements exist for the purpose of improving efficiency in performing channel functions and achieving greater marketing effectiveness. These arrangements are called vertical marketing systems. **Vertical marketing systems** are professionally managed and centrally coordinated marketing channels designed to achieve channel economies and maximum marketing impact.[6] Figure 15–6 depicts the three major types of vertical marketing systems: corporate, contractual, and administered.

Corporate Systems The combination of successive stages of production and distribution under a single ownership is a *corporate vertical marketing system*. For example, a producer might own the intermediary at the next level down in the channel. This practice, called *forward integration*, is exemplified by Ralph Lauren, which manufactures clothing and also owns apparel shops. Other examples of forward integration include Goodyear, Apple, and Sherwin-Williams. Alternatively, a retailer might own a manufacturing operation, a practice called *backward integration*. For example, Kroger supermarkets operate manufacturing facilities that produce everything from aspirin to cottage cheese for sale under the Kroger label. Tiffany &

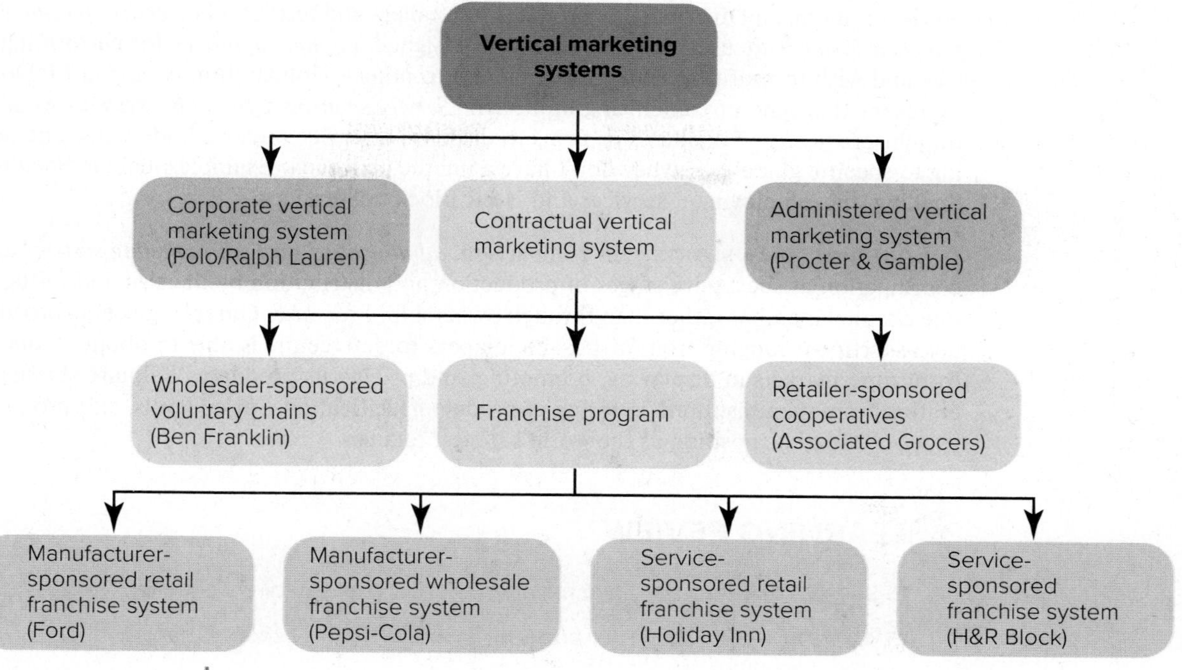

FIGURE 15–6

There are three major types of vertical marketing systems—corporate, contractual, and administered. Contractual systems are the most popular for reasons described in the text.

Co., the exclusive jewelry retailer, manufactures about half of the fine jewelry items for sale through its over 250 specialty stores and boutiques worldwide.

Companies seeking to reduce distribution costs and gain greater control over supply sources or resale of their products pursue forward and backward integration. However, both types of integration increase a company's capital investment and fixed costs. For this reason, many companies favor contractual vertical marketing systems to achieve channel efficiencies and marketing effectiveness.

Contractual Systems Under a *contractual vertical marketing system*, independent production and distribution firms integrate their efforts on a contractual basis to obtain greater functional economies and marketing impact than they could achieve alone. Contractual systems are the most popular among the three types of vertical marketing systems.

Three variations of contractual systems exist. *Wholesaler-sponsored voluntary chains* involve a wholesaler that develops a contractual relationship with small, independent retailers to standardize and coordinate buying practices, merchandising programs, and inventory management efforts. With the organization of a large number of independent retailers, economies of scale and volume discounts can be achieved to compete with chain stores. IGA and Ben Franklin variety and craft stores represent wholesaler-sponsored voluntary chains. *Retailer-sponsored cooperatives* exist when small, independent retailers form an organization that operates a wholesale facility cooperatively. Member retailers then concentrate their buying power through the wholesaler and plan collaborative promotional and pricing activities. Examples of retailer-sponsored cooperatives include Associated Grocers and Ace Hardware.

The most visible variation of contractual systems is franchising. *Franchising* is a contractual arrangement between a parent company (a franchisor) and an individual or firm (a franchisee) that allows the franchisee to operate a certain type of business under an established name and according to specific rules.

Four types of franchise arrangements are most popular. *Manufacturer-sponsored retail franchise systems* are prominent in the automobile industry, where a manufacturer such as Ford licenses dealers to sell its cars subject to various sales and service conditions. *Manufacturer-sponsored wholesale franchise systems* exist in the soft-drink industry. For example, Pepsi-Cola licenses wholesalers (bottlers) that purchase concentrate from Pepsi-Cola and then carbonate, bottle, promote, and distribute its products to retailers and restaurants. *Service-sponsored retail franchise systems* are used by firms that have designed a *unique approach* for performing a service and wish to profit by selling the franchise to others. Holiday Inn, Avis, and McDonald's represent this type of franchising approach. *Service-sponsored franchise systems* exist when franchisors license individuals or firms to dispense a service under a trade name and according to specific guidelines. They don't have a unique approach. Examples include Snelling and Snelling, Inc. employment services and H&R Block tax services.

Administered Systems In comparison, *administered vertical marketing systems* achieve coordination at successive stages of production and distribution by the size and influence of one channel member rather than through ownership. Procter & Gamble, given its broad product assortment ranging from disposable diapers to detergents, is able to obtain cooperation from supermarkets in displaying, promoting, and pricing its products. Walmart obtains cooperation from manufacturers in terms of product specifications, price levels, and promotional support due to its position as the world's largest retailer.

LEARNING REVIEW

15-3. What is the difference between a direct and an indirect channel?

15-4. Why are channels for business products typically shorter than channels for consumer products?

15-5. What is the principal distinction between a corporate vertical marketing system and an administered vertical marketing system?

MARKETING CHANNEL CHOICE AND MANAGEMENT

LO 15-3
Describe factors that marketing executives consider when selecting and managing a marketing channel, including legal restrictions.

Marketing channels not only link a producer to its buyers but also provide the means through which a firm implements various elements of its marketing strategy. Therefore, choosing a marketing channel is a critical decision.

Factors Affecting Channel Choice and Management

Marketing executives consider three questions when choosing a marketing channel and intermediaries:

1. Which channel and intermediaries will provide the best coverage of the target market?
2. Which channel and intermediaries will best satisfy the buying requirements of the target market?
3. Which channel and intermediaries will be the most profitable?

Target Market Coverage Achieving the best coverage of the target market requires attention to the *density*—that is, the number of stores in a geographical area—and type of intermediaries to be used at the retail level of distribution. Three degrees of distribution density exist: intensive, exclusive, and selective.

Intensive distribution means that a firm tries to place its products and services in as many outlets as possible. Intensive distribution is usually chosen for convenience products or services such as candy, fast food, newspapers, and soft drinks. For example, Coca-Cola's retail distribution objective is to place its products "within an arm's reach of desire." Cash, yes cash, is distributed intensively by Visa. It operates over 1.8 million automated teller machines in more than 200 countries.

Exclusive distribution is the extreme opposite of intensive distribution because only one retailer in a specific geographical area carries the firm's products. Exclusive distribution is typically chosen for specialty products or services, such as some women's fragrances and men's and women's apparel and accessories. Gucci, one of the world's leading luxury products companies, uses exclusive distribution in the marketing of its Yves Saint Laurent, Sergio Rossi, Boucheron, Opium, and Gucci brands.

Retailers and industrial distributors prefer exclusive distribution for two reasons. First, it limits head-to-head competition for an identical product. Second, it provides a point of difference for a retailer or distributor. For instance, luxury retailer Saks Inc. seeks exclusive product lines for its stores. According to the company CEO, "It's incumbent on us not to be just a place where you can buy the big brands. Those brands are still critical—the Chanels, the Pradas, the Guccis—but even with those brands, we need to find things unique to us."[7]

Selective distribution lies between these two extremes and means that a firm selects a few retailers in a specific geographical area to carry its products. Selective distribution weds some of the market coverage benefits of intensive distribution to the control over resale evident with exclusive distribution. For example, Dell Technologies chose selective distribution when it decided to sell selected products through U.S. retailers along with its direct channel.[8] According to Michael Dell, the company CEO, "There were plenty of retailers who said, 'sell through us,' but we didn't want to show up everywhere." The company now sells a limited range of its products through Walmart, Sam's Club, Best Buy, and Costco. Dell's decision was consistent with current trends. Today, selective distribution is the most common form of distribution intensity.

The growth of online buying has lessened, but not eliminated, the role of geography in determining target market coverage. The significance of geography in target market coverage is evident in multichannel marketing where a physical retail presence is important. This topic is explored further in Chapter 17 in the discussion on multichannel marketing given the popularity of cross-channel shopping.

Buyer Requirements A second consideration in channel choice is gaining access to channels and intermediaries that satisfy at least some of the interests buyers might want fulfilled when they purchase a firm's products or services. These interests fall into four broad categories: (1) information, (2) convenience, (3) variety, and (4) pre- or postsale services. Each relates to customer experience.

Information is an important requirement when buyers have limited knowledge or desire specific data about a product or service. Properly chosen intermediaries communicate with buyers through in-store displays, demonstrations, and personal selling. Apple has about 500 retail outlets in 25 countries staffed with highly trained personnel to communicate how its products can better satisfy each customer's needs.

Which buying requirements are satisfied by Jiffy Lube? Read the text to find out.

Country Gate Productions/ Shutterstock

Convenience has multiple meanings for buyers, such as proximity or driving time to a retail outlet. For example, 7-Eleven stores, with more than 60,000 outlets worldwide, many of which are open 24 hours a day, satisfy this interest for buyers. Candy and snack-food firms benefit by gaining display space in these stores. For other consumers, convenience means a minimum of time and hassle. Jiffy Lube, which promises to change engine oil and filters quickly, appeals to this aspect of convenience. For Internet shoppers, convenience means that websites must be easy to locate and navigate, and image downloads must be fast. A commonly held view among website developers is the "eight second rule": Consumers will abandon their efforts to enter or navigate a website if download time exceeds eight seconds.[9]

Variety reflects buyers' interest in having numerous competing and complementary items from which to choose. Variety is evident in the breadth and depth of products and brands carried by intermediaries, which enhances their attraction to buyers. Thus, manufacturers of pet food and supplies seek distribution through pet superstores such as Petco and PetSmart, which offer a wide array of pet products and services.

Applying **Marketing Metrics**

Channel Sales and Profit at Charlesburg Furniture

Charlesburg Furniture is one of 1,000 wood furniture manufacturers in the United States. The company sells its furniture through furniture store chains, independent furniture stores, and department store chains, mostly in the southern United States. The company has traditionally allocated its marketing funds for cooperative advertising, in-store displays, and retail sales support on the basis of dollar sales by channel.

Your Challenge

As the vice president of sales and marketing at Charlesburg Furniture, you have been asked to review the company's sales and profit in its three channels and recommend a course of action for 2020. The question: Should Charlesburg Furniture continue to allocate its marketing funds on the basis of channel dollar sales or profit?

Your Findings

Charlesburg Furniture tracks the sales and profit from each channel (and individual customer) and the three-year trend of sales by channel on its marketing dashboard. This information is displayed in the marketing dashboards below.

Several findings stand out. Furniture store chains and independent furniture stores account for 85.2 percent of Charlesburg Furniture sales and 93 percent of company profit. These two channels also evidence growth as measured by annual percentage change in sales. By comparison, the annual percentage sales growth of department store chains has declined, recording negative growth in 2019. This channel accounts for 14.8 percent of company sales and 7 percent of company profit.

Your Action

Charlesburg Furniture should consider abandoning the practice of allocating marketing funds solely on the basis of channel sales volume. The importance of independent furniture stores to Charlesburg's profitability warrants further spending, particularly given this channel's favorable sales trend. Doubling the percentage allocation for marketing funds for this channel may be too extreme, however. Charlesburg Furniture might also consider the longer-term role of department store chains as a marketing distribution channel.

Channel	Channel Sales and Profit (% of total): Sales	Profit
Furniture Store Chains	62.5%	48%
Independent Furniture Stores	22.7%	45%
Department Store Chains	14.8%	7%

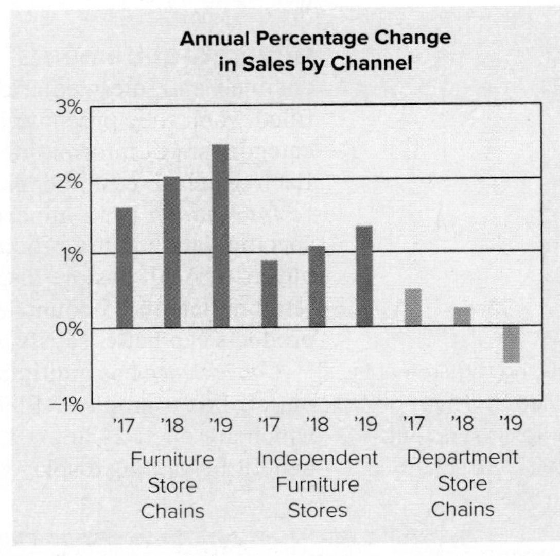

Pre- or postsale services provided by intermediaries are an important buying requirement for products such as large household appliances that require delivery, installation, and credit. Therefore, Whirlpool seeks dealers that provide such services.

Profitability The third consideration in choosing a channel is profitability, which is determined by the margins earned (revenue minus cost) for each channel member and for the channel as a whole. Channel cost is the critical dimension of profitability. These costs include distribution, advertising, and selling expenses associated with different types of marketing channels. The extent to which channel members share these costs determines the margins received by each member and by the channel as a whole.

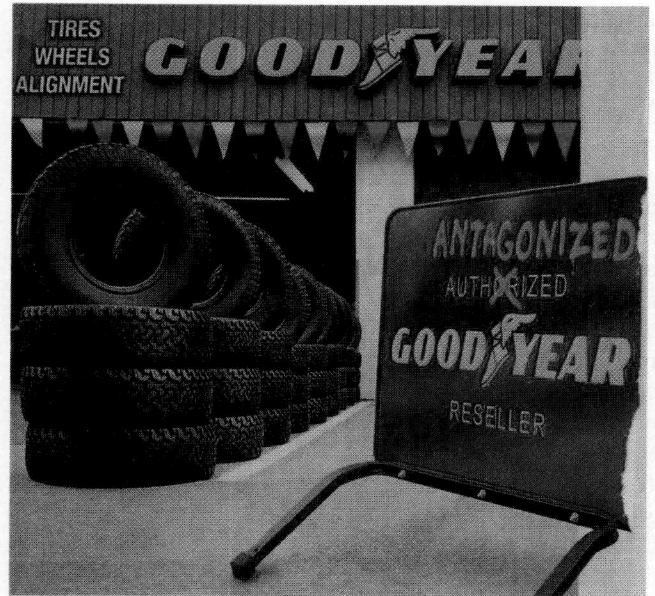

Channel conflict is sometimes visible to consumers. Read the text to learn what type of channel conflict has antagonized this independent Goodyear tire dealer.
Joe & Kathy Heiner/Lindgren & Smith, Inc.

Companies routinely monitor the performance of their marketing channels. Read the Applying Marketing Metrics box to see how Charlesburg Furniture views the sales and profit performance of its marketing channels.

Managing Channel Relationships: Conflict and Cooperation

Unfortunately, because channels consist of independent individuals and firms, there is always the potential for disagreements concerning who performs which channel functions, how profits are allocated, which products and services will be provided by whom, and who makes critical channel-related decisions. These channel conflicts necessitate measures for dealing with them.

Sources of Conflict in Marketing Channels **Channel conflict** arises when one channel member believes another channel member is engaged in behavior that prevents it from achieving its goals. Two types of conflict occur in marketing channels: vertical conflict and horizontal conflict.

Vertical conflict occurs between different levels in a marketing channel—for example, between a manufacturer and a wholesaler or retailer or between a wholesaler and a retailer. Three sources of vertical conflict are most common.[10] First, conflict arises when a channel member bypasses another member and sells or buys products direct, a practice called **disintermediation**. For example, conflict occurred when American Airlines decided to terminate its relationship with Orbitz and Expedia, two online ticketing and travel sites, and sell directly through AA Direct Connect. Second, conflict occurs due to disagreements over how profit margins are distributed among channel members. This happened when Amazon and the Hachette Book Group, the third-largest trade book and educational publisher, engaged in a seven-month dispute about how e-book revenue should be divided between the two companies. A third conflict situation arises when manufacturers believe wholesalers or retailers are not giving their products adequate attention. For example, Newell Brands, Inc. stopped shipping its popular Sharpie brand pens and markers to Office Depot because it believed Office Depot was not spending what the two companies agreed on for showcasing and marketing Sharpies.

Horizontal conflict occurs between intermediaries at the same level in a marketing channel, such as between two or more retailers (Target and Kmart) or two or more wholesalers that handle the same manufacturer's brands. Two sources of horizontal conflict are common.[11] First, horizontal conflict arises when a manufacturer increases its distribution coverage in a geographical area. For example, a franchised Cadillac dealer in Chicago might complain to General Motors that another franchised Cadillac dealer has located too close to its dealership. Second, dual distribution causes conflict when different types of retailers carry the same brands. When independent Goodyear tire dealers learned that Goodyear Tire Company decided to sell its brands through Walmart and Sam's Club, many dealers switched to competing tire makers. Likewise, when Under Armour began selling its athletic wear to department stores, sporting goods retailers became irate and began promoting their own store brands over Under Armour products.

Securing Cooperation in Marketing Channels Conflict can have destructive effects on the workings of a marketing channel so it is necessary to secure cooperation among channel members. One means is through a *channel captain*, a channel member that coordinates, directs, and supports other channel members. Channel captains can be producers, wholesalers, or retailers. P&G assumes this role because it has a strong consumer following in brands such as Crest, Tide, and Pampers. Therefore, it can set policies or terms that supermarkets will follow. McKesson, a pharmaceutical drug wholesaler, is a channel captain because it coordinates and supports the product flow from numerous small drug manufacturers to drugstores and hospitals nationwide. Walmart is a retail channel captain because of its strong consumer image, number of outlets, online presence, and purchasing volume.

A firm becomes a channel captain because it is the channel member with the ability to influence the behavior of other members. Influence can take four forms. First, economic influence arises from the ability of a firm to *reward* other members given its strong financial position or customer franchise. Microsoft Corporation, Amazon, and Walmart have such influence. *Expertise* is a second source of influence. For example, American Hospital Supply helps its customers (hospitals) manage inventory and streamline order processing for hundreds of medical supplies. Third, *identification* with a particular channel member can create influence for that channel member. For instance, retailers may compete to carry the Ralph Lauren line, or clothing manufacturers may compete to be carried by Neiman Marcus, Nordstrom, or Bloomingdale's. In both instances, the desire to be identified with a channel member gives that firm influence over others. Finally, influence can arise from the *legitimate right* of one channel member to direct the behavior of other members. This situation is likely to occur in contractual vertical marketing systems where a franchisor can legitimately direct how a franchisee behaves.

Legal Considerations Conflict in marketing channels is typically resolved through negotiation or the exercise of influence by channel members. Sometimes conflict produces legal action. Therefore, knowledge of legal restrictions affecting channel strategies and practices is important. Some restrictions were described in Chapter 14, namely vertical price fixing and price discrimination. However, other legal considerations are unique to marketing channels.

In general, suppliers can select whomever they want as channel intermediaries and may refuse to deal with whomever they choose. However, the Federal Trade Commission and the Justice Department monitor channel practices that restrain competition, create monopolies, or otherwise represent unfair methods of competition under the Sherman Act (1890) and the Clayton Act (1914). Six channel practices have received the most attention (see Figure 15–7).

Dual distribution, although not illegal, can be viewed as anticompetitive in some situations. The most common situation arises when a manufacturer distributes through its own vertically integrated channel in competition with independent wholesalers and retailers that also sell its products. If the manufacturer's behavior is viewed as an attempt to lessen competition by eliminating wholesalers or retailers, then such action would violate both the Sherman and Clayton Acts.

Vertical integration is viewed in a similar light. Although not illegal, this practice is sometimes subject to legal action under the Clayton Act if it has the potential to lessen competition or foster monopoly.

FIGURE 15–7
Channel strategies and practices are affected by legal restrictions. The Clayton Act and the Sherman Act restrict specific channel strategies and practices.

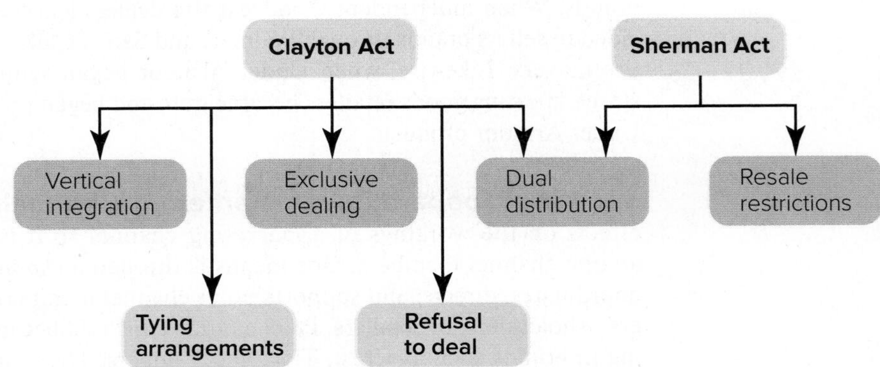

The Clayton Act specifically prohibits exclusive dealing and tying arrangements when they lessen competition or create monopolies. *Exclusive dealing* exists when a supplier requires channel members to sell only its products or restricts distributors from selling directly competitive products. *Tying arrangements* occur when a supplier requires a distributor purchasing some products to buy others from the supplier. These arrangements often arise in franchising. They are illegal if the tied products could be purchased at fair market values from other suppliers at desired quality standards of the franchisor. *Full-line forcing* is a special kind of tying arrangement. This practice involves a supplier requiring that a channel member carry its full line of products in order to sell a specific item in the supplier's line.

Even though a supplier has a legal right to choose intermediaries to carry and represent its products, a *refusal to deal* with existing channel members may be illegal under the Clayton Act. *Resale restrictions* refer to a supplier's attempt to stipulate to whom distributors may resell the supplier's products and in what specific geographical areas or territories they may be sold. These practices have been prosecuted under the Sherman Act. Today, however, the courts apply the "rule of reason" in such cases and consider whether such restrictions have a "demonstrable economic effect."

LEARNING REVIEW

15-6. What are the three questions marketing executives consider when choosing a marketing channel and intermediaries?

15-7. What are the three degrees of distribution density?

LOGISTICS AND SUPPLY CHAIN MANAGEMENT

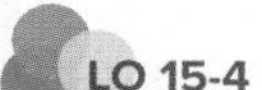

LO 15-4
Explain what supply chain and logistics management are and how they relate to marketing strategy.

A marketing channel relies on logistics to make products available to consumers and industrial users. **Logistics** involves those activities that focus on getting the right amount of the right products to the right place at the right time at the lowest possible cost. The performance of these activities is *logistics management*, the practice of organizing the cost-effective flow of raw materials, in-process inventory, finished goods, and related information from point of origin to point of consumption to satisfy *customer requirements*.

Three elements of this definition deserve emphasis. First, logistics deals with decisions needed to move a product from the source of raw materials to consumption—that is, the *flow* of the product. Second, those decisions have to be *cost effective*. Third, while it is important to drive down logistics costs, there is a limit: A firm needs to drive down logistics costs as long as it can deliver expected *customer service*, which means satisfying customer requirements.

The role of management is to see that customer needs are satisfied in the most cost-effective manner. When properly done, the results are spectacular. Consider Procter & Gamble. The company set out to meet consumer needs more effectively by collaborating with its suppliers and retailers to ensure that the right products reached store shelves at the right time and at a lower cost. The effort was judged a success when, during an 18-month period, P&G's retail customers posted a $65 million savings in logistics costs and customer service increased. When done improperly, disaster can result. KFC in the United Kingdom is an example. The company switched food distributors to reduce costs only to find that it couldn't deliver chickens on time or in sufficient quantities to its stores. KFC had to close 80 percent of its stores for the better part of a week due to no chickens.[12]

Companies today recognize that getting the right items needed for consumption or production to the right place at the right time in the right condition at the right cost is often beyond their individual capabilities and control. Instead, collaboration, coordination, and information sharing among manufacturers, suppliers, and distributors are necessary to create

KFC in the United Kingdom had to apologize to British consumers with this full-page advertisement in major British newspapers. Read the text to learn why KFC created this ad.
Source: Yum! Brands, Inc.

a seamless flow of products and services to customers. This perspective is represented in the concept of a supply chain and the practice of supply chain management.

Supply Chains versus Marketing Channels

A **supply chain** refers to the various firms involved in performing the activities required to create and deliver a product or service to consumers or industrial users. It differs from a marketing channel in terms of the firms involved. A supply chain includes suppliers that provide raw material inputs to a manufacturer as well as the wholesalers and retailers that deliver finished products to consumers. The management process is also different.

Supply chain management is the integration and organization of information and logistics activities *across firms* in a supply chain for the purpose of creating and delivering products and services that provide value to consumers. The relation among marketing channels, logistics management, and supply chain management is shown in Figure 15–8. An important feature of supply chain management is its application of sophisticated information technology that allows companies to share and operate systems for order processing, transportation scheduling, and inventory and facility management.

Sourcing, Assembling, and Delivering a New Car: The Automotive Supply Chain

All companies are members of one or more supply chains. A supply chain is essentially a series of linked suppliers and customers in which every customer is, in turn, a supplier to another customer until a finished product reaches the ultimate consumer. Even the simplified supply chain diagram for carmakers shown in Figure 15–9 illustrates how complex a supply chain can be.[13] A carmaker's supplier network includes thousands of firms that provide the 2,000 functional components, 30,000 parts, and 10 million lines of software code in a typical automobile. They provide items ranging from raw materials, such as steel and rubber, to components, including transmissions, tires, brakes, and seats, to complex subassemblies such as chassis and suspension systems that make for a smooth, stable ride. The process of coordinating and scheduling the flow of materials and components for their assembly into actual automobiles by carmakers is heavily dependent on logistical activities, including transportation, order processing, inventory control, materials handling, and information technology. A central link is the carmaker's supply chain manager, who is responsible for translating customer requirements into actual orders and arranging for delivery dates and financial arrangements for automobile dealers.

FIGURE 15–8
Relating logistics management and supply chain management to supplier networks and marketing channels.

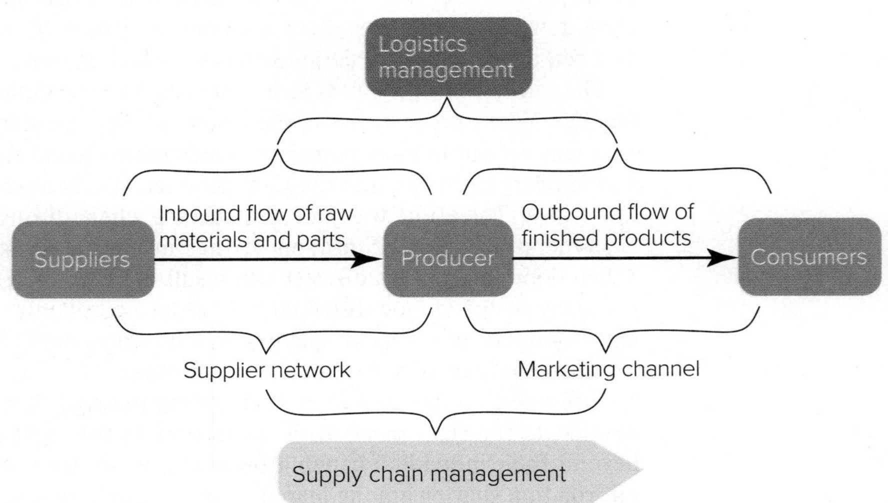

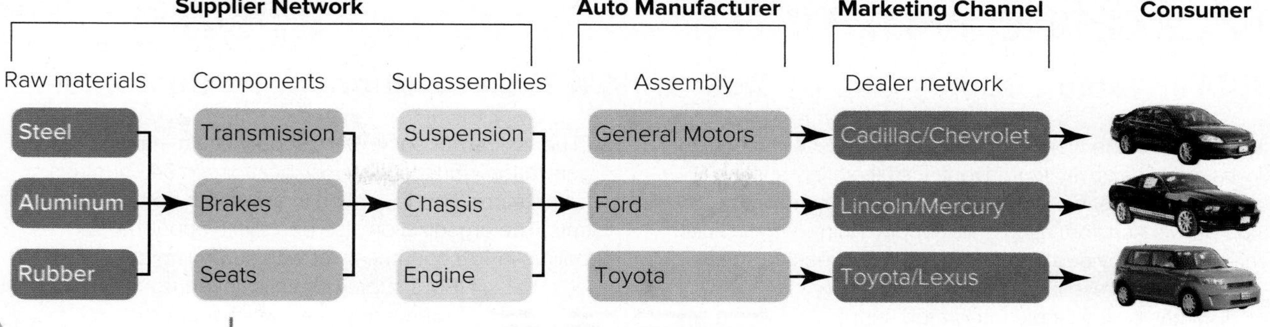

FIGURE 15–9

The automotive supply chain includes thousands of firms that provide the functional components, software codes, and parts in a typical car.

(Photos): Mike Hruby/ McGraw-Hill Education

Logistical aspects of the automobile marketing channel are also an important part of the supply chain. Major responsibilities include transportation (which involves the selection and oversight of external carriers–trucking, airline, railroad, and shipping companies–for cars and parts to dealers), the operation of distribution centers, the management of finished goods inventories, and order processing for sales. Supply chain managers also play an important role in the marketing channel. They work with car dealer networks to ensure that the right mix of automobiles is delivered to each location. In addition, they make sure that spare and service parts are available so that dealers can meet the car maintenance and repair needs of consumers. All of this is done with the help of information technology that links the entire automotive supply chain. What does all of this cost? It is estimated that logistics costs represent 25 to 30 percent of the retail price that you pay for a new car.

Supply Chain Management and Marketing Strategy

VIDEO 15-2
IBM
kerin.tv/15e/v15-2

The automotive supply chain illustration shows how information and logistics activities are integrated and organized across firms to create and deliver a car to you, the consumer. What's missing from this illustration is the linkage between a specific company's supply chain and its marketing strategy. Just as companies have different marketing strategies, they also design and manage supply chains differently. The goals to be achieved by a firm's marketing strategy determine whether its supply chain needs to be more responsive or efficient in meeting customer requirements.

Aligning a Supply Chain with Marketing Strategy There are a variety of supply chain configurations, each of which is designed to perform different tasks well. Marketers today recognize that the choice of a supply chain follows from a clearly defined marketing strategy and involves three steps:[14]

1. *Understand the customer.* To understand the customer, a company must identify the needs of the customer segment being served. These needs, such as a desire for a low price or convenience of purchase, help a company define the relative importance of efficiency and responsiveness in meeting customer requirements.
2. *Understand the supply chain.* Second, a company must understand what a supply chain is designed to do well. Supply chains range from those that emphasize being responsive to customer requirements and demand to those that emphasize efficiency with a goal of supplying products at the lowest possible delivered cost.
3. *Harmonize the supply chain with the marketing strategy.* Finally, a company needs to ensure that what the supply chain is capable of doing well is consistent with the targeted customer's needs and its marketing strategy. If a mismatch exists between what the supply chain does particularly well and a company's marketing strategy, the company will need to either redesign the supply chain to support the marketing strategy or change the marketing strategy. Read the Marketing Matters box on the next page to learn how IBM overhauled its complete supply chain to support its marketing strategy.[15]

Marketing Matters — Customer Value

IBM's Watson Supply Chain—Delivering a Total Solution for Its Customers

IBM is one of the world's great business success stories because of its ability to reinvent itself to satisfy shifting customer needs in a dynamic global marketplace. The company's transformation of its supply chain using artificial intelligence provided by Watson, its path-breaking supercomputer, is a case in point.

IBM has built a single integrated supply chain that can handle raw material procurement, manufacturing, logistics, customer support, order entry, and customer fulfillment across all of IBM—something that has never been done before. Why would IBM undertake this task? According to IBM's former CEO, Samuel J. Palmisano, "You cannot hope to thrive in the IT industry if you are a high-cost, slow-moving company. Supply chain is one of the new competitive battlegrounds. We are committed to being the most efficient and productive player in our industry."

rvlsoft/Shutterstock

The task is not easy. IBM's supply chain management organization works out of 360 locations in 64 countries, tracking more than 1.5 million in assets for both IBM and its clients. The organization also deals with about 17,000 suppliers in 100 countries. Yet with surprising efficiency, IBM's supply chain is linked from raw material sourcing to post-sales support.

Today, IBM is uniquely poised to configure and deliver a tailored mix of hardware, software, and service to provide a total solution for its customers using Watson. Watson is IBM's supercomputer that combines artificial intelligence and sophisticated software and is now being used to improve the performance of its supply chain. Not surprisingly, IBM's supply chain is heralded as one of the best in the world!

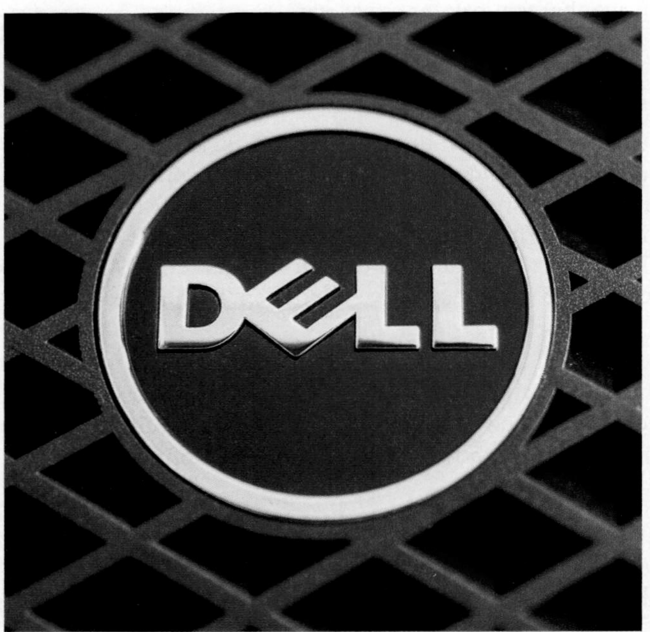

Hadrian/Shutterstock

How are these steps applied and how are efficiency and responsiveness considerations built into a supply chain? Let's look at how two well-known companies–Dell Technologies and Walmart–have harmonized their supply chain and marketing strategy.[16]

Dell: A Responsive Supply Chain The Dell Technologies marketing strategy primarily targets customers who desire having the most up-to-date computer systems customized to their needs. These customers are also willing to (1) wait to have their customized computer system delivered in a few days, rather than picking out a model at a retail store, and (2) pay a reasonable, though not the lowest, price in the marketplace. Given Dell's customer segment, the company has the option of adopting an efficient or responsive supply chain.

An efficient supply chain may use inexpensive, but slower, modes of transportation, emphasize economies of scale in its production process by reducing the variety of system configurations offered, and limit its assembly and inventory storage facilities to a single location. If Dell opted only for efficiency in its supply chain, it would be difficult to satisfy its target customers' desire for rapid delivery and a wide variety of customizable products.

Dell instead has opted for a responsive supply chain. It relies on more expensive express transportation for receipt of components from suppliers and delivery of finished products to customers. The company achieves product variety and manufacturing efficiency by designing common platforms across several products and using common components. Also, Dell has invested heavily in information technology to link itself with suppliers and customers.

Walmart: An Efficient Supply Chain Now let's consider Walmart. Walmart's marketing strategy is to be a reliable, lower-price retailer for a wide variety of mass consumption consumer products. This strategy favors an efficient supply chain designed to deliver

Lester Balajadia/Shutterstock

products to 245 million consumers each week at the lowest possible cost. Efficiency is achieved in a variety of ways. For instance, Walmart keeps relatively low inventory levels, and most of it is stocked in stores available for sale, not in warehouses gathering dust. The low inventory arises from Walmart's use of *cross-docking*—a practice that involves unloading products from suppliers, sorting products for individual stores, and quickly reloading products onto its trucks for a particular store. No warehousing or storing of products occurs, except for a few hours or, at most, a day. In fact, Walmart fines suppliers who deliver products early! Cross-docking allows Walmart to operate only a small number of distribution centers relative to its vast network of Walmart stores, Supercenters, Neighborhood Markets, Marketside stores, and Sam's Clubs, which contributes to efficiency.

Walmart has invested much more than its competitors in information technology to operate its supply chain. The company feeds information about customer requirements and demand from its stores back to its suppliers, which manufacture only what is being demanded. This large investment has improved the efficiency of Walmart's supply chain and made it responsive to customer needs.

Three lessons can be learned from these two examples. First, there is no one best supply chain for every company. Second, the best supply chain is the one that is consistent with the needs of the customer segment being served and complements a company's marketing strategy. And finally, supply chain managers need to be prepared to make trade-offs between efficiency and responsiveness on various elements of a company's supply chain.

TWO CONCEPTS OF LOGISTICS MANAGEMENT IN A SUPPLY CHAIN

The objective of logistics management in a supply chain is to minimize total logistics costs while delivering the appropriate level of customer service.

Total Logistics Cost Concept

For our purposes, **total logistics cost** includes expenses associated with transportation, materials handling and warehousing, inventory, stockouts (being out of inventory), order processing, and return products handling. Note that many of these costs are interrelated, so changes in one will impact the others. For example, if a company attempts to reduce its transportation costs by shipping in larger quantities, it will increase its inventory levels. While larger inventory levels will increase inventory costs, they should also reduce stockouts. It is important, therefore, to study the impact on all of the logistics decision areas when considering a change.

Customer Service Concept

Because a supply chain is a *flow*, the end of it—or *output*—is the service delivered to customers. Within the context of a supply chain, **customer service** is the ability of logistics management to satisfy users in terms of time, dependability, communication, and convenience. As suggested by Figure 15-10 on the next page, a supply chain manager's key task is to balance these four customer service factors against six total logistics cost factors.

Time In a supply chain setting, time refers to *order cycle* or *replenishment* time for an item, which means the time between the ordering of an item and when it is received and ready for use or sale. The various elements that make up the typical order cycle include recognition of the need to order, order transmittal, order processing, documentation, and transportation. A current emphasis in supply chain management is to reduce order cycle time so that the inventory levels of customers may be minimized. Another emphasis is to

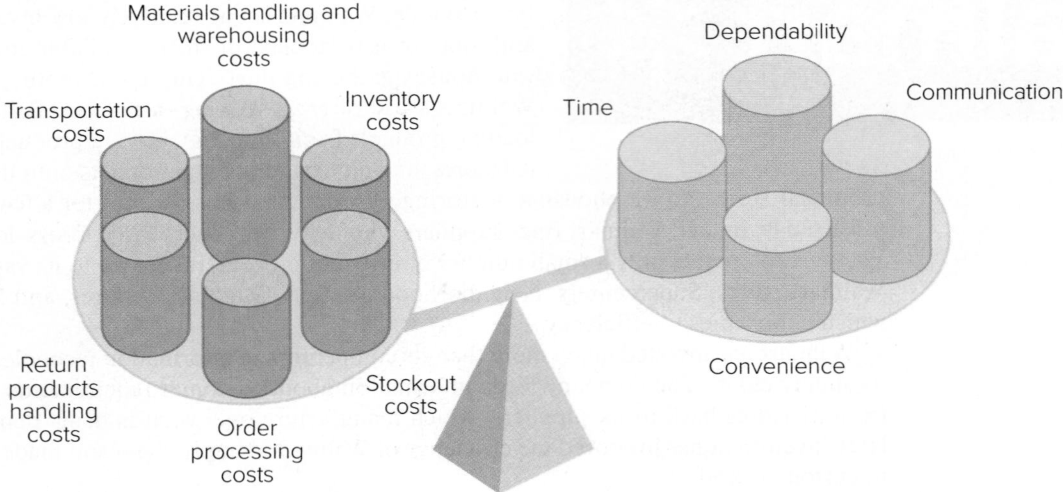

FIGURE 15–10
Supply chain managers balance total logistics cost factors against customer service factors.

make the process of reordering and receiving products as simple as possible, often through inventory systems called *quick response* and *efficient consumer response* delivery systems. For example, at Saks Fifth Avenue, point-of-sale scanner technology records each day's sales. When stock falls below a minimum level, a replenishment order is automatically produced. Vendors such as Donna Karan (DKNY) receive the order, which is processed and delivered within 48 hours.[17]

Dependability Dependability is the consistency of replenishment. This is important to all firms in a supply chain–and to consumers. How often do you return to a store if it fails to have in stock the item you want to purchase? Dependability can be broken into three elements: consistent lead time, safe delivery, and complete delivery. Consistent service allows planning (such as appropriate inventory levels), whereas inconsistencies create surprises. Intermediaries may be willing to accept longer lead times if they know about them in advance and can thus make plans.

Communication Communication is a two-way link between the buyer and supplier that helps in monitoring service and anticipating future needs. Status reports on orders are a typical example of communication between the buyer and seller.

Convenience The concept of convenience for a supply chain manager means that there should be a minimum of effort on the part of the buyer in doing business with the seller. Is it easy for the customer to order? Are the products available from many outlets? Will the seller arrange all necessary details, such as transportation? This customer service factor has promoted the use of **vendor-managed inventory (VMI)**, whereby the *supplier* determines the product amount and assortment a customer (such as a retailer) needs and automatically delivers the appropriate items.

Campbell Soup's system illustrates how VMI works.[18] Every morning, retailers electronically inform the company of their demand for all Campbell products and the inventory levels in their distribution centers. Campbell uses that information to forecast future demand and determine which products need replenishment based on upper and lower inventory limits established with each retailer. Trucks leave the Campbell shipping plant that afternoon and arrive at the retailer's distribution centers with the required replenishments the same day.

Making Responsible Decisions

Sustainability

Reverse Logistics and Green Marketing Go Together at Hewlett-Packard: Recycling e-Waste

About 50 megatons (1 megaton = 1 million tons) of electronics and electronic equipment find their way to landfills around the world annually. In 2018, Americans alone discarded over 400 million analog TV sets and computer monitors and Japanese consumers trashed more than 610 million cell phones. The result? Landfills are seeping lead, chromium, mercury, and other toxins prevalent in digital debris into the environment.

Fortunately, Hewlett-Packard has taken it upon itself to act responsibly and address this issue through its highly regarded reverse logistics program. Hewlett-Packard has recycled computer and printer hardware since 1987 and is an industry leader in this practice. The company's recycling service is available today in more than 73 countries, regions, and territories. Hewlett-Packard has recycled about 3 billion pounds of used electronic products and supplies to be refurbished for resale or donation or for recovery of materials.

Source: Hewlett-Packard Development Company, L.P.

The recycling effort at Hewlett-Packard is also part of the company's product development program. Among other initiatives in this program, emphasis is placed on product and packaging changes to reduce reverse supply chain and environmental costs. For example, more than 75 percent of the company's ink cartridges and 24 percent of its LaserJet toner cartridges are now manufactured with recycled plastic.

CLOSING THE LOOP: REVERSE LOGISTICS

The flow of products in a supply chain does not end with the ultimate consumer or industrial user. Companies today recognize that a supply chain can work in reverse. **Reverse logistics** is a process of reclaiming recyclable and reusable materials, returns, and reworks from the point of consumption or use for repair, remanufacturing, redistribution, or disposal. The effect of reverse logistics can be seen in the reduced waste in landfills and lowered operating costs for companies. The Making Responsible Decisions box describes the successful reverse logistics initiative at Hewlett-Packard.[19]

VIDEO 15-3
UPS
kerin.tv/15e/v15-3

Companies such as Motorola and Nokia (return and reuse of mobile phones); Caterpillar, Xerox, and IBM (remanufacturing and recycling); and Amazon (returns and redistribution) have implemented acclaimed reverse logistics programs. Other firms have enlisted third-party logistics providers such as UPS, FedEx, and Penske Logistics to handle this process along with other supply chain functions.[20]

LEARNING REVIEW

15-8. What is the principal difference between a marketing channel and a supply chain?

15-9. The choice of a supply chain involves what three steps?

15-10. A manager's key task is to balance which four customer service factors against which six logistics cost factors?

LEARNING OBJECTIVES REVIEW

LO 15-1 *Explain what is meant by a marketing channel of distribution and why intermediaries are needed.*
A marketing channel of distribution, or simply a marketing channel, consists of individuals and firms involved in the process of making a product or service available for use or consumption by consumers or industrial users. Intermediaries make possible the flow of products from producers to buyers by performing three basic functions. The transactional function involves buying, selling, and risk taking because intermediaries stock merchandise in anticipation of sales. The logistical function involves the gathering, storing, and dispensing of products. The facilitating function assists producers in making products and services more attractive to buyers. The performance of these functions by intermediaries creates time, place, form, and possession utility for consumers.

LO 15-2 *Distinguish among traditional marketing channels, digital marketing channels, and different types of vertical marketing systems.*
Traditional marketing channels describe the route taken by products and services from producers to buyers. This route can range from a direct channel with no intermediaries, because a producer and the ultimate consumer deal directly with each other, to indirect channels where intermediaries (agents, wholesalers, distributors, or retailers) are inserted between a producer and consumer and perform numerous channel functions. Digital marketing channels employ the Internet to make products and services available for consumption or use by consumer or business buyers. Vertical marketing systems are professionally managed and centrally coordinated marketing channels designed to achieve channel economies and maximum marketing impact. There are three major types of vertical marketing systems (VMSs). A corporate VMS combines successive stages of production and distribution under a single ownership. A contractual VMS exists when independent production and distribution firms integrate their efforts on a contractual basis to obtain greater functional economies and marketing impact than they could achieve alone. An administered VMS achieves coordination at successive stages of production and distribution by the size and influence of one channel member rather than through ownership.

LO 15-3 *Describe factors that marketing executives consider when selecting and managing a marketing channel, including legal restrictions.*
Marketing executives consider three questions when selecting and managing a marketing channel and intermediaries. (1) Which channel and intermediaries will provide the best coverage of the target market? Marketers typically choose one of three levels of market coverage: intensive, selective, or exclusive distribution. (2) Which channel and intermediaries will best satisfy the buying requirements of the target market? These buying requirements fall into four categories: information, convenience, variety, and pre- or postsale services. (3) Which channel and intermediaries will be the most profitable? Here marketers look at the margins earned (revenues minus cost) for each channel member and for the channel as a whole.

LO 15-4 *Explain what supply chain and logistics management are and how they relate to marketing strategy.*
A supply chain refers to the various firms involved in performing the various activities required to create and deliver a product or service to consumers or industrial users. Supply chain management is the integration and organization of information and logistics across firms for the purpose of creating value for consumers. Logistics involves those activities that focus on getting the right amount of the right products to the right place at the right time at the lowest possible cost. Logistics management includes the coordination of the flows of both inbound and outbound products, an emphasis on making these flows cost effective, and customer service. A company's supply chain follows from a clearly defined marketing strategy. The alignment of a company's supply chain with its marketing strategy involves three steps. First, a supply chain must reflect the needs of the customer segment being served. Second, a company must understand what a supply chain is designed to do well. Supply chains range from those that emphasize being responsive to customer requirements and demands to those that emphasize efficiency with the goal of supplying products at the lowest possible delivered cost. Finally, a supply chain must be consistent with the targeted customer's needs and the company's marketing strategy. The Dell Technologies and Walmart examples in the chapter illustrate how this alignment is achieved by two market leaders.

LEARNING REVIEW ANSWERS

15-1 What is meant by a marketing channel?
Answer: A marketing channel consists of individuals and firms involved in the process of making a product or service available for use or consumption by consumers or industrial users.

15-2 What are the three basic functions performed by intermediaries?
Answer: Intermediaries perform transactional, logistical, and facilitating functions.

15-3 What is the difference between a direct and an indirect channel?
Answer: A direct channel is one in which a producer of consumer or business products and services and ultimate consumers or industrial users deal directly with each other. In an indirect channel, intermediaries are inserted between the producer and ultimate consumers or industrial users and perform numerous channel functions.

15-4 Why are channels for business products typically shorter than channels for consumer products?
Answer: Business channels are typically shorter than consumer channels because business users are fewer in number, tend to be more concentrated geographically, and buy in larger quantities.

15-5 What is the principal distinction between a corporate vertical marketing system and an administered vertical marketing system?
Answer: A corporate vertical marketing system combines successive stages of production and distribution under a single ownership. An administered vertical marketing system achieves coordination by the size and influence of one channel member rather than through ownership.

15-6 What are the three questions marketing executives consider when choosing a marketing channel and intermediaries?
Answer: The three questions to consider when choosing a marketing channel and intermediaries are: (1) Which will provide the best coverage of the target market? (2) Which will best satisfy the buying requirements of the target market? (3) Which will be the most profitable?

15-7 What are the three degrees of distribution density?
Answer: intensive; exclusive; selective

15-8 What is the principal difference between a marketing channel and a supply chain?
Answer: A marketing channel consists of individuals and firms involved in the process of making a product or service available for use or consumption by consumers or industrial users. A supply chain differs from a marketing channel in terms of membership. It includes suppliers who provide raw materials to a manufacturer as well as the wholesalers and retailers—the marketing channel—that deliver the finished goods to ultimate consumers.

15-9 The choice of a supply chain involves what three steps?
Answer: (1) Understand the customer. (2) Understand the supply chain. (3) Harmonize the supply chain with the marketing strategy.

15-10 A manager's key task is to balance which four customer service factors against which six logistics cost factors?
Answer: The four customer service factors are time, dependability, communication, and convenience. The logistics cost factors are transportation costs, materials handling and warehousing costs, inventory costs, stockout costs (being out of inventory), order processing costs, and return products handling costs.

FOCUSING ON KEY TERMS

channel conflict p. 415
customer service p. 421
direct to consumer marketing channels p. 408
disintermediation p. 415
dual distribution p. 409
exclusive distribution p. 412
intensive distribution p. 412
logistics p. 417
marketing channel p. 404
multichannel marketing p. 409
reverse logistics p. 423
selective distribution p. 413
supply chain p. 418
total logistics cost p. 421
vendor-managed inventory (VMI) p. 422
vertical marketing systems p. 410

APPLYING MARKETING KNOWLEDGE

1 A distributor for Celanese Chemical Company stores large quantities of chemicals, blends these chemicals to satisfy the requests of customers, and delivers the blends to a customer's warehouse within 24 hours of receiving an order. What utilities does this distributor provide?

2 Suppose the president of a carpet manufacturing firm has asked you to look into the possibility of bypassing the firm's wholesalers (who sell to carpet, department, and furniture stores) and selling direct to these stores. What caution would you voice on this matter, and what type of information would you gather before making this decision?

3 What type of channel conflict is likely to be caused by dual distribution, and what type of conflict can be reduced by direct distribution? Why?

4 How does the channel captain idea differ among corporate, administered, and contractual vertical marketing systems with particular reference to the use of the different forms of influence available to firms?

5 List the customer service factors that would be vital to buyers in the following types of companies: (*a*) manufacturing, (*b*) retailing, (*c*) hospitals, and (*d*) construction.

BUILDING YOUR MARKETING PLAN

Does your marketing plan involve selecting channels and intermediaries? If the answer is "no," read no further and do not include this element in your plan. If the answer is "yes":

1. Identify which channel and intermediaries will provide the best coverage of the target market for your product or service.
2. Specify which channel and intermediaries will best satisfy the important buying requirements of the target market.
3. Determine which channel and intermediaries will be the most profitable.
4. Select your channel(s) and intermediary(ies).
5. If inventory is involved, (*a*) identify the three or four major kinds of inventory needed for your organization (retail stock, finished products, raw materials, supplies, and so on), and (*b*) suggest ways to reduce their costs.
6. (*a*) Rank the four customer service factors (time, dependability, communication, and convenience) from most important to least important from your customers' point of view, and (*b*) identify actions for the one or two factors that are the most important in regard to your product or service.

VIDEO CASE 15 Amazon: Delivering the Earth's Biggest Selection!

"The secret is we are on our seventh generation of fulfillment centers and we have gotten better every time," explains Jeff Bezos, CEO of Amazon.com, Inc. The global online retailer is a pioneer of fast, convenient, low-cost shopping that has attracted millions of consumers. Of course, while Amazon has changed the way many people shop, the company still faces the traditional and daunting task of creating a seamless flow of deliveries to its customers—often millions of times each day.

VIDEO 15-4
Amazon Video Case
kerin.tv/15e/v15-4

THE COMPANY

Bezos started Amazon.com with a simple idea: Use the Internet to transform book buying into the fastest, easiest, and most enjoyable shopping experience possible. The company was incorporated in 1994 and launched its website in July 1995. At the forefront of a huge growth of dot-com businesses, Amazon pursued a get-big-fast business strategy. Sales grew rapidly and Amazon began adding products and services other than books. In fact, Amazon soon set its goal on being "Earth's most customer-centric company, where customers can find and discover virtually anything they might want to buy online."

Today Amazon.com continues to grow by providing low prices, vast selection, and convenience. Its selection of products covers a broad range of categories including: Books; Movies, Music & Games; Electronics & Computers; Home, Garden & Tools; Beauty, Health & Grocery; Toys; Clothing, Shoes & Jewelry; Sports & Outdoors; and Automotive & Industrial. In addition, Amazon offers digital music, an app store for Android, Amazon Cloud Drive, Kindle e-readers, Kindle Fire tablets, Amazon Fire TV, and the Amazon Fire phone. Other services allow customers to:

- Search for a product or brand using all or part of its name.
- Place orders with one click using the "Buy Now with 1-Click" button on the website and the "Mobile 1-Click" button for phones.
- Receive personalized recommendations based on past purchases through opt-in e-mails.

These products and services have attracted millions of people around the globe. Further, the company's growth has made Amazon.com, along with its international sites in Australia, Brazil, Canada, China, France, Germany, India, Italy, Japan, Mexico, Spain, and the United Kingdom, the world's largest online retailer.

Amazon's e-commerce platform is also used by more than 2 million small businesses, retail brands, and individual sellers. For example, programs such as Selling on Amazon, Fulfillment by Amazon, Amazon Webstore, and Checkout by Amazon allow small businesses to use Amazon's e-commerce platform to facilitate sales. Online retailers store their products at Amazon's fulfillment centers and when they sell a product, Amazon ships it! Amazon.com also operates retail websites for brands such as bebe, Marks & Spencer, Lacoste, and AOL's Shop@AOL. Individual sellers use the Amazon network to reach millions of potential customers. These business partnerships all contribute to Amazon's sales, which now exceed $75 billion.

Bezos defines Amazon by its "big ideas, which are customer centricity, putting the customer at the center of

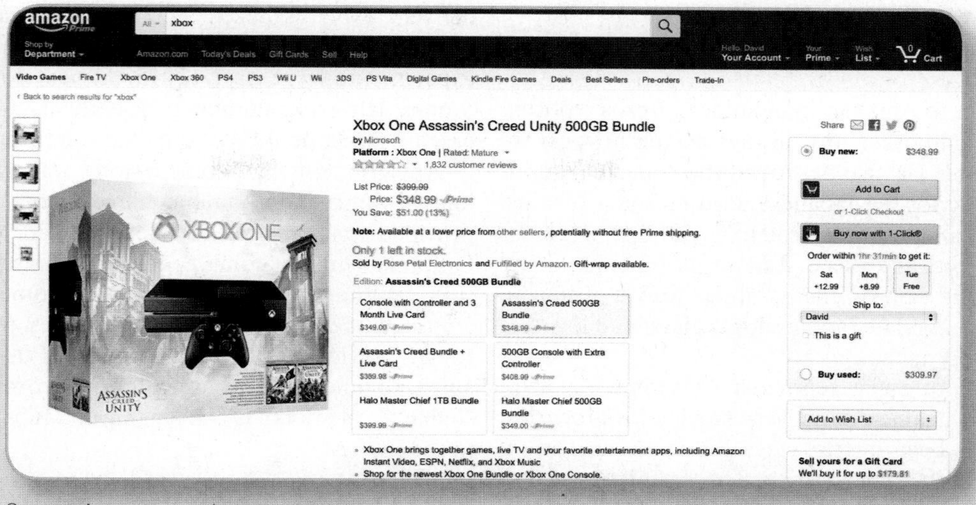

Source: Amazon.com, Inc.

everything we do, and invention—we like to pioneer, we like to explore." Amazon's success is also the result of an intense focus on cost and efficiency that leads to lower prices. More specifically, Amazon is exceptional at managing the elements of its supply chain, which make up one of the most complex and expensive aspects of the company's business.

SUPPLY CHAIN AND LOGISTICS MANAGEMENT AT AMAZON.COM

What happens after an order is submitted on Amazon's website but before it arrives at the customer's door? A lot. Amazon.com maintains huge distribution, or "fulfillment," centers where it keeps inventory of millions of products. This is one of the key differences between Amazon.com and some of its competitors—it actually stocks products. Bezos describes how they have improved: "Years ago, I drove the Amazon packages to the post office every evening in the back of my Chevy Blazer. My vision extended so far that I dreamed we might one day get a forklift. Fast-forward to today and we have 96 fulfillment centers." So Amazon must manage the flow of products from its 15 million-plus suppliers to its U.S. and international fulfillment centers with the flow of customer orders from the fulfillment centers to individuals' homes or offices.

The process begins with the suppliers. Amazon collaborates with its suppliers to increase efficiencies and improve inventory turnover. For example, Amazon uses software to forecast purchasing patterns by region, which allows it to give its suppliers better information about delivery dates and volumes. After the products arrive at the fulfillment center they are scanned and placed on shelves in what often appear to be haphazard locations. That is, books may be on the same shelf next to toys and kitchen utensils. Dave Clark, vice president of worldwide operations and customer service at Amazon, explains: "If you look at how these items fit in the bin, they are optimized to utilize the available space, we have computers and algorithms that tell people the areas of the building that have the most space to put the product that's coming in at that time." Clark observes that one of its 1-million-square-foot fulfillment centers (the size of more than 20 football fields) represents a "physical manifestation of earth's biggest selection."

At the same time, Amazon has been improving the part of the process that sorts the products into the individual orders. Once an order is placed in the computer system, sophisticated software generates a map of the location of each product and a "pick ambassador" walks the aisles to select the products. Each item is scanned as it is selected so that inventory levels and locations are always up-to-date. Packers ensure that all items are included in the box before it is taped and labeled. The boxes then travel along a conveyor belt and are diverted into groups based on the delivery location. A network of trucks and regional postal hubs then conclude the process with delivery of the order. Amazon actually uses more trucks than planes!

The success of Amazon's logistics and supply chain management activities may be most evident during the year-end holiday shopping season. Amazon received orders for 36.8 million items on Cyber Monday (the Monday following Thanksgiving), including orders for Xbox and PlayStation gaming consoles that reached more than 1,000 units per minute. During the entire holiday season Amazon shipped orders to 185 countries. Well over 99 percent of the orders were shipped and delivered on time.

CONTINUOUS IMPROVEMENT AT AMAZON

In a recent letter to Amazon shareholders, Bezos reported that Amazon employees are "always asking how do we make this better?" He also described the Amazon Kaizen program (named for the Japanese term meaning "change for the better") and how it is used to streamline processes and reduce defects and waste. As a result there are many new changes and improvements under way at Amazon, many of which are related to its supply chain and logistics management approach.

One example of a new service at Amazon is Amazon Fresh, its online, same-day-delivery service for groceries. The service has been in trial stage in Seattle for several years and recently expanded to Los Angeles and San Francisco. The success of the service in these cities is likely to influence how quickly Amazon expands into other cities. Another new service at Amazon is based on its agreement with the United States Postal Service to offer Sunday delivery to select cities. The demand for this service in the trial cities will also influence how quickly it is rolled out to other cities. Finally, Amazon received a lot of attention when it revealed that it is developing unmanned aerial drones that could fly small shipments to customers within 30 minutes. "We can carry objects up to 5 pounds which covers 86 percent of the items that we deliver," explains Bezos. The Federal Aviation Administration (FAA) granted Amazon permission to fly drones experimentally in early 2015. Expect to see Amazon drones delivering shipments as early as 2020 in some areas, assuming final FAA approvals on this practice.

Amazon.com has come a long way since 1995. Its logistics and supply chain management activities have provided Amazon with a cost-effective and efficient distribution system that combines automation and communication technology with superior customer service. To continue its drive to increase future sales, profits, and customer service, Amazon continues to use its inventive spirit to encourage innovation. According to Bezos, "What we are doing is challenging and fun—we get to work in the future."[21]

Questions

1 How do Amazon.com's logistics and supply chain management activities help the company create value for its customers?

2 What systems did Amazon develop to improve the flow of products from suppliers to Amazon fulfillment centers? What systems improved the flow of orders from the fulfillment centers to customers?

3 Why will logistics and supply chain management play an important role in the future success of Amazon.com?

Chapter Notes

1. Eddie Bauer, "Our Guarantee," accessed 2019, https://www.eddiebauer.com/custserv/customer-service-our-guarantee.jsp.
2. www.eddiebauer.com, accessed April 18, 2019; "Eddie Bauer CEO Offers Inside Tour of Epic Turnaround Campaign," presentation at the University of Washington Foster School of Business, March 16, 2017; "A Lost Eddie Bauer Returns to Its Roots Outdoors," www.forbes.com, November 10, 2016; and "Eddie Bauer in Early Stages of Turnaround," www.wwd.com, February 15, 2014.
3. "How to Make Multichannel Marketing Work," www.emarketer.com, June 10, 2016.
4. "A Lost Eddie Bauer Returns to Its Roots Outdoors," www.forbes.com, November 10, 2016.
5. *General Mills 2018 Annual Report* (General Mills, Inc.: Golden Valley, MN, 2019); "General Mills with Nestlé Is Trying to Make Cereal More Popular Overseas," www.startribune, May 15, 2015; and "Cereal Marketers Race for Global Bowl Domination," *Advertising Age,* August 20, 2012, pp. 12–13.
6. For an overview of vertical marketing systems, see Lou Pelton, Martha Cooper, David Strutton, and James R. Lumpkin, *Marketing Channels,* 3rd ed. (Burr Ridge, IL: McGraw-Hill/Irwin, 2005).
7. Rachel Dodes, "Saks to Add Exclusive Lines," *The Wall Street Journal,* February 25, 2010, p. B2.
8. "Dell Treads Carefully into Selling PCs in Stores," *The Wall Street Journal,* January 3, 2008, p. B1.
9. "8-second rule," www.pcmag.com/encyclopedia/term, accessed May 1, 2018.
10. "American Airlines Yanks Its Flights off Travel Sites," www.usatoday.com, December 23, 2010; "Amazon, Hachette Reach a Truce," *The Wall Street Journal,* November 14, 2014, pp. B1, B2; and "Sales Took Back Seat in Sharpie Spat," *The Wall Street Journal,* March 27, 2018, p. B4.
11. For an extensive discussion on channel member conflict and influence, see Robert W. Palmatier, Eugene Sivadas, Louis W. Stern, and Adel I. El-Ansary, *Marketing Channel Strategy,* 9th ed. (New York: Routledge, 2020), Chapters 10 and 11. The examples in this section come from this source and "Under Armour Does Itself Harm," *The Wall Street Journal,* August 18, 2017, p. B12.
12. These examples are from David Simchi-Levi, Philip Kaminsky, and Edith Simchi-Levi, *Designing and Managing the Supply Chain,* 4th ed. (Burr Ridge, IL: McGraw-Hill/Irwin, 2011); and "At KFC, a Bucketful of Trouble," *Bloomberg Businessweek,* March 5, 2018, pp. 20–21.
13. Patrick Burnson, "Auto Industry Supply Chain Managers Should Take Hard Look at Analytics," *Supply Chain Management,* October 2015, pp. 3–7; and John Paul MacDuffie and Takahiro Fujimoto, "Why Dinosaurs Will Keep Ruling the Automobile Industry," *Harvard Business Review,* June 2010, pp. 23–25.
14. Portions of this discussion are based on Sunil Chopra and Peter Meindl, *Supply Chain Management: Strategy, Planning, and Operations,* 6th ed. (Upper Saddle River, NJ: Prentice Hall, 2016), Chapters 1–3.

15. "IBM Rolls Out Supply Chain Insights," www.logisticsmgmt.com, October 1, 2018; and "Watson Supply Chain," www.ibm/supply-chain.com, accessed August 15, 2019; "IBM Rolls Out Watson Supply Chain Insights," www.logisticsmgmt.com, October 1, 2018.
16. Theodore Stank et al., *The Supply Chain Game Changers* (Upper Saddle River, NJ: Pearson and FT Press, 2017); Dave Blanchard, "Top 25 Supply Chains of 2019," www.industryweek.com, June 6, 2019; "The 2014 Supply Chain Top 25: Leading the Decade," *Supply Chain Management Review,* September–October, 2014, pp. 8–17; "Walmart Will Punish Its Suppliers for Delivering Early," www.msn.com, July 12, 2017; and Sunil Chopra and Peter Meindl, *Supply Chain Management: Strategy, Planning, and Operations,* 6th ed. (Upper Saddle River, NJ: Prentice Hall, 2016).
17. "Retailers Aim to Turn Minutes into Millions," *The Wall Street Journal,* December 19, 2012, pp. B1, B2; and Christina Passariello, "Logistics Are in Vogue with Designers," *The Wall Street Journal,* June 27, 2008, p. B1.
18. Stank et al., *The Supply Chain Game Changers*.
19. "War Declared on World's Growing E-Waste Crisis," phy.org/news, January 24, 2019; and "Product Return and Recycling," www.hp.com, May 10, 2019.
20. "The Corner Stone of the Circular Economy," www.supplychain247.com, February 8, 2019.
21. Amazon: This case was written by Steven Hartley. Sources: Tim Worstall, "Both Amazon and Walmart Are Really Logistics Companies, Not Retailers," www.forbes.com, April 11, 2014; Dan Mitchell, "Next Up for Disruption: The Grocery Business," www.fortune.com, April 4, 2014; Mae Anderson, "Amazon's Bezos Outlines Grocery, Drone Plans," Businessweek.com, April 10, 2014; Jeff Bercovici, "The Same-Day War: Amazon, Google and Walmart Race to Bring Your Groceries," *Forbes,* May 5, 2014; and Brad Stone, "Why Amazon's Going Up in the Air," *Bloomberg Businessweek,* December 9–15, 2013, pp. 12–13.

Retailing and Wholesaling

LEARNING OBJECTIVES

After reading this chapter you should be able to:

LO 16-1 Identify retailers in terms of the utilities they provide.

LO 16-2 Explain the alternative ways to classify retail outlets.

LO 16-3 Describe the many methods of nonstore retailing.

LO 16-4 Classify retailers in terms of the retail positioning matrix, and specify retailing mix actions.

LO 16-5 Explain changes in retailing with the wheel of retailing and the retail life-cycle concepts.

LO 16-6 Describe the types of firms that perform wholesaling activities and their functions.

Generation Z Loves Shopping in Malls!

The popularity and growth of online shopping, and the declining interest in brick-and-mortar retailers may lead you to think that malls are becoming less important. That conclusion, however, is incorrect. The reason? In a three-month period, 95 percent of the Generation Z cohort will visit a mall, compared with just 58 percent of the Generation X cohort. It turns out, Generation Z loves shopping in malls!

This is a surprise for marketers who assumed that consumers who grew up in a digital marketplace would prefer online experiences. These young consumers, however, have developed new shopping preferences that integrate traditional and contemporary shopping. Malls have noticed, and their combination of technology and retailing is creating a new way to change and improve the customer journey—the smart mall!

Smart malls use a variety of technical solutions to enhance the shopping experience. For example, they are beginning to use the Internet of Things (IoT), and smartphone apps such as FastMall, to help shoppers find and remember the location of a parking place, guide them to stores with an interactive map, and solicit feedback about their shopping experience. In addition, retailers are adding technology to become "smart stores." They are adding point-of-purchase displays that use biometric scanners to detect when a customer approaches and activate a customized video based on their personal characteristics. Similarly, virtual reality and 3D modeling tools allow stores to show customers visual depictions of products, such as appliances or furniture, in settings like their home. Potential benefits of the combination of these smart technologies include more efficient in-mall "navigation," personalized messaging, faster decision making, and higher customer satisfaction.

Social media are also becoming part of the shopping experience. Forever 21, for example, offers customers a 21 percent discount if they take a picture of themselves in a Forever 21 outfit and post it with the #f21promo hashtag. There are currently more than 20,000 of these posts on Instagram and Twitter! Similarly, Macy's has added a shop-in-a-shop called Story that is completely changed to a new theme every two months, perfect for frequent selfies. And because Generation Z is interested in personalization, stores such as American Eagle Outfitters and Levi Strauss have tailors to add patches, paint, embossing, and monogram stitching.

Smart malls and stores are also incorporating wearable technology, such as smartwatches, into the shopping experience. Smartwatches can provide information about deals, the location of products, and the use of near field communication (NFC) products such as Apple Pay, Android Pay, and PayPal's mobile wallet, which permit consumers to pay by holding a device near a payment terminal.[1]

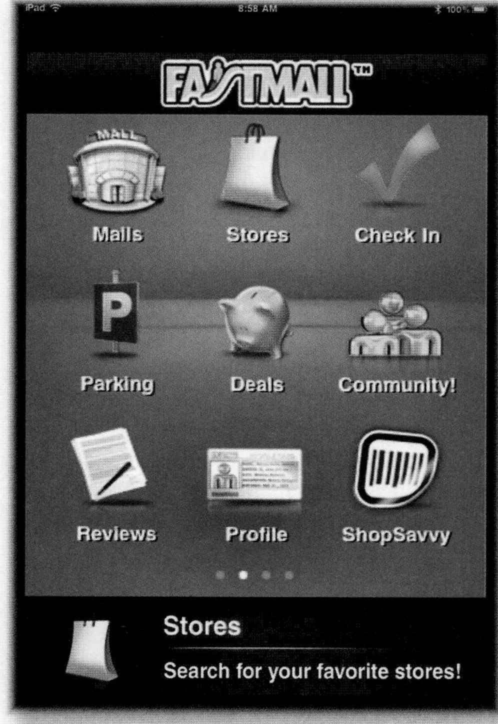

(Left) Source: MindSmack; (Center): J. Vespa/WireImage/Getty Images; (Right): Jesus Aranguren/AP Images

VIDEO 16-1
Generation Z Shopping Video
kerin.tv/15e/v16-1

These are just a few examples of the many exciting changes occurring in retailing today. This chapter examines the critical role of retailing in the marketplace and the challenging decisions retailers face as they strive to create value for customers.

What types of products will consumers buy on their smartphone, from catalogs, television, or the Internet? In what type of store will consumers look for products they don't buy directly? How important is the location of the store? Will customers expect services such as alterations, delivery, installation, or repair? What price should be charged for each product? These are difficult and important questions that are an integral part of retailing. In the channel of distribution, retailing is where the customer meets the product. It is through retailing that exchange (a central aspect of marketing) occurs. **Retailing** includes all activities involved in selling, renting, and providing products and services to ultimate consumers for personal, family, or household use.

THE VALUE OF RETAILING

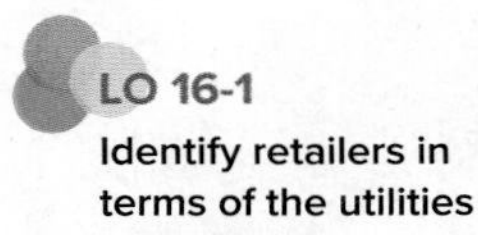

LO 16-1
Identify retailers in terms of the utilities they provide.

Retailing is an important marketing activity. Not only do producers and consumers meet through retailing actions, but retailing also creates customer value and has a significant impact on the economy. To consumers, the value of retailing is in the form of utilities provided (see Figure 16–1). Retailing's economic value is represented by the people employed in retailing as well as by the total amount of money exchanged in retail sales (see Figure 16–2).

Consumer Utilities Offered by Retailing

The utilities provided by retailers create value for consumers. Time, place, form, and possession utilities are offered by most retailers in varying degrees, but one utility is often emphasized more than others. Look at Figure 16–1 to see how well you can match the retailer with the utility being emphasized in the description.

VIDEO 16-2
CarMax
kerin.tv/15e/v16-2

Providing branch offices and ATMs, as Wells Fargo does, puts the bank's products and services close to the consumer, providing place utility. By providing financing or leasing and taking used cars as trade-ins, CarMax makes the purchase easier and provides possession utility. Form utility—production or alteration of a product—is offered by Ralph Lauren through its online *The Polo Custom Shop* program, which offers shirts that meet each customer's specifications. Finding the right sporting equipment during the off-season is the time utility provided by Dick's Sporting Goods. Many retailers offer a combination of the four basic utilities. Some supermarkets, for example, offer convenient locations (place utility); are open 24 hours a day (time utility); customize purchases in the bakery, deli, and florist (form utility); and allow several payment and credit options (possession utility).

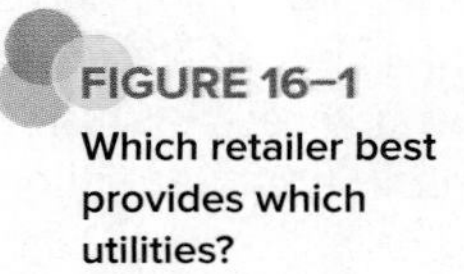

FIGURE 16–1
Which retailer best provides which utilities?

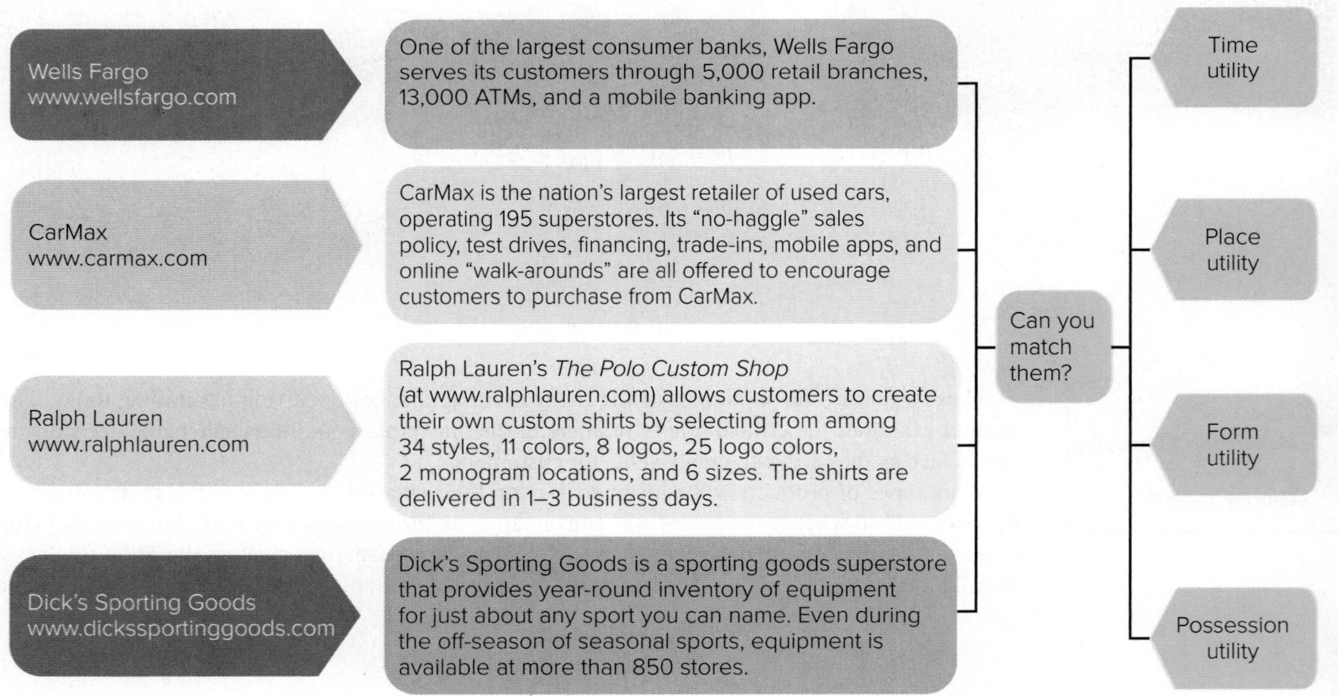

Type of retailer	Sales ($ in billions)
Sporting goods, hobby, music, and book stores	87
Electronics and appliance stores	99
Furniture and home furnishings stores	111
Florists, office supply, misc.	122
Clothing and accessory stores	260
Health and personal care stores	327
Building material and garden stores	349
Gasoline stations	419
Nonstore retailers	561
General merchandise stores	677
Food and beverage stores	701
Motor vehicle and parts dealers	1,144

0 200 400 600 800 1,000 1,200

Sales ($ in billions)

FIGURE 16–2
Are you surprised by the relative sales of different types of retailers?

The Global Economic Impact of Retailing

Retailing is important to the U.S. and global economies. Five of the forty largest businesses in the United States are retailers (Walmart, Amazon, Costco, Home Depot, and Target). Walmart's $514 billion in annual sales in 2018 surpassed the gross domestic product of all but 24 countries for that same year. Walmart, Amazon, Costco, Home Depot, and Target together have more than 3.8 million employees—more than the combined populations of Jacksonville, Florida; Austin, Texas; Kansas City, Missouri, and San Jose, California.[2] Figure 16–2 shows that many types of retailers, including food stores, automobile dealers, and general merchandise outlets, are also significant contributors to the U.S. economy.[3]

Tesco is one of the largest retailers outside the United States.
Ceri Breeze/Shutterstock

Outside the United States large retailers include Aeon in Japan, Carrefour in France, Metro Group in Germany, and Tesco in Britain.[4] In emerging economies such as China and Mexico, a combination of local and global retailers is evolving. Walmart, for example, has more than 6,000 stores outside the United States, including stores in Argentina, China, India, Japan, Mexico, and the United Kingdom. Despite the presence of these large retailers, however, most international markets are dominated by local retailers.[5]

LEARNING REVIEW

16-1. When Ralph Lauren makes shirts to a customer's exact preferences, what utility is provided?

16-2. Two measures of the impact of retailing in the global economy are ______________ and ______________.

CLASSIFYING RETAIL OUTLETS

LO 16-2
Explain the alternative ways to classify retail outlets.

For manufacturers, consumers, and the economy, retailing is an important component of marketing that has several variations. Because of the large number of alternative forms of retailing, it is easier to understand the differences among retail institutions by recognizing that outlets can be classified in several ways. First, **form of ownership** distinguishes retail outlets based on whether independent retailers, corporate chains, or contractual systems own the outlet. Second, **level of service** is used to describe the degree of service provided to the customer. Three levels of service are provided by self-, limited-, and full-service retailers. Finally, the type of **merchandise line** describes how many different types of products a store carries and in what assortment. The alternative types of outlets are discussed in greater detail in this section. For many consumers today, retail outlets are also evaluated in terms of their environmentally friendly, or green, activities, in addition to their level of service and merchandise line. The Making Responsible Decisions box gives examples of the green activities of several retailers.[6]

Form of Ownership

There are three general forms of retail ownership—independent retailer, corporate chain, and contractual systems.

Independent Retailer One of the most common forms of retail ownership is the independent business owned by an individual. Independent retailers account for most of the 3.8 million retail establishments in the United States and include hardware stores, convenience stores, clothing stores, and electronics stores. In addition, there are 47,500 furniture stores, 106,400 gas stations, and 118,000 car dealerships. For the independent retailer, the advantage of this form of ownership is simple: The owner is the boss. For customers, the independent store can offer convenience, personal service, and lifestyle compatibility.[7]

Corporate Chain A second form of ownership, the corporate chain, involves multiple outlets under common ownership. Macy's, Inc., for example, operates 640 Macy's department stores in 43 states. Macy's also owns 38 Bloomingdale's, which compete with other chain stores such as Saks Fifth Avenue and Neiman Marcus. Finally, Macy's recently acquired Bluemercury, which includes 163 specialty beauty and spa services stores.

In a chain operation, centralization in decision making and purchasing is common. Chain stores have advantages in dealing with manufacturers, particularly as the size of the chain grows. A large chain can bargain with a manufacturer to obtain good service or volume discounts on orders. Target's large volume makes it a strong negotiator with manufacturers of most products. For consumers, the buying power of chains translates into lower prices compared with other types of stores. Consumers also benefit in dealing with chains because there are multiple outlets with similar merchandise and consistent management policies.

Shutterstock/digitalreflections

Retailing has become a high-tech business for many large chains. Walmart, for example, has developed a sophisticated inventory management and cost control system that allows rapid price changes for each product in every store. In addition, retailers are implementing pioneering new technologies such as Cloud-based Internet-of-Things platforms combined with radio frequency identification (RFID) tags to improve the quality of information available about the shopping experience in their stores.

Contractual Systems Contractual systems involve independently owned stores that band together to act like a chain. Recall that in Chapter 15, we described three kinds of contractual vertical marketing systems: retailer-sponsored

Making Responsible Decisions

Sustainability

How Green Is Your Retailer? The Rankings Are Out!

A recent Nielsen report indicates that more than 80 percent of global consumers believe that companies should help improve the environment. In response, many retailers are "going green" and developing comprehensive and sophisticated business practices that reflect a new focus on sustainability and environmental responsibility. The trend has become so important that *Newsweek* evaluates eight indicators of environmental performance to provide annual "green rankings" of large companies.

Some sustainability practices are intuitive and simple, such as encouraging the use of reusable shopping bags, installing LED lighting, and using nontoxic cleaning products. Many retailers are even using recyclable materials for credit and gift cards, rather than plastic. Other practices, such as reducing CO_2 emissions with economical delivery vehicles, using rainwater for landscape maintenance, or finding alternative uses for landfill waste, require a larger effort. Very often, however, these environmental initiatives also have financial benefits. When Home Depot switched light displays to compact fluorescent (CFL) and LED light bulbs, painted the roofs of stores white, and installed solar panels, it reduced its energy use by 20 percent.

Shopping malls are adopting the practices also. In Syracuse, New York, for example, Destiny USA mall implemented water harvesting, air quality protection, landfill reclamation, and energy conservation practices to become the largest LEED (Leadership in Energy and Environmental Design) certified retail building in the world. Similarly, Walgreens became the first retailer to construct a Net Zero Energy store by using solar panels, wind turbines, daylight harvesting, and energy-efficient building materials. To expand retailers' sustainability practices even further, some states such as California are adding "zero-waste" laws that require actions such as composting restaurant waste.

Do sustainability practices such as these influence your purchase decisions? If the answer is yes, you may want to review the green rankings at https://www.newsweek.com/green-rankings-2017-18. Are your favorite retailers "green"?

cooperatives, wholesaler-sponsored voluntary chains, and franchises (see Figure 15-6). One retailer-sponsored cooperative is Associated Grocers, which consists of neighborhood grocers that all agree with several other independent grocers to buy their goods directly from food manufacturers. In this way, members can take advantage of volume discounts commonly available to chains and also give the impression of being a large chain, which may be viewed more favorably by some consumers. Wholesaler-sponsored voluntary chains such as Independent Grocers Alliance (IGA) try to achieve similar benefits.

Orangetheory Fitness is a popular franchisor.
BrandonKleinVideo/Shutterstock

In a franchise system, an individual or firm (the franchisee) contracts with a parent company (the franchisor) to set up a business or retail outlet. The franchisor usually assists in selecting the location, setting up the store or facility, advertising, and training personnel. The franchisee usually pays a one-time franchise fee and an annual royalty, usually tied to the franchise's sales.

Franchising is attractive because it offers an opportunity for people to enter a well-known, established business for which managerial advice is provided. Also, the franchise fee may be less than the cost of setting up an independent business. The International Franchise Association recently estimated that there are 759,000 franchised businesses in the United States, which generate $757 billion in annual sales and employ more than 8.1 million people. Franchising is popular in international markets also: More than half of all U.S. franchisors have operations in other countries. What is one of the fastest-growing franchises? Orangetheory Fitness now has 1,000 locations, including 115 stores outside the United States.[8]

Franchise fees paid to the franchisor can range from $15,000 for a Subway franchise to $75,000 for a Hampton hotel franchise. When the fees are combined with other costs such as real estate and equipment, however, the total investment can be much higher. Franchisees also pay an ongoing royalty fee that ranges from 5 percent for a Papa John's pizza franchise to

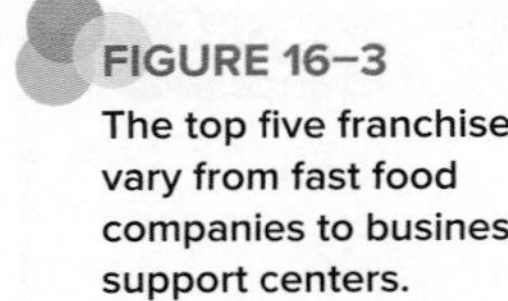

FIGURE 16–3
The top five franchises vary from fast food companies to business support centers.

Franchise	Type of Business	Total Start-Up Cost	Number of Franchises
McDonald's	Hamburgers	$1,058,000–$2,230,000	37,406
Dunkin' Donuts	Bakery	$ 228,621–$1,717,103	12,871
Sonic Drive-In	Fast food	$ 865,000–$3,641,300	3,593
Taco Bell	Mexican food	$ 525,000–$2,622,400	6,905
The UPS Store	Business support center	$ 168,885–$ 398,323	5,071

30 percent for an H&R Block tax preparation franchise. Figure 16–3 shows the top five franchises, as rated by *Entrepreneur* magazine, based on factors such as size, financial strength, stability, years in business, and costs. By selling franchises, an organization reduces the cost of expansion but loses some control. A good franchisor, however, will maintain strong control of the outlets in terms of delivery and presentation of merchandise and try to enhance recognition of the franchise name.[9]

Level of Service

Although most customers have little reason to notice form of ownership differences among retailers, they are typically aware of differences in terms of level of service. In some department stores, such as T.J. Maxx, very few services are provided. Some grocery stores, such as the Save-A-Lot chain, encourage customers to bring their bags from home. In contrast, outlets such as Neiman Marcus provide a wide range of customer services, from gift wrapping to wardrobe consultation.

Self-Service Self-service requires that customers perform many functions during the purchase process. Warehouse clubs such as Costco, for example, are usually self-service, with all nonessential customer services eliminated. Many gas stations, supermarkets, and airlines today also have self-service lanes and terminals. Video retailer Redbox has 40,000 kiosks throughout the United States—and operates without a single clerk. New forms of self-service are being developed at convenience stores, fast-food restaurants, and even car rentals. Amazon, for example, is opening new cashierless convenience stores called Amazon Go—just walk in, pick up your product, and walk out! At Zipcar you sign up, receive a Zipcard, book a car online, walk to a car, scan your card across a reader on the windshield to open the door, and drive away. In general, the trend is toward retailing experiences that make customers cocreators of the value they receive. Even banks are trying to change ATMs from being simple cash dispensers to serving as smart self-service devices.[10]

Amazon Go provides a service without clerks.
MariaX/Shutterstock

Limited Service Limited-service outlets provide some services, such as credit and merchandise return, but not others, such as clothing alterations. General merchandise stores such as Walmart, Kmart, and Target are usually considered limited-service outlets. Customers are responsible for most shopping activities, although salespeople are available in departments such as consumer electronics, jewelry, and lawn and garden.

Full Service Full-service retailers, which include most specialty stores and department stores, provide many services to their customers. Neiman Marcus, Nordstrom, and Saks Fifth Avenue, for example, all rely on better service to sell more distinctive, higher-margin goods and to retain their customers. Nordstrom offers a wide variety of services, including on-site alterations and tailoring; free exchanges and easy returns; gift cards; credit cards through Nordstrom Bank; a seven-days-a-week customer service line; a live chat line with beauty, design, and wedding specialists; online shopping with in-store pickup; catalogs; and a four-level loyalty program called The Nordy Club. During the next few years the company plans to invest in additional services and improvements such as personalized messages via a messenger app, "geofencing" so salespeople know when a customer is nearing the store to try on an online order, and "smart" fitting rooms. The full-service orientation has helped Nordstrom earn the title of most popular retailer for six consecutive years in an annual industry survey.[11]

Type of Merchandise Line

Retail outlets also vary by their merchandise lines, the key distinction being the breadth and depth of the items offered to customers (see Figure 16–4). **Depth of product line** means the store carries a large assortment of each item, such as a shoe store that offers running shoes, dress shoes, and children's shoes. **Breadth of product line** refers to the variety of different items a store carries, such as appliances and books.

Staples is the category killer in office supplies because it dominates the market in that category.
McGraw-Hill Education

Depth of Line Stores that carry a considerable assortment (depth) of a related line of items are limited-line stores. Dick's Sporting Goods stores carry considerable depth in sports equipment ranging from weight-lifting accessories to running shoes. Stores that carry tremendous depth in one primary line of merchandise are single-line stores. Victoria's Secret, a nationwide chain, carries great depth in women's lingerie. Both limited- and single-line stores are often referred to as *specialty outlets*.

Specialty discount outlets focus on one type of product, such as electronics (Best Buy), office supplies (Staples), or books (Barnes & Noble), at very competitive prices. These outlets are referred to in the trade as *category killers* because they often dominate the market. Best Buy, for example, is the largest consumer electronics retailer with more than 1,500 stores, Staples also operates more than 1,500 office supply stores, and Barnes & Noble is the largest book retailer. Interesting trends in this form of retailing include the use of price matching to compete with online retailers, improved websites and mobile apps, and shipping directly from any store with inventory rather than just warehouses.[12]

Breadth of Line Stores that carry a broad product line, with limited depth, are referred to as *general merchandise stores*. For example, large department stores such as Dillard's, Macy's, and Neiman Marcus carry a wide range of different types of products but not unusual sizes. The breadth and depth of merchandise lines are important decisions for a retailer. Traditionally, outlets carried related lines of goods. Today, however, **scrambled merchandising**, offering several unrelated product lines in a single store, is common. For example, the modern drugstore carries food, cosmetics, magazines, paper products, toys, small hardware items, and pharmaceuticals. Supermarkets sell flowers, school supplies, greeting cards, and pharmaceuticals, in addition to selling groceries.

FIGURE 16–4
Stores vary in terms of the breadth and depth of their merchandise lines.

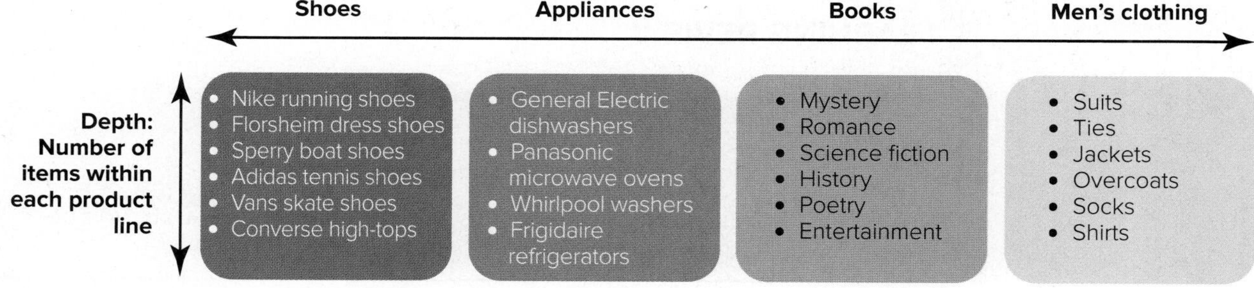

	Hypermarket		Supercenter	
Region of popularity	Europe		United States	
Average size	90,000–300,000 sq. ft.		100,000–215,000 sq. ft.	
Number of products	20,000–80,000		35,000	
Annual revenue	$100,000,000 per store		$60,000,000 per store	

Photos: (Left): PhotoStock10/Shutterstock; (Right): Marek Slusarczyk/123RF

FIGURE 16–5
Hypermarkets are popular in Europe, and supercenters are popular in the United States.

A form of scrambled merchandising, the **hypermarket**, has been successful in Europe. Hypermarkets are large stores (often more than 200,000 square feet) based on a simple concept: Offer "everything under one roof," thus eliminating the need to stop at more than one location. These stores provide variety, quality, and low prices for groceries and general merchandise items. Carrefour, one of the largest retailers in this category, has 1,507 hypermarkets, including 243 in France, 458 in the rest of Europe, 338 in Latin America, and 370 in Asia. Hypermarkets are also adding online, delivery, and smart store capabilities. Carrefour, for example, recently announced a partnership with Google to allow customers to place orders through its digital assistant, and it opened its first smart store in Shanghai that features facial recognition payment, mobile app product scanning, and personalized advertising.[13]

VIDEO 16-3
Walmart
kerin.tv/15e/v16-3

In the United States, retailers have discovered that shoppers are uncomfortable with the huge size of hypermarkets. In response, they have developed a variation of the hypermarket called the *supercenter*, which combines a typical merchandise store with a full-sized grocery store. Walmart and Target now use this concept at 3,570 Walmart Supercenters and more than 251 SuperTarget stores. Due to the increasing popularity of online retailers, however, the large size of these supercenters is no longer a certain advantage; Amazon.com, for example, is able to offer an even larger selection than these huge stores. Also, due to modern supply chain management techniques, smaller retailers are now able to keep shelves stocked without a lot of inventory. As customer interest shifts, retailers are modifying the supercenter concept to accommodate consumers' interest in smaller, more convenient stores. Walmart, for example, is expanding the number of its smaller-sized grocery stores, Walmart Neighborhood Markets, and Target has announced that it will be opening more than 100 new small-format stores in locations such as city centers, urban neighborhoods, and college campuses. Figure 16–5 shows the differences between the supercenter and hypermarket concepts.[14]

Scrambled merchandising is convenient for consumers because it eliminates the number of stops required in a shopping trip. However, for the retailer this merchandising policy means there is competition between very dissimilar types of retail outlets, or **intertype competition**. A local bakery may compete with a department store, discount outlet, or even a local gas station. Scrambled merchandising and intertype competition make it more difficult to be a retailer.

LEARNING REVIEW

16-3. Centralized decision making and purchasing are an advantage of ________________ ownership.

16-4. What are some examples of new forms of self-service retailers?

16-5. A shop for big men's clothes carries pants in sizes 40 to 60. Would this be considered a broad or a deep product line?

NONSTORE RETAILING

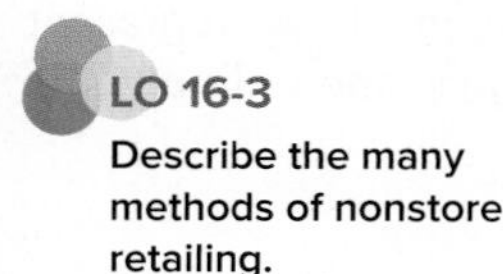

LO 16-3
Describe the many methods of nonstore retailing.

Most of the retailing examples discussed thus far in the chapter, such as corporate chains, department stores, and limited- and single-line specialty stores, involve store retailing. Many retailing activities today, however, are not limited to sales in a store. Nonstore retailing occurs outside a retail outlet through activities that involve varying levels of customer and retailer involvement. Figure 16–6 shows six forms of nonstore retailing: automatic vending, direct mail and catalogs, television home shopping, online retailing, telemarketing, and direct selling.

Automatic Vending

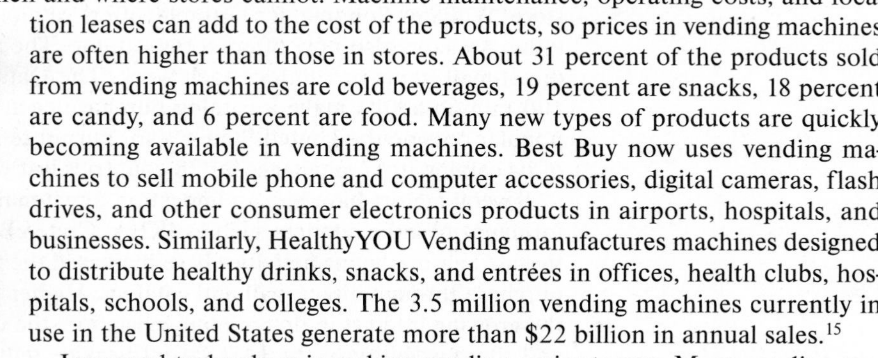

Nonstore retailing includes vending machines, or *v-commerce*, which make it possible to serve customers when and where stores cannot. Machine maintenance, operating costs, and location leases can add to the cost of the products, so prices in vending machines are often higher than those in stores. About 31 percent of the products sold from vending machines are cold beverages, 19 percent are snacks, 18 percent are candy, and 6 percent are food. Many new types of products are quickly becoming available in vending machines. Best Buy now uses vending machines to sell mobile phone and computer accessories, digital cameras, flash drives, and other consumer electronics products in airports, hospitals, and businesses. Similarly, HealthyYOU Vending manufactures machines designed to distribute healthy drinks, snacks, and entrées in offices, health clubs, hospitals, schools, and colleges. The 3.5 million vending machines currently in use in the United States generate more than $22 billion in annual sales.[15]

Vending machines offer a variety of products. Which types of products are most common in a vending machine? For the answer, see the text.
Rick Kern/Getty Images

Improved technology is making vending easier to use. Many vending machines now have touchscreens and credit card readers. In addition, some vending machine companies are testing wireless technology to allow consumers to make vending machine purchases using their mobile phones. Wireless technology is also being used by companies to monitor sales; this information is used to schedule trips to restock machines when items are sold out. Another improvement in vending machines is the trend toward "green" machines, which consume less energy by using more efficient compressors, more efficient lighting, better insulation, and sensors to detect when the surrounding area is vacant of

FIGURE 16–6
Many retailing activities do not involve a store. How many forms of nonstore retailing have you used?

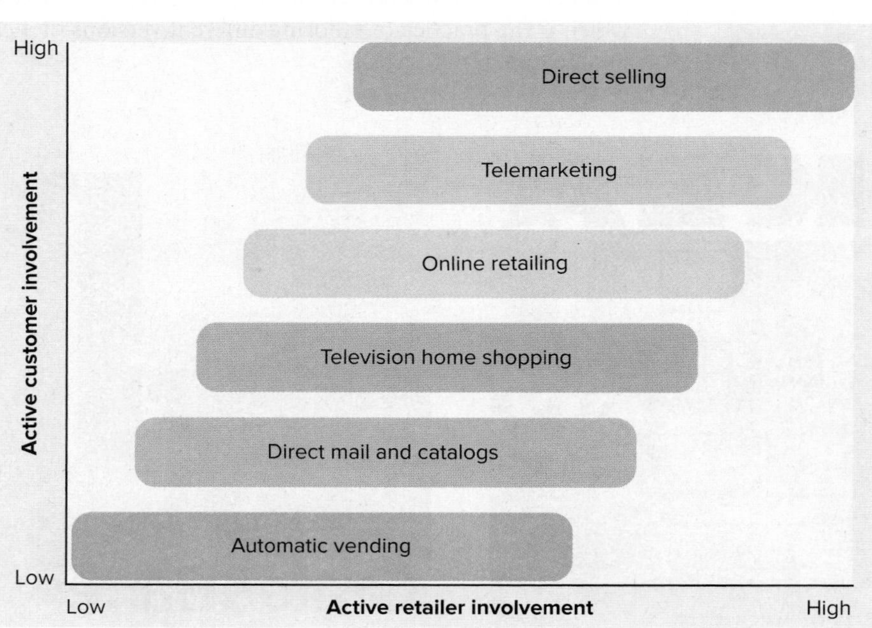

customers. Vending machines are popular with consumers; recent consumer satisfaction research indicates that 82 percent of consumers believe purchasing from a vending machine is equal to or superior to a store purchase. For today's consumers, vending machines represent an extension of brands that are already available in stores, through catalogs, and online.[16]

Direct Mail and Catalogs

VIDEO 16-4
IKEA
kerin.tv/15e/v16-4

Direct-mail and catalog retailing has been called "the store that comes to the door." It is attractive for several reasons. First, it can eliminate the cost of a store and clerks. Dell Technologies, for example, is one of the largest computer and information technology retailers, and it does not have any stores. Second, direct mail and catalogs improve marketing efficiency through segmentation and targeting, and they create customer value by providing a fast and convenient means of making a purchase. Finally, many catalogs now serve as an element of a multichannel strategy designed to encourage consumers to visit a website, a social media page, or even a store. Williams Sonoma, for example, offers catalog, online, and in-store shopping. Online retailer Amazon also now offers a toy catalog. The average U.S. household today receives 12 direct-mail items or catalogs each week. The Data & Marketing Association estimates that 100 million adults make a catalog purchase each year. Direct-mail and catalog retailing is popular outside the United States, also. Furniture retailer IKEA delivered millions of copies of its catalog in 17 languages for 28 countries last year.[17]

Several factors have had an impact on direct-mail and catalog retailing in recent years. The influence of large retailers such as IKEA, Crate&Barrel, L.L.Bean, and others has been positive as their marketing activities have increased the number and variety of products consumers purchase through direct mail and catalogs. Higher paper costs and increases in postage rates, the growing interest in do-not-mail legislation, the concern for "green" mailings and catalogs, and the possibility of the U.S. Postal Service reducing delivery to five days, however, have caused direct-mail and catalog retailers to search for ways to provide additional customer value. One approach has been to focus on proven customers rather than prospective customers. Another successful approach used by many catalog retailers is to send specialty catalogs to market niches identified in their databases. L.L.Bean, for example, has developed an individual catalog for fly-fishing enthusiasts.

New, creative forms of direct-mail and catalog retailing are also being developed. For example, retailers are adding content such as stories, images, and profiles of celebrity endorsers to catalogs to engage consumers. Williams Sonoma includes recipes in its catalogs, next to the products needed to cook them. In the future, you will also see merchants using "versioning," which is the practice of tailoring different versions of a catalog to different segments by varying the number of pages.[18]

Specialty catalogs appeal to market niches. They create value by providing a fast and convenient way to shop.

(Left): Source: Inter IKEA Systems B.V.; (Middle): Source: Crate and Barrel; (Right) Source: L.L.Bean Inc.

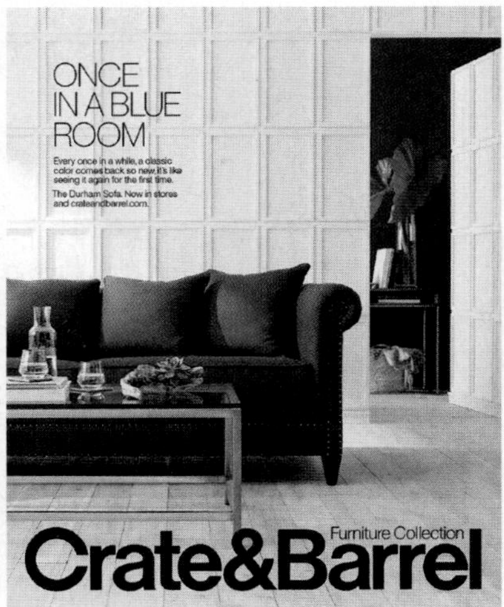

Television Home Shopping

Television home shopping is possible when consumers watch a shopping channel on which products are displayed; orders are then placed over the telephone or via the Internet. Currently, the three largest channels are QVC, HSN, and ShopHQ. QVC ("quality, value, convenience") broadcasts live 24 hours each day, 364 days a year, and reaches 370 million homes in the United States, United Kingdom, Germany, Japan, Italy, and China. The company generates sales of $8.8 billion from its 13 million customers by offering more than 800 products each week. The television home shopping channels offer apparel, jewelry, cooking and home improvement products, electronics, toys, and even food. The channels are facing new competition as YouTube begins to stream live shows, such as *Today's Shopping Choice*, a 24-hour, seven-day-a-week broadcast.[19]

Television home shopping programs serve millions of customers each year. See the text to learn how they are attracting new customers.
Source: QVC, Inc.

In the past, television home shopping programs attracted mostly 35- to 64-year-old women. To attract a younger audience, QVC has invited celebrities onto the show. For example, Ellen DeGeneres has been on the show promoting home furnishings, and Jonathan and Drew Scott have been hosts selling their Scott Living line. Broadcasting events, such as the *Red Carpet Style* show at the Four Seasons Hotel in Beverly Hills, also help attract new customers. In addition, QVC supports its television programming with retail stores, a website, mobile apps, text alerts, and the recently purchased flash sale shopping portal Zulily. QVC recently introduced Q Anytime as an iPhone app to provide a mobile shopping option. Similarly, Home Shopping Network now offers a multiplatform shopping experience. Some experts suggest that television shopping programs are becoming a modern version of door-to-door retailing by combining elements of reality TV programs, talk shows, and infomercials.[20]

Online Retailing

Online retailing allows consumers to search for, evaluate, and order products through the Internet. For many consumers, the advantages of this form of retailing are the 24-hour access, the ability to comparison shop, in-home privacy, and variety.

Online retail purchases can be the result of several very different approaches. First, consumers can pay dues to become members of an online discount service such as www.netmarket.com. The service offers thousands of products and hundreds of brand names at very low prices to its subscribers. Another approach to online retailing is to use a shopping "bot" such as www.mysimon.com. This site searches the Internet for a product specified by the consumer and provides a report listing retailers with the best prices. Consumers can also use the Internet to go directly to online malls (www.pricegrabber.com), apparel retailers (www.gap.com), bookstores (www.barnesandnoble.com), computer manufacturers (www.dell.com), grocery stores (www.peapod.com), and travel agencies (www.travelocity.com). Another approach is the online auction such as www.ebay.com, where 180 million buyers from 190 markets bid on more than 1.2 billion listings.[21] A final approach to online retailing are the "flash sales" featured at sites such as www.gilt.com and www.hautelook.com, which send text messages announcing limited-time offers at big discounts.[22]

One of the biggest problems online retailers face is that nearly two-thirds of online shoppers make it to "checkout" and then leave the website to compare shipping costs and prices on other sites. Of the shoppers who leave, many do not return as purchase propensity increases in later site visits. One way online retailers are addressing this issue is to offer consumers a comparison of competitors' offerings. At Allbookstores.com, for example, consumers can use a "comparison engine" to compare prices with Amazon.com, Barnesandnoble.com, and as many as 25 other bookstores. Experts suggest that online retailers should think of their websites as dynamic billboards if they are to attract and retain customers, and they should be easy to use, customizable, and facilitate interaction to enhance the online

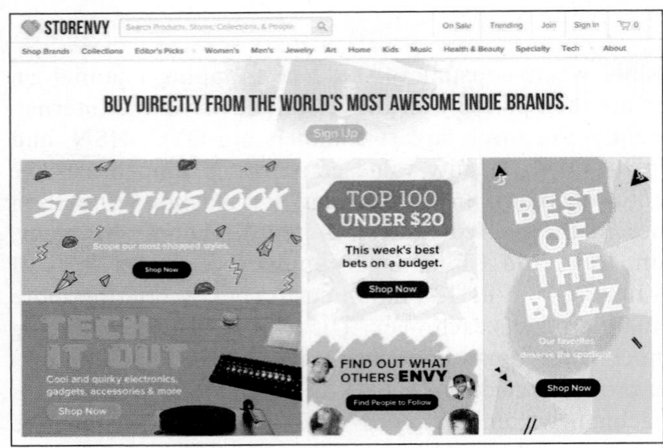

Shopping "marketplaces" like storenvy.com provide an easy way to set up online stores. Read the text to learn more!
Source: Storenvy

customer experience.[23] For example, BMW, Mercedes, and Jaguar encourage website visitors to "build" a vehicle by selecting interior and exterior colors, packages, and options; view the customized virtual car; and then use Facebook, Twitter, or e-mail to share the configuration with friends.

Online retailing is also evolving to include social shopping options, including: *intermediaries*, such as Groupon and LivingSocial, which match consumers with merchants; *marketplaces*, such as Storenvy, which provide self-service sites for online stores; and *aggregators*, such as Clarkdeals, which crawl the Web to find deals to list on their own site. Many consumers also use online resources as price comparison sites, influencing their offline shopping at local stores.[24]

Online retailing is again discussed in Chapter 17 in the context of interactive and multichannel marketing. The challenge of merging store and nonstore retailing is also discussed.

Telemarketing

Another form of nonstore retailing, called **telemarketing**, involves using the telephone to interact with and sell directly to consumers. Compared with direct mail, telemarketing is often viewed as a more efficient means of targeting consumers. Insurance companies, brokerage firms, and newspapers have often used this form of retailing as a way to cut costs but still maintain access to their customers. According to the Data & Marketing Association, more than 40 percent of businesses use telemarketing as a means of reaching consumers.[25]

The telemarketing industry has gone through dramatic changes as a result of legislation related to telephone solicitations. Issues such as consumer privacy, industry standards, and ethical guidelines have encouraged discussion among consumers, Congress, the Federal Trade Commission, and businesses. As a result, legislation created the National Do Not Call Registry (www.donotcall.gov) for consumers who do not want to receive telephone calls related to company sales efforts. The Registry now lists over 235 million telephone numbers. Currently the FTC and industry leaders are discussing measures to curb robocalls, or the use of autodialers to deliver a prerecorded message.[26]

Direct Selling

Mark A. Dierker/McGraw-Hill

Direct selling, sometimes called door-to-door retailing, involves direct sales of products and services to consumers through personal interactions and demonstrations in their home or office. A variety of companies, including familiar names such as Avon, Fuller Brush, and Mary Kay Cosmetics have created an industry with more than $35 billion in U.S. sales, and $189 billion worldwide, by providing consumers with personalized service and convenience. In the United States, there are more than 18.6 million direct salespeople working full time and part time in a variety of product categories, including wellness, home durables, and personal care.[27]

Growth in the direct-selling industry is the result of two developments. First, many direct-selling retailers have expanded into markets outside the United States. Avon, for example, has 6 million sales representatives in 80 countries. More than one-third of Amway's $8.8 billion in sales now comes from China and 90 percent comes from outside the United States. Similarly, other retailers such as Herbalife and Electrolux are rapidly expanding into new markets.[28] Direct selling is likely to continue to grow in markets where the lack of effective distribution channels increases the importance of door-to-door convenience and where the lack of consumer knowledge about products and brands increases the need for a person-to-person approach.

The second development is the growth in the number of companies that are using direct selling to reach consumers who prefer one-on-one customer service and a social shopping experience rather than online shopping or big discount stores. The Direct Selling Association reports that the number of companies using direct selling is increasing. Pampered Chef, for example, has 40,000 independent sales reps who sell the company's products at more than 1 million in-home "Cooking Shows" each year. Interest among potential sales representatives is growing because direct selling offers more independence and control of their work activities. Millennials, in particular, have observed that they can create a lifestyle that doesn't require a traditional nine-to-five routine.[29]

LEARNING REVIEW

16-6. Successful catalog retailers often send ________________ catalogs to ________________ markets identified in their databases.

16-7. How are retailers increasing consumer interest and involvement in online retailing?

16-8. Where are direct-selling retail sales growing? Why?

FORMULATING A RETAIL STRATEGY

LO 16-4
Classify retailers in terms of the retail positioning matrix, and specify retailing mix actions.

This section describes how a retailer develops and implements a retailing strategy. Research suggests that factors related to market and competitor characteristics may influence strategic choices and that the combination of choices is an important consideration for retailers.[30] Figure 16–7 identifies the relationship between strategy, positioning, and the retailing mix.

Positioning in a Retail Setting

Retail store positioning begins with a clearly defined consumer value proposition, as described in Chapter 2. Ulta Beauty, Inc., the largest beauty retailer in the United States with over 1,100 stores located in convenient and high-traffic power centers, is a case in point. The company's value proposition is straightforward: "All Things Beauty. All in One Place.™"[31] Ulta Beauty offers more than 20,000 premium and mass-market cosmetics, fragrances, and skin and hair care products. It also provides a value-added full-service salon in every store featuring hair and skin care services.

Ulta Beauty's store positioning is clear cut in the **retail positioning matrix** developed by the MAC Group, Inc., a management consulting firm.[32] This matrix positions retail outlets on two dimensions: breadth of product line and value added. As defined previously, *breadth of product line* is

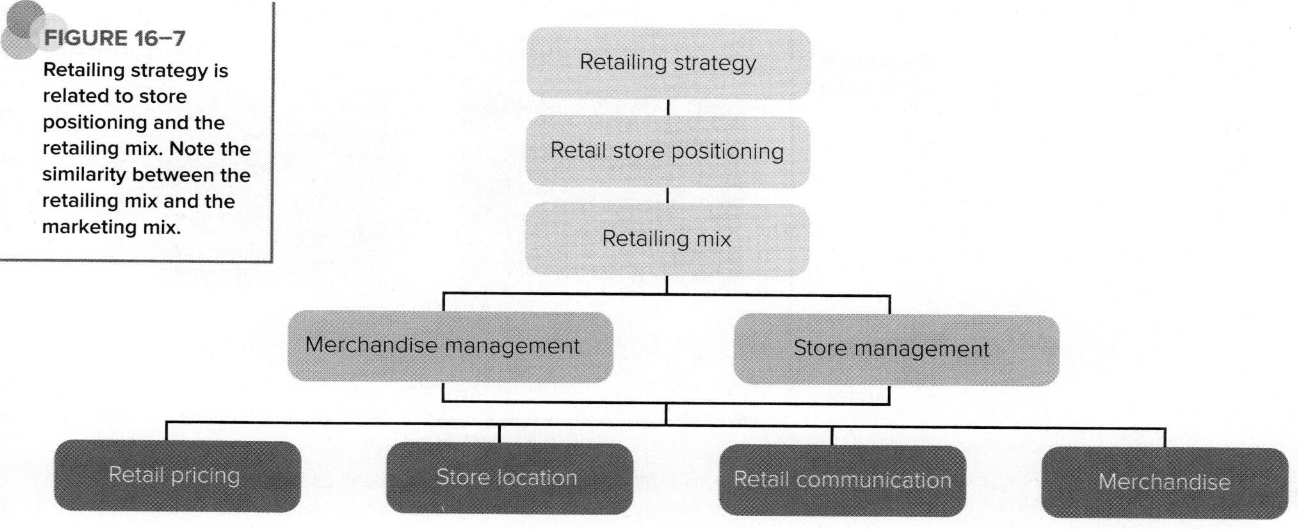

FIGURE 16–7
Retailing strategy is related to store positioning and the retailing mix. Note the similarity between the retailing mix and the marketing mix.

the range of products sold through each outlet. The second dimension, *value added*, includes elements such as convenient location, consistent product reliability, prestige, or customer service. Ulta Beauty successfully positions itself as a high value added, broad product line retailer.

The retail positioning matrix in Figure 16–8 shows four possible positions. An organization can be successful in any position, but unique strategies are required within each quadrant. Consider the four retailers shown in the matrix:

1. Bloomingdale's provides high value added and a broad product line. Retailers in this quadrant pay great attention to store design and product lines. Merchandise often has a high margin of profit and is of high quality. The stores in this position typically provide high levels of service.
2. Walmart has low value added and a broad product line. Walmart and similar firms typically trade a lower price for increased volume in sales. Retailers in this position focus on price with low service levels and an image of being a place for bargains.
3. Tiffany & Co. has high value added and a narrow product line. Retailers of this type typically sell a very restricted range of products that are high in status and quality. Customers are also provided with high levels of service.
4. DSW (short for Designer Shoe Warehouse) positions itself as a discount brand-name footwear retailer with a limited assortment of women's accessories. On the value-added and breadth of product line dimensions, DSW focuses on self-service and a narrow product line.

Retailing Mix

In developing a retailing strategy, managers work with the **retailing mix**, which includes activities related to managing the store and the merchandise in the store. The retailing mix is similar to the marketing mix and includes retail pricing, store location, retail communication, and merchandise (see Figure 16–7).

Retail Pricing In setting prices for merchandise, retailers must decide on the markup, markdown, and timing for markdowns. As mentioned in Appendix B (following Chapter 14),

FIGURE 16–8 Positioning strategies for retailers are based on breadth of product line and value added.

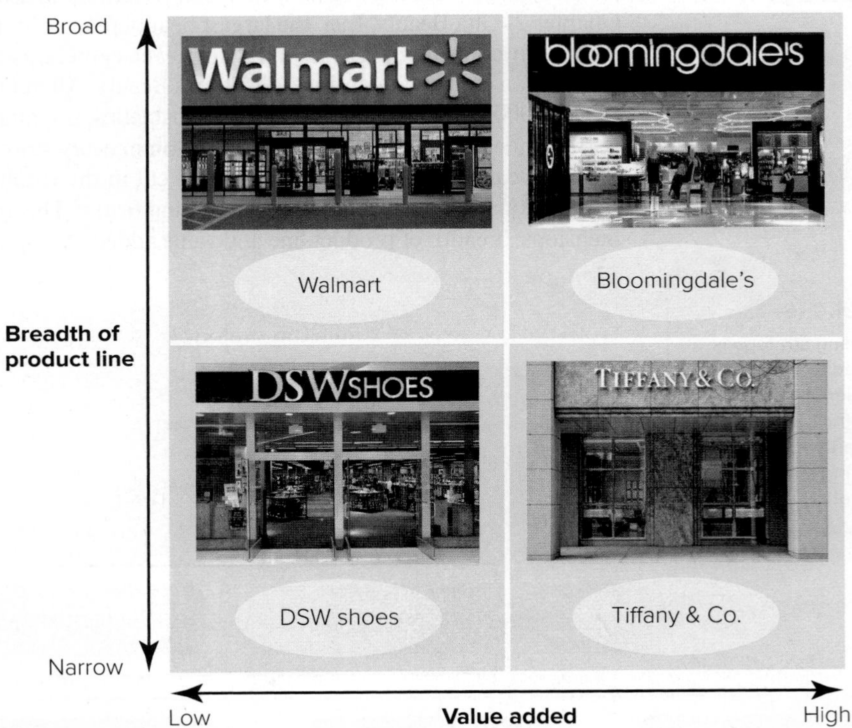

(Top left): Marek Slusarczyk/123RF; (Top right): Michael Gordon/Shutterstock; (Bottom left): Jeff Bukowski/Shutterstock; (Bottom right): Shutterstock/pio3

the *markup* refers to how much should be added to the cost the retailer paid for a product to reach the final selling price. Retailers decide on the *original markup*, but by the time the product is sold, they end up with a *maintained markup*. The original markup is the difference between retailer cost and initial selling price. When products do not sell as quickly as anticipated, their price is reduced. The difference between the final selling price and retailer cost is the maintained markup, which is also called the *gross margin*.

Rob Wilson/Shutterstock

Discounting a product, or taking a *markdown*, occurs when the product does not sell at the original price and an adjustment is necessary. Often new models or styles force the price of existing models to be marked down. Discounts may also be used to increase store traffic or demand for complementary products.[33] For example, retailers might take a markdown on the price of cake mix to generate frosting purchases.

The *timing* of a markdown can be important. Many retailers take a markdown as soon as sales fall off to free up valuable selling space and cash. However, other stores delay markdowns to discourage bargain hunters and maintain an image of quality. There is no clear answer, but retailers must consider how the timing might affect future sales. Research indicates that frequent promotions increase consumers' ability to remember regular prices.[34]

Although most retailers plan markdowns, many retailers use price discounts as part of their regular merchandising policy. Walmart and The Home Depot, for example, emphasize consistently low prices and eliminate most markdowns with a strategy often called *everyday low pricing (EDLP)*. Walmart is also developing a strategy it calls EDLP 2.0, which enables consumers to reduce their price through product bundling and payment and shipping options. Research indicates that consumer expectations about price are influenced by the store format. Specialty stores, drugstores, and convenience stores, for example, have a high price image, while online stores and mass merchants have a low price image.[35]

At off-price retail stores like T.J. Maxx, prices are low but selection may be unpredictable.
QualityHD/Shutterstock

Off-price retailing is a retail pricing practice that is used by retailers such as T.J. Maxx, Burlington Coat Factory, and Ross Stores. **Off-price retailing** involves selling brand-name merchandise at lower than regular prices. The difference between the off-price retailer and a discount store is that off-price merchandise is bought by the retailer from manufacturers with excess inventory at prices below wholesale prices. The discounter, however, buys at full wholesale prices but takes less of a markup than traditional department stores. Because of this difference in the way merchandise is purchased by the retailer, selection at an off-price retailer is unpredictable, and searching for bargains has become a popular activity for many consumers. Savings to the consumer at off-price retailers are reportedly as high as 70 percent off the prices of a traditional department store.

There are several variations of off-price retailing. One is the *warehouse club*. These large stores (75,000 to 190,000 square feet) are rather stark outlets that typically lack elaborate displays, customer service, or home delivery. Warehouse clubs require an annual membership fee (ranging from $45 to $110) for the privilege of shopping there. While a typical Walmart stocks 30,000 to 60,000 items, warehouse clubs carry 3,700 to 8,000 items and usually stock just one brand of appliance or food product. Customers are attracted by the ultra-low prices and surprise deals on selected merchandise. Service is minimal as the clubs focus on operational efficiency rather than the customer experience; however, several of the clubs have recently started to add ancillary services such as optical shops, photo departments, and pharmacies to differentiate themselves from competitors. The major warehouse clubs in the United States include Walmart's Sam's Club, BJ's Wholesale Club, and Costco. Sales of off-price retailers have grown to approximately $294 billion annually. A growing form of competition for warehouse clubs are online membership clubs such as Amazon Prime.[36]

Off 5th provides an outlet for excess merchandise from Saks Fifth Avenue.
JHVEPhoto/Shutterstock

A second variation is the *outlet store*. Factory outlets, such as Van Heusen Factory Store, Bass Shoe Outlet, and Gap Factory Store, offer products for 25 to 75 percent off the suggested retail price. Manufacturers use the stores to clear excess merchandise and to reach consumers who focus on value shopping.

Retail outlets such as Nordstrom Rack and Off 5th (an outlet for Saks Fifth Avenue) allow retailers to sell excess merchandise and still maintain an image of offering merchandise at full price in their primary store. Increasingly, retailers are offering merchandise made expressly for the outlet division. The growth of "bargain shopping" has increased demand for this type of off-price retailing, and many retailers have responded by opening more outlet stores. For example, Bloomingdale's recently opened several new outlets, bringing its total to 17. According to Bloomingdale's CEO, "Outlets deliver a compelling combination of fashion, quality, and value." Today there are approximately 216 outlet centers in the United States.[37]

A third variation of off-price retailing is offered by *single-price*, or *extreme value*, *retailers* such as Family Dollar, Dollar General, and Dollar Tree. These stores attract customers who want value and a "corner store" environment rather than a large supercenter experience. Some experts predict extraordinary growth of these types of retailers. Dollar General, for example, has 15,000 stores in 44 states and plans to open more.[38]

Store Location A second aspect of the retailing mix involves choosing a location and deciding how many stores to operate. Department stores, which started downtown in most cities, have followed customers to the suburbs, and in recent years more stores have been opened in large regional malls. Most stores today are near several others in one of five settings: the central business district, the regional center, the community shopping center, the strip mall, or the power center.

The **central business district** is the oldest retail setting, the community's downtown area. Until the regional outflow to suburbs, it was the major shopping area, but the suburban population has grown at the expense of the downtown shopping area. Consumers often view central business district shopping as less convenient because of lack of parking, higher crime rates, and exposure to the weather. Many cities such as Louisville, Denver, and San Antonio have implemented plans to revitalize shopping in central business districts by attracting new offices, entertainment, and residents to downtown locations.

Regional shopping centers consist of 50 to 150 stores that typically attract customers who live or work within a 5- to 10-mile range. These large shopping areas often contain two or three *anchor stores*, which are well-known national or regional stores such as Nordstrom, Saks Fifth Avenue, and Bloomingdale's. The largest variation of a regional center in North America is the West Edmonton Mall in Alberta, Canada. This shopping center is a conglomerate of more than 800 stores, the world's largest indoor amusement park, more than 100 restaurants, a movie complex, and two hotels, all of which attract 30 million visitors each year.[39]

A more limited approach to retail location is the **community shopping center**, which typically has one primary store (usually a department store branch) and often about 20 to 40 smaller outlets. Generally, these centers serve a population of consumers who are within a 10- to 20-minute drive.

Not every suburban store is located in a shopping mall. Many neighborhoods have clusters of stores, referred to as a **strip mall**, to serve people who are within a 5- to 10-minute drive. Gas station, hardware, laundry, grocery, and pharmacy outlets are commonly found in a strip mall. Unlike the larger shopping centers, the composition of these stores is usually unplanned. A variation of the strip mall is called the **power center**, which is a huge shopping strip with multiple anchor (or national) stores such as T.J. Maxx, Ulta, Ross Dress for Less, or Pier 1 Imports. Power centers combine the convenience of location provided by strip malls with the power of national stores. These large strip malls often have two to five anchor stores and contain a supermarket, which brings the shopper to the power center on a weekly basis.[40]

Shutterstock/QualityHD

Retail Communication A retailer's communication activities can play an important role in positioning a store and creating its image. The typical elements of communication and promotion are discussed in Chapter 19 (advertising, sales promotion, and public relations), Chapter 20 (social media), and Chapter 21 (personal selling); however, the message communicated by the many other elements of the retailing mix is also important.

Deciding on the image of a retail outlet is an important retailing mix factor that has been widely recognized. *Retail image* is often described as the way in which the store is defined in the shopper's mind, partly by its functional qualities and partly by an aura of psychological attributes. In this definition, *functional* refers to mix elements such as price ranges, store layouts, and breadth and depth of merchandise lines. The psychological attributes are the intangibles such as a sense of belonging, excitement, style, or warmth. Image has been found to include impressions of the corporation that operates the store, the category or type of store, the product categories in the store, the brands in each category, merchandise and service quality, and the marketing activities of the store.[41]

Closely related to the concept of image is the store's atmosphere, or ambience. Many retailers believe that sales are affected by layout, color, lighting, music, scent,[42] and other elements of the retail environment. This concept leads many retailers to use **shopper marketing**—the use of displays, coupons, product samples, and other brand communications to influence shopping behavior in a store. Shopper marketing can also influence behavior in an online shopping environment and when shoppers use smartphone apps to identify shopping needs or make purchase decisions. In creating the right image and atmosphere, a retail store tries to attract a target audience and fortify beliefs about the store, its products, and the shopping experience in the store. While store image perceptions can exist independently of shopping experiences, consumers' shopping experiences influence their perceptions of a store.[43]

Merchandise The final element of the retailing mix is the merchandise offering. Managing the breadth and depth of the product line requires retail buyers who are familiar with both the needs of the target market and the alternative products available from the many manufacturers that might be interested in having a product available in the store. A popular approach to managing the assortment of merchandise today is called **category management**. This approach assigns a manager the responsibility for selecting all products that consumers in a market segment might view as substitutes for each other, with the objective of maximizing sales and profits in the category. For example, a category manager might be responsible for shoes in a department store or paper products in a grocery store. As such, he or she would consider trade deals, order costs, and the between-brand effects of price range changes to determine brand assortment, order quantities, and prices. In addition, category managers must consider the impact of the location and assortment of other product categories if they share limited space (e.g., the checkout aisle) in a store.[44]

Retailers have a variety of marketing metrics that can be used to assess the effectiveness of a store or retail format. First, there are measures related to customers, such as the number of transactions per customer, the average transaction size per customer, the number of customers per day or per hour, and the average length of a store visit. Second, there are measures related to the stores and the products, such as level of inventory, number of returns, inventory turnover, inventory carrying cost, and average number of items per transaction. Finally, there are financial measures, such as gross margin, sales per employee, return on sales, and markdown percentage. The two most popular measures for retailers are *sales per square foot* and *same-store sales growth*. The Applying Marketing Metrics box on the next page describes the calculation of these measures for Apple Stores.[45]

LEARNING REVIEW

16-9. What are the two dimensions of the retail positioning matrix?

16-10. How does original markup differ from maintained markup?

16-11. A huge shopping strip mall with multiple anchor stores is a(n) ____________________ center.

Applying **Marketing Metrics**

Why Apple Stores May Be the Best in the United States!

How effective is my retail format compared to other stores? How are my stores performing this year compared to last year? Information related to these questions is often displayed in a marketing dashboard using two measures: (1) sales per square foot and (2) same-store sales growth.

Your Challenge

You have been assigned to evaluate the Apple Store retail format. The store's simple, inviting, and open atmosphere has been the topic of discussion among many retailers. To allow an assessment of Apple Stores, use *sales per square foot* as an indicator of how effectively retail space is used to generate revenue and *same-store sales growth* to compare the increase in sales of stores that have been open for the same period of time. The calculations for these two indicators are:

$$\text{Sales per square foot} = \frac{\text{Total sales}}{\text{Selling area in square feet}}$$

$$\text{Same-store sales growth} = \frac{\text{Store sales in year 2} - \text{Store sales in year 1}}{\text{Store sales in year 1}}$$

Your Findings

You decide to collect sales information for Target, Neiman Marcus, Best Buy, Tiffany, and Apple Stores to allow comparisons with other successful retailers. The information you collect allows the calculation of *sales per square foot* and *same-store sales growth* for each store. The results are then easy to compare in the graphs below.

Your Action

The results of your investigation indicate that Apple Stores' sales per square foot ($5,546) are higher than any of the comparison stores. In addition, Apple's same-store sales growth rate (20 percent) is higher than all of the other retailers. You conclude that the elements of Apple's format are very effective and even indicate that Apple may currently be the best retailer in the United States.

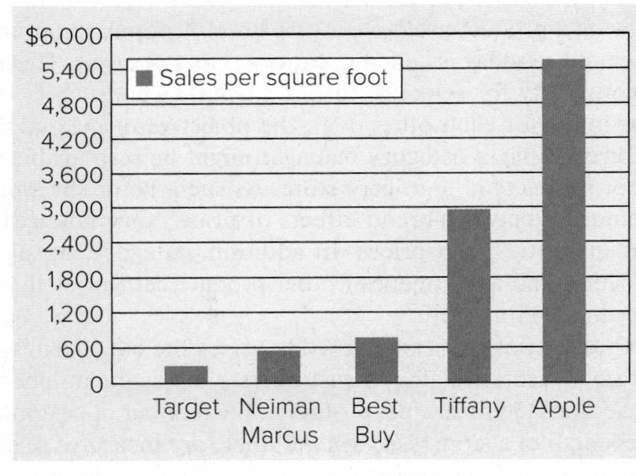

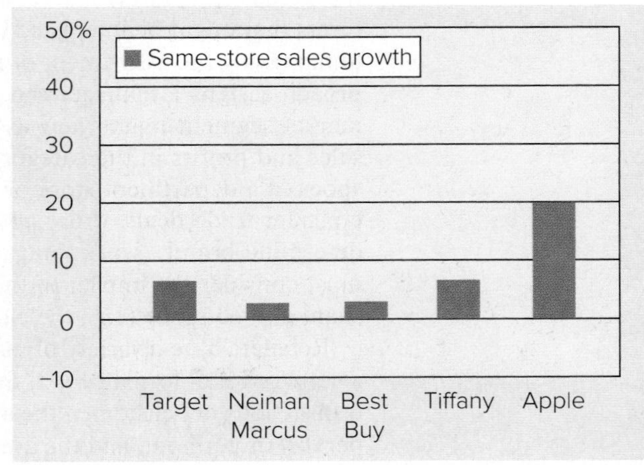

THE EVOLUTION OF RETAILING

LO 16-5

Explain changes in retailing with the wheel of retailing and the retail life-cycle concepts.

Retailing is the most dynamic aspect of a channel of distribution. New types of retailers are always entering the market, searching for a new position that will attract customers. The reason for this continual change is explained by two concepts: the wheel of retailing and the retail life cycle.

The Wheel of Retailing

The **wheel of retailing** describes how new forms of retail outlets enter the market.[46] Usually they enter as low-status, low-margin stores such as a drive-in hamburger stand with no indoor

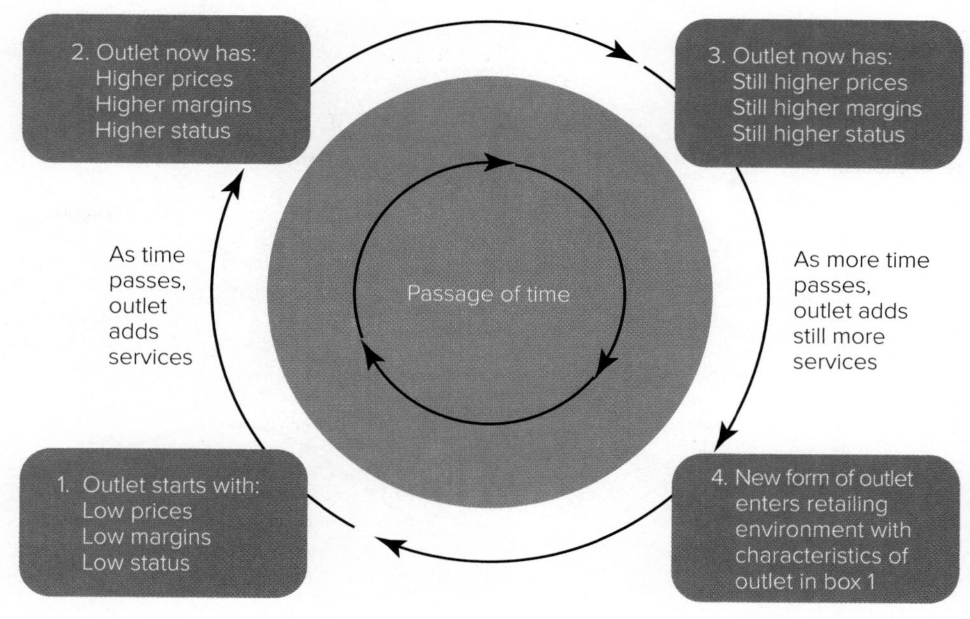

FIGURE 16–9
The wheel of retailing describes how retail outlets change over time. Read the text to find out the position of McDonald's and Checkers on the wheel of retailing.

seating and a limited menu (Figure 16–9, box 1). Gradually these outlets add fixtures and more embellishments to their stores (in-store seating, plants, and chicken sandwiches as well as hamburgers) to increase the attractiveness for customers. With these additions, prices and status rise (box 2). As time passes, these outlets add still more services and their prices and status increase even further (box 3). These retail outlets now face some new form of retail outlet that again appears as a low-status, low-margin operator (box 4), and the wheel of retailing turns as the cycle starts to repeat itself.

VIDEO 16-5
McDonald's
kerin.tv/15e/v16-5

When Ray Kroc bought McDonald's in 1955, it opened shortly before lunch and closed just after dinner, and it offered a limited menu for the two meals without any inside seating for customers. Over time, the wheel of retailing has led to new products and services. McDonald's introduced the Egg McMuffin and turned breakfast into a fast-food meal. Today, McDonald's offers an extensive menu, including oatmeal and premium coffee, and it provides seating and services such as wireless Internet connections and kid-friendly PlayPlaces. For the future, McDonald's is testing new food products, including snow crab on a sourdough bun, garlic fries, and fresh-beef Quarter Pounders, and new services, such as self-serve kiosks, mobile ordering, and table service.[47]

These changes are leaving room for new forms of outlets such as Checkers Drive-In Restaurants. The Checkers chain opened fast-food stores that offered only basics—burgers, fries, and cola, a drive-thru window, and no inside seating—and now has more than 700 stores. The wheel is turning for other outlets, too—Boston Market has added pickup, delivery, and full-service catering to its original restaurant format, and it also provides Boston Market meal solutions through supermarket delis and Boston Market frozen meals in the frozen food sections of groceries. For still others, the wheel has come full circle. Taco Bell is now opening small, limited-offering outlets in gas stations, discount stores, or "wherever a burrito and a mouth might possibly intersect."[48]

Outlets such as Checkers enter the wheel of retailing as low-status, low-margin stores.
Milesbeforelsleep/Shutterstock

The wheel of retailing is also evident in retail outlets outside the restaurant industry. Discount stores were once a major new retailing form and priced their products below those of department stores. As prices in discount stores rose, they found themselves overpriced compared with a new form of retail outlet—the warehouse club. Today, off-price retailers and factory outlets are offering prices even lower than warehouse clubs.

FIGURE 16–10
The retail life cycle describes stages of growth and decline for retail outlets.

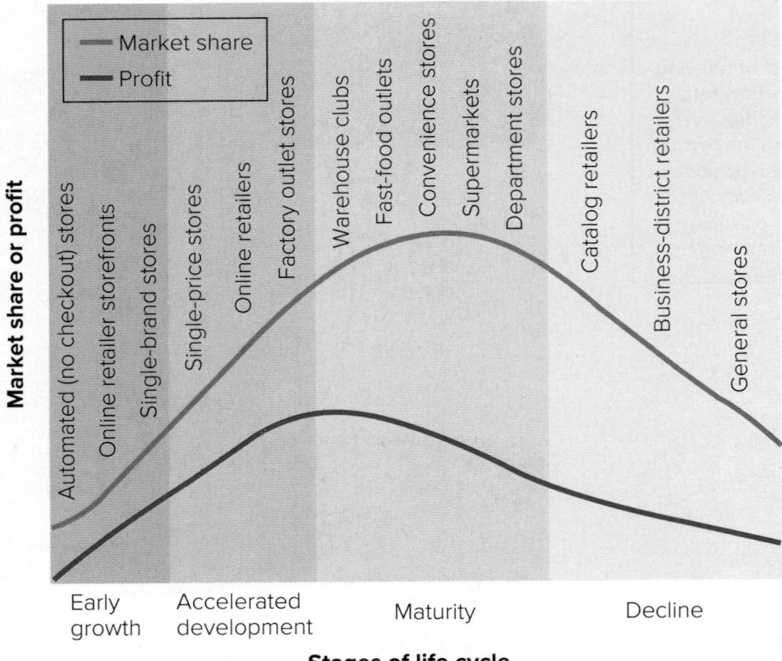

The Retail Life Cycle

The process of growth and decline that retail outlets, like products, experience is described by the **retail life cycle**.[49] Figure 16–10 shows the stages of the retail life cycle and where various forms of retail outlets are currently positioned along its spectrum. *Early growth* is the stage of emergence of a retail outlet, with a sharp departure from existing competition. Market share rises gradually, although profits may be low because of start-up costs. One form of new retail outlets includes online retailers such as Untuckit, Outdoor Voices, Adore Me, and thredUP, which are now opening storefronts. In the next stage, *accelerated development*, both market share and profit achieve their greatest growth rates. Usually multiple outlets are established as companies focus on the distribution element of the retailing mix. In this stage, some later competitors may enter. Wendy's, for example, appeared on the hamburger chain scene almost 20 years after McDonald's had begun operation. The key goal for the retailer in this stage is to establish a dominant position in the fight for market share.

The battle for market share is usually fought before the *maturity stage*, and some competitors drop out of the market. In the war among hamburger chains, Jack in the Box, Gino's Hamburgers, and Burger Chef used to be more dominant outlets. In the maturity stage, new retail forms enter the market (such as Fatburger and In-N-Out Burger in the hamburger chain industry), stores try to maintain their market share, and price discounting occurs.

The challenge facing retailers is to delay entering the *decline stage*, where market share and profit fall rapidly. Specialty apparel retailers such as Gap, Benetton, and Ann Taylor have experienced a decline in market share, department stores such as Macy's and Sears have closed hundreds of locations, and retailers such as Toys"R"Us, The Limited, Payless ShoeSource, RadioShack, and many others have closed or filed for bankruptcy. Industry analysts predict that almost 10 percent of the one million retail stores in the United States today will close by 2026.[50]

CURRENT TRENDS IN RETAILING

Two current trends in retailing–the growth of multichannel retailing and the increasing use of data analytics–are likely to lead to many more changes for retailers and consumers in the future.

Marketing Matters

Customer Value

The Multichannel Marketing Multiplier

Multichannel marketing is the blending of different communication and delivery channels that are mutually reinforcing in attracting, retaining, and building relationships with consumers who shop and buy in the traditional marketplace and marketspace. Industry analysts refer to the complementary role of different communication and delivery channels as an *influence effect*.

Retailers that integrate and leverage their stores, catalogs, and websites have seen a sizable lift in yearly sales recorded from individual customers. Eddie Bauer is a good example. Customers who shop only one of its channels spend $100 to $200 per year. Those who shop in two channels spend $300 to $500 annually. Customers who shop all three channels—store, catalog, and website—spend $800 to $1,000 per year. Moreover, multichannel customers have been found to be *three times* as profitable as single-channel customers.

JCPenney has seen similar results. The company is a leading multichannel retailer and reports that a JCPenney customer who shops in all three channels—store, catalog, and website—spends *four to eight times* as much as a customer who shops in only one channel, as shown in the chart.

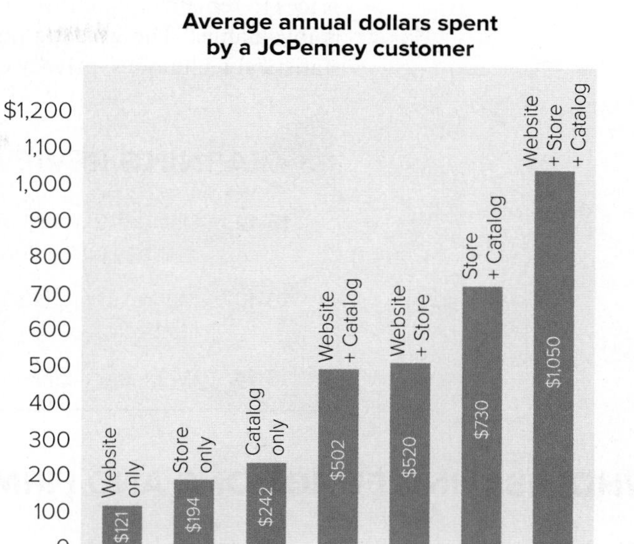

Multichannel Retailing

The retailing formats described previously in this chapter represent an exciting menu of choices for creating customer value in the marketplace. Each format allows retailers to offer unique benefits and meet the particular needs of various customer groups. While each format has many successful applications, retailers now combine many of the formats to offer a broader spectrum of benefits and experiences and to appeal to different segments of consumers. These **multichannel retailers** utilize and integrate a combination of traditional store formats and nonstore formats such as catalogs, television home shopping, and online retailing. Similarly, Crate&Barrel has integrated its store, catalog, and Internet operations, and Amazon has opened physical stores in six states, with more coming soon.

Multichannel retailers must be attentive to the different impacts of marketing activities in different channels, and the potential benefit of sharing information among the different channel operations. Recent research, for example, suggests that traditional store customers value the quality of the shopping experience while online customers are often motivated by convenience. Online retailers have recognized that the Internet often serves as a source of information and a transactional tool rather than a relationship-building medium, and they are working to find ways to complement traditional customer interactions. The benefits of this practice are also apparent in the spending behavior of consumers, as described in the Marketing Matters box.[51]

Crate&Barrel has integrated its store, catalog, and Internet channels of distribution.
Source: Crate and Barrel

Data Analytics

Data analytics has been described as the "new science of retailing." Data now available from the use of wearable technology (described earlier in this chapter) and the growth of multichannel marketing complement the substantial amounts of data already collected through scanner and loyalty card systems. The combination of these data sources has the potential to enable a new, comprehensive, and integrated analytical tool for retailers. In fact, a survey of 418 managers in eight industries indicated that firms in the retail industry have the most to gain from deploying customer analytics.

The use of data analytics can benefit retailers in at least three ways. First, understanding how consumers use multiple channels, information sources, and payment options can help retailers predict shopping behavior. Second, detailed customer-specific data allow merchants to provide personalized, real-time messaging and promotions. Finally, tracking customer needs allows retailers to offer innovative products, maintain optimal inventory levels, and manage prices to remain competitive and profitable. As one retailing expert explains, "this information is invaluable." The growing importance of data analytics is also increasing the attention to statistical techniques, privacy concerns, and ethical issues.[52]

LEARNING REVIEW

16-12. Using the wheel of retailing, describe the characteristics of a new retail form that has just entered the market.

16-13. Market share is usually fought out before the ________ stage of the retail life cycle.

16-14. What is an influence effect?

WHOLESALING FUNCTIONS AND FIRMS

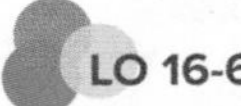

LO 16-6
Describe the types of firms that perform wholesaling activities and their functions.

Many retailers depend on intermediaries that engage in wholesaling activities—selling products and services for the purposes of resale or business use. There are several types of intermediaries, including wholesalers and agents (described briefly in Chapter 15), as well as manufacturers' sales offices, that are important to understand as part of the retailing process.

Merchant Wholesalers

Merchant wholesalers are independently owned firms that take title to the merchandise they handle. They go by various names, including *industrial distributor*. Most firms engaged in wholesaling activities are merchant wholesalers.

Merchant wholesalers are classified as either full-service or limited-service wholesalers, depending on the number of functions performed. Two major types of full-service wholesalers exist. *General merchandise* (or *full-line*) *wholesalers* carry a broad assortment of merchandise and perform all channel functions. This type of wholesaler is most prevalent in the hardware, drug, and clothing industries. However, these wholesalers do not maintain much depth of assortment within specific product lines. *Specialty merchandise* (or *limited-line*) *wholesalers* offer a relatively narrow range of products but have an extensive assortment within the product lines carried. They perform all channel functions and are found in the health foods, automotive parts, and seafood industries.

Two prominent types of limited-service wholesalers exist. *Rack jobbers* furnish the racks or shelves that display merchandise in retail stores, perform all channel functions, and sell on consignment to retailers, which means they retain the title to the products displayed and bill retailers only for the merchandise sold. Familiar products such as hosiery, toys, housewares, and health and beauty items are sold by rack jobbers. *Cash and carry wholesalers* take title to merchandise but sell only to buyers who call on them, pay cash for merchandise, and furnish their own transportation for merchandise. They carry a limited product assortment and do not make deliveries, extend credit, or supply market information. This type of wholesaler is common in electrical supplies, office supplies, hardware products, and groceries.

Agents and Brokers

Unlike merchant wholesalers, agents and brokers do not take title to merchandise and typically perform fewer channel functions. They make their profit from commissions or fees paid for their services, whereas merchant wholesalers make their profit from the sale of the merchandise they own.

Manufacturers' agents and selling agents are the two major types of agents used by producers. **Manufacturers' agents**, or *manufacturers' representatives*, work for several producers and carry noncompetitive, complementary merchandise in an exclusive territory. Manufacturers' agents act as a producer's sales arm in a territory and are principally responsible for the transactional channel functions, primarily selling. They are used extensively in the automotive supply, footwear, and fabricated steel industries. The Manufacturers' Agents National Association (MANA) facilitates the process of matching manufacturers' representatives with logical products and companies.

Courtesy of Manufacturers' Agents National Association

By comparison, *selling agents* represent a single producer and are responsible for the entire marketing function of that producer. They design promotional plans, set prices, determine distribution policies, and make recommendations on product strategy. Selling agents are used by small producers in the textile, apparel, food, and home furnishings industries.

Brokers are independent firms or individuals whose principal function is to bring buyers and sellers together to make sales. Brokers, unlike agents, usually have no continuous relationship with the buyer or seller but negotiate a contract between two parties and then move on to another task. Brokers are used extensively by producers of seasonal products (such as fruits and vegetables) and in the real estate industry.

A unique broker that acts in many ways like a manufacturer's agent is a food broker, representing buyers and sellers in the grocery industry. Food brokers differ from conventional brokers because they act on behalf of producers on a permanent basis and receive a commission for their services. For example, Nabisco uses food brokers to sell its candies, margarine, and Planters peanuts, but it sells its line of cookies and crackers directly to retail stores.

Manufacturers' Branches and Offices

Unlike merchant wholesalers, agents, and brokers, manufacturers' branches and sales offices are wholly owned extensions of the producer that perform wholesaling activities. Producers assume wholesaling functions when there are no intermediaries to perform these activities, customers are few in number and geographically concentrated, or orders are large or require significant attention. A *manufacturer's branch office* carries a producer's inventory and performs the functions of a full-service wholesaler. A *manufacturer's sales office* does not carry inventory, typically performs only a sales function, and serves as an alternative to agents and brokers.

LEARNING REVIEW

16-15. What is the difference between merchant wholesalers and agents?

16-16. Under what circumstances do producers assume wholesaling functions?

LEARNING OBJECTIVES REVIEW

LO 16-1 *Identify retailers in terms of the utilities they provide.*
Retailers provide time, place, form, and possession utilities. Time utility is provided by stores with convenient time-of-day (e.g., open 24 hours) or time-of-year (e.g., seasonal sports equipment available all year) availability. Place utility is provided by the number and location of the stores. Possession utility is provided by making a purchase possible (e.g., financing) or easier (e.g., delivery). Form utility is provided by producing or altering a product to meet the customer's specifications (e.g., custom-made shirts).

LO 16-2 *Explain the alternative ways to classify retail outlets.*
Retail outlets can be classified by their form of ownership, level of service, and type of merchandise line. The forms of ownership include independent retailers, corporate chains, and contractual systems that include retailer-sponsored cooperatives, wholesaler-sponsored voluntary chains, and franchises. The

levels of service include self-service, limited-service, and full-service outlets. Stores classified by their merchandise line include stores with depth, such as sporting goods specialty stores, and stores with breadth, such as large department stores.

LO 16-3 *Describe the many methods of nonstore retailing.*
Nonstore retailing includes automatic vending, direct mail and catalogs, television home shopping, online retailing, telemarketing, and direct selling. The methods of nonstore retailing vary by the level of involvement of the retailer and the level of involvement of the customer. Vending, for example, has low involvement, whereas both the consumer and the retailer have high involvement in direct selling.

LO 16-4 *Classify retailers in terms of the retail positioning matrix, and specify retailing mix actions.*
The retail positioning matrix positions retail outlets on two dimensions: breadth of product line and value added. There are four possible positions in the matrix–broad product line/low value added (Walmart), narrow product line/low value added (DSW), broad product line/high value added (Bloomingdale's), and narrow product line/high value added (Tiffany & Co.). Retailing mix actions are used to manage a retail store and the merchandise in a store. The mix variables include pricing, store location, communication activities, and merchandise. Two common forms of assessment for retailers are sales per square foot and same-store sales growth.

LO 16-5 *Explain changes in retailing with the wheel of retailing and the retail life-cycle concepts.*
The wheel of retailing concept explains how retail outlets typically enter the market as low-status, low-margin stores. Over time, stores gradually add new products and services, increasing their prices, status, and margins and leaving an opening for new low-status, low-margin stores. The retail life cycle describes the process of growth and decline for retail outlets through four stages: early growth, accelerated development, maturity, and decline.

LO 16-6 *Describe the types of firms that perform wholesaling activities and their functions.*
There are three types of firms that perform wholesaling functions. First, merchant wholesalers are independently owned and take title to merchandise. They include general merchandise wholesalers, specialty merchandise wholesalers, rack jobbers, and cash and carry wholesalers. Merchant wholesalers can perform a variety of channel functions. Second, agents and brokers do not take title to merchandise and primarily perform marketing functions. Finally, manufacturers' branches, which may carry inventory, and sales offices, which perform sales functions, are wholly owned by the producer.

LEARNING REVIEW ANSWERS

16-1 When Ralph Lauren makes shirts to a customer's exact preferences, what utility is provided?
Answer: form utility–involves the production or alteration of a product

16-2 Two measures of the impact of retailing in the global economy are ___________ and ___________.
Answer: (1) the total annual sales–5 of the 40 largest businesses in the United States are retailers; and (2) the number of employees working at large retailers

16-3 Centralized decision making and purchasing are an advantage of ___________ ownership.
Answer: corporate chain

16-4 What are some examples of new forms of self-service retailers?
Answer: New forms of self-service are being developed at warehouse clubs, gas stations, supermarkets, airlines, convenience stores, fast-food restaurants, and even coffee shops.

16-5 A shop for big men's clothes carries pants in sizes 40 to 60. Would this be considered a broad or a deep product line?
Answer: deep product line; the range of sizes relates to the assortment of a product item (pants) rather than the variety of product lines (pants, shirts, shoes, etc.)

16-6 Successful catalog retailers often send ___________ catalogs to ___________ markets identified in their databases.
Answer: specialty; niche

16-7 How are retailers increasing consumer interest and involvement in online retailing?
Answer: Retailers have improved the online retailing experience by adding experiential or interactive activities to their websites, allowing customers to "build" virtual products by customizing their purchases. Also, to minimize consumers leaving a website to compare prices and shipping costs on other sites, some firms now offer shoppers the ability to compare competitors' offerings.

16-8 Where are direct-selling retail sales growing? Why?
Answer: Direct-selling retailers are (1) expanding into global markets outside the United States and (2) reaching consumers who prefer one-on-one customer service and a social shopping experience rather than shopping online or at big discount stores.

16-9 What are the two dimensions of the retail positioning matrix?
Answer: The two dimensions of the retail positioning matrix are: (1) breadth of product line, which is the range of products sold through each outlet; and (2) value added, which includes elements such as location, product reliability, or prestige.

16-10 How does original markup differ from maintained markup?
Answer: The original markup is the difference between retailer cost and initial selling price, whereas maintained markup is the difference between the final selling price and retailer cost, which is also called the gross margin.

16-11 A huge shopping strip mall with multiple anchor stores is a(n) ___________ center.
Answer: power

16-12 Using the wheel of retailing, describe the characteristics of a new retail form that has just entered the market.
Answer: a low-status, low-margin, low-price outlet

16-13 Market share is usually fought out before the ___________ stage of the retail life cycle.
Answer: maturity

16-14 What is an influence effect?
Answer: An influence effect is the complementary role that different communication and delivery channels have on sales.

16-15 What is the difference between merchant wholesalers and agents?
Answer: Merchant wholesalers are independently owned firms that take title to the merchandise they handle and make their profit from the sale of merchandise they own. Agents do not take title to merchandise, typically perform fewer channel functions, and make their profit from commissions or fees paid for their services.

16-16 Under what circumstances do producers assume wholesaling functions?
Answer: Producers assume wholesaling functions when there are no intermediaries to perform these activities, customers are few in number and geographically concentrated, or orders are large or require significant attention.

FOCUSING ON KEY TERMS

breadth of product line p. 437
brokers p. 453
category management p. 447
central business district p. 446
community shopping center p. 446
depth of product line p. 437
form of ownership p. 434
hypermarket p. 438
intertype competition p. 438
level of service p. 434
manufacturers' agents p. 453
merchandise line p. 434
merchant wholesalers p. 452
multichannel retailers p. 451
off-price retailing p. 445
power center p. 446
regional shopping centers p. 446
retail life cycle p. 450
retail positioning matrix p. 443
retailing p. 432
retailing mix p. 444
scrambled merchandising p. 437
shopper marketing p. 447
strip mall p. 446
telemarketing p. 442
wheel of retailing p. 448

APPLYING MARKETING KNOWLEDGE

1 Discuss the impact of the growing number of dual-income households on (*a*) nonstore retailing and (*b*) the retail mix.
2 How does value added affect a store's competitive position?
3 In retail pricing, retailers often have a maintained markup. Explain how this maintained markup differs from original markup and why it is so important.
4 What are the similarities and differences between the product and retail life cycles?
5 How would you classify Walmart in terms of its position on the wheel of retailing versus that of an off-price retailer?
6 Develop a chart to highlight the role of each of the four main elements of the retailing mix across the four stages of the retail life cycle.
7 Refer to Figure 16–8 and review the position of DSW (Designer Shoe Warehouse) on the retail positioning matrix. What strategies should DSW follow to move itself into the same position as Tiffany & Co.?
8 Breadth and depth are two important components in distinguishing among types of retailers. Discuss the breadth and depth implications of the following retailers discussed in this chapter: (*a*) Nordstrom, (*b*) Walmart, (*c*) L.L.Bean, and (*d*) Best Buy.
9 According to the wheel of retailing and the retail life cycle, what will happen to factory outlet stores?
10 The text discusses the development of online retailing in the United States. How does the development of this retailing form agree with the implications of the retail life cycle?
11 Comment on this statement: "The only distinction among merchant wholesalers and agents and brokers is that merchant wholesalers take title to the products they sell."

BUILDING YOUR MARKETING PLAN

Does your marketing plan involve using retailers? If the answer is "no," read no further and do not include a retailing element in your plan. If the answer is "yes":

1 Use Figure 16–8 to develop your retailing strategy by (*a*) selecting a position in the retail positioning matrix and (*b*) specifying the details of the retailing mix.
2 Develop a positioning statement describing the breadth of the product line (broad versus narrow) and value added (low versus high).
3 Describe an appropriate combination of retail pricing, store location, retail communication, and merchandise assortment.
4 Confirm that the wholesalers needed to support your retailing strategy are consistent with the channels and intermediaries you selected in Chapter 15.

VIDEO CASE 16 Mall of America®: America's Biggest Mall Knows the Secret to Successful Retailing!

The secret to success at Mall of America is continually creating "new experiences for our guests," explains Jill Renslow, senior vice president of business development and marketing. "We want to make not only our locals, but also our tourists have a unique experience every time they come and visit," she adds.

> **VIDEO 16-6**
> **Mall of America Video Case**
> kerin.tv/15e/v16-6

That's an ambitious undertaking for any retailer, but it is particularly challenging for Mall of America because it attracts more than 40 million guests each year. To create new experiences the mall uses a combination of constantly changing retail offerings, entertainment options, and special attractions. From new stores, to musical acts, to celebrity book signings, to fashion shows, and even two appearances by Taylor Swift, Mall of America has become the "Hollywood of the Midwest." "The key truly is being fresh and exciting," says Renslow.

THE BIG IDEA FOR A BIG MALL

The concept of a huge mall was the result of several trends. First, covered shopping centers began to replace downtown main-street shopping areas in the United States. Second, retail developers observed that casinos were adding non-gambling activities to attract entire families. Taking their cue from Las Vegas, a Canadian family, the Ghermezians, built the West Edmonton Mall as a destination venue with shopping, restaurants, hotels, and a theme park. The success of the West Edmonton Mall led to the search for another location for the destination mall concept, and soon Mall of America was under construction in Minneapolis, Minnesota!

According to Dan Jasper, vice president of communications at Mall of America, the Ghermezians are a "wonder family that are visionaries." "They dream really big dreams, and they bring them to reality; they did that in Edmonton with the West Edmonton Mall, and they did that here in Minnesota with Mall of America," he explains. Today Mall of America is the largest mall in the United States with 4.8 million square feet of shopping and entertainment space. And it's getting bigger! "We're opening our new grand front entrance and that will bring us to 5.5 million square feet, making us by far not only the busiest, not only the most successful, but the largest, most massive mall in the nation," says Jasper.

Executives at Mall of America face several important challenges. First, they must keep a huge and diverse portfolio of retailers and attractions in the mall. Second, they must attract millions of visitors each year. Finally, they must increase its marketing and social media presence in the marketplace. The combination of these three activities is essential to the mall's continued success. This is particularly true at a time when e-commerce and online shopping are growing in popularity.

MANAGING THE MALL

The size of Mall of America is difficult to comprehend. There are more than four miles of storefront in an area the size of 88 football fields. Two anchor stores–Macy's and Nordstrom–are complemented by more than 500 specialty stores. The diversity of the retail offerings is equally amazing. The types of stores range from familiar names such as Banana Republic, Apple, and True Religion to unique stores such as Games by James, which offers thousands of board games and puzzles, and the LEGO® Store, which offers exclusive building kits and a giant pick-a-brick wall. According to Renslow, "That's what's special about Mall of America, that's what attracts people from around the world."

To encourage entrepreneurs to come to the mall there is a specialty leasing program that offers the new retailers an affordable entry-level lease in exchange for flexibility related to their location. New stores and attractions at the mall, for example, include b8ta, an electronics and technology store with the latest innovations; Baking Betty's, a store with hand-crafted cookies, pastries and ice cream; and the Void, a whole-body, fully immersive VR experience.

Mall of America also includes more than 20 restaurants, the House of Comedy for touring comedians, and an American Girl store with a doll hair salon and party facilities. The 14 theaters at Mall of America include a 200-seat 3D theater equipped with D-Box motion seating, and a 148-seat theater for guests 21 and older.

Additional unique features of Mall of America include:

- Nickelodeon Universe®, a seven-acre theme park with more than 20 attractions and rides, including a roller coaster, Ferris wheel, and a water chute in a skylighted area with more than 400 trees.

Nick Lundgren/Shutterstock

- Sea Life® Minnesota aquarium, where visitors can see jellyfish, stingrays, and sea turtles, snorkel with tropical fish, or even SCUBA with sharks!
- Two connected-access hotels including a 342-room JW Marriott and a 500-room Radisson Blu.
- The Chapel of Love, which offers custom weddings and wedding packages and has performed more than 5,000 weddings in the mall!

Regular events and activities include the Art + Style Series, Toddler Tuesdays, the Mall Stars program for people who want to walk and exercise in the mall, and the Mall of America Music Series. Mall of America also hosts corporate events for organizations with large groups. There are more than 12,000 free parking spaces available to accommodate any size group!

THE MARKET

From its opening day, visitors have been going to Mall of America at the extraordinary rate of 10,000 visitors per day. This is possible because the mall attracts shoppers from more than 18 states–including Minnesota, Wisconsin, Kentucky, Michigan, Ohio, and Pennsylvania–and from more than 11 countries–including Canada, Great Britain, France, Mexico, Germany, Scandinavia, Italy, the Netherlands, Japan, China, and Spain. The mall has worked closely with airlines and other partners to offer "Shop 'Til You Drop" packages that bring shoppers from around the world.

As Renslow explains: "Mall of America shoppers are literally from ages 3 to 83, which is a great opportunity for us but also a challenge. We need to be able to make sure that we communicate with each one of our guests. So we focus on the local market, which makes up 60 percent of our shoppers, and we also focus on our tourists who are 40 percent of our shoppers, and we have different messages to those different audiences." Another key target audience for the mall includes young women. Unmarried women have disposable income and like to travel, and married women are the primary purchase decision makers in their households and often bring their spouses, children, and girlfriends to the mall.

MARKETING, SOCIAL MEDIA, AND MALL OF AMERICA

Another key to Mall of America's success has been its ability to manage its presence in the marketplace. According to Sarah Schmidt, public relations manager for Mall of America, "A typical campaign for Mall of America includes TV, radio, and print, and we also include social media campaigns." A recent campaign called "The Scream Collector," for example, started with a TV ad and then followed up with progress reports on billboards. Another campaign created a blizzard in the mall. The "blizzard was a tweet-powered blizzard where guests had to tweet #twizzard, and once it hit a certain number of tweets it started snowing in the mall," Schmidt says.

Social media are important elements of Mall of America campaigns. Dan Jasper explains, "Mall of America is at the forefront of social media and digital technology

Jeffrey J Coleman/Shutterstock

within the retail industry; for shopping malls nobody has us beat." The mall has created a communication hub that integrates social media, texting, phone, and security all in a single system. "What that allows us to do is to speak with one voice, and to give real-time answers, suggestions, and advice to consumers," he says.

What is in the future for Mall of America? According to Jasper the answer is an even bigger mall. "In the coming years we're going to double the size of Mall of America," he says. So, prepare yourself for an even more extraordinary retailing experience![53]

Questions

1 What is the key to success at Mall of America?

2 What trends contributed to the idea for the Mall of America? How did it get started?

Chapter Notes

1. Jordyn Holman, Tiffany Kary, and Kim Bhasin, "A New Crop of Mall Rats," *Bloomberg Businessweek*, April 29, 2019, pp. 13–14; Samantha Kalany, "Smart Malls: IOT Is Impacting Retail Further," www.vartechnation.bluestarinc.com, April 3, 2019; "Apple Pay Leads the Way in Merchant Acceptance," www.mobilpaymentstoday.com, February 27, 2017; "Smart Stores," www.designretailonline.com, June 2016, p. 8; Pat Dermody, "Mobile Alters Customer Journey," *MMR*, March 7, 2016, p. 8; and Bob Violino, "Wearable Device Market to More Than Double over Next Five Years," www.information-management.com, October 6, 2016.
2. "The Fortune 500," *Fortune,* June 1, 2019, p. F-1; "GDP," The World Bank, data.worldbank.org, accessed September 19, 2019; "Annual Estimates of the Resident Population for Incorporated Places of 50,000 or More, Ranked by July 1, 2018 Population," American FactFinder, U.S. Census Bureau, factfinder.census.gov; and "GDP by Country 2019," www.worldpopulationreview.com, accessed May 18, 2019.
3. "Estimated Annual Sales of U.S. Retail and Food Service Firms by Kind of Business," 2016 Annual Retail Trade Survey, Washington, DC: U.S. Department of Commerce, Bureau of the Census, March 21, 2018.
4. "The Fortune Global 500," *Fortune*, August 1, 2018, p. F1.
5. "Location Facts," Walmart website, http://corporate.walmart.com/our-story/our-locations, accessed May 18, 2019; and Marcel Corstjens and Rajiv Lal, "Retail Doesn't Cross Borders," *Harvard Business Review,* April 2012, pp. 104–11.
6. "Sustainable Shoppers Buy the Change They Wish to See in the World," www.nielsen.com, November 8, 2018; Edmund Mander, "When Going Green Gets Rough," *Shopping Centers Today*, January 2017, p. 12; Lori Lovely, "A Net Zero Energy Retail Store in Chicago: A Walgreens Project Profile," www.foresternetwork.com, July 25, 2017; and "Newsweek Green Rankings 2017 Methodology," https://www.newsweek.com/newsweek-green-rankings-2017-methodology-739761, December 7, 2017.
7. "Industries at a Glance," Bureau of Labor Statistics, United States Department of Labor, www.bls.gov, May 18, 2019; "Retail Service Spotlight," www.selectusa.gov, May 17, 2019; and "The Economic Impact of the U.S. Retail Industry," PricewaterhouseCoopers and the National Retail Federation, 2014, p. 12.
8. "Franchise Business Economic Outlook for 2018," International Franchise Association, IHS Markit Economics, January 2018.
9. "2019 Franchise 500 Ranking," *Entrepreneur,* http://www.entrepreneur.com/franchise500.
10. Dennis Green, "Amazon Exec Reveals One of the Biggest Things the Company Has Learned about Shoppers at Its Cashierless Go Stores," www.businessinsider.com, May 19, 2019; Robert Channick, "Despite Growth of Streaming, Redbox CEO Sees Future in DVD Rentals," *Chicago Tribune*, July 20, 2017; and Antonella Comes, "Unlocking the Potential of Self-Service with Smart ATMs," *ATMmarketplace.com*, April 4, 2017.
11. "Nordstrom Again Ranks as Consumers' Favorite Premium Fashion Retailer," www.marketforce.com, February 1, 2018; and Phil Wahba, "Why Nordstrom Is Betting on High-Touch Tech," www.fortune.com, May 25, 2018.
12. Khadeeja Safdar, "Best Buy, after Turnaround, to Switch Leaders; CEO Hubert Joly Hands Top Job to Finance Chief Corie Barry," *Wall Street Journal Online*, April 15, 2019; and Miriam Gottfried, "How to Fight Amazon.com, Best Buy-Style," *The Wall Street Journal Online*, November 20, 2016.
13. Brittany Shoot, "Google Gets into Groceries by Partnering with France's Carrefour for Online Food Delivery," www.fortune.com, June 11, 2018; "Carrefour Opens Its First Smart Store in Shanghai," *Checkout*, June 2018, p. 16; and "Hypermarkets," Carrefour website, http://www.carrefour.com/content/hypermarkets, accessed May 18, 2019.
14. "Small-Format Stores Create New Possibilities," *MMR*, May 21, 2018, p. 65; Marianne Wilson, "Target Goes Next-Gen," www.chainstoreage.com, May/June 2017, p. 14; and Walmart website, https://corporate.walmart.com/our-story/our-business, accessed May 18, 2019.
15. Emily Refermat, "Annual Report: State of the Industry Annual Report," *Automatic Merchandiser,* June/July 2018.
16. John Bailey, "How Green Are Your Vending Machines?" *Vending International*, January/February 2016, p. 27.
17. "Annual and Sustainability Summary Report," INGKA Group, 2018; "About IKEA Catalogue," https://www.ikea.com/ms/en_JP/customer_service/faq/help/about_ikea/ikea_catalogue.html, accessed May 18, 2019; "Trends from 2017 DMA Statistical Fact Book," Direct Mail Statistics, Data and Marketing Association, https://thedma.org, accessed September 19, 2017; and John Mazzone and Samie Rehman, "The Household Diary Study," United States Postal Service, February 2017.
18. Denise Lee Yohn, "Why the Print Catalog Is Back in Style," *Harvard Business Review* online, February 25, 2015.
19. Bridget McCrea, "The 'Amazon-ing' of Home Shopping," *Response*, November 2016, pp. 32–36; and "Fact Sheet" from the QVC website, https://corporate.qvc.com/wp-content/uploads/qvc-corporate/2018/06/VVZaRExU.pdf, accessed May 19, 2019.
20. Dan O'Shea, "QVC Launches Mobile App with Shoppable Video, Unveils New Logo," www.retaildive.com, February 7, 2019; and Paul Ziobro, "Is There Time for QVC in the Age of Amazon?" *The Wall Street Journal*, January 9, 2017.
21. "Who We Are," eBay website, https://www.ebayinc.com/our-company/who-we-are/, accessed May 19, 2019.
22. Jacqueline Curtis, "How to Use the Best Flash Sale Sites to Score Deals," *Money Crashers,* February 20, 2013.
23. Chang Hee Park, "Online Purchase Paths and Conversion Dynamics across Multiple Websites," *Journal of Retailing*, September 2017, pp. 253–65; Susan Rose, Moira Clark, Phillip Samouel, and Neil Hair, "Online Customer Experience in e-Retailing: An Empirical Model of Antecedents and Outcomes," *Journal of Retailing* 2 (2012), pp. 308–22; and Feng Zhu and Xiaoquan (Michael) Zhang, "Impact of Online Consumer Reviews on Sales: The Moderating Role of Product and Consumer Characteristics," *Journal of Marketing* 74 (March 2010), pp. 133–48.
24. Onur H. Bodur, Noreen M. Klein, and Neeraj Arora, "Online Price Search: Impact of Price Comparison Sites on Offline Price Evaluations," *Journal of Retailing,* March 2015, pp. 125–39; and In Lee and Kyoochun Lee,

"Social Shopping Promotions from a Social Merchant's Perspective," *Business Horizons,* October 2012, pp. 441–51.

25. "Marketing Vehicle Frequency," *Statistical Fact Book* (New York: Direct Marketing Association, 2015), p. 24.
26. Katherine Skiba, "Do Not Call Registry Rises as Robocalls Drop," www.aarp.org, December 13, 2018; and Leonard Klie, "Apple, Google, Verizon, and Others Join Fight against Robocalls," *Customer Relationship Management*, November 2016, p. 18.
27. "Global Retail Sales of the Direct Selling Market," *Statista*, 2019; "Retail Sales of the Direct Selling Industry in the United States," *Statista*, 2019; "Direct Selling in the United States," Direct Selling Association, 2018; and Sharon Terlep, "Avon Ladies, Backed by Private Equity, Aim to Reconquer Middle America," *The Wall Street Journal*, March 21, 2017.
28. Eric Pfanner, "Avon Is Trying to Give Itself a Makeover," *Bloomberg Businessweek*, July 17, 2018; "Amway Reports Sales of $8.8 Billion USD in 2018," news release, www.amwayglobal.com, February 1, 2019; Phil Wahba, "Amway Boss Defends Direct Selling, Touts 'Made in the USA,'" www.fortune.com, December 11, 2014; and "Herbalife Plans Expansion of Manufacturing Capabilities in China," *Asia Pacific Biotech News,* September 2014, p. 22.
29. Amanda Shapiro, "Whatever Happened to Pampered Chef? I Hosted a Party to Find Out," www.bonappetit.com, March 26, 2018; and "Company Facts," The Pampered Chef website, https://www.pamperedchef.com/pws/baileehilt/company-facts, accessed May 19, 2019.
30. Dinesh Kumar Gauri, Minakshi Trivedi, and Dhruv Grewal, "Understanding the Determinants of Retail Strategy: An Empirical Analysis," *Journal of Retailing,* September 2008, p. 256.
31. "The Company," *ultabeauty.com*, April 4, 2019.
32. The following discussion is adapted from William T. Gregor and Eileen M. Friars, *Money Merchandizing: Retail Revolution in Consumer Financial Services* (Cambridge, MA: Management Analysis Center, Inc., 1982).
33. Dinesh K. Gauri, Brian Ratchford, Joseph Pancras, and Debabrata Talukdar, "An Empirical Analysis of the Impact of Promotional Discounts on Store Performance," *Journal of Retailing*, September 2017, pp. 283–303; Francis J. Mulhern and Robert P. Leon, "Implicit Price Bundling of Retail Products: A Multiproduct Approach to Maximizing Store Profitability," *Journal of Marketing,* October 1991, pp. 63–76.
34. Marc Vanhuele and Xavier Dreze, "Measuring the Price Knowledge Shoppers Bring to the Store," *Journal of Marketing,* October 2002, pp. 72–85.
35. Anthony Koschmann and Mathew S. Isaac, "Retailer Categorization: How Store-Format Price Image Influences Expected Prices and Consumer Choices," *Journal of Retailing* 94, no. 4 (2018), pp. 364–79; "Walmart Enables Customers to Play a Role in EDLP 2.0," *MMR,* December 19, 2016, p. 59; and "Are Sales a Thing of the Past?" *Newstex,* www.jennstrathman.com, January 10, 2013.
36. "2019 U.S. Industry & Market Report: Warehouse Clubs & Superstores Industry," C. Barnes & Co., 2019; "Warehouse Clubs & Superstores," *Hoover's,* www.hoovers.com, June 2, 2017; and "After Four Decades, Club Format Still a Hit," *MMR,* May 22, 2017, p. 101.
37. Liz Wolf, "Can Outlet Centers Continue to Succeed by Luring Shoppers with Bargains and 'Experience?'" www.nreionline.com, September 13, 2018; and "Bloomingdale's The Outlet," Macy's website, https://www.macysinc.com/brands/bloomingdales, accessed May 19, 2019.
38. "About Us," Dollar General website, https://aboutus.dollargeneral.com, accessed May 19, 2019.
39. "About WEM," West Edmonton Mall website, http://www.wem.ca/about-wem/overview, accessed June 2, 2017.
40. John Tennant, "Power Centers Boom in Secondary Markets," *Shopping Center Business*, September 21, 2016, p. 70; and "Power Centers Lead U.S. Sectors," *Shopping Centers Today*, July 2014, p. 58.
41. Julie Baker, Dhruv Grewal, and A. Parasuraman, "The Influence of Store Environment on Quality Inferences and Store Image," *Journal of the Academy of Marketing Science,* Fall 1994, pp. 328–39; Susan M. Keaveney and Kenneth A. Hunt, "Conceptualization and Operationalization of Retail Store Image: A Case of Rival Middle-Level Theories," *Journal of the Academy of Marketing Science,* Spring 1992, pp. 165–75; and James C. Ward, Mary Jo Bitner, and John Barnes, "Measuring the Prototypicality and Meaning of Retail Environments," *Journal of Retailing,* Summer 1992, pp. 194–207.
42. Andreas Herrmann, Manja Zidansek, David E. Sprott, and Eric R. Spangenberg, "The Power of Simplicity: Processing Fluency and the Effects of Olfactory Cues on Retail Sales," *Journal of Retailing* 1 (2013), pp. 30–43.
43. Roger A. Kerin, Ambuj Jain, and Daniel L. Howard, "Store Shopping Experience and Consumer Price-Quality-Value Perceptions," *Journal of Retailing,* Winter 1992, pp. 376–97.
44. Sungtak Hong, Kanishka Misra, and Naufel J. Vilcassim, "The Perils of Category Management: The Effect of Product Assortment on Multicategory Purchase Incidence," *Journal of Marketing*, September 2016, pp. 34–52.
45. Chance Miller, "Apple Again Found to Be the World's Top Retailer in Sales per Square Foot," www.9to5mac.com, July 29, 2017; Walter Loeb, "Why Productivity in Retail Sales Matters," www.forbes.com, April 24, 2017; Shari Water, "How Same-Store Sales Figures Are Used in Retail," www.the balancesmb.com, January 30, 2019; and Neil T. Bendle, Paul W. Farris, Phillip E. Pfeifer, and David J. Reibstein, *Marketing Metrics,* 3rd ed. (Upper Saddle River, NJ: Pearson Education, 2015).
46. The wheel of retailing theory was originally proposed by Malcolm P. McNair, "Significant Trends and Developments in the Postwar Period," in *Competitive Distribution in a Free, High-Level Economy and Its Implications for the University,* ed. A. B. Smith (Pittsburgh: University of Pittsburgh Press, 1958), pp. 1–25; also see Stephen Brown, "The Wheel of Retailing—Past and Future," *Journal of Retailing,* Summer 1990, pp. 143–49; and Malcolm P. McNair and Eleanor May, "The Next Revolution of the Retailing Wheel," *Harvard Business Review,* September–October 1978, pp. 81–91.
47. "McDonald's Tests Crab on Sourdough," www.QSRweb.com, March 1, 2017, p. 56; Bill Peters, "McDonald's Will Serve Fresh-Beef Quarter Pounders," *Investors Business Daily*, March 30, 2017, p. 20; "Bronx McDonald's Introduces Self-Service Kiosks," www.KioskMarketplace.com, February 1, 2017, p. 1; and Johnathan Maze, "McDonald's Adds Mobile Ordering, Table Service," *Nation's Restaurant News*," December 12, 2016, pp. 46–47.
48. "Our Story," Checkers website, http://checkerscompany.com/our_story, accessed June 12, 2015; and "Story," Boston Market website, http://www.bostonmarket.com/ourStory/index.jsp?page=story, accessed June 12, 2015.
49. William R. Davidson, Albert D. Bates, and Stephen J. Bass, "Retail Life Cycle," *Harvard Business Review,* November–December 1976, pp. 89–96.
50. Lauren Thomas, "Watch Out for These 8 Retailers—They're Ready to Grow in the US," www.cnbc.com, May 26, 2018; and "Retail Downsizing Will Accelerate, with UBS Predicting 75,000 Stores Will Be Forced to Close by 2026," *forbes.com*, April 10, 2019.
51. G. Tomas M. Hult, Pratyush Nidhi Sharma, Forrest V. Morgeson III, and Jufei Zhang, "Antecedents and Consequences of Customer Satisfaction: Do They Differ across Online and Offline Purchases?" *Journal of Retailing* 95, no. 1 (2019), pp. 10–23; Robert Berner, "J.C. Penney Gets the Net," *BusinessWeek,* May 7, 2007, p. 70; *Multi-Channel Integration: The New Retail Battleground* (Columbus, OH: PricewaterhouseCoopers, March 2001); and Richard Last, "JC Penney Internet Commerce," presentation at Southern Methodist University, February 12, 2001.
52. Eric T. Bradlow, Manish Gangwar, Praveen Kopalle, Sudhir Voleti, "The Role of Big Data and Predictive Analytics in Retailing," *Journal of Retailing*, March 2017, pp. 79–95; and "Are You Sitting on a Data Goldmine? What All Retail Brands Need to Know," www.RetailCustomerExperience.com, May 25, 2017.
53. Mall of America: This case was written by Steven Hartley. Sources: Jennifer Latson, "Why America's Biggest Mall Is Getting Bigger," www.Time.com, August 12, 2015; Samuel Greengard, "Mall of America Increases Its Social Presence," *CIO Insight*, July 28, 2015, p. 2; "JW Mall of America Hotel Set to Open in November," *Travel Weekly*, April 9, 2015, p. 17; and the Mall of America website, http://www.mallofamerica.com/.

Chapter 17 Implementing Interactive and Multichannel Marketing

LEARNING OBJECTIVES

After reading this chapter you should be able to:

LO 17-1 Describe what interactive marketing is and how it creates customer value, customer relationships, and customer experiences.

LO 17-2 Explain why certain types of products and services are particularly suited for interactive marketing and online shopping and buying.

LO 17-3 Describe why consumers shop and buy online and how marketers influence online purchasing behavior.

LO 17-4 Define cross-channel consumers and the role of multichannel marketing in reaching these consumers.

Seven Cycles Delivers Just One Bike. Yours.

"One Bike. Yours."[1] is the company tagline for Seven Cycles, Inc., located in Watertown, Massachusetts. And for good reason.

Seven Cycles is the world's largest custom bicycle frame builder. The company produces a broad range of road, mountain, cyclocross, tandem, touring, single-speed, and commuter bikes annually, and no two bikes are exactly alike. This feat is all the more impressive because Seven Cycles has sold over 30,000 custom-made bicycles since its founding 24 years ago. Custom bikes do come at a premium. Prices start at around $4,000.

At Seven Cycles, attention is focused on each customer's unique cycling experience through the optimum fit, function, performance, and comfort of his or her very own bike. According to one satisfied customer, "Getting a Seven is more of a creation than a purchase."

While Seven Cycles does offer stock frames in more than 200 sizes, each is still built to order and a full 95 percent of the bicycle frames that Seven ships are completely custom made. Customized elements include frame size, frame geometry, tubing diameters, and wall thickness, as well as countless options such as cable routing, water bottle mounts, paint color, and decal color. Every custom option is available at no additional charge, and the number of combinations is virtually infinite.

The marketing success of Seven Cycles is due to its state-of-the-art custom-built carbon, titanium, and steel bicycle frames. But as Rob Vandermark, company founder and president, says, "Part of our success is that we are tied to a business model that includes the Internet."

Seven uses its multilanguage (English, German, Swedish, Italian, Chinese, Japanese, Korean, and Flemish) website (www.sevencycles.com) to let customers get deeply involved in the frame-building process and the selection of components to outfit their complete bike. It enables customers to collaborate on the design of their own bike using the company's Custom Kit fitting system, which considers the rider's size, aspirations, and riding habits. Then customers can monitor their bike's progress through the development and production process by clicking "Where's My Frame?" on the Seven Cycles website.

This customization process and continuous feedback make for a collaborative relationship between Seven Cycles and its 200 authorized retailers in the United States. Some 30 international distributors and customers in 40 countries account for about 40 percent of the company's bike sales. "Our whole process is designed to keep the focus on the rider the bike is being built for, so it ends up being a very different and more interactive experience than most people are used to. That experience is a large part of the value we sell, above and beyond the bike," explains Jennifer Miller, co-founder and chief financial officer at Seven Cycles.

seven 7 cycles

Courtesy of Seven Cycles, Inc.

In addition to the order process, website visitors can peruse weekly news stories and learn about new product introductions to get a unique perspective on the business. They can read employee biographies online to learn more about the people who build the bikes. The website also offers a retailer-specific section as a 24/7 repository of updated information for the company's channel partners.

Beyond the website, current Seven owners can interact with the company on the Seven Cycles blog to learn about its activities and products. Seven Cycles also uses its company Facebook page, Instagram, and Twitter to post brief and timely updates and build a stronger sense of community around the brand.[2]

This chapter describes how companies design and implement interactive marketing programs. It begins by explaining how Internet technology can create customer value, build customer relationships, and produce customer experiences in novel ways. Next, it describes how Internet technology affects and is affected by consumer behavior and marketing practices. Finally, the chapter shows how marketers integrate and leverage their communication and delivery channels to implement multichannel marketing programs to better serve cross-channel consumers.

CREATING CUSTOMER VALUE, RELATIONSHIPS, AND EXPERIENCES IN A DIGITAL ENVIRONMENT

LO 17-1

Describe what interactive marketing is and how it creates customer value, customer relationships, and customer experiences.

Consumers and companies populate two market environments today. One is the traditional *marketplace*. Here buyers and sellers engage in face-to-face exchange relationships in a material environment characterized by physical facilities (stores and offices) and mostly tangible objects. The other is the *digital marketspace*, a digitally enabled environment characterized by face-to-screen exchange relationships and electronic images and offerings.

Marketing Challenges in Two Environments

The existence of two market environments is a boon for consumers. Many consumers browse and buy in both market environments. More are expected to do so in the future as mobile devices, notably smartphones, expand their capabilities.

About 90 percent of Internet users aged 15 and older have shopped online in the United States. They are expected to buy over $500 billion worth of products and services in 2022 (excluding travel, automobile, and prescription drugs).[3]

Nevertheless, marketing in two market environments poses significant challenges for companies based on their origin in the traditional marketplace and digital marketspace. In fact, the challenge of marketing in two environments has revolutionized marketing channel and supply chain systems and traditional retailing.

Legacy Companies Legacy companies that trace their origins to the traditional marketplace, such as Procter & Gamble, Walmart, and General Motors, are continually challenged to define the nature and scope of their marketspace presence. These companies consistently refine the role of digital technology in attracting, retaining, and building consumer relationships to improve their competitive positions in the traditional marketplace while also bolstering their marketspace presence. Other companies with marketplace origins have chosen not to participate in the marketspace. Luxury fashion designs, for the most part, don't sell their products online. According to the founder of Prada, "We think that, for luxury, it's not right. Personally, I'm not interested."[4] Not surprisingly, over 90 percent of luxury fashion merchandise is sold exclusively through retail stores.

Digital Natives On the other hand, digital natives with marketspace origins, including Amazon.com, Google, eBay, E*TRADE, and others, are challenged to continually refine, broaden, and deepen their marketspace presence. At the same time, these and other companies must consider what role, if any, the traditional marketplace will play in their future. For example, eyeglass online retailer Warby Parker, online mattress seller Casper Sleep, clothing online retailer Bonobos, jewelry online retailer Blue Nile, and, yes, Amazon, have opened physical showrooms that give shoppers an opportunity to experience the company's products in person before purchasing them online.

Regardless of origin, a company's success in achieving a meaningful marketspace presence hinges largely on (1) its ability to design and execute a marketing program that capitalizes on the unique value creation and (2) the relationship-building capabilities of digital technology in delivering a favorable customer experience.

Creating Customer Value in a Digital Environment

Why has the marketspace captured the eye and imagination of marketers worldwide? Recall that marketing creates time, place, form, and possession utilities, thereby creating value for consumers. Marketers believe that the possibilities for customer value creation are greater in the digital marketspace than in the physical marketplace.

Consider place and time utility. In marketspace, the provision of direct, on-demand information is possible from marketers *anywhere* to customers *anywhere, at any time*. Why? Operating hours and geographical constraints do not exist in marketspace. For example, Recreational Equipment, Inc. (www.rei.com), an outdoor gear marketer, reports that 35 percent of its orders are placed between 10:00 P.M. and 7:00 A.M., long after and before retail stores are open for business. Similarly, a U.S. consumer from Chicago can access Marks & Spencer (www.marks-and-spencer.co.uk), the well-known British department store, to shop for clothing as easily as a person living near London's Piccadilly Square. Cross-border sales will account for 20 percent of worldwide online sales in 2022.[5]

Possession utility—getting a product or service to consumers so they can own or use it—is accelerated in marketspace. Airline, car rental, and lodging electronic reservation systems such as Orbitz (www.orbitz.com) allow comparison shopping for the lowest fares, rents, and rates and almost immediate access to and confirmation of travel arrangements and accommodations.

The greatest marketspace opportunity for marketers, however, lies in its potential for creating form utility. Communication capabilities in marketspace invite consumers to tell marketers specifically what their requirements are, making customization of a product or service to fit their exact needs possible. Today, 35 percent of online consumers are interested in customizing product features or in purchasing build-to-order products that use their specifications.[6] At Seven Cycles, customers can arrange for a custom-made bike to fit their specifications, as described in the chapter-opening example.

Interactivity and Individuality Create Customer Relationships

Marketers benefit from two unique capabilities of digital technology that promote and sustain customer relationships. One is *interactivity*; the other is *individuality*.[7] Both capabilities are

Seven Cycles offers form utility by creating customized bikes for customers in over 40 countries.
Courtesy of Seven Cycles, Inc.

Seven Cycles, Inc.
www.sevencycles.com

important building blocks for buyer–seller relationships. For these relationships to occur, companies interact with their customers by listening and responding to their needs. Marketers must also treat customers as individuals and empower them to (1) influence the timing and extent of the buyer–seller interaction and (2) have a say in the kind of products and services they buy, the information they receive, and in some cases, the prices they pay.

Digital technology allows for interaction, individualization, and customer relationship building to be carried out on a scale never before available and makes interactive marketing possible. **Interactive marketing** involves two-way buyer–seller electronic communication in which the buyer controls the kind and amount of information received from the seller. Interactive marketing is characterized by sophisticated choiceboard and personalization systems that transform information supplied by customers into customized responses to their individual needs.

Mars, Inc. uses choiceboard technology to decorate M&M's candies with personal photos and messages.
McGraw-Hill Education

Mars, Inc.
www.mymms.com

VIDEO 17-1
My M&M's®
kerin.tv/15e/v17-1

Choiceboards A **choiceboard** is an interactive, digitally enabled system that allows individual customers to design their own products and services by answering a few questions and choosing from a menu of product or service attributes (or components), prices, and delivery options. Customers today design their own computers with Dell's online configurator, custom fit their clothing at www.indochino.com, assemble their own investment portfolios with Schwab's mutual fund evaluator, build their own bicycle at www.sevencycles.com, and decorate M&M's with photos of themselves and unique messages at www.mymms.com. Because choiceboards collect precise information about the preferences and behavior of individual buyers, a company becomes more knowledgeable about a customer and better able to anticipate and fulfill that customer's needs.

Most choiceboards are essentially transaction devices. However, companies have expanded the functionality of choiceboards using collaborative filtering technology. **Collaborative filtering** is a process that automatically groups people with similar buying intentions, preferences, and behaviors and predicts future purchases. For example, say two people who have never met buy largely the same music over time. Collaborative filtering software is programmed to reason that these two buyers might have similar musical tastes: If one buyer likes a particular music, then the other will like it as well. The outcome? Collaborative filtering gives marketers the ability to make a dead-on sales recommendation to a buyer in *real time*. You see collaborative filtering applied each time you view a selection at Amazon.com and see "Customers who bought this (item) also bought . . . ." About 35 percent of Amazon's revenue comes from its product recommendations.

Personalization Choiceboards and collaborative filtering are marketer-initiated efforts to provide customized responses to the needs of individual buyers. By comparison, personalization systems are typically buyer-initiated efforts. **Personalization** is the consumer-initiated practice of generating content on a marketer's website that is custom tailored to an individual's specific needs and preferences. Today, one-half of the largest online retailers in the United States use sophisticated personalization systems based on data mining results and predictive modeling techniques described in Chapter 8.[8]

Sunglass Hut is a case in point. When a shopper visits its website (www.sunglasshut.com) and clicks on a pair of sunglasses, a "see similar styles" option is shown. This option uses image recognition and artificial intelligence technology to show other sunglasses that might be suitable choices for the shopper. So instead of suggesting what the shopper might want based on what other people have purchased, which is the case with choiceboards and collaborative filtering, the shopper is shown items that fit his or her preferences and features.

Personalization techniques are welcomed by consumers. Still, companies acknowledge the need to balance a consumer's desire to be catered to on a one-to-one basis and concerns about

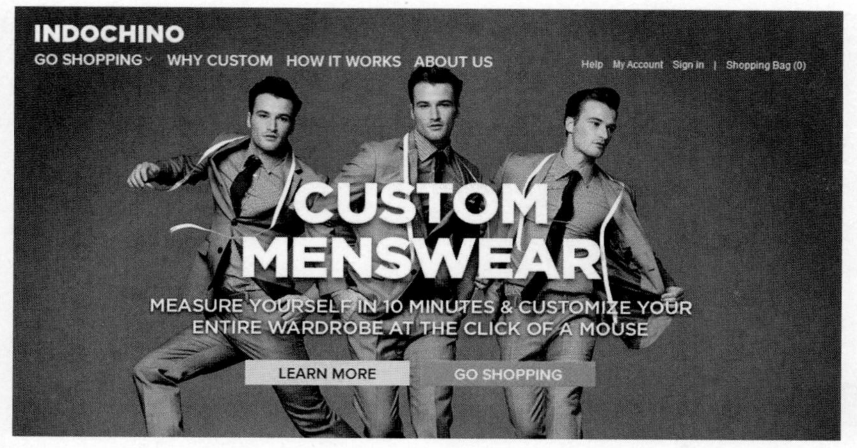

Indochino uses choiceboard technology to create customized menswear for its customers.
Source: Indochino Inc.

Indochino
www.indochino.com

intrusion. Research shows that about 40 percent of consumers feel "slightly creepy" when personalization technology correctly reads and anticipates their needs.[9]

An important aspect of personalization is a buyer's willingness to have tailored communications brought to his or her attention. Obtaining this approval is called **permission marketing**—the solicitation of a consumer's consent (called *opt-in*) to receive e-mail and advertising based on personal data supplied by the consumer. Permission marketing is a proven vehicle for building and maintaining customer relationships, provided it is properly used.

Companies that successfully employ permission marketing adhere to three rules.[10] First, they make sure opt-in customers receive only information that is relevant and meaningful to them. Second, their customers are given the option to *opt-out*, or change the kind, amount, or timing of information sent to them. Finally, their customers are assured that their name or buyer profile data will not be sold or shared with others. This assurance is important because a significant portion of adult Internet users are concerned about the privacy of their personal information and wish to protect it.[11]

Creating a Compelling Online Customer Experience

A continuing challenge for companies is the design and execution of marketing programs that capitalize on the unique customer value-creation capabilities of digital technology. Companies realize that applying this technology to create time, place, form, and possession utility is just a starting point. Today, the quality of the customer experience delivered by a company is the standard by which a meaningful marketspace presence is measured.

From an interactive marketing perspective, *customer experience* is defined as the sum total of the interactions that a customer has with a company's website, from the initial look at a home page through the entire purchase decision process.[12] Seven fundamental website design elements contribute to a customer experience. These elements are context, content, community, customization, communication, connection, and commerce. Each is described below and summarized in Figure 17-1 on the next page.

Context *Context* refers to a website's aesthetic appeal and the functional look and feel of the site's layout and visual design. A functionally oriented website focuses largely on the company's offering, be it products, services, or information. Deal-oriented travel websites, such as Priceline.com, tend to be functionally oriented with an emphasis on destinations, scheduling, and prices. In contrast, beauty websites, such as Revlon.com, are more aesthetically oriented. As these examples suggest, context conveys the core consumer benefit provided by the company's offerings.

Content *Content* applies to all digital information on a website, including the presentation form—text, video, audio, and graphics. Content relevance and presentation along with context dimensions combine to engage a website visitor and provide a platform for the five remaining design elements. The importance of content in website design is reflected in the mantra "Content is king."

Customization Website *customization* is the ability of a site to modify itself to, or be modified by and for, each individual user. Customization involves moving items around to reflect a consumer's priorities or selecting topics of interest to them. This design element is prominent in websites that offer personalized content, such as My eBay and My Amazon.

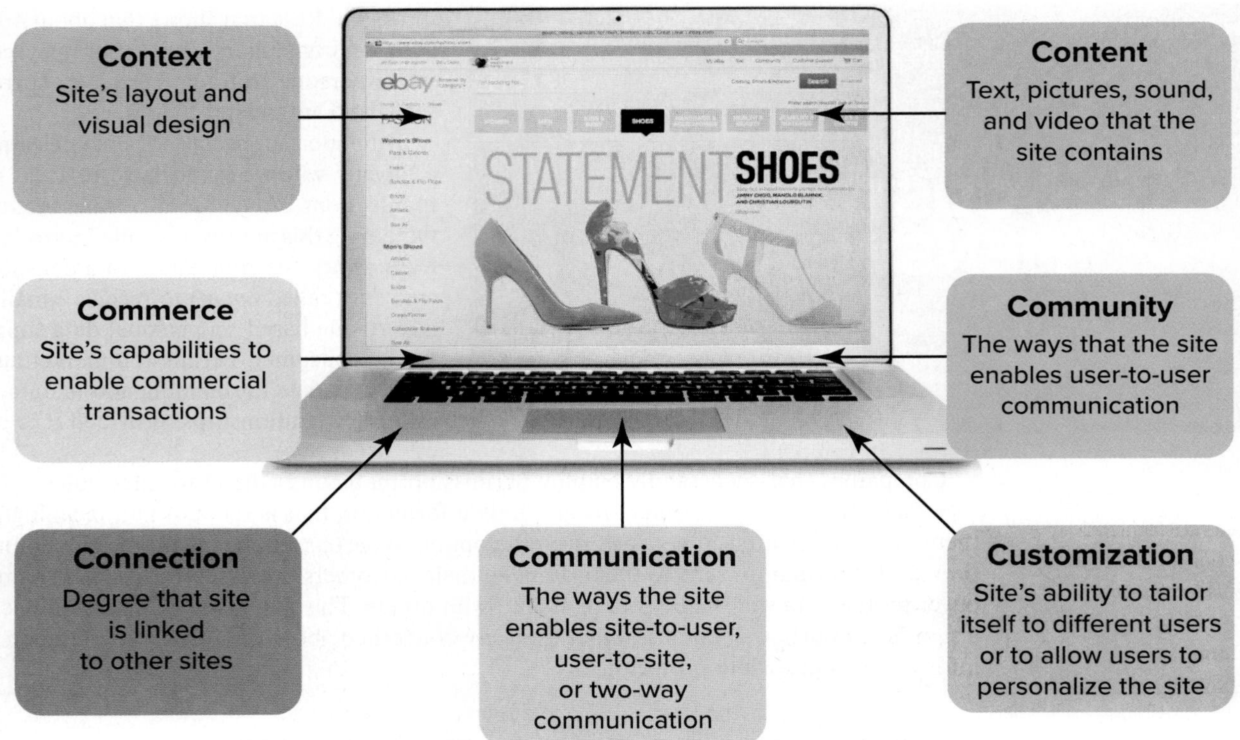

FIGURE 17–1
Seven website design elements that drive customer experience.
(Photo): NetPhotos/ Alamy Stock Photo

Connection The *connection* element is the network of linkages between a company's website and other sites. These links are embedded in the website; appear as highlighted words, a picture, or graphic; and allow a user to effortlessly visit other sites with a mouse click. For example, companies routinely display links to their Facebook, Instagram, and Twitter accounts. Connection is a major design element for informational websites such as *The New York Times*. Users of NYTimes.com can access the book review section and link to Barnes & Noble to order a book or browse related titles without ever visiting a store.

Communication *Communication* refers to the dialogue that unfolds between the website and its users. Consumers now expect communication to be interactive and individualized in real time, much like a personal conversation. Many websites enable a user to talk directly with a customer representative while shopping the site. However, an increasing number of websites use *chatbots*—sophisticated computer programs that mimic human conversation using artificial intelligence.

Community In addition, many company websites encourage user-to-user communications hosted by the company to create virtual communities, or simply *community*. This design element is popular because it has been shown to enhance customer experience and build favorable buyer–seller relationships. Examples of communities range from the Pampers Village hosted by Procter & Gamble (www.pampers.com) to the Harley Owners Group (HOG) sponsored by Harley-Davidson (www.harley-davidson.com).

Travelocity pays close attention to creating a favorable customer experience by employing all seven website design elements.
©Roberts Publishing Services. All rights reserved.

Travelocity
www.travelocity.com

Applying Marketing Metrics

Sizing Up Site Stickiness at Sewell Automotive Companies

Automobile dealerships have invested significant time, effort, and money in their websites. Why? Car browsing and shopping on the Internet is now commonplace.

Dealerships commonly measure website performance by tracking visits, visitor traffic, and "stickiness"—the amount of time per month visitors spend on their website. Website design, easy navigation, involving content, and visual appeal combine to enhance the interactive customer experience and website stickiness.

To gauge stickiness, companies monitor the average time spent per unique monthly visitor (in minutes) on their websites. This is done by tracking and displaying the average visits per unique monthly visitor and the average time spent per visit, in minutes, in their marketing dashboards. The relationship is as follows:

Average time spent per unique monthly visitor (minutes) =

$$\left(\begin{array}{c}\text{Average visits per}\\ \text{unique monthly visitor}\end{array}\right) \times \left(\begin{array}{c}\text{Average time spent}\\ \text{per visit (minutes)}\end{array}\right)$$

Your Challenge

As the manager responsible for Sewell.com, the Sewell Automotive Companies' website, you have been asked to report on the effect that recent improvements in the company's website have had on the amount of time per month visitors spend on the website. Sewell ranks among the largest U.S. automotive dealerships and is a recognized customer service leader in the automotive industry. Its website reflects the company's commitment to an unparalleled customer experience at its family of dealerships.

Your Findings

Examples of monthly marketing dashboard traffic and time measures are displayed for June 2017, three months before the website improvements were made (green arrow), and June 2018, after the improvements were made (red arrow).

The average time spent per unique monthly visitor increased from 8.5 minutes in June 2017 to 11.9 minutes in June 2018—a sizable jump. The increase is due primarily to the upturn in the average time spent per visit from 7.1 minutes to 8.5 minutes. The average number of visits also increased, but the percentage change was much less.

Your Action

Improvements in the website have noticeably "moved the needle" on average time spent per unique monthly visitor. Still, additional action may be required to increase average visits per unique monthly visitor. These actions might include an analysis of Sewell's Web advertising program, search engine initiatives with Google, links to automobile manufacturer corporate websites, and broader print and electronic media advertising.

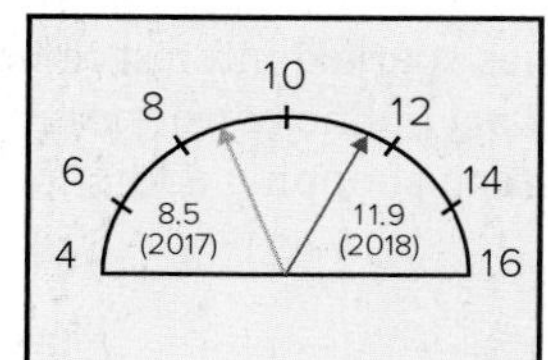

Average Time Spent per Unique Monthly Visitor (minutes)

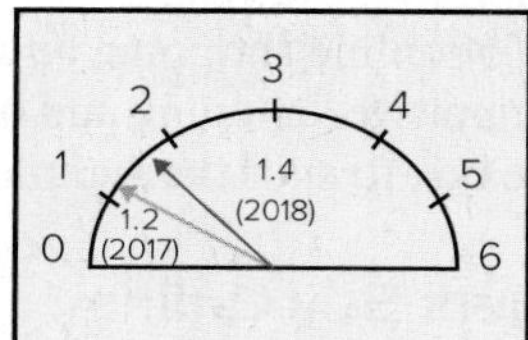

Average Visits per Unique Monthly Visitor

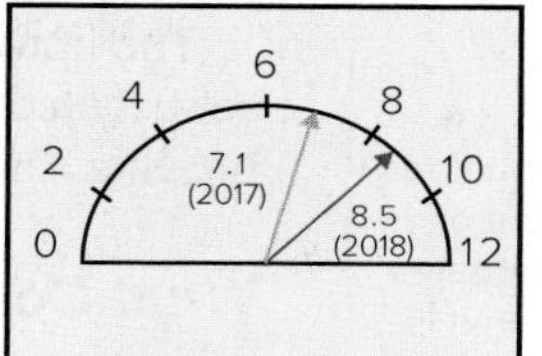

Average Time Spent per Visit (minutes)

Commerce The seventh design element is *commerce*–the website's ability to conduct sales transactions for products and services. Online transactions are quick and simple in well-designed websites.

Most websites do not include every design element. Although every website has context and content, they differ in the use of the remaining five elements. Why? Websites have different purposes. For example, only websites that emphasize the actual sale of products and services include the commerce element. Websites that are used primarily for advertising and promotion purposes emphasize the communication and connection elements.

Companies use a broad array of measures to assess website performance. For example, the amount of time per month visitors spend on their website, or "stickiness," is used to gauge customer experience.[13] Read the Applying Marketing Metrics box to learn how stickiness is measured and interpreted at one of the largest automobile dealerships in the United States.[14]

LEARNING REVIEW

17-1. The consumer-initiated practice of generating content on a marketer's website that is custom tailored to an individual's specific needs and preferences is called ______________.

17-2. What are the seven website design elements that companies use to produce a customer experience?

ONLINE CONSUMER BEHAVIOR AND MARKETING OPPORTUNITIES AND PRACTICES

Who are online consumers, and what do they buy? Why, when, and how do they choose to shop and purchase products and services in the digital marketspace rather than (or in addition to) the traditional marketplace? Answers to these questions have a direct bearing on marketing practices.

LO 17-2
Explain why certain types of products and services are particularly suited for interactive marketing and online shopping and buying.

Who Is the Online Consumer?

Online consumers are the subsegment of all Internet users who employ this technology to research products and services and make purchases. As a group, online consumers are equally likely to be women and men and tend to be better educated, younger, and more affluent than the general U.S. population. The average U.S. household spends about $5,200 online. Even though online shopping and buying is popular, a small percentage of online consumers still account for a disproportionate share of online retail sales in the United States. It is estimated that 20 percent of online consumers account for 69 percent of total consumer online sales. Also, while women and men shop online with equal frequency, men tend to spend more per purchase transaction than women.[15]

The prevalence of online shopping and buying has sparked interest in how the Internet has contributed to compulsive shopping and buying among online consumers. Read the Marketing Insights About Me box to spot the symptoms of online shopping addiction.[16]

What Consumers Buy Online

Five broad product classes or categories account for almost 70 percent of online consumer buying today and for the foreseeable future, as shown in Figure 17–2.[17] These categories share

FIGURE 17–2
Five product categories account for about 70 percent of U.S. online retail sales today—a trend that is projected to continue in the future.

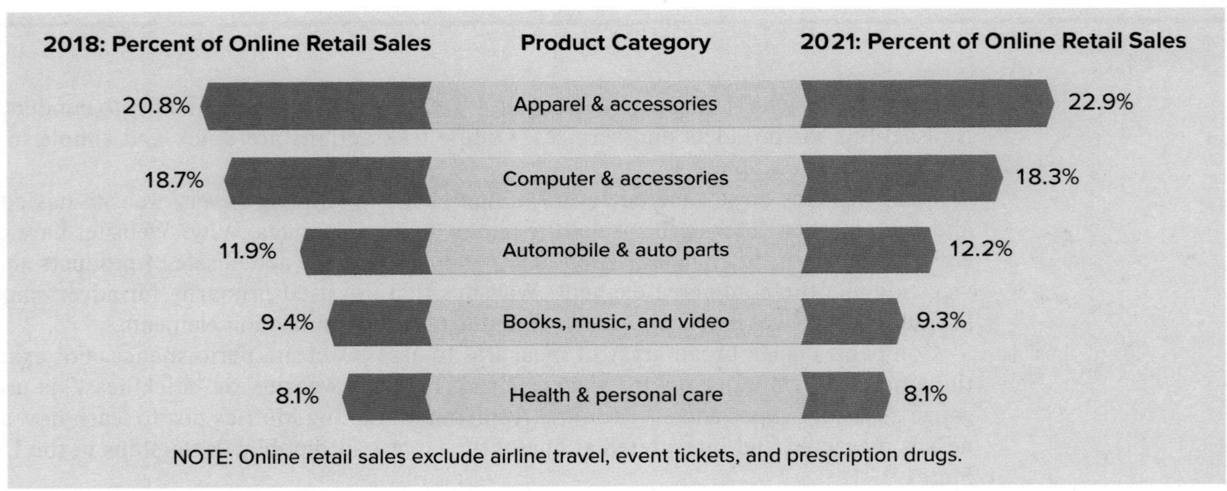

Marketing Insights About Me

Am I Addicted to Online Shopping?

Online shopping is now commonplace. For some consumers, however, online shopping has become an addiction. If you exhibit seven or more of the following symptoms, you may be addicted:

1. You spend more time than you should shopping online.
2. You promise yourself to limit ordering online, but are unable to resist.
3. Your frequent purchases and spending cause financial problems and relationship troubles.
4. When you are not shopping online, you are planning your next online shopping spree.
5. Online shopping has a negative impact on other parts of your life, such as work, school, friendships, and family.
6. Online shopping makes you feel good or relaxed.
7. You get grumpy if you can't shop online.
8. You feel guilty after online shopping.
9. You hide things you buy online because you are concerned that others will think they are unreasonable or a waste of money.
10. You buy things online you don't need or spend more than planned.

Alex Slobodkin/iStock/Getty Images

Online shopping addiction is considered an aspect of compulsive buying amplified by Internet technology. PsychCentral has an online, interactive quiz to test whether your Internet behavior is, or is becoming, an addiction. Visit the PsychCentral website at www.psychcentral.com/netaddiction/quiz/ and get your Internet addiction score.

one or more product characteristics. One product characteristic consists of items for which product information is an important part of the purchase decision but prepurchase trial is not necessarily critical. Items such as computers, computer accessories, and consumer electronics are examples.

A second kind of product characteristic includes items that can be delivered digitally, including computer software, books, music, and video. A third kind of product or service characteristic includes items that are regularly purchased and where convenience is very important. These include health care and personal care items. A final grouping consists of highly standardized products for which information about price is important. Automotive products and casual apparel and accessories are examples.

LO 17-3
Describe why consumers shop and buy online and how marketers influence online purchasing behavior.

Why Consumers Shop and Buy Online

Why do consumers shop and buy online? Marketers emphasize the customer value-creation possibilities; the importance of interactivity, individuality, and relationship building; and the ability to produce a compelling customer experience. Consumers typically refer to six reasons why they shop and buy online: convenience, choice, customization, communication, cost, and control (Figure 17–3 on the next page).

Convenience Online shopping and buying is *convenient*. Consumers can visit Walmart at www.walmart.com to scan and order from among thousands of displayed products without fighting traffic, finding a parking space, walking through long aisles, and standing in store checkout lines. Alternatively, online consumers often use **bots**, electronic shopping agents or robots that search websites to compare prices and product or service features. In either instance, an online consumer has never ventured into a store. However, for convenience to remain a source of customer value creation, websites must be easy to locate and navigate, and image downloads must be fast.

A commonly held view among online marketers is the **eight-second rule**: Customers will abandon their efforts to enter and navigate a website if download time exceeds eight seconds.

FIGURE 17–3
Why do consumers shop and buy online? Read the text to learn how convenience, choice, customization, communication, cost, and control result in a favorable customer experience.
(Photo): Fuse/Getty Images

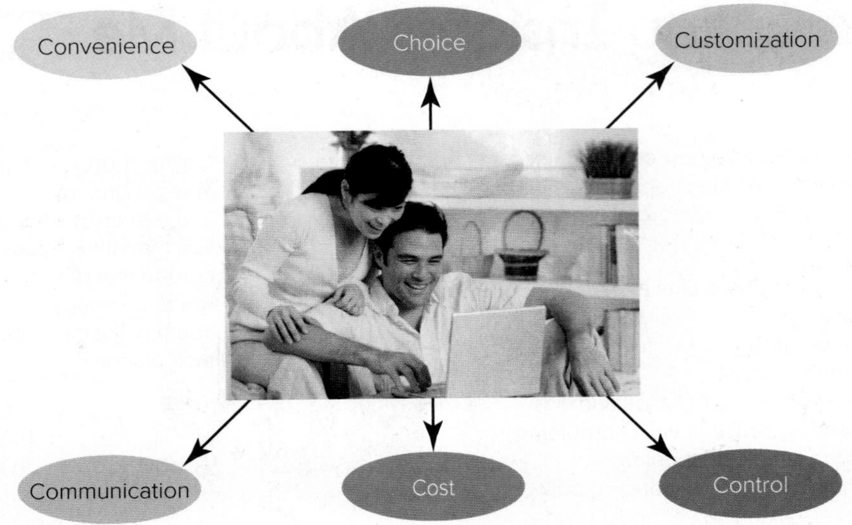

Furthermore, the more clicks and pauses between clicks required to access information or make a purchase, the more likely it is a customer will exit a website.

Choice *Choice*, the second reason consumers shop and buy online, has two dimensions. First, choice exists in the product or service selection offered to consumers. Buyers desiring selection can avail themselves of more than 1 billion websites worldwide for almost anything they want. For instance, online buyers of consumer electronics can shop individual manufacturers, such as Bose (www.bose.com), and QVC.com, a general merchant that offers more than 100,000 products.

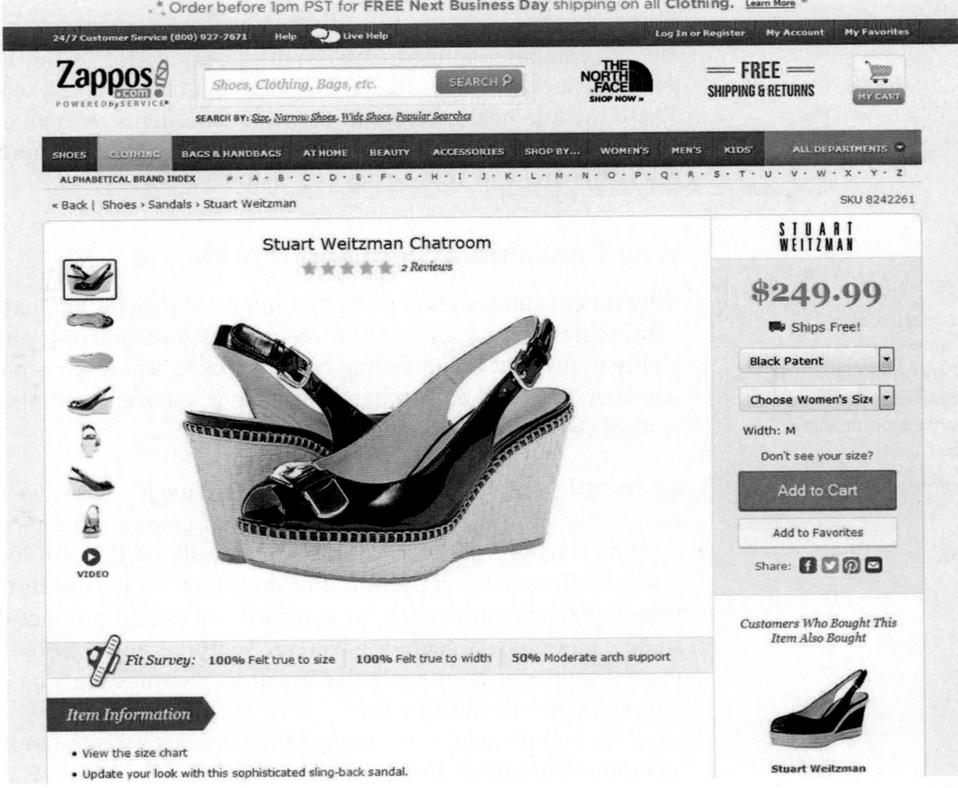

Zappos.com is successful because it meets all the requirements necessary for consumers to shop and buy online. In less than 10 years, the company has posted significant annual sales of shoes, apparel, bags, accessories, housewares, and jewelry.

Zappos.com
www.zappos.com

Choice assistance is the second dimension. Here, choiceboard and personalization technologies invite customers to engage in an electronic dialogue with marketers for the purpose of making informed choices. Choice assistance is one of the reasons for the continued success of Zappos.com. The company offers an online chat room that enables prospective buyers to ask questions and receive answers in real time. In addition, carefully designed search capabilities permit consumers to review products by brand and particular items.

Staffers in Gatorade's "Mission Control" room in Chicago, Illinois, monitor Internet and social media outlets, such as Facebook and Twitter, 24 hours a day. Whenever someone uses Twitter to say he or she is drinking a Gatorade or mentions the brand on Facebook or in a blog, it pops up on-screen at Mission Control. In this way, conversations featuring Gatorade provide useful consumer insights into how the brand is viewed and used.
Clayton Hauck Photography

Gatorade
www.gatorade.com

Customization Even with a broad selection and choice assistance, some customers prefer one-of-a-kind items that fit their specific needs. *Customization* arises from digital capabilities that make possible a highly interactive and individualized information and exchange environment for shoppers and buyers. Remember the earlier Indochino, Schwab, Dell, and Seven Cycles examples? To varying degrees, online consumers also benefit from **customerization**—the practice of not only customizing a product or service but also personalizing the marketing and overall shopping and buying interaction for each customer.[18]

Customerization seeks to do more than offer consumers the right product, at the right time, and at the right price. It combines choiceboard and personalization systems to expand the exchange environment beyond a transaction and makes shopping and buying an enjoyable, personal experience.

Communication Online consumers particularly welcome the *communication* capabilities of Internet-enabled technologies. This communication can take three forms: (1) marketer-to-consumer e-mail notifications, (2) consumer-to-marketer buying and service requests, and (3) consumer-to-consumer chat rooms and instant messaging, in addition to social networking websites such as Twitter, Instagram, and Facebook.

Communication has proven to be a double-edged sword for online consumers. On the one hand, the interactive communication capabilities increase consumer convenience, reduce

information search costs, and make choice assistance and customization possible. Communication also promotes the development of company-hosted and independent **Web communities**—websites that allow people to congregate online and exchange views on topics of common interest. For instance, Coca-Cola hosts MyCoke.com, and iVillage.com is an independent Web community for women and includes topics such as career management, personal finances, parenting, relationships, beauty, and health.

Web logs, or blogs, are another form of communication. A *blog* is a web page that serves as a publicly accessible personal journal for an individual or organization. Blogs are popular because they provide online forums on a wide variety of subjects ranging from politics to car repair. Companies such as Hewlett-Packard, PepsiCo, and Harley-Davidson routinely monitor blogs and social media posts to gather customer insights.[19]

VIDEO 17-2
Frito-Lay
kerin.tv/15e/v17-2

On the other hand, communications can take the form of electronic junk mail or unsolicited e-mail, called **spam**. In fact, 67 percent of e-mail messages sent in the world are spam.[20] The prevalence of spam has prompted many online services to institute policies and procedures to prevent spammers from spamming their subscribers, and several states have anti-spamming laws. The 2003 CAN-SPAM (Controlling the Assault of Non-Solicited Pornography and Marketing) Act restricts information collection and unsolicited e-mail promotions on the Internet.

Digitally enabled communication capabilities also make possible *buzz*, a popular term for marketplace word-of-mouth behavior. Chapter 5 described the importance of word of mouth in consumer behavior. Internet technology has magnified its significance. According to Jeff Bezos, the founder of Amazon.com, "If you have an unhappy customer on the Internet, he doesn't tell his six friends, he tells his 6,000 friends!"[21] Buzz is particularly influential for toys, cars, sporting goods, movies, apparel, consumer electronics, pharmaceuticals, health and beauty products, and health care services. Some marketers have capitalized on this phenomenon by creating buzz through viral marketing.

Viral marketing is a digitally enabled promotional strategy that encourages individuals to forward marketer-initiated messages to others via e-mail, social networking websites, and blogs. There are three approaches to viral marketing. First, marketers can embed a message in the product or service so that customers hardly realize they are passing it along. The classic example is Hotmail, which was one of the first companies to provide free, Internet-based e-mail. Each outgoing e-mail message had the tagline: "Get Your Private, Free Email from MSN Hotmail." This effort produced more than 350 million users.

Second, marketers can make the website content so compelling that viewers want to share it with others. Careerbuilder.com has done this with its Monk-e-mail site, which allows users to send personalized, private-themed e-cards for all occasions. More than 100 million Monk-e-mails have been sent in the past decade. Finally, marketers can offer incentives (discounts, sweepstakes, or free merchandise). For example, Burger King asked, "What do you love more, your friend or the Whopper?" in its Whopper Sacrifice campaign. Facebook users were asked to "unfriend" 10 people from their Facebook friends list in exchange for a free burger.[22]

Careerbuilder.com, an online career placement company, has produced a great viral marketing success with its Monk-e-mail featuring talking monkeys. People can stylize their monkeys by choosing headgear, clothes, glasses, backgrounds, and other features. They can also record a message using one of four monkey voices or their own voice. Monk-e-mail can be sent to friends or posted on Twitter.

CareerBuilder
www.careerbuilder.com

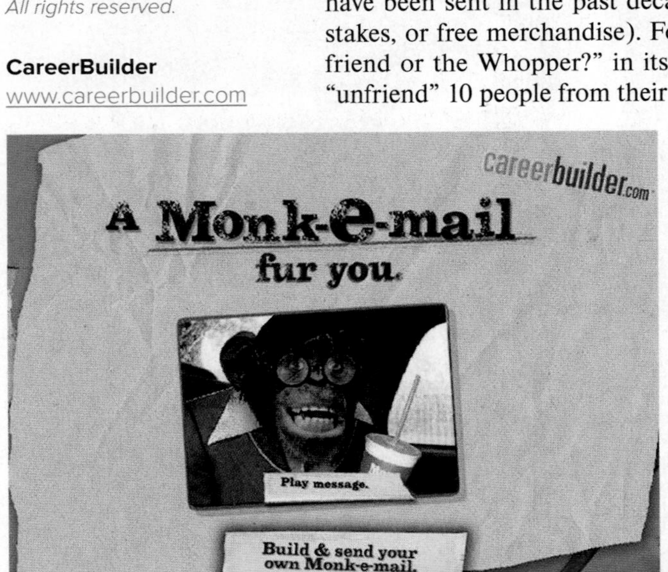

Cost Consumer *cost* is a fifth reason for online shopping and buying. Many popular items bought online can be purchased at the same price or cheaper than in retail stores.[23] Lower prices also result from sophisticated software that permits **dynamic pricing**, the practice of changing prices for products and services in real time in response to supply and demand conditions. As described in Chapter 14, dynamic pricing is a form of flexible pricing and can often result in lower prices. It is typically used for pricing time-sensitive items such as airline seats, scarce items found at art or collectible auctions, and out-of-date items such as last year's models of computer equipment and accessories.

A consumer's cost of external information search, including time spent and often the hassle of shopping, is also reduced. Greater shopping convenience and lower external

Making Responsible Decisions

Ethics

Who Is Responsible for Internet Privacy and Security?

Privacy and security are two key reasons consumers are leery of online shopping and buying. A recent Pew Internet & American Life Project poll reported that 76 percent of online consumers have privacy and security concerns about the Internet. And 73 percent of online consumers consider it an invasion of privacy if a search engine tracks their activity to personalize future search results. Even more telling, many have stopped shopping a website or forgone an online purchase because of these concerns. Industry analysts estimate that over $30 million in e-commerce sales are lost annually because of privacy and security concerns among online shoppers.

Consumer concerns are not without merit. According to the Federal Trade Commission, 46 percent of fraud complaints are Internet-related, costing consumers $560 million. In addition, consumers lose millions of dollars each year due to identity theft resulting from breaches in company security systems.

A percolating issue is whether the U.S. government should pass more stringent Internet privacy and security laws. About 70 percent of online consumers favor such action. Companies, however, favor self-regulation. For example, TrustArc (www.trustarc.com) awards its trademark to company websites that comply with standards of privacy protection and disclosure. Still, consumers are ultimately responsible for using care and caution when engaging in online behavior, including e-commerce and social media. Consumers have a choice of whether or not to divulge personal information and are responsible for monitoring how their information is being used.

Brain light/Alamy Stock Photo

What role should the U.S. government, company self-regulation, and consumer vigilance play in dealing with privacy and security issues in the digital marketspace?

search costs are two major reasons for the popularity of online shopping and buying among women—particularly those who work outside the home.

Control The sixth reason consumers prefer to buy online is the *control* it gives them over their shopping and purchase decision process. Online shoppers and buyers are empowered consumers. They seek information, evaluate alternatives, and make purchase decisions on their own time, terms, and conditions. For example, studies show that automobile shoppers spend an average of 11 hours researching cars online before setting foot in a showroom.[24] The result of these activities is a more informed and discerning shopper.

Even though consumers have many reasons for shopping and buying online, a segment of Internet users refrains from making purchases for privacy and security reasons. These consumers are concerned about a rarely mentioned seventh C—cookies.

Cookies are computer files that a marketer can download onto the computer and mobile phone of an online shopper who visits the marketer's website. Cookies allow the marketer's website to record a user's visit, track visits to other websites, and store and retrieve this information in the future. Cookies also contain visitor information such as expressed product preferences, personal data, passwords, and credit card numbers.

Cookies make possible customized and personal content for online shoppers. They also make possible the practice of behavioral targeting for marketers. **Behavioral targeting** uses information provided by cookies to direct online advertising from marketers to those online shoppers whose behavioral profiles suggest they would be interested in such advertising. A controversy surrounding cookies is summed up by an authority on the technology: "At best cookies make for a user-friendly web world: like a salesclerk who knows who you are. At worst, cookies represent a potential loss of privacy."[25] Read the Making Responsible Decisions box to learn more about privacy and security issues.[26]

When and Where Consumers Shop and Buy Online

Shopping and buying also happen at different times in the digital marketspace than in the traditional marketplace.[27] About 80 percent of online retail sales occur Monday through Friday. The busiest shopping day is Wednesday. By comparison, 35 percent of retail store sales are registered on the weekend. Saturday is the most popular shopping day. Monday through Friday online shopping and buying often occur during normal work hours–some 30 percent of online consumers say they visit websites from their place of work, which partially accounts for the sales level during the workweek.

Favorite websites for workday shopping and buying include those featuring event tickets, auctions, online periodical subscriptions, flowers and gifts, consumer electronics, and travel. Websites offering health and beauty items, apparel and accessories, and music and video tend to be browsed and bought from a consumer's residence.

How Consumers Shop and Buy Online

How online consumers shop and buy has evolved with changing technology. The majority of online consumers prefer using their laptop and desktop computers (60 percent). Six percent prefer their tablet computer. Five percent prefer their smartphones for shopping and buying. And 29 percent of online consumers have no particular preference and use multiple devices for shopping and buying.[28]

With evolving technology, notably the prevalence of smartphones and social media platforms, online shopping and buying has become more social. Today, about 75 percent of online consumers rely on social media for product and service ideas, referrals, and reviews. And an increasing number of these consumers are making purchases on social media without going to a company's website to conduct business. The use of social networks for browsing and buying is called **social commerce**. Facebook, Twitter, and Pinterest have taken the lead in promoting social commerce. Social commerce and social shopping are discussed further in Chapter 20.

Today, 15 percent of online consumers rely on subscriptions to shop and buy online.[29] **Subscription commerce** involves the payment of a fee to have products and services delivered on a recurring schedule. Amazon Prime, Dollar Shave Club, and Netflix represent three prominent examples. Convenience, lower prices, and greater personalization have fueled the popularity of subscription commerce, which now accounts for 10 percent of total U.S online sales.

LEARNING REVIEW

17-3. What are the six reasons consumers prefer to shop and buy online?

17-4. What is the eight-second rule?

CROSS-CHANNEL CONSUMERS AND MULTICHANNEL MARKETING

LO 17-4

Define cross-channel consumers and the role of multichannel marketing in reaching these consumers.

Consumers often shop and buy in both online and offline environments. Individuals who move effortlessly between these environments have given rise to the cross-channel consumer and the importance of multichannel marketing.

Who Is the Cross-Channel Consumer?

Cross-channel consumers are online consumers who shop online but buy offline, or shop offline but buy online. They differ from exclusive online consumers and exclusive offline

FIGURE 17–4
Cross-channel consumers engage in "showrooming" and "webrooming" depending on how they shop and buy online and offline.

consumers (see Figure 17–4). These distinctions will vary by the products or services shopped and bought.[30] For example, e-books are shopped and purchased by exclusive online consumers. Expensive, custom-made furniture and home furnishings are typically shopped and purchased by an exclusive offline consumer.

Showrooming Cross-channel consumers who shop offline but buy online engage in **showrooming**—the practice of examining products in a store and then buying them online for a cheaper price. While obtaining a lower price is a primary motivation for showrooming, showroomers often gather additional product information, look for online promotions or deals, and check product reviews and ratings on social media. About three-fourths of online consumers have engaged in showrooming for one or more products. Consumer electronics and home appliances are the most popular showrooming product categories.

Webrooming Cross-channel consumers who shop online but buy offline engage in **webrooming**—the practice of examining products online and then buying them in a store. While lower price is again a significant motivator for webrooming, webroomers cite other factors as well: avoiding shipping costs, gaining immediate possession of a product, and allowing for easier returns. About 80 percent of online consumers have engaged in webrooming for one or more products. Automobiles and auto parts, apparel (including shoes), and home office equipment are popular webrooming product categories.

Recent research indicates that 6 in 10 webroomers have showroomed while 9 in 10 showroomers have webroomed. Cross-channel consumers overall account for a significant amount of online activity and sales. Retail sales from cross-channel consumers is estimated to be about five times greater than from online-only retail sales.

Implementing Multichannel Marketing

The prominence of cross-channel consumers has focused increased attention on multichannel marketing. Recall from Chapter 15 that *multichannel marketing* is the blending of different communication and delivery channels that are mutually reinforcing in attracting, retaining, and building relationships with consumers who shop and buy in the traditional marketplace and the digital marketspace—the cross-channel consumer.

Efforts to implement multichannel marketing involve three steps. First, it is necessary to document cross-channel consumer behavior. Second, marketers should employ communication and delivery channels that are mutually reinforcing in attracting, retaining, and building relationships with their current and potential consumers. Finally, companies should monitor and measure multichannel marketing performance.

Document the Cross-Channel Consumer Journey Marketers have found that the identification of a consumer journey and consumer touchpoints are invaluable for multichannel

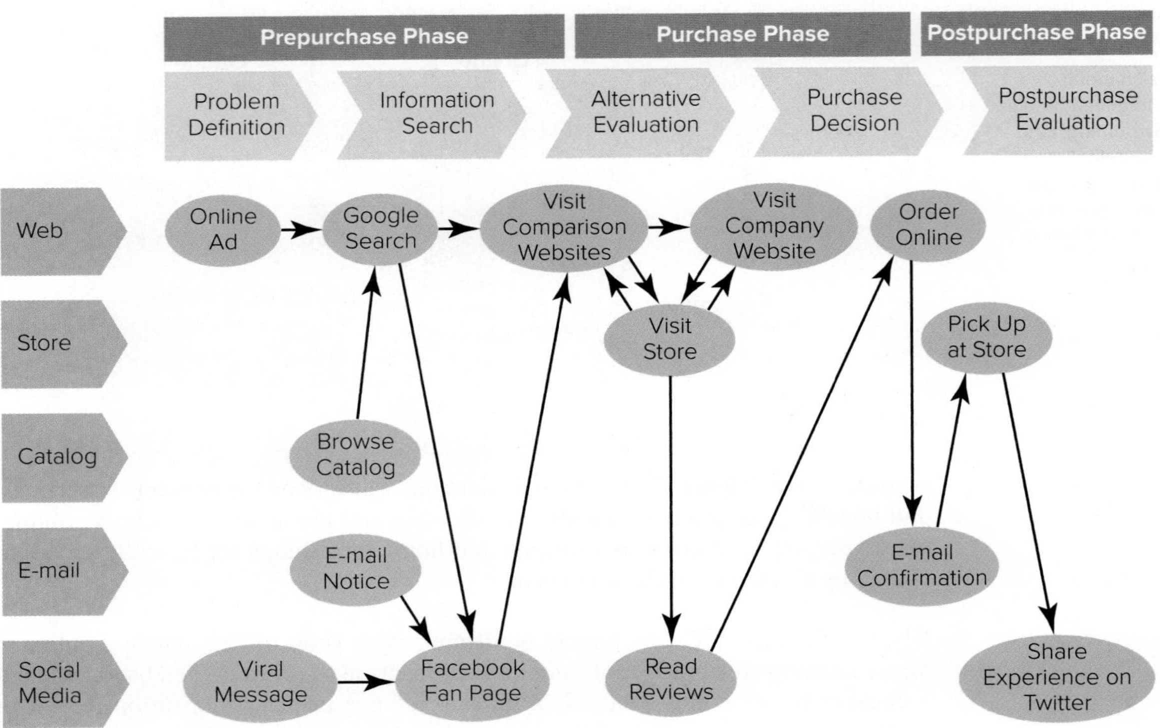

FIGURE 17–5 Illustrative Cross-Channel Consumer Journey Map

marketing to succeed. As described in Chapter 5, consumer journey maps and consumer touchpoints detail the time and place consumers and companies (brands) engage to exchange information, provide service, or handle buying transactions.

Figure 17–5 sketches a generic cross-channel consumer journey map. Three insights can be gained from such a map. First, the map identifies the communication and delivery channels engaged by cross-channel consumers. Second, the map shows the links between communication and delivery channels across the prepurchase, purchase, and postpurchase phases of the consumer purchase decision process. Finally, the map highlights consumer touchpoints that are outside the control of the company, such as comparison websites and social media. These touchpoints can form or change a cross-channel consumer's impression about a particular product, service, brand, or company.

Employ Channels That Are Mutually Reinforcing in Attracting, Retaining, and Building Relationships with Consumers There is no one best approach to multichannel marketing. The configuration of communication and delivery channels employed depends on the channels used by current and potential consumers of a company's products, brands, and services and their information-gathering and purchase preferences. It also depends on how different channels mutually reinforce one another in attracting, retaining, and building relationships with consumers. This is done by conveying a consistent customer experience through consumer touchpoints and messages across channels.

For example, as described earlier in this chapter, many companies that originally built their businesses online now operate retail stores and showrooms. They are now multichannel marketers. Similarly, the Clinique division of Estée Lauder Companies, which built its business in traditional department stores, reports that 80 percent of current customers who visit its website (www.clinique.com) later purchase a Clinique product at a department store. Equally important, 37 percent of non-Clinique consumers make a Clinique purchase after visiting the company's website.[31]

Monitor and Measure Multichannel Marketing Performance The third step in implementing multichannel marketing is monitoring and measuring performance. This step has proven difficult for marketers for two reasons. First, the magnitude of data corresponding to which channel(s) each consumer accesses during each stage in the purchase decision process has made data difficult to assemble and integrate. Second, the task of assigning the proportional credit to each channel and consumer touchpoint across all online and offline channels for a desired consumer action is extremely complex. The practice and techniques used to credit or value a particular channel and consumer touchpoint is called **marketing attribution**.

Nevertheless, progress has been made in monitoring and measuring performance.[32] For example, companies routinely track their website visitors who buy in retail stores or in catalogs. Google, which monitors online shopping behavior across the Web, now applies statistical methods to measure the extent to which online advertising leads to store purchases for individual companies. Still, a comprehensive approach for monitoring and measuring a company's multichannel marketing performance across channels and consumer touchpoints remains elusive.

Despite the challenges, the popularity of multichannel marketing is apparent in its growing impact on online retail sales.[33] Fully 70 percent of U.S. online retail sales are made by companies that practice multichannel marketing.

LEARNING REVIEW

17-5. A cross-channel consumer is ________________.

17-6. Efforts to implement multichannel marketing involve what three steps?

LEARNING OBJECTIVES REVIEW

LO 17-1 *Describe what interactive marketing is and how it creates customer value, customer relationships, and customer experiences.*
Interactive marketing involves two-way buyer–seller electronic communication in a computer-mediated environment in which the buyer controls the kind and amount of information received from the seller. It creates customer value by providing time, place, form, and possession utility for consumers. Customer relationships are created and sustained through two unique capabilities of Internet technology: interactivity and individuality. From an interactive marketing perspective, customer experience represents the sum total of the interactions that a customer has with a company's website, from the initial look at a home page through the entire purchase decision process. Companies produce a customer experience through seven website design elements: context, content, community, customization, communication, connection, and commerce.

LO 17-2 *Explain why certain types of products and services are particularly suited for interactive marketing and online shopping and buying.*
Certain product and service classes seem to be particularly suited for interactive marketing. One category consists of items for which product information is an important part of the purchase decision but prepurchase trial is not necessarily critical. A second category contains items that can be digitally delivered. Unique items represent a third category. A fourth category includes items that are regularly purchased and where convenience is very important. A fifth category consists of highly standardized items for which information about price is important.

LO 17-3 *Describe why consumers shop and buy online and how marketers influence online purchasing behavior.*
There are six reasons consumers shop and buy online. They are convenience, choice, customization, communication, cost, and control. Marketers have capitalized on these reasons through a variety of means. For example, they provide choice assistance using choiceboard and collaborative filtering technology, which also provides opportunities for customization. Company-hosted Web communities and viral marketing practices capitalize on the communications dimensions of digital technologies. Dynamic pricing provides real-time responses to supply and demand conditions, often resulting in lower prices for consumers. Permission marketing is popular given consumer interest in control.

LO 17-4 *Define cross-channel consumers and the role of multichannel marketing in reaching these consumers.*
A cross-channel consumer is an online consumer who shops online but buys offline (called webrooming), or shops offline but buys online (called showrooming). These cross-channel consumers are reached through multichannel marketing. Multichannel marketing continues to grow in popularity, despite the challenges involved in measuring multichannel marketing performance across channels and touchpoints.

LEARNING REVIEW ANSWERS

17-1 **The consumer-initiated practice of generating content on a marketer's website that is custom tailored to an individual's specific needs and preferences is called ___________.**
Answer: personalization

17-2 **What are the seven website design elements that companies use to produce a customer experience?**
Answer: From an interactive marketing perspective, customer experience is defined as the sum total of the interactions that a customer has with a company's website, from the initial look at a home page through the entire purchase decision process. Companies produce a customer experience through seven website design elements, which are: (1) context–a website's aesthetic appeal and functional look and feel reflected in site layout and visual design; (2) content–all digital information on a website, including the text, video, audio, and graphics; (3) community–the user-to-user communications hosted by the company to create virtual communities; (4) customization–the ability of a site to modify itself to, or be modified by, each individual user; (5) communication–the dialogue that unfolds between the website and its users; (6) connection– the network of linkages between a company's site and other sites; and (7) commerce–the website's ability to conduct sales transactions for products and services. Most websites do not include every design element. Although every website has context and content, they differ in the use of the remaining five elements.

17-3 **What are the six reasons consumers prefer to shop and buy online?**
Answer: The six reasons consumers prefer to shop and buy online are: convenience, choice, customization, communication, cost, and control. A reason consumers avoid shopping and buying online is the security threat posed by cookies.

17-4 **What is the eight-second rule?**
Answer: The eight-second rule is a view that customers will abandon their efforts to enter and navigate a website if download time exceeds eight seconds.

17-5 **A cross-channel consumer is ___________.**
Answer: an online consumer who shops online but buys offline or who shops offline but buys online

17-6 **Efforts to implement multichannel marketing involve what three steps?**
Answer: The three steps are: (1) document cross-channel consumer behavior; (2) employ channels that are mutually reinforcing in attracting, retaining, and building relationships with consumers; and (3) monitor and measure multichannel marketing performance.

FOCUSING ON KEY TERMS

behavioral targeting p. 473
bots p. 469
choiceboard p. 464
collaborative filtering p. 464
cookies p. 473
cross-channel consumer p. 474
customerization p. 471
dynamic pricing p. 472
eight-second rule p. 469
interactive marketing p. 464
marketing attribution p. 477
online consumers p. 468
permission marketing p. 465
personalization p. 464
showrooming p. 475
social commerce p. 474
spam p. 472
subscription commerce p. 474
viral marketing p. 472
Web communities p. 472
webrooming p. 475

APPLYING MARKETING KNOWLEDGE

1 Have you made an online purchase? If so, why do you think so many people who have access to the Internet are not also online buyers? If not, why are you reluctant to do so? Do you think that electronic commerce benefits consumers even if they don't make a purchase?

2 Like the traditional marketplace, the digital marketspace offers marketers opportunities to create time, place, form, and possession utility. How do you think Internet-enabled technology rates in terms of creating these values? Take a shopping trip at a virtual retailer of your choice (don't buy anything unless you really want to). Then compare the time, place, form, and possession utility provided by the virtual retailer to that provided by a traditional retailer in the same product category.

3 Visit Amazon.com (www.amazon.com) or Barnes & Noble (www.barnesandnoble.com). As you tour the website, think about how shopping for books online compares with a trip to your university bookstore to buy books. Specifically, compare and contrast your shopping experiences with respect to convenience, choice, customization, communication, cost, and control.

4 You are planning to buy a new car so you visit www.edmunds.com. Based on your experience visiting that site, do you think you will enjoy more or less control in negotiating with the dealer when you actually purchase your vehicle?

5 Visit the website for your university or college. Based on your visit, would you conclude that the site is a transactional site or a promotional site? Why? How would you rate the site in terms of the seven website design elements that affect customer experience?

BUILDING YOUR MARKETING PLAN

Does your marketing plan involve a marketspace presence for your product or service? If the answer is "no," read no further and do not include this element in your plan. If the answer is "yes," then attention must be given to developing a website in your marketing plan. A useful starting point is to:

1. Describe how each website element—context, content, community, customization, communication, connection, and commerce—will be used to create a customer experience.
2. Identify a company's website that best reflects your website conceptualization.

VIDEO CASE 17 Pizza Hut and imc²: Becoming a Multichannel Marketer

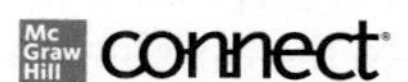

It's no surprise that Pizza Hut is the world's largest pizza chain, with more than 10,000 restaurants in 100 countries. But did you know that Pizza Hut has become one of the top U.S. Internet retailers?

VIDEO 17-3 Pizza Hut Video Case kerin.tv/15e/v17-3

According to Brian Niccol, Pizza Hut's chief marketing officer (CMO), "We've done what many would say is impossible. We successfully built an online business in three years that produces hundreds of millions of dollars in annual revenue. Today, Pizza Hut is a category leader in the interactive and emerging marketplace." So how did the company do it? Pizza Hut simply revolutionized the quick serve restaurant (QSR) world through a multichannel marketing approach that created a customer experience and a customer engagement platform that was second to none.

THE RETAIL PIZZA BUSINESS

With three national competitors dominating the marketplace, the pizza business is very competitive. Even customers who could be considered heavy users of a particular brand regularly purchase from competitors on the basis of timing, pricing, and convenience.

In general, Pizza Hut's most frequent customers (and likely those of the other two major competitors) can be divided into two categories: (1) families, primarily time-starved mothers, looking for a quick and simple mealtime solution; and (2) young adult males who fuel their active lifestyle with one of the world's most versatile and convenient foods (no cooking, no utensils, no cleanup, and leftovers are perfect for breakfast). While these two groups could not be more dissimilar on the surface, value and convenience are important for both groups. Cost-conscious mothers look for a good quality product and a hassle-free eating experience. Deal-seeking young adult males seek more of the food they love with less time and cash invested in the process.

Source: Pizza Hut, Inc.

The importance of the take-home and delivery segment of the U.S. pizza market is illustrated by the fact that Pizza Hut's principal national competitors focus exclusively on this aspect of the business. Most take-home and delivery sales are ordered before a customer enters the restaurant. In addition, a growing number of retail pizza customers had become comfortable ordering pizza online. Pizza ordering, as it turned out, was an ideal product for the digital world. People understood the basic menu, generally knew that they could customize their order in a variety of ways, and were accustomed to not being in the store when ordering. Brand retail presence and established customer delivery networks also made the shift to online ordering easier for national pizza chains than other national quick serve restaurants. But, as Pizza Hut understood, there is still an incredible level of complexity in making something truly sophisticated simple and easy for the customer.

CREATING A PLAN OF ACTION

For the most part, the intent of online ordering for the pizza business was to make transactions with the customer easier and cheaper for the brand. Pizza Hut recognized the opportunity to engage people with its brand and with other people directly and do something special—namely, build sustainable relationships with its customers and enable Pizza Hut to engage people in a more meaningful and profitable way. In short, Pizza Hut set about to reinvent the retail pizza business by breaking away from a transactional platform to an efficient and powerful customer engagement platform by reaching out to customers' kitchens and couches to offer a better mealtime ordering, delivery, and dining experience.

Pizza Hut selected imc² as one of its lead agencies to plan a comprehensive interactive strategy that focused first on the redesign of the Pizza Hut corporate website (including redefining the customer experience online and across all of the brand's touchpoints) and then on a series of progressively sophisticated and industry-leading customer engagement strategies. imc² brought 15 years of experience in interactive marketing and brand engagement to the assignment.

PIZZAHUT.COM, CUSTOMER EXPERIENCE, AND BRAND ENGAGEMENT

Pizza Hut and imc² executives agreed that the strategy for reinventing the retail pizza business would involve developing opportunities for customers to engage with the brand by using the right technologies to enable and encourage interaction. A new website was necessary to better address all major design elements. How Pizza Hut and imc² executed these design elements not only created value for its customers but also served as a basis for differentiation in the retail pizza business. Let's look at these design elements and PizzaHut.com's performance.

The Pizza Hut website was completely redesigned to support nationwide online ordering (including all franchise locations for the first time) and is updated frequently to keep up with the company's fast-paced marketing strategy and ambitious product innovation roll-out schedule. Since promotions are an important expectation in pizza purchasing and speak to the brand's consumers in a language that clearly connects with their desire for value, the website *context* and *content* balance the ability to shop for a deal with quick and easy ordering access for people who arrive at PizzaHut.com ready to purchase. The site presents a number of Pizza Hut's current offers in the central viewing window as well as through the rolling navigation directly underneath the main content. Primary navigation for information, such as the menu, locations, and nutrition facts, are displayed horizontally across the top of the rotating content.

Website *customization* is achieved in several ways, but the primary utility is to simplify ordering. For customers who have already registered, there are several personalization options, including rapid ordering called *Express Checkout*–a feature that's based on saved preferences similar to a "playlist." For example, if you have a group of friends that likes to watch movies together, you might create an order named *Movie Night* that has your group's favorite pizzas. Using the *Express Checkout* option accessible directly on the home page, you can select *Movie Night*, quickly review the order, click the "submit" button, and the pizzas are on their way, relying on saved delivery

Source: Pizza Hut, Inc.

GET THE KILLER APP FOR YOUR APPETITE!

Source: Pizza Hut, Inc.

and payment options through a stored *cookie* (a piece of digital code that is used to identify previous visitors) to speed the transaction. With this type of functionality, you can think of convenience as an investment that creates loyalty and somewhat insulates the brand against switching down the line when customers would have to register with and learn a competitor's system, and where access to their favorite features might not be available.

Website *content* and *communications* are integrated with the company's overall communications programs—including traditional media—with product innovations, promotions, and special events shared across platforms. True to the brand, communications are fun and energetic, matching bold images and vibrant color with a smart, clever, and lighthearted voice. One noteworthy example includes an April Fools' Day rebranding of the company as "Pasta Hut" to coincide with the launch of the brand's innovative line of Tuscani Pastas. This campaign included online support in the form of display media (banner ads) and the temporary rebranding of PizzaHut.com as PastaHut.com with special imagery and copy supporting the name change. Not only did the brand get plenty of coverage in the press, but it deepened the connection with customers by showing a willingness to be spontaneous and fun, inviting people to play along with the joke.

Pizza Hut's integrated marketing communications approach enables the company to easily test and incorporate other items and brands under the larger corporate umbrella, such as the WingStreet operation and the pasta extension. This demonstrates the brand's ability to stretch the QSR concept way beyond its pizza roots and suggests the kind of direction the company may pursue in the future.

PizzaHut.com and the brand's other online assets are all about getting the world's favorite pizza and signature products into the hands and stomachs of customers. Since *commerce* is a huge consideration on the site, there are multiple pathways for ordering, including several on-site methods, a Facebook app (the first national pizza chain to produce an ordering application for the world's leading social networking site), a branded desktop widget, mobile ordering (also known as Total Mobile Access, which includes both a WAP [wireless application protocol] site and text ordering), and a sophisticated and simple iPhone app that lets customers build and submit their order visually. Additional revenue streams can also be quickly built online, as demonstrated by the eGift Card program conceived and implemented by imc^2.

Realizing that it did not make sense for the company or its customers to create a *community* on the site, Pizza Hut tapped into Facebook to achieve results in a very cost-effective manner. With approximately 1 million fans and the first-of-its-kind Facebook ordering application, the brand can efficiently engage a huge group of people in a very natural way without disrupting their daily routine. Again, the brand understands that if you make something convenient, you can increase trust while securing greater transactional loyalty. Pizza Hut's program to identify a summer intern, or *Twintern*, responsible for monitoring and encouraging dialogue on Twitter and other social media networks is another example of how the brand is building on existing platforms and making effective use of the massive social marketing infrastructure.

PizzaHut.com connects mobile, desktop, social networks, and other digital gateways to complement traditional media and its retail presence. So when Pizza Hut thinks about the *connection* design element, it includes more than just linking to other websites online. Rather, it provides a comprehensive approach to creating a seamless customer experience wherever and whenever people want to engage with the brand.

PERFORMANCE MEASUREMENT AND OUTCOMES

Pizza Hut diligently measures the performance of PizzaHut.com. The company created a customized marketing dashboard that allows the Pizza Hut management team to monitor various aspects of the brand's marketing program and provides an almost constant stream of fresh information that it can use to optimize engagement with people or tweak various aspects of performance.

The results have been remarkable, but understand that due to the highly competitive nature of the industry, they are fluid and represent only a moment in time. Consider, for example:

1. PizzaHut.com dominates the pizza category with number one rankings in website traffic and search volume. According to comScore, a global leader in digital analytics and measurement, the Pizza Hut site achieves the most traffic per online dollars spent in the pizza category.

2. PizzaHut.com has become one of the top Internet retailers in the United States.
3. Pizza Hut's iPhone app had more than 100,000 downloads in the first two weeks after release.

WHAT'S NEXT

So what's next for PizzaHut.com? While the brand has made huge gains in a very short time period, staying on top in the rapidly evolving digital marketplace requires constant attention. Pizza Hut envisions that its online business will surpass the $1 billion mark and that digital transactions will lead all revenue within a decade.

While understandably protective of the company's future strategy, Pizza Hut CMO Niccol has ambitious goals and he's not joking when he deadpans, "I want Pizza Hut to become the Amazon of food service and be pioneers for the digital space. I do not want us to be a brick-and-mortar company that just dabbles in the space." The transition to something along the lines of the Amazon model suggests that the brand might further evolve its identity as a pizza business and stretch or completely redefine the QSR model.

Most brands that want to grow in the evolving economy will have to think and plan long term and be able to act swiftly as marketplace conditions change. imc^2 Chief Marketing Officer Ian Wolfman, when assessing the future of marketing, sums up the opportunity neatly: "Our agency believes that marketing's current transformation will result in a complete reorientation of how brands and companies engage with their consumers and other stakeholders. Brands that thrive will be those, like Pizza Hut, that can efficiently build sustainable relationships with people—relationships that have both high trust and high transactions" (see Figure 1). He goes on to explain that "brands taking a longer view have an unexpected advantage over traditional models that often focus too tightly on hitting near-term quarterly targets." Referring to research his agency has done on the subject, Wolfman points out that the most successful brands in the future will likely be those that resonate with people on a deeply emotional level and operate with a clearly defined sense of purpose.

Pizza Hut, with its focus on digitally enabled customer convenience and category innovation, is ideally positioned to connect with people on a level that builds trust and increases transactions. Referring to the initial time investment, however modest, that customers have to make in registering with the system and enabling various devices, Niccol sees the landscape as very promising for brands that put their customers' interests and preferences first. "If we do our job right—creating authentic engagement and making it convenient and valuable for people to interact with the brand—the numbers follow."[34]

FIGURE 1

imc² Brand Sustainability Map

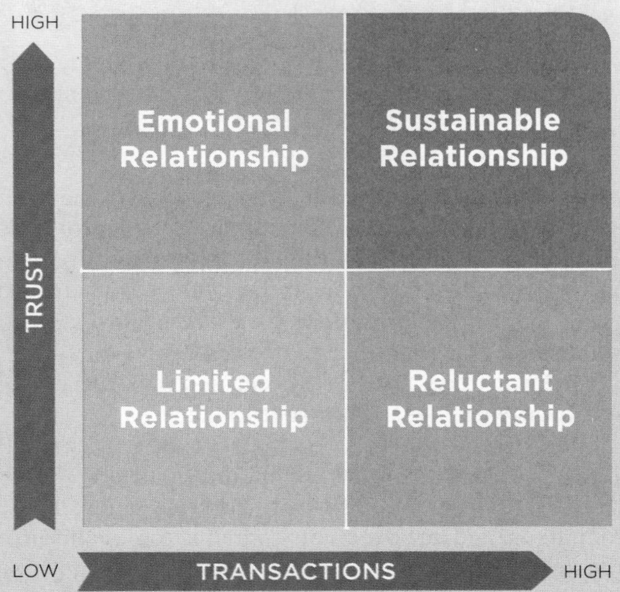

Questions

1 What kind of website is PizzaHut.com?
2 How does PizzaHut.com incorporate the seven website design elements?
3 How are choiceboard and personalization systems used in the PizzaHut.com website?

Chapter Notes

1. Seven Cycles, "Seven," http://sevencycles.com/Webdata/_archive/SevenBrochure09.pdf.
2. Interview with John Lewis, account executive and marketing manager at Seven Cycles, Inc.; www.sevencycles.com, April 20, 2019; "Seven Cycles Celebrates 20th Anniversary," *bicycleretailer.com,* February 2, 2017; and "Made in Massachusetts: Seven Cycles," www.wcvb.com/article/made-in-massachusetts-seven-cycles, January 12, 2016.
3. "U.S. Online Retail Forecast: 2017–2022," www.forrester.com, March 22, 2018.
4. "Transaction Denied," *Bloomberg Businessweek,* July 13, 2014, p. 90.
5. "For Many Retailers, the Lure of Cross-Border Ecommerce Is Profit," *emarketer.com*, March 25, 2018.
6. Rupal Parekh, "Personalized Products Please but Can They Create Profit?" *Advertising Age,* May 21, 2015, p. 4.

7. Rafi A. Mohammed, Robert J. Fisher, Bernard J. Jaworski, and Gordon J. Paddison, *Internet Marketing: Building Advantage in a Networked Economy,* 2nd ed. (Burr Ridge, IL: McGraw-Hill/Irwin, 2004).
8. "Models Will Run the World," *The Wall Street Journal,* August 20, 2018, p. A17; and "Recommended Just for You: The Power of Personalization," www.forbes.com, May 13, 2017.
9. "Consumers Don't Want Personalization to Get Too Personal," *emarketer.com,* April 14, 2018.
10. "Consumers Love Personalized Offers, but Only If They Opt In," *emarketer.com,* May 16, 2018; Manfred Kraft, Christine M. Arden, and Peter Verhoef, "Permission Marketing and Privacy Concerns: Why Do Customers (Not) Grant Permissions?" *Journal of Interactive Marketing* 39 (2017), pp. 39–54; and "Is This Really 'Opting In'?" *Advertising Age,* October 3, 2016, pp. 4ff.
11. Kelly D. Martin and Patrick E. Murphy, "The Role of Data Privacy in Marketing," *Journal of the Academy of Marketing Science,* March 2017, pp. 135–55.
12. This discussion is drawn from Jeffrey F. Rayport and Bernard J. Jaworski, *e-Commerce,* 2nd ed. (Burr Ridge, IL: McGraw-Hill/Irwin, 2004). Also see Alexander Bleier, Colleen M. Hameling, and Robert W. Palmatier, "Creating Effective Online Customer Experience," *Journal of Marketing,* March 2019, pp. 98–119.
13. Larry Freed, *Innovating Analytics* (Hoboken, NJ: Wiley, 2013).
14. This example and its data are provided courtesy of The Sewell Automotive Companies.
15. *The Truth about Online Consumers: 2017 Global Online Consumer Report,* KPMG White Paper, January 2017.
16. "10 Signs You're Addicted to Online Shopping," www.psychologytoday.com, November 4, 2015.
17. The data represent an average of estimates and forecasts provided by "U.S. E-commerce Performance StatPack," www.emarketer.com, January 30, 2019, and "Forecast Data: Online Retail Forecast, 2018 to 2024," www.forrester.com, May 2019.
18. Jerry Wind and Arvind Ranaswamy, "Customerization: The Next Wave in Mass Customization," *Journal of Interactive Marketing,* Winter 2001, pp. 13–32; and Amy Schade, "Customization vs. Personalization in the User Experience, www.nngroup.com, July 10, 2016.
19. Valerie Bauerkin, "Gatorade's Mission: Sell More Drinks," *The Wall Street Journal,* September 14, 2010, p. B6.
20. "Global Spam Volume as a Percentage of Total E-mail Traffic," www.internetlivestats.com, August 1, 2019.
21. Quoted in Judy Strauss, Adel El-Ansary, and Raymond Frost, *E-Marketing,* 5th ed. (Upper Saddle River, NJ: Prentice Hall, 2009), p. 357.
22. Victoria Taylor, "The Best-Ever Social Media Campaigns," www.forbes.com, August 17, 2017.
23. "Showrooming Hits Luxury Fashion," *The Wall Street Journal,* April 10, 2014, pp. B1, B2.
24. "Say Goodbye to the Car Salesman," *The Wall Street Journal,* November 21, 2013, pp. B1, B2; and "Death of a Car Salesman," *The Economist,* August 22, 2015, pp. 52–53.
25. Jennifer Valentino-DeVries and Emily Steel, "Cookies Cause Bitter Backlash," *The Wall Street Journal,* September 20, 2010, https://www.wsj.com.
26. "Be Afraid, Be Very Afraid," *Advertising Age,* January 8, 2018, pp. 17–19; "How Dirty Is Your Data?" www.forresterresearch.com, May 3, 2016; and "2019 Internet Crime Report," www.ic3.gov.
27. "Online Shopping Part of the Office Routine," *Dallas Morning News,* December 13, 2015, p. 2D; and Kathleen Kim, "More Employers Letting Employees Shop Online at Work," www.inc.com, November 14, 2012.
28. "How Consumers across the Globe Use Multiple Devices to Shop and Buy," www.emarketer.com, July 20, 2016.
29. "The Subscription Addiction," *The Economist,* April 7, 2018, p. 58; "Consumer Giants Spurn Risks to Chase Online Subscribers," www.msn.com, January 20, 2019.
30. The remainder of this discussion is based on the following sources: "Here's Why Stores Still Matter in the Digital Age," www.emarketer.com, March 26, 2019; "Survey: Customers Rely on Mobile while Shopping in Physical Stores," www.emarketer.com, May 14, 2019; Sonja Gensler, Scott Neslin, and Peter Verhoef, "The Showrooming Phenomenon: It's More Than Just about Price," *Journal of Interactive Marketing,* May 2017, 29–43; and "Webrooming and Showrooming in 2019," *multichannelmerchant.com,* January 19, 2019.
31. "The Global House of Prestige Beauty," *The Estée Lauder Companies 2016 Annual Report,* March 2017.
32. "Fewer Than 10% of U.S. Marketers Think Their Company's Attribution Knowledge Is Excellent," www.emarketer.com, March 1, 2019; and "Now Google Can Tell If Its Ads Send Us to Stores," *Dallas Morning News,* May 24, 2017.
33. Kristin Naragon, "Getting Multichannel Marketing Right," *hbr.org,* May 29, 2019; and "Clicks to Bricks," *DMNews,* March 2017, pp. 26–30.
34. Pizza Hut: Source: This case was prepared by Pizza Hut and imc^2 and Roger A. Kerin for exclusive use in this text.

Chapter 18 Integrated Marketing Communications and Direct Marketing

LEARNING OBJECTIVES

After reading this chapter you should be able to:

LO 18-1 Discuss integrated marketing communications and the communication process.

LO 18-2 Describe the promotional mix and the uniqueness of each component.

LO 18-3 Select the promotional approach appropriate to a product's target audience, life-cycle stage, and characteristics, as well as stages of the buying decision and channel strategies.

LO 18-4 Describe the elements of the promotion decision process.

LO 18-5 Explain the value of direct marketing for consumers and sellers.

At Taco Bell Every Day Is Taco Tuesday™!

Every Tuesday millions of Mexican food lovers celebrate the day with a taco. You may be one of them! "Of course we love that there is a day of the week dedicated to tacos," says Taco Bell's chief global brand officer, Marisa Thalberg. However, Taco Bell's new campaign, "Taco reBELLion," hopes to encourage you to think of tacos any day!

The campaign includes television ads that show three taco gangs–the Hard Shells, the Soft Shells, and Los Locos–as they rebel against the tradition of tacos on Tuesdays. The campaign also includes five types of Party Packs that contain a combination of 10 tacos and burritos; the introduction of a line of reBELLious merchandise available on the Taco Shop website (www.tacobelltacoshop.com), including shirts, swimwear, hats, and a variety of accessories; and a 15 percent off promotion for a Party Pack. Other marketing activities include announcements that "The taco #reBELLion has begun" on Twitter, posting videos on YouTube, and writing an open letter to fans.

Taco Bell's customers are independent, a little cult-like, and definitely interested in a "cool" factor so the company also uses many other forms of promotion to keep its customers engaged. Radio, outdoor, and cinema ads are common, as are news releases and public relations support. You might remember that Taco Bell teamed up with T-Mobile to run a television ad during the Super Bowl. Taco Bell also recently announced Grubhub delivery service, vegetarian menu items, and the incredible success of its Nacho Fries. Special promotions include collaborations with Microsoft to give Taco Bell diners the chance to win a special-edition Xbox One that makes Taco Bell's famous "ring" when powered on; with the MLB to give away free tacos to all store visitors if a player steals a base during the World Series; and with a Palm Springs hotel to create a Taco Bell Hotel and Resort, complete with taco-themed rooms. Taco Bell even offers a $600 wedding package at its Las Vegas Strip store!

Of course social media play an important role in Taco Bell campaigns also. Taco Hacks, for example, are a series of videos posted on Taco Bell's YouTube channel about unique ways to order from the Taco Bell menu. Similarly, The Taco Bell Clip Show posts content ranging from Taco Bell wedding proposals to sauce packet trick shots to drive-thru pranks. Taco Bell's Facebook page and Twitter account have 9.9 million and 1.9 million followers, respectively.[1]

Taco Bell's successful marketing campaigns demonstrate the opportunity for engaging potential customers and the importance of integrating the various elements of a marketing communication program. Promotion represents the fourth element in the marketing mix. The promotional element consists of five communication tools, including advertising, personal selling, sales promotion, public relations, and direct marketing. The combination of one or more of these communication tools is called the **promotional mix**. All of these tools can be used to (1) inform prospective buyers

Source: Taco Bell Corp.

about the benefits of the product, (2) persuade them to try it, and (3) remind them later about the benefits they enjoyed by using the product. In the past, marketers often viewed these communication tools as separate and independent. The advertising department, for example, often designed and managed its activities without consulting departments or agencies that had responsibility for sales promotion or public relations. The result was often an overall communication effort that was uncoordinated and, in some cases, inconsistent. Today, the concept of designing marketing communications programs that coordinate all promotional activities–advertising, personal selling, sales promotion, public relations, and direct marketing–to provide a consistent message across all audiences is referred to as **integrated marketing communications (IMC)**. This coordination is increasingly important as new media options, interactions between traditional and contemporary media, the need for client and advertising agency collaboration, and shifting consumer communication patterns all make optimal communication more challenging. In addition, by taking the consumer journey and consumer expectations into consideration, IMC is a key element in a company's customer experience management strategy.[2]

This chapter provides an overview of the communication process, a description of the promotional mix elements, several tools for integrating the promotional mix, and a process for developing a comprehensive promotion program. One of the promotional mix elements, direct marketing, is also discussed in this chapter. Chapter 19 covers advertising, sales promotion, and public relations; Chapter 20 covers social media; and Chapter 21 discusses personal selling.

THE COMMUNICATION PROCESS

LO 18-1
Discuss integrated marketing communications and the communication process.

Communication is the process of conveying a message to others, and it requires six elements: a source, a message, a channel of communication, a receiver, and the processes of encoding and decoding[3] (see Figure 18–1). The **source** may be a company or person who has information to convey. The information sent by a source, such as a description of a new smartphone, forms the **message**. The message is conveyed by means of a **channel of communication** such as a salesperson, advertising media, or public relations tools. Consumers who read, hear, or see the message are the **receivers**.

Encoding and Decoding

Encoding and decoding are essential to communication. **Encoding** is the process of having the sender transform an idea into a set of symbols. **Decoding** is the reverse, or the process of having the receiver take a set of symbols, the message, and transform the symbols into an idea. Look at the North Face advertisement: Who is the source, and what is the message?

VIDEO 18-1
The North Face
kerin.tv/15e/v18-1

Decoding is performed by the receivers according to their own frame of reference: their attitudes, values, and beliefs.[4] The North Face is the source and the advertisement is the message, which appeared in *Wired* magazine (the channel). How would you interpret (decode) this advertisement? The picture and text in the advertisement show that the source's intention is to generate interest in its product with the headline "I Live On The Edge. Never Stop Exploring"—a statement the source believes will appeal to the readers of the magazine.

The process of communication is not always a successful one. Errors in communication can happen in several ways. The source may not adequately transform the abstract idea into an effective set of symbols, a properly encoded message may be sent through the wrong channel and never make it to the intended receiver, the receiver may not properly transform the set of symbols into the correct abstract idea, or finally, feedback may be so delayed or distorted that it is of no use to the sender. Although communication appears easy to perform, truly effective communication can be very difficult.

For the message to be communicated effectively, the sender and receiver must have a mutually shared **field of experience**—a similar understanding and knowledge they apply to the message. Figure 18–1 shows two circles representing the fields of experience of the sender and receiver, which overlap in the message. Some of the better-known message problems have occurred when U.S. companies have taken their messages to cultures with different fields of experience. Many misinterpretations are merely the result of bad translations. For example, KFC made a mistake when its "finger-lickin' good" slogan was translated into Mandarin Chinese as "eat your fingers off"![5]

FIGURE 18–1
The communication process consists of six key elements. See the text to learn about factors that influence the effectiveness of the process.

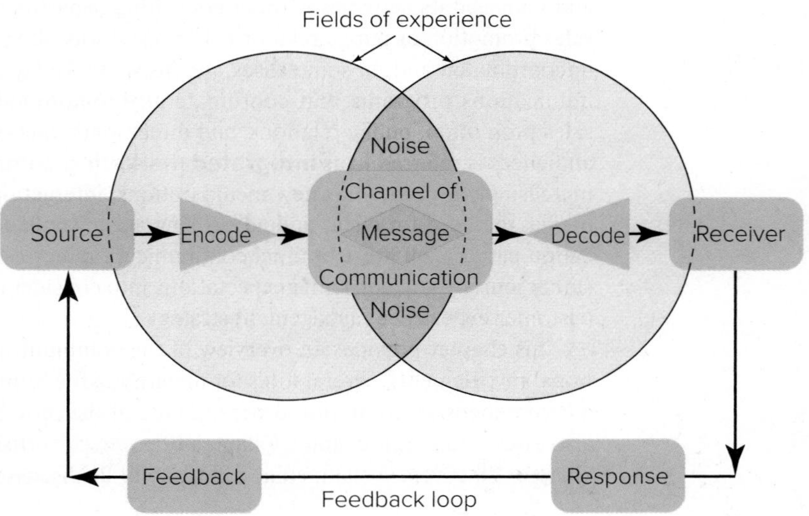

How would you decode this ad? What message is The North Face trying to send?
Source: The North Face

The North Face
www.thenorthface.com

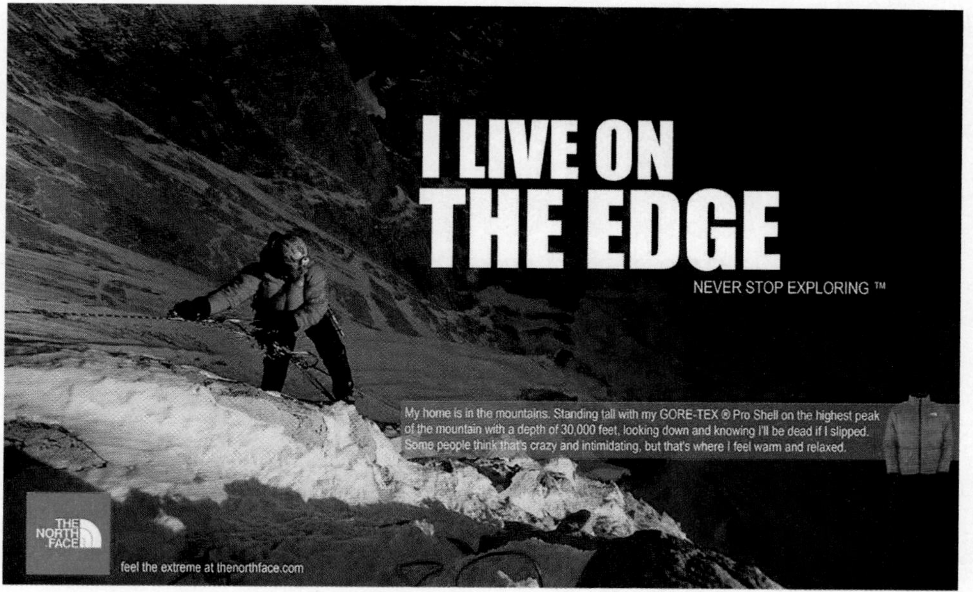

Feedback

Figure 18–1 shows a line labeled *feedback loop*, which consists of a response and feedback. A **response** is the impact the message had on the receiver's knowledge, attitudes, or behaviors. **Feedback** is the sender's interpretation of the response and indicates whether the message was decoded and understood as intended. Chapter 19 reviews approaches called *pretesting*, which ensure that messages are decoded properly.

Noise

Noise includes extraneous factors that can work against effective communication by distorting a message or the feedback received (Figure 18–1). Noise can be a simple error, such as a printing mistake that affects the meaning of a newspaper advertisement or the use of words or pictures that fail to communicate the message clearly. Noise can also occur when a salesperson's message is misunderstood by a prospective buyer, such as when a salesperson's accent, use of slang terms, or communication style make hearing and understanding the message difficult.

LEARNING REVIEW

18-1. What six elements are required for communication to occur?

18-2. A difficulty for U.S. companies advertising in international markets is that the audience does not share the same ______________.

18-3. A misprint in a newspaper ad is an example of ______________.

THE PROMOTIONAL ELEMENTS

LO 18-2
Describe the promotional mix and the uniqueness of each component.

To communicate with consumers, a company can use one or more of five promotional alternatives: advertising, personal selling, public relations, sales promotion, and direct marketing. Figure 18–2 on the next page summarizes the distinctions among these five elements. Three of these elements—advertising, sales promotion, and public relations—are often said to use *mass selling* because they are used with groups of prospective buyers. In contrast, personal selling uses *customized interaction* between a seller and a prospective buyer. Personal selling activities include face-to-face, telephone, and interactive electronic communication. Direct marketing also uses messages customized for specific customers.

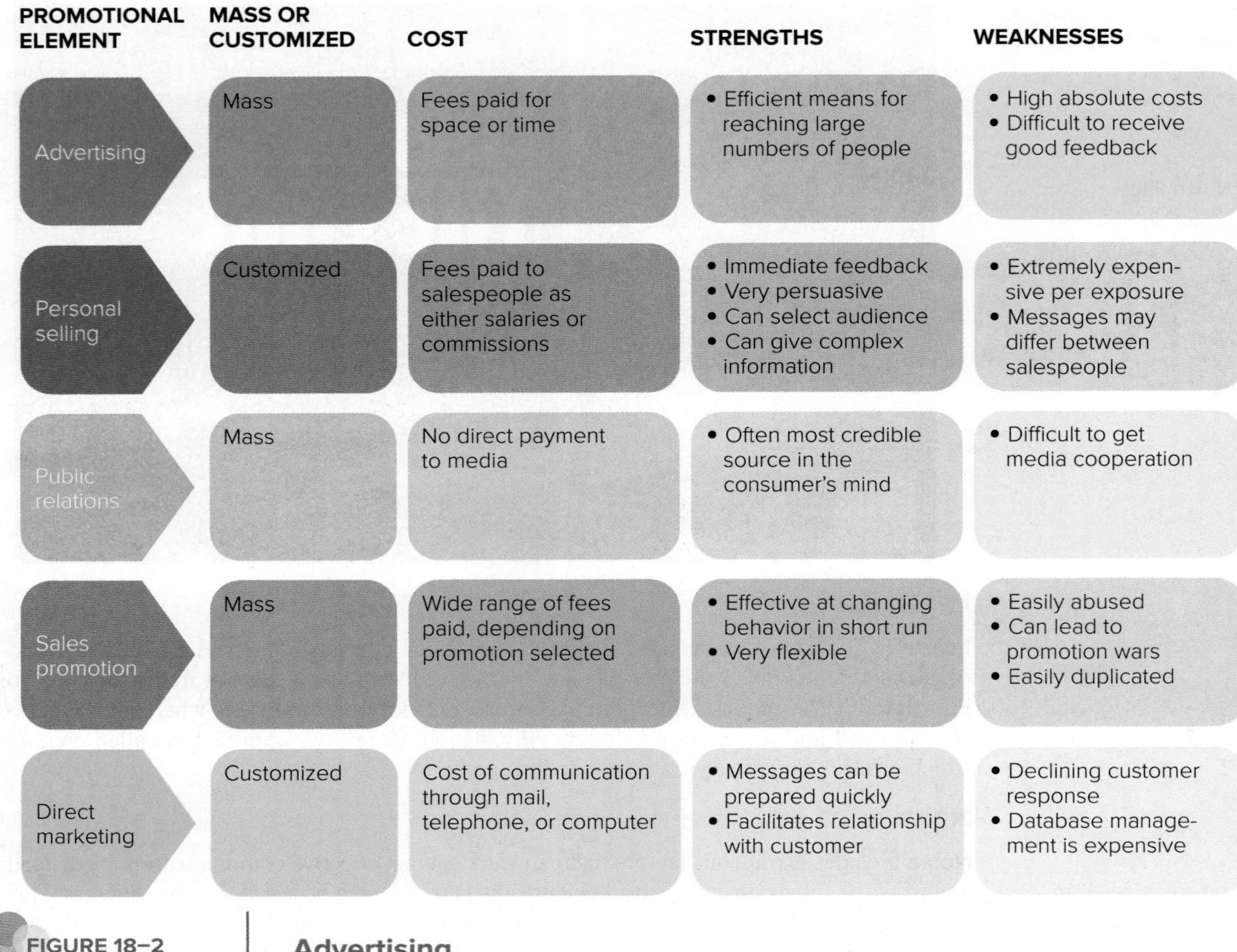

PROMOTIONAL ELEMENT	MASS OR CUSTOMIZED	COST	STRENGTHS	WEAKNESSES
Advertising	Mass	Fees paid for space or time	• Efficient means for reaching large numbers of people	• High absolute costs • Difficult to receive good feedback
Personal selling	Customized	Fees paid to salespeople as either salaries or commissions	• Immediate feedback • Very persuasive • Can select audience • Can give complex information	• Extremely expensive per exposure • Messages may differ between salespeople
Public relations	Mass	No direct payment to media	• Often most credible source in the consumer's mind	• Difficult to get media cooperation
Sales promotion	Mass	Wide range of fees paid, depending on promotion selected	• Effective at changing behavior in short run • Very flexible	• Easily abused • Can lead to promotion wars • Easily duplicated
Direct marketing	Customized	Cost of communication through mail, telephone, or computer	• Messages can be prepared quickly • Facilitates relationship with customer	• Declining customer response • Database management is expensive

FIGURE 18–2
Each of the five elements of the promotional mix has strengths and weaknesses.

Advertising

Advertising is any paid form of nonpersonal communication about an organization, product, service, or idea by an identified sponsor. The *paid* aspect of this definition is important because the space for the advertising message normally must be bought. A full-page, four-color ad in *Time* magazine, for example, costs $265,100. An occasional exception is the public service announcement, where the advertising time or space is donated. The *nonpersonal* component of advertising is also important. Advertising involves mass media (such as TV, radio, and magazines), which are nonpersonal and do not have an immediate feedback loop as does personal selling. So before the message is sent, marketing research plays a valuable role; for example, it determines that the target market will actually see the medium chosen and that the message will be understood.

There are several advantages to a firm using advertising in its promotional mix. It can be attention-getting–as with the Oculus ad–and also communicate specific product benefits to prospective buyers. By paying for the advertising space, a company can control *what* it wants to say and, to some extent, to *whom* the message is sent. Advertising also allows the company to decide *when* to send its message (which includes how often). The nonpersonal aspect of advertising also has its advantages. Once the message is created, the same message is sent to all receivers in a market segment. If the pictorial, text, and brand elements of an advertisement are properly pretested, an advertiser can ensure the ad's ability to capture consumers' attention and trust that the same message will be decoded by all receivers in the market segment.[6]

Advertising has some disadvantages. As shown in Figure 18–2 and discussed in depth in Chapter 19, the costs to produce and place a message are significant, and the lack of direct feedback makes it difficult to know how well the message was received.

Magazines are a mass media outlet for advertising.
Source: Meredith Corporation

Personal Selling

The second major promotional alternative is **personal selling**, which is the two-way flow of communication between a buyer and seller designed to influence a person's or group's purchase decision. Unlike advertising, personal selling is usually face-to-face communication between the sender and receiver. Why do companies use personal selling?

There are important advantages to personal selling, as summarized in Figure 18–2. A salesperson can control to *whom* the presentation is made, reducing the amount of *wasted coverage* or communication with consumers who are not in the target audience. The personal component of selling has another advantage in that the seller can see or hear the potential buyer's reaction to the message. If the feedback is unfavorable, the salesperson can modify the message.

The flexibility of personal selling can also be a disadvantage. Different salespeople can change the message so that no consistent communication is given to all customers. The high cost of personal selling is probably its major disadvantage. On a cost-per-contact basis, it is generally the most expensive of the five promotional elements.

VIDEO 18-2
McDonald's
kerin.tv/15e/v18-2

Public Relations

Public relations is a form of communication management that seeks to influence the feelings, opinions, or beliefs held by customers, prospective customers, stockholders, suppliers, employees, and other publics about a company and its products or services.[7] Many tools, such as special events, lobbying efforts, annual reports, press conferences, social media (including Facebook and Twitter), and image management, may be used by a public relations department, although publicity often plays the most important role.[8] **Publicity** is a nonpersonal, indirectly paid presentation of an organization, product, or service. It can take the form of a news story, editorial, or product announcement. A difference between publicity and both advertising and personal selling is the "indirectly paid" dimension. With publicity a company does not pay for space in a mass medium (such as television or radio) but attempts to get the medium to run a favorable story on the company. In this sense, there is an indirect payment for publicity in that a company must support a public relations staff.

An advantage of publicity is credibility. When you read a favorable story about a company's product (such as a glowing restaurant review), there is a tendency to believe it. Travelers throughout the world have relied on Lonely Planet's guides such as *Italy*. These books describe out-of-the-way, inexpensive restaurants and hotels, giving invaluable publicity to these

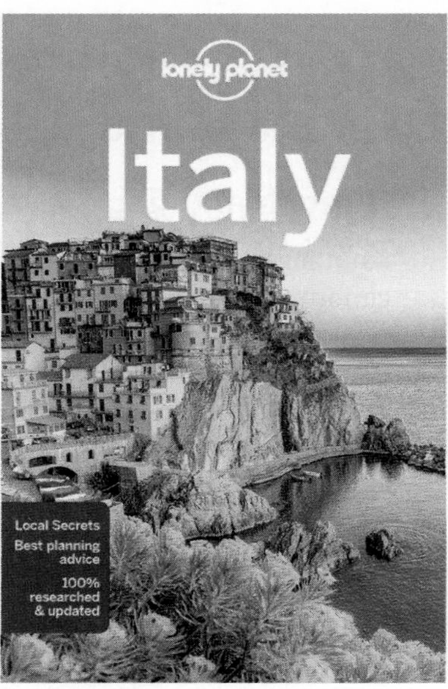

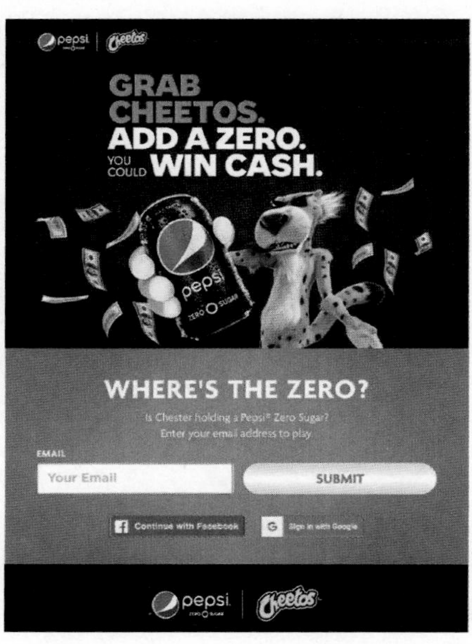

Which three elements of the promotional mix are represented by the Oculus ad, the Lonely Planet's travel guide to Italy, and the Pepsi/Cheetos sweepstakes? Read the text to find out.
Sources: (Left): Oculus VR/Facebook, Inc.; (Middle): Lonely Planet; (Right): PepsiCo, Inc.

McDonald's
514.2K Tweets
Follow
McDonald's
@McDonalds
Welcome to McDonald's USA Twitter page! Follow @McDonaldsCorp for company + biz updates. For customer support use the link below.
mcdonalds.com/us/en-us/conta...
Joined September 2009
14.1K Following 3.6M Followers
Not followed by anyone you're following
Tweets
Tweets & replies
Media
Likes
McDonald's @McDonalds · Jul 24
Is there anything better than rolling down your window and being handed
? #NationalDriveThruDay
No
35%
Definitely no
65%
2,397 votes · Final results
134
40
201

McDonald's facilitates online discussions with Twitter.
Source: McDonald's/Twitter

establishments. Such businesses do not (nor can they) buy a mention in the guide. Publicity is particularly effective when consumers lack prior knowledge of the product or service.[9]

The disadvantage of publicity relates to the lack of the user's control over it. A company can invite media to cover an interesting event such as a store opening or a new-product release, but there is no guarantee that a story will result, that it will be positive, or that the target audience will receive the message. Social media such as Facebook, Twitter, and topic-specific blogs have grown dramatically and allow public discussions of almost any company activity. Many public relations departments now focus on facilitating and responding to online discussions. McDonald's, for example, replies to tweets on its customer service Twitter account, which has more than 3.6 million followers. Generally, publicity is an important element of most promotional campaigns, although the lack of control means that it is rarely the primary element. Research related to the sequence of IMC elements, however, indicates that publicity followed by advertising with the same message increases the positive response to the message.[10]

Sales Promotion

A fourth promotional element is **sales promotion**, a short-term inducement of value offered to arouse interest in buying a product or service. Used in conjunction with advertising or personal selling, sales promotions are offered to intermediaries as well as to ultimate consumers. Coupons, rebates, samples, contests, and sweepstakes, such as the Pepsi/Cheetos promotion on the previous page, are just a few examples of sales promotions discussed later in this chapter.

The advantage of sales promotions is that the short-term nature of these programs (such as a coupon or sweepstakes with an expiration date) often stimulates sales for their duration. Offering value to the consumer in terms of a cents-off coupon or rebate may increase store traffic from consumers who are not store-loyal.[11]

Sales promotions cannot be the sole basis for a campaign because gains are often temporary and sales drop off when the deal ends. Advertising support is needed to convert the customer who tried the product because of a sales promotion into a long-term buyer. If sales promotions are conducted continuously, they lose their effectiveness. Customers begin to delay purchase until a coupon is offered, or they question the product's value. Some aspects of sales promotions also are regulated by the federal government.[12] These issues are reviewed in detail in Chapter 19.

MarsBars/iStock/Getty Images

Direct Marketing

Another promotional alternative, **direct marketing**, uses direct communication with consumers to generate a response in the form of an order, a request for further information, or a visit to a retail outlet. The communication can take many forms, including face-to-face selling, direct mail, catalogs, telephone solicitations, direct response advertising (on television and radio and in print), and online marketing.[13] Like personal selling, direct marketing often consists of interactive communication. It also has the advantage of being customized to match the needs of specific target markets. Messages can be developed and adapted quickly to facilitate one-to-one relationships with customers.

While direct marketing has been one of the fastest-growing forms of promotion, it has several disadvantages. First, most forms of direct marketing

VIDEO 18-3
Data & Marketing Association
kerin.tv/15e/v18-3

require a comprehensive and up-to-date database with information about the target market. Developing and maintaining the database can be expensive and time-consuming. In addition, growing concern about privacy has led to a decline in response rates among some customer groups. The importance of data in direct marketing efforts, however, is emphasized by the Data & Marketing Association, which advocates "innovative and responsible use of data-driven marketing." Companies with successful direct marketing programs are sensitive to these issues and often use a combination of direct marketing alternatives together, or direct marketing combined with other promotional tools, to increase value for customers.

LEARNING REVIEW

18-4. Explain the difference between advertising and publicity when both appear on television.

18-5. Cost per contact is high with the ________________ element of the promotional mix.

18-6. Which promotional element should be offered only on a short-term basis?

INTEGRATED MARKETING COMMUNICATIONS—DEVELOPING THE PROMOTIONAL MIX

LO 18-3
Select the promotional approach appropriate to a product's target audience, life-cycle stage, and characteristics, as well as stages of the buying decision and channel strategies.

A firm's promotional mix is the combination of one or more of the promotional tools it chooses to use. In putting together the promotional mix, a marketer must consider two issues. First, the balance of the elements must be determined. Should advertising be emphasized more than personal selling? Should a promotional rebate be offered? Would public relations activities be effective? Several factors affect such decisions: the target audience for the promotion, the stage of the product's life cycle, the characteristics of the product, the decision stage of the buyer, and even the channel of distribution. Second, because the various promotional elements are often the responsibility of different departments, coordinating a consistent promotional effort is necessary. A promotional planning process designed to ensure integrated marketing communications (IMC) can facilitate this goal.

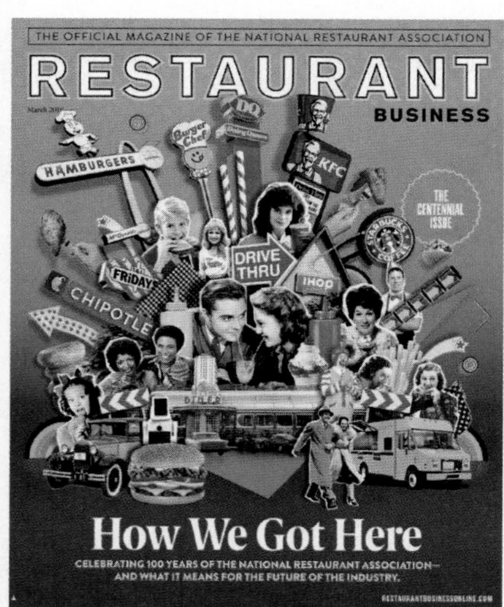

Publications such as *Restaurant Business* reach business buyers.
Source: Winsight, LLC.

The Target Audience

Promotional programs are directed to the ultimate consumer, to an intermediary (retailer, wholesaler, or industrial distributor), or to both. Promotional programs directed to buyers of consumer products often use mass media because the number of potential buyers is large. Personal selling is used at the place of purchase, generally the retail store. Direct marketing may be used to encourage first-time or repeat purchases. Combinations of many media alternatives are a necessity for some target audiences today. The Marketing Matters box on the next page describes how today's college students can be reached through mobile marketing programs.[14]

Advertising directed to business buyers is used selectively in trade publications such as *Restaurant Business* magazine for buyers of restaurant equipment and supplies. Because business buyers often have specialized needs or technical questions, personal selling is particularly important. The salesperson can provide information and the necessary support after the sale.

Intermediaries are often the focus of promotional efforts. As with business buyers, personal selling is the major promotional ingredient. The salespeople assist intermediaries in making a profit by coordinating promotional campaigns sponsored by the manufacturer and providing marketing advice and expertise. Intermediaries' questions often pertain to the allowed markup, merchandising support, and return policies.

Marketing Matters — Technology

Marketers Want to Go to College, and on Spring Break, with You!

There are approximately 20 million students in college in the United States today, and they represent an attractive target market for many businesses for several reasons. First, they are early adopters shaping spending habits that could lead them to become lifelong customers. Second, experts estimate that their annual spending power is $574 billion. The challenge for marketers is that students, who are primarily from the millennial and Generation Z cohorts, are tech-savvy, hyperconnected, and demanding. In an effort to reach students marketers are tailoring their activities to match these unique characteristics.

College students consist of "digital natives" who have grown up with smartphones and Internet access all of their lives. In fact, a recent study of university students indicated that more than half of their purchases are made online. They access Instagram, YouTube, and Twitter; they download apps, coupons, and information 24/7; and they communicate with text messages, e-mail, and blogs. For many businesses, these facts suggest that marketing through cell phones, or mobile marketing, will be an essential element in integrated marketing communications campaigns in the future.

Several guidelines help ensure the success of mobile marketing to students. First, it is important to be familiar with six-second pre-roll ads, class accounts, and chat groups on social media. In addition, communication must be honest, authentic, and transparent about the purpose and value of the brand. Finally, mobile marketing campaigns should facilitate multitasking. According to one expert, marketers "should picture students looking at texts and images while traveling on a bus, rushing to a lecture, or out socializing."

Marketers even look for ways to reach students during spring break where they might be using ad-free streaming services while sitting on the beach. So many brands are also using brand ambassadors and "influencers" to help communicate their messages.

Watch for other brands that use mobile marketing as part of their campaigns to reach college students in the future.

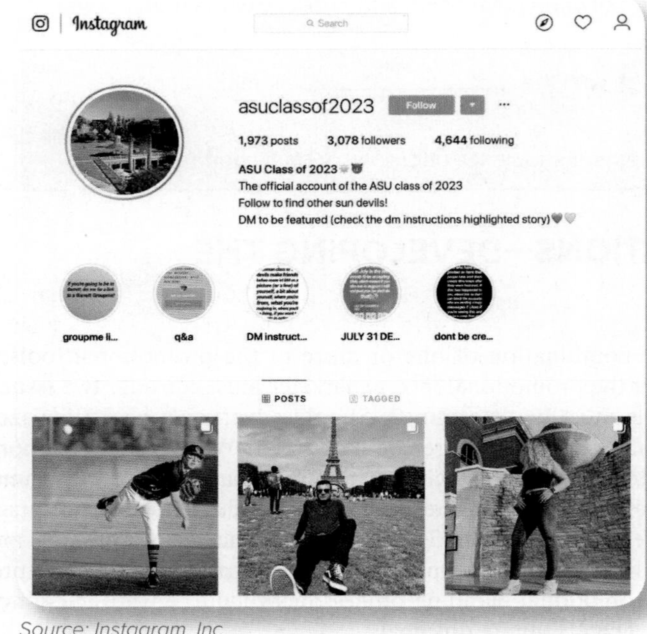

Source: Instagram, Inc

The Product Life Cycle

All products have a product life cycle (see Chapter 11), and the composition of the promotional mix changes over the four life-cycle stages, as shown in Figure 18–3.

Introduction Stage Informing consumers in an effort to increase their level of awareness is the primary promotional objective in the introduction stage of the product life cycle. In general, all the promotional mix elements are used at this time, although the use of specific mix elements during any stage depends on the product and situation. News releases about a new dog food, for example, are sent to veterinary magazines, trial samples are sent to registered dog owners, advertisements are placed in *Dogster* magazine, and the salesforce begins to approach supermarkets and pet stores to get orders. Advertising is particularly important as a means of reaching as many people as possible to build awareness and interest. Publicity may even begin slightly before the product is commercially available.

Growth Stage The primary promotional objective of the growth stage is to persuade the consumer to buy the product rather than substitutes, so the marketing manager seeks to gain brand preference and solidify distribution. Sales promotion assumes less importance in this stage, and publicity is not a factor because it depends on novelty of the product. The primary

FIGURE 18–3
The product life cycle illustrates how promotional objectives and activities change over the four stages.

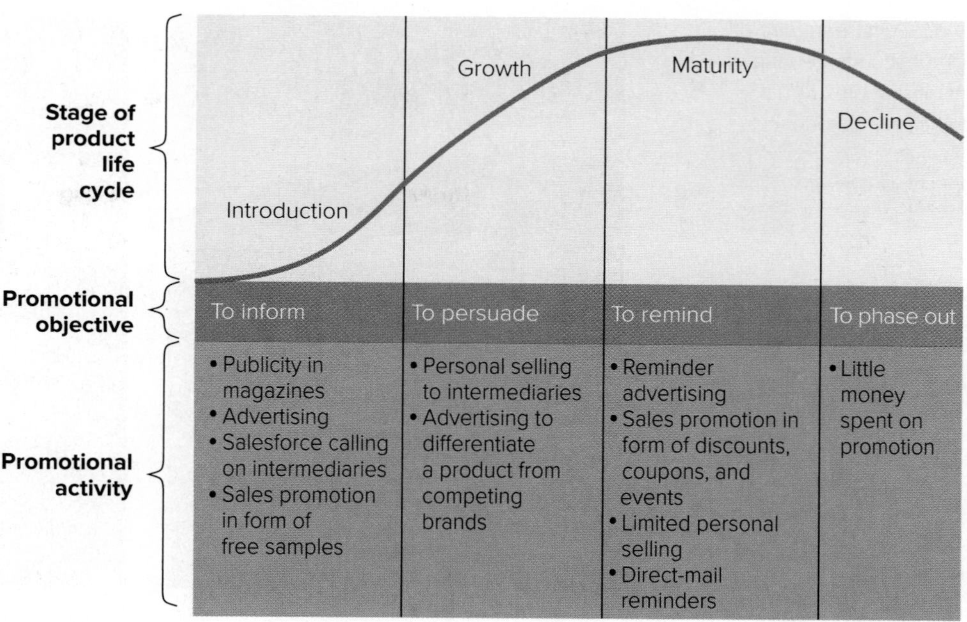

Advertising in *Dogster* can build awareness of a new dog food.
Source: I-5 Publishing, LLC.

promotional element is advertising, which stresses brand differences. Personal selling is used to solidify the channel of distribution. For consumer products such as dog food, the salesforce calls on the wholesalers and retailers in hopes of increasing inventory levels and gaining shelf space. For business products, the salesforce often tries to get contractual arrangements to be the sole source of supply for the buyer.

Maturity Stage In the maturity stage, the need is to maintain existing buyers, and advertising's role is to remind buyers of the product's existence. Sales promotion, in the form of discounts and coupons offered to both ultimate consumers and intermediaries, is important in maintaining loyal buyers. In a test of one mature consumer product, it was found that 80 percent of the product's sales at this stage resulted from sales promotions.[15] Sponsoring events can also help maintain loyalty. For more than 20 years, Purina has sponsored the Purina Pro Plan Incredible Dog Challenge, which is covered by a live stream for online viewers. In addition, Purina has developed an iPhone app called P5 to teach viewers how to train their dogs in the events they see performed during the Challenge.[16] Direct marketing actions such as direct mail are used to maintain involvement with existing customers and to encourage repeat purchases. Price cuts and discounts can also significantly increase a mature brand's sales. The salesforce at this stage seeks to satisfy intermediaries. An unsatisfied customer who switches brands is hard to replace.

Decline Stage The decline stage of the product life cycle is usually a period of phaseout for the product, and little money is spent in the promotional mix. The rate of decline can be rapid, as is the case when a product is replaced by an improved or lower-cost product, for example, or slow, as often happens when a group of loyal customers exists.

Product Characteristics

The proper blend of elements in the promotional mix also depends on the type of product. Three specific characteristics should be considered: complexity, risk, and ancillary services. *Complexity* refers to the technical sophistication of the product and hence the amount of understanding required to use it. It's hard to provide much information in a one-page magazine ad or a 30-second television ad, so the more complex the product, the greater the emphasis on personal selling. Gulfstream asks potential customers to call a representative identified in its

How do Gulfstream aircraft and Tabasco sauce differ in terms of complexity, risk, and ancillary services?

(Left): Source: Gulfstream Aerospace Corporation; (Right): Source: McIlhenny Company

ads. On the other hand, very little information is provided for simple products such as Tabasco pepper sauce.

A second element is the degree of risk represented by the product's purchase. *Risk* for the buyer can be assessed in terms of financial risk, social risk, and physical risk. A private jet, for example, might represent all three risks–it is expensive, employees and customers may see and evaluate the purchase, and safety and reliability are important. Although advertising helps, the greater the risk, the greater the need for personal selling. Consumers are unlikely to associate any of these risks with a candy bar.

The level of ancillary services required by a product also affects the promotional strategy. *Ancillary services* pertain to the degree of service or support required after the sale. This characteristic is common to many industrial products and consumer purchases. Who will provide maintenance for the plane? Advertising's role is to establish the seller's reputation. Direct marketing can be used to describe how a product or service can be customized to meet individual needs. However, personal selling is essential to build buyer confidence and provide evidence of customer service.

Stages of the Consumer Journey

Knowledge of the consumer journey can also affect the promotional mix. Figure 18–4 shows how the importance of the promotional elements varies with the three stages in the consumer journey.

Prepurchase Stage In the prepurchase stage, advertising is more helpful than personal selling because advertising informs the potential customer of the existence of the product and the seller. Sales promotion in the form of free samples also can play an important role to gain low-risk trial. When the salesperson calls on the customer after heavy advertising, there is some recognition of what the salesperson represents. This is particularly important in industrial settings in which sampling of the product is usually not possible.

Purchase Stage At the purchase stage, the importance of personal selling is highest, whereas the impact of advertising is lowest. Sales promotion in the form of coupons, deals, point-of-purchase displays, and rebates can be very helpful in encouraging demand. In this stage, social media can play an important role in the final decision by delivering promotions and giving consumers control of the process. Research indicates that direct marketing activities shorten the time consumers take to adopt a product or service.[17]

FIGURE 18–4
The importance of promotional elements varies during the stages of the consumer journey.

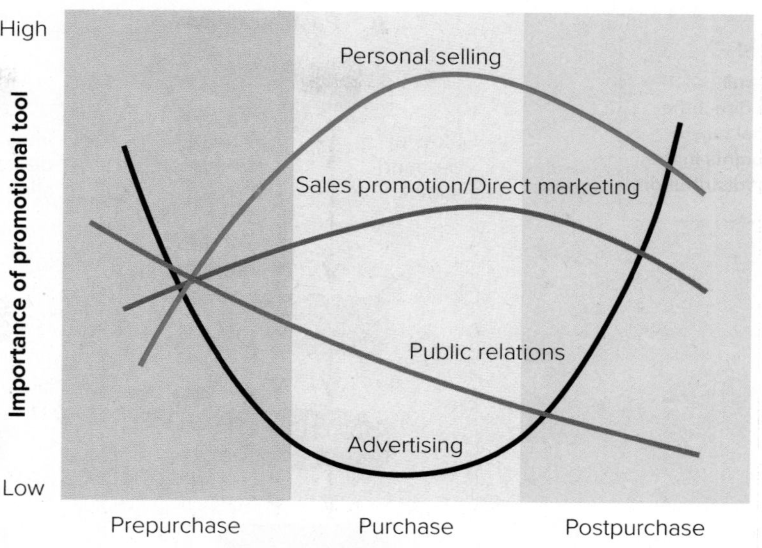

Postpurchase Stage In the postpurchase stage, the salesperson is still important. In fact, the more personal contact after the sale, the more the buyer is satisfied. Advertising is also important to assure the buyer that the right purchase was made. Advertising and personal selling help reduce the buyer's postpurchase anxiety. Sales promotion in the form of coupons and direct marketing reminders can help encourage repeat purchases from satisfied first-time triers. Public relations plays a small role in the postpurchase stage.[18]

Channel Strategies

Chapter 15 discussed the channel flow from a producer to intermediaries to consumers. Achieving control of the channel is often difficult for the manufacturer, and promotional strategies can assist in moving a product through the channel of distribution. This is where a manufacturer has to make an important decision about whether to use a push strategy, pull strategy, or both in its channel of distribution.[19]

Why does this ad suggest readers should "Ask your doctor about Otezla"? For the answer, see the text.
Source: Celgene

Push Strategy Figure 18–5A shows how a manufacturer uses a **push strategy**, directing the promotional mix to channel members to gain their cooperation in ordering and stocking the product. In this approach, personal selling and sales promotions play major roles. Salespeople call on wholesalers to encourage orders and provide sales assistance. Sales promotions, such as case discount allowances (20 percent off the regular case price), are offered to stimulate demand. By pushing the product through the channel, the goal is to get channel members to push it to their customers.

Ford Motor Company, for example, provides support and incentives for its 3,100 Ford dealers. Through a multilevel program, Ford provides incentives to reward dealers for meeting sales goals. Dealers receive an incentive when they are near a goal, another when they reach a goal, and an even larger one if they exceed sales projections. Ford also offers some dealers special incentives for maintaining superior facilities or improving customer service. All of these actions are intended to encourage Ford dealers to "push" the Ford products through the channel to consumers.[20]

Pull Strategy In some instances, manufacturers face resistance from channel members who do not want to order a new product or increase inventory levels of an existing brand. As

FIGURE 18–5
Push and pull strategies direct the promotional mix to different points in the channel of distribution.

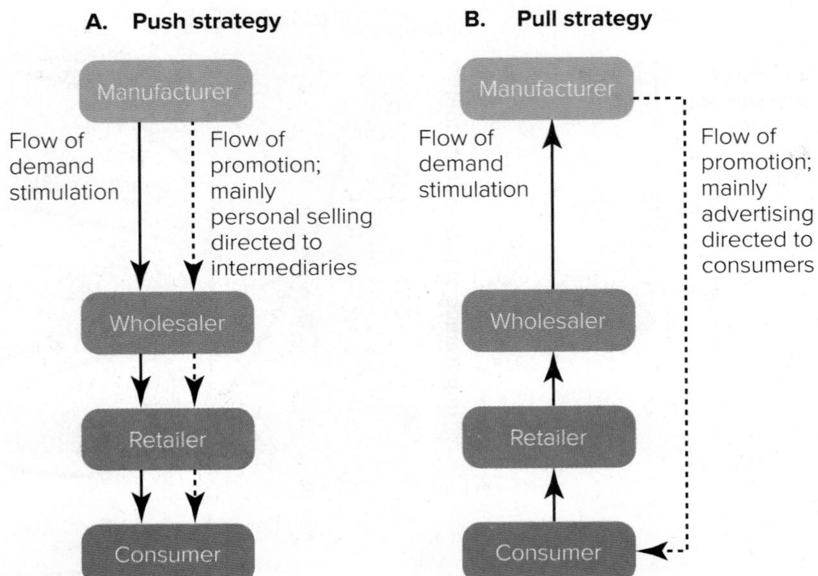

shown in Figure 18–5B, a manufacturer may then elect to implement a **pull strategy** by directing its promotional mix at ultimate consumers to encourage them to ask the retailer for a product. Seeing demand from ultimate consumers, retailers order the product from wholesalers and thus the item is pulled through the intermediaries. Pharmaceutical companies, for example, now spend more than $9.6 billion annually on *direct-to-consumer* prescription drug advertising, to complement traditional personal selling and free samples directed only at doctors. The strategy is designed to encourage consumers to ask their doctor for a specific drug by name—pulling it through the channel. Successful campaigns, such as the print ad for Otezla, which says "Ask your doctor about Otezla," can have dramatic effects on the sales of a product. Recent studies indicate that more than 40 percent of direct-to-consumer ads also emphasize a social relationship in the message.[21]

LEARNING REVIEW

18-7. Describe the promotional objective for each stage of the product life cycle.

18-8. At what stage of the consumer purchase decision process is the importance of personal selling highest? Why?

18-9. Explain the differences between a push strategy and a pull strategy.

DEVELOPING AN INTEGRATED MARKETING COMMUNICATIONS PROGRAM

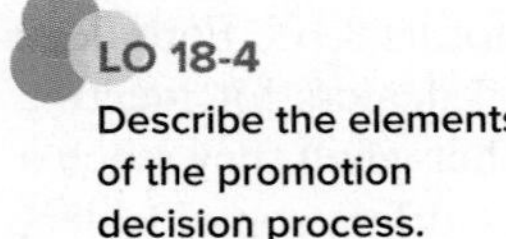
LO 18-4
Describe the elements of the promotion decision process.

Because media costs are high, promotion decisions must be made carefully, using a systematic approach. Paralleling the planning, implementation, and evaluation steps described in the strategic marketing process (Chapter 2), the promotion decision process is divided into (1) developing, (2) executing, and (3) assessing the promotion program (see Figure 18–6). Development of the promotion program focuses on the four *W*s:

- *Who* is the target audience?
- *What* are (1) the promotion objectives, (2) the amounts of money that can be budgeted for the promotion program, and (3) the kinds of promotion to be used?
- *Where* should the promotion be run?
- *When* should the promotion be run?

FIGURE 18–6 The promotion decision process includes planning, implementation, and evaluation.

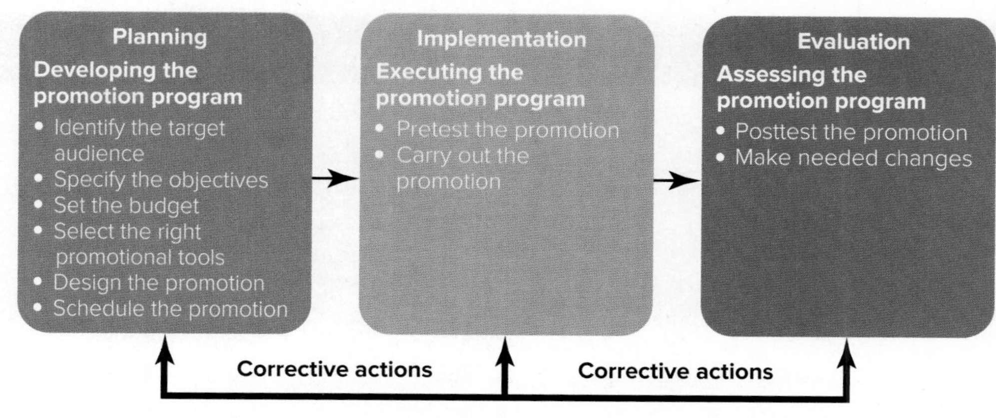

Identifying the Target Audience

The first step in developing the promotion program involves identifying the *target audience*, the group of prospective buyers toward which a promotion program will be directed. To the extent that time and money permit, the target audience for the promotion program is the target market for the firm's product, which is identified from primary and secondary sources of marketing information. The more a firm knows about its target audience—including demographics, interests, preferences, media use, and purchase behaviors—the easier it is to develop a promotional program. A firm might use a profile based on gender, age, lifestyle, and income, for example, to place ads during specific TV programs or in particular magazines. Similarly, a firm might use *online behavioral targeting*—collecting information about your Web-browsing behavior to personalize the banner and display ads that you will see as you surf the Web. Behavioral targeting was also discussed in more detail in Chapter 17.[22]

Specifying Promotion Objectives

After the target audience has been identified, a decision must be reached on what the promotion should accomplish. Consumers can be said to respond in terms of a customer path, or a **hierarchy of effects**, which is the sequence of stages a prospective buyer goes through from initial awareness of a product to eventual action. The five stages are:

- *Awareness*—the consumer's ability to recognize and remember the product or brand name.
- *Interest*—an increase in the consumer's desire to learn about some of the features of the product or brand.
- *Evaluation*—the consumer's appraisal of the product or brand on important attributes.
- *Trial*—the consumer's actual first purchase and use of the product or brand.
- *Adoption*—through a favorable experience on the first trial, the consumer's repeated purchase and use of the product or brand.

For a totally new product, the sequence applies to the entire product category, but for a new brand competing in an established product category, it applies to the brand itself. In addition, the popularity of social media sometimes leads to an "advocacy" stage where loyal consumers recommend brands they have adopted. These steps can serve as guidelines for developing promotion objectives.[23]

Although sometimes an objective for a promotion program involves several steps in the hierarchy of effects, it often focuses on a single stage. Regardless of what the specific objective might be, from building awareness to increasing repeat purchases, promotion objectives should possess three important qualities. They should (1) be designed for a well-defined target audience, (2) be measurable, and (3) cover a specified time period.

Rank	Company	Advertising ($ in millions)	+	All Other Promotion ($ in millions)	=	Total ($ in millions)
1	Comcast	$1,709		$4,413		$6,122
2	AT&T	$1,992		$3,370		$5,362
3	Amazon	$1,508		$2,962		$4,470
4	Procter & Gamble	$2,814		$1,491		$4,305
5	General Motors	$1,523		$1,616		$3,139
6	Walt Disney	$1,135		$1,997		$3,132
7	Charter Communication	$ 366		$2,676		$3,042
8	Alphabet (Google)	$ 651		$2,309		$2,960
9	American Express	$ 309		$2,489		$2,798
10	Verizon Communications	$1,090		$1,592		$2,682

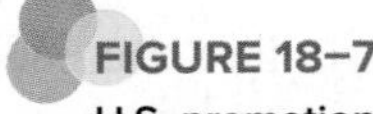

FIGURE 18–7

U.S. promotion expenditures of the top 10 companies. Note that 9 of the 10 companies spend more on promotion than on advertising.

(Both): rvlsoft/Shutterstock

Setting the Promotion Budget

From Figure 18–7, it is clear that the promotion expenditures needed to reach U.S. households are enormous. Note that each of the companies spends a total of more than $2.5 billion annually on promotion.[24]

After setting the promotion objectives, a company must decide how much to spend. Determining the ideal amount for the budget is difficult because there is no precise way to measure the exact results of spending promotion dollars. However, several methods can be used to set the promotion budget.[25]

Percentage of Sales In the **percentage of sales budgeting** approach, funds are allocated to promotion as a percentage of past or anticipated sales, in terms of either dollars or units sold. A common budgeting method, this approach is often stated in terms such as, "Our promotion budget for this year is 3 percent of last year's gross sales."[26] The advantage of this approach is obvious: It is simple and provides a financial safeguard by tying the promotion budget to sales. However, there is a major fallacy in this approach: Percentage of sales budgeting implies that sales *cause* promotion. Using this method, a company may reduce its promotion budget because of a downturn in past sales or an anticipated downturn in future sales–situations in which it may need promotion the most. See the Applying Marketing Metrics box for an application of the promotion-to-sales ratio to the restaurant industry.[27]

Competitive Parity A second common approach, **competitive parity budgeting**, is matching the competitor's absolute level of spending or the proportion per point of market share. This approach has also been referred to as *matching competitors* or *share of market*. It is important to consider the competition in budgeting. Consumer responses to promotion are affected by competing promotional activities, so if a competitor runs 30 radio ads each week, it may be difficult for a firm to get its message across with only 5 ads. The competitor's budget level, however, should not be the only determinant in setting a company's budget. The competition might have very different promotional objectives, which require a different level of promotion expenditures.[28]

All You Can Afford Common to many small businesses is **all-you-can-afford budgeting**, in which money is allocated to promotion only after all other budget items are covered. As one company executive said in reference to this budgeting process, "Why, it's simple. First, I go upstairs to the controller and ask how much they can afford to give us this year. She says a million and a half. Later, the boss comes to me and asks how much we should spend, and I say, 'Oh, about a million and a half.' Then we have our promotion appropriation."[29]

Fiscally conservative, this approach has little else to offer. Using this budgeting philosophy, a company acts as though it doesn't know anything about a promotion-sales relationship or what its promotion objectives are.

Applying Marketing Metrics

How Much Should You Spend on IMC?

Integrated marketing communications (IMC) programs coordinate a variety of promotion alternatives to provide a consistent message across audiences. The amount spent on the various promotional elements, or on the total campaign, may vary depending on the target audience, the type of product, where the product is in the product life cycle, and the channel strategy selected. Managers often use the promotion-to-sales ratio on their marketing dashboard to assess how effective the IMC program expenditures are at generating sales.

Your Challenge

As a manager at Dunkin' Donuts, you've been asked to assess the effectiveness of all promotion expenditures during the past year. The promotion-to-sales ratio can be used to make year-to-year comparisons of a company's promotional programs, to compare the effectiveness of a company's program with competitors' programs, or to make comparisons with industry averages. You decide to calculate the promotion-to-sales ratio for Dunkin' Donuts. In addition, to allow a comparison, you decide to make the same calculation for two of your competitors—Starbucks and Chick-fil-A—and for the entire restaurant chain industry. The ratio is calculated as follows:

Promotion-to-sales ratio =
Total promotion expenditures ÷ Total sales

Your Findings

The information needed for these calculations is readily available from trade publications and annual reports. The following graph shows the promotion-to-sales ratio for Dunkin' Donuts, Starbucks, Chick-fil-A, and the entire restaurant chain industry. Dunkin' Donuts spent $143 million on its promotion program to generate $8.58 billion in sales for a ratio of 1.67 (percent). In comparison, Starbucks's ratio was 0.40, Chick-fil-A's ratio was 0.80, and the industry average was 1.13.

Your Action

Dunkin' Donuts's promotion-to-sales ratio is higher than both of its competitors and higher than the industry average. This suggests that the current mix of promotional activities and the level of expenditures may not be creating an effective IMC program. In the future, you will want to monitor the factors that may influence the ratio.

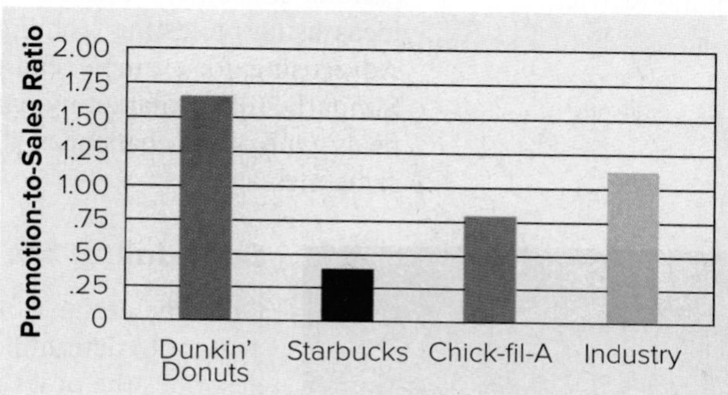

Objective and Task The best approach to budgeting is **objective and task budgeting**, whereby the company (1) determines its promotion objectives, (2) outlines the tasks it will undertake to accomplish those objectives, and (3) determines the promotion cost of performing those tasks.[30] This method takes into account what the company wants to accomplish and requires that the objectives be specified.[31] Strengths of the other budgeting methods are integrated into this approach because each previous method's strength is tied to the objectives. For example, if the costs are beyond what the company can afford, objectives are reworked and the tasks revised. The difficulty with this method is the judgment required to determine the tasks needed to accomplish objectives.

Selecting the Right Promotional Tools

Once a budget has been determined, the combination of the five basic IMC tools–advertising, personal selling, sales promotion, public relations, and direct marketing–can be specified. While many factors provide direction for selection of the appropriate mix, the large number of possible combinations of the promotional tools means that many combinations can achieve the same objective. Therefore, an analytical approach and experience are particularly important in this step of the promotion decision process. The specific mix can vary from a simple program using a single tool to a comprehensive program using all forms of promotion.

The Olympics have become a very visible example of a comprehensive integrated communications program. Because the Games are repeated every two years, the promotion is

VIDEO 18-4
Olympics
kerin.tv/15e/v18-4

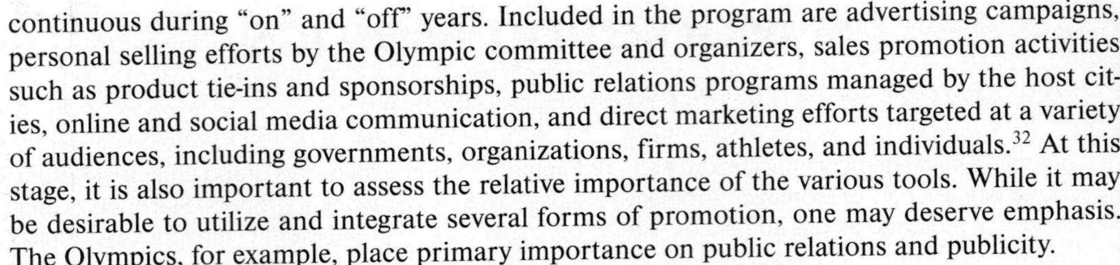

continuous during "on" and "off" years. Included in the program are advertising campaigns, personal selling efforts by the Olympic committee and organizers, sales promotion activities such as product tie-ins and sponsorships, public relations programs managed by the host cities, online and social media communication, and direct marketing efforts targeted at a variety of audiences, including governments, organizations, firms, athletes, and individuals.[32] At this stage, it is also important to assess the relative importance of the various tools. While it may be desirable to utilize and integrate several forms of promotion, one may deserve emphasis. The Olympics, for example, place primary importance on public relations and publicity.

This logo for the 2022 Winter Olympics in Beijing, China, is part of a comprehensive IMC program.
Source: The International Olympic Committee

Designing the Promotion

The central element of a promotion program is the promotion itself. Advertising consists of advertising copy and the artwork that the target audience is intended to see or hear. Personal selling efforts depend on the characteristics and skills of the salesperson. Sales promotion activities consist of the specific details of inducements such as coupons, samples, and sweepstakes. Public relations efforts are readily seen in tangible elements such as news releases, and direct marketing actions depend on written, verbal, and electronic forms of delivery. The design of the promotion will play a primary role in determining the message that is communicated to the audience. This design activity is frequently viewed as the step requiring the most creativity. Successful designs are often the result of a creative process that includes obtaining insight regarding consumers' interests and purchasing behavior, idea generation, and validation of the ideas using pretesting techniques. All of the promotion tools have many design alternatives. Advertising, for example, can utilize fear, humor, attractiveness, or other themes in its appeal. Similarly, direct marketing can be designed for varying levels of personal or customized appeals. One of the challenges of IMC is to design each promotional activity to communicate the same message.[33]

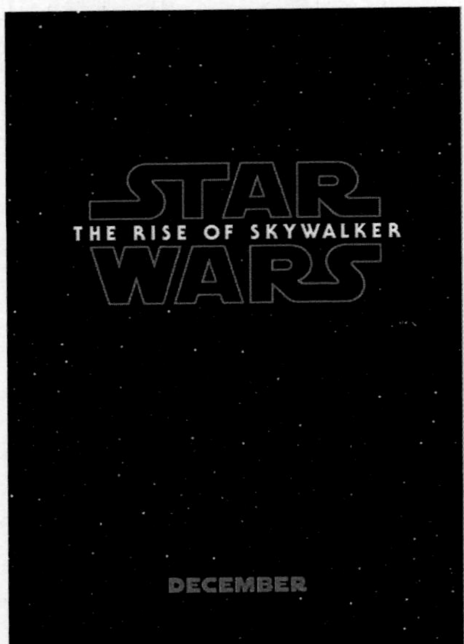

What promotional tools did Disney use to support the release of *Star Wars: The Rise of Skywalker*? Read the text to find out.
Source: Lucasfilm/The Walt Disney Studios

Scheduling the Promotion

Once the design of each of the promotional program elements is complete, it is important to determine the most effective timing of their use. The promotion schedule describes the order in which each promotional tool is introduced and the frequency of its use during the campaign.

The Walt Disney Company and Lucasfilm, for example, use a schedule of promotional tools for their movies. To generate interest in *Star Wars: The Rise of Skywalker*, the director, J.J. Abrams, announced that filming was completed and posted a photo of the movie characters on the movie set. Several months later the first trailer for the movie was posted to the Lucasfilm website, starwars.com, and a panel discussion by actors Daisy Ridley, John Boyega, Oscar Isaac, and others was hosted by Stephen Colbert at *Star Wars* Celebration Chicago. Disney also opened its new theme park, Star Wars: Galaxy's Edge; introduced the new Star Wars live-action television series, *The Mandalorian*; released a new video game, *Star Wars Jedi: Fallen Order*, on Xbox One and PlayStation 4; and announced a new Star Wars trilogy to follow *The Rise of Skywalker*. Actors from the film made promotional appearances on television talk shows and were highlighted in several magazine cover stories. Disney then revealed the packaging for a line of toys and products featuring movie characters Rey, Finn, and Poe. The campaign culminated with a celebration called Force Friday where collectibles, housewares, books, and apparel went on sale at stores around the world. The results of the movie release were record box office sales in the United States and worldwide![34]

Overall, the scheduling of the various promotions was designed to generate interest, bring consumers into theaters, and then encourage additional purchases after seeing the movie. Several factors such as seasonality and competitive promotion activity can also influence the promotion schedule. Businesses such as ski resorts, airlines, and professional sports teams are likely to reduce their promotional activity during the off-season. Similarly, restaurants, retail stores, and health clubs are likely to increase their promotional activity when new competitors enter the market.

EXECUTING AND ASSESSING THE PROMOTION PROGRAM

VIDEO 18-5
Assembly Media
kerin.tv/15e/v18-5

Carrying out the promotion program can be expensive and time-consuming. One researcher estimates that "an organization with sales less than $10 million can successfully implement an IMC program in one year, one with sales between $200 million and $500 million will need about three years, and one with sales between $2 billion and $5 billion will need five years." In addition, firms with a market orientation are more likely to implement an IMC program, and firms with support from top management have more effective IMC programs.[35] To facilitate the transition, approximately 200 integrated marketing communications agencies are in operation. In addition, some of the largest agencies are adopting approaches that embrace "total communications solutions."

E*TRADE
@etrade
Follow
Don't get mad at your boss for making more than you. Get E*TRADE.
THE HARDER YOU WORK, THE NICER THE VACATION YOUR BOSS GOES ON.
DON'T GET MAD GET E*TRADE
The Original Place To Invest Online
us.etrade.com

Read the text to learn how an integrated campaign helped E*TRADE acquire new accounts.
*Source: E*TRADE Financial Corporation*

Media agency Assembly, which recently won *Advertising Age* magazine's Media Agency of the Year award, for example, is part of a national network of 500 people who "want to do things a little differently and do the kind of work they believe in." In fact, the agency website proclaims that "Our team of advertising technologists aim to redefine what a modern agency should be for a new era of communication. We strive to blend media arts with data science to create enduring communications."[36] Assembly's clients include E*TRADE, 21st Century Fox, FX, Red Robin, and the PGA tour. One of its integrated campaigns for E*TRADE electronic trading platform included the development of "predictive models that created better accuracy." The "Don't Get Mad, Get E*TRADE" campaign, which included an ad on the Super Bowl, led to new highs in the number of account openings. Assembly provides advertising, data and analytics, direct marketing, e-commerce, search, social media, and influencer marketing services. While many agencies may still be specialists, the trend today is clearly toward an integrated perspective that includes all forms of promotion. Agencies can accomplish this by including account managers, channel experts, media specialists, and planning personnel in their campaign design efforts.[37]

An important factor in developing successful IMC programs is to create a process that facilitates their design and use. A tool used to evaluate a company's current process is the IMC audit. The audit analyzes the internal communication network of the company; identifies key audiences; evaluates customer databases; assesses messages in recent advertising, public relations releases, packaging, websites, e-mail and social media communication, signage, sales promotions, and direct mail; and determines the IMC expertise of company and agency personnel.[38] This process is becoming increasingly important as consumer-generated media such as blogs, RSS, podcasts, and social networks become more popular and as the use of search engines increases. Now, in addition to ensuring that traditional forms of communication are integrated, companies must be able to monitor consumer content, respond to inconsistent messages, and even answer questions from individual customers. According to Professor Judy Franks, marketers should also be cognizant of consumers she calls "accelerators." These individuals easily move content from medium to medium—from TV to YouTube to a mobile phone text message, for example—without any influence or control from the message source.[39]

As shown earlier in Figure 18-6, the ideal execution of a promotion program involves pretesting each design before it is actually used to allow for changes and modifications to improve its effectiveness. Similarly, posttests are recommended to evaluate the impact of each promotion and the contribution of the promotion toward achieving the program objectives. The most sophisticated pretest and posttest procedures have been developed for advertising and are discussed in Chapter 19. Testing procedures for sales promotion and direct marketing efforts currently focus on comparisons of different designs or responses of different segments. To fully benefit from IMC programs, companies must create and maintain a test-result database that allows comparisons of the relative impact of the promotional tools and their execution

Baka Sobaka/Shutterstock

options in varying situations. Information from the database will allow informed design and execution decisions and provide support for IMC activities during internal reviews by financial or administrative personnel. The San Diego Padres baseball team, for example, developed a database of information relating attendance to its integrated campaign, which included a new logo, special events, merchandise sales, and a loyalty program.

As many as three-fourths of businesses may individually test new communication elements such as digital advertising, while one-fourth of all businesses may assess "most of their communication tactics" using new and traditional measures of effectiveness.[40] For most organizations, the assessment focuses on trying to determine which element of promotion works better. In an integrated program, however, media advertising might be used to build awareness, sales promotion to generate an inquiry, direct mail to provide additional information to individual prospects, and a personal sales call to complete the transaction. The tools are used for different reasons, and their combined use creates a synergy that should be assessed on criteria such as coverage, cost, and contribution, as well as complementarity, and cross-effects. In addition, the effectiveness of IMC programs is strongly related to overall company performance.[41] Another level of assessment is necessary when firms have international promotion programs.

LEARNING REVIEW

18-10. What are the characteristics of good promotion objectives?

18-11. What is the weakness of the percentage of sales budgeting approach?

18-12. How have advertising agencies changed to facilitate the use of IMC programs?

DIRECT MARKETING

LO 18-5
Explain the value of direct marketing for consumers and sellers.

Direct marketing takes many forms and utilizes a variety of media. Several forms of direct marketing–direct mail and catalogs, television home shopping, telemarketing, and direct selling–were discussed as methods of nonstore retailing in Chapter 16. Interactive marketing is discussed in detail in Chapter 17. In addition, although advertising is discussed in Chapter 19, a form of advertising–direct response advertising–is an important form of direct marketing. In this section, the growth of direct marketing, its value for consumers and sellers, and key global, technological, and ethical issues are discussed.

The Growth of Direct Marketing

The increasing interest in customer relationship management is reflected in the growth of direct marketing. The ability to customize communication efforts and create one-to-one interactions is appealing to most marketers, particularly those with IMC programs, because it leads to more favorable attitudes from the recipients. While many direct marketing methods are not new, the ability to design and use them has increased with the availability of customer information databases and new media such as Instagram and Snapchat. In fact, as ad blocking and skipping tools have become more prevalent, many marketers are adding emphasis to direct "opt-in" approaches to reaching consumers. Figure 18–8 shows the annual expenditures on four popular forms of direct marketing and their typical response rates. For example, marketers spend more than $44 billion on direct mail each year, and direct mail generates a 5.1 percent response rate.[42]

Most campaigns use several direct marketing methods. JCPenney, for example, is one company that has integrated its direct marketing activities. The company begins a campaign by sending coupons to customers through e-mail and text messages. Consumers also receive direct-mail postcards and digital "Look Books" that invite them to visit the company's e-commerce website www.jcpenney.com or mobile commerce site https://m.jcpenney.com/. A special social commerce app is also available for purchases on JCPenney's Facebook "Fan" page. Many companies

FIGURE 18–8
Business expenditures and response rates of four popular forms of direct marketing. Read the text to learn why the use of direct marketing is increasing.

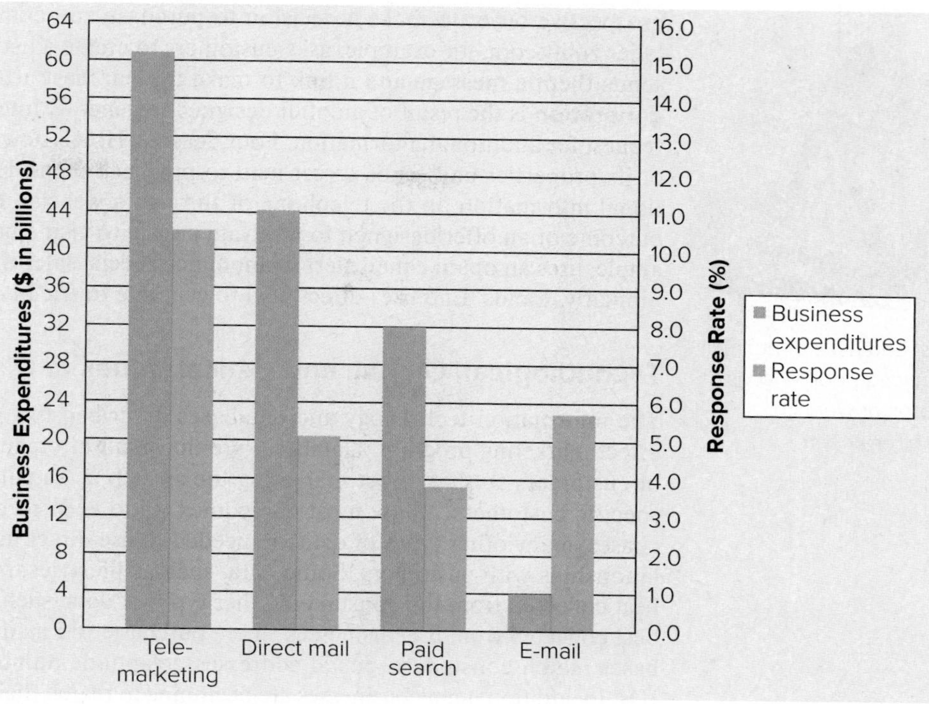

Facebook is one of many activities in JCPenney's direct marketing campaign.
Source: JCP Media, Inc/ Facebook

also integrate their direct marketing with other forms of promotion. Porsche, for example, recently launched a campaign to change consumer perceptions that its 911 model was uncomfortable and a poor choice for everyday use. The campaign consisted of TV commercials, a video contest, direct mail brochures, and a mobile-ready website. The ads, contest, and brochures all directed consumers to the website where they could view videos, photos, and testimonials from current owners about the everyday use of their cars. In addition, visitors to the website could submit their e-mail address to be contacted by a Porsche dealership. Mobile direct marketing sales and online direct marketing sales are growing at 33 percent and 20 percent, respectively–the fastest of all direct marketing tools.[43]

The Value of Direct Marketing

One of the most visible indicators of the value of direct marketing for consumers is its level of use in its various forms. For example, each year the USPS delivers more than 80 billion pieces of direct mail, including more than 9 billion catalogs. A study by the USPS found that 84 percent of millennials "look through" their mail, and 64 percent prefer scanning for information in the mail rather than e-mail. Direct marketing through e-mail, however, is also substantial as 89 percent of all e-mail delivers a marketing message. In addition, e-mail is very effective as it has the lowest cost of acquiring a new customer at approximately $10. Finally, more than $60 billion is spent on telemarketing each year.

For consumers, direct marketing offers a variety of benefits, including: They don't have to go to a store; they can usually shop 24 hours a day; buying direct saves time; they avoid hassles with salespeople; they can save money; it's fun and entertaining; and it offers more privacy than in-store shopping. Many consumers also believe that direct marketing provides excellent customer service. Toll-free telephone numbers, online help links, customer service representatives with access to information regarding purchasing preferences, delivery services, and unconditional guarantees all help create value for direct marketing customers. At Landsend.com, when customers need assistance they can click the "Chat" icon to receive help from a sales representative on the phone or through online chat or online video until the correct product is found. "It's like we were walking down the aisle in a store!" says one Lands' End customer.[44]

The value of direct marketing for sellers can be described in terms of the responses it generates. **Direct orders** are the result of offers that contain all the information necessary for a prospective buyer to make a decision to purchase and complete the transaction. Online retailer zulily.com, for example, asks customers to create a list of their favorite brands and then sends them a message and a link to make the purchase when the brands are on sale. **Lead generation** is the result of an offer designed to generate interest in a product or service and a request for additional information. Four Seasons Hotels now sells private residences in several of its properties and sends direct mail to prospective residents asking them to request additional information on the telephone or through a website. Finally, **traffic generation** is the outcome of an offer designed to motivate people to visit a business. The Home Depot, for example, uses an opt-in e-mail alert to announce special sales that attract consumers to the store. Similarly, Lands' End uses direct mail to generate traffic in its stores and on its website.[45]

Lands' End uses direct mail to motivate people to visit its stores or website.
Source: Lands' End

Technological, Global, and Ethical Issues in Direct Marketing

The information technology and databases described in Chapter 8 are key elements in any direct marketing program. Databases are the result of organizations' efforts to create profiles of customers so that direct marketing tools, such as e-mail and catalogs, can be directed at specific customers. While most companies try to keep records of their customers' past purchases, many other types of data are needed to use direct marketing to develop one-to-one relationships with customers. Some data, such as lifestyles, media use, and demographics, are best collected from the consumer. Other types of data, such as price, quantity, and brand, are best collected from the businesses where purchases are made. New integrated marketing databases match consumers' postal addresses, telephone numbers, e-mail addresses, and device IDs. In addition, many businesses are beginning to match their customer records with Facebook profiles, Twitter following behavior, and Google search activity.[46]

Increases in printing and postage rates have also increased the importance of information related to the cost of direct marketing activities. For example, the Data & Marketing Association estimates that e-mail advertising expenditures outperform social media advertising by a ratio of 3-to-1. Similarly, catalog businesses have found they can reduce the cost of printing by using innovations such as soy-based ink and recycled paper, and they can reduce postage fees through database list analysis. Related to postage fees, many direct marketers are assessing the potential impact of the USPS plan for a five-day mail delivery cycle.[47]

Direct marketing faces several challenges and opportunities in global markets today. Many countries, including the United Kingdom, Australia, the European Union, and Japan, have requirements for a mandatory "opt-in"—that is, potential customers must give permission to be included on a list for direct marketing solicitations. In addition, the mail, telephone, and Internet systems in many countries are not as well developed as they are in the United States. The need for improved reliability and security in these countries has slowed the growth of direct mail, while the dramatic growth of mobile phone penetration has created an opportunity for direct mobile marketing campaigns. Another issue for global direct marketers is payment. The availability of credit and credit cards varies throughout the world, creating the need for alternatives such as C.O.D. (cash on delivery), bank deposits, and online payment accounts such as PayPal and Venmo.[48]

Global and domestic direct marketers both face challenging ethical issues today. Concerns about privacy, for example, have led to various attempts to provide guidelines that balance consumer and business interests. The European Union passed a consumer privacy law, called the *Data Protection Directive*, after several years of discussion with the Federation of European Direct Marketing and the UK's Direct Marketing Association. A new version of the law, called the *General Data Protection Regulation* (*GDPR*), addresses new developments such as social networks and Cloud computing. Similarly, the *California Consumer Privacy Act* (*CCPA*) provides consumers with the right to know what personal data are being collected about them and the option to say no to the sale of the information.

The Federal Trade Commission and the U.S. legislature have also been concerned about privacy. Several bills that call for a do-not-mail registry similar to the Do Not Call Registry have been discussed. Similarly, there are growing concerns about Web "tracking" tools used by direct marketers to segment consumers and match them with advertising. The Making Responsible Decisions box describes some of the issues under consideration.[49]

VIDEO 18-6
Ad Choices
kerin.tv/15e/v18-6

Making Responsible Decisions

Ethics

What Is the Future of Your Privacy?

In 2003, the Federal Trade Commission opened the National Do Not Call Registry to give Americans a tool for maintaining their privacy on home and cellular telephone lines. More than 70 percent of all Americans registered. Since then, several state legislatures have also passed laws to create do-not-call lists for automated (robo) telephone calls. In addition, new discussions about privacy related to mail and computer use are now taking place.

Generally, the question being debated is, "What information is private?" Are telephone numbers, addresses of residences, and online activities private or public information? Proponents of a do-not-mail registry argue that, like telephone calls, citizens should be able to stop unsolicited mail. Proponents of do-not-track regulations suggest that website owners who use cookies to collect information about consumers' shopping habits should do so only with a consumer's consent. Marketers counter that consumers who share this information are more likely to receive messages and advertising that better match their interests.

Courtesy of Digital Advertising Alliance.

The Data & Marketing Association currently advocates several solutions. First, it has created DMAchoice, an online tool to help consumers manage the types of mail and e-mail they receive. Second, the organization is part of an advertising coalition, the Digital Advertising Alliance, that endorses a self-regulatory program for online behavioral advertising (OBA) that encourages advertisers to include the "Ad Choices" icon in the corner of online ads to allow consumers to opt out of having data collected about their online activities. Moving beyond self-regulation, the European Union recently passed the *E-Privacy Directive* to provide explicit laws for website owners. And in the United States, the Senate is evaluating the Do Not Track Online Act although it did not receive support from the FCC. These guidelines and regulations, of course, have huge implications for advertisers, portals such as Facebook and Google, and consumers.

What is your opinion? What types of information should be private? Can we find a balance between self-regulation and legislation?

LEARNING REVIEW

18-13. The ability to design and use direct marketing programs has increased with the availability of ______________ and ______________.

18-14. What are the three types of responses generated by direct marketing activities?

LEARNING OBJECTIVES REVIEW

LO 18-1 *Discuss integrated marketing communications and the communication process.*
Integrated marketing communications is the concept of designing marketing communications programs that coordinate all promotional activities—advertising, personal selling, sales promotion, public relations, and direct marketing—to provide a consistent message across all audiences. The communication process conveys messages with six elements: a source, a message, a channel of communication, a receiver, and encoding and decoding. The communication process also includes a feedback loop and can be distorted by noise.

LO 18-2 *Describe the promotional mix and the uniqueness of each component.*
There are five promotional alternatives. Advertising, sales promotion, and public relations are mass selling approaches, whereas personal selling and direct marketing use customized messages. Advertising can have high absolute costs but reaches large numbers of people. Personal selling has a high cost per contact but provides immediate feedback. Public relations is often difficult to obtain but is very credible. Sales promotion influences short-term consumer behavior. Direct marketing can help develop customer relationships, although maintaining a database can be very expensive.

LO 18-3 *Select the promotional approach appropriate to a product's target audience, life-cycle stage, and characteristics, as well as stages of the buying decision and channel strategies.*
The promotional mix depends on the target audience. Programs for consumers, business buyers, and intermediaries might emphasize advertising, personal selling, and sales promotion, respectively. The promotional mix also changes over the product

life-cycle stages. During the introduction stage, all promotional mix elements are used. During the growth stage advertising is emphasized, while the maturity stage utilizes sales promotion and direct marketing. Little promotion is used during the decline stage. Product characteristics also help determine the promotion mix. The level of complexity, risk, and ancillary services required will determine which element is needed. Knowing the customer's stage in the buying process can help marketers select appropriate promotions. Advertising and public relations can create awareness in the prepurchase stage, personal selling and sales promotion can facilitate the purchase, and advertising can help reduce anxiety in the postpurchase stage. Finally, the promotional mix can depend on the channel strategy. Push strategies require personal selling and sales promotions directed at channel members, while pull strategies depend on advertising and sales promotion directed at consumers.

LO 18-4 *Describe the elements of the promotion decision process.*
The promotional decision process consists of three steps: planning, implementation, and evaluation. The planning step consists of six elements: (1) identifying the target audience, (2) specifying the objectives, (3) setting the budget, (4) selecting the right promotional elements, (5) designing the promotion, and (6) scheduling the promotion. The implementation step includes pretesting. The evaluation step includes posttesting.

LO 18-5 *Explain the value of direct marketing for consumers and sellers.*
The value of direct marketing for consumers is indicated by its increasing level of use. For example, each year the USPS delivers more than 80 billion pieces of direct mail, including more than 9 billion catalogs. The value of direct marketing for sellers can be measured in terms of three types of responses: direct orders, lead generation, and traffic generation.

LEARNING REVIEW ANSWERS

18-1 What six elements are required for communication to occur?
Answer: The six elements required for communication to occur are: (1) a source, which is a company or person who has information to convey; (2) a message, which is the information sent; (3) a channel of communication, which is how the information is conveyed; (4) a receiver, which is the consumer who reads, hears, or sees the message; and the processes of (5) encoding, in which the sender transforms the idea into a set of symbols; and (6) decoding, in which the receiver takes the symbols, or the message, and transforms it back into an idea.

18-2 A difficulty for U.S. companies advertising in international markets is that the audience does not share the same ______________.
Answer: field of experience, which is a similar understanding and knowledge that is applied to a message

18-3 A misprint in a newspaper ad is an example of ______________.
Answer: noise—the extraneous factors that distort a message

18-4 Explain the difference between advertising and publicity when both appear on television.
Answer: Since advertising space on TV is paid for, a firm can control what it wants to say and to whom and how often the message is sent over a broadcast, cable, satellite, or local TV network. Since publicity is an indirectly paid presentation of a message about a firm or its products or services, the firm has little control over what is said to whom or when. Instead, it can only suggest to the TV medium that it run a favorable story about the firm or its offerings.

18-5 Cost per contact is high with the ______________ element of the promotional mix.
Answer: personal selling

18-6 Which promotional element should be offered only on a short-term basis?
Answer: sales promotion

18-7 Describe the promotional objective for each stage of the product life cycle.
Answer: Introduction—to inform consumers of the product's existence; growth—to persuade consumers to buy the product; maturity—to remind consumers that the product still exists; and decline—to phase out the product.

18-8 At what stage of the consumer purchase decision process is the importance of personal selling highest? Why?
Answer: Personal selling is most important at the purchase stage of the consumer purchase decision process because salespeople can provide sales assistance to prospective customers and negotiate terms of the sale.

18-9 Explain the differences between a push strategy and a pull strategy.
Answer: In a push strategy, a firm directs the promotional mix to channel members to gain their cooperation in ordering and stocking the product. In a pull strategy, a firm directs the promotional mix at ultimate consumers to encourage them to ask retailers for the product, who then order it from wholesalers or the firm itself.

18-10 What are the characteristics of good promotion objectives?
Answer: Promotion objectives should possess three important qualities. They should (1) be designed for a well-defined target audience, (2) be measurable, and (3) cover a specified time period.

18-11 What is the weakness of the percentage of sales budgeting approach?
Answer: In the percentage of sales budgeting approach, funds are allocated to promotion based on a percentage of past or anticipated dollar or unit sales. The major fallacy of this method is that sales cause promotion. By using this method, a company may reduce its promotion budget because of actual or projected downturns in past or future sales—situations where promotion may be needed the most.

18-12 How have advertising agencies changed to facilitate the use of IMC programs?
Answer: Some agencies have adopted: (1) a total communications solutions approach; (2) an integrated perspective that includes all forms of promotion; (3) an IMC audit to analyze the internal communication network of the company to identify key audiences, evaluate customer databases, assess messages contained in recent advertising, press releases, packaging, websites, social media, direct marketing, and so on, and determine the IMC expertise of company and agency personnel; and (4) strategies to monitor consumer content, respond to inconsistent messages, and answer questions from individual customers.

18-13 The ability to design and use direct marketing programs has increased with the availability of ______________ and ______________.
Answer: customer information databases; new printing technologies

18-14 What are the three types of responses generated by direct marketing activities?
Answer: They are: (1) direct orders, the result of offers that contain all the information necessary for a prospective buyer to make a decision to purchase and complete the transaction; (2) lead generation, the result of an offer designed to generate interest in a product or service and a request for additional information; and (3) traffic generation, the outcome of an offer designed to motivate people to visit a business.

FOCUSING ON KEY TERMS

advertising p. 488
all-you-can-afford budgeting p. 498
channel of communication p. 486
communication p. 486
competitive parity budgeting p. 498
decoding p. 486
direct marketing p. 490
direct orders p. 503
encoding p. 486
feedback p. 487
field of experience p. 486
hierarchy of effects p. 497
integrated marketing communications (IMC) p. 485
lead generation p. 504
message p. 486
noise p. 487
objective and task budgeting p. 499
percentage of sales budgeting p. 498
personal selling p. 489
promotional mix p. 484
public relations p. 489
publicity p. 489
pull strategy p. 496
push strategy p. 495
receivers p. 486
response p. 487
sales promotion p. 490
source p. 486
traffic generation p. 504

APPLYING MARKETING KNOWLEDGE

1 After listening to a recent sales presentation, Mary Smith signed up for membership at the local health club. On arriving at the facility, she learned there was an additional fee for racquetball court rentals. "I don't remember that in the sales talk; I thought they said all facilities were included with the membership fee," complained Mary. Describe the problem in terms of the communication process.

2 Develop a matrix to compare the five elements of the promotional mix on three criteria—to *whom* you deliver the message, *what* you say, and *when* you say it.

3 Explain how the promotional tools used by an airline would differ if the target audience were (*a*) consumers who travel for pleasure and (*b*) corporate travel departments that select the airlines to be used by company employees.

4 Suppose you introduced a new consumer food product and invested heavily both in national advertising (pull strategy) and in training and motivating your field salesforce to sell the product to food stores (push strategy). What kinds of feedback would you receive from both the advertising and your salesforce? How could you increase both the quality and quantity of each?

5 Fisher-Price Company, long known as a manufacturer of children's toys, has introduced a line of clothing for children. Outline a promotional plan to get this product introduced in the marketplace.

6 Many insurance companies sell health insurance plans to companies. In these companies the employees pick the plan, but the set of offered plans is determined by the company. Recently, Blue Cross–Blue Shield, a health insurance company, ran a television ad stating, "If your employer doesn't offer you Blue Cross–Blue Shield coverage, ask why." Explain the promotional strategy behind the advertisement.

7 Identify the sales promotion tools that might be useful for (*a*) Tastee Yogurt, a new brand introduction; (*b*) 3M self-sticking Post-it® Notes; and (*c*) Wrigley's Spearmint gum.

8 Design an integrated marketing communications program—using each of the five promotional elements—for Spotify, the online music streaming service.

9 BMW recently introduced its first sports activity vehicle, the X6, to compete with other popular crossover vehicles such as the Mercedes-Benz R-Class. Design a direct marketing program to generate (*a*) leads, (*b*) traffic in dealerships, and (*c*) direct orders.

10 Develop a privacy policy for database managers that provides a balance of consumer and seller perspectives. How would you encourage voluntary compliance with your policy? What methods of enforcement would you recommend?

BUILDING YOUR MARKETING PLAN

To develop the promotion strategy for your marketing plan, follow the steps suggested in the planning phase of the promotion decision process described in Figure 18–6.

1 You should (*a*) identify the target audience, (*b*) specify the promotion objectives, (*c*) set the promotion budget, (*d*) select the right promotion tools, (*e*) design the promotion, and (*f*) schedule the promotion.

2 Also specify the pretesting and posttesting procedures needed in the implementation and evaluation phases.

3 Finally, describe how each of your promotion tools is integrated to provide a consistent message.

VIDEO CASE 18 Taco Bell: Using IMC to Help Customers Live Más!

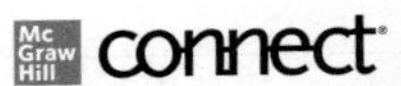

"Every touchpoint is considered," explains Stephanie Perdue, Taco Bell's senior director of marketing, "from the posters in the restaurants down to the packaging, and all of the different media channels." Stephanie is describing the integrated marketing communications (IMC) approach used by Taco Bell, the nation's leading Mexican-style quick service restaurant. IMC is one of the key factors that has contributed to the extraordinary success of the food chain, which serves more than 36 million customers each week!

VIDEO 18-7
Taco Bell Video Case
kerin.tv/15e/v18-7

THE COMPANY

The story behind Taco Bell and its success is fascinating. After World War II, a young marine named Glen Bell returned to his home state of California with an entrepreneurial spirit and an observation that people were hungry for fast, good food. He opened his first restaurant, Bell's Burgers, based on the simple concept that customers might want to walk up and get their food from a service window. Not far away, two brothers named McDonald were operating their new restaurant using a "drive-in" concept. For several years, Bell and the McDonald brothers enjoyed friendly competition as pioneers of the growing fast-food industry. However, when the burger restaurant market became crowded with competitors, Bell decided to try something new—tacos!

Tacos were new to most Americans so Bell experimented with many concepts. First he developed a crunchy taco shell and opened a restaurant called Taco Tia. His marketing activities consisted of handing out sombreros and having mariachis play outside the restaurant. Next, Bell started another restaurant, El Taco, with a group of celebrity partners. Finally, after a friend suggested that Glen should use his name in his business, the first Taco Bell was opened in Downey, California.

calimedia/Shutterstock

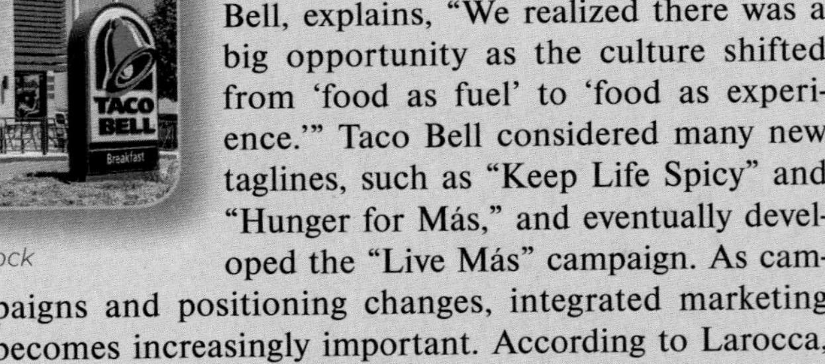

Taco Bell grew quickly, and as Bell began opening additional locations he decided that the restaurants should resemble the appearance of California's historic missions. With the help of an architect he created an inviting design based on an adobe-like exterior with a red clay-tile roof. The name and logo utilized a mission-style bell, a version of which is still in use today. Through franchises and additional corporate locations Taco Bell soon reached from coast to coast.

Today Taco Bell is a subsidiary of Yum! Brands, which also owns and operates KFC, Pizza Hut, and WingStreet. Taco Bell now has more than 7,000 locations and $10 billion in sales. Many locations are co-branded with KFC, Pizza Hut, and Long John Silver stores. Taco Bell also operates Taco Bell Express locations in convenience stores, truck stops, shopping malls, and airports.

INTEGRATED MARKETING COMMUNICATIONS AT TACO BELL

From its beginning, Taco Bell has used very creative promotional activities. For example, when the Mir space station was about to reenter Earth's atmosphere, Taco Bell placed a target in the Pacific Ocean and announced that every person in the United States would receive a free taco if any piece of the falling space station hit the target. Similarly, in its "Steal a Base, Steal a Taco" promotion, Taco Bell promises to give everyone a free taco if any player steals a base in the World Series. While the space station did not hit the target, several players have stolen bases in the World Series, leading to free tacos for everyone! Taco Bell has also offered special promotions with Mountain Dew, partnered with the NBA as its official fast food, and created videos for movie-theater advertising.

You might remember some of Taco Bell's past advertising campaigns, such as "Yo quiero Taco Bell," "Grand Taste. Loco Value," or "Get it at The Bell." The more recent "Think Outside the Bun" campaign was designed for millennials. Then as that group changed, Taco Bell executives recognized that they had an opportunity to reposition the chain. Tracee Larocca, brand creative director at Taco Bell, explains, "We realized there was a big opportunity as the culture shifted from 'food as fuel' to 'food as experience.'" Taco Bell considered many new taglines, such as "Keep Life Spicy" and "Hunger for Más," and eventually developed the "Live Más" campaign. As campaigns and positioning changes, integrated marketing becomes increasingly important. According to Larocca, "as the brand's creative director, my job is to make sure that all of our communications have the same look, tone, and feel across all platforms, making sure we maintain consistency in our brand voice no matter what we're doing internally or externally."

Advertising Age magazine recently named Taco Bell the winner of its Marketer of the Year award for its extraordinary use of integrated marketing in the launch of its Doritos Locos Tacos. The new product went through three years of development and 45 prototypes before its launch, which led to sales of 100 million units in its first

10 weeks. Taco Bell allocates approximately 70 percent of its budget to traditional media, 20 percent to digital media, and 10 percent to new media where it can "explore." The traditional media budget included a Super Bowl ad utilizing the "Live Más" theme. "It was all about a mindset and not necessarily an age range or a demographic," explains Larocca. The ad, called "Forever Young," showed "a group of old people breaking out of a retirement home and having a great night on the town," she adds.

The social media component of the campaign included Facebook, Twitter, Vine, Snapchat, and Instagram. The Twitter campaign, for example, included a Hometown Tweet-off where anyone could send a tweet saying why a Taco Bell truck should visit their hometown. Similarly, Taco Bell posted pictures to Facebook and watched the responses in the comments and the "likes." Some of the new media budget was used to try things such as Taco Bell's own video channels for Web and mobile, and a live stream to a billboard in Times Square. As Rob Poetsch, director of public affairs and engagement, observed about the Doritos Locos Tacos launch, "for the first time, we had a fully integrated plan that engaged all of our constituents."

THE FUTURE AT TACO BELL

Taco Bell continues to develop new products, brand concepts, and promotions. For example, naked egg tacos, Cinnabon Delights, and the breakfast Crunchwrap are new additions to the menu. In addition, a new brand concept called Taco Bell Cantina, which is testing its first locations in Chicago and San Francisco, will offer "tapas-style" appetizers for customers to share, and beer and wine, in an urban setting. In addition, Taco Bell announced its plan to award $10 million in Live Más Scholarships by 2022 to "innovators, creators and dreamers" aged 16–24. All of these activities are contributing to the company's continued growth. Yum! Brands expects Taco Bell's domestic sales to double by 2021![50]

Questions

1 What factors contributed to Taco Bell's early success?

2 Which of the promotional elements described in Figure 18–2 were used by Taco Bell in its Doritos Locos Tacos campaign?

3 How does Taco Bell ensure the continued success of the food chain?

Chapter Notes

1. "Forget Tacos on Tuesdays. Taco Bell Wants Fans to ReBELL and Enjoy Tacos Any Day," Taco Bell press release, www.tacobell.com, April 18, 2019; Nancy Luna, "Taco Bell," *Nation's Restaurant News*, May 6, 2019; Chris Morris, "Taco Bell Is Planning a Palm Springs Hotel and Resort," www.fortune.com, May 16, 2019; "Taco Bell Tests American Vegetarian Association-Certified Menu," www.qsrweb.com, April 2, 2019; "Taco Bell Kicks Off US Grubhub Delivery with Free Delivery Offer," www.qsrweb.com, February 7, 2019; "She Wore a Teeny-Weeny Taco Bell Bikini," www.qsrweb.com, May 2, 2019; "Taco Bell 'Steal-a-Base' Promo Back for World Series," www.qsrweb.com, October 15, 2018; "Taco Bell Giving Away Limited Edition Xbox in Effort to Increase Chalupas," www.qsrweb.com, October 17, 2018; and Patricia Odell, "Taco Bell—Cult-Like and Performing Weddings," *Promotional Marketing*, February 16, 2017, p. 2.
2. Sally Laurie and Kathleen Mortimer, "How to Achieve True Integration: The Impact of Integrated Marketing Communication on the Client/Agency Relationship," *Journal of Marketing Management* 35, no. 3–4 (2019), pp. 231–52; Rajeev Batra and Kevin Lane Keller, "Integrating Marketing Communications: New Findings, New Lessons, and New Ideas," *Journal of Marketing*, November 2016, pp. 122–45; Sita Mishra and Sushma Muralie, "Managing Dynamism of IMC—Anarchy to Order," *Journal of Marketing and Communication*, September 2010, pp. 29–37; Philip J. Kitchen, Ilchul Kim, and Don E. Schultz, "Integrated Marketing Communications: Practice Leads Theory," *Journal of Advertising Research*, December 2008, pp. 531–46; and Bob Liodice, "Essentials for Integrated Marketing," *Advertising Age*, June 9, 2008, p. 26.
3. Wilbur Schramm, "How Communication Works," in *The Process and Effects of Mass Communication*, Wilbur Schramm, ed. (Urbana: University of Illinois Press, 1955), pp. 3–26.
4. E. Cooper and M. Jahoda, "The Evasion of Propaganda," *Journal of Psychology* 22 (1947), pp. 15–25; H. Hyman and P. Sheatsley, "Some Reasons Why Information Campaigns Fail," *Public Opinion Quarterly* 11 (1947), pp. 412–23; and J. T. Klapper, *The Effects of Mass Communication* (New York: Free Press, 1960), Chapter VII.
5. "Mistakes in Advertising," on the Learn English website, http://www.learnenglish.de/mistakes/HorrorMistakes.htm, accessed March 18, 2013; and Bianca Bartz, "International Ads Lost in Translation," TrendHunter Marketing website, http://www.trendhunter.com/trends/advertising-bloopers-international-ads-lost-in-translation, accessed March 18, 2013; KFC slogan.
6. Rik Pieters and Michel Wedel, "Attention Capture and Transfer in Advertising: Brand, Pictorial, and Text-Size Effects," *Journal of Marketing*, April 2004, pp. 36–50.
7. Adapted from American Marketing Association, Resource Library Dictionary, http://www.marketingpower.com/layouts/Dictionary.aspx?dLetter=P, accessed March 18, 2013.
8. Dave Folkens, "3 Ways Social Media Is Changing Public Relations," *Online Marketing Blog*, February 17, 2011; Michael Bush, "How Social Media Is Helping the Public-Relations Sector Not Just Survive, but Thrive," *Advertising Age*, August 23, 2010, p. 1; David Robinson, "Public Relations Comes of Age," *Business Horizons* 49 (2006), pp. 247–56; and Dick Martin, "Gilded and Gelded: Hard-Won Lessons from the PR Wars," *Harvard Business Review*, October 2003, pp. 44–54.
9. Martin Eisend and Franziska Kuster, "The Effectiveness of Publicity versus Advertising: A Meta-Analytic Investigation of Its Moderators," *Journal of the Academy of Marketing Science*, December 2011, pp. 906–21; and Joan Stewart, "Pros and Cons of Free Publicity in Newspapers, Magazines," www.Business2Community.com, January 30, 2013.
10. "The Public Relations Metamorphosis: Social Media Is Here to Stay," www.Business2Community.com, December 21, 2012; Piet Levy, "CSR Take Responsibility," *Marketing News*, May 30, 2010, p. 20; Jooyoung Kim, Hye Jin Yoon, and Sun Young Lee, "Integrating Advertising and Publicity: A Theoretical Examination of the Effects of

Exposure Sequence, Publicity Valence, and Product Attribute Consistency," *Journal of Advertising*, Spring 2010, p. 97; and Marsha D. Loda and Barbara Carrick Coleman, "Sequence Matters: A More Effective Way to Use Advertising and Publicity," *Journal of Advertising Research* 45 (December 2005), pp. 362–71.

11. Kusum L. Ailawadi, Scott A. Neslin, and Karen Gedenk, "Pursuing the Value-Conscious Consumer: Store Brands versus National Brand Promotions," *Journal of Marketing*, January 2001, pp. 71–89.
12. Nikki Hopewell, "The Rules of Engagement: A Bevy of Rules and Best Practices Govern Promotions and Contests," *Marketing News*, June 1, 2008, p. 6; and Gerard Prendergast, Yi- Zheng Shi, and Ka-Man Cheung, "Behavioural Response to Sales Promotion Tools," *International Journal of Advertising* 24 (2005), pp. 467–86.
13. Adapted from American Marketing Association, Resource Library Dictionary, http://www.marketingpower.com/layouts/Dictionary.aspx?dLetter=D, accessed March 18, 2013.
14. "Marketing to College Students," www.sheerid.com, January 25, 2019; Charlotte Zoda, "How to Reach Gen Z during Spring Break," www.mssmedia.com, March 25, 2019; Alex Kronman, "Five Things to Consider When Marketing to College Students," www.martechseries.com, September 14, 2018; Taylor Lorenz, "Re-Creating Facebook on Instagram," www.theatlantic.com, April 8, 2019; and "Back-to-School and College Spending to Reach $82.8 Billion," *National Retail Federation*, July 12, 2018.
15. Dunn Sunnoo and Lynn Y. S. Lin, "Sales Effects of Promotion and Advertising," *Journal of Advertising Research* 18 (October 1978), pp. 37–42.
16. Lori Corbin, "Purina Pro Plan Incredible Dog Challenge Returns to Huntington Beach for Western Regionals," www.abc7.com, May 29, 2015; and Don Kaplan, "Every Dog Has Its Day at Purina Challenge," *Daily News*, January 12, 2013, p. 1.
17. Todd Powers, Dorothy Advincula, Manila S. Austin, Stacy Graiko, and Jasper Snyder, "Digital and Social Media in the Purchase Decision Process," *Journal of Advertising Research*, December 2012, pp. 479–89; and Remco Prins and Peter C. Verhoef, "Marketing Communication Drivers of Adoption Timing of a New E-Service among Existing Customers," *Journal of Marketing* 71 (April 2007), pp. 169–83.
18. Anders Parment, "Distribution Strategies for Volume and Premium Brands in Highly Competitive Consumer Markets," *Journal of Retailing and Consumer Services*, July 2008, p. 250; and R. Srinivasan and Archana K. Murthy, "Integrated Brand Building Process: A Special Case," *International Journal of Business Research*, June 1, 2008, p. 174.
19. "Push vs. Pull Strategies," *Daily News*, May 3, 2011; "Question: Should B2B Be Focusing All Its Efforts on 'Pull' Marketing Therefore Turning Its Back on 'Push' Marketing Techniques?" *B2B Marketing Magazine*, September 2009; and Michael Levy, John Webster, and Roger Kerin, "Formulating Push Marketing Strategies: A Method and Application," *Journal of Marketing*, Winter 1983, pp. 25–34.
20. Michael Martinez, "Ford: Dealers Get On Board for Rewards Program," *Automotive News*, February 4, 2019, p. 42; Michael Martinez, "Ford Plans Regional Incentives for Dealers," *Automotive News*, March 20, 2017, p. 4; and "Working with Ford Dealers," *Sustainability Report 2015/16*, http://corporate.ford.com/microsites/sustainability-report-2015-16/people-dealers.html.
21. Megan C. Good and Bruce A. Huhmann, "Social Relationships and Social Anxiety Appeals in Direct-to-Consumer Advertising," *Journal of Marketing Communications* 24, no. 4 (2018), pp. 393–411; Andrew Dunn, "Pharma DTC Spending Outpaces Rest of Medical Marketing, JAMA Study Finds," www.biopharmadive.com, January 7, 2019; and Fusun F. Gonul, Franklin Carter, Elina Petrova, and Kannan Srinivasan, "Promotion of Prescription Drugs and Its Impact on Physicians' Choice Behavior," *Journal of Marketing*, July 2001, pp. 79–90.
22. Sophie C. Boerman, Sanne Kruikemeier, and Frederik J. Zuiderveen Borgesius, "Online Behavioral Advertising: A Literature Review and Research Agenda," *Journal of Advertising* 46, no. 3 (2017), pp. 363–76; Don E. Shultz, Martin P. Block, and Kaylan Raman, "Understanding Consumer-Created Media Synergy," *Journal of Marketing Communications*, July 2012, pp. 173–87; "Why Behavioral Targeting Is Effective," www.Business2Community.com, January 15, 2013; Lauren Drell, "4 Ways Behavioral Targeting Is Changing the Web," *Mashable*, April 26, 2011; and adapted from American Marketing Association, Resource Library Dictionary, http://www.marketingpower.com/_layouts/Dictionary.aspx?dLetter=B, accessed April 2, 2013.
23. Philip Kotler, Hermawan Kartajaya, and Iwan Setiawan, *Marketing 4.0* (Hoboken, NJ: John Wiley & Sons, 2017); Robert J. Lavidge and Gary A. Steiner, "A Model for Predictive Measurement of Advertising Effectiveness," *Journal of Marketing*, October 1961, p. 61; and C. H. Patti, S. W. Hartley, M. M. van Dessel, and D. W. Baack, "Improving Integrated Marketing Communications Practices: A Comparison of Objectives and Results," *Journal of Marketing Communications* 23, no. 4 (2017), pp. 351–70.
24. "Leading National Advertisers," *Advertising Age Fact Pack*, June 24, 2019, p. 5.
25. George S. Low and Jakki J. Mohr, "Setting Advertising and Promotion Budgets in Multi-Brand Companies," *Journal of Advertising Research*, January–February 1999, pp. 67–78; Don E. Schultz and Anders Gronstedt, "Making Marcom an Investment," *Marketing Management*, Fall 1997, pp. 41–49; and J. Enrique Bigne, "Advertising Budget Practices: A Review," *Journal of Current Issues and Research in Advertising*, Fall 1995, pp. 17–31.
26. John Philip Jones, "Ad Spending: Maintaining Market Share," *Harvard Business Review*, January–February 1990, pp. 38–42; and Charles H. Patti and Vincent Blasko, "Budgeting Practices of Big Advertisers," *Journal of Advertising Research* 21 (December 1981), pp. 23–30.
27. "U.S. Market Leaders," *Advertising Age*, June 25, 2018, p. 28.
28. Brenda Marlin, "Adding It Up: You Can Save Time by Trying One of Three Short-Cut Approaches to an Annual Budget," *ABA Banking*, October 1, 2007, p. 36; James A. Shroer, "Ad Spending: Growing Market Share," *Harvard Business Review*, January–February 1990, pp. 44–48; and Jeffrey A. Lowenhar and John L. Stanton, "Forecasting Competitive Advertising Expenditures," *Journal of Advertising Research* 16, no. 2 (April 1976), pp. 37–44.
29. Daniel Seligman, "How Much for Advertising?" *Fortune*, December 1956, p. 123; and "All-You-Can-Afford Budgeting," common language dictionary, https://marketing-dictionary.org/a/all-you-can-afford-budgeting/, accessed September 18, 2019.
30. James E. Lynch and Graham J. Hooley, "Increasing Sophistication in Advertising Budget Setting," *Journal of Advertising Research* 30 (February–March 1990), pp. 67–75.
31. Jimmy D. Barnes, Brenda J. Muscove, and Javad Rassouli, "An Objective and Task Media Selection Decision Model and Advertising Cost Formula to Determine International Advertising Budgets," *Journal of Advertising* 11, no. 4 (1982), pp. 68–75.
32. "The Olympic Brand Maintains Its Global Strength and Recognition," *States News Service*, February 12, 2013; Graham Ruddock, "London Olympics Sponsors Are Already into Their Stride," *The Daily Telegraph*, May 6, 2011, p. 8; "The Olympics Come but Once Every Two Years," *Marketing News*, November 1, 2008, p. 12; "Olympics Will Bring Online Opportunities for Many Brands," *Revolution*, July 14, 2008, p. 13; and Don E. Schultz, "Olympics Get the Gold Medal in Integrating Marketing Event," *Marketing News*, April 27, 1998, pp. 5, 10.
33. S. Turnbull and C. Wheeler, "The Advertising Creative Process: A Study of UK Agencies," *Journal of Marketing Communications* 23, no. 2 (2017), pp. 176–94; "It's Time to Take an Integrated Marketing Approach," www.Business2Community.com, January 22, 2013; "Integrated Marketing: One Message, Many Media," *Marketing Week*, September 18, 2008, p. 31; and Cornelia Pechman, Guangzhi Zhao, Marvin E. Goldberg, and Ellen Thomas Reibling, "What to Convey in Antismoking Advertisements for Adolescents: The Use of Protection Motivation Theory to Identify Effective Message Themes," *Journal of Marketing*, April 2003, pp. 1–18.
34. Brian Raftery, "That's a Wrap: J.J. Abrams Posts Photo from Last Day of 'Star Wars: Episode IX' Filming," www.fortune.com, February 15,

2019; Chris Morris, "Watch the First Trailer for 'Star Wars: The Rise of Skywalker' Here," www.fortune.com, April 12, 2019; Christopher Palmeri, "Star Wars Fans Snatch Up Reservations for Galaxy's Edge within Two Hours," www.fortune.com, May 2, 2019; Eliana Dockterman, "Everything We Know about the Star Wars TV Show The Mandalorian," www.time.com, May 2, 2019; "Respawn Debuts Star Wars Jedi: Fallen Order," *Multimedia Publisher*, May 2019; Nick Turner, "Disney Announces New 'Star Wars' Films and Delays 'Avatar 2' Release," www.fortune.com, May 7, 2019; "SWCC 2019: 13 Things We Learned from the *Star Wars: The Rise of Skywalker* Panel," press release, www.starwars.com, April 12, 2019; and starwars.com, accessed September 19, 2019.

35. Sabine A. Einwiller and Michael Boenigk, "Examining the Link between Integrated Communication Management and Communication Effectiveness in Medium-Sized Enterprises," *Journal of Marketing Communications*, December 2012, pp. 335–61; and Mike Reid, "Performance Auditing of Integrated Marketing Communication (IMC) Actions and Outcomes," *Journal of Advertising* 34 (Winter 2005), p. 41.

36. MDC&Partners, https://www.mdc-partners.com.

37. Megan Graham, "Media Agency of the Year: Assembly," *Ad Age*, February 19, 2018, p. 38; and Assembly website, https://www.mdc-partners.com/agency/assembly, accessed May 26, 2019.

38. "Integrated Marketing: The Benefits of Integrated Marketing," *Marketing Week*, September 18, 2008, p. 33; and Tom Duncan, "Is Your Marketing Communications Integrated?" *Advertising Age*, January 24, 1994, p. 26.

39. Don E. Schultz, "The Media Circuits Evolution," *Marketing News*, March 30, 2011, p. 11; "Integrated Marketing: Digital Fuels Integration Boom," *Marketing Week*, December 11, 2008, p. 27; Don E. Schultz, "IMC Is Do or Die in New Pull Marketplace," *Marketing News*, August 15, 2006, p. 7; and Don E. Schultz, "Integration's New Role Focuses on Customers," *Marketing News*, September 15, 2006, p. 8.

40. Yunjae Cheong, John D. Leckenby, and Tim Eakin, "Evaluating the Multivariate Beta Binomial Distribution for Estimating Magazine and Internet Exposure Frequency Distributions," *Journal of Advertising*, Spring 2011, p. 7; and Jack Neff, "Copy Testing Coming to Digital Marketing," *Advertising Age*, February 28, 2011, p. 18.

41. Kevin Lane Keller, "Unlocking the Power of Integrated Marketing Communications: How Integrated Is Your IMC Program?" *Journal of Advertising* 45, no. 3 (2016), pp. 286–301; T. Reinold and J. Tropp, "Integrated Marketing Communications: How Can We Measure Its Effectiveness?" *Journal of Marketing Communications*, April 2012, pp. 113–32; and Maria Angeles Navarro-Bailon, "Strategic Consistent Messages in Cross-Tool Campaigns: Effects on Brand Image and Brand Attitude," *Journal of Marketing Communications*, July 2012, pp. 189–202.

42. Toby Eberly, "Inbound Is Hot, but Direct Response Marketing Is Still a Proven Revenue Booster," www.hanloncreative.com, July 31, 2018; and *Statistical Fact Book* (New York: Data and Marketing Association, 2018).

43. "JCPenney Debuts New Brand Promise 'Style and Value for All,'" press release, www.companyblog.jcpnewsroom.com, March 12, 2018; "Porsche–Integrated Marketing Communications," www.brandmanagement2017.com, October 10, 2017; and "Direct Mail Strategy: JCPenney's New Postcard Campaign," www.Business2Community.com, April 18, 2012.

44. *Statistical Fact Book* (New York: Data & Marketing Association, 2018); "Marketing Fact Pack 2019," *Ad Age*, December 17, 2018; and "Six Ways Lands' End Makes Online Shopping a Joy," *PR Newswire*, November 21, 2007.

45. Daniela Forte, "Why Large Retailers Are Acquiring Flash Sale Sites," www.multichannelmerchant.com, June 20, 2016; and Theresa Howard, "E-mail Grows as Direct-Marketing Tool: They're Quicker to Make, Cheap to Send," *USA Today*, November 28, 2008, p. 5B.

46. Evan Neufeld, "Cross-Device and Cross-Channel Identity Measurement Issues and Guidelines," *Journal of Advertising Research*, March 2017, pp. 109–17; Cotton Delo, "Facebook Testing Effort to Match Offline Purchases to Online Profiles," *Advertising Age*, February 25, 2013, p. 6; Michael Learmonth, "Facebook Goes the Route of Direct Marketing, While Twitter Plays It Safe with Focus on User Interests," *Advertising Age*, September 10, 2012, p. 20; and "Infogroup Targeting Solution Launches Sapphire™, a New Integrated Marketing Database," *GlobeNewswire*, August 7, 2012.

47. Sapna Maheshwari and Matt Townsend, "BC-E-MAIL-MARKETING-RETA," *Postmedia Breaking News*, March 14, 2013; "A-Catalog-Printer.com Uses Revolutionary Soy Ink Technology to Help the Environment and Reduce Costs of Printing," *SBWire*, March 22, 2013; Charley Howard, "Help USPS Help You: 3 Ways to Cut Mail Costs through Workshare Discounts," http://www.targetmarketingmag.com/article/3-ways-cut-mail-costs-throughworkshare-discounts-417119/1#, February 2011; and "How Much Will Postal Cuts Hurt?" *Advertising Age*, February 11, 2013, p. 3.

48. "Companies Opposing Anti-Spam Laws," *The Toronto Star*, February 9, 2013, p. B5; Beth Negus Viveiros, "New Bill Takes Permission beyond Opt-In in EU," *Chief Marketer*, April 19, 2011; "China: New Media Blossoming as Business Models Revamp," *BBC Monitoring World Media*, December 9, 2008; "The Data Dilemma," *Marketing Direct*, February 6, 2007, p. 37; and Marc Nohr, "South Africa–A Worthy Contender," *Marketing Direct*, March 5, 2007, p. 20.

49. Sean Michael Kerner, "What FCC's Move against 'Do Not Track' Means," *eWeek*, November 9, 2015; "Protecting Your Identity and Your Privacy," *Targeted News Service*, March 1, 2013; "The Do Not Track Online Act Was Reintroduced in Congress," *The Business Insider*, March 1, 2013; "Online Behavioral Advertising," in the DMA OBA Guidelines, Direct Marketing Association website, http://thedma.org/issues/dma-oba-guidelines, accessed April 6, 2013; Don E. Schultz, "The Bugaboo of Behaviors," *Marketing Management*, Summer 2011, pp. 10–11; "Cell Phones Now Protected by the Do Not Call List," *States News Service*, May 16, 2011; Jonathan Brunt, "'Do Not Mail' Can't Gain Traction," *Spokesman Review*, May 5, 2010, p. 7; "DMA: 'Do Not Track Online Act' Is Unnecessary," *States News Service*, May 9, 2011; "DMA Updates Its 'Guidelines for Ethical Business Practice,'" *States News Service*, May 25, 2011; Martin Courtney and Tony Lock, "Keep It Safe, Keep It Legal," *Computing*, May 26, 2011; Siobhain Butterworth, "Cookie Law Shambles Really Takes the Biscuit," *Guardian Unlimited*, May 27, 2011; and Lara O'Reilly, "New Cookie Law: What You Need to Know," *Marketing Week*, May 26, 2011.

50. Taco Bell: This case was written by Steven Hartley. Sources: Samantha Scelzo, "I Tried the Naked Egg Taco from Taco Bell and Had the Most Sophisticated Experience," *Mashable*, www.mashable.com, August 17, 2017; "August Was a Big Month for the Taco Bell Foundation's Live Más Scholarship," press release, www.tacobell.com, September 20, 2017; Maureen Morrison, "In Breakfast Wars, Taco Bell's Bold Marketing Pays Off with Big Sales," *Advertising Age*, July 28, 2014, p. 6; "Taco Bell Serving Alcohol in Wicker Park Officially Opens Tuesday," WLS-TV, September 22, 2015; Maureen Morrison, "Taco Bell's New Concept: Designer Tacos in California," *Advertising Age*, April 28, 2014, p. 4; Vanessa Wong, "Taco Bell's Secret Recipe for New Products," *Bloomberg Businessweek*, June 2–8, 2014, pp. 18–20; Maureen Morrison, "Marketer of the Year 2013," *Advertising Age*, September 2, 2013, p. 15; Mark Brandau, "Yum Plans to Double U.S. Taco Bell Sales," *Restaurant News*, May 22, 2013; "The Glen Bell Legacy," www.tacobell.com/static_files/TacoBell/StaticAssets/documents/GlenBellLegacy.pdf; "Taco Bell," http://www.yum.com/brands/tb.asp; and interviews with Taco Bell executives.

Chapter 19 Advertising, Sales Promotion, and Public Relations

LEARNING OBJECTIVES

After reading this chapter you should be able to:

LO 19-1 Explain the differences between product advertising and institutional advertising and the variations within each type.

LO 19-2 Describe the steps used to develop, execute, and evaluate an advertising program.

LO 19-3 Explain the advantages and disadvantages of alternative advertising media.

LO 19-4 Discuss the strengths and weaknesses of consumer-oriented and trade-oriented sales promotions.

LO 19-5 Recognize public relations as an important form of communication.

Consumers Are Going "Over The Top." So Advertisers Are Too!

There is a huge shift underway in how consumers receive video programming. The traditional system relied on cable, satellite, or over-the-air (OTA) services to deliver content. Today, however, millions of people are "cutting the cord" and now view movies, TV series, and videos through the Internet and a "connected" device. In marketing terminology, these consumers have gone "over-the-top" (OTT)!

So exactly how does OTT work? There are three elements. First users must have access to a broadband or Internet service. Second, they need a connected device such as a smart TV (e.g., Google TV), a gaming console (e.g., Xbox One, PlayStation 4, Switch), a smart set-top box (e.g., Roku, Google Chromecast, Apple TV), a desktop or laptop computer, a tablet, or a smartphone. Finally, consumers need a streaming service app such as Hulu or Netflix.

As consumers move to this new form of media delivery, advertisers are also making the move. In fact, the change to OTT programming represents an exciting opportunity for advertisers to improve the effectiveness of their ads and to provide greater value for viewers. In the past, advertisers selected programs, or content, in which to embed their ads. All viewers of that program saw the same advertising. The connected devices and streaming services that make OTT possible, however, create what is called "addressable television." This means advertisers can show different ads to different viewers during the same program.

Matching the advertising to specific viewers eliminates exposure to irrelevant ads. For example, addressable television capabilities allow viewers with dogs to see dog food ads while viewers with cats see only cat food ads. In addition, as more information about the viewers becomes available, artificial intelligence and machine learning enable advertisers to create more customized ads. Cadillac, for example, created 330 versions of a particular ad that were matched to specific characteristics of the viewers. The result was a 15 percent uptick in the number of viewers who watched the entire ad, and a 45 percent increase in click-throughs to the brand website.

Similarly, Toyota often starts its advertising production process by shooting a large amount of video with the intention that it will be edited into multiple ads (like the RAV4 ads shown). Addressable television advertisers face two challenges–personalization and scale. While the ideal situation would be to completely personalize each ad, current technology segments viewers based only on attributes such as job, location, and purchase history. Further, as segments get more specific, advertisers begin to worry about scale–or the number of people each ad can influence. Nonetheless, advertisers already spend more than $2.5 billion on addressable advertising to reach the 75 percent of households with OTT capabilities.

The digital technologies that enable addressable television are likely to lead to other new changes also. Ad length will vary from 15 seconds to 60 seconds depending on past

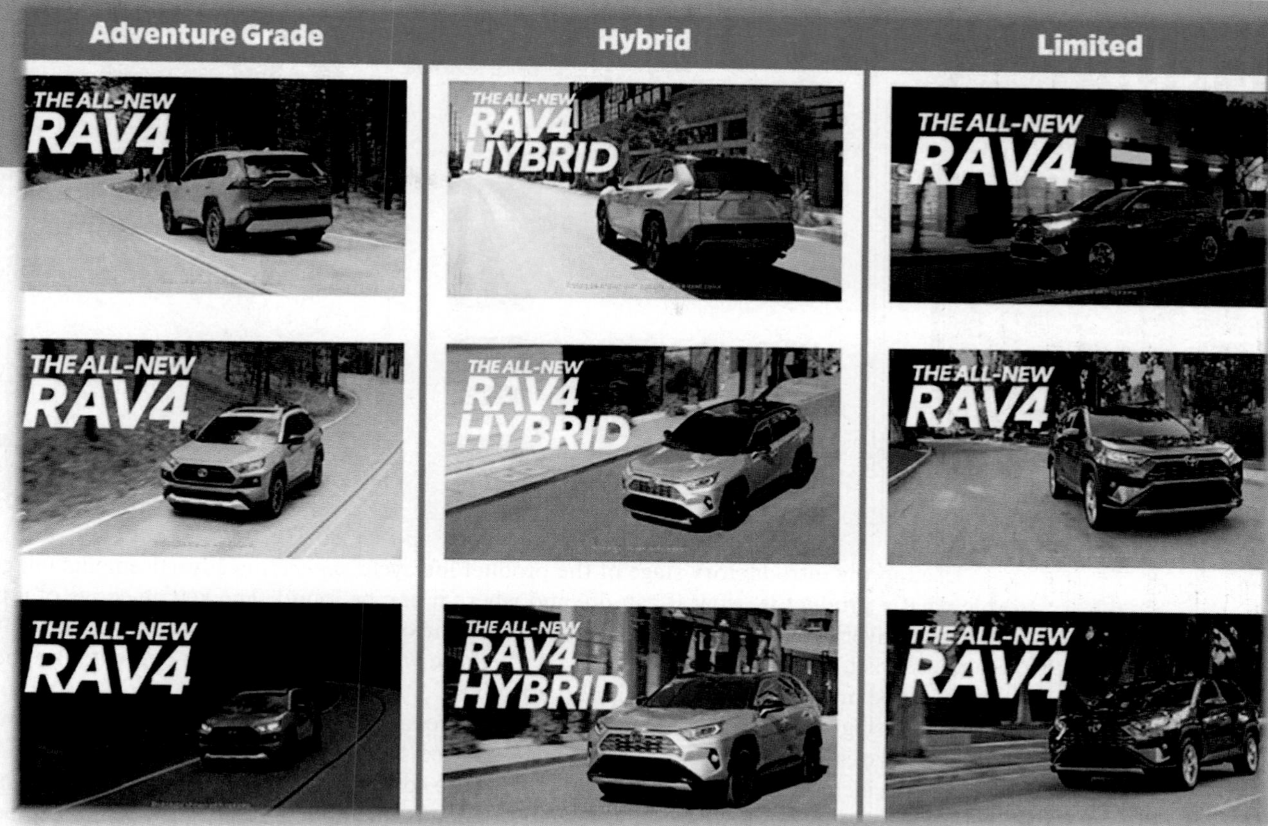

Source: Toyota Motor Sales, U.S.A., Inc.

responses. Augmented reality (AR) and virtual reality (VR) will allow new immersive, high-engagement forms of advertising. Voice recognition and search will add another layer of sophistication to addressable ads. And increased attention to privacy and personal data collection will necessitate anonymity and opt-out features.[1]

VIDEO 19-1
Virtual Reality
kerin.tv/15e/v19-1

The growth of addressable advertising is just one of the many exciting changes occurring in the field of advertising today and illustrates the importance of advertising as one of the five promotional mix elements in marketing communications programs. This chapter describes three of the promotional mix elements–advertising, sales promotion, and public relations. Direct marketing was covered in Chapter 18, and personal selling is covered in Chapter 21.

TYPES OF ADVERTISEMENTS

LO 19-1
Explain the differences between product advertising and institutional advertising and the variations within each type.

Chapter 18 described **advertising** as any paid form of nonpersonal communication about an organization, product, service, or idea by an identified sponsor. As you scan ads on your smartphone, look through any magazine, watch television, listen to the radio, or browse the Internet, the variety of advertisements you see or hear may give you the impression that they have few similarities. Advertisements are prepared for different purposes, but they basically consist of two types: product advertisements and institutional advertisements.

Product Advertisements

Focused on selling a product or service, **product advertisements** take three forms: (1) pioneering (or informational), (2) competitive (or persuasive), and (3) reminder. Look at the ads on the next page for Hyundai, Progressive, and Flowers Victoria to determine the type and objective of each ad.

Product advertisements take three forms—pioneering, competitive, or reminder—depending on their objective. See if you can correctly identify the ads shown here.

(Left): Source: Hyundai Motor Company; (Middle): Source: Progressive; (Right): Source: Flowers Victoria

Used in the introductory stage of the product life cycle, *pioneering* advertisements tell people what a product is, what it can do, and where it can be found. The key objective of a pioneering advertisement (such as the Hyundai ad introducing its new Venue) is to inform the target market. Informational ads, particularly those with specific message content, have been found to be interesting, convincing, and effective.[2]

Advertising that promotes a specific brand's features and benefits is *competitive*. The objective of these messages is to persuade the target market to select the firm's brand rather than that of a competitor. An increasingly common form of competitive advertising is *comparative* advertising, which shows one brand's strengths relative to those of competitors.[3] The Progressive ad, for example, highlights its competitive rates compared to other auto insurers. Studies indicate that comparative ads attract more attention and increase the perceived quality of the advertiser's brand although their impact may vary by product type, message content, and audience gender.[4] Firms that use comparative advertising need marketing research to provide legal support for their claims.[5]

Reminder advertising is used to reinforce previous knowledge of a product. The Flowers Victoria ad reminds consumers not to forget flowers on Valentine's Day. Reminder advertising is good for products that have achieved a well-recognized position and are in the mature phase of their product life cycle. Another type of reminder ad, *reinforcement*, is used to assure current users they made the right choice. For example, consider the tagline used in Dial soap advertisements: "Aren't you glad you use Dial? Don't you wish everybody did?"[6]

Institutional Advertisements

The objective of **institutional advertisements** is to build goodwill or an image for an organization rather than promote a specific product or service. Institutional advertising has been used by companies such as Texaco, Pfizer, and IBM to build confidence in the company name.[7] Often this form of advertising is used to support the public relations plan or counter adverse publicity. Four alternative forms of institutional advertisements are often used:

VIDEO 19-2
Chevron
kerin.tv/15e/v19-2

1. *Advocacy* advertisements state the position of a company on an issue. Chevron's "We Agree" campaign placed ads stating its position on issues such as renewable energy, protecting the planet, and community development. Another form of advocacy advertisement is used when organizations make a request related to a particular action or behavior, such as a request by IBM for gender equality in business leadership.
2. *Pioneering institutional* advertisements, like the pioneering ads for products discussed earlier, are used for announcements about what a company is, what it can do, or where it is located. Recent Bayer ads stating "We cure more headaches than you think" are intended to inform consumers that the company produces many products in addition to aspirin. KPMG uses pioneering institutional ads to inform people about its expertise with data and analytics.

Congratulations. Business leadership is now gender equal.*
*At current rates, this will be true in the year 2073.
With your help, we can make sure it won't take 54 years to reach gender parity. Be Equal promotes the advancement of gender equality in business leadership—for everyone, of any gender. It's part of our decades-long commitment to nondiscrimination in the workplace. It's why we are constantly developing technologies that help businesses combat unconscious bias and promote equal opportunity.
Business leaders around the world have already joined us in this promise to take action.
Make your pledge today at ibm.com/BeEqual
IBM

Be Equal

Source: IBM

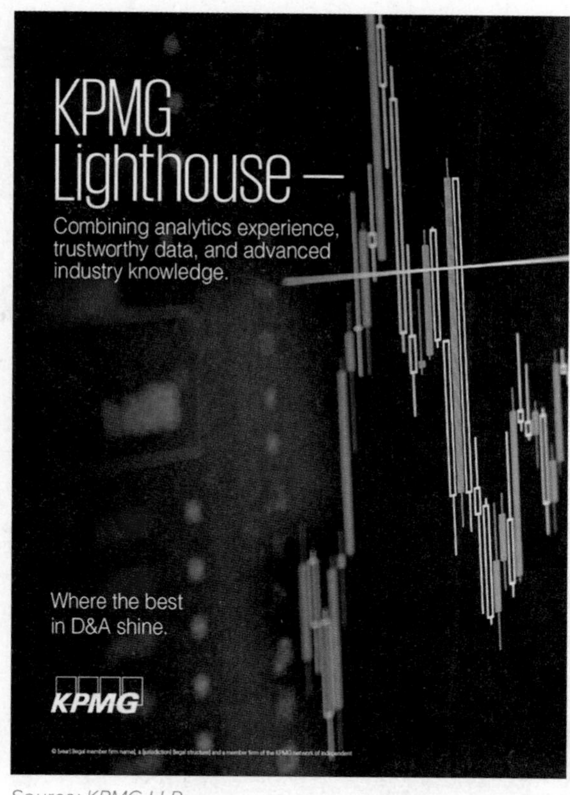

Source: KPMG LLP

IBM uses advocacy to make a request for gender equality in business leadership. KPMG uses a pioneering ad to inform readers about its expertise with data and analytics.

3. *Competitive institutional* advertisements promote the advantages of one product class over another and are used in markets where different product classes compete for the same buyers. America's milk processors and dairy farmers use their "Milk Life" campaign to increase demand for milk as it competes against other beverages.
4. *Reminder institutional* advertisements, like reminder ads for products, simply bring the company's name to the attention of the target market again. The Army branch of the U.S. military sponsors a campaign to remind potential recruits of the opportunities available in the Army.

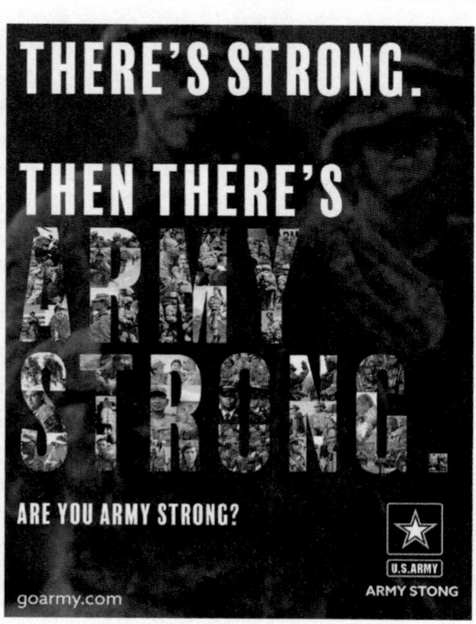

A competitive institutional ad by dairy farmers tries to increase demand for milk, and a reminder institutional ad by the U.S. Army tries to keep the attention of the target market.
(Left): Source: America's Milk Processors; (Right): Source: U.S. Army

LEARNING REVIEW

19-1. What is the difference between pioneering and competitive ads?

19-2. What is the purpose of an institutional advertisement?

DEVELOPING THE ADVERTISING PROGRAM

LO 19-2
Describe the steps used to develop, execute, and evaluate an advertising program.

The promotion decision process described in Chapter 18 can be applied to each of the promotional elements. Advertising, for example, can be managed by following the three steps (developing, executing, and evaluating) of the process.

Identifying the Target Audience

To develop an effective advertising program, advertisers must identify the target audience. All aspects of an advertising program are likely to be influenced by the characteristics of the prospective consumer. Understanding the lifestyles, attitudes, and demographics of the target market is essential. Mountain Dew, for example, is targeted at young males, while Kraft's Crystal Light Liquid is targeted at calorie-conscious women. Both campaigns emphasize advertising techniques that match their target audiences. To appeal to young males, Mountain Dew spends 40 percent of its budget investing in partnerships with Twitch, placing ads targeted at video game players on Facebook, and sponsoring sports TV channel Cheddar. Meanwhile, to attract calorie-conscious women, Crystal Light began providing nutritional information on Target.com and offering a free T-shirt with purchase.

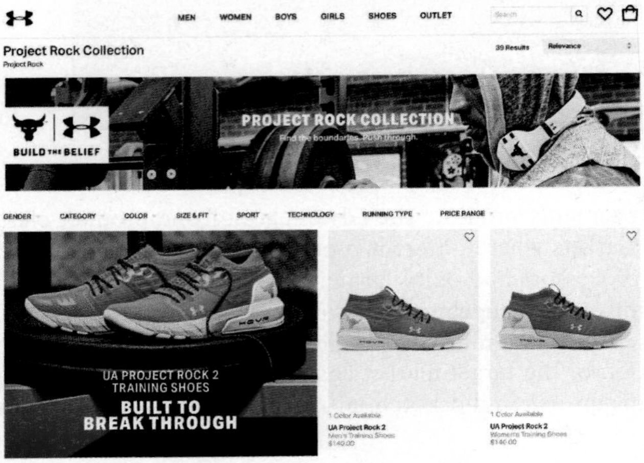

Under Armour places its ads to reach current and potential new customers.
Source: Under Armour, Inc.

Similarly, the placement of the advertising depends on the audience. When Under Armour introduced its "Project Rock" collection of athletic training apparel, shoes, and earbuds, it included a mix of videos on social media and in-store merchandising. The first video post featuring Dwayne Johnson had more than 1 million views in 15 minutes. In addition, messages featuring popular athletes, such as Olympic gold medalist Lindsey Vonn, were placed on Instagram to reach current and potential consumers. Even scheduling can depend on the audience. Nike schedules advertising, sponsorships, deals, and endorsements to correspond with the Olympics to appeal to amateur, college, and professional athletes.[8]

To eliminate possible bias that might result from subjective judgments about some population segments, the Federal Communications Commission suggests that advertising program decisions be based on marketing research about the target audience.[9]

Specifying Advertising Objectives

The guidelines for setting promotion objectives described in Chapter 18 also apply to setting advertising objectives. This step helps advertisers with other choices in the promotion decision process, such as selecting media and evaluating a campaign. Advertising with an objective of creating awareness, for example, would be better matched with a magazine than a directory such as the yellow pages. The Association of Magazine Media believes objectives are so important it created the Kelly Awards program to recognize magazine advertising campaigns that demonstrate both creative excellence and effectiveness in meeting campaign objectives. Purina was a recent winner for its "Pawsitive Moments" campaign that appeared in *Time*, *Life*, *Real*

Simple, *Southern Living*, and *People* magazines. Similarly, the Advertising Research Foundation sponsors research to advance the practice of measuring and evaluating the effectiveness of advertising and marketing communication.[10]

Experts believe that factors such as product category, brand, and consumer involvement in the purchase decision may change the importance—and, possibly, the sequence—of the stages of the hierarchy of effects (see Chapter 18). Snickers, for example, knew that its consumers were unlikely to engage in elaborate information processing when it designed a recent campaign. The result was ads with a simple humorous message, "You're not you when you're hungry," rather than extensive factual information. New managerial perspectives also consider that advertising can have a long-term impact on the financial value of the organization.[11]

FIGURE 19–1
The Super Bowl delivers a huge audience, if you can afford the cost of placing an ad.
(Photo): Robert Sullivan/ EPA/Shutterstock

Setting the Advertising Budget

In 2000, advertisers paid $2.1 million to place a 30-second ad during the Super Bowl. By 2019, the cost of placing a 30-second ad during Super Bowl LIII had more than doubled to $5.25 million (see Figure 19–1). The escalating cost is related to the large number of viewers: 98.2 million people watched the game. In addition, the audience is attractive to advertisers because

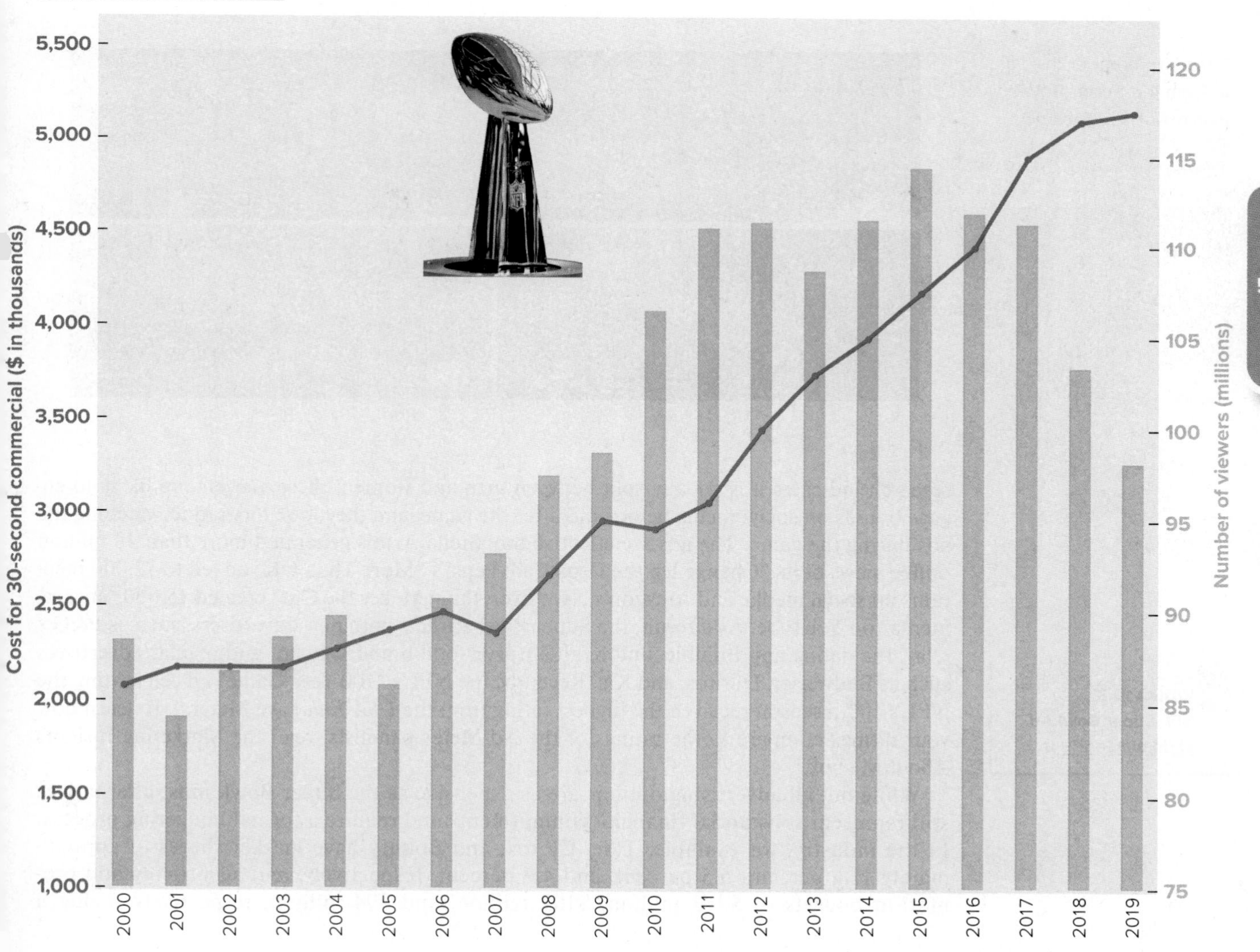

Marketing Insights About Me

Are You an Expert at Picking the Best Super Bowl Ads?

Let's compare your selection of the best Super Bowl ads with the experts. First go to www.ispot.tv/events to view the advertisements that appeared during the last Super Bowl. As you watch each ad, evaluate the elements that you think create good advertising and then select your top 10 ads. Now visit *USA Today*'s Ad Meter at http://admeter.usatoday.com/. Ad Meter ranks the Super Bowl ads each year based on the votes from 7,000 panelists. For example, some of the top ads from previous years included Amazon's "Alexa Loses Her Voice," Kia's "Hero's Journey," and Hyundai's "First Date." So how did you do? Did you pick the same ads as Ad Meter? If you matched on five or more ads consider yourself an expert! To really test yourself, look at the winning commercials since 1989 and see if you agree!

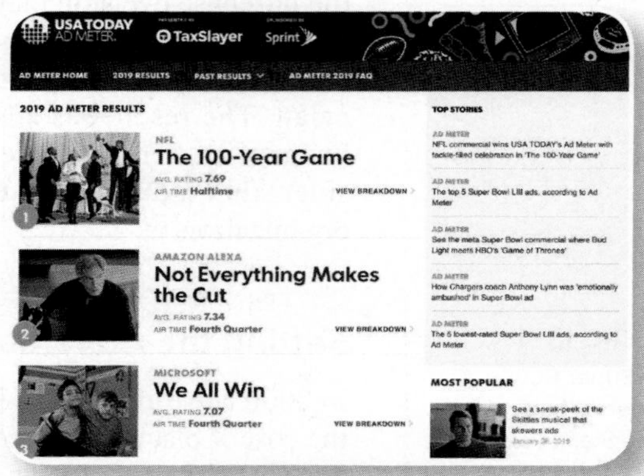

Source: Gannett Satellite Information Network, LLC

Do you remember this NFL ad from the Super Bowl?

Source: National Football League

research indicates it is equally split between men and women; these viewers are likely to engage brands on social media before and after the game; and they look forward to watching the ads during the game. The ads are effective too: Stella Artois generated more than 48 million online views of its "Change Up the Usual" ad; Pepsi's "More Than OK" ad led to 72,000 mentions on social media; and Amazon's "Not Everything Makes the Cut" created 15,000 "engagements" on YouTube. As a result, the Super Bowl attracts both new advertisers, such as P&G's Olay, the dating app Bumble, and Kraft's frozen-food brand Devour, and regular advertisers such as Budweiser, Doritos, and Kia. Recently, the NFL's "100-Year Game" ad celebrating the NFL's 100th season received the highest rating from the *USA Today* Ad Meter.[12] To learn how your ratings compare to the ratings of the Ad Meter panelists, read the Marketing Insights About Me box.[13]

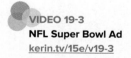

VIDEO 19-3
NFL Super Bowl Ad
kerin.tv/15e/v19-3

While not all advertising options are as expensive as the Super Bowl, most alternatives still represent substantial financial commitments and require a formal budgeting process. In the industry, for example, Tide, Clorox, and Bounty have market shares of approximately 11.6 percent, 5.5 percent, and 4.7 percent, respectively, and advertising and promotion budgets of $233 million, $109 million, and $94 million, respectively. Using a competitive parity budgeting approach, each company spends approximately $20 million for each percent of market share. Using an objective and task approach, Colgate allocated $125,000 to public relations and $300,000 to advertising for its Smart Toothbrush, which uses AI to provide brushing recommendations to users.[14]

Designing the Advertisement

An advertising message usually focuses on the key benefits of the product that are important to a prospective buyer in making trial and adoption decisions. The message depends on the general form or appeal used in the ad and the actual words included in the ad.

Message Content Most advertising messages are made up of both informational and persuasive elements. These two elements are so intertwined that it is sometimes difficult to tell them apart. For example, basic information such as the product name, benefits, features, and price can be presented in a way that tries to attract attention and encourage purchase. On the other hand, even the most persuasive advertisements have to contain at least some basic information to be successful.

Information and persuasive content can be combined in the form of an appeal to provide a basic reason for the consumer to act. Although the marketer can use many different types of appeals, common advertising appeals include fear, sex, and humor.

Fear appeals suggest to the consumer that he or she can avoid some negative experience through the purchase and use of a product or service, a change in behavior, or a reduction in the use of a product. Examples with which you may be familiar include automobile safety ads that depict an accident or injury; political candidate endorsements that warn against the rise of other, unpopular ideologies; or social cause ads warning of the serious consequences of drug and alcohol use. Life insurance companies often try to show the negative effects on the relatives of those who die prematurely without carrying enough life or mortgage insurance. Food producers encourage the purchase of low-carb, low-fat, and high-fiber products as a means of reducing weight, lowering cholesterol levels, and preventing a heart attack. Allstate has run a series of ads with a character called Mayhem who uses fear appeals to raise concerns about fires, auto theft, natural disasters, and crime, and then concludes that Allstate customers will be "better protected from mayhem . . . like me."

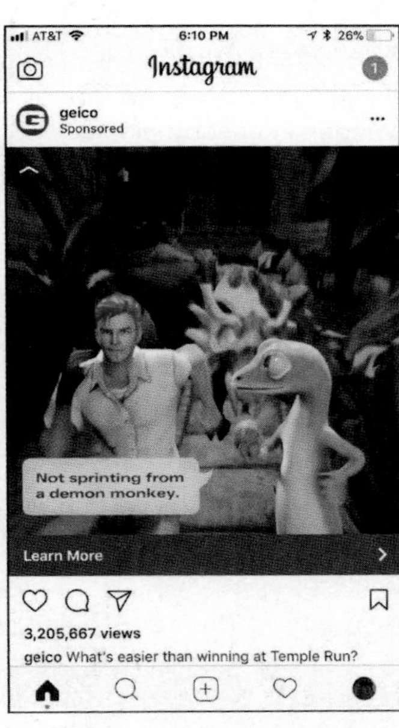

Read the text to learn why Allstate, Louis Vuitton, and GEICO use fear, sex, and humor appeals.

(Left): Source: Allstate Insurance Co.; (Middle): Source: Louis Vuitton; (Right): Source: GEICO

When using fear appeals, the advertiser must be sure that the appeal is strong enough to get the audience's attention and concern but not so strong that it will lead them to tune out the message. Research suggests that overly threatening messages have a negative effect on the intention to adapt behavior. In fact, research on antismoking ads indicates that stressing the severity of long-term health risks may actually enhance smoking's allure among youth.[15]

In contrast, *sex appeals* suggest to the audience that the product will increase the attractiveness of the user. Sex appeals can be found in almost any product category, from automobiles to toothpaste. Consumers, however, are redefining what is acceptable use of sex appeals. There is growing interest in positive messages about female and male roles, and views on gender identity are changing. Abercrombie & Fitch, for example, has moved away from overly "sexualized" campaigns, CoverGirl has named its first male ambassador, and brands such as Zara, Guess, and Mattel's Barbie are using gender-neutral ads. Louis Vuitton featured male model Jaden Smith in a women's wear ad campaign, and the fast-fashion retailer H&M recently launched a gender-neutral collection of workwear consisting of jackets, sweaters, tees, and denim jeans where "styles span genders." Studies indicate that sex appeals generate a greater response than other appeals, and they increase attention by helping advertising stand out in today's cluttered media environment. Unfortunately, sexual content does not always lead to changes in recall, recognition, or purchase intent. Experts suggest that sexual content is most effective when there is a strong fit between the use of a sex appeal in the ad and the image and positioning of the brand.[16]

Humorous appeals imply either directly or subtly that the product is more fun or exciting than competitors' offerings. As with fear and sex appeals, the use of humor is widespread in advertising and can be found in many product categories. You may have smiled at the popular GEICO ads that use a talking gecko, or a group of robbers ordering a getaway car with an app, or a group of pigeons on a wire talking about GEICO. These ads use humor to differentiate the company from its competitors. GEICO has also created viral videos and posted them on video-sharing websites such as YouTube, where millions of viewers watch them within days.[17] You may have a favorite humorous ad character, such as the Energizer Bunny, the Old Spice man, the AFLAC duck, or Travelocity's gnome. Advertisers believe that humor improves the effectiveness of their ads, although some studies suggest that humor wears out quickly, losing the interest of consumers. Another problem with humorous appeals is that their effectiveness may vary across cultures if used in a global campaign.[18]

Creating the Actual Message Advertising agency Wieden+Kennedy was recently designated number one on *Advertising Age* magazine's A-List (Agency of the Year) for doing "work that influences culture and builds business value." Examples of the agency's approach include its "Built to Be a Better Big" campaign for Ford's redesigned Expedition, the "Ingredients" campaign for Bud Light, the "A Coke is a Coke" campaign for Coca-Cola, and a creative campaign for dating app OkCupid. Wieden+Kennedy's best-known work, however, may be for Nike. The agency created the "Dream Crazy" campaign featuring Colin Kaepernick, an NFL quarterback who had expressed concern about police violence in communities of color. The contentious nature of the issue led to positive and negative reactions from Nike fans but fit with the agency's perspective on advertising. In fact, the agency's website describes its core mission as "building strong and provocative relationships between good companies and their customers."[19]

The "Dream Crazy" campaign for Nike helped Wieden+Kennedy win *Advertising Age*'s Agency of the Year award.
Source: Nike, Inc.

If they think your dreams are crazy,
show them what crazy dreams can do.
Just do it.

Wieden+Kennedy and other agencies use many forms of advertising to create their messages. A very popular form of advertising today is the use of a celebrity spokesperson. For example, Wieden+Kennedy uses tennis player Serena Williams and basketball player

VIDEO 19-4
Wieden+Kennedy
kerin.tv/15e/v19-4

LeBron James in its Nike ads, and rapper and actor Ice-T in its RXBar ads. Many companies use athletes, film and television stars, musicians, and other celebrities to talk to consumers through their ads.

Advertisers who use a celebrity spokesperson believe that the ads are more likely to influence brand equity and sales, particularly as the popularity of social media increases. These ads feature a wide variety of celebrities, among them singer Beyoncé (Pepsi), actors Jennifer Garner and Samuel L. Jackson (Capital One), and athlete Michael Jordan (Nike). L'Oréal Paris recently signed singer Celine Dion as a spokeswoman for the company and its brands. Pierre Angeloglou, global brand president, explains that Celine was selected because she "builds on our mission of aligning with spokeswomen who are strong, self-empowered, assertive, diverse and inclusive." Who is the most effective spokesperson? A recent report indicates that Zoe Saldana (Campari), Reese Witherspoon (Crate&Barrel), Gabrielle Union (New York & Company), Dwayne Johnson (Under Armour), Drew Barrymore (Crocs), and George Clooney (Nespresso) are among the top endorsers. Another group of spokespersons, including Hailey (Baldwin) Bieber, Vogue Williams, and Kendall Jenner, are influential because of their visibility on social media. Baldwin, for example, has more than 1.35 million Twitter followers and more than 705,000 Facebook followers. Recent research suggests that CEOs and founders may also serve as effective endorsers.[20]

One potential shortcoming of this form of advertising is that the spokesperson's image may change over time, becoming inconsistent with the image of the company or brand. For example, Olympic gold medalist swimmer Ryan Lochte and Tour de France cyclist Lance Armstrong lost endorsement contracts with Nike, golf pro Tiger Woods lost contracts with AT&T and Accenture, and spokesperson Jared Fogle lost his contract with Subway after they received negative public attention. Many companies now probe the backgrounds of potential endorsers and consider retired athletes and legacy (deceased) athletes who are low risk and still have lasting appeal in the marketplace. Some companies are also using licensing agreements where the spokesperson's compensation is directly related to the success of the product they endorse.[21]

Another issue involved in creating the message is the complex process of translating the copywriter's ideas into an actual advertisement. Designing quality artwork, layout, and production for advertisements can be costly—as much as $500,000—and time-consuming. The American Association of Advertising Agencies observes that marketers often produce episodic videos, in several locations, and in several languages. In addition, advertisers frequently need content for various platforms, including websites, online video channels, and digital place-based media, to complement traditional TV commercials.[22]

LEARNING REVIEW

19-3. What other decisions can advertising objectives influence?

19-4. What is a potential shortcoming of using a celebrity spokesperson?

Selecting the Right Media

Every advertiser must decide where to place its advertisements. The alternatives are the *advertising media*, the means by which the message is communicated to the target audience. Newspapers, magazines, radio, and TV are examples of advertising media. Media selection is related to the target audience, type of product, nature of the message, campaign objectives, available budget, and the costs of the alternative media. Figure 19–2 on the next page shows the share of the $209 billion spent on advertising by medium.[23]

Choosing a Medium and a Vehicle within That Medium In deciding where to place advertisements, a company has several media to choose from and a number of

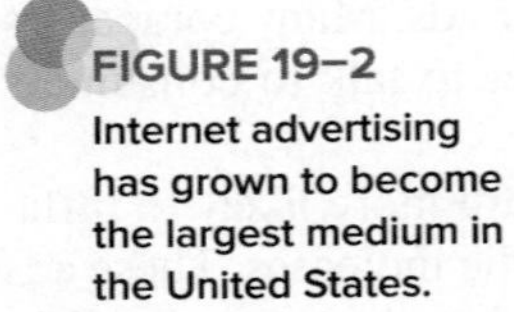

FIGURE 19–2

Internet advertising has grown to become the largest medium in the United States.

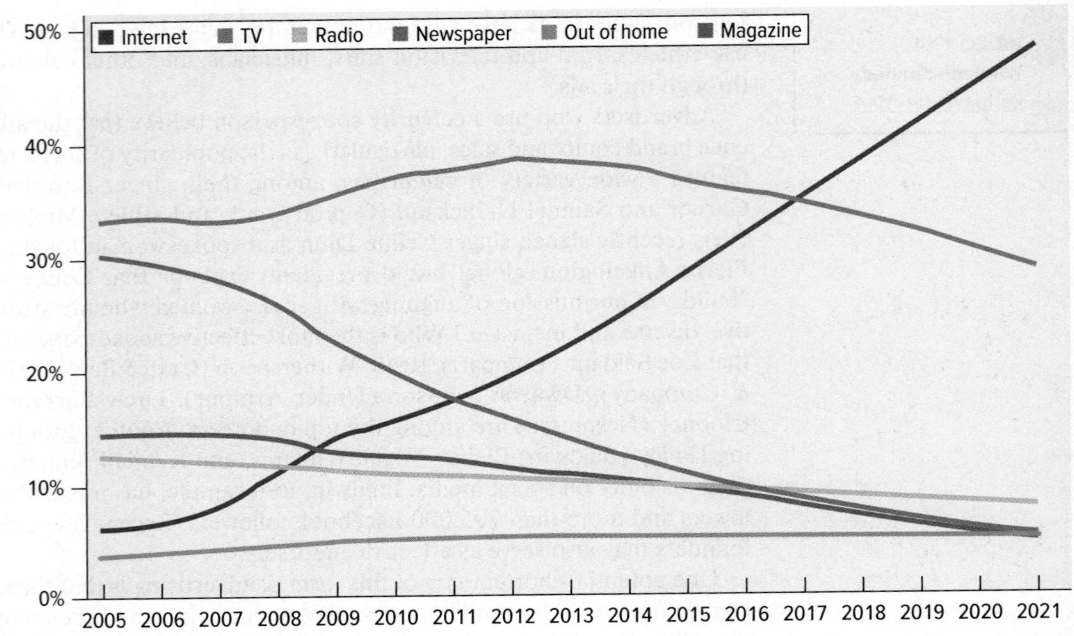

alternatives, or vehicles, within each medium. Often advertisers use a mix of media forms and vehicles to maximize the exposure of the message to the target audience while at the same time minimizing costs. These two conflicting goals are of central importance to media planning.

Basic Terms Media buyers speak a language of their own, so all advertisers involved in selecting the right media for their campaigns must be familiar with some common terms used in the advertising industry.

Because advertisers try to maximize the number of individuals in the target market exposed to the message, they must be concerned with reach. **Reach** is the number of different people or households exposed to an advertisement. The exact definition of reach sometimes varies among alternative media. Newspapers often use reach to describe their total circulation or the number of different households that buy the paper. Television and radio stations, in contrast, describe their reach using the term **rating**–the percentage of households in a market that are tuned to a particular TV show or radio station. In general, advertisers try to maximize reach in their target market at the lowest cost.

Although reach is important, advertisers are also interested in exposing their target audience to a message more than once. This is because consumers often do not pay close attention to advertising messages, some of which contain large amounts of relatively complex information. When advertisers want to reach the same audience more than once, they are concerned with **frequency**, the average number of times a person in the target audience is exposed to a message or advertisement. Like reach, greater frequency is generally viewed as desirable. Studies indicate that with repeated exposure to advertisements consumers respond more favorably to brand extensions.[24]

When reach (expressed as a percentage of the total market) is multiplied by frequency, an advertiser will obtain a commonly used reference number called **gross rating points (GRPs)**. To obtain the appropriate number of GRPs to achieve an advertising campaign's objectives, the media planner must balance reach and frequency. The balance will also be influenced by cost. **Cost per thousand (CPM)** refers to the cost of reaching 1,000 individuals or households with the advertising message in a given medium (*M* is the Roman numeral for 1,000). See the Applying Marketing Metrics box for an example of the use of CPM in media selection.

Applying Marketing Metrics

What Is the Best Way to Reach 1,000 Customers?

Marketing managers must choose from many advertising options as they design a campaign to reach potential customers. Because there are so many media alternatives (television, radio, magazines, etc.) and multiple options within each medium, it is important to monitor the efficiency of advertising expenditures on your marketing dashboard.

Your Challenge

As the marketing manager for a company about to introduce a new soft drink into the U.S. market, you are preparing a presentation in which you must make recommendations for the advertising campaign. You have observed that competitors use magazine ads, newspaper ads, and even Super Bowl ads! To compare the cost of some of the alternatives, you decide to use one of the most common measures in advertising: cost per thousand impressions (CPM). The CPM is calculated as follows:

$$CPM = \left(\frac{\text{Cost of ad}}{\text{Audience size}}\right) \times 1{,}000$$

Your challenge is to determine the most efficient use of your advertising budget.

Your Findings

Your research department helps you collect cost and audience size information for three options: full-page color ads in *Time* magazine and the *USA Today* newspaper, and a 30-second television ad during the Super Bowl. With this information you are able to calculate the cost per thousand impressions for each alternative.

Media Alternative	Cost of Ad	Audience Size	Cost per Thousand Impressions
Time (magazine)	$ 265,100	2,000,000	$ 132
USA Today (newspaper)	$ 199,000	866,791	$229
Super Bowl (television)	$5,250,000	98,200,000	$ 53

Your Action

Based on the calculations for these options, you see that there is a large variation in the cost of reaching 1,000 potential customers (CPM) and also in the absolute cost of the advertising. Although advertising during the Super Bowl has the lowest CPM, $53 for each 1,000 impressions, it also has the largest absolute cost! Your next step will be to consider other factors such as your total available budget, the profiles of the audiences each alternative reaches, and whether the type of message you want to deliver is better communicated in print or on television.

Different Media Alternatives

LO 19-3
Explain the advantages and disadvantages of alternative advertising media.

Figure 19–3 on the next page summarizes the advantages and disadvantages of the major advertising media, which are described in more detail below. For detailed coverage of direct mail, refer to Chapter 18.

Television Television is a valuable medium because it communicates with sight, sound, and motion. Print advertisements alone could never give you the sense of a sports car accelerating from a stop or cornering at high speed. In addition, television reaches more than 96 percent of all households—119.9 million, including households that receive programming delivered over the Internet. There are also many opportunities for out-of-home TV viewing, as televisions are present in many bars, fitness centers, hotels, offices, airports, and college campuses.[25]

Several aspects of traditional television viewing are changing. First, research at the Nielsen Company indicates that the amount of time allocated to television viewing is a substantial part of each day and week. American viewers spend 35 hours each week watching television programming on multiple screens, including traditional TVs, computers, tablets, and smartphones. In addition, viewers are increasingly time shifting their viewing with DVRs, DVDs, subscription services such as Netflix, and Internet options such as Hulu and Apple TV. In fact, the availability of streaming services has led to two trends: canceling pay-TV services, or "cord-cutting," and watching multiple episodes of a series in a short period of time, or "binge watching." Technologies are changing, too. In recent years, many consumers have purchased high-definition televisions. The future, however, will include 8K, OLED, QLED, ULED, flexible, and glassless 3D televisions, which are four to eight times as sharp as high-definition

MEDIUM	ADVANTAGES	DISADVANTAGES
Television	Reaches extremely large audience; uses picture, print, sound, and motion for effect; can target specific audiences	High cost to prepare and run ads; short exposure time and perishable message; difficult to convey complex information
Radio	Low cost; can target specific local audiences; ads can be placed quickly; can use sound, humor, and intimacy effectively	No visual element; short exposure time and perishable message; difficult to convey complex information
Magazines	Can target specific audiences; high-quality color; long life of ads; ads from print versions can be clipped and saved; can convey complex information	Long time needed to place ad; relatively high cost; competes for attention with other magazine features
Newspapers	Excellent coverage of local markets; ads can be placed and changed quickly; ads can be saved; quick consumer response; low cost	Ads compete for attention with other newspaper features; short life span; poor color in print versions
Directories	Excellent coverage of rural and older segments; long use period; print and digital versions available 24 hours/365 days	Public concern over environmental impact of print versions; both print and online versions compete with Google, Angie's List, etc.
Internet	Video and audio capabilities; animation can capture attention; ads can be interactive and link to advertiser	Can be complicated with many search, display, and payment options. Advertising fatigue is common.
Outdoor	Low cost; local market focus; high visibility; opportunity for repeat exposures	Message must be short and simple; low selectivity of audience; criticized as a traffic hazard
Direct mail	High selectivity of audience; can contain complex information and personalized messages; high-quality graphics	High cost per contact; poor image (junk mail)

FIGURE 19–3
Advertisers must consider the advantages and disadvantages of the many media alternatives.

television, can convert ordinary television into 3D, offer voice-activated and motion controls, and allow the viewer to watch two programs simultaneously. Smart TVs combined with services such as AI-enabled digital assistants and Amazon Prime will soon provide the opportunity for purchase-based target advertising.[26]

Television's major disadvantage is cost: The price of a prime-time, 30-second ad can range from $665,667 to run on *Sunday Night Football*, to $135,960 to run on *NCIS*, to $56,270 to run on *America's Funniest Home Videos*. Because of these high charges, many advertisers choose less expensive "spot" ads, which run between programs, or 15-second ads, rather than investing in ads that run the more traditional length of 30 or 60 seconds. In fact, approximately 44 percent of all TV ads are now 15 seconds long. Recent studies suggest that the placement of an ad within a program, and longer ads relative to other ads in a sequence of ads, may influence the ad's effectiveness. In addition, there is some indication that advertisers are shifting their interest to live events rather than programs that might be watched on a DVR days later.[27]

Another problem with television advertising is the likelihood of *wasted coverage*—having people outside the target market for the product see the advertisement. The cost and wasted coverage problems of TV advertising can be reduced through the specialized channels. Advertising time is often less expensive on cable and satellite channels than on the broadcast

ESPN is one of many specialized channels available to advertisers on cable networks.
Paul Spinelli/AP Images

networks. According to the Internet and Television Association, there are hundreds of cable channels such as Disney, ESPN, History, MTV, Oxygen, and Lifetime. Cable channels are also using "dynamic ad insertion" to allow advertisers to match their ads with the scenes in a program and with the demographics of the viewers. Advertisements for golf equipment, for example, might be inserted after a scene that shows characters playing golf or targeted to viewers who are likely golfers.[28]

Another popular form of television advertising is the infomercial. **Infomercials** are program-length (30-minute) advertisements that take an educational approach to communication with potential customers. You may remember seeing infomercials for the Magic Bullet, ThighMaster, and OxiClean products, using Ron Popeil, Suzanne Somers, and Anthony Sullivan, respectively, as the spokesperson.

Infomercials are increasingly popular because they can be both informative and entertaining, and because the average cost of a 30-minute block of television time is only $425. Each month, JWgreensheet.com publishes a list of the top 10 infomercials from the past four weeks. Recent popular infomercials included LifeLock identity theft protection products, Total Gym exercise equipment, and Crepe Erase anti-aging skin care. The industry generates more than $250 billion in annual sales and has facilitated the long-term success of many products. The Total Gym infomercials featuring Chuck Norris and Christie Brinkley, for example, have led to more than $1.2 billion in sales![29]

Radio The United States has more than 15,500 broadcast radio stations. These stations consist of approximately 4,613 AM stations and 10,901 FM stations. In addition, there are thousands of webcast Internet radio stations. The major advantage of radio is that it is a segmented medium. For example, the American Forces Network, the Family Life Network, Business Talk Radio, and the Performance Racing Network are all listened to by different market segments. Satellite radio service SiriusXM offers more than 175 commercial-free, digital, coast-to-coast channels to consumers for a monthly fee, and Internet radio services such as Pandora, Spotify, and SoundCloud offer personalized channels to each listener. The large number of media options today has reduced the amount of time spent listening to radio, although radio still reaches 90 percent of all adults weekly. Millennials listen to radio an average of 10 hours each week, making radio an important medium for businesses with college students and recent graduates as a target market.[30]

Magazines such as *Bumble Mag* appeal to narrowly defined segments such as singles who use Bumble's dating app service.
Source: Bumble

A disadvantage of radio is that it has limited use for products that must be seen. Another problem is the ease with which consumers can tune out a commercial by switching stations. Radio is also a medium that competes for people's attention as they do other activities, such as driving, working, or relaxing. Radio listening time reaches its peak during the morning drive time (7 to 8 A.M.), remains high during the day, and then begins to decline in the afternoon (after 4 P.M.) as people return home and start evening activities.[31]

Magazines Magazines have become a very specialized medium. In fact, there are currently more than 7,176 consumer magazines. Some 134 new magazines were introduced last year, including *Bumble Mag*, a lifestyle magazine offered by the dating app of the same name to create a tangible way for users to engage the brand; *Sports History*, a magazine designed to engage readers with articles and photos related to sports history; and *Oh So*, a magazine dedicated to female skateboarders and their stories. Many publishers are also taking interest in influencer-based magazines such as *Living Inspired*, a magazine launched by *Shark Tank* star Lori Greiner to offer advice and insight on money, investing, and work–life balance; *The Magnolia Journal* featuring HGTV stars Chip and Joanna Gaines; Oprah's *O* magazine, Gwyneth Paltrow's *Goop*, and Ree Drummond's *The Pioneer Woman*. Many print magazines, of course, are also available in digital versions than can be read on their websites through an iPad or a smartphone. Some magazines, such as *Auto Trader* and *Computer Weekly*, are dropping their print format to offer only a digital version. Finally, magazines such as *Good Housekeeping* and *Elle* are adding voice user interface (VUI) versions of their publications so the content will be available on voice assistant devices such as Amazon's Alexa and Apple's Siri.[32]

The marketing advantage of this medium is the great number of special-interest publications that appeal to narrowly defined segments. Runners read *Runner's World*, sailors buy *Yachting*, gardeners subscribe to *Garden Design*, and children peruse *Sports Illustrated for Kids*. Popular categories of magazines include arts and antiques, fashion, travel, cooking, automobiles, sports, and health. Each magazine's readers often represent a unique profile. Take the *Rolling Stone* reader, who tends to listen to music more than most people. SiriusXM Satellite Radio knows an ad in *Rolling Stone* is reaching the desired target audience. In addition, recent studies comparing advertising in different media suggest that magazine advertising is perceived to be more "inspirational" than other media.[33]

The cost of advertising in national magazines is a disadvantage, but many national publications publish regional and even metro editions, which reduces the absolute cost and wasted coverage. *Time* publishes well over 400 editions, including Latin American, Canadian, Asian, South Pacific, European, and U.S. editions. The U.S. editions include geographic and demographic options. In addition to cost, another limitation to magazines is their infrequency. At best, magazines are printed on a weekly basis, with many specialized publications appearing only monthly or less often. Although specialization can be an advantage of this medium, consumer interests can be difficult to translate into a magazine theme–a fact made clear by the hundreds of magazine failures during the past decade. *Self, U.S. News and World Report, NASCAR Illustrated, CosmoGirl, PC Magazine, Men's Vogue, Gourmet,* and *Mental Floss*, for example, all failed to attract and keep a substantial number of readers or advertisers. Which magazine has the highest circulation? It's *AARP The Magazine*, with a circulation of 23 million![34]

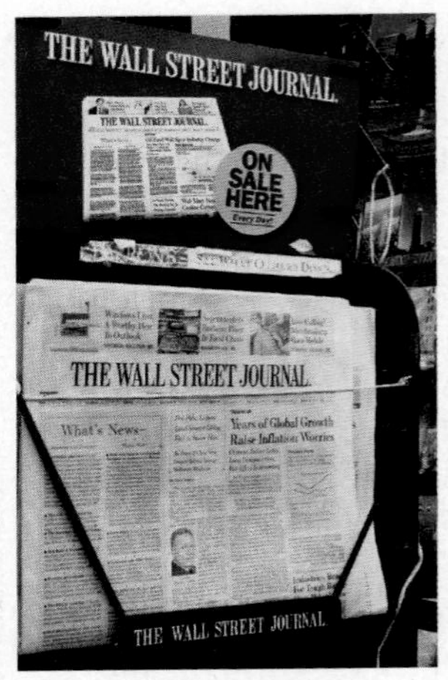

Shaul Schwarz/Getty Images

Newspapers Newspapers are an important local medium with excellent reach potential. Daily publication allows advertisements to focus on specific current events, such as a 24-hour sale. Local retailers often use newspapers as their sole advertising medium. Newspapers are rarely saved by the purchaser, however, so companies are generally limited to ads that call for an immediate customer response (although customers can clip and save ads they select). Companies also cannot expect newspapers to offer the same quality color reproduction available in most magazines.

National advertising campaigns rarely include this medium except in conjunction with local distributors of their products. In these instances, both parties often share the advertising costs using a cooperative advertising program, which is described later in this chapter. Another exception is the use of newspapers such as *The Wall Street Journal* and *USA Today*, which have national print circulation of more than 1,011,200 and 866,791 readers, respectively. One newspaper, *Metro*, offers a global audience of 18 million daily readers in Boston, New York, Philadelphia, and 100 cities in Europe, North and South America, and Asia.[35]

Several important trends are influencing newspapers today. First is the decline in circulation and advertising revenue. A recent report by the Pew Research Center showed that circulation has declined for the past 20 years. Further, although total U.S. daily circulation was recently 31 million for weekday papers and 34 million for Sunday papers, both declined approximately 10 percent during the past year. The shift is attributed to readers' growing preference for free websites and mobile services, as half of all Americans now get some form of local news on a mobile device. In addition, advertising revenue has declined as Craigslist and similar sites have become more popular with consumers.

Metro offers a global audience of daily readers.

Bill Greene/The Boston Globe via Getty Images

The second trend is the growth in digital newspapers. Today, hundreds of newspapers, including *The New York Times, The Wall Street Journal, Chicago Sun-Times*, and the *San Francisco Chronicle*, offer digital versions of their printed newspapers. In fact, digital subscriptions account for 16 percent of all newspaper subscriptions. *The New York Times* now has more digital subscribers than print subscribers. Many newspapers also have online readers who are not subscribers. *USA Today*, for example, reports that it has 32 million readers on the free portion of its website. A final trend is the growth in new types of news organizations such as *The Huffington Post*, which covers entertainment, media, living, business, and politics and has more than 11 million Twitter followers, and *Examiner.com*, which utilizes a large group of freelance reporters.[36]

Directories Directories, often called *yellow pages*, represent an advertising media alternative comparable to outdoor advertising and public relations in terms of expenditures—about $7.9 billion in the United States. According to the Local Search Association, 40 percent of U.S. consumers turn to print directories at least once a year and 25 percent use online directories (desktop, tablet, and mobile) each month. While the print directories are used by older demographics and in rural areas, their overall use is declining. In fact, several directory producers such as Hibu (Yellow Pages) have decided to discontinue their print directories to focus on their online directories. Directories are a "directional" medium because they direct consumers to where purchases can be made after other media have created awareness and demand.

Online yellow pages are used more than 11 billion times each year. See the text for advantages and disadvantages of this media alternative.
Source: DexYP

The yellow pages face several disadvantages today. First, relative to other advertising options, the yellow pages have limited accountability and ROI metrics. Many advertisers believe that yellow pages need to improve their audience measurement research and circulation auditing practices. Second, both print and digital versions of yellow pages face competition from convenient alternatives such as Google and Angie's List. Finally, yellow pages publishers are facing increasing public concern about the environmental impact of the print directories. One response from the industry is a website, www.yellowpagesoptout.com, that allows consumers to have an opt-out option if they prefer not to receive print directories.[37]

Internet The Internet represents a relatively new medium for many advertisers, although it has already attracted a wide variety of industries. Online advertising is similar to print advertising in that it offers a visual message. It has additional advantages, however, because it can also use the audio and video capabilities of the Internet. Sound and movement may simply attract more attention from viewers, or they may provide an element of entertainment to the message. Online advertising also has the unique feature of being interactive. Called *rich media*, these interactive ads have drop-down menus, built-in games, or search engines to engage viewers. Online advertising also offers an opportunity to reach younger consumers who have developed a preference for online communication.

There are a variety of online advertising options. The most popular options are paid search, display (banner) ads, classified ads, and video. Paid search is one of the fastest-growing forms of Internet advertising, as approximately 80 percent of all Internet traffic begins at a search engine such as Google, Microsoft's Bing, or Oath (see Figure 19–4). Experts estimate that consumers

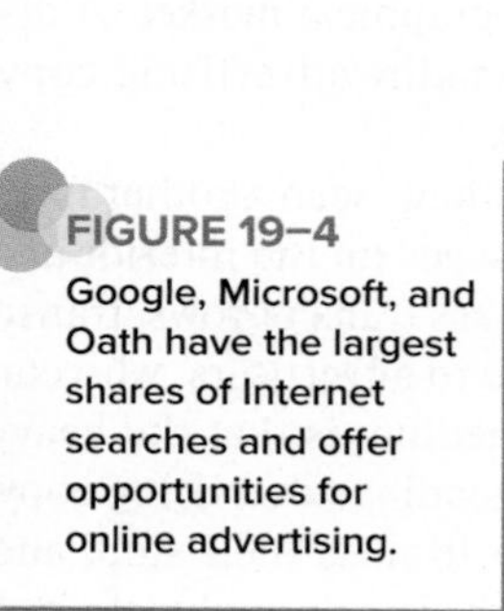

FIGURE 19–4
Google, Microsoft, and Oath have the largest shares of Internet searches and offer opportunities for online advertising.

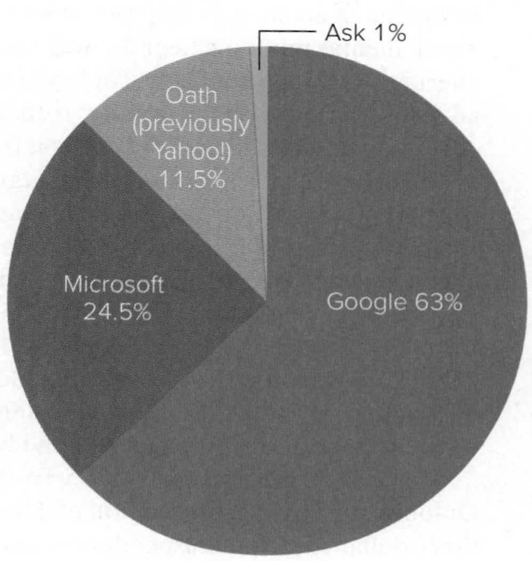

conduct 20 billion searches each month. Now search engine agencies help firms add tags, wikis, and RSS (rich site summary) to the content of a site to increase search rankings. While the use of banner ads is growing also, there is some concern that consumers are developing "banner blindness" because the click-through rate has been declining to its current level of 0.1 percent. The effectiveness of the ads can be improved with targeted advertising, and research indicates that online visitors are more likely to consent to provide information needed for targeting if the websites suggest it is a form of reciprocity or exchange for the use of free websites.

Classified ads, such as those on Craigslist, and video ads also contribute to the growth of online advertising by providing many of the advantages and characteristics of other media such as directories, magazines, newspapers, and television. Video ads also have the benefit of "going viral" when people share the ads with friends. The widespread availability of Internet access and the popularity of smartphones means that online advertising also provides the unique characteristic of being mobile. In fact, **mobile marketing** now includes the broad set of interactive messaging options that enable organizations to communicate and engage with consumers through any mobile device. Recent research indicates that the location data available from mobile devices can substantially increase the effectiveness of mobile marketing efforts.[38]

comScore's service can provide an assessment of the effectiveness of a website by measuring its impact on the digital audience.
Source: comScore, Inc.

One disadvantage of online advertising is that because the medium is relatively new, technical and administrative standards for the various formats are still evolving. This situation makes it difficult for advertisers to run national online campaigns across multiple sites. The Interactive Advertising Bureau provides "Guidelines, Standards & Best Practices" and creative guidelines to facilitate the use and growth of online advertising.

Another disadvantage to online advertising is the difficulty of measuring impact. Several companies are testing methods of tracking where viewers go on their computer in the days and weeks after seeing an ad. Nielsen's online rating service, for example, measures actual Internet use through meters installed on the computers of 500,000 individuals in 20 countries. Measuring the relationship between online and offline behavior is also important. Research by comScore, which studied 139 online ad campaigns, revealed that online ads didn't always result in a "click," but they increased the likelihood of a purchase by 17 percent and they increased visits to the advertiser's website by 40 percent.[39] The Making Responsible Decisions box describes how click fraud is increasing the necessity of assessing online advertising effectiveness.[40]

Outdoor A very effective medium for reminding consumers about your product is outdoor advertising, such as the scoreboard at San Diego's SDCCU Stadium. The most common form of outdoor advertising, called *billboards*, often result in good reach and frequency and have been shown to increase purchase rates, particularly when the billboards provide useful information in an entertaining way, in relevant locations.[41] The visibility of this medium is good supplemental reinforcement for well-known products, and it is a relatively low-cost, flexible alternative. Also, a company can buy space in a specific, targeted geographical market. A disadvantage to billboards, however, is that no opportunity exists for lengthy advertising copy. Also, a good billboard site depends on traffic patterns and sight lines.

If you have ever lived in a metropolitan area, chances are you might have seen another form of outdoor advertising, *transit advertising*. This medium includes messages on the interior and exterior of buses, subway and light-rail cars, and taxis. As the use of mass transit grows, transit advertising may become increasingly important. Selectivity is available to advertisers, who can buy space by neighborhood or bus route. One disadvantage to this medium is that the heavy travel times, when the audiences are the largest, are not conducive to reading advertising copy. People are standing shoulder to shoulder on the subway, hoping not to miss their stop, and little attention is paid to the advertising. Other forms of outdoor advertising include street furniture such as bus stop benches and bus shelters.

The outdoor advertising industry has experienced a growth surge recently. According to the Outdoor Advertising Association of America, outdoor advertising generates $5.97 in sales for every dollar spent–and expenditures have grown to $10 billion annually. Much of the growth

Making Responsible Decisions

Ethics

Who Is Responsible for Preventing Click Fraud?

Spending on Internet advertising now exceeds $87 billion as many advertisers shift their budgets from print and TV to the Internet. For most advertisers one advantage of online advertising is that they pay only when someone clicks on their ad. Unfortunately, the growth of the medium has led to "click fraud," which is the deceptive clicking of ads solely to increase the amount advertisers must pay. There are several forms of click fraud. One method is the result of Paid-to-Read (PTR) websites that recruit and pay members to simply click on ads. Another method is the result of "clickbots," which are software programs that produce automatic clicks on ads, sometimes through mobile devices. The activity is difficult to detect and stop. Google, for example, recently discovered 41 apps with hidden "adware" that had been downloaded 36 million times over a one-year period. Experts estimate that up to 20 percent of clicks may be the result of fraud and may be costing advertisers as much as $5.8 billion each year!

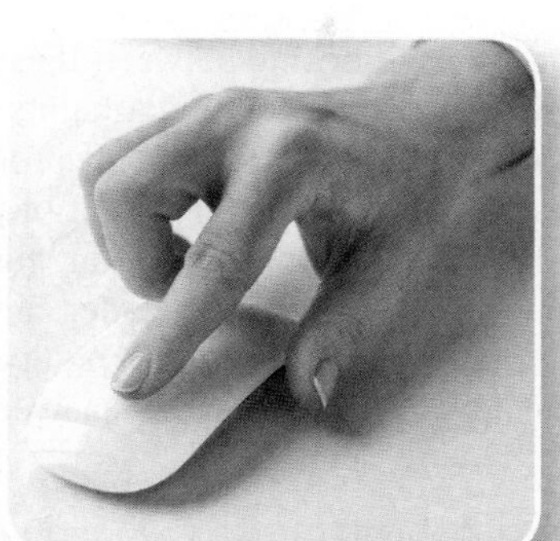

Aleksandra H. Kossowska/ Shutterstock

Investigations of the online advertising industry have discovered a related form of click fraud that occurs when legitimate website visitors click on ads without any intention of looking at the site. As one consumer explains, "I always try and remember to click on the ad banners once in a while to try and keep the sites free." Stephen Dubner calls this "webtipping"!

As the Internet advertising industry grows, it will become increasingly important to resolve the issue of click fraud. Consumers, advertisers, websites that carry paid advertising, and the large Web portals are all involved in a complicated technical, legal, and social situation. The advertising industry's Media Ratings Council has suggested a possible solution: that 50 percent of a display ad must be in view for one second to be an impression that brands pay for. Some advertisers such as Unilever, however, require 100 percent viewability. Similarly, some advertisers are now requesting "smart-pricing," which means that they pay less if the click does not lead to a consumer action such as a purchase or an information request. Finally the Interactive Advertising Bureau is advocating the use of ads.txt files that help identify legitimate ad views.

Who should lead the way in the effort to find a solution to click fraud? What actions do you suggest for the advertising industry, websites, and consumers?

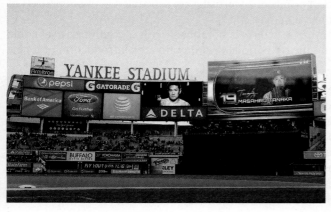

Outdoor advertising can be an effective medium for reminding consumers about a product.
Jim McIsaac/Getty Images

is the result of creative forms of outdoor advertising and the conversion to digital billboards, which allow advertisers to quickly present *conditional content*. Conditional content ads are based on current events, weather, business conditions, and even sports scores. Radio stations, for example, can display the title of the song currently playing on their station, newspapers can display current headlines, and retailers can advertise umbrellas or sunscreen based on the weather forecast.

Digital billboard companies have also donated billboard time to display public service announcements. For example, in Minnesota digital billboards display National Weather Service tornado warnings, and in Houston messages from the police department are displayed to help apprehend fugitives. In addition, as digital billboard technology improves, advertisers are contemplating using billboards to convert windows and entire storefronts into "digital engagement solutions." While these are positive trends, the outdoor advertising industry also faces important environmental concerns. For example, several states have banned billboards, a judge recently ordered two billboard companies in Los Angeles to turn off about 80 digital signs, and a district court upheld a ban on mobile billboards.[42]

Other Media As traditional media have become more expensive and cluttered, advertisers have been attracted to a variety of nontraditional advertising options called out-of-home advertising, or *place-based media*. Messages are placed in locations that attract a specific target

Out-of-home advertising such as this outdoor display is becoming interactive to engage consumers.
©Brent Jones

audience such as airports, doctors' offices, health clubs, theaters (where ads are played on the screen before the movies are shown), grocery stores, storefronts, and even the bathrooms of bars, restaurants, and nightclubs. Soon there will be advertising on video screens on gas pumps, ATMs, and in elevators, and increasingly it will be interactive.

The $2.5 billion industry has attracted advertisers such as AT&T and JCPenney, which use in-store campaigns, and GEICO, Sprint, and FedEx, which use out-of-home advertising to reach mobile professionals in health clubs, airports, and hotels. Research suggests that creative use of out-of-home advertising, such as preshow theater ads, enhances consumer recall of the ads.[43]

Selection Criteria Choosing between these alternative media is difficult and depends on several factors. First, knowing the media habits of the target audience is essential to deciding among the alternatives. Second, occasionally product attributes necessitate that certain media be used. For example, if color is a major aspect of product appeal, radio is excluded. Newspapers allow advertising for quick actions to confront competitors, and magazines are more appropriate for complicated messages because the reader can spend more time reading the message. The final factor in selecting a medium is cost. When possible, alternative media are compared using a common denominator that reflects both reach and cost–a measure such as CPM.

Scheduling the Advertising

There is no correct schedule to advertise a product, but three factors must be considered. First is the issue of *buyer turnover*, which is how often new buyers enter the market to buy the product. The higher the buyer turnover, the greater the amount of advertising required. A second issue in scheduling is the *purchase frequency*; the more frequently the product is purchased, the less repetition is required. Finally, companies must consider the *forgetting rate*, the speed with which buyers forget the brand if advertising is not seen.

Setting schedules requires an understanding of how the market behaves. Most companies tend to follow one of three basic approaches:

1. *Continuous (steady) schedule*. When seasonal factors are unimportant, advertising is run at a continuous or steady schedule throughout the year.
2. *Flighting (intermittent) schedule*. Periods of advertising are scheduled between periods of no advertising to reflect seasonal demand.
3. *Pulse (burst) schedule*. A flighting schedule is combined with a continuous schedule because of increases in demand, heavy periods of promotion, or introduction of a new product.

For example, products such as breakfast cereals have a stable demand throughout the year and would typically use a continuous schedule of advertising. In contrast, products such as snow skis and suntan lotions have seasonal demands and receive flighting-schedule advertising during the seasonal demand period. Some products such as toys or automobiles require pulse-schedule advertising to facilitate sales throughout the year and during special periods of increased demand (such as holidays or new car introductions). Some evidence suggests that pulsing schedules are superior to other advertising strategies.[44] In addition, research indicates the effectiveness of a particular ad wears out quickly and, therefore, many alternative forms of a commercial may be more effective.[45]

LEARNING REVIEW

19-5. You see the same ad in *Time* and *Fortune* magazines and on billboards and TV. Is this an example of reach or frequency?

19-6. Why has the Internet become a popular advertising medium?

19-7. What factors must be considered when choosing among alternative media?

EXECUTING THE ADVERTISING PROGRAM

Executing the advertising program involves pretesting the advertising copy and actually carrying out the advertising program. John Wanamaker, the founder of Wanamaker's Department Store in Philadelphia, remarked, "I know half my advertising is wasted, but I don't know what half." By evaluating advertising efforts, marketers can try to ensure that their advertising expenditures are not wasted.[46] Evaluation is done usually at two separate times: before and after the advertisements are run in the actual campaign. Several methods used in the evaluation process at the stages of idea formulation and copy development are discussed below.

Pretesting the Advertising

To determine whether the advertisement communicates the intended message or to select among alternative versions of the advertisement, **pretests** are conducted before the advertisements are placed in any medium.

Portfolio Tests Portfolio tests are used to test copy alternatives. The test ad is placed in a portfolio with several other ads and stories, and consumers are asked to read through the portfolio. Afterward, subjects are asked for their impressions of the ads on several evaluative scales, such as from "very informative" to "not very informative."

Jury Tests Jury tests involve showing the ad copy to a panel of consumers and having them rate how they liked it, how much it drew their attention, and how attractive they thought it was. This approach is similar to the portfolio test in that consumer reactions are obtained. However, unlike the portfolio test, a test advertisement is not hidden within other ads.

Theater Tests Theater testing is the most sophisticated form of pretesting. Consumers are invited to view new television shows or movies in which test commercials are also shown. Viewers register their feelings about the advertisements either on handheld electronic recording devices used during the viewing or on questionnaires afterward.

Carrying Out the Advertising Program

The responsibility for actually carrying out the advertising program can be handled in one of three ways, as shown in Figure 19–5. The **full-service agency** provides the most complete range of services, including marketing research, media selection, copy development, artwork, and production. The most common form of compensation for an agency is a fee-based model, although recent surveys by the Association of National Advertisers (ANA) indicate that there

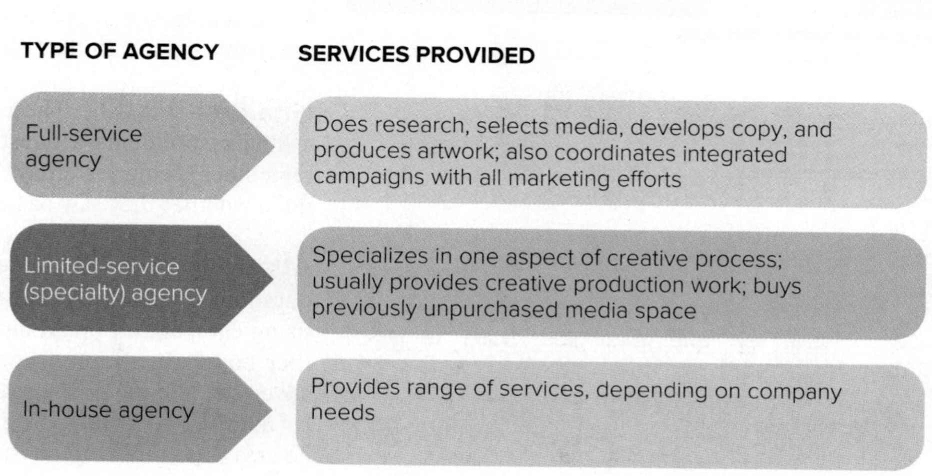

TYPE OF AGENCY
SERVICES PROVIDED
Full-service agency
Does research, selects media, develops copy, and produces artwork; also coordinates integrated campaigns with all marketing efforts
Limited-service (specialty) agency
Specializes in one aspect of creative process; usually provides creative production work; buys previously unpurchased media space
In-house agency
Provides range of services, depending on company needs

FIGURE 19–5 Alternative structures of advertising agencies used to carry out the advertising program.

may be a shift away from this method. Another form of compensation is a commission-based model which pays a percentage of the value of media costs. Finally, advertisers that have implemented integrated marketing communication approaches have utilized incentive-based models. These plans typically link compensation to specific performance goals. The use of incentive-based models may be declining also, however, because they can become very complex with traditional and digital marketing elements.

Coca-Cola recently announced a new approach to compensating its advertising agencies called "value based compensation." The approach is not based on time or cost but, rather, on value. The components of value, according to Coca-Cola, will include the work's strategic importance, the talent requirements, and whether other agencies could duplicate the work. Coca-Cola's director of worldwide media and communication, Sarah Armstrong, explains that "we want our agencies to earn their profitability, but it's not guaranteed." This approach will add additional emphasis on agency contributions beyond advertising. The ANA surveys indicate a growing interest in this form of compensation for agencies.[47]

Limited-service agencies specialize in one aspect of the advertising process, such as providing creative services to develop the advertising copy, buying previously unpurchased media (media agencies), or providing Internet services (Internet agencies). Limited-service agencies that deal in creative work are compensated by a contractual agreement for the services performed. Finally, **in-house agencies** made up of the company's own advertising staff may provide full services or a limited range of services.

ASSESSING THE ADVERTISING PROGRAM

The advertising decision process does not stop with executing the advertising program. The advertisements must be evaluated to determine whether they are achieving their intended objectives, and results may indicate that changes must be made in the advertising program.

Posttesting the Advertising

An advertisement may go through **posttests** after it has been shown to the target audience to determine whether it accomplished its intended purpose. Five approaches common in posttesting are discussed here.[48]

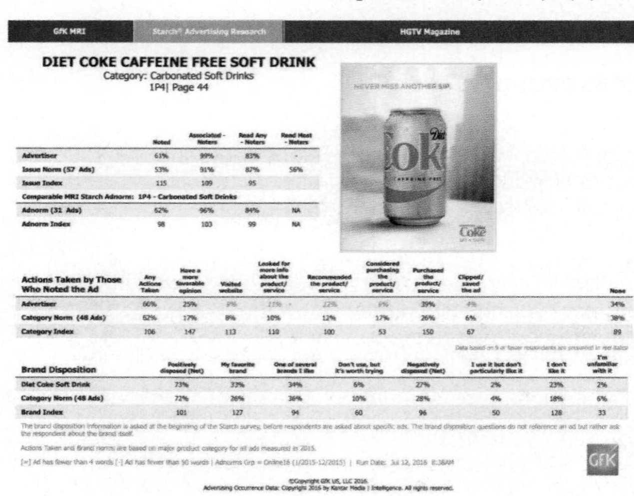

GfK MRI | Starch® Advertising Research | HGTV Magazine

DIET COKE CAFFEINE FREE SOFT DRINK

Category: Carbonated Soft Drinks

1P4| Page 44

	Noted	Associated - Noters	Read Any - Noters	Read Most - Noters
Advertiser	61%	99%	83%	-
Issue Norm (57 Ads)	53%	91%	87%	56%
Issue Index	115	109	95	
Comparable MRI Starch Adnorms: 1P4 - Carbonated Soft Drinks				
Adnorm (31 Ads)	62%	96%	84%	NA
Adnorm Index	98	103	99	NA

Actions Taken by Those Who Noted the Ad	Any Actions Taken	Have a more favorable opinion	Visited website	Looked for more info about the product/service	Recommended the product/service	Considered purchasing the product/service	Purchased the product/service	Clipped/saved the ad	None
Advertiser	66%	25%	9%	11%	12%	9%	39%	4%	34%
Category Norm (48 Ads)	62%	17%	8%	10%	12%	17%	26%	6%	38%
Category Index	106	147	113	110	100	53	150	67	89

Data based on 9 or fewer respondents are presented in red italics

Brand Disposition	Positively disposed (Net)	My favorite brand	One of several brands I like	Don't use, but it's worth trying	Negatively disposed (Net)	I use it but don't particularly like it	I don't like it	I'm unfamiliar with it
Diet Coke Soft Drink	73%	33%	34%	6%	27%	2%	23%	2%
Category Norm (48 Ads)	72%	26%	36%	10%	28%	4%	18%	6%
Brand Index	101	127	94	60	96	50	128	33

The brand disposition information is asked at the beginning of the Starch survey, before respondents are asked about specific ads. The brand disposition questions do not reference an ad but rather ask the respondent about the brand itself.

Actions Taken and Brand norms are based on major product category for all ads measured in 2015.

[*] Ad has fewer than 4 words [-] Ad has fewer than 50 words | Adnorms Grp = Online16 (1/2015-12/2015) | Run Date: Jul 12, 2016 8:38AM

GfK

The Starch test uses aided recall to evaluate an ad on four dimensions. See the text to learn more.

Courtesy of GfK North America

Aided Recall After being shown an ad, respondents are asked whether their previous exposure to it was through reading, viewing, or listening. The Starch test shown in the accompanying photo uses aided recall to determine the percentage of those who (1) remember seeing a specific ad (*noted*), (2) saw or read any part of the ad identifying the product or brand (*associated*), (3) read any part of the ad's copy (*read any*), and (4) read at least half of the ad (*read most*). Elements of the ad are then tagged with the results, as shown in the photo.[49]

Unaided Recall The unaided recall approach involves asking respondents a question such as, "What ads do you remember seeing yesterday?" without any prompting to determine whether they saw or heard advertising messages.

Attitude Tests Attitude tests involve asking respondents questions to measure changes in their attitudes after an advertising campaign. For example, they might be asked whether they now have a more favorable attitude toward the product advertised. Research suggests that attitudes can be influenced by many factors, including the increasingly popular use of co-creation to develop consumer-generated ads.[50]

Inquiry Tests Inquiry tests involve offering additional product information, product samples, or premiums to an ad's readers or viewers. Ads generating the most inquiries are presumed to be the most effective.

Sales Tests Sales tests involve studies such as controlled experiments (e.g., using radio ads in one market and newspaper ads in another and comparing the results) and consumer purchase tests (measuring retail sales that result from a given advertising campaign). The most sophisticated experimental methods today allow a manufacturer, a distributor, or an advertising agency to manipulate an advertising variable (such as schedule or copy) through cable systems and observe subsequent sales effects by monitoring data collected from checkout scanners in supermarkets.[51]

Making Needed Changes

Results of posttesting the advertising copy are used to reach decisions about changes in the advertising program. If the posttest results show that an advertisement is doing poorly in terms of awareness, cost efficiency, or sales, it may be dropped and other ads run in its place in the future. On the other hand, sometimes an advertisement may be so successful it is run repeatedly or used as the basis for a larger advertising program.

LEARNING REVIEW

19-8. Explain the difference between pretesting and posttesting advertising copy.

19-9. What is the difference between aided and unaided recall posttests?

SALES PROMOTION

LO 19-4
Discuss the strengths and weaknesses of consumer-oriented and trade-oriented sales promotions.

Sales promotion is a key element of the promotional mix today; it now accounts for more than $85 billion in annual expenditures. In a recent forecast by Zenith Media Services, sales promotion expenditures accounted for 18 percent of all promotional spending.[52] The large allocation of marketing expenditures to sales promotion reflects the trend toward integrated marketing communications programs, which often include a variety of sales promotion elements. Selection and integration of the many promotion techniques require a good understanding of the advantages and disadvantages of each kind of sales promotion. Sales promotions can have a positive influence on brand loyalty, perceptions of quality, purchase intentions, and sales.[53] The two major kinds of sales promotions, consumer-oriented and trade-oriented, are discussed below.

Consumer-Oriented Sales Promotions

Directed to ultimate consumers, **consumer-oriented sales promotions**, or simply *consumer promotions*, are sales tools used to support a company's advertising and personal selling. A variety of consumer-oriented sales promotion tools may be used, including coupons, deals, premiums, contests, sweepstakes, samples, loyalty programs, point-of-purchase displays, rebates, and product placements (see Figure 19–6 on the next page).

Coupons Coupons are sales promotions that usually offer a discounted price to the consumer, which encourages trial. Approximately 256 billion coupons worth $400 billion are distributed in the United States each year. More than 93 percent of all coupons are distributed as freestanding inserts in newspapers. Research indicates that consumer use of coupons is

KIND OF SALES PROMOTION	OBJECTIVES	ADVANTAGES	DISADVANTAGES
Coupons	Stimulate demand	Encourage retailer support	Consumers delay purchases
Deals	Increase trial; retaliate against competitor's actions	Reduce consumer risk	Consumers delay purchases; reduce perceived product value
Premiums	Build goodwill	Consumers like free or reduced-price merchandise	Consumers buy for premium, not product
Contests	Increase consumer purchases; build business inventory	Encourage consumer involvement with product	Require creative or analytical thinking
Sweepstakes	Encourage present customers to buy more; minimize brand switching	Get customer to use product and store more often	Sales drop after sweepstakes
Samples	Encourage new-product trial	Low risk for consumer	High cost for company
Loyalty programs	Encourage repeat purchases	Help create loyalty	High cost for company
Point-of-purchase displays	Increase product trial; provide in-store support for other promotions	Provide good product visibility	Hard to get retailer to allocate high-traffic space
Rebates	Encourage customers to purchase; stop sales decline	Effective at stimulating demand	Easily copied; steal sales from future; reduce perceived product value
Product placements	Introduce new products; demonstrate product use	Positive message in a noncommercial setting	Little control over presentation of product

FIGURE 19–6
Consumer-oriented sales promotion makes use of many different tools to achieve a variety of objectives.

steady at approximately 92 percent. Consumers redeemed 1.7 billion of the coupons last year, for a savings of approximately $2.7 billion.

Companies that have increased their use of coupons include Procter & Gamble, Nestlé, and Kraft, while the top retailers for coupon redemption were Walmart, Kroger, and Target. The number of coupons generated at Internet sites (e.g., www.valpak.com and www.coupons.com) and on mobile phones has been increasing as well, although they account for less than 1 percent of all coupons. The redemption rate for online coupons—approximately 12 percent—however, is substantially higher than other forms of coupons. Daily deal sites like Groupon.com and LivingSocial.com have helped fuel the growth in couponing. Today, coupons are available in almost every product category and they are used by men and women of all ages.[54]

Do coupons help increase sales? Studies suggest that market share does increase during the period immediately after coupons are distributed.[55] There are also indications, however, that couponing can reduce gross revenues by lowering the price paid by already-loyal consumers.[56] Therefore, the 9,000 manufacturers that currently use coupons are particularly interested in

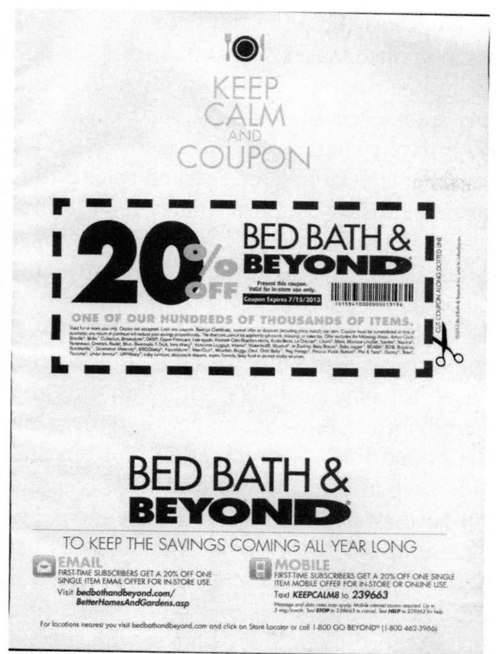

Coupons encourage trial by offering a discounted price. See the text to learn if coupons increase sales.
Mike Hruby/McGraw-Hill Education

coupon programs directed at potential first-time buyers. One means of focusing on these potential buyers is through electronic in-store coupon machines that match coupons to your most recent purchases.

Coupons are often far more expensive than the face value of the coupon; a 25-cent coupon can cost three times that after paying for the advertisement to deliver it, dealer handling, clearinghouse costs, and redemption. In addition, misredemption, or attempting to redeem a counterfeit coupon or a valid coupon when the product was not purchased, should be added to the cost of the coupon. The Coupon Information Corporation estimates that companies pay out refunds worth hundreds of millions of dollars each year as a result of coupon fraud. Recent growth in coupon fraud has marketers considering adding holograms and visual aids to help cashiers identify valid coupons.[57]

Deals Deals are short-term price reductions, commonly used to increase trial among potential customers or to retaliate against a competitor's actions. For example, if a rival manufacturer introduces a new cake mix, the company responds with a "two packages for the price of one" deal. This short-term price reduction builds up the stock on the kitchen shelves of cake mix buyers and makes the competitor's introduction more difficult.

Premiums A promotion tool often used with consumers is the premium, which consists of merchandise offered free or at a significant savings over its retail price. This latter type of premium is called *self-liquidating* because the cost charged to the consumer covers the cost of the item. McDonald's, for example, used a free premium in a promotional partnership with Disney during the release of *Avengers: Endgame*. Collectible toys that portrayed one of seven Avengers characters were given away free with the purchase of a Happy Meal. What are the most popular premiums? According to the Promotional Products Association International, the top premiums are apparel, writing instruments, shopping bags, cups and mugs, and desk accessories. By offering a premium, companies encourage customers to return frequently or to use more of the product. Research suggests that deal-prone consumers and value seekers are attracted to premiums.[58]

Kellogg's Mystery Flavor Contest offered a $10,000 prize.
Source: Kellogg NA Co.

Contests As shown in Figure 19–6, contests are another sales promotion tool used with consumers. Contests encourage consumers to apply their skill or analytical or creative thinking to try to win a prize. This form of promotion has been growing as requests for videos, photos, and essays are a good match with the trend toward consumer-generated content. For example, Kellogg's sponsored the Pringles Mystery Flavor Contest, giving people the chance to guess a new flavor of Pringles chips. To enter the contest, consumers purchased a can of the chips, registered for the Kellogg's Family Rewards program, and uploaded a picture of their receipt along with their guess. Correct guesses moved to a final round where one finalist was selected to win $10,000! If you like contests, you can enter online now at websites such as www.contestbee.com.[59]

Sweepstakes Sweepstakes are sales promotions that require participants to submit some kind of entry but are purely games of chance requiring no analytical or creative effort by the consumer. Popular sweepstakes include the HGTV "Dream Home Giveaway," which receives more than 90 million entries each year, and McDonald's Monopoly, which offers a grand prize of $1 million.[60]

Two variations of sweepstakes are popular now. First are sweepstakes that offer products that consumers value as prizes. Mars Chocolate, for example, created a sweepstakes where consumers enter a UPC code from M&M's products for a chance to win one of five Toyota automobiles. Pepsi created a similar sweepstakes called "Pepsi Fire" that allowed consumers to use Snapchat to submit codes from bottles of Pepsi and Pepsi Fire to win prizes.

The second type of sweepstakes offers an "experience" as the prize. For example, one of television's most popular series, *The Voice*, and Nissan sponsored a sweepstakes for a chance to win a trip for two to the season finale of *The Voice* in Los Angeles. Similarly, for each of the past five years, People Entertainment Network has sponsored the Oscars Fan Experience Sweepstakes for a chance to win a trip to the Oscars in Hollywood.

Federal laws, the Federal Trade Commission, and state legislatures have issued rules covering sweepstakes, contests, and games to regulate fairness, ensure that the chance for winning is represented honestly, and guarantee that the prizes are actually awarded. Several well-known sweepstakes created by Publishers Clearing House and *Reader's Digest* have paid fines and agreed to new sweepstakes guidelines in response to regulatory scrutiny.[61]

Samples Another common consumer sales promotion is sampling, which is offering the product free or at a greatly reduced price. Often used for new products, sampling puts the product in the consumer's hands. A trial size is generally offered that is smaller than the regular package size. If consumers like the sample, it is hoped they will remember and buy the product. Taco Bell has offered free tacos nationwide several times in the past to encourage customers to try new products. Recently, Taco Bell gave away free Doritos Locos tacos because the Golden State Warriors "stole" an away game in the NBA finals. The taco has become the company's most successful new product. Similarly, Ben & Jerry's offers a complimentary scoop of ice cream on "Free Cone Day." Some consumers watch for free samples online at sites such as www.freesamples.org. According to Stacy Fisher, who started trying free samples in college and now blogs about them, free samples are "a great way to try new things and save money."[62]

Loyalty Programs Loyalty programs are a sales promotion tool used to encourage and reward repeat purchases by acknowledging each purchase made by a consumer and offering a premium as purchases accumulate. The most popular loyalty programs today are credit card reward programs. More than 75 percent of all cards offer incentives for use of their card. Citibank, for example, offers "Thank You" points for using Citi credit or debit cards. The points can be redeemed for books, music, gift cards, cash, travel, and special limited-time rewards. Airlines, retailers, hotels, and grocery stores also offer popular loyalty programs. Specialty retailers such as Bed Bath & Beyond and Best Buy have enhanced their reward programs to add value to their offerings as they compete with low-cost merchandise. The rewards program at

Ben & Jerry's free samples encourage customers to try new flavors, while the Starbucks Rewards program rewards customers for repeat purchases.

(Left): Sources: Ben & Jerry's Homemade, Inc.; (Right): Source: Starbucks Coffee Company

Starbucks lets you earn "stars" that can be redeemed for drinks, food, and merchandise and also offers benefits such as refills and a free birthday treat. There are now more than 3.3 billion loyalty program memberships, for an average of 29 for each household in the United States, with point balances exceeding $50 billion.[63]

One trend in loyalty programs today is to customize the rewards and benefits for different segments of program members. This approach leads to promotions targeted at new members, members with unique purchase histories, or members who have self-selected into "elite" status groups. American Airlines, for example, has offered bonus points for new members, an additional 50 percent of award points for members who fly first class, and special benefits for members who join the American Airlines Admirals Club. Another trend is the shift away from programs where points and rewards can be earned from only one operator to an "open economy" for loyalty where points and rewards can be earned from many interchangeable programs. An example of a program moving in this direction is the Chase Ultimate Rewards program, which was recently rated highest in terms of overall customer satisfaction.[64]

Point-of-purchase displays help increase consumers' attention in a store.
McGraw-Hill Education

Point-of-Purchase Displays In a store aisle, you often encounter a sales promotion called a point-of-purchase display. These product displays take the form of advertising signs, which sometimes actually hold or display the product, and are often located in high-traffic areas near the cash register or the end of an aisle. The point-of-purchase display for new movies is designed to maximize the consumer's attention to DVDs and provide storage for the products. Annual expenditures on point-of-purchase promotion are expected to grow as point-of-purchase becomes integrated with all forms of promotion.

Some studies estimate that one-third of a consumer's buying decisions are made in the store. Grocery product manufacturers want to get their message to you at the instant you are next to their brand in your supermarket aisle, perhaps through a point-of-purchase display. At a growing number of supermarkets, this may be done with digital signage. Whole Foods Market, for example, is replacing printed and written displays with digital signage that educates shoppers about the sustainable growing practices of its suppliers. The advantage of this method of promotion is that it does not rely on the consumers' ability to remember the message for long periods. Other in-store promotions such as interactive kiosks are also becoming popular.[65]

Rebates Another consumer sales promotion tool in Figure 19–6, the cash rebate, offers the return of money based on proof of purchase. For example, T-Mobile recently offered a $360 to $390 rebate to smartphone owners who would trade in their phone and add a new line. When a rebate is offered on lower-priced items, the time and trouble of mailing in a proof of purchase to get the rebate check often means that many buyers never take advantage of it. However, this "slippage" is less likely to occur with frequent users of rebate promotions. In addition, online consumers are more likely to take advantage of rebates.[66]

Product Placements A final consumer promotion tool, **product placement**, involves the use of a brand-name product in a movie, television show, video game, or commercial for another product. It was Steven Spielberg's placement of Hershey's Reese's Pieces in *E.T. the Extra Terrestrial* that first brought a lot of interest to the candy. Similarly, when Tom Cruise wore Bausch and Lomb's Ray-Ban sunglasses in *Risky Business* and its Aviator glasses in *Top Gun*, sales skyrocketed from 100,000 pairs to 7,000,000 pairs in five years. After *Toy Story*, Etch-A-Sketch sales increased 4,500 percent and Mr. Potato Head sales increased 800 percent.

More recently you might remember seeing products from Tabasco, Sony, and Barnum's (Animal Crackers) in *Captain Marvel*; Harley-Davidson, Samsung, Apple, and Gibson (guitars) in *A Star Is Born*; and Dell, CNN, and BMW in *Mission: Impossible - Fallout*. Which brand has the highest level of product placement in films? It's Apple, with 3.5 hours of screen time in 52 top films. And which film has the most product placements? *Jurassic World: Fallen Kingdom*, with $51 million of advertising value for brands such as Nike, Cessna, Swatch, and Ford.

Product placement can take many forms today. Are you familiar with these examples?

(Left): Paramount Pictures/Photofest; (Top right): AF archive/Alamy Stock Photo; (Bottom right): DGA Photo/Alamy Stock Photo

The annual value of all product placements has grown to an estimated $10 billion as consumer resistance to traditional advertising has led advertisers to try new forms of promotion. Complaints that product placement has become excessive have led the Federal Communications Commission to begin developing guidelines for TV product placements. Meanwhile, the British government recently passed a law allowing product placement only if a bold "P" logo is shown before and after the program. Research suggests that a product placement disclosure such as this may lead to less favorable attitudes toward the products.[67]

New forms of product placement may appear to be integrated into the program. An episode of *Modern Family*, for example, includes a scene in an Apple store. Some programs have recently begun digital product placement in programs after they have been filmed. Similarly, some companies such as Amway are creating partnerships with game developers in order to be included in video games, which can be effective if competing products are not also in the game. A variation of product placement, called *reverse product placement*, brings fictional products to the marketplace. Bertie Bott's Every Flavour Beans, for example, began as an imaginary brand in *Harry Potter* books. Similarly, the movie *Forrest Gump* led to the Bubba Gump Shrimp Company restaurant chain. And fans of *The Office* can purchase Dunder Mifflin office supplies from www.quill.com![68]

Trade-Oriented Sales Promotions

Trade-oriented sales promotions, or simply *trade promotions*, are sales tools used to support a company's advertising and personal selling directed to wholesalers, retailers, or distributors. Some of the sales promotions just reviewed are used for this purpose, but three other common approaches are targeted uniquely to these intermediaries: (1) allowances and discounts, (2) cooperative advertising, and (3) training of distributors' salesforces.

Allowances and Discounts Trade promotions often focus on maintaining or increasing inventory levels in the channel of distribution. An effective method for encouraging such increased purchases by intermediaries is the use of allowances and discounts. However, overuse of these price reductions can lead to retailers changing their ordering patterns in the expectation of such offerings. Although there are many variations that manufacturers can use with discounts and allowances, three common approaches are the merchandise allowance, the case allowance, and the finance allowance.[69]

Reimbursing a retailer for extra in-store support or special featuring of the brand is a *merchandise allowance*. Performance contracts between the manufacturer and trade member usually specify the activity to be performed, such as a picture of the product in a newspaper with a coupon good at only one store. The merchandise allowance then consists of a percentage deduction from the list case price ordered during the promotional period. Allowances are not paid by the manufacturer until it sees proof of performance (such as a copy of the ad placed by the retailer in the local newspaper).

A second common trade promotion, a *case allowance*, is a discount on each case ordered during a specific time period. These allowances are usually deducted from the invoice. A variation of the case allowance is the "free goods" approach, whereby retailers receive some amount of the product free based on the amount ordered, such as 1 case free for every 10 cases ordered.[70]

A final trade promotion, the *finance allowance*, involves paying retailers for financing costs or financial losses associated with consumer sales promotions. This trade promotion is regularly used and has several variations. One type is the floor stock protection program—manufacturers give retailers a case allowance price for products in their warehouse, which prevents shelf stock from running down during the promotional period. Also common are freight allowances, which compensate retailers that transport orders from the manufacturer's warehouse.

Cooperative Advertising Resellers often perform the important function of promoting the manufacturer's products at the local level. One common sales promotional activity is to encourage both better quality and greater quantity in the local advertising efforts of resellers through **cooperative advertising**. These are programs by which a manufacturer pays a percentage of the retailer's local advertising expense for advertising the manufacturer's products.

Usually, the manufacturer pays a percentage, often 50 percent, of the cost of advertising up to a certain dollar limit, which is based on the amount of the manufacturer's products purchased by the retailer. In addition to paying for the advertising, the manufacturer often furnishes the retailer with a selection of different ad executions, sometimes suited for several different media. A manufacturer may provide, for example, several different print layouts as well as a few broadcast ads for the retailer to adapt and use.[71]

Training of Distributors' Salesforces One of the many functions the intermediaries perform is customer contact and selling for the producers they represent. Both retailers and wholesalers employ and manage their own sales personnel. A manufacturer's success often rests on the ability of the reseller's salesforce to represent its products. Thus, it is in the best interest of the manufacturer to help train the reseller's salesforce.

Because the reseller's salesforce is often less sophisticated and knowledgeable about the products than the manufacturer might like, training can increase their sales performance. Training activities include producing manuals and brochures to educate the reseller's salesforce. The salesforce then uses these aids in selling situations. Other activities include national sales meetings sponsored by the manufacturer and field visits to the reseller's location to inform and motivate the salesperson to sell the products. Manufacturers also develop incentive and recognition programs to motivate a reseller's salespeople to sell their products.

LEARNING REVIEW

19-10. What is the difference between a coupon and a deal?

19-11. Which sales promotion tool is most common for new products?

19-12. Which trade promotion approach focuses on maintaining or increasing inventory levels?

PUBLIC RELATIONS

LO 19-5
Recognize public relations as an important form of communication.

As noted in Chapter 18, public relations is a form of communications management that seeks to influence the image of an organization and its products and services. Public relations efforts may utilize a variety of tools and may be directed at many distinct audiences. While public relations personnel usually focus on communicating positive aspects of the business, they may also be called on to minimize the negative impact of a problem or crisis. Companies that have received substantial negative publicity include BP (the worst oil spill in U.S. history), Samsung (faulty smartphone batteries that started fires), and United Airlines (forcibly removing a passenger from an overbooked flight). The most frequently used public relations tool is publicity, which can often provide stronger marketing impact than advertising.[72]

Publicity Tools

In developing a public relations campaign, several **publicity tools**—methods of obtaining nonpersonal presentation of an organization, product, or service without direct cost—are available to the public relations director. Many companies frequently use the *news release*, consisting of an announcement regarding changes in the company or the product line. The objective of a news release is to inform a newspaper, radio station, or other medium of an idea for a story.

Daisy Ridley receives publicity for her movies by visiting programs such as *The Tonight Show Starring Jimmy Fallon.*
Theo Wargo/Getty Images

A second common publicity tool is the *news conference*. Representatives of the media are all invited to an informational meeting, and advance materials regarding the content are sent. This tool is often used when new products are introduced or significant changes in corporate structure and leadership are being made.

Nonprofit organizations rely heavily on *public service announcements (PSAs)*, which are free space or time donated by the media. For example, the charter of the American Red Cross prohibits any local chapter from advertising, so to solicit blood donations local chapters often depend on PSAs on radio or television to announce their needs.

Finally, today many high-visibility individuals are used as publicity tools to create visibility for their companies, their products, and themselves. Richard Branson uses visibility to promote the Virgin Group, Daisy Ridley uses it to promote her movies, and U.S. senators use it to promote themselves as political candidates. These publicity efforts are coordinated with news releases, conferences, advertising, donations to charities, volunteer activities, endorsements, and any other activities that may have an impact on public perceptions.[73]

INCREASING THE VALUE OF PROMOTION

Today's customers seek value from companies that provide leading-edge products, hassle-free transactions at competitive prices, and customer intimacy.[74] Promotion practices have changed dramatically to improve transactions and increase customer intimacy by (1) emphasizing long-term relationships and (2) increasing self-regulation.

Building Long-Term Relationships

Many changes in promotional techniques have been driven by marketers' interest in developing long-term relationships with their customers. Promotion can contribute to brand and store loyalty by improving a company's ability to target individual preferences and by engaging customers in valuable and entertaining communication. New social and mobile media have provided immediate opportunities for personalized promotion activities. In addition, technological developments have helped traditional media such as TV and radio focus on individual preferences through services such as Apple TV and SiriusXM Satellite Radio. Although the future holds extraordinary promise for the personalization of promotion, the industry will need to manage and balance consumers' concerns about privacy as it proceeds.

Changes that help engage consumers have also been numerous. Marketers have attempted to utilize interactive technologies and to integrate new media and technologies into the overall creative process. Ad agencies are increasingly integrating public relations, direct marketing, advertising, and sales promotion into comprehensive IMC campaigns. In fact, some experts predict that advertising agencies will soon become "communications consulting firms." Further, increasingly diverse and global audiences necessitate multimedia approaches and communication techniques that engage the varied groups.[75] Overall, companies hope that these changes will build customer relationships for the long term—emphasizing a lifetime of purchases rather than a single transaction.

Self-Regulation

Unfortunately, over the years, many consumers have been misled, or even deceived, by some promotions. Examples include sweepstakes in which the gifts were not awarded, rebate offers that were a terrible hassle, and advertisements whose promises were great, until the buyer read the small print. In one of the worst scandals in promotion history, McDonald's assisted an FBI investigation of the firm responsible for the fast-food chain's sweepstakes because the promotion agency security director was suspected of stealing winning game pieces.[76]

Promotions targeted at special groups such as children and the elderly also raise ethical concerns. For example, providing free samples to children in elementary schools or linking product lines to TV programs and movies has led to questions about the need for restrictions on promotions.[77] Although the Federal Trade Commission (FTC) does provide some guidelines to protect consumers and special groups from misleading promotions, some observers believe more government regulation is needed.

Formal regulation of all promotional activities by federal, state, and local governments would be very expensive. As a result, advertising agencies, trade associations, and marketing organizations are increasing their efforts toward *self-regulation*.[78] By imposing standards that reflect the values of society on their promotional activities, marketers can (1) facilitate the development of new promotional methods, (2) minimize regulatory constraints and restrictions, and (3) help consumers gain confidence in the communication efforts used to influence their purchases. As organizations strive for effective self-regulation, marketing executives will need to make sound ethical judgments about the use of existing and new promotional practices.

LEARNING REVIEW

19-13. What is a news release?

19-14. What is the difference between government regulation and self-regulation?

LEARNING OBJECTIVES REVIEW

LO 19-1 *Explain the differences between product advertising and institutional advertising and the variations within each type.*
Product advertisements focus on selling a good or service and take three forms: Pioneering advertisements tell people what a product is, what it can do, and where it can be found; competitive advertisements persuade the target market to select the firm's brand rather than a competitor's; and reminder advertisements reinforce previous knowledge of a product. Institutional advertisements are used to build goodwill or an image for an organization. They include advocacy advertisements, which state the position of a company on an issue, and pioneering, competitive, and reminder advertisements, which are similar to the product ads but focus on the institution.

LO 19-2 *Describe the steps used to develop, execute, and evaluate an advertising program.*
The promotion decision process can be applied to each of the promotional elements. The steps to develop an advertising program include the following: identify the target audience, specify the advertising objectives, set the advertising budget, design the advertisement, create the message, select the media, and schedule the advertising. Executing the program requires pretesting, and evaluating the program requires posttesting.

LO 19-3 *Explain the advantages and disadvantages of alternative advertising media.*
Television advertising reaches large audiences and uses picture, print, sound, and motion; its disadvantages, however, are that it is expensive and perishable. Radio advertising is inexpensive and can be placed quickly, but it has no visual element and is perishable. Magazine advertising can target specific audiences and can convey complex information, but it takes a long time to place the ad and is relatively expensive. Newspapers provide excellent coverage of local markets and can be changed quickly, but they have a short life span and poor color. Directories have a long use period and are available 24 hours per day; their disadvantages, however, are that they face competition from convenient alternatives such as Angie's List and raise concerns about the environmental impact of print directories. Internet advertising can be interactive, but its effectiveness is difficult to measure. Outdoor advertising provides repeat exposures, but its message must be very short and simple. Direct mail can be targeted at very selective audiences, but its cost per contact is high.

LO 19-4 *Discuss the strengths and weaknesses of consumer-oriented and trade-oriented sales promotions.*
Coupons encourage retailer support but may delay consumer purchases. Deals reduce consumer risk but also reduce perceived value. Premiums offer consumers additional merchandise they want, but they may be purchasing only for the premium. Contests create involvement but require creative thinking. Sweepstakes encourage repeat purchases, but sales drop after the sweepstakes. Samples encourage product trial but are expensive. Loyalty programs help create loyalty but are expensive to run. Displays provide visibility but are difficult to place in retail space. Rebates stimulate demand but are easily copied. Product placements provide a positive message in a noncommercial setting that is difficult to control. Trade-oriented sales promotions include (*a*) allowances and discounts, which increase purchases but may change retailer ordering patterns; (*b*) cooperative advertising, which encourages local advertising; and (*c*) salesforce training, which helps increase sales by providing the salespeople with product information and selling skills.

LO 19-5 *Recognize public relations as an important form of communication.*
Public relations activities usually focus on communicating positive aspects of the business. A frequently used public relations tool is publicity. Publicity tools include news releases and news conferences. Nonprofit organizations often use public service announcements.

LEARNING REVIEW ANSWERS

19-1 What is the difference between pioneering and competitive ads?
Answer: Pioneering (or informational) ads, used in the introductory stage of the product life cycle, tell people what a product is, what it can do, and where it can be found. The key objective of a pioneering ad is to inform the target market. Competitive (or persuasive) ads promote a specific brand's features and benefits to persuade the target market to select the firm's brand rather than that of a competitor. A form of a competitive ad is the comparative ad that shows one brand's strengths relative to those of competitors.

19-2 What is the purpose of an institutional advertisement?
Answer: The purpose of an institutional advertisement is to build goodwill or an image for an organization rather than a specific offering. This form of advertising is often used to support the public relations plan or counter adverse publicity.

19-3 What other decisions can advertising objectives influence?
Answer: Advertising objectives can influence decisions such as selecting media and evaluating an advertising campaign.

19-4 What is a potential shortcoming of using a celebrity spokesperson?
Answer: The spokesperson's image may change to be inconsistent with the image of the company or brand.

19-5 You see the same ad in *Time* and *Fortune* magazines and on billboards and TV. Is this an example of reach or frequency?
Answer: This is an example of frequency—reaching the same audience more than once.

19-6 Why has the Internet become a popular advertising medium?
Answer: The Internet offers a visual message, can use both audio and video, is interactive through rich media, and tends to reach younger consumers.

19-7 What factors must be considered when choosing among alternative media?
Answer: Choosing among alternative media depends on: knowing the media habits of the target audience; understanding the product's attributes (such as color), the competitive situation, and the need for a complicated message; and the cost, as measured by CPM.

19-8 Explain the difference between pretesting and posttesting advertising copy.
Answer: Pretests are conducted before ads are placed in any medium to determine whether they communicate the intended message or to select among alternative versions of the ad. Posttests are conducted after the ads are shown to the target audience to determine whether they accomplished their intended purpose.

19-9 What is the difference between aided and unaided recall posttests?
Answer: Aided and unaided recall posttests are conducted after the ads are shown to the target audience. Aided recall involves showing an ad to respondents who then are asked if their previous exposure to it was through reading, viewing, or listening. Aided recall is used to determine the percentage of those (1) who remember seeing a specific magazine ad (noted), (2) who saw or read any part of the ad identifying the product or brand (seen-associated), (3) who read any part of the ad's copy (read some), and (4) who read at least half of the ad (read most). Unaided recall involves specifically asking respondents if they remember an ad without any prompting to determine if they saw or heard its message.

19-10 What is the difference between a coupon and a deal?
Answer: Coupons and deals are consumer-oriented sales promotion tools used to support a company's advertising and personal selling. A coupon usually offers a discounted price to encourage trial. A deal is a short-term price reduction used to increase trial among potential customers or to retaliate against a competitor's actions.

19-11 Which sales promotion tool is most common for new products?
Answer: A product sample (or sampling) is a consumer-oriented sales promotion tool that is given to consumers through the use of a trial-size package, which is generally smaller than the regular size.

19-12 Which trade promotion approach focuses on maintaining or increasing inventory levels?
Answer: Allowances and discounts encourage increased purchases by intermediaries to maintain or increase inventory levels in the channel of distribution.

19-13 What is a news release?

Answer: A news release is a publicity tool that consists of an announcement regarding changes in the company or the product line to inform the media of an idea for a story.

19-14 What is the difference between government regulation and self-regulation?

Answer: Government regulation involves laws or other controls that are set by an agency of local, state, or federal government and restrict some promotion activities. The Federal Trade Commission (FTC) issues guidelines to protect consumers from misleading promotions. Self-regulation involves imposing standards and ethical guidelines for the promotional activities of advertising agencies, trade associations, and marketing organizations that reflect the values of society.

FOCUSING ON KEY TERMS

advertising p. 513
consumer-oriented sales promotions p. 533
cooperative advertising p. 539
cost per thousand (CPM) p. 522
frequency p. 522
full-service agency p. 531
gross rating points (GRPs) p. 522
infomercials p. 525
in-house agencies p. 532
institutional advertisements p. 514
limited-service agencies p. 532
mobile marketing p. 528
posttests p. 532
pretests p. 531
product advertisements p. 513
product placement p. 537
publicity tools p. 540
rating p. 522
reach p. 522
trade-oriented sales promotions p. 538

APPLYING MARKETING KNOWLEDGE

1 How does competitive product advertising differ from competitive institutional advertising?

2 Suppose you are the advertising manager for a new line of children's fragrances. Which form of media would you use for this new product?

3 You have recently been promoted to be director of advertising for the Timkin Tool Company. In your first meeting with Mr. Timkin, he says, "Advertising is a waste! We've been advertising for six months now and sales haven't increased. Tell me why we should continue." Give your answer to Mr. Timkin.

4 A large life insurance company has decided to switch from using a strong fear appeal to a humorous approach. What are the strengths and weaknesses of such a change in message strategy?

5 Some national advertisers have found that they can have more impact with their advertising by running a large number of ads for a period and then running no ads at all for a period. Why might such a flighting schedule be more effective than a continuous schedule?

6 Which medium in the table to the right has the lowest cost per thousand (CPM)?

Medium	Cost of Ad	Audience Size
TV show	$5,000	25,000
Magazine	2,200	6,000
Newspaper	4,800	7,200
FM radio	420	1,600

7 Each year, managers at Bausch and Lomb evaluate the many advertising media alternatives available to them as they develop their advertising program for contact lenses. What advantages and disadvantages of each alternative should they consider? Which media would you recommend to them?

8 What are two advantages and two disadvantages of the advertising posttests described in the chapter?

9 Federated Banks is interested in consumer-oriented sales promotions that would encourage senior citizens to direct deposit their Social Security checks with the bank. Evaluate the sales promotion options, and recommend two of them to the bank.

10 How can public relations be used by Firestone and Ford following investigations into complaints about tire failures?

11 Describe a self-regulation guideline you believe would improve the value of (*a*) an existing form of promotion and (*b*) a new promotional practice.

BUILDING YOUR MARKETING PLAN

To augment your promotion strategy from Chapter 18:

1 Use Figure 19–3 to select the advertising media you will include in your plan by analyzing how combinations of media (e.g., television and Internet advertising, radio and directory advertising) can complement each other.

2 Use Figure 19–6 to select your consumer-oriented sales promotion activities.

3 Specify which trade-oriented sales promotions and public relations tools you will use.

VIDEO CASE 19 Fallon Worldwide: Creating a Competitive Advantage with Creativity

"We're an advertising agency for companies who want to outsmart the competition, not outspend them," explains Andy Rhode, director of media at Fallon Worldwide. "People think about Fallon as a creative agency, and for us that's just how we get to success," he adds. In fact, Fallon's Web page proclaims, "We believe that creativity is the last legal means to an unfair advantage"!

VIDEO 19-5
Fallon Video Case
kerin.tv/15e/v19-6

THE COMPANY

Fallon Worldwide was founded by Pat Fallon and four other partners who wanted to challenge the prevailing practices in the advertising industry. According to Fallon, "our aim was to build a culture of respect, transparency, optimism, honesty, fun, resilience and generosity and by so doing, give ourselves a competitive advantage." The culture created a unique community of advertising professionals and led to a philosophy they called "family as a business model," says Rhode. The approach was an immediate success as the agency attracted national clients such as *The Wall Street Journal*, Ralston Purina, Lee Jeans, Timex, and *Rolling Stone* magazine. Fallon went on to win the Agency of the Year award from *Advertising Age* magazine—three times!

The focus on creativity influences all aspects of the agency. "We've always positioned ourselves as a creative idea-led agency, and I think that informs all of our disciplines," says Rhode. "We think about creative creatively, and we also think about strategy creatively," he explains. Fallon has offices in Minneapolis, New York, and London. Each office utilizes a straightforward structure. According to Rhode, "we have a creative department that is copywriters, we have a production department that truly produces a lot of what we make, we have a media department composed of media planners and buyers, we have a strategy department where the research really lives, and then we have an operations arm that's finance, accounting, and billing,"

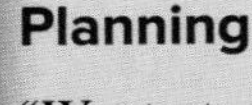

Source: Fallon Worldwide

Today Fallon is owned by a holding company called Publicis Group, which also owns Leo Burnett, Saatchi & Saatchi, Marcel, Starcom, Spark, Digitas, and several other agencies. "The value of a holding company like Publicis is the technology they are able to bring, and the scale in terms of research," says Rhode. "For global pitches, there is also the size we are able to tap into, so we certainly look at Publicis as a big advantage for us," he adds.

DEVELOPING AN ADVERTISING CAMPAIGN AT FALLON

Consumers who simply see an online video or a print ad or an endorsement from an influencer typically don't understand the many hours of work that went into an advertising campaign. At Fallon, the sequence of activities generally includes three steps: planning, implementation, and evaluation.

Planning

"We start with the planning department, and from there we engage creative, we engage account people, we engage production, and we just start working," says Jordan Hoffarber, group account director at Fallon. "Every campaign is usually rooted in some sort of human truth and that human truth has to come out of research, so research plays a big role," she adds. In fact, research is essential to understanding the customer journey and how advertising might influence prepurchase, purchase, and postpurchase activities. The planning process also involves engaging the client to ensure a mutual understanding of the campaign objectives.

Account managers are responsible for coordinating the planning activities. "As an account manager you are responsible for leading our client's business and leading our internal creative business. That means that we are not just about client service, but we're about business leadership. What are the objectives? How are we going to achieve those objectives? What are the budget parameters? And then how do we get the campaign made and out into the world? Account managers lead that process and touch every single part of that process," explains Hoffarber.

The research, strategy, and objectives help the creative team create the messaging. "As creatives it's our job to decide what is most interesting or compelling, and how we deliver that nugget of truth about a brand or a product," says Charlie Wolff, creative director at Fallon. The creative department consists of copywriters, art directors, and technologists. According to Wolff, "art directors are typically considered to be more conceptual, copywriters are ultimately responsible for the words, and technologists enlighten us to all the things that transcend words and pictures."

Implementation

The creative team also works with the agency's media planners and buyers to select and schedule the media to deliver the message to the target audience. "We like to be able to work hand-in-hand with media," says Wolff. "Especially with the way that people consume media today, it is always best when media is brought in as soon as possible in the process," he adds. Media include many alternatives such as TV, print, social, and events. While all advertising competes with messaging from other brands, social media messages have a unique challenge. "Your competitors on social are no longer your competitors in your category," explains Wolff, "Your competitors are everything in someone's social feed, it's whatever's happening in the political landscape, a friend's baby, or any other thing that is happening in the news."

Evaluation

The agency and its client want to know if a campaign is accomplishing its objectives. According to Hoffarber, "Every campaign is supposed to drive results, and results at the end of the day should be sales. However, there are a lot of other metrics that we measure, things like click-through rates, and awareness, and shareability" (how many times a message was shared with friends). Evaluation of the various measures of results allows Fallon to work with its clients to fine-tune messaging and media selection for the campaign.

DEVELOPING THE ARBY'S "WE HAVE THE MEATS" CAMPAIGN

Arby's executives came to Fallon with a simple question: What is Arby's reason for existing? Research indicated that Arby's was best known for its roast beef sandwich. However, the emphasis on roast beef was also limiting the number of new customers. Fallon called this "the roast beef riddle." "How often is somebody in the mood for a roast beef sandwich?" says Charlie Wolff, "Not very often."

So, the campaign development process began with a brief description of their challenge: change the positioning of Arby's from a place for just roast beef to a place where everybody can find something to eat. The general objective of the campaign was to expand consumer interest from a single product, roast beef, to all the other proteins that were available in Arby's sandwiches. With that as a starting point, the research, strategy, and creative teams began a discussion that led to many ideas on a massive whiteboard. Charlie Wolff explains the process: "In the case of Arby's, deciding on the specific message was a collaborative thing. We were sitting in a conference room and we would talk about each of the ideas on the board. Then we put stickers on the ones we liked and asked, 'Why do we like this?' and 'Why does this feel right?'" At the end of the process the team selected the tagline "We Have the Meats"!

The creative and media teams then invited the Arby's executive chef to Fallon. He set up in the Fallon kitchen with the different types of proteins and started slicing the meat. Rhode observes, "That's interesting to see in its whole form because it makes me trust that the food you're making is legitimate." As a result the Fallon team decided to kick off the "We Have the Meats" campaign with a television ad showing a man in a chef's coat slicing the meats available in Arby's sandwiches. "We focused on their product," says Rhode, "and I think it found a really special tone of voice that was funny without being a joke."

The assessment phase of the Arby's campaign is ongoing. Different types of sandwiches and sandwich names are tested in separate markets. In addition, promotions such as Arby's offer of a "One-day $6 trip to Hawaii" to eat Arby's sandwiches supplement the "We Have the Meats" campaign. Arby's and Fallon also monitor daily sales reports, which indicate the campaign is a huge success!

Source: Arby's IP Holder, LLC

THE FUTURE OF ADVERTISING AT FALLON

How will Fallon continue its success? There are many possibilities, but it's clear that the advertising industry is evolving and Fallon is ready for the changes. "Media is ever-changing, and that's why I got into it," says Tiffany Luong, digital media supervisor at Fallon. Of course traditional media such as TV and print still have an important role, while many new digital options are becoming more popular and creating new experiences for consumers. "What we're doing here is creatively thinking about how to tap into those new experiences when it's right for the brand, but also look at the old ways of how we've done things and creatively work in old channels," explains Luong.

The changes are not just in technology and media; consumers are changing also. "It's my job to know what excites people. It's my job to know what they are passionate about, why they're passionate about it, and how to really interact with them in a way that is helpful to a client," says Luong. "The way people work is ever changing, and the way we interact with each other is constantly changing. So that's why I'm excited to have the job I have now," Luong continues. "I want to be on the leading edge of where it will go!"

The future of advertising is going to be dynamic and exciting and likely to change our culture. According to Luong, "I think that's the beauty of what advertising can do. It can show you something within society that you didn't know, but at the same time it can create something within yourself that you didn't know!"[79]

Questions

1 What is Fallon's philosophy regarding its business model and culture?

2 Describe the steps Fallon uses to develop a campaign for a client.

3 What factors contributed to the success of the Arby's campaign?

4 What skills and interests will help future advertising professionals?

Chapter Notes

1. Shasha Deng, Chee-Wee Tan, Weijun Wang, and Yu Pan, "Smart Generation System of Personalized Advertising Copy and Its Application to Advertising Practice and Research," *Journal of Advertising*, August 2019, pp. 356–65; George P. Slefo, "The Ins and Outs of 1:1," *Ad Age*, April 29, 2019, p. 9; Charles Taylor, "Addressable TV Is Creating New Advertising Capabilities . . . and They Are Not Going Away," www.forbes.com, March 18, 2019; Charles Taylor, "Over the Top, Connected, Programmatic and Addressable Television! What Does It All Mean? Definitions and a Call for Research," *International Journal of Advertising*, May 20, 2019, pp. 343–44; Katherine Hays, "Advertising Trends You Should Consider in 2019," www.entrepreneur.com, January 17, 2019; Ted Korte, "Over the Top and Through AI to Big Data's House We Go," *TvEurope*, May 2019; Kelby Clark, "Addressable TV: How Advertising Is Evolving with Television," www.viacom.com, March 14, 2019; and Erik J. Martin, "How Virtual and Augmented Reality Ads Improve Consumer Engagement," www.econtentmag.com, May–June 2017, pp. 4–8.
2. Karen V. Fernandez and Dennis L. Rosen, "The Effectiveness of Information and Color in Yellow Pages Advertising," *Journal of Advertising*, Summer 2000, p. 61; and David A. Aaker and Donald Norris, "Characteristics of TV Commercials Perceived as Informative," *Journal of Advertising Research* 22, no. 2 (April–May 1982), pp. 61–70.
3. Larry D. Compeau and Dhruv Grewal, "Comparative Price Advertising: An Integrative Review," *Journal of Public Policy & Marketing*, Fall 1998, pp. 257–73; and William Wilkie and Paul W. Farris, "Comparison Advertising: Problems and Potentials," *Journal of Marketing*, October 1975, pp. 7–15.
4. Chingching Chang, "The Relative Effectiveness of Comparative and Noncomparative Advertising: Evidence for Gender Differences in Information-Processing Strategies," *Journal of Advertising*, Spring 2007, p. 21; Jerry Gotlieb and Dan Sarel, "The Influence of Type of Advertisement, Price, and Source Credibility on Perceived Quality," *Journal of the Academy of Marketing Science*, Summer 1992, pp. 253–60; and Cornelia Pechmann and David Stewart, "The Effects of Comparative Advertising on Attention, Memory, and Purchase Intentions," *Journal of Consumer Research*, September 1990, pp. 180–92.
5. Kathy L. O'Malley, Jeffrey J. Bailey, Chong Leng Tan, and Carl S. Bozman, "Effects of Varying Web-Based Advertising-Substantiation Information on Attribute Beliefs and Perceived Product Quality," *Academy of Marketing Studies Journal*, 2007, p. 19; Bruce Buchanan and Doron Goldman, "Us vs. Them: The Minefield of Comparative Ads," *Harvard Business Review*, May–June 1989, pp. 38–50; Dorothy Cohen, "The FTC's Advertising Substantiation Program," *Journal of Marketing*, Winter 1980, pp. 26–35; and Michael Etgar and Stephen A. Goodwin, "Planning for Comparative Advertising Requires Special Attention," *Journal of Advertising* 8, no. 1 (Winter 1979), pp. 26–32.
6. Henkel Corporation, "70 Years of Dial," accessed June 19, 2019, https://www.dialsoap.com/about.
7. David W. Schumann, Jan M. Hathcote, and Susan West, "Corporate Advertising in America: A Review of Published Studies on Use, Measurement, and Effectiveness," *Journal of Advertising*, September 1991, p. 35; Lewis C. Winters, "Does It Pay to Advertise in Hostile Audiences with Corporate Advertising?" *Journal of Advertising Research*, June–July 1988, pp. 11–18; and Robert Selwitz, "The Selling of an Image," *Madison Avenue*, February 1985, pp. 61–69.
8. Patty Odell, "Mountain Dew Bets 40 Percent of Budget on Reaching Gamers," *Promotional Marketing*, April 30, 2019, p. 2; Lucy Handley, "Dwayne Johnson Just Dropped His Latest Under Armour Ad Campaign for Project Rock," www.cnbc.com, March 21, 2019; Kaitlyn Frey, "Lindsey Vonn Is the New Ambassador for Under Armour's Project Rock," www.people.com, March 5, 2019; and Lucy Britner, "PepsiCo Goes Mobile with Latest Global Mountain Dew Campaign," *Aroq-justdrinks.com*, January 14, 2017.
9. Ira Teinowitz, "Self-Regulation Urged to Prevent Bias in Ad Buying," *Advertising Age*, January 18, 1999, p. 4.
10. "The Association of Magazine Media Announces the 2019 Kelly Awards Winners," press release, MPA, www.magazine.org, February 5, 2019; and the Advertising Research Foundation website, https://thearf.org/submit/learn-about-arf-original-research/, accessed June 2, 2019.
11. "Snickers 'You're Not You When You're Hungry': The Best Global Campaign Ever?" www.thebrandgym.com, December 15, 2018; and Amit Joshi and Dominique M. Hanssens, "The Direct and Indirect Effects of Advertising Spending on Firm Value," *Journal of Marketing*, January 2010, pp. 20–33.

12. Brian Braiker, "Super Bowl Ad Review: Yards to Go before We Sleep," *Ad Age*, February 4, 2019, pp. 20–27; Lucy Handley, "Super Bowl Draws Lowest TV Audience in More Than a Decade," www.cnbc.com, February 5, 2019; Erik Brady, "NFL Commercial Wins USA TODAY's Ad Meter with Tackle-Filled Celebration in 'The 100-Year Game'," www.usatoday.com, February 4, 2019; "Super Bowl 2019 Data," www.marketingcharts.com, February 20, 2019; and Jeanine Poggi, "Is the Super Bowl Worth the Price? For These Advertisers, It Might Be," *Advertising Age*, February 9, 2015, p. 8.
13. See the Super Bowl Commercials website at www.superbowlcommercials.org and the *USA Today* Ad Meter website at http://admeter.usatoday.com/.
14. "Colgate Smart Electronic Toothbrush E1," www.mmaglobal.com; Christopher Null, "Review: Colgate Smart Electronic Toothbrush E1," www.wired.com, February 5, 2018; and "U.S. Market Leaders by Category," Marketing Fact Pack 2019, *Advertising Age*, December 17, 2018, p. 12.
15. Bennett Bennett, "How Allstate's Mayhem Brought Carnage and Humor to Insurance Marketing," www.thedrum.com, October 30, 2018; and Sarah De Meulenaer, Patrick De Pelsmacker, and Nathalie Dens, "Have No Fear: How Individuals Differing in Uncertainty Avoidance, Anxiety, and Chance Belief Process Health Risk Messages," *Journal of Advertising* 44, no. 2 (2015), pp. 114–25.
16. Martin Eisend, "Gender Roles," *Journal of Advertising*, January 2019, pp. 72–80; Sarah Young, "H&M Launches Gender Neutral Clothing with Cult Brand Eytys," www.independent.co.uk, January 23, 2019; Jacob Hornik, Chezy Ofir, and Matti Rachamim, "Advertising Appeals, Moderators, and Impact on Persuasion," *Journal of Advertising Research*, September 2017, pp. 305–18; Doug Lloyd, "Does Sex Still Sell in 2016?" *campaignlive.com*, September 9, 2016; and Kristina Monllos, "Brands Are Throwing Out Gender Norms to Reflect a More Fluid World," *adweek.com*, October 17, 2016.
17. Rupal Parekh, "With Strong Work for Walmart and Geico, Martin Agency Is Creating a New Specialty: Making Marketers Recession-Proof," *Advertising Age*, January 19, 2009, p. 30; and Louis Llovio, "Geico Gecko's Viral Videos," *Richmond Times Dispatch*, March 28, 2009, p. B-9.
18. Thomas W. Cline and James J. Kellaris, "The Influence of Humor Strength and Humor-Message Relatedness on Ad Memorability: A Dual Process Model," *Journal of Advertising*, Spring 2007, p. 55; Yong Zhang and George M. Zinkham, "Responses to Humorous Ads," *Journal of Advertising*, Winter 2006, p. 113; and Yih Hwai Lee and Elison Ai Ching Lim, "What's Funny and What's Not: The Moderating Role of Cultural Orientation in Ad Humor," *Journal of Advertising*, Summer 2008, p. 71.
19. E. J. Schultz, "Agency of the Year," *Advertising Age*, January 23, 2017, p. 6; Gabriel Beltrone, "The World's Top 10 Most Innovative Companies in Advertising," *Adweek*, February 13, 2014; and Anomaly website, www.anomaly.com, accessed June 12, 2017; Wieden Kennedy, https://www.wk.com.
20. Arpita Agnihotri and Saurabh Bhattacharya, "The Relative Effectiveness of Endorsers," *Journal of Advertising Research*, September 2019, pp. 357–69; "The 10 Most Valuable Celebrity Endorsers," www.azbigmedia.com, December 4, 2018; Ericka Franklin, "Celine Named New Face of L'Oréal Paris," www.hollywoodreporter.com, April 2, 2019; Jennifer Edson Escalas and James R. Bettman, "Connecting with Celebrities: How Consumers Appropriate Celebrity Meanings for a Sense of Belonging," *Journal of Advertising* 46, no. 2 (2017), pp. 297–308; and Judith Anne Garretson Folse, Richard G. Netemeyer, and Scot Burton, "Spokescharacters," *Journal of Advertising*, Spring 2012, pp. 17–32.
21. "Celebrities and the Art of High-Risk Marketing," *Postmedia Breaking News*, April 25, 2013; Chris Isidore, "Lance Armstrong: How He'll Make Money Now," *CNN Wire*, January 16, 2013; Francois A. Carrillat, Alain D'Astous, and Josianne Lazure, "For Better, for Worse? What to Do When Celebrity Endorsements Go Bad," *Journal of Advertising Research*, March 2013, pp. 15–30; and Chris Isidore, "Tiger Woods No Longer Top-Paid Athlete," *CNNMoney.com*, July 17, 2012.
22. D. Simone Kovacs, "Everything You Need to Know about Video Production Costs," *blog.storyhunter.com*, April 12, 2018; and Nikki Gilliland, "Four Examples of Brands Using an Episodic Content Marketing Strategy," *Econsultancy.com*, June 23, 2016.
23. "Zenith's 2019 U.S. Media and Marketing-Services Spending Forecast," Marketing Fact Pack 2019, *Advertising Age*, December 17, 2018, p. 14.
24. Vicki R. Lane, "The Impact of Ad Repetition and Ad Content on Consumer Perceptions of Incongruent Extensions," *Journal of Marketing*, April 2000, pp. 80–91.
25. "Out-of-Home Viewing Is Helping Boost Linear TV Viewership Amid 24/7 News Cycle," *Insights*, Nielsen website, www.nielsen.com, May 1, 2019; and "Nielsen Estimates 119.9 Million TV Homes in the U.S. for the 2018–2019 TV Season," *Insights*, Nielsen website, www.nielsen.com, September 7, 2018.
26. Andrew Lipsman, "How Amazon Will Revolutionize the Future of Television Advertising," *Journal of Advertising Research*, September 2019, pp. 259–62; "The Nielsen Total Audience Report: Q3 2018," The Nielsen Company, March 19, 2019; Will Greenwald, "8K Wasn't the Only Buzzworthy TV Tech at CES 2019," *PC Magazine*, February, 2019; and J. C. Lupis, "The State of Traditional TV," *marketingcharts.com*, April 24, 2017.
27. "Cost for a 30-Second Commercial," *Marketing Fact Pack: 2019*, December 17, 2018, pp. 18–19; Yongick Jeong, "The Impact of the Length of Preceding and Succeeding Ads on Television Advertising Effectiveness," *Journal of Marketing Communications* 23, no. 4 (2017), pp. 385–99; "How Many Minutes of Commercials Are Shown in an Average TV Hour?" *tvweek.com*, May 13, 2014; Kate Newstead and Jenni Romaniuk, "Cost per Second: The Relative Effectiveness of 15- and 30-Second Television Advertisements," *Journal of Advertising Research*, 2009, pp. 68–76.
28. "Industry Data," The Internet & Television Association, www.ncta.com, June 4, 2019; Andy Stout, "Dynamic Ad Insertion Embraces Scale, www.ibc.org, February 27, 2019; and Joanna Mullally, "Today's TV Requires Advanced Advertising," *comcasttechnologysolutions.com*, February 12, 2015.
29. "Infomercial Rankings," www.jwgreensheet.com, May 24, 2019; Lia Sestric, "The Most Profitable 'As Seen on TV' Products of All Time," www.gobankingrates.com, September 28, 2018; and "10 Best-Selling Infomercial Products," *Gizmodo*, May 1, 2013.
30. "Broadcast Station Totals," News, Federal Communications Commission, April 2, 2019; and "Radio's Year-Round Reach" and "Radio Weekly Reach," *Why Radio Fact Sheet*, Radio Advertising Bureau, March 2019.
31. "Top-Rated Hours," in *State of the Media: Audio Today*, February 2016, Nielsen, p. 10.
32. *Magazine Media Factbook 2018/2019* (New York: The Association of Magazine Media), p. 107; "April and May Brought Us 20 New Titles," Launch Monitor, mrmagazine.com, June 4, 2019; "Print Magazine Revival: What to Expect for 2019," www.lasvegascolor.com, October 25, 2018; Steve Smith, "Magazines Learn a New Language," *Media Industry Newsletter*, February 6, 2017, p. 2; and Rebecca Clancy, "*Auto Trader* Print Edition to Stop as Focus Shifts to Digital," *The Telegraph*, May 7, 2013.
33. "U.S. Print Magazines Launches by Category," *Magazine Media Factbook 2016/17*, The Association of Magazine Media, 2016; and "Magazines Mean Engagement," *Magazine Media Factbook 2012/13* (New York: The Association of Magazine Media), p. 14.
34. "Total Circulation: Consumer Magazines," Research and Data, Alliance for Audited Media, June 30, 2016; "Defunct or Suspended Magazines," The Association of Magazine Media, http://www.magazine.org/insights-resources/researchpublications/trends-data/magazine-industry-facts-data/publishing-trends.
35. "General Advertising Rate Card," *The Wall Street Journal*, January 1, 2019; "Media Kit," *USA Today*, June 13, 2017; and "About Us," *Metro* website, http://www.metro.us, June 4, 2019.
36. "Newspapers Fact Sheet," Pew Research Center, www.journalism.org, June 13, 2018; Jaclyn Peiser, "New York Times Tops 4 Million Mark in Total Subscribers," *The New York Times*, November 1, 2018; "Newspapers in the United States," MarketLine Industry Profile, *MarketLine*, March 2017; and Max Willens, "The State of News Subscriptions in 5 Charts," www.digiday.com, October 31, 2017.

37. "Zenith's 2019 U.S. Media and Marketing-Services Spending Forecast," *Marketing Fact Pack*, December 17, 2018, p. 14; Isabella Andersen, "Yellow Pages vs. Digital Marketing: Is the Phone Book Really Dead?" www.socialmediatoday.com, February 8, 2018; Anne Kadet, "Yellow Pages Hang On in Digital Age," *The Wall Street Journal*, June 17, 2016; and see National Yellow Pages Consumer Choice & Opt-Out Site, https://www.yellowpagesoptout.com/homepage.

38. "Share of Search Queries Handled by Leading U.S. Search Engine Providers," *statista.com*, January 2019; Peter Pal Zubcsek, Zsolt Katona, and Miklos Sarvary, "Predicting Mobile Advertising Response Using Consumer Colocation Networks," *Journal of Marketing*, July 2017, pp. 109–26; Jan H. Schumann, Florian von Wangenheim, and Nicole Groene, "Targeted Online Advertising: Using Reciprocity Appeals to Increase Acceptance among Users of Free Web Services," *Journal of Marketing*, January 2014, pp. 59–75; "10 Ways to Improve the Banner Ad Design and Enhance the Click Through Rate," *Tech and Techie*, May 6, 2013; "'Banner Blindness' Now a Major Marketing Concern," *Bulldog Reporter's Daily Dog*, March 29, 2013; Thales Teixeira, "The New Science of Viral Ads," *Harvard Business Review*, March 2012, pp. 25–27; and the definition of mobile marketing is adapted from the Mobile Marketing Association definition, see http://www.mmaglobal.com/news/mma-updates-definition-mobile-marketing, November 17, 2009.

39. See "Guidelines, Standards & Best Practices: Measurement," at the Interactive Advertising Bureau website, https://www.iab.com/guidelines/?topic=measurement; "IAB Measurement Guidelines," Interactive Advertising Bureau, December 20, 2016; and "Online Measurement," Nielsen website, https://www.nielsen.com/us/en/solutions/measurement/online.html.

40. Shoshana Wodinsky, "Ad Fraud Is Down, But Don't Get Too Comfortable," www.adweek.com, May 1, 2019; Thomas Fox-Brewster, "Google Just Killed What Might Be the Biggest Android Ad Fraud Ever," *Forbes.com*, May 26, 2017; Keith Weed, "We Must Beat Fraud and Demand 100% Viewability," *Marketingweek.com*, March 2017, p. 22; Tim Bourgeois, "Techniques for Combating Digital Ad Fraud, Transparency, and Viewability," *EContent*, May–June 2017, p. 23; Keith Weed, "Three Things All Marketers Can Do to Eliminate Ad Fraud," *Marketing Week*, September 22, 2016, p. 13; and Christopher Heine, "What Counts as an Online Ad View? A Standard Is Nearing, but the Fight's Not Over," *Adweek*, February 27, 2015, p. 1.

41. George R. Franke and Charles R. Taylor, "Public Perceptions of Billboards: A Meta-Analysis," *Journal of Advertising* 46, no.3 (2017), pp. 395–410.

42. "OOH Media Formats," Outdoor Advertising Association of America website, *oaaa.org*, June 13, 2017; "New Study: Out of Home Advertising Delivers $5.97 in Revenue ROI," press release, Outdoor Advertising Association of America, May 16, 2017; Bradley Cooper, "Digital Signage Future Trends Report Sets the Stage for 2017," *DigitalSignageToday.com*, December 9, 2016; and Lessing E. Gold, "Mobile Billboard Advertising and the 14th Amendment," *Security & the Law*, April 2017, p. 48.

43. "Clear Channel Outdoor Holdings Releases 'Out-of-Home Advertising and the Retail Industry' Report," *Professional Services Close-Up*, January 25, 2011; Andrew Hampp, "What's New with Outdoor Ads, and What's This Digital Out-of-Home I Keep Hearing About?" *Advertising Age*, September 27, 2010, p. 48; "The Year Ahead for . . . Outdoor," *Campaign*, January 9, 2009, p. 28; Andrew Hampp, "Digital Out of Home, That's Those Pixilated Billboards, Right?" *Advertising Age*, March 30, 2009; Andrew Hampp, "Out of Home That Stood Out," *Advertising Age*, December 15, 2008, p. 22; and Daniel W. Baack, Rick T. Wilson, and Brian D. Till, "Creativity and Memory Effects," *Journal of Advertising*, Winter 2008, p. 85.

44. Sehoon Park and Minhi Hahn, "Pulsing in a Discrete Model of Advertising Competition," *Journal of Marketing Research*, November 1991, pp. 397–405.

45. Peggy Masterson, "The Wearout Phenomenon," *Marketing Research*, Fall 1999, pp. 27–31; and Lawrence D. Gibson, "What Can One TV Exposure Do?" *Journal of Advertising Research*, March–April 1996, pp. 9–18.

46. Rik Pieters, Michel Wedel, and Rajeev Batra, "The Stopping Power of Advertising: Measure and Effects of Visual Complexity," *Journal of Marketing*, September 2010, pp. 48–60; Rob Norton, "How Uninformative Advertising Tells Consumers Quite a Bit," *Fortune*, December 26, 1994, p. 37; and "Professor Claims Corporations Waste Billions on Advertising," *Marketing News*, July 6, 1992, p. 5.

47. *Trends in Agency Compensation*, 17th Edition, Association of National Advertisers, 2017; Patty Odell, "Advertisers Simplify Agency Compensation Models," *Promotional Marketing*, May 23, 2017, p. 1; and "A New Value for Agency Compensation," *rthree.com*, June 2, 2015.

48. The discussion of posttesting is based on William F. Arens, Michael F. Weigold, and Christian Arens, *Contemporary Advertising*, 12th ed. (New York: McGraw-Hill Irwin, 2009), pp. 228–30.

49. "ROI Metric Available in MRI Starch Syndicated," Mediamark Research & Intelligence, www.mediamark.com, accessed April 23, 2009.

50. Debora V. Thompson and Prashant Malaviya, "Consumer-Generated Ads: Does Awareness of Advertising Co-Creation Help or Hurt Persuasion?" *Journal of Marketing*, May 2013, pp. 33–47; David A. Aaker and Douglas M. Stayman, "Measuring Audience Perceptions of Commercials and Relating Them to Ad Impact," *Journal of Advertising Research* 30 (August–September 1990), pp. 7–17; and Ernest Dichter, "A Psychological View of Advertising Effectiveness," *Marketing Management* 1, no. 3 (1992), pp. 60–62.

51. David Krugel, "Television Advertising Effectiveness and Research Innovation," *Journal of Consumer Marketing*, Summer 1988, pp. 43–51; and Laurence N. Gold, "The Evolution of Television Advertising Sales Measurement: Past, Present, and Future," *Journal of Advertising Research*, June–July 1988, pp. 19–24.

52. "Zenith's 2019 U.S. Media and Marketing Services Spending Forecast," *Marketing Fact Pack 2019*, December 17, 2018, p. 14.

53. Fernando de Oliveira Santini, Valter Afonso Vieira, Claudio Hoffmann Sampaio, and Marcelo Gattermann Perin, "Meta-Analysis of the Long- and Short-Term Effects of Sales Promotions on Consumer Behavior," *Journal of Promotion Management* 22, no. 3 (2016), pp. 425–42; Magid M. Abraham and Leonard M. Lodish, "Getting the Most Out of Advertising and Promotion," *Harvard Business Review*, May–June 1990, pp. 50–60; Steven W. Hartley and James Cross, "How Sales Promotion Can Work for and against You," *Journal of Consumer Marketing*, Summer 1988, pp. 35–42; and Robert D. Buzzell, John A. Quelch, and Walter J. Salmon, "The Costly Bargain of Trade Promotion," *Harvard Business Review*, March–April 1990, pp. 141–49.

54. "2K19 Valassis Coupon Intelligence Report," Valassis, March 2019; "Coupon Savings Report," Valassis, 2016; "NCH Year-End 2018 Coupon Facts" NCH Marketing Services, 2019; "Coupon Use Hits 40-Year Low," *couponsinthenews.com*, February 1, 2016; Charlie Brown, "Marketers' Coupon Strategies Deliver Increased Consumer Savings in 2014 While Staying within Budgets," *Annual Topline View CPG Coupon Facts*, NCH Marketing Services, 2015; "2012 NCH Consumer Survey: Demographic Profile of Coupon Users," NCH Marketing Services, 2012; Claudia Buck, "Coupon Industry: No Scissors Required," *The State Journal-Register*, February 24, 2013, p. 40; and "How Mobile Coupons Are Driving an Explosion in Mobile Commerce," *The Business Insider*, May 22, 2013.

55. Kapil Bawa and Robert W. Shoemaker, "Analyzing Incremental Sales from a Direct-Mail Coupon Promotion," *Journal of Marketing*, July 1998, pp. 66–78.

56. Robert A. Strang, "Sales Promotion—Fast Growth, Faulty Management," *Harvard Business Review* 54 (July–August 1976), pp. 115–24; Ronald W. Ward and James E. Davis, "Coupon Redemption," *Journal of Advertising Research* 18 (August 1978), pp. 51–58. Similar results on favorable mail-distributed coupons were reported by Alvin Schwartz, "The Influence of Media Characteristics on Coupon Redemption," *Journal of Marketing* 30 (January 1966), pp. 41–46.

57. "What Is Coupon Fraud?" The Coupon Information Corporation, http://www.couponinformationcenter.com, accessed June 14, 2017; Josh Elledge, "Coupon Fraud Hurts Us All," *Grand Rapids Press*, April 19,

2011, p. B1; and Amy Johannes, "Flying the Coup," *Promo*, July 1, 2008, p. 28.

58. FanBoy, "'Avengers: Endgame' Happy Meal Toys Arrive at McDonald's," www.laughingplace.com, April 23, 2019; "The Influence of Promotional Products on Consumer Behavior," Promotional Product Association International, November 2012; Amy Johannes, "Premium Connections," *Promo*, October 2008, p. 34; and Gerard P. Prendergast, Alex S. L. Tsang, and Derek T. Y. Poon, "Predicting Premium Proneness," *Journal of Advertising Research*, June 2008, p. 287.

59. Patty Odell, "Guess the New Flavor of Pringles Chips and You Could Win $10,000," www.today.com, May 14, 2019; and Patty Odell, "The Wonder Vault Surprises Contest Entrants," *Promotional Marketing*, June 6, 2017.

60. "Congratulations to Kathy of Alabama," HGTV Dream Home 2015, HGTV website, www.hgtv.com; "The Monopoly Game at McDonald's Returns Sept. 30," McDonald's website, http://news.mcdonalds.com/US/releases/The-MONOPOLY-Game-at-McDonald%E2%80%99s-Returns-Sept-30, September 14, 2014.

61. Tanya Dua, "Pepsi Is Putting Snapchat Barcodes on Millions of Soda Bottles," *digiday.com*, May 23, 2017; Kate Hogan, "Want a Ticket to the Oscars? People Can Hook You Up!" *people.com*, November 21, 2016; "Nissan Voice Sweepstakes 2015," *The Daily Jackpot, sweeps.thedailyjackpot.com*, December 18, 2014; and "Mars Chocolate North America Launches 5 Characters, 5 Cars Promotion," *Travel & Leisure Close-Up*, June 20, 2011.

62. Kate Taylor, "Taco Bell Is Giving Away Free Food on Tuesday," *Business Insider*, June 13, 2017; Elana Ashanti Jefferson, "Sample Hunters Offer Advice for Trying—Before You Buy," *Denver Post*, July 16, 2012, p. 3C; and Schuyler Velasco, "Ben & Jerry's Free Cone Day," *The Christian Science Monitor*, April 9, 2013.

63. "Starbucks to Enhance Industry-Leading Starbucks Rewards Loyalty Program," www.stories.starbucks.com, March 19, 2019; Tom Hoffman, "How Valuable Is a Loyalty Program?" *Customer Strategist*, Peppers & Rogers Group, April 1, 2015; and Jeff Berry, "The 2015 Colloquy Loyalty Census," *Colloquy*, February 2015.

64. Erin El Issa, "Chase Ultimate Rewards Program Review," *nerdwallet.com*, November 21, 2016; Richard Postrel and Kelly Hlavinka, "An Open Economy: The Evolution of Loyalty in the United States," *Colloquy*, September 2012, http://colloquy.com/white-view.asp?uid=38; and "Maritz Loyalty Marketing Survey Updates on Consumers' Top-Rated Loyalty Programs," *Entertainment Close-Up*, May 19, 2013.

65. David Haynes, "Whole Foods Goes Truly Digital with Signage at Seattle-Area 365 Store," *sixteen-nine.net*, September 15, 2016; and "Interactive Digital Signage Helps Shoppers Discover New Products," *screenmediadaily.com*, June 14, 2017.

66. Lucas Coll, "Save up to $950 with the Best Smartphone Deals Going on Now," www.digitaltrends.com, February 8, 2019; Nathalie Dens, Patrick De Pelsmacker, Marijke Wouters, and Nathalia Purnawirawan, "Do You Like What You Recognize?" *Journal of Advertising*, Fall 2012, pp. 35–53; "The Case for Rebates," *Chief Marketer*, July 1, 2011; and Marvin A. Jolson, Joshua L. Wiener, and Richard B. Rosecky, "Correlates of Rebate Proneness," *Journal of Advertising Research*, February–March 1987, pp. 33–43.

67. Fu Guo, Guoquan Ye, Liselot Hudders, Wei Lv, Mingming Li, and Vincent G. Duffy, "Product Placement in Mass Media: A Review and Bibliometric Analysis," *Journal of Advertising*, April 2019, pp. 215–31; Joe Mandese, "Product Placement Poised to Top $10 Billion," www.mediapost.com, June 13, 2018; "Product Placement in Movies," www.productplacementblog.com, June 6, 2019; Huan Chen and Ye Wang, "Product Placement in Top-Grossing Hollywood Movies: 2001–2012," *Journal of Promotion Management*, No. 6, 2016, pp. 835–52; Ekaterina V. Karniouchina, Can Uslay, and Grigori Erenburg, "Do Marketing Media Have Life Cycles? The Case of Product Placement in Movies," *Journal of Marketing*, May 2011, pp. 27–49; and Sophie C. Boerman, Eva A. van Reijmersdal, and Peter C. Neijens, "Using Eye Tracking to Understand the Effect of Brand Placement Disclosure Types in Television Programs," *Journal of Advertising* 44, no. 3 (2015), pp. 196–97.

68. Abe Sauer, "Announcing the 2016 Brandcameo Product Placement Awards," *brandchannel.com*, February 24, 2016; "*La La Land* Hits a High Note with Product Placement," *seesawmedia.co.uk*, January 31, 2017; Haiming Hang, "Brand-Placement Effectiveness and Competitive Interference in Entertainment Media," *Journal of Advertising Research*, July 2014, pp. 192–99; "Direct Selling Leader Amway Leverages Product Placement in the Video Gaming World," *India Retail News*, April 5, 2013; Stuart Elliott, "Expanding Line of Dunder Mifflin Products Shows Success in Reverse Product Placement," *The New York Times Blogs*, November 23, 2012; Karen Idelson, "Product Placements Don't Derail Nom Hopes," *Daily Variety*, June 1, 2011, p. A8; Andrew Hampp, "Why Viewers and Marketers Are Loving 'Modern Family,'" *Advertising Age*, April 18, 2011, p. 4; "Sky and Discovery Launch Digital Product Placement," *Broadcast*, May 17, 2011; and Amy Johannes, "Simpson Mania," *Promo*, November 1, 2008, p. 8.

69. This discussion is drawn particularly from John A. Quelch, *Trade Promotions by Grocery Manufacturers: A Management Perspective* (Cambridge, MA: Marketing Science Institute, August 1982).

70. Michael Chevalier and Ronald C. Curhan, "Retail Promotions as a Function of Trade Promotions: A Descriptive Analysis," *Sloan Management Review* 18 (Fall 1976), pp. 19–32.

71. G. A. Marken, "Firms Can Maintain Control over Creative Co-op Programs," *Marketing News*, September 28, 1992, pp. 7, 9.

72. Chris Matthews and Matthew Heimer, "The 5 Biggest Corporate Scandals of 2016," *fortune.com*, December 28, 2016; Christina Zdanowicz and Emanuella Grinberg, "Passenger Dragged Off Overbooked United Flight," *cnn.com*, April 11, 2017; Harlan E. Spotts, Marc G. Weinberger, and Michelle F. Weinberger, "How Publicity and Advertising Spending Affect Marketing and Company Performance," *Journal of Advertising Research*, December 2015, pp. 416–32; Kathleen Cleeren, Harald J. van Heerde, and Marnik G. Dekimpe, "Rising from the Ashes: How Brands and Categories Can Overcome Product-Harm Crises," *Journal of Marketing*, March 2013, pp. 58–77; "Carnival Cruises Tries to Dig Themselves Out of Another PR Crisis," *Bulldog Reporter's Daily Dog*, February 22, 2013; and Peter S. Goodman, "From Corporate Crises, a Handbook on Lost Love and Publicity: Missteps by Toyota, BP, and Goldman Show Trust Is Tough to Win Back," *The International Herald Tribune*, August 23, 2010, p. 1.

73. Irving Rein, Philip Kotler, and Martin Stoller, *High Visibility* (New York: Dodd, Mead, 1987); and Steven Colford, "Ross Perot: A Winner after All," *Advertising Age*, December 21, 1992, pp. 4, 18.

74. Michael Treacy and Fred Wiersema, "Customer Intimacy and Other Value Disciplines," *Harvard Business Review*, January–February 1993, pp. 84–93.

75. Gerry Khermouch and Tom Lowry, "The Future of Advertising," *BusinessWeek*, March 26, 2001, p. 139; and "Outlook 2001: Advertising," *Marketing News*, January 1, 2001, p. 10.

76. Betsy Spethmann, "McFallout," *Promo*, October 2001, pp. 31–38.

77. "Kid Stuff," *Promo*, January 1991, pp. 25, 42; Steven W. Colford, "Fine-Tuning Kids' TV," *Advertising Age*, February 11, 1991, p. 35; and Kate Fitzgerald, "Toys Star-Struck for Movie Tie-Ins," *Advertising Age*, February 18, 1991, pp. 3, 45.

78. Herbert J. Rotfeld, Avery M. Abernathy, and Patrick R. Parsons, "Self-Regulation and Television Advertising," *Journal of Advertising* 19, no. 4 (1990), pp. 18–26.

79. Fallon: This case was written by Steven Hartley and Roger Kerin. Sources: Interviews with Andy Rhode, Charlie Wolff, Jordan Hoffarber, and Tiffany Luong; Pat Fallon, "Fallon's Chairman on Getting Clients to Take Creative Risks," *Harvard Business Review*, October 2014, pp. 35–38; T. J. Stanley, "15,000 People Responded to Arby's Offer of a One-Day, $6 Trip to Hawaii," www.adweek.com, April 19, 2019; and information available on the company websites, www.fallon.com and www.publicisgroupe.com.

Chapter 20 Using Social Media and Mobile Marketing to Connect with Consumers

LEARNING OBJECTIVES

After reading this chapter you should be able to:

LO 20-1 Define social media and describe how they have transformed marketing communications.

LO 20-2 Identify the four most prominent social media and describe how brand managers integrate them into marketing actions.

LO 20-3 Describe the characteristics of a social media marketing program, including selecting social media and choosing social media content.

LO 20-4 Compare the performance measures of social media linked to costs (inputs) versus revenues (outputs).

LO 20-5 Identify the cause of the convergence of the real and digital worlds and how this will affect the future of social media.

Marketing's Fast Lane Is Filled with Connected Cars!

Smartphones have become an integral part of our personal and professional lives, and they bring us hundreds of "mobile moments" each day. These are the mobile marketing communications that smartphone users are exposed to through social media, messaging, or e-mail. Although marketers use the term *mobile* to refer to the portability of phones, the term is quickly taking on new meaning as connected cars–cars with Internet access–make "mobile" even more mobile!

Experts estimate that more than half of new cars will soon include connected car platforms, creating an era of smart transportation and intelligent mobility. These cars feature Cloud technology and provide communication, driver assistance, entertainment, and navigation capabilities. Ford, for example, offers Amazon Alexa in its connected vehicles, and Domino's Pizza is working with Chrysler and GM to offer its in-vehicle AnyWare pizza-ordering app. Mary Bara, chair and CEO of General Motors, observes that "the auto industry will change more in the next five to ten years than it has in the past 50."

The real-time benefits of connected vehicles allow drivers to avoid congested travel routes, time traffic lights, and exchange information with nearby vehicles and pedestrians. Restaurants, gas stations, and even the nearest Starbucks can send advertising customized to the vehicle and its occupants. Convenience stores are also getting involved. The convenience store channel is very attractive to busy millennials, who are focused on easy access and are eager to find a good deal. Almost one-half of convenience store retailers already use special advertising offers as they begin to sync with the connected car systems.

Advertising through the Internet has been growing dramatically and just recently became the largest medium, reaching $69 billion and exceeding TV advertising expenditures. While Internet advertising to desktops has been substantial, Internet advertising to mobile devices has been the primary area of growth. In fact, 61 percent of Internet advertising expenditures are now targeted at mobile devices. Phones, tablets, and cars have several channels through which ads can be received. First, social media channels such as Facebook and Twitter receive push notifications when the app has been set to receive messages. Second, e-mail continues to be the backbone of many mobile marketing campaigns. Finally, messaging apps such as WhatsApp, Talk, Facebook Messenger, WeChat, and Slack allow consumers to chat with company representatives, ask questions, and obtain personalized recommendations. These messaging options, when combined with Internet bots, are becoming a new form of shopping known as *conversational commerce*.

What can you expect in the future as connected cars and conversational commerce grow? A new, convenient, integrated path for the evolving customer journey. IBM, for example, recently created a partnership with BMW to provide a Cloud computing

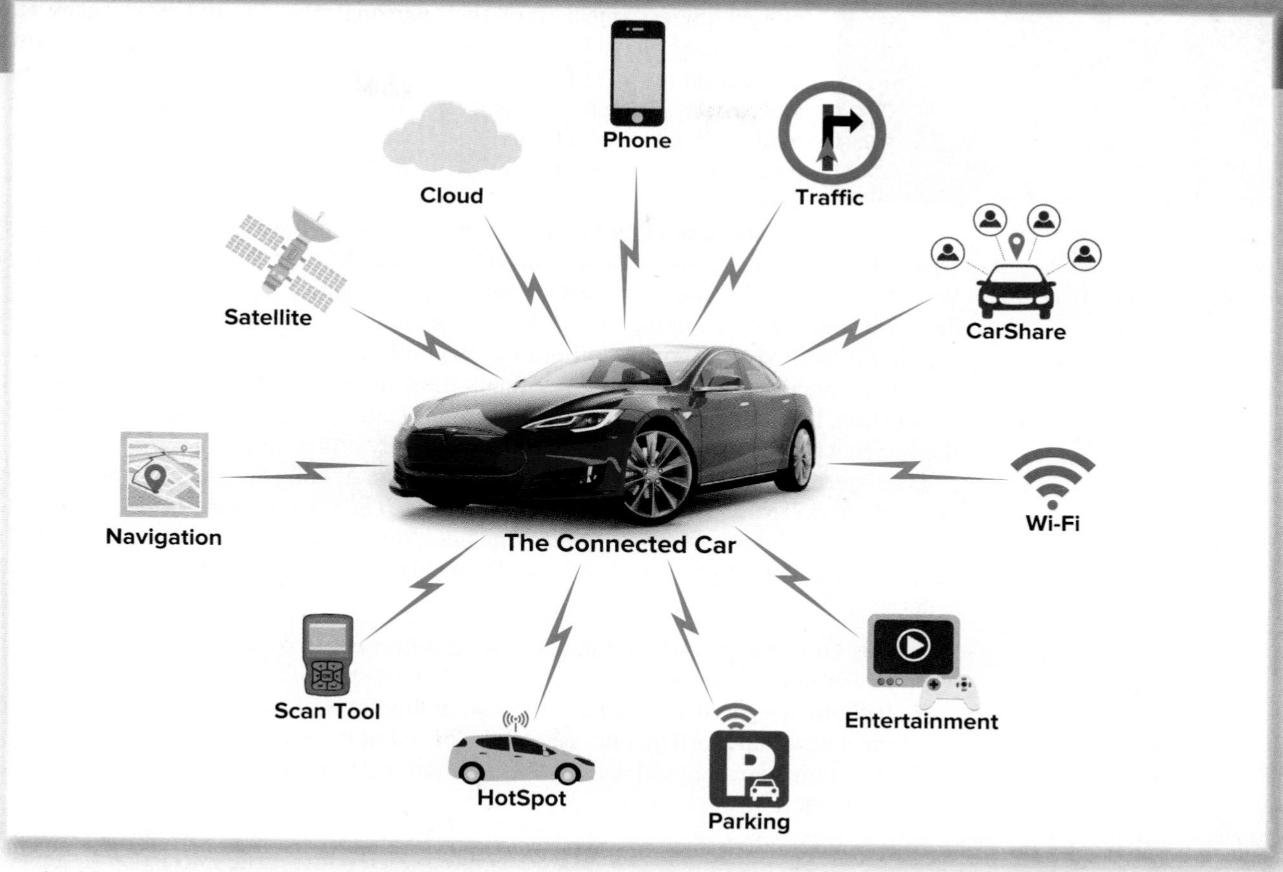

medvedsky.kz/Shutterstock

platform for 8.5 million connected vehicles. The service will allow consumers to interact with dealerships, auto insurers, repair shops, and many other businesses. Watch for other new offerings ranging from connected motorcycles, to autonomous cars, to "buy" buttons in messaging apps![1]

This chapter defines social media, describes four widely used social media, explains how organizations use them in developing marketing strategies, and considers where social media are headed in the future.

UNDERSTANDING SOCIAL MEDIA

LO 20-1
Define social media and describe how they have transformed marketing communications.

Defining *social media* is challenging, but it's necessary to help a brand or marketing manager select the right one. This section defines social media, classifies social media, and describes why and how social media have transformed marking communications.

What Are Social Media?

This section defines social media and classifies the countless social media available to assist marketing managers in choosing among them.

Defining Social Media Social media represent a unique blending of technology and social interaction to create a communal experience and personal value for users. **Social media**

The next-generation Web, Web 3.0, will be customized to each individual. Read the text to learn how!
Wright Studio/Shutterstock

are online media where users submit comments, photos, and videos—often accompanied by a feedback process to identify "popular" topics. Most social media involve a genuine online conversation among people about a subject of mutual interest, one built on their personal thoughts and experiences. However, other social media sites involve games and virtual worlds in which the online interaction includes playing a game, completing a quest, controlling an avatar, and so on. Companies also refer to social media as "consumer-generated media." A single social media site with millions of users interacting with each other, like Instagram, Facebook, Twitter, and LinkedIn, is referred to as a *social network*.

The term *social media* is sometimes used interchangeably with the terms *Web 2.0, Web 3.0,* and *user-generated content*—concepts that are the foundation of today's social media. Web 2.0 and Web 3.0 consist of technological functionalities that make possible today's high degree of interactivity among users. Web 2.0 includes functionalities that permit people to collaborate and share information online. Web 3.0, now in its application stages, includes additional functionalities that allow personalization and customization to each individual based on location, interests, and needs. It integrates new features such as Cloud computing, big data, the Internet of Things, security solutions, and privacy protection.

User-generated content (UGC) refers to any form of online media content that is publicly available and created by consumers or end users. The term *user-generated content* (also referred to as *consumer-generated content*) includes video, blogs, discussion forum posts, digital images, audio files, and related content. To qualify as UGC, content must satisfy three basic criteria:

1. It is published either on a publicly accessible website or on a social media site, so it is not simply an e-mail.
2. It shows a significant degree of original or creative effort, so it is more than simply posting a newspaper article on a personal blog without editing or comments.
3. It is consumer-generated by an individual outside of a professional or commercial organization.

Today, about 80 percent of the content appearing on social media is user-generated.[2]

Classifying Social Media Most of us would probably say that Instagram, Facebook, Twitter, LinkedIn, and YouTube are well-known social media. But marketing managers trying to reach potential customers need a system to classify the many specialized and diverse social media to select the best among them. One proposed classification system for marketers is based on two factors:[3]

1. *Media richness.* This involves the degree of acoustic, visual, and personal contact between two communication partners—face-to-face communications, say, being higher in media richness than telephone or e-mail communications. The higher the media richness and quality of presentation, the greater the social influence that communication partners have on each other's behavior.
2. *Self-disclosure.* In any type of social interaction, individuals want to make a positive impression to achieve a favorable image with others. This favorable image is affected by the degree of self-disclosure about a person's thoughts, feelings, likes, and dislikes—where greater self-disclosure is likely to increase one's influence on those reached.

How do marketing managers choose the best social media sites to reach their target markets? As a first step, the text describes how social media can be classified and how they differ from traditional media.
BigTunaOnline/Shutterstock

Figure 20–1 uses these two factors of media richness and self-disclosure to position a number of social media sites in two-dimensional space. For example, Wikipedia is a collaborative project that is low on both self-disclosure and media richness. LinkedIn, on the other hand, contains detailed career and résumé information for business networking and is high in self-disclosure but only moderate in media richness.

Marketing managers look carefully at the positioning of the social media shown in Figure 20–1 when selecting those to use in their plans. For example, LinkedIn, positioned in the Social Networking Sites segment in Figure 20–1, is a professional networking service

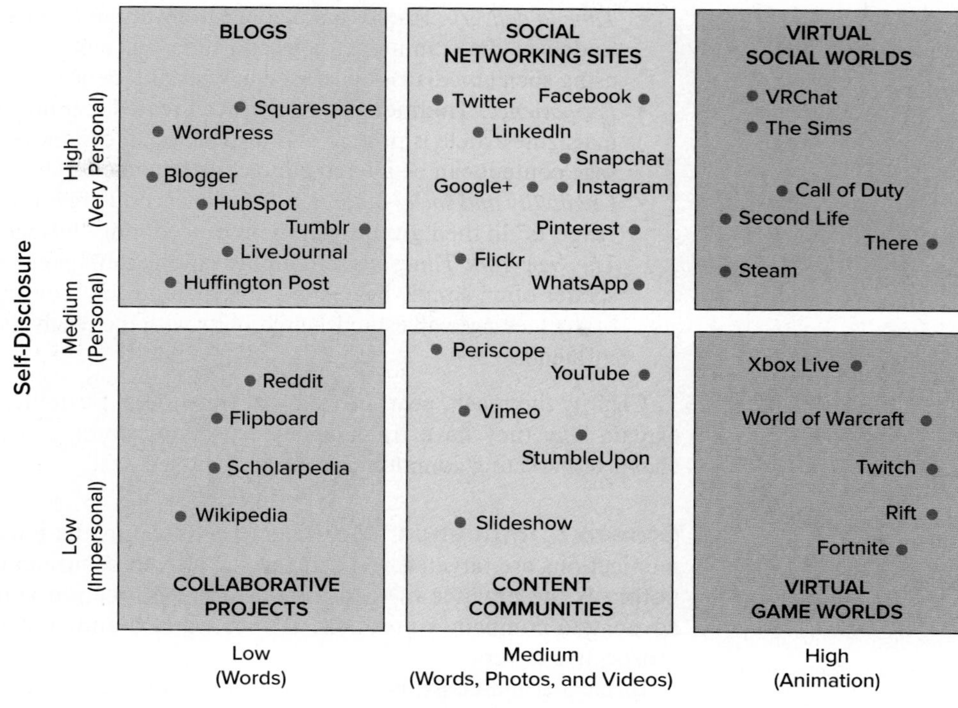

FIGURE 20–1 A sample of social media, classified by media richness and self-disclosure. Note that in moving from words to photos, videos, and animation, media richness increases. Also, in moving from very impersonal messages to highly personal ones, self-disclosure increases.

with some 610 million members in 200 countries. LinkedIn's customers include companies such as Citigroup, Microsoft, Chevron, Hewlett-Packard, and Volkswagen, which promote their companies' career opportunities to people with specific job titles, and individuals who are seeking a job or building a professional network.

Why and How Social Media Transformed Marketing Communications and Buying Behavior

Consumers receive information, news, and education from print (newspapers, magazines) and electronic (radio, television) media. These traditional media remain important elements in a company's marketing communications effort. Studies indicate that social media can complement and augment these traditional media when they are focused on brand-building, customer acquisition, and customer advocacy.

See the text for a comparison of social and traditional media.
McGraw-Hill Education

Comparing Social and Traditional Media A comparison of traditional and social media is necessary to understand why social media have transformed marketing communications. Important similarities and differences are described below:[4]

- *Ability to reach both large and niche audiences.* Both kinds of media can be designed to reach either a mass market or specialized segments.
- *Expense and access.* Messages and ads in traditional media like newspapers or television generally are expensive to produce and have restricted access by individuals. Also, traditional media are typically owned privately or by the government in some countries. In contrast, messages on social media are generally accessible everywhere, are available to anyone with a smartphone, a computer, or a tablet device, and can be produced cheaply.
- *Training and number of people involved.* Producing traditional media typically requires specialized skills and training and often involves teams of people. In contrast, sending messages on social media requires only limited skills, so practically anyone can post a message that includes words and images.

- *Time to delivery*. Traditional media can involve days or even months of continuing effort to deliver the communication, and time lags can be extensive. In contrast, individuals using social media can post virtually instantaneous content.
- *Permanence*. Traditional media, once created, cannot be altered. For example, once a magazine article is printed and distributed, it cannot be changed. But social media message content can be altered almost instantaneously by comments or editing.
- *Credibility and social authority*. Individuals and organizations can establish themselves as "experts" in their given field, thereby becoming "influencers" in that field. For example, *The New York Times* has credibility among newspaper media. But with social media, a sender often simply begins to participate in the "conversation," hoping that the quality of the message will establish credibility with the receivers, thereby enhancing the sender's influence.

Clearly, the reach, cost, investment, timeliness, flexibility, and influence of social media explain *why* they have transformed marketing communications. *How* social media have changed marketing communications is discussed next.

Kendall Jenner has more than 110 million Instagram followers. Read the text to learn how many followers she, her sisters, and mother likely have on social media.
Source: Kendall Jenner/Instagram

Growth of Influencer Marketing Social media have changed how marketing communications are targeted and spurred the growth of influencer marketing. **Influencer marketing** is the practice of focusing on the identification and recruitment of influencers to advocate a company's products, services, and brands rather than focusing exclusively on prospective buyers.

Influencer marketing is based on the concept of personal influence; namely, a consumer's purchases are often influenced by the views, opinions, or behavior of others (see Chapter 5). Influencer marketing applies this behavioral concept to social media in the presence of social networks and user-generated content. A perfect marriage!

The identification of influencers on social media is based, in large part, on the number of followers an influencer has on social networking sites such as Facebook, Instagram, and Twitter and content community sites such as YouTube. The number of followers, in turn, is often attributed to an influencer's *perceived* credibility, knowledgeability, authenticity, and reliability in providing relevant content to his or her audience. In short, social media influencers are trusted by their followers.

The recruitment of social media influencers involves partnering with individuals who are willing and able to effectively engage their followers with a product, service, or brand. These influencers are often compensated. They are paid outright, given free products or services, and reimbursed for their expenses in creating and posting content. For example, Johnson & Johnson pays some 100 influencers in North America for their baby product recommendations on Instagram, blog posts, and other Internet endorsements. The company also furnishes free samples to a similar number of parents prominent on social media.[5] It is estimated that 75 percent of large U.S. companies engage in influencer marketing and spend $1 billion on these initiatives.[6]

Social media influencers exist within specific categories. For example, the Kardashians (Kim, Kourtney, and Khloe) and Jenners (Kris, Kylie, and Kendall) are prominent influencers in the fashion, fitness, entertainment, beauty, and pop culture categories. Their combined worldwide social media followers likely exceed 500 million people. It should be no surprise that they routinely command over $100,000 for each company- or brand-sponsored post on Instagram. And Kylie Jenner makes over $1 million for each sponsored Instagram post.[7]

Emergence of Social Commerce and Social Shopping *Social commerce* was introduced in Chapter 17. Recall that social commerce involves the use of social media (notably Facebook, Instagram, Twitter, and

Pinterest) to browse and buy online without going to a company's website to conduct business. In essence, social commerce is the use of social networks in the context of e-commerce transactions. By one estimate, roughly $22 billion in annual retail sales are attributed to social commerce.[8]

Social commerce is different from social shopping. Social commerce focuses on the seller and purchase transactions. Social shopping focuses on the user or buyer shopping experience. **Social shopping** involves the use of social network services and websites by consumers to share their latest purchases, deals, coupons, product reviews, want lists, and other shopping finds with friends and contacts. The underlying idea behind social shopping is that individuals are influenced by their peers' purchases and recommendations, which can greatly influence purchase decisions. Research documents that persons identified as Generation Z and millennials are particularly active in social shopping. Their preferred social media are Instagram, Snapchat, and YouTube.[9]

LEARNING REVIEW

20-1. What are social media?

20-2. In classifying social media, what do we mean by (*a*) media richness and (*b*) self-disclosure?

20-3. Compare traditional media and social media in terms of time required to deliver the communication.

A LOOK AT FOUR PROMINENT SOCIAL MEDIA

LO 20-2
Identify the four most prominent social media and describe how brand managers integrate them into marketing actions.

Facebook, Twitter, LinkedIn, and YouTube are widely used options in the world of social media. So marketing managers need a special understanding of these four platforms as they integrate social media into their marketing strategies to supplement the traditional media they already use. This section briefly compares, defines, and explains each of these four major social media and shows how brand managers can use them. Because of its importance, Facebook merits more detailed coverage.

Comparing Prominent Social Media

Figure 20–2 on the next page compares four prominent social media (Facebook, Twitter, LinkedIn, and YouTube) from the point of view of a brand manager.[10] Facebook can increase brand exposure by enabling convenient user posting of links, photos, and videos. Twitter makes it easy to place brand messages and gain online customer support. While primarily a powerful network in helping users find jobs, LinkedIn has also found a niche in helping small businesses network to reach potential customers, as well as filling its traditional role of connecting job seekers and jobs. YouTube's videos make it especially useful in explaining a complex product.

Mark Zuckerberg is CEO of Facebook, a social network that connects more than 2.4 billion users.
Aytac Unal/Anadolu Agency/Getty Images

Facebook

Facebook is the first choice among people seeking to create and maintain online connections with others by using photos, videos, and short text entries. Facebook has also enhanced its capabilities with its purchases of Instagram (photo sharing), WhatsApp (messaging), and Oculus (virtual reality). Facebook is truly the 900-pound gorilla among all social media with these acquisitions.

BASIS OF COMPARISON	SOCIAL MEDIA facebook	twitter	LinkedIn	YouTube
Male-Female Breakdown	47% male, 53% female	66% male, 34% female	57% male, 43% female	62% male, 38% female
Brand Exposure	Powerful for gaining brand exposure through convenient user posting of links, photos, and videos.	Consistent placement of brand messages is easy with applications like Hootsuite and TweetCaster. Sponsored tweets promote brands.	Free opportunities exist, like Business Pages and LinkedIn Influencer posts. Paid Sponsored Updates provide added reach.	Powerful in gaining attention and explaining a complex product, and branding. Channels unite users on content and heighten viewership.
Customer Communication	Great for people who like your brand and want to share their opinions. Leads all social networks for this.	Twitter is powerful for gaining online customer support. Engaging one-on-one is simple and easy to track.	Half of those using social media for customer service use a LinkedIn Company Page while 40% do so with LinkedIn Groups.	YouTube gains user's ready attention in attracting customer support. Easy to allow responses to user comments and ratings.
Traffic to Website	Facebook is the traffic leader through rewording engaging content with better news feed placement. But its share of referred visits is falling.	Referral traffic from Twitter is growing faster than any other social network. Photos and videos make tweets even more clickable.	LinkedIn generates referrals—though less than many other social networks—but can be valuable for B2B and business development.	YouTube is an important source of traffic. Get traffic back to user's site by adding a hyperlink in the video description.

(Facebook logo): inbj/123RF; (Twitter logo): rvlsoft/Shutterstock; (LinkedIn logo): Artseen/Shutterstock; (YouTube logo): rvlsoft/Shutterstock

FIGURE 20-2
How brand managers can use four social media in developing their marketing strategies.

Facebook: An Overview **Facebook** is a website where users may create a personal profile, add other users as friends, and exchange comments, photos, videos, and "likes" with them. Facebook users today can keep friends and family updated on what they are thinking, doing, and feeling. In addition, users may chat with friends and create and join common-interest groups, and businesses can create Facebook Pages as a means of advertising and building relationships with customers. Facebook is open to anyone age 13 and older.

CEO Mark Zuckerberg and COO Sheryl Sandberg have managed Facebook through incredible growth. To understand the magnitude of the company, consider that Facebook:

- Grows by 8 people per second, or 7,246 people every 15 minutes.
- Processes 300 million photos, 5.7 billion likes, and 730 million comments each day.
- Has 90 percent of its users living outside the United States and Canada.
- Generates revenue from more than 2.5 million advertisers.

Half of all Facebook users have more than 200 friends in their network, and 18- to 29-year-olds have 300![11]

Facebook in a Brand Manager's Strategy Facebook Business Pages help brand managers generate awareness for their product, service, or brand within Facebook. They allow brand managers to promote their business on Facebook, separate from their private and personal profiles. Done well, these are magnets for feedback. Additionally, Facebook Business Page information is generally public and cataloged by search engines so brand managers can identify influencers within their customer base.

To generate new customers and increase traffic to their Facebook Pages, brand managers use paid ads and sponsored stories within the Facebook advertising platform. An advantage of these Facebook ads is that the content can migrate into Facebook conversations among friends–to the delight of advertisers.

The marketing challenge for an organization's Facebook Page is to post content that will generate the best response. Brand managers, however, have observed that some people do not want sponsored content on their feeds. To engage fans in a conversation on Facebook, research suggests the following guidelines:[12]

- *Be creative* in using links, photos, and videos.
- *Make it familiar, but with a twist.* Focus content strategy on imagery and messaging that is familiar to fans–punctuated with something unique. Aflac uses its Aflac Duck–the well-known "spokes-duck"–to treat fans to Aflac Duck commercials, virtual Duck gifts, and supplemental insurance offers.
- *Keep it fresh.* Redbox uses frequent posts to keep fans informed about its latest film releases.
- *Learn users' passions and let them guide content.* Taco Bell polls users to see which menu item they'd like featured in the following week's menu profile photo.

Gaining meaningful user loyalty enables a company to target promotional offers to its online fans, who typically represent about 5 percent of their customer base. Data indicate that users who "like" a brand are more likely to make a purchase because they are loyal customers. Other indicators, such as views and clicks, are also important measures of engagement.[13]

Mobile Marketing at Facebook Keeping billions of users happy is a tall order–even for Facebook. As the most common method of accessing Facebook shifts from computers to mobile smartphones, the company is continually making changes to its mobile capabilities. As CEO Mark Zuckerberg explains: "Moving from just being a single service to a family of world-class apps to help people share in different ways is the biggest shift in our strategy to connect people in many years."[14] Some recent examples include:

Facebook's dating feature is part of a family of apps designed to help connect people.
Justin Sullivan/Getty Images

- *Click-Gap metric.* As part of its effort to prevent misinformation, propaganda, hate speech, and fake news from being spread on its platform, Facebook has introduced a new metric called Click-Gap. The metric compares the popularity of links that appear in Facebook posts with the rest of the Web. If there is a disparity, Facebook will limit the post's reach.[15]
- *New privacy protections.* In response to increasing concern about privacy and the use of personal data, Facebook has several new privacy protections. For example, users are now asked to review how Facebook uses their data and are given the option to opt out of targeting based on personal profile information. In addition, Facebook will now limit the ads that can be displayed to teenagers and offer rewards for reports of data abuses.[16]
- *Dating feature.* Facebook has introduced a new feature called "Dating" that will compete with dating apps such as Tinder and Bumble. The new service allows Facebook users to create separate profiles from their main Facebook accounts and also uses a dedicated inbox that allows only text-based messages when chatting for the first time.[17]
- *E-mail marketing for Facebook app.* In a program called Custom Audiences, Facebook helps advertisers target customers as they scroll through Facebook's mobile app by matching e-mail addresses provided by the advertisers with the e-mail addresses it has for many of its users. Facebook also identifies "look-alikes," people who are similar to an advertiser's customers, for targeted ads. Currently, more than half of Facebook's sales revenues come from mobile devices.[18]

What other changes will Facebook make as part of its mobile marketing strategy? Perhaps only Mark Zuckerberg knows!

Twitter

Now that "tweets" have become part of our everyday language, it's apparent that Twitter has entered the mainstream of American life. Worldwide, Twitter now has over 321 million active monthly users who post 500 million tweets per day.[19]

Wendy's used Twitter to engage a customer in a conversation that involved millions of people and broke a world record!

(Photo): Ken Wolter/Shutterstock; (Cell): Source: Twitter

Twitter: An Overview **Twitter** enables users to send and receive *tweets*, messages up to 280 characters long. Twitter is based on the principle of "followers." So when you choose to follow another Twitter user, that user's tweets appear in reverse chronological order on your Twitter page. Twitter also offers a live video feature by clicking on the camera icon when you see the "What's happening?" message.

Because of its short message length, the ease of posting, receiving, and forwarding ("retweeting") tweets, and its convenience on a smartphone, Twitter can be a good form of communication for consumers and brands. Wendy's uses Twitter as an important tool in its social media program to communicate brand messages to its followers. As part of Wendy's social media outreach, the brand is active on Twitter with daily messages, retweets, and replies.

Teenager Carter Wilkerson, for example, asked Wendy's how many retweets it would take to receive free chicken nuggets for a year. Wendy's response led to more than 3 million retweets, a new world record for the most retweeted tweet (breaking the previous record held by Ellen DeGeneres), and a year's supply of nuggets!

Beyond sending and receiving messages, Wendy's relies on Twitter as a listening device. Wendy's social media team monitors mentions of Wendy's on Twitter to see what people are saying. If there are product concerns, Wendy's can reach out to consumers to make sure their concerns are quickly addressed.

Twitter in a Brand Manager's Strategy With the 280-character limit on tweets, brand managers cannot expect extensive comments on their brands. But they can use social media management tools like TweetDeck or Hootsuite to see what Twitter users are saying—good and bad—about both their own brands and competitive ones. They can then respond to the negative comments and retweet the positive ones. Managers can also use interactive video and live video features on Twitter to get users engaged with their brands.

Brand managers can utilize several strategies for listening to and interacting with current and potential consumers using Twitter. For example, they can:[20]

- Generate brand buzz by developing an official Twitter profile, recruiting followers, and showing photos and videos of their products.
- Follow the Twitter profiles that mention their product and monitor what is being said, responding to user criticisms to develop happier customers.
- Tweet and video stream on topics that provide information of value to their consumers.

As with Facebook, Twitter can actively engage customers if done creatively. To further enhance this engagement, Twitter recently announced that it is creating a 24-hour streaming video channel with partners such as MLB, the NFL, and Viacom. According to CEO Jack Dorsey, Twitter wants "to be the first place that anyone hears of anything going on that matters to them."[21]

LinkedIn

Unlike Facebook and Twitter, the LinkedIn site's main purpose is professional networking and job searching.

LinkedIn: An Overview **LinkedIn** is a business-oriented website that lets users post their professional profiles to connect to a network of businesspeople. These businesspeople are also called *connections*. This social network has more than 500 million registered members who conduct 6 billion professionally oriented searches annually. Because of its popularity, LinkedIn

LinkedIn Profile Checklist

College students can use the LinkedIn Profile Checklist to build an attention-getting profile page.
Source: Linkedin

has postings for more than 10 million jobs and data on more than 9 million companies. LinkedIn's international presence, too, is staggering—it is used in over 200 countries and 24 languages. LinkedIn is now owned by Microsoft.

LinkedIn in a Brand Manager's Strategy Marketing managers can use LinkedIn to promote their brand in subtle ways. This is done mainly for business-to-business (B2B) image building and networking with other professionals. Using LinkedIn Groups, managers can join groups of professionals in the same industry or with similar interests to share ideas, content, and job information and to demonstrate the organization's capabilities in particular areas.

Among small business owners, 41 percent see LinkedIn as potentially beneficial to their company—more than twice that for Facebook, Twitter, or YouTube.[22] LinkedIn recently streamlined its research process for finding qualified employees so that an employer can type its needs into the LinkedIn "search box" and receive a summary that includes people, jobs, groups, and companies. In addition, it has added a Job Matching feature to help recruiters find better matches for open positions. Brand managers also use LinkedIn for business development to identify sales leads and locate vendors.[23] Sales representatives often use LinkedIn to see the profiles of purchasing personnel or managers with whom they are meeting.

LinkedIn in a College Senior's Job Search Of growing importance, LinkedIn has over 40 million students and recent college graduates as members. College career centers and the LinkedIn student link (http://university.linkedin.com/linkedin-for-students) give key ideas for building an attention-getting LinkedIn profile for students in search of jobs:[24]

- Write an informative, short, memorable profile headline.
- Include a clear, simple, recent photo of just yourself. According to experts, your profile is more likely to be viewed if you have a photo.
- Create a professional summary—concisely giving your education, qualifications, goals, relevant work experience, and extracurricular activities.
- Fill the Skills & Expertise section with keywords and phrases the recruiters use in their searches.
- Include recommendations from people who know you well—supervisors, colleagues, instructors, and advisors.
- Set your LinkedIn profile to "public" and create a unique URL (www.linkedin.com/in/JohnSmith) that you also include in your résumé.

Finally, in your LinkedIn profile avoid these 10 most overused buzzwords: responsible, strategic, creative, effective, patient, expert, organizational, driven, innovative, and analytical.[25]

YouTube

The ability of YouTube to reach its audience stretches the imagination. Think about this: YouTube's almost 2 billion users (1) make 4 billion views per day, (2) upload 300 hours of video each minute, and (3) generate 50 percent of YouTube's traffic from mobile devices.[26]

YouTube: An Overview **YouTube** is a video-sharing website, owned by Google, in which users can upload, view, and comment on videos. YouTube uses streaming video technology to display user-generated video content that includes movie and TV clips, music videos, and original videos developed by amateurs. While most of the content is uploaded by amateurs, many companies offer material on the site through a YouTube channel.

YouTube redesigns its home page periodically to provide a more organized structure to steer users to "channels," rather than simply encouraging them to browse like in the past. Recently, YouTube also redesigned the format for its YouTube channels. These channels serve as

Marketing Matters — Technology

Vloggers Are the New Power Players, Worldwide!

The online advertising world is changing. Recent studies indicate that nearly half of all Web video ads are never seen. To further complicate the situation, it is increasingly difficult to hold the attention of the millennial and Gen Z audiences. One possible answer is that YouTube has stopped supporting 30-second unskippable ads, in favor of shorter, 6-second ads. It is video bloggers, or *vloggers*, however, who may be the secret to successful online advertising!

Marketers have observed that vloggers are becoming the online version of traditional celebrities. Zoe 'Zoella' Sugg, for example, started posting videos about cosmetics as a teenager and today has 12 million subscribers to her YouTube channel. Her audience attracts a variety of advertisers and brand collaborations, particularly since the audience is very young. Similarly, Felix Kjellberg, known online as PewDiePie, began a YouTube channel about video games in college and today has 95 million subscribers. His videos have attracted more than 14 billion views, and he was recently named one of *Time* magazine's most influential people of the year.

The influence of vloggers has become so substantial that *Forbes* magazine has published a list of the 30 Top Power Players on social media. The list includes influencers in three categories—beauty, fitness, and home—who are ranked on audience size, propensity for virality, and engagement. The members of the list are from eight different countries and between them they have 250 million social media followers from around the globe!

Watch for your favorite brands to partner with influential vloggers like these sometime soon!

home pages for organizations and individuals and allow them to upload their own videos, as well as post and share videos created by others.

What are the most-watched videos on YouTube? They are Luis Fonsi's "Despacito," Ed Sheeran's "Shape of You," and Wiz Khalifa's "See You Again" with 5.9 billion, 4.1 billion, and 4.0 billion views, respectively. All of these artists have a YouTube channel that aggregates their music and other videos they have uploaded for fans and other users to view.[27]

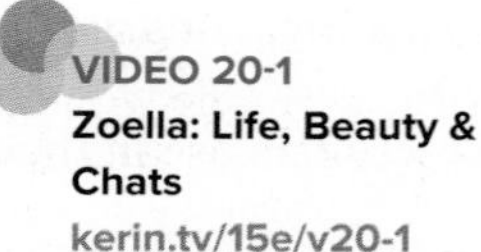
VIDEO 20-1
Zoella: Life, Beauty & Chats
kerin.tv/15e/v20-1

YouTube in a Brand Manager's Strategy YouTube offers a great opportunity for a brand manager to produce and show a video that explains the benefits of a complex product. Since YouTube is owned by Google, it incorporates a search engine, so users interested in a specific topic can find it easily. In terms of cost advantages, while a brand manager must pay the cost of creating a video, launching a new channel on YouTube is free. YouTube also offers a program to help small businesses create video ads and buy and manage keywords for their video ads on the website. For insight regarding new ways online video is becoming part of marketing strategies, see the Marketing Matters box.[28]

OK Go is an American rock band that has used YouTube to win fans, licensees, and sponsors for its music. OK Go's YouTube music videos–what it calls "treadmill videos"–are the foundation for its success. One of its first music videos, "This Too Shall Pass," won several awards and has accumulated 59 million views. One of its recent music videos, "Obsession," had 15 million views in about 16 months. OK Go is an example of musicians using YouTube to achieve music success, a route far different than trying to attract attention from a music label company.[29]

For how OK Go has used "Obsession" (15 million views) on YouTube to gain fans, licensees, live shows, and sponsors, see the text.
Source: OK Go

Guidelines for marketing and promoting a brand using YouTube videos include:[30]

- Exploit visual aspects of your message, perhaps sacrificing product messages to tell a more entertaining story.
- Create a branded channel rich in keywords to improve the odds of the video showing up in user searches. Select a viral title.
- Target viewers by using YouTube's insights and analytics research to reveal the number of views, the number of visits to your website, and what keywords are driving user visits.

Of special interest to brand managers: YouTube recently started offering advertisers the option of targeting YouTube ads based on people's Google search histories. In the past, targeting was based on the videos people had watched.[31]

LEARNING REVIEW

20-4. How is user-generated content presented by someone using Facebook?

20-5. What are some ways brand managers use Facebook to converse with a brand's fans? How does Facebook facilitate mobile marketing activities?

20-6. How can brand managers use YouTube to converse with customers? What is a new form of mobile marketing using online video?

SOCIAL MEDIA MARKETING PROGRAMS AND CUSTOMER ENGAGEMENT

LO 20-3
Describe the characteristics of a social media marketing program, including selecting social media and choosing social media content.

Experienced marketing managers understand how to use traditional media to generate sales for their brand. Some are successful, and others are less so. But many of these same managers will admit that understanding social media dynamics is a challenge and they are not often sure how to use them most effectively for their brands.

A **social media marketing program** is that portion of a company's integrated marketing communications effort designed to create and deliver online media content that attracts viewer attention and encourages readers to share it with their social network. Its purpose is to reach "active consumers" who will become "influentials" and be "delighted" with a brand and its message. These consumers will then become "evangelists" who will communicate with their online friends and the company about the joys of using a brand. Social media marketing program success depends on whether it creates and sustains **customer engagement**—the degree and depth of brand-focused interactions a customer chooses to perform online with his or her social network. The Applying Marketing Metrics box on the next page shows how different social media measure customer engagement.[32]

This section looks at (1) how to select social media, (2) the kind of social media content that is created, and (3) how to measure the results of social media programs. The section closes by describing Carmex's "Shot Seen 'Round the World" promotion. The ultimate dream for a brand manager, this Carmex-LeBronJames.com promotion went viral on YouTube!

Selecting Social Media

In using social media, a brand manager tries to select and use one or more of the options from the hundreds that exist. This often entails assessing (1) the characteristics of the website's visitors and (2) the number of users or unique visitors to the website.

Audience Data Available for Social Media Both marketing research organizations and the social media themselves provide user profile data for the social media to help brand managers choose among them. As presented earlier, the top row of Figure 20-2 shows a recent profile of the U.S. male-female audience breakdown for four major social media. As shown in the figure, Facebook users are 53 percent female and 47 percent male, while LinkedIn users are 43 percent female and 57 percent male, important differences to brand managers allocating promotion budgets.

In addition, research shows that there is substantial overlap between users of the major social media. For example, 90 percent of LinkedIn users also use Facebook and 94 percent use YouTube. Roughly three-quarters of both Twitter (73 percent) and Snapchat (77 percent) users also use Instagram.[33] This research helps to refine promotional efforts and reduce redundancy.

Applying **Marketing Metrics**

Measuring Your Customer Engagement Rate on Social Media

As a newly appointed product manager for the *FYRST* brand of athleisure men's and women's fashion apparel, you are responsible for the brand's social media program. You are interested in the customer engagement with the *FYRST* brand compared across different social media platforms and within the fashion content domain to assess the brand's social media performance.

Your Challenge

The brand's social media team reported and tracked metrics supplied by Facebook, Twitter, and Instagram. But external benchmarks to gauge the effectiveness of different social media for the brand were missing. Fortunately, published benchmark data to compare customer engagement rates are available for different social media platforms and content. The customer engagement rate (CER) measures a brand's posted content interaction with its social media followers. The customer engagement rate is calculated relative to the number of followers a company or brand has on social media. Therefore, the rate for both small and large companies and brands can be compared equally. The customer engagement rate variables and the calculations for Twitter, Facebook, and Instagram are shown below.

$$\text{Twitter customer engagement rate} = \frac{\#\text{Likes} + \#\text{Replies} + \#\text{Retweets}}{\#\text{Total impressions}} \times 100$$

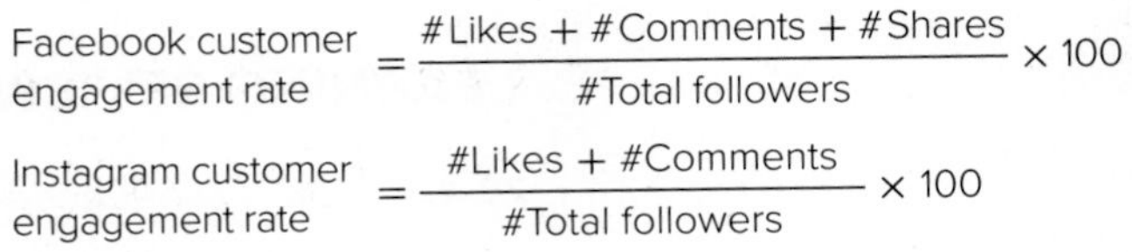

$$\text{Facebook customer engagement rate} = \frac{\#\text{Likes} + \#\text{Comments} + \#\text{Shares}}{\#\text{Total followers}} \times 100$$

$$\text{Instagram customer engagement rate} = \frac{\#\text{Likes} + \#\text{Comments}}{\#\text{Total followers}} \times 100$$

Your Findings

Based on published social media and fashion content benchmarks, a "good" CER for Twitter content posts overall is 0.10 percent, for Facebook overall, 1.0 percent, and Instagram overall, 3.0 percent. A "good" CER for fashion content is 0.12 percent for Twitter, 0.13 percent for Facebook, and 1.4 percent for Instagram. The CER for *FYRST* fashion content was 0.10 percent for Twitter, 0.13 percent for Facebook, and 1.2 percent for Instagram

Your Action

A review of the content appearing on Facebook and Instagram is needed. Instagram's customer engagement rate for the *FYRST* brand, in particular, is less than that seen on fashion content posts on this platform. (Note that Facebook's customer engagement rate for fashion content and the *FYRST* brand is the same.) The social media team needs to examine whether or not this one-year snapshot is consistent over time or is a one-time result.

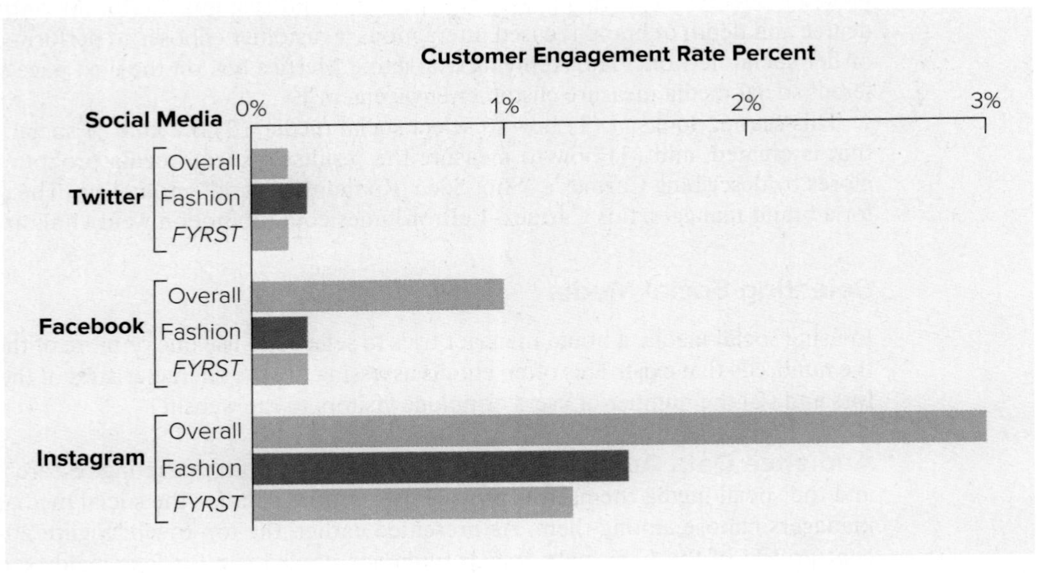

Recent Activity on the Four Social Media Figure 20–3 compares the number of users and the monthly market share of visits for Facebook, Twitter, LinkedIn, and YouTube websites. Number of users is a measure of the size of the audience. Market share is an indication of the use of the website relative to the other sites. In terms of the number of users,

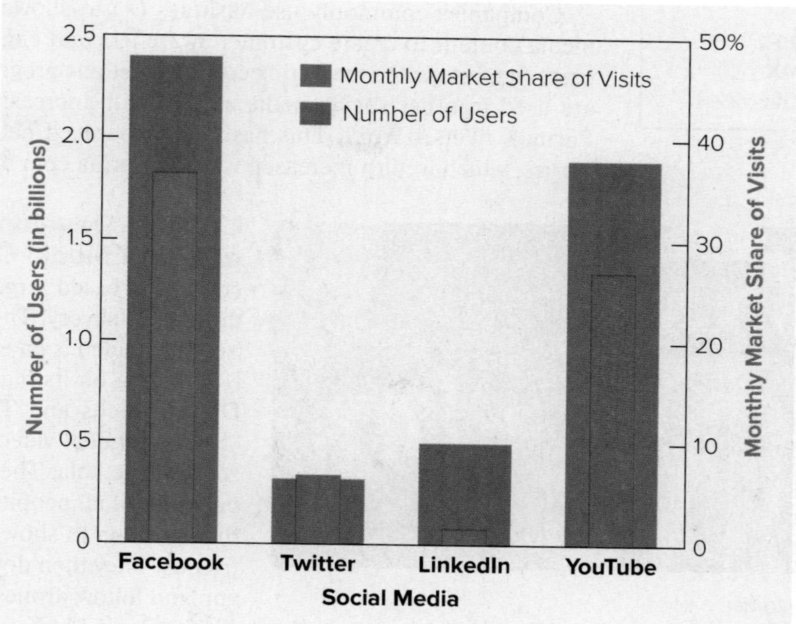

FIGURE 20-3 The number of users and monthly market share of visits for four social media sites: Facebook, Twitter, LinkedIn, and YouTube.

Facebook and YouTube have 1.9 billion or more users, although Facebook's market share is more than 35 percent larger. Similarly, Twitter and LinkedIn have between 320 and 500 million users but Twitter has a higher market share, indicating more frequent use.[34]

Selecting Social Media Content

Marketers have a variety of social media content options from which to choose. The choice of social media content is first dependent on the content's intended purpose. Is it intended to be promotional, entertaining, or educational or to serve another purpose? Second, how will social media content complement the overall integrated marketing communications effort in creating and sustaining customer engagement? Third, how will the social media content be best conveyed in different social media? Finally, content choice is also based on the characteristics of the one or more market segments a marketer wants to reach with social media. This starts with demographic characteristics like geographic region, gender, age range, and education. Additional factors like relationship status and user interests are often included as well.

Different Types of Social Media Content **Social media content** is the information and experience that are directed toward an end user or audience. Social media marketing experts typically identify seven types of social media content used by companies to create and sustain customer engagement.[35] Elements of each are described below.

- *Educational content.* This content includes infographics, FAQs, tips and tricks, and how-to posts.
- *Inspirational content.* This content includes quotes, amazing facts or trivia, personal stories of triumph, and inspirational images.
- *Interactive content.* This content includes quizzes and games, polls, virtual reality, and contests.
- *Connecting content.* This content includes stories, behind-the-scenes images, and posts that thank fans or ask for opinions and feedback.
- *Promotional content.* This content includes promotions, coupons, discounts, customer testimonials, and webinars.
- *Newsworthy content.* This content includes the latest developments regarding a brand and topical coverage about an industry, product, or service.
- *Entertaining content.* This content includes puzzles, viral videos, jokes, and comics.

VIDEO 20-2
Pepsi MAX
kerin.tv/15e/v20-2

Companies commonly use hashtags (#) to showcase product, brand, and service social media content to create customer awareness and engagement and user-generated content as part of an integrated marketing communications program. Hashtags originated on Twitter, but are used in other social media as well with increasing frequency. A successful example is Purina's #PetsAtWork. This hashtag encouraged people to post workplace pet photos and stories, which in turn increased visits to Purina.com by 34 percent.

In choosing to use a social media campaign like this Pepsi MAX video on YouTube, brand managers were able to make its diet beverage relevant to a younger target audience.
Source: PepsiCo

Creative Development, Execution, and Delivery of Social Media Content The quality of social media content is based largely on its creative development, execution, and delivery. The success of PepsiCo's "Friend Finder" YouTube video is an example.

Building on its highly successful "Uncle Drew" and "Test Drive" videos and TV ads, PepsiCo used its entertaining "Friend Finder" video to promote its Pepsi MAX beverage—a zero-calorie cola. The video begins with the observation that one-third of all people lose their friends at music festivals and then goes on to show people at a festival who have lost their friends. They then download the Pepsi MAX "Friend Finder" app and follow drones to find their friends!

"Friend Finder" was a huge hit for Pepsi MAX, with more than 5 million views on YouTube. Even better, the video reinforced the brand's global "Live For Now" tagline emphasized in its integrated marketing communications effort. As a product in the mature stage of its product life cycle, Pepsi MAX used its entertaining social media content to make its diet beverage relevant to a younger target audience. The video captured the viewer's attention by replacing some product messaging with entertainment. The Pepsi MAX success is consistent with recent studies that suggest social interactions play a key role in driving repeat purchases.[36]

Measuring the Results of Social Media Marketing Programs

LO 20-4
Compare the performance measures of social media linked to costs (inputs) versus revenues (outputs).

Performance measures for social media marketing programs can be divided into (1) those linked to inputs or costs (Figure 20–4) and (2) those tied to the outputs or revenues resulting from social media. Clearly, the ideal performance measure for both conventional and social media is one that ties actual sales revenues to the cost of the ad or other promotion. With the growth of social media, marketing and brand managers are being challenged to connect the cost of these new social media promotions to the sales they generate. The result has been an emergence of many new performance measures, often requiring a whole new language.

Performance Measures Linked to Inputs or Costs Figure 20–4 shows three performance measures for social media linked mainly to inputs or costs. Moving down the list of measures shown in Figure 20–4, one starts with a measure tied only to costs (cost per thousand, or CPM), then moves to a measure of interest in a product (cost per click, or CPC), and finally moves to a measure linked more closely to the sales revenues generated from the social media ad or action (cost per action, or CPA).

The cost per thousand (CPM) measure ties to the number of times the ad loads and a user might see it—but it does not indicate whether the user has actually reacted to it. This measure is roughly equivalent to the CPM for traditional media discussed in Chapter 19. The cost per click (CPC) measure gives the rate the advertiser pays, say to Facebook, every time a visitor clicks on the ad and jumps from that page to the advertiser's website. Finally, the cost per action (CPA) measure ties loosely to actual sales—for example, paying $5 for every purchase that originates from an ad, say, on the Facebook site. By summing up the revenues from all these purchases, a difficult task, this CPA measure most closely ties the cost of the social media ad to the sales revenues generated by the ad.

Performance Measure	Costs to Advertisers	Who Provides It	Who Uses It	An Assessment	
				Advantages	Disadvantages
Cost per thousand (CPM)	"I will pay $0.50 for every 1,000 times this ad loads, up to $100 per month."	Small websites that sell ads directly (may be using a third-party service)	Advertisers who simply want to build "awareness"	Simple to use	Impressions don't always lead to sales
Cost per click (CPC)	"I will pay $1 for every visitor who clicks on this ad and goes from your website to mine."	Most websites use this method—executed by a third party like Google/AdWords	Advertisers who want to pay for success, but may not be able to track sales from advertisement to purchase	I pay only for a visitor who has expressed an interest in my ad	Ads may not display if they are a poor fit for the viewing audience
Cost per action (CPA)	"I will pay $5 for every purchase that originates from an ad on your site."	Usually executed through third parties; Google AdSense offers this feature	Sophisticated advertisers who want to pay for success	I pay only for what works	Similar to CPC but harder to track and more expensive per action

FIGURE 20-4
Performance measures for social media linked mainly to inputs or costs, as seen by a brand manager.

Performance Measures Linked to Outputs or Revenues Many of the measures for evaluating how a brand manager's social media marketing program is doing reflect the two-way communications present in social media. These measures often tie to output results in terms of "fans," "friends," "followers," or "visitors" to a social media site, which can be a first step to estimating the sales revenue generated. From a brand manager's viewpoint, here are some of the frequently used Facebook measures, moving from the more general to the more specific:

- *Users/members.* Individuals who have registered on a social networking site by completing the process involved, such as providing their name, user ID (usually an e-mail address), and password, as well as answering a few questions (date of birth, gender, etc.).
- *Fans.* The number of people who have opted in to a brand's messages through a social media platform at a given time.
- *Share of voice.* The brand's share or percentage of all the online social media chatter related to, say, its product category or a topic.
- *Page views.* The number of times a Facebook Page is loaded in a given time period.
- *Visitors.* The total number of visitors to a Facebook Page in a given time period; if someone visits three times in one day, she is counted three times.
- *Unique visitors.* The total number of unique visitors to a Facebook Page in a given time period; if someone visits three times in one day, he is counted only once.
- *Average page views per visitor.* Page views divided by visitors in a given time period.
- *Interaction rate.* The number of people who interact with a Post ("like," make a comment, and so on) divided by the total number of people seeing the Post.
- *Click-through rate (CTR).* Percentage of recipients who have clicked on a link on the Page to visit a specific site.
- *Fan source.* Where a social network following comes from–with fans coming from a friend being more valuable than those coming from an ad.

Note that while sales revenues resulting from social media do not appear in these measures, as we move down the list, the measures are often more specific than comparable ones used in traditional media. This is because it is far simpler to electronically track the social media users who click on a website or ad than it is to track consumers who watch, listen to, or read traditional media.

Specialized Focus for Other Social Media One of the advantages of social media is that communities can form around ideas and commonalities, regardless of the physical location of their members. While major social media sites such as Facebook or YouTube may

Pinterest allows users to "pin" or share images of favorite interests on its site, which is useful for brand managers promoting their companies' products.
Source: Pinterest

garner the majority of the traffic, smaller media like Pinterest may be more successful for some products and services.

Pinterest, a virtual pinboard and content-sharing social network, allows people to "pin" or share images of their favorite things, such as clothing, craft ideas, home décor, and recipes. Pinterest members create customized, themed "boards" and categorize their images as "Odds & Ends," "Food," "Knitting," and so on. These images are shared with other members of the Pinterest community. Members can also share their pinned images on Facebook and Twitter. Similarly, content platforms such as newspapers and magazines often post on social media to generate traffic to their platforms.[37]

Pinterest has over 250 million users, 80 percent of whom are women—with 75 percent of daily traffic coming through mobile applications.[38] As a result, it has become a major sales driver for retailers and manufacturers that target women. In using Pinterest, brand managers can post images of their company's products on their Pinterest board and link them back to their websites.

VIDEO 20-3
Carmex
kerin.tv/15e/v20-3

Carmex Goes Viral with Luck and a LeBron James Bear Hug

Brand managers dream about their stars aligning—having their social media promotions go viral and reaping millions of dollars worth of free brand exposure. Carmex lip balm had this experience!

The Background As noted earlier in the chapter, Carmex has a partnership with LeBronJames.com. It started when the firm found out that LeBron James of the National Basketball Association uses Carmex in his pregame routine.

The Half-Court Hero Contest As part of their partnership, Carmex created the "Carmex and LeBronJames.com 'Half-Court Hero'" promotion. The promotion featured an online

The Shot

Nothing but Net

LeBron's Bear Hug

Achieving a brand manager's wildest dream! The text describes how the Carmex "shot seen 'round the world" achieved this dream—including 33 million YouTube viewers.

Courtesy of Altus Business Development, Inc.

entry form and weekly prizes leading up to a grand prize drawing for one lucky winner to travel to the game and have the chance to take a half-court shot worth $75,000. The "Hero" part meant that if the winner hit the shot—made the basket—Carmex would also donate $75,000 to the LeBron James Family Foundation and the Boys and Girls Clubs of America.

Michael Drysch was the lucky winner and walked to center court in front of a sold-out crowd of 20,000 fans. Michael carefully aligned himself just left of center court, took two steps, and launched a one-handed hook shot.

Nothing but net!! And $75,000 richer!

The crowd erupted as Michael turned and pumped his fist. But before he could celebrate any further, LeBron himself came running out of his team's huddle to bear hug Michael to the ground in a moment of pure jubilation.

Michael Drysch receives his reward for sinking his unlikely hook shot in the "Carmex and LeBronJames.com 'Half-Court Hero'" promotion. Also benefiting were the LeBron James Family Foundation and the Boys and Girls Clubs of America!

Courtesy of Altus Business Development, Inc.

The "Shot Seen 'Round the World" Goes Viral Instantly, the footage of Half-Court Hero winner Michael Drysch's incredible hook shot and the celebratory bear hug from LeBron James went viral online. NBATV interviewed him side-by-side with James after the game. It was the #1 Play of the Day on ESPN's *SportsCenter*. The Carmex brand team immediately arranged a public relations tour for Michael Drysch that included a trip to New York City for appearances on *Good Morning America*, *Inside Edition*, *CNN Early Start*, and dozens of local radio shows.

Meanwhile, the Carmex marketing team kept Carmex's social media accounts and website updated throughout the weekend with Twitter and Facebook Posts from the public relations tour. Within three months, Carmex's Half-Court Hero shot had been seen by over 30 million YouTube viewers and became the most-watched video of all time on the National Basketball Association's YouTube page. In all, the promotion earned Carmex over 500 million media impressions across TV, print, online, and social media.[39]

The Carmex experience is a classic "textbook example" of matching social media content and social media influencers. Its social media content was inspirational, promotional, interactive, connecting, and entertaining. The partnership with LeBron James—the most popular NBA player on social media, with more than 100 million Facebook, Twitter, and Instagram followers—was ideal.[40]

LEARNING REVIEW

20-7. What are the seven kinds of social media content?

20-8. Stated simply, how can an advertiser on Facebook expect to generate sales?

20-9. What did the Carmex team do to exploit its incredible good fortune after seeing Michael Drysch make his "Half-Court Hero" shot?

THE FUTURE: CONVERGENCE AND MOBILITY

LO 20-5
Identify the cause of the convergence of the real and digital worlds and how this will affect the future of social media.

Trends in marketing's use of social media reflect what scientists call "mirror worlds" or "smart systems" that are really the convergence of the real and digital worlds. A *smart system* is a technology- and data-based network that triggers actions by sensing changes in the real or digital world. This section discusses: (1) the convergence of real and digital worlds; (2) how this convergence links social media to marketing actions; and (3) where all this *may* be headed in *your* future.

The Convergence of Real and Digital Worlds

Source: Snapchat/Nike

Saying that our physical and virtual worlds are converging might sound like a movie plot. The convergence of real and digital worlds, however, is taking place and is the result of a proliferation of interlinked social commerce technologies, databases and algorithms, and apps. A look at several of these elements helps explain this real world–digital world convergence and what it means for marketing.

Social Commerce Technologies Social media and digital technologies are converging to change the way companies engage consumers and the way consumers communicate, shop, and pay for products and services. Snapchat, for example, recently released a link to an augmented reality image of Michael Jordan, which showed the basketball player wearing the newest model of sneakers. Users could then "walk around" Jordan, view the product, and tap into the Snap Store to make a purchase. The sneakers sold out in 23 minutes![41]

Databases and Algorithms As discussed in Chapters 8 and 9, finding prospective customers often involves market segmentation that requires databases searched with algorithms—models used to query, organize, manipulate, and present data. The owners of these databases, among them Google and Facebook, must make them as useful as possible to potential advertisers in order to succeed. Among databases, Google is the hands-down winner—indexing over 47 billion unique web pages. Its digital assistant, driven by artificial intelligence and machine learning, now gives results in answers to research queries in photos, facts, and "direct answers," and not just the "blue links" of website addresses.[42]

Facebook entered Google's territory by announcing its own search engine algorithm. Facebook users can conduct their own queries about people, places, photos, and interests. An example is "Restaurants recommended by friends." This lets Facebook give advertisers real value in the "likes" found on its site. For example, a small chocolate retail shop in New York City can target young parents who buy lots of organic food products.[43] So it's not difficult to see how a casual "like" for a brand by a user in a database's "digital world" can converge into an actual "real-world" purchase by the user through a very targeted promotion planned by a brand manager.

Read the text to learn about augmented reality on Snapchat!
Source: Snapchat/Nike

Apps The apps for smartphones are accelerating the convergence of the real and digital worlds. **Apps** (or *mobile apps* or *applications*) are small, downloadable software programs that run on smartphones and tablet devices. When Apple launched its iPhone, it didn't expect smartphone apps to be very important. Wrong! Apple's App Store currently offers more than 2.2 million apps either free or for sale, and Google Play offers more than 3 million apps for users of Android devices. With the wide array of apps to choose from, today's consumers typically spend two hours a day using about nine apps.[44]

VIDEO 20-4
Clash of Clans
kerin.tv/15e/v20-4

Many apps are video games. *Angry Birds*, for example, has been downloaded more than 3 billion times since its release, which is one reason *Angry Birds*-themed products now range from mascara to toys and entertainment parks. The 19th version of *Angry Birds* was recently released using augmented reality of the original game and visuals from the *Angry Birds Movie*. The popularity of the game is declining, though, as it enters the decline stage of its product life cycle.[45] The video games *FarmVille*, *Temple Run*, *QuizUp*, *4Pics1Word*, and *Fruit Ninja* also reveal the short product life cycle for these apps in today's tough competitive environment.

The text describes the strategy *Candy Crush Saga* uses to link the technical power of the *digital world* to the human psychology of its players in the *real world*.
alexat25/Shutterstock

Enter *Clash of Clans* and *Candy Crush Saga*. These and other successful new video games exploit the real world–digital world convergence. Today's successful new video games (1) build on a huge personal-rewards psychology for players; (2) can be played on the small smartphone screens; (3) top the most-downloaded charts of Apple iOS, Google, Android, and Facebook; and (4) often use a "freemium strategy"—where the download is free but users pay for extra features, such as for ways to speed up the game.

Time magazine analyzes how designers of the *Candy Crush* video game use its key elements to link the *digital world* of *Candy Crush* to the personal *real-world* satisfactions and rewards of its players:[46]

- *It's better with friends*. Users can give—and get—extra lives using Facebook.
- *It never ends*. There are over 5,000 levels, and designers add more almost every week.
- *It makes the player feel special*. The game gives positive feedback for nearly every click and tap.
- *It lets a player—sort of—cheat*. Players can pay for power-ups to skip past wait times.
- *It's challenging*. Increasingly varied puzzles often take multiple attempts to complete.

The *Candy Crush* app has now been installed over 2.7 billion times across Facebook, iOS, and Android devices.

Even *Angry Birds* changed its strategy from charging a download cost to using a freemium strategy when it launched *Angry Birds 2*. Sound easy to build an app? Maybe. But hundreds of creative apps die a quiet death each year!

Mobile Marketing: Tightening Links to Marketing Actions

The convergence of the real and digital worlds has also contributed to the growth of *mobile marketing*, or the broad set of interactive messaging options that are used to communicate through personal mobile devices.[47] This continuous connection present in mobile marketing has led to a variety of apps, such as:

- *Price-comparison searches*. Scan product bar codes or QR codes and research 500,000 stores, synchronizing searches between your computer, your car, and your smartphone.
- *Location-based promotions*. Use your GPS-enabled smartphone or car for location check-ins to receive discounts at stores.
- *Loyalty programs*. Win loyalty points for selecting stores and receive discounts from them.

On average, U.S. consumers of all ages check their mobile phones 47 times each day. And not surprisingly, the number of mobile shopping searches and purchases has exploded in recent years, causing huge opportunities and challenges for conventional brick-and-mortar retailers.

The clear point of difference in mobile marketing is its unique ability to empower users by connecting with them individually and continuously—learning about their likes and personal characteristics and sharing this information with online friends and (often) marketers selling products. This socially networked world will lead to connected users having more direct interactions with sellers.

The convergence of social media, smartphones, tablet devices, connected cars, and new apps will lead to companies having a more dynamic interaction with their customers. But is this an unqualified success for buyers? Consider the following perspectives.

A Consumer Purchase Where Sensors Have Some Control A vending machine scans your face to identify your age and gender and changes its display and—in the future—may give you a quantity discount for buying two of your favorite candy bars (it knows about your Facebook "likes") while showing an electronic dinner coupon for a nearby restaurant if you appear between 7:00 and 9:00 P.M. this evening. The results of the candy and dinner offer are directly measurable for marketers. While it offers unusual convenience, does this buying situation start to interfere with your personal privacy?

Too busy to visit your grocery store this week? If you are in South Korea or China, you can shop on the wall of your subway station with your smartphone—and have your purchases delivered to your door!
Imaginechina/AP Images

A Consumer Purchase Where the Buyer Controls All Some cities in South Korea and China are on the leading edge of virtual supermarket shopping. Tesco Home Plus, a global supermarket chain, provides a quick spur-of-the-moment opportunity for grocery shopping. Shoppers use their smartphones to scan images on the wall of a subway station to buy Tesco's grocery products while waiting for their train. They use the smartphone app to pay for the groceries, which are delivered to their door right after they get home.[48] In this example, buyers achieve great convenience—probably an unqualified success.

On Privacy: How Much "Convergence" Is Too Much? Smart systems are fine up to a point. For example, most of us are comfortable letting convergence find us a timely deal at a local restaurant using a location-based app on our smartphone or connected car. It may even be all right if Google's Search, Maps, Photos, Gmail, and YouTube services provide information about our geographical inquiries, recreational preferences, past travel activities, and financial circumstances to an algorithm that suggests an "ideal vacation plan."

Facebook's recent disclosures about a data breach for 87 million Facebook users, however, has many people contemplating the use and security of personal information. In fact, smartphones, cars and houses, and personal digital assistants, combined with the growing number of other connected devices (e.g., watches, refrigerators, luggage, etc.), create the potential to monitor almost all behaviors. Some numbers and facts related to privacy include:

- 2,000-plus. Estimated number of times the online activity of an average Internet user is tracked every day.
- 3,500. Number of indicators used by Acxiom Corp., a leading data broker, to predict brand affinity, preferences, and behavior.
- 2.5 billion. Approximate number of addressable consumers in the Acxiom global database.

About 68 percent of Internet users today feel that privacy laws don't protect them adequately. So 86 percent of them have used privacy technologies to take online steps to remove or mask their digital data.[49]

The future? Data privacy continues to be a topic of discussion and regulation around the globe. In 2018 the General Data Protection Regulation (GDPR) became the new legal framework governing the use of data across EU markets. In the United States, the discussion continues to try to determine the appropriate balance of the interests of consumers and businesses.

LEARNING REVIEW

20-10. What is an example of how the real (physical) and digital (virtual) worlds are converging?

20-11. What types of apps utilize the continuous connection provided by mobile marketing?

20-12. Can personal privacy become a problem as the real and digital worlds converge with smart systems?

LEARNING OBJECTIVES REVIEW

LO 20-1 *Define social media and describe how they have transformed marketing communications.*
Social media are online media where users submit comments, photos, and videos, often accompanied by a feedback process to identify "popular" topics. The reach, cost, investment, timeliness, flexibility, and influence of social media have transformed marketing communications, including the practice of influencer marketing.

LO 20-2 *Identify the four most prominent social media and describe how brand managers integrate them into marketing actions.*
Four prominent social media sites are Facebook, Twitter, LinkedIn, and YouTube. Facebook is a social network where users create a personal profile, add other users as "friends," and exchange comments, photos, videos, and "likes" with them. To increase traffic to a Facebook Page, brand managers can use paid ads and sponsored stories. Twitter enables users to send and receive "tweets," messages up to 280 characters long. For Twitter, brand managers can use monitoring programs to track what people are saying about their organization's brand. LinkedIn lets users post their personal profiles to a network of businesspeople. LinkedIn can be used to create a company profile to share brand information and career opportunities with LinkedIn users and to demonstrate the company's expertise and professionalism. YouTube is a video-sharing website where users can upload, view, and comment on videos. YouTube also allows marketers to create a brand channel to promote a product, show ads for it, and have viewers comment on it.

LO 20-3 *Describe the characteristics of a social media marketing program, including selecting social media and choosing social media content.*
A social media marketing program is that portion of a company's integrated marketing communications effort designed to create and deliver online media content that attracts viewer attention and encourages readers to share it with their social network. Selecting social media entails assessing (1) the characteristics of the website's visitors and (2) the number of users or unique visitors to the website. Choosing specific social media content from among the many options available depends on its intended purpose.

LO 20-4 *Compare the performance measures of social media linked to costs (inputs) versus revenues (outputs).*
Performance measures linked to costs (inputs) include (1) cost per thousand (similar to the CPM for a print ad), which is the number of times an ad is displayed to a user; (2) cost per click (CPC), which gives the rate the advertiser pays each time a visitor clicks on the ad and then jumps to the advertiser's web page; and (3) cost per action (CPA), which is the amount paid for every purchase that originates from an ad on a social media site. Examples of performance measures linked to revenues (outputs) include (1) users/members that have registered on social media websites; (2) the number of unique monthly users viewing the website at a given time; (3) page views, or the number of times a specific web page is loaded; and (4) visitors, or the total number of users viewing a particular web page during a specified time period.

LO 20-5 *Identify the cause of the convergence of the real and digital worlds and how this will affect the future of social media.*
The convergence of the real and digital worlds in social media is the result of the proliferation of interlinked smartphones, tablet devices, connected cars, sensors, special identification tags, databases, algorithms, apps, and other elements. This convergence will allow consumers and marketers to increase the exchange of personal and product-related information with each other. For consumers, however, this could lead to a loss of privacy and possible exploitation by unscrupulous marketers.

LEARNING REVIEW ANSWERS

20-1 What are social media?
Answer: Social media are online media where users submit comments, photos, and videos—often accompanied by a feedback process to identify "popular" topics. Business firms also refer to social media as "consumer-generated media." A single social media site with millions of users interacting with each other, like Facebook, is a *social network*.

20-2 In classifying social media, what do we mean by (*a*) media richness and (*b*) self-disclosure?
Answer: Social media can be classified based on two factors: (*a*) Media richness involves the degree of acoustic, visual, and personal contact between two communication partners. (*b*) Self-disclosure involves the degree to which an individual shares his or her thoughts, feelings, likes, and dislikes when engaged in a social interaction.

20-3 Compare traditional media and social media in terms of time required to deliver the communication.
Answer: Traditional media can involve days or even months of continuing effort to deliver the communication, and time lags can be extensive. In contrast, individuals using social media can post virtually instantaneous content.

20-4 How is user-generated content presented by someone using Facebook?
Answer: User-generated content (UGC) refers to the various forms of online media content that are publicly available and created by end users. Facebook users create a personal profile, add other users as friends, and exchange comments, photos, videos, and "likes" with them. Additionally, users may chat with friends and create and join common-interest groups.

20-5 What are some ways brand managers use Facebook to converse with a brand's fans? How does Facebook facilitate mobile marketing activities?
Answer: A brand manager can create awareness for a product, service, or brand by creating a Facebook Page for it. To generate new customers and increase traffic to their Facebook Pages, brand managers can use paid ads and sponsored stories within the Facebook advertising platform. The marketing challenge for a Facebook Page is to post and create the content that will generate the best response. Facebook facilitates mobile marketing with new initiatives, such as Facebook Live, Instant Articles, Moments, and Custom Audiences.

20-6 How can brand managers use YouTube to converse with customers? What is a new form of mobile marketing using online video?
Answer: YouTube allows brand managers to create an actual brand channel to host their advertisements and other video clips that can explain or demonstrate complex products. YouTube can also link to a brand's website. YouTube, because it is a visual medium, allows a brand manager to entertain as well as inform users about the brand. A new form of mobile marketing is the use of vloggers (video bloggers) to reach online audiences.

20-7 What are the seven kinds of social media content?
Answer: The seven kinds of social media content are: educational, inspirational, interactive, connecting, promotional, newsworthy, and entertaining.

20-8 Stated simply, how can an advertiser on Facebook expect to generate sales?
Answer: The brand manager composes a title, ad copy, and images or photos for an ad to be placed on Facebook. A website address links the ad to the brand's website or its Facebook Page. To encourage and produce new sales that can be tracked, the brand manager might also link the ad to a coupon code or some other promotional offer.

20-9 What did the Carmex team do to exploit its incredible good fortune after seeing Michael Drysch make his "Half-Court Hero" shot?
Answer: At an NBA basketball game, Michael Drysch did the impossible and made Carmex's Half-Court Hero basketball shot. Instantly, the footage of Half-Court Hero winner Michael Drysch's incredible hook shot went viral online. The Carmex brand team immediately arranged a public relations tour for Drysch that included a trip to New York City for appearances on several TV and radio shows. Meanwhile, the Carmex marketing team kept Carmex's social media accounts and website updated throughout the weekend with Twitter and Facebook posts from the public relations tour. Within three months, Carmex's Half-Court Hero shot had been seen by over 30 million YouTube viewers.

20-10 What is an example of how the real (physical) and digital (virtual) worlds are converging?
Answer: The convergence of real and digital worlds is the result of a proliferation of interlinked smartphones, tablet devices, connected cars, sensors, special identification tags, databases, algorithms, apps, and other elements. In addition, apps for smartphones are accelerating the convergence of the real and digital worlds as they make the devices more productive and provide users with entertainment. Finally, marketers can tailor specific messages to targeted users by using their personal data and preferences so that they can order products and services as a result of receiving these offers.

20-11 What types of apps utilize the continuous connection provided by mobile marketing?
Answer: Apps that offer (*a*) price comparison searches, (*b*) location-based promotions, and (*c*) loyalty programs utilize the continuous connection feature of mobile marketing. Mobile shopping searches and purchases have grown, and are creating opportunities and challenges for conventional retailers.

20-12 Can personal privacy become a problem as the real and digital worlds converge with smart systems?
Answer: The convergence of social media, smartphones, tablet devices, and new apps will lead to companies having a more dynamic interaction with their customers. This convergence allows for the collection of users' personal data, preferences, and behaviors, which allows marketers to tailor offerings based on these data. The issue is, do we want others to know all this information about us?

FOCUSING ON KEY TERMS

apps p. 568
customer engagement p. 561
Facebook p. 556
influencer marketing p. 554
LinkedIn p. 558
social media p. 551
social media content p. 563
social media marketing program p. 561
social shopping p. 555
Twitter p. 558
user-generated content (UGC) p. 552
YouTube p. 559

APPLYING MARKETING KNOWLEDGE

1 In your new job as a retail store manager you decide to add mobile marketing to your promotional campaign. Describe how ads directed at connected cars could increase sales in your store.

2 You and three college friends have decided to launch an online business selling clothes college students wear—T-shirts, shorts, sweats, and so on. You plan to use Facebook ads. What "likes" or interests do (*a*) college men and (*b*) college women have that might help you in planning your Facebook strategy?

3 You are about to graduate from college and want a job in marketing research or sales. Go to the LinkedIn site, register, and determine what information you would put on your LinkedIn profile to help you find a new job.

4 What is the significance of user-generated content when contrasted with social media and traditional media?

5 You are a brand manager for a sneaker manufacturer like Nike or New Balance and you are trying to use Facebook to reach (*a*) college-aged women and (*b*) men over 55 years of age. What three or four "likes" or interests would you expect each segment to have when you try to reach it with Facebook?

6 In measuring the results of social media, what are the (*a*) advantages and (*b*) disadvantages of performance measures linked directly to revenues versus costs?

BUILDING YOUR MARKETING PLAN

Remembering the target market segments you identified in Chapter 9 for your marketing plan:

1 (*a*) Identify which one of the four social media described in the chapter would be most useful and (*b*) give your reasons. Would you consider other social media like Pinterest? Why or why not?

2 Briefly describe (*a*) how you would use this website to try to increase sales of your products and (*b*) why you expect target market customers to respond to it.

VIDEO CASE 20 Body Glove: Helping Consumers Do What They Love!

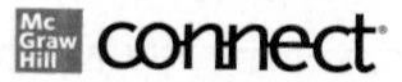

How did Body Glove® become one of the most recognizable outdoor sports brands in the world? Well, the story begins in Missouri, where twin brothers, Bob and Bill Meistrell, taught themselves to swim in a pond on their family farm. Their interest in water led them to California where they opened the Dive N' Surf sports shop in Redondo Beach with $1,800 they borrowed from their mother. They grew the business with a simple philosophy of quality products, great customer service, and a fair price. The real secret to their success, though, may have been their personal approach to business and life. Billy Meistrell, son and nephew of the founders, explains, "I constantly heard my dad and uncle say, 'Do what you love and love what you do!'"

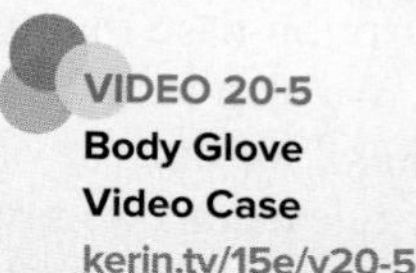

VIDEO 20-5
Body Glove
Video Case
kerin.tv/15e/v20-5

THE BODY GLOVE BRAND

The combination of their approach to business and being pioneers in diving and surfing was a powerful business model for the Meistrell brothers. According to Billy, "their work was their playground, and with that came so much passion and creativity that they developed many new products which gave everybody a much richer lifestyle in the water." One of their first innovations, for example, was the result of using the insulation from the back of a refrigerator, neoprene, to create the first practical wetsuit, which they called the Dive N' Surf Thermocline. The name, however, was difficult to explain so they began discussing potential new brand names. An observation that the wetsuit "fit like a glove" led to the now famous name Body Glove!

The brothers realized there was a lot of potential in their idea and decided they needed help. They turned to their CPA, Russ Lesser, who eventually became president of Body Glove. One of the first things that Lesser did was recommend that they get into the wholesale business. He helped arrange the purchase of a factory and the business started to grow. "We started manufacturing wetsuits," explains Lesser, "and that helped create the whole surf lifestyle." The popularity of the brand soon allowed Body Glove to pursue licensing agreements for many other products, including bathing suits. "That's when Body Glove really took off," says Lesser, "the new bathing suits hit every fashion magazine in the world." "Now we have a whole variety of watersports products. We have wet suits, we have boogie boards, we have surfboards, we have fins, masks, and snorkels, and we have all sorts of apparel," he adds. Annual sales in the United States soon approached $200 million.

Taking Body Glove to global markets was the next step and they needed a partner that could facilitate the growth. "We were approached by Marquee Brands who wanted to expand into the licensing business," says Lesser, and eventually Marquee acquired a majority position in the company. "I think it's a good match because they have the capital to expand and to market and they also have contacts around the world," he continues.

Today, Body Glove represents a classic success story. "Two young men with no money and no family connections created a company with millions of dollars of sales revenue and also created thousands of jobs," observes Lesser. The brand has a global following and the iconic Body Glove Hand Logo is one of the most recognized in sporting goods and watersports. In addition, the company continues its heritage as the third generations of the Meistrell families continue their involvement in the management of the brand, particularly the marketing activities.

MARKETING AT BODY GLOVE

The marketing function at Body Glove includes a senior executive at Marquee Brands, a marketing director, a brand director, and a team of marketing staff. Together they create annual marketing plans designed to grow the brand. According to Jenna Meistrell, brand director at Body Glove, "Every year we sit with our internal team and develop a marketing plan for the following year." "We set direction for the business by looking at all of our various product categories in different markets and figure out which categories need support," she adds. Each plan uses a combination of traditional and contemporary marketing tools.

"Traditional marketing will always be important to us," says Jenna. "We maintain print advertisements in *Surfer* magazine, *Wake* magazine, and *Outside*, *Elle*, and *Vogue*," she continues. Body Glove also uses out-of-home advertising such as advertising in Times Square and billboards near popular outdoor sports locations. The advertising always communicates a message that builds on the Body Glove heritage. Jenna explains, "Every year we try to do a new campaign and this year our campaign is 'Do What You Love.' The campaign is important to us because we almost use it as our mission statement. It's the foundation of the company, ensuring that our consumers are outside doing what they love and it is a great marketing campaign because it applies easily to all of our product categories."

Other marketing tools also play an important role in Body Glove's marketing plans. Distribution channels, for example, are being expanded. There are now more than 200 Body Glove stores in Southeast Asia, and a new partnership in Europe will provide distribution in more than 1,000 specialty and department stores. In addition, Body Glove has always had a team of sponsored athletes from the surfing, diving, and wakeboarding communities who serve as brand ambassadors. The company even produced three feature-length films—the Drop Zone series—which follow the company's sponsored athletes on watersports adventures. And of course there are a variety of sales promotion tools such as foam hands with the Body Glove logo, license plate frames, and bumper stickers. When Billy Meistrell drives a Body Glove vehicle, people stop him and ask for stickers!

SOCIAL MEDIA AT BODY GLOVE

To reach the growing market of Body Glove consumers around the globe, social media is playing an increasing role in the company's marketing. Nick Meistrell, director of marketing at Body Glove, explains: "We all know that content is king in this age, through digital and through social, you have to be generating some valuable content to be relevant among consumers and people that are attracted to your brand." There are a lot of social media options available today and Nick tries to use many of them. "I look at a 360-degree approach, I want to hit consumers through every possible outlet," he says.

What are some of the popular options today? Nick offers his perspective:

- *Facebook.* We look at Facebook as a platform to launch new products and really drive some click-through to our website and our e-commerce page. It can give consumers an experience and communicate the lifestyle, not just push product.
- *Twitter.* Twitter used to be a platform for us to tell consumers about new things we are doing. Today, however, it has become a customer service tool. Twitter is the foundation for our customer service function and is used more than the customer service link on our website. We get customer service inquiries on Twitter every day!
- *LinkedIn.* LinkedIn is a great platform for us to look for new talent when we are hiring. It is also a good way to talk about all the great stuff we are doing at Body Glove and to interact with other businesses and like-minded businesspeople.
- *YouTube.* YouTube is a huge platform for our brand. Content is king and we feel it is a great outlet to show our content. We have a great subscription base that is constantly hungry for new content. We also look at it as the new platform for commercials. So, instead of buying traditional commercials for television, we are buying our commercial space on YouTube to strategically target the right consumer.
- *Instagram.* Instagram is also a huge part of our marketing program. In this digital age you must generate organic, relevant content. Instagram is a great platform to show new content from photos and videos.
- *Pinterest.* We have so many unique products under our umbrella that can appeal to many types of consumers and Pinterest is a great place to post and see them. People love sharing moods and feelings about those products on Pinterest.

Each platform is unique and can accomplish different marketing objectives. Each platform is evolving and changing quickly, also. As Nick observes, "You have to stay cutting edge and stay up-to-date on all the relevant things that are happening out there."

One important aspect of social media is that it is increasingly accessed from mobile devices. "At the end of the day, 67 percent of our consumers now get their information online, mainly through a mobile device," Nick explains. Another aspect of social media that is changing is the ability to assess its effectiveness. "We find that it's really relevant to use the analytics built into each platform because each platform offers its own unique tools. When we are measuring our digital activity we look at impressions, we look at click-through rates, we look at cost per impression, and we look at revenue generated through our e-commerce platform."

THE FUTURE

Body Glove continues its support of conservation efforts that help preserve the environment, such as its participation in the Earth's Oceans Foundation. In addition, Body

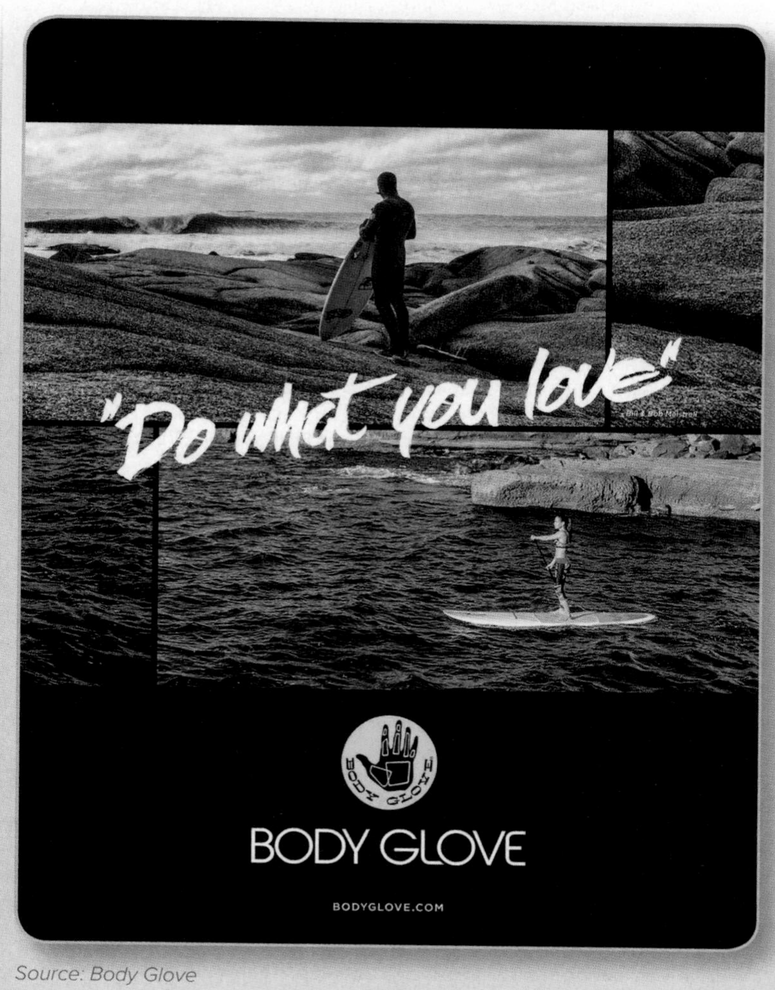

"Do what you love"
BODY GLOVE
BODYGLOVE.COM

Source: Body Glove

Glove has a variety of exciting new initiatives under way. In terms of new products, Body Glove recently introduced Body Glove Airstream Earbuds, Body Glove shoes for men and women, and an inflatable stand up paddleboard. The company also began a "Create Happiness" campaign to support a yoga and fitness initiative, and it announced a partnership with FlowRider to promote surf simulation machines. The team at Body Glove is very excited about the future. Billy smiles as he reflects, "There is no company that has put more people in the water and made so many families have a fun lifestyle than Body Glove!" So, the next time you are in or near the water, watch for Body Glove to help you "do what you love"![50]

Questions

1 How does Body Glove's heritage and philosophy contribute to its success?
2 Which of the criteria mentioned in Chapter 11 help explain why changing the brand name to Body Glove was a good decision?
3 Describe Body Glove's use of traditional marketing tools.
4 What social media platforms does Body Glove use to communicate with its customers today?
5 Why are social media and mobile marketing an increasingly important part of Body Glove's marketing plan?

Chapter Notes

1. Luke Harrison, "Connected Cars Talk of Town after 2019 Singapore Motorshow," *Enterprise Innovation*, February 10, 2019; "Domino's Teams with Xevo to Launch In-Car Ordering," www.retailcustomerexperience.com, March 27, 2019; Hans Greimel, "Nissan, Renault Ready Next-Gen Connected Car Platform," *Automotive News*, March 25, 2019, p. 16; Michele Bertoncello,, Gianluca Camplone, and Asad Husain, "Connectivity: Turbocharging the New Mobility Ecosystem," *McKinsey Quarterly*, March 2019, pp. 4-7; Sam Del Rowe, "How to Succeed at Mobile Marketing," *Customer Relationship Management,* January 2017, pp. 27-29; Renee M. Covino, "Marketing to Today's Mobile Consumer," *Convenience Store News,* May 2017, pp. 60-64; and Chester Dawson, "IBM Pairs with BMW to Market Connected Car Services," *The Wall Street Journal,* June 4, 2017.
2. "116 Amazing Social Media Statistics and Facts," *brandwatch.com*, June 15, 2018.
3. Andreas M. Kaplan and Michael Haenlein, "Users of the World, Unite! The Challenges and Opportunities of Social Media," *Business Horizons* 53, no. 1 (2010), pp. 62-64.
4. Lisette de Vries, Sonja Gensler, and Peter S. H. Leeflang, "Effects of Traditional Advertising and Social Messages on Brand-Building Metrics and Customer Acquisition," *Journal of Marketing,* September 2017, pp. 1-15; V. Kumar, JeeWon Brianna Choi, and Mallik Greene, "Synergistic Effects of Social Media and Traditional Marketing on Brand Sales: Capturing the Time-Varying Effects," *Journal of the Academy of Marketing Science,* 2017, pp. 268-88; and Chiranjeev Kohli, Rajneesh Suri, and Anuj Kapoor, "Will Social Media Kill Branding?" *Business Horizons* 58 (2015), pp. 35-44.
5. "Bringing Up Baby's Market Share," *The Wall Street Journal*, October 27/28, 2018, pp. B1, B2.
6. Christian Hughes, Vanitha Swaminathan, and Gillian Brooks, "Driving Brand Engagement through Online Social Influencers: An Empirical Investigation of Sponsored Blogging Campaigns," *Journal of Marketing,* September 2019, pp. 78-96; "Report Finds Fake Followers Are Hard to Shake," *Advertising Age,* February 4, 2019, p. 14; and "Global Influencer Marketing 2019," www.emarketer.com, May 5, 2019.
7. "Instagram Is Breaking Hearts," *The Wall Street Journal*, August 17/18, 2019.

8. Jia Wertz, "Why the Rise of Social Commerce Is Inevitable," *forbes.com*, June 25, 2019; and Daniel Keyes, "The Social Commerce Report: Inside the Fast-Developing Opportunity to Reach Billions of Consumers' Wallets Using Social Platforms," *businessinsider.com*, July 18, 2019.
9. "Study: 80% of Gen Z Purchases Influenced by Social Media," *retaildive.com*, July 17, 2019.
10. "Facebook by the Numbers: Stats, Demographics & Fun Facts," www.omnicoreagency.com, January 6, 2019; "Distribution of Twitter Users Worldwide as of April 2019, by Gender," www.statista.com, 2019; "Distribution of LinkedIn Users Worldwide as of April 2019, by Gender," www.statista.com, 2019; Zeljko Drazovic, "Eye-Opening YouTube Stats for Marketers," www.rivaliq.com, February 1, 2019.
11. "10 Facts about Americans and Facebook," www.pewresearch.org, February 1, 2019; Dan Shewan, "21 Amazing Facebook Facts You Didn't Know," *wordstream.com*, December 17, 2017; and "Stats," *newsroom.fb.com*, June 17, 2017.
12. Douglas Holt, "Branding in the Age of Social Media," *Harvard Business Review*, March 2016, pp. 40–50; and "Top 10 Ways to Engage Fans on Facebook," *Buddy Media, Inc.*, 2010.
13. Juanito Galindo, "2018: What Is the Current Value of a Facebook "Like" for Brands?" *medium.com*, January 3, 2018; and Ashish Kumar, Ram Bezawada, Rishika Rishika, Ramkumar Janakirarman, and P. K. Kannan, "From Social to Sale: The Effects of Firm-Generated Content in Social Media on Customer Behavior," *Journal of Marketing*, January 2016, pp. 7–25.
14. Deepa Seetharaman, "Facebook to Enhance Messenger App," *The Wall Street Journal*, March 26, 2015, p. B8. https://www.wsj.com.
15. Emily Dreyfuss and Issie Lapowsky, "Facebook Is Changing News Feed (Again) to Stop Fake News," www.wired.com, April 10, 2019; and "Top Facebook Updates That You Can't Afford to Miss–April 2019 Edition," www.adespresso.com, April 25, 2019.
16. "Top Facebook Updates That You Can't Afford to Miss–April 2018 Edition," www.adespresso.com, April 23, 2018.
17. Louise Matsakis, "Facebook's New 'Dating' Feature Could Crush Apps Like Tinder," *Wired.com*, May 1, 2018.
18. Rolfe Winkler and Jack Marshall, "Google Imitates Facebook with E-mail Marketing," *The Wall Street Journal*, April 15, 2015, p. B4.
19. Hamza Shaban, "Twitter Reveals Its Daily Active User Numbers for the First Time," *The Washington Post*, February 7, 2019; and "28 Twitter Statistics All Marketers Should Know in 2019," *blog.hootsuite.com*, January 16, 2019.
20. Rachel Gee, "How Twitter's Advertising Is Moving beyond 140 Characters," *Marketing Week*, October 20, 2016.
21. Todd Spangler, "Twitter Pushes Live-Video Deals with MLB, NFL, Viacom, BuzzFeed, Live Nation, WNBA and More," *Variety*, May 1, 2017; Garett Sloane, "Twitter Aims to Tame the Lions," *Advertising Age*, June 12, 2017, p. 4; and Kurt Wagner, "Twitter Is Replacing the Moments Tab with a New Explore Tab Instead," *recode.net*, January 26, 2017.
22. Steve Bygott, "Top 5 Tips for Better Branding on LinkedIn," *Best's Review*, June 2017, p. 10; and "LinkedIn Is Trying to Quicken Its Pulse," *Bloomberg Businessweek*, April 22–April 28, 2013, pp. 32–33.
23. Pedro Hernandez, "LinkedIn's Job-Matching Feature Goes Mobile," *eWeek*, May 17, 2017, p. 6.
24. Amy Segelin, "7 Ways to Get Recruiters to Notice You on LinkedIn," *fortune.com*, May 16, 2017; and "Building a Great Student Profile," LinkedIn for Students. See http://university.linkedin.com/linkedin-for-students.html.
25. Kolby Goodman, "Stand above the Rest," *Diary of Alpha Kappa Psi*, Spring 2014, pp. 12–14.
26. YouTube website, https://www.youtube.com/yt/press/statistics.html, accessed May 5, 2019.
27. "The Most Viewed YouTube Videos of All Time," www.digitaltrends.com, February 17, 2019.
28. Clare O'Connor, "Forbes Top Influencers: Meet the 30 Power Players Making a Fortune on Social Media," *forbes.com*, April 10, 2017; Clare O'Connor, "14 Big-Time Brands Paying Social Influencers to Spread Their Message," *forbes.com*, April 10, 2017; Clare O'Connor, "Forbes Top Influencers: How Zoe 'Zoella' Sugg Makes Millions from YouTube Beauty Tutorials," *forbes.com*, April 10, 2017; and Rachel Gee, "Why YouTube's Move to Ditch 30-Second Unskippable Ads Makes It 'More Powerful,'" *Marketing Week*, February 21, 2017.
29. Robin Hilton, "OK Go's New Video for 'The One Moment' Is Another Mind-Blower," *npr.org*, November 23, 2016; and Amanda Axvig, Vice President of Marketing, AOI Marketing, Inc.
30. Shalini Bisht, "How to Do Effective YouTube Marketing," *Kartrocket.com*, February 15, 2017.
31. Garett Sloane, "Advertisers Can Now Target YouTube Ads Based on People's Google Search Histories," *Advertising Age*, January 20, 2017.
32. "2019 Social Media Industry Benchmark Report," www.rivaliq.com, February 2, 2019.
33. "Social Media Use in 2018," www.pewinternet.org, March 1, 2018.
34. Alfred Lua, "21 Top Social Media Sites to Consider for Your Brand," www.buffer.com, January 24, 2019; and Priit Kallas, "Top 10 Social Networking Sites by Market Share Statistics (July 2018)," *dreamgrow.com*, August 3, 2018.
35. This discussion is based on Vinay Koshy, "7 Types of Social Media Content," https://maximzessocial business.com, accessed May 13, 2018; Melissa S. Barker et al., *Social Media Marketing: A Strategic Approach*, 2nd ed. (Boston, MA: Cengage Learning, 2017); and "Purina Launches Inaugural Pets at Work Report," company press release, June 20, 2017.
36. Christian de Looper, "Pepsi's Friend Finder Blimp Will Help You Find Your Lost Friends at a Music Festival," *Tech Times*, August 25, 2015; and Kamer Toker-Yildiz, Minakshi Trivedi, Jeonghye Choi, and Sue Ryung Chang, "Social Interactions and Monetary Incentives in Driving Consumer Repeat Behavior," *Journal of Marketing Research*, June 2017, pp. 364–80.
37. Vamsi K. Kanuri, Yixing Chen, and Shrihari Sridhar, "Scheduling Content on Social Media: Theory, Evidence, and Application," *Journal of Marketing*, November 2018, pp. 89–108; and Mae Anderson, "A Look at Why Social Media Site Pinterest Is Catnip to Retailers and Shoppers Alike," *Star Tribune*, April 25, 2014.
38. Salman Aslam, "Pinterest by the Numbers: Stats, Demographics & Fun Facts," *omnicoreagency.com*, January 23, 2017.
39. The Carmex "Half-Court Hero" example was written by Patrick Hodgdon, Manager of Digital Marketing, Bolin Marketing.
40. Gerard J. Tellis, Deborah J. MacInnis, Seshadri Tirunillai, and Yanwei Zhang, "What Drives Virality (Sharing) of Online Digital Content? The Critical Role of Information, Emotion, and Brand Prominence," *Journal of Marketing*, July 2019, pp. 1–20; and "Team LeBron Beats Team Curry in Social Media Value Faceoff," *forbs.com*, February 18, 2018.
41. Ann-Marie Alcantara, "Snapchat's Ecommerce Strategy Hit a New High When It Sold Out the New Air Jordans in Minutes," *adweek.com*, February 22, 2018.
42. "The Size of the World Wide Web (The Internet)," *worldwidewebsize.com*, June 20, 2017.
43. Evelyn M. Rusli, "Buy Signal: Facebook Widens Data Targeting," *The Wall Street Journal*, April 10, 2013, p. B4.
44. Sam Costello, "How Many Apps Are in the App Store?" *lifewire.com*, April 15, 2019; and Artyom Dogtiev, "App Download and Usage Statistics," *businessofapps.com*, February 16, 2019.
45. Andy Robertson, "'Angry Birds 2' Arrives 6 Years and 3 Billion Downloads after First Game," *forbes.com*, July 16, 2015; Juhana Rossi, "Angry Birds' Maker Perches for Global Growth Takeoff," *The Wall Street Journal*, April 4, 2013, p. B4; Spencer E. Ante, "Rovio Mines Video with 'Angry Birds Toons,'" *The Wall Street Journal*, March 12, 2013, p. B6; and John Gaudiosi, "Rovio Execs Explain What Angry Birds Toons Channel Opens Up to Its 1.7 Billion Gamers," *Forbes*, March 13, 2013. See http://www.forbes.com/sites/johngaudiosi/2013/03/11/rovio-execs-explain-what-angry-birds-toons-channel-opens-up-to-its-1-7-billion-gamers.
46. "List of Levels," Candy Crush Saga Wiki, https://candycrush.fandom.com/wiki/List_of_Levels, accessed October 4, 2019; Dean Takahashi,

"Candy Crush Saga: 2.73 Billion Downloads in Five Years and Still Counting," *venturebeat.com*, November 7, 2017; and Daniel Engher, "Why Is Candy Crush so Addictive?" *Popular Science,* July 17, 2015.

47. This discussion is based on Kieley Taylor, "On-Demanding: 12 Social Media Trends That Are Opening New Opportunities for Advertisers," *Journal of Digital & Social Media Marketing* 7, no. 1 (2019), pp. 28–34.

48. Martin Petit D'Meurville, Kimberley Pham, and Courtney Trin, "Shop on the Go," *Business Today,* February 15, 2015, pp. 113–16.

49. Christopher Mims, "Privacy Is Dead. Here's What Comes Next," *The Wall Street Journal,* May 6, 2018; and David Pierce, "How to Keep Google from Owning Your Online Life," *The Wall Street Journal,* May 8, 2018.

50. Body Glove: This case was written by Steven Hartley and Roger Kerin. Sources: Interviews with Body Glove executives Billy Meistrell, Nick Meistrell, Jenna Meistrell, and Russ Lesser; Kailee Bradstreet, "Body Glove Aims to 'Create Happiness' through Its Yoga Tour and New Fitness Initiative," *adventuresportsnetwork.com*, May 30, 2018; "New Audio Innovations from Body Glove: For People on the Move," *memebum.com*, July 2, 2018; "Body Glove Makes Waves with FlowRider," *shop-eat-surf.com*, May 8, 2018; Jim Harris,"On the Waves," *Retail-Merchandiser.com*, November/December 2017; "Marquee Brands: The Sky's the Limit," *licensemag.com*, August 2017; Kailee Bradstreet, "Body Glove Expands Distribution into Europe," *adventuresportsnetwork.com*, April 5, 2018; "Marquee Brands Acquires Body Glove," *PR Newswire,* November 2, 2016; Meghan Flynn, "Ultimate in Watersports," *Retail Merchandiser,* March/April, 2011; Frank Gromling, *Fits Like a Glove: The Bill & Bob Meistrell Story* (Flagler Beach, Florida: Ocean Publishing, 2013); and Marquee Brands website, *marqueebrands.com*.

Chapter 21 Personal Selling and Sales Management

Learning Objectives

After reading this chapter you should be able to:

LO 21-1 Discuss the nature and scope of personal selling and sales management in marketing.

LO 21-2 Identify the different types of personal selling.

LO 21-3 Explain the stages in the personal selling process.

LO 21-4 Describe the major functions of sales management.

Meet Today's Sales Professional

Have you been considering sales as a career opportunity? If so, then consider Lindsey Smith as a role model.

Lindsey Smith began her career representing Molecular Imaging Products within the Medical Diagnostics Division of GE Healthcare Americas. She joined the company right out of college with a BBA degree. The epitome of today's sales professional, she lists integrity, motivation, trust and relationship building, and a team orientation as just a few of the ingredients necessary for a successful sales career today.

As a sales professional, she recognizes the importance of constantly updating and refining her product knowledge, analytical and communication skills, and strategic thinking about opportunities to more fully satisfy each customer's clinical, economic, and technical requirements. And for good reason. Her customer contacts include physicians (radiologists, neurologists, and cardiologists), medical technologists, nurses, and health care provider CEOs, CFOs, and other administrators.

Lindsey Smith's selling orientation and customer relationship philosophy rest on four pillars:

1. *A commitment to creating value for clients.* Lindsey believes "every sales call and client interaction should create value for both the customer and the company."
2. *Seek to serve clients as a trusted consultant.* Lindsey emphasizes "being a resource for my customers by providing novel solutions for them."
3. *Reinforce the company's competitive advantage.* Lindsey continually reinforces GE Healthcare Americas's competitive advantage: "I emphasize my company's value proposition and showcase the company's product innovation, solutions, and service."
4. *Regard challenges as opportunities.* Lindsey says, "I consider challenges as opportunities to provide innovative solutions and resources to customers and to build client trust and long-term relationships."

Lindsey Smith's approach to selling and customer relationships has served her customers and her well. She is among the company's top revenue producers and has a long list of loyal customers. Ms. Smith has been a frequent recipient of the company's Commercial Excellence Award.

Not surprisingly, Lindsey Smith was promoted to senior client director at GE Healthcare Americas. This position is responsible for the entire GE Healthcare Americas company portfolio, including medical technology, health care consulting, information technology, service operations, and finance solutions for one of GE's largest strategic health care systems. This position also involves management of 75 commercial and operations personnel.[1]

Hillsman Stuart Jackson

This chapter describes the scope and significance of personal selling and sales management in marketing and creating value for customers. It first highlights the many forms of personal selling. Next, the major steps in the selling process are outlined with an emphasis on building buyer–seller relationships.

The chapter then focuses on salesforce management and its critical role in achieving a company's broader marketing objectives. Three major salesforce management functions are then detailed. They are sales plan formulation, sales plan implementation, and salesforce evaluation. Finally, technology's persuasive influence on how selling is done and how salespeople are managed is described.

SCOPE AND SIGNIFICANCE OF PERSONAL SELLING AND SALES MANAGEMENT

Chapter 18 described personal selling and management of the sales effort as being part of the firm's promotional mix. Although it is important to recognize that personal selling is a useful vehicle for communicating with present and potential buyers, it is much more. Take a moment to answer the questions in the personal selling and sales management quiz in Figure 21–1 on the next page. As you read on, compare your answers with those in the text.

FIGURE 21–1
Personal selling and sales management quiz. Check your answers as you read the chapter.

1. What percentage of chief executive officers in the largest U.S. companies have significant sales experience in their work history? (check one)

   10% ______ 30% ______ 50% ______

   20% ______ 40% ______ 60% ______

2. About what percentage of an average field sales representative's time each workweek is spent actually selling to customers by phone or face-to-face? (check one)

   40% ______ 50% ______ 60% ______

3. "A salesperson's job is finished when a sale is made." True or false? (circle one)

   True False

4. About what percentage of U.S. companies include customer satisfaction as a measure of salesperson performance? (check one)

   10% ______ 30% ______ 50% ______

   20% ______ 40% ______ 60% ______

Nature of Personal Selling and Sales Management

LO 21-1
Discuss the nature and scope of personal selling and sales management in marketing.

Personal selling involves the two-way flow of communication between a buyer and seller, often in a face-to-face encounter, designed to influence a person's or group's purchase decision. However, personal selling also takes place over the telephone and through video teleconferencing and Internet-enabled links between buyers and sellers.

Personal selling remains a highly human-intensive activity despite the use of technology. Accordingly, the people involved must be managed. **Sales management** involves planning the selling program and implementing and evaluating the personal selling effort of the firm. The tasks involved in managing personal selling include setting objectives; organizing the salesforce; recruiting, selecting, training, and compensating salespeople; and evaluating the performance of individual salespeople.

Selling Happens Almost Everywhere

"Everyone lives by selling something," wrote author Robert Louis Stevenson a century ago. This is particularly true for manufacturing sales personnel, real estate brokers, stockbrokers, and salesclerks who work in retail stores. In reality, however, virtually every occupation that involves customer contact has an element of personal selling. For example, attorneys, accountants, bankers, and company personnel recruiters perform sales-related activities, whether or not they acknowledge it.

About 20 percent of chief executive officers in the largest U.S. corporations have significant sales experience in their work history.[2] (*What percentage did you check for question 1 in Figure 21-1?*) Thus, selling often serves as a stepping-stone to top management, as well as being a satisfying career path itself.

Personal Selling in Marketing and Entrepreneurship

VIDEO 21-1
Cambridge Sales
kerin.tv/15e/v21-1

Personal selling serves three major roles in a firm's overall marketing effort. First, salespeople are the critical link between the firm and its customers. This role requires that salespeople match company interests with customer needs to satisfy both parties in the exchange process. Second, salespeople *are* the company in a consumer's eyes. They represent what a company is or attempts to be and are often the only personal contact a customer has with the company. For example, as acknowledged by IBM's former chief executive officer, the company's

Could this be a salesperson in the operating room? Read the text to find out why Medtronic salespeople visit hospital operating rooms.
Radius Images/Getty Images

Medtronic
www.medtronic.com

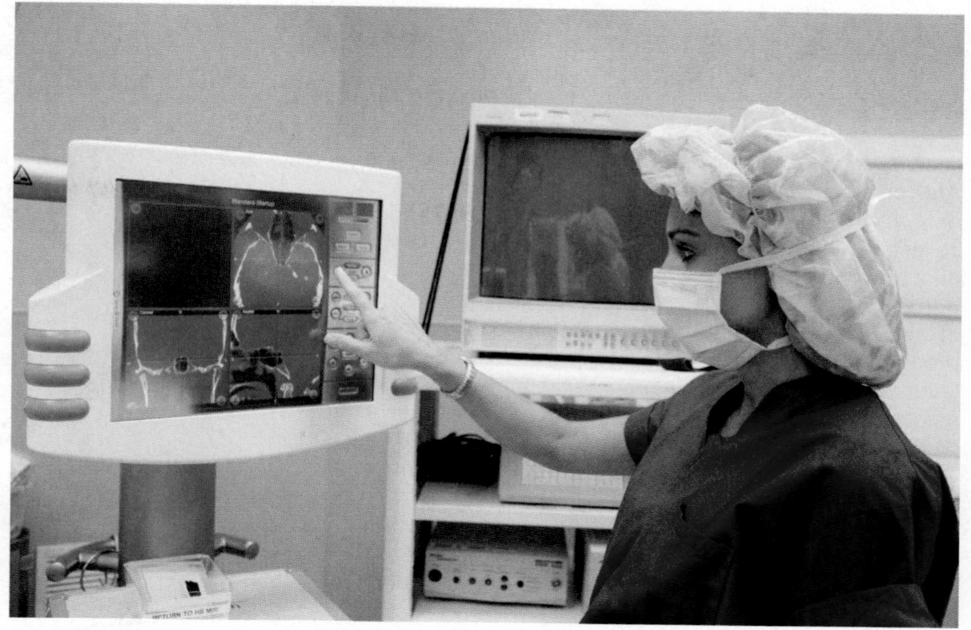

40,000-strong salesforce is "our face to the client."[3] Third, personal selling may play a dominant role in a firm's marketing program. This situation typically arises when a firm uses a push marketing strategy, described in Chapter 18. Avon, for example, pays almost 40 percent of its total sales dollars for selling expenses.

Personal selling also has been shown to be critical to successful entrepreneurial efforts for three reasons.[4] First, selling a business concept to potential investors is an entrepreneur's first sales effort. Second, selling the business concept to prospective employees necessary for the success of the venture is essential. Finally, the more traditional sales art of convincing customers to buy one's product or service, getting referrals, and building professional networks is necessary. In short, highly successful entrepreneurs have a great sales talent.

Creating Customer Solutions and Value through Salespeople: Relationship Selling

As the critical link between the firm and its customers, salespeople can create customer value in many ways. For instance, by being close to the customer, salespeople can identify creative solutions to customer problems. Salespeople at Medtronic, Inc., the world leader in the heart pacemaker market, are in the operating room for more than 90 percent of the procedures performed with their product and are on call 24 hours a day. "It reflects the willingness to be there in every situation, just in case a problem arises—even though nine times out of ten the procedure goes just fine," notes a satisfied customer.[5]

Salespeople can create value by easing the customer buying process. This happened at TE Connectivity, a producer of electrical products. Salespeople and customers had a difficult time getting product specifications and performance data on the company's 70,000 products quickly and accurately. The company now has all of its information on its website, which can be downloaded instantly by salespeople and customers.

Customer value is also created by salespeople who follow through after the sale. At Jefferson Smurfit Corporation, a multibillion-dollar supplier of packaging products, one of its salespeople juggled production from three of the company's plants to satisfy an unexpected demand for boxes from General Electric. This person's action led to the company being given GE's Distinguished Supplier Award.

Marketing Matters

Customer Value

Science and Selling: Is Customer Value Creation in Your Genes?

Is a predisposition to create customer value in your genes? Are you a born salesperson? Recent research by University of Michigan Marketing Professor Richard P. Bagozzi and his colleagues offers a novel insight into this question that may or may not surprise you.

Their research identifies a genetic marker, the 7R variant of the DRD_4 gene, that is correlated with a salesperson's predisposition or willingness to interact with customers and learn about their problems in order to meet their needs. The researchers also found that the presence of the A1 variant of the DRD_2 gene is correlated with a predisposition or tendency to try to persuade customers to buy a given product rather than listen to their needs.

These two different genetic markers help explain the difference between a salesperson's customer orientation versus sales orientation. A customer orientation is guided by such ideas as, "I try to align customers who have problems with products that will help them solve their problems," where the aim is to satisfy mutual needs and the hope is to build a long-term relationship.

In contrast, a sales orientation is driven by notions such as, "I try to sell customers all I can convince them to buy, even if I think it is more than a wise customer should buy." In this case, the motivation is to satisfy one's own short-term interests and not necessarily the needs of the customer.

Faced with a selling situation, do you have a sales orientation or a customer orientation? Customer value creation may be in your genes!

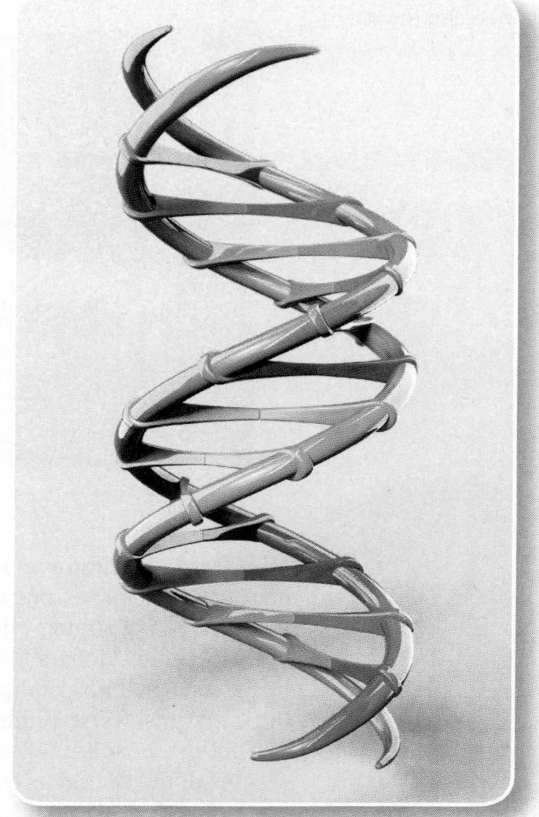

Dimitri Otis/Photographer's Choice/Getty Images

Customer value creation is made possible by **relationship selling**, the practice of building ties to customers based on a salesperson's attention and commitment to customer needs over time. Relationship selling involves mutual respect and trust among buyers and sellers. It focuses on creating long-term customers and long-run customer value, not a one-time sale. In this regard, senior sales executives consider building long-term relationships with customers to be the most important activity affecting sales performance.[6]

Relationship selling represents another dimension of *customer relationship management* first introduced in Chapter 1. It emphasizes the importance of first learning about customer needs and wants and then tailoring solutions to customer problems as a means to customer value creation. Recent research suggests that a salesperson may have a genetic predisposition to create customer value. See the Marketing Matters box for details.[7]

LEARNING REVIEW

21-1. What is personal selling?

21-2. What is involved in sales management?

THE MANY FORMS OF PERSONAL SELLING

LO 21-2

Identify the different types of personal selling.

Personal selling assumes many forms based on the amount of selling done and the amount of creativity required to perform the sales task. Broadly speaking, three types of personal selling exist: order taking, order getting, and customer sales support activities. While some firms use only one of these types of personal selling, others use a combination of all three.

Order-Taking Salespeople

Typically, an **order taker** processes routine orders or reorders for products that were already sold by the company. The primary responsibility of order takers is to preserve an ongoing relationship with existing customers and maintain sales.

Two types of order takers exist. *Outside order takers* visit customers and replenish inventory stocks of resellers, such as retailers or wholesalers. For example, Frito-Lay salespeople call on supermarkets, convenience stores, and other establishments to ensure that the company's line of snack products (such as Lay's potato chips and Doritos and Tostitos tortilla chips) is in adequate supply. In addition, outside order takers often provide assistance in arranging displays.

Inside order takers, also called *order clerks* or *salesclerks*, typically answer simple questions, take orders, and complete transactions with customers. Many retail clerks are inside order takers. Inside order takers are often employed by companies that use *inbound telemarketing*, the use of toll-free telephone numbers that customers can call to obtain information about products or services and make purchases. In business-to-business settings, order taking arises in straight rebuy situations as described in Chapter 6.

Order takers generally do little selling in a conventional sense. They engage in modest problem solving with customers. They often represent products that have few options, such as magazine subscriptions and highly standardized industrial products. Inbound telemarketing is also an essential selling activity for more "customer service" driven firms, such as Dell Technologies. At these companies, order takers undergo extensive training so that they can better assist callers with their purchase decisions.

Order-Getting Salespeople

An **order getter** sells in a conventional sense and identifies prospective customers, provides customers with information, persuades customers to buy, closes sales, and follows up on customers' use of a product or service. Like order takers, order getters can be inside (an automobile salesperson) or outside (an IBM salesperson).

Order getting involves a high degree of creativity and customer empathy and is typically required for selling complex or technical products with many options, so considerable product knowledge and sales training are necessary. In modified rebuy or new-buy purchase situations in business-to-business selling, an order getter acts as a problem solver who identifies how a particular product may satisfy a customer's need. Similarly, in the purchase of a service, such as insurance, an insurance agent can provide a mix of plans to satisfy a buyer's needs depending on income, stage of the family's life cycle, and investment objectives.

Order getting is not a 40-hour-per-week job. Industry research shows that outside order getters, or field service representatives, often work over 50 hours per week. As shown in Figure 21–2, 36 percent of an average field sales representative's time is actually spent selling by phone or face-to-face. (*What percentage did you check for question 2 in Figure 21–1?*) Another 15 percent is devoted to generating leads and researching customer accounts. The remainder of a sales representative's workweek is occupied by administrative tasks, meetings, service calls, travel, training, and customer follow-up.[8]

Order getting by outside salespeople is also expensive.[9] It is estimated that the average cost of a single field sales call on a business customer is about $500, factoring in the salesperson's compensation, benefits, and travel-and-entertainment expenses. This cost illustrates why outbound telemarketing is popular. *Outbound telemarketing* is the practice of using the telephone rather than personal visits to contact current and prospective customers. A much lower cost per sales call (from $20 to $25) and little or no field expense accounts for its widespread appeal.

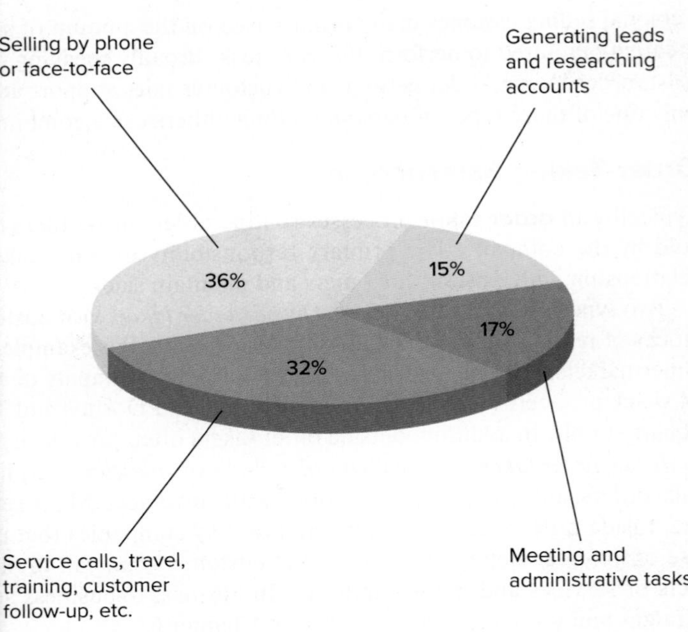

FIGURE 21–2 How do outside order-getting salespeople spend their time each week? You might be surprised after reading the text.

Photos: (Top left): Asia Images/Getty Images; (Top right): Tetra Images/Getty Images; (Bottom left): Colin Anderson Productions pty ltd/DigitalVision/Getty Images; (Bottom right): Stanley Fellerman/Corbis

Customer Sales Support Personnel

Customer sales support personnel augment the selling effort of order getters by performing a variety of services. For example, *missionary salespeople* do not directly solicit orders but rather concentrate on performing promotional activities and introducing new products. They are used in the pharmaceutical industry, where they encourage physicians to prescribe a firm's product. Actual sales are made through wholesalers or directly to pharmacists who fill prescriptions. *Sales engineers* specialize in identifying, analyzing, and solving customer problems. These salespeople bring know-how and technical expertise to the selling situation but often do not actually sell products and services. Sales engineers are popular in selling business products such as chemicals and heavy equipment.

Many firms engage in cross-functional **team selling**, the practice of using an entire team of professionals in selling to and servicing major customers.[10] Team selling is used when specialized knowledge is needed to satisfy the different interests of individuals in a customer's buying center. A selling team might consist of a salesperson, a sales engineer, a service representative, and a financial executive, each of whom would deal with a counterpart in the customer's firm.

Selling teams take different forms. In *conference selling*, a salesperson and other company resource people meet with buyers to discuss problems and opportunities. In *seminar selling*, a company team conducts an educational program for a customer's technical staff, describing state-of-the-art developments. IBM and Xerox pioneered cross-functional team selling in working with prospective buyers. Since then, other firms have embraced this practice to create and sustain value for their customers, as described in the Marketing Matters box.[11]

LEARNING REVIEW

21-3. What is the principal difference between an order taker and an order getter?

21-4. What is team selling?

Marketing Matters

Customer Value

Creating and Sustaining Customer Value through Cross-Functional Team Selling

The day of the lone salesperson calling on a customer is rapidly becoming history. Today, 75 percent of companies employ cross-functional teams of professionals to work with customers to improve relationships, find better ways of doing things, and, of course, create and sustain value for their customers.

Xerox and IBM pioneered cross-functional team selling, but other firms have been quick to follow as they spotted the potential to create and sustain value for their customers. Recognizing that corn growers needed a herbicide they could apply less often, a DuPont team of chemists, sales and marketing executives, and regulatory specialists created just the right product that recorded sales of $57 million in its first year. Procter & Gamble uses teams of marketing, sales, advertising, computer systems, and supply chain personnel to work with its major retailers, such as Walmart, to identify ways to develop, promote, and deliver products. Pitney Bowes, Inc., which produces sophisticated computer systems that weigh, rate, and track packages for firms such as UPS and FedEx, also uses sales teams to meet customer needs. These teams consist of sales personnel, "carrier management specialists," and engineering and administrative executives who continually find ways to improve the technology involved in shipping goods across town and around the world.

Efforts to create and sustain customer value through cross-functional team selling have become a necessity as customers seek greater value for their money. According to the vice president for procurement of a *Fortune* 500 company, "Today, it's not just getting the best price but getting the best value—and there are a lot of pieces to value."

Blickwinkel/Alamy Stock Photo

THE PERSONAL SELLING PROCESS: BUILDING RELATIONSHIPS

LO 21-3
Explain the stages in the personal selling process.

Selling, and particularly order getting, is a complicated activity that involves building buyer-seller relationships. Although the salesperson-customer interaction is essential to personal selling, much of a salesperson's work occurs before this meeting and continues after the sale itself. The **personal selling process** consists of six stages: (1) prospecting, (2) preapproach, (3) approach, (4) presentation, (5) close, and (6) follow-up (see Figure 21-3 on the next page).

FIGURE 21–3

Stages and objectives of the personal selling process. Each stage is critical for successful selling and building a customer relationship.

STAGE	OBJECTIVE	COMMENTS
1. Prospecting	Search for and qualify prospects	Start of the selling process; prospects produced through advertising, referrals, and cold canvassing
2. Preapproach	Gather information and decide how to approach the prospect	Information sources include personal observation, other customers, and own salespeople
3. Approach	Gain a prospect's attention, stimulate interest, and make transition to the presentation	First impression is critical; gain attention and interest through reference to common acquaintances, a referral, or product demonstration
4. Presentation	Begin converting a prospect into a customer by creating a desire for the product or service	Different presentation formats are possible; however, involving the customer in the product or service through attention to particular needs is critical; important to deal professionally and ethically with prospect skepticism, indifference, or objections
5. Close	Obtain a purchase commitment from the prospect and create a customer	Salesperson asks for the purchase; different approaches include the trial close and assumptive close
6. Follow-up	Ensure that the customer is satisfied with the product or service	Resolve any problems faced by the customer to ensure customer satisfaction and future sales possibilities

Prospecting: Identifying and Qualifying Prospective Customers

Personal selling begins with the *prospecting* stage—the search for and qualification of potential customers. There are three types of prospects. A *lead* is the name of a person who may be a possible customer. A *prospect* is a customer who wants or needs the product. If an individual wants the product, can afford to buy it, and is the decision maker, this individual is a *qualified prospect*.

Leads and prospects are generated using several sources. For example, advertising may contain a coupon or a toll-free number to generate leads. Some companies use exhibits at trade shows, professional meetings, and conferences to generate leads or prospects. Staffed by salespeople, these exhibits are used to attract the attention of prospective buyers and share information. Others utilize websites, e-mail, and social networks, such as LinkedIn, to connect to individuals and companies that may be interested in their products or services. This practice is called *social selling*.

Another approach for generating leads is through *cold canvassing* or *cold calling*, either in person or by telephone. This approach simply means that a salesperson may open a directory,

Trade shows are a popular source for leads and prospects. Companies like TSNN provide comprehensive trade show information.
Urbanmyth/Alamy Stock Photo

TSNN
www.tsnn.com

pick a name, and contact that individual or business. Despite its high refusal rate, cold canvassing can be successful.[12] However, cold canvassing is frowned upon in some cultures. For example, in most Asian and Latin American societies, personal visits, based on referrals, are expected.

Cold canvassing is often criticized by U.S. consumers and is now regulated. Research shows that 75 percent of U.S. consumers consider this practice an intrusion on their privacy, and 72 percent find it distasteful.[13] The *Telephone Consumer Protection Act* (1991) contains provisions to curb abuses such as early morning or late night calling. Additional federal regulations require more complete disclosure regarding solicitations, include provisions that allow consumers to avoid being called at any time through the Do Not Call Registry, and impose fines for violations. For example, satellite television provider Dish Network was fined $280 million for making 66 million calls to consumers who had put their telephone numbers on the Do Not Call Registry.[14]

Preapproach: Preparing for the Sales Call

Once a salesperson has identified a qualified prospect, preparation for the sale begins with the preapproach. The *preapproach* stage involves obtaining further information on the prospect and deciding on the best method of approach. Knowing how the prospect prefers to be approached and what the prospect is looking for in a product or service is essential, regardless of industry or cultural setting.

For instance, a Merrill Lynch stockbroker will need information on a prospect's discretionary income, investment objectives, and preference for discussing brokerage services over the telephone or in person. For business product companies such as Texas Instruments, the preapproach involves identifying the buying role of a prospect (for example, influencer or decision maker), important buying criteria, and the prospect's receptivity to a formal or informal presentation. Identifying the best time to contact a prospect is also important. Northwestern Mutual Life Insurance Company suggests that the following are the best times to call on people in different occupations: dentists before 9:30 A.M., lawyers between 11:00 A.M. and 2:00 P.M., and college professors between 7:00 and 8:00 P.M.

The preapproach stage is especially important in international selling, where customs dictate appropriate protocol. In many South American countries, for example, buyers expect salespeople to be punctual for appointments. However, prospective buyers are routinely 30 minutes late. South Americans take negotiating seriously and prefer straightforward presentations, but a hard-sell approach will not work.[15]

Successful salespeople recognize that the preapproach stage should never be shortchanged. Their experience coupled with research on customer complaints indicates that failure to learn as much as possible about the prospect is unprofessional and the ruin of a sales call.

Approach: Making the First Impression

The *approach* stage involves the initial meeting between the salesperson and the prospect, where the objectives are to gain the prospect's attention, stimulate interest, and build the foundation for the sales presentation itself and the basis for a working relationship. The first impression is critical at this stage, and it is common for salespeople to begin the conversation with a reference to common acquaintances, a referral, or even the product or service itself. Which tactic is taken will depend on the information obtained in the prospecting and preapproach stages.

How business cards are exchanged with Asian customers is very important. Read the text to learn the appropriate protocol in the approach stage of the personal selling process.
The Image Bank/Getty Images

The approach stage is very important in international settings.[16] In many societies outside the United States, considerable time is devoted to nonbusiness talk designed to establish a rapport between buyers and sellers. For instance, it is common for two or three meetings to occur before business matters are discussed in the Middle East and Asia. Gestures are also very important. The initial meeting between a salesperson and a prospect in the United States customarily begins with a firm handshake. Handshakes also apply in France, but they are gentle, not firm. Forget the handshake in Japan. An appropriate bow is expected. What about business cards? Business cards should be printed in English on one side and the language of the prospective customer on the other. Knowledgeable U.S. salespeople know that their business cards should be handed to Asian customers using both hands, with the name facing the receiver. In Asia, anything involving a person's name demands respect.

Presentation: Tailoring a Solution for a Customer's Needs

The *presentation* stage is at the core of the order-getting selling process, and its objective is to convert a prospect into a customer by creating a desire for the product or service. Three major presentation formats exist: (1) stimulus-response format, (2) formula selling format, and (3) need-satisfaction format.

Stimulus-Response Format The *stimulus-response presentation* format assumes that given the appropriate stimulus by a salesperson, the prospect will buy. With this format the salesperson tries one appeal after another, hoping to hit the right button. A counter clerk at McDonald's is using this approach when he or she asks whether you'd like an order of french fries or a dessert with your meal. The counter clerk is engaging in what is called *suggestive selling*. Although useful in this setting, the stimulus-response format is not always appropriate, and for many products a more formalized format is necessary.

Formula Selling Format The *formula selling presentation* format is based on the view that a presentation consists of information that must be provided in an accurate, thorough, and step-by-step manner to inform the prospect. A popular version of this format is the *canned sales presentation*, which is a memorized, standardized message conveyed to every prospect. Used frequently by firms in telephone and door-to-door selling of consumer products (for example, Kirby vacuum cleaners), this approach treats every prospect the same, regardless of differences in needs or preferences for certain kinds of information.

Canned sales presentations can be advantageous when the differences between prospects are unknown or with novice salespeople who are less knowledgeable about the product and selling process than experienced salespeople. Although it guarantees a thorough presentation, it often lacks flexibility and spontaneity. More important, it does not provide for feedback from the prospective buyer—a critical component in the communication process and the start of a relationship.

Need-Satisfaction Format The stimulus-response and formula selling formats share a common characteristic: The salesperson dominates the conversation. By comparison, the *need-satisfaction presentation* format emphasizes probing and listening by the salesperson to identify the needs and interests of prospective buyers. Once these are identified, the salesperson tailors the presentation to the prospect and highlights product benefits that may be valued by the prospect. The need-satisfaction format, which emphasizes problem solving and customer solutions, is most consistent with the marketing concept and its focus on relationship building.

Two selling styles are common with this format.[17] **Adaptive selling** involves adjusting the presentation to fit the selling situation, such as knowing when to offer solutions and when to ask for more information. Sales research and practice show that knowledge of the customer and sales situation are key ingredients for adaptive selling. Many consumer service firms such as brokerage and insurance firms and consumer product firms like Rockport, AT&T, and Gillette effectively apply this selling style.

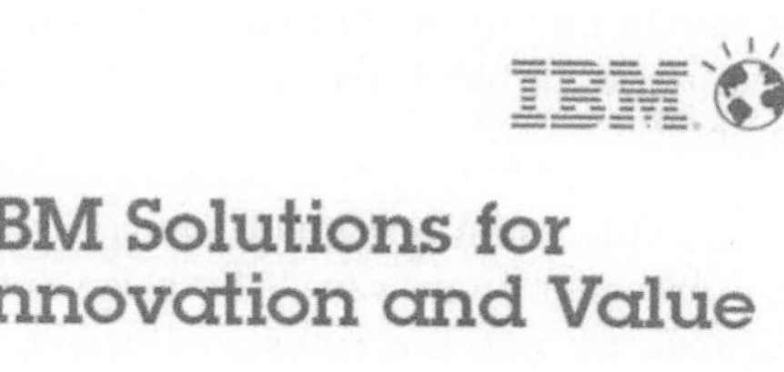

IBM is a leader in consultative selling with its focus on developing novel solutions that create customer value.
Source: IBM

Consultative selling focuses on problem identification, where the salesperson serves as an expert on problem recognition and resolution. With consultative selling, problem solution options are not simply a matter of choosing from an array of existing products or services. Rather, novel solutions often arise, thereby creating unique value for the customer.

Upselling and cross-selling is possible when a salesperson is viewed as an expert on problem recognition and resolution. *Upselling* is the practice of introducing a higher-end product solution than the one in question. *Cross-selling* is the practice of proposing related or complementary products and services. In both types of selling, the underlying intent is to create greater value for customers.

Consultative selling is prominent in business-to-business marketing. Johnson Controls's Automotive Systems Group, IBM's Global Services, DHL Worldwide Express, GE Healthcare Americas, and Xerox offer customer solutions through their consultative selling style. According to a senior Xerox sales executive, "Our business is no longer about selling boxes. It's about selling digital, networked-based information management solutions, and this requires a highly customized and consultative selling process. So we look for consultative and business-savvy salespeople." But what does a customer solution really mean? The Marketing Matters box on the next page offers a unique answer.[18]

Handling Objections A critical concern in the presentation stage is handling objections. *Objections* are excuses for not making a purchase commitment or decision. Some objections are valid and are based on the characteristics of the product or service or price. However, many objections reflect prospect skepticism or indifference. Whether valid or not, experienced

Marketing Matters — Customer Value

Imagine This . . . Putting the Customer into Customer Solutions!

Solutions to problems are what companies are looking for from suppliers. At the same time, suppliers focus on customer solutions to differentiate themselves from competitors. So what is a customer solution and what does it have to do with selling?

Sellers view a solution as a customized and integrated combination of products and services for meeting a customer's business needs. But what do buyers think? From a buyer's perspective, a solution is one that (1) meets their requirements, (2) is designed to uniquely solve their problem, (3) can be implemented, and (4) ensures follow-up.

Colin Anderson/Getty Images

This insight arose from a field study conducted by three researchers at Emory University. Their in-depth study also yielded insight into what an effective customer solution offers. According to one buyer interviewed in their study:

They (the supplier) make sure that their sales and marketing guys know what's going on. The sales and technical folks know what's going on, and the technical and support guys know what's going on with me. All these guys are in the loop, and it's not a puzzle for them.

So what does putting the customer into customer solutions have to do with selling? Three things stand out. First, considerable time and effort is necessary to fully understand a specific customer's requirements. Second, effective customer solutions are based on relationships among sellers and buyers. And finally, consultative selling is central to providing novel solutions for customers, thereby creating value for them.

Selling solutions has an added benefit to those companies that engage in this practice. Their dollar return on the sales effort is improved.

salespeople know that objections do not put an end to the presentation. Rather, techniques can be used to deal with objections in a courteous, ethical, and professional manner. The following six techniques are the most common:[19]

1. *Acknowledge and convert the objection.* This technique involves using the objection as a reason for buying. For example, a prospect might say, "The price is too high." The reply: "Yes, the price is high because we use the finest materials. Let me show you. . . . "
2. *Postpone.* The postpone technique is used when the objection will be dealt with later in the presentation: "I'm going to address that point shortly. I think my answer would make better sense then."
3. *Agree and neutralize.* Here a salesperson agrees with the objection, then shows that it is unimportant. A salesperson would say, "That's true. Others have said the same. But, they thought that issue was outweighed by other benefits."
4. *Accept the objection.* Sometimes the objection is valid. Let the prospect express such views, probe for the reason behind it, and attempt to stimulate further discussion on the objection.
5. *Denial.* When a prospect's objection is based on misinformation and clearly untrue, it is wise to meet the objection head on with a firm denial.
6. *Ignore the objection.* This technique is used when it appears that the objection is a stalling mechanism or is clearly not important to the prospect.

Each of these techniques requires a calm, professional interaction with the prospect and is most effective when objections are anticipated in the preapproach stage. Handling objections is a skill requiring a sense of timing, appreciation for the prospect's state of mind, and adeptness in communication. Objections also should be handled ethically. Lying or misrepresenting product or service features are clearly unethical practices.

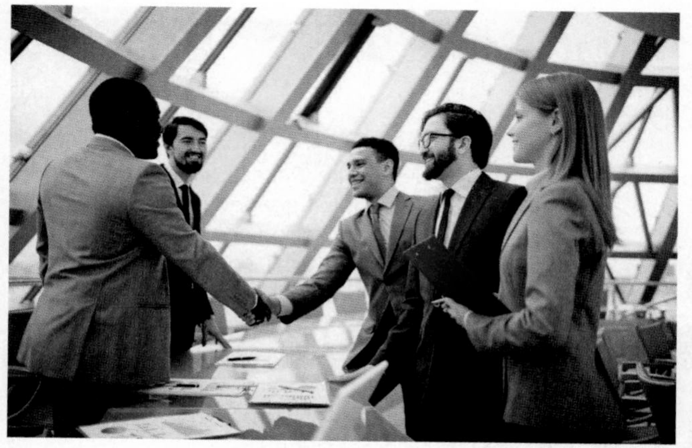

The closing stage involves obtaining a purchase commitment from the prospect. Read the text to learn how the close itself can take several forms.
shironosov/iStock/Getty Images

Close: Asking for the Customer's Order or Business

The *closing* stage in the selling process involves obtaining a purchase commitment from the prospect. This stage is the most important and the most difficult because the salesperson must determine when the prospect is ready to buy. Telltale signals indicating a readiness to buy include body language (prospect reexamines the product or contract closely), statements ("This equipment should reduce our maintenance costs"), and questions ("When could we expect delivery?").

The close itself can take several forms. Three closing techniques are used when a salesperson believes a buyer is about ready to make a purchase: (1) trial close, (2) assumptive close, and (3) urgency close. A *trial close* involves asking the prospect to make a decision on some aspect of the purchase: "Would you prefer the blue or gray model?" An *assumptive close* entails asking the prospect to consider choices concerning delivery, warranty, or financing terms under the assumption that a sale has been finalized. An *urgency close* is used to commit the prospect quickly by making reference to the timeliness of the purchase: "The low interest financing ends next week," or "That is the last model we have in stock." Of course, these statements should be used only if they accurately reflect the situation; otherwise, such claims would be unethical. When a prospect is clearly ready to buy, the final close is used, and a salesperson asks for the order.

Follow-up: Solidifying the Relationship

The selling process does not end with the closing of a sale; rather, professional selling requires customer follow-up. One marketing authority equated the follow-up with courtship and marriage by observing, "The sale merely consummates the courtship. Then the marriage begins. How good the marriage is depends on how well the relationship is managed."[20] The *follow-up* stage includes making certain the customer's purchase has been properly delivered and installed and addressing any difficulties experienced with the use of the item. Attention to this stage of the selling process solidifies the buyer–seller relationship. Research shows that the cost and effort to obtain repeat sales from a satisfied customer is roughly half of that necessary to gain a sale from a new customer.[21] In short, today's satisfied customers become tomorrow's qualified prospects or referrals. (*What was your answer to question 3 in the Figure 21-1 quiz?*)

LEARNING REVIEW

21-5. What are the six stages in the personal selling process?

21-6. What is the distinction between a lead and a qualified prospect?

21-7. Which presentation format is most consistent with the marketing concept? Why?

THE SALES MANAGEMENT PROCESS

LO 21-4
Describe the major functions of sales management.

Selling must be managed if it is going to contribute to a firm's marketing objectives. Although firms differ in the specifics of how salespeople and the selling effort are managed, the sales management process is similar across firms. Sales management consists of three interrelated functions: (1) sales plan formulation, (2) sales plan implementation, and (3) salesforce evaluation (see Figure 21-4 on the next page).

Making Responsible Decisions

Ethics

The Ethics of Asking Customers about Competitors

Salespeople are a valuable source of information about what is happening in the marketplace. By working closely with customers and asking good questions, salespeople often have firsthand knowledge of customer problems and wants. They also are able to spot the activities of competitors. However, should salespeople explicitly ask customers about competitor strategies such as pricing practices, product development efforts, and trade and promotion programs?

Gaining knowledge about competitors by asking customers for information is a ticklish ethical issue. Research indicates that 25 percent of U.S. salespeople engaged in business-to-business selling consider this practice unethical, and their companies have explicit guidelines for this practice.

It is also noteworthy that Japanese salespeople consider this practice to be more unethical than do U.S. salespeople.

Do you believe that asking customers about competitor strategies and practices is unethical? Why or why not?

Aleksandr Davydov/123RF

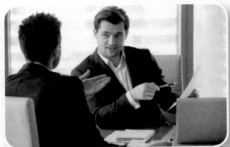

Sales Plan Formulation: Setting Direction

Formulating the sales plan is the most basic of the three sales management functions. According to the vice president of the Harris Corporation, a global communications company, "If a company hopes to implement its marketing strategy, it really needs a detailed sales planning process."[22] The **sales plan** is a statement describing what is to be achieved and where and how the selling effort of salespeople is to be deployed. Sales plan formulation involves three tasks: (1) setting objectives, (2) organizing the salesforce, and (3) developing account management policies.

Setting Objectives Setting objectives is central to sales management because this task specifies what is to be achieved. In practice, objectives are set for the total salesforce and for each salesperson.

Selling objectives can be output related and focus on dollar or unit sales volume, number of new customers added, or profit. Alternatively, they can be input related and emphasize the number of sales calls and selling expenses. Output- and input-related objectives are used for the salesforce as a whole and for each salesperson. A third type of objective that is behaviorally related is typically specific for each salesperson and includes his or her product knowledge, customer service satisfaction ratings, and selling and communication skills.

Increasingly, firms are also emphasizing knowledge of competition as an objective since salespeople are calling on customers and should see what competitors are doing. In fact, 85 percent of companies encourage their salespeople to gather competitive intelligence.[23] But should salespeople explicitly ask their customers for information about competitors? Read the Making Responsible Decisions box to see how salespeople view this practice.[24]

FIGURE 21–4

The sales management process involves sales plan formulation, sales plan implementation, and salesforce evaluation.

Sales plan formulation
- Setting objectives
- Organizing the salesforce
- Developing account management policies

→

Sales plan implementation
- Salesforce recruitment and selection
- Salesforce training
- Salesforce motivation and compensation

→

Salesforce evaluation
- Quantitative assessment
- Behavioral evaluation

Whatever objectives are set, they should be precise and measurable and specify the time period over which they are to be achieved. Once established, these objectives serve as performance standards for the evaluation of the salesforce, the third function of sales management.

Organizing the Salesforce Organizing a selling organization is the second task in formulating the sales plan. Three questions are related to organization. First, should the company use its own salesforce, or should it use independent agents such as manufacturer's representatives? Second, if the decision is made to employ company salespeople, then should they be organized according to geography, customer type, or product or service? Third, how many company salespeople should be employed?

The decision to use company salespeople or independent agents is made infrequently. The decision itself is based on an analysis of economic and behavioral factors. An economic analysis examines the costs of using both types of salespeople and is a form of break-even analysis, which was discussed in Chapter 13.

Consider a situation in which independent agents would receive a 5 percent commission on sales, and company salespeople would receive a 3 percent commission, salaries, and benefits. In addition, with company salespeople, sales administration costs would be incurred for a total fixed cost of $500,000 per year. At what sales level would independent or company salespeople be less costly? This question can be answered by setting the costs of the two options equal to each other and solving for the sales level amount (using algebra!), as shown in the equation:

$$\text{Total cost of company salespeople} = \text{Total cost of independent agents}$$
$$[0.03\ (X) + \$500{,}000] = 0.05\ (X)$$

where X = sales volume. Solving for X, sales volume equals $25 million, indicating that below $25 million in sales independent agents would be cheaper, but above $25 million a company salesforce would be cheaper. This relationship is shown in Figure 21–5.

Economics alone does not answer this question. A behavioral analysis is also necessary and should focus on issues related to the control, flexibility, effort, and availability of independent and company salespeople.[25] A firm must weigh the pros and cons of the economic and behavioral factors before making this decision.

If a company elects to employ its own salespeople, then it must choose an organizational structure based on (1) geography, (2) customer, or (3) product (see Figure 21–6 on the next page). A *geographical sales organization* is the simplest structure, where the United States, or indeed the globe, is first divided into regions and each region is divided into districts or territories. Salespeople are assigned to each district with defined geographical boundaries and call on all customers and represent all products sold by the company. College textbook publishers, such as McGraw-Hill

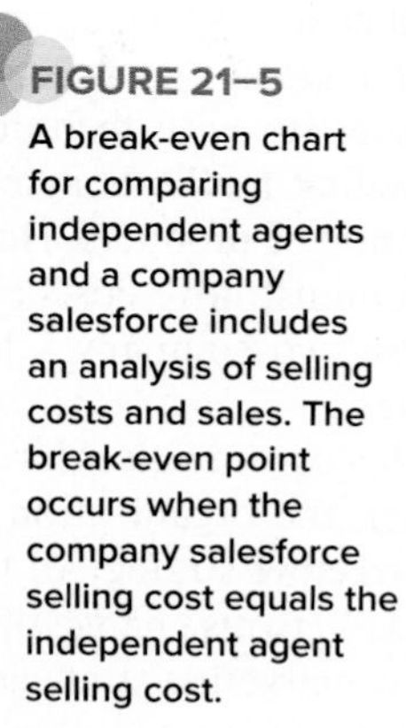

FIGURE 21–5
A break-even chart for comparing independent agents and a company salesforce includes an analysis of selling costs and sales. The break-even point occurs when the company salesforce selling cost equals the independent agent selling cost.

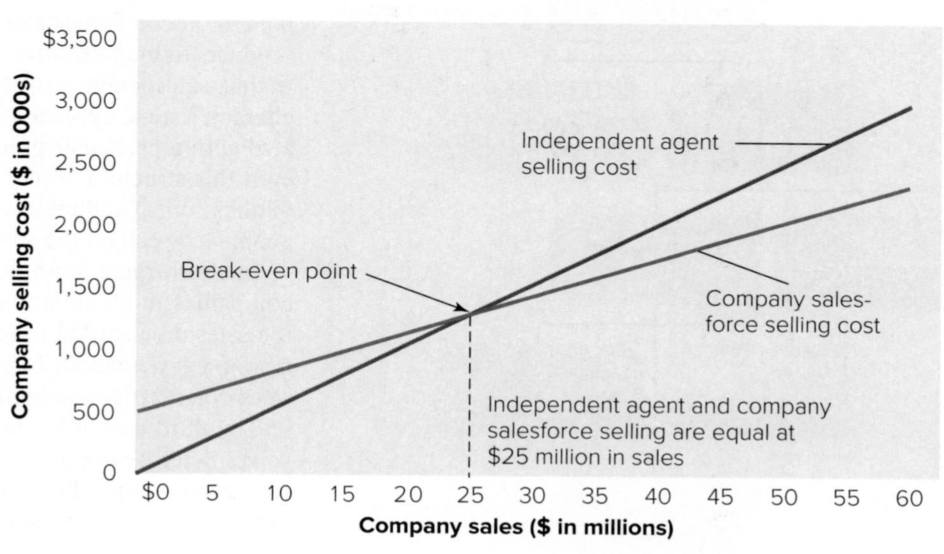

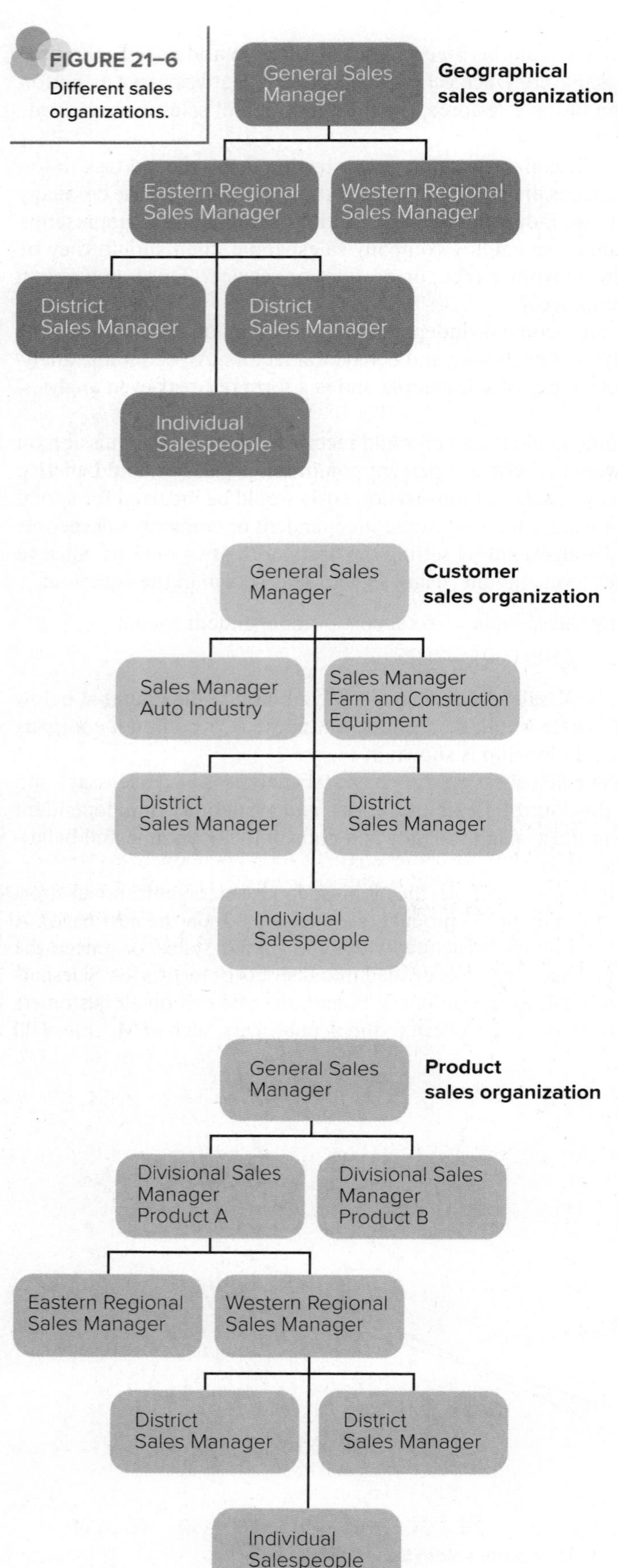

FIGURE 21–6 Different sales organizations.

Education, use this approach. An advantage of this structure is that it can minimize travel time, expenses, and duplication of selling effort. However, if a company's products or customers require specialized knowledge, then a geographical structure is unsuitable.

When different types of buyers have different needs, a *customer sales organization* is used. In practice this means that a different salesforce calls on each separate type of buyer or marketing channel. For example, Google's Cloud-computing salesforce is structured to reflect different needs of large, established companies with existing data management centers versus smaller, digital native companies that require initial installations of data centers. According to a Google senior sales executive, "A lot of our focus is making sure that our sales organization has the right background and ability to sell to different customers."[26] In general, the rationale for this approach is that more effective, specialized customer support and knowledge are provided to buyers. However, this structure often leads to higher administrative costs and some duplication of selling effort, because two or more salesforces are used to represent the same products.

An important variation of the customer organizational structure is **key account management**—the practice of using team selling to focus on important customers so as to build mutually beneficial, long-term, cooperative relationships.[27] Key account management involves teams of sales, service, and often technical personnel who work with purchasing, manufacturing, engineering, logistics, and financial executives in customer organizations. This approach, which often assigns company personnel to a customer account, results in "customer specialists" who can provide exceptional service. Procter & Gamble uses this approach with Walmart, as does Stanley Black & Decker with Home Depot.

When specific knowledge is required to sell certain types of products, then a *product sales organization* is used. For example, Maxim Steel has a salesforce that sells drilling pipe to oil companies and another that sells specialty steel products to manufacturers. The advantage of this structure is that salespeople can develop expertise with technical characteristics, applications, and selling methods associated with a particular product or family of products. However, this structure produces high administrative costs and duplication of selling effort, because two company salespeople may call on the same customer.

In short, there is no one best sales organization for all companies in all situations.[28] Rather, the organization of the salesforce should reflect the marketing strategy of the firm. Each year about 10 percent of U.S. firms change their sales organizations to implement new marketing strategies.

The third question related to salesforce organization involves determining the size of the salesforce. For example, why do you think Frito-Lay has about 18,000 route sales representatives who call on supermarkets, convenience stores, and other establishments to sell snack foods? The answer lies in the number of accounts (customers) served, the frequency of calls on accounts, the length of an average call, and the amount of time a salesperson can devote to selling.

A common approach for determining the size of a salesforce is the **workload method.** This formula-based method integrates the number of customers served, call frequency, call length, and available selling time to arrive at a figure for the salesforce size. For example, Frito-Lay needs about 18,000 route sales representatives according to the following workload method formula:

$$NS = \frac{NC \times CF \times CL}{AST}$$

Where,

NS = Number of route sales representatives

NC = Number of customers

CF = Call frequency necessary to service a customer each year

CL = Length of an average call

AST = Average amount of selling time available per year

How many route sales representatives does Frito-Lay need to sell and service its retail accounts?
David Goldman/AP Images for Frito-Lay

Frito-Lay route sales representatives sell and display products in 350,000 supermarkets, convenience stores, and other establishments. Sales representatives should call on these accounts at least once a week, or 52 times a year. The average sales call lasts an average of 83 minutes (1.38 hour). An average salesperson works 2,000 hours a year (50 weeks × 40 hours a week), but 12 hours a week are devoted to nonselling activities such as travel and administration, leaving 1,400 hours a year. Using these guidelines, Frito-Lay needs

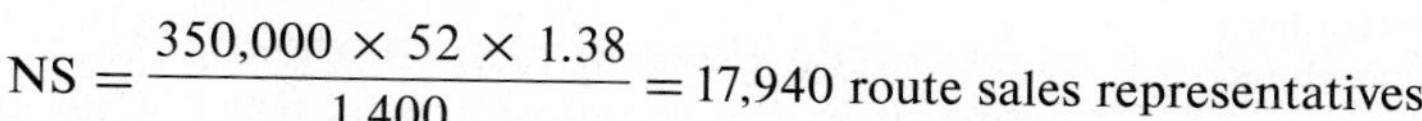

$$NS = \frac{350{,}000 \times 52 \times 1.38}{1{,}400} = 17{,}940 \text{ route sales representatives}$$

The value of this formula is apparent in its flexibility; a change in any one of the variables will affect the number of salespeople needed. Changes are determined, in part, by the firm's account management policies.

Developing Account Management Policies The third task in formulating a sales plan involves developing **account management policies** specifying whom salespeople should contact, what kinds of selling and customer service activities should be engaged in, and how these activities should be carried out. These policies might state which individuals in a buying organization should be contacted, the amount of sales and service effort that different customers should receive, and the kinds of information salespeople should collect before or during a sales call.

An example of an account management policy in Figure 21–7 on the next page shows how different accounts or customers can be grouped according to level of opportunity and the firm's competitive sales position.[29] When specific account names are placed in each cell, salespeople clearly see which accounts should be contacted, with what kind of selling and service activity, and how to deal with them. Accounts in cells 1 and 2 might have high frequencies of personal sales calls and increased time spent on a call. Cell 3 accounts will have lower call frequencies, and cell 4 accounts might be contacted through telemarketing or direct mail rather than in person. For example, Union Pacific Railroad put its 20,000 smallest accounts on a telemarketing program. A subsequent survey of these accounts indicated that 84 percent rated Union Pacific's sales effort "very effective" compared with 67 percent before the switch.

Sales Plan Implementation: Putting the Plan into Action

The sales plan is put into practice through the tasks associated with sales plan implementation. Whereas sales plan formulation focuses on "doing the right things," implementation

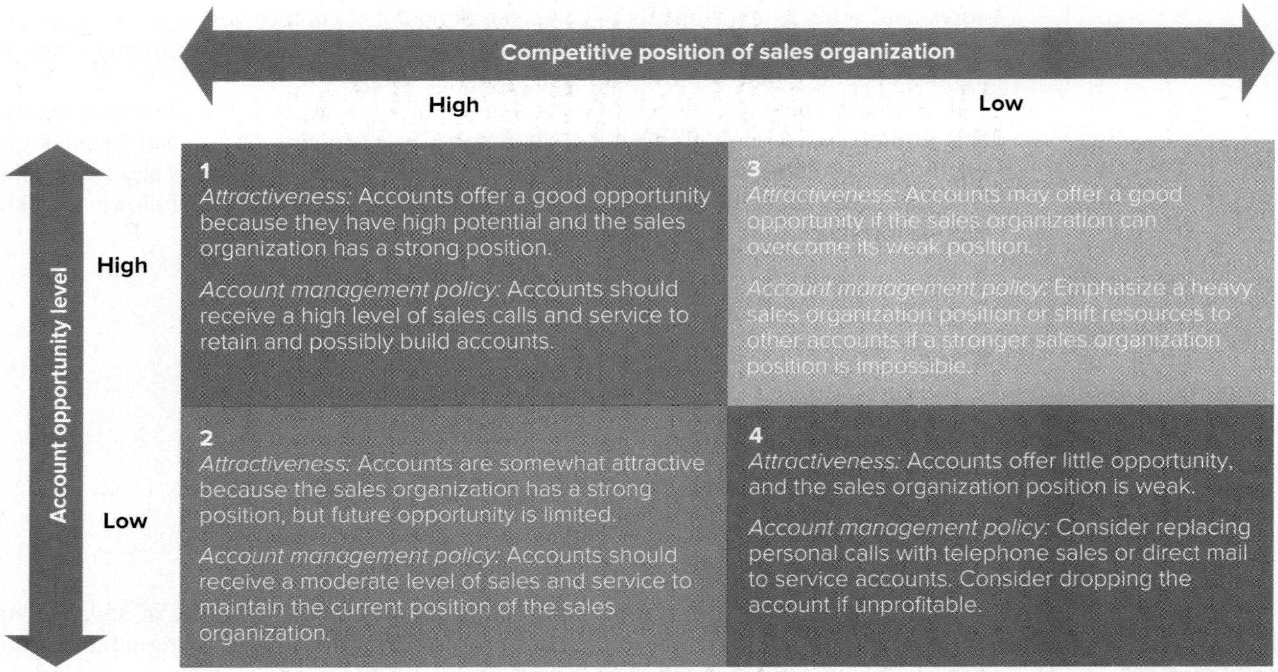

Competitive position of sales organization

Account opportunity level	High	Low
High	**1** *Attractiveness:* Accounts offer a good opportunity because they have high potential and the sales organization has a strong position. *Account management policy:* Accounts should receive a high level of sales calls and service to retain and possibly build accounts.	**3** *Attractiveness:* Accounts may offer a good opportunity if the sales organization can overcome its weak position. *Account management policy:* Emphasize a heavy sales organization position or shift resources to other accounts if a stronger sales organization position is impossible.
Low	**2** *Attractiveness:* Accounts are somewhat attractive because the sales organization has a strong position, but future opportunity is limited. *Account management policy:* Accounts should receive a moderate level of sales and service to maintain the current position of the sales organization.	**4** *Attractiveness:* Accounts offer little opportunity, and the sales organization position is weak. *Account management policy:* Consider replacing personal calls with telephone sales or direct mail to service accounts. Consider dropping the account if unprofitable.

FIGURE 21–7
An account management policy grid grouping customers according to level of opportunity and the firm's competitive sales position.

emphasizes "doing things right." The three major tasks involved in implementing a sales plan are (1) salesforce recruitment and selection, (2) salesforce training, and (3) salesforce motivation and compensation.

Salesforce Recruitment and Selection Effective recruitment and selection of salespeople is one of the most crucial tasks of sales management. It entails finding people who match the type of sales position required by a firm. Recruitment and selection practices will differ greatly between order-taking and order-getting sales positions, given the differences in the demands of these two jobs. Therefore, recruitment and selection begin with a carefully crafted job analysis and job description followed by a statement of job qualifications.

A *job analysis* is a study of a particular sales position, including how the job is to be performed and the tasks that make up the job. Information from a job analysis is used to write a *job description*, a written document that describes job relationships and requirements that characterize each sales position. It explains (1) to whom a salesperson reports, (2) how a salesperson interacts with other company personnel, (3) the customers to be called on, (4) the specific activities to be carried out, (5) the physical and mental demands of the job, and (6) the types of products and services to be sold.

The job description is then translated into a statement of job qualifications, including the aptitudes, knowledge, skills, and a variety of behavioral characteristics considered necessary to perform the job successfully. Qualifications for order-getting sales positions often mirror the expectations of buyers: (1) imagination and problem-solving ability, (2) strong work ethic, (3) honesty, (4) intimate product knowledge, (5) effective communication and listening skills, and (6) attentiveness reflected in responsiveness to buyer needs and customer loyalty and follow-up. Firms use a variety of methods for evaluating prospective salespeople. Personal interviews, reference checks, and background information provided on application forms are the most frequently used methods.[30]

Successful selling also requires a high degree of emotional intelligence. **Emotional intelligence** is the ability to understand one's own emotions and the emotions of people with whom one interacts on a daily basis. These qualities are important for adaptive selling and often spell the difference between effective and ineffective order-getting salespeople.[31] Are you interested in what your emotional intelligence might be? Read the Marketing Insights About Me box and test yourself.

Marketing Insights About Me

What Is Your Emotional Intelligence? You Might Be Surprised.

A person's success at work depends on many talents, including intelligence and technical skills. Recent research indicates that an individual's emotional intelligence or EI is also important, if not more important!

Evidence suggests that emotional intelligence is two times more important in contributing to performance than intellect and expertise alone. Emotional intelligence has five dimensions: (1) self-motivation skills; (2) self-awareness, or knowing one's own emotions; (3) the ability to manage one's emotions and impulses; (4) empathy, or the ability to sense how others are feeling; and (5) social skills, or the ability to handle the emotions of other people.

What is your emotional intelligence? Visit the website at https://globalleadershipfoundation.com/geit/eitest.html and answer 40 short questions to learn how you score on certain emotional intelligence dimensions and obtain additional insights.

Courtesy of DTS International

Salesforce Training Whereas the recruitment and selection of salespeople is a one-time event, salesforce training is an ongoing process that affects both new and seasoned salespeople.[32] Sales training covers much more than selling practices. For example, IBM Global Services salespeople, who sell consulting and various information technology services, take at least two weeks of in-class and Internet-based training on both consultative selling and the technical aspects of the business.

Training new salespeople is an expensive process. Salespeople in the United States receive employer-sponsored training annually at a cost of over $15 billion per year. On-the-job training is the most popular type of training, followed by individual instruction taught by experienced salespeople. Formal classes, seminars taught by professional sales trainers, and computer-based training are also popular.

Salesforce Motivation and Compensation A sales plan cannot be successfully implemented without motivated salespeople. Research on salesperson motivation suggests that (1) a clear job description, (2) effective sales management practices, (3) a personal need for achievement, and (4) proper compensation, incentives, or rewards will produce a motivated salesperson.[33]

The importance of compensation as a motivating factor means that close attention must be given to how salespeople are financially rewarded for their efforts. Salespeople are paid using one of three plans: (1) straight salary, (2) straight commission, or (3) a combination of salary and commission. Under a *straight salary compensation plan*, a salesperson is paid a fixed fee per week, month, or year. With a *straight commission compensation plan*, a salesperson's earnings are directly tied to the sales or profit generated. For example, an insurance agent might receive a 2 percent commission of $2,000 for selling a $100,000 life insurance policy. A *combination compensation plan* contains a specified salary plus a commission on sales or profit generated.

Mary Kay, Inc. offers unique nonmonetary rewards to recognize its successful sales consultants, including cars. The color pink used by Mary Kay, Inc. on its cars is unique to the company.
Courtesy of Mary Kay, Inc.

Mary Kay Cosmetics, Inc.
www.marykay.com

Each compensation plan has its advantages and disadvantages.[34] A straight salary plan is easy to administer and gives management a large measure of control over how salespeople allocate their efforts. However, it provides little incentive to expand sales volume. This plan is used when salespeople engage in many nonselling activities, such as account or customer servicing. A straight commission plan provides the maximum amount of selling incentive but can discourage salespeople from providing customer service. This plan is common when nonselling activities are minimal. Combination plans are most preferred by salespeople and attempt to build on the advantages of salary and commission plans while reducing the potential shortcomings of each. A majority of companies use combination plans today.

Nonmonetary rewards are also given to salespeople for meeting or exceeding objectives. These rewards include trips, honor societies, distinguished salesperson awards, and letters of commendation. Some unconventional rewards include a new pink Cadillac, Porsche, Buick, and BMW automobile, and jewelry given by Mary Kay Cosmetics to outstanding salespeople and sales directors.[35]

Effective recruitment, selection, training, motivation, and compensation programs combine to create a productive salesforce. This is particularly important for Generation Z salespeople who value transparency in their relationship with their employer. Ineffective practices often lead to costly salesforce turnover. The expense of replacing and training a new salesperson, including the cost of lost sales, can be high. Also, new recruits are often less productive than seasoned salespeople.[36]

Salesforce Evaluation: Measuring Results

The final function in the sales management process involves evaluating the salesforce. It is at this point that salespeople are assessed as to whether sales objectives were met and account management policies were followed. Both quantitative and behavioral measures are used to tap different selling dimensions.

Quantitative Assessments Quantitative assessments are based on input- and output-related objectives set forth in the sales plan. Input-related measures focus on the actual activities performed by salespeople such as those involving sales calls, selling expenses, and account management policies. The number of sales calls made, selling expense related to sales made, and the number of reports submitted to superiors are frequently used input measures.

Output measures often appear in a sales quota. A **sales quota** contains specific goals assigned to a salesperson, sales team, branch sales office, or sales district for a stated time period. Dollar or unit sales volume, last year/current year sales ratio, sales of specific products, new accounts generated, and profit achieved are typical goals. The time period can range from one month to one year.

Behavioral Evaluation Behavioral measures are also used to evaluate salespeople. These include assessments of a salesperson's attitude, attention to customers, product knowledge, selling and communication skills, appearance, and professional demeanor. Even though these assessments are sometimes subjective, they are frequently considered and are, in fact, inevitable, in salesperson evaluation. Why? These factors are often important determinants of quantitative outcomes.

About 60 percent of U.S. companies now include customer satisfaction as a behavioral measure of salesperson performance. (*What percentage did you check for question 4 in*

Applying Marketing Metrics

Tracking Salesperson Performance at Moore Chemical & Sanitation Supply, Inc.

Moore Chemical & Sanitation Supply, Inc. (MooreChem) is a large midwestern supplier of cleaning chemicals and sanitary products. MooreChem sells to janitorial companies that clean corporate and professional office buildings.

MooreChem recently installed a sales and account management planning software package that included a dashboard for each of its sales representatives. Salespeople had access to their dashboards as well. These dashboards included seven metrics—sales revenue, gross margin, selling expense, profit, average order size, new customers, and customer satisfaction. Each metric was gauged to show actual salesperson performance relative to target goals.

Your Challenge

As a newly promoted district sales manager at MooreChem, your responsibilities include tracking each salesperson's performance in your district. You are also responsible for directing the sales activities and practices of district salespeople.

In anticipation of a performance review with one of your salespeople, Brady Boyle, you review his dashboard for the previous quarter. This information can be used to provide a constructive review of his performance.

Your Findings

Brady Boyle's quarterly performance is displayed. Boyle has exceeded targeted goals for sales revenue, selling expenses, and customer satisfaction. All of these metrics show an upward trend. He has met his target for gaining new customers and average order size. But, Boyle's gross margin and profit are below targeted goals. These metrics evidence a downward trend as well. Brady Boyle's mixed performance requires a constructive and positive correction.

Your Action

Brady Boyle should already know how his performance compares with targeted goals. Remember, Boyle has access to his dashboard. Recall that he has exceeded his sales target, but is considerably under his profit target. Boyle's sales trend is up, but his profit trend is down.

You will need to focus attention on Boyle's gross margin and selling expense results and trend. Boyle, it seems, is spending time and money selling lower-margin products that produce a targeted average order size. It may very well be that Boyle is actually expending effort selling more products to his customers. Unfortunately, the product mix yields lower gross margins, resulting in a lower profit.

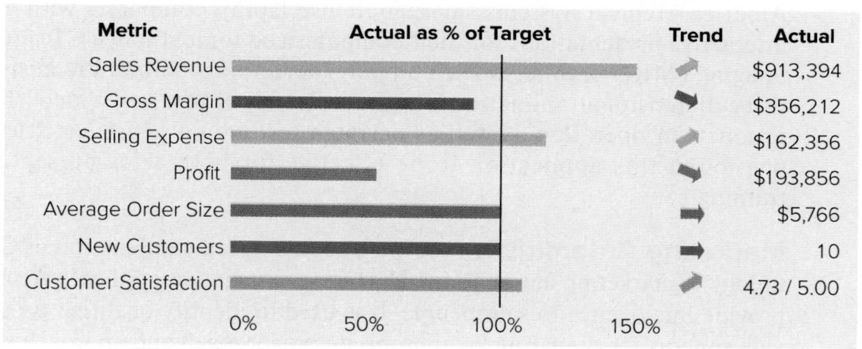

Figure 21-1?) The relentless focus on customer satisfaction by Eastman Chemical Company salespeople is an example.[37] Eastman surveys its customers with multiple versions of its customer satisfaction questionnaire delivered in nine languages. Some 25 performance items are studied, including on-time and correct delivery, product quality, pricing practice, and sharing of market information. Salespeople review the results with customers. Eastman salespeople know that "the second most important thing they have to do is get their customer satisfaction surveys out to and back from customers," says Eastman's sales training director. "Number one, of course, is getting orders."

Increasingly, companies are using marketing dashboards to track salesperson performance for evaluation purposes. An illustration appears in the Applying Marketing Metrics box.

Customer relationship management (CRM) systems and technology combine computer, information, communication, and Internet technologies to transform the selling and sales management function. U.S. companies spend upward of $37 billion each year on CRM applications.
Shironosov/iStock/Getty Images

Customer Relationship Management Systems and Technology

Personal selling and sales management have undergone a revolution with the use of customer relationship management (CRM) systems and technology. In fact, the convergence of computer, information, communication, and Internet technologies has transformed the selling and sales management function in many companies. CRM systems and technology consolidate customer and sales information in a single database so that salespeople and sales managers can more easily access, analyze, and manage a company's relationship with individual customers or accounts. These systems and technologies are designed with the goal of improving business relationships with customers, creating value for customers, assisting in new customer acquisition and current customer retention, and achieving profitable sales growth for companies.[38]

Customer relationship management systems and technologies are tailored to the needs of companies. As a rule, these systems and technologies automate workflow processes and focus on salesforce automation, marketing automation, and customer service and support automation.

Salesforce Automation The most basic application of CRM systems and technologies, and the one most applicable to selling and sales management, is salesforce automation. **Salesforce automation (SFA)** is the use of various technologies to make the selling function more effective and efficient. Examples of salesforce automation include computer hardware and software for account development and analysis (including an account's purchase history and preferences), time management, order processing, delivery and follow-up, proposal generation, and product and sales training. Its application is designed to free time for salespeople to be with customers building relationships, designing solutions, and providing service.

Sales presentation hardware and software are another application. For example, Toshiba America Medical Systems salespeople use laptop computers with capabilities to provide interactive presentations for their computerized tomography (CT) and magnetic resonance imaging (MRI) scanners. The computer technology allows the customer to see elaborate three-dimensional animations, high-resolution scans, and video clips of the company's products in operation as well as narrated testimonials from satisfied customers. Toshiba has found this application to be effective for both sales presentations and salesforce training.

Marketing Automation A more sophisticated combination of CRM systems and technology is marketing automation. *Marketing automation* applies systems and technologies to provide intelligence to salespeople. It is used to identify qualified prospects from leads, provide support for preparing an appropriate preapproach and approach strategy for a customer, track the customer buying process, and identify opportunities for upselling and cross-selling a company's products and services to new and existing customers.

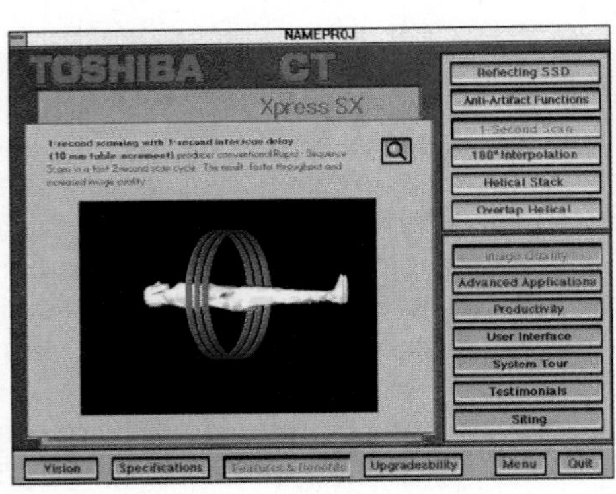

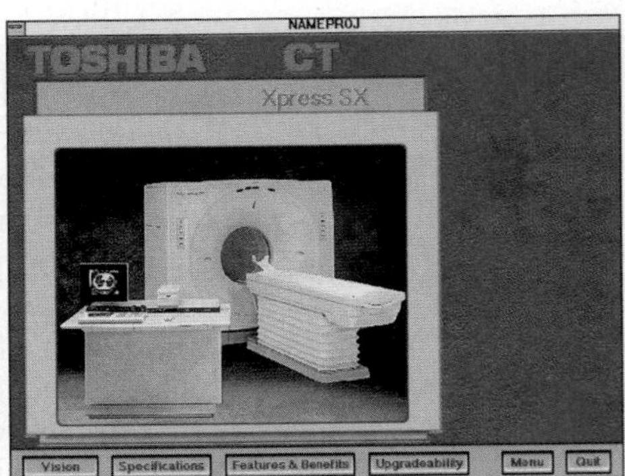

Toshiba America Medical Systems salespeople have found salesforce automation to be an effective sales presentation tool and training device.
Source: Toshiba America Medical Systems

Toshiba America Medical Systems
www.toshiba.com

Marketing automation emphasizes sophisticated analytical techniques and computer software. For example, these techniques use tracking codes in social media, e-mail, and websites to track the behavior of anyone showing an interest in a product or service to gain a measure of intent to buy. Customer leads and prospects are scored, based on their activities, and automatically sent highly targeted product and service information through social media and e-mail. If you've ever researched a product or service online and shortly thereafter received messages from suppliers of that product or service, you've seen marketing automation at work.

Customer Service and Support Automation The third most prominent application of customer relationship management processes and technology is customer service and support automation. *Customer service and support automation* consists of processes and technologies that supply customers with information about postsale activities, including installation, repair, replacement, and replenishment, and technical expertise pertaining to products. Two features of successful customer service and support automation are the availability of "live chat" opportunities and the ability to provide a single source for customer problem solving. Both features attempt to overcome customer frustration with having to contact multiple service and support personnel to solve any, and all, problems.

Customer relationship management processes and technology are clearly changing how selling is done and how salespeople are managed. U.S. companies spend upward of $37 billion annually on CRM applications. These applications promise to boost selling productivity, improve customer relationships, and decrease selling and customer service costs. Nevertheless, one-half of senior sales and marketing executives in the United States believe that CRM processes and technologies have not yet achieved their full potential.[39]

LEARNING REVIEW

21-8. What are the three types of selling objectives?

21-9. What three factors are used to structure sales organizations?

21-10. How does emotional intelligence tie to adaptive selling?

LEARNING OBJECTIVES REVIEW

LO 21-1 *Discuss the nature and scope of personal selling and sales management in marketing.*
Personal selling involves the two-way flow of communication between a buyer and seller, often in a face-to-face encounter, designed to influence a person's or group's purchase decision. Sales management involves planning the selling program and implementing and controlling the personal selling effort of the firm. The scope of selling and sales management is apparent in three ways. First, virtually every occupation that involves customer contact has an element of personal selling. Second, selling plays a significant role in a company's overall marketing effort. Salespeople occupy a boundary position between buyers and sellers; they *are* the company to many buyers and account for a major cost of marketing in a variety of industries. Salespeople also can create value for customers. Finally, through relationship selling, salespeople play a central role in tailoring solutions to customer problems as a means to customer value creation.

LO 21-2 *Identify the different types of personal selling.*
Three types of personal selling exist: (*a*) order taking, (*b*) order getting, and (*c*) customer sales support activities. Each type differs from the others in terms of actual selling done and the amount of creativity required to perform the sales task. Order takers process routine orders or reorders for products that were already sold by the company. They generally do little selling in a conventional sense and engage in only modest problem solving with customers. Order getters sell in a conventional sense and identify prospective customers, provide customers with information, persuade customers to buy, close sales, and follow up on customers' use of a product or service. Order getting involves a high degree of creativity and customer empathy and is typically required for selling complex or technical products with many options. Customer sales support personnel augment the sales effort of order getters by performing a variety of services. Sales support personnel are prominent in cross-functional team

selling, the practice of using an entire team of professionals in selling to and servicing major customers.

LO 21-3 *Explain the stages in the personal selling process.* The personal selling process consists of six stages: (1) prospecting, (2) preapproach, (3) approach, (4) presentation, (5) close, and (6) follow-up. Prospecting involves the search for and qualification of potential customers. The preapproach stage involves obtaining further information on the prospect and deciding on the best method of approach. The approach stage involves the initial meeting between the salesperson and prospect. The presentation stage involves converting a prospect into a customer by creating a desire for the product or service. The close involves obtaining a purchase commitment from the prospect. The follow-up stage involves making certain that the customer's purchase has been properly delivered and installed and addressing any difficulties experienced with the use of the item.

LO 21-4 *Describe the major functions of sales management.* Sales management consists of three interrelated functions: (*a*) sales plan formulation, (*b*) sales plan implementation, and (*c*) salesforce evaluation. Sales plan formulation involves setting objectives, organizing the salesforce, and developing account management policies. Sales plan implementation involves salesforce recruitment, selection, training, motivation, and compensation. Salesforce evaluation involves the use of quantitative and behavioral measures to assess the performance of the salesforce. Finally, customer relationship management systems and technologies are becoming increasingly important in sales management, boosting selling productivity, improving customer relationships, and decreasing selling and customer service costs.

LEARNING REVIEW ANSWERS

21-1 What is personal selling?
Answer: Personal selling involves the two-way flow of communication between a buyer and seller, often in a face-to-face encounter, designed to influence a person's or group's purchase decision.

21-2 What is involved in sales management?
Answer: Sales management involves planning the selling program and implementing and evaluating the personal selling effort of the firm. The tasks involved in managing personal selling include setting objectives; organizing the salesforce; recruiting, selecting, training, and compensating salespeople; and evaluating the performance of individual salespeople.

21-3 What is the principal difference between an order taker and an order getter?
Answer: An order taker processes routine orders or reorders for products that were already sold by the company. The primary responsibility of order takers is to preserve an ongoing relationship with existing customers and maintain sales. An order getter sells in a conventional sense and identifies prospective customers, provides customers with information, persuades customers to buy, closes sales, and follows up on customers' use of a product or service. Order getting involves a high degree of creativity, customer empathy, considerable product knowledge, and sales training.

21-4 What is team selling?
Answer: Team selling is the practice of using an entire team of professionals in selling to and servicing major customers. Team selling is used when specialized knowledge is needed to satisfy the different interests of individuals in a customer's buying center.

21-5 What are the six stages in the personal selling process?
Answer: The six stages in the personal selling process are: (1) prospecting–searching for qualified potential customers; (2) preapproach–obtaining further information on prospects and deciding on the best method of approach; (3) approach–setting up the first meeting between the salesperson and the prospect to gain his/her attention, stimulate interest, and establish a foundation for the relationship and eventual sales presentation; (4) presentation—converting a prospect into a customer by creating a desire for the offering; (5) close–obtaining a purchase commitment from the prospect; and (6) follow-up—delivering, installing, and/or resolving any difficulties with the purchase.

21-6 What is the distinction between a lead and a qualified prospect?
Answer: A lead is the name of a person who may be a possible customer, whereas a qualified prospect is an individual who wants the product, can afford to buy it, and is the decision maker.

21-7 Which presentation format is most consistent with the marketing concept? Why?
Answer: The need-satisfaction presentation format emphasizes probing and listening by the salesperson to identify the needs and interests of prospective buyers and then tailors the presentation to the prospect and highlights product benefits, which is consistent with the marketing concept and its focus on relationship building.

21-8 What are the three types of selling objectives?
Answer: The three types of selling objectives are: (1) output-related (dollars or unit sales, number of new customers, profit); (2) input-related (number of sales calls, selling expenses); and (3) behavior-related (product and competitive knowledge, customer service satisfaction ratings, selling and communication skills).

21-9 What three factors are used to structure sales organizations?
Answer: Three questions need to be answered when structuring a sales organization: (1) Should the company use its own salesforce or independent agents such as manufacturer's representatives? (2) If the decision is made to employ company salespeople, then should they be organized according to geography, customer type, or product or service? (3) How many company salespeople should be employed?

21-10 How does emotional intelligence tie to adaptive selling?
Answer: Emotional intelligence is the ability to understand one's own emotions and the emotions of people with whom one interacts on a daily basis. Evidence suggests that emotional intelligence is two times more important in contributing to performance than intellect and expertise alone. Emotional intelligence has five dimensions: (1) self-motivation skills; (2) self-awareness, or knowing one's own emotions; (3) the ability to manage one's emotions and impulses; (4) empathy, or the ability to sense how others are feeling; and (5) social skills, or the ability to handle the emotions of other people. These qualities are important for adaptive selling.

FOCUSING ON KEY TERMS

account management policies p. 595
adaptive selling p. 589
consultative selling p. 589
emotional intelligence p. 596
key account management p. 594
order getter p. 583
order taker p. 583
personal selling p. 580
personal selling process p. 585
relationship selling p. 582
sales management p. 580
sales plan p. 592
sales quota p. 598
salesforce automation (SFA) p. 600
team selling p. 584
workload method p. 595

APPLYING MARKETING KNOWLEDGE

1 Jane Dawson is a new sales representative for the Charles Schwab brokerage firm. In searching for clients, Jane purchased a mailing list of subscribers to *The Wall Street Journal* and called them all regarding their interest in discount brokerage services. She asked if they have any stocks and if they have a regular broker. Those people without a regular broker were asked their investment needs. Two days later, Jane called back with investment advice and asked if they would like to open an account. Identify each of Jane Dawson's actions in terms of the personal selling process.

2 For the first 50 years of business, the Johnson Carpet Company produced carpets for residential use. The salesforce was structured geographically. In the past five years, a large percentage of carpet sales have been to industrial users, hospitals, schools, and architects. The company also has broadened its product line to include area rugs, Oriental carpets, and wall-to-wall carpeting. Is the present salesforce structure appropriate, or would you recommend an alternative?

3 Where would you place each of the following sales jobs on the order-taker/order-getter continuum shown below? (*a*) Burger King counter clerk, (*b*) automobile insurance salesperson, (*c*) Hewlett-Packard computer salesperson, (*d*) life insurance salesperson, and (*e*) shoe salesperson.

Order taker —————————————— Order getter

4 Listed here are two different firms. Which salesforce compensation plan would you recommend for each firm, and what reasons would you give for your recommendations? (*a*) A newly formed company that sells lawn care equipment on a door-to-door basis directly to consumers; and (*b*) the Nabisco Company, which sells heavily advertised products in supermarkets by having the salesforce call on these stores and arrange shelves, set up displays, and make presentations to store buying committees.

5 Tyler Automotive, Inc. supplies 1,000 independent auto parts stores throughout the United States. Each store is called on 12 times a year, and the average sales call lasts 30 minutes. Assuming a salesperson works 40 hours a week, 50 weeks a year, and devotes 75 percent of the time to actual selling, how many salespeople does Tyler Automotive need?

6 A furniture manufacturer is currently using manufacturer's representatives to sell its line of living room furniture. These representatives receive an 8 percent commission. The company is considering hiring its own salespeople and has estimated that the fixed cost of managing and paying their salaries would be $1 million annually. The salespeople would also receive a 4 percent commission on sales. The company has sales of $25 million, and sales are expected to grow by 15 percent next year. Would you recommend that the company switch to its own salesforce? Why or why not?

7 Suppose someone said to you, "The only real measure of a salesperson is the amount of sales produced." How might you respond?

BUILDING YOUR MARKETING PLAN

Does your marketing plan involve a personal selling activity? If the answer is "no," read no further and do not include a personal selling element in your plan. If the answer is "yes":

1 Identify the likely prospects for your product or service.
2 Determine what information you should obtain about the prospect.
3 Describe how you would approach the prospect.
4 Outline the presentation you would make to the prospect for your product or service.
5 Develop a sales plan, focusing on the organizational structure you would use for your salesforce (geographic, product, or customer).

VIDEO CASE 21 Cascade Maverik: Creating an Amazing Success Story with Exceptional Salespeople

"We've worked hard to ensure that we surround ourselves with really strong, talented, curious people, and our salesforce exemplifies that," says Tim Ellsworth, Global Business Director for Cascade Maverik Lacrosse.

VIDEO 21-2
Cascade Maverik Video Case
kerin.tv/15e/v21-2

Tim Ellsworth has managed many aspects of the business that have helped the company become the number one brand in lacrosse equipment. "We have a sales organization, a marketing organization, a manufacturing organization, and an R&D organization; it's very interdisciplinary," he explains. World-class product development, designs that are "powered by the player," rapid U.S. production facilities, and a passion for athlete safety are all important parts of the message the salesforce brings to market.

THE SPORTING GOODS INDUSTRY AND THE GROWTH OF LACROSSE

The sporting goods industry generates about $100 billion in retail equipment sales for all sports, and is expected to grow for the next five years. Industry growth is driven by technological advancements and customization, increases in consumer discretionary income, and shifts in the popularity of different sports. Sporting goods manufacturers sell products through sporting goods retailers, department stores, mass merchandisers, and directly online.

Source: Cascade Maverik Lacrosse, LLC

Source: Cascade Maverik Lacrosse, LLC

Participation rates in many sports are changing. Tackle football and soccer have experienced declines in youth participation. At the same time, other sports such as inline skating, skateboarding, mountain biking, snowboarding, parkour, and base jumping are becoming more popular. While basketball is the most popular team sport, baseball, ice hockey, and lacrosse have been growing. In fact, during the past two decades lacrosse has been the fastest-growing team sport among male and female players at the youth, high school, college, and professional levels. According to Ellsworth, "Lacrosse is still a relatively small sport compared to basketball, baseball, and football, but the sport is really contagious. People are getting addicted to our sport once they engage and understand a little bit about it!"

THE SALES MANAGEMENT PROCESS AT CASCADE MAVERIK

To achieve the company objective to be "the fastest supplier of high-performance lacrosse gear," Cascade Maverik utilizes a rigorous sales management process. The process addresses several key tasks including organizing the salesforce. According to Debbie Errante, sales manager at Cascade Maverik, the "salesforce is broken out by geographic territories throughout the U.S., and key accounts, typically based in highly populated areas, are also supported by the salesforce." Other sales management tasks include recruiting and selecting new salespeople, training sales representatives, and designing a compensation program.

The recruitment and selection process requires finding people who match the culture and requirements at Cascade Maverik. Errante explains: "we have a lot of people on the road who are not based out of our corporate offices and therefore they need to be self-motivated, and a good teammate. Most of our employees are actually coming out of playing some type of sport so they understand the team mentality." Other important attributes include computer skills, communication skills, and particular personality traits. "We are looking for sales representatives that are personable, that can communicate, are self-motivated and have a positive attitude, showing a smile, coming in well-dressed, and looking like they're prepared for the day and ready to be a go-getter," says Errante. The application process at Cascade Maverik usually begins with an online application, then an online interview, and finally a face-to-face meeting that may include a presentation. Errante observes that it is "important that a sales representative is comfortable in front of a room."

Salesforce training at Cascade Maverik consists of corporate office training and on-the-job training. "Our training process starts by meeting some of your key team members as well as getting some background information on your key accounts," explains Errante. New sales representatives also spend time learning the administrative activities that take place in the office. The on-the-job component of the training includes participating in sales calls and presentations with senior salespeople. "Whatever it takes to make sure that they feel confident once we send them out into the marketplace to be successful at their job," says Errante.

At Cascade Maverik, compensation is a combination of salary and commission. According to Errante, "salary allows our employees to step into their role confidently, and commission is about motivation." Providing an incentive for serving new customers and being completely up-to-date is particularly important as the sport grows and changes. "The growth of the sport as well as new rules, regulations, and products are something the sales team needs to take into consideration. If they can't sell the product, then we can't be successful as a team," says Errante.

THE SELLING PROCESS AT CASCADE MAVERIK

The personal selling process at Cascade Maverik focuses on building customer relationships. Laura Edward, a territory sales representative for Cascade Maverik, explains:

Source: Cascade Maverik Lacrosse, LLC

"It's extremely important to establish a relationship with the person you're selling to. When I'm building a relationship with a coach, it's extremely important to get to know them a little bit. I think that's important for a long-lasting relationship rather than just one sale." Sales representatives typically follow the steps identified in Figure 21-3 to build relationships.

The process begins with prospecting, or identifying new customers. "I spend about 25 percent of my time prospecting, finding potential leads, talking to coaches," says Edward. "You really have to hit the road to find the coaches that we want to sell to." The second step is to gather information about the prospects' needs. "I want to understand their equipment needs and how our products can align with those needs," explains Edward. The next steps are to arrange a meeting and make a presentation. According to Edward, "once I've set up a time and place to meet with a coach, it's time to present our product line and the benefits that we can bring. It's important to cater to the coaches and their schedules." Step five is to "close" by asking for an order and obtaining a purchase commitment from the coach. Finally, sales representatives must follow up to ensure that the customer is satisfied. "Once the product is delivered you want to follow up with the coach or athletic director to see how the equipment is meeting their expectations," says Edward. "It's our goal to have every coach extremely satisfied.

Cascade Maverik sales representatives also use the selling process to maintain relationships with existing customers. Information about past purchases help the team evaluate future needs. Cascade Maverik's commitment to its customers and the sport are creating an exciting success story. Watch for a lacrosse game coming to your community soon![40]

Questions

1 What factors are contributing to the growth of lacrosse and lacrosse equipment?

2 What are some of Cascade Maverik's success factors?

3 How does Cascade Maverik approach sales management functions such as recruiting, training, and compensation?

4 How does Laura Edward create customer value through the personal selling process?

Chapter Notes

1. Interview with Lindsey Smith, GE Healthcare Americas, March 6, 2017.
2. *Route to the Top: 2018* (Chicago: Heidrick & Struggles International, 2018).
3. Jessi Hempel, "IBM's All-Star Salesman," www.cnnmoney.com, September 26, 2008.
4. Jim Clifton and Sangeeta Bharadwaj Badal, *Entrepreneurial StrengthsFinder* (New York: Gallup Press, 2014); "The Five Sales Tactics Every Entrepreneur Must Master," *forbes.com,* January 30, 2013; and Waverly Deutsch, "What Great Entrepreneurs, Salespeople, and Business Leaders Have in Common," *CHICAGOBOOTHREVIEW*, August 2018.
5. "Guess Who Else Is in on the Operation?" *The Dallas Morning News*, November 27, 2016.
6. Mark W. Johnston and Greg W. Marshall, *Contemporary Selling: Building Relationships, Creating Value,* 5th ed. (New York: Routledge, 2016).
7. Richard P. Bagozzi et al., "Genetic and Neurological Foundations of Customer Orientation: Field and Experimental Evidence," *Journal of the Academy of Marketing Science,* September 2012, pp. 639–58; "Does Your Salesperson Have the Right Genes?" *Harvard Business Review,* April 2013, p. 24; and Giorgio Apollinari, et al., "Polymorphisms of the IXTR Gene Explain Why Sales Professionals Love to Help Customers," *Frontiers of Behavioral Neuroscience*, November 2013, pp. 1-12.
8. Salesforce Research, "State of Sales," 3rd edition, *salesforce.com*, 2018.
9. "The New Willy Loman Survives by Staying Home," *Bloomberg Businessweek,* January 14–January 20, 2013, pp. 16-17.
10. For an overview of team selling, see Eli Jones, et al., "Key Accounts and Team Selling: A Review, Framework, and Research Agenda," *Journal of Personal Selling & Sales Management,* Spring 2005, pp. 181-98; Ryan R. Mullins and Nikolaos G. Panagopoulos, "Understanding the Theory and Practice of Team Selling: An Introduction to the Special Section and Recommendations on Advancing Sales Team Research," *Industrial Marketing Management*, February 2019, pp. 1-3; and related articles in this section.
11. Eric Baron, *Innovative Team Selling* (New York: John Wiley & Sons, 2013); and "Team Selling Works!" www.sellingpower.com, March 24, 2013.
12. "Is Everything You Were Taught about Cold Calling Wrong?" www.forbes.com, August 28, 2018.
13. Jim Edwards, "Dinner, Interrupted," *BrandWeek,* May 26, 2003, pp. 28-32.
14. "Those Pesky Unwanted Calls Won't Go Away," *The Wall Street Journal,* September 9-10, 2017, p. A2.
15. Paul A. Herbing, *Handbook of Cross-Cultural Marketing* (New York: Haworth Press, 1998).
16. Philip R. Cateora, Mary C. Gilly, John L. Graham, and R. Bruce Money, *International Marketing,* 17th ed. (Burr Ridge, IL: McGraw-Hill/Irwin, 2016).
17. This discussion is based on Mark W. Johnston and Greg W. Marshall, *Contemporary Selling: Building Relationships, Creating Value,* 5th ed. (New York: Routledge, 2016).
18. Kapil R. Tuli, Ajay K. Kohli, and Sundar G. Bharadwaj, "Rethinking Customer Solutions: From Product Bundles to Relational Processes," *Journal of Marketing,* July 2007, pp. 1-17. Also, see Stefan Worm, Sundar G. Bharadwaj, Wolfgang Ulaga, and Werner J. Reinartz, "When and Why Do Customer Solutions Pay Off in Business Markets?" *Journal of the Academy of Marketing Science*, July 2017, pp. 490-512.
19. For an extensive discussion of objections, see Charles M. Futrell, *Fundamentals of Selling,* 13th ed. (Burr Ridge, IL: McGraw-Hill/Irwin, 2014), Chapter 12.
20. Theodore Levitt, *The Marketing Imagination* (New York: Free Press, 1983), p. 111.
21. Stephen B. Castleberry and John F. Tanner Jr., *Selling: Building Partnerships,* 10th ed. (Burr Ridge, IL: McGraw-Hill, 2019).
22. *Management Briefing: Sales and Marketing* (New York: Conference Board, October 1996), pp. 3-4.
23. Christopher Murphy, *Competitive Intelligence: Gathering, Analyzing, and Putting It to Work* (New York: Routledge, 2016).
24. Joel LeBon, *Competitive Intelligence and the Sales Force* (New York: Business Expert Press, 2013); and Douglas E. Hughes, Joel LeBon, and Adam Rapp, "Gaining and Leveraging Customer-Based Competitive Intelligence: The Pivotal Role of Social Capital and Salesperson Adaptive Selling Skills," *Journal of the Academy of Marketing Science*, January 2013, pp. 91-110.
25. See Mark W. Johnston and Greg W. Marshall, *Sales Force Management,* 11th ed. (Burr Ridge, IL: McGraw-Hill/Irwin, 2014), pp. 100-4; and William T. Ross Jr., Frederic Dalsace, and Erin Anderson, "Should You Set Up Your Own Sales Force or Should You Outsource It? Pitfalls in the Standard Analysis," *Business Horizons,* January–February 2005, pp. 23-36.
26. "Google Cloud's Chief Plans to Catch Amazon and Microsoft Sales Reps," *The Wall Street Journal*, February 12, 2019, p. B2.
27. Eli Jones, et al., "Key Accounts and Team Selling: A Review, Framework, and Research Agenda," *Journal of Personal Selling & Sales Management,* Spring 2005, pp. 181-98. Also see Aditya Gupta, Alok Kumar, Rajdeep Grewal, and Gary L. Lilian, "Within-Seller and Buyer-Seller Network Structures and Key Account Profitability," *Journal of Marketing*, January 2019, pp. 108-32.
28. William L. Cron and David W. Cravens, "Sales Force Strategy," in Robert A. Peterson and Roger A. Kerin, eds., *Wiley International Encyclopedia of Marketing: Volume 1–Marketing Strategy* (West Sussex, UK: John Wiley & Sons, Ltd., 2011), pp. 197-207.
29. This discussion is based on William L. Cron and Thomas E. DeCarlo, *Dalrymple's Sales Management,* 10th ed. (Hoboken, NJ: John Wiley & Sons, Inc., 2009).
30. René Y. Darmon, *Leading the Sales Force* (New York: Cambridge University Press, 2007).
31. Jeb Blount, *Sales EQ: How Ultra High Performance Salespeople Leverage Sales-Specific Emotional Intelligence to Close the Complex Deal* (Hoboken, NJ: John Wiley & Sons, 2017); Richard D. McFarland, Joseph C. Rode, and Tassadduq A. Shirvani, "A Contingency Model of Emotional Intelligence in Professional Selling," *Journal of the Academy of Marketing Science*, January 2016, pp. 108-18; "Look for Employees with High EQ over IQ," *forbes.com,* March 18, 2013; and Blair Kidwell, David M. Hardesty, Brian R. Murtha, and Shibin Sheng, "Emotional Intelligence in Marketing Exchanges," *Journal of Marketing,* January 2011, pp. 78-93.
32. Rosann L. Spiro, Gregory A. Rich, and William J. Stanton, *Management of a Sales Force,* 12th ed. (Burr Ridge, IL: McGraw-Hill/Irwin, 2008), Chapter 7; and Thomas L. Powers, Thomas E. DeCarlo, and Gouri Gupte, "An Update on the Status of Sales Management Training," *Journal of Personal Selling & Sales Management,* Fall 2010, pp. 319-26.
33. Rushana Khusainova, et al., "(Re) defining Salesperson Motivation: Current Status, Main Challenges, and Research Directions," *Journal of Personal Selling & Sales Management,* March 2018, pp. 2-29; and Thomas Steenburgh and Michael Ahearne, "Motivating Salespeople: What Really Works," *Harvard Business Review*, July–August 2012, pp. 71-75.
34. This discussion is based on Mark W. Johnston and Greg W. Marshall, *Sales Force Management,* 11th ed. (Burr Ridge, IL: McGraw-Hill/Irwin, 2014), Chapter 11; and Andris Zoltners, Prabhakant Sinha, and Sally E. Lorimer, *The Complete Guide to Sales Force Incentive Compensation* (New York: AMACOM, 2006).
35. www.MaryKay.com, accessed June 5, 2019.
36. "How to Prevent Turnover on Your Sales Team," *Sales and Marketing Management Magazine*, February 2019, pp. 21-26; and Jeffrey E. Lewin

and Jeffrey K. Sager, "The Influence of Personal Characteristics and Coping Strategies on Salespersons' Turnover Intentions," *Journal of Personal Selling & Sales Management,* Fall 2010, pp. 355–70.

37. James R. Evans, *Quality and Performance Excellence*, 7th ed. (Mason, OH: Cengage, 2014).

38. Don Peppers and Martha Rogers, *Managing Customer Experience and Relationships*, 3rd ed. (Hoboken, NJ: John Wiley & Sons, 2017); and Francis Buttle and Stan Maklan, *Customer Relationship Management: Concepts and Technologies*, 3rd ed. (New York: Routledge, 2017). Also see Nathaniel N. Hartman, Heiko Wieland, and Stephan L. Vargo, "Converging on a New Theoretical Foundation for Selling," *Journal of Marketing*, March 18, 2018, pp. 1–18.

39. "Top-Five Focus Areas for Improving Sales Effectiveness Initiatives," www.accenture.com, accessed May 5, 2017.

40. Cascade Maverik: This case was written by Steven Hartley and Roger Kerin. Sources: Interviews with Tim Ellsworth, Debbie Errante, and Laura Edward, Cascade Maverik Lacrosse; "Cascade Maverik Solidifies #1 Position in NCAA Division 1 College Lacrosse," *PR Newswire*, February 26, 2019; "Sporting Goods Manufacturing," *First Research Industry Profile*, June 3, 2019; "2017 Participation Survey," *USLacrosse.org*; Marisa Lifschutz, "Athletic & Sporting Goods Manufacturing in the US," *IBISWorld*, www.ibisworld.com, May 2019; and information available on the company websites, www.maveriklacrosse.com and www.cascadelacrosse.com.

Pulling It All Together: The Strategic Marketing Process

LEARNING OBJECTIVES

After reading this chapter you should be able to:

LO 22-1 Explain how marketing managers allocate resources.

LO 22-2 Describe the generic business strategy and blue ocean strategy planning frameworks.

LO 22-3 Explain what makes an effective marketing plan.

LO 22-4 Describe the levels and functions of an organization's marketing department.

LO 22-5 Explain the use of marketing ROI, metrics, and dashboards in evaluating marketing programs.

At General Mills, Its "Consumer First" Approach to Strategic Marketing Is the Key to Success!

How can a company with billions in sales and thousands of employees continue to grow in a rapidly changing and very competitive marketplace? The answer to this question at General Mills is a process it calls "Consumer First." This agile approach uses a deep understanding of the consumer to develop new ideas, favors fast-to-market testing, and utilizes iterations of feedback before a full-scale rollout.

As vice president of the Center for Learning and Experimentation at General Mills, Vivian Milroy Callaway is responsible for helping uncover and introduce new-product ideas for the company. The strategic marketing process–planning, implementation, and evaluation–is essential to her job and recently played an important role in the development of a new dessert concept called Warm Delights.

To start the process, Callaway did not look at the new dessert concept alone–but in relation to all the other sweet treats people were eating. "One of my challenges," she says, "is that consumers often say one thing in marketing research studies and then do something else when facing a supermarket shelf." To overcome this problem, Callaway and her team ran marketing experiments that involved putting a prototype dessert in a store, measuring the results, improving the prototype, and then repeating the process.

The research helped General Mills understand many aspects of the product that were important to consumers. For example, the research revealed that extending the black microwavable bowl outside the edges of the Warm Delights package would better communicate its cooking convenience to prospective buyers. So the unique packaging with the bowl edges exposed was adopted. After many additional experiments, the result was a successful nationwide launch of Warm Delights microwavable desserts, followed quickly by a product line extension, Warm Delights Minis. Growth of both products suggests that the process provided a good match with consumer tastes![1]

Planning for Even More Change

General Mills's U.S. retail sales now exceed $15 billion from five food categories: cereal, ice cream, yogurt, convenient meals, and snacks. While consumer tastes in each category are changing, a quick environmental scan of the largest division, cereal, shows how important a good strategic marketing process is for the company. Consider the following:

- *Expense.* The launch of a new cereal typically costs up to $30 million and usually involves replacing one of more than 300 competing breakfast cereals already sitting on retailers' shelves.

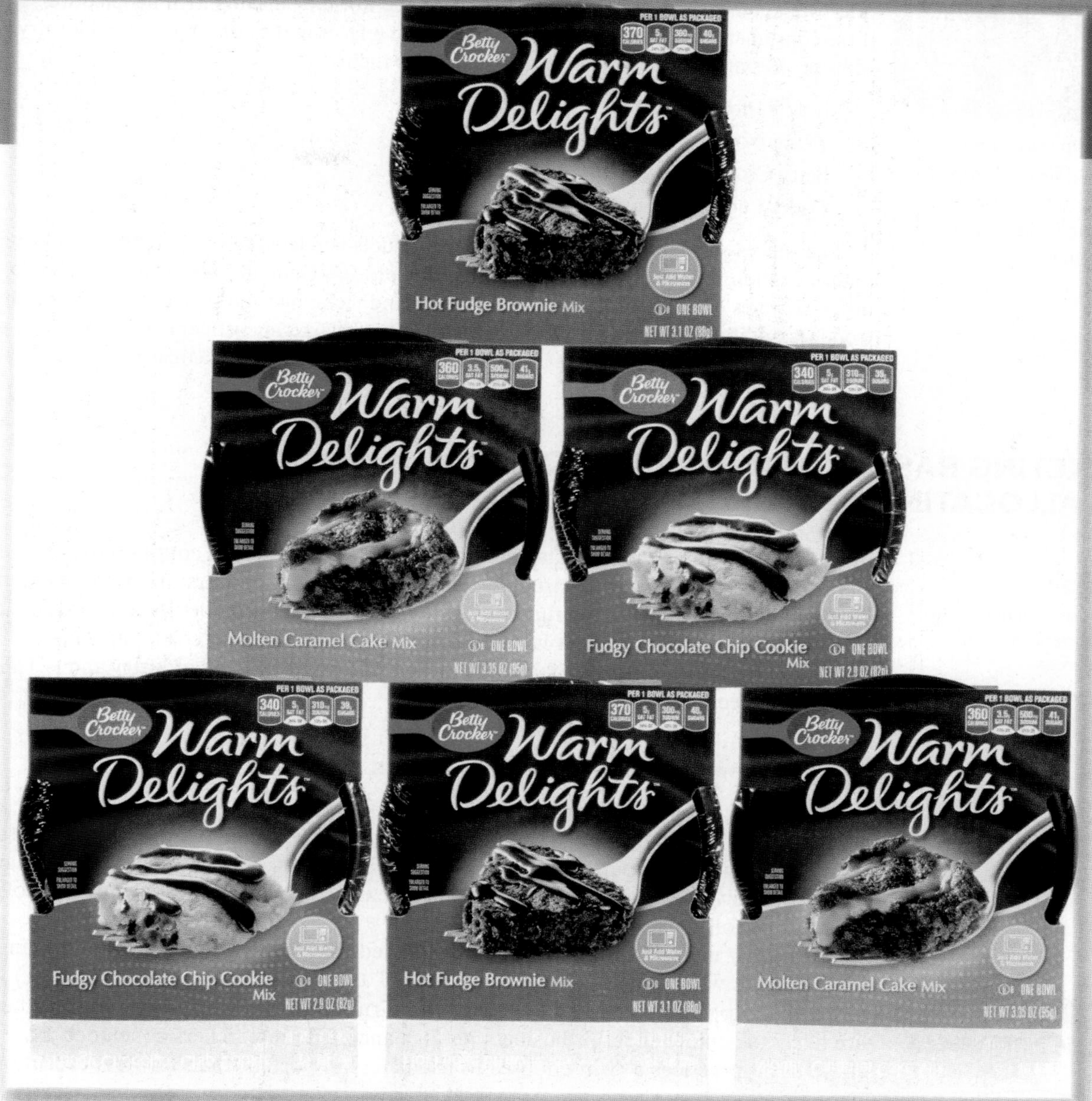

McGraw-Hill Education

- *Success rate*. Only one out of four brands "succeeds," which is defined as maintaining distribution for three to four years in the $10 billion-a-year U.S. ready-to-eat (RTE) cereal market. Adding to the challenge: Retail food industry sales did not grow while costs increased.

VIDEO 22-1
General Mills
kerin.tv/15e/v22-1

- *Market trends*. The lack of growth in the RTE cereal market is being caused by several factors including (1) consumers are moving away from products with sugar, genetically modified ingredients, or artificial food dyes, and toward products perceived as healthy, natural, or organic; and (2) consumers are eating more breakfasts at fast-food and fast-casual restaurants rather than eating cereal at home.[2]

Creative Initiatives at General Mills

General Mills introduces more than 300 new food products each year in response to consumers' changing tastes. In fact, the company website emphasizes the perspective that drives it to continually

Changes in consumers' tastes led General Mills to offer gluten-free, low-in-sugar Epic protein bars.
McGraw-Hill Education

offer what consumers are asking for: "We serve the world by making food people love." In light of these consumer trends and the intense competition it faces in the consumer foods industry, General Mills is offering a variety of new products, among them:

Epic Performance Bars
YQ by Yoplait
Betty Crocker Mug Treats
Fruity Lucky Charms[3]

The success or failure of these and other products is related to the planning, implementation, and evaluation phases of the strategic marketing process General Mills uses. This chapter revisits and elaborates on some of the behavioral issues and techniques presented in Chapter 2. It also introduces additional perspectives and tools that chief marketing officers and marketing, product, and brand managers apply in the challenging and ever-changing marketplace.

MARKETING BASICS: DOING WHAT WORKS AND ALLOCATING RESOURCES

LO 22-1
Explain how marketing managers allocate resources.

As noted in Chapter 2, corporate and marketing executives search continuously to find a competitive advantage–a unique strength relative to what competitors are doing now and what they will likely be doing in the future.[4] Having identified this competitive advantage, they then must figure out how to exploit it, often by creating a compelling customer journey.[5] This involves (1) finding and using what works for their organization and industry and (2) allocating resources effectively.

Finding and Using What Really Works

As marketing managers attempt to create competitive advantage they often ask what business practices lead to organizational success. To answer the question, researchers conducted an in-depth analysis of 160 companies and more than 200 management tools and techniques. Their findings? Individual management tools and techniques had no direct relationship to superior business performance in the companies.[6]

What *does* matter? The researchers concluded that four basic business and management practices are what matter–"what really works," to use their phrase. These are (1) strategy, (2) execution, (3) culture, and (4) structure. Firms with excellence in all four of these areas are likely to achieve superior business performance. The researchers concluded that which of these basic practices a firm chooses to use is less important than flawless execution of the ones it does use.

Costco and Toyota achieve excellence with two key business practices—a clear, focused strategy (Costco) and a performance-oriented culture (Toyota).
(Top): IgorGolovniov/Shutterstock; (Bottom): rvlsoft/Shutterstock

Industry leaders such as Home Depot do all four of the basic practices extremely well, not just two or three, and are vigilant about continuing to do them well when conditions change. In contrast, Sears, Fitbit, and Groupon are struggling today to get these basics right and regain their past success. Let's look at companies that stand out today in each of the four key business practices:

- *Strategy: Devise and maintain a clearly stated, focused strategy.* While Walmart may be the unstoppable force in mass-merchandise retailing, its Sam's Club comes up short in warehouse club retailing. The winner: Costco Wholesale, the largest membership warehouse club chain in the United States. A key reason is its focused strategy that provides more product selection. Costco's strategy: Expand into product categories that consumers are likely to buy in bulk.[7]
- *Execution: Develop and maintain flawless operational execution.* Toyota is generally acknowledged as the best in the world in revolutionizing auto manufacturing. It created the doctrine of *kaizen*, or continuous improvement, which is now used throughout the auto industry. It has also launched a new version of the Toyota Production System (TPS) that

has reduced the average time to deliver a project from 186 days to 69 days to help make "what is needed, when it is needed, and in the amount needed."[8]

VIDEO 22-2
Skunk Works
kerin.tv/15e/v22-2

- *Culture: Develop and maintain a performance-oriented culture. Fortune*, LinkedIn, and Glassdoor regularly rank Google as one of the best companies to work for. Its culture is based on several key principles including: "Focus on the user and all else will follow" and "Great just isn't good enough." The performance result? High employee job satisfaction, 16 percent growth in sales, and a 19 percent profit margin.[9]
- *Structure: Build and maintain a fast, flexible, flat organization.* Successful small organizations often grow into bureaucratic large ones with layers of managers and red tape that slow decision making. The unquestioned all-time leader in delivering world-class aircraft with only a small team of engineers, designers, and machinists: Lockheed Martin's Skunk Works. Discussed later in the chapter, its first director set key organizational guidelines, like "use a small number of good people who can talk to anyone in the organization to solve a problem."[10]

Of course, in practice a firm cannot allocate unlimited resources to achieving each of these business basics. It must make choices based on where its resources can produce the greatest return, the topic of the next section.

Allocating Marketing Resources Using Sales Response Functions

A **sales response function** relates the expense of the marketing effort to the marketing results obtained.[11] To simplify the examples that follow, only the effects of annual marketing effort on annual sales revenue will be analyzed, but keep in mind that the concept also applies to other measures of marketing success–such as profit or units sold.

Maximizing Incremental Revenue Minus Incremental Cost Economists give managers a specific guideline for optimal resource allocation: Allocate the firm's marketing, production, and financial resources to the markets and products where the excess of incremental revenues over incremental costs is greatest. This parallels the marginal revenue-marginal cost analysis discussed in Chapter 13.

Figure 22–1 illustrates the resource allocation principle that is inherent in the sales response function. The firm's annual marketing effort, such as advertising, personal sales, sales promotion, direct marketing, and public relations expenses, is plotted on the horizontal axis. As the annual marketing effort increases, so does the resulting annual sales revenue, which is plotted on the vertical axis. The relationship is assumed to be S-shaped, showing that an additional $1 million of marketing effort, from $3 million to $4 million at Point A, results in a far greater increase of sales revenue in the midrange ($20 million) of the curve than at either end.

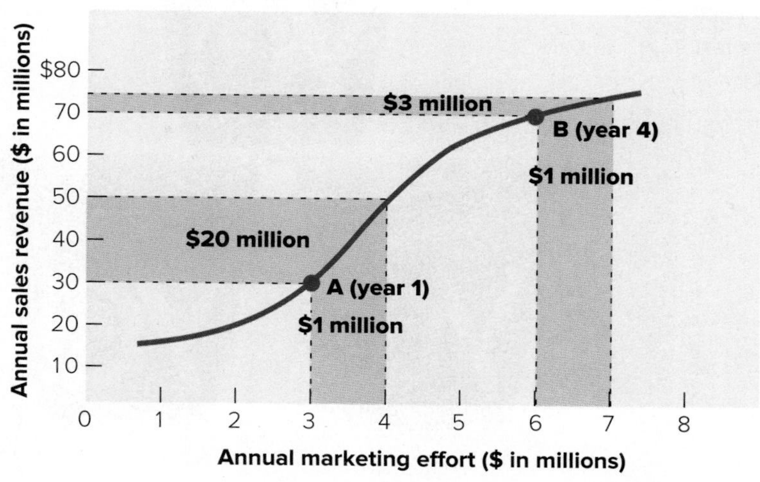

FIGURE 22–1
A sales response function shows the impact of various levels of marketing effort on annual sales revenue for two different years.

This is because at the left end of the S-curve, the cost of the marketing effort to gain new customers is high for they must be made aware of the product. In contrast, at the right end of the S-curve, the easy-to-get customers are already buying the product and gaining new customers is again very costly—as illustrated by Point B at the right end.

An Example of Resource Allocation Suppose Figure 22–1 shows the situation for a new General Mills product such as Blueberry Cheerios, a mainstream cereal featuring natural fruit juice coloring, that is also gluten-free. It is targeted at health-conscious consumers who want a great-tasting cereal. Blueberry Cheerios is an extension of Cheerios, the best-selling cereal brand in the United States.[12]

Also assume that the sales response function in Figure 22–1 doesn't change through time as a result of changing consumer tastes and incomes. Point A shows the position of the firm in year 1, whereas Point B shows it three years later in year 4. Now suppose General Mills decides to launch new advertising and sales promotions that increase its marketing effort for the brand from $3 million to $6 million a year. If the relationship in Figure 22–1 holds true and is a good picture of consumer purchasing behavior, the sales revenues of Blueberry Cheerios should increase from $30 million to $70 million a year.

Let's look at the major resource allocation question: What are the probable increases in sales revenue for Blueberry Cheerios in year 1 and year 4 if General Mills spends an additional $1 million in marketing effort? As Figure 22–1 reveals,

Year 1

Increase in marketing effort from $3 million to $4 million = $1 million.
Increase in sales revenue from $30 million to $50 million = $20 million.
Ratio of incremental sales revenue to effort = $20 million:$1 million = 20:1.

Year 4

Increase in marketing effort from $6 million to $7 million = $1 million.
Increase in sales revenue from $70 million to $73 million = $3 million.
Ratio of incremental sales revenue to effort = $3 million:$1 million = 3:1.

Thus, in year 1 a dollar of extra marketing effort returned $20 in sales revenue, whereas in year 4 it returned only $3. If no other expenses are incurred, it might make sense to spend $1 million in year 4 to gain $3 million in incremental sales revenue. However, it may be far wiser

How should General Mills decide how to allocate resources to products such as Blueberry Cheerios and YQ by Yoplait? For the answer, see the text.
McGraw-Hill Education

for General Mills to invest the money in one of its other brands, such as its new YQ by Yoplait.

The essence of resource allocation is simple: Put incremental resources where the incremental returns are greatest over the foreseeable future. For General Mills, this means that it must allocate its available resources (talent and dollars) more efficiently when developing its broad portfolio of products and brands and creating the marketing actions required to reach their respective target market segments. Low interest rates have created an environment where the cost of financial resources is very low.

Allocating Marketing Resources in Practice General Mills, like many firms in the consumer packaged foods industry, does extensive analysis using **share points,** or percentage points of market share, as the common basis of comparison to allocate marketing resources effectively for different product lines within the same firm. This practice allows the company to explore questions like, "How much is it worth to us to try to increase our market share by another 1 (or 2, or 5, or 10) percentage point(s)?"

This analysis enables higher-level managers to make resource allocation trade-offs among different kinds of strategic business units owned by the company. To make these resource allocation decisions, marketing managers must estimate: (1) the market share for the product; (2) the revenues associated with each point of market share (a share point in breakfast cereals may be five times what it is in cake mixes); (3) the contribution to overhead and profit (or gross margin) of each share point; and (4) possible cannibalization effects on other products in the line (for example, sales of Blueberry Cheerios might reduce sales of regular Cheerios).

Resource Allocation and the Strategic Marketing Process Company resources are allocated effectively in the strategic marketing process by converting marketing information into marketing actions. Figure 22–2 summarizes the strategic marketing process introduced in Chapter 2, along with the pertinent marketing actions and information. Figure 22–2 is a simplification of the actual strategic marketing process. In practice, marketing actions and the information needed to develop them overlap throughout the three phases of the strategic marketing process.

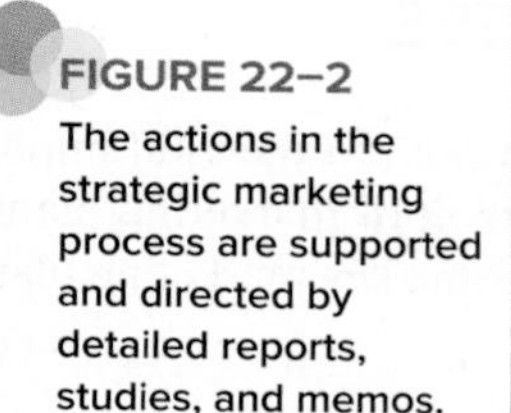
FIGURE 22–2
The actions in the strategic marketing process are supported and directed by detailed reports, studies, and memos.

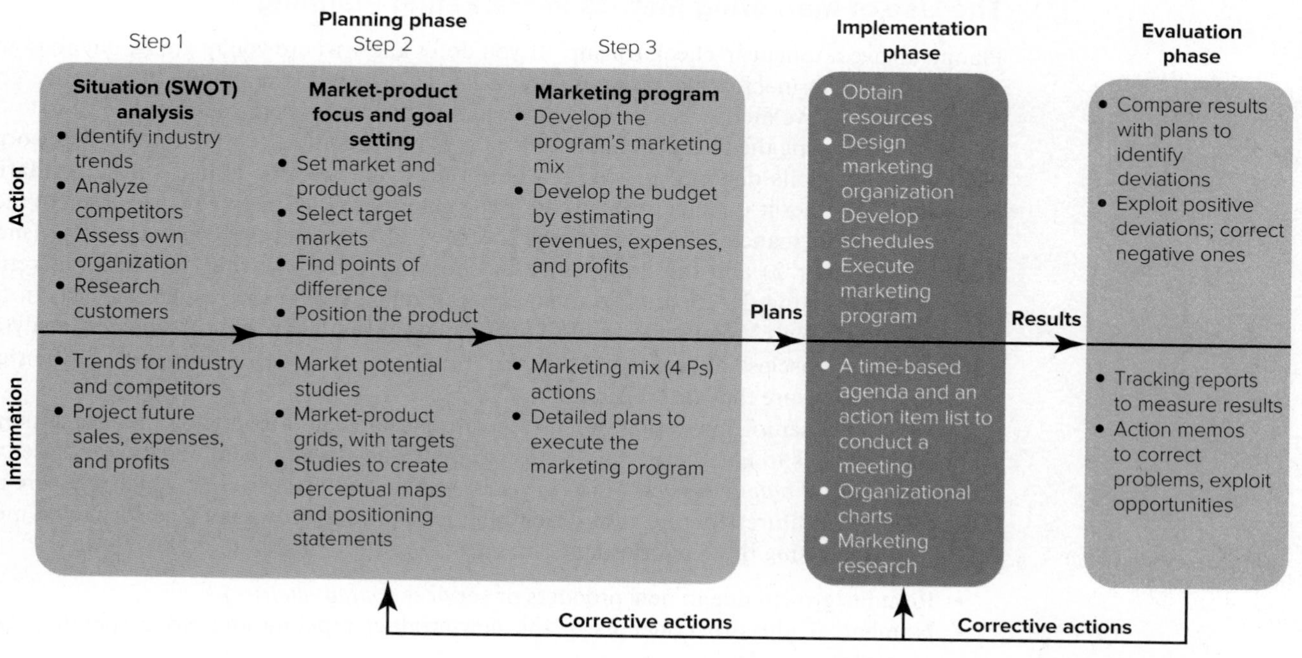

The upper half of each box in Figure 22-2 highlights the actions involved in that part of the strategic marketing process, and the lower half summarizes the information and reports used. Note that each phase has an output report, as shown below:

Phase	Output Report
Planning	Marketing plans (or programs) that define goals (with pertinent marketing metrics) and the marketing mix strategies to achieve them
Implementation	Action memos that tell (1) *who* is (2) to do *what* (3) by *when*
Evaluation	Corrective action memos, triggered by comparing results with goals, often using the firm's marketing metrics and displayed in marketing dashboards

The corrective action memos become feedback loops in Figure 22-2 that help improve decisions and actions in earlier phases of the strategic marketing process.

LEARNING REVIEW

22-1. What are the four basic practices "that really work" that characterize industry-leading firms?

22-2. What is the significance of the S-shape of the sales response function in Figure 22–1?

THE PLANNING PHASE OF THE STRATEGIC MARKETING PROCESS

Four aspects of the strategic marketing process deserve special mention: (1) the vital importance of marketing metrics in marketing planning; (2) the time horizon of marketing plans; (3) competing planning frameworks that have proven useful; and (4) some key marketing planning and strategy lessons.

The Use of Marketing Metrics in Marketing Planning

Planners have a tongue-in-cheek truism: "If you don't know where you're going, any road will get you there." In making marketing plans, the "road" chosen is really the quantitative goal *plus* the quantitative metric used to measure whether the goal is being achieved.

Today, measuring the results of marketing actions has become a central focus in many organizations. This boils down to defining "where the organization is going"—the quantitative goals—and "whether it is really getting there"—the quantitative marketing metrics used to measure actual performance. This emphasizes the need for data-driven decision making (mentioned in Chapter 2) and the importance of choosing and displaying the right marketing metrics in marketing dashboards so managers can quickly view the results and act. In the words of Coca-Cola's Vice President of Global Knowledge and Analytics: "The best analytics in the world are useless if we don't get the right information to the right people at the right time, and then ensure they take action."[13]

For example, senior marketing executives who prefer that "a company undertake major strategic initiatives to enhance its innovation and product-development capabilities" use two kinds of metrics:[14] *output metrics*, which measure results, and *input metrics*, which measure the effort and expenditures that go into developing new products. Areas of performance most often measured using these metrics are:

- Revenue growth due to new products or services (*output metrics*).
- Number of ideas or concepts in the new-product pipeline and R&D spending as a percentage of sales (*input metrics*).

Using only one of these two metrics gives an incomplete picture of a company's product development capabilities. When combined, these two metrics display marketing inputs and outputs and provide a basis for evaluating performance.

The Time Horizon of Marketing Plans

The planning phase of the strategic marketing process usually results in a marketing plan that sets the direction for the marketing activities of an organization. As noted earlier in Appendix A, a marketing plan is the heart of a business plan. Like business plans, marketing plans aren't all from the same mold; they vary with the length of the planning period, their purpose, and their audience. Let's look briefly at two kinds: long-range and annual marketing plans.

Long-Range Marketing Plans Typically, long-range marketing plans cover marketing-related investments and programs two to five years into the future. These plans consider what products and services to keep, add, and delete in the future using a portfolio analysis described in Chapter 2. They also present new marketing initiatives and address marketing organization topics. For example, a recent Frito-Lay long-range marketing plan focused on growth outside its existing snack business and augmenting its ongoing internal product development activities. This initiative, in turn, resulted in a dedicated team within its marketing organization with a formal charge: "To drive significant Frito-Lay growth by seeking new business platforms and products which combine the best of Frito-Lay advantages with high impact consumer food solutions."[15]

Long-range plans originate at the CMO level in companies. They are directed at other senior-level executives, such as the CEO and chief financial officer, and the board of directors. Importantly, long-range marketing plans give direction and a context for annual marketing plans described next.

Consumer packaged goods firms like Campbell Soup Company create detailed annual marketing plans to focus their strategies.
McGraw-Hill Education

Annual Marketing Plans Annual marketing plans are usually developed by a marketing or product manager. These plans detail marketing goals and strategies for a product, product line, or entire firm for a single year. Annual plans place a heavy emphasis on segmentation, targeting, and positioning; elements of the marketing mix; and revenue and expense projections. Suppose Campbell Soup Company's annual planning cycle starts with a detailed marketing research study of current users and ends after 24 weeks with the approval of the plan by the division general manager, 10 weeks before the fiscal year starts. Between these points there are continuing efforts to uncover key issues with specialists both inside and outside the firm. The plan is fine-tuned through a series of reviews by several levels of management, which leaves few surprises and little to chance. Attention to sales response functions and budgeting is critical in annual marketing plans.

Competing Planning Perspectives for Pursuing Growth and Profit

LO 22-2
Describe the generic business strategy and blue ocean strategy planning frameworks.

Planning efforts in companies are directed at finding the means for bolstering sales growth and profits. Two competing planning frameworks that help executives make important resource allocation decisions are (1) generic business strategies and (2) blue ocean strategies. Both strategies consider planning from the perspective of achieving marketplace differentiation and cost advantages resulting in sales growth and profit. However, their approaches differ.

Generic Business Strategies As shown in Figure 22-3 on the next page, there are four generic business strategies related to marketplace differentiation and cost advantages in an industry.[16] A **generic business strategy** is one that can be adopted by any firm, regardless of the product or industry involved, to achieve a competitive advantage.

In this framework, the columns identify the two fundamental alternatives a firm can use in seeking a competitive advantage: (1) It can become the low-cost producer within the markets in which it competes, or (2) it can differentiate itself from competitors by developing points of difference in its product offerings or marketing programs. In contrast, the rows identify the

FIGURE 22–3 Four generic business strategies involve combinations of (1) competitive scope, or the breadth of the target markets; and (2) a stress on lower cost versus product differentiation.

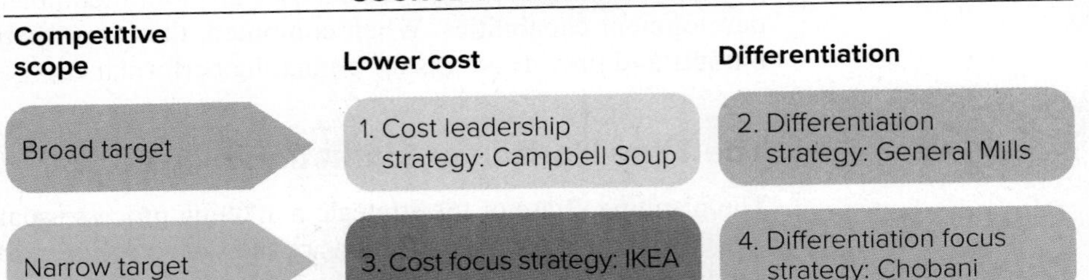

competitive scope: Choosing a broad target means the firm will be competing in many market segments, whereas choosing a narrow target means the firm will be competing in only a few segments or even a single segment. The columns and rows result in four generic business strategies, which can provide a competitive advantage among similar strategic business units in the same industry. These four strategies are as follows:

Which generic strategy is IKEA using? For the answer and a discussion of these strategies, see the text and Figure 22–3.
Source: IKEA

1. A **cost leadership strategy** (cell 1) focuses on reducing expenses and, in turn, lowers product prices while targeting a broad array of market segments. This may be done by securing less expensive raw materials from lower-cost suppliers or investing in new production equipment to reduce unit costs and improve quality. Campbell Soup's sophisticated product development and supply chain systems have led to huge cost savings. So its cost leadership strategy has resulted in lower prices for customers—causing its market share to increase to approximately 60 percent of the soup market.
2. A **differentiation strategy** (cell 2) requires products to have significant points of difference—product offerings, brand image, higher quality, advanced technology, or superior service—to charge a higher price while targeting a broad array of market segments. This strategy allows the firm to charge a price premium. General Mills uses this strategy in stressing its nutritious, high-quality brands in reaching a diverse array of customer segments.
3. A **cost focus strategy** (cell 3) involves controlling expenses and, in turn, lowering product prices targeted at a narrow range of market segments. Retail chains targeting only a few market segments in a restricted group of products often use a cost focus strategy successfully. IKEA has become the world's largest furniture retailer by selling flat-pack, self-assembly furniture, accessories, and bathroom and kitchen items to cost-conscious consumers.
4. Finally, a **differentiation focus strategy** (cell 4) requires products to have significant points of difference in order to target one or only a few market segments. Chobani Greek Yogurt, discussed in Chapter 1, uses a differentiation focus strategy. Its launch of a healthy, high-quality, great-tasting yogurt using natural ingredients successfully reached the segment of consumers who favor Greek-style yogurt.

In summary, the generic business strategy framework focuses on achieving a competitive advantage in defined industries or markets in which a company is currently operating. It also highlights the trade-off between pursuing either a product or marketing differentiation strategy or a cost-based strategy as a pathway for growth and profit.

Blue Ocean Strategy A blue ocean strategy offers a more expansive perspective on the pursuit of sales growth and profit.[17] By comparison with the generic business strategy framework, a **blue ocean strategy** emphasizes the simultaneous pursuit of product or marketing program differentiation *and* lower cost in newly configured industries and markets envisioned by marketing strategists and entrepreneurs alike. Companies (and entrepreneurs) are challenged to reimagine the marketplace. They are advised to (1) look across traditional industry or market boundaries, (2) combine complementary products and services, and (3) create new

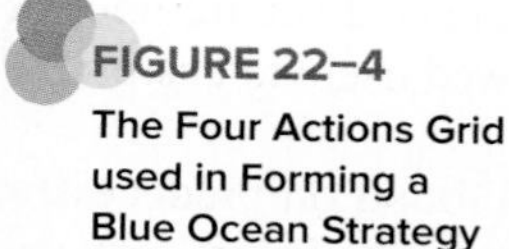

FIGURE 22–4
The Four Actions Grid used in Forming a Blue Ocean Strategy

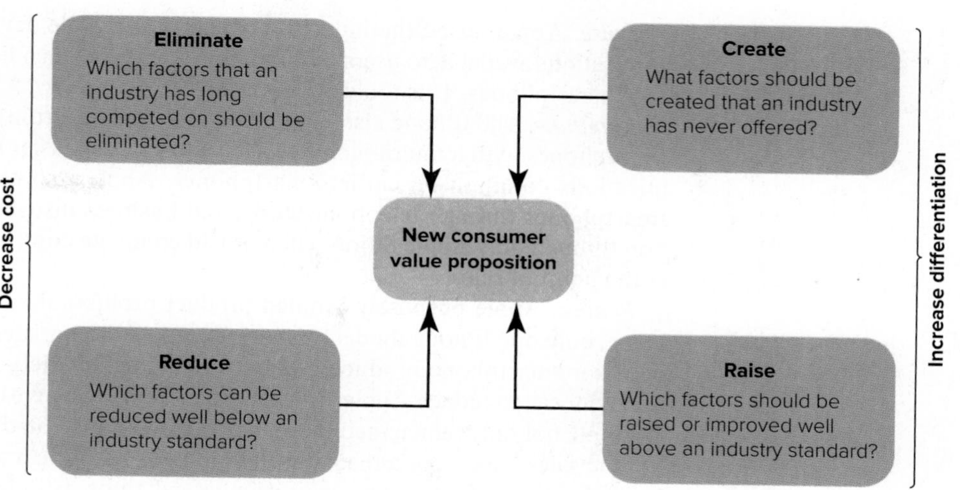

buyer and user experiences for the purpose of fashioning new industries and markets and adopting business practices that foster new consumer value propositions.

The Four Actions Grid A central framework in forming a blue ocean market strategy is the Four Actions Grid shown in Figure 22–4. This framework focuses on increasing product and marketing program differentiation by creating and raising industry factors that are new and improved relative to existing conditions in the marketplace. At the same time, the framework focuses on decreasing cost by eliminating and reducing prevailing industry factors that are no longer necessary or can be provided or performed below current industry standards. By increasing marketplace differentiation and decreasing cost at the same time, new consumer value propositions become possible.

Reimagining Smartphones The Four Actions Grid can be brought to life by describing the smartphone industry and Apple's role in its formation. At the time Apple developed its iPhone, the company competed in the highly competitive desktop, laptop, and tablet computing industry and in the portable music player market with its iPod devices. It is important to note that Apple did not invent the smartphone concept. Rather, smartphone predecessors included several efforts to merge the technologies behind personal digital assistants (mobile devices with Internet access) and mobile cell phones. These products had a very short battery life, were bulky, contained small screens, lacked wireless data services, featured raised keyboard buttons, and offered limited applications for users who were mostly businesspeople.

In developing the iPhone, Apple redefined industry and market boundaries. It *looked across industry and market boundaries*. Instead of limiting itself to the boundaries of the mobile phone industry and its competitive business practices, Apple looked across the then nascent smartphone industry, the portable music industry, and the Internet communication device industry. Apple iPhone was the first mobile phone to integrate the core functions of these three product categories into a single device. Apple also *looked across complementary product and service offerings*. The iPhone was equipped with an operating system also used in related company products; namely its Mac line of computers and iPod. It was also able to recruit its network of app developers that made the App Store one of its key differentiation elements. Finally, Apple product designers focused on *enhancing the buyer and user experience*. Unlike its predecessors, the iPhone targeted consumers rather than businesses, emphasized simplicity and ease of use, and provided entertainment (Apple iTunes) along with voice and Internet connectivity.

Apple's success with the iPhone can be further clarified in the context of the Four Actions Grid. A brief overview of each action is described below.

Create. Apple was able to create a smartphone that no one expected. The iPhone's slim rectangular form with square icons and a vivid screen brought an innovative look and a user-friendly feel to mobile phones, which at the time were bulky and unattractive.

Raise. Apple raised the industry standard for mobile devices. It increased the number of applications available to users through its App Store, which in turn allowed users to customize their smartphones. This too was a first.

Eliminate. The iPhone also eliminated a physical (button) keyboard found on predecessor smartphones with a multitouch interface allowing for easier use. It removed business-only applications common on earlier smartphones. Apple also eliminated the practice of selling smartphones through telephone stores and business distributors. It limited iPhone distribution through only Apple Stores where it had complete control over merchandising and pricing at the point of sale.

Reduce. Apple purposely avoided product proliferation. For the first 10 years of its existence, only one iPhone model was introduced, with upgrades, of course. By comparison, predecessor smartphone producers were introducing a variety of models. The net effect of this decision was to reduce Apple R&D and marketing resources, thus reducing cost.

Apple not only reimagined the smartphone, but it created the industry familiar to all today. iPhone sales have been a mainstay of Apple for more than a decade. But Apple is not alone. Consider the entrepreneurs who reimagined the taxi industry (Uber), the hotel industry (Airbnb), and retailing (Amazon).

LEARNING REVIEW

22-3. What is the difference between an input metric and an output metric?

22-4. Describe generic business strategy and blue ocean strategy as planning frameworks.

Some Marketing Planning and Strategy Lessons

LO 22-3
Explain what makes an effective marketing plan.

Applying marketing planning frameworks is not automatic; in fact, it requires a great deal of managerial judgment. Commonsense requirements of an effective marketing plan are discussed next, followed by problems that can arise.

Guidelines for an Effective Marketing Plan President Dwight D. Eisenhower once made a now classic observation about planning when he said, "Plans are nothing; planning is everything." It is the process of careful planning that focuses an organization's efforts and leads to success. The plans themselves, which change with events, are often secondary. Effective planning and plans are inevitably characterized by identifiable objectives, specific strategies or courses of action, and the means to execute them. Here are some guidelines for developing effective marketing plans:[18]

- *Set measurable, achievable goals.* Ideally, goals should be quantified and measurable in terms of what is to be accomplished and by when. So, "Increase market share from 18 percent to 22 percent by December 31, 2021," is preferable to "Maximize market share given our available resources." Also, to motivate people, the goals must be achievable.
- *Use a base of facts and valid assumptions.* The more a marketing plan is based on facts and valid assumptions, rather than guesses, the less uncertainty and risk are associated with executing it. Good marketing research helps.
- *Utilize an open strategy formulation process.* A transparent and inclusive process will lead to more ideas, enhance engagement, and increase the chances for successful implementation.
- *Use simple, but clear and specific, plans.* Effective execution of plans requires that people at all levels in the firm understand what, when, and how they are to accomplish their tasks. Involve people with the right skills and experience in the planning effort.

- *Have complete and feasible plans.* Marketing plans must incorporate all the key marketing mix factors and be supported by adequate resources.
- *Make plans controllable and flexible.* Marketing plans must enable results to be compared with planned targets, often using precise marketing metrics. This allows the flexibility to alter the original plans based on recent results.
- *Find the right person to implement the plans.* But make sure that person is heavily involved in making the plans.

VIDEO 22-3
Papa John's
kerin.tv/15e/v22-3

Problems That Plague Marketing Planning and Strategy Marketing planning and strategy initiatives are often plagued by problems in their development and assessment. Seasoned marketing executives typically cite four major problems that emerge when companies engage in the strategic marketing process:

1. *Plans may be based on presumed knowledge or poor assumptions about environmental forces*, especially future economic conditions and competitors' actions. Marketers for the most part did not expect the "Great Recession of 2008" and taxi and hotel companies did not expect, or downplayed the effect of, Uber and Airbnb, respectively, on their business and marketing plans. Both developments should have been identified or at least alluded to in the situation analysis phase of the strategic marketing process.
2. *Planners and their plans may have lost sight of their customers' needs.* But not at the Papa John's pizza chain. The "better ingredients, better pizza" slogan[19] is a concern for competing Pizza Hut executives. The reason is that this Papa John's slogan reflects the firm's obsessive attention to detail, which is stealing market share from the much-bigger Pizza Hut. Sample detail: If the cheese on the pizza shows a single air bubble or the crust is not golden brown, the offending pizza is not served to the customer.
3. *Too much time and effort may be spent on data collection and writing formal plans that are too complex to implement.* One firm cut its planning instructions "that looked like an auto repair manual" to five or six pages for operating units.
4. *Line operating managers often feel no sense of ownership in implementing the plans.* Andy Grove, when he was CEO of Intel, observed, "We had the very ridiculous system . . . of delegating strategic planning to strategic planners. The strategies these [planners] prepared had no bearing on anything we actually did."[20] The solution was to assign more planning activities to line operating managers—the people who actually carry them out.

THE IMPLEMENTATION PHASE OF THE STRATEGIC MARKETING PROCESS

The postgame summary provided by a losing football coach often runs something like, "We had an excellent game plan; we just didn't execute it." The planning-versus-execution issue applies to the strategic marketing process as well: When a marketing plan fails, it's difficult to determine whether the failure is due to a poor plan or poor implementation.

Is Planning or Implementation the Problem?

Effective managers tracking progress on a struggling plan first try to identify whether the problems involve (1) the plan and strategy, (2) its implementation, or (3) both, and then they try to correct the problems. But as discussed earlier in the chapter, research on what really works shows that successful firms have excellence on both the planning and strategy side and the implementation and execution side.

At the other extreme, most of the hundreds of start-up firms that fail have both planning *and* implementation problems. Their bad planning often results from their focus on getting start-up money from investors rather than providing real value to customers. Poor implementation by some of these firms leads to their spending huge sums on wasteful marketing to try to promote their business idea. Also, many of these firms don't understand key implementation issues that involve inventories, warehouses, and physical distribution.

Increasing Emphasis on Marketing Implementation

A recent survey of strategic marketing planning executives suggests that only 50 percent of marketing strategies are implemented as planned. Similarly, a Bain & Company report suggests that executives believe about 40 percent of a strategy's potential is lost due to poor implementation. As a result there is growing emphasis on the implementation phase of the strategic marketing process. Today, the implementation involves creating an organization-wide ownership of planning objectives. This level of ownership often requires that planning activities are shared throughout the organization, from planners to the line managers responsible for implementing the plans. In addition, the emphasis on implementation has encouraged frequent assessment and adjustment of marketing actions.[21]

Improving Implementation of Marketing Programs

No magic formula exists to guarantee the effective implementation of marketing plans. In fact, the answer seems to be a balance between good management skills and good practices, from which have come some guidelines for improving program implementation.

Open communications at Lockheed Martin's Skunk Works have led to state-of-the-art aircraft like this F-35 Lightning II Joint Strike Fighter.
Source: U.S. Navy photo courtesy Lockheed Martin

Take Action and Avoid Paralysis by Analysis Management experts warn against "paralysis by analysis," the tendency to excessively analyze a problem instead of taking action. To overcome this pitfall, they call for a "bias for action" and recommend a "do it, fix it, try it" approach.[22] Their conclusion: Perfectionists finish last, so getting it 90 percent perfect and letting the marketplace help in the fine-tuning makes good sense in implementation.

Lockheed Martin's Skunk Works got its name from the comic strip *L'il Abner*. Led by Kelly Johnson, Skunk Works developed its legendary reputation for achieving superhuman technical feats by stressing teamwork and working within the constraints of small budgets and tight deadlines. Under Johnson, the Skunk Works turned out a series of world-class aircraft. Two of Kelly Johnson's basic tenets: (1) Make decisions promptly, and (2) avoid paralysis by analysis. One U.S. Air Force audit showed that Johnson's Skunk Works could carry out a program on schedule with 126 people, whereas a competitor in a comparable program was behind schedule with 3,750 people.[23]

VIDEO 22-4
F-35
kerin.tv/15e/v22-4

Surface Problems with Open Communications Two more Kelly Johnson axioms from Lockheed Martin's Skunk Works apply here: (1) When trouble develops, surface the problem immediately, and (2) get help—don't keep the problem to yourself. Success often lies in fostering a work setting that is open enough so employees are willing to speak out when they see problems, without fear of punishment. The focus is placed on trying to solve the problem as a group rather than finding someone to blame. In this "open communications" environment, solutions are solicited from anyone who has a creative idea to suggest—from the janitor to the president.

Toyota's new service center uses the genchi genbutsu—"go and see"—principle to train its new mechanics.
Yuri Kageyama/AP Images

Communicate Goals and the Means of Achieving Them Those called on to implement plans need to understand both the goals sought and how they are to be accomplished. Historically, Toyota's growth has been built on a foundation of QDR—quality, dependability, and reliability. Besides emphasizing "always better cars" under CEO Akio Toyoda, the Toyota design team encourages a more "emotional" link between buyers and Toyota vehicles. And it continues to stress genchi genbutsu—"go and see"—a principle that suggests that to truly understand a situation you need to go to the source and see it for yourself. For example, Toyota engineers observe production on the factory floor and drive vehicles in real-use situations. The genchi genbutsu principle was the driving force behind the construction of Toyota's Tajimi Service Center, which simulates 13 driving conditions to train 4,800 mechanics each year.[24]

Have a Responsible Program Champion Willing to Act Successful programs almost always have a **program champion,** a person who is willing and able to "cut the red tape" to move the program forward. Such a person often has the uncanny ability to move back and forth between the "big picture" and the specific details as the situation warrants. Program champions can be notoriously brash in overcoming organizational hurdles. The U.S. Navy's Admiral Grace Murray Hopper gave the world not only an early computer language but also her famous advice for cutting through an organization's red tape: "Better to ask forgiveness than permission."

Founder Sara Blakely launched Spanx with a simple mantra: "Failure just leads you to the next great thing."

Will Vragovic/Tampa Bay Times/ZUMAPRESS.com/ Alamy Stock Photo

Reward Success but Don't Punish Failure Sara Blakely, founder and 100 percent owner of Spanx, has a simple mantra: "Failure just leads you to the next great thing"–so learn takeaway lessons from your failures. Her vision for her start-up was to eliminate "visible panty lines" when women dressed in stylish outfits. So she cut the feet off her control-top pantyhose, wrote her own patent application, and made all her initial sales calls. Customers were thrilled and thanked Blakely for "creating something they didn't even know they needed and now they can't live without." Today, Spanx has 200 products, including a men's line of undershirts, underwear, and socks, and Blakely recently appeared on *Forbes*'s list of America's Richest Self-Made Women.[25]

When an individual or a team is rewarded for achieving an organization's goal, they have maximum incentive to see a program implemented successfully because they have personal ownership and a stake in that success. At the same time, many firms owe their success to learning important lessons from their failures.

LEARNING REVIEW

22-5. What is the meaning and importance of a program champion?

22-6. Describe one or two lessons from Lockheed Martin's Skunk Works that can be applied to implementing marketing programs.

Organizing for Marketing

A marketing organization is needed to implement the firm's marketing plans. Today's marketing organizations understand: (1) the evolving role of the chief marketing officer and (2) how line versus staff positions and divisional groupings interrelate to form a cohesive marketing organization.

LO 22-4
Describe the levels and functions of an organization's marketing department.

The Evolving Role of the Chief Marketing Officer The senior executive responsible for a firm's marketing activities shown in Figure 22-5 on the next page is increasingly given the title of chief marketing officer (CMO) rather than vice president of marketing. This reflects the broadening of the CMO's role as the inside-the-company "voice of the consumer." So today, it is critical that CMOs understand (1) the changing characteristics of domestic and global consumers, (2) the role of digital media and mobile marketing in integrated marketing efforts, and (3) how to validate decisions with the many new sources of data, information, and

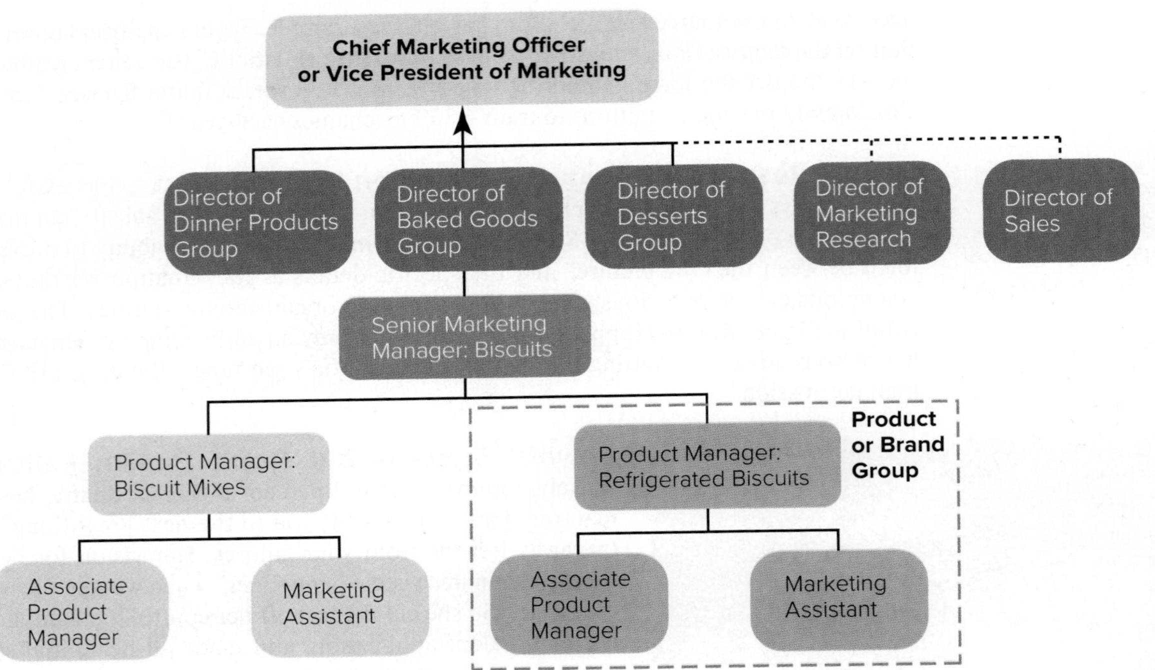

FIGURE 22–5 This organization of a strategic business unit in a typical consumer packaged goods firm shows two product or brand groups—biscuit mixes and refrigerated biscuits.

artificial intelligence. These broadened responsibilities have led to increasing influence. Recent surveys indicate that CMOs are responsible for budgets that represent more than 10 percent of company revenue, 60 percent of CMOs report directly to the CEO or COO, and CMOs are typically retained in their positions for six years.[26]

Line versus Staff and Divisional Groupings Although simplified, Figure 22–5 shows the organization of a typical strategic business unit in a consumer packaged goods firm like Procter & Gamble, Kraft, or General Mills. It consists of the Dinner Products, Baked Goods, and Desserts groups and highlights the distinction between line and staff positions. Managers in *line positions*, such as the senior marketing manager for Biscuits, have the authority and responsibility to issue orders to people who report to them, such as the two product managers shown in Figure 22–5. In this organizational chart, line positions are connected with solid lines. People in *staff positions* (connected by dotted lines) have the authority and responsibility to advise people in line positions but cannot issue direct orders to them.

Most marketing organizations use divisional groupings–such as product line, functional, geographical, and market-based–to implement plans and achieve objectives. Only the first of these appears in the organizational chart in Figure 22–5. The top of the chart shows organization by *product line groupings* in which a unit is responsible for specific product offerings, such as Dinner Products or Desserts.

At higher levels than what is shown in Figure 22–5, grocery products firms are organized by *functional groupings*–such as manufacturing, marketing, and finance–that represent the different departments or business activities within a firm.

Most grocery products firms use *geographical groupings*, in which sales territories are subdivided according to geographical location. Each director of sales has several regional sales managers reporting to him or her, such as western, southern, and so on. These, in turn, have district managers reporting to them, with the field sales representatives operating at the lowest level.

A fourth method of organizing a company is to use *market-based groupings*, which utilize specific customer segments, such as the banking, health care, or manufacturing segments. When this method of organizing is combined with product groupings, the result is a *matrix organization*.

A relatively new position in consumer products firms is the *category manager* (the senior marketing manager in Figure 22–5), who is responsible for an entire product line–all biscuit brands, for example. These marketers attempt to reduce the possibility of one brand's actions hurting another brand in the same category. Procter & Gamble uses category managers to organize by "global business units," such as baby care and beauty care. Cutting across country boundaries, these global business units implement standardized worldwide pricing, promotion, and distribution.

THE EVALUATION PHASE OF THE STRATEGIC MARKETING PROCESS

LO 22-5
Explain the use of marketing ROI, metrics, and dashboards in evaluating marketing programs.

Evaluation, the final phase of the strategic marketing process, involves (1) the marketing evaluation process itself and (2) the use of marketing ROI, metrics, and dashboards. We conclude this section with a look at how General Mills uses marketing metrics and dashboards.

The Marketing Evaluation Process

The essence of marketing evaluation involves (1) comparing results with planned goals to identify deviations and then (2) taking corrective actions.

Identifying Deviations from Goals Marketing plans made in the planning phase have both quantified goals and a specific marketing metric used to measure whether the goal is actually achieved. Marketing actions are taken in the implementation phase to attempt to achieve the goals set in the planning phase. In the evaluation phase, as Figure 22–6 shows, the quantitative results are measured using the marketing metrics and compared with the actual results of the marketing actions. For speed and efficiency, the results are compared with goals and often shown to marketing managers on marketing dashboards to enable them to take timely actions.

Acting on Deviations from Goals A marketing manager interprets the marketing dashboard information using *management by exception*, which involves identifying results that deviate from plans to diagnose their causes and take new actions. The marketing manager looks for two kinds of deviations, each triggering a different kind of action:

- *Actual results exceed goals.* In this case, marketing must act quickly to exploit unforeseen opportunities. In the past year Starbucks has added new flavors such as Dragon Drink and S'mores Frappuccino, opened new Reserve Roastery stores, began testing of new compostable cups and strawless lids, and launched a new loyalty program with tiered rewards and customizable options. It also upgraded its Mobile Order and Pay app to allow customers to click "trace now" to discover information about the grower of their coffee beans. The result? At its annual meeting of shareholders, Starbucks reported sales grew to more than $24 billion from 30,000 stores in 76 countries. Having exceeded its goals,

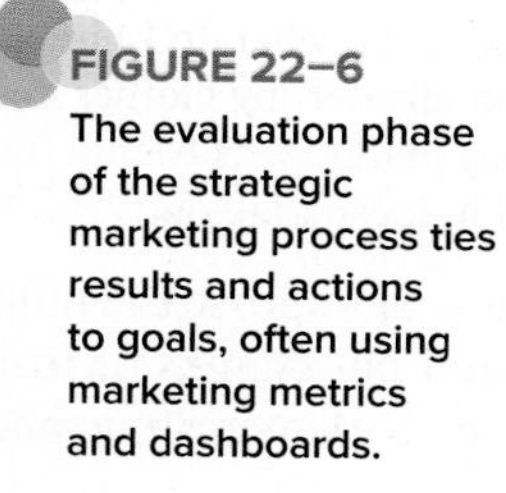

FIGURE 22–6
The evaluation phase of the strategic marketing process ties results and actions to goals, often using marketing metrics and dashboards.

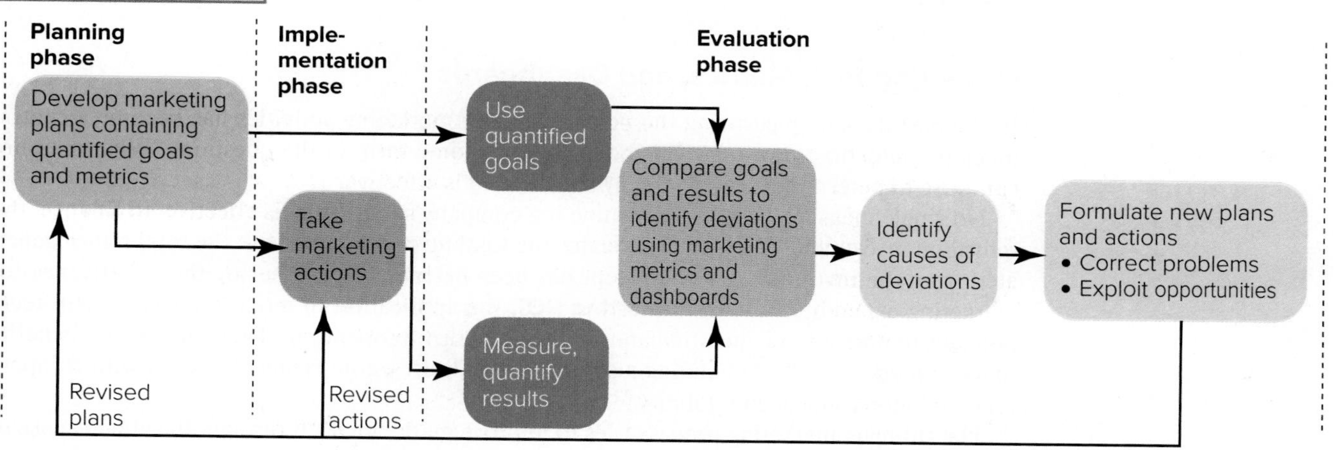

With 30,000 stores in 76 countries, Starbucks is still growing and plans to hire 25,000 veterans and military spouses.

Stephen Brashear/AP Images

Starbucks announced plans to build 10,000 "greener" stores by 2025; test a partnership with Uber Eats called Starbucks Delivers; and hire 25,000 veterans and military spouses.[27]

- *Actual results fall short of goals.* This requires a corrective action. One of America's favorite snacks, Hostess Twinkies, was first produced in 1930 and eventually generated $1 billion in sales from 14 plants and 9,000 employees. As consumers became more health-conscious, however, sales began to decline. Dean Metropoulos, who has made a career of saving distressed brands, bought Hostess, modernized the manufacturing, doubled the product's shelf life, and capitalized on the pop culture status of the Twinkie. Today, Twinkies are available in all Walmart and Sam's Club stores, 100,000 convenience stores, and vending machines and sales have exceeded the goals in the business plan.[28]

"Hiring a Milkshake" and Digging beneath the Numbers The "goals" used in marketing metrics are almost always *quantitative* goals. But sometimes the numbers can hide what is really happening and digging beneath the surface is needed to reveal the insights that lead to better marketing actions. A product and service example illustrates this issue.

A fast-food chain asked a team of consultants to beef up sales of its milkshakes. The chain had huge files about the likes of loyal milkshake customers. Changing the milkshakes based on those likes had no impact on sales. So consultants tried a different approach and asked: "What job is a customer trying to do when he hires a milkshake?" After looking at the results, the consultants found that (1) half the milkshakes were bought by men in the early morning; (2) it was the only thing they bought; and (3) they then drove off in their car with it.

Research on why these customers "hired the milkshake" revealed they (1) all had a similar job (2) with a long, boring drive to work and (3) needed something to do while driving.

> One hand had to be on the wheel, but, jeez, somebody gave me another hand and there isn't anything in it. And I'm not hungry yet but I know I'll be hungry by ten o'clock. So what do I hire? If you promise not to tell my wife, I hire doughnuts a lot, but they crumb all over my clothes and they're gone too fast. . . . But, let me tell you, this milkshake is so viscous that it takes twenty-five minutes to suck it up that little straw. And you can turn it sideways and it doesn't fall out![29]

By understanding what job the customers were trying to get done, how to improve the milkshake product became clear: You make the milkshake more viscous and put chunks of fruit into it to make sucking through a straw on the commute more unpredictable, interesting, and rewarding!

Marketing ROI, Metrics, and Dashboards

In the past decade, measuring the performance of marketing activities has become a central focus in many organizations. This boils down to some form of the question, "What measure can I use to determine if my company's marketing is effective?"

No single measure exists to determine if a company's marketing is effective. In finance, the return on investment (ROI) metric relates the total investment made to the total return generated from the investment. The concept has been extended to measuring the effectiveness of marketing expenditures with **marketing ROI,** the application of modern measurement technologies to understand, quantify, and optimize marketing spending. There are several benefits to using marketing ROI, including justifying expenditures, comparing efficiency with competitors, and increasing accountability.[30]

The strategic marketing process tries to improve marketing ROI through the effective use of marketing metrics and dashboards:

- *Marketing metrics*. Depending on the specific goal or objective sought, one or a few key marketing metrics are chosen, such as market share, marketing ROI, cost per sales lead, cost per click, sales per square foot, and so on. This is step 2 (set market and product goals) of the planning phase shown in Figure 22–2.
- *Marketing dashboards*. Ideally, the marketing metrics are displayed—often daily or weekly—on the marketing dashboard on the manager's computer. With today's syndicated scanner data, website hits, and TV viewership tracking, the typical manager faces information overload. So an effective marketing dashboard highlights actual results that vary significantly from plans. This alerts the manager to potential problems.

FIGURE 22–7
As a member of the Warm Delights team at General Mills, here is the marketing dashboard you see on your computer screen. You can use this dashboard to update the distribution channels strategy for the recently introduced line of Warm Delights Minis.
Source: Nelson Ng, Data Visualization Advisor, Dundas Data Visualization, Inc.

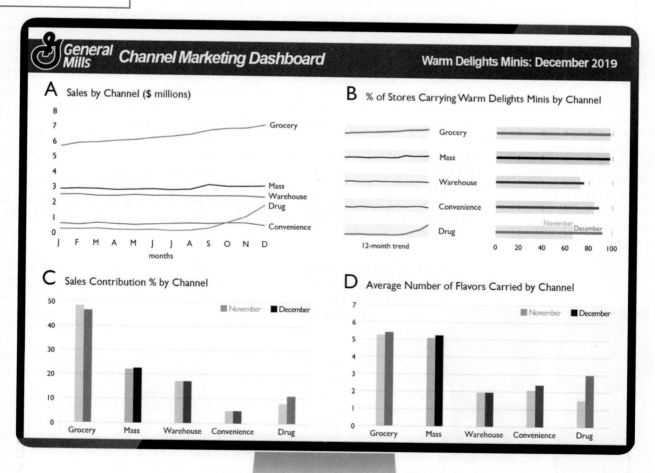

These highlighted exceptions or deviations from the marketing plan (shown in the evaluation phase in Figure 22–2) are the immediate focus of the marketing manager, who then tries to improve the firm's marketing ROI.

Evaluation Using Marketing Metrics and Marketing Dashboards at General Mills

Let's assume it is mid-January and you are part of Vivian Callaway's Warm Delights team at General Mills. Your team is using the marketing data and metrics shown in the marketing dashboard in Figure 22–7. We can summarize the evaluation step of the strategic marketing process using this dashboard and the three-step Challenge–Findings–Actions format used in the Applying Marketing Metrics boxes in the book.

The Distribution Challenge for Warm Delights Minis You've been asked to analyze the channel of distribution strategy of the Warm Delights Minis product. This hypothetical example is based on the type of scanner data that might appear in a computer display used by General Mills. However, details have been modified to simplify the data and analysis.

The marketing dashboard in Figure 22–7 focuses on the distribution of Warm Delights Minis.[31] As with all new grocery products, the challenge is to gain distribution on retailers' shelves. So the marketing metrics in Figure 22–7 show the distribution of Warm Delights Minis in the five main channels of distribution used by General Mills. These five channels and their shortened names in Figure 22–7 are:

- Grocery stores/supermarkets—Grocery
- Mass merchandisers—Mass
- Warehouse/club stores—Warehouse
- Convenience stores—Convenience
- Drugstores/pharmacies—Drug

The Findings for Warm Delights Minis The Figure 22–7 marketing dashboard describing the performance of Warm Delights Minis is divided into four charts, each with different marketing metrics:

- *Chart A: Monthly Sales by Channel ($ millions).* This shows the sales revenues for warehouse and convenience stores are flat or trending downward while those for mass merchandisers and grocery are up slightly. The grocery channel is clearly the most important. But the really encouraging news is the jump in sales in the drugstore channel from September to December.
- *Chart B: Percentage of Stores Carrying Warm Delights Minis by Channel.* The horizontal bar chart—a narrow December bar within the wider November bar—explains much of the major increase in September to December drugstore dollar sales seen in Chart A. Chart B shows that from November to December the percentage of drugstores carrying the Warm Delights Minis jumped from about 64 percent to 91 percent.
- *Chart C: Sales Contribution % by Channel.* The monthly bars total 100 percent. While the chart shows the importance of the grocery channel, it also shows the increased monthly sales revenue in the drugstore channel.
- *Chart D: Average Number of Flavors Carried by Channel.* This paints the picture more clearly. An important reason for the increased dollar sales from the drug channel is due to increasing the average number of flavors carried in a drugstore from 1.4 to 3.0 from November to December.

You've eaten healthy all day and now you want something quick and tasty to satisfy your sweet tooth. Try Warm Delights Minis—the 150-calorie, microwavable dessert! Just add water in the container and cook for 1 minute. Then, enjoy!
McGraw-Hill Education

The Actions for Warm Delights Minis Further analysis of the marketing dashboard showing the sales by channel of individual flavors of Warm Delights Minis reveals the jump in sales in the drugstore channel is because (1) a major chain (like Walgreens) added the line and (2) drugstores are embracing the new flavors, which is very important because they are now actively selling many food lines.

Your investigation also reveals a different situation for the four channels other than drugstores. The minor changes in sales there are due to the two new flavors simply replacing older, slower-moving ones.

Hot desserts normally experience an increased seasonal demand in winter. So because sales and distribution are growing, you decide to invest in the brand and schedule additional national TV advertising in late January and throughout February to exploit both the seasonal demand and recent sales trends. Seeing the jump in sales from adding a major drugstore chain, you research ways to attract other potential chains in each of the five main channels Warm Delights Minis uses.

LEARNING REVIEW

22-7. What are four groupings used within a typical marketing organization?

22-8. How do marketing metrics tie the goal-setting element of the planning phase of the strategic marketing process to the evaluation phase?

LEARNING OBJECTIVES REVIEW

LO 22-1 *Explain how marketing managers allocate resources.*
Marketing managers use the strategic marketing process and marketing information, such as marketing plans, sales reports, and action memos, to effectively allocate their scarce resources to exploit the competitive advantages of their products. Marketers may use techniques like sales response functions or market share (share point) analysis to help them assess what the market's response will be to additional marketing efforts and expenditures.

LO 22-2 *Describe the generic business strategy and blue ocean strategy planning frameworks.*
Generic business strategies involve combinations of competitive scope, broad or narrow, and the basis for competitive advantage—low cost or differentiation. There are four generic business strategies that firms can adopt: (1) a cost leadership strategy, (2) a differentiation strategy, (3) a cost focus strategy, and (4) a differentiation focus strategy. A blue ocean strategy advises companies to (1) look across traditional industry boundaries, (2) combine complementary products and services, and (3) create new user experiences. The strategy suggests managers create, raise, reduce, and eliminate factors related to the consumer value proposition.

LO 22-3 *Explain what makes an effective marketing plan.*
An effective marketing plan has measurable, achievable goals; uses facts and valid assumptions; is simple, clear, and specific; is complete and feasible; and is controllable and flexible.

LO 22-4 *Describe the levels and functions of an organization's marketing department.*
First, marketing departments must distinguish between line positions, those individuals who have the authority and responsibility to issue orders to people who report to them, and staff positions, those individuals who have the authority and responsibility to advise but cannot directly order people in line positions to do something.

Second, marketing organizations use one of four divisional groupings to implement marketing plans: product line groupings, which are responsible for specific product offerings; functional groupings, which represent the different departments and business activities within a firm; geographical groupings, in which sales territories are subdivided on a geographical basis; and market-based groupings, which utilize specific customer segments.

LO 22-5 *Explain the use of marketing ROI, metrics, and dashboards in evaluating marketing programs.*
The evaluation phase of the strategic marketing process involves measuring the results of the marketing actions from the implementation phase and comparing them with goals set in the planning phase. Marketing metrics, used to help quantify the goals in the planning stage, are of two kinds: input metrics and output metrics. The marketing manager then takes action to exploit positive deviations from the plan and to correct negative ones. Today, managers want an answer to the question, "Are my marketing activities effective?" One answer is in using marketing ROI, which is the application of modern measurement technologies to understand, quantify, and optimize marketing spending. Quantifying a marketing goal with a carefully defined output metric and tracking this metric on a marketing dashboard can improve marketing ROI.

LEARNING REVIEW ANSWERS

22-1 What are the four basic practices "that really work" that characterize industry-leading firms?
Answer: The four basic business and management practices that matter are: (1) strategy–devise and maintain a clearly stated, focused strategy; (2) execution–develop and maintain flawless operational execution; (3) culture–develop and maintain a performance-oriented culture; and (4) structure–build and maintain a fast, flexible, flat organization.

22-2 What is the significance of the S-shape of the sales response function in Figure 22-1?
Answer: The sales response function relates the expense of marketing effort to the marketing results obtained. Different levels of marketing effort will cause different rates of sales revenue growth. In Figure 22-1, an additional $1 million of marketing effort results in far greater increases of sales revenue in the midrange of the curve than at either end. At the left end of the S-curve, the cost of the marketing effort to gain new customers is high for they must be made aware of the product. In contrast, at the right end of the S-curve, the easy-to-get customers are already buying the product and getting every new one is again very costly.

22-3 What is the difference between an input metric and an output metric?
Answer: Marketing metrics are used to measure actual organizational performance–whether its goals have been achieved. An output metric is a measure of actual results, such as sales revenues due to new offerings and customer satisfaction with new offerings during a specified time period. An input metric measures the efforts that go into

developing new offerings, such as the number of ideas or concepts in the new-product pipeline and R&D spending as a percentage of sales.

22-4 Describe generic business strategy and blue ocean strategy planning frameworks.
Answer: The generic business strategy framework rests on four distinct differentiation and cost strategies to achieve a competitive advantage in current industries or markets: (1) *cost leadership strategy*, which focuses on reducing expenses and, in turn, lowers product prices while targeting a broad array of market segments; (2) *differentiation strategy*, which requires products to have significant points of difference to charge a higher price while targeting a broad array of market segments; (3) *cost focus strategy*, which involves controlling expenses and, in turn, lowering product prices targeted at a narrow range of market segments; and (4) *differentiation focus strategy*, which requires products to have significant points of difference to target one or only a few market segments. The blue ocean strategy framework also rests on differentiation and cost strategies, but with a focus on envisioning new industries or markets and developing innovative consumer value propositions. Using a Four Actions Grid, differentiation is derived from creating or raising industry factors that are new and improve existing conditions in the marketplace. Decreasing cost results from eliminating and reducing prevailing industry factors that are no longer necessary or can be performed below current industry standards.

22-5 What is the meaning and importance of a program champion?
Answer: A program champion is able and willing to cut red tape and move the program forward to get it implemented. Such a person often has the uncanny ability to move back and forth between the "big picture" and the specific details as the situation warrants. Program champions can be notoriously brash in overcoming organizational hurdles. An adage voiced by a program champion: "Better to ask forgiveness than permission."

22-6 Describe one or two lessons from Lockheed Martin's Skunk Works that can be applied to implementing marketing programs.
Answer: Examples of lessons from Lockheed's Skunk Works are: (1) make decisions promptly; (2) avoid "paralysis by analysis," which is the tendency to excessively analyze a problem instead of taking action; (3) when trouble develops, surface the problem immediately; (4) get help—don't keep the problem to yourself; (5) hold weekly meetings using a time-based agenda, which is one that shows the running time allocated to each agenda item; and (6) create an action item list.

22-7 What are four groupings used within a typical marketing organization?
Answer: The four marketing organizational groupings are: (1) product line, in which a unit is responsible for specific product offerings; (2) functional, where different departments or business activities within a firm are represented, such as manufacturing, marketing, and finance; (3) geographical, in which sales territories are subdivided according to geographical location; and (4) market-based, which uses specific customer segments. When this method of organizing is combined with product groupings, the result is a matrix organization.

22-8 How do marketing metrics tie the goal-setting element of the planning phase of the strategic marketing process to the evaluation phase?
Answer: For each marketing plan goal developed in the planning phase for an organization's offering, a marketing metric is created to measure whether the goal actually has been achieved. Marketing actions are then taken in the implementation phase with these goals in mind. In the evaluation phase, actual results are measured using this marketing metric to compare the established goal with the results to identify any deviations that need to be either exploited or corrected when revising the marketing plans for the next period.

FOCUSING ON KEY TERMS

blue ocean strategy p. 616
cost focus strategy p. 616
cost leadership strategy p. 616
differentiation focus strategy p. 616
differentiation strategy p. 616
generic business strategy p. 615
marketing ROI p. 624
program champion p. 621
sales response function p. 611
share points p. 613

APPLYING MARKETING KNOWLEDGE

1 Assume a firm faces an S-shaped sales response function. What happens to the ratio of incremental sales revenue to incremental marketing effort at the (*a*) bottom, (*b*) middle, and (*c*) top of this curve?

2 What happens to the ratio of incremental sales revenue to incremental marketing effort when the sales response function is an upward-sloping straight line?

3 Assume General Mills has to decide how to invest millions of dollars to try to expand its dessert and yogurt businesses. To allocate this money between these two businesses, what information would General Mills like to have?

4 The first Domino's Pizza restaurant was near a college campus. What implementation problems are (*a*) similar and (*b*) different for restaurants near a college campus versus a military base?

5 A common theme among managers who succeed repeatedly in program implementation is fostering open communication. Why is this so important?

6 In the organizational chart for the consumer packaged goods firm in Figure 22-5, where do product line, functional, and geographical groupings occur?

7 Why are quantified goals in the planning phase of the strategic marketing process important for the evaluation phase?

BUILDING YOUR MARKETING PLAN

Do the following activities to complete your marketing plan:

1. Draw a simple organizational chart for your organization.
2. Develop a Gantt chart (see Chapter 2) to schedule the key activities required to implement your marketing plan.
3. In terms of the evaluation, list (*a*) the four or five critical factors (such as revenues, number of customers, variable costs) and (*b*) how frequently (monthly, quarterly) you will monitor them to determine if special actions are needed to exploit opportunities or correct deviations.
4. Finalize your marketing plan based on the outline presented in Appendix A.

VIDEO CASE 22 General Mills Warm Delights: Indulgent, Delicious, and Gooey!

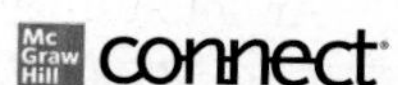

Vivian Milroy Callaway, vice president for the Center for Learning and Experimentation at General Mills, retells the story for the "indulgent, delicious, and gooey" Warm Delights product. She summarizes, "When you want something that is truly innovative, you have to look at the rules you have been assuming in your category and break them all!"

VIDEO 22-5
Warm Delights Video Case
kerin.tv/15e/v22-5

When a new business achieves a breakthrough, it looks easy to outsiders. The creators of Betty Crocker Warm Delights stress that if the marketing decisions had been based on the traditions and history of the cake category, a smaller, struggling business would have resulted. The team chose to challenge the assumptions and expectations of accumulated cake category business experience. The team took personal and business risks, and Warm Delights became a roaring success.

PLANNING PHASE: INNOVATION, BUT A SHRINKING MARKET

"In the typical grocery store, the baking mix aisle is a quiet place," says Callaway. Shelves display many flavors, types, and brands. Prices are low, but there is little consumer traffic. Cake continues to be a tradition for birthdays and social occasions. But, consumer demand has declined. The percentage of U.S. households that bought at least one baking mix in 2000 was 80 percent. Fifteen years later the percentage was about 62 percent, a very significant decline.

Today, a promoted price of 89 cents to make a 9 × 12 inch cake is common. Many choices, but little differentiation, gradually falling sales, and low uniform prices are the hallmarks of a mature category. But it's not that consumers don't buy cake-like treats. In fact, indulgent treats are growing. The premium prices for ice cream ($3.00 a pint) and chocolate ($3.00 a bar) are not slowing consumer purchases.

The Betty Crocker marketing team challenged the food scientists at General Mills to create a great-tasting, easy-to-prepare, single-serve cake treat. The goal: Make it indulgent, delicious, and gooey. The team focused the scientists on a product that would have:

- Consistent great taste.
- Quick preparation.
- A single portion.
- No cleanup.

The food scientists delivered the prototype! Now, the marketing team began hammering out the four Ps. They started with the descriptive name "Betty Crocker Dessert Bowls" and a plan to shelve it in the "quiet" cake aisle. This practical approach would meet the consumer need for a "small, fast, microwave cake" for dessert. Several marketing challenges emerged:

- *The comparison problem*. The easy shelf price comparison to 9 × 12 inch cakes selling for 89 cents would make it harder to price Dessert Bowls at $2.00.
- *The communication problem*. The product message "a small, faster-to-make cake" wasn't compelling. For example, after-school snacks should be fast and small, but "dessert" sounds too indulgent.
- *The quiet aisle problem*. The cake-aisle shopper is probably not browsing for a cake innovation.
- *The dessert problem*. Consumers' on-the-go, calorie-conscious meal plans don't generally include a planned dessert.
- *The microwave problem*. Consumers might not believe it tastes good.

In sum, the small, fast-cake product didn't resonate with a compelling consumer need. But it would be a safe bet because the Dessert Bowl positioning fit nicely with the family-friendly Betty Crocker brand.

IMPLEMENTATION PHASE: LEAVING BEHIND THE SECURITY OF FAMILY

The consumer insights team really enjoyed the hot, gooey cake product. But they feared it would languish in the cake aisle under the "Dessert Bowl" name since this didn't capture the essence of what the food delivered. They explored who the indulgent treat customers really are. The data revealed that the heaviest buyers of premium treats are women without children. This focused the team on a target consumer: "What does she want?" They enlisted an ad agency and consultants to come up with a name that would appeal to "her." Several independently suggested the "Warm Delights" name, which became the brand name.

An interesting postscript to the team's brand name research: A competitor apparently liked not only the idea of a quick, gooey, microwavable dessert but also the "Dessert Bowls" name! You may now see its competitive product on your supermarket's shelves.

Targeting on-the-go women who want a small, personal treat had marketing advantages:

- The $2.00 Warm Delights price compared favorably to the price of many single-serve indulgent treats.
- The product food message "warm, convenient, delightful" is compelling.
- On-the-go women's meal plans do include the occasional delicious treat.

©Daniel Hundley/Token Media

One significant problem remained: The cake-aisle shopper is probably not browsing for an indulgent, single-serve treat.

The marketing team solved this shelving issue by using advertising and product point-of-purchase displays outside the cake aisle. This would raise women's awareness of Warm Delights. Television advertising and in-store display programs are costly, so Warm Delights sales would have to be strong to pay back the investment.

Vivian Callaway and the team turned to market research to fine-tune the plan. The research put Warm Delights (and Dessert Bowls) on the shelf in real grocery stores. A few key findings emerged. First, the name "Warm Delights" beat "Dessert Bowls." Second, the Warm Delights with nuts simply wasn't easy to prepare, so nuts were removed. Third, the packaging with a disposable bowl beat the typical cake-mix packaging involving using your own bowl. Finally, by putting the actual product on supermarket shelves and in displays in these stores, sales volumes could be analyzed.

EVALUATION PHASE: TURNING THE PLAN INTO ACTION!

The marketing plan isn't action. Sales for Warm Delights required the marketing team to (1) get the retailers to stock the product, preferably somewhere other than the cake aisle, and (2) appeal to consumers enough to have them purchase, like, and repurchase the product.

The initial acceptance of a product by retailers is important. But each store manager must experience good sales of Warm Delights to be motivated to keep its shelves stocked with the product. Also, the Warm Delights team must monitor the display activity in the store. Are the displays placed in the locations as expected? Do the sales increase when a display is present? Watching distribution and display execution on a new product is very important so that sales shortfalls can be addressed proactively.

Did the customer buy one or two Warm Delights? Did the customer return for a second purchase a few days later? The syndicated services that sell household panel purchase data can provide these answers. The Warm Delights team evaluates these reports to see if the number of people who tried the product matches with expectations and how the repeat purchases occur. Often, the "80/20 rule" applies. So, in the early months, is there a group of consumers who buy repeatedly and will fill this role?

For ongoing feedback, calls by Warm Delights consumers to the toll-free consumer information line are monitored. This is a great source of real-time feedback. If a pattern emerges and these calls are mostly about the same problem, that is bad. However, when consumers call to say "thank you" or "it's great," that is good. This is an informal quick way to identify if the product is on track or further investigation is warranted.

GOOD MARKETING MAKES A DIFFERENCE

The team took personal and business risks by choosing the Warm Delights plan over the more conservative Dessert Bowls plan. Today, General Mills has loyal Warm Delights consumers who are open to trying new flavors, new sizes, and new forms. If you were a consultant to the Warm Delights team, what would you do to grow this brand in terms of product line and brand extensions?[32]

Questions

1 What is the competitive set of desserts in which Warm Delights is located?

2 (*a*) Who is the target market? (*b*) What is the point of difference on the positioning for Warm Delights? (*c*) What are the potential opportunities and hindrances of the target market and positioning?

3 (*a*) What marketing research did Vivian Callaway execute? (*b*) What were the critical questions that led her to conduct research and seek expert advice? (*c*) How did this affect the product's marketing mix price, promotion, packaging, and distribution decisions?

4 (*a*) What initial promotional plan directed to consumers in the target market did Callaway use? (*b*) Why did this make sense to Callaway and her team when Warm Delights was launched?

5 If you were a consultant to Vivian Callaway, what product changes would you recommend to increase sales of Warm Delights?

Chapter Notes

1. Eric Schroeder, "General Mills Sees 'Clear Improvement' in U.S. Operations," www.bakingbusiness.com, February 20, 2019; "General Mills 'Consumer First' Push Brings New Products and Focus," www.brandchannel.com, July 11, 2108; and personal interviews with Vivian Milroy Callaway.
2. "Company Profile: General Mills Inc.," *MarketLine*, November 16, 2018; Brittany Shoot, "General Mills Prices Have Gone Up," www.fortune.com, March 21, 2019; Simon Harvey, "CAGNY 2019—General Mills' Focus Remains on Organic Growth Struggle," www.Just-Food.com, February 20, 2019; "Cereal Sales Slump Amid Changing Diets and Other Breakfast Options," www.cbsnews.com, June 28, 2018; and General Mills Annual Report 2018.
3. "Our New Products Are There for Those Moments," news release, www.generalmills.com, July 10, 2018; and Rebekah Schouten, "Slideshow: New Products from General Mills, Kellogg, Post," www.foodbusinessnews.net, December 28, 2018.
4. Hugh Courtney, John T. Horn, and Jayanti Kar, "Getting into Your Competitor's Head," *The McKinsey Quarterly*, February 2009.
5. Nicolaj Siggelkow and Christian Terwiesch, "The Age of Continuous Connection," *Harvard Business Review*, May 2019, pp. 64–73; David C. Edelman and Marc Singer, "Competing on Customer Journeys," *Harvard Business Review*, November 2015, pp. 88–100; Roger A. Kerin, P. Rajan Varadarajan, and Robert A. Peterson, "First-Mover Advantage: A Synthesis, Conceptual Framework, and Research Proposition," *Journal of Marketing*, October 1992, pp. 33–52; and Pankaj Ghemawat, "Sustainable Advantage," *Harvard Business Review*, September–October 1986, pp. 53–58.
6. Nicholas Bloom, Raffaella Sadun, and John Van Reenen, "Does Management Really Work?" *Harvard Business Review*, November 2012, pp. 76–82; and Nitin Nohria, William Joyce, and Bruce Roberson, "What Really Works," *Harvard Business Review*, July 2003, pp. 42–52.
7. Sean Bryant, "Costco vs Sam's Club: What's the Difference?" www.investopedia.com, April 20, 2019; and "Costco Brand of Retailing Continues to Resonate," *MMR*, May 25, 2015, p. 56.
8. Jill Jusko, "TPS in the Age of Disruption," www.industryweek.com, February 19, 2019; and David Sedgwick, "Toyota's New Plan: Design Parts, Then Cars," *Automotive News*, June 15, 2015, p. 33.
9. "Key Statistics: Alphabet Inc.," www.finance.yahoo.com, May 6, 2019; and Pavel Krapivin, "How Google's Strategy for Happy Employees Boosts Its Bottom Line," www.forbes.com, September 17, 2018.
10. Sebastien Roblin, "Skunk Works: They Helped Create the F-22, F-35, U-2 Spyplane, and F117 Stealth Fighter," www.nationalinterest.org, May 4, 2019; Ben R. Rich and Leo Janos, *Skunk Works* (Boston: Little, Brown and Company, 1994).
11. Murali K. Mantrala, Probhakant Sirha, and Andris A. Zoltners, "Impact of Resource Allocation Rules on Marketing Investment-Level Decisions and Profitability," *Journal of Marketing Research*, May 1992, pp. 162–75.
12. Erica Chayes Wida, "Blueberry Cheerios Are Hitting Store Shelves This Spring," www.today.com, April 10, 2019.
13. Martyn Crook, "Putting Analytics into Action," presented at the Marketing Science Institute Conference, April 3–5, 2019.
14. Renee Dye and Olivier Sibony, "How to Improve Strategic Planning," *The McKinsey Quarterly*, August 2007; and Jacques Bughin, Amy Guggenheim Shenkan, and Marc Singer, "How Poor Metrics Undermine Digital Marketing," *The McKinsey Quarterly*, October 2008.
15. "Frito-Lay Company: Cracker Jack," in Roger A. Kerin and Robert A. Peterson, *Strategic Marketing Problems: Cases and Comments*, 13th ed. (Upper Saddle River, NJ: Pearson Education, 2013), pp. 253–80.
16. Michael E. Porter, *Competitive Advantage: Creating and Sustaining Superior Performance* (New York: The Free Press, a Division of Simon & Schuster, 1985), adapted with permission.

17. This discussion is based on W. Chan Kim and Renee Mauborgne, *Blue Ocean Strategy* (Boston: Harvard Business School Publishing, 2015) and *Blue Ocean Strategy Shift* (New York: Hachette Book Group, 2017).
18. Henry Adobor, "Opening Up Strategy Formulation: Benefits, Risks, and Some Suggestions," *Business Horizons*, May 2019, pp. 383–93; Several of the items in the list are adapted from Massimo Garbuio, Dan Lovallo, and Patrick Viguerie, "How Companies Make Good Decisions," *The McKinsey Quarterly*, December 2008; Renee Dye and Olivier Sibony, "How to Improve Strategic Planning," *The McKinsey Quarterly*, August 2007; and Jungkiu Choi, Dan Lovallo, and Anna Tarasova, "Better Strategy for Business Units," *The McKinsey Quarterly*, June 2007.
19. Papa John's, "Our Pizza," https://www.papajohns.com.
20. Stratford Sherman, "How Intel Makes Spending Pay Off," *Fortune*, February 22, 1993, pp. 57–61.
21. Brian D. Smith, "Between Saying and Doing Is the Ocean: An Empirical Exploration of the Gap between Strategic Marketing Plans and Their Implementation in the Life Sciences Industry," *Journal of Strategic Marketing* 27, no. 1 (2019), pp. 38–49; and Michael Mankins, "5 Ways the Best Companies Close the Strategy-Execution Gap," www.hbr.org, November 20, 2017.
22. Stuart Crainer, "In Search of Excellence: 30 Years On," *Business Strategy Review*, Fall 2012, pp. 78–80.
23. Ben R. Rich and Leo Janos, *Skunk Works* (Boston: Little, Brown and Company, 1994), pp. 51–53.
24. "Genchi-genbutsu Renewed," *Industrial Engineer*, September 2013, p. 11; and Geoff Colvin, "How It Works," *Fortune*, February 27, 2012, p. 75.
25. Ruthie Ackerman, "Fashioning a Whole New Industry: The Founders of Rent the Runway and Spanx Share Their Tips for True Disruption," www.forbes.com, October 2, 2018; "America's Richest Self-Made Women," *Forbes*, July 11, 2018; Haley Draznin, "Spanx Founder: It's Fun to Make Money—And to Give It Away," *money.cnn.com*, May 5, 2017; and the Spanx website, www.spanx.com.
26. Marty Swant, "Survey Finds CMOs Spent Less in 2019 but Will Increase Spend in 2020," www.forbes.com, October 2, 2019; *CMO Survey Report: Highlights and Insights*, *cmosurvey.org*, February 2017; and Caren Fleit, "The Evolution of the CMO," *Harvard Business Review*, July–August 2017, p. 60.
27. Nancy Luna, "5 Big Takeaways from Starbucks' Annual Meeting," *Nation's Restaurant News*, April 15, 2019, p. 1; Joanna Fantozzi, "The Evolution of the Starbucks Loyalty Program," *Nation's Restaurant News*, April 15, 2019, p. 1; "Starbucks Tests Compostable Cup in Several Major Cities," *Waste360*, March 25, 2019, p. 1; Laura Stampler, "Starbucks Adds Hot Pink Dragon Drink to Menu," www.fortune.com, April 30, 2019; and Kate Rogers, "Starbucks to Build 10,000 'Greener' Stores by 2025," www.cnbc.com, September 13, 2018.
28. Steven Bertoni, "The Twinkie Miracle," *Forbes*, May 4, 2015, pp. 74–82.
29. Larissa MacFarquhar, "When Giants Fail," *The New Yorker*, May 14, 2012, pp. 81–95.
30. Amy Gallo, "A Refresher on Marketing ROI," *Harvard Business Review*, *hbr.org*, July 25, 2017; and James D. Lenskold, *Marketing ROI* (New York: McGraw-Hill, 2003).
31. The illustrative example of using a marketing dashboard at General Mills was developed by David Ford and Vivian Milroy Callaway.
32. Warm Delights: This case was prepared by Roger Kerin, Steven Hartley, and William Rudelius.

APPENDIX

C PLANNING A CAREER IN MARKETING

GETTING A JOB: THE PROCESS OF MARKETING YOURSELF

Getting a job is usually a lengthy process, and it is exactly that—a *process* that involves careful planning, implementation, and evaluation. You may have everything going for you: a respectable grade point average (GPA), relevant work experience, several extracurricular activities, superior communication skills, and demonstrated leadership qualities. Despite these, you still need to market yourself systematically, aggressively, and authentically; after all, even the best products lie dormant on retailers' shelves unless marketed effectively. As authors Reid Hoffman and Ben Casnocha suggest, think of finding your first job as "The Start-Up of You!"

The process of getting a job involves the same activities marketing managers use to develop key brand characteristics and introduce successful products into the marketplace.[1] The only difference is that you are marketing yourself, not a product. You need to conduct marketing research by analyzing your personal qualities (performing a self-audit) and by identifying job opportunities.

Rafal Olechowski/Alamy Stock Photo

Based on your research results, select a target market—those job opportunities that are compatible with your interests, goals, skills, and abilities—and design a marketing mix around that target market. *You* are the "product"; you must decide how to "position" and "brand" yourself in the job market.[2]

The price component of the marketing mix is the salary range and job benefits (such as health and life insurance, vacation time, and retirement benefits) that you hope to receive. Promotion involves communicating with prospective employers through written and electronic correspondence (advertising) and job interviews (personal selling). The place element focuses on how to reach prospective employers—at the career services office, job fairs, or online, for example.

This appendix will assist you in career planning by (1) providing information about careers in marketing and (2) outlining a job search process.

CAREERS IN MARKETING

The diversity of marketing opportunities is reflected in the many types of marketing jobs, including digital marketing, product management, marketing research, and public relations. While many of these jobs are found at traditional employers such as manufacturers, retailers, and advertising agencies, there are also many opportunities in a variety of other types of organizations.

Professional services such as law, accounting, and consulting firms, for example, have a growing need for marketing expertise. Similarly, nonprofit organizations such as universities, the performing arts, museums, and government agencies are developing marketing functions. Event organizations such as athletic teams, golf and tennis tournaments, and the Olympics are also new and visible sources of marketing jobs.

The diversity of marketing jobs is also changing because of changes in the marketing discipline. The growth of influencer marketing, mobile marketing, and social media has created a variety of new jobs including brand ambassadors, marketing analysts, content marketing specialists, and social media managers. The growth of multichannel and omnichannel marketing has led to the need for channel integration specialists. The increasing involvement and engagement of consumers has required public relations personnel to become social networking experts and consumer-generated content managers. Other specialties in demand now include customer relations management (CRM), customer experience management (CEM), multicultural marketing, and viral marketing.[3]

Examples of companies that have opportunities for graduates with degrees in marketing include AT&T, Capital One, Century Link, E*TRADE, Ford, Home Depot, Kaiser Permanente, Ocean Spray, O'Reilly Automotive, Pepsi, Pfizer, Ricoh, Wayfair, and Wells Fargo.[4] Most of these career opportunities offer a chance to work with interesting people on stimulating and rewarding problems. One product manager comments, "I love marketing as a career because there are different challenges every day."[5]

Recent studies of career paths and salaries suggest that marketing careers can also provide excellent opportunities for advancement and substantial pay. For example, one of every four chief executive officers (CEOs) held positions in marketing before becoming CEO.[6] Similarly, reports of average starting salaries of college graduates indicate that salaries in marketing compare favorably with those in many other fields. The average starting salary of new marketing undergraduates in 2019 was $56,186, compared with $52,909 for advertising majors and $52,303 for journalism majors.[7] The future is likely to be even better. The U.S. Department of Labor reports that employment of advertising, promotion, and marketing managers is expected to grow at a rate of 10 percent through 2026. This growth is being spurred by the introduction of new products to the marketplace and the growing need to "manage digital media campaigns, which often target customers through the use of websites, social media, and live chats."[8]

VIDEO C-1
Careers
kerin.tv/15e/vC-1

Figure C-1 describes marketing occupations in seven major categories: product management and physical distribution, sales, nonprofit marketing, global marketing, advertising and promotion, retailing, and marketing research. One of these may be right for you. Additional sources of marketing career information are provided at the end of this appendix.

Product Management and Physical Distribution

Many organizations assign one manager the responsibility for a particular product. For example, Procter & Gamble (P&G) has separate managers for Tide, Cheer, Gain, and Bold. Product or brand managers are involved in all aspects of a product's marketing program, such as marketing research, sales, sales promotion, advertising, and pricing, as well as manufacturing. Managers of similar products typically report to a category manager, or marketing director, and may be part of a *product management team* to encourage interbrand cooperation.[9]

College graduates with bachelor's and master's degrees—often in marketing and business—enter P&G as assistant brand managers, the only starting position in its product or brand groups. As assistant brand managers, their responsibilities include developing a detailed marketing plan for a specific brand and learning consumer, shopper, and customer insights. With good performance and demonstrated leadership, after three to six years the assistant brand manager is promoted to brand manager, then after four to eight years to associate marketing director, and after three to eight years to marketing director. These promotions often involve several brand groups. For example, a new employee might start as assistant brand manager for Folger's coffee, be promoted to brand manager for Crest toothpaste, become an associate marketing director for P&G's soap products, and finally a marketing director for a different brand group. Other positions important at P&G include launch leader, account manager, and market manager.[10]

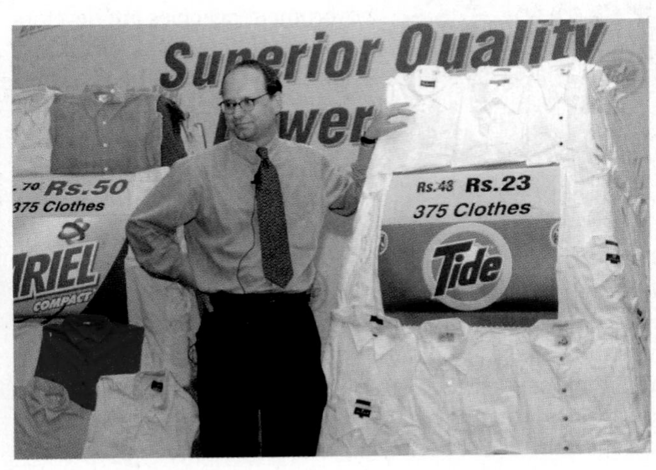

Product or brand managers are involved in all aspects of a product's marketing program.
Dibyangshu Sarkar/AFP/Getty Images

Several other jobs related to product management (see Figure C-1) deal with physical distribution issues such as storing the manufactured product (inventory), moving the product from the firm to the customers (transportation), and engaging in many other aspects of the manufacture and sale of goods. Prospects for these jobs are likely to increase as a wider range of products and technologies lead to increased demand. In addition, as manufacturers cut costs, they are increasingly shifting more responsibilities to wholesalers.[11]

PRODUCT MANAGEMENT AND PHYSICAL DISTRIBUTION

Product development manager creates a road map for new products by working with customers to determine their needs and with designers to create the product.

Product or brand manager is responsible for integrating all aspects of a product's marketing program, including research, sales, sales promotion, advertising, and pricing. Brand managers may utilize brand ambassadors who facilitate the use of social media, online reviews, trade show presentations, and word-of-mouth exposure.

Supply chain manager oversees the part of a company that transports products to consumers and handles customer service.

Operations manager supervises warehousing and other physical distribution functions and often is directly involved in moving products on the warehouse floor.

Inventory control manager forecasts demand for products, coordinates production with plant managers, and tracks shipments to keep customers supplied.

Physical distribution specialist is an expert in the transportation and distribution of products and also evaluates the costs and benefits of different types of transportation.

SALES

Direct or retail salesperson sells directly to consumers in the salesperson's office, the consumer's home, or a retailer's store.

Trade salesperson calls on retailers or wholesalers to sell products for manufacturers.

Industrial or semitechnical salesperson sells supplies and services to businesses.

Complex or professional salesperson sells complicated or custom-designed products to businesses. This requires understanding of the product technology.

Customer service manager maintains good relations with customers by coordinating the sales staff, marketing management, and physical distribution management.

NONPROFIT MARKETING

Marketing manager develops and directs marketing campaigns, fund-raising, and public relations.

GLOBAL MARKETING

Global marketing manager is an expert in world-trade agreements, international competition, cross-cultural analysis, and global market-entry strategies.

ADVERTISING AND PROMOTION

Account executive maintains contact with clients while coordinating the creative work among artists and copywriters. Account executives work as partners with the client to develop marketing strategy.

Media buyer deals with media sales representatives in selecting advertising media and analyzes the value of media being purchased.

Copywriter works with art director in conceptualizing advertisements and writes the text of print or radio ads or the storyboards of television ads.

Art director handles the visual component of advertisements.

Sales promotion manager designs promotions for consumer products and works at an ad agency or a sales promotion agency.

Public relations manager develops written or video messages for the public and handles contacts with the press.

Digital marketing manager develops and executes the e-business marketing plan and manages all aspects of the advertising, promotion, and content for the online business.

Social media marketing manager plans and manages the delivery of marketing messages through all social media and monitors and responds to the feedback received.

RETAILING

Buyer selects products a store sells, surveys consumer trends, and evaluates the past performance of products and suppliers.

Store manager oversees the staff and services at a store.

MARKETING RESEARCH

Project manager coordinates and oversees market studies for a client.

Account executive serves as a liaison between client and market research firm, like an advertising agency account executive.

Marketing research analyst/Data scientist analyzes consumer data to identify preferences, behavior patterns, and user profiles to create and evaluate marketing programs.

Competitive intelligence researcher uses new information technologies to monitor the competitive environment.

Marketing database manager is responsible for collection and maintenance of data and information, support of the data analytics and decision support systems, and timely and accurate report generation.

Source: Adapted from Sarah Steimer, "Marketing Job Titles," Marketing News, *May 2019, pp. 26-27; Lila B. Stair and Leslie Stair,* Careers in Marketing *(New York: McGraw-Hill, 2008); and David W. Rosenthal and Michael A. Powell,* Careers in Marketing, *©1984, pp. 352–54.*

FIGURE C–1
Seven major categories of marketing occupations.

Advertising and Promotion

Although we may see hundreds of advertisements in a day, what we can't see easily is the fascinating and complex advertising profession. The entry-level advertising positions filled every year include jobs with a variety of firms. Advertising professionals often remark that they find their jobs appealing because the days are not routine and they involve creative activities with many interesting people.

Advertising positions are available in three kinds of organizations: advertisers, media companies, and agencies. Advertisers include manufacturers, retail stores, service firms, and many other types of companies. Often they have an advertising department responsible for preparing and placing their own ads. Advertising careers are also possible with the media: television, radio stations, magazines, and newspapers. Finally, advertising agencies offer job opportunities through their use of account management, research, media, and creative services.

Starting positions with advertisers and advertising agencies are often as assistants to employees with several years of experience. An assistant copywriter facilitates the development of the message, or copy, in an advertisement. An assistant art director participates in the design of visual components of advertisements. Entry-level media positions involve buying the media that will carry the ad or selling airtime on radio or television or page space in print media. Some agencies are encouraging employees to develop skills in multiple roles. Advancement to supervisory positions requires planning skills, a broad vision, and an affinity for spotting an effective advertising idea. Students interested in advertising should develop good communication skills and try to gain advertising experience through summer employment opportunities or internships.[12]

Growing interest in integrated marketing programs has increased opportunities for sales promotion managers, public relations managers, and Internet marketing managers. These positions require an understanding of the potential synergy of all promotional tools. Responsibilities include the design and implementation of sweepstakes, sampling programs, events and partnerships, newsletters, press releases and conferences, e-mail promotions, Web-content management, and permission marketing campaigns. In addition, as advertisers increase search marketing budgets, the number of search marketing positions is increasing. Finally, many companies have decided that they need social media managers to ensure that messages can be sent to and received from the millions of people now on Facebook, Twitter, and other social media websites.[13]

Retailers such as Nordstrom offer careers in merchandise management and store management.
Source: Nordstrom, Inc

Retailing

There are two separate career paths in retailing: merchandise management and store management (see Figure C–2). The key position in merchandising is that of a buyer, who is responsible for selecting merchandise, guiding the promotion of the merchandise, setting prices, bargaining with wholesalers, training the salesforce, and monitoring the competitive environment. The buyer must also be able to organize and coordinate many critical activities under severe time constraints. In contrast, store management involves the supervision of personnel in all departments and the general management of all facilities, equipment, and merchandise displays. In addition, store managers are responsible for the financial performance of each department and for the store as a whole. Typical positions beyond the store manager level include district manager, regional manager, and divisional vice president.[14]

FIGURE C–2
Two common retailing career paths include merchandise management and store management.

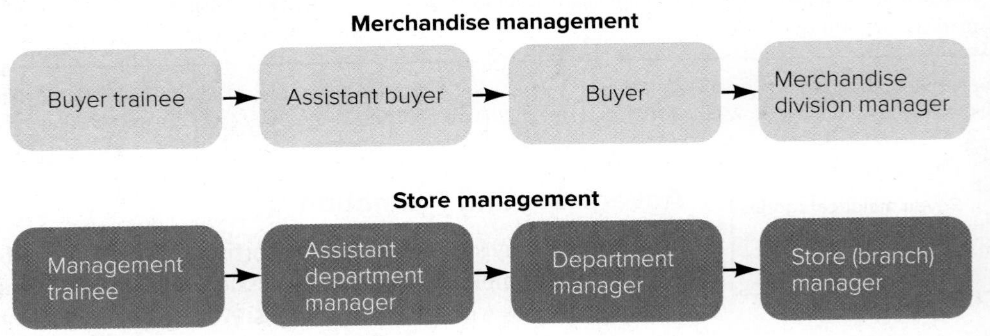

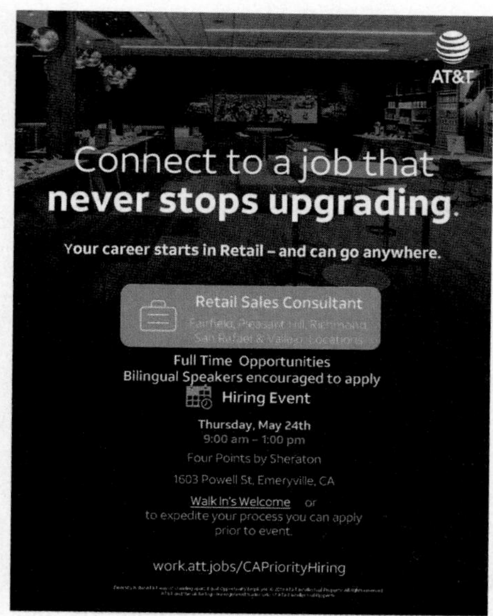

AT&T is well known for its sales career opportunities.
Source: AT&T

Most starting jobs in retailing are trainee positions. A trainee is usually placed in a management training program and then given a position as an assistant buyer or assistant department manager. Advancement and responsibility can be achieved quickly because there is a shortage of qualified personnel in retailing and because superior performance of an individual is quickly reflected in sales and profits—two visible measures of success. In addition, the growth of multichannel retailing has created new opportunities such as website management and online merchandise procurement.[15]

Sales

College graduates from many disciplines are attracted to sales positions because of the increasingly professional nature of selling jobs and the many opportunities they can provide. A selling career offers benefits that are hard to match in any other field: (1) the opportunity for rapid advancement (into marketing management or to new territories and accounts); (2) the potential for extremely attractive compensation; (3) personal satisfaction, feelings of accomplishment, and increased self-confidence; and (4) independence—salespeople often have almost complete control over their time and activities.[16]

Employment opportunities in sales occupations are found in a wide variety of organizations, including insurance agencies, retailers, and financial service firms (see Figure C–3). In addition, many salespeople work as manufacturers' representatives for organizations that have selling responsibilities for several manufacturers. Activities in sales jobs include *selling duties*, such as prospecting for customers, demonstrating the product, or quoting prices; *sales-support duties*, such as handling complaints and helping solve technical problems; and *nonselling duties*, such as preparing reports, attending sales meetings, and monitoring competitive activities. Salespeople who can deal with these varying activities and have empathy for customers are critical to a company's success. According to *Bloomberg Businessweek*, "Great salespeople feel for their customers. They understand their needs and pressures; they get the challenges of their business. They see every deal through the customer's eyes."[17]

One of the fastest areas of growth in sales is in the direct marketing industry. Interest in information technology, customer relationship management (CRM), and integrated marketing has increased the demand for contact with customers. For many firms this means increasing the amount of time salespeople spend with clients; for other firms it means increased use of Web conferencing technology; for still others it means sophisticated e-mail marketing. *Sales & Marketing Management* magazine's recent issue on sales technology describes the many new data analysis, social collaboration, and virtual meeting solutions that provide better relationships between salespeople and customers. Consultant Susan Aldrich observes that customers always say, "I want you to know about me and offer me things that are relevant to me."[18]

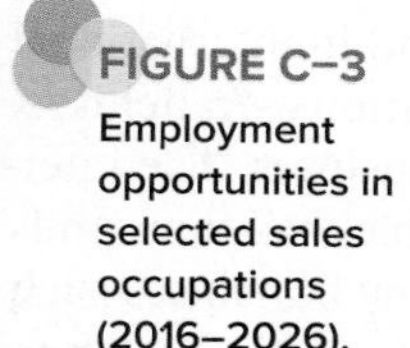

FIGURE C–3
Employment opportunities in selected sales occupations (2016–2026).

Occupation	2016 Employment	2026 Employment	Percentage Change 2016–2026	Growth
Insurance sales agents	501,400	551,200	10%	49,800
Real estate brokers and sales agents	444,100	469,000	6%	24,900
Retail salespersons	4,854,300	4,946,700	2%	92,400
Wholesale and manufacturing sales representatives	1,813,500	1,907,600	5%	94,100
Securities, commodities, and financial services sales agents	375,700	399,000	6%	23,300

Source: Occupational Outlook Handbook, 2018–19 Edition (Washington, DC: U.S. Department of Labor, Bureau of Labor Statistics).

Garmin is an example of a company that encourages students to think about a career and the culture of the company.
Source: Garmin

Marketing Research

Marketing researchers play important roles in many organizations today. In fact, *U.S. News & World Report* suggests that market research analyst positions are the number one job in business. They are responsible for obtaining, analyzing, and interpreting data to facilitate making marketing decisions. This means marketing researchers are basically problem solvers. Success in the area requires not only an understanding of statistical analysis, research methods, and programming, but also a broad base of marketing knowledge, writing and verbal presentation skills, and an ability to communicate with colleagues and clients. According to Stan Sthanunathan, vice president of marketing strategy and insights at Coca-Cola, a researcher's job "is to bring out opportunities."[19] Individuals who are inquisitive, methodical, analytical, and solution-oriented find the field particularly rewarding.

The responsibilities of the men and women currently working in the market research industry include defining the marketing problem, designing the questions, selecting the sample, collecting and analyzing the data, and, finally, reporting the results of the research. These jobs are available in three kinds of organizations. *Marketing research consulting firms* contract with large companies to provide research about their customers or products or services.[20] *Advertising agencies* may provide research services to help clients with questions related to advertising and promotional problems. Finally, some companies have an *in-house research staff* to design and execute their research projects. Online marketing research, which is likely to become the most common form of marketing research in the near future, requires an understanding of new tools such as dynamic scripting, response validation, intercept sampling, instant messaging surveys, and online consumer panels.[21]

Although marketing researchers may start as assistants performing routine tasks, they quickly advance to broader responsibilities. Survey design, interviewing, report writing, and all aspects of the research process create a challenging career. In addition, research projects typically deal with such diverse problems as consumer motivation, pricing, forecasting, and competition in domestic and international markets. Successful candidates "like what they're doing and get excited over their work, whether it be listening to a focus group or running a complex data mining model," according to Carolyn Marconi, director of marketing research for the Vanguard Group, Inc.[22]

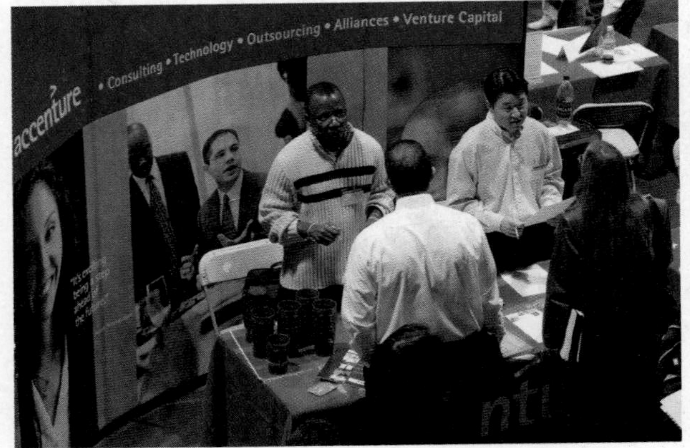

Accenture places thousands of consultants throughout the world.
Delane B. Rouse/AP Photo

International Careers

Many of the careers just described can be found in international settings–in large multinational U.S. corporations, franchises, and small- to medium-size firms with export business. The international consulting firm Accenture, for example, has thousands of consultants around the world. Similarly, many franchises such as 7-Eleven, which has 59,100 locations outside of North America, are rapidly expanding outside the United States.[23] The changes in the European Union, Brazil, Russia, India, China, and other growing markets are likely to provide many opportunities for international careers.

Several methods of gaining international experience are possible. For example, some companies may alternate periods of work at domestic locations with assignments outside the United States. In addition, working for a firm with headquarters outside the United States at one of its local offices may be appealing. In many organizations, international experience has become a necessity for promotion and career advancement. "If you are going to succeed, an expatriate assignment is essential," says Eric Kraus of Gillette Co. in Boston.[24]

Applicants for international positions need language skills and an ability to adapt to different business models, management styles, and local practices. In addition, as multinational firms use worldwide communication technologies to build global teams of people who have never met, collaboration skills become increasingly important. Accenture uses instant messaging, voice, video and online meetings, and telepresence technology to help its 459,000 employees serve clients in more than 120 countries. Similarly, IBM helps thousands of its employees be a part of "innovation jams" with a team home page on the company intranet.[25]

THE JOB SEARCH PROCESS

Activities you should consider during your job search process include assessing yourself, identifying job opportunities, preparing your résumé and related correspondence, and going on job interviews.

Assessing Yourself

You must know your product–you–so that you can market yourself effectively to prospective employers. Consequently, a critical first step in your job search is conducting a self-inquiry or self-assessment. This activity involves understanding your career vision, your passion, and your skills, abilities, personality, preferences, and individual style. You must be confident that you know what work environment is best for you, what makes you happy, the balance you seek between personal and professional activities, and how you can be most effective at reaching your goals. This process helps ensure that you are matching your profile to the right job. According to business consultant and author Debbie Qaqish, "marketers now have more career opportunities than at any other time in history," so "it is up to you to manage your career, seek these new opportunities, and enjoy an exciting and fulfilling career as a marketer."[26]

Asking Key Questions A self-analysis, in part, entails asking yourself some very important and difficult questions (see Figure C-4 on the next page). It is critical that you respond to the questions honestly, because your answers ultimately will be used as a guide in your job selection.[27] A less-than-candid appraisal of yourself might result in a job mismatch.

Identifying Strengths and Weaknesses After you have addressed the questions posed in Figure C-4, you are ready to identify your strengths and weaknesses. To do so, draw a vertical line down the middle of a sheet of paper and label one side of the paper "strengths" and the other side "weaknesses." Based on your answers to the questions, record your strong and weak points in their respective columns. Ideally, this cataloging should be done over a few days to give you adequate time to reflect on your attributes. In addition, you might seek input from others who know you well (such as parents, close relatives, friends, professors, or employers) and can offer more objective viewpoints. They might even evaluate you on the questions in Figure C-4, and you can compare the results with your own evaluation. Finally, to help identify additional strengths, you might purchase a copy of the very popular book *StrengthsFinder 2.0* by Tom Rath. A hypothetical list of strengths and weaknesses is shown in Figure C-5 on the next page.

stuartmiles99/Getty Images

What skills are most important? The answer, of course, varies by occupation and employer. Recent studies, however, suggest that problem-solving skills, communication skills, interpersonal skills, data and analytical skills, and leadership and motivation skills are all valued by employers. LinkedIn's Global Talent Trends Report indicates that 80 percent of recruiters believe that "soft" skills such as creativity, persuasion, collaboration, and adaptability

INTERESTS

- How do I like to spend my time?
- Do I enjoy working with people?
- Do I like working with tangible things?
- Do I enjoy working with data?
- Am I a member of many organizations?
- Do I enjoy physical activities?
- Do I like to read?

ABILITIES

- Am I adept at analysis?
- What are my hardware, software, and operating system skills?
- Do I have good verbal and written communication skills?
- What special talents do I have?
- At which abilities do I wish I were more adept?

EDUCATION

- How have my courses and extracurricular activities prepared me for a specific job?
- Which were my best subjects?
- My worst?
- Is my GPA a good indication of my academic ability? Why?
- Do I aspire to a graduate degree?
- Is this something I want to pursue before beginning my job? Or after?
- Why did I choose my major?

PERSONAL GOALS

- What are my short-term and long-term goals? Why?
- Am I career oriented, or do I have broader interests?
- What are my career goals?
- What jobs are likely to help me achieve my goals?
- What do I hope to be doing in 5 years? In 10 years?
- What do I want out of life?
- What work-life balance do I prefer?

PERSONALITY

- What are my good and bad traits?
- Am I competitive?
- Do I work well with others?
- Am I outspoken?
- Am I a leader or a follower?
- Do I work well under pressure?
- Do I work quickly, or am I methodical?
- Do I get along well with others?
- Am I ambitious?
- Do I work well independently of others?

DESIRED JOB ENVIRONMENT

- Am I willing to relocate? Why?
- Do I have a geographical preference? Why?
- Would I mind traveling in my job?
- Do I have to work for a large or nationally known firm to be satisfied?
- Must my job offer rapid promotion opportunities?
- If I could design my own job, what characteristics would it have?
- How important is high initial salary to me?

EXPERIENCE

- What previous jobs have I held?
- What were my responsibilities in each job?
- What internships or co-op positions have I held?
- What were my responsibilities?
- What volunteer positions have I held?
- What were my responsibilities?
- Were any of my jobs or positions applicable to positions I may be seeking? How?
- What did I like the most about my previous jobs?
- What did I like the least?
- If I had it to do over again, would I work in these jobs? Why?

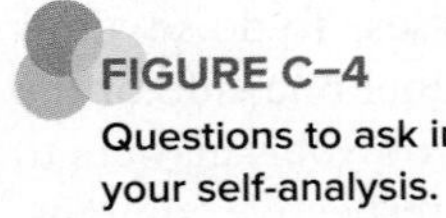
FIGURE C–4 Questions to ask in your self-analysis.

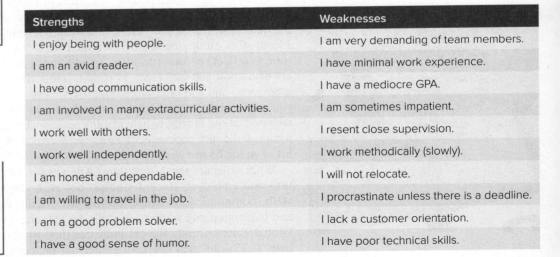

Strengths	Weaknesses
I enjoy being with people.	I am very demanding of team members.
I am an avid reader.	I have minimal work experience.
I have good communication skills.	I have a mediocre GPA.
I am involved in many extracurricular activities.	I am sometimes impatient.
I work well with others.	I resent close supervision.
I work well independently.	I work methodically (slowly).
I am honest and dependable.	I will not relocate.
I am willing to travel in the job.	I procrastinate unless there is a deadline.
I am a good problem solver.	I lack a customer orientation.
I have a good sense of humor.	I have poor technical skills.

FIGURE C–5 Hypothetical list of a job candidate's strengths and weaknesses.

are growing in importance. Personal characteristics employers seek in a job candidate include honesty, integrity, motivation, initiative, self-confidence, flexibility, and enthusiasm. Finally, most employers also look for work experience, practicum projects, internships, or co-op experience. These activities "give you hands-on experience and make you a stronger job candidate," explains Arlene Hill, director of career development at American University's Kogod School of Business. Candidates who are pursuing digital marketing positions must have skills related to search engine optimization (SEO), search engine marketing (SEM), mobile marketing, social media, and content management.[28]

Taking Job-Related Tests Personality and vocational interest tests, provided by many colleges and universities, can give you other ideas about yourself. After tests have been administered and scored, test takers meet with testing service counselors to discuss the results. Test results generally suggest jobs for which students have an inclination. The most common tests at the college level are the Strong Interest Inventory and the Campbell Interest and Skill Survey. Some counseling centers and career coaches also use the Myers-Briggs® Type Indicator personality inventory and the Peoplemap™ assessments to help identify professions you may enjoy.[29] If you have not already done so, you may wish to see whether your school offers such testing services.

Identifying Your Job Opportunities

To identify and analyze the job market, you must conduct some marketing research to determine what industries *and* companies offer promising job opportunities that relate to the results of your self-analysis. Several sources that can help in your search are discussed next.

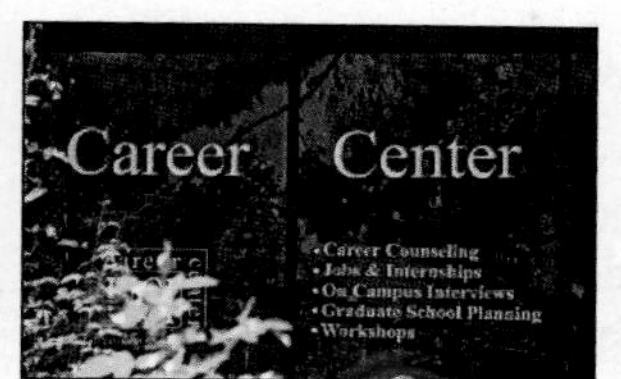

Campus career centers are excellent sources of job information.
GIPhotoStock Z/Alamy Stock Photo

Career Services Office Your campus career services office is an excellent source of job information. Personnel in that office can (1) inform you about which companies will be recruiting on campus; (2) alert you to unexpected job openings; (3) advise you about short-term and long-term career prospects; (4) offer advice on résumé construction; (5) assess your interviewing strengths and weaknesses; and (6) help you evaluate a job offer. Career services offices are also expanding to help students connect with companies that might not recruit on campus.[30] In addition, the office usually contains a variety of written materials focusing on different industries and companies and tips on job hunting.

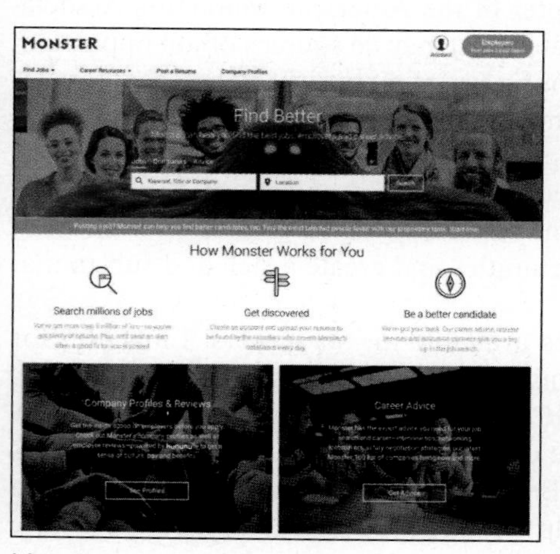

Monster.com is a popular employment website where students can match their skills and interests with job openings.
Source: Monster.com

Online Career and Employment Services Many companies no longer make frequent on-campus visits. Instead, they may use the many online services available to advertise an employment opportunity or to search for candidate information. The National Association of Colleges and Employers, for example, maintains a site called NACElink Network (www.nacelink.com). Similarly, Monster.com, Glassdoor.com, and Careerbuilder.com are online databases of employment ads, candidate résumés, and other career-related information. Some of the information resources include career guidance, a cover letter library, occupational profiles, résumé templates, and networking services.[31] Employers may contact students directly when the candidate's qualifications meet their specific job requirements. The advantage of this system for students is that regardless of the size or location of the campus they are attending, many companies have access to their résumé. Some job boards even allow applicants to post audio and video clips of themselves. One advantage for recruiters is that some of the job boards utilize software for performing background verification.[32] Your school's career center may also have a home page that offers online job search information and links to other Internet sites.

Library The public or college library can provide you with reference material that, among other things, describes successful firms and their operations, defines the content of various jobs, and forecasts job opportunities. For example, *Fortune* publishes a list of the 1,000 largest

U.S. and global companies and their respective sales and profits, and Dun & Bradstreet publishes directories of more than 26 million companies in the United States. The *Occupational Outlook Handbook* is an annual publication of the U.S. Department of Labor that provides projections for specific job prospects, as well as information pertaining to those jobs. A librarian can indicate reference materials that will be most pertinent to *your* job search.

Advertisements Help-wanted advertisements provide an overview of what is happening in the job market. Local newspapers (particularly Sunday editions), college newspapers, trade publications (such as *Marketing News* or *Advertising Age*), and business magazines contain classified advertisement sections that generally have job opening announcements, often for entry-level positions. Reviewing the want ads can help you identify what kinds of positions are available and their requirements and job titles, which firms offer certain kinds of jobs, and levels of compensation.

Employment Agencies An employment agency can make you aware of several job opportunities very quickly because of its large number of job listings available through computer databases. Many agencies specialize in a particular field (such as sales and marketing). The advantages of using an agency include that it (1) reduces the cost of a job search by bringing applicants and employers together, (2) often has exclusive job listings available only by working through the agency, (3) performs much of the job search for you, and (4) tries to find a job that is compatible with your qualifications and interests.[33] In the past, some employment agencies have engaged in questionable business practices, so check with the Better Business Bureau (www.bbb.org) or your business contacts to determine the quality of the various agencies.

Personal Contacts and Networking An important source of job information that students often overlook is their personal contacts. People you know often may know of job opportunities, so you should advise them that you're looking for a job. Relatives and friends might aid your job search. Instructors you know well and business contacts can provide a wealth of information about potential jobs and even help arrange an interview with a prospective employer. They may also help arrange *informational interviews* with employers that do not have immediate openings. These interviews allow you to collect information about an industry or an employer and give you an advantage if a position does become available. It is a good idea to leave your résumé with all your personal contacts so they can pass it along to those who might be in need of your services.

Student organizations (such as the student chapter of the American Marketing Association and Pi Sigma Epsilon, the professional sales fraternity) may be sources of job opportunities, particularly if they are involved with the business community. Local chapters of professional business organizations (such as the American Marketing Association and Sales and Marketing Executives International) also can provide job information; contacting their chapter president is a first step in seeking assistance from these organizations. According to career consultant Lydia Lazar, "Proactive, consistent networking is the most important strategy to master if you want to find exciting job opportunities and create a rich and substantial career over your lifetime."[34]

Artseen/Shutterstock

There are many popular social networking sites available to job seekers. LinkedIn, for example, has more than 500 million users, including recruiters. Other sites include Twitter, Jobster, Facebook, Craigslist, MyWorkster, VisualCV, and Jobfox. Some of the sites allow users to create and post a traditional résumé while others facilitate personalized web pages with video, audio, images, and even work samples. BranchOut.com can link to Facebook and pull education and work history from pages to help identify a network of friends who have worked for a specific company. Even Instagram and Pinterest have job-related postings and personal-brand pinboards. Using all or many of these sites provides greater exposure. Remember, however, to be consistent in the image and information presented online.[35]

State Employment Office State employment offices have listings of job opportunities in their state and counselors to help arrange a job interview for you. Although state employment offices perform functions similar to employment agencies, they differ in listing only job opportunities in their state and providing their services free of charge.

Direct Contact Another means of obtaining job information is direct contact—personally communicating to prospective employers (either by mail, e-mail, or in person) that you would be interested in pursuing job opportunities with them. Often you may not even know whether jobs are available in these firms. If you correspond with the companies in writing, a letter of introduction and an attached résumé should serve as your initial form of communication. One way to make direct contact with companies is to attend a career or job fair. These events allow many employers, recruiters, and prospective job seekers to meet in one location.[36] Your goals in direct contact are to create a positive impression and, ultimately, to arrange a job interview.

Writing Your Résumé

A résumé is a document that communicates to prospective employers who you are. An employer reading a résumé is looking for a snapshot of your qualifications to decide if you should be invited to a job interview. It is imperative that you design a résumé that presents you in a favorable light and allows you to get to that next important step. Job search website Glassdoor reports that companies receive an average of 250 résumés for every job posting, and that from that pool four to six candidates are interviewed.[37] Personnel in your career services office can provide assistance in designing résumés.

The Résumé Itself A well-constructed résumé generally contains up to nine major sections: (1) identification (name, address, telephone number, and e-mail address); (2) job or career objective; (3) educational background; (4) honors and awards; (5) work experience or history; (6) skills or capabilities (that pertain to a particular kind of job for which you may be interviewing); (7) extracurricular activities; (8) personal interests; and (9) personal references.[38]

There is no universally accepted format for a résumé, but three are more frequently used: chronological, functional, and targeted. A *chronological* format presents your work experience and education according to the time sequence in which they occurred (i.e., in chronological order). If you have had several jobs or attended several schools, this approach is useful to highlight what you have done. With a *functional* format, you group your experience into skill categories that emphasize your strengths. This option is particularly appropriate if you have no experience or only minimal experience related to your chosen field. A *targeted* format focuses on the capabilities you have for a specific job. This alternative is desirable if you know what job you want and are qualified for it.

In any of the formats, if possible, you should include quantitative information about your accomplishments and experience, such as "increased sales revenue by 20 percent" for the year you managed a retail clothing store. A résumé that illustrates the chronological format is shown in Figure C-6 on the next page.[39]

There are several other important considerations as you prepare your résumé. First, remember that your résumé is a marketing tool and its purpose is to present you for a particular job or role. Therefore, anticipate that you will have more than one version of your résumé, or more likely, a customized résumé for each job opportunity you are considering. Second, although traditional printed versions of résumés can be created with visually appealing fonts and graphics, a simpler, digital version of your résumé is also a necessity. A digital résumé should use a popular font (e.g., Times New Roman) and relatively large font size (e.g., 10–14 pt.) and avoid italic text, shading, or underlining. Finally, your résumé should accommodate employers who use applicant tracking software (ATS) to search for keywords. You should identify potential keywords for each job posting and include them within your experience, accomplishments, and education descriptions.[40]

Related to the use of technology, video résumés are becoming increasingly popular as a means for job seekers to communicate their personality to employers with job opportunities in customer-facing roles such as sales and public relations. In addition, don't forget that many

FIGURE C–6

A chronological résumé presents your education and work experience in the sequence in which they occurred.

Sally Winter

Campus address (until 6/1/2020):
Elm Street Apartments, #2B
College Town, OH 44042
Mobile phone: (555) 424-1648
Email: swinter@osu.stu.edu
LinkedIn: www.linkedin.com/in/sallywinter

Home address:
123 Front Street
Teaneck, NJ 07666
Phone: (555) 836-4995

Education

B.S. in Business Administration, Ohio State University, 2020, cum laude
3.3 overall GPA—3.6 GPA in major

Work Experience

Paid for 70 percent of my college expenses through the following part-time and summer jobs:

Summer 2019 Legal Secretary, Smith, Lee & Jones, Attorneys at Law, New York, NY

- Took dictation and transcribed tapes of legal proceedings
- Typed contracts and other legal documents
- Reorganized client files for easier access
- Answered the phone and screened calls for the partners

2017–2019 Academic Years Salesclerk, College Varsity Shop, College Town, Ohio

- Helped customers with buying decisions
- Arranged stock and helped with window displays
- Assisted with website design and content management
- Took over responsibilities of store manager when she was on vacation or ill

2014–2017 Assistant Manager, Treasure Place Gift Shop, Teaneck, NJ

- Supervised two salesclerks
- Helped select merchandise at trade shows
- Handled daily accounting
- Worked comfortably under pressure during busy seasons

Campus Activities

- Elected captain of the women's varsity tennis team for two years
- Worked as a reporter and night editor on campus newspaper for two years
- Elected historian for Mortar Board chapter, a senior women's honorary society

Technical Skills

- Microsoft Office, Google Analytics, WordPress, HTML5, Wix

Personal Interests

- Collecting antique clocks, listening to jazz, swimming

References Available on Request

employers may visit social networking sites such as Facebook or may simply "Google" your name to see what comes up. Review your online profiles before you start your job search to provide a positive and accurate image![41]

Letter Accompanying a Résumé The letter accompanying a résumé, or cover letter, serves as the job candidate's introduction. As a result, it must gain the attention and interest of the reader or it will fail to give the incentive to examine the résumé carefully. In designing a letter to accompany your résumé, address the following issues:[42]

- Address the letter to a specific person.
- Identify the position for which you are applying and how you heard of it.

- Indicate why you are applying for the position.
- Summarize your most significant credentials and qualifications.
- Refer the reader to the enclosed résumé.
- Request a personal interview, and advise the reader when and where you can be reached.

Emphasizing unique attributes can be helpful. According to Caroline Taylor, vice president of global marketing at IBM, "Being just like everyone else is probably the most career-limiting thing you can do." A sample letter comprising these six factors is presented in Figure C–7.

Interviewing for Your Job

The job interview is a conversation between a prospective employer and a job candidate that focuses on determining whether the employer's needs can be satisfied by the candidate's qualifications. The interview is a "make or break" situation: If the interview goes well, you have increased your chances of receiving a job offer; if it goes poorly, you probably will be eliminated from further consideration.

FIGURE C–7
A sample letter accompanying a résumé provides the job candidate's introduction.

Sally Winter
Elm Street Apartments, #2B
College Town, OH 44042
January 31, 2020

Mr. J. B. Jones
Sales Manager
Hilltop Manufacturing Company
Minneapolis, MN 55406

Dear Mr. Jones:

Dr. William Johnson, Professor of Business Administration at the Ohio State University, recently suggested that I write to you concerning your opening and my interest in a sales position. With a B.S. degree in business administration and courses in personal selling and sales management, I am confident that I could make a positive contribution to your firm.

During the past four years, I have been a salesclerk in a clothing store and an assistant manager in a gift shop. These two positions required my performing a variety of duties including selling, purchasing, stocking, and supervising. As a result, I have developed an appreciation for the viewpoints of the customer, salesperson, and management. Given my background and high energy level, I feel that I am particularly well qualified to assume a sales position in your company.

My enclosed résumé better highlights my education and experience. My extracurricular activities should strengthen and support my abilities to serve as a sales representative.

I am eager to talk with you because I feel I can demonstrate to you why I am a strong candidate for the position. I have friends in Minneapolis with whom I could stay on weekends, so Fridays or Mondays would be ideal for an appointment. I will call you in a week to see if we can arrange a mutually convenient time for a meeting. I am hopeful that your schedule will allow this.

Thank you for your kind consideration. If you would like some additional information, please feel free to contact me at (555) 424-1648. I look forward to talking with you.

Sincerely,

Sally Winter

enclosure

Preparing for a Job Interview To be successful in a job interview, you must prepare for it so you can exhibit professionalism and indicate to a prospective employer that you are serious about the job. When preparing for the interview, several critical activities need to be performed.

Before the interview, gather facts about the industry, the prospective employer, and the job. Relevant information might include the general description for the occupation; the firm's products or services; the firm's size, number of employees, and financial and competitive position; the requirements of the position; and the name and personality of the interviewer. Obtaining this information will provide you with additional insight into the firm and help you formulate questions to ask the interviewer. This information might be gleaned, for example, from corporate annual reports, *The Wall Street Journal*, Moody's manuals, Standard & Poor's *Register of Corporations, Directors, and Executives, The Directory of Corporate Affiliations*, selected issues of *Bloomberg Businessweek*, or trade publications. In addition, you should look at comments on the company review website Glassdoor. You should also study the LinkedIn profiles, Twitter feeds, and blogs of the people you'll be meeting. If information is not readily available, you could call the company and indicate that you wish to obtain some information about the firm before your interview.[43]

Preparation for the job interview should also involve role-playing or pretending that you are in the "hot seat" being interviewed. Before role-playing, anticipate questions interviewers may pose and how you might address them (see Figure C–8). Do not memorize your answers, though, because you want to appear spontaneous, yet logical and intelligent. Nonetheless, it is helpful to practice how you might respond to the questions. In addition, develop questions you might ask the interviewer that are important and of concern to you (see Figure C–9). Asking

FIGURE C–8

Anticipate questions frequently asked by interviewers and practice how you might respond.

Interviewer Questions
1. How would you describe yourself?
2. What do you consider to be your greatest strengths and weaknesses?
3. Describe your most rewarding college experiences.
4. What do you see yourself doing in 5 years? In 10 years?
5. What are three important leadership qualities that you have demonstrated?
6. What do you really want out of life?
7. What are your long-range and short-range career goals?
8. Why did you choose your college major?
9. In which extracurricular activities did you participate? Why?
10. What jobs have you enjoyed the most? The least? Why?
11. How has your previous work experience prepared you for a marketing career?
12. Why do you want to work for our company?
13. What qualifications do you think a person needs to be successful in a company like ours?
14. Describe a creative idea you produced that led to the success of a project.
15. What criteria are you using to evaluate the company for which you hope to work?
16. Describe a project where you worked as part of a team.
17. What can I tell you about our company?
18. Are you willing to relocate?
19. Are you willing to spend at least six months as a trainee?
20. Why should we hire you?

FIGURE C–9

Interviewees should develop questions about topics that are important to them.

Interviewee Questions
1. Why would a job candidate want to work for your firm?
2. What makes your firm different from its competitors?
3. What is the company's promotion policy?
4. Describe the typical first-year assignment for this job.
5. How is an employee evaluated?
6. What are the opportunities for personal growth?
7. Do you have a training program?
8. What are the company's plans for future growth?
9. What is the retention rate of people in the position for which I am interviewing?
10. How can you use my skills?
11. Why is this position vacant?
12. How would you describe the ideal candidate?
13. Why do you enjoy working for your firm?
14. How much responsibility would I have in this job?
15. What is the corporate culture in your firm?

good questions can make you stand out from other candidates. "It's an opportunity to show the recruiter how smart you are," comments one recruiter.[44]

When role-playing, you and someone with whom you feel comfortable should engage in a mock interview. Afterward, ask the stand-in interviewer to candidly appraise your interview content and style. You may wish to make a video of the mock interview.

Before the job interview you should attend to several details. Know the exact time and place of the interview; write them down–do not rely on your memory. If your initial interview is a video interview, test your Internet connection, software (e.g., Skype), camera, and lighting.[45] Get the full company name straight. Find out what the interviewer's name is and how to pronounce it. Have a notepad and a pen at the interview in case you need to record anything. Make certain that your appearance is clean, neat, professional, and conservative. And be punctual; arriving tardy to a job interview gives you an appearance of being unreliable.

Succeeding in Your Job Interview You have done your homework, and at last the moment arrives and it is time for the interview. Although you may experience some apprehension, view the interview as a conversation between the prospective employer and you. Both of you are in the interview to look over the other party, to see whether there might be a good match. When you meet the interviewer, greet him or her by name, be cheerful, smile, and maintain good eye contact (in the case of a video interview, look at the camera!). Take your lead from the interviewer at the outset. Sit down after the interviewer has offered you a seat. Sit up straight in your chair, and look alert and interested at all times. Appear relaxed, not tense. Be enthusiastic.

During the interview, be yourself. If you try to behave in a manner that is different from the real you, your attempt may be transparent to the interviewer or you may ultimately get the job but discover that you aren't suited for it. However, remember that the interview is not the time to tweet, text, or take a telephone call.[46] In addition to assessing how well your skills match those of the job, the interviewer will probably try to assess your long-term interest in the firm.

As the interview comes to a close, leave it on a positive note. Thank the interviewer for his or her time and the opportunity to discuss employment opportunities. If you are still interested in the job, express this to the interviewer. The interviewer will normally tell you what the employer's next step is–probably a visit to the company.[47] Rarely will a job offer be made at

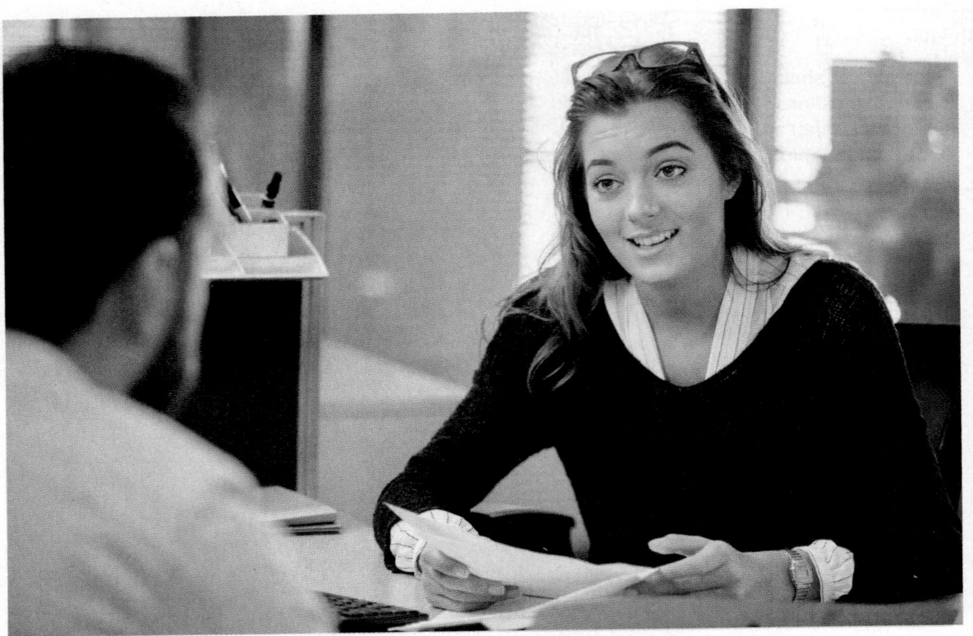

View the interview as a conversation between the prospective employer and you.
sturti/Getty Images

the end of the initial interview. If it is and you want the job, accept the offer; if there is any doubt in your mind about the job, however, ask for time to consider the offer.

Following Up on Your Job Interview After your interview, send a thank-you note to the interviewer and indicate whether you are still interested in the job. If you want to continue pursuing the job, polite persistence may help you get it. The thank-you note is a gesture of appreciation and a way of maintaining visibility with the interviewer. (Remember the adage, "Out of sight, out of mind.") Even if the interview did not go well, the thank-you note may impress the interviewer so much that his or her opinion of you changes.

After you have sent your thank-you note, you may wish to call the prospective employer to determine the status of the hiring decision. If the interviewer told you when you would hear from the employer, make your telephone call *after* this date (assuming, of course, that you have not yet heard from the employer); if the interviewer did not tell you when you would be contacted, make your telephone call a week or so after you have sent your thank-you note. While e-mail is a common form of communication today, it is often viewed as less personal than a letter or telephone call, so be confident that e-mail is preferred before using it to correspond with the interviewer.[48]

As you conduct your follow-up, be persistent but polite. If you are too eager, one of two things could happen to prevent you from getting the job: The employer might feel that you are a nuisance and would exhibit such behavior on the job, or the employer may perceive that you are desperate for the job and thus are not a viable candidate.

Handling Rejection You have put your best efforts into your job search. You developed a well-designed résumé and prepared carefully for the job interview. Even the interview appears to have gone well. Nevertheless, a prospective employer may send you a rejection letter. ("We are sorry that our needs and your superb qualifications don't match.") Although you will probably be disappointed, not all interviews lead to a job offer because there normally are more candidates than there are positions available.

If you receive a rejection letter, you should think back through the interview. What appeared to go right? What went wrong? Perhaps personnel from your career services office can shed light on the problem, particularly if they are accustomed to having interviewers rate each interviewee. Try to learn lessons to apply in future interviews. Keep interviewing and gaining interview experience; your persistence will eventually pay off.

SELECTED SOURCES OF MARKETING CAREER INFORMATION

The following is a selected list of marketing information sources that you should find useful during your academic studies and professional career.

Business and Marketing Publications

John A. Davis, *Measuring Marketing: The 100+ Essential Metrics Every Marketer Needs*, 3rd ed. (Boston: Walter de Gruyter Inc., 2018). This book offers readers an informative guide to important analytical tools and marketing metrics needed to quantify success in today's dynamic business world.

Encyclopedia of Business Information Sources, 36th ed. (Detroit: Gale Group, 2019). A bibliographic guide to more than 35,000 citations covering more than 1,100 subjects of interest to business personnel.

Craig S. Fleisher and Babette E. Bensoussan, *Business and Competitive Analysis: Effective Application of New and Classic Methods*, 2nd ed. (New Jersey: Pearson Education, 2015). This book provides a practical primer on the competitive analysis process and detailed descriptions of classic analytical approaches as well as new techniques emerging from multiple disciplines.

Paul Hague, Julia Cupman, Matthew Harrison, and Oliver Truman, *Market Research in Practice: An Introduction to Gaining Greater Market Insight*, 3rd ed. (Philadelphia: Kogan Publishers, 2016). This book offers a practical guide to the basics of marketing research. Filled with real-world applications and important details, the book presents a step-by-step approach to conducting primary research, from planning a project through execution, analysis, and presentation of findings.

Cassandra J. Hartnett, Andrea L. Sevetson, and Eric J. Forte, *Fundamentals of Government Information: Mining, Finding, Evaluating, and Using Government Resources*, 2nd ed. (New York: Neal-Schuman Publishers, Inc., 2016). This manual provides the background knowledge and tools needed to access online and print government information resources. Key topics include consumer information, census data, and summaries from the *Statistical Abstract of the United States*.

Hoover's Handbook of World Business (Austin, TX: Mergent, Inc., 2018). A detailed source of information about companies outside the United States, including firms from Canada, Europe, Japan, China, India, and Taiwan.

Marketing Dictionary (American Marketing Association). This online resource contains definitions of marketing phrases and terms and is continually adding new terms to keep marketers up to date. See https://marketing-dictionary.org.

Jadish Sheth and Naresh Malhotra, eds., *International Encyclopedia of Marketing* (West Sussex: John Wiley & Sons Ltd., 2011). This six-volume reference contains 360 entries from over 500 global experts. Entries are arranged alphabetically within each subject volume, and each volume carries an index.

Career Planning Publications

Richard N. Bolles, *What Color Is Your Parachute? 2020: A Practical Manual for Job-Hunters and Career-Changers* (Berkeley, CA: Ten Speed Press, 2019). A companion workbook is also available. See www.jobhunters-bible.com.

Reid Hoffman and Ben Casnocha, *The Start-Up of You: Adapt to the Future, Invest in Yourself, and Transform Your Career* (New York: Crown Publishing Group, 2012).

Miriam Salpeter, *Social Networking for Career Success* (New York: Learning Express, 2013).

Sheryl Sandberg, *Lean In for Graduates* (New York: Knopf, 2014).

Martin Yate, *Knock 'em Dead: The Ultimate Job Search Guide* (Holbrook, MA: Adams Media Corporation, 2017).

Websites: Resources on job searches, résumé writing, interviewing, and U.S. and international job postings:

www.careerbuilder.com
www.careeronestop.org
www.careers-in-marketing.com
www.careers.org
www.glassdoor.com
www.idealist.org
www.indeed.com
www.job.com
www.monster.com
www.simplyhired.com
www.studentcentral.com
www.usajobs.gov
www.vault.com
www.ziprecruiter.com

Selected Periodicals

Adweek, Nielsen Business Media, Inc. (weekly). See www.adweek.com. (subscription rates: $149 per year, print and digital; $99 digital edition)

Ad Age, Crain Communications, Inc. (24 times per year). See www.adage.com. (all access subscription rate: $2.10/week)

Barron's, Dow Jones & Co., Inc. (weekly). See http://online.barrons.com/homepage. (student subscription rate: $16 for 15 weeks or $52 for 52 weeks)

Bloomberg Businessweek, McGraw-Hill Companies (weekly). See www.businessweek.com. (student subscription rate: $9.99/month)

Business Horizons, Indiana University c/o Elsevier Science Publishing (bimonthly). See www.elsevier.com. (subscription rate: $167/year)

Chain Store Age, Lebhar-Friedman, Inc. (monthly). See www.chainstoreage.com. (subscription: call 847-564-1468)

eCommerce Times, ECT News Network, Inc. (daily). See www.ecommercetimes.com. (free web access)

Forbes, Forbes Inc. See www.forbes.com. (subscription rate: $20/year)

Harvard Business Review, Harvard University (six times per year). See www.hbr.org. (subscription rate: $12/month for print and digital, $10/month for digital only)

Health Marketing Quarterly, Taylor and Francis (quarterly). See www.tandfonline.com. (subscription rate: $127 print; $146 print and online)

Industrial Marketing Management, Elsevier Science Publishing (8 issues). See www.elsevier.com. (subscription rate: $225)

International Journal of Electronic Commerce, Taylor & Francis Group (quarterly). See http://www.ijec-web.org/. (subscription rate: $135 print)

Journal of Consumer Marketing, Emerald Group Publishing, Ltd. (7 issues). See www.emeraldinsight.com. (subscription rate: free web access)

Journal of Consumer Research, Journal of Consumer Research, Inc. See www.ejcr.org. (subscription rates: $184 online; $215 print; $29 student online; $42 student print)

Journal for the Advancement of Marketing Education, Marketing Management Association. See http://www.mmaglobal.org/publications/jame/. (subscription rate: free web access)

Journal of Interactive Marketing, Direct Marketing Educational Foundation (quarterly). See www.elsevier.com. (subscription rate: $299)

Journal of International Marketing, American Marketing Association (quarterly). See www.ama.org. (subscription rates: $140 digital; $152 print; $155 print and online)

Journal of Marketing, American Marketing Association (quarterly). See www.ama.org. (subscription rates: $171 digital; $186 print; $190 print and online)

Journal of Marketing Communications, Taylor & Francis Publishing (8 issues per year). See www.tandfonline.com. (subscription rate: $318)

Journal of Marketing Education, Sage Publications (three times per year). See www.sagepub.com. (subscription rate: $138)

Journal of Marketing Research, American Marketing Association (bimonthly). See www.ama.org. (subscription rates: $171 digital; $186 print; $190 print and online)

Journal of Personal Selling and Sales Management, American Marketing Association (quarterly). See www.jpssm.org. (subscription rate: $112)

Journal of Public Policy and Marketing, American Marketing Association (semiannually). See www.ama.org. (subscription rates: $99 digital; $108 print; $110 print and online)

Journal of Retailing, Elsevier Science Publishing (quarterly). See www.elsevier.com. (subscription rate: $209)

Journal of the Academy of Marketing Science, Springer Science and Business Media LLC (6 issues). See www.springer.com/jams. (subscription rate: $91)

Marketing Education Review, CTC Press (three times per year). See www.marketingeducationreview.com. (subscription rate: free web access)

Marketing News, American Marketing Association (biweekly). See www.ama.org/marketing-news-home/. (subscription rate: free web access)

PR Week, Haymarket Media (weekly). See www.prweek.com/us. (subscription rate: $348 print and digital; $298 digital only)

Sales & Marketing Management, Lakewood Media Group, LLC. See www.salesandmarketing.com. (subscription rate: free)

Stores, National Retail Federation (monthly). See www.nrf.com or www.stores.org. (free web access)

The Wall Street Journal, Dow Jones & Company, Inc. (daily). See www.wsj.com. (student subscription rate: $4/month digital; $10/month digital and print)

Professional and Trade Associations

American Advertising Federation
1101 Vermont Ave. N.W., 5th Floor
Washington, DC 20005-6306
(202) 898-0089
www.aaf.org

American Association of Advertising Agencies
1065 6th Ave.
New York, NY 10018
(212) 682-2500
www.aaaa.org

American Marketing Association
130 E. Randolph St., 22nd Floor
Chicago, IL 60601
(800) AMA-1150 or (312) 542-9000
www.ama.org

American Production and Inventory Control Society (APICS)
8430 West Bryn Mawr Ave., Suite #1000
Chicago, IL 60631
(800) 444-2742
www.apics.org

ANA Business Marketing
155 E. 44th Street
New York, NY 10017
(212) 697-5950
www.marketing.org

Data & Marketing Association
225 Reinekers Lane, Suite 325
Alexandria, VA 22314
(212) 768-7277
www.thedma.org

Direct Selling Association
1667 K Street N.W., Suite 1100
Washington, DC 20006
(202) 452-8866
www.dsa.org

Insights Association
1156 15th St. N.W., Suite 700
Washington, DC 20005
(202) 800-2545
www.insightsassociation.org

International Franchise Association
1900 K Street N.W., Suite 700
Washington, DC 20006
(202) 662-0767
www.franchise.org

International News Media Association
P.O. Box 740186
Dallas, TX 75374
(214) 373-9111
www.inma.org

Internet Marketing Association
10 Mar Del Rey
San Clemente, CA 92673
(949) 443-9300
www.imanetwork.org

Marketing Science Institute
1000 Massachusetts Ave.
Cambridge, MA 02138-5396
(617) 491-2060
www.msi.org

Mobile Marketing Association
41 E. 11th St., 11th Floor
New York, NY 10003
(646) 257-4515
www.mmaglobal.com/

National Retail Federation
1101 New York Ave. N.W., Suite 1200
Washington, DC 20005
(202) 783-7971
www.nrf.com

Product Development and Management Association
1000 Westgate Drive, Suite 252
St. Paul, MN 55114
(651) 290-6280
www.pdma.org

Professional Association for Customer Engagement
5250 E. US 36, #1102B
Avon, IN 46123
(317) 816-9336
http://www.paceassociation.org/

Public Relations Society of America
120 Wall St., 21st Floor
New York, NY 10005
(212) 460-1400
www.prsa.org

Sales and Marketing Executive International
P.O. Box 1390
Suma, WA 98295-1390
(312) 893-0751
www.smei.org

Society for Marketing Professional Services
123 North Pitt St., Suite 400
Alexandria, VA 22314
(703) 549-6117
www.smps.org

Strategic and Competitive Intelligence Professionals
7550 IH 10 West, Suite 400
San Antonio, TX 78229
(703) 739-0696
https://www.scip.org

Appendix Notes

1. William Arruda, "Personal Branding in the Digital World," *Talent Management*, February 2019, pp. 42–47; David Hagenbuch, "The Three C's of Personal Branding," *Marketing News*, July 2017, pp. 52–53; Reid Hoffman and Ben Casnocha, *The Start-Up of You* (New York: Crown Publishing, 2012); Joann S. Lublin, "The Year Ahead: Your 'Personal Brand' May Need Some Work," *The Wall Street Journal*, January 2, 2014, p. B4; Catherine Kaputa, *You Are a Brand! How Smart People Brand Themselves for Business Success* (Boston: Nicholas Brealey Publishing, 2010); and Diane Brady, "Creating Brand You," *Bloomberg Businessweek*, August 22, 2007, pp. 72–73.
2. Debra Wheatman, "Seven Tips for Conducting a Targeted Career Campaign," *Marketing News*, January 2015, p. 62; Morag Cuddeford-Jones, "Managing a Marketing Career Is Academic," *Marketing Week*, January 16, 2013; Linda J. Popky, *Marketing Your Career: Positioning, Packaging and Promoting Yourself for Success* (Woodside Business Press, 2009); Marianne E. Green, "Marketing Yourself: From Student to Professional," *Job Choices for Business & Liberal Arts Students*, 50th ed., 2007, pp. 30–31; and Joanne Cleaver, "Find a Job through Self-Promotion," *Marketing News*, January 31, 2000, pp. 12, 16.
3. Gordon Wyner, "Navigating a Marketing Career," *Marketing News*, March 2017, pp. 24–25; Michelle Boggs, "Hiring Trends for the Year Ahead," *Marketing News*, April 2015, p. 63; Kevin Cochrane, "The 21st Century Marketer," *Marketing News*, March 30, 2011, p. 22; and John N. Frank, "Stand Out from the Crowd, Landing a Marketing Job Today Means Touting Your Specialty and Staying Positive," *Marketing News*, January 30, 2009, p. 22.
4. *Job Outlook 2019* (Bethlehem, PA: National Association of Colleges and Employers, November 2018); www.Monster.com, accessed June 9, 2019; and Michael C. Bush and Christopher Tkaczyk, "100 Best Companies to Work For," *Fortune*, March 1, 2019, pp. 57–80.
5. Nicholas Basta, "The Wide World of Marketing," *BW's Guide to Careers*, February–March 1984, pp. 70–72.
6. Hal Conick, "Study Finds One Quarter of CEOs Have a Marketing or Sales Background," *Marketing News*, February 18, 2017; Anjali Bansal, David S. Daniel, John T. Mitchell, and Patrick B. Walsh, "The CEO Today: Sharing Leadership at the Top," *Research & Insight*, SpencerStuart, March 2013, http://www.spencerstuart.com/research/articles/1642/; Jonathan Harper and Frank Birkel, "From CMO to CEO: The Route to the Top," *Research & Insight*, SpencerStuart, December 2009, http://www.spencerstuart.com/research/articles/1329/; and "Leading CEOs: A Statistical Snapshot of S&P 500 Leaders," *Research & Insight*, SpencerStuart, December 2008, http://www.spencerstuart.com/research/ceo/975/.
7. *Salary Survey* (Bethlehem, PA: National Association of Colleges and Employers, Winter 2019), pp. 9, 10.
8. "Advertising, Promotions, and Marketing Managers," *Occupational Outlook Handbook*, 2018–19 Edition (Washington, DC: U.S. Department of Labor), http://www.bls.gov/ooh/management/advertising-promotions-and-marketing-managers.htm, accessed June 9, 2019.
9. Matthew Creamer, "P&G Primes Its Pinpoint Marketing," *Advertising Age*, May 7, 2007.
10. "P&G Profiles," P&G website, http://www.experiencepg.com/our-people/profiles.aspx, accessed June 3, 2013.
11. "Wholesale and Manufacturing Sales Representatives," *Occupational Outlook Handbook*, 2014–15 Edition (Washington, DC: U.S. Department of Labor), http://www.bls.gov/ooh/sales/wholesale-and-manufacturing-sales-representatives.htm#tab-6, accessed July 14, 2015.
12. "Freedom to Explore Different Career Paths Makes for a More Well-Rounded, Dedicated Staff," *Advertising Age*, March 26, 2012, p. 14; and S. William Pattis, *Careers in Advertising* (New York: McGraw-Hill, 2004).
13. "13 Professional Skills for a Rewarding Career in Digital Marketing," *Business2Community.com*, January 9, 2013; Sarah Lundy, "Job Opportunities Multiply in Social Media: With More People Connecting Online, Businesses Rush to Join the Party," *Buffalo News*, January 10, 2011, p. C1; Duane Forrester, "Search Can Offer Jobs, Decent Salaries," *Advertising Age*, May 26, 2008, p. 28; and Tanya Lewis, "Talent in Demand," *PRWeek Career Guide*, 2006, pp. 4–6.
14. Ellen Davis, "The Increasing Scope of Retail Careers" *Stores Magazine*, July 31, 2014, p. 73; and Roslyn Dolber, *Opportunities in Retailing Careers* (New York: McGraw-Hill, 2008).
15. Peter Coy, "Help Wanted," *Bloomberg Businessweek*, May 11, 2009, pp. 40–46; and "The Way We'll Work," *Time*, May 25, 2009, pp. 39–50.
16. Jeff S. Johnson and Joseph M. Matthes, "Study Reveals Secrets of Successful Sales-to-Marketing Transitions," *Marketing News*, May 2019, pp. 16–17.
17. "Wholesale and Manufacturing Sales Representatives," *Occupational Outlook Handbook*, 2018–19 Edition (Washington, DC: U.S. Department of Labor), http://www.bls.gov/ooh/sales/wholesale-and-manufacturing-sales-representatives.htm, accessed June 9, 2019; and Jack and Suzy Welch, "Dear Graduate . . . To Stand Out among Your Peers, You Have to Overdeliver," *Bloomberg Businessweek*, June 19, 2006, p. 100.
18. "The Tech Effect," *Sales & Marketing Management*, July–August 2015, pp. 40–41; and Elisabeth A. Sullivan, "One-to-One," *Marketing News*, June 15, 2009, pp. 10–13.
19. Carol Shea, "Career Advice for New Marketing Researchers," *Marketing News*, July 2015, p. 61; Piet Levy, "10 Minutes with Stan Sthanunathan, Vice President of Marketing Strategy and Insights, The Coca-Cola Co.," *Marketing News*, February 28, 2011, p. 34; and Edmund Hershberger and Madhav N. Segal, "Ads for MR Positions Reveal Desired Skills," *Marketing News*, February 1, 2007, p. 28.
20. Zach Brooke, "An Internal Success Story," *Marketing News*, August 2017, pp. 52–54; Nielsen company website, http://www.nielsen.com/us/en/about-us.html; and "Market Research Analyst," in Les Krantz, ed., *Jobs Rated Almanac*, 6th ed. (New York: St. Martin's Press, 2002).
21. Deborah L. Vence, "In an Instant, More Researchers Use IM for Fast, Reliable Results," *Marketing News*, March 1, 2006, p. 53; and Joshua Grossnickle and Oliver Raskin, "What's Ahead on the Internet," *Marketing Research*, Summer 2001, pp. 9–13.
22. Matt Valle, "Eight Reasons to Choose Market Research as a Career," *Marketing Insights*, April 2014, pp. 12–13; and Carolyn D. Marconi, "Desperately Looking for New Talent Is a Recurring Theme," *Marketing Research*, Spring 2000, pp. 4–6.
23. "2019 Franchise 500," *Entrepreneur* website, www.entrepreneur.com, accessed October 5, 2019.
24. Lisa Bertagnoli, "Marketing Overseas Excellent for Career," *Marketing News*, June 4, 2001, p. 4.
25. "Accenture Broadcast Services: A Global Communications Capability," Accenture website, https://www.accenture.com/us-en/success-accenture-broadcast-services-global-communications-capability, July 14, 2015; "Global Consulting Firm Accenture Opens Office in Calgary," *Postmedia Breaking News*, February 6, 2013; and "Managing Collaborators No Matter Where They Sit," *The Huffington Post*, April 17, 2013.
26. Debbie Qaqish, "How to Take Control of Your Marketing Career," *Marketing News*, May 2019, pp. 50–51.
27. Robin T. Peterson and J. Stuart Devlin, "Perspectives on Entry-Level Positions by Graduating Marketing Seniors," *Marketing Education Review*, Summer 1994, pp. 2–5.
28. Hal Conick, "If the Marketing Career Fits," *Marketing News*, October 2019, pp. 51–55; "Soft Skills Set You Apart," *Marketing News*, May 2019, pp. 30–31; Leslie Kendrick, "The Value of Student-Integrated Practicum Projects," *Marketing News*, May 2019, pp. 52–53; and Avi Levine, "Seven Skills You Need to Land a High-Paying Digital Marketing Job," *Marketing News*, May 2015, p. 58.
29. Barbara Flood, "Turbo Charge Your Job Search, Job Searching and Career Development Tips," *Information Outlook*, May 1, 2007, p. 40.

30. "More MBA Grads Take the Road Less Traveled," *Bloomberg Businessweek*, April 18–24, 2011, p. 53.
31. Susan Adams, "Secrets of Making the Most of Job Search Websites," *Forbes.com*, January 15, 2014, p. 13; and Francine Russo, "The New Online Job Hunt," *Time*, October 3, 2011, pp. B14–B16.
32. Peter Cappelli, "Making the Most of On-Line Recruiting," *Harvard Business Review*, March 2001, pp. 139–46.
33. Ronald B. Marks, *Personal Selling: A Relationship Approach*, 6th ed. (New York: Pearson, 1996).
34. Lydia Lazar, "Golden Guide Career Advice," *Marketing News*, June 2019, pp. 78–79; Chris Farrell, "It's Not What Grads Know, It's Who They Know," *Bloomberg Businessweek*, June 18, 2012, pp. 9–10; Sima Dahl, "A New Job Is No Excuse to Ease Up on Networking," *Marketing News*, February 28, 2011, p. 4; and Wayne E. Baker, *Networking Smart* (New York: McGraw-Hill, 1994).
35. Jessica Schaeffer, "How to Use Social Media to Scope Your Next Job," *Marketing News*, April–May 2017, pp. 65–66; "Careers in Marketing: Utilizing Social Networking to Improve Your Job Prospects," *CareerAlley*, July 22, 2012; "Finding Job Candidates Who Aren't Looking," *Bloomberg Businessweek*, December 17, 2012, pp. 41–42; Sima Dahl, "Pinning Your Career Hopes on Pinterest," *Marketing News*, May 15, 2012, p. 5; Tim Post, "New Graduates Use Social Media to Look for Jobs," *St. Paul Pioneer Press*, June 3, 2011; Susan Berfield, "Dueling Your Facebook Friends for a New Job," *Bloomberg Businessweek*, March 7, 2011, p. 35; and Dan Schawbel, "Top 10 Social Sites for Finding a Job," *Mashable*, February 24, 2009.
36. Stacie Garlieb, "How to Fare Well at a Job Fair," *Marketing News*, May 2014, p. 60; and "Stand Out at the Career Fair," *Job Choices for Business & Liberal Arts Students: 2009*, 52nd ed. (Bethlehem, PA: National Association of Colleges and Employers, 2008), pp. 22–23.
37. Hal Conick, "8 Ways Marketers Can Improve Their Resumes," *Marketing News*, May 2019, pp. 10–11; and Amy Diepenbrock, "Will Your Resume Open the Door to an Interview?" *Job Choices for Business & Liberal Arts Students, 2011*, National Association of Colleges and Employers, p. 31.
38. Marianne E. Green, "Resume Writing: Sell Your Skills to Get the Interview!" *Job Choices for Business & Liberal Arts Students*, 50th ed., 2007, pp. 39–47.
39. C. Randall Powell, "Secrets of Selling a Résumé," in Peggy Schmidt, ed., *The Honda How to Get a Job Guide* (New York: McGraw-Hill, 1984), pp. 4–9.
40. Sarah Steimer, "Are Creative Resumes Risky for Marketers?" *Marketing News*, January 2017, p. 53; Debra Wheatman, "Resume Trends Worth Following," *Marketing News*, July 2014, p. 63; Karla Ahern and Naomi Keller, "Expert Advice: Your Resume Questions Answered," *Marketing News*, September 2014, p. 61; and Sima Dahl, "Social Media and Your Job Search: How the Age of the Referral May Impact Your Career," *Marketing News*, September 30, 2012, p. 6.
41. Hal Conick, "6 Ways to Make (or Break) Your Career on Twitter," *Marketing News*, May 2016, pp. 52–53; Lydia Stockdale, "How to Make a Great Video CV," *The Guardian*, February 27, 2014; Robert Klara, "These Guys Want to Clean Up Your Reputation," *Adweek*, March 3, 2014, p. 22–23; "Post with Caution: Your Online Profile and Our Job Search," *Job Choices for Business & Liberal Arts Students: 2009* (Bethlehem, PA: National Association of Colleges and Employers, 2008), p. 30; and "If I 'Google' You, What Will I Find?" *Job Choices for Business and Liberal Arts Students*, 50th ed., 2007, p. 16.
42. Charlotte Rogers, "Badge of Honour," *marketingweek.com*, March 2017, pp. 12–13; William J. Banis, "The Art of Writing Job-Search Letters," *Job Choices for Business and Liberal Arts Students*, 50th ed., 2007, pp. 32–38; and Arthur G. Sharp, "The Art of the Cover Letter," *Career Futures* 4, no. 1 (1992), pp. 50–51.
43. Zach Brooke, "How to Make Glassdoor Work for You," *Marketing News*, June 2017, pp. 88–89; Lindsey Pollak, "The 10 Commandments of Social Media Job Seeking," *Job Choices for Business & Liberal Arts Students, 2011*, National Association of Colleges and Employers, p. 20; Alison Damast, "Recruiters' Top 10 Complaints," *Bloomberg Businessweek*, April 26, 2007; and Marilyn Moats Kennedy, "'Don't List' Offers Important Tips for Job Interviews," *Marketing News*, March 15, 2007, p. 26.
44. Tom Gimbel, "How to Stand Out as a Marketing Job Applicant," *Marketing News*, February 2017, pp. 61–62; Sima Dahl, "Where Do You See Yourself in Five Years?" *Marketing News*, November 15, 2010, p. 4; and Dana James, "A Day in the Life of a Corporate Recruiter," *Marketing News*, April 10, 2000, pp. 1, 11.
45. Meghan Casserly, "'You Look Like a Convict' and the Most Common Pitfalls of Interviewing over Skype," *Forbes.com*, October 3, 2012.
46. Paul Davidson, "Managers to Millennials: Job Interview No Time to Text," *USA Today*, April 29, 2013.
47. Robert M. Greenberg, "The Company Visit–Revisited," *NACE Journal*, Winter 2003, pp. 21–27.
48. Mary E. Scott, "High-Touch vs. High-Tech Recruitment," *NACE Journal*, Fall 2002, pp. 33–39.

GLOSSARY

80/20 rule A concept that suggests 80 percent of a firm's sales are obtained from 20 percent of its customers. p. 244

above-, at-, or below-market pricing Setting a market price for a product or product class based on a subjective feel for the competitors' price or market price as the benchmark. p. 377

account management policies Policies that specify whom salespeople should contact, what kinds of selling and customer service activities should be engaged in, and how these activities should be carried out. p. 595

adaptive selling A need-satisfaction presentation format that involves adjusting the presentation to fit the selling situation, such as knowing when to offer solutions and when to ask for more information. p. 589

advertising Any paid form of nonpersonal communication about an organization, product, service, or idea by an identified sponsor. p. 488, 513

all-you-can-afford budgeting Allocating funds to promotion only after all other budget items are covered. p. 498

apps Small, downloadable software programs that can run on smartphones and tablet devices. Also called *mobile apps* or *applications*. p. 568

attitude A "learned predisposition to respond to an object or class of objects in a consistently favorable or unfavorable way." p. 137

baby boomers Includes the generation of 76 million children born between 1946 and 1964. p. 77

back translation The practice where a translated word or phrase is retranslated into the original language by a different interpreter to catch errors. p. 187

balance of trade The difference between the monetary value of a nation's exports and imports. p. 177

barriers to entry Business practices or conditions that make it difficult for new firms to enter the market. p. 90

barter The practice of exchanging products and services for other products and services rather than for money. p. 348

basing-point pricing Selecting one or more geographical locations (basing point) from which the list price for products plus freight expenses are charged to the buyer. p. 386

behavioral targeting Uses information provided by cookies to direct online advertising from marketers to those online shoppers whose behavioral profiles suggest they would be interested in such advertising. p. 473

beliefs A consumer's subjective perception of how a product or brand performs on different attributes based on personal experience, advertising, and discussions with other people. p. 137

blended family A family formed by merging two previously separated units into a single household. p. 80

blue ocean strategy A strategy that emphasizes the simultaneous pursuit of product or marketing program differentiation and lower cost in newly configured industries and markets envisioned by marketing strategists and entrepreneurs alike. p. 616

bots Electronic shopping agents or robots that search websites to compare prices and product or service features. p. 469

brand community A specialized group of consumers with a structured set of relationships involving a particular brand, fellow customers of that brand, and the product in use. p. 142

brand equity The added value a brand name gives to a product beyond the functional benefits provided. p. 303

brand licensing A contractual agreement whereby one company (licensor) allows its brand name(s) or trademark(s) to be used with products or services offered by another company (licensee) for a royalty or fee. p. 306

brand loyalty A favorable attitude toward and consistent purchase of a single brand over time. p. 136

brand name Any word, device (design, sound, shape, or color), or combination of these used to distinguish a seller's products or services. p. 303

brand personality A set of human characteristics associated with a brand name. p. 303

brand purpose The reason why a brand exists, the place it has in consumers' lives, the solution it provides to consumers, and the brand's role in making society better off. p. 304

branding A marketing decision in which an organization uses a name, phrase, design, symbols, or combination of these to identify its products and distinguish them from those of competitors. p. 303

breadth of product line The variety of different product items a store carries. p. 437

break-even analysis A technique that analyzes the relationship between total revenue and total cost to determine profitability at various levels of output. p. 360

break-even chart A graphic presentation of the break-even analysis that shows when total revenue and total cost intersect to identify profit or loss for a given quantity sold. p. 361

break-even point (BEP) The quantity at which total revenue and total cost are equal. p. 360

brokers Independent firms or individuals whose principal function is to bring buyers and sellers together to make sales. p. 453

bundle pricing The marketing of two or more products in a single package price. p. 372

business The clear, broad, underlying industry or market sector of an organization's offering. p. 32

business analysis The stage of the new-product development process that specifies the features of the product and the marketing strategy needed to bring it to market and make financial projections. p. 279

business plan A road map for the entire organization for a specified future period of time, such as one year or five years. p. 56

business portfolio analysis A technique that managers use to quantify performance measures and growth targets to analyze their firms' strategic business units (SBUs) as though they were a collection of separate investments. p. 37

business products Products organizations buy that assist in providing other products for resale. Also called *B2B products* or *industrial products*. p. 266

business-to-business marketing The marketing of products and services to companies, governments, or not-for-profit organizations for use in the creation of products and services that they can produce and market to others. p. 155

buy classes Consist of three types of organizational buying situations: straight rebuy, new buy, and modified rebuy. p. 164

buying center The group of people in an organization who participate in the buying process and share common goals, risks, and knowledge important to a purchase decision. p. 163

capacity management Integrating the service component of the marketing mix with efforts to influence consumer demand. p. 334

category management An approach to managing the assortment of merchandise in which a manager is assigned the responsibility for selecting all products that consumers in a market segment might view as substitutes for each other, with the objective of maximizing sales and profits in the category. p. 447

cause marketing Occurs when the charitable contributions of a firm are tied directly to the customer revenues produced through the promotion of one of its products. p. 114

caveat emptor The legal concept of "let the buyer beware" that was pervasive in the American business culture prior to the 1960s. p. 106

central business district The oldest retail setting, usually located in the community's downtown area. p. 446

channel conflict Arises when one channel member believes another channel member is engaged in behavior that prevents it from achieving its goals. p. 415

channel of communication The means (e.g., a salesperson, advertising media, or public relations tools) of conveying a message to a receiver during the communication process. p. 486

choiceboard An interactive, digitally enabled system that allows individual customers to design their own products and services by answering a few questions and choosing from a menu of product or service attributes (or components), prices, and delivery options. p. 464

code of ethics A formal statement of ethical principles and rules of conduct. p. 108

collaborative filtering A process that automatically groups people with similar buying intentions, preferences, and behaviors and predicts future purchases. p. 464

commercialization The stage of the new-product development process that positions and launches a new product in full-scale production and sales. p. 281

communication The process of conveying a message to others that requires six elements: a source, a message, a channel of communication, a receiver, and the processes of encoding and decoding. p. 486

community shopping center A retail location that typically has one primary store (usually a department store branch) and often 20 to 40 smaller outlets, serving a population of consumers who are within a 10- to 20-minute drive. p. 446

competition The alternative firms that could provide a product to satisfy a specific market's needs. p. 89

competitive parity budgeting Allocating funds to promotion by matching the competitor's absolute level of spending or the proportion per point of market share. Also called *matching competitors* or *share of market*. p. 498

constraints In a decision, the restrictions placed on potential solutions to a problem. p. 209

consultative selling A need-satisfaction presentation format that focuses on problem identification, where the salesperson serves as an expert on problem recognition and resolution. p. 589

consumer behavior The actions a person takes in purchasing and using products and services, including the mental and social processes that come before and after these actions. p. 125

Consumer Bill of Rights An outline presented by President John F. Kennedy in 1962 that codified the ethics of exchange between buyers and sellers, including the rights to safety, to be informed, to choose, and to be heard. p. 106

consumer ethnocentrism The tendency to believe that it is inappropriate, indeed immoral, to purchase foreign-made products. p. 188

consumer journey map A visual representation of all the touchpoints a consumer comes into contact with before, during, and after a purchase. p. 132

consumer-oriented sales promotion Sales tools used to support a company's advertising and personal selling directed to ultimate consumers. Also called *consumer promotions*. p. 533

consumer products Products purchased by the ultimate consumer. p. 266

consumer touchpoints A marketer's product, service, or brand points of contact with a consumer from start to finish in the purchase decision process. p. 131

consumerism A grassroots movement started in the 1960s to increase the influence, power, and rights of consumers in dealing with institutions. p. 91

contribution margin (CM) Expressed on a per unit basis as the difference between unit selling price (**P**) and unit variable cost (**UVC**), or as a percent: $CM = \frac{UVC}{P} \times 100$ p. 359

convenience products Items that the consumer purchases frequently, conveniently, and with a minimum of shopping effort. p. 267

cookies Computer files that a marketer can download onto the computer and mobile phone of an online shopper who visits the marketer's website. p. 473

cooperative advertising Advertising programs whereby a manufacturer pays a percentage of the retailer's local advertising expense for advertising the manufacturer's products. p. 539

core values The fundamental, passionate, and enduring principles of an organization that guide its conduct over time. p. 31

cost focus strategy A generic business strategy that involves controlling expenses and, in turn, lowering product prices targeted at a narrow range of market segments. p. 616

cost leadership strategy A generic business strategy that focuses on reducing expenses and, in turn, lowers product prices while targeting a broad array of market segments. p. 616

cost per thousand (CPM) The cost of reaching 1,000 individuals or households with the advertising message in a given medium (*M* is the Roman numeral for 1,000). p. 522

cost-plus pricing Summing the total unit cost of providing a product or service and adding a specific amount to the cost to arrive at a price. p. 373

countertrade The practice of using barter rather than money for making global sales. p. 177

cross-channel consumer A consumer who shops online but buys offline, or shops offline but buys online. p. 474

cross-cultural analysis The study of similarities and differences among consumers in two or more nations or societies. p. 185

cross tabulation A method of presenting and analyzing data involving two or more variables to discover relationships in the data. Also known as *cross tab*. p. 222

cultural symbols Things that represent ideas and concepts in a specific culture. p. 186

culture The set of values, ideas, and attitudes that are learned and shared among the members of a group. p. 82

currency exchange rate The price of one country's currency expressed in terms of another country's currency. p. 190

customary pricing Setting a price that is dictated by tradition, a standardized channel of distribution, or other competitive factors. p. 377

customer contact audit A flowchart of the points of interaction or "service encounters" between consumers and a service provider. p. 328

customer engagement The degree and depth of brand-focused interactions a customer chooses to perform online with his or her social network. p. 561

customer experience The internal response that customers have to all aspects of an organization and its offering. p. 16

customer experience management (CEM) The process of managing the entire customer experience with the company. p. 333

customer lifetime value (CLV) Represents the financial worth of a customer to a company over the course of their relationship. p. 245

customer relationship management (CRM) The process of identifying prospective buyers, understanding them intimately, and developing favorable long-term perceptions of the organization and its offerings so that buyers will choose them in the marketplace and become advocates after their purchase. p. 16

customer service The ability of logistics management to satisfy users in terms of time, dependability, communication, and convenience. p. 421

customer value The unique combination of benefits received by targeted buyers that includes quality, convenience, on-time delivery, and both before-sale and after-sale service at a specific price. p. 11

customer value proposition The cluster of benefits that an organization promises customers to satisfy their needs. p. 43

customerization The growing practice of not only customizing a product or service but also personalizing the marketing and overall shopping and buying interaction for each customer. p. 471

customs What is considered normal and expected about the way people do things in a specific country. p. 185

data The facts and figures related to the project that are divided into two main parts: secondary data and primary data. p. 210

decoding The process of having the receiver take a set of symbols, the message, and transform them back to an idea during the communication process. p. 486

demand curve A graph that relates the quantity sold and price, showing the maximum number of units that will be sold at a given price. p. 356

demand factors Factors that determine consumers' willingness and ability to pay for products and services. p. 356

demographics Describing a population according to selected characteristics such as age, gender, ethnicity, income, and occupation. p. 76

depth of product line The store carries a large assortment of each product item. p. 437

derived demand The demand for industrial products and services that is driven by, or derived from, the demand for consumer products and services. p. 157

development The stage of the new-product development process that turns the idea on paper into a prototype. p. 280

differentiation focus strategy A generic business strategy that requires products to have significant points of difference to target one or only a few market segments. p. 616

differentiation strategy A generic business strategy that requires products to have significant points of difference to charge a higher price while targeting a broad array of market segments. p. 616

direct marketing A promotional alternative that uses direct communication with consumers to generate a response in the form of an order, a request for further information, or a visit to a retail outlet. p. 490

direct orders The result of direct marketing offers that contain all the information necessary for a prospective buyer to make a decision to purchase and complete the transaction. p. 503

direct to consumer marketing channels Allow consumers to buy products by interacting with various print or electronic media without a face-to-face meeting with a salesperson. p. 408

discretionary income The money that remains after paying for taxes and necessities. p. 85

disintermediation A source of channel conflict that occurs when a channel member bypasses another member and sells or buys products direct. p. 415

disposable income The money a consumer has left after paying taxes to use for necessities such as food, housing, clothing, and transportation. p. 85

diversification analysis A technique that helps a firm search for growth opportunities from among current and new markets as well as current and new products. p. 40

dual distribution An arrangement whereby a firm reaches different buyers by employing two or more different types of channels for the same basic product. p. 409

dynamic pricing The practice of changing prices for products and services in real time in response to supply and demand conditions. p. 472

dynamic pricing policy Setting different prices for products and services in real time in response to supply and demand conditions. Also called a *flexible-price policy*. p. 379

economic espionage The clandestine collection of trade secrets or proprietary information about a company's competitors. p. 107, 184

economy Pertains to the income, expenditures, and resources that affect the cost of running a business and household. p. 84

eight-second rule A view that customers will abandon their efforts to enter and navigate a website if download time exceeds eight seconds. p. 469

electronic commerce The activities that use electronic communication in the inventory, promotion, distribution, purchase, and exchange of products and services. Also called *e-commerce*. p. 88

e-marketplaces Online trading communities that bring together buyers and supplier organizations to make possible the real-time exchange of information, money, products, and services. Also called *B2B exchanges* or *e-hubs*. p. 166

emotional intelligence The ability to understand one's own emotions and the emotions of people with whom one interacts on a daily basis. p. 596

encoding The process of having the sender transform an idea into a set of symbols during the communication process. p. 486

environmental forces The uncontrollable forces that affect a marketing decision and consist of social, economic, technological, competitive, and regulatory forces. p. 11

environmental scanning The process of continually acquiring information on events occurring outside the organization to identify and interpret potential trends. p. 74

ethics The moral principles and values that govern the actions and decisions of an individual or group. p. 104

everyday low pricing (EDLP) The practice of replacing promotional allowances with lower manufacturer list prices. p. 384

exchange The trade of things of value between buyer and seller so that each is better off after the trade. p. 6

exclusive distribution A level of distribution density whereby only one retailer in a specific geographical area carries the firm's products. p. 412

experience curve pricing A method of pricing based on the learning effect, which holds that the unit cost of many products and services declines by 10 percent to 30 percent each time a firm's experience at producing and selling them doubles. p. 374

exporting A global market-entry strategy in which a company produces products in one country and sells them in another country. p. 192

Facebook A website where users may create a personal profile, add other users as friends, and exchange comments, photos, videos, and "likes" with them. p. 556

family life cycle The distinct phases that a family progresses through from formation to retirement, each phase bringing with it identifiable purchasing behaviors. p. 143

feedback In the feedback loop, the sender's interpretation of the response, which indicates whether a message was decoded and understood as intended during the communication process. p. 487

field of experience A mutually shared understanding and knowledge that the sender and receiver apply to the message so that it can be communicated effectively during the communication process. p. 486

fixed cost (FC) The sum of the expenses of the firm that are stable and do not change with the quantity of a product that is produced and sold. p. 359

fixed-price policy Setting one price for all buyers of a product or service. Also called a *one-price policy*. p. 379

FOB origin pricing The "free on board" (FOB) price the seller quotes that includes only the cost of loading the product onto the vehicle and specifies the name of the location where the loading is to occur (seller's factory or warehouse). p. 384

Foreign Corrupt Practices Act (1977) A law, amended by the International Anti-Dumping and Fair Competition Act (1998), that makes it a crime for U.S. corporations to bribe an official of a foreign government or political party to obtain or retain business in a foreign country. p. 186

form of ownership Distinguishes retail outlets based on whether independent retailers, corporate chains, or contractual systems own the outlet. p. 434

four I's of services The four unique elements to services: intangibility, inconsistency, inseparability, and inventory. p. 321

frequency The average number of times a person in the target audience is exposed to a message or an advertisement. p. 522

full-service agency An advertising agency that provides the most complete range of services, including marketing research, media selection, copy development, artwork, and production. p. 531

gap analysis A type of analysis that compares the differences between the consumer's expectations about and experiences with a service based on dimensions of service quality. p. 327

Generation X Includes the 55 million people born between 1965 and 1980. Also called the *baby bust*. p. 77

Generation Y Includes the 62 million Americans born between 1981 and 1996. Also called the *echo-boom*. p. 78

Generation Z The post-millennial generation, which includes consumers born between 1997 and 2010. p. 78

generic business strategy A strategy that can be adopted by any firm, regardless of the product or industry involved, to achieve a competitive advantage. p. 615

global brand A brand marketed under the same name in multiple countries with similar and centrally coordinated marketing programs. p. 183

global competition Exists when firms originate, produce, and market their products and services worldwide. p. 181

global consumers Consumer groups living in many countries or regions of the world who have similar needs or seek similar features and benefits from products or services. p. 183

global marketing strategy A strategy used by transnational firms that employ the practice of standardizing marketing activities when there are cultural similarities and adapting them when cultures differ. p. 182

globalization The focus on creating economic, cultural, political, and technological interdependence among individual national institutions and economics. p. 178

goals Statements of an accomplishment of a task to be achieved, often by a specific time. Also called *objectives*. p. 33

green marketing Marketing efforts to produce, promote, and reclaim environmentally sensitive products. p. 113

gross income The total amount of money made in one year by a person, household, or family unit. Also known as *money income* at the Census Bureau. p. 85

gross rating points (GRPs) A reference number used by advertisers that is obtained by multiplying reach (expressed as a percentage of the total market) by frequency. p. 522

hierarchy of effects The sequence of stages a prospective buyer goes through from initial awareness of a product to eventual action that includes awareness, interest, evaluation, trial, and adoption of the product. p. 497

hypermarket A form of scrambled merchandising, which consists of a large store (more than 200,000 square feet) that offers everything in a single outlet, eliminating the need for consumers to shop at more than one location. p. 438

idea generation The stage of the new-product development process that develops a pool of concepts to serve as candidates for new products, building upon the previous stage's results. p. 276

idle production capacity Occurs when the service provider is available but there is no demand for the service. p. 322

influencer marketing The practice of focusing on the identification and recruitment of influencers to advocate a company's products, services, and brands rather than focusing exclusively on prospective buyers. p. 554

infomercials Program-length (30-minute) advertisements that take an educational approach to communication with potential customers. p. 525

information technology Includes all of the computing resources that collect, store, and analyze data. p. 220

in-house agencies Consist of the company's own advertising staff, who may provide full services or a limited range of services. p. 532

institutional advertisements Advertisements designed to build goodwill or an image for an organization rather than promote a specific product or service. p. 514

integrated marketing communications (IMC) The concept of designing marketing communications programs that coordinate all promotional activities–advertising, personal selling, sales promotion, public relations, and direct marketing–to provide a consistent message across all audiences. p. 485

intensive distribution A level of distribution density whereby a firm tries to place its products and services in as many outlets as possible. p. 412

interactive marketing Two-way buyer–seller electronic communication in which the buyer controls the kind and amount of information received from the seller. p. 464

internal marketing The notion that a service organization must focus on its employees, or internal market, before successful programs can be directed at customers. p. 333

Internet of Things (IoT) The network of products embedded with connectivity-enabled electronics. p. 88

intertype competition Competition between very dissimilar types of retail outlets that results from a scrambled merchandising policy. p. 438

involvement The personal, social, and economic significance of the purchase to the consumer. p. 129

joint venture A global market-entry strategy in which a foreign company and a local firm invest together to create a local business in order to share ownership, control, and profits of the new company. p. 193

key account management The practice of using team selling to focus on important customers so as to build mutually beneficial, long-term, cooperative relationships. p. 594

label An integral part of the package that typically identifies the product or brand, who made it, where and when it was made, how it is to be used, and package contents and ingredients. p. 310

laws Society's values and standards that are enforceable in the courts. p. 104

lead generation The result of a direct marketing offer designed to generate interest in a product or service and a request for additional information. p. 504

learning Those behaviors that result from (1) repeated experience and (2) reasoning. p. 136

level of service Describes the degree of service provided to the customer from three types of retailers: self-, limited-, and full-service. p. 434

limited-service agencies Advertising agencies that specialize in one aspect of the advertising process, such as providing creative services to develop the advertising copy, buying previously unpurchased media space, or providing Internet services. p. 532

LinkedIn A business-oriented website that lets users post their professional profiles to connect to a network of businesspeople, who are also called *connections*. p. 558

logistics Those activities that focus on getting the right amount of the right products to the right place at the right time at the lowest possible cost. p. 417

loss-leader pricing Deliberately selling a product below its customary price, not to increase sales, but to attract customers' attention to it in hopes that they will buy other products with large markups as well. p. 377

manufacturers' agents Agents who work for several producers and carry noncompetitive, complementary merchandise in an exclusive territory. Also called *manufacturers' representatives*. p. 453

market People with both the desire and the ability to buy a specific offering. p. 9

market modification Strategies by which a company tries to find new customers, increase a product's use among existing customers, or create new use situations. p. 301

market orientation An organization with a market orientation focuses its efforts on (1) continuously collecting information about customers' needs, (2) sharing this information across departments, and (3) using it to create customer value. p. 15

market-product grid A framework to relate the market segments of potential buyers to products offered or potential marketing actions. p. 238

market segmentation Involves aggregating prospective buyers into groups, or segments, that (1) have common needs and (2) will respond similarly to a marketing action. p. 43, 237

market segments The relatively homogeneous groups of prospective buyers that (1) have common needs and (2) will respond similarly to a marketing action. p. 13

market share The ratio of sales revenue of the firm to the total sales revenue of all firms in the industry, including the firm itself. p. 33

market testing The stage of the new-product development process that exposes actual products to prospective consumers under realistic purchase conditions to see if they will buy. p. 280

marketing The activity, set of institutions, and processes for creating, communicating, delivering, and exchanging offerings that have value for customers, clients, partners, and society at large. p. 5

marketing attribution The practice and techniques used to credit or value a particular channel and consumer touchpoint. p. 477

marketing channel Consists of individuals and firms involved in the process of making a product or service available for use or consumption by consumers or industrial users. p. 404

marketing concept The idea that an organization should (1) strive to satisfy the needs of consumers while also (2) trying to achieve the organization's goals. p. 15

marketing dashboard The visual display of the essential information related to achieving a marketing objective. p. 34

marketing metric A measure of the quantitative value or trend of a marketing action or result. p. 35

marketing mix The controllable factors—product, price, promotion, and place—that can be used by the marketing manager to solve a marketing problem. p. 10

marketing plan A road map for the marketing actions of an organization for a specified future time period, such as one year or five years. p. 34, 56

marketing program A plan that integrates the marketing mix to provide a good, service, or idea to prospective buyers. p. 13

marketing research The process of defining a marketing problem and opportunity, systematically collecting and analyzing information, and recommending actions. p. 206

marketing ROI The application of modern measurement technologies to understand, quantify, and optimize marketing spending. p. 624

marketing strategy The means by which a marketing goal is to be achieved, usually characterized by a specified target market and a marketing program to reach it. p. 46

marketing tactics The detailed day-to-day operational marketing actions for each element of the marketing mix that contribute to the overall success of marketing strategies. p. 46

marketspace An information- and communication-based electronic exchange environment mostly occupied by sophisticated computer and telecommunication technologies and digital offerings. p. 88

measures of success Criteria or standards used in evaluating proposed solutions to the problem. p. 208

merchandise line Describes how many different types of products a store carries and in what assortment. p. 434

merchant wholesalers Independently owned firms that take title to the merchandise they handle. p. 452

message The information sent by a source to a receiver during the communication process. p. 486

mission A statement of the organization's function in society that often identifies its customers, markets, products, and technologies. Often used interchangeably with *vision*. p. 32

mixed branding A branding strategy where a firm markets products under its own name(s) and that of a reseller because the segment attracted to the reseller is different from its own market. p. 309

mobile marketing The broad set of interactive messaging options that enable organizations to communicate and engage with consumers through any mobile device. p. 528

moral idealism A personal moral philosophy that considers certain individual rights or duties as universal, regardless of the outcome. p. 109

motivation The energizing force that stimulates behavior to satisfy a need. p. 133

multibranding A branding strategy that involves giving each product a distinct name when each brand is intended for a different market segment. p. 308

multichannel marketing The blending of different communication and delivery channels that are mutually reinforcing in attracting, retaining, and building relationships with consumers who shop and buy in traditional intermediaries and online. p. 409

multichannel retailers Retailers that utilize and integrate a combination of traditional store formats and nonstore formats such as catalogs, television home shopping, and online retailing. p. 451

multicultural marketing Combinations of the marketing mix that reflect the unique attitudes, ancestry, communication preferences, and lifestyles of different races. p. 81

multidomestic marketing strategy A strategy used by multinational firms that have as many different product variations, brand names, and advertising programs as countries in which they do business. p. 182

multiproduct branding A branding strategy in which a company uses one name for all its products in a product class. p. 307

new-product development process The seven stages an organization goes through to identify opportunities and convert them into salable products or services. p. 275

new-product strategy development The stage of the new-product development process that defines the role for a new product in terms of the firm's overall objectives. p. 275

noise Extraneous factors that can work against effective communication by distorting a message or the feedback received during the communication process. p. 487

North American Industry Classification System (NAICS) Provides common industry definitions for Canada, Mexico, and the United States. p. 156

objective and task budgeting Allocating funds to promotion whereby the company: (1) determines its promotion objectives; (2) outlines the tasks to accomplish those objectives; and (3) determines the promotion cost of performing those tasks. p. 499

objectives Statements of an accomplishment of a task to be achieved, often by a specific time. Also called *goals*. p. 33

observational data Facts and figures obtained by watching how people actually behave, using mechanical, personal, or neuromarketing data collection methods. p. 212

odd-even pricing Setting prices a few dollars or cents under an even number. p. 372

off-peak pricing Charging different prices during different times of the day or during different days of the week to reflect variations in demand for the service. p. 331

off-price retailing Selling brand-name merchandise at lower than regular prices. p. 445

online consumers The subsegment of all Internet users who employ this technology to research products and services and make purchases. p. 468

open innovation Practices and processes that encourage the use of external as well as internal ideas and internal as well as external collaboration when conceiving, producing, and marketing new products and services. p. 273

opinion leaders Individuals who exert direct or indirect social influence over others. p. 139

order getter Sells in a conventional sense and identifies prospective customers, provides customers with information, persuades customers to buy, closes sales, and follows up on customers' use of a product or service. p. 583

order taker Processes routine orders or reorders for products that were already sold by the company. p. 583

organizational buyers Those manufacturers, wholesalers, retailers, service companies, not-for-profit organizations, and government agencies that buy products and services for their own use or for resale. p. 18, 155

organizational buying behavior The decision-making process that organizations use to establish the need for products and services and identify, evaluate, and choose among alternative brands and suppliers. p. 162

organizational culture The set of values, ideas, attitudes, and norms of behavior that is learned and shared among the members of an organization. p. 32

packaging A component of a product that refers to any container in which it is offered for sale and on which label information is conveyed. p. 310

penetration pricing Setting a low initial price on a new product to appeal immediately to the mass market. p. 370

perceived risk The anxiety felt because the consumer cannot anticipate the outcomes of a purchase but believes there may be negative consequences. p. 135

percentage of sales budgeting Allocating funds to promotion as a percentage of past or anticipated sales, in terms of either dollars or units sold. p. 498

perception The process by which an individual selects, organizes, and interprets information to create a meaningful picture of the world. p. 134

perceptual map A means of displaying in two dimensions the location of products or brands in the minds of consumers to enable a manager to see how they perceive competing products or brands, as well as the firm's own product or brand. p. 256

permission marketing The solicitation of a consumer's consent (called "opt-in") to receive e-mail and advertising based on personal data supplied by the consumer. p. 465

personal selling The two-way flow of communication between a buyer and seller, often in a face-to-face encounter, designed to influence a person's or group's purchase decision. p. 489, 580

personal selling process Sales activities occurring before, during, and after the sale itself, consisting of six stages: (1) prospecting,

(2) preapproach, (3) approach, (4) presentation, (5) close, and (6) follow-up. p. 585

personality A person's consistent behaviors or responses to recurring situations. p. 134

personalization The consumer-initiated practice of generating content on a marketer's website that is custom tailored to an individual's specific needs and preferences. p. 464

points of difference Those characteristics of a product that make it superior to competitive substitutes. p. 43

posttests Tests conducted after an advertisement has been shown to the target audience to determine whether it accomplished its intended purpose. p. 532

power center A retail location consisting of a huge shopping strip with multiple anchor (or national) stores. p. 446

predatory pricing The practice of charging a very low price for a product with the intent of driving competitors out of business. p. 387

prestige pricing Setting a high price so that quality- or status-conscious consumers will be attracted to the product and buy it. p. 371

pretests Tests conducted before an advertisement is placed in any medium to determine whether it communicates the intended message or to select among alternative versions of the advertisement. p. 531

price (P) The money or other considerations (including other products and services) exchanged for the ownership or use of a product or service. p. 348

price discrimination The practice of charging different prices to different buyers for products of like grade and quality. p. 387

price elasticity of demand The percentage change in quantity demanded relative to a percentage change in price. p. 357

price fixing A conspiracy among firms to set prices for a product. p. 386

price lining Setting the price of a line of products at a number of different specific pricing points. p. 371

price war Successive price cutting by competitors to increase or maintain their unit sales or market share. p. 381

pricing constraints Factors that limit the range of prices a firm may set. p. 352

pricing objectives Specifying the role of price in an organization's marketing and strategic plans. p. 351

primary data Facts and figures that are newly collected for the project. p. 210

private branding A branding strategy used when a company manufactures products but sells them under the brand name of a wholesaler or retailer. Also called *private labeling* or *reseller branding.* p. 309

product A good, service, or idea consisting of a bundle of tangible and intangible attributes that satisfies consumers' needs and is received in exchange for money or something else of value. p. 18, 266

product advertisements Advertisements that focus on selling a product or service and which take three forms: (1) pioneering (or informational), (2) competitive (or persuasive), and (3) reminder. p. 513

product class Refers to the entire product category or industry. p. 297

product differentiation A marketing strategy that involves a firm using different marketing mix actions to help consumers perceive a product as being different and better than competing products. p. 238

product form Pertains to variations of a product within the product class. p. 297

product item A specific product that has a unique brand, size, or price. p. 268

product life cycle Describes the stages a new product goes through in the marketplace: introduction, growth, maturity, and decline. p. 292

product line A group of product or service items that are closely related because they satisfy a class of needs, are used together, are sold to the same customer group, are distributed through the same outlets, or fall within a given price range. p. 268

product-line pricing The setting of prices for all items in a product line to cover the total cost and produce a profit for the complete line, not necessarily for each item. p. 379

product mix Consists of all the product lines offered by an organization. p. 268

product modification Involves altering one or more of a product's characteristics, such as its quality, performance, or appearance, to increase the product's value to customers and increase sales. p. 301

product placement A consumer sales promotion tool that uses a brand-name product in a movie, television show, video game, or a commercial for another product. p. 537

product positioning The place a product occupies in consumers' minds based on important attributes relative to competitive products. p. 255

product repositioning Changing the place a product occupies in a consumer's mind relative to competitive products. p. 255

profit The money left after a for-profit organization subtracts its total expenses from its total revenues—and the reward for the risk it undertakes in marketing its offerings. p. 28

profit equation Profit = Total revenue − Total cost; or Profit = (Unit price × Quantity sold) − (Fixed cost + Variable cost). p. 350

program champion A person who is willing and able to "cut the red tape" to move the program forward. p. 621

promotional allowances Cash payments or an extra amount of "free goods" awarded sellers in the marketing channel for undertaking certain advertising or selling activities to promote a product. p. 384

promotional mix The combination of one or more communication tools used to: (1) inform prospective buyers about the benefits of the product, (2) persuade them to try it, and (3) remind them later about the benefits they enjoyed by using the product. p. 484

protectionism The practice of shielding one or more industries within a country's economy from foreign competition through the use of tariffs or quotas. p. 178

protocol A statement that, before product development begins, identifies: (1) a well-defined target market; (2) specific customers' needs, wants, and preferences; and (3) what the product will be and do to satisfy consumers. p. 271

public relations A form of communication management that seeks to influence the feelings, opinions, or beliefs held by customers, prospective customers, stockholders, suppliers, employees, and other publics about a company and its products or services. p. 489

publicity A nonpersonal, indirectly paid presentation of an organization, product, or service. p. 489

publicity tools Methods of obtaining nonpersonal presentation of an organization, product, or service without direct cost, such as news releases, news conferences, and public service announcements (PSAs). p. 540

pull strategy Directing the promotional mix at ultimate consumers to encourage them to ask the retailer for a product. p. 496

purchase decision process The five stages a buyer passes through in making choices about which products and services to buy: (1) problem recognition, (2) information search, (3) alternative evaluation, (4) purchase decision, and (5) postpurchase behavior. p. 125

push strategy Directing the promotional mix to channel members to gain their cooperation in ordering and stocking the product. p. 495

quantity discounts Reductions in unit costs for a larger order. p. 382

questionnaire data Facts and figures obtained by asking people about their attitudes, awareness, intentions, and behaviors. p. 214

quota A restriction placed on the amount of a product allowed to enter or leave a country. p. 179

rating The percentage of households in a market that are tuned to a particular TV show or radio station. p. 522

reach The number of different people or households exposed to an advertisement. p. 522

receivers Consumers who read, hear, or see the message sent by a source during the communication process. p. 486

reference groups People to whom an individual looks as a basis for self-appraisal or as a source of personal standards. p. 142

regional shopping centers A retail location consisting of 50 to 150 stores that typically attract customers who live or work within a 5- to 10-mile range, often containing two or three anchor stores. p. 446

regulation Restrictions state and federal laws place on a business with regard to the conduct of its activities. p. 90

relationship marketing Links the organization to its individual customers, employees, suppliers, and other partners for their mutual long-term benefit. p. 12

relationship selling The practice of building ties to customers based on a salesperson's attention and commitment to customer needs over time. p. 582

response In the feedback loop, the impact the message had on the receiver's knowledge, attitudes, or behaviors during the communication process. p. 487

retail life cycle The process of growth and decline that retail outlets, like products, experience, consisting of the early growth, accelerated development, maturity, and decline stages. p. 450

retail positioning matrix A matrix that positions retail outlets on two dimensions: breadth of product line and value added, such as location, product reliability, or prestige. p. 443

retailing All activities involved in selling, renting, and providing products and services to ultimate consumers for personal, family, or household use. p. 432

retailing mix The activities related to managing the store and the merchandise in the store, which include retail pricing, store location, retail communication, and merchandise. p. 444

reverse auction In an e-marketplace, an online auction in which a buyer communicates a need for a product or service and would-be suppliers are invited to bid in competition with each other. p. 167

reverse logistics A process of reclaiming recyclable and reusable materials, returns, and reworks from the point of consumption or use for repair, remanufacturing, redistribution, or disposal. p. 423

sales forecast The total sales of a product that a firm expects to sell during a specified time period under specified environmental conditions and its own marketing efforts. p. 227

sales management Planning the selling program and implementing and evaluating the personal selling effort of the firm. p. 580

sales plan A statement describing what is to be achieved and where and how the selling effort of salespeople is to be deployed. p. 592

sales promotion A short-term inducement of value offered to arouse interest in buying a product or service. p. 490

sales quota Specific goals assigned to a salesperson, sales team, branch sales office, or sales district for a stated time period. p. 598

sales response function Relates the expense of the marketing effort to the marketing results obtained. p. 611

salesforce automation (SFA) The use of various technologies to make the sales function more effective and efficient. p. 600

scrambled merchandising Offering several unrelated product lines in a single store. p. 437

screening and evaluation The stage of the new-product development process that internally and externally evaluates new-product ideas to eliminate those that warrant no further effort. p. 278

secondary data Facts and figures that have already been recorded prior to the project at hand. p. 210

selective distribution A level of distribution density whereby a firm selects a few retailers in a specific geographical area to carry its products. p. 413

self-regulation An alternative to government control whereby an industry attempts to police itself. p. 93

service continuum The range of offerings companies bring to the market, from the tangible to the intangible or the product-dominant to the service-dominant. p. 323

services Intangible activities or benefits that an organization provides to satisfy consumers' needs in exchange for money or something else of value. p. 266, 319

seven Ps of services marketing An expanded marketing mix concept for services that includes the four Ps (product, price, promotion, and place or distribution) as well as people, physical environment, and process. p. 331

share points An analysis that uses percentage points of market share as the common basis of comparison to allocate marketing resources effectively for different product lines within the same firm. p. 613

shopper marketing The use of displays, coupons, product samples, and other brand communications to influence shopping behavior in a store. p. 447

shopping products Items for which the consumer compares several alternatives on criteria such as price, quality, or style. p. 267

showrooming The practice of examining products in a store and then buying them online for a cheaper price. p. 475

situation analysis Taking stock of where the firm or product has been recently, where it is now, and where it is headed in terms of the organization's marketing plans and the external forces and trends affecting it. p. 42

skimming pricing Setting the highest initial price that customers really desiring the product are willing to pay when introducing a new or innovative product. p. 370

social audit A systematic assessment of a firm's objectives, strategies, and performance in terms of social responsibility. p. 114

social class The relatively permanent, homogeneous divisions in a society into which people sharing similar values, interests, and behaviors can be grouped. p. 143

social commerce The use of social networks for browsing and buying. p. 474

social forces The demographic characteristics of the population and its culture. p. 76

social media Online media where users submit comments, photos, and videos–often accompanied by a feedback process to identify "popular" topics. p. 551

social media content The information and experience that are directed toward an end user or audience. p. 563

social media marketing program That portion of a company's integrated marketing communications effort to create and deliver compelling online media content that attracts viewer attention and encourages readers to share it with their social network. p. 561

social responsibility The idea that organizations are part of a larger society and are accountable to that society for their actions. p. 112

social shopping The use of social network services and websites by consumers to share their latest purchases, deals, coupons, product reviews, want lists, and other shopping finds with friends and contacts. p. 555

societal marketing concept The view that organizations should satisfy the needs of consumers in a way that provides for society's well-being. p. 17

source A company or person who has information to convey during the communication process. p. 486

spam Communications that take the form of electronic junk mail or unsolicited e-mail. p. 472

specialty products Items that the consumer makes a special effort to search out and buy. p. 267

standard markup pricing Adding a fixed percentage to the cost of all items in a specific product class. p. 373

strategic marketing process The process whereby an organization allocates its marketing mix resources to reach its target markets and achieve a competitive advantage. p. 41

strategy An organization's long-term course of action designed to deliver a unique customer experience while achieving its goals. p. 28

strip mall A retail location consisting of a cluster of neighborhood stores to serve people who are within a 5- to 10-minute drive. p. 446

subcultures Subgroups within the larger, or national, culture with unique values, ideas, and attitudes. p. 145

subscription commerce The payment of a fee to have products and services delivered on a recurring schedule. p. 474

supply chain The various firms involved in performing the activities required to create and deliver a product or service to consumers or industrial users. p. 418

sustainable development Conducting business in a way that protects the natural environment while making economic progress. p. 115

sustainable marketing The effort to meet today's (global) economic, environmental, and social needs without compromising the opportunity for future generations to meet theirs. p. 113

SWOT analysis An acronym describing an organization's appraisal of its internal **S**trengths and **W**eaknesses and its external **O**pportunities and **T**hreats. p. 42

target market One or more specific groups of potential consumers toward which an organization directs its marketing program. p. 10

target pricing Consists of (1) estimating the price that ultimate consumers would be willing to pay for a product, (2) working backward through markups taken by retailers and wholesalers to determine what price to charge wholesalers, and then (3) deliberately adjusting the composition and features of the product to achieve the target price to consumers. p. 372

target profit pricing Setting an annual target of a specific dollar volume of profit. p. 374

target return-on-investment pricing Setting a price to achieve an annual target return on investment (ROI). p. 375

target return-on-sales pricing Setting a price to achieve a profit that is a specified percentage of the sales volume. p. 375

tariffs Government taxes on products or services entering a country that primarily serve to raise prices on imports. p. 178

team selling The practice of using an entire team of professionals in selling to and servicing major customers. p. 584

technology Inventions or innovations from applied science or engineering research. p. 87

telemarketing Using the telephone to interact with and sell directly to consumers. p. 442

total cost (TC) The total expense incurred by a firm in producing and marketing a product. Total cost is the sum of fixed cost and variable cost. p. 359

total logistics cost The expenses associated with transportation, materials handling and warehousing, inventory, stockouts (being out of inventory), order processing, and return products handling. p. 421

total revenue (TR) The total money received from the sale of a product. p. 358

trade-oriented sales promotions Sales tools used to support a company's advertising and personal selling directed to wholesalers, distributors, or retailers. Also called *trade promotions*. p. 538

trade war A situation in which countries try to damage each other's trade, typically by imposition of tariff and quota restrictions. p. 179

trading down Reducing a product's number of features, quality, or price. p. 302

trading up Adding value to the product (or line) through additional features or higher-quality materials. p. 302

traditional auction In an e-marketplace, an online auction in which a seller puts an item up for sale and would-be buyers are invited to bid in competition with each other. p. 167

traffic generation The outcome of a direct marketing offer designed to motivate people to visit a business. p. 504

triple bottom line The recognition of the need for organizations to improve the state of people, the planet, and profit simultaneously if they are to achieve sustainable, long-term growth. p. 113

Twitter A website that enables users to send and receive "tweets," messages up to 280 characters long. p. 558

ultimate consumers The people who use the products and services purchased for a household. Also called *consumers, buyers,* or *customers*. p. 18

uniform delivered pricing The price the seller quotes that includes all transportation costs. p. 385

unit variable cost (UVC) Variable cost expressed on a per unit basis for a product. p. 359

unsought products Items that the consumer does not know about or knows about but does not initially want. p. 267

usage rate The quantity consumed or patronage (store visits) during a specific period. *Frequency marketing* focuses on usage rate. p. 243

user-generated content (UGC) The various forms of online media content that are publicly available and created by consumers or end users. Also called *consumer-generated content*. p. 552

utilitarianism A personal moral philosophy that focuses on "the greatest good for the greatest number" by assessing the costs and benefits of the consequences of ethical behavior. p. 110

utility The benefits or customer value received by users of the product. p. 18

value The ratio of perceived benefits to price; or Value = (Perceived benefits ÷ Price). p. 349

value consciousness The concern for obtaining the best quality, features, and performance of a product or service for a given price that drives consumption behavior. p. 84

value pricing The practice of simultaneously increasing product and service benefits while maintaining or decreasing price. p. 350

variable cost (VC) The sum of the expenses of the firm that vary directly with the quantity of a product that is produced and sold. p. 359

vendor-managed inventory (VMI) An inventory management system whereby the supplier determines the product amount and assortment a customer (such as a retailer) needs and automatically delivers the appropriate items. p. 422

vertical marketing systems Professionally managed and centrally coordinated marketing channels designed to achieve channel economies and maximum marketing impact. p. 410

viral marketing A digitally enabled promotional strategy that encourages individuals to forward marketer-initiated messages to others via e-mail, social networking websites, and blogs. p. 472

Web communities Websites that allow people to congregate online and exchange views on topics of common interest. p. 472

webrooming The practice of examining products online and then buying them in a store. p. 475

wheel of retailing A concept that describes how new forms of retail outlets enter the market. p. 448

whistle-blowers Employees who report unethical or illegal actions of their employers. p. 109

word of mouth The influencing of people during conversations. p. 140

workload method A formula-based method for determining the size of a salesforce that integrates the number of customers served, call frequency, call length, and available selling time to arrive at a figure for the salesforce size. p. 595

World Trade Organization (WTO) A permanent institution that sets rules governing trade between its members through panels of trade experts who decide on trade disputes between members and issue binding decisions. p. 179

yield management pricing The charging of different prices to maximize revenue for a set amount of capacity at any given time. p. 373

YouTube A video-sharing website in which users can upload, view, and comment on videos. p. 559

NAME INDEX

A

B

C

D

E

F

G

H

I

J

K

L

M

N

O

P

Q

R

S

T

U

V

W

Z

COMPANY/PRODUCT INDEX

A

B

C

D

E

F

G

H

I

J

K

L

M

N

O

P

Q

R

S

T

U

V

W

Z

SUBJECT INDEX

A

D

E

F

G

H

I

J

K

N

O

P

Q

S

T

U

V

W